Patterns of World History

Patterns of World History

Volume One to 1600

Third Edition

Peter von Sivers
University of Utah

Charles A. Desnoyers
La Salle University

George B. Stow
La Salle University

New York Oxford
OXFORD UNIVERSITY PRESS

Oxford University Press is a department of the University of Oxford. It furthers the University's objective of excellence in research, scholarship, and education by publishing worldwide. Oxford is a registered trade mark of Oxford University Press in the UK and certain other countries.

Published in the United States of America by Oxford University Press
198 Madison Avenue, New York, NY 10016, United States of America.

For titles covered by Section 112 of the US Higher Education Opportunity Act, please visit www.oup.com/us/he for the latest information about pricing and alternate formats.

Library of Congress Cataloging-in-Publication Data

Names: Von Sivers, Peter, author. | Desnoyers, Charles, 1952- author. | Stow, George B., author. | Perry, Jonathan Scott, author.

Title: Patterns of world history, with sources / Peter von Sivers, University of Utah; Charles A. Desnoyers, La Salle University; George B. Stow, La Salle University; with the assistance of Jonathan S. Perry, University of South Florida, Sarasota-Manatee.

Description: Third edition. | New York, NY : Oxford University Press, 2017. | Includes bibliographical references and index.

Identifiers: LCCN 2017005347 (print) | LCCN 2017006181 (ebook) | ISBN 9780190693602 (pbk. : alk. paper) | ISBN 9780190693619 (pbk. : alk. paper) | ISBN 9780190693626 (pbk. : alk. paper) | ISBN 9780190693633 (updf) | ISBN 9780190693640 (updf) | ISBN 9780190693657 (updf)

Subjects: LCSH: World history--Textbooks. | World history—Sources.

Classification: LCC D21 .V67 2017 (print) | LCC D21 (ebook) | DDC 909—dc23 LC record available at https://lccn.loc.gov/2017005347

9 8 7 6 5 4 3 2 1

Printed by LSC Communications, United States of America

Coniugi Judithae dilectissimae

—PETER VON SIVERS

To all my students over the years,
who have taught me at least as much as I've taught them;
and most of all to my wife, Jacki, beloved in all things,
but especially in her infinite patience and fortitude
in seeing me through the writing of this book.

—CHARLES A. DESNOYERS

For Susan and our children, Meredith and Jonathan.

—GEORGE B. STOW

—I hear and I forget; I see and I remember; I do and I understand
(Chinese proverb) 我听见我忘记;我看见我记住;我做我了解

Brief Contents

MAPS xvii
STUDYING WITH MAPS xix
PREFACE xx
NOTE ON DATES AND SPELLINGS xxviii
ABOUT THE AUTHORS xxix

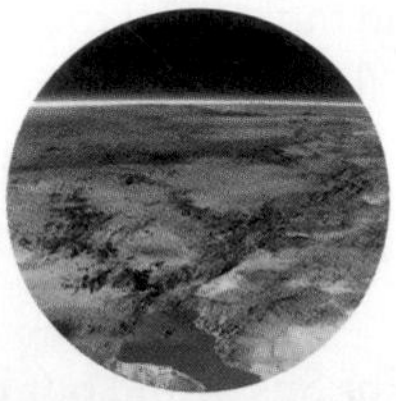

PART 1: From Human Origins to Early Agricultural Centers

Prehistory–600 BCE 2

1. The African Origins of Humanity, Prehistory–10,000 BCE 4
2. Agrarian–Urban Centers of the Middle East and Eastern Mediterranean, 11,500–600 BCE 30
3. Shifting Agrarian Centers in India, 3000–600 BCE 64
4. Agrarian Centers and the Mandate of Heaven in Ancient China, 5000–481 BCE 90
5. Origins Apart: The Americas and Oceania, 16,000–600 BCE 118

PART 2: The Age of Empires and Visionaries

600 BCE–600 CE 146

6. Chiefdoms and Early States in Africa and the Americas, 600 BCE–600 CE 148
7. Interaction and Adaptation in Western Eurasia: Persia, Greece, and Rome, 550 BCE–600 CE 178
8. Empires and Visionaries in India, 600 BCE–600 CE 214
9. China: Imperial Unification and Perfecting the Moral Order, 722 BCE–618 CE 242

PART 3: The Formation of Religious Civilizations

600–1450 CE 270

10. Islamic Civilization and Byzantium, 600–1300 CE 272

11. Innovation and Adaptation in the Western Christian World, 600–1450 CE 308

12. Sultanates, Song, and the Mongol Super Empire: Contrasting Patterns in India, China, and Inner Asia, 600–1600 CE 342

13. Religious Civilizations Interacting: Korea, Japan, and Vietnam, 550–1500 CE 370

14. Patterns of State Formation in Africa, 600–1450 CE 400

15. The Rise of Empires in the Americas, 600–1550 CE 428

PART 4: Interactions across the Globe

1450–1750 456

16. Western European Expansion and the Ottoman–Habsburg Struggle, 1450–1650 458

17. The Renaissance, New Sciences, and Religious Wars in Europe, 1450–1750 490

18. New Patterns in New Worlds: Colonialism and Indigenous Responses in the Americas, 1500–1800 524

FURTHER RESOURCES R-1

CREDITS C-1

SOURCE INDEX SI-1

SUBJECT INDEX I-1

Contents

MAPS xvii
STUDYING WITH MAPS xix
PREFACE xx
NOTE ON DATES AND SPELLINGS xxviii
ABOUT THE AUTHORS xxix

PART ONE
From Human Origins to Early Agricultural Centers
PREHISTORY–600 BCE 2

Chapter 1
Prehistory–10,000 BCE
The African Origins of Humanity 4

The Origins of Humanity 5
Hominins: No Longer Chimpanzees but Not Yet Human 6

Human Adaptations: From Africa to Eurasia and Australia 10
The African Origins of Human Culture 10
Migration from South Asia to Australia 14
Migration from Asia to Europe 18

The Ice Age Crisis and Human Migration to the Americas 20
The Ice Age 20

Putting It All Together 27

PATTERNS OF EVIDENCE: **Sources for Chapter 1**
1.1—*Shell bead jewelry from the Grotte des Pigeons, Taforalt, Morocco* •
1.2—*Python-shaped ornamented rock found in the Rhino Cave, Botswana* •
1.3—*Paintings in the Cave of Altamira, Santillana del Mar, Spain* •
1.4—*Flax fibers found at the Dzudzuana Cave, Republic of Georgia, Caucasus Mountains*

Features:
Patterns Up Close:
The Disappearance of Neanderthals 22
Against the Grain:
The Hobbits of Flores Island 29

Chapter 2
11,500–600 BCE
Agrarian–Urban Centers of the Middle East and Eastern Mediterranean 30

Agrarian Origins in the Fertile Crescent, ca. 11,500–1500 BCE 31
Sedentary Foragers and Foraging Farmers 31
The Origin of Urban Centers in Mesopotamia and Egypt 35
Kingdoms in Mesopotamia, Egypt, and Crete 39

Interactions among Multiethnic and Multireligious Empires, ca. 1500–600 BCE 46
The Hittite and Assyrian Empires, 1600–600 BCE 47
Small Kingdoms on the Imperial Margins, 1600–600 BCE 51

Religious Experience and Cultural Achievements 55

Features:
Patterns Up Close:
Babylonian Law Codes 42
Against the Grain:
Akhenaten the Transgressor 62

Putting It All Together 60

PATTERNS OF EVIDENCE: Sources for Chapter 2

2.1—*Law Code of Hammurabi* • 2.2—*Babylonian Poem of the Righteous Sufferer* • 2.3—*Advice from a royal scribe to his apprentice, Middle Kingdom Egypt, Twelfth Dynasty* • 2.4—*Sketch of the palace complex at Knossos, Minoan Crete* • 2.5—*The Great Hymn to the Aten*

Chapter 3
3000–600 BCE

Shifting Agrarian Centers in India 64

The Vanished Origins of Harappa, 3000–1500 BCE 65

The Region and People 66

Adapting to Urban Life in the Indus Valley 68

The Collapse of the Cities 73

Interactions in Northern India, 1500–600 BCE 74

The Vedic World, 1750–800 BCE 75

Statecraft and the Ideology of Power, 800–600 BCE 79

Indian Society, Culture, and Religion, 1500–600 BCE 81

Society and Family in Ancient India 81

Cultural Interactions to 600 BCE 84

Putting It All Together 86

PATTERNS OF EVIDENCE: Sources for Chapter 3

3.1—*Hymns to Agni, from the* Rig-Veda, *Book 2* • 3.2—*The Bhagavad Gita* • 3.3—*The Brihadaranyaka Upanishad* • 3.4—The Code of Manu • 3.5—*Image of Draupadi and the Pandava, from the Dashavatara Temple, Deogarh, India*

Features:

Patterns Up Close:
The Caste System 76

Against the Grain:
A Merchants' Empire? 88

Chapter 4
5000–481 BCE

Agrarian Centers and the Mandate of Heaven in Ancient China 90

The Origins of Yellow River Cultures, 5000–1766 BCE 91

Geography and Climate 92

The Origins of Neolithic Cultures 94

The Age of Myth and the Xia Dynasty, 2852–1766 BCE 97

The Interactions of Shang and Zhou History and Politics, 1766–481 BCE 99

The Shang Dynasty, 1766–1122 BCE 99

The Mandate of Heaven: The Zhou Dynasty to 481 BCE 102

Economy, Society, and Family Adaptation in Ancient China 105

Shang Society 106

Interactions of Zhou Economy and Society 107

Gender and the Family 109

Interactions of Religion, Culture, and Intellectual Life in Ancient China 110

Features:

Patterns Up Close:
The Chinese Writing System 112

Against the Grain:
Women's Voices 116

Oracle Bones and Early Chinese Writing 110
Adaptations of Zhou Religion, Technology, and Culture 114

Putting It All Together 115

PATTERNS OF EVIDENCE: Sources for Chapter 4

4.1—The Zuo Commentary (Zuozhuan) • 4.2—*Excerpts from* The Book of Odes *(Shijing)* • 4.3—The Book of Lord Shang (Shangjun Shu) • 4.4—The Canon of Shun • 4.5—*Iron sword with jade handle, earliest cast-iron object (Western Zhou), from Henan Museum, Guo state, Sanmenxia city*

Chapter 5
16,000–600 BCE

Origins Apart: The Americas and Oceania 118

The Americas: Hunters and Foragers, 16,000–600 BCE 120
The Environment 121
Human Migrations 124

Agriculture, Villages, and Urban Life 126
The Neolithic Revolution in the Americas 127
The Origins of Urban Life 129
The First Mesoamerican Settlements 134
Foraging and Farming Societies Outside the Andes and Mesoamerica 136

The Origins of Pacific Island Migrations 139
Lapita and Cultural Origins 140
Creating Polynesia 141

Putting It All Together 142

PATTERNS OF EVIDENCE: Sources for Chapter 5

5.1—Quipu *from the Caral-Supe culture, Peru* • 5.2—*Textile fragment from Chavín de Huántar, Peru* • 5.3—*Burial Mound at L'Anse Amour, Labrador, Canada* • 5.4—*Lapita pot shards, found in Vanuatu, western Pacific*

Features:
Patterns Up Close:
The Origin of Corn 130
Against the Grain:
Thor Heyerdahl 144

PART TWO

The Age of Empires and Visionaries
600 BCE–600 CE 146

Chapter 6
600 BCE–600 CE

Chiefdoms and Early States in Africa and the Americas 148

Agriculture and Early African Kingdoms 149
Saharan Villages, Towns, and Kingdoms 150
The Kingdom of Aksum 153

The Spread of Villages in Sub-Saharan Africa 155
West African Savanna and Rain-Forest Agriculture 155
The Spread of Village Life to East and South Africa 157
Patterns of African History, 600 BCE–600 CE 160

Early States in Mesoamerica: Maya Kingdoms and Teotihuacán 161
The Maya Kingdoms in Southern Mesoamerica 161
The Kingdom of Teotihuacán in the Mexican Basin 166

Features:
Patterns Up Close:
The Mayan Ball Game 168
Against the Grain:
Nazca Lines and Speculation 176

The Andes: Moche and Nazca 170
The Moche in Northern Peru 171
Paracas and the Nazca in Southern Peru 172

Putting It All Together 174

PATTERNS OF EVIDENCE: **Sources for Chapter 6**
6.1—*Relief sculpture from Meroë, Sudan* • 6.2—*Cosmas Indicopleustes (Cosmas the India-Voyager),* Christian Topography • 6.3—*The market at Jenné-jeno, Mali* • 6.4—*Limestone panel from a Mayan temple, Palenque*

Chapter 7
550 BCE–600 CE

Interaction and Adaptation in Western Eurasia: Persia, Greece, and Rome 178

Features:
Patterns Up Close:
The Plague of Justinian 194
Against the Grain:
Women in Democratic Athens 212

Interactions between Persia and Greece 179
The Origins of the Achaemenid Persian Empire 180
Greek City-States in the Persian Shadow 183
Alexander's Empire and Its Successor Kingdoms 185

Interactions between the Persian and Roman Empires 186
Parthian Persia and Rome 187
The Sasanid Persian and Late Roman Empires 192

Adaptations to Monotheism and Monism in the Middle East 197
Challenge to Polytheism: The Origins of Judaism, Zoroastrianism, and Greek Philosophy 198
Toward Religious Communities and Philosophical Schools 201

The Beginnings of Science and the Cultures of Kings and Citizens 204
The Sciences at the Library of Alexandria 204
Royal Persian Culture and Arts 205
Greek and Roman Civic Culture and Arts 206

Putting It All Together 210

PATTERNS OF EVIDENCE: **Sources for Chapter 7**
7.1—*The Cyrus Cylinder* • 7.2—*Herodotus,* Histories • 7.3—*1 Maccabees* • 7.4—*Graffiti from the walls of Pompeii* • 7.5—*The murder of the philosopher Hypatia, Alexandria, Egypt*

Chapter 8
600 BCE–600 CE

Empires and Visionaries in India 214

Features:
Patterns Up Close:
The Global Trade of Indian Pepper 234
Against the Grain:
India's Ancient Republics 240

Patterns of State Formation in India: Republics, Kingdoms, and Empires 215
The Road to Empire: The Mauryas 216
The Classical Age: The Gupta Empire 220
The Southern Kingdoms, ca. 300–600 CE 222

The Vedic Tradition and Its Visionary Reformers 223
Reforming the Vedic Tradition 224
The Maturity of Hinduism: From the Abstract to the Devotional 229

Stability amid Disorder: Economy, Family, and Society 231
Tax and Spend: Economy and Society 231
Caste, Family Life, and Gender 233

Strength in Numbers: Art, Literature, and Science 237

Putting It All Together 239

PATTERNS OF EVIDENCE: Sources for Chapter 8

8.1—*The Seven Pillar Edicts of King Ashoka* • 8.2—The Questions of King Milinda (The Milindapanha) • 8.3—*Bamiyan Buddhas, Afghanistan* • 8.4—*Seated Buddha, from the Gandhara culture, Afghanistan-Pakistan* • 8.5—*Kalidasa,* The Cloud Messenger

Chapter 9 **722 BCE–618 CE**

China: Imperial Unification and Perfecting the Moral Order 242

Visionaries and Empire 243

Confucianism, Legalism, and Daoism 244

The Qin Dynasty 248

The Han Dynasty 251

The Domestic Economy: Society, Family, and Gender 256

Industry and Commerce 256

Gender Roles 260

Intellectual Trends, Aesthetics, Science, and Technology 262

Confucianism, Education, and History during the Han 262

Buddhism in China 264

Intellectual Life 265

Putting It All Together 266

PATTERNS OF EVIDENCE: Sources for Chapter 9

9.1—Analects (Lunyu) *of Confucius* • 9.2—Book of Mencius *(Mengzi)* • 9.3—*Li Si, "Memorial on the Burning of Books," from the* Shiji • 9.4—Han Shu (History of the Former Han Dynasty) • 9.5—*Ban Zhao,* Admonitions for Women *(Nüjie)*

Features:

Patterns Up Close: The Stirrup 254

Against the Grain: Yang Zhu and Mo Di 268

PART THREE

The Formation of Religious Civilizations

600–1450 CE 270

Chapter 10 **600–1300 CE**

Islamic Civilization and Byzantium 272

The Formation of Islamic Religious Civilization 273

The Beginnings of Islam 274

Islamic Theology, Law, and Politics 277

Eastern Christian Civilization in Byzantium 282

Byzantium's Difficult Beginnings 282

The Seljuk Invasion and the Crusades 287

Islamic and Eastern Christian Civilizations at Their Height 291

State and Society in Mamluk Egypt 291

Byzantine Provincial and Central Organization 294

Commercial Relations from the Atlantic to the South China Sea 296

Religion, Sciences, and the Arts in Two Religious Civilizations 298

Islamic Culture: Intellectual and Scientific Expressions 298

Features:

Patterns Up Close: Byzantine Icons and Islamic Miniatures 302

Against the Grain: Did Ibn Taymiyya "Have a Screw Loose"? 306

Artistic Expressions in Islamic Civilization 300
Learning and the Arts in Byzantium 301

Putting It All Together 304

» PATTERNS OF EVIDENCE: **Sources for Chapter 10**

10.1—*Excerpts from the Quran,* Sura 2 *"The Cow"* • 10.2—*Documents related to the iconoclasm controversy* • 10.3—*Memoirs of Usama Ibn Munqidh* • 10.4—*A Jewish engagement contract from Fustat (Old Cairo)* • 10.5—The Alchemy of Happiness, *by Abd al-Hamid al-Ghazali*

Chapter 11
600–1450 CE

Innovation and Adaptation in the Western Christian World 308

Features:
Patterns Up Close:
The Gothic Cathedral 326
Against the Grain:
The Cathar Heresy 340

The Formation of Christian Europe, 600–1000 309
Frankish Gaul and Latin Christianity 309

Recovery, Reform, and Innovation, 1000–1300 315
The Political Recovery of Europe 315
The Economic and Social Recovery of Europe 317
Religious Reform and Expansion 321
Intellectual and Cultural Developments 327

Crisis and Creativity, 1300–1415 330
The Calamitous Fourteenth Century 330
Signs of a New Era in the Fifteenth Century 335

Putting It All Together 338

» PATTERNS OF EVIDENCE: **Sources for Chapter 11**

11.1—*Einhard's* Life of Charlemagne • 11.2—*Feudal contracts and the swearing of fealty* • 11.3—*Peter Abelard,* The Story of My Misfortunes • 11.4—*Giovanni Boccaccio,* The Decameron, *"Putting the Devil Back in Hell"* • 11.5—*Flagellants attempt to ward off the Black Death in Germany and in England*

Chapter 12
600–1600 CE

Sultanates, Song, and the Mongol Super Empire 342

Features:
Patterns Up Close:
Gunpowder 356
Against the Grain:
Empress Wu 368

India: The Clash of Cultures 343
Buddhist and Hindu India after the Guptas 344
Islam in India, 711–1398 346
Toward the Mughal Era, 1398–1450 348

Interactions and Adaptations: From Buddhism to Neo-Confucian Synthesis in China 349
Creating a Religious Civilization under the Tang 350
The Song and Yuan Dynasties, 960–1368 354
The Ming to 1450: The Quest for Stability 360
Society, Family, and Gender 362
Perceptions of Perfection: Intellectual, Scientific, and Cultural Life 364

Putting It All Together 366

» PATTERNS OF EVIDENCE: **Sources for Chapter 12**

12.1—*The* Chachnamah • 12.2—*Harsha Vardhana,* The Lady of the Jewel Necklace • 12.3—*Poetry of the Tang Dynasty* • 12.4—*Marco Polo, "Kubilai Khan at War"* • 12.5—*Model of a Ming ship in the flotilla of Zheng He*

Chapter 13
550–1500 CE

Religious Civilizations Interacting: Korea, Japan, and Vietnam 370

Korea to 1450: Innovation from Above 371

People and Place: The Korean Environment 371

Conquest and Competition: History and Politics to 1450 372

Economy, Society, and Family 376

Religion, Culture, and Intellectual Life 378

Japan to 1450: Selective Interaction and Adaptation 379

The Island Refuge 379

Adaptation at Arm's Length: History and Politics 379

Economy, Society, and Family 386

Religion, Culture, and Intellectual Life 388

Vietnam: Human Agency and State Building 391

The Setting and Neolithic Cultures 391

Economy, Society, and Family 394

Religion, Culture, and Intellectual Life 395

Putting It All Together 397

Features:

Patterns Up Close:
Printing 380

Against the Grain:
Zen and Bushido 398

» PATTERNS OF EVIDENCE: **Sources for Chapter 13**

13.1—*Murasaki Shikibu,* The Tale of Genji • 13.2—Haedong kosŭng chŏn, *on Buddhism in Korea* • 13.3—Nihongi (Chronicles of Japan) • 13.4—*P'i Jih-hsiu, "Three Poems of Shame"* • 13.5—*Copper head of Bodhisattva Avalokiteshvara, Vietnam*

Chapter 14
600–1450 CE

Patterns of State Formation in Africa 400

Christians and Muslims in the Northeast 401

Nubia in the Middle Nile Valley 401

Ethiopia in the Eastern Highlands 405

Adaptation to Islam: City-States and Kingdoms in East and Southern Africa 409

The Swahili City-States on the East African Coast 409

Traditional Kingdoms in Southern and Central Africa 413

Central African Chiefdoms and Kingdoms 415

Cultural Encounters: West African Traditions and Islam 417

The Kingdom of Ancient Ghana 417

The Empire of Mali 420

Rain-Forest Kingdoms 423

Putting It All Together 424

Features:

Patterns Up Close:
The Sculptures of Ife 422

Against the Grain:
Sundiata's Rise to Power 426

» PATTERNS OF EVIDENCE: **Sources for Chapter 14**

14.1—The Fetha Nagast, *Ethiopia* • 14.2—*Ibn Battuta on Mali, from the* Rihla • 14.3—*Golden Bracelets from the "Lost City" of Mapungubwe, South Africa* • 14.4—*'Abd al-'Azīz al-Bakrī,* Description of West Africa • 14.5—*Walls and moats at Sungbo's Eredo, Nigeria*

Chapter 15
600–1550 CE

The Rise of Empires in the Americas 428

The Legacy of Teotihuacán and the Toltecs in Mesoamerica 429
Militarism in the Mexican Basin 430
Late Maya States in Yucatán 432

The Legacy of Tiwanaku and Wari in the Andes 434
The Expanding State of Tiwanaku 434
The Expanding City-State of Wari 436

American Empires: Aztec and Inca Origins and Dominance 438
The Aztec Empire of Mesoamerica 438
The Inca Empire of the Andes 441

Imperial Society and Culture 446
Imperial Capitals: Tenochtitlán and Cuzco 447
Power and Its Cultural Expressions 450

Putting It All Together 452

PATTERNS OF EVIDENCE: **Sources for Chapter 15**
15.1—*The Temple of the Jaguars, Chichén Itzá* • 15.2—*Skeletons in a Wari royal tomb site, El Castillo de Huarmey, Peru* • 15.3—*Bernal Díaz,* The Conquest of New Spain • 15.4—*Pedro Cieza de León on Incan roads* • 15.5—*Garcilaso de la Vega, "The Walls and Gates of Cuzco"*

Features:
Patterns Up Close:
Human Sacrifice and Propaganda 450
Against the Grain:
Amazon Rain-Forest Civilizations 454

PART FOUR

Interactions across the Globe
1450–1750 456

Chapter 16
1450–1650

Western European Expansion and the Ottoman–Habsburg Struggle 458

The Muslim–Christian Competition in the East and West, 1450–1600 459
Iberian Christian Expansion, 1415–1498 460
Rise of the Ottomans and Struggle with the Habsburgs for Dominance, 1300–1609 464

The Centralizing State: Origins and Interactions 475
State Transformation, Money, and Firearms 475

Imperial Courts, Urban Festivities, and the Arts 480
The Ottoman Empire: Palaces, Festivities, and the Arts 480
The Spanish Habsburg Empire: Popular Festivities and the Arts 483

Putting It All Together 486

PATTERNS OF EVIDENCE: **Sources for Chapter 16**
16.1—*Christopher Columbus,* The Book of Prophecies • 16.2—*Thomas the Eparch and Joshua Diplovatatzes, "The Fall of Constantinople"* • 16.3—*Evliya Çelebi, "A Procession of Artisans at Istanbul"* • 16.4—*Ogier Ghiselin de Busbecq, "The Court of Suleiman the Magnificent"* • 16.5—*Janissary musket*

Features:
Patterns Up Close:
Shipbuilding 466
Against the Grain:
Tilting at Windmills 488

Chapter 17
1450–1750

The Renaissance, New Sciences, and Religious Wars in Europe 490

Cultural Transformations: Renaissance, Baroque, and New Sciences 492
The Renaissance and Baroque Arts 492
The New Sciences 495
The New Sciences and Their Social Impact 498
The New Sciences: Philosophical Interpretations 502

Centralizing States and Religious Upheavals 504
The Rise of Centralized Kingdoms` 504
The Protestant Reformation, State Churches, and Independent Congregations 507
Religious Wars and Political Restoration 512

Putting It All Together 521

PATTERNS OF EVIDENCE: Sources for Chapter 17

17.1—*Examination of Lady Jane Grey, London* • 17.2—*Sebastian Castellio,* Concerning Whether Heretics Should Be Persecuted • 17.3—*Duc de Saint-Simon, "The Daily Habits of Louis XIV at Versailles"* • 17.4—*Giorgio Vasari,* The Life of Michelangelo Buonarotti • 17.5—*Galileo Galilei, Letter to the Grand Duchess Christina de' Medici*

Features:
Patterns Up Close: Mapping the World 504
Against the Grain: The Digger Movement 523

Chapter 18
1500–1800

New Patterns in New Worlds: Colonialism and Indigenous Responses in the Americas 524

The Colonial Americas: Europe's Warm-Weather Extension 525
The Conquest of Mexico and Peru 526
The Establishment of Colonial Institutions 531

The Making of American Societies: Origins and Transformations 541
Exploitation of Mineral and Tropical Resources 541
Social Strata, Castes, and Ethnic Groups 545
The Adaptation of the Americas to European Culture 551

Putting It All Together 554

PATTERNS OF EVIDENCE: Sources for Chapter 18

18.1—*Hernán Cortés,* Second Letter from Mexico to Emperor Charles V • 18.2—*Marina de San Miguel's Confessions before the Inquisition, Mexico City* • 18.3—*Nahuatl Land Sale Documents, Mexico* • 18.4—The Jesuit Relations, *French North America* • 18.5—*The Salem Witch Trials, British North America*

Features:
Patterns Up Close: The Columbian Exchange 542
Against the Grain: Juana Inés de la Cruz 556

FURTHER RESOURCES R-1
CREDITS C-1
SOURCE INDEX SI-1
SUBJECT INDEX I-1

Maps

Map 1.1 Early Human Origins to 3 Million Years Ago 8
Map 1.2 Human Migration Out of Africa 14
Map 1.3 The Ice Age 21
Map 1.4 Human Migration to the Americas 26
Map 2.1 Farming and Settlement in the Ancient Middle East and Eastern Mediterranean 32
Map 2.2 Urban Centers in Mesopotamia and Egypt, 5500–3500 BCE 36
Map 2.3a The Akkadian Kingdom 40
Map 2.3b Kingdom of Babylonia 40
Map 2.4 Old Kingdom Egypt, ca. 2613–2160 BCE 45
Map 2.5 The Hittite Empire and Eastern Mediterranean, ca. 1500 BCE 48
Map 2.6 The Assyrian Empire 51
Map 3.1 India: Physical Features and the Monsoon Cycle 67
Map 3.2 Harappan Civilization, ca. 2300 BCE 69
Map 3.3 Mohenjo-Daro 70
Map 3.4 Northern India, ca. 600 BCE 82
Map 4.1 Early China: Geography and Climate 93
Map 4.2 Shang China 100
Map 4.3 Zhou China 103
Map 5.1 The Environment of the Americas 122
Map 5.2 Early Urban Centers in the Andes 129
Map 5.3 Major Corn-Producing Regions of the World 131
Map 5.4 Olmec Civilization 135
Map 5.5 Adena and Hopewell Cultures 138
Map 5.6 The Colonization of the Pacific 140
Map 6.1 The Kingdoms of Meroë and Aksum, ca. 650 BCE–600 CE 152
Map 6.2 Villages and Settlements in Sub-Saharan Africa, 600 BCE–600 CE 158
Map 6.3 Mayan Civilization, ca. 200 BCE–800 CE 162
Map 6.4 Teotihuacán, ca. 100 CE–500 CE 170
Map 6.5 Andean Centers, 600 BCE–600 CE 173
Map 7.1 Achaemenid Persian Empire 181
Map 7.2 Greece in the Sixth Century BCE 183
Map 7.3a,b Alexander's Empire (a) and Successor Kingdoms after the Breakup of Alexander's Empire (b) 187
Map 7.4 Roman Empire at the Time of Augustus 191
Map 7.5 The Plague of Justinian 194
Map 7.6 Nomadic Invasions and Barbarian Migrations into the Roman Empire, 375–450 CE 196
Map 7.7 The Sasanid Empire 197
Map 7.8 Jewish Communities and Greek Philosophical Schools, ca. 100 CE 201
Map 8.1 Northern India, ca. 400 BCE 216
Map 8.2 The Mauryan Empire under Ashoka, 273–231 BCE 218
Map 8.3 The Gupta Empire 221
Map 8.4 The Spread of Buddhism to 600 CE 229
Map 8.5 Asian Trade Routes, ca. 100 CE 235
Map 9.1 The Qin Empire 249
Map 9.2 The Han Empire 252
Map 9.3 China in 589 CE 254
Map 9.4 Industry and Commerce under the Han 258
Map 9.5 The Silk Road, ca. 150 CE 260
Map 10.1 Arab Conquests to 750 276
Map 10.2 The Early Abbasid City of Baghdad 279
Map 10.3 The Islamic Commonwealth, ca. 1022 CE 281
Map 10.4 The Byzantine Empire, ca. 1025 CE 284
Map 10.5 The Seljuk Empire in 1092 CE 287
Map 10.6 The Crusader Kingdoms, ca. 1140 CE 290
Map 10.7 The Afro-Eurasian World Commercial System, ca. 1300 297
Map 11.1 The Empire of Charlemagne 313
Map 11.2 Mediterranean Trade in the Twelfth and Thirteenth Centuries 319
Map 11.3 The First Crusade, 1095–1099 325
Map 11.4 The Spread of the Black Death in Europe 332
Map 11.5 The Hundred Years' War, 1337–1453 334
Map 11.6 The Great Western Schism, 1378–1417 336
Map 12.1 Harsha's Empire, ca. 645 CE 344
Map 12.2 Eurasian Trade Routes, ca. 1000 CE 346
Map 12.3 India under the Sultanate of Delhi 348
Map 12.4 East and Central Asia, 618–960 352
Map 12.5 East Asia in 1150 355
Map 12.6 The Mongol Empire 359
Map 12.7 Voyages of Zheng He, 1405–1433 361
Map 13.1 Korea: Topography and Precipitation 373
Map 13.2 Korea, ca. 500 CE 374
Map 13.3 Korea under the Koryo, 936–1392 375
Map 13.4 Japan: Topography and Climate 382
Map 13.5 Heian Japan 384
Map 13.6 Japan, ca. 1350 386
Map 13.7 Southeast Asia: The Physical Setting 392
Map 13.8 Vietnam, ca. 1428 394
Map 14.1 Long-Distance Trade in Northeast Africa and the Middle East, 800–1200 404
Map 14.2 The Ethiopian Highlands, ca. 1450 408
Map 14.3 Swahili City-States, ca. 1400 412
Map 14.4 Great Zimbabwe, ca. 1450 416
Map 14.5 The Luba Kingdom, ca. 1400 417
Map 14.6 West African States, 600–1450 420
Map 15.1 North America and Mesoamerica, ca. 1100 431
Map 15.2 Tiwanaku and Wari, ca. 1000 437
Map 15.3 The Aztec Empire, ca. 1520 440
Map 15.4 The Inca Empire, ca. 1525 442
Map 15.5 Tenochtitlán and the Valley of Mexico 447
Map 15.6 Cuzco 61
Map 16.1 Africa, the Mediterranean, and the Indian Ocean, 1415–1498 469
Map 16.2 The Ottoman Empire, 130 471
Map 16.3 Europe and the Medit ca. 1560 473
Map 16.4 Ottoman–Po in the I 499
Map 17.1 Ce

Map 17.2	European Warfare, 1450–1750	507
Map 17.3	The Protestant Reformation, ca. 1580	511
Map 17.4	Europe in 1648	517
Map 17.5	The Expansion of Russia, 1462–1795	520
Map 18.1	The European Exploration of the Americas, 1519–1542	529
Map 18.2	The Colonization of Central and South America to 1750	533
Map 18.3	The Colonization of North America to 1763	538
Map 18.4	The Columbian Exchange	543

Studying with Maps

MAPS

World history cannot be fully understood without a clear comprehension of the chronologies and parameters within which different empires, states, and peoples have changed over time. Maps facilitate this understanding by illuminating the significance of time, space, and geography in shaping the patterns of world history.

Global Locator

Many of the maps in *Patterns of World History* include *global locators* that show the area being depicted in a larger context.

Projection

A map *projection* portrays all or part of the earth, which is spherical, on a flat surface. All maps, therefore, include some distortion. The projections in *Patterns of World History* show the earth at global, continental, regional, and local scales.

Topography

Many maps in *Patterns of World History* show *relief*—the contours of the land. Topography is an important element in studying maps because the physical terrain has played a critical role in shaping human history.

Scale Bar

Every map in *Patterns of World History* includes a *scale* that shows distances in both miles and kilometers, and in some instances in feet as well.

Map Key

Maps use symbols to show the location of features and to convey information. Each symbol is explained in the map's *key*.

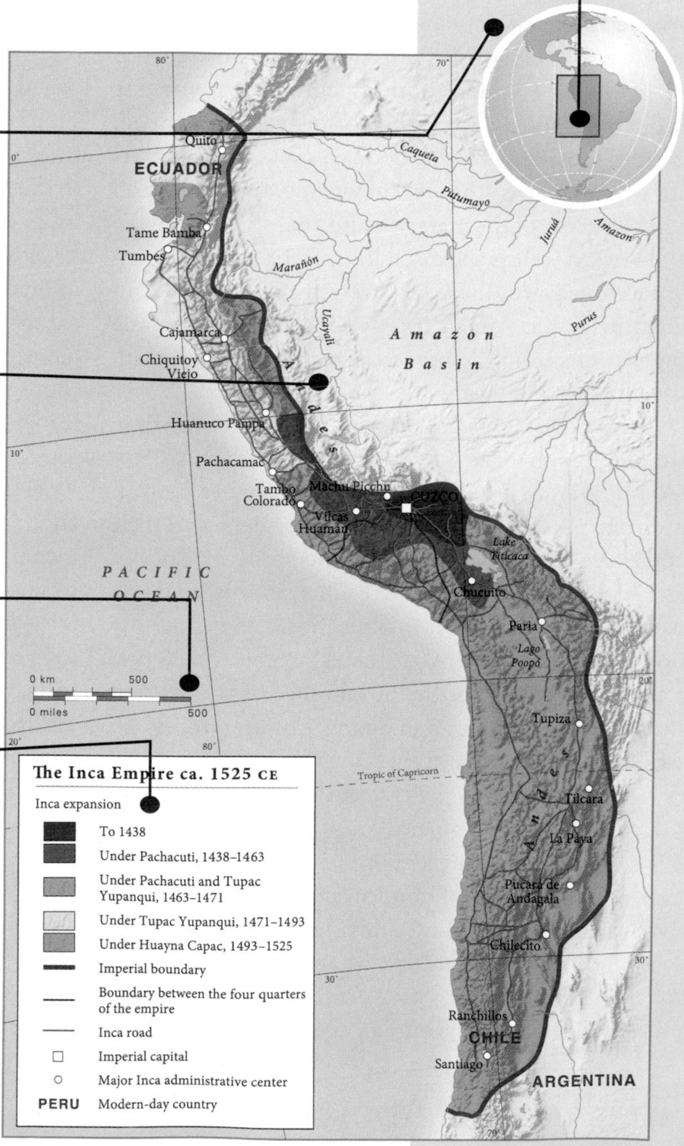

One map in each chapter is accompanied by an icon that indicates that the map can be analyzed in an interactive fashion (see pages xxv–xxvi).

Preface

The response to the first two editions of *Patterns of World History* has been extraordinarily gratifying to those of us involved in its development. The diversity of schools that have adopted the book—community colleges as well as state universities; small liberal arts schools as well as large private universities—suggests to us that its central premise of exploring *patterns* in world history is both adaptable to a variety of pedagogical environments and congenial to a wide body of instructors. Indeed, from the responses to the book we have received thus far, we expect that the level of writing, timeliness and completeness of the material, and analytical approach will serve it well as the discipline of world history continues to mature. These key strengths are enhanced in the third edition of *Patterns* by constructive, dynamic suggestions from the broad range of students and instructors who are using the book.

It is widely agreed that world history is more than simply the sum of all national histories. Likewise, *Patterns of World History*, Third Edition, is more than an unbroken sequence of dates, battles, rulers, and their activities, and it is more than the study of isolated stories of change over time. Rather, in this textbook we endeavor to present in a clear and engaging way how world history "works." Instead of merely offering a narrative history of the appearance of this or that innovation, we present an analysis of the process by which an innovation in one part of the world is diffused and carried to the rest of the globe. Instead of focusing on the memorization of people, places, and events, we strive to present important facts in context and draw meaningful connections, analyzing whatever patterns we find and drawing conclusions where we can. In short, we seek to examine the interlocking mechanisms and animating forces of world history, without neglecting the human agency behind them.

The *Patterns* Approach

Our approach in this book is, as the title suggests, to look for patterns in world history. We should say at the outset that we do not mean to select certain categories into which we attempt to stuff the historical events we choose to emphasize, nor do we claim that all world history is reducible to such patterns, nor do we mean to suggest that the nature of the patterns determines the outcome of historical events. We see them instead as broad, flexible organizational frameworks around which to build the structure of a world history in such a way that the enormous sweep and content of the past can be viewed in a comprehensible narrative, with sound analysis and ample scope for debate and discussion. In this sense, we view them much like the armatures in clay sculptures, giving support and structure to the final figure but not necessarily preordaining its ultimate shape.

From its origins, human culture grew through interactions and adaptations on all the continents except Antarctica. A voluminous scholarship on all regions of the world has thus been accumulated, which those working in the field have to attempt to master if their explanations and arguments are to sound even remotely persuasive. The sheer volume and complexity of the sources, however, mean that even the knowledge and expertise of the best scholars are going to be incomplete. Moreover, the humility with which all historians must approach their material contains within it the realization that no historical explanation is ever fully satisfactory or final: As a driving force in the historical process, creative human agency moves events in directions that are never fully predictable, even if they follow broad patterns. Learning to discern patterns in this process not only helps novice historians to appreciate the complex challenges (and rewards) of historical inquiry; it also develops critical thinking abilities in all students.

As we move through the second decade of the twenty-first century, world historians have long since left behind the "West plus the rest" approach that marked the field's early years, together with economic and geographical reductionism, in the search for a new balance between comprehensive cultural and institutional examinations on the one hand and those highlighting human agency on the other. All too often, however, this is reflected in texts that seek broad coverage at the expense of analysis, thus resulting in a kind of "world history lite." Our aim is therefore to simplify the study of the world—to make it accessible to the student—without making world history itself simplistic.

Patterns of World History, Third Edition, proposes the teaching of world history from the perspective of the relationship between continuity and change. What we advocate in this book is a distinct intellectual framework for this relationship and the role of innovation and historical change through patterns of origins, interactions, and adaptations. Each small or large technical or cultural innovation originated in one geographical center or independently in several different centers. As people in the centers interacted with their neighbors, the neighbors adapted to, and in many cases were transformed by, the innovations. By "adaptation" we include the entire spectrum of human responses, ranging from outright rejection to creative borrowing and, at times, forced acceptance.

Small technical innovations often went through the pattern of origin, interaction, and adaptation across the world without arousing much attention, even though they had major consequences. For example, the horse collar, which originated in the last centuries BCE in China and allowed for the replacement of oxen with stronger horses, gradually improved the productivity of agriculture in eleventh-century western Europe. More sweeping intellectual–cultural innovations, by contrast, such as the spread of universal religions like Buddhism, Christianity, and Islam and the rise of science, have often had profound consequences—in some cases leading to conflicts lasting centuries—and affect us even today.

Sometimes change was effected by commodities that to us seem rather ordinary. Take sugar, for example: It originated in Southeast Asia and was traded and grown in the Mediterranean, where its cultivation on plantations created the model for expansion into the vast slave system of the Atlantic basin from the fifteenth through the nineteenth centuries, forever altering the histories of four continents. What would our diets look like today without sugar? Its history continues to unfold as we debate its merits and health risks and it supports huge multinational agribusinesses.

Or take a more obscure commodity: opium. Opium had been used medicinally for centuries in regions all over the world. But the advent of tobacco traded from the Americas to the Philippines to China, and the encouragement of Dutch traders in the region, created an environment in which the drug was smoked for the first time. Enterprising rogue British merchants, eager to find a way to crack closed Chinese markets for other goods, began to smuggle it in from India. The market grew, the price went down, addiction spread, and Britain and China ultimately went to war over China's attempts to eliminate the traffic. Here, we have an example of an item generating interactions on a worldwide scale, with impacts on everything from politics to economics, culture, and even the environment. The legacies of the trade still weigh heavily on two of the rising powers of the recent decades: China and India. And opium and its derivatives, like morphine and heroin, continue to bring relief as well as suffering on a colossal scale to hundreds of millions of people.

What, then, do we gain by studying world history through the use of such patterns? First, if we consider innovation to be a driving force of history, it helps to satisfy an intrinsic human curiosity about origins—our own and others. Perhaps more importantly, seeing patterns of various kinds in historical development brings to light connections and linkages among peoples, cultures, and regions—as in the aforementioned examples—that might not otherwise present themselves.

Second, such patterns can also reveal differences among cultures that other approaches to world history tend to neglect. For example, the differences between the civilizations of the Eastern and Western Hemispheres are generally highlighted in world history texts, but the broad commonalities of human groups creating agriculturally based cities and states in widely separated areas also show deep parallels in their patterns of origins, interactions, and adaptations. Such comparisons are at the center of our approach.

Third, this kind of analysis offers insights into how an individual innovation was subsequently developed and diffused across space and time—that is, the patterns by which the new eventually becomes a necessity in our daily lives. Through all of this we gain a deeper appreciation of the unfolding of global history from its origins in small, isolated areas to the vast networks of global interconnectedness in our present world.

Finally, our use of a broad-based understanding of continuity, change, and innovation allows us to restore culture in all its individual and institutionalized aspects—spiritual, artistic, intellectual, scientific—to its rightful place alongside technology, environment, politics, and socioeconomic conditions. That is, understanding innovation in this way allows this text to help illuminate the full range of human ingenuity over time and space in a comprehensive, evenhanded, and open-ended fashion.

Options for Teaching with *Patterns of World History*, Third Edition

In response to requests from teachers who adopted the previous editions, *Patterns of World History* includes a selection of primary-text and visual sources after every chapter. This section, called "Patterns of Evidence," enhances student engagement with key chapter patterns through contemporaneous voices and perspectives. Each source is accompanied by a concise introduction to provide chronological and geographical context; "Working with Sources" questions after each selection prompt students to make critical connections between the source and the main chapter narrative.

For the convenience of instructors teaching a course over two 15-week semesters, both versions of *Patterns* are limited to 31 chapters. For the sake of continuity and to accommodate the many different ways schools divide the midpoint of their world history sequence, Chapters 15–18 overlap in both volumes; in Volume 2, Chapter 15 is given as a "prelude" to Part Four. Those using a trimester system will also find divisions made in convenient places, with Chapter 10 coming at the beginning of Part Two and Chapter 22 at the beginning of Part Five. Finally, a Brief Edition of *Patterns* is also available. The Brief Edition is 25 percent shorter in length and does not include end-of-chapter primary sources..

Patterns of Change and Six Periods of World History

Similarly, *Patterns* is adaptable to both chronological and thematic styles of instruction. We divide the history of the world into six major time periods and recognize for each period one or two main patterns of innovation, their spread through interaction, and their adoption by others. Obviously, lesser patterns are identified as well, many of which are of more limited regional interactive and adaptive impact. We wish to stress again that these are broad categories of analysis and that there is nothing reductive or deterministic in our aims or choices. Nevertheless, we believe the patterns we have chosen help to make the historical process more intelligible, providing a series of lenses that can help to focus the otherwise confusing facts and disparate details that comprise world history.

Part One (Prehistory–600 BCE): Origins of human civilization—tool making and symbol creating—in Africa as well as the origins of agriculture, urbanism, and state formation in the three agrarian centers of the Middle East, India, and China.

Part Two (600 BCE–600 CE): Emergence of the axial-age thinkers and their visions of a transcendent god or first principle in Eurasia; elevation of these visions to the status of state religions in empires and kingdoms, in the process forming multiethnic and multilinguistic polities.

Part Three (600–1450): Disintegration of classical empires and formation of religious civilizations in Eurasia, with the emergence of religiously unified regions divided by commonwealths of multiple states.

Part Four (1450–1750): Rise of new empires; interaction, both hostile and peaceful, among the religious civilizations and new empires across all continents of the world. Origins of the New Science in Europe, based on the use of mathematics for the investigation of nature.

Part Five (1750–1900): Origins of scientific–industrial "modernity," simultaneous with the emergence of constitutional and ethnic nation-states, in the West (Europe and North America); interaction of the West with Asia and Africa, resulting in complex adaptations, both coerced as well as voluntary, on the part of the latter.

Part Six (1900–Present): Division of early Western modernity into the three competing visions: communism, supremacist nationalism, and capitalism. After two horrific world wars and the triumph of nation-state formation across the world, capitalism remains as the last surviving version of modernity. Capitalism is then reinvigorated by the increasing use of social networking tools, which popularizes both "traditional" religious and cultural ideas and constitutionalism in authoritarian states.

Chapter Organization and Structure

Each part of the book addresses the role of change and innovation on a broad scale in a particular time and/or region, and each chapter contains different levels of exploration to examine the principal features of particular cultural or national areas and how each affects, and is affected by, the patterns of origins, interactions, and adaptations:

- *Geography and the Environment*: The relationship between human beings and the geography and environment of the places they inhabit is among the most basic factors in understanding human societies. In this chapter segment, therefore, the topics under investigation involve the natural environment of a particular region and the general conditions affecting change and innovation. Climatic conditions, earthquakes, tsunamis, volcanic eruptions, outbreaks of disease, and so forth all have obvious effects on how humans react to the challenge of survival. The initial portions of chapters introducing new regions for study therefore include environmental and geographical overviews, which are revisited and expanded in later chapters as necessary. The larger issues of how decisive the impact of geography on the development of human societies is—as in the commonly asked question "Is geography destiny?"—are also examined here.
- *Political Developments:* In this segment, we ponder such questions as how rulers and their supporters wield political and military power. How do different political traditions develop in different areas? How do states expand, and why? How do different political arrangements attempt to strike a balance between the rulers and the ruled? How and why are political innovations transmitted to other societies? Why do societies accept or reject such innovations from the outside? Are there discernible patterns in the development of kingdoms or empires or nation-states?
- *Economic and Social Developments*: The relationship between economics and the structures and workings of societies has long been regarded as crucial by historians and social scientists. But what patterns, if any, emerge in how these relationships develop and function among different cultures? This segment explores such questions as the following: What role does economics play in the dynamics of change and continuity? What, for example, happens in agrarian societies when merchant classes develop? How does the accumulation of wealth lead to social hierarchy? What forms do these hierarchies take? How do societies formally and informally try to regulate wealth and poverty? How are economic conditions reflected in family life and gender relations? Are there patterns that reflect the varying social positions of men and women that are characteristic of certain economic and social institutions? How are these in turn affected by different cultural practices?
- *Intellectual, Religious, and Cultural Aspects*: Finally, we consider it vital to include an examination dealing in some depth with the way people understood their existence and life during each period. Clearly, intellectual innovation—the generation of new ideas—lies at the heart of the changes we have singled out as pivotal in the patterns of origins, interactions, and adaptations that form the heart of this text. Beyond this, those areas concerned with the search for and construction of meaning—particularly religion, the arts, philosophy, and science—not only reflect shifting perspectives but also, in many cases, play a leading role in determining the course of events within each form of society. All of these facets of intellectual life are in turn manifested in new perspectives and representations in the cultural life of a society.

Features

- **Seeing Patterns/Thinking Through Patterns:** "Seeing Patterns" and "Thinking Through Patterns" use a question–discussion format in each chapter to pose several broad questions ("Seeing Patterns") as advance organizers for key themes, which are then matched up with short essays at the end ("Thinking Through Patterns") that examine these same questions in a sophisticated yet student-friendly fashion.

- **Patterns Up Close:** Since students frequently apprehend macro-level patterns better when they see their contours brought into sharper relief, "Patterns Up Close" essays in each chapter highlight a particular innovation that demonstrates origins, interactions, and adaptations in action. Spanning technological, social, political, intellectual, economic, and environmental developments, the "Patterns Up Close" essays combine text, visuals, and graphics to consider everything from the pepper trade to the guillotine.
- **Against the Grain:** These brief essays consider counterpoints to the main patterns examined in each chapter. Topics range from visionaries who challenged dominant religious patterns, to women who resisted various forms of patriarchy, to agitators who fought for social and economic justice.
- **Marginal Glossary:** To avoid the necessity of having to flip pages back and forth, definitions of key terms are set directly in the margin at the point where they are first introduced.

Today, more than ever, students and instructors are confronted by a vast welter of information on every conceivable subject. Beyond the ever-expanding print media, the Internet and the Web have opened hitherto unimaginable amounts of data to us. Despite such unprecedented access, however, all of us are too frequently overwhelmed by this undifferentiated—and all too often indigestible—mass. Nowhere is this more true than in world history, by definition the field within the historical profession with the broadest scope. Therefore, we think that an effort at synthesis—of narrative and analysis structured around a clear, accessible, widely applicable theme—is needed, an effort that seeks to explain critical patterns of the world's past behind the billions of bits of information accessible at the stroke of a key on a computer keyboard. We hope this text, in tracing the lines of transformative ideas and things that left their patterns deeply imprinted into the canvas of world history, will provide such a synthesis.

Changes to the Third Edition

Streamlined narrative and sharpened focus To facilitate accessibility, we have shortened the text wherever possible. This reduction has not come at the expense of discarding essential topics. Instead, we have tightened the narrative, focusing even more on key concepts and (with the guidance of reviewers) discarding extraneous examples. We are profoundly grateful to the reviewers who pointed out errors and conceptual shortcomings. Factual accuracy and terminological precision are extremely important to us.

Updated scholarship All chapters were revised and updated, in accordance with recent developments and new scholarship. Here is a chapter-by-chapter overview that highlights the changes we made in the third edition:

- **Part One** Chapter 1 includes three major changes: a discussion of the new stone tool finds in Kenya, dated to 3.3 million years ago; revisions to our understanding of the Neanderthals, on the basis of the new Bruniquel Cave finds; and revisions to our understanding of the human settlement of the Americas, resulting from new genetic studies (2015–2016). Chapter 2 clarifies the conceptual transition from nature spirituality to what is commonly called polytheism. Chapter 3 updates the material on ancient India and Harappans, and the "Patterns Up Close" in Chapter 5 adds the results of a new 2016 genetic study on corn.
- **Part Two** The title of Chapter 7 has been changed to "Interaction and Adaptation in Western Eurasia: Persia, Greece, and Rome" to more emphatically show the interactions among these cultural zones. Chapter 8 contains a revised section on Jainism, and Chapter 9 adds a survey of the contemporary debate about the "Han Synthesis."
- **Part Three** Chapter 10 offers clearer discussions of the Arab conquests of the Middle East, North Africa, and Iberia during the 600s and early 700s as well as of the composition of Islamic salvation history in the 800s, including the biography of the Prophet Muhammad. The coverage of

Byzantium is improved with a discussion of iconoclasm and the split between Catholicism and Greek Orthodoxy in 1054. Chapter 12 focuses more strongly on the Mongol interval and adds specificity to the discussion of Neo-Confucian philosophy. The coverage of the Mongols has been increased in Chapter 12, and the new chapter title, "Contrasting Patterns in India, China, and Inner Asia," reflects these changes.

- **Part Four** In Chapter 17 we eliminated considerable detail from the presentation of the European religious wars and broadened the focus in the English case to include the War of the Three Kingdoms. Chapter 21 updates the discussion of the Chinese rural economy and the debate about the High Level Equilibrium Trap. It also improves the discussion of Qing concepts of multicultural empire.
- **Part Five** In Chapter 22 the basic concepts of modern nationalism are reformulated: We now distinguish between the patterns of constitutionalism and ethnic nationalism as keys for the understanding of political modernity. In addition, the process of Italian ethnic nationalist unification is presented more clearly. Chapter 23 is completely reorganized, emphasizing in addition the significance of the Paraguayan War of 1864–1870. In Chapter 24, the role of the Hakkas in the Taiping movement is described more clearly. Chapter 26 emphasizes the importance of the steam engine in the Industrial Revolution more strongly and reconceptualizes the nineteenth-century class structure in the emerging industrial societies. Chapter 27 defines more sharply the pattern of the New Imperialism during the nineteenth century.
- **Part Six** Chapter 29 updates the "Patterns Up Close" feature on the Non-Aligned Movement. In Chapter 30 we shortened the text so as to create room for an improved coverage of the Lebanese civil war, the Iranian Islamic Revolution, the US Vietnam War, and the Brazilian economic miracle. In Chapter 31, we similarly removed text and replaced it with paragraphs on the travails of the Arab Spring, the new military regime in Egypt, the "Islamic State" of Iraq and Syria, the failed coup d'état in Turkey, as well as the new populist anti-globalism, complete with "Brexit" in Europe and Donald J. Trump's electoral victory in the United States. The "Patterns Up Close" essay on information technology was updated to include IT's misuse by terrorists.

Ensuring Student Success

Oxford University Press offers instructors and students a comprehensive ancillary package for qualified adopters

- **Dashboard:** Simple, informative, and mobile, Dashboard is an online learning and assessment platform tailored to your textbook that delivers a simple, informative, and mobile experience for professors and students. It offers quality content and tools to track student progress in an intuitive, web-based learning environment; features a streamlined interface that connects students and instructors with the most important course functions; and simplifies the learning experience to save time and put student progress first. Dashboard for *Patterns of World History,* Third Edition, includes:

- An embedded e-book that integrates multimedia content, providing a dynamic learning space for both students and instructors. Each chapter in *Patterns of World History* includes:

  - image analysis
  - document analysis
  - map analysis, interactive timelines, and interactive concept maps
  - Many chapters also include video analysis
  - audio flashcards

- Three sets of quizzes per ch... both low stakes and high stakes t... quizzes are aligned according t... taxonomy: quiz

1 tests basic concepts and terminologies; quiz 2 provides questions that test both basic facts and ability to apply concepts; quiz 3 tests ability to evaluate and analyze key concepts.

- The complete set of questions from the testbank (1,500 questions), that provide for each chapter, approximately 40 multiple-choice, short-answer, true-or-false, and fill-in-the-blank as well as approximately 10 essay questions.

For more information about Dashboard, contact your Oxford University Press Representative or call 800.280.0280.

- **Ancillary Resource Center (ARC):** This online resource center, available to adopters of *Patterns of World History,* includes:
- **Instructor's Resource Manual:** Includes, for each chapter, a detailed chapter outline, suggested lecture topics, learning objectives, map quizzes, geography exercises, classroom activities, "Patterns Up Close" activities, "Seeing Patterns and Making Connections" activities, "Against the Grain" exercises, biographical sketches, and suggested Web resources and digital media files. Also includes for each chapter approximately 40 multiple-choice, short-answer, true-or-false, and fill-in-the-blank as well as approximately 10 essay questions.
- **Oxford World History Video Library:** Includes short, two- to three-minute videos that offer overviews of such key topics as the the Golden Age of Islam, Genghis Khan, the steam engine, and the atomic age.
- **PowerPoints:** Includes PowerPoint slides and JPEG and PDF files for all the maps and photos in the text, an additional 400 map files from *The Oxford Atlas of World History,* and approximately 1000 additional PowerPoint-based slides from OUP's Image Bank Library, organized by themes and topics in world history.
- **Computerized testbank:** Includes approximately 1,500 questions that can be customized [illegible] the instructor.
- [illegible] **cartridges** containing student and in[illegible] [illegible]sources are available for the most com[illegible] [illegible]ourse management systems.

Additional Learning Resources

- ***Sources in Patterns of World History:* Volume 1: To 1600:** Includes approximately 75 text and visual sources in world history, organized by the chapter organization of *Patterns of World History.* Each source is accompanied by a headnote and reading questions.
- ***Sources in Patterns of World History:* Volume 2: Since 1400:** Includes approximately 90 text and visual sources in world history, organized by the chapter organization of *Patterns of World History.* Each source is accompanied by a headnote and reading questions.
- ***Mapping Patterns of World History,* Volume 1: To 1600:** Includes approximately 50 full-color maps, each accompanied by a brief headnote, as well as blank outline maps and Concept Map exercises.
- ***Mapping Patterns of World History,* Volume 2: Since 1400:** Includes approximately 50 full-color maps, each accompanied by a brief headnote, as well as blank outline maps and Concept Map exercises.
- ***Now Playing: Learning World History Through Film:*** Designed specifically to accompany Patterns of World History, this free supplement examines thirty-two films to show how key themes in world history play out in a variety of time periods and contexts.
- **Open Access Companion Website (www.oup.com/us/vonsivers):** Includes quizzes, notetaking guides, and flashcards.
- **E-book for Patterns of World History:** E-books of all the volumes, at a significant discount, are available for purchase at www.redshelf.com or www.vitalsource.com.

Bundling Options

Patterns of World History can be bundled at a significant discount with any of the titles in the popular Very Short Introductions, World in a Life, or Oxford World's Classics series, as well as other titles from the Higher Education division world history catalog (www.oup.com/us/catalog/he). Please contact your OUP representative for details.

Patterns of World History, Brief Third Edition

A brief edition of *Patterns of World History* based on the same content as this volume is available. Please contact your local Oxford University Press representative for additional information.

Acknowledgments

Throughout the course of writing, revising, and preparing *Patterns of World History* for publication we have benefited from the guidance and professionalism accorded us by all levels of the staff at Oxford University Press. John Challice, vice president and publisher, had faith in the inherent worth of our project from the outset and provided the initial impetus to move forward. Meg Botteon guided us through the revisions and added a final polish, often helping us with substantive suggestions. Katherine Schnakenberg carried out the thankless task of assembling the manuscript and did so with generosity and good cheer, helping us with many details in the final manuscript. Keith Faivre steered us through the intricacies of production with the stoicism of a saint.

Most of all, we owe a special debt of gratitude to Charles Cavaliere, our editor. Charles took on the daunting task of directing the literary enterprise at a critical point in the book's career. He pushed this project to its successful completion, accelerated its schedule, and used a combination of flattery and hard-nosed tactics to make sure we stayed the course. His greatest contribution, however, is in the way he refined our original vision for the book with several important adjustments that clarified its latent possibilities. From the maps to the photos to the special features, Charles's high standards and concern for detail are evident on every page.

Developing a book like *Patterns of World History* is an ambitious project, a collaborative venture in which authors and editors benefit from the feedback provided by a team of outside readers and consultants. We gratefully acknowledge the advice that the many reviewers, focus group participants, and class testers (including their students) shared with us along the way. We tried to implement all of the excellent suggestions. We owe a special debt of thanks to Evan R. Ward, who provided invaluable guidance for the revision of the coverage of Latin America and the Caribbean in Part 5, and to Jonathan S. Perry, who deftly assembled the documents. Of course, any errors of fact or interpretation that remain are solely our own.

Reviewers of the Third Edition

Kevin Eoff, Palo Verde College

Christina Firpo, CalPoly University

Aaron Hagler, Troy University

Ephraim Harel, Montgomery College, Rockville

Michael Markus, Alabama State University

Scott Merriman, Troy University

Curtis Morgan, Lord Fairfax Community College

Joanna Neilson, Lincoln Memorial University

Jahan Salehi, Central Piedmont Community College

William Skiles, California State University, San Marcos

Marika Snider, Miami University

Daniel Stephen, Colorado State University

Jason Tatlock, Armstrong State University

Michael Thensted, Mississippi Gulf Coast Community College

Walter Ward, University of Alabama at Birmingham

Paul Tenkotte, Northern Kentucky University

Daniel R. Pavese, Wor-Wic Community College

and one anonymous reviewer.

Please let us know your experiences with *Patterns of World History* so that we may improve it in future editions. We welcome your comments and suggestions.

Peter von Sivers
pv4910@xmission.com

Charles A. Desnoyers
desnoyer@lasalle.edu

George B. Stow
gbsgeorge@aol.com

Note on Dates and Spellings

In keeping with widespread practice among world historians, we use "BCE" and "CE" to date events and the phrase "years ago" to describe developments from the remote past.

The transliteration of Middle Eastern words has been adjusted as much as possible to the English alphabet. Therefore, long vowels are not emphasized. The consonants specific to Arabic (alif, dhal, ha, sad, dad, ta, za, `ayn, ghayn, and qaf) are either not indicated or rendered with common English letters. A similar procedure is followed for Farsi. Turkish words follow the alphabet reform of 1929, which adds the following letters to the Western alphabet or modifies their pronunciation: *c* (pronounced "j"), *ç* (pronounced "tsh"), *ğ* (not pronounced but lengthening of preceding vowel), *ı* ("i" without dot, pronunciation close to short e), *i/İ* ("i" with dot, including in caps), ö (no English equivalent), *ş* ("sh"), and *ü* (no English equivalent). The spelling of common contemporary Middle Eastern and Islamic terms follows daily press usage (which, however, is not completely uniform). Examples are "al-Qaeda," "Quran," and "Sharia."

The system used in rendering the sounds of Mandarin Chinese—the northern Chinese dialect that has become in effect the national spoken language in China and Taiwan—into English in this book is *hanyu pinyin,* usually given as simply pinyin. This is the official romanization system of the People's Republic of China and has also become the standard outside of Taiwan, Republic of China. Most syllables are pronounced as they would be in English, with the exception of the letter *q,* which has an aspirated "ch" sound; ch itself has a less aspirated "ch" sound. *Zh* carries a hard "j" and *j* a soft, English-style "j." Some syllables also are pronounced—particularly in the regions around Beijing—with a retroflex r so that the syllable *shi,* for example, carries a pronunciation closer to "shir." Finally, the letter *r* in the *pinyin* system has no direct English equivalent, but an approximation may be had by combining the sounds of "r" and "j."

Japanese terms have been romanized according to a modification of the Hepburn system. The letter *g* is always hard; vowels are handled as they are in Italian—*e,* for example, carries a sound like "ay." We have not, however, included diacritical markings to indicate long vowel sounds for *u* or *o.* Where necessary, these have been indicated in the pronunciation guides.

For Korean terms, we have used a variation of the McCune-Reischauer system, which remains the standard romanization scheme for Korean words used in English academic writing, but eliminated any diacritical markings. Here again, the vowel sounds are pronounced more or less like those of Italian and the consonants, like those of English.

For Vietnamese words, we have used standard renditions based on the modern Quoc Ngu ("national language") system in use in Vietnam today. The system was developed by Jesuit missionaries and is based on the Portuguese alphabet. Once more, we have avoided diacritical marks, and the reader should follow the pronunciation guides for approximations of Vietnamese terms.

Latin American terms (Spanish, Nahua, or Quechua) generally follow local usage, including accents, except where they are Anglicized, per the *Oxford English Dictionary.* Thus, the Spanish-Quechua word "Tiahuanacu" becomes the Anglicized word "Tiwanaku."

We use the terms "Native American" and "Indian" interchangeably to refer to the peoples of the Americas in the pre-Columbian period and "Amerindian" in our coverage of Latin America since independence.

In keeping with widely recognized practice among paleontologists and other scholars of the deep past, we use the term "hominins" in Chapter 1 to emphasize their greater remoteness from apes and proximity to modern humans.

Phonetic spellings often follow the first appearance of a non-English word whose pronunciation may be unclear to the reader. We have followed the rules for capitalization per *The Chicago Manual of Style.*

About the Authors

Peter von Sivers is associate professor of Middle Eastern history at the University of Utah. He has previously taught at UCLA, Northwestern University, the University of Paris VII (Vincennes), and the University of Munich. He has also served as chair of the Joint Committee of the Near and Middle East, Social Science Research Council, New York, 1982–1985; editor of the *International Journal of Middle East Studies*, 1985–1989; member of the board of directors of the Middle East Studies Association of North America, 1987–1990; and chair of the SAT II World History Test Development Community of the Educational Testing Service, Princeton, NJ, 1991–1994. His publications include *Caliphate, Kingdom, and Decline: The Political Theory of Ibn Khaldun* (1968), several edited books, and three dozen peer-reviewed chapters and articles on Middle Eastern and North African history, as well as world history. He received his Dr. phil. from the University of Munich.

Charles A. Desnoyers is professor of history and director of Asian Studies at La Salle University in Philadelphia. He has previously taught at Temple University, Villanova University, and Pennsylvania State University. In addition to serving as History Department chair from 1999–2007, he was a founder and long-time director of the Greater Philadelphia Asian Studies Consortium, and president (2011–2012) of the Mid-Atlantic Region Association for Asian Studies. He has served as a reader, table leader, and question writer for the AP European and World History exams. He served as editor of the organization's *Bulletin* from 1995–2001. In addition to numerous articles in peer-reviewed and general publications, his work includes *Patterns of Modern Chinese History* (2016, Oxford University Press) and *A Journey to the East: Li Gui's "A New Account of a Trip Around the Globe"* (2004, University of Michigan Press). He received his PhD from Temple University.

George B. Stow is professor of ancient and medieval history and director of the graduate program in history at La Salle University, Philadelphia. His teaching experience embraces a variety of undergraduate and graduate courses in ancient Greece and Rome, medieval England, and world history, and he has been awarded the Lindback Distinguished Teaching Award. Professor Stow is a member of the Medieval Academy of America and a Fellow of the Royal Historical Society. He is the recipient of a National Defense Education Act Title IV Fellowship, a Woodrow Wilson Foundation Fellowship, and research grants from the American Philosophical Society and La Salle University. His publications include a critical edition of a fourteenth-century monastic chronicle, *Historia Vitae et Regni Ricardi Secundi* (University of Pennsylvania Press, 1977), as well as numerous articles and reviews in scholarly journals including *Speculum*, *The English Historical Review*, the *Journal of Medieval History*, the *American Historical Review*, and several others. He received his PhD from the University of Illinois.

Patterns of World History

PART ONE

From Human Origins to Early Agricultural Centers

PREHISTORY–600 BCE

World history is the discipline that tells us what humans had in common as they evolved both materially and mentally from prehistory to the present. When we study these common patterns, we find that the first period of world history (prehistory–600 BCE) can be subdivided into three wide-ranging phases, which we will discuss very broadly in this part-opening essay. We will return to these same patterns as they develop—and discover new, more complex patterns—in Chapters 1–5.

The Origins of Modern Humanity

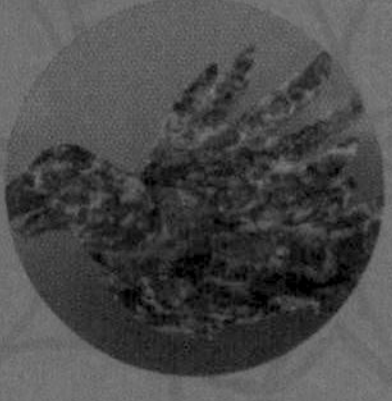

The first phase (6.5 million years ago–8500 BCE) began with the origins and evolution of humanity in Africa. After about 5.5 million years, around 80,000–50,000 BCE, groups of modern humans left Africa and began carrying their civilization of stone tools, shell jewelry, figurines, carvings, rock paintings, and religious symbols across the entire world.

Technologically, the modern humans who left Africa had already acquired the skills to make tools from stone, bone, and wood. Mentally, they were also creating artifacts to which they attributed symbolic meaning, such as seashell necklaces and stone surfaces incised with geometric figures. The tools and artifacts of our earliest ancestors were obviously far less sophisticated than ours today. But they nevertheless defined a fully human civilization that spread across the globe—until the last Ice Age (32,000–12,000 years ago) put a stop to much of their interactions. Separated by impenetrable ice or desert barriers and existing without much contact for thousands of years, modern human groups developed their own distinct regional technologies and cultures.

Wherever our forager forebears were, they organized themselves into larger lineage societies with shared initiation rites and members who mediated the material and spiritual worlds. Even the stone tools, jewelry, figurines, and rock images displayed remarkable similarities across their respective regions. In short, African-originated material technology and mental culture dominated the world.

Origins, Interactions, and Adaptations

7 million years ago
Toumaï, oldest possibly hominin fossil to date

300,000 years ago
Homo sapiens, or Modern Human, emerges in East Africa

15,500 years ago
Earliest archaeological evidence of humans in the Americas

9500 BCE
End of last ice age

The Origins of Agricultural Centers

The second phase (8500–3300 BCE) began once the global climate normalized, after the "great thaw," when agricultural centers originated in the Middle East, South and East Asia, and the Americas. In the Middle East, foragers resumed their migratory patterns, carrying their languages into regions opened up by receding glaciers and deserts. Between 8500 and 7000 BCE, foragers settled in permanent villages situated below mountain ranges, where seasonal runoff water supported rich forests and meadows. They grew skilled in the collection of plant seeds, which they developed, through selective breeding, into domesticated wheat, barley, rice, millet, and corn. They also captured young animals and domesticated them in their houses and pens for their meat, milk, and hair.

Some of the early hill farmers moved into river valleys and deltas, where they expanded irrigation systems, supporting the rise of cities and kingdoms. The first agrarian–urban centers of the Middle East, India, China, and the Americas originated in irrigated river valleys between 3500 and 2500 BCE. Structured societies emerged in which kings, claiming divine mandates, and administrative and military ruling classes governed craftspeople and farmers.

The Origins of Empires

In the third phase, people outside the Eurasian agrarian centers adapted to agriculture through interaction with the agrarian–urban centers (3300–600 BCE). Steppe peoples, who controlled the mines containing the raw materials for making bronze alloys, used their horses and bronze weapons to migrate to, conquer, or establish new, distant kingdoms. Through their migrations or conquests, the nomadic steppe peoples of Europe and central Asia connected the three agrarian centers of the Middle East, India, and China. A pattern was established whereby the three centers were continuously adapting to each other's technological and cultural achievements, with steppe nomads functioning as their intermediaries.

From 1100 BCE onward the three Asian agrarian centers gradually replaced bronze with a cheaper metal, iron, as the principal material for weapons and tools. As a result, political and military competitiveness among kingdoms escalated dramatically. The first empires—that is, assemblages of conquered kingdoms under a king-of-kings or emperor—appeared; for example, the Neo-Assyrian Empire in the Middle East. Meanwhile, in some regions of the more sparsely populated continents of Africa and the Americas, agrarian centers grew more slowly, from villages to towns and, in a few places, even small kingdoms.

Thinking Like a World Historian

- What is the best way to describe the three early phases of world history?
- Why and how do we differentiate "modern" humans from earlier ancestors?
- What adaptations were necessary to improve agriculture? How did improvements in agriculture affect the development of society?
- What adaptations changed the methods of early warfare? How did developments in warfare affect regional interactions among civilizations?
- How did regional interactions with agricultural centers give rise to early kingdoms?

8500 BCE Beginnings of agriculture in Fertile Crescent

ca. 7000 BCE First evidence of rice cultivation in Yangzi valley

3000 BCE–200 CE Lapita cultural complex in western Pacific

ca. 2700 BCE First American city at Caral-Supe in Peru

2500–1700 BCE Flourishing of Harappan culture in Indus River valley, India

1766–1122 BCE Traditional dates for the Shang dynasty

1650 BCE Hittite Empire

1200 BCE Beginning of Iron Age

750–600 BCE Greek city-states: from aristocrats to citizen assemblies

interactive timeline

Chapter 1 **PREHISTORY–10,000 BCE**

The African Origins of Humanity

When Donald Johanson awoke in his tent on the morning of November 30, 1974, he felt that this was the day on which something "terrific" might happen. He and Tom Gray got into their Land Rover and drove for about a half hour to "locality 162" at Hadar in the Afar desert of Ethiopia in northeastern Africa. Once there, the two men walked about, checking the ground carefully for fossils of human predecessors. Members of the expedition had gone over the ground twice before but failed to find anything beyond animal bones.

After 2 hours of fruitless searching, with the temperature now soaring to 110 degrees Fahrenheit, the two took a final glance at a gully the team had visited not long before. Amid the heat waves shimmering off the baked ground, Johanson found himself squinting at something out of place and called out, "That's a bit of an [hominin] arm." With growing excitement, he and Gray began to locate other bones nearby. "An unbelievable, impermissible thought flickered through my mind," Johanson remembered. "Suppose all these fitted together? Could they be parts of a single, extremely primitive skeleton? No such skeleton had ever been found—anywhere." The two raced back to the camp, sharing their excitement with the other scientists and local Afar workers. When night fell and the camp was rocking with joy, a tape recorder was playing the Beatles' song "Lucy in the Sky with Diamonds"; so fossil Hadar AL 288-1, dated to 3.2 million years ago, became known ever after as "Lucy."

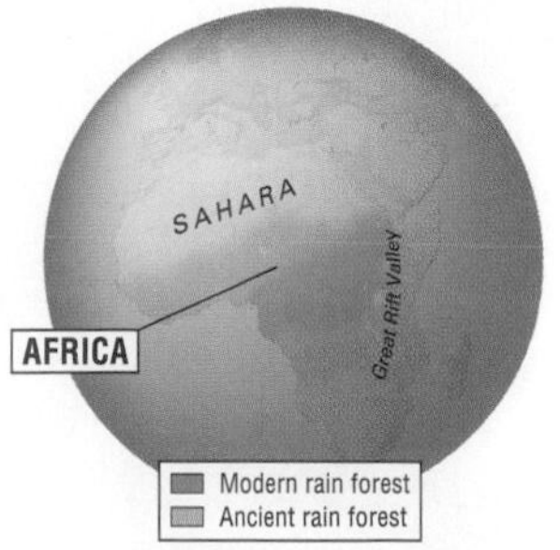

***ABOVE:* Satellite View Southward Across the African Rift Valley.**

Today, a quarter century later, Lucy is neither the oldest nor the most significant skeleton ever found. She remains the most famous, however. Many of the local people in the Afar region still think of Lucy as the ancestor of all humankind. Cafés in Ethiopia carry the name "Lossy" in her honor. Her image has appeared on stamps, and her name is a staple in crossword puzzles. For many people Lucy—the petite female buried for 3.2 million years in a sandbank on the edge of a former lake or stream—is all they know about human origins.

The story of Lucy provides our entry into the study of the origins and evolution of humankind. In the course of millions of years of interactions among cooling climates, more differentiated environments, and genetic changes favoring larger brains, splits among hominin lineages produced lines of early humans who could fashion at first simple, and later more sophisticated, stone tools. From among other lineages back in Africa, finally the line of anatomically and intellectually modern humans evolved who fashioned cultural artifacts such as jewelry, geometric figures cut into stone, and rock drawings. Once more, humans left Africa and settled the world, not only Eurasia but also Australia and the Americas. For the first time in the history of life on earth, a single species was no longer completely bound to the forces of evolution and its interplay between environment and genetics. These first modern humans had become cultural beings, by means of which they had acquired a measure of freedom from evolution: Instead of nature writing their history, they could create their own human history—the world history you are about to enter with this book.

Seeing Patterns

» **What made it possible for *Homo sapiens* to survive in a dangerous environment? Why is it difficult to imagine life as a prehistoric forager?**

» **Where did humans go when they left Africa, and what kinds of lives did they establish for themselves in the areas where they settled? Which were the most important social patterns that evolved, and how were the humans impacted by the worsening Ice Age?**

» **Why did early humans create cave paintings and figurines? Do these show patterns that can be interpreted?**

The Origins of Humanity

Becoming human was a long and arduous journey. In the interactions between climate, environment, and genes, every evolutionary step had to build successively on every preceding one so that *anatomically*, as well as *intellectually*, fully evolved modern humans could emerge in Africa about 100,000 years ago. Nothing in this journey was predetermined, but it was also not accidental, given what we know about the genetic architecture of human DNA. It is open ended, as is the human history which followed the emergence of modern humans. Both evolution and history display recognizable patterns, but these patterns neither were preprogrammed nor occurred by happenstance—they included both predictable and spontaneous occurrences resulting from the constraints and opportunities offered by the interaction of climate, environment, and genes. As we will see throughout this book, however, history equally depends on human agency and its resulting actions. Human prehistory is significant for us today because, thanks to much work done by archaeologists and anthropologists, we are beginning to recognize the complexity of all that had to happen on our evolutionary path to make us fully human: to reach the point where we could become the active creators of our world.

"Not all Hominids are Human Beings," David Johanson and Maitland A. Edey

Chapter Outline

- The Origins of Humanity
- Human Adaptations: From Africa to Eurasia and Australia
- The Ice Age Crisis and Human Migration to the Americas
- Putting It All Together

Hominins: Forerunners of humans after genetically splitting from the chimpanzees.

Hominins: No Longer Chimpanzees but Not Yet Human

Modern humans are the descendants of long lines of early human-like primates called **hominins**, which in the distant past lived in East Africa. The line of hominins split from that of the other apes sometime around 5 million years ago, but the fossil record is still too poor to allow definite conclusions. Equally unclear is the parentage among the 20 or so species of hominins coming thereafter, which paleoanthropologists (as the archaeologists and researchers of fossils are called) have discovered so far. The fog begins to lift only around 1.8 million years ago, with the emergence of *Homo erectus*, the first hominin that left Africa and was adaptable to many new environments in Eurasia. It thus took some 3 million years of dead ends as well as environmentally more adaptable forerunners of humans to pave the way for the human species to emerge.

Many historians view the *pre*history of humans as a field belonging to archaeologists and anthropologists. For these historians, *history* begins only with the rise of the first cities in Mesopotamia around 3500 BCE in which scribes created written documents. This view is unfortunate since historians routinely take the findings of scholars in other disciplines, such as archaeology, anthropology, climatology, geography, medicine, and sociology, into consideration when they write histories on topics after about 3500 BCE. Since written records, furthermore, are highly unreliable documents—subject to manipulation by human hand subsequent to their original production—historians regularly take recourse to the more reliable findings of other disciplines wherever they can. Indeed, in the twenty-first century historians with broad visions have pleaded persuasively for eliminating the artificial distinction between prehistory and history. They speak instead—as the medieval cultural historian Daniel Lord Smail does—of the "deep history" of humanity.

Oldest Stone Tools to Date. Discovered in Kenya at the Lomekwi 3 archaeological site in the Turkana Basin, these tools are 3.3 million years old.

Who Are Our Ancestors? The specific environmental and genetic interactions favorable for the split between hominin and other ape lines are complex. We know that changes in the climate between warm and cool cycles played a part, which were reflected in the African rain forest advancing and retreating. It is also known that it took about 1 million years, from 5 to 4 million years ago according to the genetic clock, and a fairly large population of 50,000–70,000 animals for the split between the chimpanzees in the ape line and the first hominins to begin and be completed. The genetic clock, however, is not only not beyond controversy; it is also not synchronized with the three oldest known tropical African fossils which seem to depart from the rest of the ape line. The Toumaï skull (7–6 million years old), Orrorin femurs (6.1–5.7 million years old), and Kaddaba teeth (5.8–5.4 million years) seem to indicate hominin features. But whether the three can be counted as having belonged to human ancestors is still fiercely debated.

Firmer ground on the road to humanity is reached with Ardi (*Ardipithecus ramidus,* 4.5–4.3 million years ago), a descendant of Kaddaba. If the genetic clock is correct, the members of this lineage lived on the hominin side of the chimpanzee–hominin split. In their home in the tropical rain forests and savannas of East Africa, their capability for straight-limbed tree-walking allowed them to move easily back and forth between these two environments. In the dense rain forest, most apes flexed their hind legs as they stood on branches, hanging on with one hand to the tree while reaching with the other hand for fruits or for branches of the next tree to swing to. In the less dense savanna tree stands, hominins could lean over and reach farther by standing on straight legs. Ardis with their straight legs transferred their branch-walking to the ground, which allowed them to step out of the rain forest and walk upright in the savanna for extended periods. They thereby substantially increased their adaptability to a variety of environments, especially during dry periods when the rain forest shrank. Most other apes, by contrast, stayed on their traditional home turf of rain forest, where they learned how to knuckle-walk on the ground for short distances, between more distant trees.

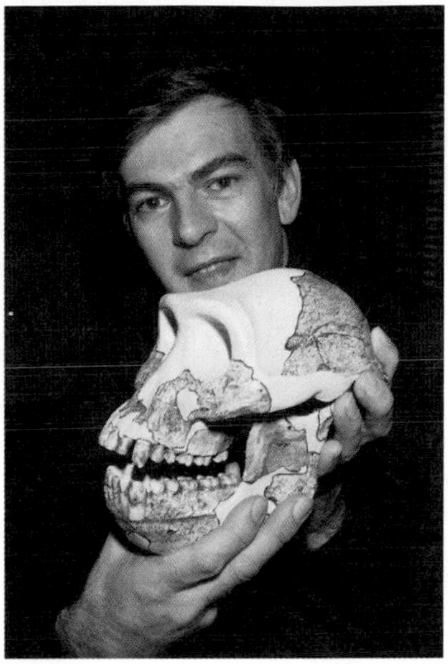

Human Origins. Donald Johanson with Lucy.

Ardis apparently were not able yet to venture very far into drier environments. After only 200,000 years they were replaced by a different species, the **australopiths** (scientific name *Australopithecus*). These hominins date to 3.9–1.8 million years ago and were widespread, with hundreds of fossil sites ranging from Ethiopia to South Africa (see Map 1.1). We are fairly certain of these date ranges and regional distributions because of a couple of key paleoanthropological finds, which have been widely publicized: (1) a set of fossilized footprints uncovered in Kenya and (2) an almost complete skeleton found in Ethiopia, which has become known as "Lucy" (see the vignette at the beginning of the chapter). The footprints reveal how much improved the australopiths were as walkers on the ground, but they were still also very much at home in the rain forest.

Australopiths: Prehuman species of the genus *Australopithecus* that existed before those classed under the genus *Homo*.

Bipedalism: The first human characteristic of hominins, specifically, the ability to walk for short periods or distances on hind legs.

Environmental Adaptability Improved upright walking, or **bipedalism,** became a key evolutionary advantage to hominins. Walking on two feet is more

7–5.4 million years ago
Toumaï, Orrorin, and Kaddaba, possibly hominin fossils

5 million years ago
Split of the chimpanzee–hominin lines, as indicated by the genetic clock

4.5 million years ago
Ardi hominins, first assumed human ancestor line

4.2–1.8 million years ago
Multiple lines of australopith hominins

1.8 million years ago
Homo erectus, present in Asia and Africa

interactive timeline

300,000 years ago
Homo sapiens, or Modern Human, emerges in East Africa

80,000–60,000 years ago
Modern humans migrate from East Africa to Asia

60,000–50,000 years ago
Modern humans migrate to Australia

35,000 years ago
Earliest evidence of modern humans in Europe and Siberia

13,500–13,000 years ago
Traditional assumption of human arrival in the Americas

9,400–9,300 years ago
"Spirit Cave mummy" and "Kennewick Man" in the North American West

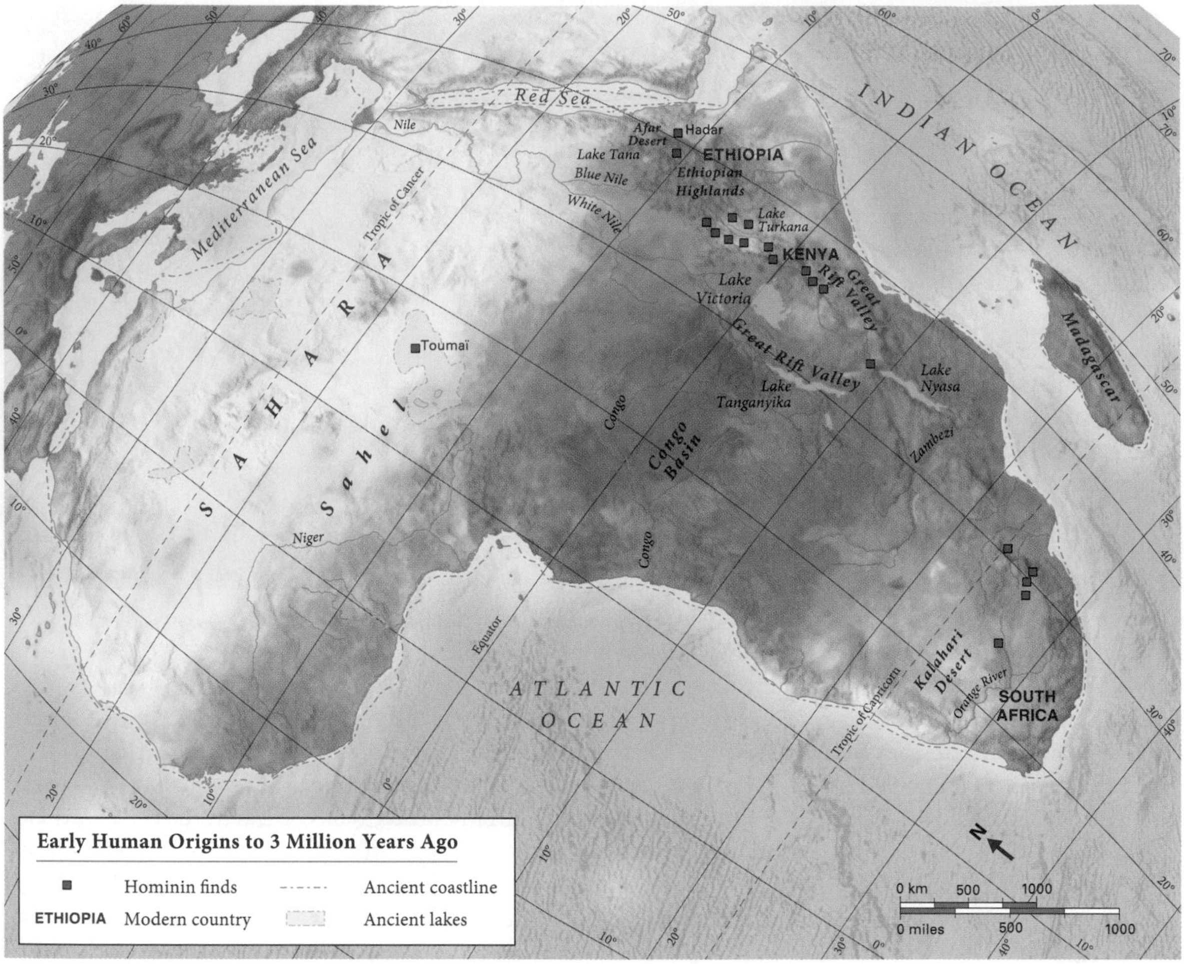

MAP 1.1 **Early Human Origins to 3 Million Years Ago.**

Savanna: Broken forests with interspersed bush and grasslands.

Oldowan toolmaking: Early stone-carving technique, which consisted of splitting a stone into two, thereby producing sharp edges on both fragments. See also **Acheulian** and **Levallois toolmaking.**

energy efficient than knuckle-walking and frees the arms to do something else. Being upright exposes a smaller body surface to the sun, a factor important for venturing out from the rain forest into the **savanna** and steppe. Partaking of the plant resources available in these environments made hominins gradually more flexible than other apes, which were limited to their rain-forest habitat. On the one hand, the rain forest abounded with fruits and nuts, but on the other hand, the savanna offered grasses and seeds. It was in the savanna environment, today the Kenyan Turkana steppe basin, that hominins around 3.3 million years ago fashioned the first stone tools, that is, rocks split in such a way that the broken pieces had sharp edges. The discovery of these tools, made in 2011, dethrones the 2.5-million-year-old Oldowan tools, also unearthed in the Turkana Basin in 1936, from their place as the oldest tools. It now appears that first evidence of awakening intelligence has to be located in the earliest hominins, rather than in their successors.

On the Threshold of Humanity The making of tools became more refined and widespread about 2.5 million years ago in the hands of australopith successor lineages. These younger flaked stones are called **Oldowan** tools (after the

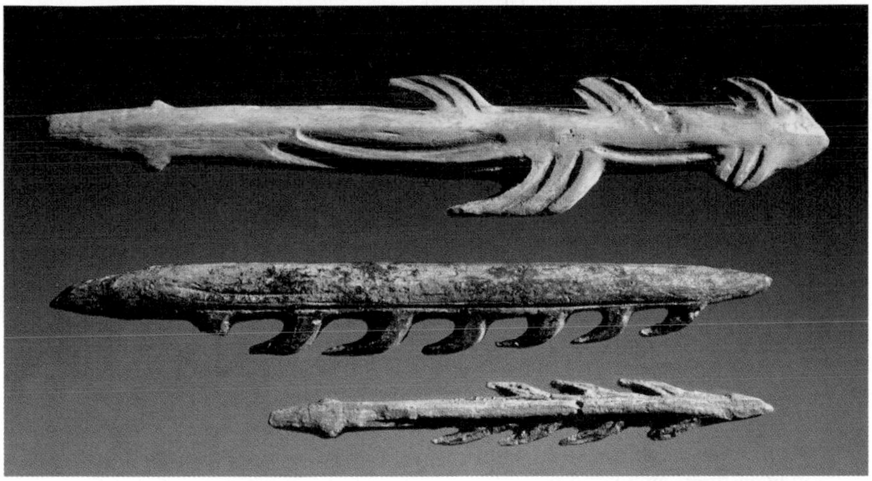

Acheulian Toolkit. The preferred materials for Acheulian axes were obsidian, chert, and flint. The stone scraper on the left shows the Levallois technique, in which the edges of a stone are trimmed and flaked. Harpoons like the ones shown at the top left were made from reindeer antlers. On the right is a spear thrower from France that dates to about 14,000 years ago. Spear throwers gave hunters the ability to propel their missiles with surer aim. Note the horse-shaped handle.

Olduvai region in the Tanzanian Great Rift Valley) and enabled the hominins to broaden their diet from vegetarian foods to more or less regular meals of meat. Hominins became omnivores, partaking of a broader range of nutrition available in nature. The making of stone tools marks the beginning of the **Paleolithic**, or Old Stone Age, in prehistory, which lasted until about 11,500 years ago.

A cool, dry spell of the climate about 1.8 million years ago made mobility again very important. A new hominin line, *Homo erectus (Upright Human)*, evolved that no longer climbed trees, was fully stabilized on its feet, and was capable of walking long distances. It could deal equally with the demands of rain forest, savanna, grasslands, and now also steppe habitats. It mastered the control of fire 1 million years ago, as announced in 2004 on the basis of finds in South Africa. Small groups of perhaps two-dozen hominins, so scholars assume, formed camp groups, huddling around fires at cave entrances or under rock overhangs. The brain size of *H. erectus* was about half of that of the fully evolved *H. sapiens*. This new line of hominins was the first to adopt habits that we can recognize as human.

Paleolithic: Old Stone Age, 2.5 million–11,500 years ago.

H. erectus was the creator of vastly improved stone tools in most places where the line lived. Instead of continuing to use the simple Oldowan stones with sharp edges, *H. erectus* created the new **Acheulian** [ah-SHOI-lee-yan] stone technology, around 1.8–1.6 million years ago. (This technology was named after Saint-Acheul, a suburb of Amiens in northern France where the first finds were made in the nineteenth century.) Acheulian tools were oval or pear-shaped hand axes cut with the help of hammer stones from larger cores, or they were one or more flakes split from cores. When the edges of these hand axes became dull, *H. erectus* split further, smaller flakes away to resharpen the edges. A simple visual comparison of Oldowan and Acheulian tools reveals how much the manual skills of early humans advanced in about a million years.

Acheulian toolmaking: A technique which consisted of flaking a hard piece of rock (especially flint, chert, or obsidian) on both sides into a triangle-shaped hand axe, with cutting edges, a handheld side, and a point.

Fossils from around 1.8 million years ago indicate the almost simultaneous presence of *H. erectus* in East Africa, the Caucasus region in eastern Europe, and Java in the southeast Asian archipelago. Stone tools in India, dated to 1.8–1.6 million years ago, can be similarly interpreted as indicators of the presence of *H. erectus* in the subcontinent. Given this astounding simultaneity, scholars are beginning to waver concerning the traditional "out-of-Africa" theory assumed for *H. erectus*. Until the early 2000s scholars assumed that it was a group of this line that led the first great wave of hominins leaving Africa for the Middle East and Asia. But now it seems possible that one or several of the predecessor lines accomplished this feat several hundred thousand years earlier.

The *H. erectus* fossils from the Dmanisi Cave in Georgia in the Caucasus, discovered in 2005, are of central importance for this revision of the theory of *H. erectus* as the first hominin out of Africa. The cave contained five sets of fully preserved skulls and bones, the anatomies of which were very different from each other. Had they been found individually in caves distant from each other, researchers would have viewed them as belonging to five different lines of early *Homo*. Instead, in an important article of 2013, an international team of researchers came to the conclusion not only that the five fossils belong to the same line but that numerous other fossils found in Africa as well as Asia and dated to around 1.8 million years ago are members of the same hominin line. The ancestor clearly came from Africa, but the line of *H. erectus* itself was perhaps of non-African origin.

Human Adaptations: From Africa to Eurasia and Australia

H. erectus was the ancestor of *H. sapiens* ("Wise Human," "Modern Human" in this chapter), the species of modern humans to which we belong. Scholars are far from agreed, however, as to how many intermediate lineages existed between then and now. When *H. sapiens* emerged in Africa about 300,000 years ago two characteristics distinguished this human being from its less evolved forerunners: (1) rapidly developing *technical skills* and (2) *cultural creativity*. These two characteristics represent a fundamental transformation of hominins that placed them on a path toward full liberation from the determinism of nature. The timing of this liberation is still debated by scientists, but world historians generally assume that when *H. sapiens* created a recognizable culture in Africa, it became at least partially the free creator of a new direction in natural history.

The African Origins of Human Culture

The oldest specimen of a *H. sapiens* found so far is a jawbone with teeth recovered from the site of Jebel Irhoud in Morocco. It was dated in 2017 to about 300,000 years ago. The archaeological record documenting modern humans in Africa is still spotty, but the 17 sites containing bone and skull remnants of *H. sapiens* as well as a half dozen sites with human artifacts allow for at least one important conclusion: *H. sapiens*, in a process of gradual development in Africa, became physically and intellectually fully human, capable of the basics of culture. While humans continued to remain subject to the natural interaction between environment and genes, requiring constant updates in adaptation, culture gave them the freedom to accept and reject—a completely new dimension largely independent from nature.

Livelihood Early hominins, as discussed earlier, did not hunt; they scavenged meat from animals killed and only partially eaten by predators. Alternatively, hominins purposely followed predators and chased them away after the kill. Stone scrapers, once invented, greatly facilitated the separation of meat from carcasses. An elusive post–*H. erectus* line introduced spears in the form of sharpened sticks some 400,000 years ago and thus allowed the transition from scavenging to hunting.

Really effective spears had to await *H. sapiens* as the creator of the much refined new stoneworking technique, the **Levallois** [le-val-WAH], derived from the name of a suburb of Paris, France, where in the nineteenth century the first spear points were found. With this technique, a craftsperson chipped off small flakes from the edges of a prepared stone core and then hammered a larger flake—flat on the bottom, domed on the top, and sharpened by the small flakes around the edge—from the center, leaving a more or less deep indentation in the spent core. These center flakes could be as large as hand axes and meat cutters or as small as spear points. The appearance of spear points and increasingly large numbers of animal bones in the archaeological sites was an indicator that *H. sapiens* was emerging as an efficient hunter of animals. The hunt, requiring strength as well as endurance, tended to be the province of males—and remained a prestige occupation for much of human history. But it provided no more than a supplement to *H. sapiens*' nutrition, which remained plant based.

Levallois toolmaking: A stone technique where stone workers first shaped a hard rock into a cylinder or cone.

The combination of the male-dominated hunt with the communal gathering of plant foods defines what is called "forager society." Foraging, formerly called "hunting and gathering," was the dominant pattern of human history for the longest period—several hundred thousand years. It is also the least documented period, requiring for its understanding a combination of archaeology with the anthropological insights gained from observation of surviving foraging societies in the nineteenth and twentieth centuries. Thus, the descriptions of such societies we offer are unavoidably somewhat speculative.

H. sapiens continued to live in sheltered places provided by cave entrances and rock overhangs, the source of the popular stereotype of the "caveman." But there were also campsites with hut-like shelters made from branches. Clothing consisted of skins and furs acquired through hunting and slung around the body. Hearths, in which *H. sapiens* could build fires at will, served as places for the roasting of meat or the provision of warmth during cold nights or in the winter. Anthropological studies suggest that extended families congregated around the hearths to groom each other or give each other comfort and companionship. In the vicinity of the campsite, a total of a dozen dispersed families were in touch with one another, forming a clan, among which sexual partners were chosen.

Around 120,000 years ago, food gathering and preparation appear to have become considerably more varied. *H. sapiens* began to include shellfish collected on beaches and in lagoons in their diets. A little later, humans began catching fish on the coasts and in the lakes and rivers of Africa, using tools carved from bone, such as hooks and barbed points mounted on spears. With the help of grindstones, men and women pulverized hard seeds for consumption or storage. Plaster-lined storage pits appeared in the camps, as did separate refuse dumps. And as the settlements became more numerous, trade networks sprang up, providing toolmakers with obsidian mined as far as 200 miles away. Obsidian is a glass-like hard rock found near volcanoes and therefore relatively rare, so it was much sought after. We may also see this initial period of trade as marking the beginning of thousands of years of increasing human *interaction*—a process vital to the transferring of cultural and technological innovation among human groups.

Gender Relations A central element in human culture is the relationship between men and women. Unfortunately, archaeology is unable to reveal anything decisive about this relationship in Paleolithic forager society. Obviously, the roles of men and women were less specialized among foragers than in agrarian–urban society: Males and females spent most of their time collecting and preparing vegetal foods together, and the male-dominated hunt was a supplemental occupation. But how much these occupations furthered a male–female balance or allowed for one of the two genders to become dominant is not easy to determine.

With the rise of feminism in academia scholars revived the idea, popular in the nineteenth century, of an early female-centered society. Marija Gimbutas (1921–1994), a Lithuanian-born archaeologist, published several books in the 1970s and 80s on what she assumed was a "matristic" society in Russia prior to 4500 BCE. This society, so she asserted, was egalitarian, peaceful, and goddess oriented. It was by this time agrarian, but by implication matristic culture was assumed to have had deep roots in the preceding forager stage of human life. In her view, aggressive, warlike male dominance came about only with the rise of horseback-riding herders from the southern Russian steppes who were bent on conquest.

Other anthropologists, instead, assumed that male dominance began at about the same time that warring kingdoms emerged in the Middle East. War captives became slaves, and elaborate hierarchies emerged in which women, in turn, found themselves relegated to inferior positions. However the origins of patriarchy are explained, there is little controversy over its connection with agrarian–urban life. What came before, however, and was prevalent during the Paleolithic forager period of human history is impossible to determine one way or the other. While patriarchy was part and parcel of the agrarian–urban pattern, what we know of the preceding forager society so far does not indicate a prevalence of matriarchy. In African Paleolithic forager society, females and males differed in their functions but not so decisively that the one or the other could easily become dominant.

Creation of Symbols Parallel to the development of foraging, hunting, and beginning gender roles, there were also first signs of a development of *H. sapiens*' mental life. Activity in the camps expanded from the craftsmanship of tools to that of nonutilitarian objects. This expansion was perhaps the decisive step with which *H. sapiens* left the worlds of animals and other early humans behind and became truly modern. Around 135,000 years ago, humans in what is today Morocco in northwest Africa took seashells and fragments of ostrich eggshell, perforated them, and strung them on leather strips as pendants and necklaces. The significance of this step cannot be overemphasized. By themselves, seashells and ostrich eggshells are natural objects of no particular distinction, but as jewelry they have the meaning of beauty for their wearer: In the form of jewelry they are *symbols,* which are mental concepts distinct from shells found as objects in nature (see Source 1.1).

H. sapiens was the first and only being that did not think only in the concrete, practical terms of toolmaking but also in *abstract* symbolic terms by using something to express something else, such as jewelry for the concept of beauty. This vital transformation may be seen as the root of the human capacity to conceptualize and, with it, the foundation of art, religion, philosophy, science, and all other intellectual pursuits.

Archaeological examples for the emergence of abstract symbolic thinking in Africa are not yet very numerous. But taken together they powerfully suggest an intellectual modernity emerging to match the anatomical modernity of African *H. sapiens*. From about 90,000 years ago, for example, we begin to see gravesites, indicators of reflection on the significance of life, death, ancestral dignity, and generational continuity. Humans added jewelry as the preferred grave gift, suggesting the contemplation of an afterlife or spirit world.

Even more recognizably abstract are the early symbols appearing on a 70,000-year-old small piece of ochre excavated in 1991 from Blombos Cave and on 60,000-year-old ostrich eggshell fragments excavated in 1996 from Diepkloof Rock Shelter, both in South Africa. They display geometrically arranged engravings, the meaning of which is unknown. Ochre is a soft, reddish form of rock easily ground into powder and as such often found as a gift in prehistoric graves, symbolizing blood with its power of life. Ostrich eggshells served as containers or flasks which could be adorned with engravings similar to etchings on crystal. Even today, engravings or etchings distinguish artistically sophisticate crystal from ordinary glass containers.

Finally, a small stone plaque from Apollo 11 Cave in Namibia discovered in 1969–1972, containing the image of a rhinoceros, is of particular importance for the appreciation of the African origin of *H. sapiens*. The plaque is estimated to be 25,000 years old. Collectively, the preceding examples can be taken as a confirmation of *H. sapiens* not only as a technically versatile toolmaker but also as the one animal capable of creating symbols that signify something beyond the materials from which they were made (see Source 1.2).

Migration from Africa Once the *H. sapiens* lineage was fully equipped with practical skills and the foundations of culture, it was adaptable to almost any environment. In 2016, three teams of genetic researchers working independently from each other came to the conclusion that all non-Africans in the world today descend from groups of Africans who left the continent between 80,000 and 50,000 years ago. Many scholars assume that these groups left Africa for Asia by crossing the straits between Ethiopia and Yemen and between Oman and Iran. The members of this group, so it is thought, drifted like beachcombers along the coast, making their way to India, Malaysia, and Indonesia perhaps about 77,000 years ago. Some of their descendants seem to have kept on moving, reaching China about 70,000 years ago, sailing to Australia sometime after 60,000 years ago, and crossing from Korea over a then existing land bridge to Japan about 30,000 years ago. Eventually, modern humans from South Asia migrated northwestward to Europe and northeastward to Siberia, where they arrived around 44,000 years ago. The Siberian groups then made their way to Alaska in North America 16,000 years ago, completing the journey around the world in 70,000 years (see Map 1.2).

Apollo 11 Cave, Namibia. An animal depicted on a stone slab, from about 25,000 years ago. Together with the Blombos Cave ochre, this artwork is evidence of early humans' ability to create symbols.

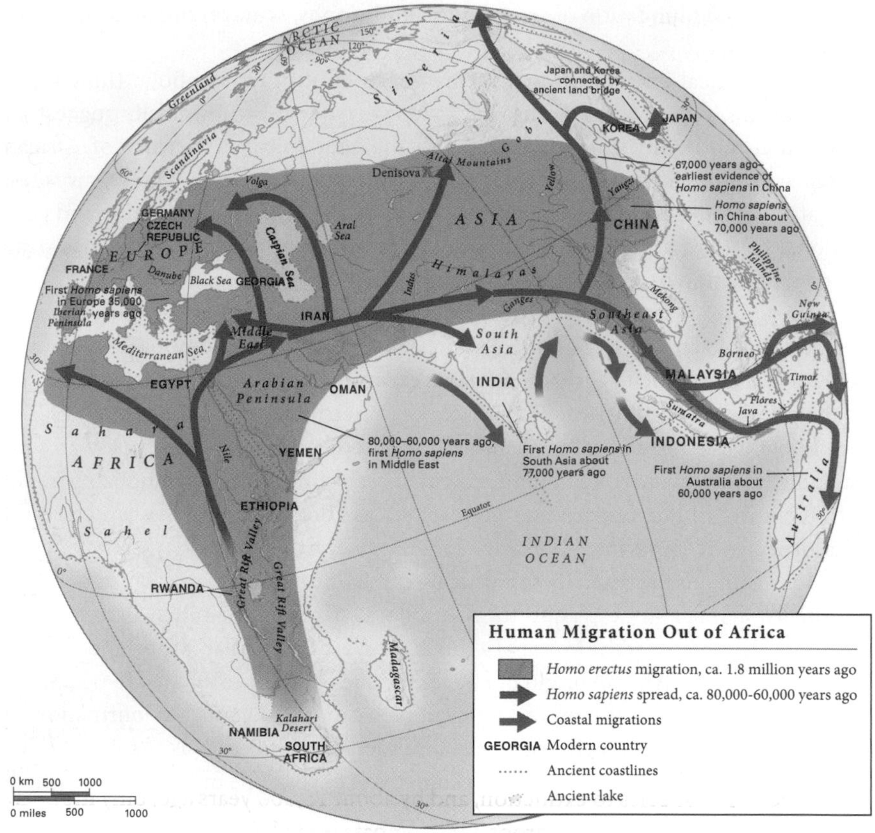

map analysis

MAP 1.2 Human Migration Out of Africa.

Migration from South Asia to Australia

The migration of human groups from south Asia to Australia deserves a closer look within the context of foraging society as the original mode of human social organization. Australia was the only large world region where foraging remained dominant until the modern scientific–industrial age and, therefore, could be studied almost until today. Largely isolated from the rest of the world until the eighteenth century, the Australian foragers developed a distinct culture of their own. But since they shared the same *H. sapiens* genes as their foraging relatives on the Afro-Eurasian continent, the life patterns of both also remained fundamentally similar, in terms of foraging, social organization, and symbolical expression.

Geography and Migration Although it is the smallest of the earth's continents, Australia extends across a variety of geographical zones. In the north, rain forest became dominant. In eastern Australia, various mixtures of forest, savanna, and steppe evolved. The center and most of the west of the continent developed a mixture of steppes, deserts, and lakes. The south (today's southeastern Australia and Tasmania) became temperate, with an almost South African or Mediterranean climate. Small pockets of mountain vegetation came into existence only in what are today the central parts of eastern Australia and southern Tasmania. They displayed geological formations and climate zones corresponding to those of Africa south of the Sahara.

These geographical environments became the homes to modern humans, who descended originally from Africa and had adapted to life in South Asia.

During an ice age 70,000–60,000 years ago, South Asia and most of the northern islands of Indonesia were connected by land bridges. Farther south, island chains where one could travel by raft without losing sight of land encouraged the idea of further travel. Inevitably, the mariners reached a point where land was no longer visible on the horizon. About 60,000 years ago, the distance from the island of Timor to Australia was 65 miles. Scholars have speculated that smoke rising from lightning-produced brush fires in the south could have suggested to some enterprising mariners that there was land beyond the horizon. Whatever motivated them to take to the sea, they evidently succeeded in crossing it.

Settlement of the Continent As *H. sapiens* groups arrived on the Australian continent, presumably in the northwest, they fanned out eastward and southward, slowly populating it. The descendants of the original settlers became known in our own time as **Aboriginals**. Bringing their African and south Asian foraging customs with them, the settlers hunted the Australian animals and gathered what was edible of its plant life. Australia's animals, as they are today, were very different from those in Africa and South Asia: On account of the continent's early connection with Antarctica and South America, its game animals were largely marsupials, carrying their newborns in protective pouches during the nursing phase. Unlike in Africa and Eurasia, with their profusion of dangerous animals, there were few marsupial predator species to threaten these first humans. The Aboriginal peoples gradually hunted the largest marsupial species to extinction, and by about 16,000 years ago, only medium and small animals, such as kangaroos and wombats, were left to hunt.

Aboriginals: The original settlers of Australia, who arrived some 60,000–50,000 years before the arrival of European settlers at the end of the eighteenth century CE.

As elsewhere in foraging societies, men were the hunters. They used spears and spear throwers—short sticks with a curve or hook on the end to extend the length of the thrower's arm and give additional power to the flight of the spear. Bows and arrows, which appeared for the first time in South Africa 64,000 years ago, probably were too late for the migrants to take with them on their journey to Australia. In southern Australia, eel was a major protein staple. Men trapped this fish in rivers and human-made river basins, using nets made of bulrush fiber. In Tasmania the main meat source was the seal. Once the large marsupials were gone, hunting became a highly diversified set of activities for the Aboriginals.

Women, and secondarily men, were responsible for gathering plant foods. The basic staples were wild millet and rice. The main fruits and vegetables were the solanum [sow-LAH-num], a tomato-like fruit rich in vitamin C; the yam daisy, a sweet, milky tuber with yellow, daisy-like flowers; and the quandong [KWAN-dong] fruit, also abounding in vitamin C, which was collected from trees and then dried. Women used grindstones to prepare hard seeds and vegetables, such as pine nuts, flax and acacia seeds, as well as bracken (a large fern) and bindweed (a family of vines). Yam, taro, and banana thrived only in the northeast.

Eucalyptus, a native of Australia found nearly everywhere on the continent, served for firewood in the stone-built hearths. People also used fire as a hunting tool and to promote revegetation. Controlled grass fires and brush fires drove animals in the desired direction where strategically positioned hunting parties could slaughter them. Fires were used to synchronize more closely the production and collection of nuts and fruits on trees, thereby increasing the efficiency of harvests. Over time, the Aboriginals developed a keen sense of how to exploit nature efficiently, while consciously setting about preserving it.

Australia was less rich in grasses suitable for grain cultivation than southwest Asia. For example, Australia had only two types of edible grass seeds; in southwest Asia, there were around 40 types. Thus, it should come as no surprise that foraging remained the dominant mode of subsistence, even if people stayed in their camps for long periods of time before moving them. Only in the south, where eel trapping was the main form of livelihood, did permanent villages appear, similar in many ways to their counterparts in late forager Africa, Europe, North America, and Japan. Aboriginals thus remained closely adapted to the basic, relatively modest patterns of forager livelihood until the first English settlers arrived at the end of the eighteenth century CE.

Social Structures and Cultural Expressions Since modern-day Aboriginals remained faithful to their traditional forms of life, a great deal about their social structures and organization is known. Australian anthropologists have collected a wealth of data, observing forager culture as it existed in the nineteenth and early twentieth centuries. Unfortunately, today foraging is disappearing before our eyes at an accelerated rate. But the existing literature contains much that is rooted in the distant past, even though, of course, the Aboriginals changed in the course of world history just like humans on all other continents.

According to this literature, in the traditional Aboriginal society of the nineteenth century or earlier, marriages were predominantly *monogamous*—that is, they consisted of a husband and wife. Some men who not only were successful hunters but also became wealthy through trade could acquire additional wives. Families that camped together and assisted each other in hunting and food gathering formed *clans*, which were units in which all families considered themselves to be descendants of a common ancestor. Groups of clans formed a lineage of between 500 and 1,500 members. Generally, lineages were too large to camp or move about together. They were, rather, loose associations of clans living miles apart but from which they selected their marriage partners. Marriages took place among members of one group of clans and members of another group. Lineages met collectively once a year at one of the sacred places of their land to celebrate shared rituals and ceremonies.

The Dreamtime Despite this loose social organization, lineage members considered themselves trustees of clearly marked parcels of ancestral land. Typical markers were identifiable features of the landscape, such as rocks, rivers, or trees. *Taboos*—things or practices that were forbidden—and myths surrounded both land and markers. People venerated them through rituals, ceremonies, dances, and recounting the myths. Respected elders, who commanded a particularly high degree of regard, presided over the rituals. An elder was venerated when he had a large number of sons, family alliances, and valuable artifacts acquired through trade. The most esteemed elders possessed a deep knowledge of the clan's past in the **Dreamtime**, the name given to the ancient period in which the lineage's past was embedded.

Dreamtime: In the Australian Dreamtime, the shaman constructs an imaginary reality of the lineage's origins and roots, going back to the time when the world was created and the creator devised all customs, rituals, and myths.

More specifically, the Dreamtime consisted of the stories, customs, and laws which defined the lineage in its original, perfect state at the time of creation. Elders acquired access to this time through trance states, requiring many years of initiation, training, and practice. Their knowledge of the Dreamtime, it was believed, gave them access to creation's hidden powers, enabling them to read other people's minds, recognize their secret concerns, and heal illnesses. Elders, however, did not possess a monopoly on knowledge of nature's hidden powers. All members of the clan had access to its sacred heritage and could use it to practice magic, experiment with sorcery, or cast spells.

Aboriginal elders never were able to wield political power through armed forces within their own lineages. Since there was no agriculture and, therefore, no agricultural surplus, and since trade did not evolve beyond the exchange of obsidian, tools, and weapons, elders could not acquire enough wealth to pay fighters. Only on the continent's northern coast was there a modest trade in local pearls for knives, pottery, cloth, sails, and canoes from Timor; but it too did not support the rise of powerful chiefdoms. Aboriginal society thus remained "stateless" in the sense of possessing no administrative institutions. Elders in positions of authority used persuasion, not force, to keep the peace.

Australian Rock Art How much the Dreamtime involved rock paintings, existing in large numbers in Australia, is unfortunately not known. Rock art is the one form of cultural expression where historical change in the otherwise slow-paced Aboriginal culture is evident: Contemporary Aboriginals are unable to interpret the meaning of early rock paintings. There are many more recent than early rock paintings, but they are very different in content and style from the earlier ones. Changing climatic conditions leading to different migration patterns are presumably responsible for modern Aboriginals losing their familiarity with the rich culture of ancient Australian rock art.

The best-known Australian rock images are the so-called Bradshaw paintings in the Kimberley region of northwest Australia, which probably date to a period of 30,000–20,000 years ago. Between two ice ages, this region had a fairly even, year-round climate with sufficient rainfall to support foraging and, hence, the presence of human groups practicing rock art. At present, scholars work with a classification dividing the Bradshaw paintings into two major stylistic periods, beginning with (1) indentations, grooves, and animals, and followed by (2) elongated human figures with tassels or sashes, fruits and vegetables resembling human figures, and clothespin and stick figures.

The two periods are very difficult to date, since so far none of the places where they have been found have yielded any material that could be reliably carbon dated. Only one Bradshaw painting has been dated so far to some 17,500 years ago, thanks to a wasp nest on top of it that contained sand grains suitable for thermoluminescent dating. The painting could be much older, of course, depending on when the wasp settled on it. Scholars generally assume that the proliferation of Bradshaws was roughly contemporary with the efflorescence of prehistoric rock art in Europe.

Australian Shamans in a Trance. These "Bradshaw" figures are usually interpreted as showing movements and communication with the spirits of animated cosmic nature.

The striking parallelism between Australian and European rock art demonstrates that humans did not have to interact to express themselves culturally in similar ways. Similar forager patterns could evolve without mutual contact. The fact that a great proliferation of rock paintings occurred simultaneously in Australia and Europe leads to the conclusion that none of the human groups migrating away from Africa was privileged over any other. This cultural parity among foragers needs to be kept in mind as we turn to African *H. sapiens* migrating to Europe.

Migration from Asia to Europe

There was a gap of at least 30,000 years between groups of modern humans leaving Africa (80,000–60,000 years ago) and migrating to Europe (44,000 years ago). Scholars assume that these humans settled first in central Asia before their descendants fanned out to Europe as well as East Asia. By that time, *H. sapiens* was well adapted to the cool and dry climate of the savannas and steppes with their large herds of bison, horses, and reindeer. Little is known about the migratory path these descendants chose as they walked across the Asian interior to Europe. It is generally assumed that they moved from the region around the Urals west to the Black Sea and into Europe (see Map 1.2).

Hybrid Imagery. Two lion-headed figurines, one apparently dancing, described by the excavator, archaeologist Nicholas Conard, as a "depiction of mythical imagery," although he does not indicate of which myths. The ca. 32,000-year-old figurines were found in two caves in southwestern Germany.

Neanderthals and Other Lines When *H. sapiens* arrived in Europe around 44,000–35,000 years ago, this region was already settled by another human line, that of the **Neanderthals** [nay-AN-der-tall, after a valley in northwest Germany where the first specimen was found in the nineteenth century]. This line is assumed to have descended from a successor to *H. erectus* 300,000 years ago, although the exact descent is unclear. In fact, on the basis of fossil finds in Spain (Sima de los Huesos) and Siberia (Denisova), as well as subsequent DNA analyses of these finds during 2010–2013, scholars now speak of several successor lineages, coexisting and interbreeding as well as perhaps even overlapping with *H. erectus* in Europe and Asia.

So far, however, Neanderthals are the best-documented Paleolithic fossil humans in Europe and western Asia, with over 600 finds. The fossils range in age from 230,000 to 24,000 years old and are widely distributed geographically among western Europe, the Altai Mountains in eastern Asia, and the Middle East. Early European *H. sapiens*—or **Crô-Magnon** [crow-MAG-non, after the name of the cave in southwestern France where, in the nineteenth century, European *H. sapiens* bones were first found]—was clearly an intruder in an inhabited, if still sparsely settled, human landscape.

In their forager livelihood, the two species were very similar. The former, however, were smaller and more heavily boned than modern humans. Neanderthals were probably able to talk, albeit in a rudimentary way since they did not yet possess the throat structures of *H. sapiens*. They buried their dead without gifts of jewelry. But sprinklings of red ochre, a symbol of lifeblood, which modern humans often included in their graves, were found in at least one Neanderthal grave. The stone and bone toolkits of the two were alike, but whether Neanderthals created paintings is at present not certain, in spite of some contrary claims (for example, for the image of two seals in a cave near Málaga, Spain, dated in 2012 to 43,000 years ago; hand stencils and disks in the cave of El Castillo, Spain, redated in 2012 to 40,800 years ago; and a cross in Gorham's Cave, Gibraltar, dated in 2014 to 39,000 years ago). Most intriguing is the discovery, publicized in 2016, of the cave of Bruniquel in southwestern France. At a distance of 1,100 feet from the entrance, some 176,000 years ago Neanderthals broke off stalagmites from the floor and arranged them in one large and one incomplete small circle. Burned bones testify to the use of fire (for lighting?) in the cave. Slowly, we are beginning to receive a more detailed idea of the depth of Neanderthal life and culture in Europe and Asia.

Rock Paintings and Figurines *H. sapiens*' cultural creativity, which had burst forth in Africa, continued after the migration into Asia and Europe. On the latter continent, there are some 700 caves with rock paintings and engravings, as well as aboveground sites with small figurines. Currently, the oldest known artifacts are the paintings of El Castillo, previously mentioned, and a small ivory figurine of a mammoth dating to 35,000 years ago and found in 2007 in Vogelherd Cave in southwestern Germany. Two slightly more recent, equally small ivory statuettes of humans with lion heads, one of them apparently dancing, were also found in southwestern Germany. The mammoth legs have holes, leading to the speculation that this artifact was sewn to garments. Other figurines might have been worn as pendants.

Several thousand years later, an entire class of female figurines, some thin and delicate and others bulging and coarse, called "Venuses," appeared all over western Europe. These figurines were made of stone or bone, and one of them, unearthed in the Czech Republic, was formed of fired clay ca. 26,000 years ago. The creation of the first ceramic pieces was thus a Paleolithic invention, even though the regular production of pottery appeared only some 17,000 years later in agrarian society. All figurines were small, fitting comfortably into the palm of a hand, and therefore easily transportable. The bulging Venuses have been interpreted as fertility goddesses, indicating an early matriarchy, but this interpretation is questionable, given the great variety of female and male figurines of the Venus type. Other scholars view these figurines as dolls for children in the camps or as representatives of relatives or ancestors in camp rituals. Hard proof, however, is still outstanding, if it is even possible.

The great majority of rock paintings in Europe show animals, usually from their most easily identifiable profiles. The animals appear alone or in herds, at rest or in motion, either chasing or fleeing other beasts, or locked in conflict with each other. The oldest paintings found so far are of grass-eating steppe animals, such as reindeer, horses, cattle, aurochs, bison, mammoths, or rhinoceroses, with which modern humans, migrating from the Russian steppes into central and western Europe, were familiar. Dating to 30,000 years ago, they were discovered in 1994 in Chauvet [show-VAY] Cave in southern France. One intriguing image in this cave depicts a figure with the head and torso of a bison and the legs of a human. A similarly intriguing image from 13,000 years ago, found in the Trois-Frères [trwah-FRAIR] Cave in southwestern France, is known as "the sorcerer," an upright being with human hands and legs but also equipped with reindeer ears and antlers, a bird face, a fox tail, and a phallus. These images of hybrid beings are rare, however; only some 200 are known to exist, in contrast to the tens of thousands of large, mostly herbivore mammals on which the painters concentrated.

Depictions of humans are also rare. The best known, at Lascaux [las-COE] in southwestern France and dated to 17,000 years ago, is that of a bison, perhaps hit by a spear and standing in front of a human stick figure, prostrate with an erect penis. A spear with a bird on top and a rhinoceros face away from the human. A set of 15,000-year-old engravings on slabs used to cover the floor of La Marche [la-MARSH] Cave in west-central France consists of expertly executed, realistic sketches of young and old males and females, dressed in boots, robes, and hats. These sketches could easily be modern cartoons: They demonstrate that there is little that separates contemporary humans from those who lived 15,000 years ago.

image analysis

Venus Figurine. This is the oldest known figurine made of fired clay. It was excavated at Dolní Věstonice, Czech Republic, in 1925. Many more broken figurines were found near the kiln. They perhaps represented family members during rituals and, as bearers of their spirits, had to be destroyed at the end of the rituals so as to end their influence.

Modern chemical analyses have shown that the rock painters knew how to grind and mix minerals to make different colors. They mixed charcoal and manganese dioxide to outline their paintings in black. To add color, they used other ground minerals, such as hematite for red, mixed in various finely graded proportions. Painters carefully sketched the images before filling them in with paint and shading the figures. They often used protrusions in the rock walls to enhance three-dimensionality

Lascaux Cave, France. This figure shows a bison, apparently disemboweled by a spear and standing in front of a human stick figure, prostrate with an erect penis. This 17,000-year-old image could be interpreted as depicting the scene of a mortally wounded, angry animal attacking a defenseless human. Alternatively, it might also depict a human in deep sleep or trance (hence the erect penis) in the presence of one of the most common steppe animals, also with an enlarged sexual organ. The interest in sexuality, also reflected in the Venus figures, might represent a growing awareness not only of a common spirituality in humans, animals, and plants, but also of a common vitality animating the world.

and augment the technique of shading. In a number of images, frontal and lateral views are combined. One image depicts a bison with six legs, evidently simulating its swift motion. Thus, the thematic diversity of images had its complement in technical versatility.

The main places with rock art are halls and domes deep inside often miles-long caves. The complete darkness inside was illuminated with torches and grease-filled bowls with wicks. Flutes, made of swan bones, and stalagmites, tapped as percussion instruments, testify to the presence not only of painters but also of musicians. To judge by the extant footprints, teenagers as well as adults, men as well as women assembled inside the caves. Modern scholars, such as the South African archaeologist J. David Lewis-Williams, speculate that the caves were places for rituals, perhaps even shamanic assemblies, in which elders, in trance, entered a spiritual world shared with other living beings. Hints of the human mind reflecting on such a shared spiritual world can perhaps be found in the hybrid lion man, bison man, and sorcerer figurines and images previously mentioned. The Australian Bradshaw figures, showing swaying humans with plant-like features, may similarly point in the direction of such a reflection. It is possible to recognize in the Paleolithic artifacts the beginnings of religious thought, specifically the idea of a spiritual nature connecting humans, animals, and plants with each other (see Source 1.3).

The Ice Age Crisis and Human Migration to the Americas

In the course of its natural history, the earth has traversed many ice ages. Modern humans experienced two. The first one, 70,000–60,000 years ago, created land bridges that enabled humans to cross much of the Indonesian archipelago on foot and travel the rest of the distance by boat to Australia. This ice age was comparatively mild and brief, in contrast to the last ice age of the world's history, 30,000–13,500 years ago, which severely altered the flora and fauna on all continents. Humans, although suffering through it, exploited it for one major achievement: their migration from Siberia to the Americas.

The Ice Age

Humans created many of the figurines and cave paintings previously discussed when Europe's climate was steadily getting colder. The end of the Paleolithic era occurred during one of the climatically most inhospitable periods in world history. Large parts of the world either descended into a deep freeze or became bone dry. The northern zone of Eurasia, from England to Siberia, changed into a desolate wasteland, partially covered with gigantic ice sheets. The central zone, from southern France to Mongolia, consisted of semiarid steppe lands. The southern zone, from Iberia (today's Spain and Portugal) to southern China, was temperate but semidry, with grasslands and pockets of woodlands.

In Africa and Australia, the rain forest was reduced to a few areas in central Africa and the northern tip of Australia, leaving the rest of those continents largely exposed to drought. The northern Sahara and southern Kalahari in Africa as well as the interior of Australia were giant deserts, cutting deep into what were once rich savannas and rain forest. Life for modern humans in Eurasia, Africa, and Australia during this ice age was an arduous struggle for daily survival (see Map 1.3).

Difficult Living Conditions Signs of stress and even desperation testify to the harsh conditions of the Ice Age. For example, human bone remnants from a number of ancient campsites in modern-day Russia display signs of malnutrition and disease. Because of the difficult conditions, humans abandoned the northern European and Russian plains, which remained uninhabited for 15 millennia. Central European settlements were hemmed in between Scandinavian and Alpine glaciers. In an important development, humans domesticated the dog sometime around 15,000 years ago, probably to help in hunting. Many animal species, adapted to warmer weather (including Neanderthals; see "Patterns Up Close"), did not take the Ice Age well, and died out. Species that thrived in colder weather (such as woolly mammoths, mastodons, woolly rhinoceroses, and giant deer) failed to adjust after the end of the Ice Age when the weather became warm again. Whether humans hastened the disappearance of the latter animals through overhunting is a matter of dispute among scholars. Ultimately, most of these huge beasts died out around 6,000–4,000 years ago.

"Little Sorcerer." The meaning of this cave drawing from Trois-Frères, France, continues to baffle. The figure combines traits of a deer, an owl, a fox, and a human. It could be a hunter stalking prey. The combining of animal and human qualities characterizes some 200 examples of Ice Age art.

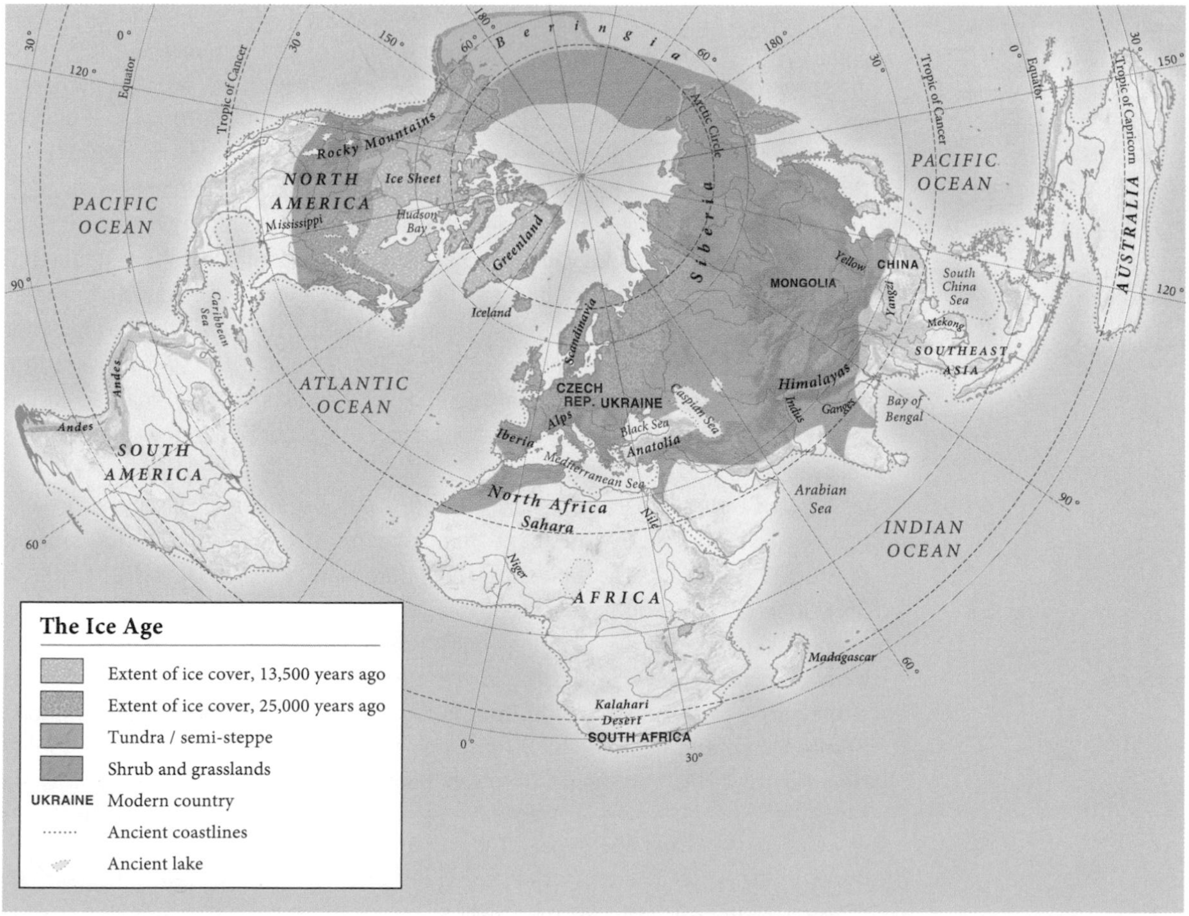

MAP 1.3 The Ice Age.

Patterns Up Close

The Disappearance of Neanderthals

The lineage *Homo neanderthalensis* flourished in Eurasia between 300,000 and 110,000 years ago, at a time when (with one interruption around 140,000 years ago) a generally warm and wet climate supported dense woodlands and savanna much more extensive than today. Neanderthals frequently had their camps at the edges of wetlands, lakes, and rivers. As hunters, they typically stalked and ambushed animals from behind trees with thrusting spears. They were therefore not well adapted to the colder and drier steppe lands, which during this time were limited to the eastern reaches of central Asia and which they generally avoided.

Donaña National Park in southwestern Spain.

Beginning about 110,000 years ago the climate gradually changed from warm and wet to cold and dry, bringing about an increase in steppe and open grasslands. This gradual increase, however, often reversed for periods of varying length. During times of greater fluctuation, sometimes within three or four generations, Neanderthals had to adjust their hunting style to open landscapes where larger hunting parties and throwing spears were required. Neanderthals never felt comfortable with throwing spears, however, and certainly did not use bows and arrows, which were developed only later by *H. sapiens*. During a time of respite about 75,000–44,000 years ago when the climate and environment stabilized at a relatively warm and wet level, Neanderthals happily returned to their accustomed forms of livelihood.

Unfortunately, the subsequent period, when the climate resumed its shift from warm and wet to cold and dry, brought havoc to Neanderthal populations in Europe. As open grassland, and eventually steppe, replaced forest and savanna, Neanderthals retreated from north to south. At the same time, *H. sapiens* advanced together with grassland and steppe from southern central Asia and Russia westward into Europe. Scholars assume that the migration of *H. sapiens*, fully adapted to life in open landscapes, into central and western Europe occurred along the Danube valley, around 35,000 years ago.

The bone record of *H. sapiens*, however, is still extremely poor, and at present there is only one *H. sapiens* fossil from Romania that has been securely dated to 34,000 years ago. The earliest western European fossils of *H. sapiens* date to 30,000 years ago, and at present it is impossible to determine who the creators of the figurines and cave paintings during a critical period of about 4,000 years were. *H. neanderthalensis* and *H. sapiens* clearly coexisted, but the fossil record is entirely that of Neanderthals. In fact, in 2010, the Swedish-born paleogeneticist Svante Pääbo and his team based in Leipzig, Germany, completed an analysis of Neanderthal DNA (from bones from Croatian Neanderthals) and found that there was interbreeding with modern humans: Some 1–4 percent of Neanderthal genes were absorbed into the modern human genome. What the nature of this coexistence was—peaceful or hostile—became a major point of contention toward the end of the twentieth century.

At this time, the general scholarly opinion was that Neanderthals disappeared from the European scene around 30,000 years ago. But in 1999 a Portuguese team published an analysis of a 25,000-year-old fossil of a child discovered at Abrigo Lagar do Velho [VEL-yo] in central Portugal. The team suggested, on anatomical grounds, that this child was born of "admixed" Neanderthal and *H. sapiens* parentage. Apparently the Neanderthals existed for a while longer, in retreat to the far west of the continent.

This impression was confirmed in 2006 when a British team published the results of excavations in Gorham's Cave, Gibraltar, according to which tools found in the cave can be ascribed to Neanderthals who lived there as recently as 28,000–24,000 years ago. At that time, southern Spain was the last remnant of the warm and wet environment of lush forests and savannas, populated by carnivores (leopards, lions, hyenas, lynxes, and brown bears) as well as herbivores (red deer, boar, aurochs, horse, rhino, and elephant) in which Neanderthals thrived. As always, the Neanderthals of the final years still preferred to hunt smaller- to intermediate-sized game, such as rabbits (80 percent of all bones in the Gibraltar cave), birds, mussels, seals, and dolphins. Soon after 24,000 years ago, Gibraltar was hit by the full blast of the Ice Age. Neanderthals could not adjust, but *H. sapiens*—steppe runner and big-game hunter—survived.

More refined carbon measurements, however, published in 2014, suggest that earlier dating methods tended to systematically underestimate the age of Neanderthal fossils. As a result, a number of scholars now believe that Neanderthal disappeared already around 40,000 years ago. Their interbreeding with *H. sapiens* must have occurred in western Asia where their coexistence lasted the longest. In southern Spain, where *H. sapiens* appeared the latest, the extended survival of Neanderthals to 28,000–24,000 years ago is now in doubt, although for the time being no new dates have been offered.

Ultimately, it was the environment, not defeat by more resourceful modern humans, that did the Neanderthals in. It just so happened that when climate change resulted in a cold and dry steppe environment, as well as the Ice Age that dominated world history from 30,000 to 13,000 years ago, the more versatile *H. sapiens* was poised to master the challenge.

Questions

- Before reading this essay, what misconceptions did you have about Neanderthals?
- Is it important for world historians to study the history of Neanderthals? If yes, for which reasons?

Although life was not easy, *H. sapiens* possessed the technological and mental resources to survive even the worst climate conditions. The modern humans had at their disposal a great variety of implements for catching fish, snaring birds, and hunting animals, including harpoons, fishhooks, and darts made of bone; fishnets; and bird traps. Boomerangs, invented independently in Europe and Australia, were also used for hunting larger fowl. Wooden handles attached to large stone axe heads increased the efficiency of cutting meat or wood. In a situation of increasingly scarce large animals, *H. sapiens* became efficient at hunting small animals. In this, they were aided by dogs which thus became the earliest domesticated animals, as previously mentioned.

Human mobility increased substantially. Canoes took the form of dugouts or were constructed of bone and wood frames covered with skins. As a result of innovations like the canoe, the range for trading expanded. Baltic *amber* (fossilized tree resin prized for making jewelry) was found 600 miles away in southern Europe, and Mediterranean shells were carried by traders to the Ukraine, 800 miles to the northeast.

Ice Age humans dressed themselves warmly, wearing hooded fur coats stitched together with bone needles, using thin leather strips, as evidenced by figurines discovered in Siberia. An imprint left on kiln-fired clay, found in the Czech Republic, indicates that humans also began to weave woolen cloth on looms, another historical first (see also Source 1.4). No doubt, *H. sapiens* groups were decimated by the impact of the Ice Age, but groups of hardy survivors were still tenaciously hanging on when the world finally warmed up again and became wetter around 14,500 years ago.

The Beringia Land Bridge During the coldest period of the Ice Age, around 19,000 years ago, global sea levels dropped by some 450 feet, increasing the landmass of the continents by about 100 miles in all directions and exposing land bridges connecting Indonesia to Malaysia, Japan to Korea, and Asia to North America. The land bridge connecting Asia and North America to Siberia and the Americas was Beringia, a large landmass of some half a million square miles, which today has been reduced to the area of what is Alaska and northwestern Canada.

Tundra: Landscape in which the topsoil unfreezes during the summer and supports dwarf shrubs, sedges and grasses, mosses, and lichens.

Northern Beringia was covered with ice and **tundra**, but the southern rim was apparently ice free. Sediment cores taken from the seabed off Alaska contain pollen as well as plant and insect fossils, suggesting the existence of shrublands and forests of birch, willow, and alder. Therefore, it was possible for humans and animals to survive along the southern rim of Beringia. A few stone tool and spear point finds in Alaska lend weight to the human survival theory.

But, as research published in 2014 argues, survival would have been at the cost of isolation, with humans cut off from both Siberia and the lower Americas for some 10,000 years. Indeed, genetics points to such an isolation, since the mitochondrial DNA (genetic information passed on by mothers) taken from present-day Native Americans indicates that their genome emerged in Siberia about 25,000 years ago, but did not spread within the Americas until about 15,000 years ago. Thus, Beringia would have been the only refuge for early humans in a for the most part barren or ice-covered, uninhabitable, northern hemisphere stretching from Scandinavia and Siberia to Canada and Greenland.

Migration to the Americas Around 13,500 years ago, it is thought that the ice sheet in what is today the Canadian province of Alberta split, creating a narrow passageway that made a human pathway from Alaska possible. If there was indeed a migration, it must have occurred soon after the passageway opened. Since many of the thousands of spear points that have been found all over North America south of the ice sheet—the so-called Clovis points (see Chapter 5)—go as far back as

13,000 years ago, there were about 500 years for humans to migrate from Alaska to North America. Traditionally, scholars have thought it plausible that it was at this time that humans settled the Americas.

In the 1990s and early 2000s, however, a number of spear points and human settlements older than 13,000 years ago were discovered. Sites at Monte Verde in Chile, Meadowcroft in Pennsylvania, Topper in South Carolina, Cactus Hill in Virginia, Buttermilk Creek in Texas, Taíma Taíma [ta-EE-ma] in Venezuela, and Santana de Riacho [ree-ACHO] and Lapa do Boquete [bo-KET] in Brazil have been reliably dated to 14,000–16,000 years ago. The effect of the new research has been that the arrival of humans prior to 13,500 years ago is no longer mere speculation but is fast becoming the scientific consensus (see Map 1.4).

Long-distance ocean travel in ancient times was perhaps less difficult than has been previously assumed. After all, *H. sapiens* had already traveled by raft or boat from Indonesia to Australia 60,000 years ago. Could modern humans have sailed along the Pacific coastline from Beringia to what is today the state of Washington about 16,000 years ago? Proof of such a journey would, unfortunately, be difficult to come by, since the coastline was some 50 miles farther out in the Pacific than it is today and any settlement traces would now be submerged below sea level. In the absence of underwater archaeology so far, nothing is known about such settlements.

An American Water Nymph A possible answer to the question of migrations prior to that of the Clovis spear-point people ca. 13,500 years ago can be gleaned from the genetic study of two human teeth recovered in 2007 from a cavernous sinkhole on the Yucatán peninsula. The teeth were from an almost perfectly preserved skeleton of a 15- or 16-year-old girl named Naia (from Gr., *naias*, water nymph) who had fallen into the sinkhole. According to the study, published in 2014, Naia's skeleton dates to 13,000–12,000 years ago. Her mitochondrial DNA—as well as that of the "Anzick-1" fossil of the same age found in Montana also published in 2014—is closely related to that of the groups of Siberian *H. sapiens* which had migrated to Beringia during the Ice Age.

It appears, therefore, that members from one single, genetically uniform population in Beringia have populated the Americas from at least ca. 16,000 years ago, that is, if one accepts the pre-Clovis archaeological record. Two papers published in 2016 confirm the assumption of a genetically uniform population of first settlers coming from Beringia. This population is related to Siberians but has small DNA admixtures (1–2 percent) pointing to people from the Andaman islands (west of Malaysia), New Guinea, and Australia. The two papers agree that these admixtures happened prior to the arrival of the above population in the Americas but differ on how early and directly these admixtures took place. Prior to 13,500 years ago these Beringians must have traveled by boat along the Pacific coast. Then, around 13,500 years ago they likely walked through the Alberta split in the North American ice shield.

Native Americans or Amerindians In 1996, two brothers discovered a skull on one of the banks of the Columbia River near Kennewick, Washington, when they were sneaking into the annual hydroplane show. Scared by their discovery, they alerted the authorities. Subsequently, the archaeologist James Chatters found most of the bones belonging to the skull nearby and dubbed the fossil "Kennewick Man." A California lab dated them to about 9,000 years ago.

According to US law, ancient remains found on federal land (which is the case in Kennewick) belong to the Native American tribe that can prove parentage. An Oregon

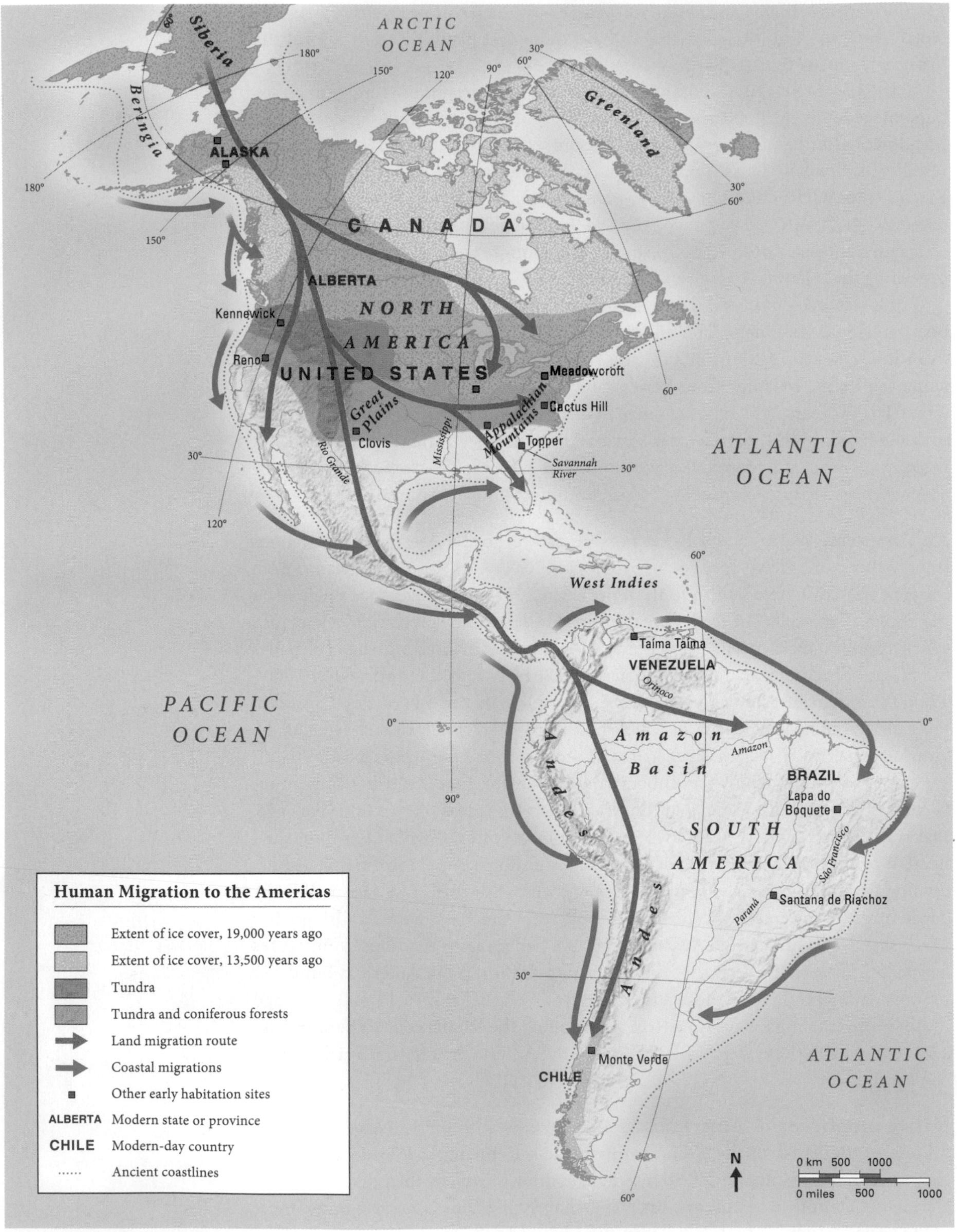

MAP 1.4 **Human Migration to the Americas.**

tribe claimed the bones, and a lengthy lawsuit ensued among several tribes, backed by the US government, and a number of archaeologists concerned to have scientific access to the fossil. The lawsuit was settled in 2004 in favor of the archaeologists who claimed that the cranial features of Kennewick Man pointed more to a person of Ainu descent in Japan than to Native American parentage. New DNA tests in 2015, however, determined that Kennewick Man is definitely Native American, even if his skull seems to be different. Therefore, the US Army Corps of Engineers in 2016 began procedures to determine which Native American group may rebury Kennewick Man's remains.

It is thus clear today the original settlers of the Americas are descendants of a single population that had moved from Siberia to Beringia some 23,000 years ago. During various stages of the thaw after the Ice Age (16,000–13,500 years ago) groups from among this population traveled by boat or on foot to the Americas, where they dispersed rapidly and also diversified genetically. We call these settlers today Native Americans or Amerindians (the terminology is still fluid).

Putting It All Together

The time it took from Ardi to the first modern humans in East Africa was slightly less than 7 million years. Another 100,000 years elapsed before modern humans peopled the earth, down to Clovis and the transition to agriculture in the Fertile Crescent of the Middle East. From there, in another 10,000 years we reached our own time. The time proportions are staggering: The history from Clovis and the Fertile Crescent to the present is a mere 0.02 percent of the time from Ardi to the present and 4 percent of that from the first *H. sapiens* fossil to the present. Practically the entire time we needed to become genetically human is buried in the "deep history" mentioned at the beginning of this chapter.

interactive concept map

Nearly as deeply buried is the process during which we began to carve out the space for culture, which we possess within the frameworks of our genes and the environment. Realizing how long these genetic and cultural time spans of prehistory are is what matters for us today: The 10,000 years of history from the shift of forager to agrarian–urban and eventually scientific–industrial society represent a breathtakingly short time of development yet one that is so overwhelmingly complex that we have great difficulty understanding it. When we step back from this frenetically paced world history of the past 10,000 years and consider the much slower deep history of humanity, we become aware that, had it not been for this slow, tortuous, and often dead-end incubation, we would never have been able to sustain the speed of the later history of which we are the current product.

The principal reason for the slow pace of deep history was the conscious effort of foragers to limit population growth as well as the size of their groups. Women as well as men, constantly on the move in search for food, had a strong interest in having few children and nursing them for several years so as to extend birth spacing. Of course, Paleolithic populations grew over the course of the millennia; otherwise, there would not have been a pattern shift from foraging to agrarian–urban life. Thus, even though the culture of foraging sought to inhibit population growth, this culture was not so rigid that people under climatologically and environmentally benign circumstances were not open to material and cultural change. It was under these circumstances at the end of the Ice Age 13,500 years ago that humans in some parts of the world gradually abandoned foraging and began adapting to agriculture.

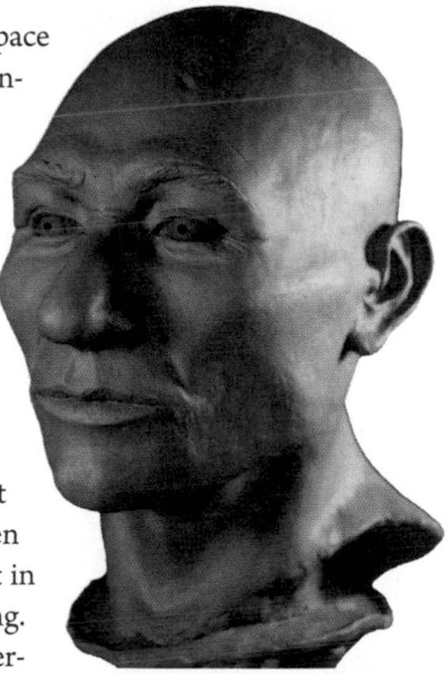

Reconstruction of the Facial Features of Kennewick Man (9,300 Years Ago). Initially declared to be of Ainu-Japanese descent on the basis of his facial features, DNA tests of 2015 determined that he is Native American.

Review and Relate

Thinking Through Patterns

Examine the ways historians approach the big questions of this chapter.

What made it possible for *H. sapiens* to survive in a dangerous environment? Why is it difficult to imagine life as a prehistoric forager?

We are twice removed from the world of foragers: After foraging came farming, which is also difficult to understand, because today's pattern of life is part of scientific–industrial civilization. Even those among us who practice wilderness survival still have a lifeline to modern civilization through cell phones, GPS, etc. *H. sapiens* foragers in prehistory, by contrast, relied on their stone tools, bows and arrows, rock shelters, clan members, and unsurpassed knowledge of animals, berry bushes, fruit and nut trees, mushroom patches, and grass fields to guide them through their daily lives. Collecting vegetables, catching fish, and killing the occasional animal did not take as much of an effort as farming later did, and foragers had more leisure time than farmers engaged in the annual agricultural cycle.

Where did humans go when they left Africa, and how did they establish themselves in the areas where they settled? How did they adapt to the worsening Ice Age?

After modern humans left East Africa, probably in several waves between 80,000 and 60,000 years ago, in all likelihood they first went to northern India, before fanning out in all directions to Australia, Siberia, and Europe. They encountered *H. erectus* and successors, such as Neanderthals, and interbred with the latter. The modern humans who settled in Australia remained foragers because the Australian flora did not include grasses that could be cultivated through selective breeding into grains. From the complex lineage societies into which they evolved, we can see that forager life could acquire a differentiated culture, expressed in the so-called Dreamtime. However, when the Ice Age hit, forager clans and lineages had to adapt to harsh environmental conditions and retreat southward. Foremost among the adaptations were the abilities to make protective woolen clothing and build boats with which to travel to more favorable places.

Why did early humans create cave paintings and figurines? Do they show patterns that can be interpreted?

The existence of tens of thousands of prehistoric cave paintings and figurines found on all continents attests to the great importance *H. sapiens* gave to the representation of humans, animals, plants, and hybrid figures with which they shared the natural world. The attention they paid to these beings—be they at rest or in motion, alone or in groups, in outline or full detail—shows how important it was to them to identify the inhabitants of their world accurately and to teach the young how to recognize them in nature. Beyond the precise representations, early humans evidently also wanted to demonstrate that their identities were not necessarily fixed. The examples of humans depicted with the features of lions, bisons, stags, or even plants suggest the idea that humans could assume the identity of other beings in nature. In later periods of history, masks of animals or human ancestors, worn by humans in the performance of rituals, expressed similar concepts of interchangeable identities. In other words, as important as it was to have an accurate knowledge of visible things, these early humans also conceived of an invisible world in which identities could be exchanged, shared, or merged. In this sense, prehistoric art can be seen as the first expression of spiritual experience, where humans expressed an awareness not only of the visible world in all its diversity but also an invisible world of other identities.

Against the Grain

Consider this as a counterpoint to the main patterns examined in this chapter.

The Hobbits of Flores Island

In 2003, an Australian–Indonesian team unearthed the partial fossils of 13 hominins in a cave on the island of Flores in the southern archipelago of Indonesia. The fossils were of beings that measured only 3–4 feet high and had brains no larger than those of chimpanzees or some australopiths. Layers of earth in which the fossils were discovered seemed to date to fairly recent times, and, accordingly, their owners were declared to have lived as late as 18,000 years ago. Their closest relatives seemed to be members of the species *H. erectus*, and to the astonishment of the scholarly world this diminutive new type of hominin, dubbed *H. floresiensis*, appeared to have survived well into the period of modern humans, even if isolated from mainland Asia.

Given their small size and late survival, the hominins of the island entered popular imagination as the "Hobbits of Flores," on account of their seeming similarities with the diminutive characters in J. R. R. Tolkien's *Lord of the Rings* novels. Did these hobbits perhaps survive even later than 18,000 years ago? Researchers cited oral history among the modern inhabitants of Flores, recorded by ethnologists, which included stories about small creatures in remote parts of the island stealing food and snatching children around the time of the Portuguese arrival in the sixteenth century. It looked like evolution had reversed itself.

In 2016, however, new and improved measurements of the layers of soil surrounding the fossils revealed that the hobbit finds were much older than originally calculated: The hominins lived actually on the island between 100,000 and 60,000 years ago. Nevertheless, even if—disappointingly—hobbit islanders and *H. sapiens* on the way to Australia did not meet, the long survival of *H. erectus* still remains remarkable indeed.

- The story of *H. floresiensis* is a story of overlapping species. Which other examples of species overlapping each other are there?
- Improved measurement technologies require constant revisions. Which cases of revision, in addition to that of *H. floresiensis*, come to mind?

Key Terms

audio flashcards

Aboriginals 15
Acheulian toolmaking 9
Australopiths 7
Bipedalism 7
Dreamtime 16
Hominins 6
Levallois toolmaking 11
Oldowan toolmaking 8
Paleolithic 9
Savanna 8
Tundra 24

For additional resources, please go to **www.oup.com/us/vonsivers.**
Please see the Further Resources section at the back of the book for additional readings and suggested websites.

» PATTERNS OF EVIDENCE |

Sources for Chapter 1

SOURCE 1.1

Shell bead jewelry from the Grotte des Pigeons, Taforalt, Morocco

ca. 82,000–75,000 BCE

The discovery of 13 shells in a cave in eastern Morocco in 2007 has led to a discussion about the oldest known form of human ornamentation. Because each shell contains a pierced hole and traces of red ochre (a pigment derived from a type of rock), archaeologists concluded that the shells had been strung together as necklaces or bracelets. Another important detail is that the shell is from a genus of marine snail called *Nassarius*. The closest this snail is found to the site (at least today) is an island off the coast of Tunisia, more than 800 miles away.

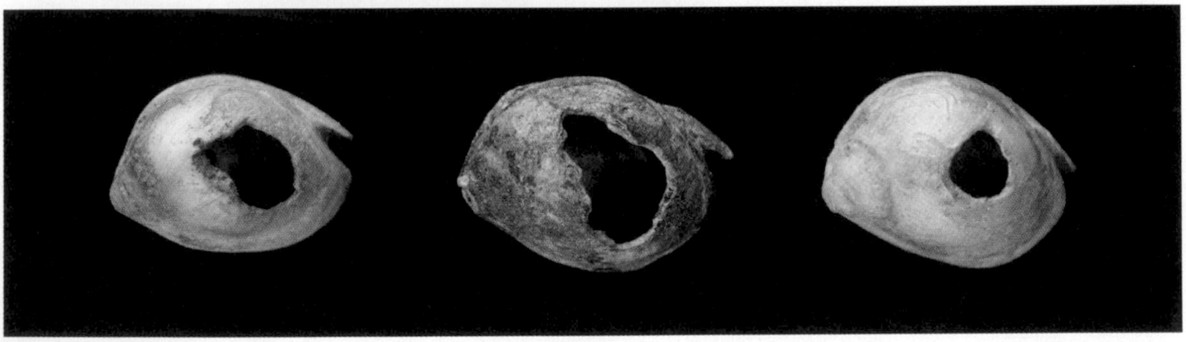

» Working with Sources

1. **Why is the creation of jewelry a significant step in the development of human society?**
2. **What might this find indicate about trade patterns and networks in northern Africa around 80,000 years ago?**

Source: *Smithsonian Institution, National Museum of Natural History*, http://humanorigins.si.edu/category/tags/292

SOURCE 1.2

Python-shaped ornamented rock found in the Rhino Cave, Botswana

ca. 70,000 BCE

Archaeologists working in the Tsodilo Hills of Botswana in 2006 may have found the oldest evidence of a form of human ritual behavior. One cavern contains a large rock, roughly 20 feet long and 6.5 feet wide, that resembles a giant python, with the natural features of the stone forming its eye and mouth. While its resemblance to a reptile may be natural, there are also several hundred man-made grooves along its side, indicating an attempt to replicate scales with fashioned tools. Spearheads were also found at the site, and similar ones in the area have been dated to 77,000 years ago. Researchers have concluded that this was a worship site for the inhabitants of the region in this period.

» Working with Sources

1. **What symbolic connections might early humans have attributed to snakes, and why might snakes have been depicted and worshipped?**
2. **What does the growth of "abstract symbolic thinking" suggest about the development of early *H. sapiens* societies?**

Source: *National Geographic*, http://news.nationalgeographic.com/news/2006/12/061222-python-ritual.html

SOURCE 1.3

Paintings in the Cave of Altamira, Santillana del Mar, Spain

ca. 24,000–16,000 BCE

Silex: Finely ground stone used as pigment in paint.

Inspired by the excitement attending the discovery of prehistoric cave paintings in France, amateur Spanish archaeologist Marcelino Sanz de Sautuola (1831–1888) conducted work on a Spanish cave in which similar paintings had been found. A series of excavations have been undertaken in the years since, leading to the discovery of many objects made from **silex**, bone, and horn at various levels of the cave system. The paintings—of horses, deer, bison, and human hands—were made throughout the cave's occupation, and the images are generally outlined in a black charcoal pigment and filled in with red or yellow paint.

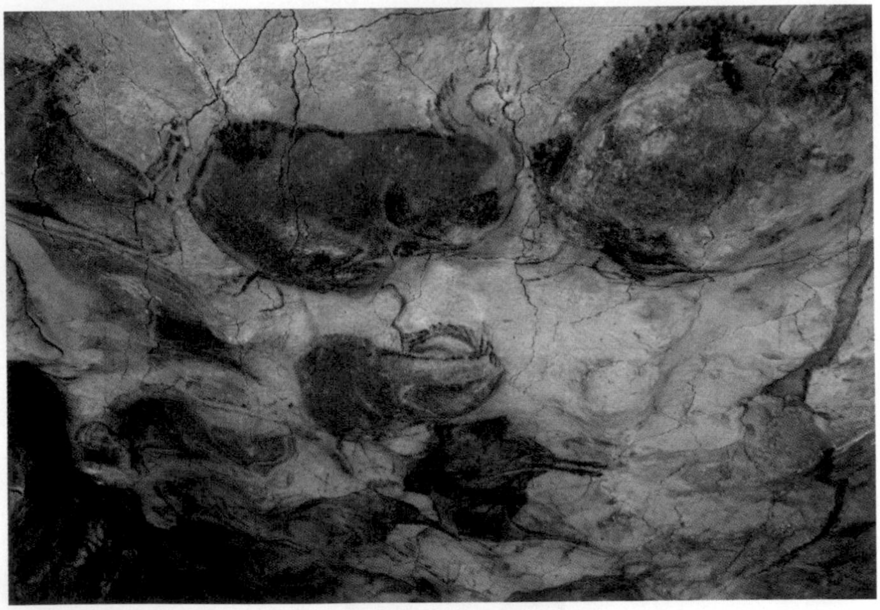

» Working with Sources

1. **What do these images depict, and how can they be compared with the paintings found at Lascaux and Trois-Frères, France (see pp. 19 and 21)?**
2. **What do the artistic and technical accomplishments of these artists indicate about the cultural creativity of early humans?**

Source: *Museo de Altamira*, Spain, http://en.museodealtamira.mcu.es/Prehistoria_y_Arte/index.html

SOURCE 1.4

Flax fibers found at the Dzudzuana Cave, Republic of Georgia, Caucasus Mountains

ca. 30,000 BCE

A 2009 paper in *Science* announced the identification of at least 488 fibers of flax attached to clay samples found in a cave in Georgia, in the Caucasus Mountains. Some of these fibers had been spun and dyed, and one of the threads (no. 8 in the figure) had been twisted. The applied colors, ranging from black to gray to turquoise, may indicate that the inhabitants of the cave were engaged in producing colorful textiles. The presence of spores in the cave indicates that fungus was probably already growing on the clothes and progressively breaking them down.

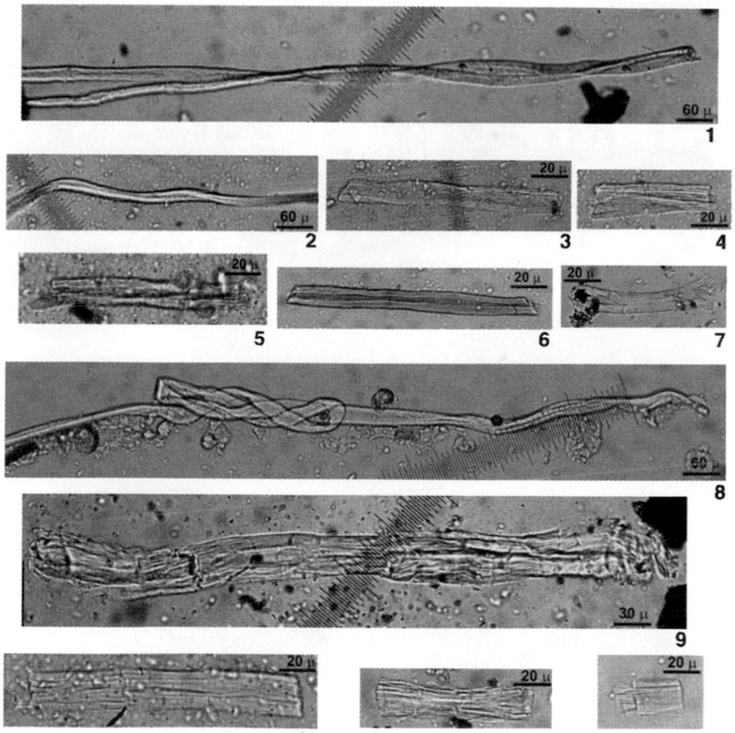

» Working with Sources

1. **What does the manufacture of clothing suggest about the sophistication of Upper Paleolithic human societies?**
2. **Can the manufacture of textiles in this period be compared to other forms of handcraft in the same era?**

Source: *Science Magazine*, September 11, 2009, http://www.sciencemag.org/content/325/5946/1359.full#xref-ref-2-1

Chapter 2 11,500–600 BCE

Agrarian–Urban Centers of the Middle East and Eastern Mediterranean

She was the first writer in world history we know by name. The high priestess Enheduanna [en-hay-doo-AN-nah] lived at the end of the third millennium BCE and was a daughter of Sargon of Akkad, ruler of Mesopotamia's first recorded kingdom. Amazingly, her writings are still available today in translation. Her best-known poem, "The Exaltation of Inanna," was written after a rebel leader had deposed Enheduanna as high priestess. In the poem Enheduanna sadly wonders why Inanna (also later known as Ishtar), the goddess of love, fertility, and war, has abandoned her: She has fulfilled all rituals and sacrifices and yet she is exiled from her goddess. Imploring Inanna to take her back into her good graces, Enheduanna marshals all her poetic powers.

After reciting prayerful poems night and day, Enheduanna finally succeeded. Inanna accepted her priestess' appeals and the rightful ruler returned Enheduanna to her temple position.

Agrarian–urban society: A type of society characterized by intensive agriculture and people living in cities, towns, and villages.

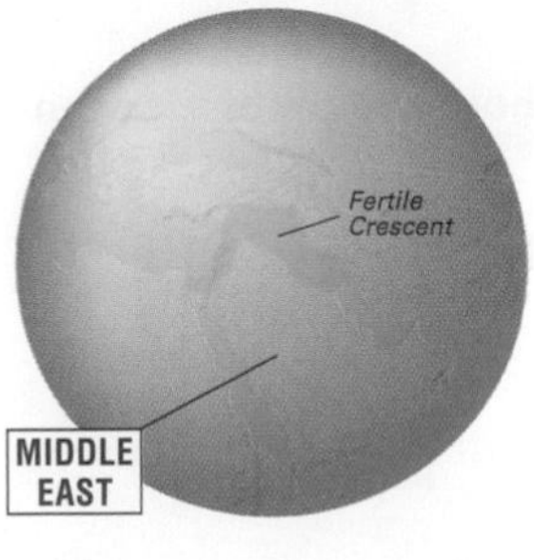

The end of the third millennium BCE, when Enheduanna lived, was a time when **agrarian–urban society**, with its villages and cities, had become well established in several different areas. Foragers had pioneered agriculture and village settlements during a long period of 5,000 years in the Fertile Crescent of the Middle East, a region particularly favored by climate, vegetation,

***ABOVE:* Standard of Ur in Mesopotamia, showing the so-called Peace/Banquet scene, with the king (first row, third from left) observing a variety of urban and rural activities.**

and animal populations. Once these early inhabitants had become farmers, they began interacting with foragers in the marshes of the Mesopotamian river delta, where—with the help of river water conducted via canals to the fields for irrigation—the groups merged. This combined population used the bountiful harvests for the foundation of cities in which craftspeople, priests and priestesses, merchants, kings, and rebels mingled, creating the fundamentals of the urban amenities of contemporary civilization: comfortable houses, places of worship, administrative centers, public archives, taverns, workshops, and markets. Many of these urban achievements are still crucial to our lives today. This chapter will trace the origins of farming, villages, cities, kingdoms, and empires in the Middle East, the first of the agrarian–urban centers in world history.

Seeing Patterns

- **What are the main factors that enabled the transition from foraging to farming?**
- **Where did the pattern of agricultural life first emerge and why?**
- **How did the creation of agrarian–urban society—what we commonly call "civilization"—make for an entirely new pattern of world history?**

Agrarian Origins in the Fertile Crescent, ca. 11,500–1500 BCE

The movement from foraging to agriculture—one of the most pivotal patterns in world history—was a slow process, covering several millennia. During this time, farmers built villages, in which they worked small garden-like plots and depended on annual rains for the growth of their crops. Farming gathered momentum as people mastered increasingly complex methods of irrigation. Farmers began to settle in the two great river valleys of the Tigris–Euphrates [you-FRAY-teez], in present-day Turkey, Syria, and Iraq, and of the Nile in Egypt. In these valleys, irrigation using river water allowed for larger plots and bigger harvests. Nutrient-rich river silt from the regular floods made the fields even more fertile and provided for often considerable surpluses of grain. These surpluses allowed populations to build cities and states, with ruling institutions composed of kings, advisors, armies, and bureaucracies.

Sedentary Foragers and Foraging Farmers

The region of the Middle East and the eastern Mediterranean stretches over portions of three continents—eastern Europe, southwestern Asia, and northeastern Africa. Historically, this region has always formed a single geographical unit within which there was extensive circulation of goods and ideas, although it did not constitute a single cultural zone. After the rise of the political institution of the empire, from about 1100 BCE, areas in the Middle East and the eastern Mediterranean were often also in competition with each other.

Geography and Environment To understand how people in the Middle East and eastern Mediterranean adopted farming and settlement, we need to look first at the geography of the region. The western half includes Thrace and Greece in the north, together with numerous islands in the Aegean Sea, a branch of the Mediterranean Sea. The terrain on the mainland as well as the islands is mostly mountainous, covered with forests or brushwood. To the east, adjacent to Thrace and Greece, lies Anatolia, which comprises most of modern Turkey. Anatolia is a peninsula consisting of a central high plain which is ringed by mountain chains and traversed by rivers.

South of Anatolia and lying on the eastern shore of the Mediterranean Sea is the Levant (from French for "rising [sun]"), encompassing modern Syria, Lebanon, Israel, and Palestine. Along the coastline is a mountain chain reaching from Mount

Chapter Outline

- Agrarian Origins in the Fertile Crescent, ca. 11,500–1500 BCE
- Interactions among Multiethnic and Multireligious Empires, ca. 1500–600 BCE
- Religious Experience and Cultural Achievements
- Putting It All Together

Lebanon in the north to the hill country of Palestine in the south. Mount Lebanon was covered at the time with huge cedars, of which only remnants survive today. The Levant, the Taurus Mountains of southeastern Anatolia, and the Zagros Mountains of southwestern Iran are often referred to as the "Fertile Crescent," to indicate its role as the birthplace of agriculture (Map 2.1).

To the east of the mountain chain extends the Syrian steppe, which gradually gives way on the south to the Arabian Desert. South of the Levant on the African continent are Egypt and Nubia (today's northern Sudan) on both sides of the Nile River. Both are largely covered by desert but bisected by the fertile Nile valley. This valley is wide and swampy in Sudan and narrow in Egypt, except for the Fayyum Depression and the Nile's Mediterranean delta. Also in the Middle East are three smaller regions:

- Persia (modern-day Iran), stretching from the Caspian Sea southward to the Persian Gulf
- Mesopotamia, "the land between the rivers," namely, the Euphrates and Tigris in present-day Iraq and Kuwait
- the Arabian Peninsula, consisting of modern Saudi Arabia, the United Arab Emirates, Qatar, Oman, and Yemen

Recent historical climate research has established that between the end of the Ice Age (around 11,500 BCE) and 4000 BCE monsoon rain patterns extended farther west than they do today. Monsoon rain currently forms in the summer in southern Africa and moves northeastward along East Africa before moving to India and China. When the monsoon still covered the Middle East, from the Mediterranean coast to the Persian Gulf, verdant vegetation covered land that is desert today. At

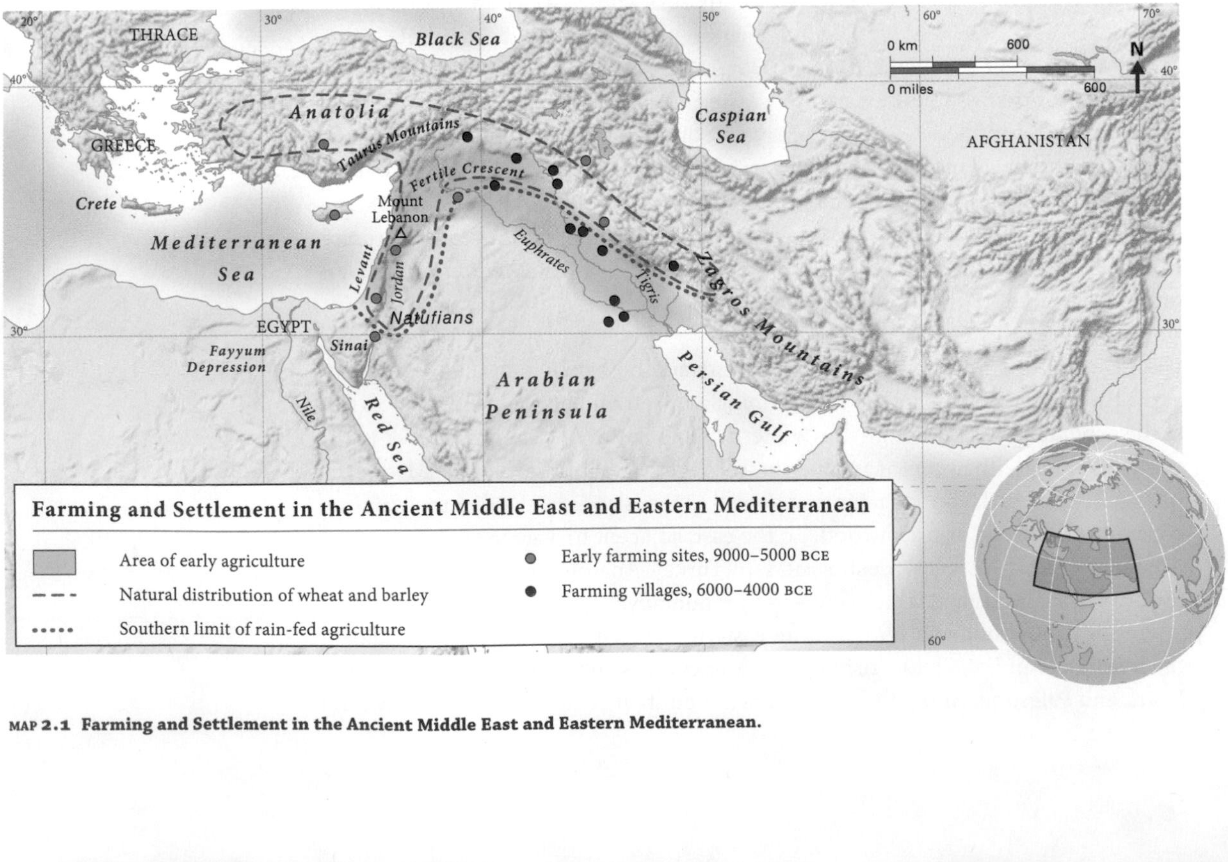

MAP 2.1 Farming and Settlement in the Ancient Middle East and Eastern Mediterranean.

present, only the highlands of Yemen and mountain rings around the central salt desert of Iran receive enough rain to sustain agriculture. At the eastern end of the Middle East is Afghanistan, a country with steppe plains and high mountains bordering on India—like the Fertile Crescent and Mesopotamia. It was also a center of early **agrarian society**.

Agrarian society: At a minimum, people engaged in farming cereal grains on rain-fed or irrigated fields and breeding sheep and cattle.

Agriculture first appeared in the Fertile Crescent for several reasons: its moderate climate, its fertile soil, and its access to abundant water sources (the Tigris and Euphrates) for irrigation. Other advantages enjoyed by this region included large areas of wild grains, primarily wheat and barley, as well as a variety of domesticated animals, including cows and sheep, along with donkeys and horses to transport goods from one region to the other. Finally, because of its location, agricultural advances were easily transmitted from the Fertile Crescent to Egypt in the West and to India and China in the East.

The Natufians The richness of the Fertile Crescent in plants and animals during the early centuries after the end of the Ice Age seems to have encouraged settlement. Foragers found everything they wanted within a radius of a few miles: wild grains, legumes such as lentils and chickpeas, and game. Nature replenished its ample resources year after year. Semipermanent hamlets, forming the Natufian culture (11,500–9500 BCE), arose in the Jordan and upper Euphrates valleys.

Each hamlet of the Natufians, consisting of about 60 inhabitants, contained a few semicircular pit houses made up of a stone foundation, posts, thatched walls, and a thatched roof. Sometimes their homes would even become their final resting places—the Natufians buried their dead underneath the floors of abandoned houses or along the edges of settlements. Some graves contained ornaments, and at least two persons have been found buried with their dogs. Later Natufians often removed the skulls of their ancestors—whether before or after the burial of the body is unknown—and venerated them in altar niches in their houses. Thus began an important ancestral cult that spread across the Middle East and lasted for several millennia.

To gather food, the Natufians went out into the woods with baskets and obsidian-bladed sickles. Wild cereal grains had evolved over the millennia so that their seeds scattered easily upon ripening, furthering the growth of new crops. Gatherers carefully tapped plants whose seeds had not yet scattered and collected the grains in baskets. Back in the hamlets, the grain was ground with pestles on

interactive timeline

- **11,500 BCE** End of last ice age
- **9500 BCE** Beginnings of agriculture in Fertile Crescent
- **4300 BCE** City-state of Uruk; introduction of the plow and wheel
- **3500 BCE** Temples in Mesopotamia and Egypt
- **3100 BCE** Unified kingdom of Upper and Lower Egypt
- **2340 BCE** Kingdom of Akkad; era of poetess Enheduanna
- **2000 BCE** Babylonian kingdom; palace-state of the Minoans

- **1900 BCE** Egyptian *Book of the Dead*
- **1650 BCE** Hittite Empire
- **1450 BCE** Palace-states of Mycenae in Greece
- **1350 BCE** Assyrian Empire in southwest Asia
- **1200 BCE** Bronze Age collapse; Phoenician, Philistine, and Israelite kingdoms
- **1100 BCE** *Enuma Elish*, Mesopotamian creation myth
- **750–600 BCE** Greek city-states: from aristocrats to citizen assemblies

grindstones. Storage seems to have been minimal, limited to portable containers, such as baskets. The abundant food supply, however, did not last. A near-glacial cold and dry period from 10,900 to 9600 BCE, called the "Younger Dryas" (named after a cold-resistant mountain flower), caused wild cereal stands to wither and game animals to drift away to warmer climes. Most of the sedentary foragers deserted their hamlets and returned to a fully migratory life of foraging. The short-lived, semisettled culture of the Natufians collapsed.

In the few hamlets that survived, people turned to storing grain in plastered pits or stone silos in order to cope with the harsher winters. In spring, they planted some of their stored grain to thicken the sparse wild stands. When warmer and more humid weather returned, a new era began, the **Neolithic**, or New Stone Age. Scholars use this designation for the period from about 9600 to 4500 BCE in the Middle East because it was characterized by innovations such as polished stone implements (spades and sickles), the introduction of agriculture, animal domestication, sun-dried bricks, plaster, and pottery—in short, most of the key elements of agrarian society.

Neolithic Age: Period from ca. 9600 to 4500 BCE when stone tools were adapted to the requirements of agriculture through the making of sickles and spades.

Selective Breeding of Grain and Domestic Animals Climatically, the Neolithic Age began with a metaphorical bang. Within just a few generations, summer temperatures increased by an extraordinary 7 degrees. Thereafter, temperatures continued to rise, at a more modest rate, for another 2,000 years. In this balmy climate, both old and newly established hamlets expanded quickly into villages of around 300–500 inhabitants. People continued to collect grain but also began to plant fields. In the early summer, they waited for the moment when almost all the grain was still in its ears. Through selective breeding, they gradually weeded out early-ripening varieties and began harvesting fields in which all grain ripened at the same time. The kernels of these first wheat and barley varieties were still small, and it took until about 7000 BCE in the Middle East before farmers had bred the large-grained wheat and barley of today.

Parallel to the selective breeding of grain, farmers also domesticated *pulses*—the edible seeds of pod-bearing plants—beginning with chickpeas and lentils. Pulses had the advantage of helping with the refertilization of the grain fields: Pods, stalks, and roots contain nitrogen needed by all plants to grow. Farmers continued to hunt, but they also captured young wild goats and sheep and through selective breeding accustomed them to live with humans in their houses and pens—the first domestication of livestock. For two millennia, this kind of early farming remained essentially garden farming, with handheld implements, such as digging sticks, spades, and sickles.

The original agriculture—the cultivation of grain and pulses and the domestication of goats and sheep—relied on annual rains in the Fertile Crescent and became more widespread when farmers tapped creeks for the irrigation of their fields during dry months. Inhabitants of this region discovered the benefits of rotating their crops and driving goats and sheep over the stubble of harvested grain fields, using the animals' droppings for refertilization and leaving the fields fallow for a year. Around 6500 BCE, these peoples added cattle, pigs, donkeys (domesticated first in Nubia), and pottery (clay vessels fired in kilns) to their farms. For the first time in world history, the epic transition from foraging to farming had been completed.

The Origin of Urban Centers in Mesopotamia and Egypt

During the fifth millennium BCE, the climate of the Middle East and eastern Mediterranean changed from one with monsoon rains falling during the summer to one with wet winters and dry summers in the west and north and general dryness prevailing in the east and south. Most of the Arabian Peninsula began to dry up. In lower Mesopotamia, drier conditions forced settlers coming from upstream to pay closer attention to irrigation. All of these changes would contribute to the rise of the first agrarian–urban centers founded along rivers—in the Middle East, Egypt, the Indus valley in the Indian subcontinent, and later the Yellow River valley in China.

Euphrates and Nile Floods The Tigris River in eastern Mesopotamia, with its turbulent waters and high banks, did not lend itself early on to the construction of irrigation canals. The Euphrates River in western Mesopotamia, however, flowed more tranquilly and closer to the surface of the land, providing favorable conditions for irrigated farming. At its lower end, in present-day Iraq, the Euphrates united with the Tigris and dispersed out into swampland, lagoons, and marshes, which supported a rich plant and animal life. It was here that the first farmers from the Fertile Crescent settled, establishing the Ubaid culture of villages (6000–4000 BCE).

The annual snowmelt in the mountains of northeastern Anatolia caused the Euphrates and Tigris to carry often devastating deluges of water down into the plain. The floods arrived in early spring just as the first grain was ready for harvest, forcing the farmers into heroic efforts to keep the ripening grain fields from being inundated by water. And yet the spring floods helped prepare the fields for the growing of smaller crops, such as chickpeas, peas, lentils, millet, and animal fodder. The floods also softened hardened soils and sometimes leached them of salt deposits. Thus, in spite of some drawbacks, irrigated farming in lower Mesopotamia, with its more predictable water supplies, was more productive and reliable than was the more irregular rain-fed agriculture in the Taurus–Zagros–Levant region to the north.

The Egyptian Nile originates in regions of East Africa where the rains hit during the early summer. Much of this rain is collected in Lake Victoria, from which the White Nile flows northward. In the Sudan it unites with the Blue Nile, which carries water and fertile silt down from the Ethiopian mountains. The Nile usually begins to swell in July, crests in August–September, and recedes during October. For the Neolithic inhabitants of Egypt these late-summer and fall floods created conditions quite different from those of lower Mesopotamia, which depended on the spring floods.

In Egypt, the floods coincided with the growing season of winter barley and wheat. Silt carried by the Nile fertilized the fields every year prior to planting. Because of the steeper descent in both the long valley and short delta of the Nile, the water table was lower and the danger of salt rising to the surface was less than in Mesopotamia, where, over time, large areas became infertile. The first agricultural settlements appeared in the Fayyum [fay-YOOM], a swampy depression off the Nile southwest of modern Cairo, around 5200 BCE. By about 3500 BCE, agriculture had spread south along the Nile and north into the delta.

Early Towns Between 5500 and 3500 BCE, villages in lower Mesopotamia and Upper Egypt developed into towns. They were composed of a few thousand

Assembly: Gathering of either all inhabitants or the most influential persons in a town; later, in cities, assemblies and kings made communal decisions on important fiscal or juridical matters.

Sharecroppers: Farmers who received seed, animals, and tools from landowners in exchange for up to two-thirds of their harvest and access to land.

Nomads: People whose livelihood was based on the herding of animals, such as sheep, goats, cattle, horses, and camels; moving with their animals from pasture to pasture according to the seasons, they lived in tent camps.

inhabitants, with markets where farmers exchanged surplus food staples and traders offered goods not produced locally. The Mesopotamian towns administered themselves through local **assemblies**, in which male adults came together to decide on communal matters such as mutual help during the planting and harvesting seasons, the digging of canals, punishments for criminal acts by townspeople, and relations with other towns and villages. For nearly two millennia towns in this region regulated their irrigated agriculture through communal cooperation (see Map 2.2).

In Mesopotamian and Egyptian towns an irrigated field produced about twice as much wheat or barley as did a rain-fed field. Indeed, irrigation made it possible for townspeople to accumulate an agricultural surplus that protected them against famines and allowed for population increases. Some people accumulated more grain than others, and the first social distinctions along the lines of wealth appeared. Gradually, wealthy families became owners of land beyond their family properties. **Sharecroppers** who worked these lands were perhaps previously landowners who had fallen into debt and now paid rent (in the form of grain) to the new landowners. Other landless farmers left agriculture altogether and became **nomads**, breeding *onagers* (ancestors of donkeys), sheep, and goats on steppe lands unsuited to cultivation. Wealthy landowners appropriated the places of ritual and sacrifice in the villages and towns and constructed elaborate temples, mansions, workshops, and granaries.

Eventually, the landowning priestly families stopped not only farming their own land but also making tools, pottery, cloth, and leather goods, turning the production of these goods over to specialized craftspeople, such as toolmakers (for stone, bone,

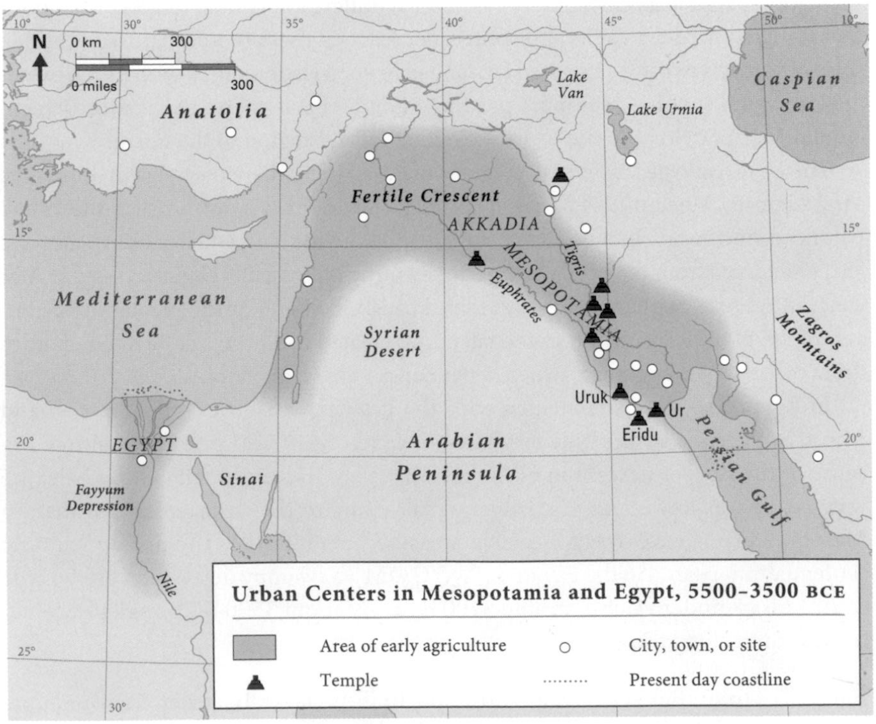

map analysis

MAP 2.2 Urban Centers in Mesopotamia and Egypt, 5500–3500 BCE.

or wood tools), potters, weavers, or cobblers, and paying them with grain rations. The landowners employed traders who traveled to other areas with crafts (pottery, cloth, leather goods), trading them for raw materials. Mesopotamian merchants traveled with cloth and tools to villages and towns in the Zagros Mountains and returned with timber, stone, obsidian, and copper. Egyptian villagers traded textiles with villagers in the Sinai Peninsula in return for copper and with Nubian villagers in return for gold.

Around 4300 BCE, some mountain people in the region had mastered the crafts of mining and smelting copper. This metal was too soft to replace obsidian, but the many other uses to which it was put have led scholars to mark the middle of the fifth millennium BCE as the moment when the Neolithic, or New Stone Age, of polished stone tools came to an end and the *Chalcolithic*, or Copper Age, began.

Temples In the course of the fifth millennium BCE, wealthy landowners gained control over the communal grain stores and clan shrines and enlarged these into town shrines. In Eridu, the shrine, originally a mud brick structure with an offering table for sacrifices, grew over the millennia through a dozen superimpositions into a monumental temple. Adjacent to the early temples were kilns, granaries, workshops, breweries, and administrative buildings. The wealthy landowners, presiding over the temples as priests, were responsible for the administration of all aspects of cult ritual in the temples, as well as the provision of labor in the temple fields, which included the digging and cleaning of irrigation canals; the planting, harvesting, transporting, and storing of crops; and the pasturing, stabling, and breeding of animals.

City, city-state: A place of more than 5,000 inhabitants with nonfarming inhabitants (craftspeople, merchants, administrators), markets, and a city leader capable of compelling obedience to his decisions by force.

In Upper Egypt, landowner-priests presided over the construction of the first temples around 3500 BCE, together with elegantly embellished tombs for themselves. The decorations in both temples and tombs depict boats, animals, and humans. One such painting shows a leader carrying out an expedition on the Nile upstream to Nubia, returning with gold, ebony, and diorite (black rock used for statues) to create elaborate ornaments for his temple and tomb. Unfortunately, the sparse archaeological record in Egypt at this point presents few details concerning the transition from village to town.

The World's First Cities In contrast to a town, a **city** (or **city-state**, if the surrounding villages are included) is defined as a place of more than 5,000 inhabitants, with a number of nonfarming inhabitants, such as craftspeople, merchants, and administrators. The latter lived on the food they received in exchange for their own handiwork, such as pottery, textiles, and traded goods. To keep order in such a large place where many people did not know each other, the dominant landowner-priest created a personal entourage of armed men, wielding police power. The first place in Mesopotamia to fit the definition of a city was Uruk, founded near Eridu around 4300 BCE.

The Temple at Eridu. Artist's reconstruction of the temple at Eridu. Note the immense platform supporting the temple and the sacred enclosure, which measured 200 square yards.

Within a millennium, it was a city of 50,000–80,000 inhabitants with a mixture of palaces, multistory administrative buildings, workshops, residences, palace estates, and villages clustered around the city with both large and small individual farms.

The people of Uruk were important pioneers of technical and intellectual innovations. It was here that the first known plow was found. Mesopotamian plows were sophisticated wooden constructions with seeder funnels on top and pulled by pairs of oxen or donkeys. Plowing and controlled sowing allowed for much larger harvests. Uruk craftspeople introduced the potter's wheel, which accelerated and made more precise the manufacture of earthenware and ceramics. The sizes of jars, pots, and bowls gradually became standardized, simplifying the storage of grain and its distribution in the cities.

At the same time, two- and four-wheeled carts pulled by oxen expedited the transportation of large quantities of grain from the fields to the city. The grain was made into bread, to conveniently feed the populace, and beer, which like bread became a source of calories and a safe, potable, and easily storable drink of choice among urban dwellers. By some estimates, more than 40 percent of Mesopotamia's grain was committed to beer production, and archaeologists have unearthed numerous recipes for the brew.

Another particularly serviceable invention was bronze, the world's first *alloy*—that is, a blending of two or more metals in the smelting process. Bronze is an alloy of copper and arsenic or tin; it is a hard, although relatively expensive, metal that could be used in tools and weapons. Bronze became so useful in the Middle East and eastern Mediterranean during the following centuries that it replaced stone and copper implements for all but a few purposes in daily life, leading historians to refer to this as the *Bronze Age* (in the Middle East from 3300 to 1200 BCE). Bronze became one of the hallmarks of agrarian–urban life as its use spread or was independently developed in other places in Eurasia.

Cuneiform Writing The administrators in the bureaucracy, who were responsible for the accounting and distribution of grain, animals, ceramics, textiles, and imported raw materials, greatly simplified their complicated tasks around 3450 BCE by inventing a form of writing. Scribes wrote in cuneiform [kyoo-NEE-uh-form] (from the Latin, meaning "wedge-shaped") script on clay tablets, using signs denoting objects and sounds from the spoken language. Small stone or clay tokens indicating different types of grain or goods on baskets or containers had been ubiquitous in the Middle East since the late Paleolithic. These tokens with a variety of engraved or imprinted signs might have been precursors of cuneiform writing. Historians are still researching and arguing these points. However the debate is eventually settled, it is obvious that writing was a major expansion of the conceptual horizon of humankind that reached back to the first flaked stones, ornaments, figurines, and cave paintings in the Paleolithic. For the first time, scribes could not only write down the languages they spoke but also clarify for future generations the meaning of the sculpted and painted artifacts which would otherwise have been mute witnesses of history. With the advent of writing, record keeping, communication, increasingly abstract thought, and, for the first time, history could all be recorded.

Kingdoms in Mesopotamia, Egypt, and Crete

With the introduction of the plow and increasing numbers of metal tools, city leaders greatly expanded their landholdings. They employed large groups of laborers to cut canals through riverbanks onto virgin lands. Vast new areas of lowlands, situated at some distance from riverbanks, became available for farming. Portions of this land served as overflow basins for floodwaters, to protect the ripening grain fields. Craftspeople invented lifting devices to channel water from the canals into small fields or gardens. As a result of this field and irrigation expansion, the grain surpluses of both temples and villages increased enormously.

Kingship in Mesopotamia A consequence of the expansion of agriculture was the rise of nearly two-dozen cities in lower and central Mesopotamia. As cities expanded and multiplied, the uncultivated buffer lands which had formerly separated them disappeared. People drew borders, quarreled over access to water, made deals to share it, and both negotiated and fought over the ownership of wandering livestock.

When it became impossible to contain conflicts and wars broke out, city dwellers built walls and recruited military forces from among their young population. The commanders, often of modest origins, used their military positions to acquire wealth and demanded to be recognized as leaders. They challenged the authority of the priests, who had been the traditional heads of villages and towns. Depending on circumstances, the Mesopotamian city assemblies chose their leaders from either the self-made or the priestly leaders, calling the former "great man" (*lugal*) and the latter "king" (*en*).

Once in power, a royal leader sought to make his position independent from the assemblies and impose dynastic or family rule on the city. To set himself apart from his assembly colleagues, he claimed divine or sacred sanction for his kingship. The King List of 2125 BCE, in which the reigns of all early kings in lower Mesopotamia were coordinated, begins: "After the kingship descended from heaven, the kingship was in Eridu." In other words, the kings argued that as divinely ordained rulers they no longer needed the consensus of the assemblies for their power or that of their sons and grandsons. The earliest king known by name and attested in the archaeological record was Enmebaragesi [en-me-ba-ra-GAY-see] of Kish, who reigned around 2500 BCE. Later kings are known for all the nearly two-dozen cities of Mesopotamia.

Cuneiform Script. Scribes impressed the syllables on the wet clay with a wedge-shaped reed stylus.

Akkadia and Babylonia During the 2000s BCE, these Mesopotamian cities began competing against each other for military supremacy. The first royal dynasty to bring them together in a unified territorial state or empire—numbering about 2 million inhabitants—was that of Akkadia (ca. 2340–2150 BCE). Sargon ("The Great"), the first major king (r. 2334–2279 BCE), commanded several thousand foot soldiers armed with bronze helmets, leather coats, spears, and battle-axes. At its height, Sargon's Akkadian polity stretched from Mesopotamia into Asia Minor and Syria, earning him the distinction of creating the world's first empire. Sargon's grandson, Naram-Sin, added the

Zagros Mountains and Syria to the Akkadian empire and claimed to be the "king of the four (world) shores." He considered his state to be an open-ended kingdom stretching in all four directions and limited only by the sea which surrounded the earth. Naram-Sin was the first king to conceive of a grand imperial design which would lead to the unification of the ethnically, linguistically, and religiously diverse peoples of the Middle East, with or without their consent. However, he did not yet possess the military means to embark on large-scale conquests and **empire** building (see Map 2.3).

Empire: Large multiethnic, multilinguistic, multireligious state consisting of a conquering kingdom and several defeated kingdoms.

A later major Mesopotamian kingdom was Babylonia. Its best-known king was Hammurabi (r. 1792–1750 BCE), who ordered the engraving of the entire code of Babylonian law onto a 7-foot slab of basalt. Like so many rulers in Mesopotamia and, indeed, in cultures around the world, Hammurabi saw himself as the executor of a stern, divinely sanctioned law that punished evildoers and rewarded the righteous. By today's standards, Hammurabi's laws were harsh, threatening severe punishments for crimes against property, land, and commerce. For example, tavern owners who overcharged customers or who failed to notify the police of the presence of criminals on their property were to be drowned. Priestesses caught in taverns were to be burned to death. The law of Mesopotamia was no longer the customary law of villages and towns but the royal writ, divinely ordained and backed by military force (see "Patterns Up Close").

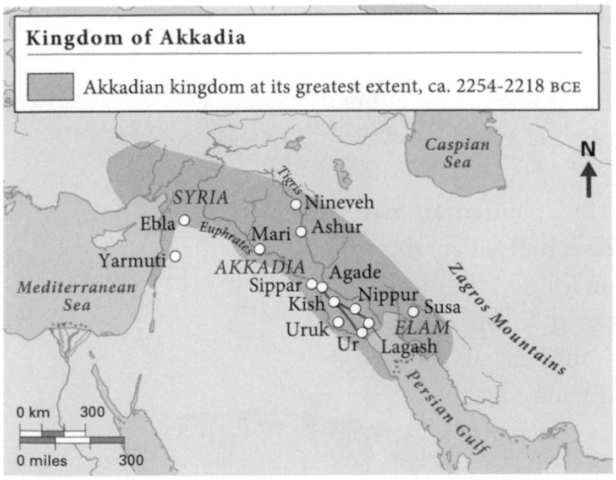

(a)

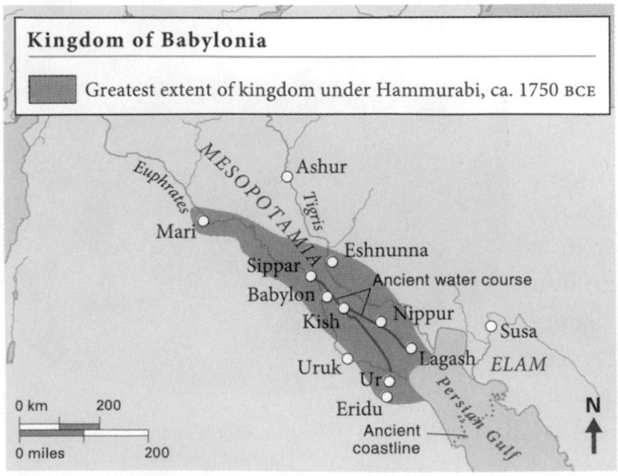

(b)

MAP 2.3 **(a) The Akkadian Kingdom. (b) Kingdom of Babylonia.**

Patriarchy and Gender The pattern of state formation from villages to kingdoms contained in itself another pattern crucial in the development of society in the Middle East and beyond: the increasingly pronounced patriarchal structure of society. As we have seen in Chapter 1, the archaeological evidence does not allow many conclusions concerning gender functions in Paleolithic society. The Lascaux image of the injured bull charging its hunter, who is depicted as a stick figure with a phallus, is a rare exception. The gathering and preparation of vegetal food was an occupation that required the communal cooperation of all and probably more than balanced the special occupation of males in the hunt. The Neolithic rise of agriculture does not seem to have changed much in these largely unstructured gender relations.

The wars among the city-states and kingdoms were important events in the creation of new patterns of gender relations. Large numbers of war captives, providing cheap labor as slaves in temple households and wealthy residences, gave the priestly and self-made kings a decisive edge in beginning the restructuring of agrarian–urban society. A ruling class emerged, composed of dynastic families who collaborated with other landowning and priestly families. One rank below the ruling class were the merchants and craftspeople, who formed a hierarchy among themselves, with merchants and jewelry makers at the top and tanners—because of the unpleasant odor of their manufacturing processes—in the lower ranks. At the bottom of this increasingly structured, hierarchical society were slaves and other marginal urban groups, such as day laborers and prostitutes.

The transition from agrarian societies to urban civilizations had several implications for gender roles. In more egalitarian agricultural societies there was little room for gender distinctions; women served vital roles in the planting and gathering of grains and in caring for children, while men hunted large game. This changed with the growth of urban centers, which resulted in varieties of social stratification. New arrangements were required to accommodate the political, economic, military, and religious changes brought about by urban life. Each of these changing spheres was dominated by males. Men developed and administered military affairs, and fighting forces were restricted to males. Men also emerged as rulers and high-ranking administrators, regulated commercial and trading matters, and formed the ranks of scribes, priests, and other functionaries.

Another factor of urban life was the emergence of wealth and property rights, which gave rise to the need to ensure inheritance of private property through male descent. Because this required both establishing and maintaining the legitimacy of the male line, sexual activities of women were restricted. As a result, women's roles were confined to household functions, thereby subordinating their social status to males.

The formation of hierarchical social structures did not stop with the rise of social classes. As we shall see in later chapters, men assumed legal power over women on all levels of society in nearly every agrarian–urban civilization. At first, the patriarchy was still relatively mild. In the ruling classes of Mesopotamia, female members held high positions as priestesses, queen consorts, and in a few cases even queens, but only as extensions of male dynastic rule. Enheduanna, in the vignette at the beginning of this chapter, was an example of a highborn woman unhappily dependent on the decisions of the male members of her family. As attested in the law code of Hammurabi, married women enjoyed some legal rights, including the right to sue for divorce if they could prove mistreatment. In general, however, wives were in many ways considered the property of their husbands, who could divorce their wives in cases of neglect of the household without returning dowries and who could engage in sexual relations with mistresses and prostitutes—while wives caught in adultery were thrown in the river along with their lovers.

Women in Egyptian society fared better in some ways than their Mesopotamian counterparts. Although they existed in a male-dominated society, women were accorded more respect in marriage, and they had more legal rights; they could own and transfer property, and they could sue for divorce. A few women in Egyptian royalty were considered nearly equal to men. In New Kingdom Egypt (1550–1070 BCE), princesses had the same rights of divine descent as princes. Sisters and brothers or half-brothers sometimes married each other, reinforcing the concept that their lineage was divine and pure. A famous example is Hatshepsut [hat-SHEP-soot], who was married to her half-brother. She was a strong-willed woman who became "king" (the title of "queen" did not exist) after the death of her husband, ruling for over two decades (r. ca. 1479–1457 BCE), before a son from one of her former husband's concubines succeeded her.

Patterns Up Close

Babylonian Law Codes

In addition to the invention of cuneiform writing and the use of the wheel, the Babylonians in lower Mesopotamia produced the earliest known collections of written laws. Because of their formal, written nature, these law codes differed from earlier oral and customary law common to all early cultures. When did these laws originate, how did they develop across time, and what was their influence on later ages?

The origin and evolution of the legal tradition are intertwined with developments associated with the complexity of urban life. In order to sustain sufficient agricultural production, people devised an intricate system of irrigation and drainage canals, along with dikes and dams, to control the often unpredictable flooding of the Tigris and Euphrates Rivers. All of this necessitated not only extensive planning and maintenance but also the allotment of plots of land, some closer to and others farther from water sources. In addition, the emergence of complex political, economic, and social relationships—fraught with disputes and inequalities—called for the establishment of a set of centrally administered rules and regulations in order to provide for conflict resolution as well as retribution for wrongdoing.

Across a span of nearly 500 years, from the earliest codification of King Urukagina of Lagash in ca. 2350 BCE to the monumental Code of Hammurabi in 1750 BCE (see Source 2.1), law developed through a successive series of increasingly comprehensive and refined legal codes consistent with developing complexities of urban expansion. Consequently, evolving law codes address correspondingly wider audiences, they cover a broader spectrum of social classes, and they present more complex examples of potential infractions as well as more nuanced resolutions. Most legal codes open with a prologue, which is followed by a body of laws, and close with an epilogue. In terms of format, Sumerian laws follow the format of "if this, then that" regarding violations and ensuing punishments, and punishments are meted out with reference to social status. Finally, they pay growing attention to the importance of irrigation, with more and more references to the maintenance of river dikes and irrigation canals, along with harsh consequences for neglecting this.

The law code of Hammurabi, king of Babylon (r. 1792–1750 BCE), represents the first complete written and well-organized code of law. An amalgamation of

In later millennia, after empires formed, noble women disappeared from their male-dependent public positions and lived in secluded areas of the palaces. Men tightened the law, relegating women to inferior family positions. Patriarchy was thus a product not of agrarian but of urban society in city-states and kingdoms of Mesopotamia and, a little later, Egypt.

Egyptian Kingdoms In Egypt, the first city was Hierankopolis [hee-ran-KO-po-lis], founded around 3000 BCE. Smaller cities dotted the river downstream to the delta. As in Mesopotamia, the rulers of cities began to develop into small-scale kings. Among the first of these we know by name were Menes, Narmer, and Aha. Whoever among these three was the first king, he unified all Egyptian lands—stretching from Upper Egypt down the Nile to the delta—and established the first dynasty of Egypt's Early Dynastic period (ca. 3100–2613 BCE), choosing Memphis, near

earlier Sumerian precepts, the code exceeds them in its extensions and embellishments; whereas earlier codifications list around 40 laws, those of Hammurabi number fully 282. Like earlier models, the code acknowledges distinctions in social categories along with inequalities among them but goes beyond them in addressing more social classes and grouping the classes according to relative wealth and social standing. Also, like previous collections, the code is broken down into several categories, including issues related to property and family law; but here again it covers many more possible scenarios in an effort to close previous loopholes.

Unlike its Sumerian predecessors, however, the code departs significantly when it comes to retribution in that it calls for more extreme punishments according to the principle of *lex talionis* ("an eye for an eye"). Thus, "If a man put out the eye of another man, his eye shall be put out." Further, the importance of maintaining irrigation systems is consistent with earlier themes but expressed in more nuanced terms: "If anyone open his ditches to water his crop, but is careless, and the water flood the field of his neighbor, then he shall pay his neighbor [grain] for his loss."

The long-term influence of Sumerian and Babylonian legal codes—particularly Hammurabi's code—extends far beyond ancient Mesopotamia. Many of its concepts and precepts served as predecessors of Hittite, Egyptian, and Assyrian laws. Instances of its influence appear in the development of biblical law, and striking similarities to the notion of *lex talionis* are found in Jewish law. The code was carried westward across the Mediterranean, where many of its principles found their way into Roman law, especially the organized codification of civil cases.

Questions

- What do the first law codes tell us about ancient Sumerian and Babylonian societies?
- Are the legacies of these first law codes still evident in modern Western legal practice today?

Stele with Hammurabi's Code.

modern Cairo, as his capital. At first, lesser rulers continued their reigns in the other cities. They even rebelled against the king from time to time. Therefore, the early policies of the Egyptian kings were focused almost exclusively on the unification of Egypt. Since it was not easy to subjugate the lesser rulers in a country 650 miles in length, unification was a protracted process.

The first king claimed divine birth from Egypt's founder god, Horus, the falcon-headed deity. As god on earth, the king upheld the divine order (*ma'at* [ma-AHT]) of justice and peace for all. For their part, the inhabitants of his kingdom were no more than humble servants whose duty was to provide for the king's earthly and heavenly life by paying him taxes and constructing an opulent palace and tomb for him. Of course, in practice this royal supremacy was far from complete. Even during times of strong centralization there were always some powerful figures—provincial landowners and governors, for example—who held title to their properties in their

Egyptian Hieroglyphs, Luxor, Valley of the Kings; Carved into the Wall and Colored.

own names and collected rents from the farmers working on these properties. As in Mesopotamia, the claim of the kings to divine sanction or even divinity did not keep rivals from bidding for supreme power.

Hieroglyphs, Bureaucracy, and Pyramids As with cuneiform in Mesopotamia, the Egyptian kings were greatly aided in the process of unification by the introduction of a system of accounting and writing. Around 3500–3200 BCE, administrators and scribes developed *hieroglyphic* writing in Egypt. In this system, formalized pictures symbolizing objects and syllables were used to represent words; hieroglyphic writing was limited to royal inscriptions. The writing material used in Egypt was papyrus, which was more expensive but less cumbersome than the Mesopotamian clay tablets. Papyrus was made from a special kind of Egyptian reed, the core of which was cut into strips, laid out crosswise, and pressed into textured sheets. First documented around 2700 BCE, papyrus became a major export item in the following millennium.

In addition to aiding in communication, writing—as it did in Mesopotamia—lent itself to a larger and more efficient bureaucracy in Egypt. At the beginning of the Old Kingdom (ca. 2613–2160 BCE), heavy Nile flooding enabled the Egyptian kings to expand agriculture on their lands. The royal palace and temple became large, elaborately hierarchical organizations in which everything was minutely regulated, including the food rations distributed to the palace administrators, priests, craftspeople, and laborers. Using arithmetic manuals, scribes calculated the quantities of bread, beer, and meat rations to be distributed; of timber for the shipyards; and of flax for the linen-weaving workshops (see Source 2.3). In its complexity, the Egyptian bureaucratic system of the Old Kingdom easily surpassed that of lower Mesopotamia during the contemporaneous Akkadian period (see Map 2.4).

The most astounding bureaucratic achievement of the Old Kingdom was the construction by Khufu (r. 2589–2566 BCE) of a pyramid near modern Cairo as a funerary monument for himself. Along with two other pyramids, Khufu's Great Pyramid makes up the famous Giza pyramids, which served as tombs for the bodies of later kings. By the orders of Khufu, stone workers quarried local limestone from cliffs along the Nile for the central portion of each of the pyramids. Finer, less brittle casing stones came from quarries upstream on the Nile. Ramparts of chipped stone and other debris, as well as sledges, rollers, and heavy levers made of timber, helped laborers move the stone blocks into place, as much as 479 feet high. After the completion of the pyramid, the construction machinery was dismantled, and today sand covers what were once the workers' camps.

Great Pyramid of Giza and Sphinx. The pyramid of Khafre, one of the three pyramids at Giza, was constructed during the Old Kingdom (ca. 2500 BCE). The Sphinx, shown in the foreground, has the body of a lion and the face of a man, perhaps that of Khafre.

The workforce, perhaps as many as 10,000 laborers, consisted of farmers who were working off their annual 1-month labor service owed to the king. A special labor office made sure that the withdrawal of groups of laborers from the villages was staggered in such a way that regular field labor was disrupted as little as possible. Foremen administered the groups of laborers. Other officials provided rations for them

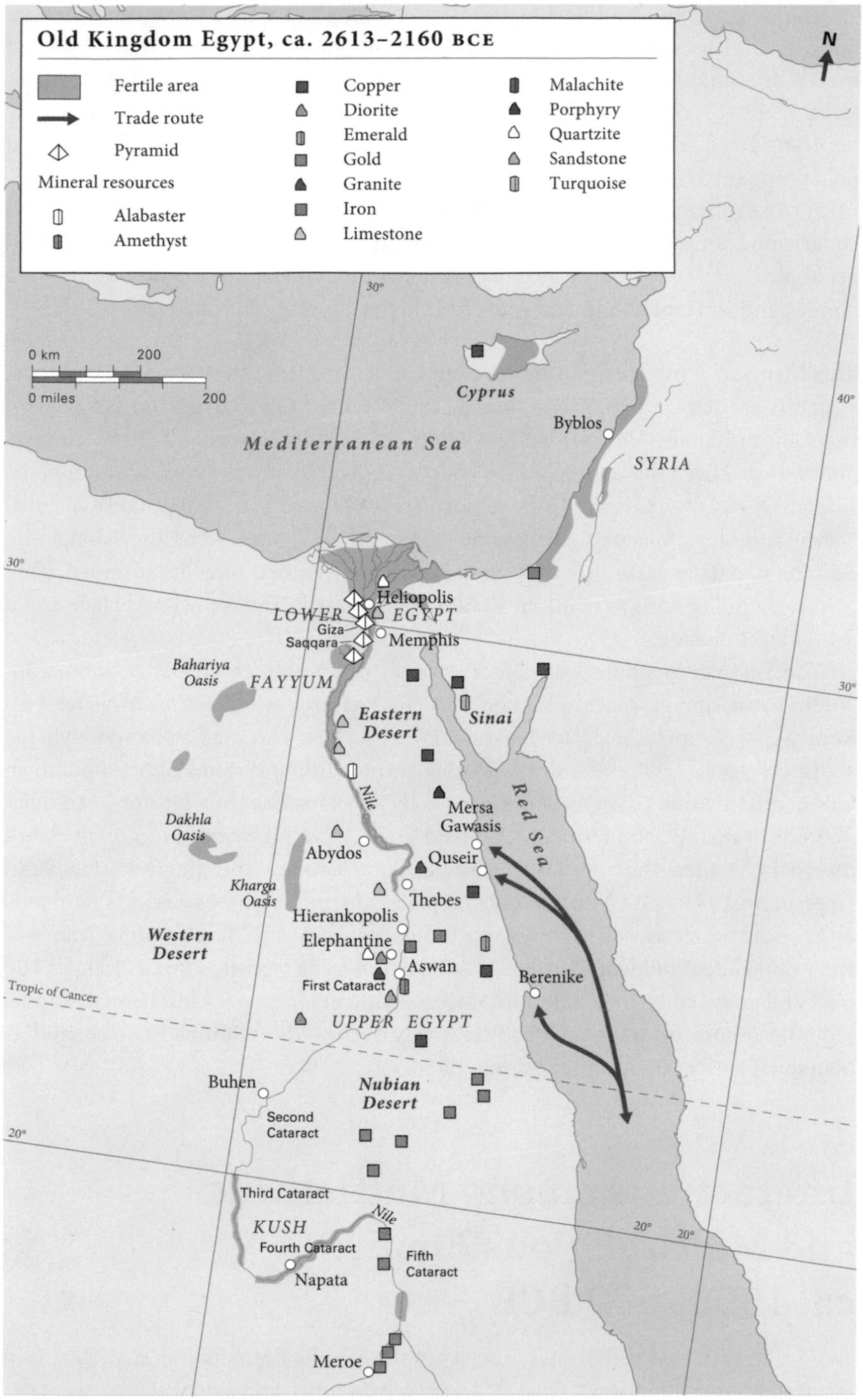

MAP 2.4 **Old Kingdom Egypt, ca. 2613–2160 BCE.**

in their camps. Although the workers were strictly supervised, we know that they also occasionally went on strike. Labor unrest, however, could easily be suppressed by the Egyptian army, which was composed of up to 20,000 soldiers, mostly Nubian archers.

The kings of the Middle Kingdom (ca. 2040–1750 BCE) were more modest builders and focused instead on large-scale agricultural projects, the mining of metals in Sinai, and long-distance trade. During Amenemhet III's long reign (r. ca. 1843–1796 BCE), Egypt reached the peak of its internal development. Workers transferred from Syria drained the Fayyum Depression and created irrigated fields similar to those found around many cities in Mesopotamia. Merchants developed close relations with other merchants in the Levant, from where they imported cedar wood for ships, roofs, and coffins. Egyptian exports consisted of jewelry and art objects made of gold. By the end of Amenemhet's reign, the kingdom numbered about 1 million inhabitants and was a formidable power.

The Minoan Kingdom After farming had spread from the Levant to Anatolia, seafarers carried the practice westward around 6500 BCE to mainland Greece and the Aegean islands. They settled first on the islands of Cyprus and Crete. Crete is about 170 miles long and 35 miles wide at its widest point. Over the millennia, some of the early villages of Crete grew into towns, and by around 2000 BCE small states with kings, spacious palaces, and surrounding villages were flourishing. The dominant **palace-state** was that of the Minoans (named after its founder, King Minos), a polity with as many as 12,000 inhabitants in the sprawling palace and a few villages outside.

Palace-state: A city or fortified palace with surrounding villages.

The Minoan kingdom was centered on a palace with hundreds of rooms, including vast storage spaces for food and cisterns for the collection of water (see Source 2.4). Among the palace personnel were scribes who used a pictorial-syllabic script on clay tablets similar to the writing and recording systems of Mesopotamia. Unfortunately, this script, called *Linear A* by scholars, has thus far not been deciphered. In the villages, farmers produced grain, olive oil, wine, and honey. Royal merchants traded these products for obsidian, copper, and tin from mainland Greece, Anatolia, and Cyprus. Craftspeople made pottery, bronze vessels, and jewelry for the palace as well as for export to Egypt, Syria, and Mesopotamia. Minoans were skilled boatbuilders who constructed oceangoing vessels, some as long as 100 feet, and powered by both sails and rowers. Minoan Crete was closely related to its older neighbors, from whom it had creatively borrowed—but it had also created its own independent trade and seafaring traditions.

Interactions among Multiethnic and Multireligious Empires, ca. 1500–600 BCE

From around 1700 to 1000 BCE, society in the Middle East and the Mediterranean changed in important ways. Chariot warfare, iron tools, and iron weapons were developed and refined. Agriculture spread from the original core of Syria, Mesopotamia, and Egypt to the periphery in Greece, central Anatolia, central Asia, and Arabia. The peoples in this peripheral area adapted the basic agricultural methods acquired from the core area but also introduced contributions of their own, especially military and transport technologies. On the basis of these contributions, conquerors built large empires in which a small, ethnically defined ruling class ruled over collections of other ethnic groups, speaking a multiplicity of languages and sacrificing to a multiplicity of gods.

The Hittite and Assyrian Empires, 1600–600 BCE

Agriculture spread from the Middle East to foragers in western Europe and central Asia. Villagers in central Asia, known as "Proto-Indo-Europeans," domesticated the horse and used it for pulling chariots. Later, Indo-Europeans migrated with their horses and chariots to the Middle East, India, and western Europe, where they settled as ruling classes among the indigenous villagers.

Horses and Chariots from Central Asia The spread of agriculture into Europe and central Asia had major consequences for the Middle East and the eastern Mediterranean. Shortly after 3000 BCE, in the region around the Ural Mountains in central Asia, local Proto-Indo-European villagers domesticated the horse, using it for its meat and for transporting heavy loads. Around 2000 BCE, after villages in the southern Ural Mountains had been transformed into towns through trade, town leaders emerged who were equipped with horse-drawn chariots, as well as with composite bows, made of a combination of grooved wood and horn carefully glued together. With a length of 4 feet and a range of 150 yards, this bow was much more powerful than the existing simpler and shorter bows dating back to the Paleolithic. A chariot could accommodate two or three warriors, one to guide the horses with leather reins and bronze bits and the others to shoot arrows with the composite bow. Around 1700 BCE, both chariot and composite bow made their entry into the Middle East and eastern Mediterranean. They contributed to a major transformation of the kingdoms that had hitherto relied solely on foot soldiers.

The Hittite Empire The first rulers in the Middle East to make use of chariots and composite bows for their military were the Hittites (1650–1182 BCE), Indo-Europeans settling in central Anatolia. This area, one of the richest mining regions in the Middle East, had large iron deposits. Iron was a by-product of copper smelting but was initially considered useless since it manifested itself in the form of "bloom iron," a soft substance with an abundance of ore impurities. Only after prolonged forging (that is, of hammering during which the bloom iron had to be kept red hot) were smiths able to remove the impurities and increase carbon content for hardening. By around 1500 BCE, smiths in Anatolia had fully mastered the art of iron making. The Hittites incorporated iron into the equipment of their chariot armies, in the form of swords, helmets, and protective armor. The combination of these military elements gave the Hittites an early advantage, which they used to become the pioneers of a new type of conquering polity—an "empire" consisting of many different peoples, languages, and temple religions. At its peak, the Hittite Empire stretched from Anatolia to northern Syria, comprising peoples of many languages and religions (see Map 2.5).

To distinguish themselves from ordinary kingdoms, the Hittite kings called themselves "great kings." In their capital, Hattusa, they ruled with an assembly (*panku*) of their principal administrators, recruited from the aristocracy. When they conquered rival kingdoms, they left the lesser, conquered kings in place as provincial rulers. The core of Hittite armies consisted of a nobility of highly trained, disciplined, and

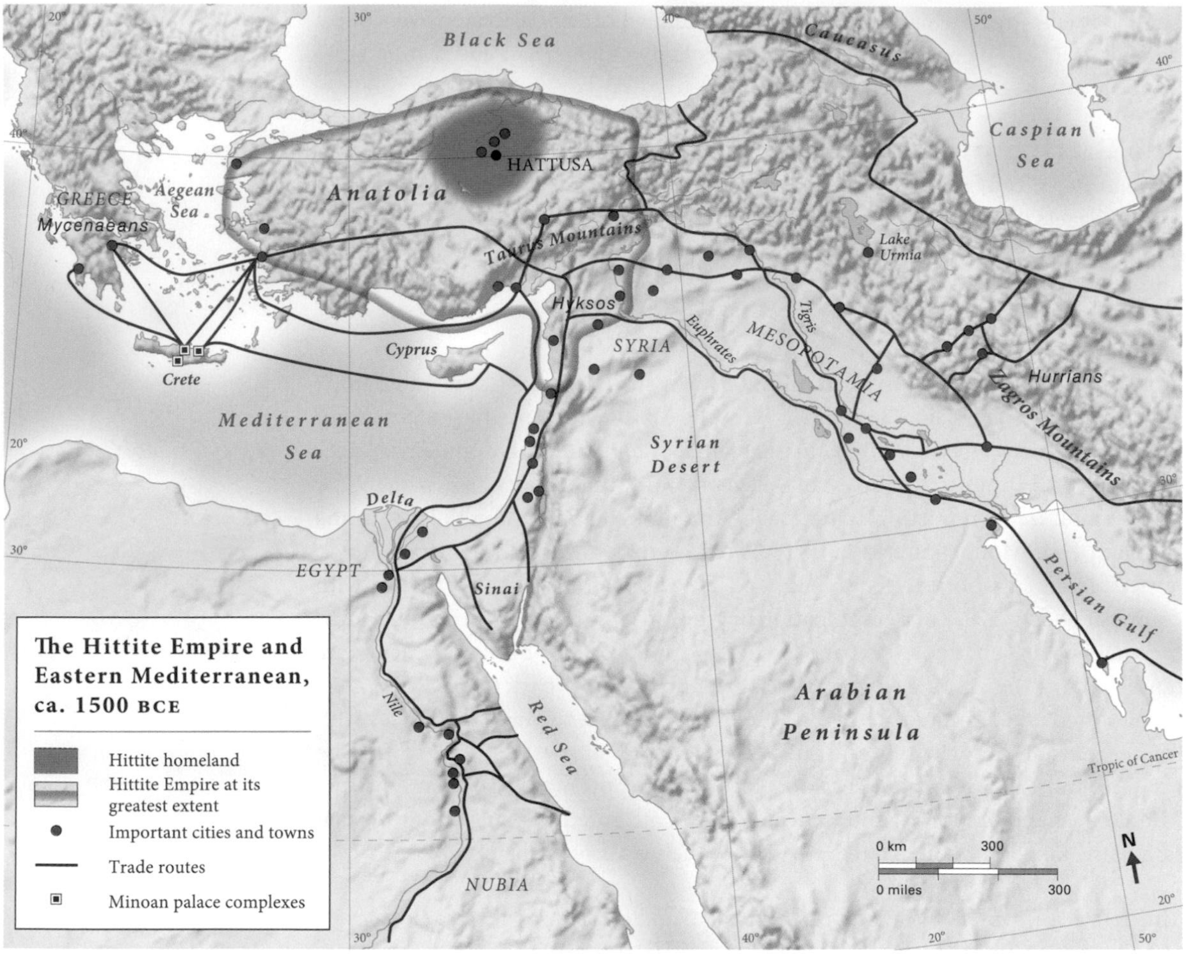

MAP 2.5 The Hittite Empire and Eastern Mediterranean, ca. 1500 BCE.

mobile chariot warriors. Mercenary foot soldiers, acting as skirmishers, protected the chariots from direct attacks by enemy infantry. These skirmishers were enrolled from among mountaineers, herders, and nomads for the duration of campaigns.

In the conquered lands, the "great kings" placed nobles in strategic garrisons to keep the local, non-Hittite rulers in check. Since the imperial warehouses held limited amounts of foodstuffs, the nobility received land grants, using the rents they extracted from the towns and villages for their livelihood. This Hittite system of employing both its nobility and local rulers was to become the model of organization for all subsequent Middle Eastern and eastern Mediterranean empires.

The practice of imposing an empire on many regional kingdoms did not make for stable politics. People to the east of the Hittites, the Hurrians in the Zagros Mountains, who also had a king and ruling class equipped with chariots, repeatedly invaded their western neighbors. At one point, in the early sixteenth century BCE, they vied with the Hittites for control of Syria. Their struggle dislodged a Syrian, chariot-equipped people, the Hyksos, who migrated to Egypt where they established a kingdom in the Nile delta. As a result of losing the delta, the Egyptians adopted chariot warfare and imperialism as well. Under the eighteenth dynasty, ca.

image analysis

Tutankhamen (1336–1327 BCE) of Egypt in Full Battle Regalia. The pharaoh, accompanied by skirmishers (*far left*), is aiming at deer in a herd fleeing from his galloping horses.

1550–1086 BCE, they inaugurated the New Kingdom, which devoted its military energies to the conquest of Nubia in the south and Palestine and Syria in the north.

Imperial Egypt During the New Kingdom (ca. 1550–1070 BCE), the Egyptians vigorously pushed their border with the Hittites as far north as possible, building garrisons and collecting tributes from a number of coastal cities in southern Syria (modern Palestine) and Lebanon. The Egyptians eventually clashed with the Hittites at Qadesh [kah-DISH] in northern Syria (1274 BCE), where they engaged in the largest chariot battle ever fought in the Middle East. Neither side prevailed, and in the earliest known peace treaty—the Treaty of Kadesh—the two empires decided to curb their imperialism and coexist diplomatically with each other, with Syria divided between them.

A short time later, this coexistence was shattered by invasions of the "Sea Peoples" from the Aegean Sea. Originally a mixture of former foot soldiers, mountaineers, and herders from northern Greece had raided the Mycenaean [my-sen-EE-yan] kingdoms of southern Greece, as we discuss later in this chapter. These people, joined by survivors of the collapsing kingdoms, took to the sea (hence their name "Sea Peoples") and sailed to the wealthy kingdoms of the Levant. One group of Sea Peoples, presumably remnants of one of the Mycenaean kingdoms, destroyed the Hittite Empire in 1207 BCE, reducing it to a few small fragments. The Egyptian Empire lost southern Syria to another set of seafaring invaders, the Pelesets [PE-le-sets] (Philistines) and retreated to Sinai, abandoning its imperial ambitions.

The invasions by Sea Peoples triggered the so-called **Bronze Age collapse** of ca. 1200 BCE with which the **Iron Age** in the Middle East and eastern Mediterranean began. The collapse is explained as a crisis in which the overextended early empires of the Hittites and Egyptians were unable to sustain the enormous expenses required for chariot warfare. With the decline in the numbers of chariots, large numbers of skirmishers became jobless. Scholars assume that most of the destruction and diminishment of these early kingdoms was due to marauding or migrating skirmishers like the Pelesets and Ahhiyawa , who were unemployed.

Bronze Age collapse: Around 1200 BCE, resulting from the collapse of the Hittite Empire and the weakening of the Egyptian New Kingdom; chariot warfare had become unsustainable in these early kingdoms.

Iron Age: Around 1500–1200 BCE, smiths were able to produce sufficiently high temperatures to smelt iron bloom, a mixture of iron and a variety of impurities.

The Assyrians Emerging after the Bronze Age collapse, the Assyrians (ca. 1350–607 BCE) founded a new empire, which like the Hittite Empire was also based on rain-fed agriculture. Its capital was Assur, a city founded in upper Mesopotamia around 2000 BCE on an island in the Tigris River. Originally, Assur's farming base was too limited to support territorial conquests. Instead, its inhabitants enriched themselves through trade. They built trading outposts as far away as central Anatolia and exchanged textiles for timber, copper, tin, and silver, much of which they sold to the Babylonians in the south. In the fourteenth century BCE, the Assyrian kings began to use Assur's commercial riches to finance their first large-scale conquests.

The Assyrians expanded into both the Zagros Mountains and Syria, reaching the borders of the Hittite Empire and claiming equal status with them. The great king of the Hittites, however, haughtily rejected the upstart's claim: "On what account should I write to you about brotherhood? Were you and I born from the same mother?" Stopped at the Hittite borders, Assyrian troops turned southeastward and expanded into lower Mesopotamia. Here, they occupied Babylon for a short period, humiliating their wealthy neighbors by carrying away the statue of the city god.

After some severe military setbacks, during which Assyria was reduced to its upper Mesopotamian center, ambitious kings renewed Assyrian expansion, creating Neo-Assyria (New Assyria), which lasted from 934 to 607 BCE. They embarked on conquests as had no other kings before them, systematically and ruthlessly conquering the lands around them. The core of the Neo-Assyrian armies consisted of small chariot forces and larger regiments of a new type of warrior—horsemen, chosen from among the nobility. These horsemen rode without stirrups on saddlecloths and fought using bows and arrows. The conquered peoples were forced to contribute soldiers to the Assyrian infantry, thus replenishing and multiplying the ranks of the largest and most expendable forces. Iron swords, iron-tipped lances, full-length

Ashurbanipal Hunting Lions in Chariot. Note the driver holding the reins, accompanied by the archer, presumably Ashurbanipal. Note also the powerful flex of the composite bow, as well as the quivers of arrows mounted on the sides of the chariot.

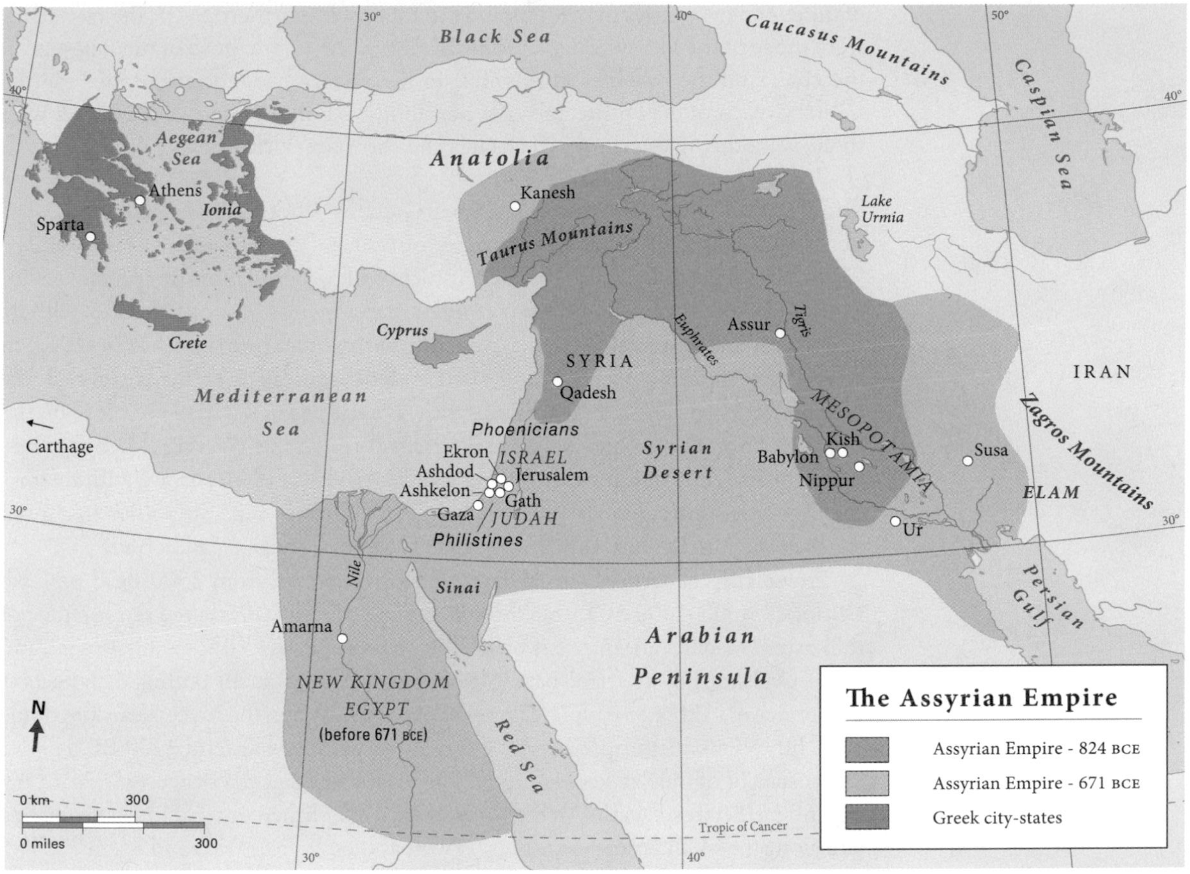

MAP 2.6 The Assyrian Empire.

scale armor (iron platelets sewn on leather shirts), and iron helmets were now common and helped the Assyrians to become the most formidable empire builders of their day.

In fact, the Assyrians were among the most ruthless campaigners in recorded history. They destroyed temples, razed cities, and forcibly deported the defeated inhabitants of entire provinces to other parts of the empire. Scholars have estimated that hundreds of thousands of deportees, the men among them often in chains, had to walk hundreds of miles through the countryside before being settled in new villages. At the peak of their conquests (745–609 BCE), the Assyrian rulers became the first to unify all of the Middle East, a dream first expressed by King Naram-Sin of Akkad centuries earlier. This same accomplishment would be repeated many more times in years to come (see Map 2.6).

Small Kingdoms on the Imperial Margins, 1600–600 BCE

Syria was a region between the Hittite (or, later, Assyrian) Empire in the north and the Egyptian Empire in the south. The dominant form of political organization in this region was the city-state under a royal dynasty. These city-states were located on the coast and had harbors, a number of surrounding villages, and a larger hinterland of independent villages in the hills and mountains. In northern Syria, the city-states were those of the Phoenicians; in southern Syria, they were those of the Pelesets on the coast and the Israelites in the hills. In the eastern Mediterranean, outside the military reach of the Hittite and Assyrian Empires but in commercial contact with them, were the Mycenaean palace-states and early Greek city-states.

The Phoenicians The people known in Greek as "Phoenicians" and by the Egyptians as "Canaanites" held the city-states of Byblos (modern Jubeil [joo-BALE]), Sidon, and Tyre (ca. 1600–300 BCE), each with a population of several tens of thousands. The Phoenicians also controlled the slopes of Mount Lebanon, with its famous cedars. These valuable trees, together with timber from Anatolia, were much sought after in the Middle East and eastern Mediterranean as construction material for buildings and ships. No less important was a species of sea snail collected on the beaches, from which a highly valued purple textile dye was extracted. Urban craftspeople made ceramics, textiles, leather goods, jewelry, and metalware with distinctive Phoenician designs, destined for sale abroad. More than any other territorial states in the Middle East, the Phoenician city-states were engaged in trade.

Phoenicians as traders appear in the historical record from 2500 BCE onward. During ca. 1600–1200 BCE, the Phoenicians and Mycenaeans shared the sea trade of the eastern Mediterranean, transporting their own goods as well as metals, timber, and stone. On land, they preferred paying tribute to, and occasionally putting their fleets at the service of, Hittite or Egyptian imperial overlords. When the Mycenaean kingdoms and Hittite Empire collapsed and the Egyptians withdrew around 1200 BCE under the onslaught of the Sea Peoples, the Phoenicians seized their chance. Systematically expanding their reach in the Mediterranean, they established trade outposts on islands and along the Mediterranean coast as far west as modern Morocco and Spain.

In addition to founding numerous ports and outposts around the Mediterranean (one of which, Carthage, would later become the center of a powerful city-state on its own), the Phoenicians acquired world-historical importance through their introduction of the letter alphabet. People in Syria had been familiar with the Mesopotamian cuneiform and Egyptian hieroglyphic writing systems for centuries. Both systems were complicated, however, and required many years of training to learn. From rock inscriptions discovered in 1998 in Egypt it appears that Phoenician (or Syrian) merchants began experimenting around 1900–1800 BCE with a much simplified writing system. In this system letters replaced the traditional signs and syllables, with each letter standing for a spoken consonant. Subsequently, in various parts of Syria, fully developed alphabets with letters for about 30 spoken consonants appeared (the vowels were not written). The Phoenician alphabet of ca. 1200 BCE was the most widely used, becoming the ancestor of all alphabetical scripts.

The Pelesets and Israelites During its imperial phase (ca. 1550–1200 BCE), Egypt controlled the Palestinian towns of Gaza, Ashkelon, Ashdod, Gath, and Ekron. Occasionally, the Egyptian kings aided their governors in these towns by carrying out punitive campaigns. After one such campaign, a defeated people in southern Syria was "stripped bare, wholly lacking seed," as an Egyptian inscription of 1207 BCE recorded. The name used in the inscription for this people was "Israel," the first time this name appeared in the records. "Israel" seems to refer to some sort of tribal alliance among Canaanite villagers and herders in the hills.

When the Pelesets, or Philistines, took over southern Syria and Egypt withdrew a short time later, agriculture and trade quickly recovered from heavy Egyptian taxation. The coastal Philistines established garrisons among the Israelites in order to secure trade routes through the highlands and along the Jordan valley. In response, as is recorded in the Hebrew Bible (the Old Testament in Christian usage), a military leader named Saul and a number of tribal leaders recruited a military force that began a war of liberation against the Philistines. According to this scripture, Saul was killed during the early stages of the war, and his successor, David, completed the liberation, establishing himself as king in Jerusalem shortly after 1000 BCE.

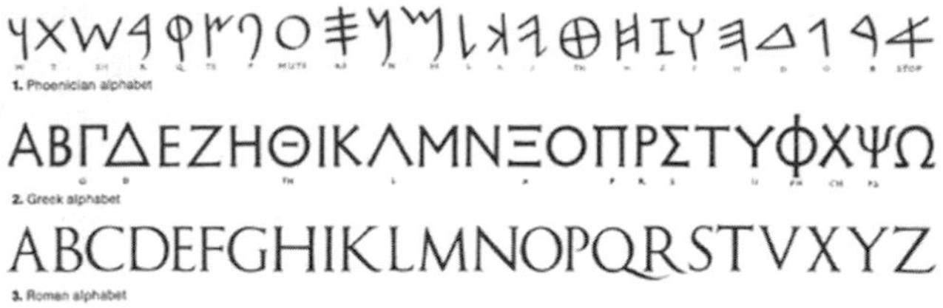

Phoenician, Greek, and Roman Alphabets. This illustration reveals similarities among the Phoenician, Greek, and Roman alphabets. Phoenician traders carried the alphabet across the Mediterranean, where it was adopted by Greeks. Subsequent interactions among Greeks, Etruscans, and Romans resulted in the transition to Roman letter forms, which in turn ultimately provided the foundation for English characters.

According to the Hebrew Bible, Jerusalem was a town on top of a mountain spur in southern Syria. David's son Solomon is said to have greatly enlarged the town, constructing a palace, the famous temple, and administrative buildings. To date, archaeologists have found few traces of Solomon's constructions except a few foundation walls and terraces on the eastern slope of present-day Jerusalem. Moreover, they have not even been able to confirm the rise of Jerusalem from village to city level. For historians, therefore, the biblical account, like that of many ancient texts, is perhaps best understood not as history but as a religious foundation story, demonstrating God's providence.

According to the Hebrew Bible, the two states that emerged after Solomon, Israel in the north (930–722 BCE) and Judah in the south (930–587 BCE), enjoyed only short periods of independence after being liberated from the coastal Philistines. The empire of Assyria and its successor, Neo-Babylonia (626–539 BCE), conquered the two kingdoms in the eighth to seventh centuries BCE. Thousands of members of the two royal families, priests, scribes, landowners, and craftspeople had to resettle in other parts of Syria or in Mesopotamia. The Philistines, together with people in the Syrian steppes (collectively called "Arabs"), suffered similar fates of defeat and deportation. In their place, Anatolian and Iranian populations settled in Syria. The final wave of Israelite deportations, under the Neo-Babylonians in 597–582 BCE, became the infamous "Babylonian captivity" (*gola*) mourned by several prophets in the Hebrew Bible.

The Mycenaeans and Early Greeks Parallel to the Phoenicians, Pelesets/Canaanites, and Israelites in Syria, the Mycenaeans arose in Greece and the eastern Mediterranean during the middle of the second millennium BCE. After the adaptation to farming, demand for specialized agricultural products (such as olive oil, wine, dried fruits, and nuts) among the villages had advanced sufficiently to result in the emergence of towns and cities which traded in these goods as well as in copper and bronze wares. Around 1700 BCE, in Attica and the Peloponnesus, two peninsulas with relatively large plains suitable for agriculture, leaders built forts as refuges in times of war for their fellow villagers. The best known among these forts were Mycenae, Tiryns, Pylos, Sparta, and Athens.

Two centuries later, the forts evolved into palaces with warrior lords and kings, as well as administrative offices, surrounded by clusters of villages. In these palace-states, scribes introduced a new, cuneiform-derived script, which has been identified as Greek, and unlike the Linear A of the Minoans, has been deciphered. This *Linear B* script provides us with invaluable information for understanding early Greek culture. About 1450 BCE, chariot and bronze weapon–equipped Mycenaean warriors sailed to Minoan Crete and conquered the island. The Mycenaeans were a major seafaring power in the eastern Mediterranean, establishing trading outposts in competition with the Phoenicians.

The Mycenaean palace-states were short lived. When an earthquake hit around 1250 BCE, the walls of many palaces collapsed. Former mercenaries (skirmishers in the chariot armies of the Hittites) joined by herders from northern Greece raided the weakened Mycenaean palace-states. A century later most palaces had disappeared, together with their administrators, scribes, and archives. The descendants of the kings, however, managed to salvage some wealth, as evidenced by their tombs. Iron swords and jewelry found in these tombs were of Phoenician origin and indicate that some sea trade continued even after the destruction of the Mycenaean states.

A general recovery in Greece began during the eighth century BCE. Trade in agricultural goods such as grain, olive oil, and honey was revived in new market outposts in Anatolia, Syria, and Egypt. The Anatolian craft of ironworking spread to Greece. Literacy returned as the Greeks adopted the Phoenician alphabet, adding vowels to the existing consonants to create the Greek alphabet. The population increased, often so quickly that many people were unable to find employment. After 750 BCE, many unemployed or adventurous Greeks seeking new challenges emigrated to the Anatolian west coast or as far as Italy and the Black Sea to colonize the land and establish new cities. As these cities developed into city-states of their own, the region along the Anatolian coast became known as "Ionia."

The distinctive mark of the new city-states was the absence of palaces. Instead, a sacred precinct in a city's center served as an open space for general assemblies. Contained within this space were a temple and administrative buildings with porches supported by rows of pillars. The construction techniques and styles for these temples and pillars came from Egypt. Farmers in villages outside the city walls produced grain, vegetables, olive oil, and wine for the urban dwellers. A city with surrounding villages formed a city-state, or *polis*. Each of these new city-states administered its own internal and external affairs, although they also formed alliances or pursued hostilities with each other.

Initially, kings from among the landowning families were responsible for the administration of the city-states. Their forerunners had been the warrior lords and the landowning families of the post-Mycenaean period and made up what the Greeks called the "aristocracy" of the states. During the period 750–600 BCE, conflict often broke out between the aristocracy and the common folk—merchants, traders, craftspeople, and free farmers—over the distribution of wealth in the growing cities. Some aristocrats exploited these tensions and allied themselves with groups of commoners. Once allied, these aristocrats assumed power as tyrants, who attempted to create family dynasties. Many of the would-be dynasts sponsored festivals, public work projects, and artists; but their popularity rarely lasted beyond the sons who succeeded them.

Other aristocrats opposed the tyrants and agreed to power sharing with the commoners. Through trade, many commoners were becoming wealthier than the aristocrats. Both aristocrats and commoners served as foot soldiers in the city-states' defense forces. These armies relied not on charioteers but on foot soldiers, who were heavily armed with shields, lances, and swords, all made of iron. Their battle order was the *phalanx*—that is, a block of eight or more rows of soldiers marching forward shoulder to shoulder, each man holding a shield in the left hand, helping to guard the man to his left, while in his right hand he held a lance or pike.

In the narrow valleys and defiles of Greece and Ionia these bristling "hedgehog" formations were nearly impossible to break with archers, infantry, or cavalry—if each man held his position and the men in the back moved up to take the place of those who fell. In these phalanxes it was not individual aristocratic valor that counted but the courageous willingness of each citizen-soldier to support and protect the other. Thus, as many ordinary city dwellers became the military equals of the aristocracy in the crucible of battle, they quite naturally began to demand an equal share of political power in times of peace.

Political reformers in the sixth century BCE gave commoners their first basic political rights. The best-known reforms were those introduced in Athens and Sparta, the city-states with the largest agricultural territories. In Athens, aristocratic rule was replaced with political rights distributed according to levels of property ownership. The poorest class had the right to participate in the citizen assembly, cast votes, and sit on juries; members of the wealthier classes could run for a variety of leadership and temple offices. A written law code curbed arbitrariness. With these assemblies, the Greek city-states continued the Mesopotamian and Hittite systems of assemblies discussed earlier. Whether the Greeks developed their assemblies independently or adopted them from their predecessors is not known. What can be debated, however, is how deeply the idea of political participation is rooted in the region of the Middle East and the eastern Mediterranean, reaching back to 3500 BCE. In Greece, and later Rome, these traditions would evolve into the ancestral forms of many of the political institutions we live under today, particularly **republican** and **democratic** offices.

Republicanism: A system of government in which, in the place of kings, the people are sovereign, electing representatives to executive and legislative offices.

Democracy: A system of government in which most or all of the people elect representatives and in some cases decide on important issues themselves.

In Sparta, the traditional rule by two coequal kings was held in check through a newly created board of five officers elected annually from among the popular assembly. These officers were responsible for the administration of day-to-day affairs in Sparta. The assembly was made up of all landowners wealthy enough to live in town because of the revenue they collected from their legally indentured (unfree) tenant farmers in the surrounding villages. These political reforms, however, did not prevent new tyrants from rising up in periodic takeover attempts. Thus, in the middle of the first millennium BCE, Greeks were still struggling to find a consistent direction for their political development.

Religious Experience and Cultural Achievements

By around 5500 BCE, when agriculture had replaced foraging, many human groups began to move from naturalism to polytheism as their new form of religion. In *naturalism* people experience an awe and reverence toward the creatures and forces of the natural world. However, there is no indication in the available archaeological record that people identified these creatures and forces with particular deities. With the rise of cities and the development of writing, these forces received names. *Polytheism* is the general term used to denote religions of personified forces in nature. Artists depicted and sculpted the deities as well as the rulers who derived their mandates from these gods. Writers recorded myths and hymns exploring the relationship between humans and gods. Administrators, responsible for constructing architectural monuments, calculating the calendar, and assessing the taxes, laid the foundations of the mathematical and physical sciences. Since many of the religious and cultural achievements were expressed in writing, we can evaluate them today with far better understanding than the culture of the foragers and early farmers.

Toward Polytheism The creators of the Paleolithic rock paintings in Africa, Europe, and Australia (discussed in Chapter 1) have left us few hints of their spiritual preoccupations in their world full of dangerous animals. The depictions of "lionman," "bisonman," and "sorcerer" are but a few examples where the human and animal worlds are merged, presumably with people in the cave rituals experiencing this merger, with the purpose of influencing the animal world. In the Neolithic transition period from foraging to agriculture, the principal change was the transfer of ritual from caves to aboveground sanctuaries and towns.

An example of the transfer to a sanctuary was Göbekli Tepe in southern Anatolia, a place where foragers came together for rituals during 9000–6000 BCE. Excavations begun in 1995 are still in progress, but a rich imagery of animals, mostly in the form of reliefs, has already been unearthed. It shows that naturalism was still in force, even if the venue was no longer a cave. The oldest example documenting the transfer of ritual from the cave to the town is Çatal Hüyük [Tsha-TAL Hoo-YOOK] (7500–5700 BCE) in southern Anatolia, excavated in the 1960s and 1990s. At its height, the town had 5,000 inhabitants, who lived in densely packed houses accessible only from the top with ladders. The inhabitants farmed fields outside of town, using irrigation water from the Taurus Mountains, and hunted extensively. Probably communal rooms in town contained a concentration of artifacts, among which Venus-type figurines and reliefs and wall paintings of animals, especially of *aurochs* (ancestors of cattle), are prominent. The imagery is reminiscent of that of the Paleolithic foragers, but the emergence of urban places of ritual indicates that humans were far along in the transition from nature to civilization.

In Ubaid Mesopotamia (6000–4000 BCE), urban places of ritual evolved into temples. Urban dwellers then took the decisive steps of transition from naturalism to polytheism in the period 3500–2500 BCE when forces of nature began to lose influence and to spark fear in daily life. With the advent of an emerging partnership with nature in the production of abundant food supplies instead of hunting and gathering, as well as kings ruling cities and the appearance of writing, the transition from naturalism to polytheism was begun. This connection among writing, kingship, and gods is crucial for an understanding of polytheism and religion in general: Prior to 3500 BCE, religion tended to be an impersonal and nameless naturalism; thereafter, it was the polytheism of kings with often colorful personalities, told in myths and epics. Writing made it possible to record the names of individuals, kings viewed themselves as the guarantors of urban life, and gods were the powers that endowed kings with the authority to prevent urban life from slipping back into preurban culture. In the cities, people were no longer in awe of wild animals, as they had been during forager days. But they were still in awe of nature's powers, as they had been during the earlier Neolithic village life, when nature could be benevolent through bounty and fertility as well as wrathful through floods, storms, droughts, or blights.

Polytheism began when kings became individuals—through adopting patron deities—and associated the awe-inspiring natural powers and phenomena with these deities. Or perhaps polytheism evolved the other way around: Villagers created rituals to please the awe-inspiring anonymous forces of nature, and after the introduction of writing and kingship, these forces became deities. Either way, the rise of polytheism depended crucially on writing and kingship.

In polytheistic empires, rulers were very tolerant toward the phenomenon of multiple gods, even though they had a personal relationship with only one god, their patron deity, and the priesthood of their deity's temple. Even strong rulers never had the power to force the many temple priesthoods of their empire to give up their gods. Egyptian kings, however, unified Egypt more thoroughly than their Mesopotamian counterparts, who never overcame the long city-state tradition of their region. Under royal influence, therefore, Egyptian priesthoods devised a hierarchically organized pantheon of all gods, along with elaborate stories about these gods.

During the New Kingdom period (ca. 1550–1070 BCE) kings and priests came into close contact with other empires of the Middle East. They developed an understanding that all gods taken together were really only a few deities, or even only one, with many different manifestations—an understanding quite similar to that of Vedic India. One theologically well-versed king, Akhenaten (1353–1336 BCE), went even further, conceiving of the Sun as the only god, to the exclusion of the pantheon, to whom all Egyptians were henceforth to pray. The new Sun religion—not quite true monotheism yet, where God the One would have to be both personal and invisible—was too radical to survive Akhenaten. But its brief appearance demonstrates the full range of meaning which polytheism as a religion could acquire. (See "Against the Grain.")

Akhenaten and His Family. This wall painting shows Akhenaten, the 18th Dynasty (New Kingdom) Egyptian pharaoh, and his family worshiping Aten (see Source 2.5). Images like these were designed to broadcast Akhenaten's devotion to the solar disc among his subjects.

Mesopotamian and Egyptian Literature

Among the earliest writings in the world exploring religious themes are the *Epic of Gilgamesh* and the myth of *Enuma Elish*. These had their origins in third-millennium BCE Mesopotamia but were not recorded for another millennium. The first is the story of Gilgamesh, who was a mythical king in early Sumer. Gilgamesh, according to the epic, ruled Uruk and built its walls. Like the Chinese sage kings we will meet in Chapter 4, he fought many battles and performed heroic deeds in both this world and the underworld but failed in his

excerpt from the *Epic of Gilgamesh*

ultimate quest to find immortality. In the end, Gilgamesh could not escape the fate of all mortals and had to suffer death as well.

Flood stories featured prominently in these early texts; and there are several similarities between those conveyed in the Epic of Gilgamesh and Genesis, the first book of the Hebrew Bible. In each the gods unleashed a gigantic flood as punishment for sinful behavior, whereupon a righteous figure is directed to build a boat and to fill it with select humans and animals in order to escape the deluge. After they land on a mountaintop, sacrifices are offered, which appease the Creator's wrath.

The myth of *Enuma Elish* (named after its first line, which means "when on high . . .") tells the story of creation, beginning with a time when nothing existed but Father Abzu (the Depth or Abyss) and Mother Tiamat (Ocean) and their numerous children, who were the city gods of Mesopotamia. The raucous behavior of his children enraged Abzu. He tried to kill them but was instead murdered by one of them. Tiamat [tee-ya-MAT] and her second husband continued the violent domestic battle, finally driving the children away. Marduk [MAR-dook], alone among the children, eventually returned and slaughtered both his mother and stepfather. He split Tiamat's body into halves, which became heaven and earth. From the blood of the stepfather he made humankind, whom he predestined to serve the gods. One senses how the unknown authors of this text struggle with the question of power in nature—at times benevolent and at times violent, always unpredictable, even as one sacrifices to please it.

The Egyptian version of the creation myth, like that of the Mesopotamians, also begins with an original ocean. In the Egyptian telling, an island arose from the depth of this ocean. The ruler of this island was the creator god Atum, who contained all the qualities of nature in himself. He created things in pairs, one after the other, beginning with air and water and finishing his handiwork with the male and female of the human race. This Egyptian creation myth is more explicit than its Mesopotamian cousin about the infinity of the original "depth" and "ocean," out of which earth and heaven were created. It is also far less violent, a reflection of the more gradual and harmonious growth of the Egyptian kingdom and empire.

Sculptures and Paintings Mesopotamian and Egyptian rulers wanted to impress those who observed them as severe, powerful, and pious persons. Early Mesopotamian kings had massive statues made of themselves, showing them posed in prayer. In Egypt, compact, block-like royals stand freely or sit impassively on their thrones. Statues in both regions often have wide, oversized eyes that stare sternly at the viewer. On many high-relief sculptures carved into stone, larger-than-life-size kings with bulging muscles trample victoriously over diminutive enemies. In all these sculptures the primary objective of the artists was not photographic realism but a rendering of the gulf between gods and kings on the one hand and subjects on the other.

Wall paintings were highly popular among Mesopotamians, Egyptians, and Minoans. Unfortunately, in the more humid region of lower Mesopotamia, few such paintings survived. By contrast, in the dry climate of Egypt (except for the delta), a large number still exist. Paintings filled the interior of tombs, illustrating scenes from their owners' lives. The painters' point was not only to show their royal features but also to draw them from all angles: Looking at the images from the perspective of eternal life, the kings should be able to see themselves in all their earthly aspects simultaneously. Accordingly, face, arms, and legs were painted in profile; eyes, shoulders, and upper body appear frontally; and the waist was half frontal but turned to reveal the navel. Later, as more nonroyal people built tombs for themselves, the complex multi-angled royal perspective gave way to a simpler, single-angle realism.

The Greek arts began in the Minoan and Mycenaean city-states. Minoan wall paintings, stylistically related to those of the Egyptian New Kingdom (ca. 1550–1070 BCE), show realistic scenes with vegetation, birds, dolphins, and bulls. The art of Mycenae is mostly known to us from small sculptures, masks, drinking vessels, and jewelry found in the tombs of royal warriors. Through their close contact with the Assyrians, the Greeks in their growing city-states (during the period ca. 750–600 BCE) learned not only about Mesopotamian literature but also about their arts. Winged and fighting animals, as well as muscular gods and heroes, appear in vase paintings. Egypt was the inspiration for the development of sculptures, which initially were block like, wide eyed, and stylized. Gradually, however, with the decline of the aristocracy, stylized representation was replaced by realism. By the 500s BCE, the heavy and stern-looking kings were succeeded by well-proportioned, smoothly muscled, and slightly smiling figures depicted as one would encounter them in the market.

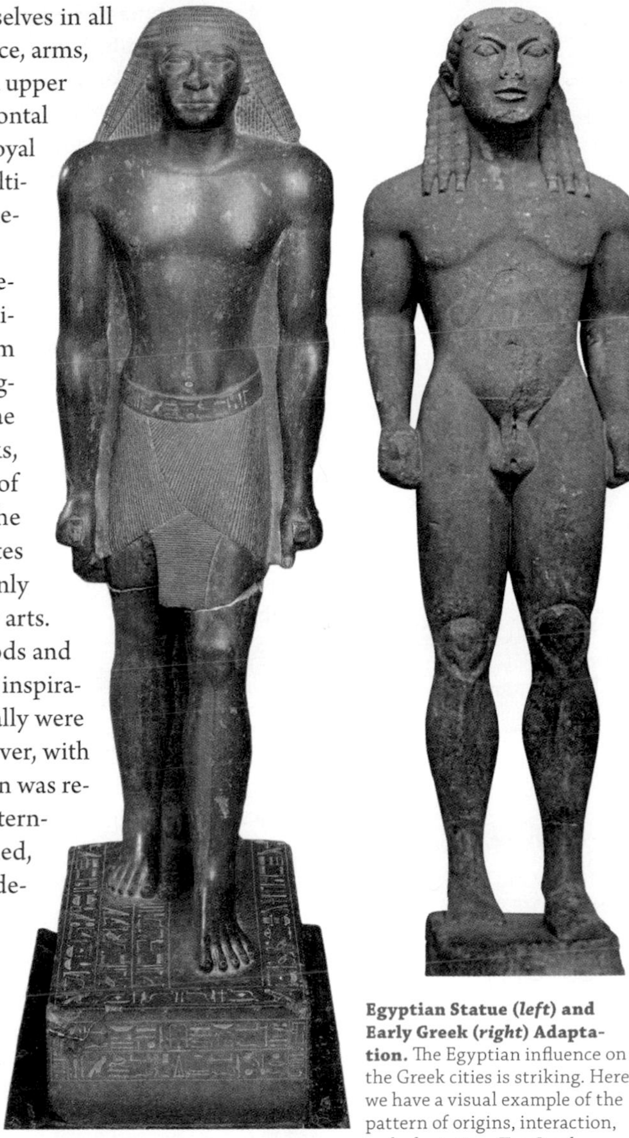

Egyptian Statue (*left*) and Early Greek (*right*) Adaptation. The Egyptian influence on the Greek cities is striking. Here we have a visual example of the pattern of origins, interaction, and adaptation. The Greek example is a creative adaptation of an Egyptian model.

Scientific Beginnings In both Mesopotamia and Egypt, conceptualization of reality advanced substantially from Old and New Stone Age imagery. For the first time we get glimpses of humans constructing abstract ideas, without recourse to the senses—for example, in mathematics. Mathematical calculations, such as addition and subtraction, began in Mesopotamia even before the first writing system was introduced.

Subsequently, scribes developed tables for multiplication and division, squares, cubes, square roots, cube roots, and reciprocal and exponential functions. They calculated numerical approximations for the square roots of 2 and 3. Exercise texts from the Old Babylonian period (ca. 2000–1600 BCE) pose such problems as: "Beyond the ditch I made a dike, one cubit per cubit is the inclination of this dike. What is the base, the top and the height of it? And what is its circumference?" Babylonian mathematical interests focused primarily on the roots of algebra. Scribes also laid the foundations for geometry and astronomy by devising the system of 60 degrees for arcs, angles, and time—all still in use today.

Babylonian world map

In Egypt, the *Rhind Mathematical Papyrus* (ca. 1550 BCE) is an early handbook of geometric and algebraic questions typically used by scribes and administrators.

It teaches the apprentice scribe how to calculate the volume of rectangles, triangles, and pyramids and how to measure the slopes of angles. Algebraic operations are illustrated through examples such as "[animal] fat [worth] ten gallons [of grain] is issued for one year; what is its share per day?" As in Mesopotamia, Egyptian mathematics implicitly employed important mathematical principles without yet stating them explicitly.

The *Kahun* (ca. 1825 BCE) and *Edwin Smith* (ca. 1534 BCE) *Papyri* are the best-known texts on the applied science of medicine. They cover diagnosis, prescriptions, and surgery. In the latter text we find the earliest distinction between supernatural and natural causes of illness, disease, or injury.

A few examples illustrate ancient Egyptian medical standards. Headache is diagnosed as "half head," which the Greeks translated as "*hemikrania*," from which our English word "migraine" is derived. Remedies for treating stiffness of limbs, pregnancy, birth complications, and childhood diseases, as well as advice on birth control and abortion, include mixtures of homeopathic herbs and elements. Surgeons received advice on how to use copper knives for male and female circumcision and needles for stitching up wounds. During their work, physicians were encouraged to repeat magic healing formulas that encouraged their patients to use their own self-healing powers.

Putting It All Together

interactive concept map

The beginning of the agrarian age in the Middle East and eastern Mediterranean was marked by agricultural surpluses, especially in irrigated areas. Depending on the size of the surplus, a pattern of state formation became visible along which city-states, kingdoms, and empires emerged in the various areas of the region. The central concern of the rulers in these small and large states was establishing and maintaining their authority, which included the use of military force—something not always easy to justify, especially when trade and ruling-class cooperation were also important. Therefore, the rulers appealed to gods—that is, personalized forces in nature stronger than rulers. The will of these forces was conceived as being expressed in the law code of each state. Gods were lawgivers, and their law possessed divine authority; thus, rulers became the executors of the god-given law.

Although "divine," the rulers' mandate was never absolute. Popular or aristocratic assemblies from preroyal times of tribal or clan organization survived stubbornly or were revived in the Greek *poleis*. Although the Hittite and Assyrian kings succeeded in marginalizing these assemblies during periods of empire building, the divine mandate was not exclusively theirs, and they had to share power, if only to a limited degree. It is important to note that this tradition of assemblies, which we often associate solely with Greece, was widespread in the Middle East. This awareness is necessary to understand the period after 600 BCE when individuals arose with messages of personal salvation and announced that it was not simply fate or misfortune to live and die under these often harsh imperial powers. Instead, they insisted that the destiny of humanity *transcended* these all-too-human institutions.

Review and Relate

Thinking Through Patterns

Examine the ways historians approach the big questions of this chapter.

» What are the main factors that enabled the transition from foraging to farming?

One crucial factor in this pattern was the environment of the Taurus–Zagros–Levant region, the Fertile Crescent. Adequate rainfall, abundant edible plants suitable for domestication, and several animals that proved useful and easy to domesticate characterized the region. But had it not been for human beings mastering irrigation, such a transition might have remained confined to small microclimatic regions. Populations in the great riverine agricultural areas in Mesopotamia and Egypt (and, as we will see in the following chapters, India and China) took as their task the mastery of the fertility of river valleys and the use of reliable river water for irrigation, rather than relying on rainfall. Here was a system adaptable to a variety of climates, as witnessed by the fact that these four early agricultural civilizations arose in dry climates watered by large river systems.

» Where did the pattern of agrarian life first emerge and why?

While scholars still debate the absolute origins of the domestication of plants and animals, most are in agreement that the Fertile Crescent is central to this process. Here, experimentation with local grains, leaf plants, and pulses during the Neolithic helped humans develop more reliable and better-yielding crops, which were then traded locally and, through regional trade, farther afield. The climatic zones of Eurasia were especially well suited to this because of the long east–west axis. Animals like sheep, goats, and cattle were similarly found over wide areas and were easy to trade, which led to the sharing of information about raising livestock. Another important factor was that as populations grew as a result of the stability of food production by agriculture, groups split off and started their own communities, carrying the new techniques with them. Thus, by about 5000 BCE, the basic techniques and species of Eurasian and North African domestication were well established.

» How did the creation of agrarian–urban society—what we commonly call "civilization"—make for an entirely new pattern of world history?

The ability of humans to create large food surpluses encouraged a considerable degree of settlement. Such stability enabled the nonproducing part of the population to occupy themselves with creating nonagricultural things—buildings, religious centers, defensive works, dwellings. As these elements of villages and towns grew and became more complex, they allowed the cumulative knowledge and production of human beings to enlarge in these sites. In short, cities created an entirely new kind of society with elaborate class hierarchies built on power and efficiency. Rivalry and competition among cities required ever more powerful defenses to protect the people, their wealth, and their trade. From this period, the patterns of urban life and of state formation were established, patterns we readily recognize today as our own.

Against the Grain

Consider this as a counterpoint to the main patterns examined in this chapter.

Akhenaten the Transgressor

- Why was Akhenaten's revolt against prevailing religious practices considered so revolutionary?
- Are there any possible similarities between Akhenaten's approach to monotheism and later examples found in either early Judaism or Zoroastrianism?

As early as the Old Kingdom (ca. 2686–2181 BCE) Re, the sun god, was well established as the supreme deity (sometimes referred to as the "Father of the Gods") in the Egyptian polytheistic pantheon. Re was closely associated with kings, who were often depicted as his sons. During the Middle Kingdom, Amenhotep III ("Amun is satisfied") (1386–1349 BCE) promoted the worship of Amun-Re as the focus of Egyptian religion. It was therefore assumed that Amenhotep's son and successor, Amenhotep IV (1353–1336 BCE), would follow in his father's footsteps.

For reasons that are not altogether clear, Amenhotep IV took the radical step of repudiating the cult of Amun-Re in favor of a new object of devotion, that of the Aten (the solar disc). To drive home the point, early in his reign ***Amen***hotep IV changed his name to Akhen***aten*** ("devoted adherent of Aten"). Thus, in place of Amun as the *supreme* god among all the gods, Aten was now designated as the *sole* god for all Egyptians.

Akhenaten quickly instituted policies in order to officially replace worship of Amun-Re with devotion to the Aten. Masons were ordered to chisel out all references to Amun in temples and other monuments, while scribes were directed to delete similar references in official documents. Then, after closing down all temples of Amun, Akhenaten constructed a new capital at Akentaten, hundreds of miles north of Thebes, the center of the priestly cult attending Amun-Re. Here, the new temples to Aten were designed as sun temples, facing east in order to admit the light of the rising sun into the interior. Moreover, in various forms the Aten was depicted as a solar disc, whose rays of light were directed to the hands of Akhenaten and his queen, Nefertiti, who would presumably then share the beneficence of the sun's life-giving rays with their subjects (see page 57).

Akhenaten's experiment at overturning existing orthodoxy was short lived. His successor (possibly his own son), given the name Tutenkh***aten***, quickly reverted to the previous cult of Amun-Re, taking the name Tutenkh***amen*** (1336–1327 BCE). Nevertheless, Akhenaten's radical revolution has generated considerable scholarly conjecture. Among explanations for his motives, it has been thought that his intention was to undermine the growing political power of the priests of Amun-Re. Alternatively, perhaps Akhenaten was determined to replace polytheism with an early form of monotheistic religion devoted to *his* power and not to the solar disc. A more benevolent theory suggests that Akhenaten was interested in opening up religion (formerly restricted to a select few who followed the commands of the priests of Amun-Re) to wider participation by all Egyptians. Perhaps the most provocative of speculations concerns whether Akhenaten was the forebear of later monotheistic worship in the ancient Near East.

Key Terms

audio flashcards

Agrarian society 33
Agrarian–urban society 30
Assembly 36
Bronze Age collapse 49
City, city-state 37
Democracy 55
Empire 40
Iron Age 49
Neolithic Age 34
Nomads 36
Palace-state 46
Republicanism 55
Sharecroppers 36

For additional resources, please go to
www.oup.com/us/vonsivers.
Please see the Further Resources section at the back of the book for additional readings and suggested websites.

PATTERNS OF EVIDENCE | Sources for Chapter 2

SOURCE 2.1 Law Code of Hammurabi

ca. 1772 BCE

In order to "cause justice to prevail in the land" and to "further the welfare of the people," the Amorite King Hammurabi (ca. 1792–1750 BCE), having made Babylon his capital and having conquered Mesopotamia, issued a comprehensive code of laws. He caused them to be inscribed on stones that were erected at crossroads and in marketplaces throughout his kingdom, so that all his subjects would understand the penalties that their actions might incur. This document survives on one of these stones, topped by an illustration showing Hammurabi receiving the order to write as directed by the sun god Shamash. The stone was discovered by French archaeologists in 1901–1902, and it remains one of the treasures of the Louvre Museum in Paris.

1. If a man accuse a man, and charge him with murder, but cannot convict him, the accuser shall be put to death.

3. If a man in a case before the court offer testimony concerning deeds of violence, and do not establish the testimony he has given . . . the man shall be put to death.

53. If a man neglect to strengthen his dike, and do not strengthen his dike, and a break be made in his dike and he let the water carry away farmland, then the man in whose dike the break has been made shall restore the grain which he has damaged.

54. If he be not able to restore the grain, they shall sell him and his goods, and the farmers whose grain the water has carried away shall divide the results of the sale.

104. If a merchant give an agent grain, wood, oil, or goods of any kind with which to trade, the agent shall write down the money received and return it to the merchant. The agent shall take a sealed receipt for the money which he gives to the merchant.

105. If the agent be careless and do not take a receipt for the money which he has given to the merchant, the money not receipted for shall not be placed to his account.

196. If a man destroy the eye of another man, they shall destroy his eye.

Source: Nels M. Bailkey and Richard Lim, eds., *Readings in Ancient History: Thought and Experience from Gilgamesh to St. Augustine*, 6th ed. (Boston: Houghton Mifflin, 2002), 28–36.

197. If he break a man's bone, they shall break his bone.

198. If he destroy the eye of a common man or break a bone of a common man, he shall pay one *mina* of silver.

199. If he destroy the eye of a man's slave or break a bone of a man's slave, he shall pay one-half his price.

206. If a man strike another man in a quarrel and wound him, that man shall swear, "I did not strike him intentionally," and he shall be responsible for the physician.

207. If he die as a result of the blow, he shall swear as above, and if it were the son of a gentleman, he shall pay one-third *mina* of silver.

228. If a builder erect a house for a man and complete it, he shall give him two shekels of silver per *sar* of house as his wage.

229. If a builder erect a house for a man and do not make its construction firm and the house which he built collapse and cause the death of the owner of the house, that builder shall be put to death.

233. If a builder erect a house for a man and do not surround it with walls of proper construction, and a wall fall in, that builder shall strengthen that wall at his own expense.

253. If a man hire a man to oversee his farm and furnish him the seed-grain and entrust him with oxen and contract with him to cultivate the field, and that man steal either the seed or the crop and it be found in his possession, they shall cut off his fingers.

From the Epilogue:

The great gods proclaimed me, and I am the guardian shepherd whose scepter is righteous and whose beneficent shadow is spread over my city. In my bosom I carried the people of the land of Sumer and Akkad; under my protection I brought their brethren into security; in my wisdom I sheltered them.

That the strong might not oppress the weak, and that they should give justice to the orphan and the widow. . . .

» Working with Sources

1. **When are financial and capital punishments applied in the code, and is there a consistent principle at work here?**
2. **Why is Hammurabi concerned with the regulation of business transactions, and particularly when they have to do with agriculture?**

SOURCE 2.2 Babylonian Poem of the Righteous Sufferer

ca. 2000–1600 BCE

Composed in Akkadian and consisting of 480 lines distributed over four tablets, this poem is a protest against one man's undeserved suffering. The author is tormented but cannot determine the cause, and he feels that the god Marduk is not responding adequately to his lamentation. Because he has always been faithful to his god and assiduous in his worship, the Sufferer begins to speculate that the gods are not concerned with human pain at all. Even more, they may engage in this sort of torment for their own benefit. The figure of the "Righteous Sufferer" is frequently compared to the biblical figure Job. While this "Babylonian Job" is eventually delivered from his sufferings, perhaps his complaints linger on.

My god has forsaken me and disappeared,
My goddess has failed me and keeps at a distance.
The benevolent angel who walked beside me has departed,
My protecting spirit has taken to flight, and is seeking someone else.
My strength is gone; my appearance has become gloomy;
My dignity has flown away, my protecting made off. . . .
The king, the flesh of the gods, the sun of his peoples,
His heart is enraged with me, and cannot be appeased.
The courtiers plot hostile action against me,
They assemble themselves and give utterance to impious words. . . .
They combine against me in slander and lies.
My lordly mouth have they held as with reins,
So that I, whose lips used to prate, have become like a mute.
My sonorous shout is reduced to silence,
My lofty head is bowed down to the ground,
Dread has enfeebled my robust heart. . . .
If I walk the street, ears are pricked;
If I enter the palace, eyes blink.
My city frowns on me as an enemy;
Indeed my land is savage and hostile.

. . .

Source: Nels M. Bailkey and Richard Lim, eds., *Readings in Ancient History: Thought and Experience from Gilgamesh to St. Augustine*, 6th ed. (Boston: Houghton Mifflin, 2002), 20–22.

My ill luck has increased, and I do not find the right.
I called to my god, but he did not show his face,
I prayed to my goddess, but she did not raise her head.
The diviner with his inspection has not got to the root of the matter,
Nor has the dream priest with his libation elucidated my case.
I sought the favor of the ***zaqiqu*-spirit**, but he did not enlighten me;
And the incantation priest with his ritual did not appease the divine wrath against me.
What strange conditions everywhere!
When I look behind, there is persecution, trouble.

. . .

For myself, I gave attention to supplication and prayer:
To me prayer was discretion, sacrifice my rule.
The day for reverencing the god was a joy to my heart;
The day of the goddess' procession was profit and gain to me.
The king's prayer—that was my joy,
And the accompanying music became a delight for me.
I instructed my land to keep the god's rites,
And provoked my people to value the goddess' name.
I made praise for the king like a god's
And taught the populace reverence for the palace.
I wish I knew that these things were pleasing to one's god!
What is proper to oneself is an offense to one's god,
What in one's heart seems despicable is proper to one's god.
Who knows the will of the gods in heaven?
Who understands the plans of the underworld gods?
Where have mortals learnt the way of a god?
He who was alive yesterday is dead today.
For a minute he was dejected, suddenly he is exuberant.
One moment people are singing in exaltation,
Another they groan like professional mourners.

***Zaqiqu*-spirit:** The god of dreams.

Working with Sources

1. **What is the responsibility of the gods to this worshipper, and what can he do if the gods renege on the contract?**
2. **How are the priestly establishment and the king connected to this man? Have these institutions also failed him?**

SOURCE 2.3

Advice from a royal scribe to his apprentice, Middle Kingdom Egypt, Twelfth Dynasty

ca. 1878–1839 BCE

The Papyrus Lansing is a letter of instruction from the royal scribe (and "chief overseer of the cattle of Amun-Re, King of Gods") Nebmare-nakht to his apprentice Wenemdiamun. It seems to date from the reign of the pharaoh Senusret III (Sesostris III). The letter conveys a great deal of practical advice to an up-and-coming scribe—as well as warnings about what temptations he must avoid to be successful. While Nebmare-nakht is clearly proud of the status his work has earned him, he also illuminates the specific duties and responsibilities of a royal official in this period.

The scribe of the army and commander of the cattle of the house of Amun, Nebmare-nakht, speaks to the scribe Wenemdiamun, as follows. Be a scribe! Your body will be sleek; your hand will be soft. You will not flicker like a flame, like one whose body is feeble. For there is not the bone of a man in you. You are tall and thin. If you lifted a load to carry it, you would stagger, your legs would tremble. You are lacking in strength; you are weak in all your limbs; you are poor in body.

Set your sight on being a scribe: a fine profession that suits you. You call for one; a thousand answer you. You stride freely on the road. You will not die like a hired ox. You are in front of others.

I spend the day instructing you. You do not listen! Your heart is like an empty room. My teachings are not in it. Take their meaning to yourself!

The marsh thicket is before you each day, as a nestling is after its mother. You follow the path of pleasure; you make friends with revelers. You have made your home in the brewery, as one who thirsts for beer. You sit in the parlor with an idler. You hold the writings in contempt. You visit the prostitute. Do not do these things! What are they for? They are of no use. Take note of it!

Furthermore. Look, I instruct you to make you sound; to make you hold the palette freely. To make you become one whom the king trusts; to make you gain entrance to treasury and granary. To make you receive the ship-load at the gate of the granary. To make you issue the offerings on feast days. You are dressed in fine clothes; you own horses. Your boat is on the river; you are supplied with attendants. You stride about inspecting. A mansion is built in

---

Source: Translated by A. M. Blackman and T. E. Peet, *Journal of Egyptian Archaeology* 11 (1925): 284–298, as quoted by Miriam Lichtheim, *Ancient Egyptian Literature* (Berkeley and Los Angeles: University of California Press, 1973), vol. 2, 171–172.

your town. You have a powerful office, given you by the king. Male and female slaves are about you. Those who are in the fields grasp your hand, on plots that you have made. Look, I make you into a staff of life! Put the writings in your heart, and you will be protected from all kinds of toil. You will become a worthy official.

Do you not recall the fate of the unskilled man? His name is not known. He is ever burdened [like an ass carrying] in front of the scribe who knows what he is about.

Come, let me tell you the woes of the soldier, and how many are his superiors: the general, the troop-commander, the officer who leads, the standard-bearer, the lieutenant, the scribe, the commander of fifty, and the garrison-captain. They go in and out in the halls of the palace, saying, "Get laborers!". . . .

His march is uphill through mountains. He drinks water every third day; it is smelly and tastes of salt. His body is ravaged by illness. The enemy comes, surrounds him with missiles, and life recedes from him. He is told: "Quick, forward, valiant soldier! Win for yourself a good name!" He does not know what he is about. His body is weak, his legs fail him. When victory is won, the captives are handed over to his majesty, to be taken to Egypt. The foreign woman faints on the march; she hangs herself on the soldier's neck. His knapsack drops, another grabs it while he is burdened with the woman. . . .

Be a scribe, and be spared from soldiering! You call and one says: "Here I am." You are safe from torments. Every man seeks to raise himself up. Take note of it!

» Working with Sources

1. **How does Nebmare-nakht attempt to make the life of a diligent scribe attractive to his apprentice? How does he use negative examples to steer Wenemdiamun in the right direction?**
2. **Why is the position of scribe so prominent in Middle Kingdom Egypt? What role does a scribe play in relation to the Pharaoh?**

SOURCE 2.4

Sketch of the palace complex at Knossos, Minoan Crete

ca. 1700–1400 BCE

In 1900, Sir Arthur Evans discovered the remains of a vast palace complex on the island of Crete in the southern Aegean Sea. Christening the civilization "Minoan" after the legendary King Minos of Crete, Evans continued to excavate at Knossos and at other sites around the island. The palace at Knossos seems to have contained hundreds of rooms, including a throne room and storage spaces for food and cisterns for the collection of water. The

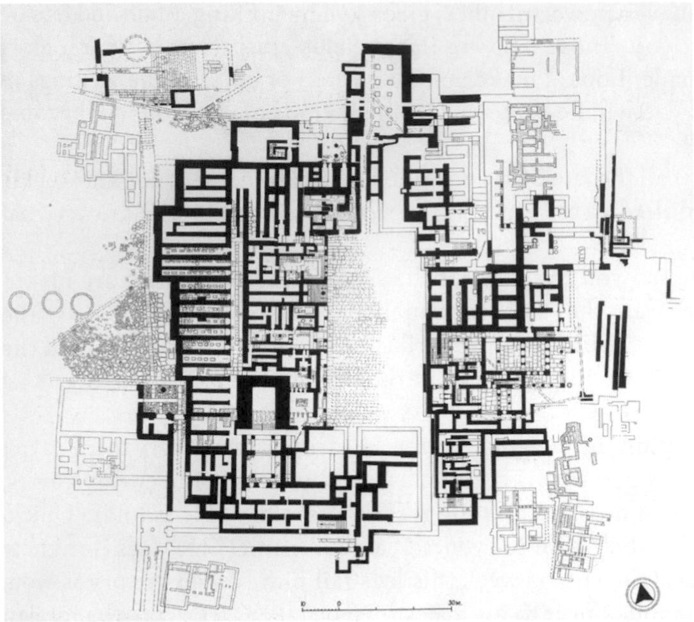

legacy of Evans's work can be viewed at the visual archive held at the Ashmolean Museum in Oxford, England (http://sirarthurevans.ashmus.ox.ac.uk/), and there is a virtual tour of the site, provided by the British School at Athens (http://www.bsa.ac.uk/knossos/vrtour/).

Working with Sources

1. **Can the palace complex at Knossos be compared with palace sites in Mesopotamia and Egypt in the second millennium BCE? In what respects?**
2. **What do you think the palace complex suggests about the structure of Minoan society?**

SOURCE 2.5

The Great Hymn to the Aten

ca. 1353–1336 BCE

This hymn to the Egyptian sun god Aten has been attributed to King Akhenaten ("the devoted adherent of Aten"), the pharaoh formerly known as Amenhotep IV. While Akhenaten's experiment in monotheism was short lived, the poem reflects the connections this revolutionary religious thinker attempted to forge between himself and an all-powerful deity. Note that he also solicits the blessings of Aten for himself, as leader of the Egyptian people, and for his wife, the famous Nefertiti.

Splendid you rise in heaven's
lightland,
O living Aten, creator of life!
When you have dawned in eastern
lightland,
You fill every land with your beauty.

Source: Translated by J. A. Wilson, as quoted by Miriam Lichtheim, *Ancient Egyptian Literature*, vol. 2, 96–99.

Neferkheprure, Only-one-of-Re: Akhenaten.

You are beauteous, great, radiant,
High over every land;
Your rays embrace the lands,
To the limit of all that you made.

. . .

When you set in western lightland,
Earth is in darkness as if in death;
One sleeps in chambers, heads covered,
One eye does not see another.
Were they robbed of their goods,
That are under their heads,
People would not remark it.
Every lion comes from its den,
All the serpents bite;
Darkness hovers, earth is silent,
As their maker rests in lightland.

. . .

Ships fare north, fare south as well,
Roads lie open when you rise;
The fish in the river dart before you,
Your rays are in the midst of the sea.
Who makes seed grow in women,
Who creates people from sperm;
Who feeds the son in his mother's womb,
Who soothes him to still his tears.
Nurse in the womb,
Giver of breath,
To nourish all that he has made.

. . .

Maat: balance, law, justice.

You are in my heart,
There is no other who knows you,
Only your son, ***Neferkheprure, Only-one-of-Re***,
Whom you have taught your ways and your might.
[Those on] earth come from your hand as you made them,
When you have dawned they live,
When you set they die;
You yourself are lifetime, one lives by you.
All eyes are on your beauty until you set.
All labor ceases when you rest in the west;
When you rise you stir [everyone] for the King,
Every leg is on the move since you founded the earth.
You rouse them for your son who came from your body,
The King who lives by Maat, the Lord of the Two Lands,
Neferkheprure, Only-one-of-Re,
The Son of Re who lives by **Maat**, the Lord of crowns,
Akhenaten, great in his lifetime;
And the great Queen whom he loves, the Lady of the Two Lands,
Nefer-nefru-Aten Nefertiti, living forever.

» Working with Sources

1. **How does the hymn reflect on the practical advantages provided by the sun?**
2. **How does the hymn reinforce the power of Aten in political terms?**

Chapter 3 3000–600 BCE

Shifting Agrarian Centers in India

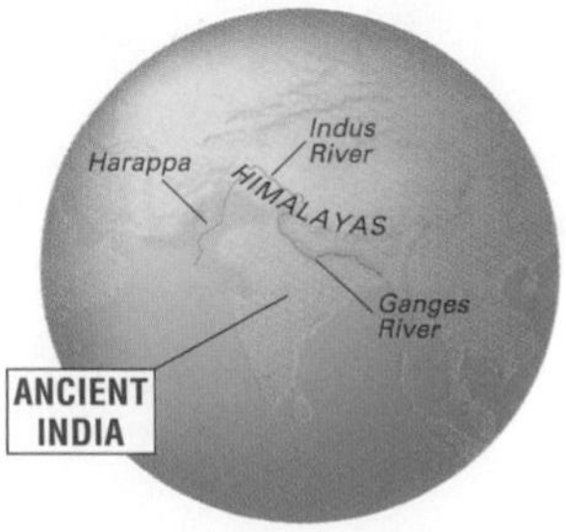

The objects were beyond curious. They appeared to be ancient seals, but the inscriptions were completely unlike anything General Alexander Cunningham had seen before in India. Some years previously, in 1856, British engineers working on an extension of the East India Railway near the Ravi River, a tributary of the great Indus system, had found ancient mounds stuffed with uniform, fire-baked bricks. Regarding these sturdy bricks as a godsend for supporting their railroad tracks, they proceeded to loot the mounds of their available building materials. Fortunately, the men noticed that some of the bricks contained these puzzling signs and sent them to Cunningham, who had already built a reputation for his archaeological work at several north Indian Buddhist sites. Intrigued by their obvious antiquity and aghast at the destruction already visited upon the mounds, he had the sites placed under protection. The tracks of the railroad, it turned out, were being supported by the remains of one of the world's most ancient cities! Identifying the civilization that created it, however, would prove to be one of archaeology's greatest challenges.

It was well into the next century before scholars really began to understand the place of this "lost city" of Harappa—the center of one of the world's oldest and most mysterious societies. And although a full program of archaeological investigation has been under way at Harappa and dozens of similar sites throughout the Indus valley since the 1920s, some

***ABOVE:* The animal depicted in this Harrappan "unicorn seal" is still elusive and remains the subject of considerable debate.**

of the most basic questions about this society remain to be answered. For example, how did their writing system—composed of the symbols carved on the seals first brought to Cunningham—work? Unlike other early civilizations, which endured for thousands of years, Harappan society was relatively short lived, lasting perhaps 600 years before vanishing almost entirely; why did it disappear? And while scholars believe the structures of Harappan village life set many of the patterns for later Indian rural society, exactly how did these structures develop over the intervening generations? Indeed, how and why did urban societies reemerge later along the Ganges River, setting so many of the patterns of south Asian history? In short, what were the fundamental patterns that marked these founding cultures, and how did these patterns change the lives of the peoples in the region and come to be adopted and adapted by them?

One important pattern marking the history of northern India, like that of Mesopotamia, lies in regular rhythms of migration and invasion, interchanges of innovation, assimilation of peoples, and the expansion of ideas. In contrast to the long history of political unification in Egypt or China, all of India did not experience rule by a single regime until the nineteenth century CE. Yet considerable cultural and religious unity had already been created thousands of years earlier under the influence of newly emerging states along the Ganges River. The ability to maintain this cultural continuity while creating social systems with the flexibility to manage innovation from outside has marked India to the present day. Among their most significant achievements, the social, philosophical, and political challenges facing these early Ganges states resulted in some of the world's most important religious movements: Hinduism, Jainism, and the most widespread and influential religious movement in Asia, Buddhism.

Seeing Patterns

» Who were the Harappans? Where did they come from? What evidence exists for their origins?

» What explanations have been offered for the collapse of Harappan society? How well do the rival theories hold up, given what scholars and archaeologists have discovered?

» How can we know about the newcomers to northern India? What sources exist for historians to examine?

» What patterns can we see evolving in the Ganges River states that will mark the subsequent development of Indian civilization?

The Vanished Origins of Harappa, 3000–1500 BCE

Since the first intensive archaeological work of the 1920s, the sites of the Indus valley have been imbued with all the romance of "lost civilizations." Unlike Egypt (see Chapter 2), where the patterns of society remained remarkably stable for thousands of years, or Mesopotamia, which spawned a succession of states and empires, the cities of the Indus valley flourished for less than 1,000 years—from about 2500 to 1700 BCE—before vanishing almost without a trace. Anchored by two major cities—Harappa [hah-RAP-uh] in the north and Mohenjo-Daro [moe-hen-joe DAH-roe] in the southwest—and extending from the upper Ganges River to the Arabian Sea, a dense network of small cities, towns, and villages marked by a remarkable consistency of architecture and artifact occupied the largest cultural area of the third millennium BCE: twice the size of the Old Kingdom of Egypt and four times that of the empire of Sargon in Mesopotamia. Trade with southwest Asia and Egypt extended Harappan influence even farther.

Chapter Outline

- The Vanished Origins of Harappa, 3000–1500 BCE
- Interactions in Northern India, 1500–600 BCE
- Indian Society, Culture, and Religion, 1500–600 BCE
- Putting It All Together

Yet this "Harappan," or "Indus valley," culture, as archaeologists have named it, remains by far the most mysterious of the early centers of agriculturally supported urban society. The sophistication and precision of its urban planning, the standardization of weights and measures, and the attention to cleanliness and comfort all suggest an elaborate system of social organization, yet we know virtually nothing of its arrangement. Scholars have labored for nearly a century to unlock the secrets of the Harappan pictographic symbols, yet they remain mostly undeciphered. Most tantalizing of all is the fundamental question: Why, as the new mode of urban society gathered momentum elsewhere, did the inhabitants of this one abandon their cities and disappear from the historical record? To look at what we can and do know about these mysterious people, we must start with the geography of the Indus and its region.

The Region and People

Geographers define the region encompassed by the modern states of India, Pakistan, and Bangladesh as a *subcontinent*—a large, distinct area of land somewhat smaller than a continent. While the region is attached to the Eurasian landmass, it is almost completely cut off from it by some of the most forbidding physical barriers on earth. The lower two-thirds of India form a vast peninsula surrounded on three sides by the Arabian Sea, the Indian Ocean, and the Bay of Bengal. To the north of the bay, extending from Bangladesh through the Indian province of Assam to the north and east and deep into Myanmar (formerly Burma), are continuous ranges of heavily forested mountains. Some of the world's highest annual rainfall totals—over 100 inches—are regularly recorded here.

Forming the northeastern border of the subcontinent above the rain belt is the "roof of the world," the Himalayan Mountains. These meet another set of formidable peaks, the Hindu Kush, which extends into Pakistan and, with the Sulaiman and Kirthar ranges, marks the northwestern border of the region. Access to the Indian peninsula by land is thus limited to a handful of mountain passes through the Himalayas and the more substantial Khyber and Bolan Passes of the northwest. Historically, these have been the main avenues of trade, migration, and, frequently, invasion (see Map 3.1).

Topography: The physical features—mountains, rivers, deserts, swamps, etc.—of a region.

The Monsoon System As the region is surrounded by water and framed by high mountains, India's internal **topography** also has a considerable influence on its climate. The Deccan Plateau, Vindhya Range, and other internal highland areas tend to both trap tropical moisture against the west coast and funnel it toward the region drained by the Ganges River in the northeast. The moisture itself comes from the summer winds of the monsoon system, a term derived from the Arabic word *mausim*, for "season." The winds carry moisture generated from the heat of central and southern Africa as they flow southwest to northeast over the Indian Ocean from June through October and govern the climatic cycles of southeastern Asia, Indonesia, and southern China as well as India. In the winter months the winds reverse direction and pull hot, dry air down from central Asia. During this dry season, rainfall is scant or nonexistent over large areas of south Asia.

The extremes of the monsoon cycle, as well as its regularity, exert a powerful influence on Asian agriculture. This is particularly the case in India, where the monsoon rainfall amounts differ widely from region to region. Because even minor variations in the timing of the cycle or the volume of rain may spell potential flood or

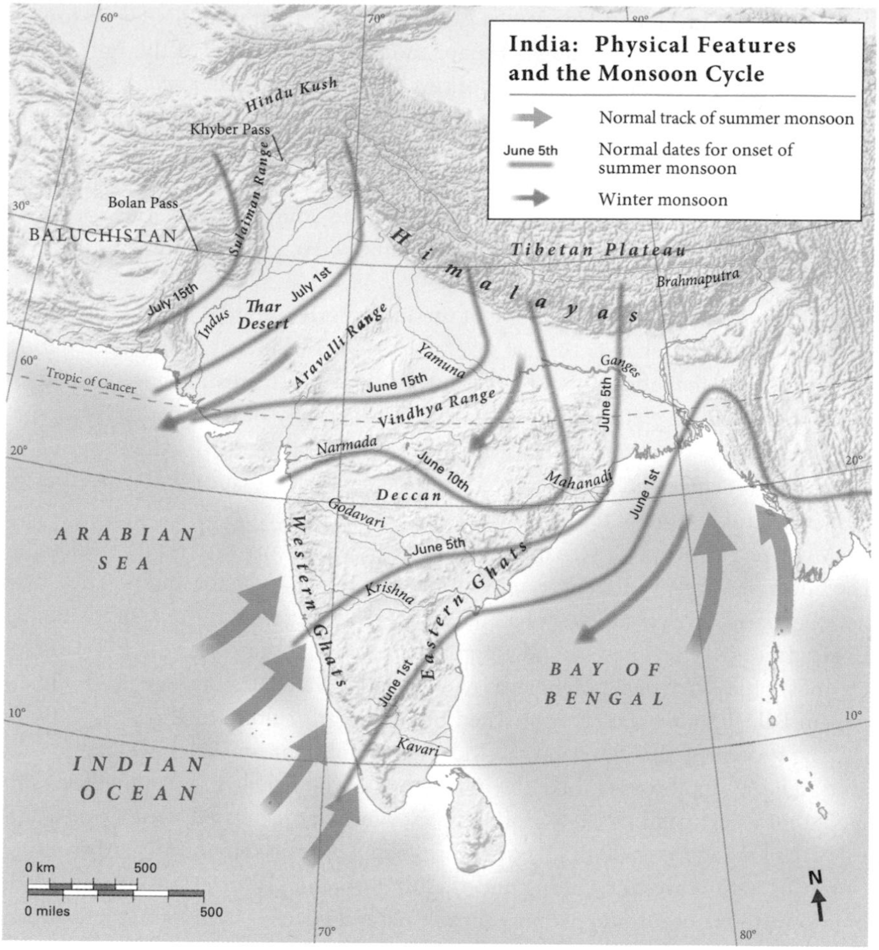

MAP 3.1 India: Physical Features and the Monsoon Cycle.

famine, the arrival of the monsoon is even today greeted with nervous anticipation. Generally speaking, the subcontinent becomes drier as one moves farther north and west until one reaches the Thar, or Great Indian, Desert and the plain of Sind, the site of some of the hottest temperatures ever recorded on earth—nearly 130 degrees Fahrenheit. It is this arid region bordered by mountains and watered by the Indus River system that saw the rise of the first Indian cities.

interactive timeline

6500–3000 BCE
Mehrgarh Neolithic culture in areas west of the Indus River

2500–1700 BCE
Mature Harappan period

1700–1300 BCE
Late Harappan period

1500–1200 BCE
Indo-European migrations enter northern India

1400–800 BCE
Composition of the Vedas by the Indo-European migrants

600–500 BCE
Development of the written language of Sanskrit

600–400 BCE
Composition of the Upanishads

800–500 BCE
Reemergence of urban life, now centered along the Ganges

ca. 600 BCE
Essential structures of *varna* and *jati* (caste) social systems in place

As the Greek historian Herodotus called Egypt "the gift of the Nile," so too, as archaeologists have noted, should Harappan civilization be called the "gift of the Indus." A vast river system composed of seven main branches in ancient times, the Indus has a slow, meandering course that for millennia has left behind rich deposits of fertile soil, by some estimates twice as much as those of the Nile. Moreover, like the Yellow River in China, the constant buildup of silt in the riverbed periodically caused the water to overflow its banks and change course—dangerous for those living close by but an effective means of spreading soil over a wide area.

Mehrgarh Culture The peopling of the Indian subcontinent has been the subject of intense research over the last several decades. The advent of advanced dating techniques and the refinement of DNA analysis and genetic testing have yielded an incredibly complex picture of the historical demography of the region. Groups of people in India's extreme south still chant prayers so ancient that the meaning of the words has long been lost. Recent testing has suggested that they may be directly descended from some of the earliest migrants out of Africa.

More recent peoples, perhaps speakers of a parent language termed "Elamite-Dravidian," are believed to have moved into the region near the Indus. They may have been part of a wave of early agriculturalists emerging from the area of the Fertile Crescent. Researchers have found a number of Neolithic sites near the river, one of the most productive being Mehrgarh [MARE-gar], located near a strategic mountain pass in Baluchistan. Scholars have dated the Mehrgarh culture to about 6000 BCE, making it perhaps the oldest on the Indian subcontinent for which we have a reliable archaeological record. Like the inhabitants of the Fertile Crescent, villagers in Neolithic Baluchistan raised wheat and barley and domesticated sheep, goats, and cattle. As long ago as 5500 BCE, pottery was being produced in the area. Also dating from this period are the crafting and trading of fine *lapis lazuli* (an opaque, dark blue gemstone) beadware, or "microbeads," later a coveted item among Harappan luxury goods. Significantly, even the earliest Baluchistani dwellings are made of mud brick, a material that with greater scope and sophistication became a hallmark of the Harappan cityscape. For all of these reasons, some archaeologists have viewed Mehrgarh culture as a possible precursor to Harappa.

Scholars agree that by about 3000 BCE a culture of villages and towns with elaborate trade networks, sophisticated pottery, and a substantial array of domesticated plants and animals had long been established in the hills of Baluchistan adjacent to the Indus and its western tributaries. Attracted, most likely, by the comparative ease of growing staple crops in the reliably fertile river valleys, the inhabitants of these hill sites extended their settlements eastward sometime before 2600 BCE and began a rapid phase of consolidation, which culminated in the region's first cities.

Adapting to Urban Life in the Indus Valley

By about 2300 BCE the two major cities of Harappa and Mohenjo-Daro—separated by 350 miles—marked the poles of a system of small cities, towns, and villages sprawled across an area estimated to be between 650,000 and 850,000 square miles (see Map 3.2). At its height, the city of Harappa had a population of over 40,000—comparable to that of the largest Mesopotamian cities of the period—and its defensive walls measured 3.5 miles in circumference. The location of these cities on a floodplain, moreover, dictated that they be built on enormous artificial hills

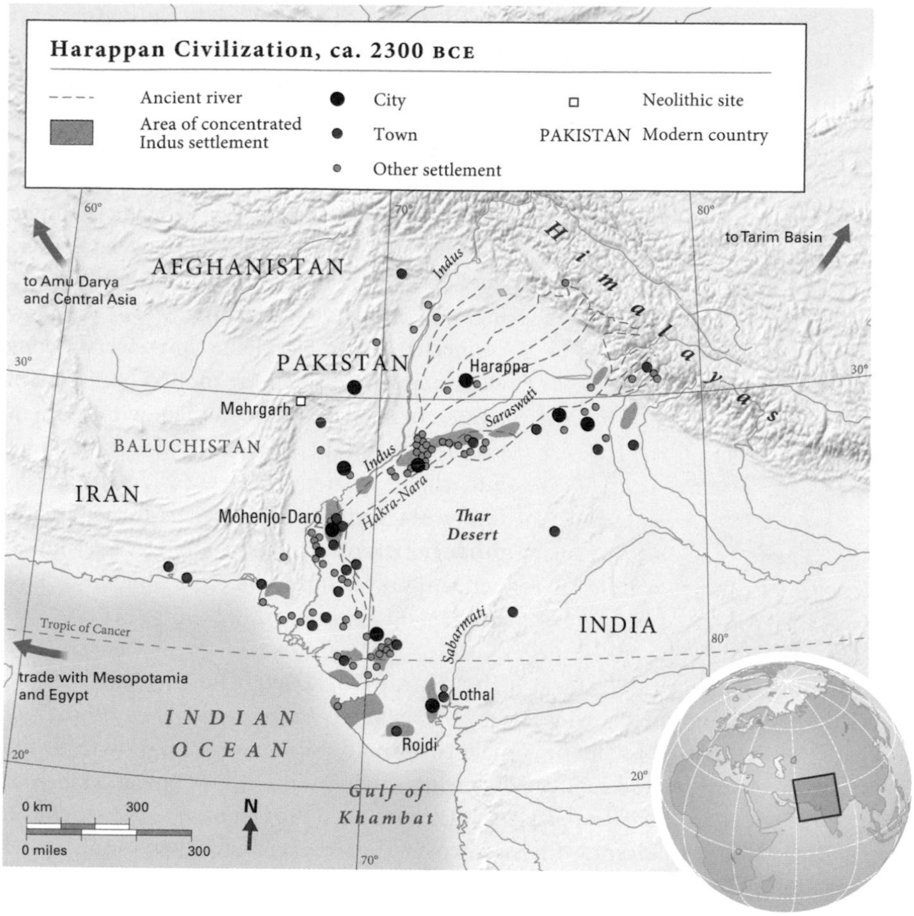

MAP 3.2 Harappan Civilization, ca. 2300 BCE.

map analysis

to protect them from damage during times that the rivers overflowed their banks. Mohenjo-Daro, for example, with an estimated 3,000 dwellings and a population of about 41,000, was built on two 40-foot mounds separated by a channel 200 yards wide for easy access to the Indus. More remarkable than the sheer size of these cities, however, are their similarities to each other.

Harappan Uniformity While all the cities of Mesopotamia and Egypt contained architectural features that make them a recognizable part of their respective cultures, Harappan cities seem almost to have been designed by the same hand. Harappa and Mohenjo-Daro, as well as several smaller cities and numerous towns, are laid out according to a rigorously surveyed and meticulously planned grid, with major thoroughfares running on north/south and east/west axes and squares, public buildings, and markets at regular, convenient locations. The larger streets are paved with brick and remarkably straight. They are laid out according to standard widths, and most have drains and gutters connected to what may be the most elaborate urban sewer system of ancient times (see Map 3.3). The bricks themselves were produced according to a uniform ratio of 4:2:1. Moreover, the Harappans developed perhaps the world's first decimal system and used it in designing highly refined scales of weights

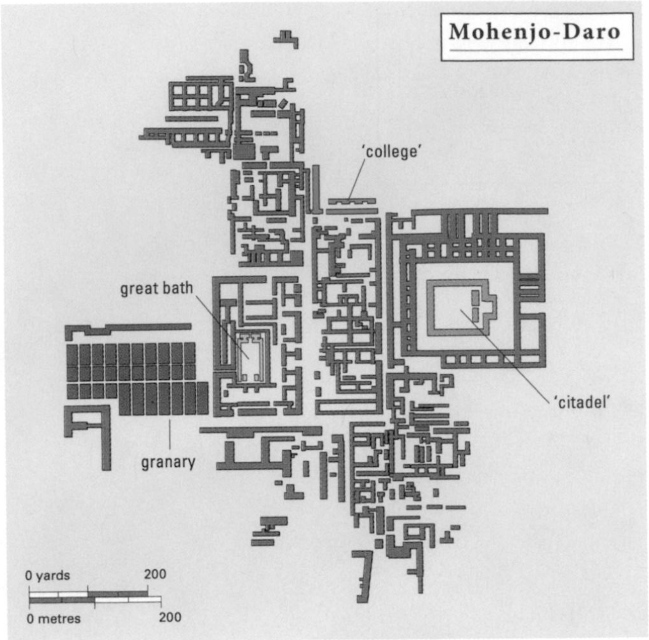

MAP 3.3 **Mohenjo-Daro.**

Cesspits: Deep holes or trenches used to deposit human waste and refuse; in the case of Harappa, they were flushed with water into city sewers and drains, ultimately leading to the adjacent river.

and measures. The smallest scale division yet uncovered among any culture of this period was found in Lothal: 1.704 millimeters.

This uniformity appears to have extended into the personal realm as well. Houses of several stories were made of brick and plastered with gypsum, their floor plans strikingly similar even at widely spaced sites. Many had brick-lined indoor wells and primitive toilets emptying into terra-cotta **cesspits** whose overflow connected to the city's drains and sewers. Nearly all dwellings had a bathing room reminiscent of a modern shower stall, complete with a waterproof floor and drain system to direct the water into channels in the street. Inside the dwellings, a staggering array of wheel-turned, mass-produced clay pots, jars, cooking vessels, copperware and bronzeware, and even toys have been found at various sites.

The Harappan Diet The rich alluvial soil of the region supported a wide variety of fruits, vegetables, and grains. Wheat and barley were staple crops, but peas, melons, figs, and sesame were also produced. The recovery of cotton seeds and small patches of cloth and fishing line at Mohenjo-Daro suggests that the Harappans may also have been the first people to raise cotton for use in clothing. Recent work has uncovered signs of elaborate and sophisticated irrigation systems designed to conserve water during dry periods. Cattle appear to have been the chief domestic animals, and indications of the large herds kept in some areas imply that they were seen as signs of wealth. It is not clear, however, whether they were used principally for food and milk or as work animals, as were water buffaloes. Whatever the case, some scholars see in their importance at this early time the origins of the later centrality of the cow in Indian culture and religion.

Sheep and pigs were also widespread and appear to have been an important part of the Harappan diet. Seal carvings and figurines suggest that the Harappans were sophisticated dog breeders, with some of the animals wearing what appear to be collars and depictions of a variety of different sizes and snout and tail configurations. It is also thought that the chicken was first domesticated here in Neolithic times. Rice, which figures so prominently in later Indian agriculture, may have also been grown but, because of the relatively arid climate, does not appear to have been a staple.

Harappan Identity and Government But who were they? Even today, evidence concerning the identity of the Harappans is obscure and contradictory. Everyday items and statuary offer few clues. Samples of symbols, most of which are found on what are believed to be merchant seals, were believed by some to hold tenuous links to a "Proto-Dravidian" language group distantly related to that of most modern south Indian peoples. Scholars have also suggested that the Harappans may have been an eastern branch of a people called "Proto-Mediterraneans," who ranged widely across southwest Asia. More recently, as previously noted, their predecessors in the region may have been the Elamite-Dravidian speakers from the area around the Fertile Crescent/Zagros Mountains. Complicating the matter further, archaeologists have identified an urban society designated as the "Bactria-Margiana Archaeological Complex" (BMAC) to the northwest of the Indus valley culture that shares some technological features with the Harappans but thus far no other obvious connections beyond some evidence of trade. Such findings are thus intriguing, but the uniqueness of Harappan urban life argues against any theory of simple cultural diffusion.

As with other early urban cultures, there appears to have been a close relationship among the religious, political, and social spheres of Harappan society. Nevertheless, the clues, while suggestive, again yield little that is definitive. For example, the replication of city plans and architecture throughout such a wide area might indicate the kind of strong central authority and bureaucratic control typically found in a kingdom or empire. Yet we know virtually nothing of how it might have been organized. Indeed, there seems to be an absence of the kind of monumental architecture of palaces and temples so characteristic of other wealthy, centralized states. Moreover, some departures from the otherwise rigorous uniformity of previous sites found in recent work at Rojdi [ROEJ-dee] have led scholars to amend this picture in favor of one of overall unity marked by discernible regional styles. This modified view, along with findings that suggest that a number of pockets of Harappan culture survived the collapse of the cities by many centuries, would, in light of the apparent self-sufficiency of these areas, seem to work against theories of highly centralized control.

The Horned God. The figure on this seal found at Mohenjo-Daro may be a depiction of a Harappan deity. Its cross-legged "lotus" position and multiple faces prompted archaeologist Sir John Marshall to theorize in the 1930s that it was an early version of the Hindu god Shiva. More recently, some scholars have moved away from this claim, noting that mention of Shiva does not occur for another 1,000 years during the Vedic period. Above the figure is a typically short sample of the pictographic Harappan script.

Harappan Trade The ability to mass-produce a vast array of articles implies specialization, regulation, and an occupation-based class system. Moreover, elaborate port facilities suggest the prominence of a merchant class with overseas connections. Mesopotamian records from about 2300 BCE tell of a people called "Meluha," now believed to be the Harappans, who carried on extensive seaborne trade and maintained colonies of merchants in several of their cities.

Harappan seals have been found at Ur in Mesopotamia, and there is evidence of Harappan merchandise being traded as far away as Egypt and central Asia. Because of the apparent occupational specialization of the Harappans, some scholars have theorized that they may have belonged to *guilds*, organizations whose members all pursue the same trade or craft. However, the plainness and uniformity of Harappan dwellings, in contrast to the pervasiveness of their amenities—generous living quarters, indoor plumbing, and so forth—defy any easy generalizations about class structure.

The Harappans appear to have maintained complex trade networks both within their cultural sphere and outside of it. Fortified border settlements, evidently trading posts, extended their influence to the borders of modern Iran and as far north as the Amu Darya, or Oxus, River, the region of the BMAC. Curiously, however, we see virtually no evidence of foreign trade goods such as handicrafts in the Indus cities, suggesting perhaps tight government control over outside influences.

In addition to bulk foodstuffs such as grain, the Mesopotamian records of the Meluha note that their merchants dealt in beadwork, lapis lazuli, pearls, rare woods, cotton cloth, and dog and cat figurines. Due in part to our inability to decipher the Harappan symbols, we know much less about their imports, though bulk goods such as foodstuffs, oils, and cloth seem to be among them. The network of cities along the Indus also seems to have been pivotal in the long-distance trade of copper from Baluchistan and in the exchange of gold, silver, semiprecious stones, shells, and timber throughout an extensive area north and west into Afghanistan and east to central Asia. Harappan figurines have been found along a broad front of nomadic routes from the Tarim Basin west. In addition, their sophistication and realism is striking among their contemporaries.

Lothal The complexity of these questions of trade and social organization may be seen quite vividly at Lothal [LOW-tall]. Located several miles up the Sabarmati River from the Gulf of Khambat (Cambay), Lothal was a large—perhaps the chief—Harappan seaport. Recent work has shown it to be not only a vital link in Harappan maritime trade in the Arabian Sea and points west but an important manufacturing center of various trade items as well.

Lothal's central structure is an enormous basin, approximately 120 feet long and 70 feet wide, which was once connected to an inlet of the river. Most researchers believe that this was a dock for oceangoing ships—perhaps the oldest yet discovered—though some contend instead that it was a reservoir for water storage. Nearby are a number of structures believed to have been warehouses, each with numerous cubicles marked with what appear to be the stamps and seals of various merchants.

But Lothal was also a famous regional craft center, with microbeads used for decorative craft items and jewelry as its chief product for internal trade and export. Indeed, scholars theorize that the city's site may have been chosen precisely because of its proximity to convenient sources of precious stones for bead making. The site, with the precise city planning and water systems typical of Harappan cities, is also notable for its numerous specialized pottery kilns and bead "factories," complete with worker housing. Yet, for all this wealth of artifacts, such questions as who the merchants or workers were, how they were organized and governed, what levels of mobility there might have been among different classes, and even precisely what those classes might have been remain elusive.

Phallic stones: Stones in the shape of or meant to evoke the male sex organ; Indian religions use a host of phallic images, or *lingams*, in shrines, rituals, and festivals to symbolize the male, or active, forces of both natural and supernatural creation.

Harappan Religion Clues about Harappan religion are equally tantalizing. The swastika, a symbol long associated with the cyclical nature of life in Indian and Buddhist art before its appropriation by the Nazis in the twentieth century, is first found in the cities of the Indus. Moreover, recent scholarship has suggested that the entire Harappan system of symbols, always assumed to be a form of writing, may instead be best understood as a form of religious shorthand for use in the multiethnic and multilingual Indus society. Figurines depicting cows, buffaloes, tigers, crocodiles, elephants, assorted animals from surrounding regions, and even mythical ones such as unicorns have also been found. Along with female figurines and **phallic stones**, these perhaps connote a type of fertility religion. Like many Neolithic and agrarian–urban cultures, the Harappans interred their dead with ornaments and pottery and perhaps food. Such practices have led scholars to speculate that the Harappans may have believed in an afterlife. All of these finds have also led scholars to see deep continuities with later Hindu practices.

Dockyard at Lothal. While some scholars maintain that this structure was a holding tank or reservoir for the local irrigation system, the current consensus is that it was in fact a technologically advanced area for loading and unloading oceangoing ships. A sophisticated system of channels kept it flooded to the proper level, prevented overflow, and, with locks and gates, allowed access to the river and sea.

The prominence of such combined dualities as male and female or plant and animal may imply a principal deity embodying a unity of opposites, perhaps prefiguring later Indian religious conceptions. Likewise, the central importance of the Indus River and the considerable attention paid to personal bathing are believed to be symbolically linked with a great ritual bath in the center of Mohenjo-Daro, perhaps adding yet another ritual dimension to the picture. Here again, however, the details are obscure, and, for the moment, the nature of Harappan religion remains an open question.

The Collapse of the Cities

Around 1900 BCE the major cities of Harappan society appear to have been in decline. Structures of inferior quality seem to have been constructed on top of earlier buildings, suggesting a drop in population with a consequent loss of maintenance and services. By 1700 BCE the great cities appear to have been all but abandoned, their people moving to smaller outlying towns and villages, many returning to farming or becoming herders.

Some recent interpretations of Harappan urban decline attribute it to ecological collapse. The surrounding land—overgrazed, stripped of trees, and reliant upon the river for fertilization—had reached the limits of its capacity to support large cities. Perhaps increased flooding or weather-related problems stretched these limits even further. One theory holds that a prolonged regional drought—extending even to Mesopotamia—occurred around 2200 BCE, resulting in a drying up of vital branches of the Indus watershed. Some scholars have proposed that increasing salt levels in the Indus played a role, perhaps as the result of diverting too much of its water for irrigation and supplying the cities; one study places part of the blame on earthquakes, which may have partially diverted the river's flow around 1800 BCE. We do know that the Hakra-Nara River was abruptly shunted into the Indus by the early eighteenth century BCE, resulting in a progressive drying up of its old watershed and increased flooding on the lower Indus.

Recent work at sites in the area south of the Indus valley indicates a longer period of survival for some of the smaller late Harappan towns in the region. Nevertheless, by about 1500 BCE it appears that remnants of Indus civilization were to be found only within isolated regional cultures that blended Harappan influences with those of neighboring peoples. The expansion of Harappan village agriculture to the east and south, however, continued. Indeed, the firm base that had made Harappan urban life possible—the cultivation of regionally appropriate staple crops and animals domesticated by people organized in villages—might justly be called the foundation of Indian social history. In that sense, though its cities were long since abandoned, the culture that produced this pattern of world history can hardly be considered "lost." It would be centuries, however, before India again saw the rise of cities.

Interactions in Northern India, 1500–600 BCE

The "villains" of the Harappan collapse were long considered to be Indo-European-language-speaking migrants from the north who called themselves "Aryans" (Sanskrit, "the noble ones")—a term which, through a series of twisted associations and garbled history, Adolf Hitler and the Nazis later identified with Germans. The identification of the Indo-European family of languages with the peoples of northern Europe in the nineteenth century prompted the Nazi appropriation of the term "Aryan" for those of Germanic ethnicity in the 1930s and 1940s. The tales associated with them recount their movement south and east through the Khyber Pass and across the Punjab between 1700 and 1400 BCE. Their accounts of epic battles had formerly been assumed to refer to their conquest of the Harappans. The earliest of their religious texts, the *Rig-Veda* [rig VAY-duh], refers to a short, dark-skinned people whom the Aryans contemptuously called *dasas*, or "the others," a term later used to denote servants or slaves. It also mentions conflicts with sedentary phallus-worshipping people living in cities and manning fortifications, which would certainly seem to describe the Harappans.

These works, however, were not written down until centuries after the events may have occurred, and whether their references date from the mid-second millennium BCE or were added later on is still not resolved. Moreover, while battles undoubtedly did occur, long periods of peaceful migration and settlement appear to have taken place as well. Perhaps the most significant problem, however, is that the Harappan cities appear to have been largely abandoned by the time the newcomers arrived on the scene.

In addition, the relative lack of Aryan artifacts; conflicts of interpretation among archaeologists, classical scholars, and linguists; and a growing body of scholarship by Indian researchers have produced in recent years a comprehensive questioning of the narrative of the role of Aryan migration altogether. Indeed, some scholars have suggested that long-held assumptions about the Aryans grew out of nineteenth-century beliefs of European superiority supported by the British occupation of India. Their contention is that the roots of Vedic society came not with invaders from the north but from peoples—perhaps the remnant of the Harappans themselves—already long established in the Punjab and, later, along the Ganges River. One problem with this interpretation, however, is that the society depicted in the Vedas—highly male centered, aristocratic, centralized—appears to bear little resemblance to the urban, egalitarian-appearing Harappans. The importance of the horse to later Vedic society also suggests a close connection to the Indo-Europeans as the people who appear to have domesticated the horse. Some scholars feel that the cultural discrepancy can at least be explained by the necessity of a societal shift as the Harappan remnant migrated east, ultimately settling around the Ganges. Since the debate, in any case, has loomed increasingly large in revisiting broad currents of Indian history and identity, it most likely will remain unresolved for some time to come.

Woolen Trousers. These trousers, at more than three thousand years old, are believed to be the oldest extant pair. Discovered in the ancient Yanghai graveyard of the Tarim Basin in 2014, they are believed to have been developed by early horse-riding peoples in central Asia.

The Vedic World, 1750–800 BCE

Most scholars, however, still assign a prominent, if not predominant, role to the Indo-European migrants. While, as we have seen, their exact homeland is unknown, scholars believe it to be in central Asia in the area around the Caspian Sea. Groups of nomadic peoples speaking a set of languages that linguists have designated "Proto-Indo-European" appear to have migrated along a broad front into Asia Minor, the eastern Mediterranean, Iran, and deep into central Asia, as evidenced by the so-called Tocharian texts and the recent find of the Tarim Basin mummies. In all these areas they proved to be important catalysts in the diffusion of such technologies as ironworking and the use of the horse and chariot.

Indo-European Origins Their ancestors had already played an extensive role in the spreading of items and ideas throughout Eurasia long before the Aryans arrived in India. Indeed, recent European scholarship has suggested that their presence predated the Neolithic settlement of the continent. More recently, branches are believed to have migrated east and west across the continent from perhaps 4000 to 2500 BCE. In the course of their travels they were active agents in collecting, refining, and spreading a host of Bronze Age technologies. They are believed to have been the people who introduced the domestication of the wild horses of the central Asian steppes on a wide scale, along with such items as bridles and weapons for use on horseback. Similarly, it seems likely that they were instrumental in moving the technology of the chariot along a wide front, ranging from the Mediterranean to China. As we saw in Chapter 2, around 1000 BCE various Indo-European-descended groups, most prominently the Hittites, brought the techniques of ironmaking out of Anatolia, ultimately taking them as far as the western reaches of the Yellow River basin.

Scholars have long identified a Proto-Indo-European language these groups are believed to have spoken as the parent tongue of a family of languages that includes Latin, German, Greek, the Slavic languages, Celtic languages such as Gaelic, and what became the Indian literary language, Sanskrit. A number of words with common roots for certain basic objects or concepts may be found among these languages. Examples include *pater* (Latin), *Vater* (German), and *pitar* (Sanskrit) for "father"; *septem* (Latin) and *sapta* (Sanskrit) for "seven"; and the place name "Iran" (from "Aryan"). However, a new group of scholars has argued for a "Paleolithic continuity theory," in which these groups had already begun to differentiate linguistically by the beginning of the Neolithic period and were not involved in massive "invasions" on the continent from the fifth to the third millennium BCE.

Patterns Up Close | The Caste System

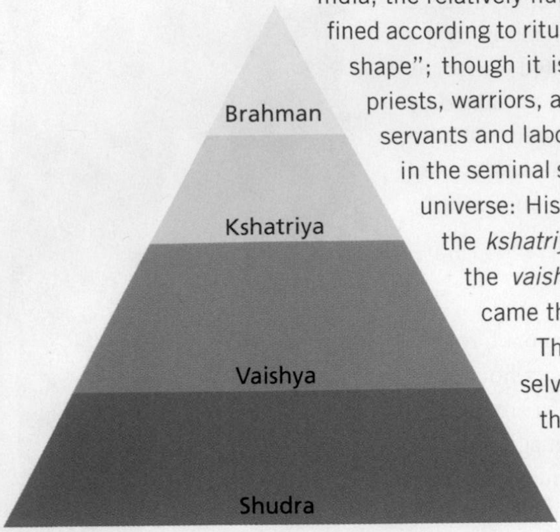

More than any other agrarian states, the *janapadas* developed an interlocking social order based on ethnicity and occupation. As the Vedic peoples settled into northern India, the relatively fluid divisions of their nomadic society became more firmly defined according to ritual position and occupational status as the four *varnas* ("form; shape"; though it is also sometimes interpreted as "color"): the first three for priests, warriors, and commoners, respectively, and a fourth that included both servants and laborers. The origin of the *varnas*, according to the *Rig-Veda*, lay in the seminal sacrifice of the cosmic being Purusha, which gave form to the universe: His mouth became the Brahmans, or priests; his arms became the *kshatriyas* [kuh-SHA-tree-yahs]—kings and warriors; his two thighs the *vaishyas* [vy-SHEE-yahs], or merchants; and from his two feet came the *shudra*, or peasants, servants, and laborers.

The newcomers' task of establishing and maintaining themselves as an elite class over the indigenous peoples meant that the system had to be expanded to accommodate all but with tight restrictions placed on social mobility. Thus, it appears that intermarriage was forbidden between the new elites and *dasas*, the term used for non-Aryans, and the latter were incorporated into the peasant/laborer/servant *varna*. By the sixth century BCE it appears that divisions between Aryans and non-Aryans that might have originally been based on ethnicity or locale were giving way to ones based on occupation. An elaborate *jati*, or caste, system—a term derived from the Portuguese word *casta*, for "breed" or "race," which they mistakenly believed governed these social arrangements—was already developing.

Based on the original divisions of the four *varnas*, each caste was theoretically divisible into an infinite number of subcastes finely graded according to hereditary occupations. A new category of "excluded" castes—the so-called untouchables (today called Dalits)—was added, comprising people whose occupations were considered

The Vedas Scholars believe that sometime around 2000 BCE a linguistic group designated "Indo-Aryans" had already split off from the Indo-Iranian subgroup and began moving toward the passes leading to northern India. As noted earlier, however, the confusing written record, the lack of firm archaeological sites, and national politics have made this history extraordinarily difficult to unravel. Some scholars see the Indo-Aryans as emerging from the BMAC culture; others see them as engaging in wars within the BMAC against the indigenous settled inhabitants; still others see them as migrating into the Punjab long after the Harappan cites had been in decline. In this context, they view their accounts of great "battles" and storming "citadels" as in reality cattle raids and attacks on village corrals.

In any case, the migrants appear to have carried with them an oral tradition of epic poetry, hymns, prayers, and heavily allegorical myth and history that would be carefully cultivated and preserved until it was committed to writing after 600 BCE. The core works, composed from around 1400 to 800 BCE, are the religious hymns

ritually unclean: butchers, refuse collectors, privy cleaners, leather workers, and those involved with tending to the dead. The excluded castes also came to include "outcasts," people who for various offenses had "lost caste" and were therefore placed on the fringes of society. Perhaps a lingering vestige of early Vedic attempts at ethnic separation, stringent prohibitions were imposed on sexual relations between *shudras* and members of the castes within the first three "twice-born" (Aryan) *varnas*—so called because they alone were permitted to undergo the ceremony of the "sacred thread" and be "reborn" as initiates to the mysteries of the Vedic scriptures.

1805 French Lithograph of Indian Funeral (*top*) and Upper-Caste Dress (*bottom*).

The evolving *jati* system, with its precarious balance of flexibility and stability, expanded southward as the Ganges River states pushed farther and farther into these areas. Eventually, it incorporated villages, clans, and sometimes even entire tribal groups into their own *jatis*. Though highly restrictive in terms of social mobility, these arrangements guaranteed a prescribed place for everyone in society, with at least a minimal degree of mutual support. Moreover, the idea of movement between castes became a vital part of Indian religious traditions through the doctrines of continual rebirth and the transmigration of souls. Thus, the evolving Indian innovation in response to the problem of incorporating a staggering multiplicity of ethnic, linguistic, and religious groups into its expanding culture was to create a space in society for each, while ensuring stability by restricting the social mobility of individuals and encouraging good behavior through the hope of a higher place in the next life. The fact that the system continues today despite its dissolution by the Indian government is testimony to its tenacious cultural roots and long-standing social utility.

Questions

- How is the caste system a cultural adaptation?
- How does the persistence of the caste system today demonstrate its social utility?

known as the Vedas ("knowledge" or "truths"). Like the *Iliad* and *Odyssey* for Homeric Greece, the Vedas are still the principal window through which we can glimpse the world of early northern India.

The *Rig-Veda*, the earliest of the Vedas, is currently believed to have been composed between about 1400 and 900 BCE. Some scholars, however, have suggested that some of the references contained in it point to much more ancient indigenous origins for it. Its verses were customarily memorized and passed from generation to generation by priests and their successors until after 1400 CE. The oldest recorded poetry in any Indo-European language, the *Rig-Veda*'s 1,028 verses provide an idealized and allegorical vision of a society led by hard-fighting, lusty warrior chieftains and priests, and composed of herders, cultivators, artisans, and servants. These groups became the prototypes of the four early social divisions, or *varnas*—priests, warriors, merchants, and commoners (see "Patterns Up Close"). Material wealth and skill in battle were the most valued attributes of Vedic culture. This emphasis on struggle and daring is seen as evidence of a strongly *patriarchal*, or male-led, society with an elaborate hierarchy based on kinship and prowess.

Early North Indian Society and Economics Though a nomadic people, the Indo-Europeans possessed a high degree of technical skill. Not only had they benefited from the diffusion of earlier Bronze Age crafts, but, as we have seen, they were also important agents in distributing these crafts throughout Eurasia. They were particularly proficient in weaponry, and their bronze spear tips, arrowheads, and blades, in addition to the mobility of their chariots and horseborne warriors, very likely gave them a pronounced advantage over those of the village communities they encountered. After the beginning of the first millennium BCE, they also helped spread the use of iron.

Excellent horsemen, the Vedic peoples made extensive use of horse-drawn wagons and chariots in battle. The earliest migrants may have introduced the horse to northern India, and it is likely that they first brought the chariot to late Xia or early Shang China. Elaborate equipment such as bridles, yokes, harnesses, and other items related to the use of horses have been found at a number of sites. The horse was so potent a symbol of power and well-being in Vedic culture and religion that its sacrifice became the most sacred of all ceremonies.

Ranging across vast stretches of grassland, the early Vedic peoples carried much of their food supply with them in the form of domestic animals. As with the Harappans, cattle were the chief measure of wealth, thus continuing the centrality of the "sacred cow" to the Indian religious experience. As skilled cultivators as well as herdsmen, the migrants adapted easily to a wide range of environments. Sheep and goats were also mainstays of their livestock, while milk and butter, particularly the clarified butter called "ghee" [gee, with a hard "g"], occupied a prominent place in their religious symbolism.

As a highly refined product of the cow, ghee came to signify a rain that was at once purifying and fruitful. Even today ghee is used in daily household rituals. In the *Rig-Veda*, it acquired *cosmological* significance; that is, it was seen as something that helps to reveal the underlying meaning and structure of the universe. As with so many aspects of the deeper Indian past, ghee provides tantalizing clues about ancient practices but still leaves a tightly drawn veil over everyday life.

The Settlement of Northern India While the Vedas provide a rich literary account of Indo-European conceptions of society and religion, the history of the settlement of northern India is far more obscure. Evidence from assorted sites suggests that there was a prolonged period of migration and settlement in the northwest of the subcontinent marked by a gradual transition of the Vedic peoples from a nomadic and pastoral life to a settled and agricultural one. As early as 1000 BCE, evidence of large towns appears in the area around present-day Delhi. An important catalyst in bringing about the conditions necessary for the reemergence of large cities, however, was the beginning of widespread rice cultivation in the newly opened lands to the east.

First domesticated in Neolithic southeast Asia and south-central China, rice proved well suited to the warm temperatures, monsoon rains, and high fertility of the Ganges basin once the forests had been cleared. Here, it seems evident that the introduction of iron tools such as plows and axes was instrumental in preparing the land. High yields and a climate warm enough to permit two crops per year helped ensure the surpluses necessary to support an increasingly dense network of villages, towns, and cities, sometimes called by archaeologists India's "second urbanization."

However, the meticulous, intensive labor required at every stage of the rice plant's growth cycle required many hands for its successful cultivation. The plants must be grown in shallow water of a carefully prescribed depth and must be transplanted before the grain is harvested. Hence, the elaborate infrastructure of rice culture—the dikes, drainage ditches, terraces, raised paths, and other items related to water control—demanded a high degree of cooperation and increasingly sophisticated social organization. From roughly 800 BCE, we can trace the development of strong agrarian-based states called *janapadas* [jah-nah-PAH-duhs] ("populated territories" or "clan [*jana*] territories") in northern and northeastern India.

Statecraft and the Ideology of Power, 800–600 BCE

By the sixth century BCE the *janapadas* had encompassed the entire Ganges valley and were leading the way toward a cultural, if not a military, conquest of the subcontinent. Supported by the growing agricultural wealth and trade of the region, their influence was crucial in spreading their increasingly elaborate religion steadily east and south. Sixteen large states, or *mahajanapadas* [MAH-hah-jah-nah-PAH-duhs], now dominated northern India from the Bay of Bengal to the foothills of the Himalayas. The four largest—Avanti, Vatsa, Kosala, and Magadha—grew increasingly powerful, rich, and contentious along the Ganges. Buoyed by large revenues from agricultural and trade taxes and supported by theories that accorded kingship an almost divine status, their respective quests for domination grew as they absorbed their weaker neighbors. In this respect, as we shall see in Chapter 4, these states shared much in common with their contemporaries, the states of Zhou China.

Centralization and Power among the Ganges States The growing power and prosperity of the larger states tended to push them toward increasing centralization so that their resources might be used to maximal effect in the struggle for domination and survival. The two wealthiest *mahajanapadas*, Magadha and Kosala, found the route to consolidation through centralized kingdoms supported by the Brahmans, or priests. By the sixth century BCE this combination of state power and religion had produced kings, or *maharajas* [mah-hah-RAH-juhs], who were accorded godlike stature and wielded power that was seen as both secular and divine. For example, a number of kings, with the sanction of the priestly class, conducted increasingly elaborate horse sacrifices. The king's horse, accompanied by soldiers and royal grooms, was first made to wander the kingdom for a year, during which all land within the borders of its travels was claimed by the ruler. Its sacrifice thus became not only a supremely important religious festival but also a reminder of the king's power.

Other large states retained systems of government in which power was more diffuse, often being ruled by councils of various sorts as opposed to kings; scholars sometimes refer to these states as "republics." The most powerful of the republics, the Vajjian Confederacy, was ruled by a chief whose authority was derived from a council made up of heads or representatives of the principal clans. The council members were in turn responsible to local assemblies of clan elders and notables.

Even among the republics, the general trend appears to have been that of growing economic prosperity coupled with fierce competition among all the states for domination and survival—requiring ever greater efficiency in collecting revenue and spending for defense—pushing them toward either monarchy or absorption. The Vajjian Confederacy, for example, was eventually absorbed by Magadha during its drive for empire in northern India.

Thus, by the sixth century BCE, these states, like the Greek *poleis* and the states of late Zhou China, found themselves embroiled in continual political crises. Alliances between the states were sought and abandoned as the situation warranted; attempts to create a balance of power repeatedly failed as the largest states relentlessly vied for control. Increasing sophistication in strategy, tactics, and military technology—now including iron weapons, massed cavalry, perhaps the earliest use of war elephants, and even giant bows—put a premium on manpower and revenue, thus giving the larger states further advantages. By the late fourth century BCE, when these armies faced the threat of invasion by the forces of Alexander the Great and his successor Seleucus, they would number in the hundreds of thousands of men.

The Ideology of Rulership Warfare conducted by kings vested with godlike status raised a number of ethical and practical questions about the nature of kingship, the responsibilities of rulers to their subjects, and their role as agents of a universal order. For example, how should a ruler monitor the activities of his subjects? What are the bounds of behavior in terms of diplomacy, espionage, the conduct of conflict, and the long-term welfare of the kingdom? Under what conditions may the rules be broken? In short, how should the ideal ruler comport himself for the good of his kingdom, subjects, and himself in accordance with his divine mission?

The growing size, wealth, and power of the Ganges states made these questions increasingly important as all struggled to expand—or merely survive. By 600 BCE, all the Gangetic rulers were, roughly speaking, in the situation later described by the political strategist Kautilya [kaw-TEEL-yuh] of Magadha in his grimly realistic, pioneering political treatise, the *Arthashastra* [ar-tah-SHAS-truh]. In this constant war of all against all, says Kautilya, the wise ruler understands that those who encircle him on all sides and "prevail in the territory adjacent to his are . . . known as the enemy." On the other hand, those who control the territory "that is separated from the conqueror's territory by one [namely, the enemy's territory] is the constituent known as friend." Hence, one's policy toward neighboring states should be opportunistic: Attack the weak, seek allies against the strong, bide one's time with equals, and practice duplicity wherever and whenever necessary. As we shall see, there are many parallels with late Zhou Chinese treatises such as Sun Zi's *Art of War*. The prime purpose of such action, however, must always be the welfare of one's subjects by means of the survival and prosperity of the state.

This grim vision of the evolving world of statecraft was tempered somewhat by the themes depicted in the epics, composed during the Vedic period, though committed to writing only in the third century BCE, of which the two most famous are the Mahabharata [Mah-hah-BAH-rah-tuh] and the Ramayana [Rah-muh-YAH-nuh]. Perhaps the world's longest poem—at 100,000 verses in 18 books, it is many times longer than the Bible—the Mahabharata centers on the struggles among the descendants of the king Bharat, and especially on the conflicting obligations imposed on the individual by state, society, and religion. The sixth book, the Bhagavad Gita [BAH-guh-vahd GEE-tuh] (Song of the Lord), has been called the "Indian gospel" because of its concentration on the tense and intricate balance of ethics and action.

Illustration from the Mahabharata. The stories of the Mahabharata continue to be among the most popular forms of entertainment in India today. In this 1598 CE painting, Arjuna confronts his relatives on the battlefield.

On the eve of a battle in which the enemy includes his relatives and former companions, Arjuna, the protagonist, agonizes over fighting against his family and friends. His charioteer—actually the god Krishna in disguise—reminds him of the need to fulfill his duty according to *dharma* [DAR-mah] (literally "that which is firm"). To act according to dharma means following one's prescribed role according to one's place in society and in the natural order. As a warrior and ruler, therefore, Arjuna cannot leave the field of battle because of his personal connections to his opponents. Krishna tells him that the higher law of dharma demands that he put aside his personal reservations and fulfill his larger obligation to fight and win. Hence, Arjuna is urged to perform his duty without attachment as the agent of forces that transcend the immediate ties of friendship or family. Thus, if Arjuna forces himself to do his duty because it must be done, abandoning his attachment to the result—whatever it may be—then, according to Krishna, he is acting wisely and advancing the course of the universe.

By about 600 BCE, the largest of the northern Indian states, especially Magadha and Kosala, were attempting both to expand southward and to absorb their neighbors along the Ganges. In this volatile political environment, they developed ideologies of kingship and power based on a common understanding of the religious and cultural implications of the Vedas and a realistic appraisal of their respective political environments. At once supported and trapped by the idea of dharma as it relates to kingship, they would struggle for the next several centuries until Magadha incorporated the northern third of the subcontinent into an empire (see Map 3.4).

Indian Society, Culture, and Religion, 1500–600 BCE

The first chronicles of Indian history do not make their appearance until well after the beginning of the Common Era. Because of this, such documentary evidence as we have about social history, especially that of families or village organization, is found in religious and literary texts, law codes, and the collections of folktales and genealogies called the *Puranas* [poor-AH-nuhs] ("legends"), which date from about 500 BCE.

Society and Family in Ancient India

While part of Indian religious thought was becoming increasingly concerned with the nature of the absolute and ways to connect with it (see Chapter 8), much of the

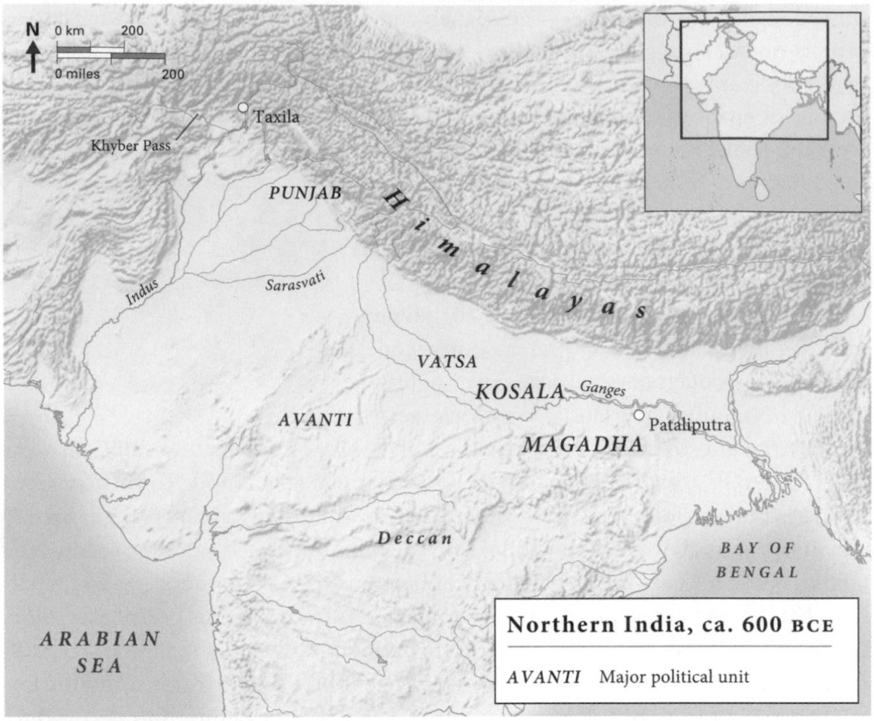

MAP 3.4 Northern India, ca. 600 BCE.

rest dealt with the arrangement of society, law, and duty; the role of the family and its individual members; and relationships between men and women.

Dharma and Social Class For example, the Bhagavad Gita contains numerous illustrations of the dilemmas that come from following one's dharma: duty in accordance with one's capabilities and the requirements of one's place in society. Krishna outlines these duties quite succinctly to Arjuna in the Bhagavad Gita in a set of passages that closely echo the structure of the *varnas*: "Tranquility, control, penance, purity, patience, and honesty, knowledge, judgment, and piety are intrinsic to the action of a priest," he notes, while "heroism, fiery energy, resolve, skill, refusal to retreat in battle, charity, and majesty in conduct are intrinsic to the action of the warrior." The activities that support the subsistence of society such as farming, herding cattle, and commerce "are intrinsic to the action of a commoner," while "action that is essentially service is intrinsic to the servant."

The great majority of Indians followed Krishna's last two sets of injunctions. Although one of the distinctive developments in the rise of the Gangetic states had been the rebirth of urban life in India, the village remained the center of the social world for perhaps 80–90 percent of the subcontinent's inhabitants—as it largely does to this day. In pursuing various tasks such as tending cattle and water buffalo, raising a variety of crops such as rice, wheat, barley, millet, and, in the southern areas, spices, medicinal herbs and barks, and forest products the villagers were organized by clan and *jati*, or **caste** (see "Patterns Up Close").

Caste: A system in which people's places in society—how they live, the work they do, and whom they marry—are determined by heredity.

Though arranged according to a rigid hierarchy, the social system based on *jati* ("to be born into") functioned in many ways as a kind of extended family, each with its own clans, villages, local dialects, gods, laws, advisory councils, and craft and work specializations. Thus, as the organization of society became more complex—owing to the demands of increased size, trade, population diversity, and urbanization—the ritual importance of the four *varnas* of the Vedas was slowly giving way to the occupational emphasis of *jati* in the new agrarian–urban order.

As the system expanded south, it incorporated many local leaders, clan elders, and other notables into the higher castes. Sometimes entire villages were accorded their own castes on the basis of lineage or occupational specialty. At its peak, the number of castes and subcastes may have exceeded 3,000. As the various peoples of the subcontinent were brought into the structure, the older ritual divisions of the early Vedic era were slowly broken down even further, though their traces remain even to the present.

The all-pervasive force of dharma extended into the personal realm as well as that of politics. Behavior in village society and the family, and even the possibilities for religious fulfillment, hinged upon understanding and carrying out the demands of dharma. These demands, however, varied greatly according to an individual's social standing, gender, and place in the family.

Gender Roles: Men and Women in Society The importance of family life in India is readily evident in religious scriptures and the law codes, or *smriti* [SMER-tee]. By 600 BCE, *artha* [AHR-tah], the pursuit of subsistence and prosperity, was recognized as a moral course of action necessary to sustain family position and harmony. In addition to tending to the extensive ritual demands of daily life, the male householder of the upper caste was expected to "cast food on the ground for dogs, untouchables [the excluded castes], and crows." Moreover, according to the *smriti*, "Children, married daughters living in the father's house, old relatives, pregnant women, sick persons, and girls, as also guests and servants—only after having fed these should the householder and his wife eat the food that has remained." Thus, the male householder must be willing to habitually sacrifice his own needs for those of his family and dependents.

The position of women in the Indian family and in Indian society is more difficult to determine. At once partner and property, the center of the family, yet burdened with complex restrictions over education and marriage, adult women seem simultaneously to occupy several separated rungs on the hierarchies of family and society. Unswerving loyalty and devotion on the part of wives and daughters was demanded and highly prized. For example, a large part of the epic of the Ramayana, an allegorical account of the conquest of the peoples of the south, centers on the obsessive, though ultimately groundless, suspicion of the hero Rama [RAH-mah] about the faithfulness of his kidnapped wife, Sita. The reciprocal aspect of the demand for loyalty and devotion, as the Code of Manu advises, is that, "regarding this as the highest dharma of all four classes, husbands . . . must strive to protect their wives." Thus, a great part of Rama's behavior toward Sita springs from his self-reproach over his failure to fulfill his most basic responsibility of protecting his wife. At the same time, Sita's loyalty to Rama makes her an exemplary model of dharma.

In household matters a wife should be engaged "in the collection and expenditure of . . . (the husband's) wealth, in cleanliness, in dharma, in cooking food for the family, and in looking after the necessities of the household." The position of women in this context, the code says, is "deserving of worship."

Coupled with this ideal of domesticity is a concept of women and women's sexuality as simultaneously compelling and threatening. The idea of *kama,* as encapsulated in the later *Kama Sutra,* included the enjoyment of a wide variety of sexual pleasures by men and women as part of a balanced social and religious life. Much Indian literature, both sacred and secular, as well as motifs, symbols, and statuary associated with shrines and temples, graphically celebrates the union of male and female as the conduit for the primal creative force of the universe. Female beauty itself is identified with beneficial natural phenomena.

Later on, during the period of Classical Hinduism, numerous temples would have carvings depicting men and women in all phases of sexual activity, and even today small local temples feature phallic stones which worshipers periodically anoint with milk and flowers.

In contrast to this concept of truth and purity arising from naked innocence was the idea that the material world in general, and sexuality in particular as its most enticing aspect, could divert a person from fulfilling his or her dharma. As such, it poses a threat to the social and natural order if not properly controlled. The close relationship between society and religion in this regard provided considerable latitude for men to explore ways of going "beyond" the material and sexual world by engaging in solitary, often celibate, religious practices. On the other hand, it also bolstered the idea that a woman without the protection of a husband or family was a danger to herself and a source of temptation to others. For both men and women, independence from the social system of family, clan, or caste—unless channeled into an approved religious or social practice—was subject to severe sanction. But, because of the concept that the family was the foundation of society as a whole and the place of women was at the center of family life, the burdens of supporting the system and the penalties for failing to do so fell far more heavily on women than on men.

Cultural Interactions to 600 BCE

The social system of *varna* and *jati* held together as the religion of the Vedas expanded into the diverse body of beliefs, practices, and philosophy that would later be referred to by outsiders as "Hinduism." The term is derived from the Persian word *hindu,* taken from the Sanskrit *sindhu,* or "rivers," in reference to the inhabitants of the Indus valley.

Gods and Priests Though principally the embodiments or controllers of natural forces, the gods had human personalities as well. Indra, for example, was a swashbuckling warrior with a taste for *soma,* an intoxicating drink used in religious rituals. Varuna was the regulator of cosmic affairs and the lawgiver. Agni encompassed all the forces of light, sun, and fire and was, in a sense, the messenger of the gods, carrying the sacrifices of humans to the other deities.

The prestige of the Brahmans (priests), as members of the most important and respected *varna,* grew as they monopolized the performance of ever more elaborate rituals and sacrifices. The priests carefully maintained the oral tradition of the Vedas, taking extreme care to pass on the exact formulas of the old rituals, while also creating new, increasingly elaborate ones centered on the needs of a more sedentary, agrarian people. The growing emphasis on the precise details of various rituals, as codified in the Vedic commentaries called Brahmanas, spurred the development of education among the men of the upper castes. By the sixth century BCE, the major works of the Vedic and Brahmanic oral tradition were being committed to writing in Sanskrit, from this time forward the sacred language of Indian scriptures.

Toward New Religious Directions At the same time, this trend contributed to an increasing *formalism* within the Vedic-Brahmanic tradition: the belief that only the precise observance of all the proper forms of ritual behavior—prayers, sacrifices, daily and seasonal ceremonies—could ensure their effectiveness. Since the formulas for these rituals were for the most part accessible only to the "twice-born" or upper *varnas*, a small percentage of the population, and considered the special province of the Brahmans, there was considerable social and religious exclusiveness attached to the tradition as well. Indeed, the punishment prescribed for the non-twice-born overhearing the inner secrets of Brahmanic ritual was to have molten lead poured into their ears.

A movement away from this restrictive formalism was already apparent by 600 BCE. Instead of appeasing the gods through the precise performance of ritual as a means of ensuring the cosmic order, some in the upper *varnas* began seeking the forces behind that order and trying to achieve communion with them. Two paths within the Vedic-Brahmanic tradition became discernible in this regard.

image analysis

One path was *asceticism*, full or partial renunciation of the material world, which, because of its impermanence, was seen as an impediment to a deeper understanding of reality. The Vedic tradition had long held a special reverence for hermits and those who fled society in order to purify themselves. The many schools of ascetic practice held that the multiple distractions of making a living, raising a family, and even the body itself hindered the quest for one's spiritual essence. These schools developed a variety of strategies for uncovering the unchanging, and thus real, "self" removed from a world where everything is impermanent and, hence, illusory.

The practices of certain schools of *yoga* ("discipline"), for example, were based on the belief that mastery of the body allowed the adept to leave the restrictions of the material world and achieve communion with this inner self. Since the body, as part of the physical world, is subject to constant change, the discipline of postures, breathing, and meditation allows the practitioner to go beyond its limitations and find that which is unchanging within.

The other emerging path to a deeper spiritual reality was scriptural. Between the seventh and fifth centuries—though perhaps from as early as 800 BCE—a diverse group of writings called the Upanishads [hoo-PAHN-ee-shahds] ("secret knowledge") marked a dynamic new direction within the Vedic tradition. The Upanishads represented the Vedanta, the "fulfillment" of the Vedas, in which the hidden symbolism was revealed, layer by layer, and apparent inconsistencies were reconciled. While different levels of understanding the "true" principles of the Vedas were

Asceticism. For millennia great respect has been accorded those who withdraw from the lure of the material world and seek the unchanging within. Here, a modern "world renouncer," or *sannyasi*, is shown.

Bathing in the Ganges at Varanasi. The sacred character of rivers in the Indian religious experience may go back all the way to the Harappans. As the multiple religious traditions we know as Hinduism developed in the Ganges valley, that river assumed a position of central importance in terms of ritual purification. Here, bathers are shown on the ghats—steps built on the riverbank—of the city of Varanasi, also known as Benares, site of some of Hinduism's holiest shrines.

to be expected of those with limited access to the scriptures, a slavish reliance on the formal aspects of sacrifice was clearly subject to criticism.

The material world was increasingly regarded as extraneous as well. The individual "self" (*atman*) was ultimately to become identified with the cosmic "essence" (*brahman*—note that this usage is different from the same term used to describe the priestly *varna*).

Karma-Samsara Though the full impact of these trends would be felt only in succeeding centuries, speculation about the nature of individual and universal "essence" was already beginning to be reflected more broadly in culture and society. The elaboration of the idea of caste and its accompanying obligations carried with it the development of *karma-samsara,* the transmigration of souls and reincarnation. Though few references to these concepts are found in the Vedas, by the sixth century BCE the two ideas appear to have been widely accepted. The concept of a nonmaterial essence or "soul" carrying with it the residue of one's deeds—*karma*—is coupled with the idea of the rebirth of the soul into a new body—*samsara.* The fidelity with which a person pursues his or her dharma within the context of the caste system ensures an advance in caste in the next life. Ultimately, the doctrine provided for *moksha*—release from the karmic cycle and the achievement of a state of complete understanding in this world—for those who are fully able to grasp the principles of *atman: brahman* and *dharma.*

Putting It All Together

interactive concept map

In the Indus valley, as we have already seen in Egypt and Mesopotamia, a critical mass of factors required for the transition to agrarian-based cities had come together sometime around 2500 BCE. Yet our inability to decipher the symbols of the Harappans has proven to be a powerful impediment to our understanding of how their society worked and, equally important, why it fell. We are accustomed to thinking of history as a series of thresholds through which human societies pass in linear, progressive fashion—from forager society to agrarian to urban society, for example—without any substantial backtracking. And yet there are the Harappans, who, for whatever reason, abandoned their splendid cities for, we must suppose, village agriculture or life in the forest.

Invasion by mobile nomads had formerly been seen as the cause, and this pattern of struggle between the settled and the nomadic will continue in various parts of the world for thousands of years. For the Harappans, however, the coming of the nomadic Indo-Europeans may not actually have had much of an impact, making the questions of interaction and adaptation that much more intriguing.

In India, the interruption in urban life lasted nearly 1,000 years. When cities again arose, they were centered hundreds of miles from the old, now forgotten

Harappan sites. Instead of the apparent uniformity of the earlier society, the new one was to be marked by the struggle of individual states for advantage and supremacy. Yet, although these Gangetic states lacked political unity, their cultural and religious similarity remained an important factor throughout Indian history. Their unique innovation of the *jati* system was to act like a great flexible mold within which Indian society was increasingly cast into ever more complex sections.

Not surprisingly, this unsettled period of interaction and adaptation for the Gangetic societies was marked by widespread questioning of social, political, and religious arrangements. In the India of 600 BCE, the beginnings of an important redirection of the Vedic tradition were already under way through the speculations of the earliest Upanishads, which mark a pivotal development in the history of abstract religious and philosophical conceptualization. Moreover, amid the rich diversity of ascetic religious experience, some visionaries were shortly to map the direction of entirely new religious paths. One of these, Buddhism, may be seen as perhaps the first avowedly *universal* religious system and, thus, the beginning of a vitally important new pattern of world history.

Review and Relate

Thinking Through Patterns

Examine the ways historians approach the big questions of this chapter.

» Who were the Harappans? Where did they come from? What evidence exists for their origins?

The riddle of the origins of the Harappans has remained unsolved for close to 100 years. Most scholars believe their ancestors had been in the Indus region or nearby Baluchistan for millennia. Some also see them as perhaps related to extremely ancient peoples inhabiting the region around modern Kerala. Clues for this include archaic chants still practiced in Kerala that contain words that are believed to be so ancient that no one knows their meaning anymore. Carbon-14 dating, linguistic tracking, DNA surveys, and sedimentary analysis of ruins have all enhanced our understanding. One large impediment, however, remains: deciphering Harappan script—or, as we noted in this chapter, even judging whether the symbols the Harappans left behind are in fact a form of writing. Thus, a powerful analytic tool for understanding any civilization, the literary record, remains elusive.

» What explanations have been offered for the collapse of Harappan society? How well do the rival theories hold up, given what scholars and archaeologists have discovered?

Why do civilizations rise and fall? This is a key question for archaeologists and historians. Collapse can come from predictable causes—war, famine, ecological degradation—or random ones like earthquakes or volcanic eruptions. For the Harappans, the literary record of the Indo-Europeans long suggested that they conquered the Harappans, but it seems in conflict with more recent discoveries about the flooding patterns of the Indus, the sedimentary analysis of building and rebuilding of structures, and salinization levels at various points in the river. As is most often the case, historians generally expect to find no single *sufficient cause*—one that by itself led to the collapse—but rather a number of *necessary causes*—those that contributed but were not capable of causing the collapse all by themselves.

➢ How can we know about the newcomers to northern India? What sources exist for historians to examine?

Another ongoing debate revolves around the identity and nature of the newcomers into northern India. Here, as noted in the previous discussion, the literary record of the Vedas, particularly the oldest, the *Rig-Veda*, appears in conflict with much of the archaeological evidence. While the Vedas are quite clear about where the newcomers ended up, they are tantalizingly vague about where they originated. Indo-European-speaking peoples ranged widely across Eurasia, which we can tell from the vast legacy of the spread of their languages, and the kinds of technologies associated with them: horse equipment, chariots, iron. But because they left little in the way of archaeological sites, piecing together their story from their material culture is extremely challenging. For the moment, much of the most productive work is being done through genetic analysis of the area's modern inhabitants, as well as increasingly refined linguistic techniques of *glottochronology*—the tracing of language change over time and space.

➢ What patterns can we see evolving in the Ganges River states that will mark the subsequent development of Indian civilization?

Since one of our primary tasks in this text is to help you look for patterns surrounding origins, interactions, and adaptations, the question arises about the nature of patterns we see evolving among the early north Indian states. Not all these states were monarchies, but the religious aura of the monarchs and its relationship to the first stirrings of what will become Hinduism is striking. The permeation of society by religion is certainly a pattern that continues to this day, as is the desire for transcending the bounds of the material world by a variety of ascetic or scholarly methods. The most pervasive pattern lies in the development of the caste system as the basic social structure of society, which tenaciously endures even today in the face of a constitutional ban.

Against the Grain

Consider this as a counterpoint to the main patterns examined in this chapter.

A Merchants' Empire?

- What similarities and differences do you see among the Harappans and other river-based agrarian–urban societies?

Despite their unique cultural aspects, patterns of development among the land-based agrarian–urban civilizations we have examined so far share an important quality: The Mesopotamians, the Egyptians, the Gangetic states, and (as we will see in Chapter 4) the states arising in ancient China were all dependent on rivers for the fertility of their soil, for irrigation, and for transport, among other necessities. Indeed, scholars have repeatedly cited the centrality of rivers among these civilizations as a powerful conditioning factor in shaping the form and structure of their early institutions. Such riverine societies, which need large-scale public works projects to control the rivers on which they depend, develop powerful central governments (with kings or emperors wielding power through state bureaucracies or dependent local rulers) capable of directing such enormously complex undertakings. Such governments thus control vast labor resources and tend to display their power by means of monumental architecture (such as palaces and religious centers) and other visible signs of state and religious unity and harmony.

The great exception to this pattern appears to be the Harappan system of cities in the Indus valley. Although the Indus cities were at least as reliant on the river as the cities of these other agrarian–urban civilizations, we see practically no evidence of a central government of any kind, aside from the striking uniformity of buildings and materials. We see no monumental palaces or tombs. Apart from what may be modest temples and baths, we see little in the way of any kind of state religion or cult, though religious objects themselves are quite numerous. In other words, we see little that we can point to with certainty to suggest a large state presence of any kind as reflected in the categories of artifacts found in, say, Egypt or Mesopotamia.

So how did things function? One intriguing (if still unproven) theory suggests that, rather than having a powerful central government and bureaucracy to marshal the resources of the state, the Harappan cities were part of a well-integrated merchants' empire. This possibility is supported in part by the vast amount of trade articles recovered in the Indus region, by the many apparent craft factories and warehouses, by the harbor and docking facilities, and by the theory that Harappan writing may in fact be nothing more than a sophisticated shorthand script used principally by merchants.

If this is indeed the case, it not only goes "against the grain" of the early patterns of riverine civilization but against the trends of world history in general. One thinks of the Republic of Venice, 3,000 years later, as another trading empire, run by a merchant aristocracy for the benefit of its traders. It may well have been that the Harappan system was organized and run along similar lines. If so, its size and influence make it unique in its mode of operation—as it appears to be in so many other ways.

- Based on your reading of this chapter, is there evidence that works against the theory of a "merchants' empire" to explain the apparent differences between the Indus valley and other early river civilizations?

Key Terms

audio flashcards

Caste 82
Cesspits 70
Phallic stones 72
Topography 66

For additional resources, please go to **www.oup.com/us/vonsivers.**
Please see the Further Resources section at the back of the book for additional readings and suggested websites.

PATTERNS OF EVIDENCE | Sources for Chapter 3

SOURCE 3.1 Hymns to Agni, from the *Rig-Veda*, Book 2

ca. 1400–900 BCE

The worship of Agni, as the fire principle animating a burnt offering to the gods, features prominently in the *Rig-Veda*. The voice of Agni was thought to be heard in the crackling of the fire beneath a sacrifice, and it was a crucial element of Vedic tradition that the priest perform the ritual correctly. Fire was conflated with the emanations of the sun, and the priestly *varna*, or caste, was thought to be the community's best representative to the god.

HYMN I. Agni.

1. THOU, Agni, shining in thy glory through the days, art brought to life from out of the waters, from the stone: From out of the forest trees and herbs that grow on ground, thou, Sovereign Lord of men art generated pure.

2. Thine is the Herald's task and Cleanser's duly timed; Leader art thou, and Kindler for the pious man. Thou art Director, thou the ministering Priest: thou art the Brahman, Lord and Master in our home.

3. Hero of Heroes, Agni! Thou art Indra, thou art Viṣṇu of the Mighty Stride, adorable: Thou, Brahmaṇaspati, the Brahman finding wealth: thou, O Sustainer, with thy wisdom tendest us.

4. Agni, thou art King Varuṇa whose laws stand fast; as Mitra, Wonder-Worker, thou must be implored. Aryaman, heroes' Lord, art thou, enriching all, and liberal Aṁśa in the synod, O thou God.

. . .

12. Thou, Agni, cherished well, art highest vital power; in thy delightful hue are glories visible. Thou art the lofty might that furthers each design: thou art wealth manifold, diffused on every side.

13. Thee, Agni, have the Ādityas taken as their mouth; the Pure Ones have made thee, O Sage, to be their tongue. They who love offerings cling to thee at solemn rites: by thee the Gods devour the duly offered food.

14. By thee, O Agni, all the Immortal guileless Gods eat with thy mouth the oblation that is offered them. By thee do mortal men give sweetness to their drink. Pure art thou born, the embryo of the plants of earth. . . .

Source: *The Hymns of the Rigveda*, trans. Ralph T. H. Griffith (Benares: E. J. Lazarus, 1889), 333–338.

HYMN II. Agni.

1. WITH sacrifice exalt Agni who knows all life; worship him with oblation and the song of praise, Well kindled, nobly fed; heaven's Lord, Celestial Priest, who labors at the pole where deeds of might are done.

2. At night and morning, Agni, have they called to thee, like milk-cattle in their stalls lowing to meet their young. As messenger of heaven thou lightest all night long the families of men. Thou Lord of precious boons.

3. Him have the Gods established at the region's base, doer of wondrous deeds, Herald of heaven and earth; Like a most famous car, Agni the purely bright, like Mitra to be glorified among the people.

4. Him have they set in his own dwelling, in the vault, like the Moon waxing, fulgent, in the realm of air. Bird of the firmament, observant with his eyes, guard of the place as it were, looking to gods and men.

5. May he as Priest encompass all the sacrifice. Men throng to him with offerings and with hymns of praise. Raging with jaws of gold among the growing plants, like heaven with all the stars, he quickens earth and sky.

. . .

12. Knower of all that lives, O Agni, may we both, singers of praise and chiefs, be in thy keeping still. Help us to wealth exceeding good and glorious, abundant, rich in children and their progeny.

13. The princely worshippers who send to those who sing thy praise, O Agni, reward, graced with cattle and horses,—Lead thou both these and us forward to higher bliss. With brave men in the assembly may we speak aloud.

» Working with Sources

1. **Why was the priestly caste so vital to the correct performance of the ritual?**
2. **How are the powers of the sun and a sacrificial fire conflated in these hymns?**

SOURCE 3.2

The Bhagavad Gita

ca. 1750–800 BCE, written down in the third century BCE

The Bhagavad Gita comprises the sixth book, and is the central component, of the Mahabharata. Because it centers on the struggles between kings and princes, the Mahabharata can be read as a reflection of the ideological components of rulership in ancient India. At its center is a power struggle between the descendants of two brothers, culminating in a comprehensive war that ends in the victory of one branch of the

Source: *The Bhagavadgita, with the Sanatsugatiya and the Anugita*, trans. Kashinath Trimbak Telang (Oxford: Clarendon, 1882), 37, 39–41, 42, 73–75, 87–88, and 91.

family over the other. Elements of philosophy, religion, and moral behavior appear throughout the poem, and the concepts of *dharma* (natural law, correct behavior) and chaos are introduced by Krishna, the wise sage who appears at critical moments to explain the wider implications of what seems a simple battle narrative. The speakers in the following excerpt are Dhritarâshtra, a blind king in the midst of a succession crisis; Sañgaya, the visionary narrator of the battle; and Arjuna, one of the five sons of Pandu, the Pandava.

BHAGAVADGÎTÂ. CHAPTER I.

Dh*ri*tarâsh*t*ra said:

What did my (people) and the Pâ*nd*avas do, O Sañgaya! when they assembled together on the holy field of Kurukshetra, desirous to do battle?

. . .

Sañgaya said:

Thus addressed by Gu*d*âkes*a* , O descendant of Bharata! H*ri*shîkes*a* stationed that excellent chariot between the two armies, in front of Bhîshma and Dro*n*a and of all the kings of the earth, and said, O son of P*ri*thâ! Look at these assembled Kauravas.' There the son of P*ri*thâ saw in both armies, fathers, and grandfathers, preceptors, maternal uncles, brothers, sons, grandsons, companions, fathers-in-law, as well as friends. And seeing all those kinsmen standing (there), the son of Kuntî [Arjuna] was overcome by excessive pity and spake thus despondingly.

Ar*j*una said:

Seeing these kinsmen, O K*ri*sh*n*a! standing (here) desirous to engage in battle, my limbs droop down; my mouth is quite dried up; a tremor comes on my body; and my hairs stand on end; the Gâ*nd*îva (bow) slips from my hand; my skin burns intensely. I am unable, too, to stand up; my mind whirls round, as it were; O Kes*a*va! I see adverse omens and I do not perceive any good (to accrue) after killing (my) kinsmen in the battle. I do not wish for victory, O K*ri*sh*n*a! nor sovereignty, nor pleasures: what is sovereignty to us, O Govinda! what enjoyments, and even life? Even those, for whose sake we desire sovereignty, enjoyments, and pleasures, are standing here for battle, abandoning life and wealth-preceptors, fathers, sons as well as grandfathers, maternal uncles, fathers-in-law, grandsons, brothers-in-law, as also (other) relatives. These I do not wish to kill, though they kill (me), O destroyer of Madhu! Even for the sake of sovereignty over the three worlds, how much less then for this earth (alone)?

. . .

Sañgaya said:

Having spoken thus, Ar*j*una cast aside his bow together with the arrows, on the battle-field, and sat down in (his) chariot, with a mind agitated by grief.

CHAPTER VII.

The Deity said:

O son of Prithâ! now hear how you can without doubt know me fully, fixing your mind on me, and resting in me, and practicing devotion. I will now tell you exhaustively about knowledge together with experience; that being known, there is nothing further left in this world to know. Among thousands of men, only some work for perfection; and even of those who have reached perfection, and who are assiduous, only some know me truly. . . .

There is nothing else, O Dhanañgaya! higher than myself; all this is woven upon me, like numbers of pearls upon a thread. I am the taste in water, O son of Kuntî! I am the light of the sun and moon. I am 'Om' in all the Vedas, sound in space, and manliness in human beings; I am the fragrant smell in the earth, refulgence in the fire; I am life in all beings, and penance in those who perform penance. Know me, O son of Prithâ! to be the eternal seed of all beings; I am the discernment of the discerning ones, and I the glory of the glorious. I am also the strength, unaccompanied by fondness or desire, of the strong. And, O chief of the descendants of Bharata! I am love unopposed to piety among all beings. And all entities which are of the quality of goodness, and those which are of the quality of passion and of darkness, know that they are, indeed, all from me; I am not in them, but they are in me. The whole universe deluded by these three states of mind, developed from the qualities, does not know me, who am beyond them and inexhaustible; for this delusion of mine, developed from the qualities, is divine and difficult to transcend. Those cross beyond this delusion who resort to me alone. Wicked men, doers of evil (acts), who are deluded, who are deprived of their knowledge by (this) delusion, and who incline to the demoniac state of mind, do not resort to me. But, O Arjuna! doers of good (acts) of four classes worship me: one who is distressed, one who is seeking after knowledge, one who wants wealth, and one, O chief of the descendants of Bharata! who is possessed of knowledge. Of these, he who is possessed of knowledge, who is always devoted, and whose worship is (addressed) to one (Being) only, is esteemed highest.

. . .

CHAPTER X.

. . .

Arjuna said:

You are the supreme Brahman, the supreme goal, the holiest of the holy. All sages, as well as the divine sage Nârada, Asita, Devala, and Vyâsa, call you the eternal being, divine, the first god, the unborn, the all-pervading. And so, too, you tell me yourself, O Kesava! I believe all this that you tell me (to be) true; for, O lord! neither the gods nor demons understand your manifestation. You only know yourself by yourself. O best of beings! creator of all things! lord of all things! god of gods! lord of the universe! be pleased to declare without, exception your divine emanations, by which emanations you stand pervading all these worlds. How shall I know you, O you of mystic power! always meditating on you? And in what various entities, O lord! should I meditate on you? Again, O Ganârdana! do you yourself declare your powers and emanations; because hearing this nectar, I (still) feel no satiety.

The Deity said:

. . . I am the rod of those that restrain, and the policy of those that desire victory. I am silence respecting secrets. I am the knowledge of those that have knowledge And, O Arjuna! I am also that which is the seed of all things. There is nothing movable or immovable which can exist without me. O terror of your foes! there is no end to my divine emanations. Here I have declared the extent of (those) emanations only in part. Whatever thing (there is) of power, or glorious, or splendid, know all that to be produced from portions of my energy.

» Working with Sources

1. **Why does Arjuna feel compelled to act, despite the competing claims of family ties?**
2. **How does the text develop the theme of supreme knowledge and its power?**

SOURCE 3.3

The Brihadaranyaka Upanishad

ca. 600 BCE

A diverse set of writings, the Upanishads were thought to convey secret knowledge and serve as the *vedanta*, or fulfillment, of the Vedic tradition. Among these documents are the Aranyakas ("forest books"), which may have been recited originally by hermits who had retreated to forests. Throughout the Upanishads one can see the full development of the principle of the joining of the individual self (*atman*, or "soul") with the *brahman*, or "world soul"/"soul essence."

SECOND ADHYÂYA. FIRST BRÂHMANA.

1. There was formerly the proud Gârgya Bâlâki, a man of great reading. He said to Agâtasatru of Kâsi, 'Shall I tell you Brahman?' Agâtasatru said: 'We give a thousand (cows) for that speech (of yours), for verily all people run away, saying, Ganaka (the king of Mithilâ) is our father (patron).'

Source: *The Upanishads*, vol. 2, trans. F. Max Müller (Oxford: Clarendon, 1884), 100–101 and 103–105.

2. Gârgya said: 'The person that is in the sun, that I adore as Brahman.' Agâtas*a*tru said to him: 'No, no! Do not speak to me on this. I adore him verily as the supreme, the head of all beings, the king. Whoso adores him thus, becomes Supreme, the head of all beings, a king.'

3. Gârgya said: 'The person that is in the moon (and in the mind), that I adore as Brahman.' Agâtas*a*tru said to him: 'No, no! Do not speak to me on this. I adore him verily as the great, clad in white raiment, as Soma, the king.' Whoso adores him thus, Soma is poured out and poured forth for him day by day, and his food does not fail.

4. Gârgya said: 'The person that is in the lightning (and in the heart), that I adore as Brahman.' Agâtas*a*tru said to him: 'No, no! Do not speak to me on this. I adore him verily as the luminous.' Whoso adores him thus, becomes luminous, and his offspring becomes luminous.

. . .

13. Gârgya said: 'The person that is in the body, that I adore as Brahman.' Agâtas*a*tru said to him: 'No, no! Do not speak to me on this. I adore him verily as embodied.' Whoso adores him thus, becomes embodied, and his offspring becomes embodied. Then Gârgya became silent.

14. Agâtas*a*tru said: 'Thus far only?' 'Thus far only,' he replied. Agâtas*a*tru said: 'This does not suffice to know it (the true Brahman).' Gârgya replied: 'Then let me come to you, as a pupil.'

15. Agâtas*a*tru said: 'Verily, it is unnatural that a Brâhma*n*a should come to a **Kshatriya**, hoping that he should tell him the Brahman. However, I shall make you know him clearly,' thus saying he took him by the hand and rose.

Kshatriya: Second highest of the four *varnas* (castes) in Hindu society.

And the two together came to a person who was asleep. He called him by these names, 'Thou, great one, clad in white raiment, Soma, King.' He did not rise. Then rubbing him with his hand, he woke him, and he arose.

16. Agâtas*a*tru said: 'When this man was thus asleep, where was then the person (purusha), the intelligent? And from whence did he thus come back?' Gârgya did not know this?

17. Agâtas*a*tru said: 'When this man was thus asleep, then the intelligent person (purusha), having through the intelligence of the senses (prâ*n*as) absorbed within himself all intelligence, lies in the ether, which is in the heart. When he takes in these different kinds of intelligence, then it is said that the man sleeps (svapiti). Then the breath is kept in, speech is kept in, the ear is kept in, the eye is kept in, the mind is kept in.

18. But when he moves about in sleep (and dream), then these are his worlds. He is, as it were, a great king; he is, as it were, a great Brâhma*n*a; he rises, as it were, and he falls. And as a great king might keep in his own subjects, and move about, according to his pleasure, within his own domain, thus does that person (who is endowed with intelligence) keep in the various senses (prâ*n*as) and move about, according to his pleasure, within his own body (while dreaming).

19. Next, when he is in profound sleep, and knows nothing, there are the seventy-two thousand arteries called Hita, which from the heart spread through the body. Through them he moves forth and rests in the surrounding body. And as a young man, or a great king, or a great Brâhma*n*a, having reached the summit of happiness, might rest, so does he then rest.

20. As the spider comes out with its thread, or as small sparks come forth from fire, thus do all senses, all worlds, all Devas, all beings come forth from that Self. The Upanishad (the true name and doctrine) of that Self is 'the True of the True.' Verily the senses are the true, and he is the true of the true.

Working with Sources

1. **How does the text develop the principles of *brahman* and *soma* addressed in Chapter 3?**
2. **What is the responsibility of the king with respect to knowledge?**

SOURCE 3.4

The Code of Manu

ca. 100–300 CE

The *Code of Manu* deals with many different features of Hindu life, such as the proper behavior of different castes and methods for ritual purification. The "Manu" referred to in the title is the legendary "first man" of Hindu culture, also recognized as the first lawgiver. Thus, the *Code of Manu* is thought of within Hinduism as a text based on human traditions (*smriti*), but it is also believed to be consistent with the values included in texts that are divinely revealed (*shruti*), such as the "Purusha Hymn." As a result, it restates and reaffirms traditional values and structures, but it does so on the basis of religious authority.

The responsibilities described for women in the *Code of Manu* need to be understood within the context of Hinduism. As was discussed in Chapter 3, a central component of Hinduism is the concept of *dharma* ("that which is firm"). Hindus believe that by living up to the religious and social responsibilities attached to one's social position (caste and gender), one sustains the proper order of the universe and gains good *karma*, moving up the scale of reincarnation toward unity with the *brahman*, or World Soul. Composed following a period of unrest, the *Code of Manu* represents a vigorous attempt to reestablish order within the Hindu world.

Source: *The Law of Manu*, in *The Sacred Books of the East*, vol. 25, trans. G. Bühler (Oxford: Clarendon, 1886), 194–197, 328–330, 332, 335, 344–345.

Hear now the duties of women.

By a girl, by a young woman, or even by an aged one, nothing must be done independently, even in her own house.

Her lord is dead to her sons; a woman must never be independent.

She must not seek to separate herself from her father, husband, or sons; by leaving them she would make both (her own and her husband's) families contemptible.

She must always be cheerful, clever in (the management of her) household affairs, careful in cleaning her utensils, and economical in expenditure.

Him to whom her father may give her, or her brother with the father's permission, she shall obey as long as he lives, and when he is dead, she must not insult (his memory). . . .

[B]etrothal (by the father or guardian) is the cause of (the husband's) dominion (over his wife).

The husband who wedded her with sacred texts, always gives happiness to his wife, both in season and out of season, in this world and in the next.

Though destitute of virtue, or seeking pleasure (elsewhere), or devoid of good qualities, (yet) a husband must be constantly worshipped as a god by a faithful wife.

No sacrifice, no vow, no fast must be performed by women apart (from their husbands); if a wife obeys her husband, she will for that (reason alone) be exalted in heaven.

A faithful wife, who desires to dwell (after death) with her husband, must never do anything that might displease him who took her hand, whether he be alive or dead. . . . [L]et her emaciate her body by (living on) pure flowers, roots, and fruit; but she must never even mention the name of another man after her husband has died.

Until death let her be patient (of hardships), self-controlled, and chaste, and strive (to fulfill) that most excellent duty which (is prescribed) for wives who have one husband only. A virtuous wife who after the death of her husband constantly remains chaste, reaches heaven, though she have no son, just like those chaste men.

By violating her duty towards her husband, a wife is disgraced in this world, (after death) she enters the womb of a jackal, and is tormented by diseases (the punishment of) her sin. . . .

[A] female who controls her thoughts, speech, and actions, gains in this (life) highest renown, and in the next (world) a place near her husband.

Women must particularly be guarded against evil inclinations, however trifling (they may appear); for, if they are not guarded, they will bring sorrow on two families. . . . No man can completely guard women by force; but they can be guarded by the . . . (following) expedients: Let the (husband) employ his (wife) in the collection and expenditure of his wealth, in keeping (everything) clean, in (the fulfillment of) religious duties, in the preparation of his food, and in looking after the household utensils. Women, confined in the house under trustworthy and obedient servants, are not (well) guarded; but those who of their own accord keep guard over themselves, are well guarded. . . .

Through their passion for men, through their mutable temper, through their natural heartlessness, they become disloyal towards their husbands, however carefully they may be guarded in this (world).

(When creating them) Manu allotted to women (a love of their) bed, (of their) seat and (of) ornament, impure desires, wrath, dishonesty, malice, and bad conduct. . . . The production of children, the nurture of those born, and the daily life of men, (of these matters) woman is visibly the cause.

Offspring, (the due performance of) religious rites, faithful service, highest conjugal happiness and heavenly bliss for the ancestors and oneself, depend on one's wife alone.

He only is a perfect man who consists (of three persons united), his wife, himself, and his offspring; thus (says the Veda), and (learned) Brahmanas propound this (maxim) likewise, "The husband is declared to be one with the wife." . . .

The husband receives his wife from the gods, (he does not wed her) according to his own will; doing what is agreeable to the gods, he must always support her (while she is) faithful.

"Let mutual fidelity continue until death," this may be considered as the summary of the highest law for husband and wife.

» Working with Sources

1. **According to the code, how should men relate to women? In what ways are men asked, in their relationships with women, to keep order?**
2. **How are women rewarded for behaving the way the code instructs them to? How are the rewards connected with the Hindu belief in reincarnation and *karma*?**

SOURCE 3.5 Image of Draupadi and the Pandava, from the Dashavatara Temple, Deogarh, India

Late sixth century CE

This is an inscribed rendering of some of the major male and female characters of the Mahabharata. According to this legend, a king surrenders power to his blind brother and has five sons (the Pandava) by his queen, Kunti. The five brothers are collectively married to the beautiful princess Draupadi. In Indian tradition, her role is analogous to the way the palm of a hand holds together the hand's five fingers.

Source: Courtesy of Ed Sentner.

» Working with Sources

1. How is the female principle represented in this collective portrait?
2. Does this image evoke in any way the restrictions on female behavior detailed in the *Code of Manu*?

Chapter 4 **5000–481 BCE**

Agrarian Centers and the Mandate of Heaven in Ancient China

Thousands of miles east of Harappa and several centuries after its decline, the twenty-first Shang king, Wu Ding, prepared to commune with his ancestors in the hope of gaining some insight into the childbearing prospects of his pregnant wife, Fu (Lady) Hao. Fu Hao, his favorite (and most powerful) wife, had come from a noble family outside the Shang capital of Yin, near the modern city of Anyang in northern China. Well educated and highly capable as an administrator, Fu Hao had even on occasion led Shang armies in the field. Now she was entrusted with what Wu Ding and his court considered to be the most important duty of all: continuing the line of Shang kings into the future. For the Shang kings believed that the past, present, and future rulers of their line formed an unbroken continuum, with the deceased existing in a spirit realm accessible to the living by ritual divination. Therefore, Wu Ding, whose concern for Fu Hao and her unborn child was paramount, sought the advice of the ancestors about her condition and that of her child to come. Wu Ding and his chief diviner, Que [chway], intoned their questions and held a cleaned and dried shoulder blade of an ox over heat. The diviner then tapped it carefully with a bronze rod and attempted to read the meaning of the cracks as they appeared in the hot bone. As a final step, they incised Que's name as diviner, the date,

***ABOVE:* Skeleton and Shang War Chariot, Anyang, China.**

the question, and the ancestors' response into the bone as a permanent record of the inquiry.

Que's reading of the cracks was "It is bad; it will be a girl." Although this was considered disappointing because of the desire for a male heir, Fu Hao remained Wu Ding's most beloved wife until her death. Indeed, after she died, the despondent king frequently sought her advice through oracle bones on matters of state and private affairs. Fortunately for us, her tomb is one of the most completely preserved from the Shang era. Like the vast caches of oracle bones uncovered over the years, it tells us a great deal about society and gender, economics and trade, and the origins and interactions of Chinese states among themselves and with neighboring peoples.

Like Harappa along the Indus, the Shang state had developed in a process of growth and consolidation among the Late Neolithic settlements along China's Yellow River. But the Harappans and the Shang had begun very different historical paths for India and China. Harappa and the other cities of the Indus, as we have seen, all but disappeared, their influence detectable only within the deepest currents of later Indian society. In contrast, the foundations laid by the Shang and subsequent dynasties developing in China's Yellow River valley remained vital into the twenty-first century and profoundly influenced East and Southeast Asia. The history of India was one of infusion and synthesis, of cycles of partial political unity punctuated by long stretches of fragmentation. The political and cultural experience of China, however, was marked by relatively little outside influence and thousands of years of centralized rule. Moreover, for the great majority of its history, China would be perhaps the world's greatest exporter of ideas and goods.

Seeing Patterns

- How did the interplay of environment and climate help to influence the earliest patterns of Chinese civilization? How do historians address the question of whether "geography is destiny" in this case?
- What can the remains of Neolithic Chinese settlements tell us about the continuities and disruptions of Chinese history?
- How did the Zhou concept of the Mandate of Heaven operate?

The Origins of Yellow River Cultures, 5000–1766 BCE

> The sun beyond the mountain glows,
> The Yellow River seaward flows,
> If you want an even better sight,
> Ascend an even greater height.
>
> "CLIMBING 'STORK PAVILION,'" WANG ZHIHUAN (648–742 CE)

An observer at the site of the Stork Pavilion of poet Wang Zhihuan's reverie could justly claim to have gazed upon the heartland of Chinese history. Situated on a high bluff at Yongji in the south of the modern province of Shaanxi, the pavilion marked a celebrated scenic spot commanding a view of the Yellow River as it approaches its great bend to the east. Here it is joined by the Wei River from the west and rolls across the North China Plain in a leisurely but at times fearsome manner for another 500 miles to the Bohai Gulf, an arm of the Yellow Sea.

Over the centuries, our observer might have witnessed the origins and development of some of China's first Neolithic cultures along the river. Sixty miles up the

Chapter Outline

- The Origins of Yellow River Cultures, 5000–1766 BCE
- The Interactions of Shang and Zhou History and Politics, 1766–481 BCE
- Economy, Society, and Family Adaptation in Ancient China
- Interactions of Religion, Culture, and Intellectual Life in Ancient China
- Putting It All Together

Wei, he or she could have visited China's most famous Neolithic village at Banpo or one of dozens in between. Even today, on every side of the bend lie burial mounds from a wide selection of China's early village and town cultures. Nearby is the modern city of Xi'an [SHE-ahn], the capital of no fewer than 13 Chinese regimes during its long history. And here, too, the richest and most famous site of all attracts visitors by the millions: the sprawling tomb complex of China's first emperor, Qin Shi Huangdi [chin SHUHR hwang-DEE], packed with thousands of life-sized terra-cotta soldiers in perfect ranks marching in timeless close-order drill.

Geography and Climate

While China's natural boundaries are perhaps less dramatic than those of India, they have had an equally profound effect on its history and society. As with India, the Himalayas and Pamirs along the southern border of Tibet mark one natural barrier. River systems such as the Amur and Ussuri in the north, the Salween in the southwest, and the Red in Vietnam have also represented past borders, though not impermeable ones. The northern and western deserts—the Gobi, Ordos, and Taklamakan—have also served as natural boundaries that frequently passed in and out of the hands of successive Chinese dynasties as their emperors sought to curb the incursions of nomads or control central Asian trade routes.

The chief effect of these features, however, has been to limit the principal avenues of outside interaction to the narrow corridor running west of Xi'an, south of Mongolia, and north of the modern province of Qinghai, spanning the route of the famous Silk Road. Like the Khyber Pass in India, this route has historically been the main avenue into China; unlike the Khyber, however, it has seldom been an invasion route for outsiders. The result of this has been that, on the one hand, the origins and early development of ancient China were more isolated than those of the other Eurasian centers of civilization, but, on the other hand, the relative absence of interaction with outside competitors facilitated both cultural and political unification.

While conditioned by many of the same factors found in India, China's climate is more varied. The area south of the Qin [chin] Mountains marks the northern boundary of the region regulated by the monsoon, with warm temperatures and abundant summer rainfall. Because of the summer monsoon, rainfall amounts can range from about 40 inches per year in the eastern coastal city of Hangzhou [HAHNG-joe] to over 70 inches in the subtropical south. The suitability of the southern regions for rice cultivation, as with the Gangetic societies of India, resulted in rapid growth and high population density there. Above the monsoon line, temperatures and rainfall amounts are influenced more by the weather systems of the Eurasian interior. Thus, northern China is subject to blistering summers and frigid winters with scant and unreliable precipitation.

One result of these conditions has been that China's population has historically been concentrated in the plains along the major river valleys and the coast. Three main river systems have remained the primary avenues of agriculture and commerce: the Pearl River (Zhujiang) in the south, the Yangzi [YAHNG-zuh] River (at 3,988 miles, the third longest in the world), and the Yellow River (Huanghe), where the most influential early Chinese societies developed (see Map 4.1).

The Yellow River Rising in the highlands of Gansu and flowing north to the Ordos Desert, the Yellow River then turns south and east out of Inner Mongolia for

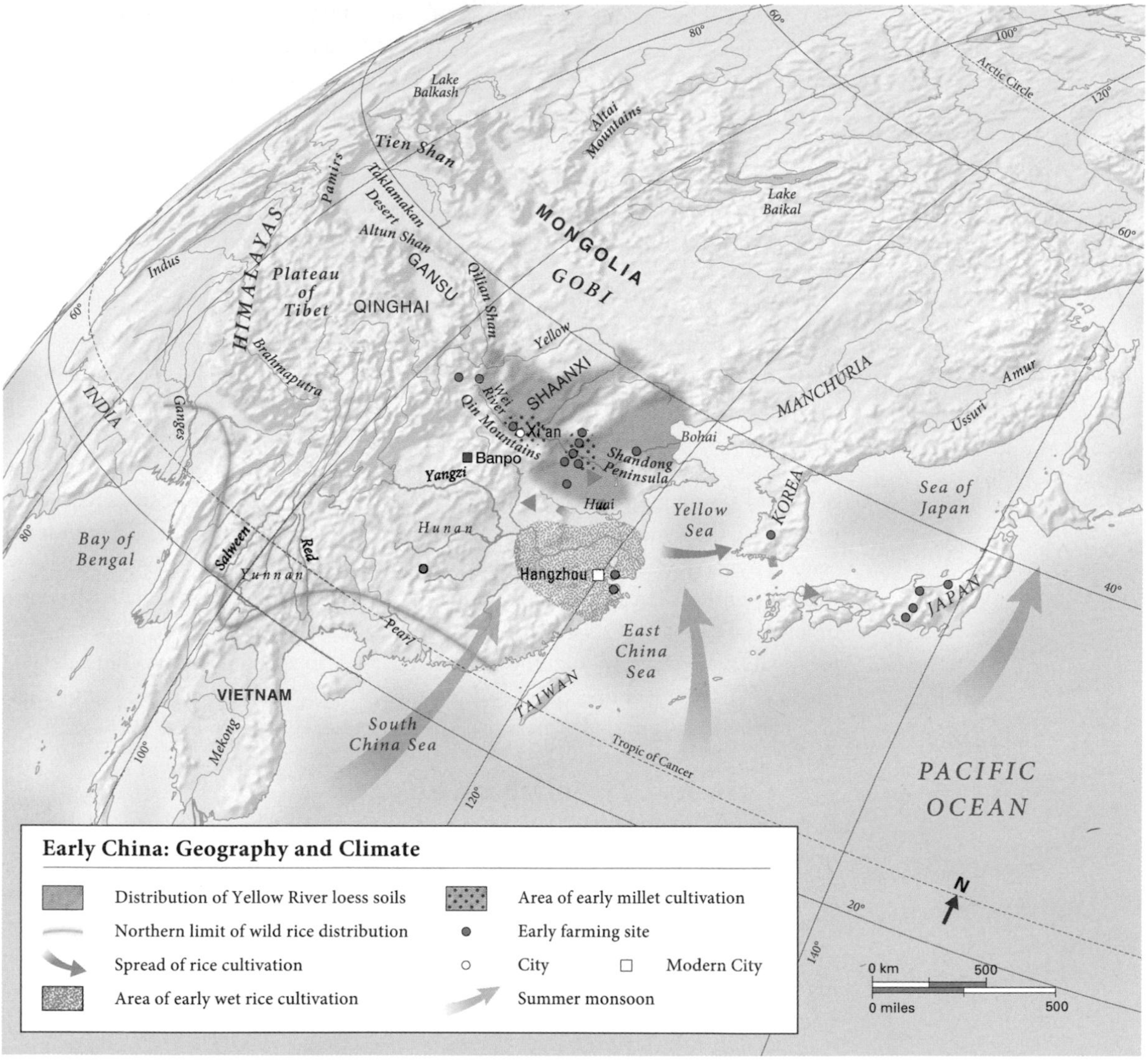

MAP **4.1 Early China: Geography and Climate.**

map analysis

10,000–8000 BCE
First Neolithic settlements in Yellow River valley

ca. 7000 BCE
First evidence of rice cultivation in Yangzi valley

5000–3500 BCE
Yangshao culture develops along upper Yellow River

4500–1500 BCE
Longshan culture develops along lower Yellow River

2852–2205 BCE
Traditional era of "culture heroes" and "sage kings"

2205–1766 BCE
Traditional dates for Xia dynasty

ca. 2000 BCE
Flourishing of Erlitou, believed to be a city and palace complex of Xia dynasty

1766–1122 BCE
Traditional dates for Shang dynasty

ca. 1400 BCE
Earliest "oracle bone" caches with archaic Chinese writing

ca. 1300 BCE
Introduction of chariot to northern China

1122–771 BCE
Western Zhou dynasty: capital located at Xi'an

770–256 BCE
Eastern Zhou dynasty: capital moved to Luoyang

722–481 BCE
Spring and Autumn period

interactive timeline

500 miles before making its bend to the east and the sea, a total distance of about 3,000 miles. The river gets its name as a result of the *loess*—a light, dry, mineral-rich soil deposited by centuries of strong winds—it picks up as it flows, giving it a yellowish tint. As with the Nile in Egypt, the rich, easily worked soil carried by the river has brought abundantly productive agriculture to arid northern China, but like the Indus, the constant buildup of silt in the riverbed also causes it to overflow its banks, resulting in the devastation of fields and villages in its path through the North China Plain, the vast flatlands lining the river course on its final run to the sea.

"China's Sorrow" This building up and bursting of natural levees, along with earthquakes and occasional human actions, such as the dynamiting of dikes during World War II to stop the Japanese invasion, have caused the Yellow River to change course 26 times over the last 3,000 years. Its mouth has shifted several times above and below the Shandong Peninsula, assuming its present course to the north following massive floods in 1854–1855. Not surprisingly, efforts to control the river have occupied a prominent place in the mythology, history, and political and social organization of the region from earliest times. For example, Yu, the supposed founder of the Xia dynasty, was said to have labored for decades to control the river's rampages. More recently, some scholars have pointed to the centralized bureaucratic structure of imperial China and suggested that it was dictated in part by the struggle for mastery of its waterways, though this has been subject to spirited debate. Thus, despite its gift of fertility over the course of thousands of years, the Yellow River's unpredictable nature has prompted writers to sometimes refer to it as "China's sorrow."

The Origins of Neolithic Cultures

Between 70,000 and 20,000 years ago, modern *Homo sapiens* became established in eastern Eurasia. Human communities that produced small, refined stone implements such as arrowheads and knives ranged across north and central China from about 30,000 years ago, marking an extensive foraging culture. Within a few millennia of the last glacial retreat, settlements began to appear in northern China containing the first traces in the region of the transition from forager society to an agrarian one, based on agriculture and the domestication of animals.

Agriculture developed very quickly in China and included a wide variety of crops and livestock. Sites of rice cultivation in central China, dating to 7000 BCE, are among the earliest in the world, while several strains of **millet** were already being grown in the north. Recent work suggests that early strains of wheat and barley, perhaps spreading from areas around the Fertile Crescent, may also have been grown. Chickens, pigs, sheep, cattle, and dogs were also widely raised. Areas along the Yellow River contain some of the earliest agricultural villages in China, and several *prototypical cultures*—those that pioneered techniques, institutions, or patterns of social organization widely copied in later years—emerged here and along the North China Plain over the next several thousand years.

Millet: A species of grass cultivated for its edible white seeds and as hay for animal feed.

Banpo Village Perhaps the most studied of the thousands of Neolithic sites across China is Banpo [BAN-paw] Village, located on the outskirts of Xi'an. Banpo Village is representative of Yangshao [YAHNG-shaow], or "painted pottery," culture, which flourished from 5000 to 3500 BCE. Although the potter's wheel had not yet been introduced from western Eurasia, Yangshao communities like Banpo had sophisticated kilns that fired a wide variety of brightly painted storage pots, vases, and so forth, decorated with animal and geometric designs. The inhabitants of Yangshao villages also produced stone implements such as axes, chisels, and knives to support the community's hunting, farming, and fishing activities.

The perimeter of the Banpo settlement is surrounded by a defensive ditch, rather than the walls characteristic of later towns and cities, with 40 homes arranged around a rectangular central structure believed to be a clan meeting house or religious site. The homes were supported by vertical posts and had thatched roofs that, along with the walls, were plastered with mud and straw. The village contains a number of features that archaeologists believe to be early forms of certain long-standing patterns of rural life in northern China. For example, some of the huts contain raised clay beds with flues laid through them—an early version of the *kang* [kahng], the heated bed still found in older northern Chinese farming homes today. Also, silkworm cocoons and crude needles suggest the early development of silk weaving. Perhaps the most exciting finds, however, are the pot shards bearing stylized pictures of animals and geometric markings that some Chinese scholars have speculated may be ancestral forms of the Chinese written language.

Interior View of Banpo Dwelling (*top*). Circular Foundation Showing Postholes (*bottom*).

Longshan Culture Settled life in villages and towns appears to have expanded greatly during the Longshan period, from about 4000 to 2000 BCE. Once thought to have grown out of Yangshao culture as it spread east to modern Shandong Province, the dates of the earliest distinct Longshan artifacts have now been pushed as far back as 4500 BCE. A later branch of Longshan culture based in what is now Henan [HEH-nahn] Province is also believed to have arisen around 2000 BCE, lasting until about 1500 BCE, when it was absorbed by the Shang dynasty.

Like their Yangshao counterparts, Longshan potters were highly skilled and pioneered forms and styles still favored by Chinese artisans today. The black-colored pottery associated with Longshan culture is particularly refined. Some of the pieces are so delicate and nearly transparent

Painted Pottery, or Yangshao, Earthenware Basin Found at Banpo Site. Contrast and compare this piece with the one from Longshan. What similarities and differences can you spot?

Longshan (Black Pottery) Culture Stemmed Beaker (*bei*), Shandong, ca. 2000 BCE.

image analysis

that they resemble the famous "eggshell porcelain" of later Chinese imperial pottery works. The introduction of the potter's wheel from the west in the mid-third millennium BCE—one of the earliest indications we have of Late Neolithic Chinese interactions with other peoples—permitted unprecedented precision, while improved kilns, reaching firing temperatures in excess of 1,800 degrees Fahrenheit, and experimentation with kaolin clays began a long process of ceramic innovation that ultimately resulted in the first porcelain thousands of years later.

After 2000 BCE, the Longshan and other Late Neolithic cultures were at a point where a transition to a society marked by large towns and even small cities supported by agriculture was becoming discernible. Towns of several thousand inhabitants have been uncovered, and a number of sites contain elaborate altars. The use of gold, copper, bronze, and jade in jewelry is also increasingly evident. Craft specialization and embryonic social classes are detectable.

Beyond the North China Plain Given the subtropical environment of the regions below the Yangzi River basin in central China, it would be surprising if archaeologists did not find remains of flourishing cultures there as well. Until recently, however, such artifacts have been marginal and fragmentary. In addition to isolated sites on the western Yangzi River, a few close to modern Shanghai and Hangzhou, and at Dalongtan in Yunnan, the most extensive distinctive culture is that of Dapenkeng [DAH-pen-keng], which flourished from 5000 to 2500 BCE. Artifacts including pot shards, arrowheads, and polished tools and axes indicate a sophisticated coastal and riverine society along an extensive corridor running from the borders of modern Vietnam along the south China coast to Fujian Province and, most strikingly, across the Taiwan Strait to the western coast of that island.

The vast reach of Dapenkeng culture and the similarity of its relatively rare artifacts over a wide area suggest extensive interaction with peoples throughout the region. While the origins of this culture may be obscure, they do appear to be quite different from those of the north. Long and patient work by linguists has established this area as part of a Proto-Austronesian-speaking region, one whose parent language is distinct from the Sino-Tibetan language group that contains the various Chinese dialects and that has strong links to the Austronesian speakers on modern Taiwan. This in turn has prompted scholars studying the origins of the Polynesian language family—which is part of the Austronesian group—to search for possible links with these people on Taiwan and along the China coast.

Origins of Rice Cultivation While the staple grain crops of the north included various strains of millet, with wheat and barley not coming into extensive cultivation until the Zhou period, the most far-reaching innovation in the regions south of the North China Plain was the development of widespread rice cultivation. Two sources have been cited as likely early centers of rice experimentation: Southeast Asia and the area extending from China's modern province of Hunan to the coastal reaches of the Yangzi River, where rice grains have been dated to 7000 BCE. While we cannot know with precision which region played the more prominent role in spreading rice cultivation and techniques throughout China, we do know that Southeast Asia remained an important source of new rice strains that allowed China's food production to keep pace with its population until well into the nineteenth century. Other food sources domesticated elsewhere making their appearance in Neolithic south

China include chickens—perhaps obtained from south Asia via Southeast Asia—and cattle, especially the water buffalo. Cattle, however, were raised primarily for farmwork rather than consumption.

Toward a Chinese Culture With these recent finds, the older view of Chinese civilization being the exclusive product of the Yellow River valley cultures, which then expanded to more distant areas, has undergone considerable modification. Instead, scholars now suggest that the area approximating modern China consisted around 3000 BCE of a collection of agrarian communities that remained distinct in their own right but whose interactions with each other began to contribute common cultural elements that ultimately became identified as "Chinese." Indeed, some scholars have adopted a view of China down through the end of the third millennium BCE as being not so far from the mythical period referred to by ancient writers as *wanguo* [WAHN-gwo]—the "ten thousand states."

Though scholars have filled in much of the picture of these ancient cultures, the precise time and duration of their transition to one marked by cities is still very much open to debate. Chinese chroniclers, however, drawing upon the world's largest and longest literary record, have long given pride of place in this regard to their first three dynasties: the Xia, Shang, and Zhou.

The Age of Myth and the Xia Dynasty, 2852–1766 BCE

The Chinese have been called the most historically minded people on earth. For thousands of years, the use of writing for purposes of record keeping has been of paramount importance, and the written word itself was considered to have a kind of inner power. For millennia, the careful study, writing, and rewriting of history have been vital elements of individual self-cultivation as well as key mechanisms for political and social control (see "Patterns Up Close").

Among the earliest collections of Chinese writings we have are those of the *Shujing* [SHOO-jeeng]. Also known as The *Book of History* or *Classic of Documents,* the *Shujing* is a detailed compilation of ancient material purportedly from 2357 to 631 BCE. Though heavily laden with material of questionable reliability, it remains a principal documentary source for information about the people, places, and events of China's first three dynasties: the Xia [she-AH], Shang [shahng], and Zhou [joe]. In a surprising number of cases, its clues have helped to illuminate the archaeological evidence in recent attempts to establish the historical existence of the Xia dynasty.

Culture Heroes and Sage Kings According to Chinese legend, mythical culture heroes and sage kings reigned from 2852 to 2205 BCE and introduced many of China's basic elements and institutions. Among the contributions attributed to the first culture hero, Fuxi, were medicine, divination, and, according to some stories, writing. His successor, Shen Nong, was credited with developing agriculture. Fire and silkworm cultivation were said to have been introduced during the reign of Huangdi, the "Yellow Emperor," whose reign followed that of Shen Nong. The Yellow Emperor's rule was followed by that of the three sage kings—Yao, Shun, and Yu—who set the example for strong moral leadership and are credited with passing the role of leadership on to the land's most worthy men instead of to their own family members.

Between Myth and History The *Shujing* acclaims Yu, the last sage king, as the tamer of the Yellow River. He is also traditionally considered to be the founder of the Xia dynasty in 2205 BCE. Because of the difficulty in establishing a clear archaeological record, however, Yu and his successors have largely remained suspended between myth and history.

Moreover, the character of the *Shujing* as a creation of later Zhou chroniclers, with a specific agenda of justifying Zhou rule, has cast a long shadow over events that allegedly took place over 1,500 years before. More generally, as the sole literary account we have of the period, it has naturally assumed a dominant and, most likely, misleading role as the master narrative of ancient Chinese history. Some scholars have even argued that the Xia were an invention of the Zhou. More recently, some have suggested that their rule was in fact a kind of Shang mythology. On the other hand, some, notably a group of Chinese archaeologists, have noted that the relative accuracy of the dates given in the *Shujing* for events in the Shang dynasty suggests a similar level of reliability for its accounts of the earlier Xia.

Recent archaeological work also has moved somewhat closer to confirming the historical existence of a widespread culture, if not yet a state, corresponding to the literary accounts of the Xia. Excavations at Erlitou [AR-lee-toe] in southern Shaanxi Province in the 1950s and 1960s revealed that artifacts at the site fall within the traditional dates given for the existence of the Xia. In addition, artifacts, particularly early bronze ritual vessels virtually identical to those at Erlitou, appear widely throughout regions described in the *Shujing* as belonging to the Xia and, in some cases, considerably beyond it.

Xia Society The small number of purported Xia sites makes it difficult to draw many firm conclusions about their society. Much of what we believe is based on the premise that the Xia was a transitional society, developing and elaborating the material culture of the late Longshan and Yangshao cultural periods. Of particular note in this transition are the growing importance of bronze casting, the increasingly complex symbols on pottery, and the widespread evidence of large-scale communal efforts at flood control, including dams, dikes, levees, and retention ponds.

As we have seen, the Yangshao and Longshan cultures stretched across a continuum from small hunting, fishing, and farming villages to substantial agriculturally supported towns. The Xia, however, though our picture of them is far from complete, appear to have reached the tipping point at which most of the hallmarks of urban society—what we commonly think of as "civilization"—began to appear. For example, excavation at the Erlitou site, dated to perhaps 2000 BCE, reveals a walled city of moderate size containing what is believed to be the foundation of China's first palace: a stamped-earth terrace extending over 100 yards on each side.

Moreover, the layout of the buildings within walled compounds dating from this time began to resemble that of later official residences. Beams supported by large wooden posts carry the weight of moderately sloped roofs with upturned ends, while "curtain walls," which bear little or none of the structure's weight, are built between the posts of plastered brick or masonry. Most of the larger buildings are also built along a north–south axis with their courtyards and entrances facing south, an orientation favored even today by Chinese builders.

Literary evidence suggests that Xia leaders exercised a strong family- or clan-based rule, and the archaeological evidence seems to support this to a considerable degree. Evidence indicating the role of the elites as mediators with the spirit world, and particularly with the ancestors of Xia rulers, is also found in abundance at Erlitou. China's first bronze ritual vessels—wine beakers on tripod stands in shapes favored throughout subsequent Chinese history—as well as jade figurines, turquoise jewelry, the world's earliest lacquered wood items, and cowry shells, a medium of exchange monopolized by the Xia rulers, all testify to their leaders' religious and social roles. Moreover, foundations of workers' residences and workshops for copper and bronze casting have also been found. As with a number of Longshan sites, extensive cemeteries outside the city suggest the development of social classes in the number and kind of burial artifacts and the position and richness of elite plots.

Though the boundaries of Chinese history have been pushed back considerably by such work, the Xia remain, like their contemporaries the Harappans, an elusive, if perhaps not a "lost," civilization. For at least one leading scholar, however, the findings at Erlitou represent not merely a regional variation among many ancient cultures, but "an early form of Chinese civilization." (Sarah Allen, "Erlitou and the Formation of Chinese Civilization," *Journal of Asian Studies*, 66:2 [May, 2007]: 490).

The Interactions of Shang and Zhou History and Politics, 1766–481 BCE

The Shang dynasty represents the first genuine flowering of urban society in East Asia. Though this development occurs somewhat later than in the other core areas of Egypt and the Mediterranean, southwest Asia, and the Indus valley, we nevertheless find here all of the attributes of such cultures elsewhere: a high degree of skill in metallurgy, a large and varied agricultural base, an increasingly centralized political and religious system, growing **social stratification**, a written language, and, of course, cities. In all of these areas the Shang made considerable contributions; in some, such as their spectacular bronzes and especially their system of written characters, they were startlingly original.

Social stratification: A hierarchical arrangement of groups or classes within a society—for example, peasants, merchants, officials, ministers, rulers.

The Shang Dynasty, 1766–1122 BCE

Unlike the idealized rule of the sage kings Yao, Shun, and Yu depicted in the *Shujing*, Shang social and political organization was based on kinship, with an emphasis on military power and efficiency of command. As in Mesopotamia, the advent of cities, with their vastly increased populations, now required rulers to wield greater power for defense and internal regulation, while at the same time appealing to an authority beyond human power for legitimacy. Thus, loyalty was pledged to the Shang king and his family. Members of the king's extended family controlled political and religious power, with more distant relatives acting as court officials.

Among the purported 31 Shang kings mentioned in literary records, rulership often passed from uncle to nephew, though sometimes it went from elder brother

Shang Weapon. A bronze ceremonial axe head with intricate decorative markings, from the thirteenth to the eleventh century BCE.

to younger. Unlike the Aryan system of *varna,* there was no rigidly defined priestly class, though spirit mediums and diviners were widely used by Shang rulers—as we saw with Wu Ding—and exercised considerable influence at court. Local leaders who controlled walled cities and towns and their surrounding lands were employed by the ruling families as regional officials, as were specially designated Shang allies, though the exact nature of these arrangements is not clearly understood.

Shang Armies and Expansion Though small compared to the forces commanded by their successors, the armies fielded by Shang rulers were the most powerful of East Asia in their day. One expeditionary force of the late thirteenth-century BCE king Wu Ding and his wife Fu Hao numbered more than 13,000 men and included both paid soldiers and local defense forces recruited from the larger walled towns. Excavations reveal that the armies were organized into companies of 100 men who wielded bronze-tipped spears and pikes topped with crescent-shaped axe heads and spear tips (see Map 4.2).

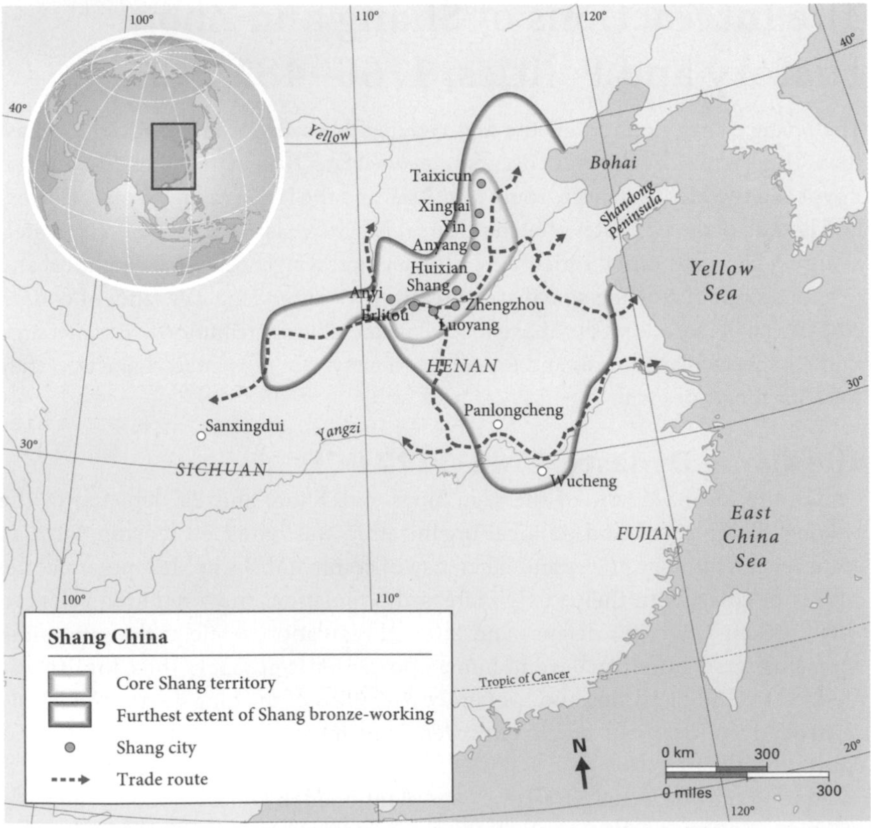

MAP 4.2 **Shang China.**

Shang Chariot. Whether used for battle or state functions, Shang-era chariots were distinctive in their wide stance, roominess, and portability. The photograph shows a careful reconstruction of a Shang chariot with authentic bronze decorations and lacquered finish. Note the linchpins holding the wheels to the axles. These could be quickly removed for ease in changing wheels or breaking down the chariot in order to carry its parts separately.

The Introduction of the Chariot Another potent weapon used by the Shang was the chariot, possibly introduced to China through interaction with Indo-Europeans around 1300 to 1200 BCE, when these vehicles first make their appearance in Shang burial sites. Chariots seem to have been shortly preceded by the widespread introduction of the horse from the west, an innovation that had already revolutionized transport and warfare through much of Eurasia. Up to this point, the small Mongolian ponies native to the northern reaches of Shang lands seem to have attracted little interest, perhaps because of their limitations as transport and draft animals. The larger and faster steeds of central Asia and the western Eurasian steppes, however, were to remain important items of trade for the Chinese for thousands of years and were celebrated in painting, poetry, and song.

Shang chariots were pulled by two horses and generally held three men. Detachable wheels held by linchpins permitted easy storage and repair. Both charioteers and infantry wielded large composite bows—so called because they were made of wood, cattle horn, and sinew. The bows were curved away from the archer in their unstrung state for additional power. As with other ancient peoples, the combination of archers with the chariot gave Shang forces considerable striking power, especially when employed against slower and more unwieldy infantry formations.

Client states: States that are dependent on or partially controlled by more powerful ones.

Shang Politics and Foreign Relations Because their prestige depended in large part on their military power and harmony with their ancestors, the Shang rulers constantly mounted campaigns for sacrifice—both material and human. Indeed, the archaeological evidence and oracle bone inscriptions suggest that the greater part of Shang foreign relations with **client states** and allies consisted of setting and enforcing levels of tribute and labor service. Shang kings, especially Wu Ding, continually led expeditions against settled peoples to the west, the most prominent of whom, the Zhou, based around modern Xi'an, were ultimately enlisted as allies and clients. Wu Ding's successors, such as Zu Geng [ZOO-gung] and Di Yin, met with less success, however, and over time shifting coalitions of former allies and client states began to encroach on Shang lands. Significantly, even to the end of the Shang period, the interior lands of the state appear to have been considered secure enough to lack walls and other defensive structures around many major towns.

Shang Interactions Throughout the span of roughly 1,200 years from the traditional beginnings of the Xia to the end of the Shang, ties between the northern Chinese states and the other Eurasian civilizational cores seems to have been tenuous at best. The most direct links appear to have been through the trade and migrations of an ethnically and culturally diverse group of nomadic–pastoral peoples who ranged along a broad northern tier of Eurasia from the steppes of modern Ukraine to the area of modern Manchuria in the east. Though they left few traces, and early Chinese accounts use a haphazard collection of names for them, scholars have theorized that these nomads included both speakers of Altaic languages—the distant ancestors of the Mongols, Manchus, Turks, and perhaps the Huns—and, perhaps more significantly at this point, the Indo-European peoples who played such an important role in spreading a host of ancient technologies throughout Eurasia.

Though direct mention of these nomadic peoples is almost completely absent from Shang records, a number of objects in Shang tombs carry clear signs of their foreign origins. For example, Fu Hao's tomb contains a number of bronze and jade objects—most significantly, bronze mirrors—which only later would come into widespread use in China. For their part, the Shang circulated local and foreign items such as bronze vessels, weapons, and jade throughout the region and beyond.

Many of these foreign items have been found as far south as northern Vietnam, and the peoples of surrounding areas acknowledged Shang predominance in wealth and culture. The picture is complicated somewhat by the recent work on cultures that show a connection to artifacts uncovered at Shang sites, and even at Erlitou, but have distinct—almost exotic—regional variations. The most intriguing example is that of the strange elongated figurines of Sanxingdui [SAN-shing-dway] in Sichuan [SIH-chwan], well out of Shang-dominated territory. On the whole, however, widespread recognition of Shang sophistication marks, with the ascendancy of the Zhou, an important example of a recurring pattern of world history, as well as that of China: conquerors on the cultural periphery interacting with and adapting to the culture of the conquered.

The Mandate of Heaven: The Zhou Dynasty to 481 BCE

Unlike the Xia and Shang dynasties, the nearly nine centuries of Zhou rule are extensively documented in such literary works as the *Zuo Zhuan* [ZWOA-jwan] (*The*

Commentaries of Mr. Zuo), the *Chunqiu* [CHWUN-chew] (*Spring and Autumn Chronicles*), and later compilations such as the *Shiji* [SHIH-jee] (*Records of the Historian*) by the second-century BCE historian Sima Qian [sih-ma-CHIEN] in addition to the *Shujing*.

Like the *Shujing*, these other Zhou records contain much of questionable value and uncertain origin. Nevertheless, they suggest both an ongoing quest for social, political, and moral order as well as institutional and intellectual experimentation on a grand scale. They also provide us, in the closing date of the *Spring and Autumn Chronicles* (481 BCE), with an important transition point with which to end this chapter. As we will see in Chapter 9, out of the increasingly fierce competition among the Zhou states for expansion and survival in the succeeding Warring States period (formally 403–256 BCE but used to encompass the entire era from 480 down to the creation of the Qin Empire in 221 BCE) came China's greatest flowering of philosophical and political theory and ultimate unification into an empire that would last, with brief interruptions, for over 2,000 years.

The Mandate of Heaven By the twelfth century BCE, it appears through the trend of oracle bone inscriptions that the size of the Shang state had shrunk considerably because of encroachment by peoples to the north and west. The oracle bones also suggest an increased concentration of power in the hands of the last Shang kings, a situation depicted in the literary record as coinciding with their dissolution and corruption. Against this backdrop, the state of Zhou to the west—which, as we have seen, had become a Shang dependency—began to take military action. The *Shujing* tells of the Zhou kings Wen, Wu, and Cheng and Cheng's regent, the Duke of Zhou, systematically pushing their holdings eastward from 1122 BCE, taking much of the Shang territory under their control. Sometime around 1045 BCE, Zhou forces captured and burned the last Shang capital and stronghold near Anyang. In doing so, the Zhou sought to portray their conquest as morally justified after an overlong interlude of Shang decadence (see Map 4.3).

Unlike the rise and fall of states in other areas, conquest by one of the three dynasties, as depicted in the literary record, did not mean exile, extinction, or enslavement for those defeated. On the contrary, the conquerors were shown as presenting their victories as acts of moral renewal for those they conquered by ridding them of oppressive or degenerate rulers and restoring leadership to the worthy. Although the attitudes of the common people toward such shifts of

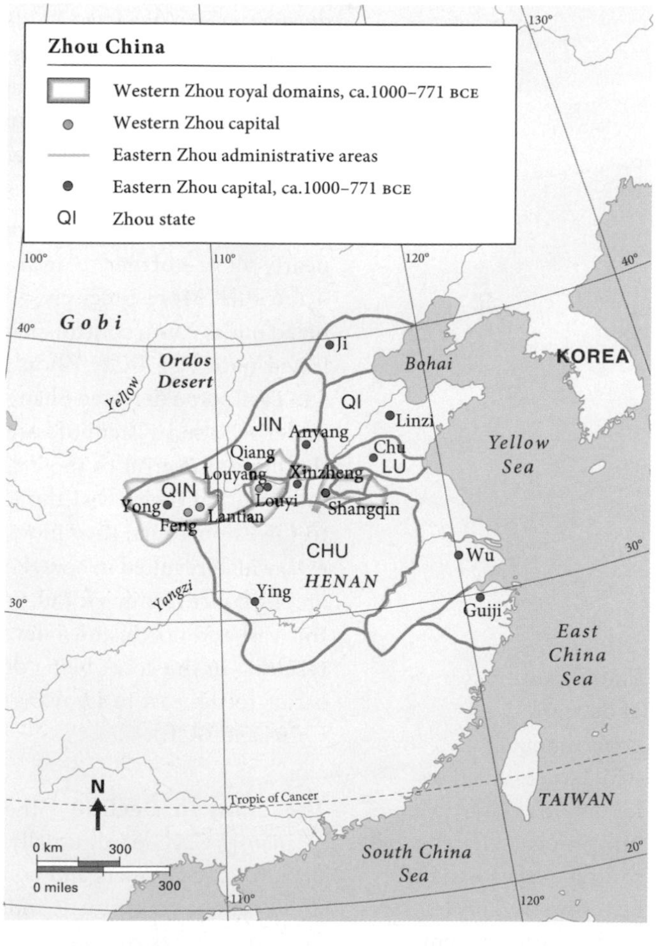

MAP 4.3 **Zhou China.**

power remain unknown, the idealized speeches of the new rulers in the *Shujing*, for example, attempt to justify their actions and seek the cooperation of all classes in the new order.

As the compilers of this literary record, the Zhou sought to place themselves firmly within it. While it is unknown whether the practices they recorded had been widespread or newly invented by the conquerors, they provided the backdrop for one of China's most enduring historical and philosophical concepts: the Mandate of Heaven.

According to this idea, a dynasty's right to rule depends on the moral correctness of its rulers. Over time, dynasties grow weaker and tend to become corrupt as individual rulers give in to the temptations of court life or different factions seek to manipulate the throne. Under such conditions, rebellion from within or conquest by outside forces becomes morally justified. The success of such actions is then seen as proof that heaven's approval or "mandate" has been taken from the old rulers and bestowed on the insurgents, who may then legitimately found a new dynasty. Ultimately, however, the new dynasty, too, will decline. Thus, the fall of the Shang dynasty, as described in the *Shujing*, sprang from a loss of virtue, similar to that of the Xia, which had earlier resulted in Shang ascendancy. The idea of such a "dynastic cycle" operating as the driving force of history was later codified by court historians during the Han dynasty (202 BCE–220 CE).

Throughout Chinese history, these concepts not only allowed political renewal to take place internally but framed a remarkably durable system within which the Chinese and outside conquerors could interact and adapt themselves to each other in maintaining governmental and societal continuity.

Western Zhou and Eastern Zhou By the end of the eleventh century BCE, nearly all of northern China as far south as the Yangzi River had come under Zhou rule. More precisely, a network of over 100 smaller territories was organized under Zhou control, marking the beginning of the Western Zhou era, which lasted until 771 BCE. Zhou rulers placed family, distinguished subjects, allies, and even some defeated Shang notables in leadership positions of these territories under a graded system of hereditary ranks. By the eighth century BCE, however, the more powerful of these territories had begun to consolidate their holdings into states of their own. Though the states would continue to pledge their loyalty to the Zhou court, they increasingly worked toward promoting their own interests, which resulted in a weakening of Zhou political power. A half century of war among court factions for ultimate rule, border struggles with nomadic peoples to the west and north, and a devastating earthquake further weakened Zhou power, resulting in the court being driven from its capital at Xi'an in 771 BCE and relocating to the east in Luoyang. This forced move began the Eastern Zhou period (770–256 BCE).

Feudalism: A system of decentralized government in which rule is held by landowners who owe obligations of loyalty and military service to their superiors and protection to those under them.

The Zhou in Decline The Zhou system of decentralized government called *fengjian* [FUNG-jien], usually rendered as "**feudalism**," gave considerable autonomy to its local rulers and was thus an important reason for the weakening of the Zhou central government and the strengthening of its dependent states. As these dependent states grew in power and their economies flourished, local rulers became less loyal to the Zhou leadership, and some rulers even went as far as naming themselves "king" (*wang*) of their own domains.

The prestige of the Zhou court was further weakened after its flight to Luoyang in 770. Continuing border problems with nomadic–pastoral peoples to the north and west around the Zhou home state and the relative isolation of its new capital drastically cut the flow of revenue from the dependent domains. This isolation was especially important since these states were in a period of tremendous economic expansion. Within a few generations of the inauguration of the Eastern Zhou in 770 BCE, Zhou control and power had significantly weakened in absolute as well as relative terms.

The Zhou decline is graphically described in the *Spring and Autumn Chronicles* and its accompanying work, *The Commentaries of Mr. Zuo*. Compiled in the Zhou state of Lu in the modern province of Shandong, these complementary works detail the maneuverings of states and individuals in northern China from 722 to 481 BCE. The world they depict is one in which repeated attempts at creating a stable political and social order among the 15 major Zhou states are frustrated by constantly shifting power dynamics and especially by the rise of dominant states on the Zhou periphery.

Early on, during the mid-seventh century, the most important of these states was Qi [chee], which dominated northeast China and much of Shandong. By shrewd diplomacy and careful use of military power, Qi became the first "senior," or *ba* [bah], state in a system of **hegemony** in which the lesser Zhou states deferred to the *ba* state as the protector of the Zhou system. The successive *ba* states mounted alliances against non-Zhou states and attempted to regulate relations among those within the system. They also presided at conferences held from the mid-sixth century BCE aimed at regularizing trade and diplomacy among the states. Qi was succeeded by Jin, which reorganized the *ba* system and, in 579 BCE, sponsored a truce and disarmament conference among the Zhou states.

Hegemony: A system of state relations in which less powerful states directly or implicitly agree to defer to the lead of the most powerful state, which is, thus, the hegemon.

By the latter part of the sixth century, a rough balance of power among the four leading states of Jin, Chu [Choo] (the premier state of the southern periphery), Qi, and Qin (a rising force in the old Zhou homeland near Xi'an) held sway. While this system functioned for several decades, new powers on the peripheries, expansion into non-Zhou lands, and civil war in Jin ultimately precipitated the partition of Jin in 403 BCE, marking the formal opening of the Warring States period. By its close, Zhou itself had been absorbed by the combatants (in 256 BCE), and Qin would emerge as not just the dominant state but the creator of a unified empire in 221 BCE.

Economy, Society, and Family Adaptation in Ancient China

From Neolithic times, the Chinese economy has been based on agriculture. It was only in early 2012 that China's urban population outstripped its rural one. Still, as of 2015 approximately 44% of China's people are involved in agricultural pursuits. From early times as well, both the Yellow River states and those in the south of China outside of the control of the Shang and Zhou dynasties relied on a peasant subsistence economy based on family and clan landownership, with much of the local political power diffused to the thousands of villages dotting the landscape. While periodic concentration of landlord power and the problems of land-centered social relationships occupied Chinese rulers over the course of millennia, China, unlike some other agriculturally based societies, never developed an extensive system of slave labor.

Family life played a dominant role among all members of ancient Chinese society. Here, in a way parallel to trends in other agrarian kingdoms, the position of women in power among the elite eroded over time, a process that would be accelerated during the long interval of imperial rule. By the late Zhou period, the hierarchy of patriarchy and the growing influence of notions of *filial piety*—a model of behavior based on relationships among members of a family headed by the father—were on their way to becoming firmly established.

Shang Society

Though Shang leaders, like those of the Xia and Zhou, frequently moved their headquarters for political and military reasons, nearly all of their newly established capitals swiftly grew to proportions comparable to those developing in India and the Mediterranean.

Erligang The capital city at Erligang [AR-lee-gahng] was characteristic of the late Xia or early Shang period. It had a defensive wall 4.5 miles in circumference, enclosing an urban center of about a square mile. The area within the walls was the province of the rulers, related families, diviners, and bronze casters and craftspeople in the direct service of the elites. Merchants and craftspeople involved in the manufacture of items other than bronze, jade, or ritual objects lived outside the city walls, as did peasants and slaves.

The life of the commoners in Erligang centered largely on communal agriculture. They tilled the soil with small plows, stone-tipped hoes, and assorted wooden implements, bronze being considered too valuable for use in agricultural tasks. They grew millet and vegetables as their staples and raised water buffalo, sheep in the more arid areas, chickens, and pigs. The pig, domesticated since at least Yangshao times, continued to be of central importance in the rural diet. Even today, the written character for "family" or "household" (家, *jia*) is represented by a character depicting a pig under a roof.

Social Class and Labor Within the towns and villages immediately outside the larger cities, a more differentiated social structure was also developing, with artisans of various trades organized according to lineage. Many families and clans tended to pursue the same occupations for generations, and craft guilds and other organizations came to be dominated by family groups, such as potters and ceramics makers, as was the case later in imperial China. The constant warfare of Shang rulers and their increasing interest in monumental projects, such as flood control along the Yellow River and its tributaries, all boosted the need for labor. Professional soldiers and local militia generally satisfied Shang military needs. Conscript labor, however, constituted an increasingly important part of the workforce.

Interactions of Zhou Economy and Society

The large size of the territory claimed by the Zhou dynasty, and the enhanced trade that this expansion entailed, added to the wealth and power of all the rulers of its increasingly autonomous dependencies. The expansion of these dependencies to the Yangzi River basin brought much of East Asia's most productive farmland under some form of Zhou control and stimulated increased interaction with the inhabitants of the region.

Innovation and Adaptation in Agriculture In the north, the introduction of the soybean from Manchuria, with its high protein content and ability to fix nitrogen in the soil, boosted crop yields and pushed growers to cultivate more marginal lands. The rotation of wheat and different varieties of millet allowed for more intensive farming. The use of more efficient ox-drawn plows and, from the fourth century BCE, iron-tipped tools, as well as increasingly elaborate irrigation and water-conservancy efforts, pushed yields even further. In the south, the Zhou dependencies, like the *janapadas* of India, developed rapidly as rice cultivation facilitated population growth. With the coming of intensive rice farming, the economic and demographic center of China moved steadily southward. By the middle of the sixth century BCE, the Zhou kingdoms taken together constituted the world's most populous, and perhaps richest, agriculturally based urban society.

Zhou Rural Society The Zhou rulers devised a system of ranks for governing their dependencies based on the size of landholdings:

- *hou* [ho], the title given to rulers of the Zhou dependencies
- *qing* [ching], the chief functionaries of the *hou*
- *shi* [shihr], a general category for lower officials, eventually including talented commoners
- *shuren* [SHOO-ren], the remainder of the commoners.

Members of the various ranks of the aristocracy were responsible for collecting taxes from their dependents and the *shuren* and were required to provide military service to those above in return for support and protection. Peasant cultivators worked their own lands, with the lands of the aristocracy often scattered in plots among those of the commoners.

The Well-Field System In an attempt to untangle the more confusing aspects of this land arrangement, the Zhou were the first among many dynasties to attempt to impose a uniform system of land tenure in China. Later writers, most notably the philosopher Mencius, would look back nostalgically on the idealized *well-field system*—a method of land division said to have been devised by the Duke of Zhou. In this arrangement, each square *li* (one *li* is about one-third of a mile), consisting of 900 *mou* (each *mou* is approximately one-sixth of an acre), was divided into a grid of nine plots. Individual families would each work one of the eight outside plots while the middle one would be farmed in common for the taxes and rents owed the landowner or local officials. The term "well-field" comes from the Chinese character for "[water] well" (井, *jing*), which resembles a grid. Whether the system as idealized by Mencius was ever widely practiced is still a matter of debate among scholars. It did, however, remain the benchmark against which all subsequent attempts at land reform were measured, even into the twentieth century.

By the late 500s BCE, a substantial change had taken place in many of the Zhou states. The needs of individual governments to use the wealth of their states to support their militaries and developing bureaucracies prompted them to institute land taxes based on crop yields and, in some cases, to commute labor obligations to direct taxes payable in kind to the state. Depending on the state and the productivity of the land, these tended to vary from 10 to 20 percent of a family holding's yield. Then, as now, the taxes tended to affect the poor the most.

The New Classes: Merchants and *Shi* Further evidence for the decline of the Zhou feudal system is the rise of new classes. For the first time, the literary record now includes references to merchants. The growing power of this new class began, among other processes, a long-term struggle with various governments for control of such vital commodities as salt and iron. It also marked the beginning of the perception of merchants as *usurpers*—a class with no ties to the land and thus no stake in upholding the values of landholders or peasants—whose drive for profit from trafficking in the goods of others endangered the stability of Zhou social institutions. Accompanying the rise of a merchant class was the steady advance of a cash economy. The coining of money was becoming widespread by the late Zhou, including the round copper "cash" with the square middle hole, symbolically depicting heaven and earth, which remained almost unchanged for over 2,000 years.

Though often viewed with distaste by the landed aristocracy, merchants, with their wealth and expertise, were increasingly seen as resources to be tapped. Their rapid rise to economic prominence, however, meant that as a group their social position lay outside the traditional structures of agrarian life. Their independence and mobility, along with the steady growth of cities as centers of trade, helped spur political and economic centralization as the rulers of Zhou territories attempted to create more inclusive systems of administration. Direct taxation by the state, uniform law codes, and administrative restructuring were increasingly altering the old arrangement of mutual obligation between aristocratic landowners and dependent peasant farmers. Here, members of the new *shi* class, drawn from the lower aristocracy and wealthier commoners, who, like merchants, were divorced somewhat from the older structures of rural life, took on the role of bureaucrats and advisors. From the ranks of the *shi* would rise many of China's most famous thinkers, starting with Confucius, and the duties and proper conduct of the *shi* would come to occupy a prominent place in their writings from the late sixth century BCE on.

Central Asian Interactions The growing wealth of north and central China spurred a dramatic increase in trade outside of the Zhou realm as well as among its constituent states, particularly in the south and along well-established routes into central Asia. As one measure of the extent of such interaction, scholars have pointed to silk threads appearing in the bindings of Egyptian mummies dated to 1000 BCE, in Greek gravesites several hundred years later, and even in central and northern European encampments from about 500 BCE. In this interchange, Zhou traders were increasingly helped by the carriers of the central Asian exchange.

By the sixth century BCE, a series of loosely related cultures along this northern front (called *Scythic* because of their broad cultural similarity to the peoples the

Greeks called "Scythians") can be clearly discerned. These peoples appear to have taken Zhou goods much farther than originally thought, and scholars are only now beginning to realize the vast extent of their trade relations. What other goods besides silk may have been involved in such exchanges remains unknown, however, until the period of officially sanctioned and better-recorded trade along the Silk Road began in the second century BCE.

Gender and the Family

While scholars have long explored the role of women and the family during China's imperial era, notably during the Song and Ming dynasties, serious study of gender roles in ancient China has only recently begun. One obvious reason for this is the relative scarcity of records from earlier times. Another is the development of women's instructional literature from roughly the first century BCE to the first century CE, a phenomenon that has provided modern scholars with an important focal point in charting a shift in perspectives of female "virtue" and proper behavior in the home and in public.

Elite Women of the Shang In marked contrast to later Chinese court life, with its tightly prescribed etiquette and seclusion of wives and concubines from the avenues of power, elite women of the Shang often participated in political, and even military, affairs. As we saw in the opening of this chapter, one of the most complete Shang burial sites is that of Fu Hao, discovered in 1975. The most prominent of the 64 wives of Wu Ding, Fu Hao was buried with artifacts—hundreds of bronze, jade, and bone ornaments, as well as the sacrificial skeletons of 16 people and six dogs—that help bring to life a woman whose existence, though well established in written records, has otherwise been elusive.

The artifacts also shed light on a number of questions regarding Shang technology and material culture, court life, and especially the position of women among the aristocracy. For example, inscriptions on oracle bones in Fu Hao's tomb indicate that she wielded considerable power and influence even before becoming Wu Ding's principal wife. Prior to coming to court at the Shang capital of Yin sometime in the late thirteenth century BCE, she owned and managed a family estate nearby and was apparently well educated in a number of areas that would make her well prepared for palace life. She both supervised and conducted religious rituals at court and during military expeditions. As Wu Ding's chief confidant she advised him on political and military strategy and diplomacy. She even conducted her own military campaigns against Shang adversaries. The king apparently considered her so wise and beloved that after her death he frequently appealed to her for guidance through divination with oracle bones.

Women's Status in Transition Elite women like Fu Hao appear to have shared a comparatively equal status with male rulers, even to the point of leading armies and practicing divination, though it should also be mentioned that their tombs tend to be smaller and less elaborate than those of males of comparable rank. To the extent that such literature as the *Book of History* and the *Poetry Classic* of the early Zhou era addresses issues of women and power, women were still depicted as occupying important positions as mentors and advisors. Women's crafts such as spinning and weaving, and especially the different skills demanded by silk production, were highly regarded. In fact, there were government offices supervised and staffed by women to oversee silk and hemp cloth weaving. The *Poetry Classic* (*Book of Odes*), in depicting the lives of ordinary people, suggests a far more egalitarian relationship between men and women than would be the case during the imperial period.

The wives and concubines of rulers in many instances had their own sets of records and genealogies as well, an important asset among the powerful in this family-conscious society. Even by the late Zhou period, as one scholar notes, a "model" woman like Lady Ji of the state of Lu was able to instruct her son, the high official Wen Bo (Earl Wen), in the arts of government by comparing the roles of different officials to the proper arrangement of the components of a loom in the process of weaving. In this role of advisor, she was much praised for her virtue by subsequent thinkers.

Yet it was also true that by this time it was Wen Bo and not Lady Ji who actually held the reins of power. Late Zhou women might be well educated and highly capable, but they seldom ruled in their own right. In fact, the treaties hammered out during the Spring and Autumn period (722–481 BCE) in many cases specifically barred women from involvement in state affairs. The same general trend may be glimpsed at other levels of society as well. The enormously complex web of family, clan, village, and class associations of the Zhou era reflects considerable respect for the wisdom and work of women, but these skills were increasingly seen as best exercised in the home instead of in the public sphere. The later development of state-sponsored Confucianism, with its preponderant emphasis on filial piety, ushered in a markedly secondary role for women.

Interactions of Religion, Culture, and Intellectual Life in Ancient China

In many respects, the evolution of Chinese religion follows a similar pattern to that of other agriculturally based urban societies. That is, like the gods of the early Mesopotamians, the first Chinese gods were local deities that inhabited a spirit world presided over by a ruling god. In China, the rulers' ancestors occupied the highest rungs of the spirit world, and worship largely consisted of communication with them by various means. Religion was not separate from everyday life but permeated all aspects of it.

While they creatively adapted and adopted many other aspects of Shang culture, the Zhou era marked a turn toward a more abstract, impersonal, and universal concept of religion. As an illustration of this, Shangdi [SHANG-dee], the chief Shang deity, and other beings with superhuman powers but human-like personalities, began to give way to the more distant Zhou concept of "heaven" (*tian* [tien]) as the animating force of the universe. As in other religious traditions, there is a movement to go beyond the invocation of gods through proper sacrifice and divination rituals—*formalism*—in order to seek insight into the forces that control the universe. By the late Zhou era, this concept of heaven as the guiding cosmic force had become central to nearly every major Chinese religious and philosophical tradition.

Oracle Bones and Early Chinese Writing

Scholars agree that samples of Shang characters found on oracle bones are examples of China's earliest known writing, representing an entirely original system. One legend has it that the cultural hero Fuxi discovered writing after seeing symbols etched on the back of a turtle, and, indeed, the oracle bones themselves are mostly the undershells of turtles and the shoulder blades of oxen.

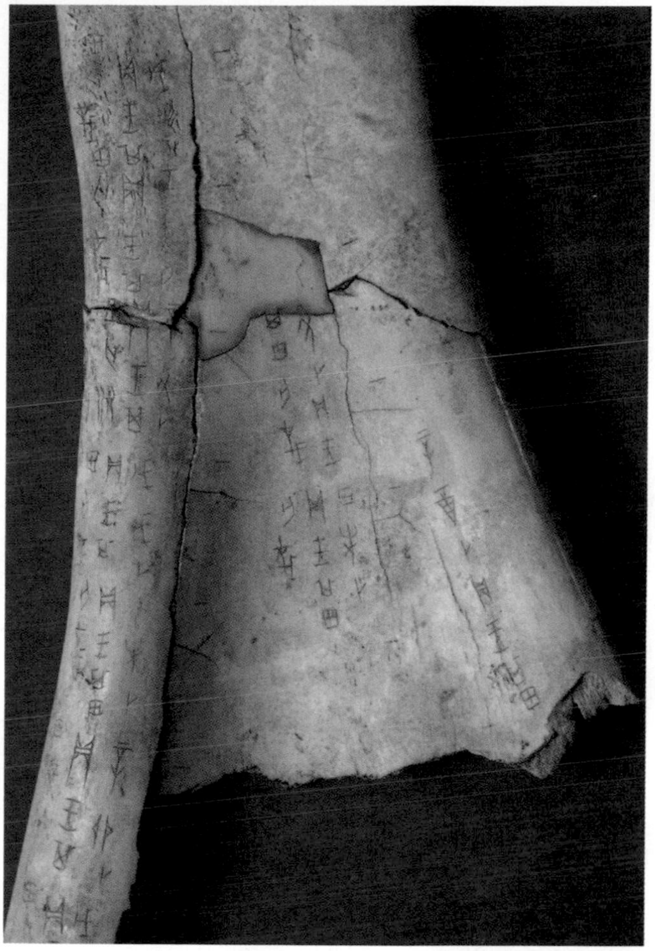

Shang Oracle Bone Inscription on Shoulder Blade of an Ox.

As we saw earlier with Wu Ding, seekers of guidance would consult the diviner, who would ask questions of the ancestors. The bones were then heated, tapped with a rod, the resulting cracks interpreted as answers, and the information incised in the bone. Several thousand distinct symbols have been identified, and many are clearly ancient versions of modern Chinese characters. More important, the principles these symbols employed as a form of writing had already moved away from those of other hieroglyphic or pictographic languages. Chinese characters became increasingly stylized and, after the Qin era (221–202 BCE), put into standard forms. But in most cases, these retained enough of their earlier character to be recognizable to later readers. Moreover, the political and religious significance of Shang and Zhou ritual vessels, which, in many cases, contained inscriptions in archaic characters, ensured that some knowledge of them would be preserved.

Shang Bronzes While it now seems that, like the potter's wheel, some of the early bronze articles and weapons found at late Longshan sites may have come by way of trade routes from western Asia, bronze-casting techniques used in China quite likely diffused northward from Southeast Asia at about the same time. The best evidence for this is that the "carved-clay" technique favored by Shang and Zhou casters, in which inner and outer molds of the object are made of clay and molten bronze is poured into the gap between them, is unique to China and radically different from the "lost wax" method of the peoples of western Eurasia. Shang and early Zhou ritual vessels themselves, with their richly stylized *taotie* [TAOW-tea-eh] motifs—fanciful abstract reliefs of real and mythical animals incorporated into the design—are utterly unlike anything outside of East Asia.

Shang Religion The use of bronze vessels with their elaborately stylized *taotie* motifs constituted a central part of Shang religious ceremonies among the elites. Offerings of meats, grains (wheat, millet, and occasionally rice), and wine were a regular part of Shang ritual. Except for some limited references in later literature to offerings of wine and millet at local shrines and ancestral graves, we know little about the religious practices of Shang commoners. However, the growing number of artifacts and oracle bones found at the gravesites of elites and at the remains of royal palaces has considerably clarified the belief system of the rulers.

Patterns Up Close

The Chinese Writing System

Of all the innovations commonly associated with China—paper, gunpowder, tea, the compass—perhaps the one with the longest-lasting impact was its unique writing system. Like many attempts at symbolic communication, such as those of the Egyptians, the Harappans, and, in the Americas, the Mayans, it was originally a system based on pictures. As with these other systems, the pictures became simplified and to some extent standardized for ease of interpretation. In its earliest form, for example, the Chinese character for the sun is a circle with a dot in the center. In its modern form it is still recognizable as 日.

Three Excellences. Chinese children learn at an early age to combine painting, poetry, and calligraphy as the highest form of self-expression.

Even in its archaic form, Chinese contained two basic types of characters: *pictographs*—pictures designating particular objects—and *ideographs*—pictures representing ideas—as well as some purely phonetic characters. Both types became increasingly elaborated and stylized, with the most basic characters acquiring phonetic components and compounds of simple characters formed to represent abstract expressions. For example, compounding the character 女, *nu* [neeu] (female or woman), with 子, *zi* [zuh] (child), created 好, *hao* [how] (good), an abstract expression symbolized quite concretely by a mother and child. Similarly, 女, *nu*, placed under the character for roof yielded the character, 安, *an* [ahn], meaning peace or contentment. The characters for sun (日) and moon (月) placed together came to mean bright, 明.

The close association of the written language with early Chinese religious practices, court ceremonial functions, and self-cultivation and character development imbued it over the centuries with a kind of spiritual dimension not usually found among the written languages of other peoples. The patience and discipline demanded by learning the thousands of characters necessary for advanced literacy and the artistic possibilities embodied in the brush and ink

The principal deity, Di or Shangdi, presided over the spirit world and governed both natural and human affairs. Shangdi was joined by the major ancestors of the dynastic line, deities believed to influence or control natural phenomena, and local gods appropriated from various Shang territories. The religious function of the Shang ruler, as it appears to have been for the Xia and would be for subsequent Chinese dynasties, was to act as the intermediary between the world of the spirits and that of humanity. Hence, rituals appear to have consisted largely of sacrifices to ancestors to ensure their benevolence toward the living. As we have seen, the Shang sought the guidance of their ancestral spirits through divination on a wide variety of human affairs, such as royal marriages and military campaigns, and on such natural phenomena as droughts, floods,

Ancestor Worship and Human Sacrifice from the *Shijing*

traditionally used to write them placed calligraphy at the top of Chinese aesthetic values. Thus, wherever written Chinese is used, skill at the three interrelated "excellences" of painting, poetry, and calligraphy is esteemed as the highest mode of self-expression.

The Chinese written language had a tremendous impact on the course of Asian history. While it requires extensive memorization compared to the phonetically written languages of other cultures, it is remarkably adaptable as a writing system because the meaning of the characters is independent of their pronunciation. Thus, speakers of non-Chinese languages could attach their own pronunciations to the characters and, as long as they understood their structure and grammar, could use them to communicate. This versatility enabled Chinese to serve as the first written language not only for speakers of the Chinese family of dialects and languages on the Asian mainland but also for the Koreans, Japanese, and Vietnamese, whose spoken languages are totally unrelated to Chinese. The pattern of interaction and adaptation prompted by the acquisition of the written language allowed the vast body of Chinese literature, philosophy, religion, history, and political theory to tie the literate elites of these states together within a common cultural sphere. In this respect, it functioned in much the same way as Latin among the educated of Europe. Even today, despite the development of written vernacular languages in all these countries, the ability to read classical Chinese is still considered to be a mark of superior education. Moreover, the cultural heritage transmitted by Chinese characters continues to inform the worldviews of these societies.

Questions

- How did the pattern of interaction and adaptation that characterized the development of the Chinese writing system bring people together into a common cultural sphere?
- How does the impact of the Chinese writing system compare to the impact other writing systems have had in other parts of the world?

plantings, and harvests. Scholars theorize that many of the animals appearing as designs on ritual vessels represent messengers from the spirit world associated with divination.

As the Shang state grew more powerful and commanded more and more resources, the size and scope of the sacrifices also increased. Like the Xia, the Shang practiced human sacrifice. Excavations at both the early capital in the Erligang district of the modern city of Zhengzhou and later capitals near Anyang have yielded numerous sites containing headless skeletons. The evidence suggests that the death of a ruler was accompanied by the slaughter of hundreds of slaves, servants, and war captives, perhaps to serve the deceased in the spirit world.

Ritual Vessel with *Taotie* Design Pattern.

Adaptations of Zhou Religion, Technology, and Culture

The Zhou, like other conquerors after them, sought to give legitimacy to their reign by adopting many of the forms of art and ritual practiced by the defeated Shang. As before, the ruler maintained his place as mediator between the human and divine worlds. But the Zhou also appear to have followed the trend toward more abstract religious ideas we have observed in other early civilizations.

Heaven The Zhou introduced the concept of *tian*, "heaven," as a relatively neutral, impersonal controlling force of the universe, which eventually replaced the more approachable, human-like Shangdi. It was this more abstract heaven whose mandate gave the right to rule to all subsequent Chinese dynasties. Thus, throughout the long history of imperial China, the emperor retained the title of *Tianzi*, "son of heaven," as a symbol of his cosmic filial piety—his obligation to fulfill heaven's mandate as a son serves his father.

Iron Casting Perhaps the most significant technological innovation introduced during the Zhou period was the use of iron. Some late Shang and Western Zhou tombs contained iron objects of foreign origin, probably obtained from Indo-European peoples ranging across central Asia. By the seventh century BCE, basic technologies for mining and working iron are in evidence in western China. Significantly, it appears that the casting techniques of bronze production were adapted to this purpose. When combined with the high-temperature technologies employed by Zhou potters, the Chinese produced the world's earliest cast iron. By the sixth century BCE, cast- and wrought-iron weapons, tools, and farm implements were in common use; even some steel objects, including a sword, have been found. As in Gangetic India, they were instrumental in opening up new lands for cultivation and multiplying the deadliness of warfare.

Folk Culture: *The Book of Songs* As noted in the previous section, we know relatively little about the lives of the common people during the period of the Xia, Shang, and Zhou dynasties. One of the few sources that do provide some clues is the *Shijing*, the *Poetry Classic*, sometimes called *The Book of Odes* or *The Book of Songs*. The subject matter covers a wide range of interest and emotion, from homely observations on the cycles of rural life to protests and cleverly veiled satire. It is believed that, in most cases, the verses were meant to be sung. Though we do not know the names of the authors of these works, it is believed that a number of them were written by women.

As historical source material as well as art, the *Shijing's* songs and poems of the lives and loves, burdens and laments of peasants and soldiers, young wives and old men are still striking in their immediacy today. One of the most famous of these is a kind of concealed lament about taxes containing the lines:

> "Big rat, big rat,
> Don't eat my millet!
> Three years I've served you
> But you won't care for me."
>
> —ODE 113: "BIG RAT," FROM *THE BOOK OF SONGS*

Putting It All Together

interactive concept map

The period from the first Neolithic settlements in the Yellow River valley to the birth of Confucius in 551 BCE witnessed the beginning of many of the foundations of the cultures of China and, through interaction with Chinese influences, East and Southeast Asia. Like the other agricultural–urban cores in Mesopotamia, along the Nile, and in the Indus valley, the society that emerged in northern China was very much a product of its major river system. As early as 10,000 BCE, the Yellow River basin saw the rise of self-sufficient agricultural villages, marking the transition from forager to agrarian society. It was the early states that developed here that came to dominate the Chinese historical record. With the rise of the Xia dynasty late in the third millennium BCE, the first evidence of Chinese cities and the first people, places, and events traceable through later literary sources all make their appearance.

The Shang conquest of the Xia, traditionally held to be in 1766 BCE, marks the first flowering of China's Bronze Age. The centering of political, military, and religious authority in one ruler; the development of a unique and versatile form of writing; the growth of cities; and the widespread use of bronze under the Shang in many ways run parallel to developments in the other early centers of civilization. In their casting techniques and design motifs of bronze ritual vessels and their system of writing, however, Shang contributions were original and long lasting.

The theme of moral renewal came with the rise of the Zhou after 1122 BCE and was perhaps applied retroactively by them as well. Nearly all of China from the Yangzi River basin north was incorporated into a decentralized governmental system centered on the Zhou court at Xi'an. But the growing power of the largest Zhou territories eventually eclipsed that of the court; this began a prolonged era of struggle between the states. The increased wealth and power of rulers, aided by the drive of new social classes such as merchants and the *shi* to share in it, contributed to the breakdown of older feudal social patterns during the Spring and Autumn period from 722 to 481 BCE. Continual warfare stimulated both a drive for political consolidation and a questioning of the foundations of society. With the ideas of Confucius, to whom we turn at the beginning of Chapter 9, a radical direction in conceiving the nature and aims of society would soon take place. His ideas, adopted by a Chinese imperial system that would last over 2,000 years, would profoundly affect hundreds of millions of people inside and outside of China in the centuries to come.

Review and Relate

Thinking Through Patterns

Examine the ways historians approach the big questions of this chapter.

How did the interplay of environment and climate help to influence the earliest patterns of Chinese

The relationship of environment to the ways in which a particular culture lives is at once seemingly obvious and quite complex. In the case of northern China, the river both allows a large, reliably fertile area for cultivation to be maintained and restricts the ability to live close to it because of flooding. Not surprisingly, the collective efforts of the early Chinese states to control the river proved central to the character

civilization? How do historians address the question of whether "geography is destiny" in this case?

of these states. But what kinds of larger conclusions can we draw? Some scholars in the past theorized that early civilizations based around rivers developed many similarities in their patterns of governing, such as centralization, bureaucracy, and elaborate labor regulations. But here the key is in the details: How similar can we say Egypt is to Shang Dynasty China? As for the larger question of geography and destiny, most historians would say that geography is an important *conditional* factor, among many others, in determining how a civilization develops.

» What can the remains of Neolithic Chinese settlements tell us about the continuities and disruptions of Chinese history?

Among other things, these remains can suggest the kinds of plants and animals that were domesticated, the kinds of shelters that housed people, how gender roles were assigned, how the people living there handled their dead, and how they defended themselves. Many of these things are open to debate, however. Scholars in the People's Republic of China, for example, argued that such Neolithic villages were matriarchal and matrilineal; those from outside are less sure of the evidence for this. If true, the later switch to the strong patriarchal tradition represents an important change in the structure of Chinese families.

» How did the Zhou concept of the Mandate of Heaven operate?

The Mandate of Heaven, as we have seen, was at once a way for the Zhou to retrospectively legitimize their conquests and to create a precedent for future moral renewal. As part of a dynastic cycle, it set the fundamental pattern for the way the Chinese tended to view history. The rule of a particular dynasty was expected to advance in reform and expansion in its early stages, reach a comfortable point of harmony in its middle stages, and go into moral and material decline in its final stages. From that point, revolt breaks out and heaven transfers its mandate to a new dynasty—*if that revolt succeeds*. If not, the rebels have committed the worst of crimes. There is a definite closed logic to this system: Heaven approves, so the rebels succeed; the rebels succeed because heaven approves. This pattern of dynastic cycle and heavenly mandate made China's historical experience—conveniently fitted to the theory—not only comprehensible but also predictable. Alert rulers constantly searched for signs that the mandate was in danger; the people themselves often speculated about portents or natural disasters as presaging dynastic change. Even China's modern rulers are heirs to this pattern: During human-made and natural disasters the Communist Party is even more alert to possible signs that the people are expecting a "dynastic" change.

Against the Grain

Consider this as a counterpoint to the main patterns examined in this chapter.

Women's Voices

- It often seems as if women had somewhat greater freedom among

While scholars still debate the extent to which the Neolithic villages like Banpo may have been matrilineal or matriarchal, there is universal agreement that by the time of the first three dynasties, the northern Chinese states and their successors were creating a rigorously patriarchal society and culture. As we shall see in Chapter 9, this will be considerably reinforced by the uses to which Confucian values were put. Yet it is a mistake to assume that women were without influence or agency in ancient China; indeed, male Confucian writers occasionally noted the exploits of outstanding women of the ancient past, even those who went beyond what ultimately came to be seen as the filial, home-centered core ideals so widely celebrated in manuals of female deportment. One need only look at the enduring tales of the woman warrior Mulan, recently popularized in the West through literature and animated film, to see a powerful counterfoil to the stereotypical subservient Chinese daughter.

Long before this period, however, the *Shijing* (*Book of Songs*), in its collections of sung poems from the common people, contained a number of compositions that, although the individual authors are unknown, show strong evidence of having been composed by women, or perhaps in some cases in the persona of women. In them we have one of the few tools available with which we can discern something of the authentic voices of ancient Chinese women. Consider this lament from a young woman facing the challenges of family expectations for marriage:

> My mind is not a mirror;
> It cannot [equally] receive [all impressions]
> I, indeed, have brothers,
> But I cannot depend on them.
> I meet with their anger . . .
> Silently I think of my case,
> And, starting as from sleep, I beat my breast. (Number 26; "Cypress Boat")

In an almost visceral way, she gives voice to the frustration of the independent mind and heart as it breaks on the shoals of family and social convention. Her song was to be a familiar one over the intervening centuries.

the earliest civilizations we have encountered than they would in the period after 600 BCE. Do you think this is a fair observation? If so, which of these societies seemed to offer the most agency to women?

- Why did China become increasingly patriarchal over time? Does the development of urban–agrarian society necessarily lead to patriarchy?

Key Terms

audio flashcards

Client states 102	Hegemony 105	Social stratification 99
Feudalism 104	Millet 94	

For additional resources, please go to **www.oup.com/us/vonsivers.**
Please see the Further Resources section at the back of the book for additional readings and suggested websites.

PATTERNS OF EVIDENCE |

Sources for Chapter 4

SOURCE 4.1 *The Zuo Commentary (Zuozhuan)*

ca. fourth century BCE

The *Spring and Autumn Annals* (*Chunqiu*), a chronicle covering the years 722–481 BCE and composed at the court of Lu (the home state of Confucius), was acknowledged even at the time to be very difficult reading. Accordingly, scholars began composing commentaries to elucidate its finer points and clarify its meaning. The third orthodox commentary, attributed to "Mr. Zuo," continues to influence historical thought about ancient China. This section concerns a conflict between the states of Qin and Jin in the seventh century BCE.

Renxu: The date of the battle.

On ***renxu*** day, they fought on the plain of Han. The warhorses of Jin were confounded by the mud and forced to halt. The Lord [of Jin] called for Qing Zheng. Qing Zheng said, "You rejected my remonstrance and disobeyed the divination. You were resolutely seeking defeat—why flee from it now?" Then he abandoned [his lord].

Liang Youmi was driving for Han Jian; Guo She was the right-hand man. They came upon the carriage of the Earl of Qin and were about to stop him. [Qing] Zheng misled them by [calling for someone] to save the Lord [of Jin]; thus they lost the Earl of Qin. Qin caught the Marquis of Jin and returned with him. The Grand Masters of Jin followed him, letting their hair loose and camping in the wilderness. The Earl of Qin sent an embassy [asking them] to desist, saying, "Gentlemen, why are you so aggrieved? I am accompanying the Lord of Jin to the west only in order to comply with the ominous dream of Jin. Would I dare do anything excessive?"

The Grand Masters of Jin paid their respects by kowtowing three times and said, "Lord, you tread on the Earth Deity and bear up August Heaven. August Heaven and the Earth Deity have surely heard your words, my Lord, so we, your flock of subjects, dare to be inspired by them beneath you."

When Lady Mu heard that the Marquis of Jin was about to arrive, she ascended a terrace with Heir Apparent Ying, [her other son] Hong, and her daughter Jianbi, and stood upon a pyre there. She sent an embassy clad in mourning cap and gown to meet [her husband], and then she said, "Heaven Above has sent down catastrophe, causing my two lords to meet each other

Source: Victor H. Mair, Nancy Shatzman Steinhardt, and Paul R. Goldin, eds., *Hawai'i Reader in Traditional Chinese Culture* (Honolulu: University of Hawai'i Press, 2005), 72–76.

without jade and silk, and to be aroused to warfare. If the Lord of Jin enters [the capital] in the morning, I and my children will die in the evening; if he enters in the evening, we will die the next morning. Only my Lord can decide [the hour of my death]!" Thereupon [the Lord of Jin] was lodged in the Spirit Terrace.

. . .

Zisang said, "If we send him home but take his heir apparent hostage, that would be the greatest accomplishment. Jin cannot be annihilated, and to kill their lord would only bring about their hatred. Moreover, Historian Yi once said, 'Do not initiate misfortune; do not await [others'] disorders; do not redouble anger.' Redoubled anger is difficult to bear, and to abuse others is inauspicious." Thereupon they granted peace with Jin.

» Working with Sources

1. **Is this merely a rousing battle story, or does the tale convey a sense of what behavior is proper in the midst of conflict?**
2. **What role does anger play in the narrative? Why?**

SOURCE 4.2 Excerpts from *The Book of Odes (Shijing)*

ca. 2852–481 BCE

Over 300 poems of various lengths were anthologized and transmitted by Confucius in the early fifth century BCE. Philosophers of the Confucian school (see Chapter 9) cherished the Odes and cited them frequently, and they have continued to entrance readers with their naturalistic imagery and personal voices. Only two samples are given here, but this rich tradition of poetry should be sampled at length.

Wild and Windy

Wild and windy was the day;
You looked at me and laughed,
But the jest was cruel, and the
  laughter mocking.
My heart within is sore.

There was a great sandstorm
  that day;
Kindly you made as though
  to come,
Yet neither came nor went away.
Long, long my thoughts.

A great wind and darkness;
Day after day it is dark.
I lie awake, cannot sleep,
And gasp with longing.

Source: Arthur Waley, trans., *The Book of Songs*, edited with additional translations by Joseph R. Allen (New York: Grove, 1996), 27 and 65.

Dreary, dreary the gloom;
The thunder growls.
I lie awake, cannot sleep,
And am destroyed with longing.

I Beg of You, Zhong Zi

I beg of you, Zhong Zi,
Do not climb into our homestead,
Do not break the willows we
have planted.
Not that I mind about the
willows,
But I am afraid of my father
and mother.
Zhong Zi I dearly love;
But of what my father and
mother say
Indeed I am afraid.
I beg of you, Zhong Zi,
Do not climb over the wall,
Do not break the mulberry-trees we
have planted.
Not that I mind about the
mulberry-trees,
But I am afraid of my brothers.
Zhong Zi I dearly love;
But of what my brothers say
Indeed I am afraid.

I beg of you, Zhong Zi,
Do not climb into our garden,
Do not break the hard-wood we
have planted.
Not that I mind about the
hard-wood,
But I am afraid of what people
will say.
Zhong Zi I dearly love;
But of all that people will say
Indeed I am afraid.

Working with Sources

1. **How do the poems deal with the theme of love, whether reciprocated or not?**
2. **What do they suggest about gender relations in ancient China?**

SOURCE 4.3

The Book of Lord Shang (Shangjun Shu)

ca. 338 BCE

This collection of sayings and reports attributed to Lord Shang (d. 338 BCE) may have been compiled by later officials, but its vision of a centralized bureaucracy was emulated at many points in China's turbulent history. The work is composed of 25 or more brief sections, some of which are lost, but the remainder address the necessity of good and competent government.

Source: Sebastian De Grazia, ed., *Masters of Chinese Political Thought: From the Beginnings to the Han Dynasty* (New York: Viking, 1973), 339–343.

The guiding principles of the people are base and they are not consistent in what they value. As the conditions in the world change, different principles are practiced. Therefore it is said that there is a fixed standard in a king's principles. Indeed, a king's principles represent one viewpoint and those of a minister another. The principles each follows are different but are one in both representing a fixed standard. Therefore, it is said: "When the people are stupid, by knowledge one may rise to supremacy; when the world is wise, by force one may rise to supremacy." That means that when people are stupid, there are plenty of strong men but not enough wise, and when the world is wise, there are plenty of clever men, but not enough strong. It is the nature of people, when they have no knowledge, to study, and when they have no strength, to submit.

. . .

A sage-prince understands what is essential in affairs, and therefore in his administration of the people, there is that which is most essential. For the fact that uniformity in the manipulating of rewards and punishments supports moral virtue is connected with human psychology. A sage-prince, by his ruling of men, is certain to win their hearts; consequently he is able to use force. Force produces strength, strength produces prestige, prestige produces virtue, and so virtue has its origin in force, which a sage-prince alone possesses, and therefore he is able to transmit benevolence and righteousness to the empire.

. . .

Of old, the one who could regulate the empire was he who regarded as his first task the regulating of his own people; the one who could conquer a strong enemy was he who regarded as his first task the conquering of his own people. For the way in which the conquering of the people is based upon the regulating of the people, is like the effect of smelting in regard to metal or the work of the potter in regard to clay; if the basis is not solid, then people are like flying birds or like animals. Who can regulate these? The basis of the people is the law. Therefore, a good ruler obstructed the people by means of the law, and so his reputation and his territory flourished.

» Working with Sources

1. **Why does Lord Shang assume there will be an antagonistic relationship between a ruler and the ruled?**
2. **Would he think it preferable for a leader to appear virtuous rather than to actually be virtuous?**

SOURCE 4.4 *The Canon of Shun*

Third millennium BCE?

Shun was thought to be one of the three "sage kings" who ruled China between 2852 and 2205 BCE, after the reign of the "Yellow Emperor." The achievements of these kings are recorded—though the exact dating of each strand of material is controversial—in the *Shujing*, or *Book of History*. The material in the compilation purportedly dates from 2357 to 631 BCE, but, regardless of its precise chronology, the "Canon" attributed to Shun reveals increased sophistication in determining the role and proper behavior of a leader.

1. Examining into antiquity, we find the emperor Shun was called Chong Hua. He corresponded to the former emperor; he was profound, wise, accomplished, and intelligent. He was mild and respectful, and entirely sincere. The report of his mysterious virtue was heard on high, and he was appointed to occupy the imperial Seat.

. . .

9. In five years there was one tour of inspection, and four appearances of the nobles at court. They set forth a report of their government in words. This was clearly tested by their works. They received chariots and robes according to their services.

10. Shun instituted the division of the land into twelve provinces, raising altars upon twelve hills in them. He likewise deepened the rivers.

11. He gave delineations of the statutory punishments, enacting banishment as a mitigation of the five great inflictions, with the whip to be employed in the magistrates' courts, the stick to be employed in schools, and money to be received for redeemable crimes. Inadvertent offenses and those which might be caused by misfortune were to be pardoned, but those who offended presumptuously or repeatedly were to be punished with death. "Let me be reverent; let me be reverent!" he said to himself. "Let compassion rule in punishment!"

. . .

24. The emperor said, "Kui, I appoint you to be Director of music, and to teach our sons, so that the straightforward may yet be mild, the gentle may yet be dignified, the strong not tyrannical, and the impetuous not arrogant. Poetry is the expression of earnest thought; singing is the prolonged utterance of that expression. The notes accompany that utterance, and they are harmonized themselves by the pitch pipes. In this way the eight different kinds of instruments can all be adjusted so that one shall not take from or interfere with another, and spirits and men will thereby be brought into harmony." Kui said, "Oh! I smite the stone; I smite the stone. The various animals lead on one another to dance."

25. The emperor said, "Long, I abominate slanderous speakers, and destroyers of right ways, who agitate and alarm my people. I appoint you to be the minister of Communication. Early and late give forth my orders and report to me, seeing that everything is true."

Source: James Legge, trans., *The Sacred Books of China: The Texts of Confucianism*, vol. 3 (Oxford: Clarendon, 1879), 38, 40–41, and 44–45.

26. The emperor said, "Ah! you, twenty and two men, be reverent, and so shall you aid me in performing the service of heaven."

27. Every three years there was an examination of merits, and after three examinations the undeserving were degraded, and the deserving promoted. By this arrangement the duties of all the departments were fully discharged. The people of San Miao were discriminated and separated.

28. In the thirtieth year of his life, Shun was called to employment. Thirty years he was on the throne with Yao. Fifty years after he went on high and died.

≫ Working with Sources

1. **How important is effective management of subordinates to the career of a king of Shun's stature?**
2. **To which particular voices should a wise king give heed?**

SOURCE 4.5

Iron sword with jade handle, earliest cast-iron object (Western Zhou), from Henan Museum, Guo state, Sanmenxia city

ca. 1046–771 BCE

When this sword was discovered in 1990, it challenged conventional wisdom about when and under what circumstances Chinese people made the first cast-iron object. The dating of the object to the Western Zhou period pushed back the earliest date of this kind of manufacture by over 200 years. The sword consists of an iron blade, a bronze handle core, and a jade handle. Embedded turquoises were also found at the joint of the blade and the handle.

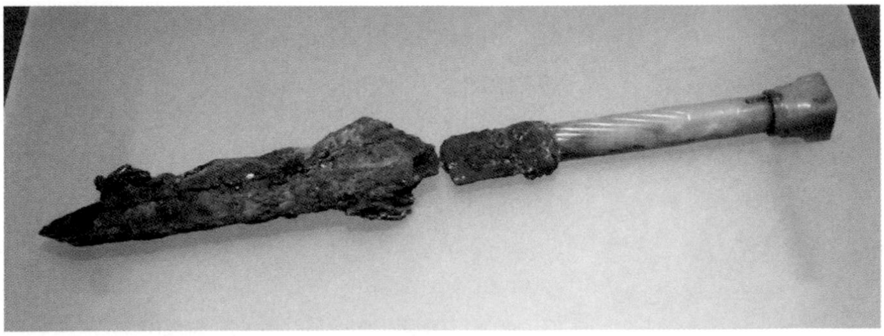

≫ Working with Sources

1. **What does this object suggest about the casting technology and metal-working prowess of workers in the Zhou dynasty?**
2. **Why would a cast-iron sword have been an especially effective weapon in this era?**

Source: Tim Hulsen - OurTravelPics.com.

Chapter 5 **16,000–600 BCE**

Origins Apart: The Americas and Oceania

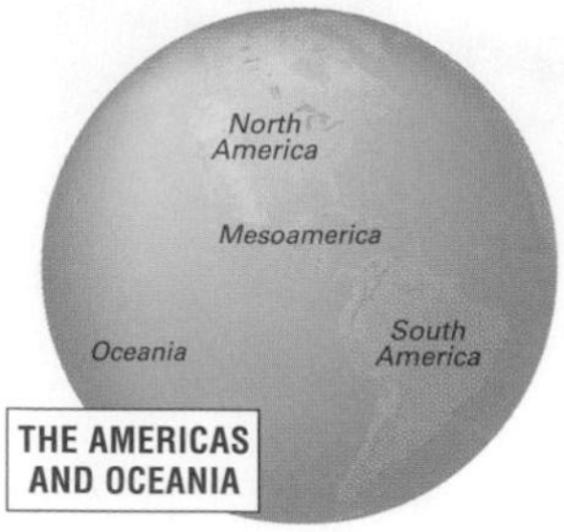

In a dramatically understated press release from the Chicago Field Museum dated April 26, 2001, anthropological archaeologists Ruth Shady Solis, Jonathan Haas, and Winifred Creamer announced a stunning discovery in the archaeology of the Americas. The scientists had just finished conducting **radiocarbon dating** tests on plant fibers taken from site excavations of Caral, in the Supe valley in Peru. Though largely ignored for over a century, the site had recently stirred considerable interest because of its immense size (over 200 acres), monumental architecture—pyramids more than 60 feet high and nearly 500 feet square at the base—and evidence of early urban living. The test results, however, now demanded a complete retelling of the main narrative of the history of civilization in the Americas.

Because earlier evidence pointed toward a relatively late arrival for modern humans in the Americas and given the difficulty of domesticating staple grain plants—corn, for example, it was believed, took some time to be bred into a useful food crop—the earliest known American civilizations had been assumed to be much more recent than their earliest Eurasian and African counterparts—until now, that is. For decades, discoveries in North and South America had strongly suggested that humans had migrated

ABOVE: **Cut from copper, this bird was made by villagers of the early American Hopewell culture (c. 200 BCE–500 CE).**

much earlier than previously thought, calling into question their puzzlingly swift occupation of the continents.

But the Caral-Supe [ka-RALL soo-PAY] results, published in the journal *Science*, put the date of the materials tested at 2627 BCE, making the city as old as the pyramids of Egypt and the most ancient Mesopotamian cities. Indeed, work at nearby sites showed that they had been occupied by substantial villages for far longer, that the entire area was supported by elaborate irrigation works, and that Caral-Supe is only one of 18 similar urban sites in the Supe valley. Clearly, the human urge to create cities, monumental architecture, and religious sites ran deep enough to manifest itself thousands of miles away from other early examples.

The Americas represent a vital counterpoint to the development of agrarian-based cities and states in Eurasia and Africa, which we have discussed in earlier chapters. In some ways, the parallels run very close:

- the role of staple food surplus accumulation
- the development of urban centers as religious and trade centers
- the kinds of buildings—pyramids, for example.

Yet some of the differences in the civilizations provide enticing puzzles. For example, Caral-Supe appears to have been thriving long before ceramics turn up in Peru, an innovation that in all cases *predated* cities in Eurasia and Africa. In addition, although there is some evidence of record keeping by ***quipu***, the much later system of knotted ropes used by the Incas, there is no writing—again, something the major Eurasian civilizations developed. Finally, as with later American civilizations, there is no evidence of the use of the wheel for transportation or mechanical work. Thus, in our search for patterns of world history, the Americas provide an entirely independent test case for examination and analysis.

- In Chapter 1, we examined the "big bang" of world history: the origins of human society in Africa and the first great pattern of human subsistence: foraging.
- In Chapter 2, we learned about the next great pattern of people moving from foraging to farming societies and some of the consequences that change brought.
- In Chapter 3, we explored how this pattern can be replayed and remixed in different ways—in some cases, like that of the Harappans, moving from an urban society back to village farming or foraging.
- In Chapter 4, we learned more about how civilizations become centralized, while at the same time regional powers can challenge the forces of centralization.

In Chapter 5, we will see examples of all of these patterns but conditioned by the key variable of *separation*. How do we explain these similarities and differences appearing in societies separated by thousands of miles of ocean and with no evidence of contact? A vital part of our examination springs from interactions and adaptations.

Seeing Patterns

» What do historians see as the advantages and disadvantages of the separation of the Americas from the societies of Eurasia and Africa?

» The wheel is often cited as the most basic human invention, yet large and sophisticated civilizations were able to flourish without this signal innovation. Why do you think it did not develop in the Americas?

» Why did no cities develop on the larger Pacific Islands?

Quipu: Spanish for Quechua *khipu*; the knots in the strings and the varying distances from each other have supposedly numerical or symbolical meanings.

How did these take place thousands of miles away in the Americas and the islands of the Pacific? (See "Against the Grain.") How do the critical elements of environment and culture play out in such societies separated from the intense direct contact among societies in Eurasia and Africa? How do they alter the patterns we have examined? How much greater or lesser bearing do environment and culture have on the human societies on the thousands of islands of Oceania? How did the peoples interact with each other and adopt or reject certain innovations? Indeed, how "isolated" were the occupants of these islands from each other and the societies of Asia, Australia, and the Americas? Finally, given the importance that we place on interaction and adaptation among peoples, what advantages and disadvantages did such separateness bring?

Chapter Outline

- The Americas: Hunters and Foragers, 16,000–600 BCE
- Agriculture, Villages, and Urban Life
- The Origins of Pacific Island Migrations
- Putting It All Together

The Americas: Hunters and Foragers, 16,000–600 BCE

The remoteness of human beings on the American continents from the larger and more interconnected societies of Eurasia and Africa raises one of the key questions of world history: What would people do in places far removed from other human communities over long periods of time? The initial great migration out of Africa had equipped human beings with an assortment of tools, practices, and habits that collectively created an effective *foraging*—or hunting and gathering—type of society. As we read in Chapter 1, human foragers spread out to populate the earth in Eurasia and Australia, and the coming of humans to the Americas in many ways represented the final stage of their great migration from Africa.

Radiocarbon dating: Sometimes referred to as "carbon dating" or "carbon-14 dating." Carbon 14 is a weak radioactive isotope of the element carbon formed by the interaction of cosmic rays and atmosperhic nitrogen. Plants absorb small doses of it during photosynthesis, and animals acquire it by eating plants or plant-eating animals. When the organism containing carbon 14 dies the isotope begins to decay at a regular rate, and scientists can use this to determine the age of the plant or animal in question. Because of carbon 14's relatively short half-life, its dating accuracy is good to only about 50,000 years.

The advances and retreats of the great ice sheets of the polar region over the last 70,000 years allowed several possible opportunities for humans to migrate from the Eurasian landmass in search of game. Exactly when *Homo sapiens* began to move into these new lands, however, has been a highly controversial question. Though some have speculated that migration might have begun as early as 40,000–30,000 years ago, we now have enough genetic and archaeological evidence to support dates from about 16,000 years ago.

As we saw in Chapter 1, studies published in 2016 have confirmed that the first inhabitants of the Americas appear to have migrated from Siberia to the southern tier of Beringia—the land bridge between Eurasia and North America exposed by the drop in sea levels during the last Ice Age—perhaps 23,000 years ago. Because of a 10,000-year gap in the genetic trail, it is believed that these Beringians stayed in place for millennia, blocked by the ice sheets in Eurasia and North America. Some may have sailed to ice-free areas down the North American coast as suggested by artifacts dated to 14,000-16,000 years ago. With the Alberta split in the North American ice shield, however, the way was open for land migration into the Americas about 13,500 years ago. After this date, the number and range of humans grew rapidly on the two continents, with inhabitants forming small, highly mobile forager bands.

Yet, even at this stage, the migrants had begun to adapt the technology of spears, bows, and other hunting equipment to the big game of the new continent with astonishing swiftness. And as the success of their hunting began to reduce the populations of their favored game, a question arises for world historians: Would they now follow the same patterns by undergoing a Neolithic revolution and developing practices and institutions similar to those of humans in Eurasia and Africa?

It does indeed appear that they did. During the period from about 6000 to 4000 BCE, in what is today Mesoamerica (Mexico and Central America) and the Andes Mountains in South America in Ecuador and Peru, people began to settle in villages. They domesticated squash, beans, corn, and, somewhat later, potatoes and founded the first forms of agrarian society in the Americas. Separated by thousands of miles and vast bodies of water from the peoples of Eurasia and Africa, they were nevertheless traveling independently along the same crucial early pattern of world history: moving from foraging to farming and to settled life—until, ultimately, they too built great cities, states, and empires. As we will see, however, there were also some important differences in their modes of subsistence and technology and the processes involved in the creation of these new societies.

The Environment

Next to Eurasia, the two continents comprising the Americas encompass the largest landmass on earth. From the perspective of Europe, they form the Western Hemisphere—that is, the western "half" of the "sphere" or globe. Located north and south of the equator, the Americas resemble geographical mirror images of each other, with somewhat similar types of landscape and climate, though their shapes differ considerably (see Map 5.1).

The Americas' most prominent geographical feature is a contiguous spine of mountain ranges, or **cordilleras** [cor-dee-YEH-ras], near or along the entire western coast. Known as the Rocky Mountains in the north, these ranges become the Sierra Madre in the center and the Andes in the south. Water from these mountains feeds nearly all river systems on the continents, of which there are eight major ones in the north and four in the south. Both continents also share low mountain systems along their eastern coasts. North and South America meet in Mesoamerica near the equator, with North America then reaching northward to the North Pole and South America extending southward almost to Antarctica. Thus, the climatic zones of both South and North America range from extreme cold to subtropical and tropical warmth.

Cordilleras: A continuous spine of mountain ranges near or along the entire western coast of the Americas.

Geographical Regions North America consists of four main geographical regions:

- The Mountain West
- The Canadian Shield, which stretches from today's Canada to Greenland
- The Great Plains and central lowlands in the center of today's United States
- The Appalachian Mountains in the east and the broad coastal plain along the Atlantic Ocean.

The four regions not only are distinct geographically but also vary considerably in precipitation and temperature. Historically, they have produced widely differing modes of subsistence and society among their inhabitants from the time of the first migrants through much of the history of present-day Canada, the United States, and Mexico, as well as among interior regions of all three countries.

Mesoamerica and South America form six distinct geographical regions:

- The Central American mainland and the Caribbean islands
- The Andes Mountain region along the west coast
- The Guyana Shield, a rocky plateau that separates the Amazon River and basin in the south from the Orinoco River

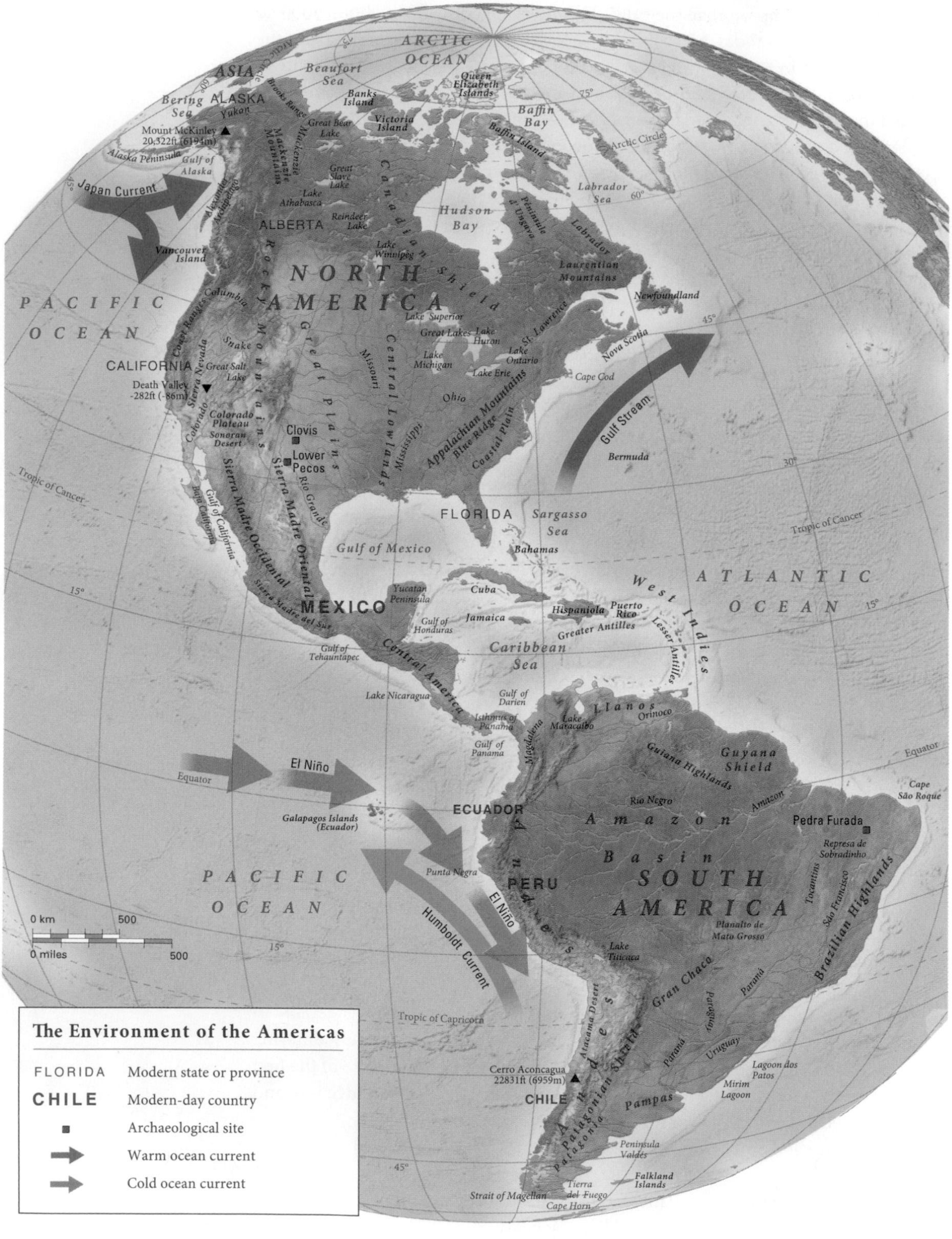

MAP 5.1 The Environment of the Americas.

- The Brazilian Shield, a rocky crust in the east jutting into the South Atlantic Ocean
- The *Gran Chaco* in the east between the Andes and Paraguay River
- The Patagonian Shield, in the center of the continent's southern tip.

Here, the size of the mountains and the extent of the rain forests dictated even greater regional separation than in North America until recent times.

During winters in North America, freezing winds from the Arctic blow south across the Canadian Shield into the central plains, or American Midwest. By contrast, at the southern tip of South America, air currents are predominantly westerly and more moderate and do not push winter frost very far northward. Thus, apart from the southern tip at Cape Horn and Tierra del Fuego—the site of some of the world's most violent seas and frequent storms—snow and frost are mostly limited to the Andes. In North America, winter and summer temperatures vary greatly, except in Florida and southern California, as do precipitation levels, especially in the western half of the continent. Generally, the eastern and midwestern regions of North America receive regular rainfall throughout the year, while the western regions and lower Pacific coast tend to be drier, with occasional droughts, and intermittently subject to massive forest fires started by lightning strikes.

In Mesoamerica, the Caribbean, and the northern two-thirds of South America, temperatures and humidity levels tend to be relatively high. Large steppe and desert areas cover the western third of North America, while in South America deserts and steppes are more limited and mostly found along the northwestern coast and in the interior of the south. Prior to modern times, large forests covered the eastern two-thirds of North America and the northern half of South America.

Ocean Currents, Hurricanes, and El Niño Like the monsoon system that wields so much influence in the agricultural life of India, China, the Indian Ocean, and western Pacific regions, large-scale weather events governed at least in part by the actions of ocean currents and continental weather systems have played historical roles in the Americas. Unlike the monsoon systems, however, their cycles have only recently come to be understood.

Running roughly parallel to the eastern coasts of northern South America and nearly all of North America, the Gulf Stream current of the Atlantic Ocean moves warm water from the South Atlantic along the Eastern Seaboard of the United States before heading northeast toward the European coast. There, it moderates the climate of northern Europe and the British Isles despite their high latitudes. In the Americas, the Gulf Stream's interactions with changing wind patterns in fall and winter in

interactive timeline

The Americas

- **16,000–13,500 BCE** Periods of possible migration to Americas from Eurasia
- **11,000–8000 BCE** Foragers fan out across the Americas
- **4000–3000 BCE** Andean and Mesoamerican agrarian villages
- **ca. 2700 BCE** First American city at Caral-Supe in Peru
- **1200–900 BCE** Olmec city at San Lorenzo on Gulf of Mexico
- **1000–200 BCE** Chavín de Huántar city site in Andes
- **ca. 1000 BCE** Inuit migrations in North America
- **ca. 1000 BCE–100 BCE** Adena villages in North America
- **900–600 BCE** Olmec city at La Venta

Oceania

- **40,000 BCE** First migrations from Taiwan
- **3000 BCE–200 BCE** Lapita cultural complex in western Pacific
- **ca. 500–200 BCE** Splitting off of first Polynesian communities
- **ca. 600 CE** Polynesian settlement of Hawaii

eastern North America frequently result in large storms called "nor'easters," a phenomenon first studied by the American scientist Benjamin Franklin.

More destructive is the frequency with which the Gulf Stream guides hurricanes into the Caribbean Sea and along the North American coast. The immense "heat pump" of the African interior and Sahara Desert continually spawns tropical disturbances in the eastern Atlantic, which gain strength over the warm waters there and the Caribbean as they move westward. Historically, the east–west winds that drive the tropical disturbances played a vital role in fostering the first European voyages to the Western Hemisphere as well as the trans-Atlantic slave trade by making navigation swift and predictable (see Chapters 16 and 19). In the case of hurricanes, however, the storms are often picked up by the Gulf Stream, fed by its warm waters, and directed north from Cuba along the North American coast, where, in modern times, they have caused immense destruction in this heavily populated area.

In the Pacific, the Humboldt and Japan Currents work in a similar fashion, though, in relation to the direction of their waters in the Americas, in reverse. That is, warm waters of the western Pacific and along the Japanese Pacific coast move northward toward the Aleutian Islands and then down the west coast of the Americas. Like the Gulf Stream, this has a considerable moderating effect on climate, particularly from the coast of southern Alaska to northern California, home to much of the world's temperate rain forests. From northern California to Chile, the currents are generally cooler than the surrounding ocean and provide important fish and marine mammal habitats. For millennia, these supplied the peoples of the west coast with sustenance and allowed settled life with a minimum of agriculture.

El Niño: A periodic reversal of the normal flow of currents in the Pacific, greatly altering weather patterns.

The Pacific region is also home to the **El Niño** phenomenon, which, though little understood until recently, plays an immense role in global climatology. In cycles that vary from 3 to 8 years, large areas of abnormally warm water appear off the coasts of Peru and Chile, which lowers barometric pressures there and raises them in the western Pacific. The results tend to vary but usually alter the jet stream patterns and cause abnormal rainfall and storm levels over large areas of the globe, particularly in the Americas. The reverse phenomenon, La Niña, occurs when the oceans in the region have large areas of abnormally cold water.

Human Migrations

One of the most hotly contested debates in modern archaeology is who exactly the first people to appear in the Americas were and where they came from. Part of the debate revolves around the authenticity of sites and the accuracy of techniques used to date them; part of it also arises from legal and political issues of who can claim to be the "first" Americans and have rights to the contents of such sites. As we saw in Chapter 1 and in the preceding discussion, however, the genetic record now suggests that the first Americans came in one migration from Beringia; all are now classified as *Native Americans* (also often called *Amerindians*).

This also, as we have seen, appears to have put to rest the controversy over the origins of Kennewick man, discovered in 1996 on the banks of the Columbia River in Washington State and dated to about 9000 years ago: Once thought to be related to the Ainu of northern Japan, he has been confirmed to be Native American.

Early Foragers One of the ways in which scientists have attempted to track and date the migrations of early Americans is through their hunting technology.

The earliest arrivals hunted with *stabbing spears*—weapons meant to be thrust into an animal's body or thrown from a very short distance. During the period from 11,000 to 8000 BCE, such spears were equipped with a stone point that was grooved, or "fluted," on both sides. These fluted sides allowed the spearhead to be inserted into a groove cut into one end of the spear and fastened there with a leather strip. As in Eurasia and Africa, the size and shape of spearheads and arrowheads provide valuable clues to regional variations in technology and, by tracking these, on migration patterns. In North America, where the spearhead flutes were oval, they are known as "Clovis points," from the town in New Mexico near where scholars identified them for the first time in the 1930s.

Clovis points image analysis

The pervasiveness of Clovis points in the north and a fishtail style of spear flutes in South America had suggested to scholars until very recently that their users were indeed the first migrants to the continents. It was also widely thought that their close dating and specialized use in big-game hunting indicated that these people had settled both continents within a few years of arriving and had, in short order, killed off most of the prehistoric big game such as mammoths, mastodons, and ground sloths. The absence of Clovis points in Eurasia and the presence of less sophisticated points and tools at the newly examined earlier sites (such as Buttermilk Creek in Texas), however, now seem to suggest that the Clovis people had already been here for some time. Indeed, these points might be seen as the first distinctively "American" innovations.

Like their counterparts we examined in Chapters 1 and 2, these early American settlers were hunters and gatherers, or *foragers*. They formed groups of extended families and lived in rock shelters, caves, and huts, moving whenever the food resources in a given territory were exhausted. Once a year, during the summer, extended families met to commemorate a common ancestor by sharing food and performing other rituals. Families held initiation ceremonies for adults, arranged marriages, and exchanged goods such as obsidian, copper, mica (a mineral that flakes off in transparent sheets), and seashells. Most of the time families stayed in their own territory, collecting wild foods such as grass seeds, roots, berries, mushrooms, fruits, and nuts.

As we have seen, the fluted spear points were designed specifically for hunting big game, such as mammoths, moose, and bison. Killing these animals would have required repeated stabbing, for which securely fastened points were necessary. The warming climate, however, favored the expansion of forests and was increasingly unfavorable to the survival of big-mammal species. As big game became scarce, hunters shifted to smaller spear points and smaller game, such as antelope, deer, and rabbit. By about 8000 BCE most big-mammal species were gone from the Americas.

Toward Settlements As larger game became increasingly scarce, people in coastal areas began relying more on fish and shellfish, and those in inland regions increased their collection of wild seeds and nuts. Hunters developed the spear thrower, a device for hurling smaller spears from a greater distance at elusive small animals. Obsidian, recovered from volcanic regions and traded over long distances, became the preferred material for spear points. Following a pattern similar to that of their distant relatives in Eurasia and Africa, humans in the Americas learned to grind, groove, and polish stone to make axes, mortars, pestles, and grindstones. Bone became an important material for spears, fishhooks, awls, needles, combs, and spatulas. Humans continued to live in rock shelters and caves, but also increasingly constructed huts made of poles and covered with skins or even more permanent

Midden: A refuse pile; archaeologists treasure such piles because a great deal can be learned about the material culture of a society by what the people threw out over long periods of time.

wooden structures. These more permanent dwelling places appeared especially along the seacoasts, the Great Lakes, and large rivers, where there were plentiful resources of fish, shellfish, and waterfowl. The first domesticated animal, the dog, appeared, perhaps descended from the wolves picking through human **middens** or perhaps accompanying hunters migrating to the new continents. As bands of hunters and gatherers acquired more household goods, they became less inclined to move about over large distances. As in Eurasia and Africa, they increasingly tended to stay close to favored long-term food sources and centers of ceremonial life.

Early Ceremonial Life As did their contemporaries in north China, more sedentary foragers began to bury their dead in cemeteries, which soon became territorial centers. Hunter–gatherers in the Americas, like those on the other continents, buried their dead with gifts of ochre, symbolizing the color of life, and tools to help them in the life after death. Leaders of forager bands were often *shamans,* elders with spiritual powers that enabled them to deal with the forces of nature. By donning animal masks, playing music on flutes and drums, and engaging in ritual dance, shamans fell into ecstatic trances. During these trances they experienced themselves merging with powerful animals or other people, charming animals into submission, exorcising evils from humans, or healing afflictions. Leaders worked together with elders, forming councils for the administration of their settlements and hunting grounds.

Shaman-led ceremonies often took place in caves or overhangs, where people painted animals and humans on the rock walls. Probably the oldest paintings are those of Pedra Furada [PAY-drah Foo-RAH-dah] in northeastern Brazil, dating to about 8000 BCE. One of the most distinctive paintings in the ceremonial vein is that of the so-called white shaman at Lower Pecos in Texas, dating to 2000 BCE. He is shown in a trance, leaving his body behind. His feet are feline, his arms are feathered, and he is surrounded during his spiritual journey by animals and humans, both dead (upside down) and alive (upright). Foragers possessed a complex culture, ranging from sophisticated gathering and hunting techniques and settlements ordered by elders to shamanic religious ceremonies.

The White Shaman, Lower Pecos, Texas, ca. 2000 BCE. The practice of *shamanism*—the belief in the ability of certain individuals to communicate with spirits or inhabit the spirits of people or animals—appears to be a common feature of many widely diverse peoples. Many scholars believe that migrants from Asia carried these religious forms with them to the Americas because of their resemblance to practices among peoples in Siberia and other areas in northern Eurasia.

Agriculture, Villages, and Urban Life

As we have seen in the preceding chapters, far-reaching changes accompanied human societies that made the transition from foraging to agriculture—from hunting and gathering to relying principally on domesticated plants and animals. The first major change we see associated with this momentous pattern is the ability to maintain large populations: to sustain villages, towns, and cities, developing increasingly complex societies with ever more diverse intellectual, cultural, and religious spheres. The second change is the opposite side of the coin: the creation of the potential for conflict and destruction on an unprecedented scale. Both of these changes grow from the Neolithic revolution (see Chapter 2). In the Americas, however, this grand pattern of world history appears to have begun somewhat later than in many areas of Eurasia and Africa.

The Neolithic Revolution in the Americas

The most noteworthy first steps toward agriculture took place in central and southern Mexico in Mesoamerica and Ecuador and Peru in the Andes. Temperatures in these regions turned warmer after about 4000 BCE. Foragers shortened their annual migrations and extended existing patches of wild bean and **teosinte,** [tay-oh-SIN-tay] (a wild grass precursor of maize [corn]) through purposeful planting. Careful harvesting and replanting, probably with obsidian-spiked sickles, led to early domesticated varieties of these plants, increasingly bearing larger kernels. Beans were domesticated first in Peru, and maize followed somewhat later in southern Mexico. By about 3000 BCE, foragers in these regions had completed their transformation into farmers (see "Patterns Up Close").

Teosinte: A wild grass native to Mesoamerica, believed to be ancestral to maize (corn).

Early Domestication of Plants and Animals Humans in Mesoamerica and the Andes exchanged their domesticated species of beans and corn within their regions and began trading other domesticated staples as well. In Mesoamerica these included squash, manioc (a root), avocado, and chili pepper; in the Andes, quinoa (a seed), amaranth (an herb), potatoes, tomatoes, and cotton. In time, these plants spread via trade throughout both regions wherever the climate and soil would support them.

The domestication of animals in the Americas, however, was more modest than that of plants. Unlike in Eurasia and Africa, the majority of large mammals had died out after the last Ice Age, with the result that no draft, pack, or riding animals of sufficient size were left to be domesticated (see Figure 5.1). The Americas thus had no

Pedra Furada, Toca do Boqueirão da Pedra Furada, Serra da Capivara National Park, Piauí, Brazil. The image in this cave (*toca*) in northeastern Brazil, dated to ca. 10,000–4000 BCE, shows crocodiles, llamas, deer, and a puma. Using carbon-14 and thermo-luminescence dating in 2003, archaeologists established the date of 58,000 BCE for hearth fire in Pedra Furada—a date considerably earlier than the currently accepted time for the arrival of humans in the Americas. North American archaeologists have been so far unable to refute either the date or the hearth fire theory, although skepticism remains.

horses or cattle until they were brought by the Spanish in the sixteenth century CE as part of the so-called Columbian exchange of plants, animals, and diseases traveling in both directions. The development of the wheel, so intimately connected with draft animals, with its nearly infinite uses on plows, chariots, carts, and other conveyances, never took place in the Americas, though some of the world's best roads were built through the Andes. The only animals suitable for domestication—besides the dog—were the llama and alpaca (both relations of the camel), guinea pig (a rodent), Muscovy duck, turkey, and honeybee. The llama, whose capacity is limited to carrying about 60 pounds for 12 miles per day, was the only animal in pre-Columbian America to provide even modest transportation services. The wool of the alpaca, together with cotton, became an important textile fiber in the Andes. In the relative absence of domesticated animals raised for meat, hunting and fishing remained important methods of obtaining food (see Figure 5.1).

Early Settlements Early agricultural settlements ranged in size from a few extended families to as many as 1,000 inhabitants. As in Neolithic China, the typical dwelling was a round, dome-shaped, wooden house with a sunken floor, stone foundation, and thatched roof. As in southwest Asia, some early American agrarian peoples mummified their dead by salting or smoking them before burial. Others buried their dead in midden piles on the outskirts of their villages or in the sand dunes along the beaches. Funerary gifts were modest, usually consisting only of the cotton clothes worn during life and a red mat—symbolizing the blood of life—wrapped around the body. In contrast to more transient hunter–gatherer settlements, agrarian villages became settled communities of the living and the dead.

Between 3000 and 2000 BCE, villagers in the lowlands along the Andes coast of Peru built rafts of balsa wood, which enabled them to fish farther from shore. They also pioneered the use of irrigation in the dozens of river deltas along the coast. With crop yields boosted by irrigation, the population of the villages increased to 2,000 or 3,000 inhabitants, and the first signs of social stratification and distinctions in wealth appeared. Scholars have speculated that upstream families had more water and thus accumulated greater food reserves than downstream families. Under the leadership of upstream elders, inhabitants of several villages pooled their labor and built monumental plazas, platforms, and terraces in central locations in their settlements.

As had other societies making the agrarian transition, Mesoamerican and Andean societies also began producing pottery, which was used in the preparation and preservation of food. The earliest known pottery dates to about 3300–3200 BCE on the northern Andean coast; by 1800 BCE pottery making had spread throughout central and southern Mexico. Cotton textiles dating to about 3000 BCE have been found along the coasts of Ecuador and Peru. Richly colored pieces of cloth served as skirts and overcoats. Condors with outstretched wings, double-headed snakes, felines, and human figures were typical motifs on the textiles.

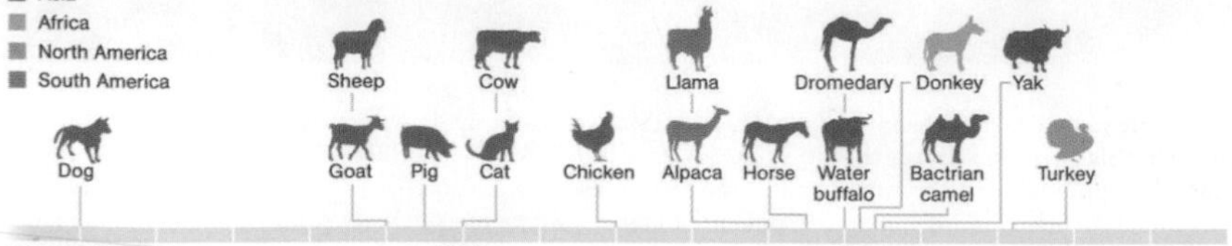

Figure 5.1 Comparative Timeline for Domestication of Animals.

The Origins of Urban Life

As we saw in the opening vignette to this chapter, in 1994, archaeologists began excavating the ruins of a large, planned city covering over 200 acres at Caral in the Supe River valley in Peru. Caral-Supe was one of at least 18 sites of a culture that flourished in the valleys descending from the Andes to the coast. Researchers were stunned at the monumental stone architecture that included what appeared to be pyramid-shaped temples, plazas, a wide variety of dwellings of different sizes, and, perhaps most intriguing of all, a large amphitheater. As important as the initial survey of the site turned out to be, its significance grew further in 2001 when carbon dating revealed the artifacts at the site to be from 2627 BCE, making this by far the oldest city in the Americas and contemporary with the early Mesopotamian cities and the Great Pyramid of Egypt. As Jonathan Haas, one of the scientists involved in the dating, noted, "This is a project that comes along once in a generation and offers opportunities rarely glimpsed in the field of archaeology."

Caral-Supe Scholars now theorize that this city, like the similarly mysterious sites along the Indus, was part of a fairly large civilization supported by intensive agriculture and fishing, with extensive trading networks and an incipient class system. They have linked the Caral-Supe culture to the ruins at Aspero, on the Peruvian coast, which contain similar pyramids but had been previously covered by centuries of trash heaps. The varied climate, ranging from the coast through lowland plains and river valleys up to mountain highlands, produced pumpkins, squash, sweet potatoes, corn, chilies, beans, and cotton, while the rivers and sea yielded a variety of edible aquatic life. The agriculture of the valley was supported by a highly complex and sophisticated irrigation system utilizing mountain runoff and directing water to individual plots (see Map 5.2).

MAP 5.2 **Early Urban Centers in the Andes.**

Patterns Up Close | The Origin of Corn

We have no idea who the originators of corn were nor exactly where they might have lived nor even exactly when the momentous event took place. We do not know whether the idea occurred to a number of people simultaneously or to one lone experimenter. We assume, given the unprepossessing nature of the plant in question, the *teosinte* grass, that it did not suggest itself as a productive food crop, or even as edible, for quite some time. Yet, when these first bold people began to cultivate it, they were unknowingly taking part in one of the most momentous revolutions in world history: a completely independent chapter in the transition from foraging to agriculture and, ultimately, to agrarian-based urban civilization. The ultimate result of their work, maize, or corn, became the staple of the great Mesoamerican civilizations, sustained the early peoples of North America, and ultimately became the world's most versatile and widely grown food crop (see Map 5.3). Indeed, ancient Mayans believed that humans themselves were made from corn.

Various Types of Corn.

The site where we believe the event took place, somewhere in what is now southern Mexico, may have been inhabited by human beings for as few as 7,000 or 8,000 years. And it was here, perhaps 6,000–7,000 years ago, that they began the process of cultivating this unpromising grass into the grain that would eventually sustain vast numbers of people. Yet, to this day, plant geneticists are still not in agreement as to how this transition took place.

It was long assumed that *teosinte* was the sole ancestor of corn and that the process was one of painstaking selection and replanting. That is, people would inspect a group of plants and search for the ones with the largest and most numerous kernels and then plant them and repeat the process over many generations, hoping over time to select for those desirable qualities. Given the *teosinte* limit of eight rows of tiny seeds, it was assumed this process would take hundreds, perhaps thousands, of years. Yet the short time between the known dates of early corn cultivation and the rise of corn-supported societies suggests that the transition was much faster. Because of this, scientists have recently theorized that corn is in fact the result of crossbreeding more than one genus of plants.

Farmers were the largest social class, with merchants, administrators, and priests also in evidence, though it is not clear at this point exactly what constituted the hierarchy. Widely varying sizes of houses suggest disparities of wealth, and the proximity of some of the houses to pyramids seems to indicate a religious or bureaucratic connection, but the exact nature of these remains the subject of speculation. Similarly, the uses to which the amphitheater was put can only be guessed, though pictures of musicians suggest that they were an important part of festivals held there.

Perhaps the most intriguing artifact of all is an intact quipu, a device of elaborate knotted ropes tied together in patterns that form a coded system of communication,

The most promising results so far were presented by plant geneticist Mary Eubanks in 2004, who attempted to experimentally trace the origins of corn. Her experiments showed convincingly that *teosinte* was, in fact, an ancestor plant of modern corn but that it had at some point been bred with *gama grass*, which contains key genes for multiplying and enlarging the kernels on each ear. Moreover, her work supported the work of other recent research that suggested that the plant had developed very rapidly into a usable staple, perhaps in less than a century.

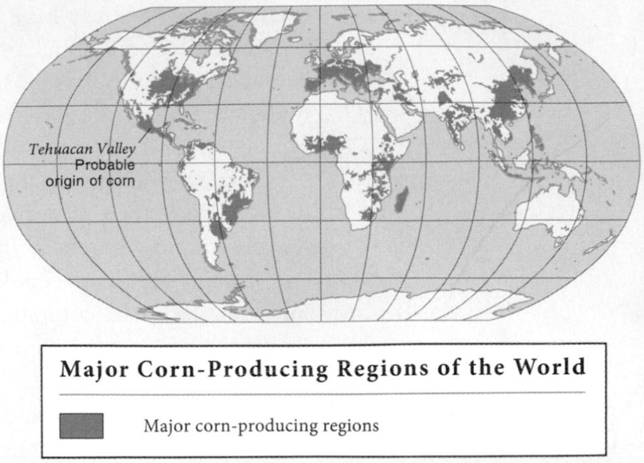

MAP 5.3 Major Corn-Producing Regions of the World.

We have to assume that this momentous feat was accomplished by plan and experimentation, given its complexity. The result was one that permanently altered the agricultural patterns of world history, particularly over the last 300 years. Corn's versatility allows it to be cultivated on every habitable continent; in dry or moist, hot or cool climates; and often on land too marginal to support any other staple crop. And corn combined with beans provides essential amino acids, which in turn negates the need for domesticated animals as a source of protein. It is widely used as human and animal food and helped to sustain population expansions in North America, Asia, and Europe. It spawned huge industries in such modern foodstuffs as corn syrup and oil and older ones like whiskey and beer. Most recently, and controversially, it has been touted as a biofuel. In short, this American innovation's uses are still unfolding as we wrestle with the problems of population, land use, and energy consumption.

Questions

- Why is the innovation of corn a "momentous revolution in world history"?
- How does the fact that this example of bioengineering occurred 6,000–7,000 years ago put today's debate on genetically modified foods into a new perspective?

a kind of writing system by means of knots. Since the quipu was also used by the Incas over 4,000 years later, it represents not only a direct connection between these two societies but one of the world's first, and oldest, systems of record keeping in continuous use.

Other Andean Cultures Of smaller scale and a somewhat later period are the structures at El Paraíso, Peru, which date from about 2000 BCE. To construct these monuments, villagers built large rectangles of locally quarried rock and mud mortar. They filled the interior of the rectangle with rock rubble encased in large mesh bags, which may have been used to measure the amount of labor each villager contributed. Multichambered and multistoried buildings made of stone occupied some of the platforms. Steep staircases led from the lower plazas up to these buildings, which were plastered and painted in primary colors. Wooden beams supported the roofs.

Charcoal-filled pits in the building chambers indicate that some form of sacrifice took place there. The chambers were small, allowing access to no more than a few prominent villagers or shamans. The rest of the villagers assembled on upper and lower platforms, according to their social status, to participate in religious functions and share communal feasts. Early sculptures dating to 1519 BCE depict ancestral warriors and suggest that villagers might also have come together for military displays.

Farmers in the Andean highlands also built ceremonial centers in their villages. As in the lowlands, these centers contained fire pits for sacrificial offerings. The buildings were much smaller, however, with only one or two chambers, and stood on modest platforms. Highlanders, in addition to farming, engaged in long-distance trade, exchanging obsidian and cotton from the highlands for lowland pottery. Sometime around 1500 BCE, highlanders developed skills in metallurgy (perhaps including smelting), thus laying the foundation for the development of exquisitely crafted metalwork, including copper, gold, and silver.

Chavín de Huántar While our understanding of the early Caral-Supe culture is still in its infancy, more extensive work on the later small highland city of Chavín de Huántar [Cha-VIN de Oo-WAN-tar] (ca. 1000–200 BCE) has yielded important insights into Andean cultural patterns. Situated in a valley high in the Andes Mountains on both banks of a tributary to the Marañón River, the modern town was dominated by a bridge, which was destroyed in a landslide in 1945. A 3-day journey from both coast and rain forest and at an elevation of 10,000 feet, Chavín carried on an organized long-distance trade, built and graded roads, protected them with retaining walls, and cleared a number of mountain paths to facilitate travel. Residents of Chavín imported obsidian, used in the making of sharp tools, and metals and exported textiles, pottery, and gold and silver artifacts.

Early Chavín was a small place of some 300 inhabitants, most of whom—including priest-rulers and craftspeople—were detached from agriculture. Another 700 full-time farmers and herders lived in outlying hamlets. Farmers grew potatoes, quinoa, and some corn on the slopes and valley floor, supplementing the rainfall with irrigation. Corn was used not only for making bread but also for brewing a type of beer, called *chicha*. On the higher grasslands, herders bred llamas and alpacas. The dried meat and wool of these animals contributed substantially to the village economy, as did the llamas' role as pack animals.

Chavín's ceremonial center consisted of U-shaped ramparts built on a plaza and lined with walls of cut and polished stone. The walls enclosed several partially interconnected underground complexes. Within the U was a round, sunken court accessible via staircase. A cross-shaped, centrally located chamber contained what is assumed to have been the center's main deity, a stone sculpture of a fanged, snarling feline creature, standing upright like a human, with one clawed paw extended upward and the other hanging down. The sculpture might have had a shamanic significance, symbolizing the priest's ability to assume or tame the powers of a wild animal.

Other underground chambers were used for sacrificial offerings. Remnants of pottery once filled with the meat and bones of animals—as well as human bones—found in these chambers suggest animal and human sacrifices. An elaborate system of canals guided water through the underground chambers. Priest-rulers and the assembled villagers used the temple complex to offer sacrifices, observe open-air rituals, celebrate feasts, dance, and perform music.

By around 500 BCE, the population had grown to about 3,000 inhabitants. Artisans living in the town began to specialize in particular crafts. Craftspeople living in one section of town made beads and pendants from seashells; artisans in another section fabricated stone tools; and a third section of the town housed those who made leather goods. Whether these craftspeople had given up agricultural labor completely is not known. Homes for the wealthy were built of stone, while the less well-off lived in houses made of adobe. The rich dined on the meat of young llamas; poorer residents subsisted on the meat of decommissioned pack animals. Around the town, there must have been a number of villages with farmers producing enough food to feed the urban dwellers.

The increased population meant larger assemblies, which in turn required bigger platforms and a larger temple for more sacrifices. Laborers added a square, sunken court, a feature common to many Andean and Mesoamerican cities, and additional underground chambers, mostly for storage. By 400 BCE, Chavín had become the culturally dominant center of the region. Large numbers of travelers, traders, and pilgrims from the coast and rain forest visited the temple. Travelers made offerings of seashells, coca leaves, and textiles to the priests in return for receiving temple blessings, presumably for their health, welfare, and safe return. Residents of Chavín provided services for the visitors, such as lodging and meals. Craftspeople produced clothing, wall hangings, banners, and pottery in what were identifiable Chavín patterns, motifs, and styles. Archaeologists have found Chavín artifacts as far away as 350 miles.

Inhabitants of Chavín pioneered new techniques in the making of textiles and in metallurgy. Textile makers combined the wool from llamas with cotton to create a new blended cloth. They decorated it using new methods of dyeing and painting adapted to wool fibers. Goldsmiths devised new methods of soldering and alloying gold and silver to make large ornamental objects. Small objects, such as golden headbands, ear spools, beads, and pins, signified prestige and wealth. Gold artifacts found in the graves of the wealthy thus attest to the high value residents of Chavín appear to have placed on gold.

Chavín came to a gradual end, perhaps declining as other centers began producing equivalent pottery, textiles, and gold jewelry, and competing in trade. In any

Chavín de Huántar, New Temple. Chavín is one of the best-studied sites and over the years has yielded considerable information about town and small-city life in the ancient Americas.

event, sometime after 500 BCE, archaeologists note a decisive trend toward militarization, with the emergence of fortified villages and forts. Possibly, the people of Chavín ultimately fell victim to a military attack. Sometime around 200 BCE, it appears that squatters invaded the largely deserted city, which subsequently fell into ruin.

The First Mesoamerican Settlements

In Mesoamerica, the first permanent villages appear to date from around 1800 BCE. The first ceremonial centers, the collaborative work of farmers from several villages, appeared along the Pacific coast of southern Mexico and Guatemala around 1500 BCE. As in the Andes, the ceremonial centers consisted of plazas, platforms, and terraces. Metallurgy, however, did not develop here for another millennium, and instead craftspeople used jade for ornaments. (The Spanish believed that this green, translucent gemstone was useful in the treatment of kidney stones.) By around 1200 BCE, agrarian society throughout the Andes and Mesoamerica was characterized by ceremonial centers centrally located among several villages, monumental structures of plazas and platforms, and an emerging craftsmanship in the production of sacred ornaments.

The Olmec The first important Mesoamerican center was that of the Olmecs at San Lorenzo (1200–900 BCE), located on the Gulf of Mexico in hot, humid, and forested coastal lowlands. The name "Olmec" means "rubber people" in the language of the later Aztecs and refers to the rubber-tree farming for which the area was later known. Farmers in these lowlands had to cut down the dense tropical rain forest with stone axes and burn it before they could plant corn. Once the riverbanks had been cleared, the silt deposited by floods during the rainy season and the rich soil created favorable agricultural conditions. As in Mesopotamia, Egypt, India, and China, the rivers here proved marvelously productive. It is estimated that farmers harvested as much as 3,200 pounds of corn per acre from the riverbanks, a yield twice as plentiful as that in the villages of the Mexican valleys and highlands to the west. The high yield allowed for the rise of wealthy ruling families, who assumed a dominant position over small farmers (see Map 5.4).

Olmec Jade Mask. Like the Chinese, Mesoamerican peoples appear to have worked jade from very ancient times.

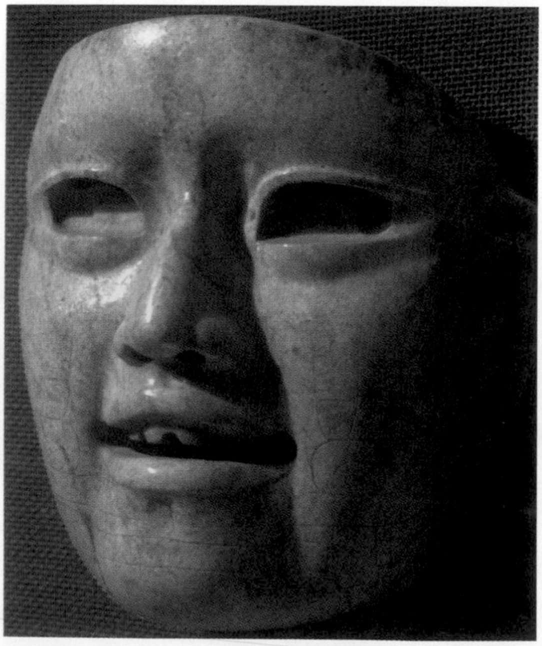

The ceremonial center of San Lorenzo was located on a plateau overlooking the surrounding rain forest, villages, and fields. On this plateau, archaeologists have so far unearthed some 60 terraced platforms, 20 ponds, countless basalt-lined drainage troughs, and the foundations of dwellings for 1,000 inhabitants. These dwellings were arranged around small family plazas. Among the household goods found in the dwellings were grindstones for preparing corn and tools for making beads and ear ornaments. The dense concentration of dwellings suggests that San Lorenzo was an urban center, inhabited by priests, administrators, and craftspeople. Based on estimates of crop yields in the area and the number of dwellings at the site, scholars believe that this center was surrounded by some 10,000 small farmers dispersed in outlying villages and hamlets and producing the surplus food needed to feed the urban center.

The priest-rulers of San Lorenzo engaged thousands of farmers as laborers to construct the plateau and its terraced platforms. Laborers quarried blocks of basalt from a mountain range 70 miles to the northwest of San Lorenzo. Large groups of workers shouldered beams from which the basalt blocks, weighing 18 tons on average, hung in slings. They carried these blocks to the coast and shipped them to San Lorenzo on rafts. There, sculptors fashioned the blocks into fierce-looking, helmeted heads, kneeling or sitting figures, and animal statues.

MAP 5.4 Olmec Civilization.

It is unknown whether these figures represented priest-rulers, gods, or divine beings. Olmec priest-rulers also commissioned sculptors to craft figurines and masks of clay. Other craftspeople made figurines from jade and serpentine. One jade figurine is that of a jaguar with a human body representing perhaps the rain god. Like the legendary *werewolf*—a human being who is transformed into a wolf when the moon is full—scholars have speculated that these figures might be *were-jaguars*. That is, the figurine might indicate rituals in which priests possessed shamanic powers shared with jaguars and other wild animals. Since jade and serpentine could be obtained only from areas some 200 miles away, San Lorenzo appears not to have been an isolated urban center with surrounding villages but a place with far-reaching trade connections.

La Venta Around 900 BCE, a mysterious event took place that destroyed San Lorenzo. Perhaps a religious calendar cycle was completed and a ruler ordered the destruction of the urban center. Perhaps there was an internal uprising, with farmers protesting their oppression by the ruling priests and administrators and then offering ritual atonement. Whatever occurred, the event left San Lorenzo's large stone sculptures mutilated and buried in carefully prepared graves, along with the sculptors' tools used in creating the images.

Following the fall of San Lorenzo, La Venta, 50 miles to the northeast, became the leading Olmec center. The first settlers at La Venta cleared the rain forest from a ridge on a swampy river island in the lowlands and then, like the Harappans on the Indus, graded the ridge to create a plateau. On the plateau they erected terraced platforms and a fluted, 100-foot-high earthen mound to establish an urban center. Burial sites at La Venta contained axes and figurines made of serpentine and jade as well as concave mirrors ground from hematite and other iron-bearing ores. Rulers' regalia included mirrors worn on the chest, but what significance these might have had is unknown.

Three of the burial sites at La Venta each contained 485 pieces of serpentine carefully arranged to form a stylized jaguar face. Only two sites contained human remains, as the extremely acid soil of La Venta dissolved most human bones. The burial gifts in the site included ochre, figurines, beads, ear ornaments, and awls made of jade. About 600 BCE La Venta ended under circumstances as mysterious as those that destroyed San Lorenzo. The next Olmec center was at Tres Zapotes, a more modest complex 70 miles to the northwest. Tres Zapotes endured from about 500 to 1 BCE, when it was eclipsed by new ceremonial centers in the highlands west of the Olmec lowlands.

Through their long-distance trade, the Olmecs left a strong cultural imprint throughout Mesoamerica. Olmec traders, probably accompanied by armed escorts, obtained the obsidian needed for making stone-sculpting tools in Guatemala and jade from mines south of the Mexican Basin and in Guatemala and Costa Rica. In exchange for these raw materials, the Olmecs exported cacao beans (from which chocolate is obtained), pottery, textiles, and jewelry. Along their trade routes, the Olmecs maintained settler outposts to supply the traders, mostly westward toward the Valley of Mexico, to which they exported their artistic styles.

Olmec Writing In 2006 an announcement came that, like the work at Caral-Supe, redefined the archaeology of the Americas. Scientists at Cascajal in Veracruz, Mexico, found a large stone with what is currently believed to be Olmec writing on it. Dating to somewhere between 1100 and 900 BCE, it appears to be the oldest writing in the Americas. Moreover, it is unlike any of the later scripts of the Mayas or Aztecs and thus seems to have died out as a system with the decline of the Olmecs.

Like Egyptian hieroglyphics and Chinese Shang-era scripts, the Olmec characters contain stylized representations of objects like fish, insects, and plants, but there are also some that seem to have a phonetic component. Unfortunately, the number of symbols contained on the Cascajal stone and a stone roller stamp dating from a few centuries later is simply too small to be deciphered. With the accumulation of other samples in the future it is hoped that the fragments of an Olmec literature may ultimately come to light. In the meantime, like the Linear A script of the Minoans and the seal figures of the Harappans, the Olmec figures present scholars with an important challenge in decoding the past.

Foraging and Farming Societies Outside the Andes and Mesoamerica

After 2000 BCE, many foragers in the forests, deserts, and tundras in North and South America had adopted agriculture as a full or partial mode of subsistence. While most societies in the Andes and Mesoamerica had become fully agrarian by around 2000 BCE, foraging groups in the places already mentioned continued to persist—in some places down to the present. Using stone tools, they hunted in the extreme north, slowly cleared some of the forests that covered the entire east and Midwest of North America, irrigated and farmed arid areas of the southwest, and foraged and farmed in the Amazon Basin of South America.

The Inuit The Inuit [INN-ooh-it] from Siberia arrived in the far northern tundra of North America around 2000 BCE. For a long period the Inuit remained traditional hunter–gatherers, hunting mammals on land and fish in the rivers and sea. Much later, during the first millennium CE, they began hunting whales. As many as 20 sailors with paddles manned a boat built of walrus ribs and skin. In the summer, boats sailed the coastal seas for weeks at a time. When sailors spotted a bowhead whale, they shot a toggling harpoon into the animal. The head of the harpoon detached, burrowing into the skin of the animal. After many more harpoon shots and a long struggle, sailors killed the whale, hauled it ashore, and stored the fat and meat in ice. A whale carcass could feed a hamlet for an entire winter.

The Inuit lived in pit houses framed by whale ribs, covered with walrus skin, and piled over with sod. The entrances were long, dipped tunnels that trapped the cold air below the floor of the house. On winter hunts for seals and walruses, people built snow houses, or *igloos*, from ice blocks. During the summer, the Inuit moved from the often waterlogged pit houses to tents. Women were expert seamstresses, using caribou sinew and seal and caribou pelts to make warm and watertight pants, parkas, and boots. For transportation on snow and ice, the Inuit used dog teams to pull sleds made with bone runners. They traded mammal teeth and carved bone artifacts for timber and earthenware from the south. By 1000 CE the Inuit had expanded from the North American Arctic eastward, eventually reaching Greenland, where the Norse from Scandinavia had established their first settlement in 982 CE.

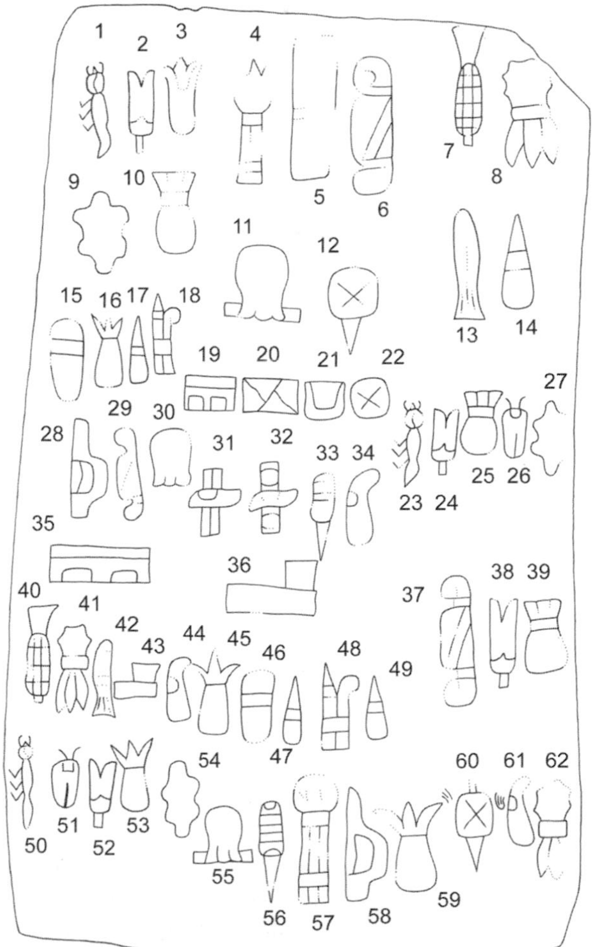

Cascajal Block. Currently the oldest example of writing found in the Americas, this sample was created by the Olmecs in the early first millennium BCE. Notice the stylized renderings of objects and placement horizontally, rather than vertically. What kinds of things do they suggest to you?

Adena and Hopewell Agricultural villages appeared in the cleared forest areas of North America by the first millennium BCE. Village inhabitants planted sunflower, goosefoot, sumpweed, and corn. The villagers of the Adena (1000–100 BCE) and Hopewell cultures (200 BCE–500 CE) pooled their labor to build ridges and mounds used in ceremonies and rituals. The phenomenon of mound building, a practice with very ancient roots, seems to have been widespread among peoples living in the east and Midwest of North America. A small mound covering a child's grave found in Labrador is estimated to be some 7,500 years old. Others, much larger and more recent (about 4,500 years old), have been found in the lower Mississippi valley; some of these mounds are more than 20 feet high. In the case of the earthworks at Hopewell, large square and circular enclosures contained multiple mounds, tens of feet high, encompassing dozens of acres of land. Research from the mid-1990s suggests that some of the Hopewell settlements were also connected by roads up to 60 miles long, perhaps serving communal purposes such as official visits and gift exchanges (see Map 5.5).

Amazonian Peoples In the floodplains of the Amazonian rain forest in South America,

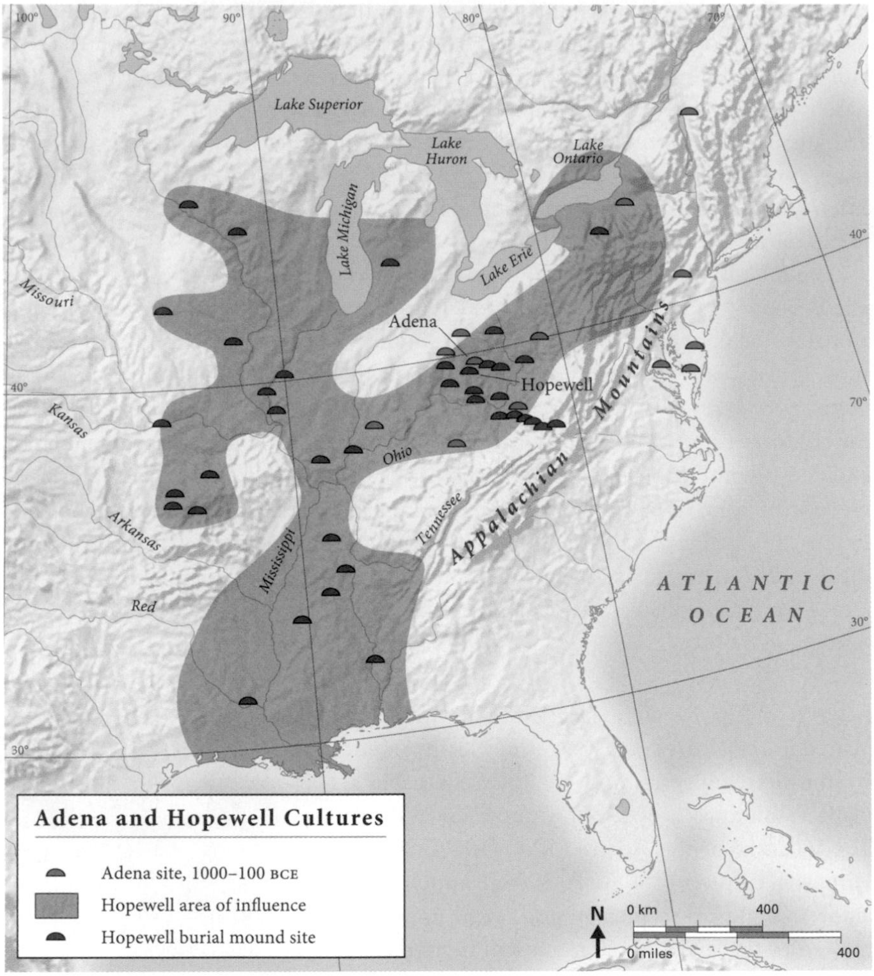

MAP 5.5 **Adena and Hopewell Cultures.**

agricultural villages also date to the first millennium BCE. The best-explored culture is that of Marajó, on a large island in the mouth of the Amazon. At its height in ca. 500 BCE, the Marajó built large funeral mounds 30 feet high and 750 feet long. Depending on their social status, the dead were buried with modest grave gifts or in richly painted, jewelry-filled urns. The cultures of the flood plains in the upper Amazon drainage are still largely unexplored. For example, at an unknown date, the people of the Baures culture in today's Bolivia established a large hydraulic complex of canals, raised fields, moat-enclosed villages with sacred precincts, and causeways connecting the villages. The complexity of this culture left a strong impression on the Spanish missionaries who visited the area in the sixteenth century CE.

The Islands of the Caribbean The earliest hunter–gatherer settlements in the rain forests of the Caribbean islands date to the fourth millennium BCE, but from where on the mainland these first settlers came is unknown. The first agricultural settlements appeared between 500 BCE and 500 CE, when migrants from the rain forests along the Orinoco River in the northeast of South America colonized the eastern Caribbean as far west as Hispaniola (today's Dominican Republic and Haiti). These people built villages and terraces on which they grew manioc. Their ceramics are in the shape of, or painted to display, a variety of animals, such as frogs, bats, and turtles, indicative of a shamanic religion. Beginning in eastern Hispaniola around 500 CE, villagers supported the emergence of the Taíno [Ta-EE-no] chieftain society that by ca. 1500 comprised nearly the entire Caribbean. Influenced by Mayan culture (see Chapter 6), some Taíno chiefs built ball courts and causeways. In their villages, the chiefs employed specialized craftspeople for the production of ceramics and cotton textiles, as well as stone and wood carvings. Sailors using canoes traveled extensively to the mainland and among the islands in search of salt, jade, and metals. These travels connected the Taíno chiefdom society with Mesoamerican societies on the mainland.

The Origins of Pacific Island Migrations

If the early societies of the Americas show how the great patterns of world history can achieve striking variations in separation from other groups, the peopling of the thousands of islands of Oceania may be seen as an extreme case of the interaction of these patterns with culture and an environment apart. In prehistoric times, Asians traveled in multiple waves not only to the Americas but also to the islands of the Pacific and Indian Oceans (see Map 5.6).

The populating of Oceania must rank as one of humankind's greatest feats. Unlike the comparatively short distances involved in establishing human societies on the islands of the Caribbean or Mediterranean, vast amounts of open ocean had to be routinely crossed among many of the island groups in the Pacific in order to settle them. Such trips were considered epic voyages as late as the eighteenth century. Yet these early seafaring people settled island after island, traveling restlessly until they had discovered nearly every island of Oceania. As we saw in Chapter 4, their homeland appears to have been Taiwan and the Indonesian-Philippine archipelagos. Using computer-assisted linguistic analysis, modern scholars have now theorized that the people of Oceania are at least partially related to Taiwan's aboriginal population (about half a million members today), mostly concentrated in the central mountains of Taiwan. About 6,000 years ago, the first seafaring people left Taiwan and, together with subsequent waves of emigrants, spread out in westerly and easterly directions. They settled in the Philippines, Indonesia, and the Malay Peninsula, bestowing their languages and ethnic identities on the aboriginal peoples of these lands.

In later times, descendants of these settlers, all speakers of languages belonging to the Austronesian family, spread farther into the Indian and Pacific Oceans. In the Indian Ocean, they sailed as far west as Madagascar, an island off the east coast of Africa, where they arrived around 200 CE and founded a number of chiefdoms. In the Pacific Ocean, they sailed to the Bismarck archipelago, off the eastern coast of New Guinea. It was on this archipelago that settlers created the Lapita culture around 1600 BCE, which was the homeland for the colonization of Oceania—that is, the islands of Polynesia, Micronesia, and parts of Melanesia. On the map, Oceania forms a huge triangle comprising Polynesia, Hawaii, New Zealand, and Easter Island, with Micronesia and Melanesia to the west.

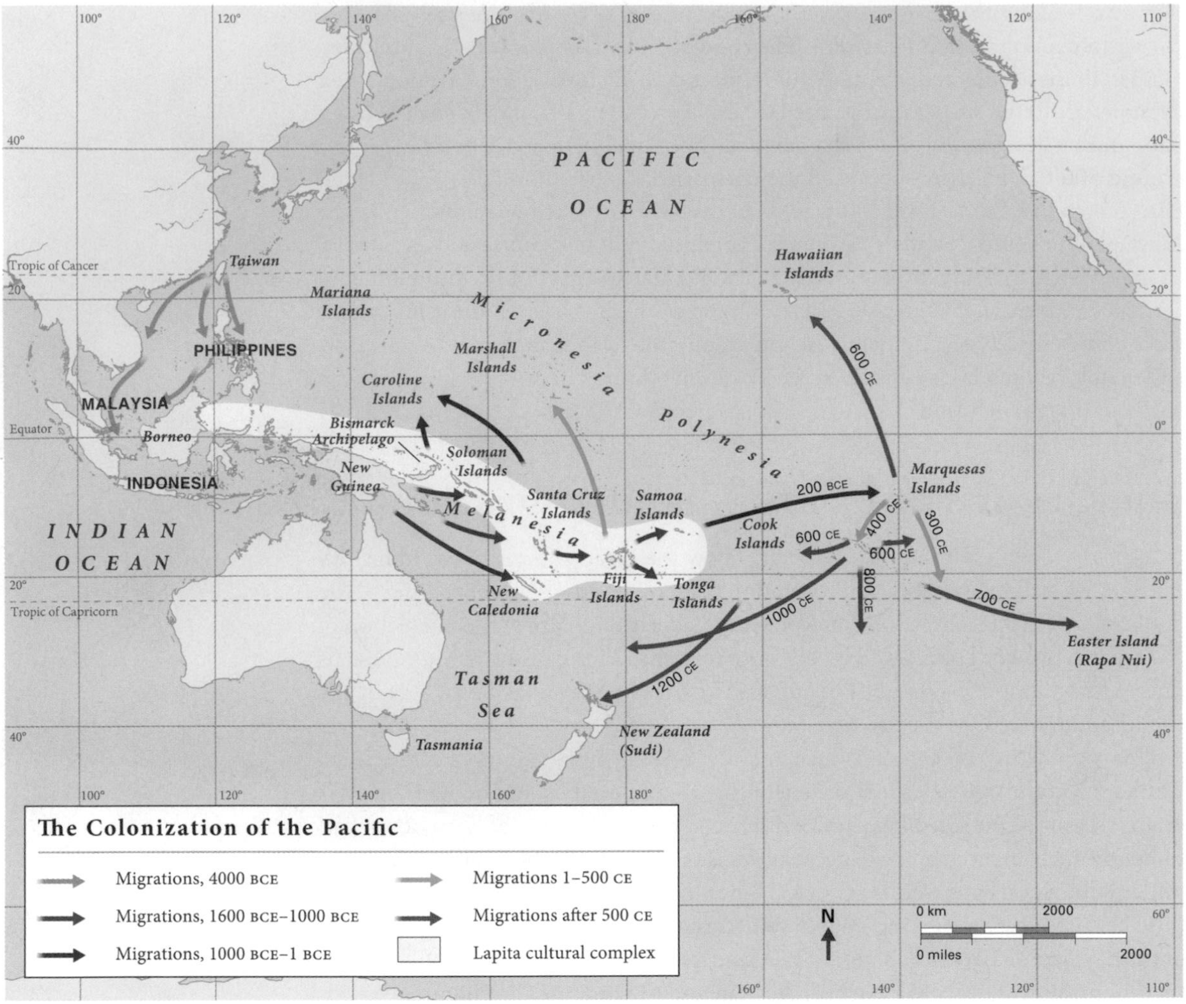

MAP 5.6 The Colonization of the Pacific.

map analysis

Lapita and Cultural Origins

By the fourth millennium BCE, a sophisticated system known as the Lapita cultural complex had already become well established. Named for a site on the island of New Caledonia, the Lapita culture was a system of kinship-based exchanges among the inhabitants of thousands of islands running from Borneo to the edge of Melanesia in the western Pacific. Of particular importance was obsidian, which, as in the Americas, was highly prized as a material for tools and weapons in the absence of workable metals. Another item in demand was a distinctive kind of pottery decorated with stamped patterns called Lapita ware, after shards located at that site.

Environment and Long-Distance Navigation By about 1600 BCE it appears that a number of further factors come together to allow for decisive innovations in long-distance navigation over hundreds of miles of open sea as well as systematic colonization of otherwise uninhabitable islands. The development of ever larger and more sophisticated sail- and paddle-driven oceangoing canoes, stabilized with outriggers or double hulls, provided reliable craft for such journeys. An extensive, orally transmitted storehouse of navigational information—much of it still retained by Polynesian elders today—enabled sailors to set their courses by the sun and stars, retain elaborate mental maps of islands visited, read winds and currents, and take advantage of seasonal reverses in prevailing wind directions.

Perhaps the most important development centered on supplying such voyages. Here, the cultivation of easily storable root crops, especially yams and taro, proved invaluable in sustaining long voyages. Among other staples circulated about the newly colonized islands were breadfruit, coconuts, and bananas, as well as such domesticated animals as pigs, chickens, and dogs, which entered the trade system from Southeast Asia, the Philippines, and Indonesia. Over the centuries from 1600 to 100 BCE, Lapita sailors moved eastward and settled the islands of Vanuatu, Tonga, Fiji, and Samoa. Archaeologists believe that Fiji may be the ultimate source of the culture that sparked the next outward migration: that of the Polynesians.

Papua New Guinea, Sorting Yams. Papua New Guinea is one of the so-called hearths of agriculture where the domestication of many plants occurred, beginning ca. 9,000–7,000 years ago. The domestication of the yam several millennia later resulted in an enduring staple crop, and their portability allowed their spread as they sustained seafarers throughout the Pacific.

Creating Polynesia

As populations grew, the primary mode of governmental and economic organization, the kinship-based chiefdom, became increasingly elaborate. On Tonga, the Society Islands, the Marquesas, and later the Hawaiian Islands, the power of local chiefs extended to nearby island systems. Even here, far removed from outside influences, the inclination of human societies toward centralization, as well as tension with smaller regional societies that we discussed in Chapter 4, is apparent.

Conflict, Interaction, and Expansion What effect such centralization and the increasingly intensified agriculture of staples in the more productive islands may have had on their inhabitants is uncertain. Up to a point, it may have made these societies more efficient as food producers. But the difficulties we have seen in other societies of sustaining large populations on limited amounts of land were undoubtedly intensified in an island society. Some researchers have theorized, for example, that environmental problems related to overpopulation may have developed in the Cook Islands and the Marquesas around 500 BCE and again in 200 BCE. Political disputes arising from the struggles between centralizing and decentralizing factions may have played a role as well. In any case, there seems to have been a break around 500 CE that resulted in the longest period of migration yet: to Hawaii around 600, Easter Island (Rapa Nui) about 700, and New Zealand by 1200. In the cooler climates of Easter Island and New Zealand the introduction of the South American sweet potato—one of the rare examples of hypothetical Polynesian interaction with continental societies—allowed for a diversity of staple crops to support the population.

Tupaia, the great Polynesian navigator

Early Pacific Seafaring Rafts. During the first millennium CE, Polynesian navigators benefited from advances in ship design as they colonized far-flung island chains. The Norwegian adventurer Thor Heyerdahl demonstrated the seaworthiness of similar designs when he constructed a replica of the type of raft utilized by aboriginal seafaring Peruvians. The raft measured approximately 45 feet by 18 feet and consisted of several large balsa tree trunks arranged in a crisscross design. The craft was outfitted with a 29-foot mast and a huge sail, along with a sizeable cabin to provide shelter for the six-man crew. For sustenance, large quantities of drinking water and food supplies—mostly coconuts, sweet potatoes, and other Peruvian staples—were carried on board.

Later Interactions By the time of the first European contact in the early sixteenth century, nearly every habitable island had been settled, and some, Hawaii and New Zealand perhaps most dramatically, had populations of many hundreds of thousands. As we shall see in subsequent chapters, however, this vast achievement of exploration and colonization would soon be threatened by disease and a new breed of conquerors and colonists. Like the Amerindian cultures of the Americas, disease would reduce the populations in some of these islands by perhaps as much as 80 percent. The next three and a half centuries of European exploration of the Pacific would carry with them untold and, all too often, disastrously unforeseen consequences.

Putting It All Together

interactive concept map

Though separated from each other by thousands of miles of ocean and spawning radically different cultures, the Americas and Oceania share common patterns with each other as well as with the cultures of Eurasia and Africa. The first pattern that historians can see is that even in such widely separated areas, human foraging communities at roughly the same time *independently began a process toward the development of agriculture and animal domestication.* While domestication of the first plants and animals and gathering into more settled village life began shortly after the last retreat of the glaciers in Eurasia, it came somewhat later in the Americas, perhaps because human groups were still rather scattered and few in number and could be sustained by large-game hunting. The many different types of plants available as food—especially legumes—were relatively high in protein, an important feature as large game became increasingly scarce. It is also the case that the plant that ultimately became a chief staple of the American societies, corn, required extensive experimentation before becoming domesticated in anything near its present form. Thus, it is only around 4000 BCE that we see its development and the beginning of its extensive domestication.

The second pattern we can see is *growth and sophistication of social structures and the development of the city and of monumental architecture for religious and political purposes.* Even in Oceania, where the critical population levels for cities were never reached, one finds the monoliths of Rapa Nui as evidence of this human pattern. In some cases, the types of structures—pyramids, terraces, and obelisks, for example—seem to follow an almost "universal" pattern, so much so that scholars still struggle to find evidence of contact among widely separated cultures where none appears to have existed.

Recent finds at the Caral-Supe sites show how rapidly the development of astonishingly sophisticated large cities took place once the threshold of plant and animal domestication was crossed. The accomplishments of the society that created Caral and the other sites uncovered so far, like those of the Indus valley, survived in the local practices of Andean peoples long after the cities themselves were abandoned. The settlements of the Olmecs on the southern Gulf coast of Mexico, though coming somewhat later, were equally imposing in their architecture, the efficacy of their farming techniques and irrigation practices, the sophistication of their social structures, and, it now appears, their development of writing. Yet it is also the case that people will not create all the aspects of "civilization" in the same ways and by the same means. One striking example of this is the use of the wheel. Rotation and cyclical motion appear to permeate the ritual lives of people all over the globe, yet the use of the wheel for conveyance and as a basic concept of technology is not universal.

Thus, as with so many human innovations, the intersection of need and opportunity led to a crucial breakthrough. Hence, despite the widespread use of ball courts employing spheres of rubber put through circular hoops as a central political and religious ceremony among Mesoamerican peoples and the enormous cyclical mathematical and timekeeping achievements of later peoples like the Mayas (and even the fact that we have evidence that American societies provided their children with toys that had wheels), the need and means for utilizing heavy-wheeled vehicles never occurred and thus never developed as it had in Eurasia and Africa.

In the case of Oceania, the peopling of the innumerable islands of the Pacific was inseparable from trade and cultural connections. Colonizing uninhabited islands could take place only when the plants and animals required could be brought along and provision could be made to trade for unavailable items. Thus, in terms of square mileage, the Lapita system was one of the world's largest trading spheres, stretching thousands of miles and including thousands of islands. Yet, for a variety of reasons—the necessities traded, the remoteness of the islands from other trade centers, the lack of connections to mainland Asia and the Americas, the unique seafaring skills of the island navigators—the peoples of Oceania remained separated from other such systems. Even here, as in the Americas, Eurasia, and Africa, we see yet another pattern emerging within the political behavior of human societies: *centralization and resistance to it.* As with other fundamental patterns of world history, we will see this one emerge repeatedly in a variety of guises as our story proceeds.

Review and Relate

Thinking Through Patterns

Examine the ways historians approach the big questions of this chapter.

What do historians see as the advantages and disadvantages of the separate evolution of the Americas?

Like the role of geography, this is a question that is often debated. For one thing, we can turn the question around and ask why we should consider the Americas as "isolated," rather than Eurasia and Africa. But it is also true that the societies were not as large or as ethnically diverse as their Eurasian counterparts. Historically, too, scholars still often view the two sets of continents as "old" and "new" and from that perspective view the Americas as "isolated." A big part of how one chooses to look at the question also revolves around how one sees the roles of invasion, infusion of innovation, and cultural competition. Some scholars have argued that the very shape of Eurasia allowed for the brisk dissemination of innovation along broad areas similarly situated in latitude and therefore climate. The Americas, by way of contrast, were more longitudinally oriented, making such diffusion more difficult. Some argue that the separateness of the Americas allowed them to hothouse distinctive cultural traits among their populations. Yet others argue that constant mixing of peoples and ideas accelerates innovation and, hence, "progress." One distinct disadvantage of isolation is that peoples become susceptible to diseases and biological changes suddenly inflicted on them. Thus, from the sixteenth to the early eighteenth centuries, virulent epidemics of Eurasian and African diseases like smallpox devastated the peoples of the Americas when introduced. Though the Americas in all likelihood introduced syphilis in return, it did not cause nearly the devastation in Eurasia and Africa that the Old World diseases did in the New World.

» Why did no cities develop on the larger Pacific Islands?

While the Pacific Islanders had abundant access to food for immediate consumption, the islands themselves were generally too small to allow the accumulation of enough surplus food to free up the numbers of nonfarmers necessary to build and maintain a city. In addition, the islands themselves contained limited amounts of building materials and fresh water, while their isolation helped guard them against attack. Culturally, the islanders also had grown to *expect* that if their numbers outran the food supply, they could simply find another island to which the excess population could migrate.

» The wheel is often cited as the most basic human invention, yet large and sophisticated civilizations were able to flourish without this signal innovation. Why do you think it did not develop in the Americas?

Historians looking at this question tend to look at it in one of two ways: culturally or practically. Some cultural scholars see a lack of deep-seated affinities for circular motion in the belief systems of the American peoples as helping to prevent them from relating to the motion of the wheel in the way that Eurasian and African peoples did. Yet American societies had toys with wheels on them, so they were not unaware of the concept of circular motion—indeed, far from it. The scholars favoring a practical or technological approach argue that the environment of the mountains close by seacoasts, rain forests, and dry, hilly regions was not conducive to bulk transport by wheeled vehicles and that the peoples there simply were never forced to look for more efficient means of transport.

Against the Grain

Consider this as a counterpoint to the main patterns examined in this chapter.

Thor Heyerdahl

- In what ways do Heyerdahl's theories represent a good example of thinking "against the grain"?

The early Americas and Oceania present an interesting exception to the principal theme of *Patterns of World History*. Because they were separated by thousands of miles of ocean from Eurasian and African developments, the peoples of the early Americas and Oceania were denied the benefits of cultural innovations resulting from interactions and adaptations. One might assume, therefore, that these isolated cultures were entirely dependent on indigenous cultural and environmental factors in the development of their emerging civilization.

Although generally accepted, the isolationist theory has not gone entirely unchallenged. Over the last few decades a few unorthodox archaeologists and historians have presented arguments and theories that oppose these traditional views. One of the earliest challengers was Thor Heyerdahl, an amateur Norwegian archaeologist. Heyerdahl set out to demonstrate that South American sailors could have established east-to-west contacts by traversing vast distances across the Pacific solely by relying on prevailing trade winds and ocean currents. In 1947 Heyerdahl successfully sailed across the Pacific from Peru to Polynesia aboard a large balsa raft named the *Kon-Tiki* (after a mythical Peruvian god), similar to those used by ancient Incans. The voyage took 101 days to complete across an expanse of nearly 5,000 miles. This startling achievement convinced Heyerdahl that the original settlers of Polynesia were ancient Peruvians. As additional support for his theory, Heyerdahl pointed out that some modern Polynesians had lighter complexions than others, possible evidence of earlier Peruvian rather than Asian descent. (See photo of Heyerdahl's journey on p. 142.)

- How do the sorts of evidence Heyerdahl and others have used to question the isolationist theory of early Oceanic and American history provide a different perspective on the types of sources most commonly associated with historical research?

Heyerdahl's theory has met with mixed reception. His assumption that some of the early Polynesians were of Peruvian descent has been generally discredited by the academic establishment. By relying on mitochondrial DNA analyses, archaeologists have argued that in fact the first settlers of Polynesia were indeed of Asian—not Peruvian—descent. And yet, intriguingly, recent scholarly opinion—based on more sophisticated genomic HLA typing as well as DNA analysis of a select group of Easter Islanders—indicates the presence of genetic traits found among Amerindians, most likely Peruvians. In addition, recent archaeological investigation has produced linguistic and material evidence in support of the diffusion of agrarian advances carried from Peru westward across the Pacific. For example, the sweet potato, indigenous to Peru, was present in Polynesia centuries before European expeditions across the Pacific. Therefore, despite its controversial approach and results, Heyerdahl's courageous adventure and radical suppositions suggest at the very least the possibility of transoceanic cultural diffusion by prehistoric Peruvian seafarers.

Key Terms

audio flashcards

Cordilleras 121
El Niño 124
Midden 126
Quipú 119
Radiocarbon dating 118
Teosinte 127

For additional resources, please go to **www.oup.com/us/vonsivers.**
Please see the Further Resources section at the back of the book for additional readings and suggested websites.

PATTERNS OF EVIDENCE |

Sources for Chapter 5

SOURCE 5.1

Quipu from the Caral-Supe culture, Peru

2600–2000 BCE

Recent archaeological discoveries in the Caral-Supe valley have pushed back the timeline of cultural development in the Andes by several millennia. A fixture of later Incan culture, the *quipu* was an elaborate series of knotted ropes that seemed to serve as a coded system of communication. Excavations have demonstrated that the *quipu* was used in the region as much as 3,000 years before its earliest previous attestation. Moreover, this *quipu* was apparently left as an offering on the stairway of a public building when another building was built on top.

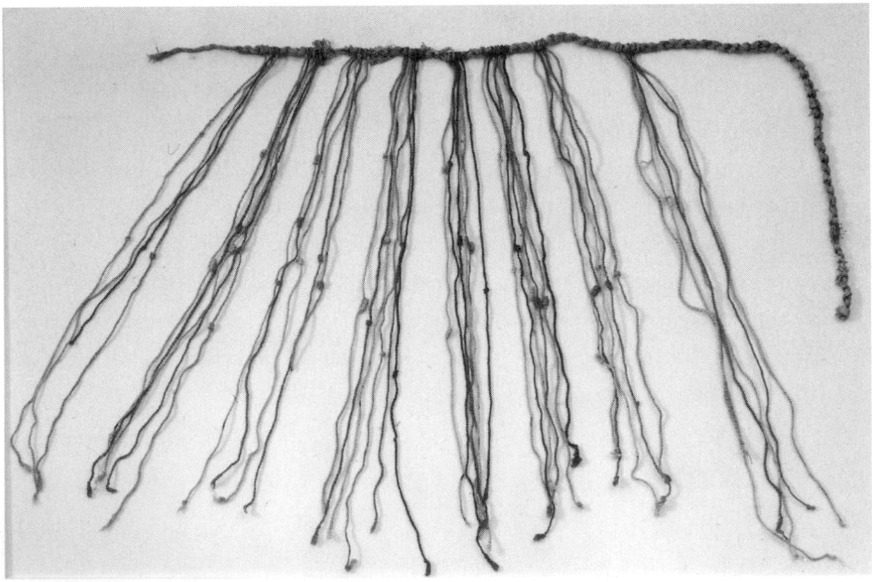

Working with Sources

1. What does this object suggest about the continuities among various Andean cultures over several thousand years?
2. What does the existence of an object used for accounting suggest about this culture's administrative and bureaucratic sophistication?

Source: © President and Fellows of Harvard College, Peabody Museum of Archaeology and Ethnology, Harvard University, PM# 2004.24.35177 (digital file# 153390016).

SOURCE 5.2

Textile fragment from Chavín de Huántar, Peru

ca. 500–200 BCE

Now housed in the Metropolitan Museum of Art in New York City, this section of an elaborately crafted and painted piece of textile attests to the manufacturing prowess of the Chavín people. In the image, a central fanged figure grasps and may be controlling a four-eyed monster. The snake-like elements of this figure have led to the conclusion that he is an ancestor of the *khipucamayuc*, the Inca name for the keeper of a *quipu*.

» Working with Sources

1. **What does the sophistication of this object indicate about the division of labor in Chavín society at its peak?**
2. **What were the likely connections between textile manufacture and the operation of *quipu* in the period?**

SOURCE 5.3 Burial mound at L'Anse Amour, Labrador, Canada

ca. 5500 BCE

This mound marks the grave of an adolescent boy from the "Maritime Archaic" people of Labrador. Roughly 7,500 years ago, his body was wrapped in a shroud of bark or hide and placed face down in the grave with his head facing to the west. At that point, a large mound of rocks was erected over his burial place.

» Working with Sources

1. **What are the similarities between this burial mound and others found in ancient North America?**
2. **What seems to have been the status of this boy, judging from the placement and the circumstances of his burial?**

Source: Courtesy of Brian Bursey

SOURCE 5.4

Lapita pot shards, found in Vanuatu, western Pacific

ca. fourth millennium BCE

Named for a site in the archipelago of New Caledonia, the Lapita culture was a system of kinship-based exchanges among the inhabitants of thousands of islands in the western Pacific. Elements of "Lapita ware," decorated with stamped patterns, were in high demand, and pots were exchanged among the inhabitants of the islands.

≫ Working with Sources

1. **What do the elaborate designs imprinted on this pot suggest about the sophistication of Lapita culture?**
2. **How can the pot be connected with the themes of navigation and gift exchange in the wider Polynesian culture?**

Source: © Philippe Métois

PART TWO

The Age of Empires and Visionaries

600 BCE–600 CE

By the middle of the first millennium BCE, two major transformations changed the course of world history. First, kingdom formation, which had begun earlier in Eurasia, became a near-universal pattern in the world, including sub-Saharan Africa and Mesoamerica. Second, visionaries emerged in Eurasia, whose formulations of monotheism and monism laid the foundations of religious civilizations that eventually emerged in the Middle East, India, China, and adjacent regions after 600 CE.

Kingdoms and Empires

Sub-Saharan Africa and the Americas. Around 600 BCE, improvements in agricultural productivity made it possible for some chiefdoms to expand into kingdoms. In sub-Saharan Africa, the kingdoms were Meroë in the steppes of the middle Nile and Aksum in the highlands of Ethiopia, and in Mesoamerica, the kingdoms were those of the Maya in the Yucatán Peninsula and Teotihuacán in the Mexican Basin.

The Middle East and the Mediterranean. After the Hittites and Neo-Assyrians, around 600 BCE the Persian Achaemenids continued the pattern of empire building. The Greeks resisted the Persians for a long time with their alternatives of city-states and elective offices. But eventually the Macedonian Greek Alexander the Great, his Hellenist successors, and the republican Romans in the western Mediterranean also adopted the imperial pattern, expanding into the Middle East. The Roman Empire competed with the two Persian successor empires of the Parthians and Sasanids for dominance of the region. The characteristic pattern of the Middle East and Mediterranean was competitive imperialism.

India and China. Intense political–military competition among small states ruled by a military class or royal dynasty led to the elimination of the weakest states and the consolidation of larger kingdoms in both India and China around 600 BCE. In contrast to the Middle East and Mediterranean, the pattern of India and China was one of rising and falling single empires, followed by long periods of decentralization before the rise of new imperial dynasties that unified much or all of the region.

ca. 800 BCE
Earliest evidence of iron smelting in sub-Saharan Africa

550–331 BCE
Achaemenid Persia

551–479 BCE
Traditional dates for life of Confucius

ca. 427–347 BCE
Plato, founder of the first philosophical school, the Academy

Interactions in Eurasia and with Africa. Merchants in the kingdoms and empires of Eurasia and sub-Saharan Africa began to interact during the period 600 BCE–600 CE. They pioneered the sea routes to southern India, China, and eastern Africa and the land routes of the Silk Road through central Asia and across the Sahara from northern to western Africa. Exchanges on these routes were not yet regular enough to lead to adaptations, for example, of technological inventions. But the trade whetted the appetites of rulers for luxury goods, such as spices, ointments, silks, and ceramics, stimulating the rise of merchant classes.

Visionaries and the Adoption of State Religions

Visionaries. At the height of the political–military competition among city-states, kingdoms, and empires around 700–500 BCE, individuals arose in Eurasia to proclaim new visions of reality. In the place of the polytheistic universe in which gods and humans mingled, they proclaimed a transcendent God or "first principle" beyond the universe. Their messages were not bound to the particular kingdoms or empires in which the visionaries lived but were addressed to anyone who would listen.

What difference did their new visions of reality make? For the first time in world history, individuals claimed to have discovered standards of truth and justice that were beyond the ever-changing circumstances of kingdoms and empires and their polytheistic pantheons. An unchanging God or first principle, so these individuals argued, was the measure for what was truthful and just. Not all agreed, however, that this measure could be translated into concrete doctrines, laws, and regulations.

Empires and the Adoption of State Religions. In the centuries after the visionaries, small groups of followers popularized the messages of monotheism and monism. They formed priestly classes, churches, and/or schools. Interaction among groups of followers led to the adaptation of some monotheisms and monisms to each other. For example, Jews adopted elements from Zoroastrianism and Greek philosophy, Buddhists influenced Confucianism and Daoism, and a group of Jews founded the reform movement of Christianity and merged it with Greek philosophy.

As one might expect, kings and emperors sought to capitalize on the unifying forces they perceived in monotheism and monism. By 600 CE, monotheism or monism had become the dominant religion, philosophy, and/or ethics of the empires and kingdoms in Eurasia and parts of sub-Saharan Africa.

Previous chapters focused on the patterns of social and political formation, from foraging to agricultural villages, as well as towns and cities, and from there to kingdoms and empires. Now—after the adoption of state religions—kings, emperors, and religious officials laid the foundations for the formation of religious civilizations which, after 600 CE, evolved into social and cultural units that were geographically larger and more enduring than kingdoms and empires—lasting, in most cases, right to the present.

Thinking Like a World Historian

» What is the connection between food, population density, and patterns of social–political formation in world history? Why did these patterns develop later in sub-Saharan Africa and the Americas?

» What elements did the visionaries of ca. 700–500 BCE share in common, and what made their visions so decisive in the course of world history?

» What is the difference between kingdoms and empires, and how did empires change as a result of the adoption of state religions?

interactive timeline

322–185 BCE Most of India united for the first time under Mauryan Empire

221–206 BCE First Chinese Empire under Qin

196 BCE–284 CE Early Roman Empire (including imperial republic)

100–750 CE Moche chiefdom in northern Peru

700 BCE–900 CE Maya kingdoms in southeastern Mexico and Central America

300–600 CE Kingdom of Aksum in northeastern sub-Saharan Africa

322–550 CE Much of India reunited under Gupta Empire

476 CE End of western Roman Empire

Chapter 6 600 BCE–600 CE

Chiefdoms and Early States in Africa and the Americas

A humble stone carving in Oaxaca, in southern Mexico, carbon-dated to about 600 BCE, is the earliest documentation for the existence of a 260-day divinatory calendar in Mesoamerica, which later played a central part in Mayan time reckoning and divination. Mexican archaeologists excavated the inscription in the 1930s, and an American archaeological team in the 1990s discovered perhaps an even earlier version of this calendar in Tabasco to the north of Oaxaca. Amazingly, this calendar system is still in use by people in southern Mexico, making it among the world's longest-lived methods of reckoning time. Similarly, an astronomical observatory in Kenya, carbon dated to 300 BCE, is the earliest example of the so-called Borana lunar calendar of 354 days. It is still in use today among the Kushite herders of East Africa. Two American anthropologists discovered the observatory in Namoratunga [nah-mow-rah-TOON-ga], Kenya, during fieldwork in 1978. The two calendars not only attest to the cultural prowess of Mesoamerica and sub-Saharan East Africa during the period of 600 BCE–600 CE but, more important, are reminders

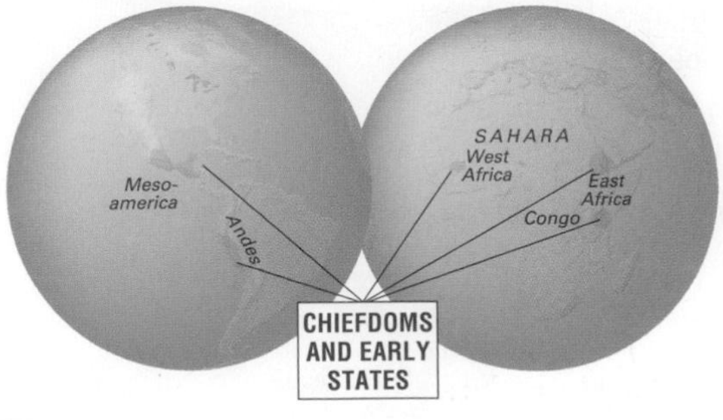

***ABOVE:* The ruins of Meroitic pyramids at Jebel Barkal in modern Sudan.**

of the diversity and relativity of all calendar systems, including the modern Western one which dominates the world today.

Interest in time reckoning was not the only similarity between the Americas and sub-Saharan Africa. During the period 600 BCE–600 CE, these regions also resembled each other in terms of patterns of agricultural development, spread of villages, emergence of chiefdoms, and early rise of kingdoms. These institutions, results of regional interactions and adaptations, evolved more slowly than in the more populated Eurasia, where kingdoms and empires already proliferated prior to 600 BCE–600 CE. Since there was little contact between Eurasia on one hand and the Americas and much of sub-Saharan Africa on the other it is all the more remarkable that the patterns of agriculture and life in villages, chiefdoms, and kingdoms were fairly consistent *within* world regions as much as *across* world regions. People did not need to be in contact with each other across the continents to build their institutions in similar ways. All they needed were sufficiently large populations for similar institutions to arise. Nevertheless, as we saw in Chapter 5, the isolated world regions, through their own internal interactions, adapted to a transition from foraging to agriculture. Indeed, as recent scholarship has revealed, urban centers like Caral-Supe appear to be of the same age as some of the earliest Old World sites.

In this chapter, we will see how, through continued internal interactions, sub-Saharan Africans and Americans blazed indigenous trails in pattern formation, from villages to **chiefdoms** and **kingdoms**. Sharing a common humanity with the Eurasians, they did not need the direct influence of those peoples to develop remarkably similar social and political patterns. The calendars of these two regions, while strikingly similar to Eurasian models in some respects, also illustrate the adaptation of the concept to local needs as well as sophistication.

Agriculture and Early African Kingdoms

Largely on account of its relative separation and lower population levels, sub-Saharan Africa (like the Americas and Oceania) transitioned from forager society to agrarian–urban society with its patterns of village, city-state, kingdom, and empire formation somewhat less rapidly or completely than Eurasia. However, on the northern rim of the Sahara Africans interacted with the Middle East and adapted to its agrarian patterns early on. They adopted village life, built cities, and created kingdoms (such as Kush and Nubia along the Nile) well before the period of 600 BCE–600 CE. After 600 CE, the kingdoms of Meroë [ME-ro-way] in the Nile valley and Aksum in the Ethiopian highlands flourished, while Africans farther south shifted from foraging to agriculture, villages, and chiefdoms. By 600 CE, urbanism had spread to West Africa and foraging had shrunk to pockets in the center and south of the continent.

Seeing Patterns

» How does comparing and contrasting sub-Saharan Africa with the Americas during 600 BCE–600 CE help in understanding the agrarian–urban patterns of social and political development across the world?

» Where did chiefdoms, cities, and kingdoms arise in sub-Saharan Africa and why? On which forms of agriculture, urbanization, and trade were they based?

» Which areas in the Americas saw the development of a corn- and potato-based agriculture that did not depend on the plow, the wheel, and ironmaking?

Chiefdom: An agricultural village or town of up to 1,000 inhabitants, in which people know each other, requiring a person of authority (an elder or the head of a large family) to keep order as a respected chief.

Chapter Outline

- Agriculture and Early African Kingdoms
- The Spread of Villages in Sub-Saharan Africa
- Early States in Mesoamerica: Maya Kingdoms and Teotihuacán
- The Andes: Moche and Nazca
- Putting It All Together

Kingdom: A city-state or territorial state of at least several thousand inhabitants in which a ruler, claiming a divine mandate and supported by a military force, keeps order and provides for the defense against outside attacks.

Saharan Villages, Towns, and Kingdoms

For many millennia, the Sahara was relatively hospitable, with savannas and steppes, furthering the pattern shift from foraging to agriculture. But when the monsoon rains shifted eastward, around 5000–3000 BCE, the desert expanded, and savannas and steppes retreated southward. Agrarian life relocated to oases and the Nile River valley. In the northeast, the kingdom of Meroë established a capital with the same name in the middle Nile basin, between the Nile and the western slopes of the northern Ethiopian highlands. The kingdom received its support from a sufficient, although not abundant, agricultural surplus produced with the help of annual Nile floods and irrigation.

Saharan Chiefdoms and Kingdoms The earliest evidence of Africans shifting from foraging to agriculture comes from the area of the middle Nile around Khartoum, the capital of modern Sudan. Archaeological sites reveal a culture of raising cattle, cultivating sorghum, and shaping distinctive pottery. Sorghum tolerates a climate of less rainfall than wheat and barley, and it is possible that farmers along the middle Nile domesticated it locally, probably after becoming familiar with Middle Eastern farming. By the period between 4000 BCE and the first written records in Egypt in 3100 BCE, a substantial chiefdom of Nilo-Saharan speakers had emerged in northern Sudan, then called "Nubia" (from the Latinized Egyptian word *nebew* for gold, which was found in a valley off the Nile). This chiefdom was based on farming, livestock raising, and trading of gold as well as rain-forest ivory and timber from farther south. Archaeologists have noted that even at this early date tombs in Nubia contained objects rivaling those of the Egyptians, including objects from southwest Asia and beyond. Moreover, Nubian military prowess emerged clearly in Egyptian records, with archers especially sought after as mercenaries. Indeed, the bow and arrow, both Paleolithic African inventions, gave their names to the state which the Egyptians called *Ta-Seti* [tah-SAY-tee], the "Land of the Bow."

After 2500 BCE, a kingdom grew in wealth and power in Nubia, building a palace, large tombs, temples, and a wall around its capital city of Kerma, the first African city outside Egypt. During 1850–1400 BCE Kerma and Egypt were rivals for the control of Nile trade, with each conquering and ruling the other for periods of time until Egypt eventually destroyed Kerma and colonized Nubia for about half a millennium. Nubia regained autonomy early in the first millennium BCE, in a state centered around the city of Napata, a new capital at some distance upstream on the Nile. Later, the Napatan kings liberated themselves from Egyptian control and even assumed the throne of their northern neighbor as the twenty-fifth dynasty (ca. 780–686 BCE). But when Assyria, the first empire to unify all of the Middle East, conquered Egypt, the defeated king retreated and relocated himself farther upstream at Meroë, south of the Nile bend in the border zone between the southern Saharan steppe and the savanna.

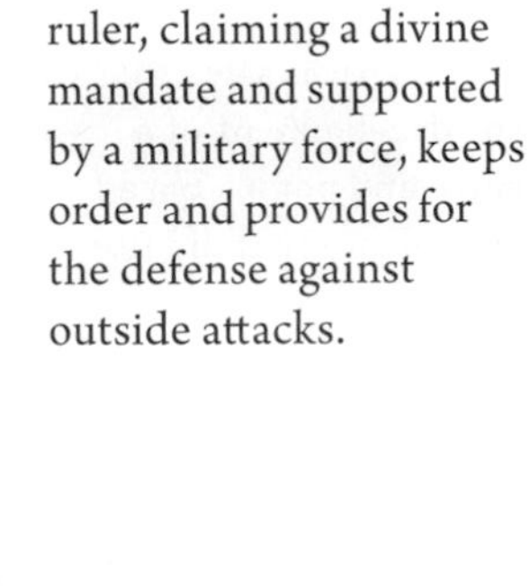

AFRICA, SHOWING SITES IN MAURETANIA 2000 BCE–600 BCE

The Villages of Tichitt-Oualata Contemporaneously with the Nubian kingdoms, villages emerged in the southeastern corner of today's Mauretania. As in Nubia, the climate in the western Sahara had changed during 5000–3000 BCE, away from the monsoon regime which since the end of the last Ice Age (12,500 BCE) had supported a steppe and savanna vegetation in what is desert today. As the monsoon patterns moved eastward, foragers retreated to shallow lakes and oases. They left behind a rich collection of cave paintings in the surrounding mountains dating to earlier times when the Sahara was still wet. During 3000–2000 BCE, these foragers—perhaps stimulated by the knowledge of Middle Eastern agriculture—domesticated pearl millet, a type of grain requiring less water than wheat or barley to grow.

Archaeological evidence published by a British team in 2004 points to the emergence of a set of sizeable villages at Dhar Tichitt [dar tee-SHEET] and Dhar Oualata [dar wah-LAH-tah] in Mauretania around 2000 BCE, which flourished until 600 BCE. There, the team identified centers with large masonry structures. Corrals held herds of cattle, and granaries held large quantities of millet. Numerous tomb mounds, perhaps for the chiefs in the villages, held beads and copper jewelry. Furnaces contained remnants of charcoal and ore, evidence of craftspeople smelting copper that was mined in the nearby Saharan mountains. While it appears that the social structure was based on wealth in livestock, exactly how society was regulated, what nature of religious order it possessed, and which form of chiefly authority ruled are still unclear. One theory holds that the people eventually retreated farther south, together with the steppe and savanna, as the Sahara continued to dry out. As we shall see in Chapter 14, these migrants might have been the founders of the kingdom of ancient Ghana.

Meroë on the Middle Nile The kings of Meroë were successors of the twenty-fifth Nubia-descended dynasty of Egypt, who, under Assyrian pressure, withdrew to the steppes of the middle Nile, about 100 miles north of present-day Khartoum. Here they built their capital, Meroë. At that time, the floodplain to the south of the capital still received sufficient monsoon rainfall during the summer to support agriculture. In addition, the kings built large water reservoirs to supply the farmers. The latter grew the African cereals sorghum and millet, but archaeological finds also include barley and wheat, all of which were planted with the plow. Presumably, the kingdom financed itself for the most part with the agricultural surplus.

At its height, from the sixth through fourth centuries BCE, the city of Meroë encompassed 20,000 inhabitants, and a substantial population lived in the provincial towns. Although the king was the recognized head of Meroë, the kingdom was largely decentralized. The provinces downstream and upstream along the Nile were autonomous, ruled by their own town chiefs who perhaps sent no more than annual presents to the capital. Outside the limited agricultural area, cattle nomads grazed their herds.

The difference in power between the kings and the chiefs was defined by the royal control over trade. Miners in the desert north of the capital produced iron ore

interactive timeline

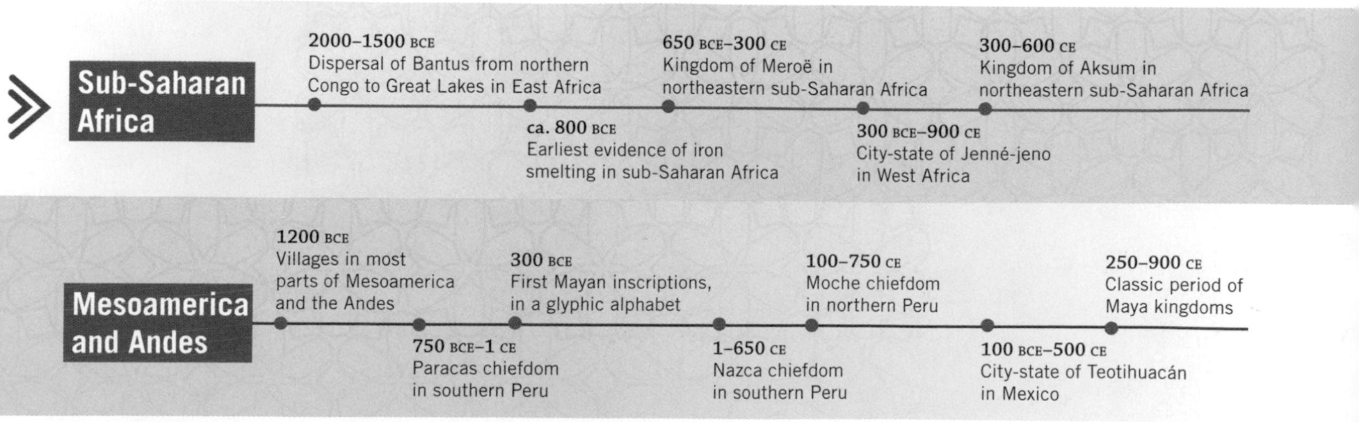

and farmers south of the capital grew cotton, both of which were important for the urban crafts. Smiths and weavers in Meroë produced weapons, hoes, utensils, and cloth, both for local consumption and for trade beyond the kingdom. Hunters in the south acquired ivory from elephants and feathers from ostriches hunted in the savanna. Traders carried these goods on donkey and camel caravans on the traditional trade route down the Nile to Egypt or across the Red Sea to Yemen by boat. In return, they brought back olive oil and wine from Egypt and frankincense and myrrh from Yemen (see Map 6.1 and Source 6.1).

From the kingdom's inception in the seventh century BCE, people in Meroë mined, smelted, and forged iron; they might have been the first to do so in sub-Saharan Africa. However, how and when the knowledge of smelting and forging iron began in sub-Saharan Africa has been a bone of contention among scholars. As is generally agreed, the craft of iron smelting evolved gradually in Hittite Anatolia during several centuries after 1500 BCE (see Chapter 2). To date, the possible spread of ironworking skills from the Middle East to Africa has not been satisfactorily proved. But the independent origin of ironworking in Africa has not been demonstrated conclusively either. Researchers such as Stanley Alpern and Jan Vansina, evaluating the evidence in the early 2000s, came to the conclusion that the earliest

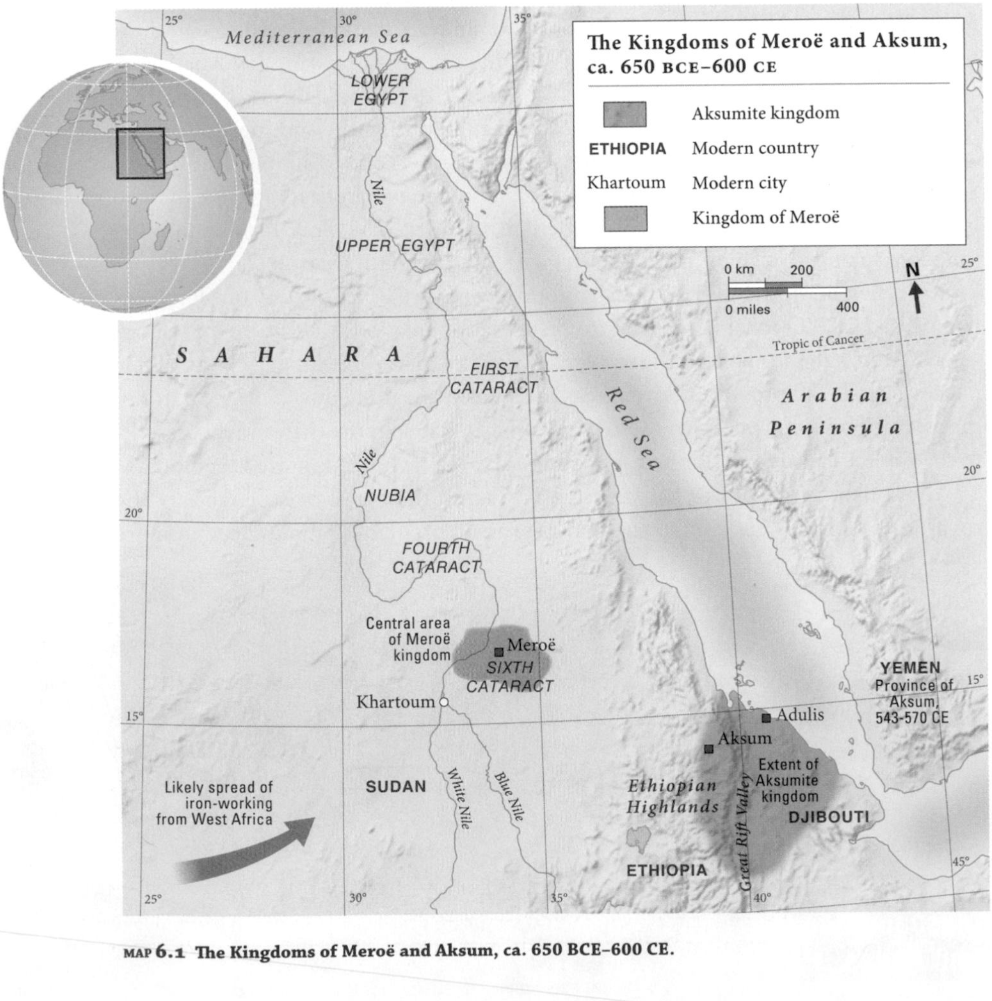

MAP 6.1 The Kingdoms of Meroë and Aksum, ca. 650 BCE–600 CE.

reliable carbon date for iron production is 839–782 BCE, in the savanna on the border between today's Central African Republic and Cameroon. If this date is correct, Meroë would have received the impetus for iron production from within sub-Saharan Africa.

Meroë's Cultural Achievements In Meroë, the kings adapted their Nubian–Egyptian heritage to the different regional circumstances of the steppe and savanna south of the Sahara. Their monuments acquired a distinct style, as is evidenced by their tombs: pyramids with flat tops and pyramids with steep angles. Although the main temple was devoted mainly to the Egyptian pantheon, the priests also added native deities, such as the lion god Apedemek. The inherited Egyptian hieroglyphics seem to have "evolved" into an alphabetic script, visible on many monuments, even though at present this script is still undeciphered.

In spite of its regional orientation, Meroë was well known to the outside world. Mediterranean travelers visited it quite frequently. In the early first century CE the kings of Meroë skirmished with Rome over border issues. And in the third century CE, when Meroë's power was already declining, Heliodorus of Emesa, a Hellenistic-Greek writer, made it the stage for the conclusion of his popular romance novel *Aethiopica*. As much as Meroë provided a physical network for regional travelers, it also provided an intellectual link between Eurasia and Africa; the people of Meroë facilitated this important cultural link through their adaptations.

The Kingdom of Aksum

Meroitic trade with the Red Sea had to cross through the Ethiopian highlands. Exposed to this trade, highlanders gradually acculturated to urbanized Meroë as well as Yemen. Sometime in the early first century CE, a king replaced the chiefdoms of the highlands and established the kingdom of Aksum (300–600 CE). Based on a relatively productive, plow-driven agriculture, this kingdom assumed control of the trade from Meroë, which declined subsequently. Aksum became the major supplier of African goods to the Roman Empire, from where it accepted Christianity in the early 300s.

Meroë's Decline and Aksum's Rise Three factors contributed to Meroë's decline in the third century CE. First, the iron industry devoured immense amounts of charcoal, which is made by burning wood in earth-covered mounds. Once the forests in the east were gone, the iron industry in the capital city was doomed, depriving the kings of a major source of their income. Second, beginning in the late 200s BCE, camel nomads from the deserts east of the Nile raided northern Meroë. Third, the eastern neighbor, Ethiopia, acculturated to Meroë, thanks to the trade that crossed its land. Ethiopian guides and owners of transportation animals became participants in the trade, and then chiefs in the agriculturally rich high plain of Aksum took it over. Aksum was located close to the coast, where the port of Adulis (today Zula) was one of the main transshipment ports in the Red Sea. Thus, a combination of agricultural and commercial wealth enabled the chiefs of Aksum to assume the succession of Meroë.

The agricultural bounty of the Ethiopian highlands southeast of Meroë was due to its plains at 5,000–6,000 feet elevation and surrounding mountains 15,000 feet high. Deep valleys, notably of the Blue Nile and of the Rift Valley, cut into these highlands, which were therefore accessible only over steep ascents. The summer monsoon from the south Atlantic brought sufficient and, in places, abundant rain to the plains and mountains and supported large forests and a productive subtropical agriculture in the lower elevations.

As in the Nile valley, agriculture in the Ethiopian highlands was of considerable age, with evidence (from a rock painting and archaeological finds) of the existence of plows, oxen, barley, and wheat going back several thousand years. In higher elevations where barley and wheat did not prosper, farmers grew teff, a high-yielding grain. Plenty of grasslands supported cattle breeding. The Red Sea coast was dry and hot, with today's Djibouti sporting the highest average temperatures in the world. The coast supported only a few ports dependent on their hinterland. Because of its elevation, Ethiopia was a largely self-contained region in Africa, remaining outside the large population movements and cultural assimilation characteristic of West and East Africa.

Aksum's Splendor Aksum, founded around 100 CE, came into its own around 300 CE. Its king, Ezana (ca. 303–350 CE), adopted Christianity as the state religion in 333 CE, thereby making Aksum the third Christian kingdom, after Armenia (301 CE) and Georgia (319 CE). Like his Armenian and Georgian counterparts and, somewhat later, the Roman emperor, Ezana replaced tolerance for a multiplicity of polytheistic religions with the requirement of conversion to a single faith (see Chapter 7). When the Roman emperors, however, embraced what would become the Roman Catholic interpretation of Christianity at the Church Council of Chalcedon (451 CE), Aksum opted for Coptic Christianity, which was dominant in Egypt. It did not break with the Roman Empire and even sided with it in the second half of the 500s CE against the Sasanid Persians, but it kept its distance.

Another centralizing policy characteristic of Aksum was the use of a gold-based currency through which the taxation of the market for the import and export of luxury goods was facilitated. The kings of Aksum acquired their gold by sending merchants, protected by accompanying troops, to the southern highlands outside the kingdom, where the gold was mined. The merchants paid with salt, iron, and cattle. Finally, a small central administration of tax collectors, tax farmers, and provincial tribute collectors ensured delivery of agricultural surplus to granaries in the towns and the capital. The provinces outside the capital, however, were in reality small kingdoms, federated with Aksum through some kind of tribute system, the details of which are unknown. Even though more centralized than Meroë, Aksum was well below the level of administrative coherence of a typical Middle Eastern or Mediterranean kingdom or empire, such as Ptolemaic Egypt (305–30 BCE) or Antigonid Greece (301–168 BCE) (see Source 6.2).

Imperialism and Crisis In the 500s CE, Aksum briefly engaged in imperialism—the only imperialism coming out of sub-Saharan Africa in its entire history. This century was a time of profound crisis in both the Roman and Sasanid Persian Empires, which were under threat by nomadic invaders from the central Asian and Russian steppes (see Chapter 7). Naval trade in the Red Sea declined, and the kingdom of Himyar in Yemen increasingly relied on camel caravan trade along the west coast of Arabia. Perhaps under the influence of Jewish communities at the northern end of the caravan route, a Yemeni usurper who had converted to

Judaism seized the throne and persecuted the Christians in his land. In response, and with the encouragement of Rome, the Aksumite king invaded Yemen and defeated the usurper. After a period of political instability, Aksum was able to make Yemen a regular province (543–570 CE).

But Aksum eventually lost this province when the Sasanid Persians invaded by land and sea in 570 CE, to establish their own proxy regime at the commercially important entrance to the Red Sea. The Sasanids had recovered earlier than the Romans from nomadic invasions and were determined to turn the long competition between the two empires (discussed in Chapter 7) to their favor. Seizing control over the entire India and East Africa trade was part of the Sasanid strategy to defeat Rome in the Middle East.

As a kingdom dependent to a considerable degree on transcontinental luxury trade, Aksum eventually became a collateral victim of this new Persian ascendancy. After 570 CE, Aksumite trade in the Red Sea declined precipitously. The capital city shrank to a shadow of itself, and in the following centuries provincial rulers in the highlands farther south rose to prominence. In addition, there were signs of internal problems: Timber resources for Aksum's iron industry in the vicinity of the capital became scarce. Although Ethiopia did not disintegrate, as Meroë had done, after 600 CE it played a much more modest regional role.

Aksumite Stela, pre-400s CE. This is the largest of hundreds of stone monoliths, some with tombs and altars, attesting to the architectural sophistication of the kingdom. Workmen transported them from quarries 3 miles away, where they had cut the stelae with iron tools. Some of the stelae, like the one above, have false windows and doors, looking like modern Art Deco buildings.

The Spread of Villages in Sub-Saharan Africa

By about 600 BCE, agriculture and pastoralism were common not only in East Africa but also in West Africa. Both emerged when a majority of people retreated from the increasingly dry Sahara southward into West Africa. They followed the gradual southward shift of West Africa's three ecological zones, stretching from west to east in the form of more or less broad bands. The first and northernmost zone was the steppe, or **Sahel** (Arabic *sahil*, or "coast" of the "sea" of the Sahara Desert). The second zone was the *savanna*, an expanse of grassland with stands of trees. The third zone was a relatively narrow (up to a 150-mile-wide) belt of rain forest along the coast from Guinea to Cameroon. Villages were dispersed by 600 BCE over all three zones, although they were most numerous in the savanna, where farming was most productive.

Sahel: An area of steppe or semidesert bordering the Sahara.

West African Savanna and Rain-Forest Agriculture

During the period 600 BCE–600 CE the densest village networks were located in the savannas of the inland delta of the Niger and middle Senegal Rivers. The village of Jenné-jeno [JEN-nay JEN-no] in the delta developed into a major urban center during 300–900 CE. Indications are that it was a chiefdom with a developing regional trade for raw materials and luxury goods. In the rain forest, the evolution of slash-and-burn agriculture is still largely undocumented by archaeology, although its end result, the so-called Bantu dispersal, with its combination of yam, taro, banana, and oil palm village agriculture, is well established.

Seated Figure, Jenné-jeno,Terra-Cotta, Thirteenth Century; New York, Metropolitan Museum. This convoluted figure, sculpted with exquisite refinement, shows a person in an apparently intense meditative pose.

Inland Delta Urbanism The river Niger originates in the far west of the West African rain forest and flows northeast from the savanna to the Sahel, before turning at a right angle southeastward in the direction of the Atlantic Ocean. Midway along its northeastern leg, it slows and divides into several branches, the 250-mile-long and 50-mile-wide inland delta. In the first millennium BCE, when the climate was still relatively humid, the delta was located entirely in the savanna, forming a huge area of canals, islands, and swamps. Villagers in the delta grew millet and African rice, the latter domesticated around 1500 BCE.

Over time, a dense network of villages developed. After 300 BCE a village division process began by which some villages, increasing to town size, became the center of satellite villages. This is how Jenné-jeno at the southern end of the delta originated. By 900 CE, so it is estimated, Jenné-jeno was a *city*—that is, a dwelling place for a nonagricultural crafts-based population—of between 5,000 and 13,000 inhabitants. A prominent craft was pottery, with some potters specializing in the creation of small terra-cotta figurines, such as horsemen, archers, and humans in convoluted poses. The city was surrounded within a circle of half a mile in diameter by 25 villages. Other towns with satellite villages developed farther downstream as well and made the delta the most populated area in West Africa.

Unfortunately, the archaeology of the period under consideration has not revealed much yet about the social stratification and power structures of Jenné-jeno. It is clear that this urban–rural center had a line of chiefs, some basic administrative offices, and craftspeople. The strongest evidence is a gold ring and many objects made of copper and bronze dated to 850–900 CE. Copper and iron ore had to be carried in by donkey or camel from a distance of 30 miles or more from mines in the desert and savanna to be smelted and manufactured in town into weapons and implements. Two chemically analyzed glass beads, dated to the pre-600 CE period, seem to have come from overseas, one from India, Southeast Asia, or East Asia and the other from Roman Italy or Egypt. Thus, trans-Saharan trade seems to have been in existence, supporting an incipient urban demand for luxuries (see Source 6.3).

Rain-Forest Settlements The earliest evidence for rain-forest agriculture comes from the Kintampo complex of 2250–750 BCE, located in today's Ghana. Here, archaeologists have found traces of wood and mud huts on stone foundations, domesticated cattle and dwarf goats, rats, pottery, terra-cotta figurines, and polished stone implements. The assumption is that the villagers practiced slash-and-burn farming, growing yams and oil palms. Unfortunately, no archaeological evidence of the cultivation of yams has been found so far, and the earliest evidence for oil palm cultivation dates to an 800 BCE site in the Atlantic Niger delta. Rain-forest archaeology, burdened by the tendency of the environment to break down the organic matter of artifacts, is lagging behind, and archaeologists have begun producing good data only from the 1990s onward.

Early Plant Domestication? A first breakthrough in tropical archaeology came in 1996 at Nkang in the Cameroons. Belgian scholars excavating this site were able to date banana **phytoliths** to about 500 BCE. Phytoliths are silica from soil sediments deposited in bananas. Their dating caused unrest among many Africanists who for decades had thought that the banana had arrived with Indonesian sailors on the East African coast sometime between 200 and 500 CE. The Ugandan scientist B. Julius Lejju caused even more surprise in 2006 when he published findings from Munsa, Uganda, with evidence from banana phytoliths dating to the fourth millennium BCE. While discussion about the validity of the new data is still continuing, it is becoming more and more evident that Indian Ocean connections between Southeast Asia and East Africa are of greater antiquity than hitherto assumed. Did domesticated bananas, yams, sugarcane stalks, and rice travel westward and domesticated sorghum and millet travel eastward already thousands of years ago, carried by intrepid Polynesian sailors?

Phytoliths: Many plants pick up silica from the soil. After these plants decay, the silica returns to the soil in the form of phytoliths, which can be analyzed microscopically. Carbon dating of soil layers provides approximate dates.

Village Farming West African slash-and-burn farming for yam, banana, and oil palm plantations consisted of clearing small areas of rain forest for the establishment of villages of up to 500 inhabitants. Virgin rain forest was relatively easy to cut, even with stone tools, prior to the arrival of iron axes in the 800s BCE. Trees between 80 and 125 feet high formed a thick canopy, allowing relatively little light to penetrate and, therefore, not much undergrowth to develop and obstruct the clearing process. Each clearing was large enough for a village of a few hundred farmers, family fields, communal fallow land, and small numbers of cattle and goats.

If a village grew beyond its population capacity, a group had to depart and select a new site in the rain forest for clearing. Yam fields could be cultivated for up to 3 years and had to lie fallow for 10–15 years. During the fallow years, the rain forest grew back, although it now no longer returned to its virgin state. A secondary rain forest developed, with few tall trees and a proliferation of medium vegetation up to 30 feet high. Given several millennia of slash-and-burn cultivation, over time nearly all virgin African rain forests were replaced by secondary forest. As in so many other places in the world, what many might perceive as pristine "jungle" was in fact the creation of human hands, as emphasized by Jan Vansina in his classic on African rain-forest settlement. The transformation of the environment by humans, for better or worse, is a process that began early on in world history.

The Spread of Village Life to East and South Africa

Groups of yam, banana, and oil palm farmers of southeast Nigeria, at the eastern end of the West African rain-forest belt, calling themselves "Bantu," meaning "the people," exhausted their area for clearings around 2000 BCE. In contrast to their westerly neighbors, they were fortunate in their search for new spaces to clear because they had the equatorial rain forest of the Congo to the southeast at their disposal. Once there, a northerly group began to disperse around 1500 BCE, this time, however, eastward into the savanna of the Great Lakes in East Africa. On their way, they adapted to the cereal agriculture and iron crafting of the savanna villagers. The Bantu villages of the Great Lakes became the center for one of the great transformation events of history. Under Bantu impact, during 600 BCE–600 CE, nearly all foragers in the southern cone of Africa became either villagers or cattle nomads and adopted Bantu languages and culture (see Map 6.2).

Inland Villagers and Nomads At the time of the northern Bantu arrival around 600 BCE, much of the land around the Great Lakes was still heavily forested

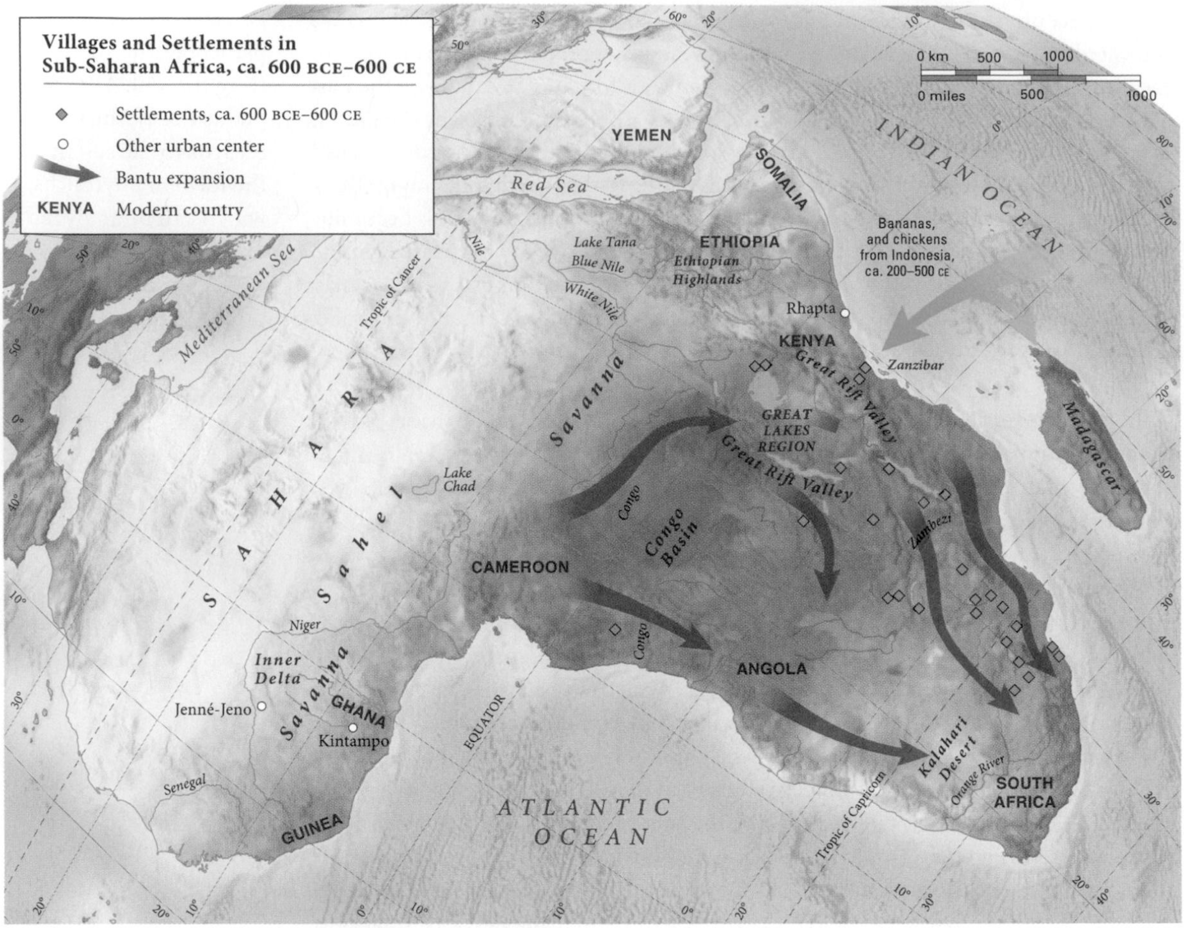

MAP 6.2 Villages and Settlements in Sub-Saharan Africa, 600 BCE–600 CE.

map analysis

Tsetse Fly: This insect can carry the virus that causes sleeping sickness, causing extreme fatigue and eventual death in humans and domesticated animals. Some animal species were able to adapt as dwarf variations, notably horses, cattle, and goats. The fly thrives in low elevations in rain forests, along rivers, and around lakes.

savanna. As the villagers cleared the forest, the threat of the **tsetse fly** diminished and nomads from the north were able to expand southward. Many nomads gave up their minimal farming, which they traditionally engaged in from campsites. As in the Middle East, these nomads entered into a symbiotic relationship with the villagers, from whom they acquired their necessary grain supplements. In the meantime, the southern migrants of the original Bantu dispersal of 2000 BCE had settled the Congo equatorial rain forest and, under the impact of their northern and eastern cousins, had complemented their yam and oil palm agriculture with millet and sorghum, as well as ironworking. Only small pockets of the original Paleolithic foragers of the virgin rain forest, the pygmies, continued their traditional lifestyle, although they eventually adopted Bantu languages.

The conversion of the foragers on the savanna south of the Congo rain forest to farming, from the Great Lakes westward to Angola and southward to the tip of South Africa, was the work of both eastern Great Lakes and western Congo branches of Bantu descendants. The foragers either retreated before the farmers with their iron implements and weapons or adapted voluntarily to farming and speaking a Bantu language. Small numbers of savanna foragers, speaking Khoisan-family languages, retreated into the Kalahari Desert and steppe in western and central South Africa, hanging on to a precarious hunting-and-gathering survival. As could be expected, the process from Bantu origins and Bantu interaction with the nomads and foragers of East and South Africa to the eventual mutual adaptations took time and was still incomplete in 600 CE.

African Traditional Rituals The results of an analysis of Bantu linguistic roots and of early Iron Age (350–900 CE) sites in South Africa provide a glimpse into traditional **African spirituality**, summarized by Jan Vansina, a pioneer of Bantu studies. In this perception of reality, Bantus distinguished between the daily world of more or less regular cycles of renewal and disintegration in the village (birth, puberty, adulthood, marriage, old age) and the fields (rain, plantation, harvest, and dry season) on one hand, and the calendar movements of heaven (described at the beginning of this chapter) on the other. Elaborate rituals, including a scrupulous observance of taboos and omens, had to be followed to keep the village and field cycles on their regular paths. For example, South African sites contain stone cairns marking the space of male circumcision lodges, stone-walled pits for rainmaking ceremonies, places with broken pots symbolizing deflowering in female puberty rites, and masks used for the representation of ancestor spirits in village feasts. Rituals guaranteed that the human and field cycles would remain in sync.

African spirituality: Perception of reality based on the concept of nature in all its manifestations (planets and stars, landscapes, trees and plants, animals and humans), pervaded by spirits and influencing each other.

Ancestor and nature spirits pervaded the village and fields, and they had to be given their due respect through regular sacrifices, lest they disrupt the cycles of renewal and disintegration. Charms, mixed from herbs, protected against unintended insults of the spirits. The worst disruption, however, threatened to come from male or female witches in the villages who, acting out of envy, vengeance, or malice, could severely harm or even kill their victims. The only way to avoid death from bewitchment was to seek a diviner or healer in the village who, through trances, dreams, oracles, or charms, was able to enter the spirit world, recognize bewitchment, and stop it through **witchcraft**. It appears that in the early African Iron Age the adoption of elaborate rituals involving the human and field cycles—and, in some places, the calendar cycle, as evidenced by the Borana calendar discussed in the vignette at the beginning of this chapter—represented the main changes in the patterns of reality conceptualizations dating back to the African origins of humanity.

Witchcraft: A belief in which an evil person (male or female) can harm an innocent victim at a distance and cause the victim to become possessed, with attendant illnesses.

Indonesian Contacts Village agriculture received a boost in 200–500 CE when Indonesian sailors brought new species of bananas and chickens to East Africa. These sailors were descendants from Austronesian farmers, who had dispersed to the islands of the Pacific, Philippines, and Indonesia, beginning around 4000 BCE, and who had probably also traveled shortly thereafter to East Africa, as discussed earlier in the chapter. The mariners of 200–500 CE sailed on large outriggers. These watercraft were rigged with canted square sails, which made it possible to sail a course at an angle from the headwind. Prevailing wind patterns in the southern Indian Ocean would otherwise have made sailing westward from Indonesia to Africa difficult. Where on the African coast the Indonesians landed is unknown, although they definitely settled the still-uninhabited tropical island of Madagascar, the fourth largest island in the world.

Incipient Urbanism on the East Coast East Africans also benefited from trade with the Middle East. Archaeological evidence points to the inclusion of the northern East African coast into the Yemeni commercial network in the last centuries BCE,

Stone Relief of a Large Outrigger Merchant Ship, Buddhist Temple of Borobudur, on the Indonesian Island of Java, ca. 800 CE. This type of ship traveled regularly from Java to East Africa on the cinnamon trade route, with its merchants exchanging spices for ivory, wild animal skins, and slaves during the early centuries of the first millennium.

which connected Meroë, Ptolemaic and Roman Egypt, Parthian and Sasanian Persia, the Indian west coast, Sri Lanka, and (indirectly) Indonesia and China. Remnants of two camps on the northern coast of Somalia, dating to 150 BCE–500 CE, contain shards of ceramics from all these places. But as impermanent fixtures, these camps do not indicate regular commercial journeys.

The mid-first century CE seems to have been the transition point in the construction of permanent ports. The *Periplus of the Erythraean Sea*, a Greek-Hellenistic source describing for the Romans the monsoon winds for journeys to and from India, mentions Yemenis intermarrying with locals in the town of Rhapta along the Kenyan coast.

The archaeological remnants of Rhapta have not yet been located, but Roman glass beads and shards found in digs on the island of Zanzibar and the nearby Tanzanian coast suggest regular journeys beginning around 200 CE. The beads and ceramics were presumably intended to be exchanged for ivory, rock crystal, ostrich feathers, and hardwood. If true, the roots of the later Swahili cities antedated the spread of Islam by several centuries—just as they did in the case of Jenné-jeno in West Africa before the rise of Islamic Saharan kingdoms.

Patterns of African History, 600 BCE–600 CE

Based on a modestly productive agriculture, sub-Saharan Africa evolved along two basic patterns in the period 600 BCE–600 CE. First, in the northeast Meroë and Aksum adapted themselves to Middle Eastern agriculture, including the plow and irrigation techniques. In addition, both African-domesticated sorghum and millet—and in Aksum teff—were grown. With the help of irrigated farming and long-distance trade, chiefs built kingdoms, which lasted as long as the urban infrastructure could be supported. The exhaustion of timber in the vicinity of the capitals ended the royal pattern of social and political evolution in the sub-Saharan northeast.

Second, in the northwest of sub-Saharan Africa inhabitants pioneered the agricultures of the steppe, savanna, and rain forest on the basis of millet, rice, yam, and the fruit of the oil palm. Millet was productive enough to support the rise of villages. In one steppe region, the inland delta of the Niger, the irrigated farming of millet and rice allowed for the rise of a dense village network, village nucleation, and eventually a city, Jenné-jeno. With its incipient long-distance trade, this city foreshadowed the post-600 rise of Saharan kingdoms. Farther south, in the rain forest, the farming of yam, banana, and oil palm supported the emergence of small and widely dispersed villages. The expansion of the Bantus and their agriculture brought village life as well as iron smelting to all parts of sub-Saharan Africa.

Africa and the Americas The Americas displayed striking similarities to the internal sub-Saharan interactions and adaptations. The latter, as we have seen, were responsible for patterns of village, city, and kingdom formation. In Mesoamerica as well as the Peruvian Andes Mountains, internal processes of interaction and adaptation based on increasingly productive agricultures also supported a pattern of village, city-state, and kingdom development from 600 BCE to 600 CE.

The principal difference, however, was that in sub-Saharan Africa this evolution gradually expanded also to the central and southern regions, whereas in the Americas no such expansion took place until after 600 CE. Social and political formation patterns spread to North America only after 600 CE, as represented by the Pueblo and Cahokia cultures in what are today the US states of Arizona, Utah, New Mexico, and Missouri.

Early States in Mesoamerica: Maya Kingdoms and Teotihuacán

In Chapter 5 we saw that the chiefdoms of Caral-Supe (2600–2000 BCE) and Chavín de Huántar (1000–200 BCE) in the Andes as well as of the Olmecs (1200–600 BCE) in Mesoamerica represent early examples of social processes of development from agriculture and villages to urbanization, chiefdoms, and kingdoms. In the period of 600 BCE–600 CE, in the southern Yucatán Peninsula of modern southeastern Mexico and the Mexican Basin in south-central Mexico, chiefdoms evolved into full-fledged kingdoms. In the Andes, urban centers continued to form under chiefly rule, although in Teotihuacán and Moche the urban culture was nearly as diversified as in the Mesoamerican kingdoms.

The Maya Kingdoms in Southern Mesoamerica

Closeness to the equator and a long rainy season supported a dense rain forest in the central Yucatán Peninsula. By creating clear-cuts and heaping up the soil on elevated fields or terraces on hill slopes, Maya villagers built a rich agriculture based on squash, beans, and corn. Around 600 BCE towns evolved into cities, where chieftains transformed themselves into kings. By organizing the labor of the farmers during slack agricultural times in the winter, they created city-states with imposing temple pyramids and palaces, surrounded by outlying villages. Among these city-states, the most powerful during the period 600 BCE–600 CE were Tikal and Kalakmul (see Map 6.3).

Mayaland on the Yucatán Peninsula The climate of the Yucatán Peninsula is subtropical, with a rainy season extending from May to September. The base of the Yucatán Peninsula consisted of rain-forest lowlands and swamps, traversed by rivers. To the south were rain-forest highlands, sloping from a chain of mountains about 80–110 miles wide, which descended gradually toward the lowlands in the north and abruptly to the Pacific coast in the south. The northern region comprised the tip of the Yucatán and consisted of dry and riverless lowlands. Maya culture began in the center and south and later radiated into the southern mountains and northern lowlands. Underlying the northern lowland areas was a limestone shelf that provided stone for construction. Here, local *chert* (a fine-grained sedimentary silica-rich rock) and flint deposits provided for the fashioning of tools with which to quarry the limestone. The volcanic south was quarried for its lava stone and was also rich in obsidian and jade. Quetzals, birds whose feathers were used for prestigious ornamentation, inhabited this region as well (see Map 6.3), which was thus rich in resources.

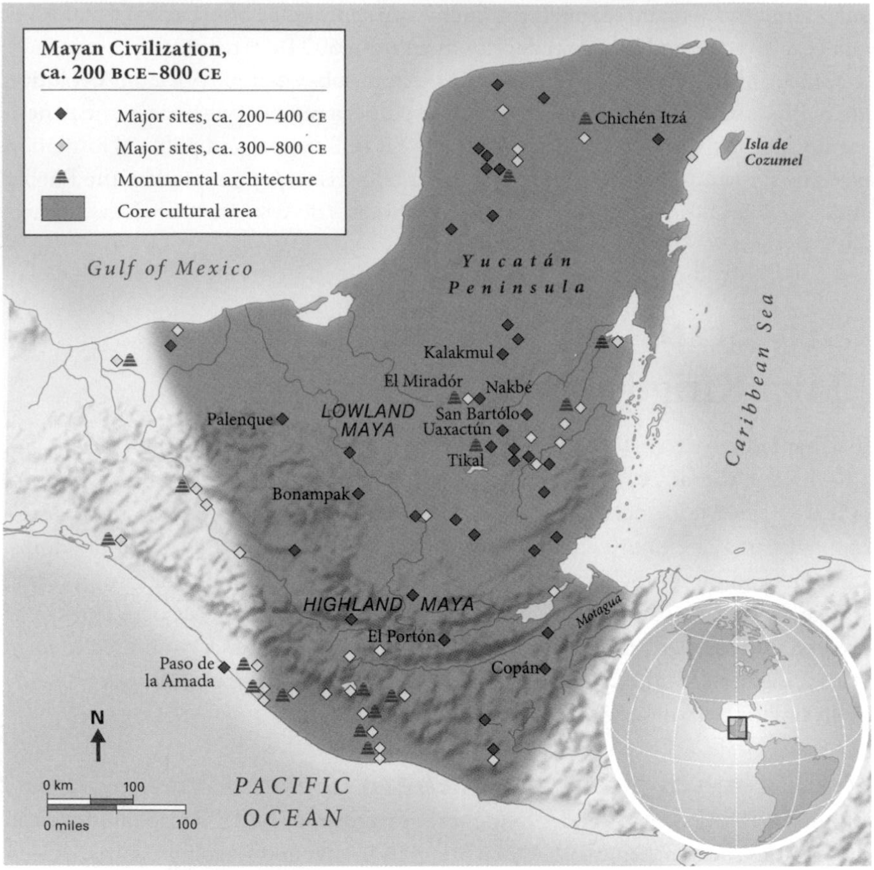

MAP **6.3 Mayan Civilization, ca. 200 BCE–800 CE.**

The people in the Yucatán highlands and lowlands spoke varieties of Mayan dialects. Even though they were exposed early on to Olmec cultural influence to the west, it does not appear that there was much Olmec immigration as Maya culture formed. As the early Mayas became sedentary in the center of the peninsula and along the Pacific, they cut down the rain forest in order to clear fields, drain swamps, and build villages on low stone platforms near water sources. Drainage ditches in fields indicate a beginning intensification of agriculture. By around 1000 BCE, some villages evolved into towns, dominating village clusters around them. Elite lineages under chieftains resided in the towns and controlled the best lands, while more humble lineages in the surrounding villages were on less productive soils. Although society continued to be organized by familial descent, social stratification by wealth began to differentiate the lineages. This stratification is archaeologically recognizable from rich tomb gifts as well as corrective dentistry: Then, as now, the wealthy had enhanced means to beautify themselves.

Early Kingdoms As in the agrarian centers of Eurasia, debt dependence was probably the earliest lever of power in the hands of the Mayan chieftains. Poor farmers, it can be assumed, borrowed seeds from rich farmers and during droughts were often unable to return what they had borrowed. Rich farmers had larger families, built bigger homes, and had more domestic workers producing pottery and textiles. They traded manufactured goods for goods not locally available, such as obsidian and jade. Thus, in the period 1000–600 BCE, these wealthy farmers transformed themselves into chieftains, exerting family rule for more or less extended periods over a central town surrounded by satellite villages.

Beginning in the seventh century BCE, chieftains in some agriculturally rich areas increased their wealth so that they could claim to be kings (sing. *ajaw*). Kings surrounded themselves with military forces through which they made themselves the ultimate arbiters in all town disputes. They began to collect taxes, enlarge their towns into *cities*—that is, centers with craftspeople and merchants who did not practice agriculture—and conquer other villages. During slack times in the agricultural cycle, these kings commanded farmers to construct the first ceremonial monuments—rectangular platforms up to 50 feet in elevation with temples and royal residences on top. Olmec-inspired stone stelae with images of human figures, dressed in Maya-style clothing, were placed around the platforms. Nakbé (700 BCE–150 CE), a city in the north of the central lowlands, was the site of the first temple pyramids on ceremonial platforms. These pyramids were stepped stone structures, as high as 200 feet, with staircases to the temples on top. In those elevated temples, kings conducted their sacrifices in tribute to the gods of the emerging divine pantheon.

A nearby town, El Miradór (600 BCE–150 CE), became a city with surrounding villages about a century after Nakbé. Perhaps favored by better trade connections than Nakbé, El Miradór gradually surpassed its neighbor in size and monumental ambitions. With about 100,000 inhabitants, hundreds of ceremonial and palatial structures on its platforms, and a 216-foot pyramid built around 300 BCE, this Mayan city was the largest early center of what ultimately were more than 4,400 Mayan urban and rural sites. Only the later Tikal (200–600 CE) reached a similar size. El Miradór was explored systematically by archaeologists for the first time only in 1978–1983 and then again beginning in 2003. To their surprise, this site turned out to be as fully Mayan, with its temple pyramids, elite structures, stelae, ball courts, sweat houses, and commoner quarters, as the later and better-known centers. Maya culture at its peak has to be considered—as it is in this chapter—within a much longer time horizon than previously assumed.

El Miradór, La Danta Temple, 600 BCE–150 CE. By height (230 feet), volume, and footprint, this pyramid was the largest of all Maya sacred structures and one of the largest buildings of the premodern world. At present, the site is only partially excavated, and archaeological work is still ongoing. The temple visible atop the pyramid is surmounted by a rooster-like roof comb, once covered by stucco figurines of Maya deities.

Progress made since the 1990s in deciphering the Maya glyphic script has allowed the conclusion that "Mayaland" consisted of some 15–17 fully evolved, dominant kingdoms in the central lowlands during the Early Classic Period, each with a capital and one or more secondary cities, plus countless towns and villages nearby. Marriage alliances among the royal lineages of the capitals and secondary cities served to maintain the cohesion of the kingdom. Rebellions by secondary cities, however, often called the power of the kings into question. Many scholars think that the frequent wars in Mayaland were either intrakingdom rebellions or wars among secondary cities in different kingdoms. The only exception was the direct military competition between the kingdoms of Tikal and Kalakmul, which endured for many centuries.

Spirituality and Polytheism The kings and their royal households lived in palaces adjacent to the temple pyramids. When they ascended the throne, in the tradition of American spirituality, kings often assumed the names of animals or combined them with the names of human-made objects—for example, "Spearthrower Owl," "Shield Jaguar," and "Smoke Squirrel." Heirs to the throne, usually the eldest sons, used the same name but with the suffix II, III, and so forth. On wall paintings, earthenware vessels, and stelae, kings were recognizable through their elaborate headdresses decorated with quetzal feathers, animal masks, and richly embroidered clothing. When sons were still minors, their mothers assumed the roles of regents. Occasionally, women ruled as queens. After death, kings were buried in pyramids or in separate tombs. Dead kings were assumed to have taken their place among the gods, residing in abodes both above and beneath the earth.

Polytheism: Personification of the forces of nature and performance of rituals and sacrifices to ensure the benevolence of the gods and goddesses.

Polytheism had begun to develop on top of traditional spirituality after the emergence of the first villages around 2500 BCE. Traditional spirituality was shared by all, commoners and chiefs. The gods of polytheism were more powerful than the spirits of ancestors. They were the embodiments of forces of nature whose favor the kings—more powerful than chiefs—curried if rich harvests were to occur and the kingdom was to flourish.

The Mayan kings considered themselves servants of the many animal, nature, star, and war gods which had come to populate the divine pantheon by the time of the Olmecs in the eleventh century BCE and continued to grow during the Maya period. They fulfilled the demands of these gods for sacrifices during daily rituals in the temples atop the pyramids. The main sacrifice was the gift of blood—a heritage from traditional spirituality: blood as the force of life—which Mayan kings drew from their earlobes, tongues, and penises. During times of war, captured enemies, from kings to commoners, were also sacrificed. Through their blood, the kings nourished nature and supported the human and divine worlds.

The Ruling Classes Apart from their temple service, kings and leading officials also assembled for the administration of justice, the collection of rents and tributes, commercial exchanges, and diplomatic relations. Many of these functions required expert knowledge of the annual calendar as labor on palaces or pyramids could be required from farmers only during specific times in the agricultural cycle. Other functions, such as military action, required divination to discover the most favorable star constellations under which to proceed. The tracking of these units of times required a specialized group of calendar specialists, mathematicians, and astronomers.

The Mayan calendar was an outgrowth of developments that began sometime after 1000 BCE in Olmec-influenced Paso de la Amada. One calendar was the 260-day, or 9-month, divinatory calendar, which scholars interpret as being related to the human gestation period. A second calendar, based on the solar year of 365 days and important for determining the beginnings of the agricultural seasons, was nearly as old. A third calendar was the Mayan Calendar Round, occurring every 52 years when the divinatory and solar calendars began on the same day. The Mayas believed that this calendar inaugurated cycles of calamitous as well as fortuitous times. The fourth calendar in use among the Mayas was the Long Count Calendar, which counted the days elapsed since the mythical origin of the universe (corresponding to August 11, 3114 BCE, in the Gregorian calendar). A sophisticated mathematics, based on a *vigesimal* system of numbers (base 20, unlike our modern base-10 system), undergirded the calculations necessary for the coordination of these four calendars.

Other activities of the royal family and leading courtiers consisted of daily processions and feasts during which copious amounts of cacao, spiced with chili, vanilla, and honey, were consumed. Alternatively, the elite consumed chocolate wafers, forerunners of our modern chocolate bars, which were also used as easily transportable nourishment on journeys. Finally, the court attended ball games in stadiums, which formed part of the temple-palace grounds. As in the kingdoms of Eurasia, but without evidence of any influence, in Maya kingdoms the occupations and functions of the ruling class were ritualized, refined pastimes far beyond the reach of common farmers and craftspeople. A stratified social hierarchy typified the Maya kingdoms (see "Patterns Up Close").

The Commoners The commoners, whose taxes supported the royal courts, lived in housing compounds of a few thatched huts or clusters of huts erected around courtyards on stone platforms, which allowed them to be above the floodwaters during the rainy season from May to September. In these houses, women were in charge of cooking, weaving, pottery making, the growing of garden vegetables and fruits, and the rearing of domestic animals (including dogs, turkeys, and pigeons). Garden fruits included avocado, guava, papaya, vanilla, and pineapple. Within the household, women and men shared the crafts of toolmaking, fabricating tools from chert, bone, and wood. In larger Maya kingdoms some households seem to have specialized more than others in tool manufacturing and weaving, with both women and men participating.

Men were in charge of growing corn in fields which were cut into the rain forest through slash-and-burn techniques. Fields near rivers and in swamps were "raised fields" (Spanish *chinampas*), rectangular islands on which the mud from adjacent canals had been heaped. The main agricultural implement was the digging stick (Mayan *kool* [kohl]), with which farmers loosened the soil and dropped corn kernels into a hole. Slopes along river valleys were terraced in order to retain rain or irrigation water. Cotton, cacao, and tobacco fields formed special plantations because of either special soil preparation or intensive labor needs. Hunting and fishing with bow and arrow, blowguns, and harpoons, skills inherited from forager times, remained important occupations among both royals and commoners.

The hard agricultural labor of the commoners produced an agricultural surplus, which supported ruling dynastic families as well as craftspeople in the cities. Craftspeople worked for the construction and maintenance of royal palaces, creating monuments, wall paintings, pottery, and inscriptions on stone pillars or stelae.

Mayan Writing Excavations in the early 2000s suggest that Mayan writing might have begun around 400–300 BCE. These early texts—although similar in appearance to the fully evolved script of the later centuries—still await decipherment. Their age raises the important question among Maya specialists of whether the notion of the late Olmecs having developed writing first can still be maintained. The Mayas might very likely have been the originators.

Mayan writing is a **glyphic** as well as a syllabic script, numbering some 800 signs. It is structurally similar to Sumerian cuneiform and Egyptian hieroglyphics. In their basic form, glyphs are *pictograms*, one-word images of the most essential features of

Glyphic script: The Maya developed a script of some 800 images. Some are pictograms standing for words; others are syllables to be combined with other syllables to form words.

what is to be depicted (for example, the glyph for a human being would be a stick figure with body, legs, arms, and a head). But gyphs were also used as syllables, consisting of one, two, or three signs combining consonants and vowels. Combinations of multiple syllabic glyphs, or *syllabaries*, are pronounced as a series of syllables. Given the mixture of pictograms and syllabaries, which is of potentially immense size, the complexity of Mayan writing appeared for a long time to be an insuperable obstacle to any effort at deciphering.

A breakthrough came only in the 1960s and 1970s when scholars successfully interpreted a number of stelae monuments as records of royal births, accessions to the throne, and deaths. First, scholars realized that Mayan writing had the previously mentioned syllabic component; then, the Russian-born American architect and Maya specialist Tatiana Proskouriakoff discovered that the inscriptions on many royal stelae contained information on dynastic dates and events. The final breakthrough came during a conference at the Maya site of Palenque in 1973 when participants recognized the syllables *k'inchi* as referring to the Mayan sun god as well as individual kings.

As first in Mesopotamia and then in many other places, kings invoked patron gods that symbolized forces in nature and thereby became founders of polytheism, as mentioned before. In one inspirational afternoon, a working group consisting of the art historian and epigrapher Linda Schele, the linguist Floyd Lounsbury, and the undergraduate Peter Mathews deciphered the king list of Palenque, containing eight rulers. Since then, scholars have assembled a dictionary of as many as 1,000 words, and it has become possible to embark on a systematic chronicling of the dynasties of Maya kingdoms (see Source 6.4).

The Crisis of the Kingdoms Spectacular building activities characterized Mayaland during ca. 400–600 CE. Ruling classes must have grown to considerable sizes, and it is possible that farmers in some kingdoms were no longer willing to produce food staples as well as provide labor for the pyramid temples and palaces. Destruction identified in some archaeological sites could be interpreted as the result of revolts. In other places, overexploitation of the soil, loss of topsoil on terraces, or salinization of lowland fields as the result of neglected drainage might have increased the imbalance between the peasants and ruling classes. Frequent wars among the kings might have reduced the size of the ruling class, but their wars clearly also had negative consequences for the farmers.

The destructive interplay among the ruling class, farmers, and the environment produced a crisis beginning in the late 500s CE and extending through the mid-600s CE. It led to the collapse of many older Mayan kingdoms and endangered the survival of the strongest newer ones in the southern lowlands. When the crisis ended, the political weight of Maya power shifted to the northern lowlands of the Yucatán Peninsula.

The Kingdom of Teotihuacán in the Mexican Basin

The subtropical climate of Yucatán extended northward into the highlands, in which the Mexican Basin was the largest agricultural region. Although the high elevation did not allow for the full breadth of Mayan agriculture, the alluvial soil and water from the surrounding mountains supported a productive agriculture of beans, squash, and corn. The northern part of the basin developed a rich village life later than the south, but its closeness to obsidian quarries gave these villages commercial advantages. Militarily and economically, the town of Teotihuacán in the north caught up to the Mayan south around the early 100s CE and developed into a city-state that became politically and culturally dominant across all of what is today Mexico.

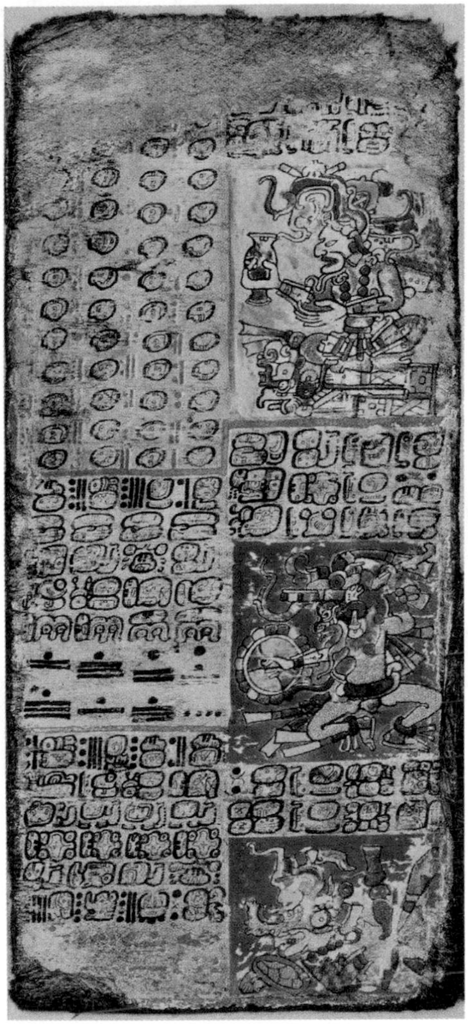

Mayan Glyphs. Beginning in the fourth century BCE, scribes in the Maya kingdoms developed a written language composed of pictograms and syllables, eventually numbering about 800 signs. This language allowed communication among educated people in the different Maya kingdoms who spoke often mutually unintelligible local languages. Because of the double meaning of each glyph as pictogram and syllable, it took most of the twentieth century for scholars to decipher the Mayan language. The example shown here is from the Dresden Codex.

image analysis

The Mexican Basin The Mexican Basin is a large, 7,400-foot-high bowl without river outlets in southern Mexico. In the center of the bowl was Lake Texcoco [tes-CO-co], nourished by rivers flowing down from 15,000-foot-high mountain chains on the eastern and western sides. As in Mayaland, the basin enjoyed a rainy season during the summer. River water, channeled through irrigation canals to terraces and the flatlands around the central lake, as well as numerous bays, supported a moderately productive agriculture.

During the period of village expansion (1200–600 BCE), many of the slopes surrounding this bowl were forested. There was plenty of firewood and timber for construction, as well as abundant wildlife for the hunt. Fish in the freshwater bays of the lake were another important food source. Clay deposits in the flatlands and obsidian quarries on the slopes of the still-active volcanoes in the northeastern mountains provided resources for the manufacture of ceramics, tools, and weapons. However, the high elevation and temperature differences between winter and summer did not allow for cultivation of cotton, cacao, vanilla, and other tropical fruits which enriched lowland Maya agriculture. These latter products had to be acquired by trade.

The principal plant fiber for the weaving of clothes came from the *maguey* [ma-GAY] plant, a large, deep-rooted, agave-like cactus that could grow in poor soil and did not need much water. The fiber was obtained from scraping the sweet-tasting flesh off the interior of the long, stalk-like leaves. The flesh contained a juice which, in its fermented state, was consumed as an alcoholic drink called *pulque* [Spanish, PULL-kay; Nahuatl, *octli*]. If people wished to manufacture clothes from cotton or acquire cacao, vanilla, jade, or quetzal feathers, they had to trade their obsidian. Commercial exchange was a necessary ingredient in the period of village expansion and played a major part in the subsequent pattern of kingdom formation.

Teotihuacán In a wide valley to the northeast of Lake Texcoco, traversed by the San Juan River and endowed with rich alluvial soil, villagers in the early centuries of the Common Era dug a large canal system with raised fields similar to those of the Maya. Around 100 BCE, villages around this canal network began to cluster, eventually forming the city of Teotihuacán. When the transition from chieftains to kings and chiefly dynasties occurred is impossible to determine on the basis of the present archaeological record. The iconic writing system, less developed than that of the Mayas and lacking syllabic elements, does not allow for identification of any rulers

Patterns Up Close

The Mayan Ball Game

One of the most remarkable features in Mesoamerica was the team ball game. Although it shares its ancient age with similar games in China, the Persian Middle East, and the Greek and Roman Mediterranean, only in Mesoamerica was it a game with formal rules, played in stadiums constructed specifically for this purpose. In Mesoamerica, archaeologists in 1985 discovered the oldest stadium to date, from 1400 BCE, in the ruins of Paso de la Amada, a chiefdom town with surrounding villages in the far southeast of today's Mexico. Adjacent to the palace of the chief, this ball court measures 260 by 23 feet, with two 7-foot-high spectator platforms on both long sides. Later on, during the Maya period, these platforms usually rose theater-style on both sides, for better viewing from farther away. Given the proximity of the ball court to the chief's residence, it is possible that other chiefdoms in the area engaged in what we would call today "league tournaments."

The Mayan Ball Game. Note the strong body protection around the midsections of the players as well as the elaborate headdresses, symbolizing animals.

The ball was made of solid rubber, from a gum- or latex-producing tree growing in the area of Paso. Balls were around 2 feet or more in diameter and weighed 8 pounds. Given these dimensions, players often wore protective gear around their hips and helmets on their heads, as shown in murals and on ceramics.

Under the Maya, who called the game *pitz* and built about

or lineages. Teotihuacán was a city-state with an anonymous dynasty, centered in a city and surrounded by villages. In its physical appearance it was even more imposing than most of the Maya kingdoms (see Map 6.4).

In the first century CE, the rulers of Teotihuacán began spectacular building projects. They laid out an urban grid along a north–south axis, dubbed the "Avenue of the Dead" by archaeologists, which included two densely constructed city quarters of some 2,200 housing units. Each unit housed a patrilineal clan of 60–100 members. Near the central avenue, closely packed and plastered adobe houses were divided by alleyways. Some 600 houses had the appearance of workshops, primarily for the making of tools from the gray and green obsidian mined near Teotihuacán. The workshops indicate a degree of nonagricultural crafts specialization, which one would expect from a city. Farther away, houses and fields were interspersed. Canals, reservoirs, and an extensive drainage system facilitated the transportation of food, the provision of drinking water, and the elimination of waste. By around 300 CE, Teotihuacán had grown to as many as 100,000 inhabitants. It was a metropolis easily comparable to Rome, Ctesiphon, and Alexandria in the Roman Mediterranean and Persian Middle East; Pataliputra in Gupta India; and Chang'an in Han China.

An aerial view of Teotihuacán's ruins conveys the vast scale on which the temple pyramids, palaces, markets, and city quarters were built. The Temples of the Moon and the Sun, built at the northern end of the city, represent the earliest structures.

1,500 courts, the rules became more formalized. A basic rule was that the ball had to be hit with the hip only and had to remain aloft. But variations are also known in which players struck the ball with forearms, bats, or hand stones. The size of a team extended from one to seven players. The team that lost was the one that dropped the ball most often.

The significance of the Mayan ball game fits into the larger picture of agrarian–urban society and its chiefdom and kingdom patterns when polytheism with its innumerable rituals and sacrificial practices assumed elaborate proportions. Although the archaeological record is debatable, it appears that ball games took place during chiefly or royal festivities and fertility rituals, and perhaps also human sacrifices. The apparent but also disputed role of some players as human sacrifices on a number of murals was a late Mayan phenomenon. Today, in scientific–industrial society, these roots of "games" in past rituals, processions, and reenactments of divine events are largely forgotten. Instead, sports have their own modern rituals, such as flag waving, parading, tailgating, and hooliganism. Whether religious or secular, rituals are permanent fixtures that follow their own patterns, parallel to those of society at large.

Questions

- How did the ball game serve as a microcosm for larger patterns in Mayan society?
- What function could the ball game have played in relations among the various Mayan chiefdoms?

They were ceremonial centers which attracted pilgrims from everywhere in the Mexican Basin and beyond. Archaeologists interpret the Temple of the Sun as a construction on top of a cave symbolizing the entrance to the nether world. In the third century CE, the temple of the god of the feathered serpent (Nahuatl *Quetzalcoatl* [ket-sal-COA]) followed, probably built in honor of the then reigning dynasty. The founding king sacrificed some 260 humans, probably war captives, to garner the good will of the god. After what appears to have been an internal uprising and change in leadership in the 400s CE, the new rulers destroyed the temple's facade and erected an attachment (Spanish *adosada*) in front of it. Colorful wall paintings and pottery, depicting rulers, priests, gods, and mythical figures in processions, rituals, and dances, still survive, attesting to a highly developed aesthetic culture. Today, after a century of intermittent excavations, much has been learned about the city's architecture, but little is yet known about its rulers and inhabitants.

The Decline of the City As in the case of the Maya kingdoms, the balance among the peasantry, urban inhabitants, dynasties, and construction programs was not always easy to maintain. Hints at an internal upheaval point to the balance being lost for a first time around 400 CE. Another such upheaval occurred in the late 500s CE, to judge from fires and destructions along the Avenue of the Dead, possibly in the course of a popular uprising against the rulers. Thereafter, the population of

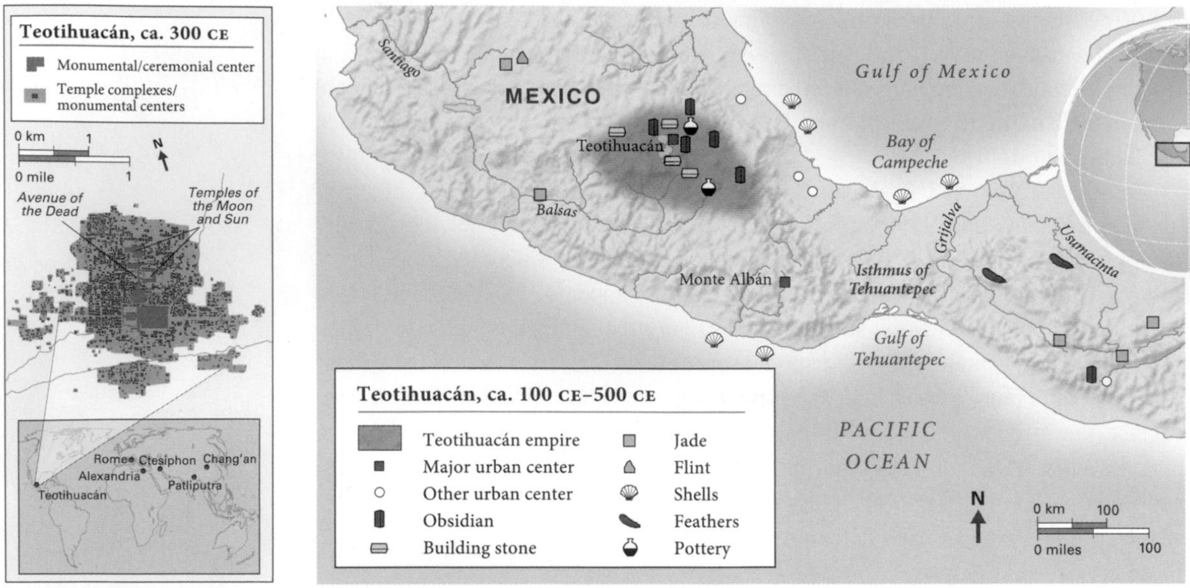

MAP 6.4 **Teotihuacán, ca. 100–500 CE.**

the central city quarters declined rapidly, although the outlying quarters continued to exist, reverting back to the village level as farming communities for centuries to come. The mid-500s CE saw prolonged periods of cooler weather and droughts and were generally a more difficult time for farming in the Americas. As we shall see in Chapter 15, in contrast to the agriculturally richer Maya kingdoms, the less endowed Mexican Basin found a return to urbanism and dynastic states more difficult.

At its height, Teotihuacán exerted a commercial, cultural, and perhaps even political influence considerably greater than the Maya kingdoms. Its trade reached deep into Mayaland and beyond, to the Isthmus of Panama. Teotihuacán exchanged its obsidian for cotton, rubber, cacao, jade, and quetzal feathers from the subtropical lowlands. Its gods, especially the deity of the feathered serpent, were sacrificed to everywhere in Mesoamerica. Similarly, Teotihuacán was instrumental in spreading the so-called *talud-tablero* architectural style (sets of inward-sloping platforms, surmounted by temples) from the Basin of Mexico to the Yucatán Peninsula. In the later 300s CE and throughout the 400s CE, Maya rulers of Tikal, Uaxactún [wa-shac-TOON], and other kingdoms claimed descent from rulers of Teotihuacán, evidently seeking to benefit from the city's prestige as a ceremonial center.

The Andes: Moche and Nazca

In Andean South America, a pattern of chiefdom formation, wherein chieftains controlled urban ceremonial centers and surrounding villages, evolved between 3000 and 2000 BCE, a millennium earlier than in Mesoamerica. Given the absence of large plains and the enormous differences in elevation within short distances, however, relatively small chiefdoms remained the dominant social formation in the Andes. Still, around 1000–200 BCE, a major ceremonial center like Chavín de Huántar (north of present-day Lima) was a town with fewer than 5,000 inhabitants, even though it was a pilgrimage site for most of the Andes. Chavín's successors, the chiefdoms of Moche and Nazca, although somewhat larger, remained within the chiefdom pattern during the period 600 BCE–600 CE.

The Moche in Northern Peru

The Moche Valley was the place of the two largest ceremonial centers in the Andes, the Temple Pyramids of the Sun and the Moon. The power of its main chiefdom must have been impressive, since large numbers of farmers had to be mobilized for the construction of these pyramids. But it remained a federation of village chiefdoms clustered around an urbanized temple center with a dominant chiefly lineage.

Moche Origins The Moche Valley was at the center of nine coastal valleys in what is today northern Peru. It had a subtropical climate south of the equator with moderately wet winters from April to November and dry summers from December to March. It was based on an irrigated agriculture of corn, pulses, cotton, and potatoes; llamas and alpacas from the highlands were domesticated for wool and light transportation. Here, the earliest evidence of the emergence of the Moche chiefdoms (100–750 CE) is the tomb of the "Lord of Sipán," dated to 50 CE. The tomb contained the chief's mummy, clad in warrior clothing and richly decorated with gold and silver necklaces, nose rings, earrings, helmets, and bracelets. Eight people were buried with him, including his wife, two other women (perhaps concubines), a military officer, a watchman, a banner holder, a child, and a dog. This chieftain was wealthy and powerful indeed.

A Federated Chiefdom Half a century later, Moche chieftains began the construction of the two Temple Pyramids of the Sun and the Moon, huge stepped structures made of adobe bricks. Markers on the bricks indicate the participation of about 100 village teams in the construction, which lasted intermittently for centuries. The platforms contain the burial places of Moche chieftains and priests and the remains of human sacrifices brought during ceremonies and rituals. At the feet of the two temples was a city that included administrative offices and workshops. Lesser chieftain lineages ruled in the more remote valleys. Altogether the chiefdoms formed a loose federation around a main ceremonial center and pilgrimage place.

Teotihuacán, Temple of the Feathered Serpent God Quetzalcóatl. This sculpture of a serpent's head with its exposed, menacing fangs and the collar made of feathers is one of many along the front wall of this temple. The hybrid deity [quetzal bird and snake (*cóatl*)] bridged the fertile earth and the planet Venus, bringer of rain in the summer.

None of the participating villages appear to have grown beyond the moderately large spaces at the mouth of valleys, and it seems that they coexisted peacefully for the most part. When the generally cooler and drier climate of the sixth century CE arrived, it had a greater negative impact on the agriculture of the central chiefdom in Moche, closer to the coast and at the end of the river streams, than on the chiefdoms upstream in the valleys. In the Moche Valley with its two huge temples the balance between chiefly elites and farmers was more difficult to maintain than in the farther valleys with smaller elites and comparatively larger peasantries. Eventually, in the early 600s CE, the Moche elite dissolved, while smaller elites in nearby valleys carried on and eventually disappeared also, sometime around 750 CE (see Map 6.5).

Paracas and the Nazca in Southern Peru

Southern Peru was much drier, and its agrarian population density lagged behind that of the north. The chiefdoms were correspondingly more modest. Nevertheless, Paracas [pa-RA-cas] represents one of the earliest burial places for mummies in the world, and Nazca offers the most elaborate petroglyphs of the Americas. The two possess, therefore, considerable cultural significance.

Moche Terra-Cotta Portrait Vessel with Handle, ca. 100–800 CE. Archaeologists assume that the vessel shows a chief. Other types of Moche vessels show deities, animals, ritual objects, sexual acts (for education?), domestic objects, and crafts activities. Potters often used stone molds for making their wares. Among the Andes peoples, the Moche potters were among the most imaginative and versatile.

Paracas Chiefs Desert conditions on the southern Peruvian coast and full dependence on runoff water from Andean snowmelt between January and March after the Andean winter required more elaborate irrigation works than on the northern coast. The patterns of social formation from foraging to villages and chiefdoms with ceremonial centers were correspondingly slower and more modest. Shamans and chiefs on the Paracas peninsula and the Ica valley set the pattern in motion when they unified a number of hamlets. Subsequently, other Paracas chiefdoms appeared in neighboring valleys, forming a loose confederation (750 BCE–1 CE).

A necropolis on the peninsula contained hundreds of mummies of chieftains, wrapped in the colorful, high-quality wool and cotton mantles still characteristic of southern Peru today. It was primarily through the icons woven into the mantles and painted on pottery that modern scholars identified the Paracas chiefs. These icons included figures—shamanic ancestors or early agricultural, polytheistic deities—holding weapons, plants, or skulls. Other icons were felines, birds, or whales, often with human-like features reminiscent of Paleolithic cave paintings in other parts of the world. Although contemporary with the Maya kingdoms in Mesoamerica, the Paracas chiefdoms in the Andes were culturally still compact.

The Nazca Ceremonial Center The transition from pottery painted after firing to predecorated or slipware ceramics defines the shift from the Paracas to the Nazca chiefdoms (1–650 CE). Nazca chiefs built ceremonial centers, not the monumental freestanding ones as on the northern Peruvian coast but more modest adobe structures, which actually covered preexisting mounds. Cahuachi [ca-wooh-WAH-chee], the main pilgrimage center, contained 40 such structures, assumed to represent the contributing chiefdoms.

During the extended cold weather and drought periods of the sixth century CE, when a number of rivers dried out, Nazca chiefs mobilized the villagers in the valleys for the construction of an extensive tunnel network for irrigation. Workers tapped underground water in the mountains and guided it onto the slopes of the valleys and into reservoirs. These highly sophisticated constructions, with intermittent shafts and manholes for cleaning and repair, were built so sturdily that many of them are still in operation today. Called *puquios* [Quechua, POO-kyos], they are reminiscent of the much later *qanat* [Arabic, ka-NAHT] structures of Islamic Iran and Morocco. In the agrarian age, chiefdoms could be technologically just as innovative as kingdoms and empires.

Geoglyphs: Long geometric lines and figures as well as outlines of animals formed in the desert by removing darker stones and exposing the lighter sand underneath.

The Nazca Geoglyphs Another Nazca innovation was the so-called Nazca **geoglyphs**, large geometric and animal figures laid out in the dry highlands and on

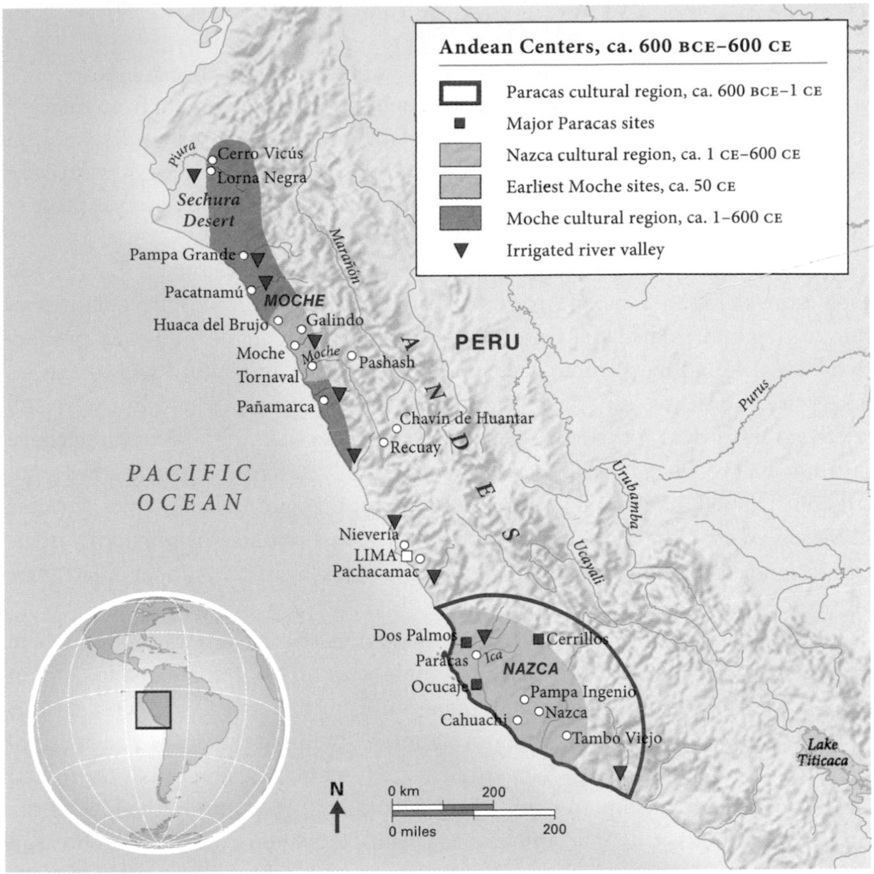

MAP 6.5 **Andean Centers, 600 BCE–600 CE.**

the valley slopes of the chiefdoms. Villagers constructed straight and zigzag lines, triangles and trapezoids, as well as images of a monkey, spider, whale, and several birds with astounding precision by removing dark-colored rocks and exposing the lighter sand underneath. These geoglyphs, totaling some 300, are unique to the Andes, and the closest parallel was not created until nearly a millennium later when the Incas arranged sacred objects (Quechua, *huacas*) outside their capital, Cuzco, in straight lines.

There are, however, vague parallels with a considerable number of undated later geoglyphs in the Great Basin and other western regions of North America. Native Americans under the leadership of shamans used these later geoglyphs during rituals in which they evoked honored figures, animals, and events of the mythical past. Processual archaeologists (archaeologists applying concepts of cultural evolutionism) relate the Nazca symbols to the abstract Paleolithic geometric cave symbols found in Africa, Europe, and Australia (see Chapter 1). But since the purpose of these symbols is also unknown, a fully convincing theory is still elusive. (See "Against the Grain: Nazca Lines and Speculation.")

Nazca Lines: A Spider. These lines can only be seen from the air—drawn perhaps in honor of a sky god who can see them from above?

Eventually, the Nazca came under the influence of the highland state of Wari, a later city-state in the Andes (see Chapter 15). This state expanded its political and cultural influence toward the southern Peruvian coast in the first half of the 700s CE and gradually transformed the identity of the Nazca chiefdoms.

Putting It All Together

interactive concept map

In the period 600 BCE–600 CE, agriculture and life in villages became nearly universal in the world. Only Australia remained outside this development from foraging to agrarian settlement. Of course, remnants of foraging societies survived, notably in sub-Saharan Africa and even more so in the Americas. But it is nevertheless striking that humans on the latter two continents developed in the same direction as those in Eurasia toward cities, kingdoms, and long-distance luxury trade.

Agrarian-based urban culture, however, was a fragile achievement in Eurasia and even more so in sub-Saharan Africa, Mesoamerica, and the Andes. Irregularities of the weather and, in the latter regions, the slow improvement of food plant productivity (as revealed by plant archaeologists) meant that agriculture was a tenuous enterprise. Corncobs, especially, had evolved toward greater length but were still relatively short during the Maya period. Only by the time of the Aztecs, selective breeding had produced corn of modern proportions. As a rule, dynastic cities regularly outstripped the natural resources of their local environments, as was the case in Meroë, Aksum, the Maya cities, and Teotihuacán. But once the possibility of urbanization had arrived, this option was usually not lost again and sooner or later new city-based states arose.

As we have seen in this chapter, the primary dynastic urban achievements were monumental architecture, sophisticated metal and textile craftsmanship, and, in some cases, forms of intellectual expression. Typical examples covered in this chapter were the remarkably similar monumental temple pyramids and stelae of the kings in northeastern sub-Saharan Africa, Mesoamerica, and the Andes. Metal and textile craftsmanship, of course, had deep village roots on both sides of the Atlantic. Gold, silver, copper, and bronze jewelry was often exquisite, and the iron manufacturing in African villages was remarkably developed. In cities these crafts became the refined products of specialized workers who did not participate in farming.

Similarly, precocious intellectual achievements appeared both in nomadic contexts (complementary to agriculture), as witnessed by the Borana calendar of the Kushite nomads in Kenya, and in small-town agricultural chiefdoms, as seen in the giant geometric lines and animal outlines created in the desert landscape by the Nazca of Peru. By comparison, the intellectual pursuits in royal cities were on a much larger scale. Here, the Mayas took the prize with their complex calendar and script, as well as their elaborate divine pantheon and cosmogony.

Altogether, evolving largely on their own, both sub-Saharan Africa and the Americas made long strides in the period 600 BCE–600 CE toward expressing the same depth of humanity which was already on display in Eurasia. They did not yet have empires or possess the literary breadth that favored the rise of the visionaries of transcendence, hallmarks of the Middle East, India, and China during 600 BCE–600 CE. But their more compact cultures were not lacking in any of the overall patterns that characterized Eurasia.

Review and Relate

Thinking Through Patterns

Examine the ways historians approach the big questions of this chapter.

Innovations in world history usually originated in one specific place and then radiated outward to new populations through interactions among different peoples. Through adaptation, the new populations incorporated innovations into their own cultures. Adaptation was never slavish imitation; it was always a creative process of shaping something from a different culture to the new culture's needs and circumstances. Sub-Saharan Africa and the Americas were partially or entirely limited to their own internal patterns of innovation, given their relative or absolute isolation from Eurasia. Encountering the same experiences and challenges as humans in Eurasia, albeit somewhat later, their responses were remarkably comparable. Thus, the history of the world was not merely the history of peoples coming into more and more intensive contact with each other. It was also the history of peoples experiencing similar challenges without transcontinental interaction.

» How does comparing and contrasting sub-Saharan Africa with the Americas during 600 BCE–600 CE help in understanding the agrarian–urban patterns of social and political development across the world?

Agrarian sub-Saharan Africa during 600 BCE–600 CE is an example where interaction with the Middle East—as well as, in some periods, the absence of interaction—formed the background for comparable processes of economic, social, and political developments. The middle Nile valley and the highlands of Ethiopia gave rise to the plow-based agrarian kingdoms of Meroë and Aksum, both receiving their original plows and grain from the Middle East and maintaining a lively trade for luxury goods with that region. By contrast, the West African inland Niger delta grew into the urbanized chiefdom of Jenné-jeno with limited external interactions. Through interaction and adaptation, forms of farming as well as iron smelting (the latter perhaps received from the Middle East) traveled south in sub-Saharan Africa, together with the Bantu expansion.

» Where did chiefdoms, cities, and kingdoms arise in sub-Saharan Africa and why? On which forms of agriculture, urbanization, and trade were they based?

Three regions in the Americas were favorable for the development of densely settled villages, some of which subsequently evolved into cities and kingdoms: Yucatán with its Maya kingdoms, the Mexican Basin with the city-state of Teotihuacán, and Peru with the Moche and Nazca chiefdoms. The Maya kingdoms were economically and culturally the most differentiated polities—and the only ones to record the histories of their kings in writing on stelae and other monuments. Highly productive farming took place on riverbanks or hill terraces, with a surplus that supported the construction of elaborate temple pyramids and structures containing painted ceramics and wall paintings.

» Which areas in the Americas saw the development of a corn- and potato-based agriculture that did not depend on the plow, the wheel, and ironmaking?

Against the Grain

Consider this as a counterpoint to the main patterns examined in this chapter.

Nazca Lines and Speculation

- Is it important to be aware of purely speculative theories of world history? For what reasons?
- What are some other feats of ancient engineering, architecture, or craft that seem to inspire speculative (or even fantastic) theories? Do historians have a particular responsibility to engage with or dispute "fringe" theories?

Peruvian archaeologist Toribio Mejia Xesspe was the first scholar to describe the Nazca geoglyphs, which he viewed in 1927 from adjacent hills. The true extent of the glyphs and its many figures, however, became known only once seen from the air. The pioneer of the aerial mapping of the site was Paul Kosok, an American historian interested in ancient irrigation systems who crisscrossed the area by plane during the 1940s. Further mapping was carried out by his assistant, Maria Reiche, a trained mathematician from Germany interned during World War II in Peru. Reiche devoted her life to recording the Nazca lines and protecting them from encroachment by road builders and squatters.

Based on the discovery that a number of lines converged at the winter and summer solstices, Reiche published her theory that the Nazca geoglyphs were elements of a complex astronomical calendar and observatory, and the animal figures represented constellations. This theory did not find much support among later scholars, who demonstrated that only 20 percent of the glyphs had an astronomical significance. Reiche's theory, however, inspired popular writers to engage in frequently outlandish speculation about the site—speculation that has only increased as the centenary of the discovery approached. For example, some have proposed that extraterrestrials created landing pads among the allegedly primitive Nazca people (Erich von Däniken, 1970 and 1972); others suggested that the Nazca were technically sophisticated people who used hot air balloons to survey the accuracy of their creations (Jim Woodman and Julian Nott, 1977). Still others have speculated that the Nazca lines were a version of GPS coordinates with which ancient civilizations encoded the locations of their sacred sites (Carl Munck, 2005); energy beams locating the earth in space (Alla Belocon, 2007); magnetic strips that in the distant past allowed a group of "Gliptolitic" earthlings to lift off to a space voyage (Kathleen Doore, 2008); or elements of an "exploded planet cult" among the Nazca (Allan Alford, 2000). Like many seemingly impossible large-scale works of engineering or art, the Nazca lines have proven particularly attractive to those who prefer outlandish speculation to evidence-based inquiry.

Key Terms

audio flashcards

African spirituality 159
Chiefdom 149
Geoglyphs 172
Glyphic script 165
Kingdom 149
Phytoliths 157
Polytheism 164
Sahel 155
Tsetse Fly 158
Witchcraft 159

For additional resources, please go to **www.oup.com/us/vonsivers.**
Please see the Further Resources section at the back of the book for additional readings and suggested websites.

» PATTERNS OF EVIDENCE |

Sources for Chapter 6

SOURCE 6.1 Relief sculpture from Meroë, Sudan

ca. 600–300 BCE

The kings of Meroë, successors of the Nubia-descended twenty-fifth dynasty of Egypt, established their capital on the Middle Nile about 100 miles north of Khartoum, Sudan. At its height, the city was home to more than 20,000 people. Its surviving buildings have qualified it as a UNESCO World Heritage Site.

» Working with Sources

1. **How does the relief reflect the ongoing influence of ancient Egyptian iconography and symbolism?**
2. **What was the extent of the empire around Meroë, and what was the source of its influence?**

Source: ©Unesco/Ron Van Oers

SOURCE 6.2

Cosmas Indicopleustes (Cosmas the India-Voyager), *Christian Topography*

ca. 550 CE

This remarkable account of a merchant's travels throughout Eastern Africa, the Arabian Peninsula, and India resulted from the singular obsession of a monk in retirement. Determined to prove that a proper understanding of earth's geography would confirm God's creation—and that the earth was a flat, oblong table surrounded by the ocean—the monk Cosmas reflected back on his extensive voyages, which had probably been undertaken to further a spice-import business. Cosmas commented on the trading practices of the Aksumites and on their wealthy culture, providing one of the few available outsider glimpses of Aksum.

The region that produces frankincense is situated at the projecting parts of Ethiopia, and lies inland, but is washed by the ocean on the other side. Hence the inhabitants of Barbaria, being near at hand, go up into the interior and, engaging in traffic with the natives, bring back from them many kinds of spices, frankincense, cassia, calamus, and many other articles of merchandise, which they afterwards send by sea to Agau, to the country of the Homerites [Yemen], to Further India, and to Persia.

This very fact you will find mentioned in the Book of Kings, where it is recorded that the Queen of Sheba, that is, of the Homerite country, whom afterwards our Lord in the Gospels calls the Queen of the South, brought to Solomon spices from this very Barbaria, which lay near Sheba on the other side of the sea, together with bars of ebony, and apes and gold from Ethiopia which, though separated from Sheba by the Arabian Gulf, lay in its vicinity. We can see again from the words of the Lord that he calls these places the ends of the earth, saying: *The Queen of the South shall rise up in judgment with this generation and shall condemn it, for she came from the ends of the earth to hear the wisdom of Solomon* (Matthew 12:42). For the Homerites are not far distant from Barbaria, as the sea which lies between them can be crossed in a couple of days, and then beyond Barbaria is the ocean, which is there called Zingion. The country known as that of Sasu is itself near the ocean, just as the ocean is near the frankincense country, in which there are many gold mines.

The King of the Aksumites, accordingly, every other year, through the governor of Agau, sends thither special agents to bargain for the gold, and these are accompanied by many other traders—upwards, say, of five hundred—bound on the same errand as themselves. They take along with them to the mining district oxen, lumps of salt, and iron, and when they reach its neighborhood they make a halt at a certain spot and form an encampment, which they fence

Source: Cosmas Indicopleustes, *Christianike Topographia*, Book 3, trans. and ed. Christopher Haas, Villanova University; available online: http://www29.homepage.villanova.edu/christopher.haas/cosmas_indicopleustes.htm.

round with a great hedge of thorns. Within this they live, and having slaughtered the oxen, cut them in pieces, and lay the pieces on the top of the thorns, along with the lumps of salt and the iron. Then come the natives bringing gold in nuggets like peas, called *tancharas,* and lay one or two or more of these upon what pleases them—the pieces of flesh or the salt or the iron, and then they retire to some distance off. Then the owner of the meat approaches, and if he is satisfied he takes the gold away, and upon seeing this, its owner comes and takes the flesh or the salt or the iron. If, however, he is not satisfied, he leaves the gold. When the native, seeing that he has not taken it comes and either puts down more gold, or takes up what he had laid down, and goes away.

Such is the mode in which business is transacted with the people of that country, because their language is different and interpreters are hardly to be found. The time they stay in that country is five days more or less, according as the natives more or less readily coming forward buy up all their wares. On the journey homeward they all agree to travel well-armed, since some of the tribes through whose country they must pass might threaten to attack them from a desire to rob them of their gold. The space of six months is taken up with this trading expedition, including both the going and the returning. In going they march very slowly, chiefly because of the cattle, but in returning they quicken their pace lest on the way they should be overtaken by winter and its rains.

For the sources of the river Nile lie somewhere in these parts, and in winter, on account of the heavy rains, the numerous rivers which they generate obstruct the path of the traveler. The people there have their winter at the time we have our summer. It begins in the month *Epiphi* of the Egyptians and continues till *Thoth,* and during the three months the rain falls in torrents, and makes a multitude of rivers all of which flow into the Nile.

» Working with Sources

1. **How does Cosmas characterize the Aksumites, and to what other peoples does he compare them?**
2. **How and why does Cosmas allude to Old and New Testament accounts in his analysis of cultures adjoining the Red Sea?**

SOURCE 6.3 The market at Jenné-jeno, Mali

founded ca. third century BCE

After extensive archaeological work was done at the site of Jenné-jeno in the 1980s, researchers concluded that the city was the oldest known in sub-Saharan Africa, and that it flourished throughout the first millennium CE. It is situated on a vast low mound at the heart of the Niger Inland Delta. The site was gradually abandoned in favor of Timbuktu during the Middle Ages.

Working with Sources

1. **How did the founders of Jenné-jeno capitalize on existing trade networks in western Africa, and what geographic factors were involved?**
2. **Examining this recent photo of Jenné-jeno, what does it say about the continuity of patterns of trade and urbanism in West Africa?**

SOURCE 6.4

Limestone panel from a Mayan temple, Palenque

ca. 490 CE

This panel from a temple in the Mayan city of Palenque contains glyphs (forming a caption) and two figures. A captive kneels before a standing warrior who holds a flint spear and wears a war headdress. The large text to the left records an event at Palenque that occurred in 490. The small text above the kneeling figure gives the name of a captive.

Working with Sources

1. **What are the likely circumstances surrounding the creation of this image?**
2. **What were the connections between Mayan temples and warfare?**

Source: (6.3, top) Photo by Rob Dougall. (6.4, bottom) The Linda Schele Drawings Collection, http://research.famsi.org/schele_list.php?_allSearch=118.

Chapter 7 550 BCE–600 CE

Interaction and Adaptation in Western Eurasia: Persia, Greece, and Rome

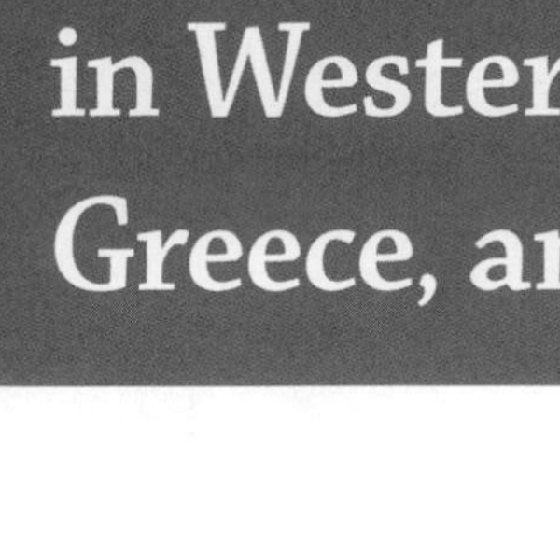

At one of his banquets after vanquishing the Achaemenid [a-KEE-ma-nid] Persian Empire in 330 BCE, the world conqueror Alexander the Great (r. 336–323 BCE) had a violent confrontation with one of his leading commanders, Cleitus. Flatterers at the banquet compared Alexander to the gods, and Alexander himself boasted that his conquests were far superior to those of his father, Philip. Cleitus, older than Alexander and an officer in Philip's army who had been engaged in the preparations for the Greek conquest of Persia, angrily interjected. It was the army that was the true victor, he objected, noting that he himself had saved Alexander's life in at least one of the battles against the Persians.

The exchange became heated, fueled by copious amounts of wine. At one point, Cleitus loudly complained about Alexander demanding that everyone, Greek and Persian, fall on their knees when entering his presence. As the shouting match continued, Alexander first threw an apple at Cleitus, then reached for his sword—which guards had prudently removed—and finally grabbed a javelin, killing Cleitus with a lightning-like thrust. Almost before the blow had

***ABOVE:* Detail from the Ara Pacis Augustae (Altar of Augustan Peace), commissioned by the Roman Senate in 13 BCE and consecrated in 9 BCE, to celebrate the end of the civil war after the triumphal return of Augustus (27 BCE–14 CE) from Spain and Gaul.**

been struck, Alexander regained his senses. Deeply remorseful, he grieved over the death of his companion; according to one source, he abstained from food and drink for several days, bewailing the loss of his veteran commander.

Although the sources that report the incident vary considerably in detail, they agree that the quarrel was about the question of Alexander remaining true to his Macedonian/Greek heritage or becoming a Persian "king of kings." Was he still a first among equals? Was he still bringing liberty to the Greeks of Asia? Or was he becoming a divinely mandated monarch who could command Persians and Greeks alike to obey him on bended knee? Not surprisingly, these questions arose right at the time that Alexander had completed the liberation of the Greeks from Persian rule, destroyed the Persian Empire, and was about to begin his conquest of India. He was on his way to becoming the exalted single ruler of the then known world, encompassing all nations, languages, and religions on earth, a world similar to that heaven where Zeus ruled all gods and goddesses (or the Libyan god Ammon, from whom Alexander believed he was descended).

Seeing Patterns

» Why should the Middle East and Mediterranean Europe during the period 600 BCE–600 CE be studied as a single unit?

» What is transcendence, and why is it important to understand its importance in world history?

» Which elements characterize the institutions that grew out of the Middle Eastern monotheisms of Judaism and Christianity and the monism of Greek philosophy and science?

The Middle East and Mediterranean during 600 BCE–600 CE was a region that was culturally diverse, as illustrated by Cleitus's contrast between Greek liberties and Achaemenid Persian royal power. It was also an area of intense military rivalry, as we see in Alexander's avenging the Persian dominance of Greece in 386 by his own conquest of Persia in 334. Later on, as we shall learn in this chapter, the successor states of Parthian and Sasanid Persia and Rome continued the rivalry. However, already in the sixth century BCE, Greek, Jewish, and Iranian visionaries introduced very similar *monotheistic* (single personal god) and *monist* (single impersonal principle) forms of thought into the region. Centuries later, in the rivalry between Persia and Rome, the opposing state religions of Christianity and Zoroastrianism also faced off against each other. In short, this chapter focuses on one single region that had evolved from its Mesopotamian and Egyptian agrarian–urban origins and shared such basic patterns as imperialism, monotheism, and monism but was also torn apart by concrete and unbridgeable political and cultural differences. Intense internal interaction and adaptation characterized the Middle East and Mediterranean in the period of 600 BCE–600 CE.

Interactions between Persia and Greece

The Achaemenid Persian conquest of the Middle East, from Anatolia and Egypt in the west to northwestern India in the east, was a relatively easy affair compared to the conquest of Greece, whose inhabitants resisted fiercely. Although Persia was able to subjugate the Greek city-states of the Anatolian coast, it proved unable to conquer the Greek mainland. A century and a half later, Alexander the Great unified Greece and led it to victory over Persia, establishing a short-lived Macedonian–Greek Empire. Alexander's generals divided the empire into three successor kingdoms under which politics stabilized until the Persians, under the Parthians and Sasanids, renewed the Persian imperial tradition.

Chapter Outline

- **Interactions between Persia and Greece**
- **Interactions between the Persian and Roman Empires**
- **Adaptations to Monotheism and Monism in the Middle East**
- **The Beginnings of Science and the Cultures of Kings and Citizens**
- **Putting It All Together**

The Origins of the Achaemenid Persian Empire

The Persians originated as agrarian villagers and nomadic horse and sheep breeders during the Bronze Age in central Asia south of the Ural Mountains. Toward the end of the third millennium BCE, groups of nomads migrated from the Urals southward and, by the middle of the second millennium BCE, reached the Aral Sea region. From here, some migrants pushed farther, establishing themselves in Upper Mesopotamia and India around 1200 BCE. The Persians were a branch that migrated sometime before the 800s BCE from the Aral Sea region to the southwestern Iranian province of Fars, from which the name "Persia" is derived.

Persian Conquests The first to appear in the historical record were the Medes, who had arrived from central Asia in southwest Iran at the end of the Bronze Age. They presided over a loosely organized kingdom with provincial vassals adjacent to the Assyrian Empire in Fars. The head of one vassal family, Cyrus II the Great (r. ca. 550–530 BCE) of the Achaemenids, assumed the crown of the Persians in 550 BCE and, in contrast to the Medes, embarked on an ambitious series of imperial conquests. Outlined in a text on a clay cylinder, Cyrus describes himself as the representative of the high god Marduk on earth and his rule as that of peace and justice everywhere. He first expanded into Anatolia (modern-day Turkey), where he conquered the kingdom of Lydia [LIH-dee-ya]. The Lydians are notable for having created in 615 BCE the first minted money in world history, coins made of silver and gold and used in trade. Next, Cyrus turned to the neighboring Greek city-states of Ionia on the southwestern Anatolian coast. His generals besieged these cities one by one, until their inhabitants either surrendered or returned to the Greek mainland.

Cyrus himself was busy with the conquest of the Iranian interior and north, as far as Afghanistan. In 540 BCE he began his campaign against Neo-Babylonia in Mesopotamia, capturing the capital of Babylon a year later. The Phoenician city-states in Syria submitted voluntarily in the following years. Within a little more than a decade, Cyrus had defeated the most important powers of the period and had unified all of the Middle East except Egypt, which Persia conquered a little later, in 525 BCE (see Map 7.1). In Jerusalem, Cyrus permitted the rebuilding of the Temple by Jews returning from Mesopotamia in 538, where their ancestors had been deported a century and a half earlier (see Chapter 2). In gratitude, the Jews gave him the title "Messiah" (Anointed One or Savior), making him the only non-Jew with this divine title.

Persian Arms The Achaemenids achieved their conquests with the help of lightly armed, highly mobile mounted archers as well as heavily armored, slow-moving **cataphracts**—horsemen with protective armor consisting of iron scales sewn on leather shirts. The archers fought with composite bows, and the cataphracts with 5-foot-long, iron-tipped lances for thrusting. Saddles and stirrups had not yet been invented, and hence the lance—requiring the mounted user to have a firm footing with which to brace himself—was still a relatively short, modest weapon. Infantry soldiers armed with bows, arrows, shields, and javelins provided support for the cavalry, complementing its tank-like thrust.

Cataphracts: Heavily armed and protected cavalry soldiers.

Early on, Persian kings supplemented their armies with heavily armored infantry recruited from among the Anatolian Greeks. These foot soldiers, called **hoplites**, fought shoulder to shoulder in ranks, called "phalanxes." They were equipped with 8-foot-long, iron-tipped thrusting spears, short iron swords, large shields held on the left forearm, helmets, and iron-scale protective armor. In close quarters, hoplite

Hoplites: Greek foot soldiers fighting in closed ranks, called "phalanxes."

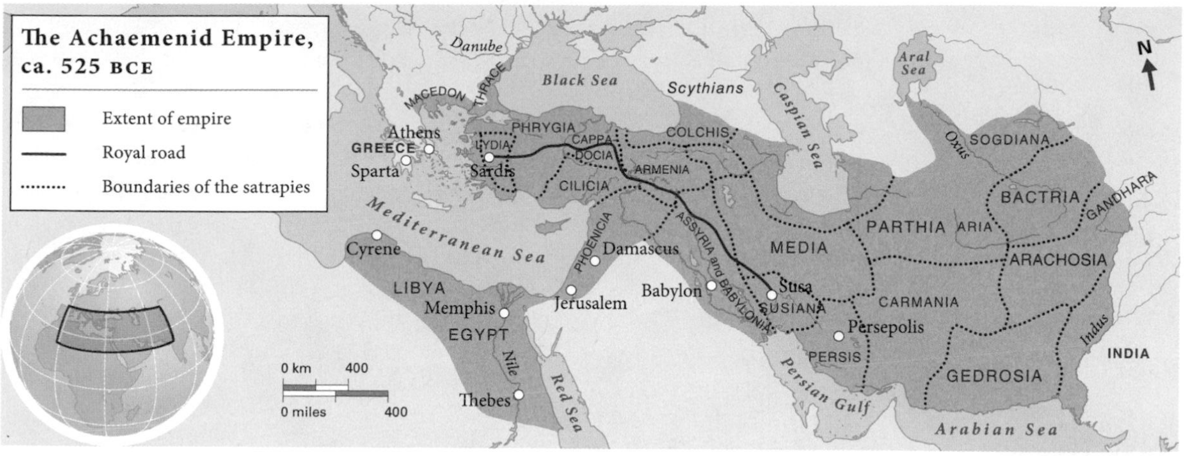

MAP 7.1 Achaemenid Persian Empire.

phalanxes were nearly invincible. Even in the open, however, phalanxes were difficult to crack, unless attacked by mounted archers on their unshielded right flank.

The Persian navy comprised as many as 1,200 galleys during its peak in the fifth century BCE. The Ionian and Phoenician provinces of the Persian Empire constructed and staffed these galleys, which were long, narrow ships, approximately 100 feet long and 15 feet wide. Apart from fighting naval battles against the Greeks, the navy also explored the western Mediterranean and even unsuccessfully attempted the circumnavigation of Africa. Altogether, the Persian military was a formidable fighting machine stationed in garrisons and ports in the various provinces of the Middle East and eastern Mediterranean.

Persian Administration The Achaemenid Persian Empire, encompassing not only the Middle Eastern agrarian centers of Mesopotamia and Egypt but also those of the Indus valley, is estimated to have had some 15 million inhabitants. The kings prided themselves on having at their palace in southwestern Iran containers of water from both the Nile and the Danube, which they served at their banquets to demonstrate their vast power. The enormous size of the Persian territories demanded creative assimilation of the institutions they inherited. The empire consisted of some 70 ethnic groups, hundreds of temple cults, a small Persian aristocracy, and a limited central bureaucracy. Most kings prayed to the god Ahuramazda (Ahu-ra MAZ-da) of the Zoroastrians, but others selected other deities from the Persian pantheon. Since the Achaemenids granted considerable autonomy to their 30 provinces, many of

interactive timeline

ca. 610–546 BCE Anaximander, Greek visionary

550–331 BCE Achaemenid Persia

490 and 480/79 BCE Persian wars against Greece

ca. 427–347 BCE Plato, founder of the first philosophical school, the Academy

336–323 BCE Alexander the Great

300s BCE Rome begins to unify the Italian peninsula

238 BCE–224 CE Parthian Persian Empire

196 BCE–284 CE Roman imperial expansion

166–40 BCE Hasmoneans (Maccabeans) rule a kingdom in Judea

224–642 CE Sasanid Persian Empire

284–640 Late Roman Empire

ca. 350–380 Zoroastrianism, preferred religion in Sasanid Empire, and Christianity, state religion in Roman Empire

370–450 Central Asian Huns invade northern Persian and Roman borders

476 End of western Roman Empire

530–580 Imperial recovery in Persia and Rome

Persepolis. This relief from the stairs that approach the royal audience hall shows ambassadors from the various lands under the power of the "king of kings" humbly offering tribute.

which retained their native ruling dynasties, temples, and legal systems, a bewildering number of languages, ethnic groups, and religious pantheons coexisted in the empire.

Around 500 BCE, the empire had become integrated enough that the kings could replace indigenous rulers with their own governors from the Persian aristocracy. These provincial governors, or *satraps,* supported by Persian troops in fortresses, were powerful rulers. They administered Persian law, to which all imperial subjects could appeal from their own legal systems (see Source 7.1). The satraps also collected tributes and taxes, with which they maintained themselves and their troops, forwarding the remainder to the kings. When called upon by the kings, the governors contributed their provincial troops to the royal army. Officially, the Achaemenid king called himself "king of kings" (**shahinshah** [SHAW-in-shaw])—that is, emperor—in order to make his elevated status clear to all princes and governors of regional and Persian aristocratic origin, as well as the populace.

Shahinshah: "King of kings," the title of Persian rulers.

The *shahinshahs* had a number of palaces in Iran and Mesopotamia, among which Persepolis [per-SEH-puh-lis] is the best known. Here, they maintained the central administration with its treasury and archive. The language used for administrative purposes was imperial Aramaic, a special bureaucratic version of the spoken and alphabetically written Aramaic that had become the predominant language of Mesopotamia and Syria in the previous centuries. Clay tablets continued to be used as writing material, particularly in Mesopotamia; but scribes preferred parchment or papyrus scrolls, which offered them more space. A basic principle of the empire's financial administration was the hoarding of all incoming silver and gold. Trade was not yet fully monetized, and the kings minted only small amounts of coins. As elsewhere in Asia, villagers continued to pay taxes or rents in kind, and local markets continued to function primarily on the basis of barter. Enormous quantities of precious metal piled up in the Persian treasuries, with no purpose yet except luxury trade and the giving of presents.

The vast size of the empire dictated that the imperial administration pay close attention to its communication networks. Thus, the Persians created their famous "royal roads," perhaps the first such highways in the world. They consisted mostly of regularly maintained paths connecting Persia with Anatolia and Mesopotamia as directly as possible. Governors provided the roads with distance markers, constructed inns and depots at regular intervals, and protected them through a chain of police and army posts. The roads were intended primarily for quick troop movements, although traders with carts and pack animals used them as well.

Greek City-States in the Persian Shadow

In the sixth century BCE, while Persia evolved into an empire, hundreds of city-states—cities (singular *polis*; plural *poleis*) with surrounding villages—dotted the landscape in Anatolia, Greece, and Italy. The most populous of these poleis were Athens and Sparta. The two competed for dominance, but neither could overcome the other, and their rivalry eventually benefited Persia in its attempt to assume power over Greece.

Athens and Sparta Most of the hundreds of city-states of which Greece was composed ruled themselves independently. The only common bonds, besides language, history, and culture, were a number of so-called **oracles** and the Olympic Games. Greeks went to the oracles to settle disputes or to divine their future. The Olympic Games, in the polis of Olympia, brought together the Greek youth for athletic competitions. Athens, with 200,000 inhabitants, and Sparta, with 140,000 inhabitants, were the largest city-states and exerted a certain dominance but ultimately accomplished little in terms of unification (see Map 7.2).

Oracles: Temples where humans could consult priests or priestesses to determine the will of the gods.

MAP 7.2 Greece in the Sixth Century BCE.

Athens is located on the small peninsula of Attica in southeastern Greece. Its limited agricultural resources forced inhabitants to specialize in the production of cash crops, such as wine, olive oil, nuts, and dried fruits. They traded these crops, together with woolen textiles and metal goods, for grain and metals from Italy, the Black Sea region, and Egypt. The growing focus on trade helped in the emergence of mercantile interests among the landowning citizenry. Disputes about representation in the ruling council and chronic debt among farmers forced the first among several reforms in 594 BCE under Solon, sole archon, or ruler for one year. In 508 BCE, Cleisthenes, a prominent landowner, forged an alliance between merchant landowners and smallholders to bring about further constitutional reforms, broadening the citizenry to include more modest property owners and ending the arbitrary rule of self-appointed strongmen. He expanded the rights of citizens to sit on juries and participate in the legislative assembly, which was enlarged to 500 members. Proposals adopted by the assembly were to be ratified by the citizenry, and executive power was vested in boards of elected magistrates. The reforms of Solon and Cleisthenes are often cited by scholars as the first steps toward the creation of Athenian democracy in the middle of the next century.

Sparta was another major city-state of Greece and Athens' principal rival. It was located on a plain in the Peloponnesus [peh-lo-po-NEE-sus] Peninsula southwest of Athens. Unlike land-poor Athens, Sparta had room to enlarge its agricultural base before eventually turning to maritime trade. Its constitutional organization preceded that of Athens by a century and, therefore, embodies more traditional traits. Citizenship was based on landownership, and Spartan citizens were entitled to stand for participation in the 30-member Council of Elders and the five-member Board of Overseers, the decisions of which were ratified by the assembly of owners of medium-sized properties. Executive power was in the hands of two hereditary kings.

Army service was of crucial importance in Sparta. At age 7, boys left home and entered military camps to train as hoplites. Until the age of 30, married soldiers were not allowed to live with their wives but received extended military leaves in order to create large families. A thoroughgoing code of male citizen discipline dominated Sparta. Women also received rigorous physical training and were fully imbued with the Spartan military ethic: Wives or mothers seeing their men off to battle customarily handed them their shields with the parting words "Come home with it or on it."

Tyrtaeus, "Praise for the Virtuosity of the Citizen Soldier"

The village farmers who tilled the land in Sparta and the other Greek city-states were noncitizens of unfree status, in contrast to the free farmers in the Middle East. In Athens, as we have already noted, small free farmers were at the center of early reform efforts. In Sparta, however the farmers, called *helots*, were the descendants of surrounding peoples conquered by Sparta during its years of expansion and tied to the land in perpetuity.

Since, in addition to villagers, women were excluded from political participation, constitutional rule benefited only small minorities in the Greek city-states. This was true even in the mid-fifth century BCE, when the final round of Athenian reforms under Pericles extended voting and office rights to all male citizens. While Athens' "golden age" of democracy was arguably the most open of the ancient world, it was still restricted to no more than one-third of the population at its height. Thus, what has been idealized by people in the modern era as a forerunner of our own institutions was in fact not very different from the urban assemblies in Mesopotamian cities and those of some of the early Indian city-states in the Ganges valley (see Chapter 3). In retrospect, Greece was thus not the only pioneer of constitutional rule: It shared this role with other societies, although each adopted rule by assemblies independently and not as a result of interaction.

Greece and Persia Their maritime commercial wealth made the Greek city-states irresistible targets of Persian imperialism. When Athens supported the Ionian revolt of the Greek city-states in 499–494 BCE, the Persian monarchy found its justification to wage war against the Greeks. They suppressed the revolt and organized two large-scale invasions of the Greek mainland in the following years (492–490 and 480–479 BCE). Both invasions were well planned and included vastly superior land and sea forces. Storms took their toll on these forces, however, and long supply lines further compromised Persian military efficiency. To meet the invasion, the Greek city-states on the mainland united under the joint leadership of Athens and Sparta. In two battles, on land at Marathon (490 BCE) and on the sea at Salamis (480 BCE), the united Greeks took advantage of their better knowledge of local conditions and the utility of the phalanx against larger massed forces in narrow areas and repelled both Persian invasions. Greece managed to preserve its liberty and escape Persian imperial dominance (see Source 7.2). Soon, however, the Greek world was plunged into a long and devastating internal conflict.

After the repulsion of the Persian invasions, Athenian–Spartan unity fell apart. As a substitute, Athens formed a league with as many as 200 poleis around the Aegean and Black Seas and for about two decades harassed the Persians in the eastern Mediterranean. When Athens diverted a portion of the league's membership contributions to the reconstruction of its Persian War–damaged citadel, the Acropolis, however, anger against this perceived self-service erupted into the Peloponnesian War (431–404 BCE). During this war, Sparta made itself the champion of liberation from what many Greek cities viewed as an Athenian empire. After depleting Athens' land forces, Sparta—with Persian financial support—built a navy, which won a brilliant victory over Athens, forcing the latter to sue for peace in 404 BCE.

Repelled by the Greeks at Marathon and Salamis, the Achaemenid Persians played their cards carefully, this time stoking fears of Spartan dominance. During yet another round of hostilities, a coalition of city-states led by Athens and backed by Persia defeated Sparta. In the King's Peace of 386 BCE, the Persians granted the Greeks in Anatolia autonomy, or self-rule, according to their city-state constitutions, provided they recognized Persia's overall dominance. Persia held the purse strings, employing some 50,000 Greek hoplite mercenaries who became jobless in Greece after the King's Peace. Persian imperial hegemony over Greece had finally become a reality, to last for about half a century.

Alexander's Empire and Its Successor Kingdoms

The one Greek area that remained outside Persian control was Macedonia, on the northern periphery of the Greek city-states. Although the Macedonians spoke a Greek dialect, the city-state Greeks considered them barbarians—that is, people mired in tribal customs and without an urban culture. In the middle of the 300s BCE, however, a king, Philip II (359–336 BCE), unified the country and provided it with a disciplined infantry army. He conquered the Greek city-states to the south, and his son Alexander continued the expansion with the conquest of Persia.

Alexander and His Successors In 337 BCE, Philip employed his greatly enhanced military strength to declare war on the Persian Empire, in revenge for the

East Meets West. A turbaned man stands next to a Corinthian capital in the Hellenistic city of Ai-Khanoum, founded in what is today northern Afghanistan—ancient Bactria—in the fourth century BCE after Alexander's conquests. Ai-Khanoum was one of the focal points of Hellenism in the East. Archaeological excavations in the 1970s revealed a flourishing city, with a Greek-style theater, a huge palace, a citadel, a gymnasium, and various temples.

Persian invasion of Macedonia and Greece a century earlier. He made himself the champion of Greek liberty in Asia, the "liberator" of the city-states in Anatolia. Just as Philip was getting ready to invade Anatolia, he was assassinated in a court intrigue. Philip's 20-year-old son Alexander took over both throne and campaign, setting off for Persia in 334 BCE. In three fiercely fought battles (334–330 BCE), Alexander outmaneuvered and defeated the Persian defenders; he prevailed because the Macedonian army was the most proficient and advanced force in the region. The Persian king was the lesser strategist and tactician, but he and the Persian aristocracy resisted tenaciously. The Persian forces retreated slowly into what is today Afghanistan. Alexander occupied the Persian royal towns and confiscated the Persian treasury, including some 7,000 tons of precious metals. During a drunken revelry in the palace town of Persepolis, Alexander had the imperial palace burned down, as a final act of vengeance for the destruction of the Acropolis by the Persians.

After finishing off the Achaemenid forces in Afghanistan and occupying Bactria (modern Uzbekistan) to the northeast, Alexander invaded India. When he reached the Ganges basin, however, persistent monsoon rains and exhausted troops forced him to retreat. As he left, he appointed governors over northwest India. Under these governors, Greek culture entered the subcontinent and exerted a palpable influence even beyond 305 BCE when the expanding Maurya Empire conquered India (see Chapter 8). Alexander returned to the Middle East and made plans to trump the Persians by executing their unfulfilled plan to circumnavigate Africa. Before he could depart, however, a fever seized him; and within 10 days, at the age of 33, Alexander was dead (323 BCE). In the stupendously short time of just 11 years, he had turned the mighty Persian Empire into a Macedonian–Greek one (see Map 7.3).

Not surprisingly, this empire did not hold together. Alexander's one legitimate son was born after his father's death and had no chance to assume the throne. Alexander's generals divided the empire among themselves, founding kingdoms, among which Antigonid Greece (276–167 BCE), Ptolemaic Egypt (305–30 BCE), and Seleucid southwest Asia (305–64 BCE) were the most important.

Hellenism: Period of Greek history from 323 BCE to 31 BCE.

Altogether, about 1 million Greeks emigrated during the 200s BCE to the Middle East, assimilating gradually into the local population of some 20 million and imprinting their **Hellenistic** (Greek-influenced) culture on urban life. Thus, even though the Macedonian–Greek Empire failed politically almost immediately, its cultural legacy lasted for centuries, even in faraway central Asia and India.

Interactions between the Persian and Roman Empires

A century after Alexander's conquests, a resurgent Persia—in the shape of Parthia—appeared in the northeastern corner of the Seleucid kingdom. This resurgence coincided with Rome's expansion after the unification of Italy. On the periphery of the

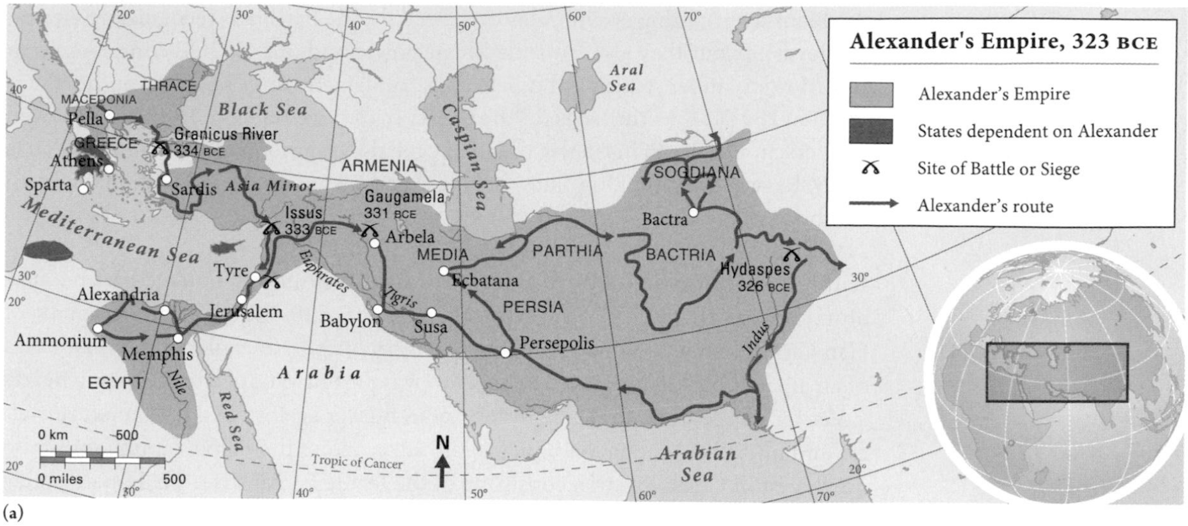

(a)

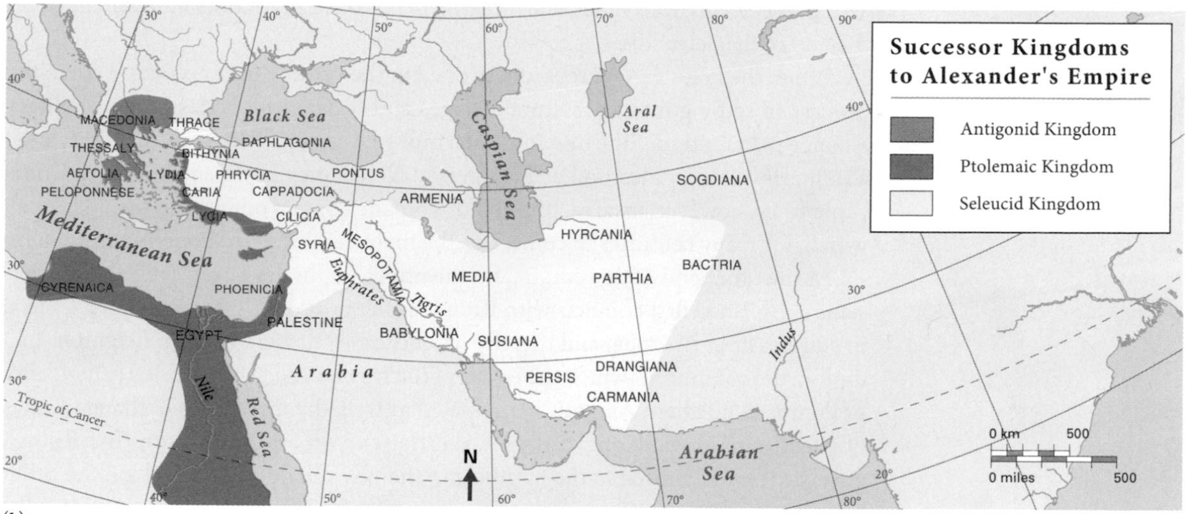

(b)

MAP 7.3 Alexander's Empire (a) and Successor Kingdoms after the Breakup of Alexander's Empire (b).

map analysis

successor kingdoms of Alexander's Macedonian–Greek Empire, both Parthia and Rome pressed against the Antigonids, Seleucids, and Ptolemies. After conquering these kingdoms, Rome and Parthia eventually came face to face in Anatolia and Syria in the early second century BCE. Neither, however, succeeded in eliminating the other, as strenuously as they tried in a long series of wars. As a result, the Middle East and the Mediterranean remained politically as divided as they had been in the previous centuries under the successor states of Alexander the Great.

Parthian Persia and Rome

Parthia was originally the name of the northeasternmost province of the Seleucid kingdom. In the 240s BCE, the tribal federation of the Parni, distant relatives of the Achaemenid Persians, migrated from the region east of the Aral Sea in central Asia to Parthia, where they defeated the Seleucid governor. The Seleucids, distracted by conflicts on their western front with Ptolemaic Egypt, were unable to prevent the

Parthians from seizing provincial power. Initially, the Parthians recognized Seleucid overlordship, but they also expanded their power and in 141 BCE conquered Iran and Mesopotamia, reducing the Seleucids to a small rump kingdom in northern Syria. In 109 BCE, Mithridates II, "the Great" (r. ca. 123–88 BCE), formally renewed the Persian Empire in his newly founded capital Ctesiphon, near where Baghdad is today, by assuming the title "king of kings" and taking over the traditional Iranian pantheon of gods.

Parthian Diplomacy Parthian Persia was a major power, in large part because of its diplomacy. In 115, Wudi [woo-DEE] (r. ca. 140–87 BCE), the emperor of Han China, sent a diplomatic mission to Mithridates II, to explore the possibilities of an alliance as well as trade. The mission was part of Wudi's efforts, lasting nearly a quarter of a century, to secure his northern border against Turkic nomadic invaders and find allies among the nomads in Bactria across the Pamir Mountains in the northwest of China. Bactria, consisting of the fertile Fergana [fer-GAH-nah] valley plain and surrounding mountain chains, had been governed previously by the Achaemenid Persians, Alexander, and Greek generals but had become independent after the end of the Seleucids.

When the first Chinese missions arrived in the valley, many nomads were in the process of settling into agricultural villages and displayed less desire for a military alliance than for trade. The missions then moved westward, where they encountered a militarily strong power in Parthian Persia. No alliance between Persia and China came to be, however. Instead, this first diplomatic contact opened up the Silk Road, which, for many centuries to come, was the main central Asian trade route.

At the other end of this empire, on the upper Euphrates River, the Parthian Persians established first contacts with Rome, which in 103 BCE had occupied Cilicia, in southeastern Anatolia, and thereby had become Parthia's western neighbor. In a diplomatic meeting, in which the envoy of the small, Persian-descended principality of Pontus in northern Anatolia participated as well, the three sides exchanged vows of friendship. The meeting, however, did not end on a positive note. The Roman governor seated himself in the middle and thereby sought to pull rank on the other two envoys, causing an infuriated Mithridates II to have his ambassador executed for allowing the Roman envoy to claim superiority. Not surprisingly, Rome and Persia soon came to blows.

Roman Republican Origins The western Mediterranean, adapting to agriculture around 3000 BCE and to the Iron Age after 1000 BCE, became part of the Middle Eastern and eastern Mediterranean agrarian centers in the course of the first millennium BCE. Phoenicians from the eastern Mediterranean established ports along the northern shores of Africa, in Spain, and on the islands of Sicily and Sardinia, attracted by the rich mineral resources there. Their principal port at the entrance to the western Mediterranean, in today's Tunisia, was Carthage. Later on, Greeks established city-states in southern Italy and Sicily. In north-central Italy was the kingdom of the Etruscans, a local people who originally came from Anatolia and the Levant and settled in Italy ca. 2000 BCE. The kingdom included Rome, founded around 1000 BCE.

Republic: State without a royal dynasty and with an elected executive.

Subsequently, around 500 BCE, the Romans made themselves independent and overthrew their kings. They created a **republic** (from Latin *res publica*, "public matter"), that is, a state without a king, electing leaders and forming a constitutional government. Around 450 BCE, the Romans adopted the Twelve Tablets, a set of laws covering a variety of legal matters, such as procedure, property, inheritance, constitution, due process, family, and crime. A chief priest was responsible for administering the cult of the patron god, Jupiter, and fixing the calendar. Later on, the Romans sacrificed to hundreds of gods, and their polytheistic religious practices acquired a close resemblance to those of the Greeks and Persians.

Paestum, Southern Italy. By the sixth century BCE, Greek city-states were flourishing across southern Italy and Sicily, including Paestum, which has some of the best-preserved temples outside of Greece, including the Temple of Hera shown here.

Expansion of the Republic In the 300s BCE, when Rome began to unify the peninsula, it organized its citizen army more formally into legions. The heavily armed infantry of **legionaries** consisted of landed citizens able to pay for their swords, javelins, helmets, shields, and scale armor. Wealthy Romans also manned the light and heavy cavalry, including cataphracts, while small landholders made up the light infantry of skirmishers. With the help of these legionaries, Rome completed the unification of Italy and in three wars (246–146 BCE) conquered its strongest rival, Carthage, across the Mediterranean in what is today Tunisia.

Legionaries: Roman foot soldiers fighting in semiclosed ranks.

Around 200 BCE, during the second war when Carthage was still surviving, it sought to protect itself against Rome through an alliance with the kingdom of Antigonid Greece. In a first expansion east, the Romans defeated the Antigonids and, in 196 BCE, issued the Isthmus Declaration, according to which the Greeks of Greece, Anatolia, and farther east were to be "free" of Antigonid overlordship and governed by their own laws. In Roman eyes, the Greek cities were now clients. When the Greeks resented this restriction of their laws and rebelled, in the middle of the second century BCE, they were ruthlessly repressed by the Romans, who eventually reduced Greece to provincial status.

The Isthmus Declaration was Rome's decisive step toward becoming an empire. It continued its republican institutions for another two centuries and never formally abolished them. Historians usually date the beginning of the Roman Empire to 27 BCE, when the Senate bestowed the title "Augustus" on Octavian. In the wake of Rome's expansion into North Africa, Greece, and Anatolia during the second and first centuries BCE, a new ruling class of wealthy landowners emerged. These consisted of Italian aristocrats who had appropriated the land of smallholders absent for extended periods during their military service as legionaries, turning these lands into large estates (*fundi*, sing. *fundus*) worked by tenant farmers or slaves for cash crops (olive oil, wine). Ruling-class members also acquired leases of conquered lands overseas, where they established estates with enslaved war captives. A Roman author of the first century CE, Pliny the Elder, observed that half of the province of North Africa (today's Libya, Tunisia, and Algeria) was owned by six landlords. As Rome transformed itself into an empire, wealthy landed aristocrats came to dominate public affairs.

Discharged legionaries and dispossessed farmers crowded Rome, while rebellious slaves on estates in southern Italy and Sicily rose up in massive revolts. The most dangerous revolt was that of Spartacus in 73–71 BCE. Spartacus was an army

Augustus. The famous Augustus of Prima Porta dated to 15 CE, and probably a copy of a bronze original commissioned by Augustus at some date after he was honored with the title "Augustus" in 27 BCE. Intended as a representation of the power and authority of Rome's first emperor, the statue depicts Augustus as barefooted, a symbolic image of gods and heroes.

deserter from Thrace in Greece who had been recaptured, enslaved, and trained as a gladiator. The sources describe Spartacus as a skillful tactician who devastated estates throughout Italy and held the Roman army in check for 3 years before it succeeded in defeating him.

Efforts by a few social reformers at improving the lot of the poor through food subsidies, land reforms, and public work projects failed against the fierce resistance of the landowners. About the only reform that succeeded was that of Marius, who was senator from 107 to 85 BCE and a successful general in North Africa. He opened the army ranks to the landless, equipped them with arms, and enlisted them for up to 20 years of service. Upon retirement, soldiers received plots of land in conquered provinces. This reform greatly benefited imperial expansion and also Romanized conquered provinces through settled veterans. But it also encouraged generals to use the now fully professionalized army for their own ambitions.

In the middle of the first century BCE, three ambitious generals were vying for control of the empire. One of them was Julius Caesar (100–44 BCE), a magistrate, from a prominent family and a successful conqueror of northwestern Europe. After his return from his conquests, in 48 BCE he defeated his last remaining rival, Pompey (106–48 BCE), also a consul and leader of the empire's strongest military forces. When Caesar then in addition to his consulate assumed several titles traditionally held by other magistrates, including that of "dictator for life," he provoked much opposition. In the Senate, several assassins eventually struck Caesar down, and a "triumvirate" of generals assumed power.

The triumvirate did not last. Civil war broke out, and the ultimate victor was Octavian (r. 31 BCE–14 CE), an adopted younger relative of Caesar whose career the latter had furthered. More subtle than Caesar, Octavian gradually created a new constitutional order with himself as leader, always maintaining the pretense of being merely the first of the citizenry *(princeps civitatis)*. In practice he possessed unlimited powers under the title of Augustus ("the Revered One"), bestowed on him in 27 BCE.

Selections from "The Achievements of the Divine Augustus"

The Augustan Age To consolidate his power, Augustus limited imperial expansion in the north to France, England, and Germany, west of the Rhine and Danube Rivers. He ordered the construction of a wall, called the *limes*, linking the two rivers, to keep the Germanic tribes on the other side at bay. In the east, a series of wars (56 BCE–1 CE) with the Persian Parthian Empire over the control of Armenia, Upper Mesopotamia, and Syria ended inconclusively. Egypt, Syria, and Judea came under direct Roman rule; Armenia became a Roman client state; Upper Mesopotamia east of the Euphrates remained Parthian; and peace reigned between Rome and Parthia for two generations. At this time, the Roman Empire had about 55 million inhabitants (see Map 7.4). It was considerably more populous than its Middle Eastern competitor, Parthia, with 10 million, but less so than its territorially smaller contemporary, Han China (202 BCE–220 CE), with 58 million. In addition, the Roman and Parthian Empires were geographically far less compact

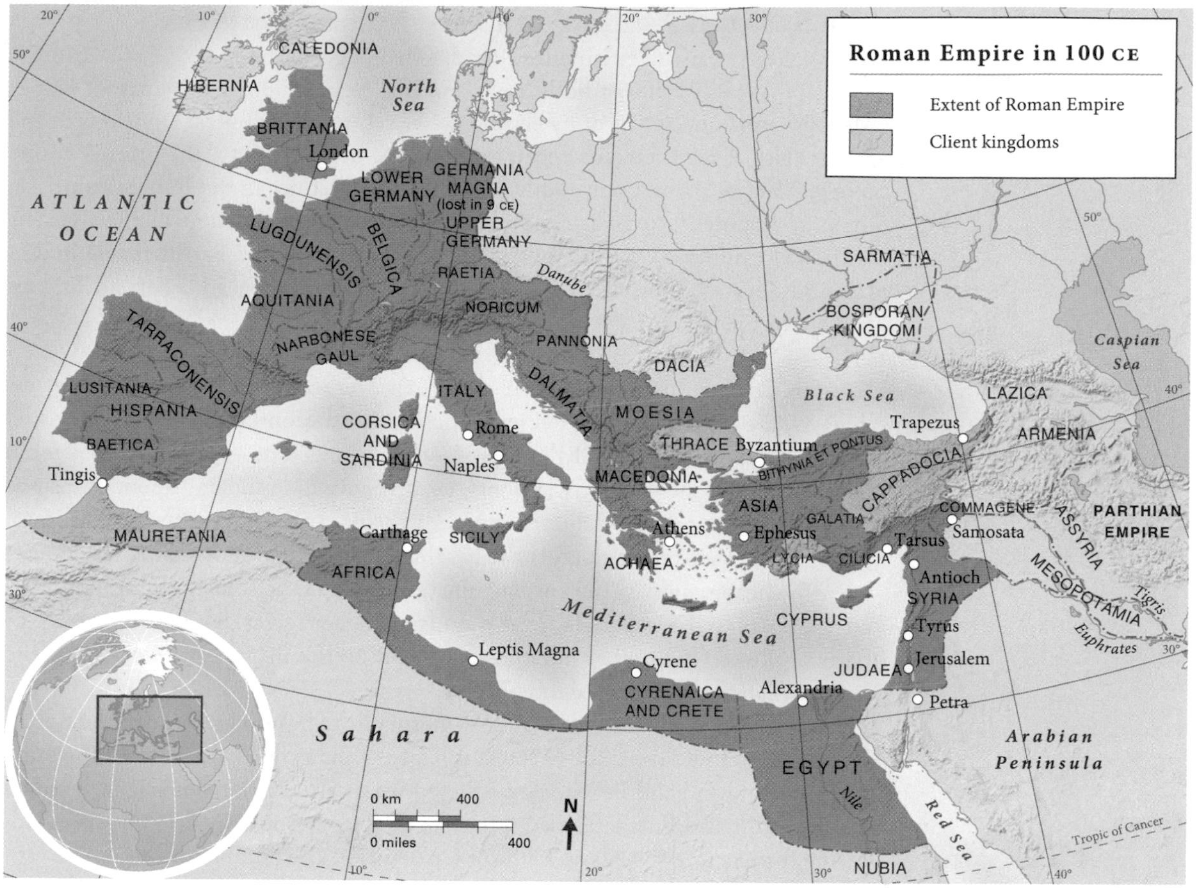

MAP 7.4 **Roman Empire at the Time of Augustus.**

and had more vulnerable borders than China, disadvantages which hampered political cohesion.

All 44 Roman provinces outside Italy had to pay heavy poll and agricultural taxes in kind and silver coins, primarily to support a standing army, which Augustus reduced to half of the size of the earlier civil war armies. Legionaries came not only from Italy but also from France and the Iberian Peninsula. In addition, tax money went into the building and upkeep of roads and ports, as well as wheat subsidies and circuses for the inhabitants of Rome and other large cities. In contrast to the huge military, the number of civilian Roman administrators in the provinces was small. The Roman Peace (*pax romana*) clearly rested more on the projection of military might than on a civilian administration, as in Han China.

The Roman Peace on the borders was rarely disrupted during the first two centuries following Augustus. Not surprisingly, the disruptions that did occur were on the border with Parthian Persia. Here, the flashpoint was the kingdom of Armenia, which both Parthia and Rome coveted as a client state. Compromise solutions collapsed twice (54–63 CE and 112–117 CE). On the second occasion, Rome came close to destroying Parthia when it succeeded in occupying Mesopotamia for a short time. The subsequent puppet kingdom, however, was unable to maintain itself, and the Parthians returned to independence.

The Sasanid Persian and Late Roman Empires

After renewing its independence, Parthia challenged Rome twice (161–166 CE and 193–198 CE). It lost both times and had to give up the province of Upper Mesopotamia and much of its economic wealth to pay tributes. Divisions in the ruling class of the Parthians began to appear. In the early 200s, the priestly family of a temple to Anahita, the goddess of water and fertility in the Iranian pantheon in Fars, assumed provincial leadership functions in opposition to the dynasty. Ardashir, a descendant of this priestly family, finally ended Parthian rule in 224 CE and declared himself king of kings, establishing the Sasanid Persian Empire (224–642 CE).

Roman Crisis Just when Persian imperial power was rejuvenated through a new dynasty, the Roman Empire fell into a political and economic crisis, which lasted half a century (234–285 CE) and profoundly changed its organization. As in all empires, the balance among war booty, tax revenue, and military expenditures was always precarious. Booty acquired in the Parthian wars kept the empire afloat until the 220s, but thereafter emperors had to dilute the silver money paid to the legionaries with cheaper metals. The ensuing inflation angered the soldiers, who supported any claimant to the imperial throne promising higher wages. Some two-dozen emperors followed each other in rapid succession on the throne, and for a while the empire even fragmented into three pieces.

In addition to the internal conflicts, Germanic tribes broke through the northern defenses and during 260–276 CE pillaged as far as northern Italy. At the same time, both Rome and Persia were afflicted by what historians of science assume was an outbreak of mass disease along the trade routes in 251–266 CE, foreshadowing the plague of 541 (see "Patterns Up Close"). The number of deaths was estimated in the hundreds of thousands. At the end of the 200s it appeared as if Rome was at its end.

Emperor Diocletian (r. 285–305 CE), however, salvaged the empire. He divided it into an eastern and a western half, doubled the number of provinces and civil administrators, and created a separate set of military districts. In addition, he ended Italy's tax exemption, regularized tax collection, increased the number of legions by one-third, and created a mobile field army under his command. Civil peace returned to the empire, albeit at the price of an increased militarization.

Adoption of Monotheism Since the early Sasanids had to consolidate their rule in a large territory, stretching from Upper Mesopotamia to Uzbekistan and northwestern India, they could not exploit the Roman crisis to the fullest. Although they led lightning invasions into Roman territories in Syria and Anatolia, acquired immense booty, received large indemnity payments, and even captured the Roman emperor Valerian in battle in 260 CE, in the end the Romans always regained control over Armenia and Upper Mesopotamia. Diocletian, after his reforms, was even able to push the border eastward to the Tigris River.

In the first half of the 300s, while the inconclusive wars between the two imperial rivals of Rome and Persia continued, both empires took first, halting steps toward a profound religious transformation—that is, a shift away from polytheism and toward the elevation of monotheism to the status of state religion. During the previous polytheist millennia in the Middle East and the Mediterranean, kings and emperors had supported imperial temple priesthoods in their capitals in return for the justification of their rule. Temples devoted to many other deities existed in their realms, and rulers did not seek their elimination. But when the Romans and Persians suffered their severe internal crises—the former nearly falling apart and the latter changing dynasties—rulers became aware of the need for a unifying single religious bond.

At the beginning of the reign of Emperor Constantine I, "the Great" (r. 306–337 CE), Christianity's adherents numbered about 10 percent of the Roman population. Christianity had begun three centuries earlier with the preaching of Jesus of Nazareth. Since Christians refused to recognize the pantheon of Roman gods, however, they were periodically persecuted, sometimes savagely. But their numbers recovered in between persecutions and by the early 300s, their existence in the empire had become visible enough for contenders to the imperial throne to take Christianity seriously as a potential source for support.

General Constantine appealed to this support when he fought his way in 312 with his army from England to power in Rome. A year later, as emperor, he issued an edict of toleration and in 325 he presided over the Council of Nicaea, which issued the **Nicene Creed** as the common doctrinal platform among Christians. He also granted tax privileges and jurisdictional powers to what was now the Christian Church. Baptized shortly before his death, Constantine can be considered the first Christian Roman emperor. Several pagan emperors succeeded Constantine before, in 380, Christianity became the sole state religion, with the closing of the Temple of Jupiter in Rome.

Nicene Creed: Basic Christian doctrine defining faith as belief in God, the Father; Jesus Christ, his son of the same substance; and the Holy Ghost.

In Persia, under the sponsorship of Shapur II (r. ca. 307–379), Zoroastrian priests began to write down the Yasht, the oldest holy scripture of Zoroastrianism. The shahinshahs, with large Jewish and Christian minorities in Mesopotamia, took the different route of making Zoroastrianism the preferential religion in ca. 350, with Christianity and Judaism being accorded a protected status. Thus, both empires sought to strengthen internal unity through the adoption of a single monotheistic faith in the course of the fourth century.

Nomadic Invasions The adoption of Christianity and Zoroastrianism to strengthen the cohesion of the Roman and Sasanid Empires came just in time, before the great migrations of peoples across Eurasia caused severe disruptions. The migrations began in the mid-300s CE when the western branch of the Huns—horse- and sheep-breeding nomads in the steppes of central Asia east of the Ural Mountains—moved westward and southward on the Silk Road. As in the case of the previous migrations out of central Asia in the second millennium BCE, the reasons that the western Huns packed up and journeyed westward remain unclear. One possible factor was the success of the Chinese in driving away nomadic invaders from their Great Wall in the north, resulting in a chain reaction of migrations among neighboring tribes, including the Huns. During their journey westward, the Huns grew into a large federation of nomads, farmers, and town dwellers of mixed ethnic and linguistic composition (Turks, Mongols, and Iranians).

As the Huns entered the Russian plains, they encountered local Germanic farming populations, whom they defeated. Other Germanic peoples, such as the Visigoths, fled from the Huns and negotiated their entry into the Roman Empire. In the early 400s CE, both Hunnish and Germanic peoples overcame the defenses

Patterns Up Close

The Plague of Justinian

At the end of the 500s, neither the Roman nor the Sasanid Empire was as populous and wealthy as before the nomadic invasions from the north. In addition, for the first time (in 541 CE), a mass epidemic, the bubonic plague, hit the world, breaking out first in the Roman Empire and traveling thereafter to Persia and, in cycles of 15 years, by the 600s CE as far as China and England. This plague, recorded as the "Plague of Justinian"—it sickened the emperor himself for several weeks—dramatically reduced population levels everywhere. The Plague of Justinian originated either in East Africa or in Burma. It reached the Mediterranean through black rats infested with fleas traveling in ships on the Indian Ocean and Red Sea.

Historians know now that for the plague to spread from fleas and rats in one of its endemic regions and become a pandemic the region's average temperatures must have declined. Fleas are most likely to jump from rats to humans at 59–68 degrees Fahrenheit. Such a temperature decline might have occurred a few years prior to 541 CE, with the eruption of the volcano Krakatau in Indonesia in 535 CE, the ashes of which obscured the sun for a number of years. Although the climate returned to normal a few years later, recurrent cycles of the plague every decade or two until well into the 700s CE prevented population levels from recovering.

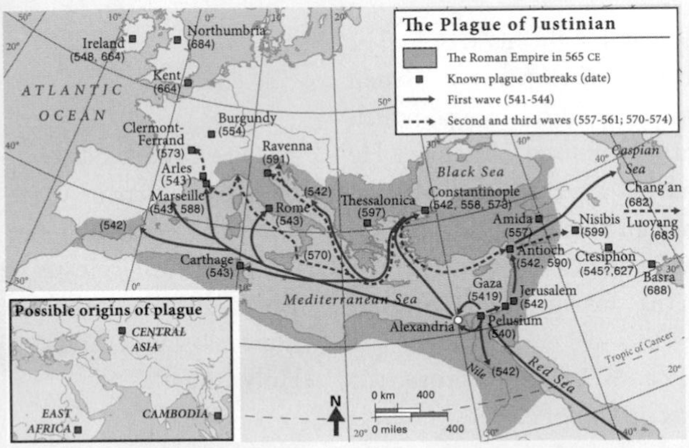

MAP 7.5 **The Plague of Justinian.**

Observers in various cities of the Roman Empire, some afflicted by the plague themselves, have left us vivid accounts. People infected by the plague bacillus typically developed a high fever, followed by

of the Romans, poured into the western half of the Roman Empire, and eventually ended the western line of emperors, an event remembered as the fall of Rome in 476 CE (see Map 7.6).

The emperors in the eastern half of the empire withstood the migrants' threat, in part because of Constantinople's strategic location. This city, made the capital by Constantine in 330 CE, was relatively close to the endangered northern and eastern borders, allowing for a more rapid deployment of troops than was possible from faraway Rome. The Sasanids initially repelled an attack by another branch of the Huns on their central Asian border in the early 400s CE but succumbed to renewed invasions in 483–485 and were forced to pay tribute for a number of years. A third branch of Huns invaded the Gupta Empire of India toward the end of the 400s CE. In the mid-500s the Sasanids eventually recovered from the invasions, but the Guptas were reduced to small remnants. Further compounding matters, plague struck the Middle East and Europe in 541 CE (see "Patterns Up close").

Roman and Persian Recovery The architect of the reconstruction of the Roman Empire was Justinian I, "the Great" (r. 527–565 CE). Although not a military

swelling of the lymph nodes in the groin, the armpits, and the neck. In great pain and delirious from fever, most people died quickly after a few days. Although the concept of quarantine was known, there was no known medicine. Survivors tried folk remedies, to no avail. Many clerical observers at the time were convinced that sinfulness was what had attracted God's wrath. For us modern observers, the most important lesson of the Plague of Justinian is the evidence it provides of how interconnected the various parts of Eurasia and Africa were toward the middle of the 500s CE (see Map 7.5).

The Plague of Justinian shows us also how climate and disease followed their own natural patterns in world history, patterns different from those of the polytheistic and monotheistic city-states, kingdoms, and empires. By killing up to one-third of the population and keeping population levels low for at least a century, the Plague of Justinian severely impacted city-state, kingdom, and empire patterns. The reduced population levels led to increased labor costs and food shortages; it also made survivors wealthier. On the other hand, since the plagues were equal-opportunity killers, they hit states and societies with impartial ferocity. Justinian's plague favored neither Rome nor Persia and thus had a more quantitative than lasting qualitative effect on the process of world history.

Questions

- What does Justinian's plague tell us about the interconnectedness of Afro-Eurasia at this time?
- How does understanding the impact of disease and climate on human societies add a new dimension to the patterns of world history?

campaigner himself, Justinian employed talented generals who reconquered most shores of the western Mediterranean from the Germanic invaders, including all of Italy. As the empire stabilized, prosperity returned. With improved tax revenues, Justinian was able to finance reform measures. The best known of these reforms was the reorganization of the legal system, based on the codification of the huge body of Roman law that had grown from the initial Twelve Tablets in republican Rome. In addition to the *Codex Justinianus* and *Digests,* he issued an instructional textbook, the *Institutions,* used by law students for centuries after Justinian's death. Originally written in Latin, Justinian's *Codex* was later translated into Greek and became the legal foundation for the Roman Empire's successor, the Byzantine Empire (610–1453 CE), as well as the Islamic empire of the Abbasids (750–1258 CE), together with Persian law.

Often considered the crown jewel among Justinian's long-lasting achievements was the construction of Hagia Sophia ("Holy Wisdom"), until the construction of Saint Peter's in Rome the largest Christian church. Begun shortly after deadly riots in 532 among factions in the population had destroyed large portions of Constantinople, Hagia Sophia represents Justinian's efforts in rebuilding the city. A magnificent architectural accomplishment, Hagia Sophia combines Roman features with

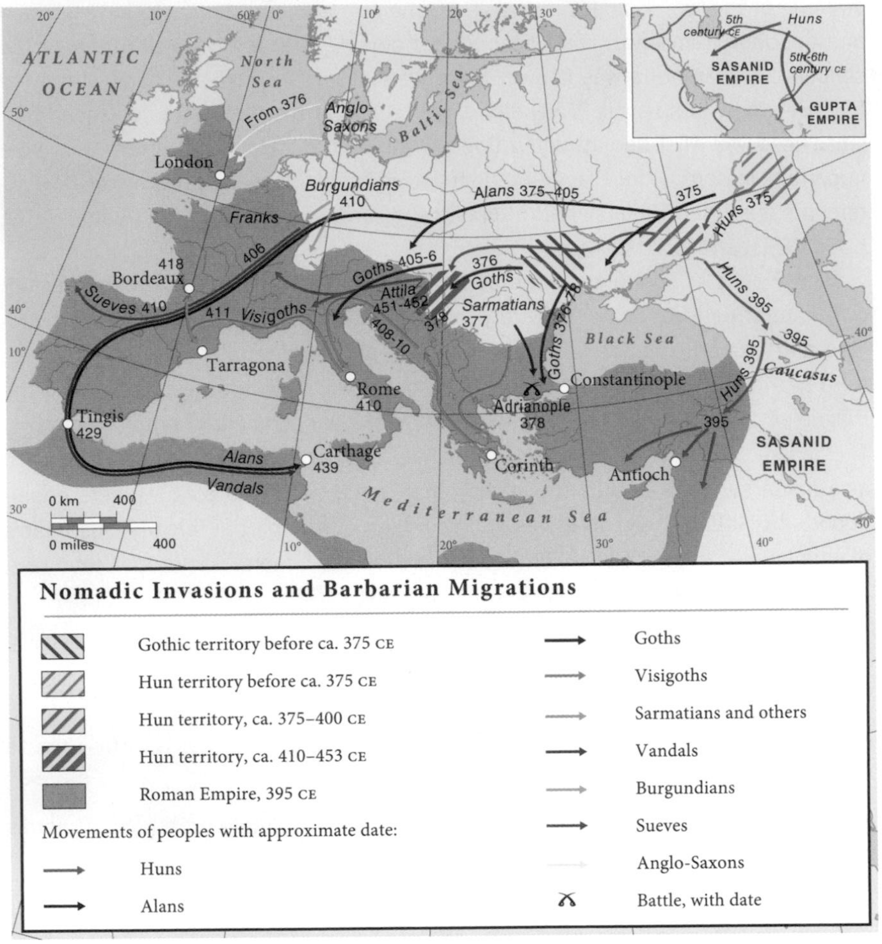

MAP 7.6 **Nomadic Invasions and Barbarian Migrations into the Roman Empire, 375–450 CE.**

new elements. It was designed to provide for a large open space, capped by a huge dome surrounded by windows that admitted light into the interior. So stunned was Justinian by the magnificence of the new church that he is said to have blurted out, "Solomon, I have outdone thee!"

In Persia, it was Khosrow I (r. 531–579) who rebuilt the Sasanid Empire (see Map 7.7). He began his rule in the aftermath of a civil war that pitted Mazdak, a renegade Zoroastrian priest and social reformer, and the dynasty against the Zoroastrian priesthood and the ruling class. In this war, the dynasty confiscated landed estates from the ruling class, opened the latter's granaries to the poor, and distributed its lands to small military landowners (*dihqans*). Khosrow, scion of the dynasty but siding with the opposing ruling class to keep the empire together, seized power and had Mazdak executed, ending the social reforms. But he maintained the military reforms in favor of the *dihqans*, thereby distancing himself from the traditional ruling class. After a census of the population, which allowed him to raise taxes and hire bureaucrats, he greatly expanded the central administration at the expense of the ruling class.

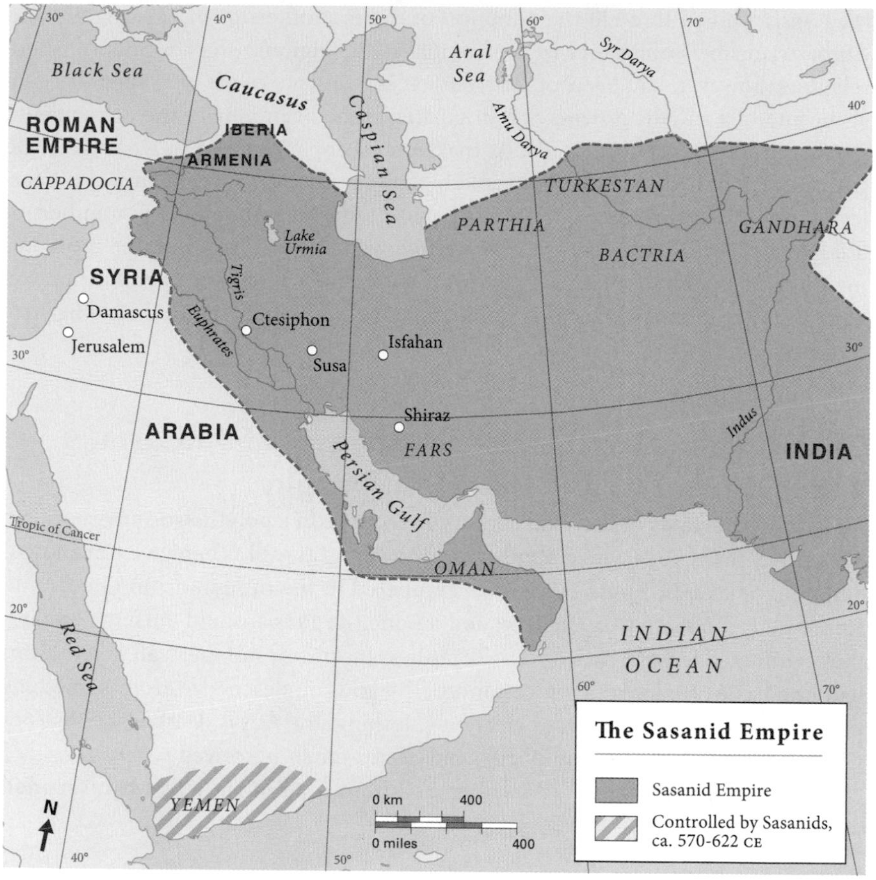

MAP 7.7 The Sasanid Empire.

Like Justinian, Khosrow also pursued military expansion. Acceding to pleas from the Armenians after a revolt against Justinian in 530 CE, Khosrow reopened hostilities against the Romans. Initially, his armies broke through to the Mediterranean and returned with rich loot, but the campaign stalled and the war once more ended in 577 CE in a draw. The Romans agreed to pay a tribute, and Khosrow returned the conquered territories. In the north, Khosrow defeated European and Turkic tribes, expanding the border eastward to Turkistan. A plea from the king of Yemen in southwestern Arabia to aid him in his efforts to repel a Roman-backed Ethiopian invasion brought Khosrow's fleet to southern Arabia in 575–577 CE. On land, Arab vassal kings established Persian control over much of the rest of Arabia. In contrast to Rome, the reach of Persia was much expanded at the end of the sixth century.

Adaptations to Monotheism and Monism in the Middle East

Although demographically weakened by plague, Rome and Sasanid Persia were comparatively strong unitary empires at the end of the 500s CE. Both had regained territories lost to the Asian tribal migrations two centuries earlier but were religiously unified through the adoption of the monotheisms of Christianity and Zoroastrianism as obligatory or preferential state religions. The adoption of these religions, however, had been of relatively recent vintage, as we have seen. It came at the end of a lengthy process that originated at the beginning of the Achaemenid Persian Empire (550–330 BCE). At that time, visionaries arose to whom a single god revealed himself or who discovered fundamental truths. At first, these visionaries of religious monotheism and philosophical monism had only small numbers of followers. It took many centuries before followers of each faith became more numerous and organized themselves in local communities dispersed over the empires' territories until the creeds achieved imperial sanction as the preferred or obligatory state religion.

Challenge to Polytheism: The Origins of Judaism, Zoroastrianism, and Greek Philosophy

Religious visionaries of the sixth century BCE arose in a polytheistic environment, a culture of many gods who embodied overpowering as well as benign natural forces and phenomena. In Egypt these gods numbered in the thousands; in Greece and Rome their numbers were smaller; and among the Persians and ancient Israelites they numbered fewer than a dozen. Regardless of specific numbers, all polytheisms had one basic characteristic in common: The gods all descended from something unnamable that existed prior to creation (Nothing, the Abyss, Darkness, Waste, or Chaos). Unity preceded multiplicity, and even though perceived reality consisted of both, in thought they could be separated from each other. Unity **transcended** multiplicity.

Transcendence: Realm of reality above and beyond the limits of sensory experience.

Judaism Remarkably, the discovery of transcendence occurred more or less simultaneously during the 600s BCE in Mesopotamia, Iran, and Anatolia. The historically most influential case was that of an anonymous Jewish visionary, whom scholars dubbed "Deutero-Isaiah" or "Second Isaiah" (fl. ca. 560 BCE) in Mesopotamia. After their deportation by the Neo-Babylonians from Palestine (597–582 BCE), as we saw in Chapter 2, a majority of Israelites lived in Babylonian exile, scattered over areas of Upper and Lower Mesopotamia as well as western Iran and earning their livelihood as scribes, craftspeople, and soldiers. After the establishment of the Achaemenid Persian Empire and its subsequent conquest of Babylonia and Syria, including Palestine, these scribes began to compile their Israelite religious traditions from Palestine into larger collections of writings. They became the founders of what is called today "Judaism," and one of them, Deutero-Isaiah, was the first to declare Yahweh [YAH-way], or God, to be the only god of the Jews.

In Deutero-Isaiah's words, there are no gods but Yahweh: "Thus says the Lord the king of Israel, and his redeemer the Lord of hosts; I am the first, and I am the last; and beside me there is no other god" (Is. 44:6–8). Yahweh is completely distinct from the traditional gods of polytheism. Yahweh is invisible and cannot be represented by visible images: "Verily you are a God who hides himself, O God of Israel, the Savior [Messiah]" (Is. 45:15). God in Deutero-Isaiah is the single, invisible creator and sustainer of the world. He is transcendent—a conceptual reality beyond the sensory or empirical reality of this world.

Some of Deutero-Isaiah's followers inserted revisions in the corpus of early scriptures that the Jews had brought with them into Babylonian exile to emphasize Yahweh's transcendence, particularly in the book of Genesis dealing with creation. (A new element they also introduced in Genesis was the 7-day calendar, an innovation which is today recognized everywhere.) Other followers petitioned the Persian king to allow them to leave for Jerusalem and restore the temple destroyed by the Neo-Babylonians. The Persian king issued the permit in 538 BCE (see previous discussion, p. 180), and a small but determined group of monotheists returned to Jerusalem to construct the Second Temple (completed in 515 BCE). A new priesthood took up residence in the Temple and, on the basis of new rituals and laws, administered the emerging monotheistic faith of Judaism.

Zoroastrianism Zoroastrians attribute their origin to Zoroaster (also called Zarathustra), who, like Moses of the Israelites, is supposed to have lived around 1200 BCE, long before the rise of monotheism. The earliest recorded references to Zoroaster's teachings, however, date only to the rise of the Achaemenid Persian Empire in 550 BCE. These teachings were handed down orally by a priestly class, the magi. The main oral text is the Avesta, a body of liturgical texts which the magi used in their religious ceremonies.

The earliest text forms the section called "Yasht" in the Avesta. Zamyad Yasht 19, or the "Hymn to the Earth," speaks of the glories of Ahuramazda (God), to whom the priests are bringing sacrifices. The last of his glories, bestowed on humankind at the end of history, is that of the savior (*saoshyant*), who will restore the world "which will [thenceforth] never grow old and never die, never decaying and never rotting, ever living and ever increasing" (Yasht 15:89–90). Other sections of the Avesta describe in considerable detail the time just prior to the arrival of the savior, a time of trial and tribulation with horrible calamities and devastations, later called the "apocalypse" (Greek *apocalypsis*, revelation). Both themes—Savior or Messiah and apocalypse—are trademarks of Zoroastrian monotheism. In later centuries they

Zoroastrian Fire Temple. Consisting of a cube with a superimposed dome, this Zoroastrian temple, one of the best preserved, is located outside Baku in present-day Azerbaijan. Zoroastrianism was prevalent in the Caucasus region until the arrival of Christianity, and then, Islam.

became central in Judaism, Christianity, and Islam. They replaced the polytheistic notion of a shadowy afterlife in the underworld with salvation of the righteous in God's transcendent kingdom.

Unfortunately, the extant sources do not present a clear picture of the evolution of Zoroastrian monotheism after the 500s BCE. It appears, however, that under the Parthians the magi introduced traditional Iranian and Anatolian cults of fire, maintained in fire temples, into Zoroastrianism. Similarly, they adopted customs of exposing the dead on rooftops to vultures before burying the bones cleansed of mortal flesh in graves. How far the fire temples evolved into congregational places for priests and laity, however, similar to Jewish synagogues, Christian churches, or Greek philosophical schools, is still a matter of conjecture among scholars.

Greek Philosophy While the author of Deutero-Isaiah and the Zoroastrian reformers of the 500s BCE are unknown to us today, the first Greek philosophers are known by name: Thales, Heraclitus, and Thales' pupil Anaximander, who lived during the first half of the 500s in the city of Miletus on the Anatolian coast. Of these, Thales of Miletus is usually credited with beginning the Greek philosophical tradition of divorcing scientific explanations of natural phenomena from mythical, supernatural forces. Anaximander, in contrast to Judaism and Zoroastrianism, formulated the impersonal, or *monist*, "principle of the infinite" (*apeiron*) as the invisible cause underlying the world (*kosmos*). A lively debate over principles ensued after Anaximander and his successors, also mostly from Anatolia, proposed several other cosmic principles. This debate became the basis for the rise of the mathematical and physical sciences in the subsequent centuries.

The Athenian Plato (ca. 427–347 BCE) was the first systematic thinker who extended the debate from principles in nature to a principle common to all areas of reality, such as politics, ethics, and the arts, calling it Being (*on*, originally coined by his predecessor Parmenides, fl. fifth century BCE). In his thinking, called "philosophy," meaning love of wisdom, Being is embodied in the three transcendent forms of Truth, Justice, and Beauty. These forms, so Plato argued, represent objective standards against which all earthly assertions about truth, justice, and beauty in daily life are to be measured. Anaximander's monism thus formed the trunk from which two major branches, science and philosophy, sprouted.

The Break from Polytheism to Monotheism The common thread linking the three visions of transcendence is that they all involve transcendent symbols, such as God or Being, which can only be thought by the mind but not experienced by the senses. For the Greek, Zoroastrian, and Jewish visionaries, reality consisted of two separate halves, the one that can be comprehended only through abstract thought and the other that can be comprehended concretely by being sensed. Polytheist reality is undivided, with gods and natural phenomena conjoined. Given this contrast, it is not surprising that monotheism was incompatible with polytheism. Deutero-Isaiah expressed this incompatibility explicitly; in Greek philosophy and Zoroastrianism it was more implicit. Nevertheless, in the long run, polytheism disappeared from the Middle East and Mediterranean, ceding its long reign to monotheism and subsequent religious civilizations.

Toward Religious Communities and Philosophical Schools

The visionaries were founders of small religious communities and philosophical schools amid an initially continuing polytheism in the Greek city-states and the Persian Empire, both in the Iranian–Mesopotamian imperial center and the Jewish province of Palestine. The small Jewish community that built the Second Temple in Jerusalem grew more rapidly than the Zoroastrian fire temple communities and Greek philosophical schools and led the way to monotheism. It furthermore spawned a Jewish reform movement, Christianity, which in turn changed the Roman Empire from polytheism to monotheism (see Map 7.8).

Judaism in Palestine The Achaemenid Persian kings allowed the Jews, who had moved from Mesopotamia to Palestine and had founded the Second Temple in Jerusalem, a large degree of autonomy. Under their successors, the Ptolemaic and Seleucid kings in the states after Alexander the Great, this autonomy declined substantially. These kings introduced Greek-Hellenistic institutions and culture into Palestine, forcing the Jews to allow the *gymnasium* (the basic school, which included Olympic sports exercises in the nude) as well as polytheism and philosophy in their midst. A majority resisted the introduction of the gymnasium and Zeus with fierce and eventually successful rebellions. As a result, the Jews established

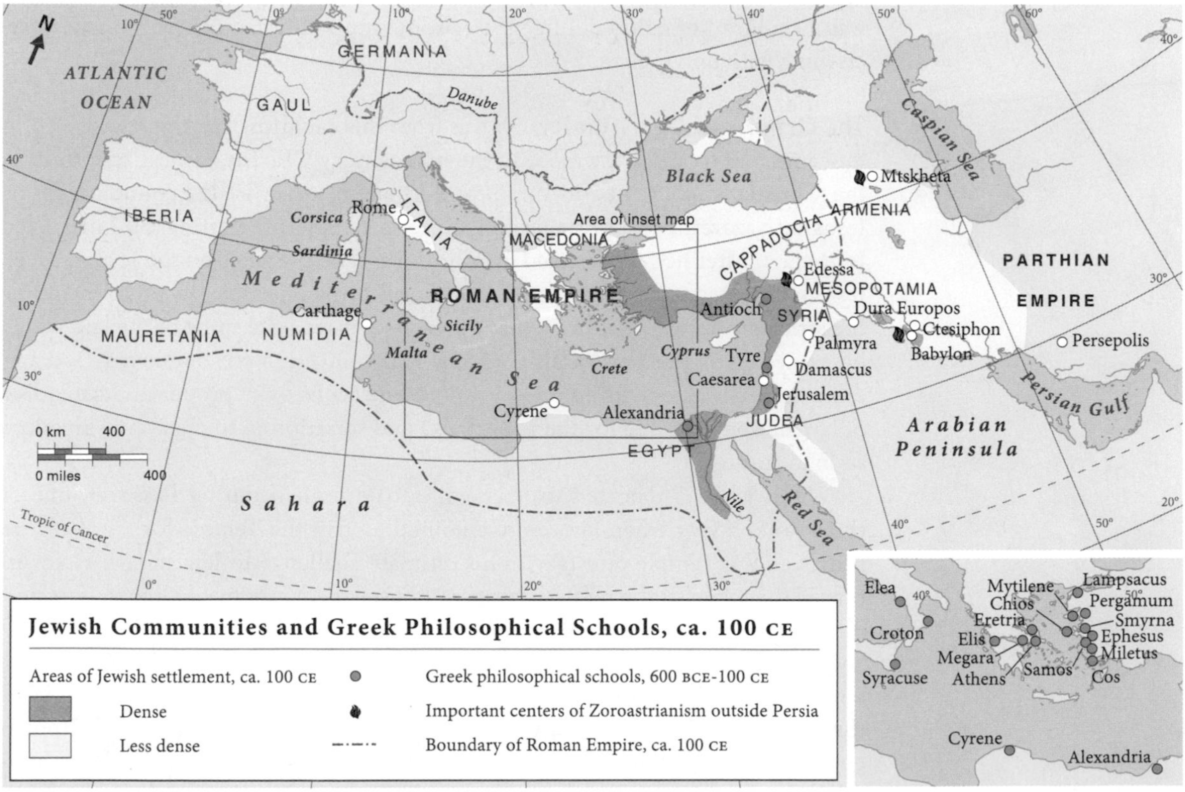

MAP 7.8 Jewish Communities and Greek Philosophical Schools, ca. 100 CE.

the autonomous Hasmonean (also called "Maccabean") kingdom (140–37 BCE), which sought to limit the Hellenization of society (see Source 7.3).

In spite of all Hasmonean attempts to keep Judaism pure, educated Jews learned Greek and read the writings of the Greek philosophers, especially the so-called Cynics, who advocated the virtues of natural simplicity far removed from power, wealth, and fame. Scribes translated Jewish scriptures into Greek, and in the second half of the 200s BCE prayer houses, called "**synagogues**," emerged in cities and towns for the study of the scriptures and of the new Jewish law that had evolved since the foundation of the Second Temple. The monotheism of Yahweh continued to be exclusively administered by priests. But preachers in the synagogues, called "Pharisees," made this monotheism an increasingly popular faith among ordinary Jews.

Synagogues: Jewish meeting places for prayer and legal consultation.

In the first century BCE, the Romans and Persian Parthians replaced the Seleucids and the Herodians replaced the Hasmoneans in Palestine. The Jews interacted not only with the culture of Hellenism but also with the culture of the Romans, their new overlords, and the Parthian Persians, their new neighbors to the east. Many Jews adapted to the Roman philosophical school of the Stoics (who, like the Cynics, advocated an ethics in harmony with the laws of nature) and to the Persian Zoroastrian-inspired apocalypse, which predicted God's final war against evil (that is, foreign domination by Rome), the resurrection of the dead, the day of judgment, and salvation in the heavenly kingdom. Elements of philosophy and the apocalypse, coming together in the teachings of the Pharisees in the synagogues, found widespread followers in the Jewish population. Palestine was a cauldron of cultural influences—some monotheistic, others monist, many clashing with polytheism.

The Origins of Christianity It was from this cauldron that the Jewish reform movement of Christianity arose in the first century CE. The earliest scriptures of the Christians, contained in the New Testament, describe the founding figure, Jesus of Nazareth, as a preacher in Galilee in northern Palestine, 50 miles from Jerusalem. After he was baptized by John, an ascetic preacher on the Jordan River, Jesus is reported to have left the Mosaic as well as the Pharisaic law aside, including the stringent purity laws, and to have preached instead the spirit of the law, which he expressed as the "law of love" (Mark 12:29–30). Only if one loved God and one's neighbor as one loved oneself would one acquire the proper understanding of law and be prepared for the apocalypse and salvation in the heavenly kingdom soon to come.

When Jesus is reported to have gone to Jerusalem during Passover, one of three times a year when Jews were enjoined to visit the Temple for sacrifices, he provoked the Temple priests with his ultimate challenge to Jewish law: He overturned the tables of the money changers and sellers of sacrificial birds to Jews performing the required animal sacrifices. For Jesus, obedience to all these detailed laws and regulations was quite unnecessary in the anticipation of the heavenly kingdom. According to the New Testament, his actions in the Temple initiated the chain of events which ended with the priests turning Jesus over to the Roman governor, Pontius Pilot. The governor understood Jesus as having declared himself king of the Jews, an act of treason in the Roman Empire punishable by death on the cross.

Again according to the New Testament, shortly after Jesus' death, miraculous resurrection, and ascension to the right hand of God, the Pharisee, Roman citizen, and philosophically trained Paul of Tarsus in Anatolia converted to Jesus' law of love. Paul dispensed with another Jewish law, circumcision, and thereby liberated Jesus' message from its last tie to Judaism: Henceforth, anyone could become a follower of Jesus. Paul retained the concept of the apocalypse with its tribulations but also argued that salvation had already begun and would soon be completed with Jesus' return—his Second Coming as the Savior (Messiah) or Anointed (Christus)—at the head of the heavenly kingdom. Paul traveled widely and preached to numerous small Christian communities, called "churches" (Greek, sing. *ekklesia*), which formed in the Roman Empire during the middle of the first century CE.

The Christian Church Paul trained the first missionaries, and after him proselytizing became a regular feature of the emerging Christian community. The missionaries preached Christianity in the Roman Empire from scriptures which evolved in the first three centuries CE. At this time, the first basic canon of accepted writings, the New Testament, was assembled. A hierarchy of bishops and priests preached from these scriptures to laypeople who congregated in local churches for regular communal services. From an early period, however, Christians were divided on how to understand the New Testament. The philosophically educated tended to interpret it figuratively—that is, by reading their philosophical concepts into scripture. Others, opposed to Greek philosophy, preferred a literal interpretation, even though Paul's Christianity was already philosophically tinged. A long struggle over the integration of scripture and philosophy into a single Christian civilization ensued in the church.

Principal figures in the struggle were theologians, called "Church Fathers." The earliest among them was Origen of Alexandria (ca. 185–254 CE), who focused not only on the allegorical but also on the ethical interpretation of scripture. The intellectually most versatile church father was Augustine (354–430 CE), from what is today Algeria. His two main works are the *Confessions*, in which he describes his conversion to Christianity and reflections on spirituality, and *The City of God*, in which he defends Christianity against the accusation by many Romans that its adoption as the state religion in 380 contributed to the decline of the empire. Although his philosophical training was limited, he was a strong proponent of the allegorical interpretation, which became a principal pillar of church doctrine. Thanks to the Church Fathers, the church was set on a path of merging monotheism and philosophy as the basis for the rise of a Christian civilization.

Mural from Dura-Europos on the Euphrates. The city, founded in 303 BCE, was home to a sizable Jewish community whose synagogue was adorned with murals in the Parthian-Hellenistic style. Shown here is a depiction of the infant Moses being rescued from the Nile.

As a result of the Church Fathers' theological works and debates in church councils during the period of ca. 400-600, three main Christian denominations evolved. The Orthodox Catholic Church, supported by the Roman emperors, patriarchs of Constantinople, and the pope in Rome adopted a Christology that defined Jesus Christ as being simultaneously fully human and fully divine. The Eastern Syriac Church, under the catholicus, adhered to nearly the same Christology but was subject to the Sasanid shahinshahs. The Coptic Church in Egypt and Jacobite Church in Syria, by contrast, defined Christ as possessing only a single, divine nature from birth ("Incarnation"). Both Copts and Jacobites, subject to the Roman emperors but bitterly opposed to the two-nature Christology of the Orthodox Catholic and Eastern Syriac Churches, represented a general tendency in early Christianity toward the divinization of Jesus. This tendency was cut short, however, in the 600s with the emergence of Islam in which Jesus is viewed as entirely human (see Chapter 10).

The Beginnings of Science and the Cultures of Kings and Citizens

Monotheism and philosophy entered society early on during the Jewish Second Temple kingdom in Palestine. In the Persian and Roman Empires this incorporation, in the form of preferred or state religions, took longer. Greek science became important in Ptolemaic Egypt (305–30 BCE). The Ptolemies provided state support for the development of mathematics, physics, astronomy, and the applied science of mechanics as new and independent fields of culture. The other, inherited forms of cultural expression—painting, sculpture, architecture, and literature—remained within traditional polytheistic confines. Nevertheless, in Greece and Rome these latter cultural forms underwent substantial innovation and differentiation, influenced by Hellenism as well as Parthian and Sasanid Persia.

The Sciences at the Library of Alexandria

In Athens and other city-states, citizens supported philosophical schools, such as the Academy of Plato or the Lyceum of Aristotle (384–322 BCE), one of Plato's students and the tutor of Alexander. These institutions were small if compared with the enormous resources the Ptolemies and their Roman successors poured into a new type of institution of Greek learning, the institute for advanced study, as we would say today. Centers of advanced study, principally libraries and museums, flourished at Pergamon, Alexandria, and elsewhere. The Library of Alexandria (280 BCE–ca. 400 CE) was devoted primarily to research in the mathematical and natural sciences. At times, some 100 resident fellows did research in its library holdings of half a million scrolls, performed dissection of corpses in laboratories, gazed at the stars in the astronomical observatory, strolled through the botanical gardens, and shared meals.

The most developed branch of the sciences at the Library was geometry. Euclid (fl. ca. 300 BCE), one of the founders of the Library, provided geometry with its basic definitions and proofs in his *Elements*, still important today. In addition to geometry, mathematicians laid the foundations for algebra. The pioneer was Diophantus (ca. 214–284 CE), with his exploration of the properties of algebraic equations. Hypatia (ca. 360–415 CE), the first known female scientist in world history, is said to have contributed further to the development of algebra, but her work is unfortunately no longer extant (see Source 7.5). In the absence of a practical Greek number system, however, algebra remained ultimately stunted in its growth in Alexandria and had to await the Muslims and the Arabic numeral system—originally devised in India—to evolve fully.

Alexandrian geographers and astronomers, trained in geometry, made important calculations of the earth's circumference and tilt and formulated the first heliocentric astronomical theory, according to which the earth spins around the sun. Unfortunately, this theory was rejected in favor of more commonsensical observations, such as the fact that an arrow shot upward falls to the same spot instead of farther to the west. Therefore, the opposite theory of the earth standing still at the center of the planetary system became dominant. Claudius Ptolemy (ca. 87–170 CE) devised such a detailed and precise geometric system of the planets' movements that his geocentrism reigned for the next millennium and a half in the astronomies of the Islamic Middle East and western European Christianity, dethroned eventually only by Copernicus in the sixteenth century.

Star lists from Ptolemy's *Almagest*

In addition to astronomy, physics also flourished at the Library. The outstanding physicist was Archimedes (287–212 BCE), who investigated the behavior of floating bodies in the new science of hydrostatics—bold investigations, which had to wait a millennium and a half before being fully appreciated in the works of Galileo Galilei, one of the pioneers of modern physics. The Library came to its end under unknown circumstances at the beginning of the 400s CE. Its legacy, however, was such that later Islamic rulers resumed the tradition of sponsoring institutes for advanced study.

Royal Persian Culture and Arts

The Achaemenid Persians arrived in Mesopotamia with their rich Indo-European traditions of divine and heroic myths, which were also characteristic of Aryan migrants to India. These myths told of deities and heroes mingling in a verdant landscape of mountains, rivers, and pastures. Major themes included the protracted, sometimes noble, and occasionally treacherous struggles between the Persians and their tribal rivals in central Asia, whom they called "Turanians." After 600 BCE, monotheistic Zoroastrians reworked the pagan myths in the Avesta so that under the one, invisible God (Ahuramazda) the other deities became lesser beings, such as angels and demons. The myths and epics were handed down orally until the 400s CE, well after the disappearance of the Achaemenids, before they were finally written down.

As heirs of both Achaemenid Persian and Greek traditions, the Parthians forged a new synthesis between inherited styles and adopted Greek-Hellenistic elements, while maintaining an overall palace-focused culture of their own. For example, courtiers listened to bards who recited the exploits of Hercules and other Greek heroes, thereby laying the foundations for the Rustam story cycle written down several centuries later. Other bards and minstrels traveled among aristocratic families, composing stories of their masters' courtly loves and intrigues or their exploits in battles against nomadic invaders from central Asia. After the Parthians, these stories were handed down orally and grew in both length and complexity. They exist today in a modern Persian version, called the *Book of Kings* (*Shahname* [Sha-ha-na-MAY]), compiled by the poet Firdosi [Feer-dow-SEE] in the eleventh century CE.

The Sasanids were major transmitters of Indian texts to the Middle East and Mediterranean. The most popular text was a translation of animal fables, known in Sanskrit as the *Five Treatises* (*Panchatantra* [Pan-cha-TAN-trah]) and in Arabic

Monumental Barrel Vault of the Sasanid Royal Reception Hall, Ctesiphon.

as *Kalila wa dimna* [ka-LEE-lah wa DIM-nah]. In these fables, animals appear in witty, cleverly constructed stories intended to teach lessons to palace courtiers and retainers. Other texts were instruction manuals on chess, a game which made its way to the West during Sasanid times. Also from India came medical texts complete with discussions of anatomy, diseases, and herbs. All these texts, which were either useful or entertaining, or both, played important roles at the Sasanid court.

In architecture, the characteristic feature of Sasanid palaces was the monumental dome and barrel vault. Arches, domes, and barrel vaulting had been pioneered in Mesopotamia in the second millennium BCE but only for small structures. Sasanid vaults and domes were massive structures. The central audience hall of the palace in the capital, Ctesiphon, built ca. 250 CE, had a barrel vault 118 feet high. Other palaces had "squinched" domes of up to 45 feet across, covering square audience and banquet halls. *Squinches* were curved triangular transition spaces between the dome and the corners of the halls. In order to counter the outward thrust of the dome's weight, buttresses supported the walls on the outside. The techniques of both barrel vaulting and the dome were transmitted from Sasanid Persia to Christian Armenia, Rome, and ultimately western Europe, where they appeared in church architecture.

Greek and Roman Civic Culture and Arts

The disappearance of kings and aristocracies in the Greek city-states during the sixth century BCE had momentous consequences for Greek culture. Instead of merely a handful of kings and aristocrats sponsoring the arts, thousands of wealthy citizens began to patronize artists or even create works of literature, sculpture, painting, and architecture themselves. A broad civic artistic creativity arose. Although polytheism, myths, and other ancient traditions remained central for the majority of the citizens and only a minority adapted to the new philosophical and scientific monism, the heritage lost its symbolical, stylized, and generic royal orientation. Instead, Greeks began to experiment with a variety of individual shapes, types, and models, seeking realistic representation in their art.

As in Mesopotamia and Egypt, seasonal festivals were of great importance in Greece. In contrast to Mesopotamia and Egypt, however, Greek city culture encouraged personal artistic expression. Given the increasing participation of commoners in the state, festivals in Greece became occasions for the composition of songs and poems whose authors were remembered by name. Festivals often had poetry contests, and Hesiod (see subsequent discussion) appears as the earliest winner of such a contest. In the following century, a writer who acquired fame outside the poetry contest circuit was Sappho. She was the instructor of female initiation groups in one of the city-states on the island of Lesbos. Her poetry reflects the experience of erotic experimentation among adolescent girls which was part of their preparation for marriage.

Greek Literature and Art The earliest Greek literature dates to the eighth century BCE. The period 750–600 BCE was a time of close cultural contact between the rising Greek city-states and the Neo-Assyrian Empire, which dominated Syria and Anatolia. Not surprisingly, therefore, the Assyrian versions of the Mesopotamian epic and creation myths, *Gilgamesh* and *Enuma Elish,* made their way to the Greeks, where they were incorporated into Greek culture.

This incorporation was the work of two gifted writers, Homer (fl. ca. 730 BCE) and Hesiod (fl. ca. 700 BCE), both from Greek city-states in Anatolia, and both familiar with Mesopotamian literature through interactions with the ancient Near East. Homer composed two epics in the form of extended poems, the tragedy *Iliad* and the narrative legend *Odyssey*. Hesiod's *Theogony* begins with "Chaos, the Abyss," out of which the earth, or Gaia, came into being. The rest of the *Theogony* is devoted to telling the stories of some 300 divinities descended from Chaos and Gaia. Three of the first four generations of deities destroyed each other violently. The fourth, the Olympians, became the present pantheon of gods, with Zeus as the patriarch.

The Greek theater emerged around 500–480 BCE out of the stylized traditions and rituals of the Dionysiac cult. Every year in March, during the Dionysiac processions, competitions took place among groups of citizens (later wealthy noncitizens also competed) for the presentation of the best tragedy or comedy. These competing groups, or *choruses,* dressed in sumptuous robes and elaborate masks to perform the chosen dramatic or comic piece through declamation and dance. In the course of time, individual actors emerged from among the chorus members and presented dialogues on which the chorus commented as the plot evolved. Tragedy developed out of Dionysiac myths and comedy from the Dionysiac processions.

Among the most important writers who composed for the early Greek stage were the tragedians Aeschylus, Sophocles, and Euripides, as well as the comedian Aristophanes. In *The Persians,* Aeschylus developed the theme of the Greeks defending their freedom from Persian tyranny, a theme which in the course of time changed into the Europeans defining their culture as superior to that of the Other, the inferior Orient. In this chapter, which focuses on Persia, Geece, and Rome as equal partners in a single, undivided region of the Middle East and the Mediterranean Sea, we seek to overcome the otherization of the Orient. In other respects as well, all four authors

Greek Realism. The Greeks used decorated stelae to mark the burial places of the dead in much the same way tombstones function today. This intimate relief, from about 450 BCE, memorializes a young girl. The treatment of the child's body is realistic—note the chubby arms—and the way the girl tenderly holds her pet doves transforms the little scene into a touching story.

of tragedies, and many of their successors, continue to exercise a profound influence on the evolution of culture today.

Just as democracy encouraged the exploration of individual character in tragedy and comedy, so it supported the search for character representation in Greek painting and sculpture. Unfortunately, no murals or panels exist today, although a few Roman reproductions survive. Vase painting gives us a good impression of scenes of daily life, even though the medium imposed severe limits of color and composition on artists. Surviving examples of sculptures are plentiful, even if primarily in the form of later Roman copies, which often lack the refinement of the original Greek models.

In the fifth century BCE, sculptors abandoned the last traces of the traditional Middle Eastern symbolic royal style that required figures to be in tranquil repose, projecting dignity and solemnity. Instead, sculptors began to explore physical movement and individual emotional states. In terms of themes, poses, and individuality, Greek vase paintings and sculptures achieved a remarkably wide range, from figures exerting themselves in their chosen sports to exquisite models of human beauty. Greek sculptors and painters abandoned symbolism and, instead, embraced realism as their style of representation (what we might call today "photographic representation").

Roman Literature and Art Greece influenced Roman culture early on. As early as the middle of the third century BCE, Romans had translated Greek plays and poetry into Latin. After the adaptation of Greek poetic metrical patterns to the Latin language, a long line of poets emerged. Prose writings on political and historical themes, also modeled on Greek precursors, appeared in large numbers. Emperor Augustus and his wealthy friend Maecenas, renowned for his sponsorship of the arts, stimulated an outburst of early imperial pride. For example, in his epic poem *The Aeneid*, Virgil (70–19 BCE) played down the influence of Greece by positing the origins of Rome in Troy, the rival of Greece. In his Odes, Horace (65–8 BCE) glorified courage, patriotism, piety, justice, and a respect for tradition, which he regarded as uniquely Roman virtues. These writers viewed Rome as the culmination of civilization.

Roman sculpture followed the Greek civic style closely by emphasizing proportion, perspective, foreshortening, and light and shadow. Among the earliest sculptures were marble busts which aristocratic Romans had made of their patriarchs, cast from wax masks and plaster models. These busts, kept in family shrines, were a central part of aristocratic life in the republic. During the imperial period prior to the establishment of Christianity as the state religion (31 BCE–380 CE), life-sized imitations of Greek and Egyptian statues were commonly found in the households of the wealthy. On columns and triumphal arches, reliefs similar to those of the Persians celebrated military victories. In contrast to the Parthians and Sasanids, civic Romans adorned their cities with numerous monumental structures and hence provided their empire with much greater visibility.

Roman pictorial art existed mostly in the form of wood panels, wall paintings, and floor mosaics. In the fifth century CE, the first illustrated book appeared, depicting scenes from Virgil's *Aeneid*. Nearly all panel paintings have perished,

Scene from the Aeneid. According to Virgil's *Aeneid*, on his journey from Troy, Aeneas landed in North Africa and fell madly in love with Dido, the queen of Carthage. One day, as they were hunting, a storm forced the two to seek shelter in a cave. Destiny, however, demanded that Aeneas travel on to Italy and found Rome. In her disconsolate grief of being without Aeneas, Dido committed suicide. The cave episode is illustrated here in a manuscript of the fifth century CE.

Pompeii: Mural Executed with Careful Attention to Perspective, Light and Shadow, and Foreshortening. An eruption of the Vesuvius volcano buried the city in 79 CE in ash and thereby preserved the murals of the city. They provide some of the best evidence we have of life in ancient Rome.

image analysis

but wall paintings have survived in larger numbers, ironically because of their preservation in Pompeii and other cities buried by the eruption of Mount Vesuvius in 79 CE. The paintings demonstrate Roman art at a remarkably skilled level, with perspective emphasized and executed just as precisely as in Greek art (see Source 7.4).

Rome's architecture was initially closely modeled on the Greek and Etruscan heritage in Italy. In the imperial age, when the desire for monumental architecture developed, the Romans—shortly after the Parthians—adopted the elements of arch and dome for large buildings. An example is the Pantheon in Rome, built in 118–126 CE. This building, a temple dedicated to all the Roman gods, consists of a dome placed on top of a drum and lit by a round open skylight at its apex (diameter and height both 142 feet). The circular foundation wall made squinches unnecessary. The courtyard of Emperor Diocletian's palace in what is now Split, Croatia (ca. 300 CE), contains the first example of arches set on pillars, which later acquired crucial importance in Islamic and medieval Christian architectures.

Beginning with the first Christian emperor, Constantine, in the early fourth century CE, there was a return from realistic to symbolical representation in the arts. The rich variety of literature shrank to the one category of religious poetry and hymns. Pagan Greek and Roman realistic artists had emphasized emotional variety in their art, playing with surface detail, perspective, foreshortening, light and shadow, and full and empty space. The representational style changed into the **hieratic style** of art, in which the sanctity of the depicted human figures is emphasized. Christian artists began to emphasize what they considered essential for sacredness. Instead of seeking emotionally diverse forms and expressions, they drew from Middle Eastern models, which retained connections to symbolism. Accordingly, characters and objects became generic and lost their detailed psychological and physical characteristics. Space became two dimensional and figures were large or small according to their religious importance, not their closeness to or distance from the viewer. What mattered was the paradigmatic saintly comportment of figures, which the believers were supposed to imitate. Religious uniformity came to dominate culture in the Roman and Sasanid Persian Empires, as it dominated their politics in the form of state religion.

Hieratic style: Representation in painting or sculpture that is highly restrained or severe in emotional import.

Putting It All Together

interactive concept map

In 590/591 the Sasanid Empire suffered a war of succession during which one of the rivals, King Khosrow II (r. 590–628), fled to the Romans. Before he arrived in Constantinople, he sent an embassy that pleaded for military support: "It is impossible for a single monarchy to embrace the innumerable cares of the organization of the universe. . . . It is never possible for the earth to resemble the unity of the divine and primary rule." As Khosrow had hoped, his ambassadors' arguments were persuasive, and he received Roman military support, with which he defeated his rival and regained the Persian throne.

Khosrow's argument is a fitting conclusion to this chapter on world empires, which began with Alexander's bold quest to unite the Mediterranean, Middle East, and India. For Alexander it was still possible to think in terms of one supreme god in heaven and one empire on earth. But after the introduction of monotheism, the situation changed. For the Persian ambassadors it was impossible for a human empire not only to ever resemble the kingdom of God but also to reign alone on earth. For the Persians and Romans—Theophylactus cites the above Persian ambassadors approvingly—the one single God anywhere and nowhere disapproves of all imperial projects on earth and prefers a commonwealth of multiple kingdoms. It is this reevaluation of politics and history which the visionaries of ca. 600 BCE can be seen as having contributed to world history. Obviously, many kings and emperors later in history did not accept the idea of the futility of empires. But after monotheism, they had to reckon with forceful critics who would cut their ambitions down to size and remind people of the fundamental difference between the imperfect earthly states and the heavenly kingdom.

Review and Relate

Thinking Through Patterns

Examine the ways historians approach the big questions of this chapter.

» Why should the Middle East and Mediterranean Europe during the period 600 BCE–600 CE be studied as a single unit?

The sharp division between Europe and the Middle East that exists today is a recent phenomenon. During the period of late multireligious and early monotheistic empires, from 600 BCE to 600 CE, the two regions were tightly intertwined. Initially, the sequence of the multireligious Persian and Macedonian Empires dominated the Middle East and eastern Mediterranean. Later, the competition between the subsequent two empires, Rome and Persia, inaugurated a pattern of urbanization, a deepening gulf between the wealthy and poor, and the immigration of tribal people from central Asia.

» What is transcendence, and why is it important to understand its importance in world history?

The awareness of transcendence exists constantly, even if it remains for the most part unexpressed and little thought about. In its most common form, it is encountered as the unknown future: You dream of getting a college degree as the entry ticket to your future academic career. After years of toil, sacrifices, and financial cost, the day of graduation arrives. In one moment, as your name is called, the transcendent expectation becomes a reality: As you clutch the diploma, a thrill goes down your spine. The same holds true for the past: You do not know from where you came and what the origin of your consciousness is. In a more general sense, the great visionaries of 700–500 BCE abstracted a separate, transcendent God or first principle from the world to explain its origin. In polytheism, there had been a single cosmos in which the high god, plus all the other gods and goddesses in heaven, intermingled with humans on earth. Following the visionaries, thinkers explored new, abstract dimensions of justice and thought in the new intellectual disciplines of science, philosophy, and theology.

Which elements characterize the institutions that grew out of the Middle Eastern monotheisms of Judaism–Christianity and monism of Greek philosophy-science?

In the Middle East and eastern Mediterranean, visionaries were the creators of bodies of transcendent thought that evolved into the Zoroastrian and Jewish religions as well as Greek philosophy and science. The visionaries and their early followers created scriptures which expounded in great detail the nature of God or the first principle. Anyone could read or listen to the scriptures, and, accordingly, the visionaries and their successors attracted communities of like-minded followers. Zoroastrianism, Judaism, and Christianity were religions of salvation: Firm believers in the power of God's forgiveness would be saved in a transcendent kingdom of heaven. For Zoroastrians, Jews, and Christians—cogs in the giant, brutal, and meaningless multireligious machines of the Persian and Roman Empires—this religious promise of salvation was the only way of making sense out of life. Eventually the emperors themselves converted, making monotheism the religion of their states.

Against the Grain

Consider this as a counterpoint to the main patterns examined in this chapter.

Women in Democratic Athens

- How does the inferior status of Athenian women represent a contradiction to the prevailing view of Athenian democracy?
- In what ways does this image of women in Athens compare and contrast with women's status in other ancient civilizations?

The word "democracy" is derived from the Greek *demos* ("the people") and *kratia* ("power" or "strength"). Yet even though democratic rule in Athens is usually cited as a model of egalitarian rule, the status of women in Athenian society reflects a glaring contradiction of this ideal depiction.

Several indicators point to policies of marked gender inequality. Athenian women could neither vote nor own property. Their marriages were often arranged, primarily for monetary gain; once married, women could not sue for divorce. Married women were under the constant control of a guardian (*kyrios*), either their husbands or nearest male relatives. Women were required to bring dowries into the marriage, which were immediately assigned to the husband's control.

For the most part, women's roles consisted of bearing and raising children, inculcating in them the moral and ethical values of the polis, and being responsible for managing the household (*oikos*). Because women were believed to be more emotional and driven by sexual passion than men, they were seen to pose a threat to the stability of both *oikos* and polis. Thus, Athenian women were largely confined to the home, although they frequented the marketplace and civic center (*agora*), and occasionally attended festivals. Women were also assigned participatory roles in funerals, weddings, and religious rituals, where they played important roles as priestesses. Educated women routinely accompanied men as companions (*hetairai*) to various social functions, such as plays and dinner parties. At the bottom of the social ladder were slave women and prostitutes (*pornai*).

Why were Athenian women relegated to second-class citizenship? In an agrarian, patriarchal society like Athens men determined cultural norms, and thus reflected prevailing views of women. For example, in Euripides' *Medea* the protagonist laments "If only children could be got by some other way without the female sex. . . . If women didn't exist, human life would be rid of all its miseries." And in his *Politics* Aristotle observes that "the male is by nature superior, and the female inferior; and the one rules, and the other is ruled; this principle, of necessity, extends to all mankind."

Key Terms

audio flashcards

Cataphracts 180
Hellenism 186
Hieratic style 210
Hoplites 180
Legionaries 189
Nicene Creed 193
Oracles 183
Republic 188
Shahinshah 181
Synagogues 202
Transcendence 198

For additional resources, please go to **www.oup.com/us/vonsivers.**
Please see the Further Resources section at the back of the book for additional readings and suggested websites.

PATTERNS OF EVIDENCE |

Sources for Chapter 7

SOURCE 7.1 The Cyrus Cylinder

539 BCE

Founder of the Achaemenid Persian Empire, Cyrus (Kurosh) the Great rose to the throne of a small kingdom in 559 BCE; by the time of his death in 529, he had brought virtually the entire Near East under his control. In 539, he conquered Babylon and drove out Nabonidus, the last of the Neo-Babylonian kings. However, he was hailed as a liberator by the priests of the Babylonian god Marduk, and he issued a remarkable document, in which he praised himself for the restoration of all temples, priesthoods, and cults in his vast empire. The text, which was publicized in Akkadian, an ancient Mesopotamian language, is preserved on a clay cylinder, today called the Cyrus Cylinder and housed in the British Museum.

. . .

On account of their complaints, the lords of the gods became furiously angry and left their [the Babylonians'] land; the gods, who dwelt among them, left their homes. . . . In all lands everywhere [the god Marduk] searched; he looked through them and sought a righteous prince after his own heart, whom he took by the hand. He called Cyrus, king of Anshan, by name; he appointed him to lordship over the whole world.

The land of Qutu, all the Umman-manda, he cast down at his feet. The black-headed people, whom he gave his hands to conquer, he took them in justice and righteousness. Marduk, the great lord, looked joyously on the caring for his people, on his pious works and his righteous heart. To his city, Babylon, he caused [Cyrus] to go; he made him take the road to Babylon, going as a friend and companion at his side. His numerous troops, in unknown numbers, like the waters of a river, marched armed at his side. Without battle and conflict, he permitted him to enter Babylon. He spared his city, Babylon, a calamity. Nabonidus, the king, who did not fear him, he delivered into his hand.

. . .

When I [Cyrus] made my triumphal entrance into Babylon, I took up my lordly residence in the royal palace with joy and rejoicing; Marduk, the great

---

Source: Cyrus Cylinder, trans. R. W. Rogers, http://www.kchanson.com/ANCDOCS/meso/cyrus.html.

lord, moved the noble heart of the residents of Babylon to me, while I gave daily attention to his worship. My numerous troops marched peacefully into Babylon. In all Sumer and Akkad I permitted no enemy to enter.

The needs of Babylon and of all its cities I gladly attended to. The people of Babylon [and . . .], and the shameful yoke was removed from them. Their dwellings, which had fallen, I restored. I cleared out their ruins. Marduk, the great lord, rejoiced in my pious deeds, and graciously blessed me, Cyrus, the king who worships him, and Cambyses, my own son, and all my troops, while we, before him, joyously praised his exalted godhead.

. . .

And the gods of Sumer and Akkad—whom Nabonidus, to the anger of the lord of the gods, had brought into Babylon—by the command of Marduk, the great lord, I caused them to take up their dwelling in residences that gladdened the heart. May all the gods, whom I brought into their cities, pray daily before Bel and Nabu for long life for me, and may they speak a gracious word for me and say to Marduk, my lord, "May Cyrus, the king who worships you, and Cambyses his son, their [. . .] I permitted all to dwell in peace [. . .]."

» Working with Sources

1. **How and why did Cyrus incorporate local deities into his public image after subjugating Babylon?**
2. **How does this document compare with other texts on peace and justice in Mesopotamia?**

SOURCE 7.2

Herodotus, *Histories*

ca. 420s BCE

Having failed to defeat the Athenians in their first attempt in 490 BCE, the Persians launched a massive invasion of the entire Greek peninsula in 480, under the leadership of Darius's successor, Xerxes. Thirty-one Greek cities agreed to band together to resist this force of (according to Herodotus) 1,700,000 Persian soldiers, in addition to a sizeable naval contingent. Herodotus envisions a conversation between Xerxes and the Spartan defector Demaratus shortly before the first major confrontation between Persia and the Greeks at Thermopylae. In answer to the king's question, Demaratus claims that the Greeks will prove more difficult to defeat than Xerxes expects.

Source: Herodotus, *The Histories*, trans. Aubrey de Sélincourt (Harmondsworth, UK: Penguin, 1954), 403–405.

Having sailed from one end to the other of the line of anchored ships, Xerxes went ashore again and sent for Demaratus, the son of Ariston, who was accompanying him in the march to Greece. "Demaratus," he said, "it would give me pleasure at this point to put to you a few questions. You are a Greek, and a native, moreover, of by no means the meanest or weakest city in that country—as I learn not only from yourself but from the other Greeks I have spoken with. Tell me, then—will the Greeks dare to lift a hand against me? My own belief is that all the Greeks and all the other western peoples gathered together would be insufficient to withstand the attack of my army—and still more so if they are not united. But it is your opinion upon this subject that I should like to hear."

. . .

"I think highly," [Demaratus said,] "of all Greeks of the Dorian lands, but what I am about to say will apply not to all Dorians, but to the Spartans only. First then, they will not under any circumstances accept terms from you which would mean slavery for Greece; secondly, they will fight you even if the rest of Greece submits. Moreover, there is no use in asking if their numbers are adequate to enable them to do this; suppose a thousand of them take the field—then that thousand will fight you; and so will any number, greater than this or less."

Xerxes laughed. "Demaratus," he exclaimed, "what an extraordinary thing to say! Do you really suppose a thousand men would fight an army like mine?"

. . .

"King," Demaratus answered, "I knew before I began that if I spoke the truth you would not like it. But, as you demanded the plain truth and nothing less, I told you how things are with the Spartans. Yet you are well aware that I now feel but little affection for my countrymen, who robbed me of my hereditary power and privileges and made me a fugitive without a home—whereas your father welcomed me at his court and gave me the means of livelihood and somewhere to live. Surely it is unreasonable to reject kindness; any sensible man will cherish it. Personally I do not claim to be able to fight ten men—or two; indeed I should prefer not even to fight with one. But should it be necessary—should there be some great cause to urge me on—then nothing would give me more pleasure than to stand up to one of those men of yours who claim to be a match for three Greeks. So it is with the Spartans; fighting singly, they are as good as any, but fighting together they are the best soldiers in the world. They are free—yes—but not entirely free; for they have a master, and that master is Law, which they fear much more than your subjects fear you. Whatever this master commands, they do; and his command never varies: it is never to retreat in battle, however great the odds, but always to remain in formation, and to conquer or die. If, my lord, you think that what I have said is nonsense—very well; I am willing henceforward to hold my tongue. This time I spoke because you forced me to speak. In any case, I pray that all may turn out as you desire."

Xerxes burst out laughing at Demaratus' answer, and good-humoredly let him go.

» Working with Sources

1. For what reasons does Demaratus think the Spartans will fight so hard to resist Xerxes?
2. What does the passage reveal concerning Herodotus' attitude toward the Greeks—and the Persians?

SOURCE 7.3

1 Maccabees

ca. 134 BCE

Just before his death in Babylon in June 323 BCE, Alexander the Great was the unrivaled conqueror of an enormous portion of the known world, counting modern Greece, Egypt, the Middle East, Iran, and Afghanistan among his possessions. However, when he died, leaving his kingdom "to the strongest," conflicts immediately broke out among his Macedonian successors to determine who that strongest man was. A part of the military and political struggle that followed was an attempt to Hellenize, with varying levels of success, the older and more entrenched cultures Alexander had defeated as he raced through Africa and Asia. This process continued for the next three centuries. In the mid-second century BCE, one of these successor kings, Antiochus IV Epiphanes, attempted a brutal imposition of Greek cultural values on the Jews in Jerusalem. This effort, and the revolt it triggered, is described in the apocryphal (i.e., not part of the standard canon) Jewish book of 1 Maccabees. Notice that the Hellenistic era did not appear to everyone to have been a fortuitous blending of disparate cultures.

1 After Alexander son of Philip, the Macedonian, who came from the land of
Kittim, had defeated King Darius of the Persians and the Medes, he succeeded
him as king. (He had previously become king of Greece.) **2** He fought many
battles, conquered strongholds, and put to death the kings of the earth. **3** He
advanced to the ends of the earth, and plundered many nations. When the
earth became quiet before him, he was exalted, and his heart was lifted up. **4**
He gathered a very strong army and ruled over countries, nations, and princes,
and they became tributary to him. **5** After this he fell sick and perceived that
he was dying. **6** So he summoned his most honored officers, who had been
brought up with him from youth, and divided his kingdom among them while
he was still alive. **7** And after Alexander had reigned twelve years, he died. **8**
Then his officers began to rule, each in his own place. **9** They all put on crowns

Source: *The Apocrypha: Revised Standard Version of the Old Testament* (New York: Thomas Nelson & Sons, 1957), 190–192.

after his death, and so did their descendants after them for many years; and they caused many evils on the earth.

10 From them came forth a sinful root, Antiochus Epiphanes, son of King Antiochus; he had been a hostage in Rome. He began to reign in the one hundred thirty-seventh year of the kingdom of the Greeks. **11** In those days certain renegades came out from Israel and misled many, saying, "Let us go and make a covenant with the Gentiles around us, for since we separated from them many disasters have come upon us." **12** This proposal pleased them, **13** and some of the people eagerly went to the king, who authorized them to observe the ordinances of the Gentiles. **14** So they built a gymnasium in Jerusalem, according to Gentile custom, **15** and removed the marks of circumcision, and abandoned the holy covenant. They joined with the Gentiles and sold themselves to do evil. **16** When Antiochus saw that his kingdom was established, he determined to become king of the land of Egypt, in order that he might reign over both kingdoms. **17** So he invaded Egypt with a strong force, with chariots and elephants and cavalry and with a large fleet. **18** He engaged King Ptolemy of Egypt in battle, and Ptolemy turned and fled before him, and many were wounded and fell. **19** They captured the fortified cities in the land of Egypt, and he plundered the land of Egypt.

20 After subduing Egypt, Antiochus returned in the one hundred forty-third year. He went up against Israel and came to Jerusalem with a strong force. **21** He arrogantly entered the sanctuary and took the golden altar, the lampstand for the light, and all its utensils. **22** He took also the table for the bread of the Presence, the cups for drink offerings, the bowls, the golden censers, the curtain, the crowns, and the gold decoration on the front of the temple; he stripped it all off. **23** He took the silver and the gold, and the costly vessels; he took also the hidden treasures that he found. **24** Taking them all, he went into his own land. He shed much blood, and spoke with great arrogance. **25** Israel mourned deeply in every community, **26** rulers and elders groaned, young women and young men became faint, the beauty of the women faded. **27** Every bridegroom took up the lament; she who sat in the bridal chamber was mourning. **28** Even the land trembled for its inhabitants, and all the house of Jacob was clothed with shame. **29** Two years later the king sent to the cities of Judah a chief collector of tribute, and he came to Jerusalem with a large force. **30** Deceitfully he spoke peaceable words to them, and they believed him; but he suddenly fell upon the city, dealt it a severe blow, and destroyed many people of Israel. **31** He plundered the city, burned it with fire, and tore down its houses and its surrounding walls. **32** They took captive the women and children, and seized the livestock. **33** Then they fortified the city of David with a great strong wall and strong towers, and it became their citadel.

. . .

44 And the king sent letters by messengers to Jerusalem and the towns of Judah; he directed them to follow customs strange to the land, **45** to forbid burnt offerings and sacrifices and drink offerings in the sanctuary, to profane sabbaths and festivals, **46** to defile the sanctuary and the priests, **47** to build altars and sacred precincts and shrines for idols, to sacrifice swine and other unclean animals, **48** and to leave their sons uncircumcised. They were to make themselves abominable by everything unclean and profane, **49** so that they would forget the law and change all the ordinances. **50** He added, "And whoever does not obey the command of the king shall die." **51** In such words he wrote to his whole kingdom. He appointed inspectors over all the people and commanded the towns of Judah to offer sacrifice, town by town. **52** Many of the people, everyone who forsook the law, joined them, and they did evil in the land; **53** they drove Israel into hiding in every place of refuge they had. **54** Now on the fifteenth day of Chislev, in the one hundred forty-fifth year, they erected a desolating sacrilege on the altar of burnt offering. They also built altars in the surrounding towns of Judah, **55** and offered incense at the doors of the houses and in the streets. **56** The books of the law that they found they tore to pieces and burned with fire. **57** Anyone found possessing the book of the covenant, or anyone who adhered to the law, was condemned to death by decree of the king. **58** They kept using violence against Israel, against those who were found month after month in the towns. **59** On the twenty-fifth day of the month they offered sacrifice on the altar that was on top of the altar of burnt offering. **60** According to the decree, they put to death the women who had their children circumcised, **61** and their families and those who circumcised them; and they hung the infants from their mothers' necks. **62** But many in Israel stood firm and were resolved in their hearts not to eat unclean food. **63** They chose to die rather than to be defiled by food or to profane the holy covenant; and they did die.

Working with Sources

1. **To what specific innovations does the writer of this document object? Why?**
2. **What evidence is contained in this document of cultural misunderstanding?**

SOURCE 7.4 Graffiti from the walls of Pompeii

ca. 79 CE

This is a small sample of the array of painted, scratched, and scribbled graffiti archaeologists have discovered on the walls of the city of Pompeii, which was sealed in ash after the eruption of Mount Vesuvius in 79 CE.

Source: Naphtali Lewis and Meyer Reinhold, eds., *Roman Civilization: Selected Readings*, vol. 2 (New York: Columbia University Press, 1990), 276–278.

I

Twenty pairs of gladiators of Decimus Lucretius Satrius Valens, life-time flamen [priest] of Nero son of Caesar Augustus [Claudius], and ten pairs of gladiators of Decimus Lucretius Valens, his son, will fight at Pompeii on April 8, 9, 10, 11, and 12. There will be a full card of wild beast combats, and awnings [for the spectators]. Aemilius Celer [painted this sign], all alone in the moonlight.

II

Market days: Saturday in Pompeii, Sunday in Nuceria, Monday in Atella, Tuesday in Nola, Wednesday in Cumae, Thursday in Puteoli, Friday in Rome.

III

6th: cheese 1, bread 8, oil 3, wine 3 [expenses in food, in coins called *asses*]
7th: bread 8, oil 5, onions 5, bowl 1, bread for the slave [?] 2, wine 2
8th: bread 8, bread for the slave [?] 4, grits 3
9th: wine for the winner 1 *denarius* [a higher denomination of coin], bread 8, wine 2, cheese 2
10th: [. . .] 1 *denarius,* bread 2, for women 8, wheat 1 *denarius,* cucumber 1, dates 1, incense 1, cheese 2, sausage 1, soft cheese 4, oil 7

IV

Pleasure says: "You can get a drink here for an as, a better drink for two, Falernian [fine quality wine] for four."

V

A copper pot is missing from this shop. 65 sesterces reward if anybody brings it back, 20 sesterces if he reveals the thief so we can get our property back.

VI

The weaver Successus loves the innkeeper's slave girl, Iris by name. She doesn't care for him, but he begs her to take pity on him. Written by his rival. So long.

[Answer by the rival:] Just because you're bursting with envy, don't pick on a handsomer man, a lady-killer and a gallant.

[Answer by the first writer:] There's nothing more to say or write. You love Iris, and she doesn't care for you.

VII

Take your lewd looks and flirting eyes off another man's wife, and show some decency on your face!

VIII

Anybody in love, come here. I want to break Venus' ribs with a club and cripple the goddess' loins. If she can pierce my tender breast, why can't I break her head with a club?

IX

I write at Love's dictation and Cupid's instruction;
But damn it! I don't want to be a god without you.

X

[A prostitute's sign:] I am yours for 2 *asses* cash.

» Working with Sources

1. **Are you surprised by what these graffiti reveal about daily life in Pompeii?**
2. **How could this material be used to assess the relative standing of women in Roman society? Should it be used in this way?**

SOURCE 7.5

The murder of the philosopher Hypatia, Alexandria, Egypt

ca. 415 CE

Born around 360 CE and instructed by her father, Theon, a mathematician and the last librarian of the famous Library of Alexandria, Hypatia directed the Platonic school in the city, teaching students who were of mixed religious commitments but were, presumably, all men. The few sources that mention her agree that she was abducted, stripped of her clothes, and stoned to death with roof tiles by a fanatical group of Christians, but the precise sequence of events that led to this atrocity has always been controversial.

Because all of these sources were composed by Christians—with the exception of her own correspondence with a former student, the bishop Synesius of Cyrene—the lynching of Hypatia may be interpreted as an instance of fanaticism attempting to destroy reason, or as the elimination of a dangerous pagan influence in the midst of a Christianizing Egypt. The latter approach has, unfortunately, been more common, given Christian influence—and misogyny—in Western societies and the installation of her main opponent, Bishop Cyril of Alexandria, as one of the "fathers of the church."

There was a woman in Alexandria named Hypatia. She was the daughter of the philosopher Theon. She had progressed so far in her education that she surpassed by far the philosophers of her time, and took over the Neoplatonic

Source: Socrates, *Ecclesiastical History* 7.15, available online at http://www.stoa.org/diotima/anthology/wlgr/wlgr-religion451.shtml.

school that derived from Plotinus, and set forth every philosophical approach to those who wanted to learn them. Accordingly people from all over who wanted to study philosophy rushed to her side. Because of the dignified reputation that derived from her education, she began (with due modesty) to address even the rulers. And she had no hesitation about being in the company of men, since they all respected her more because of her extraordinary chastity.

Then she became the subject of envy. Because she was frequently in the company of Orestes, people in the church began to slander her, as if that were what was preventing Orestes from making friends with the bishop. Some hotheaded men who agreed with this, who were led by a certain Peter the Reader, were on the lookout for the woman when she returned to her house from wherever she had been. They threw her out of her carriage, and dragged her to the church known as Caesarion. They tore off her clothing, and killed her with potsherds. When they had torn her apart limb from limb, they took the pieces of her body to the place called Cinaron, and burned them.

This act did no small amount of damage to Cyril and to the Church at Alexandria. For murder and fighting, and everything of that sort, are totally alien to those who believe in Christ. These events took place after Cyril had been bishop for four years, and Theodosius for ten [c. 415 CE], in the month of March, during Lent.

. . .

About Hypatia the philosopher. An illustration of how disorderly the Alexandrians are. She was born and raised and educated in Alexandria. She inherited her father's extraordinarily distinguished nature, and was not satisfied with the training in mathematics that she received from her father, but turned to other learning also in a distinguished way. Although she was a woman she put on a man's cloak and made her way into the center of the city and gave to those who wanted to listen public lectures about Plato or Aristotle or about some other philosophers. In addition to her teaching she also excelled in the practical arts, being just and chaste, she remained a virgin, though she was so beautiful to look at that one of her pupils fell in love with her. When he was no longer able to control his passion, he let her know how he felt about her. The uneducated stories have it that Hypatia told him to cure his disease through the study of the arts. But the truth is that he had long since given up on culture; instead, she brought in one of those women's rags and threw it at him, revealing her unclean nature, and said to him, "This is what you are in love with, young man, and not with the Beautiful," and in shame and wonder at this ugly display his soul was converted and he became more chaste.

That (according to this account) is what Hypatia was like, skilled in debate and dialectic, intelligent in her conduct and politically adept. The other citizens understandably were fond of her and accorded her the greatest respect, and the current magistrates of the town always went first to her, as used to happen also in Athens. For even though the practice had died out, the name of philosophy still seemed distinguished and impressive to the people who had primary charge of the city. It then happened that the man in charge of the opposing sect, Cyril, passed by Hypatia's house and saw a large crowd in front of the door, consisting of men and horses, some arriving, some leaving, and some waiting there. He asked what the gathering was, and why there was commotion in front of the house, and learned from his followers that the philosopher Hypatia was giving a lecture and that this was her house. And when he learned this he was very upset and soon planned her murder, the most unholy of all murders. As she was going out to lecture, as was her custom, a group of bestial men attacked her, true ruffians, who had no respect for God and no concern for men's indignation; they killed the philosopher and brought the greatest pollution and disgrace on their fatherland.

» Working with Sources

1. **Was Hypatia killed principally because she was a female philosopher or because she was a non-Christian philosopher?**
2. **How did Hypatia both refer to and transcend the boundaries placed upon women in ancient Greco-Roman society?**

Chapter 8 600 BCE–600 CE

Empires and Visionaries in India

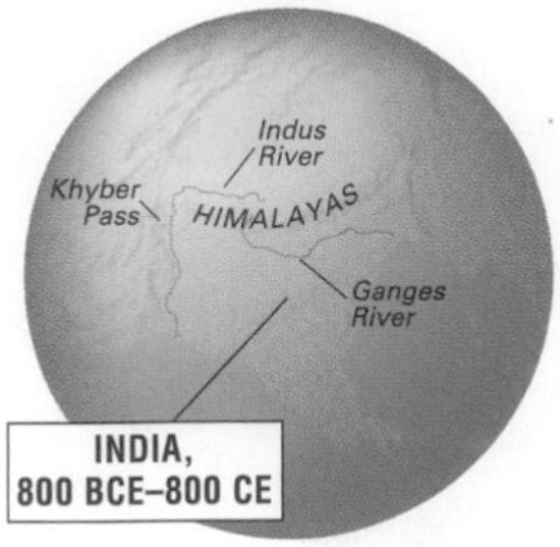

It was one of the most intriguing meetings of the ancient world, though no one could have foreseen its ultimate significance at the time. One of the participants, Alexander the Great, as we have seen, had already become by the age of 30 the most successful military leader the world had ever seen. His present interest, however—the conquest of northern India—had so far proved difficult in the face of the huge armies and terrifying ranks of war elephants massed by his opponents. Now, as he prepared to invade the most powerful Indian state, Magadha, Alexander's men were growing anxious about the seemingly insatiable ambition of their commander. Given the opposition within his own ranks and on the battlefield, Alexander had retreated to the northern city of Taxila, near the modern capital of Islamabad in Pakistan, to replenish his forces and rethink his situation.

While in Taxila, Alexander met with a man identified by his biographers simply as "Sandrokoptros," who had recently fled the Magadhan court after a failed attempt to overthrow its government. Though we can only speculate about the substance of the talks between the two men, Alexander's use of local politics in his past military campaigns suggests that he sought to take advantage of Sandrokoptros's knowledge of Magadha and its leadership in planning his attack. The intelligence Alexander obtained must have been discouraging, for he soon abandoned his plans to invade India and, facing the possibility of mutiny among his men, withdrew to the safer confines of

***ABOVE:* Buddhism in its many forms remains one of the world's most widespread religions. The Sanchi Stupa shown here is an early model of a form of sacred structure found throughout the Buddhist world.**

Persia, where he died in 323 BCE. Following Alexander's death, one of his commanders, Seleucus Nikator [si-LOO-kus Ni-KAY-tor], gained control of the eastern reaches of his empire. By 321 BCE, however, Seleucus Nikator found his territory around the Indus River threatened by a powerful new Indian state created by none other than Alexander's former ally, Sandrokoptros. But it was not until the end of the eighteenth century CE that the shadowy "Sandrokoptros" was identified by English Sanskrit scholars as Chandragupta Maurya [chahn-drah-GUP-tah MOR-y-ah], the founder of India's first and largest indigenous empire.

The meeting between Alexander and Chandragupta was significant for many reasons. For one thing, it took place between two men with similar desires for world empire, whose models of leadership inspired a host of imitators. More significant for our purposes, however, was what this meeting symbolized for the future patterns of Indian history: intensifying exchanges of ideas and goods between peoples of vastly different cultures and beliefs.

Seeing Patterns

» Think about the reasons for the spread of Buddhism inside and outside of India. How have historians seen the decline of Buddhism in India?

» What do you consider to be the most influential patterns in Indian history to this point? Why?

» Do you think some of Ashoka's ideas could be implemented by governments today? Why or why not?

Indian visionaries and innovators made contributions that would have a profound effect on patterns of world history as they made their way throughout Eurasia and North Africa. In turn, India's place as a crossroads of trade and invasion continually replenished the subcontinent with innovation from outside. Many centuries later, the lore of India's wealth and culture would fire the imaginations of Europeans and drive them to seek out the connection first established by Alexander and Chandragupta so many centuries before.

Patterns of State Formation in India: Republics, Kingdoms, and Empires

When Alexander arrived, the pattern of state formation in India had shifted permanently to the plains and hills of the Punjab and Ganges valley. As we noted in Chapter 3, the shift may have begun when tectonic movements in the Himalayas around 1900 BCE caused the drying up of the Sarasvati River in northwest India. People abandoned the agrarian–urban center of the Indus valley and migrated eastward. Much of the land to which they migrated in the Punjab and Ganges valley consisted of rain forest and marshes that required laborious land clearing. But the settlers drew on their past experience as they built the new agrarian–urban centers of northern India. In contrast to Africa and Mesoamerica where the patterns of state formation from villages and chiefdoms to kingdoms developed slowly, state formation proceeded rapidly. The earliest traces of villages date to about 1200 BCE. Thereafter, polities emerged quickly, in the form of warrior republics and kingdoms. Both flourished in the early first millennium BCE.

A gradual consolidation process set in from about 800 BCE onward, with a few kingdoms emerging as the strongest states, while the warrior republics disappeared

Chapter Outline

- Patterns of State Formation in India: Republics, Kingdoms, and Empires
- The Vedic Tradition and Its Visionary Reformers
- Stability amid Disorder: Economy, Family, and Society
- Strength in Numbers: Art, Literature, and Science
- Putting It All Together

from the scene. At the height of the wars for predominance, around 700–400 BCE, visionaries similar to those appearing at the same time in the eastern Mediterranean, the Middle East, and China offered reforms of the Vedic traditions: the Upanishads, Jainism, and Buddhism. The process of state formation reached a first peak with the Mauryan Empire, which united northern and central India and experimented with Buddhism as a privileged religion. A firm marriage between state and religion, however, occurred with the Hindu Gupta Empire (320–550 CE), which, along with its contemporary, Christian Rome, became the first empire in world history to lay the foundation for a religious civilization.

The Road to Empire: The Mauryas

In the early first millennium BCE, the emerging states along the Ganges River valley developed political systems ranging from "republics" to centralized monarchies whose rulers were accorded god-like status. The agricultural advances made in these formerly forested areas, particularly through the use of iron tools—and the dikes, ponds, flooded fields, and drainage systems necessary for growing rice—resulted in the emergence of wealthy, centralized states led by Magadha and Kosala, along with the lesser kingdoms of Vatsya and Avanti farther west (see Map 8.1).

During the half century before Alexander attempted to expand his empire into northern India, Mahapadama Nanda [mah-hah-PAH-dah-mah NAHN-dah], a member of the *shudra* (or lowest) *varna*, seized power in Magadha and embarked on a series of military campaigns against Vatsya and Avanti, both of which he conquered.

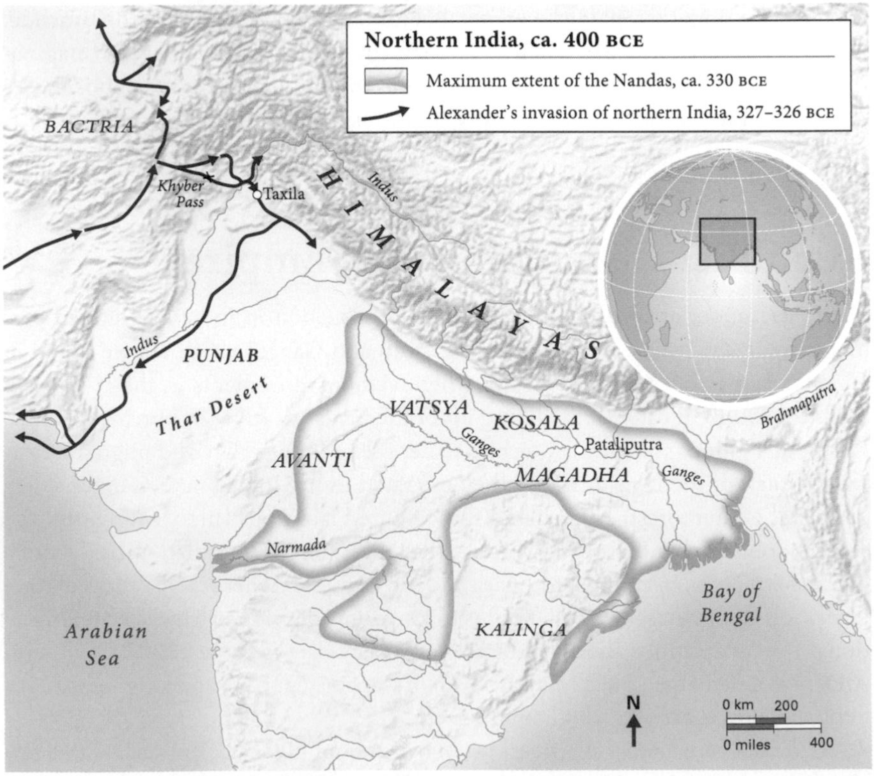

MAP 8.1 Northern India, ca. 400 BCE.

By the 330s BCE, the Magadhan state stretched across the entire breadth of northern India, and the taxes imposed by the Nandas brought unprecedented wealth to their capital of Pataliputra [pah-tah-lee-POO-trah], the modern city of Patna, on the Ganges. The Nandas, however, were not alone in their aspirations for universal empire.

Chandragupta Maurya Little is known of Chandragupta's early life. It is believed that at a young age he was put under the care of the philosopher Kautilya, whose *Arthashastra* became the most influential political treatise in Indian history (see Chapter 3). Contemporary accounts of Chandragupta's court and the structure of his government suggest a strong connection to the political practices of the idealized ruler outlined in the *Arthashastra*. At this stage, however, Kautilya was instrumental in the young Chandragupta's first attempt to seize power from the ruling Nandas. Playing on discontent over Nanda taxation and the threat to religious order posed by rulers from the lowest *shudra varna,* he used his considerable influence to back a palace revolt by the young Chandragupta. When the revolt was unsuccessful, the two fled to Taxila, a dominant trade crossroads strategically located near the Khyber Pass, where they encountered Alexander.

Kautilya and Alexander played important roles in building Chandragupta's empire, though Alexander's role is less obvious. The dislocations in the northwest caused by Alexander's attempted invasions allowed Chandragupta to pursue a patient strategy of securing the most vulnerable and least contented of the Nandas' client states while methodically surrounding and, ultimately, conquering Magadha. By 321 BCE Chandragupta had secured the capital and embarked on a campaign to enlarge his empire. Following a series of battles with Alexander's successor Seleucus Nikator, the Greeks surrendered their north Indian and Indus territories to Chandragupta. Though forced from his Indian holdings, Seleucus and his successors maintained cordial relations with the Mauryas and posted the ambassador Megasthenes to the Mauryan capital of Pataliputra. Though little survives of his reports, Megasthenes' accounts of the enormous wealth and population of the capital and the efficiency of Mauryan government formed the basis of much of the classical and medieval European understanding of India.

Although his motivations for doing so are unclear, Chandragupta stepped down from his throne around 297 BCE and joined an ascetic religious order, the Jains, formed on the basis of the teachings of the visionary Mahavira (see subsequent

interactive timeline

800–600 BCE Early patterns of state formation in the Ganges valley

700–600 BCE Upanishad reformers of Vedic tradition

600–480 BCE Mahavira, founder of Jainism, and Buddha, founder of Buddhism

324–323 BCE Alexander the Great's campaigns in northern India

321–185 BCE Most of India united for the first time under Mauryan Empire

273–231 BCE Reign of Ashoka, Mauryan emperor

ca. 90 BCE–300 CE Movements of central Asian peoples into India's northwest

78 CE–101 CE Reign of Kanishka of Kushan Empire; early Buddhist works among Bactrian Greeks; period of the flowering of Gandharan art

322–550 Much of India reunited under Gupta Empire

340–370 Flourishing of Kalidasa, poet and playwright

399–414 Journey of Buddhist monk Fa Xian throughout Asia

510 Battle of Gwalior; decline of Gupta power

450–520 Migrations of Huns into northern India

300–800 Rise of the Pallava and Chalukya kingdoms in the south

discussion). Legend has it that he ended his life in the Jain monastery at Karnataka, where, in imitation of the order's founder, he refused all food and engaged in a "fast to death" rather than consume any living thing. Chandragupta's son continued to expand the Mauryan domains to the west and south, but it was his grandson Ashoka [ah-SHOW-kah] (r. ca. 273–231 BCE), who emerged as perhaps India's most dominant ruler until the nineteenth century CE.

Ashoka Born around 304 BCE, Ashoka may have actually seized the throne from his father. Like his predecessors, he soon began a series of military ventures to drive the Mauryan Empire deeper into the south (see Map 8.2). The climax of his efforts was a fierce war he fought with the kingdom of Kalinga, the last adjacent region outside of Mauryan control, on the eastern coast. Though figures given in ancient sources must always be treated with suspicion, by Ashoka's own admission, 100,000 people were killed in the conflict. Yet it was also here, at the height of his power, that, deeply moved by the carnage in Kalinga, in around 260 BCE he abruptly abandoned the path of conquest, converted to Buddhism, and vowed to rule his kingdom by "right conduct" alone.

Scholars know perhaps more about Ashoka's reign than that of any other ancient Indian monarch. He told much of his own story and outlined his Buddhist-inspired ideas for proper behavior on inscriptions in caves and on rocks and pillars set up in strategic places throughout his empire. Written mostly in Prakrit, the parent tongue of

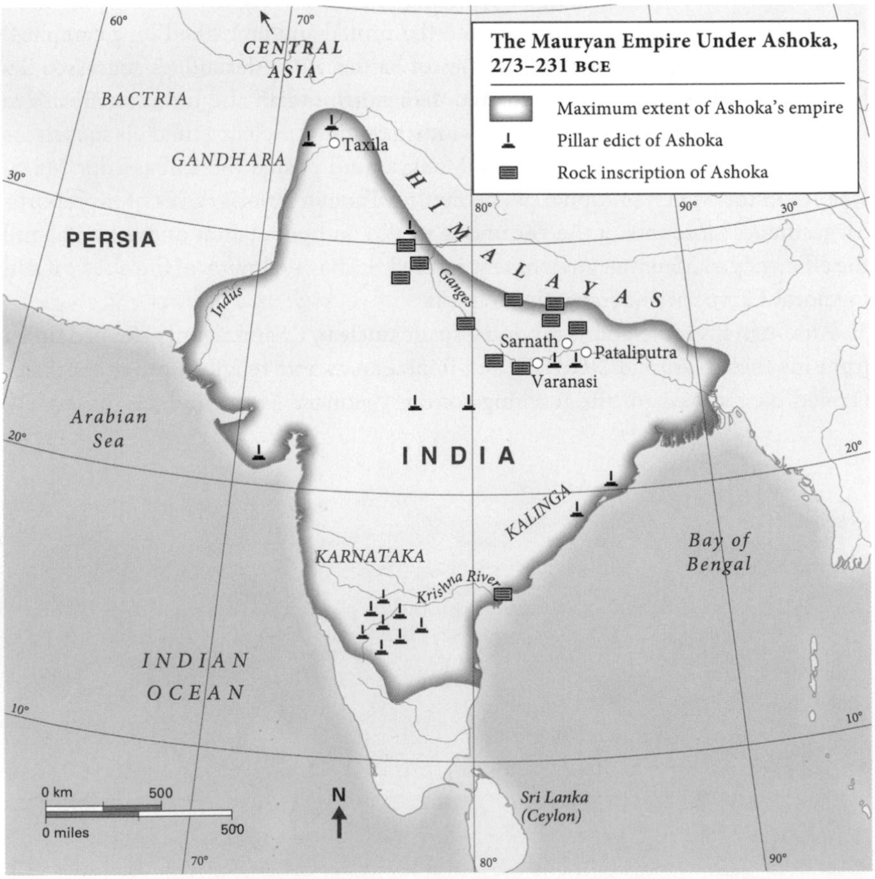

MAP 8.2 **The Mauryan Empire under Ashoka, 273–231 BCE.**

many of the modern north Indian dialects, these inscriptions present a fascinating and human glimpse of the ruler and his personal vision of the idea of dharma (see Chapter 3).

Departing somewhat from the Bhagavad Gita's concept of dharma as duty (see Chapter 3), dharma for Ashoka was simply "that which is good." Among other things, this involved living a life of "kindness, liberality, truthfulness, and purity." Moreover, he believed that following the path of dharma represented the only way one could achieve happiness. One distinctive innovation growing out of Ashoka's support of dharma was his taking up of the Buddhist concept of *ahimsa*, or nonviolence: People should be kind to the weak and disadvantaged and do no harm to any living creature. By way of setting an example, Ashoka declared dozens of animal species to be under his protection, forbade the wholesale burning of forests, and even warned his people not to burn grain husks in order to avoid injuring any creatures living within them. Ashoka's devotion to dharma even extended to sending his sons as Buddhist missionaries to Sri Lanka, where it has remained the principal faith to this day.

Although Ashoka advocated the peaceful principles of dharma, the records of his reign also indicate that his empire was, in many respects, an early kind of police state. He followed many of the political practices suggested in Kautilya's *Arthashastra*, which emphasizes that a monarch must be alert to the moods of his people, on the lookout for enemies, and ready to capitalize on opportunities to exercise power. While allowing the practice of many religions other than Buddhism, Ashoka kept a tight rein on his officials and people through a vast network of spies and informers, a practice begun by his grandfather Chandragupta. The empire itself was divided into four large regional districts, each with a governor. They and all the officials under them were subject to periodic review by roving special commissioners appointed by the throne, whose chief task was to check on everyone's adherence to dharma. Thus, the entire governmental apparatus was now geared toward uplifting the people's morality and supervising their happiness.

Ashoka also encouraged a unified system of commercial law, standardization of weights and measures, and uniform coinage throughout his realm, innovations that greatly facilitated trade and commerce. A majority of state revenues came from taxes on harvests of wheat, rice, barley, and millet plus those on internal and external trade. Under the Mauryans, India was the major crossroads in the exchange of gold and silver brought by the Hellenistic kingdoms and for the expanding maritime trade accompanying the advance of Buddhism into Southeast Asia. In the north, Taxila and the cities and towns along the caravan routes from China to the west grew wealthy from the increasing exchange of silk and other luxury goods.

Within India, the circulation of tropical fruits, medicinal barks, and innumerable other forest products augmented trade still further. Thus, the immense wealth and power flowing into Ashoka's court in Pataliputra made that city of half a million perhaps the richest in the ancient world. The wealth at Ashoka's command and his devotion to dharma allowed the government to spend lavishly in sponsoring public works—palaces, roads, rest stops and hostels for travelers, and parks—as well as temples and shrines for various religious groups.

In all, Ashoka's regime represents a pioneering attempt to construct a workable moral order, a pattern of world history that emerged repeatedly as states seeking to become world empires increasingly turned to religious and philosophical systems that proclaimed universal truths. In India, as in southwest Asia and the Mediterranean, and as we will see in China, these universal truths were proclaimed by visionaries who sensed problems developing in the old order of their respective societies. The ultimate end of this process, which we will explore in detail in Part 3, was the development of religious civilizations.

Capital of Ashoka Pillar of Sarnath. The lion motif atop the chakravartin wheel, symbolizing universal kingship, tops one of Ashoka's famous pillars. The one from which this capital was taken had been set up to commemorate the Buddha's first sermon in Sarnath's deer park.

image analysis

The Nomadic Kingdoms of the North With the end of the Mauryan Empire, northern India was transformed into a series of regional kingdoms run by local rulers. Greek-speaking peoples from Bactria—descendants of troops and colonists who had come to the area under Alexander the Great—controlled some of these territories. Their most famous ruler, Menander, achieved immortality in Buddhist literature as "King Milinda" by engaging in a debate at court with the philosopher Nagasena. Their talks, as later set down, became an important exposition of Buddhist ideas and purportedly led to Menander's conversion.

By the first years of the Common Era, the Bactrian Greek rulers of northern India confronted new nomadic groups from central Asia, who eventually put an end to Greek rule in the region. These groups had been put into motion by repeated Chinese campaigns against the Xiongnu [SHIUNG-noo] (believed by some to be the Huns) and the Yuezhi [YOO-eh-jih]. As they moved into northern India sometime around 25 CE, the Yuezhi became known as the "Kushans." Under its most famous ruler, Kanishka (r. ca. 78–101 CE), the Kushan Empire expanded into not only northern India but also much of modern Pakistan and Afghanistan. Kanishka, like Menander, adopted Buddhism and actively propagated the faith within his growing kingdom and beyond. Through his efforts, the new religion expanded along the caravan routes of central Asia and shortly afterward appears for the first time in Chinese records.

Although the continual arrival of new groups expanded the cultural resources of northern India and greatly aided the spread of Buddhism, it also worked against the development of stable states in the region. With the intensity of the migrations abating by the end of the third century, however, a new and aggressive line of rulers, the Guptas, established power in the Ganges valley and stood poised to reunite the old Mauryan heartland. Under their rule would come India's great classical age.

The Classical Age: The Gupta Empire

The origin of the Gupta line is somewhat obscure, though scholars agree that, like the Mauryans, it originated somewhere near Magadha. The first major ruler of the dynasty was Chandragupta I (r. ca. 320–335 CE; no relation to the Chandragupta of the Mauryan Empire), whose new state occupied much of the old heartland of Magadha and Kosala. With recognition of the rising power of the Guptas extending from Nepal in the north to the Shaka territories in the west, the way lay open for his successor, Samudragupta [sahm-OO-drah-gup-tah] (r. ca. 335–380 CE), to expand the borders of the empire even farther.

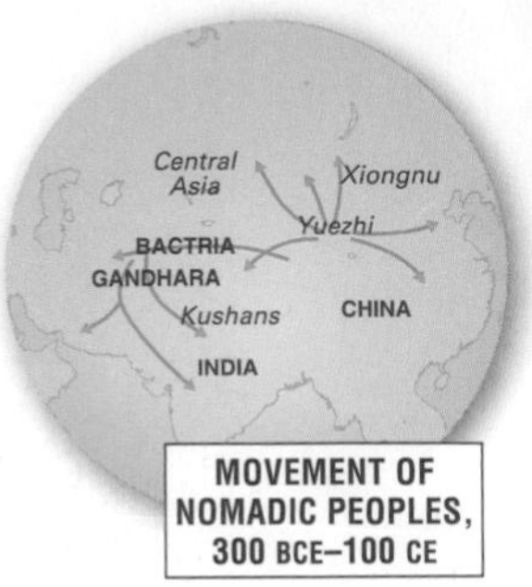

MOVEMENT OF NOMADIC PEOPLES, 300 BCE–100 CE

Under Samudragupta, the Gupta dominion extended both north and south, embracing a swath of territory extending far up the Ganges River to the borders of the Kushans south of Taxila and down the coast deep into the territory of the Pallavas in the south. Like Chandragupta I, he forged ties to regions outside of Gupta control, whose populations in turn pledged their loyalty to him. As was the case of the states of Zhou China, this arrangement has often been characterized as "feudal" in that it resembles the relationships among the states of medieval Europe, though scholars are careful not to push the parallels too far. Samudragupta's son Chandragupta II

(r. ca. 380–413 CE) seized the throne from his elder brother and continued to expand the empire, adding the southern and western Gujarati territories of the Shakas. The cumulative effect of this string of conquests over barely a century was that, once again, the Indian subcontinent stood on the threshold of unity (see Map 8.3).

Hinduism: A convenient shorthand term for the vast multiplicity of religious practices derived from the Vedic, Brahmanic, Upanishadic, and later traditions in India and those places influenced by Indian culture.

Court and Culture The Gupta era is considered to be the classical age of Indian culture and religion. During the reign of the Guptas, the collection of religious traditions called "**Hinduism**" flourished, becoming the dominant faith of the time. Indeed, the Guptas actively used the gods and practices of Hinduism, particularly in their devotion to Vishnu and Shiva, to extend their legitimacy not just as kings but as universal rulers.

Although the Guptas preferred the king-centered, hierarchical Brahmanic tradition of Hinduism, which they made the privileged religion in the state, they

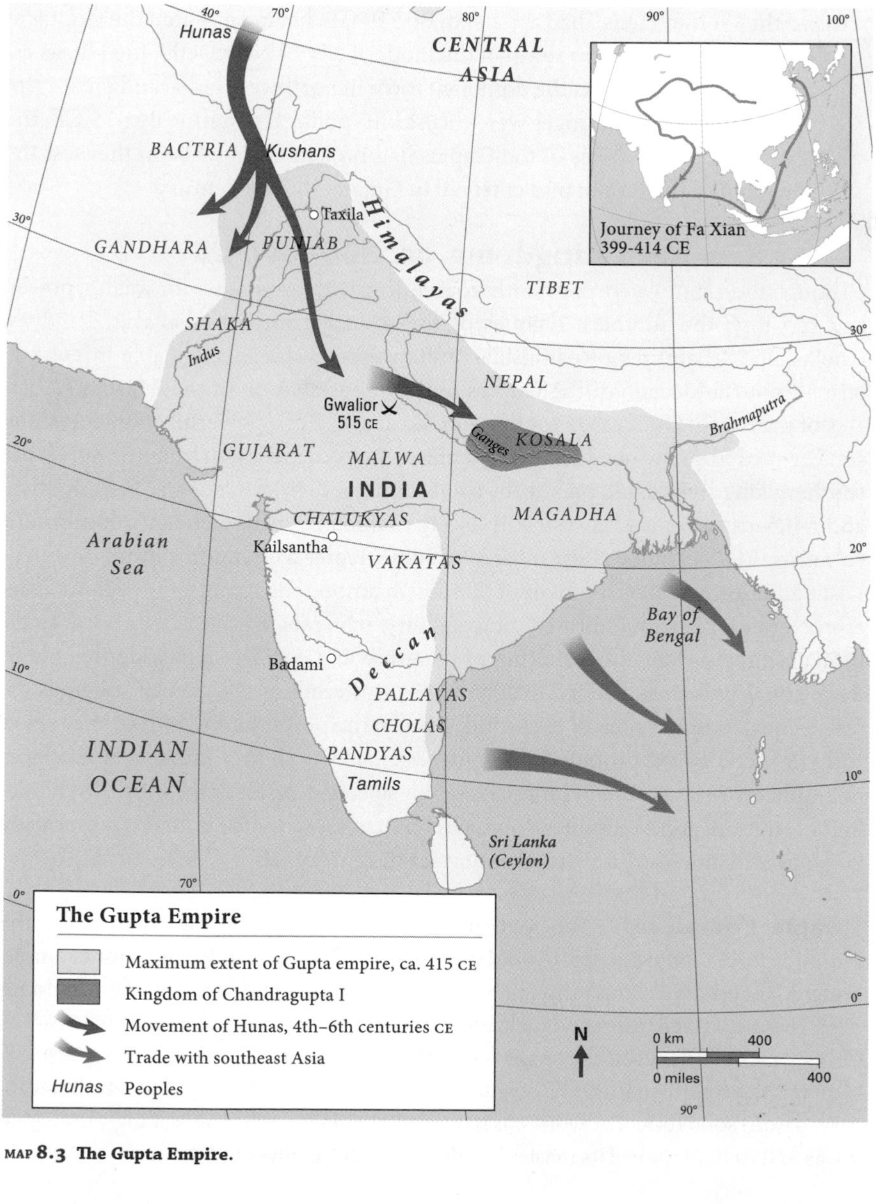

MAP 8.3 **The Gupta Empire.**

Coins of the Northwest Kingdoms, Second Century BCE and Late First Century CE. The complex history of the area encompassed by modern Afghanistan and Pakistan has been understood principally through the coins minted by the many rulers of frequently shifting territories. The silver coin (above) was minted by a Bactrian Greek king, probably in the second century BCE. The gold coin (below) with the Greek inscription was the product of the reign of the famous Buddhist king Kanishka (78–101 CE) of the Kushans and depicts the king himself.

Devotional: In the context of this chapter, belonging to a branch of Hinduism in which one dedicates oneself to practices that venerate, honor, or adore a particular god or divinity. The largest of these branches are dedicated to Vishnu and Shiva.

permitted the practice of other faiths, including both Jainism and Buddhism. Under their influence and with their financial support, the first distinctly "Hindu" art was created in the temples and shrines to a variety of deities that were built in staggering profusion. In addition, the era marked a peak of popularity for classical treatises on political and social behavior such as the *Arthashastra* and the *Kama Sutra*, the famous manual of sexual practices and personal deportment, as well as, it is often supposed, the works of the playwright and poet Kalidasa (fl. fifth century CE), sometimes called the "Indian Shakespeare."

The Waning of Gupta Power Gupta power began to fade under the reigns of Chandragupta II's son and grandson, whose weakened authority was challenged by groups seeking greater autonomy in the vicinity of Malwa, in central India. By this time, however, a new wave of central Asian nomads, the Hunas, sometimes called the "White Huns," had appeared. By 510 CE, having defeated the Guptas at Gwalior, some 200 miles south of the modern city of New Delhi, the Hunas established themselves as the dominant force in northwest India, and once again the areas along the Ganges were thrust into political disunity. By 515 CE, the eastern tributary states of the Guptas had broken away, while in the west the kingdom of the Rajputanas emerged in Gujarat by mid-century.

The Southern Kingdoms, ca. 300–600 CE

Though their states were constantly contending with each other for wealth, power, and territory, the southern regimes of the so-called imperial Pallavas, Pandyas, Cholas, and Chalukyas of peninsular India were comparatively stable in cultural terms from the decline of the Guptas until the installation of the Muslim sultanates of the north. One reason for this was the absence of a powerful empire pushing south. Freed from the need to defend themselves from incursion from the north, the southern kingdoms could pursue the pacification of their own realms. Their political and religious systems were also still largely dominated by descendants of northern colonists, so their ruling classes shared to some degree a common culture.

In addition, the development of Hinduism among the Tamils, the region's chief ethnic group, contributed to cultural stability, while its synthesis with local traditions inspired a dramatic flowering of literature and art. These include the rise of **devotional** branches of Hinduism and an outpouring of spectacular religious art rarely equaled in any area of the world. Finally, the power and wealth of the region was enhanced by the promotion of trade, especially with the "Indianized" enclaves of Southeast Asia and the Indonesian archipelago. As a result of these ties, Indian religions, culture, and economics dominated Indian Ocean trade until it was gradually taken over by the Muslims after the fourteenth century CE.

Temple Complexes The southern kingdoms' most tangible remains are the Hindu temple complexes left behind at a number of sites. The Pallavas, for example, under Mahendra Vikruma Varman I (r. ca. 590–630 CE), constructed the famous Mandapa Temple, carved from solid rock. His descendant Narasimha Varman II (r. 695–728 CE) sponsored the seven rock pagodas of Mahabali Purana. Perhaps most spectacular of all was the eighth-century CE Rashtakutra complex of Krishna I at Kailasantha, again carved from solid rock. The work was so complex, detailed, and painstakingly done that it was said to have moved its master builder to cry, "Oh, how did I do this?"

The Kailasantha Temple. Hewn from a single, solid rock, the Kailasantha Temple, part of an elaborate complex in east-central India, is considered the world's most monumental sculpture. Strongly influenced by south Indian architectural traditions, the temple complex dazzles the visitor with carvings of innumerable deities, mythic figures, and erotic imagery.

Regional Struggles The long process of interaction and adaptation in India had already created a recognizably different society as one moved south from the Ganges. In these areas the systems of *varna* and *jati* (see Chapter 3) tended to revolve more around where one lived than they did in the north. For example, there were major differentiations between those living in the cities and flatland farming communities and the "hill peoples" and "forest peoples," still considered largely uncivilized. A major division also existed between the local leaders, whose families had in many cases emigrated from the north and were members of the upper *varnas*, and their subjects. Within these divisions, rulers tended to be more predatory in their efforts to enrich themselves and their kingdoms.

The rise of the Chalukya state on the western side of the peninsula in the mid-sixth century CE, along with that of the Vakatakas of the Deccan Plateau and the Rashtakutras in the early eighth century CE, resumed the struggle for wealth and territory among the older southern kingdoms. As we will see in Chapter 13, by the middle of the eighth century CE, the Chalukya state spawned a potent rival when the areas to the north and west broke away from its grasp. The leaders there became known as the "Rashtakutras" and shortly thereafter captured the capital at Badami.

The Vedic Tradition and Its Visionary Reformers

Beginning around 700 BCE, visionaries appeared seeking to reform a Vedic tradition that they believed had grown overly formalistic and unresponsive to the needs of the people. As we noted in Chapter 3, the first of these men were the thinkers who created the Upanishads, a set of spiritual writings that laid the foundations of *monism*—the belief in a single transcendent first principle—in Hindu thought. In the next two centuries, Mahavira and the Buddha followed, becoming the founding figures, respectively, of Jainism, presently a small community in India, and Buddhism, today a major religion in Southeast Asia, China, and Japan.

Reforming the Vedic Tradition

The Vedas consisted of four books of hymns to the gods and goddesses of the Hindu pantheon and described in detail the rituals and sacrifices required to keep the world in harmony with these deities. They thus framed the culture of the period 1200–600 BCE, when the inhabitants of the Indian subcontinent initiated the pattern of Punjab and Ganges valley state formation. As we saw at the beginning of this chapter, several dozen warrior republics and kingdoms competed against each other for wealth and power, similar to the warring states of China that we will explore in Chapter 9. It was against the backdrop of this competition that visionaries critical of the polytheistic Vedic heritage arose and sought to reform it through the formulation of a single first principle. The main figures of these reform efforts were the authors of the Upanishads (ca. 700–300 BCE), Mahavira (trad. 599–527 BCE), and Gautama, the Buddha, or Enlightened One (trad. 563–483 BCE).

The Upanishad Visionaries Many authors of the more than 100 Upanishads are known to us by name. They were Brahmanic priests—and also the daughter of one—whose principal concern was to penetrate beyond the complexities of the tens of thousands of gods (as one of the Upanishads mockingly asserts) to a vision of cosmic unity. This Upanishadic vision, with its proclamation of monism, was remarkably similar to those propounded in the Middle East and China during the same time: They insisted on a transcendent first principle as universal truth, addressed to anyone anywhere.

The Indian visionaries were hermit teachers living in the forests of the Gangetic states seeking to "draw near" to themselves (one meaning of the Sanskrit *upanishad*) disciples who did not want merely to understand the transcendent unity of the universe outside of the individual but also to attain this unity by merging their personal selves (*atman*) into the universal self (*brahman*) and thereby achieving salvation. These visionaries did not develop this theme of the unity of atman–brahman systematically in the form of treatises. Instead, they concentrated on leading their disciples through brief aphorisms, paradoxes, and negations ("not this, nor that") step by step into deep meditation, which they considered the activity through which salvation could be achieved. As time went on, however, contemplation of the Upanishadic scriptures and their hidden meanings concerning the mysteries of atman–brahman also became a vital part of a new evolving tradition. In the highest state of understanding of atman–brahman, one could attain release from the bounds of the cycles of death and rebirth and thus enter into transcendence, or *moksha*.

Criticism of the Vedic Rituals and Sacrifices Although they were advocates of monism, or first principle, the authors of the Upanishads remained faithful to the Vedic rituals, sacrifices, and doctrines. Their reforms were limited to creating a meditative supplement to the Vedic religion. However, as strong kingdoms emerged in the 500s BCE and conquered smaller kingdoms and warrior republics, criticism of religious ritual grew. Urbanization and trade created new classes of inhabitants, such as merchants and craftspeople, to whom rituals and sacrifices meant far less than they did to the kings and the priestly class. The merchants and craftspeople viewed the rituals as formalistic and the sacrifices, consisting of burning large quantities of food and killing many animals, as wasteful. For the kings and priests, these religious practices were essential to legitimize their power. The Vedic doctrine that eventually caused the break between the priests and their strongest critics, however, was that of the cycle of *karma–samsara* (see Chapter 3), death and rebirth.

The Ascetic Break: Jainism The founder of the Jains, Nigantha Nataputta [nee-GAN-tah nah-tah-POO-tah], whose title of Vardhamana Mahavira means "the great hero," was born the son of a warrior chief perhaps around 540 BCE. At the age of 30 he left home and gave up all his worldly possessions to become an ascetic, and after 12 years he found meditative enlightenment. From this point on he was given the title of *jina*, or "conqueror," and from this his followers became known as Jains. For the next 40 years, he wandered throughout India without clothes or possessions, spreading the new sect's principles and practices. Finally, as the ultimate exemplar of the movement's ideal of not taking the life of any being whatsoever, Mahavira refused all food and performed a ritual fast that led to his death in Pava, near Pataliputra.

While much of the earliest Jain doctrine was lost during its first two centuries of oral transmission, it begins with a universe in which all things possess *jiva*, a kind of "soul" that yearns to be free from the prison of the material world. Jains believe that even inanimate objects, such as stones—as well as plants, human beings, and other animals—possess *jiva*, though at different levels or "senses." These "souls" are governed in turn by the degree to which a thing's past karma stands between it and its release from material bondage. For human beings, karma builds up according to the injuries one does to other beings and objects, intentionally or not. The way to enlightenment is to act in such a way that one acquires as little karma as possible, while performing actions of suffering and self-sacrifice to atone for and reduce the karma one already has. In this sense, karma might be thought of as a kind of weight on the "soul": As karma dissipates, the soul becomes lighter until, finally free, it rises to the very heights of the cosmos and lives for eternity.

Jain world map

Ahimsa Jain monks take extraordinary pains to prevent injury to any object, especially living things. For example, from the first centuries of the movement there has been a **schism** between those who insist on complete nakedness—to avoid attachment to worldly possessions as well as not injuring creatures that might be trapped in one's clothing—and those who wear a simple white robe. Other measures include wearing gauze masks to filter out invisible organisms that might be breathed in and carrying brooms to sweep small creatures out of one's path. Monks live by begging food from others—so that they themselves do not have to harvest it—and hence, kill it—and add to their karma. Because suffering reduces karma, some underwent extraordinary ordeals, such as allowing themselves to be covered with biting insects or lying on beds of nails. Such extreme forms of asceticism, especially if done for show or outside the spirit of overcoming the realm of the body, were ultimately condemned as "dark penance." Still, the most dedicated performed the supreme sacrifice and ritually fasted unto death in their later years, which, because of the intense suffering involved and the resolute refusal to harm living things, was seen as the ultimate act of ahimsa, or nonviolence. This is practiced by a handful of devotees even today, despite recent efforts in India to make it illegal.

Schism: A division; when used in a religious context it usually refers to the splitting of members of a certain religion into two or more camps over matters of doctrine, ritual, etc.

Not surprisingly, the strict practices of the Jains did not appeal to most people. As a result, an extensive laity, especially among the lower castes who identified more with the sacrifices of the monks, grew to support them. The patronage of kings, most famously Chandragupta Maurya, helped ensure the sect's vitality. As a matter of course, Jains would not take up farming, so monastic and lay followers were often involved in business, study, and writing—occupations they still favor today. Modern Jains practice a modified form of the earlier traditions, engaging in vegetarianism or veganism, though often wearing clothes indistinguishable from those of other traditions. Some also still participate in certain ceremonies in the nude or with their traditional white garments. The religion's most distinctive element, however, is that it is rigorously **atheistic**, choosing not to worship any god but insisting instead on meditatively merging into an eternal, uncreated, indifferent unity that is both universal and transcendent.

Atheistic: Not believing in a god or supreme being.

The Middle Way: Buddhism The other major movement, Buddhism, began in part as a reaction against such extreme ascetic practices. Siddhartha Gautama, whose title of "Buddha" means "the Enlightened One," is believed to have been born a prince in the Shakya republic in the Himalayan foothills. His traditional birthdate is given as 563 BCE, though recent accounts have moved it to at least the mid-400s BCE. Because of his royal pedigree, he is frequently referred to as "Sakyamuni," or prince of the Sakyas. Seeking to shelter him from the evils of the world, Gautama's father secluded him in the palace. At the age of 29, however, Gautama left his world of privilege and followed the paths of various Vedic schools. At one point, following a discipline of extreme asceticism, his path of self-deprivation led him to fast nearly to death.

During his travels, Gautama was exposed to the entire range of human suffering and death from which his father had tried so hard to shelter him. His shock and compassion for the world around him drove him to find a way to understand the endless round of death and rebirth to which all creatures were apparently subject. According to Buddhist accounts, the insight gained from his experiences and a long period of deep meditation sparked his enlightenment one day under a pipal (fig) tree in the town of Gaya. Shortly afterward, Gautama went to a deer park in Sarnath, close by the great city of Varanasi (Benares), where he found five former disciples and preached a sermon to them outlining what became known as the Middle Way—the path of moderation.

Statue of the Jain Saint Gomateshwara at Karnataka. The world's largest statue cut from a single stone, this statue was built at the site of the famous Jain monastery where, it was said, Chandragupta Maurya entered the order and fasted to death, following the example of the sect's founder, Mahavira.

The Four Noble Truths, the Eightfold Path, and Nirvana Gautama believed that the fundamental nature of the perceived universe is change. In a constantly changing world, suffering is the common lot of all beings because they attach themselves to what will ultimately be taken from them. Although they crave permanence, they rely only on their senses, which provide the illusion of stability but actually obscure the true, ever-changing nature of things. Pushed into evil deeds in pursuit of whatever they desire, they accumulate karma. Over many lifetimes, the karma they acquire stays with them even after the separation of the material "soul" from the immaterial at death. It builds up with each life and keeps them from breaking free of the cycle of death and rebirth.

In that first sermon in Sarnath, Gautama distilled these insights into what he called the Four Noble Truths:

1. All life is suffering.
2. Suffering arises from craving.
3. To stop suffering, one must stop craving.
4. One stops craving by following the Eightfold Path of right views, right resolve, right speech, right conduct, right livelihood, right effort, right mindfulness, and right concentration.

Later sermons and vast numbers of commentaries outlined the specifics of the Eightfold Path. Essentially, the path represents a course of life in which one avoids extreme behaviors of any kind, adheres to a code of conduct that favors **altruism** and respects the life of all living beings, and through meditation and "right mindfulness" reaches a state of calm nonattachment with an uncluttered mind able to grasp the universal truth. When one reaches this stage, the karmic traces of past lives are "blown out" like a lamp flame, the literal meaning of the Sanskrit word associated with this final state of enlightenment: *nirvana*, or nothingness. In Buddhism, this nothingness is a more explicit version of the logic of *moksha*—transcendence—first explored in the Upanishads.

Altruism: The practice of acting in an unselfish manner for the good of others.

Even during the Buddha's lifetime his followers had organized into a brotherhood, despite his dying instruction that the true path to enlightenment resided in them as individuals. As in other movements, the void left by the Buddha's death resulted in disputes about the authenticity of certain teachings and questions about how the group should now conduct itself. Over the following two centuries, several Buddhist councils were held, and during one of these meetings, a division developed, resulting in one group separating from the main body of adherents. The now separate group became known as Theravada [ter-rah-VAH-dah], "the teachings of the elders." Under Ashoka's influence, Theravada Buddhism became the approved sect, with the first complete surviving texts dating from this time.

the Buddha

Buddhist Texts The *Pali Canon*, written in Pali, the sacred language of Buddhism, is a collection of texts that forms the foundation of Theravada Buddhism and serves as the fundamental body of scriptures for nearly all Buddhist schools. The collection consists of the *Tripitaka* [tree-pee-TAH-kuh], or "Three Baskets"; the *Vinaya* [vee-NAI-yah], treatises on conduct and rules of discipline for monks; the *Sutras* [SOO-truhs], or "discourses," of which there are five groups, with most of them believed to have originated with the Buddha; and the *Abhidhamma* [ah-bee-DAH-mah], doctrines of philosophy and metaphysics.

As Theravada Buddhism developed and spread in northern India and beyond, a number of developments changed its character, making it more accessible to a larger group of followers. The rich cultural interaction of the many peoples encountering it resulted in a great number of religious ideas and traditions circulating around the region. Questions and problems among Buddhist adherents from these different areas required broader solutions than in earlier times. For example, stories of the Buddha's last days implied that he would save everyone who followed his path, opening the way for the potential enlightenment of all. Coupled with this was a developing tradition of the Buddha as one in a long line of past and future buddhas, suggesting the potential for a devotional component to the religion. In addition, there was the concept of the *bodhisattva* [boh-dee-SAHT-vuh]—one who, having achieved enlightenment, does not proceed to nirvana but is dedicated instead to helping the suffering achieve their own enlightenment.

Theravada and Mahayana All of these ideas took shape around the first century CE in what became the largest branch of Buddhism, Mahayana [mah-hah-YAH-nah], the "greater vehicle." Dismissing Theravada Buddhism as Hinayana [heen-ah-YAH-nah], or "the lesser vehicle," Mahayana spread along the trade routes into central Asia, into the borderlands of the Parthians, and ultimately to China, Korea, Japan, and Tibet (see Map 8.4). As it spread, its different interpretive schools were, broadly speaking, divided into *esoteric* branches—those seeking enlightenment through scriptural or other kinds of deep knowledge—and devotional branches. Of the devotional schools, that of Amitabha [ah-mee-TAH-bah], the Heavenly Buddha of the Western Paradise, is today the most popular Buddhist sect in both China and Japan (see Chapters 9 and 13).

As Buddhism was spreading across the greater part of Asia, however, its decline had, in a sense, already begun in the land of its birth. With the revitalization and

Great Buddhist Stupa at Sanchi. The need for commemorative burial mounds and reliquaries for the Buddha's relics spawned a characteristic structure called a stupa, meaning "gathered" or "heap." Brimming with symbolic motifs representing the stages of enlightenment, the structures changed considerably from this example—built in the first century BCE over an earlier one from the Mauryan period—as they spread through East Asia, where they assumed the shape of the pagoda.

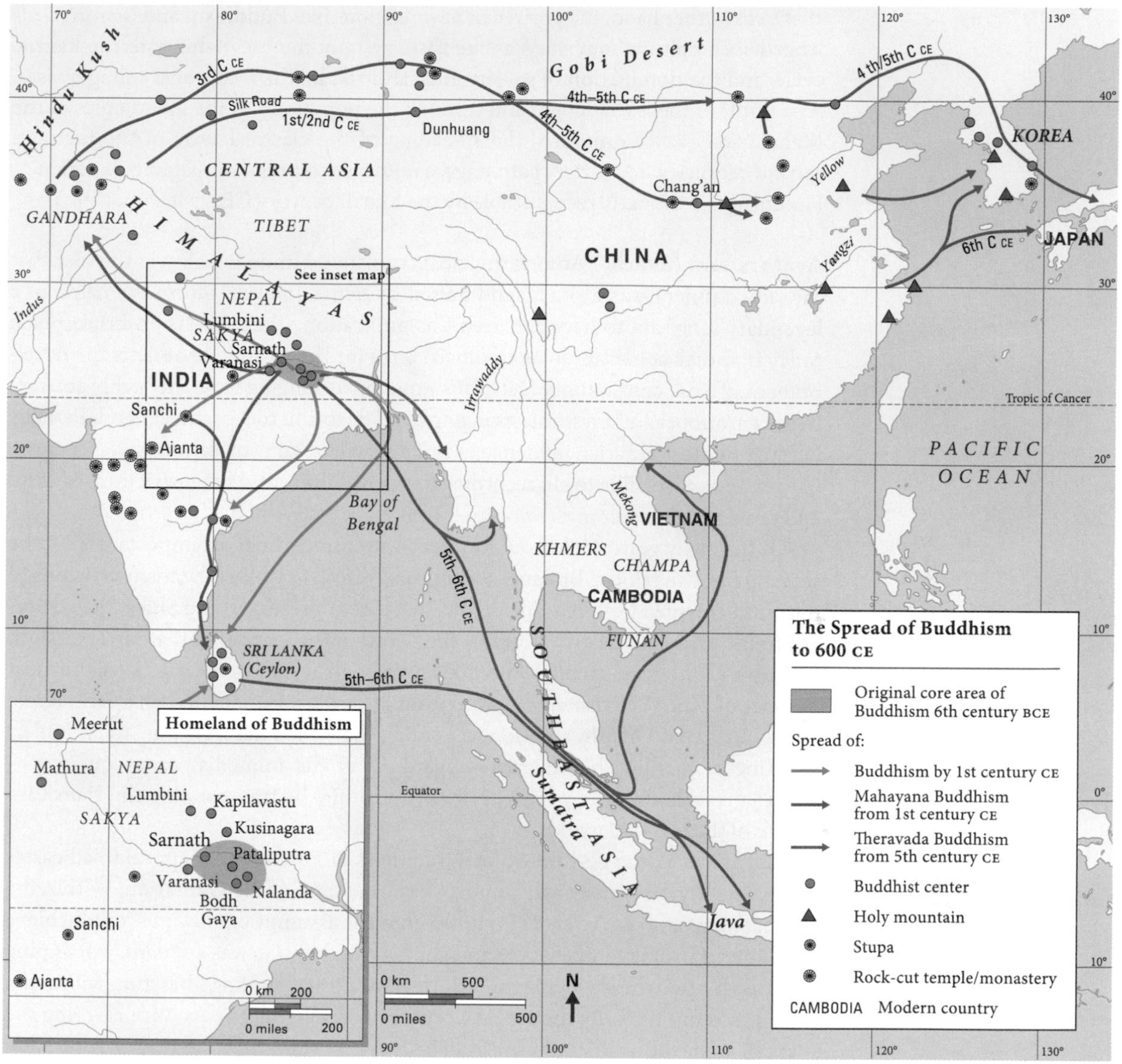

MAP **8.4 The Spread of Buddhism to 600 CE.**

map analysis

consolidation of the older Vedic and Brahmanic traditions into Hinduism, all the schools of Buddhism were to face strong competition for converts and noble patronage.

The Maturity of Hinduism: From the Abstract to the Devotional

The period from the Mauryans to the rise of the Guptas brought about a number of changes within the orthodox traditions of Indian religion. On the one hand, the continuing push of state formation to the south carried with it the older Vedic and Upanishadic traditions. Along the way, these traditions had incorporated many local deities into their pantheon of gods. Over the next several centuries these southern areas would lead in the rise of devotional cults, especially those of Vishnu and Shiva, culminating in the *bhakti* movements beginning in the seventh century CE.

On the other hand, the growth of new religions like Buddhism and Jainism challenged such cultural mainstays as the caste system, the inevitability of the karmic cycle, and the domination of society and salvation by the traditional ruling classes. As a result of these challenges and through the popularity of the grand epics of the Mahabharata and Ramayana, the spreading of the classical texts of the first and second centuries, and Gupta patronage, a rejuvenated brand of religious experience, Hinduism, is distinctly recognizable by the fourth century CE.

Avatars and Alvars Among the most consistent Hindu beliefs was the idea that the subcontinent was a single land united by faith—*Bharat*—from the name of a legendary king said to have achieved this unification. The name is enshrined even today in India's constitution as an official term for the nation. Another is the development of a full continuum of religious experience, ranging from the highly abstract to the emotional and mystical, springing from devotion to a particular god. Perhaps because of the egalitarian influence of Buddhism and Jainism, salvation was increasingly seen as accessible to all, according to one's abilities and the restrictions of caste and one's social position.

Of the many gods singled out for special attention, the most important were the so-called Indian trinity: Brahma, Vishnu, and Shiva. Of these, the main divisions of devotion emerged between Vishnu, the beneficent preserver, and Shiva, the powerful, fertile giver and destroyer of life, the "Lord of the Dance" of the universe. Both Vishnu and Shiva can manifest themselves through avatars or incarnations, the most popular of which is Krishna, an incarnation of Vishnu, who plays such a central role in the Bhagavad Gita. In addition to guiding that epic's hero, Arjuna, to an understanding of fulfilling his dharma—regardless of the immediate consequences—Krishna reveals the true power of devotion to him as transcending the transitory nature of the material world.

The ability of the new devotional traditions of Hinduism to appeal to all castes made the religion increasingly popular from the time of the Guptas on. Within the all-encompassing character of Hinduism grew the assumption that one could achieve salvation according to one's caste and ability, whether one was a *shudra*, worshiping Shiva with a pure heart, or a highly educated Brahman, finding liberation within the most profound texts. By the seventh century CE, religious poets were carrying the message of devotional Hinduism to all believers in vernacular languages. *Alvars* and *nayanars*, singers of praise for Vishnu and Shiva, respectively, created some of the most passionate and beautiful religious poetry in any language over the next five centuries and helped bond the people to the orthodox religion as a whole.

Shakti and Tantra A related development was that of Shakti, literally "power," sometimes called "tantra." Shakti practitioners often probed the darker edges of the multiple natures of the gods—especially Shiva and his consort Kali, or Durga—associated with death and destruction. Toward this end they purposely violated social norms—by eating meat, having illicit sex (even committing incest), eating human excrement, and, on rare occasions, committing ritual murder. The idea behind such perverse behavior was both to prove one's mastery over attachment to the acts themselves and to push beyond the ordinary dualities of good and evil. Such extreme activities were comparatively rare, though the idea of transcending ordinary norms also passed into Buddhism at about the same time, in the fourth and fifth centuries CE.

Here, it was also referred to as "tantra" and often as "the vehicle of the thunderbolt." In this modified form it passed into Nepal and Tibet, where its mysticism and interest in magical practices formed important elements of Tibetan Buddhism.

Stability amid Disorder: Economy, Family, and Society

Despite India's tumultuous political history, the agrarian-based economy of the subcontinent remained for 2,000 years the richest (along with China) in the world. Its agriculture was enormously productive in its most fertile areas, and the topography and climate allowed an astonishing variety of products, from fragrant woods to pepper and other tropical spices, to be produced for domestic consumption and export. As the economy flourished, society as a whole remained relatively stable. The hierarchical nature of the caste system maintained continuity through times of political turmoil, prescribing set duties and standards of behavior according to social position. Although the newly emerged religions of Buddhism and Jainism did not recognize the caste system, their appearance and spread did not fundamentally alter that system.

The relationships between men and women and among family members outlined in Chapter 3 grew increasingly complex, particularly from the classical age of the Guptas onward. Despite the trend in Buddhism—and, as we shall see in Chapters 10 and 12, in Islam—toward greater equality between men and women, beliefs such as the strictly delineated spheres of husband and wife, the idea of the female as a fundamental force of the universe, and a male vision of women as simultaneously desirable and threatening were considerably enlarged during this time.

Tax and Spend: Economy and Society

By 600 BCE, the inhabitants of the emerging Gangetic states had long since made the transition to being settled agriculturalists. With the vast majority of inhabitants of the new states being peasants from the lowest *shudra varna*, the chief form of revenue was harvest taxes. The average tax levied on the people of these early states appears to have been around one-sixth of their annual harvest.

Accelerating Taxes With the expansion of Magadha in the fifth and fourth centuries BCE, the agricultural tax increased to one-quarter of the harvest and even higher on royal lands—as much as half the cultivable land in the kingdom. By this time, the accelerating pace of urban life, the explosion of trade, and the increasingly differentiated castes expanded the economy even more, allowing whole new classes of items to be taxed. Thus, the immense wealth wielded by the Mauryans was accumulated through harvest taxes as high as one-half of all the produce raised in the empire, as well as taxes on livestock, internal trade, imports and exports, and such commodities as gold, textiles, salt, horses, and a variety of forest products and spices. Moreover, the increase in trade had led to a growing commercial class expanding beyond the traditional *Vaishya* (merchant) *varna*, while the growing need for capital and credit was met by guilds of bankers and traders in precious metals.

Agricultural taxes of about one-quarter to one-third of the harvest continued under the Guptas. The various working guilds, or *sreni,* in the major cities were highly organized. As under the Mauryans, bankers and merchants were frequently tapped by rulers for ready cash to fund armies, buy off intruders, or finance other emergency measures. Despite low **tariffs**, the Guptas enjoyed a highly favorable balance of trade. Indeed, the empire's self-sufficiency in nearly all commercial items meant that foreign traders had to pay for their goods in gold or silver. Because of this, the Romans were eventually forced to stop much of their Indian trade because of its drain on their supply of precious metals.

Tariffs: Taxes levied on imports.

Trade and Expansion By the time of Persia's invasion in the late sixth century BCE, the reputation of the wealth of northern India was already well established among the Greeks. The historian Herodotus (ca. 484–425 BCE), for example, noted that the yearly tribute of gold from the region was several times that of Persian Egypt. Interactions with the expanding Hellenistic world extended the reach of Indian markets and trade through the eastern Mediterranean and, shortly, into the expanding Roman domains.

With the decline of the Mauryans and the adoption of Buddhism by peoples of the northwest, the region around Taxila became the **nexus** of a caravan trade that from the third century BCE to the third century CE linked nearly all of Eurasia from Roman Britain to Han China and beyond through the famous Silk Road (see Chapter 9). In addition, Buddhist, Jain, and Brahmanic religious elements all spread westward over time to enrich in varying degrees the intellectual climate of the Parthians, Greeks, and Romans.

Nexus: A connection, a bond or link; also, a series of connections.

Indians also dominated the region's maritime trade until they were gradually displaced by the Arabs from the eighth to the fifteenth centuries CE and by the Europeans thereafter. The reputations of "Chryse" and "Cheronese," the lands of gold of Southeast Asia, were well established among the Romans through Indian trade by the first centuries CE, while Roman and Greek jars and coins could be found as far away as Vietnam, Cambodia, and Java. Colonies of Greek, Roman, Persian, and Arab traders clustered in the western port cities of Broach and Kalliena, trading tin, copper, hides, and **antimony** for the teak, ebony, ivory, spices, and silks available there. A testament to the importance of trade in the Greco-Roman world was the first-century guide to the Indian Ocean, the *Periplus* (marine atlas) *of the Erythrean Sea* (see "Patterns Up Close: The Global Trade of Indian Pepper").

Antimony: A metal widely used in alloys.

Indian Influence beyond India By the first century CE, this expanding trade region had established a network of outposts in Southeast Asia and the Indonesian archipelago. Buddhist influence in the area may have come soon after. Though it is unclear whether merchants or missionaries made the first contacts, a series of small settlements of Indians on the Malay Peninsula launched the founding of the first of the Indianized kingdoms in the area, that of Funan in the Mekong delta of Southeast Asia by the Brahmin Kaudinya in the second century CE. The spread of both Buddhism and the Indian system of "god-kings" soon reached the nearby Khmers [ke-MARES] and the state of Champa [KAM-puh] in modern Cambodia and Vietnam. By the seventh and eighth centuries CE, these areas became important trade centers in their own right, connecting the Indian states with Tang China and Heian Japan.

In addition, these countries formed important way stations in the expanding traffic of Buddhist pilgrims. The widespread appeal of Buddhism enhanced the Indian economy by both increasing the volume of trade on the subcontinent and providing a uniform structure for its expansion abroad. The mobility of pilgrims and monks, their role as missionaries, and their aversion to a number of lower-caste occupations made them natural candidates to assist in the increasingly far-flung circulation of goods and ideas. Monasteries served as hostels and way stations along well-traveled routes; larger complexes along branches of the Silk Road often had commercial centers grow up around them, particularly if they were destinations for pilgrims as well. The international character of Buddhism also facilitated contacts among long-distance traders. Perhaps most important, it linked India to an emerging cultural sphere that soon spanned Eurasia from the borderlands of the Persian empires to Japan. By the fourth century CE, firm trade ties had been established with the Romans, the Sasanids, the remnant states of Han China, and the Buddhist and Indianizing territories of Southeast Asia (see Map 8.5).

Caste, Family Life, and Gender

As with the economy, the basic patterns of Indian society were already being forged by the seventh century BCE. The integration of the Vedic peoples, those of northwestern India, and the early inhabitants of the Ganges valley had been largely completed. Thereafter, the fusion of Vedic traditions into a distinct form of Hindu culture, drawn heavily from the Brahmanic religious and social practices, proceeded apace. In the Gupta Empire, when Hinduism became the privileged religion of the state and the subcontinent was largely decentralized as regional kingdoms competed with each other, Hinduism evolved into a religious civilization, the pattern of social organization dominant during the period 600–1450 in world history (see Part 3).

Maturation of the Caste System Perhaps the most distinctive marker of Hinduism as a religious civilization is the caste (*jati*) system. Scholars are still uncertain as to whether this system originated with the four *varnas* in the Punjab–Ganges states or whether it evolved later. In any case, *varna* and caste seem to have merged over time to create a markedly stable, adaptable, yet also repressive system that continues even today, despite being technically unlawful under the Indian constitution. One of the caste system's chief functions was to provide a mechanism for absorbing and acculturating peoples of widely divergent languages, ethnicities, and religious practices into an integrated social whole. Within the framework of caste, all people lived within an interlocking system of reciprocal rights and responsibilities in which even those at the bottom levels had a necessary, if disagreeable, societal function.

During the Mauryan era, Ashoka's advocacy of dharma also reinforced older notions of duty according to social position, while such treatises on proper behavior as the *Code of Manu* (written down by 200 CE) helped solidify concepts of model conduct among the various classes of society. By the Gupta period, renewed interest in societal stability after nearly five centuries of disorder prompted increased attention to stricter boundaries for acceptable behaviors within the different *jati*. Indeed, genetic testing among various modern Indian groups has shown that, while there was considerable fluidity among castes and intermarriage throughout the first millennium BCE, this slowed down considerably after approximately 100 CE, even before the Hindu revival of the Gupta period. Along with this, the idea of **ritual pollution** resulting from unsanctioned contact with lower castes—requiring ever more elaborate purification rites to cleanse oneself after such contact—becomes increasingly

Ritual pollution: The act of someone or something becoming "unclean" in terms of religious taboos or prohibitions.

Patterns Up Close

The Global Trade of Indian Pepper

Pepper was perhaps the world's most sought-after commodity for thousands of years. Indeed, its primacy among such other rare spices as nutmeg, ginger, cinnamon, and cloves ultimately drove European adventurers and traders to the Americas as they sought a direct all-water route to its source in India.

The black pepper plant (*Piper nigrum*) is a vine native to the Malabar Coast of India in the modern state of Kerala. The two main varieties of pepper, white and black, are derived from the same berries: white pepper is the product of removing the black skin of the dried seeds (peppercorns) and crushing them, while black pepper comes from soaking and drying the seeds with their fruit coating still attached. As far back as the thirteenth century BCE, Egyptian records show black pepper being used in mummifications, a testament to its early place as a valued import.

Pepper Pot. The earliest records of pepper being imported into Britain are from the first century. Discovered in 1992, this exquisite pepper pot—a special container intended to hold this expensive spice—is designed in the shape of an empress and dates to the fifth century CE. Made of gold and silver, it testifies to the high value placed on such a precious commodity, especially in a remote place like Britain.

By the third century BCE, pepper had become a mainstay of south India's burgeoning Indian Ocean trade, with growing annual cargoes going to China, Southeast Asia, and Egypt. The Hellenistic cultural exchange conducted through Ptolemaic Egypt spread the use of pepper throughout the Mediterranean world. By the first century BCE, traders from Egypt, coastal Arabia, and northeast Africa were regularly availing themselves of the monsoon winds to make annual voyages to the Malabar ports for pepper. But it was after the Roman acquisition of Egypt that pepper became the subject of a kind of mania throughout their empire. Contemporary Romans like Pliny the Elder regularly complained of the huge drain of gold required to keep the empire adequately spiced, and the export of gold to India was ultimately curtailed.

How does one account for the huge popularity of a food product that has no nutritive value and burns the tongue? Initially, part of pepper's attraction may have been its exotic quality as a mysterious spice from a faraway land. But it had also long been used for medicinal purposes in India, and from Roman times through

common. This increasing trend of social segregation led to such things as small closets, nooks, and other places of concealment built into the houses of the upper castes so that their lower-caste servants could instantly hide themselves if their masters suddenly happened upon them.

Yet such repressive extremes also mask some of the strengths that gave the caste system its vitality and longevity. Like religious organizations and guilds in medieval Europe, *jati* membership provided a kind of extended family, giving each person a recognized and valued place in society, despised as they might be by their "betters." In some areas, especially in the south, entire villages or clans were incorporated into their own *jatis*; in others, ethnicity or occupation might be the determining criteria. Although the upper castes dominated the political structure of rural society, social power was in fact more diffuse than is usually appreciated. For example, the members of various caste and guild councils were customarily represented at state functions. In addition, different castes became associated with special feasts and their sponsoring gods or goddesses, giving them a degree of informal power within the larger social structure.

the European Middle Ages it was hailed in European and Arab treatises as healthful in a number of ways. Moreover, although pepper's effectiveness as a preservative is questionable, it was nonetheless highly useful as a flavor enhancer in a variety of preserved foods.

The Arab occupation of the prime transshipment areas of the eastern Mediterranean and the termini of the Silk Road and, by the fourteenth century, their domination of Indian Ocean trade caused the price of Indian commodities to soar in Europe. The urge to break the Islamic monopoly of the spice trade ultimately drove the Portuguese to sail around Africa, and Columbus to sail into the Atlantic, hoping to go directly to the Malabar Coast. The commercial network built on pepper and other spices was now positioned to drive what would grow into the world's first global trading system.

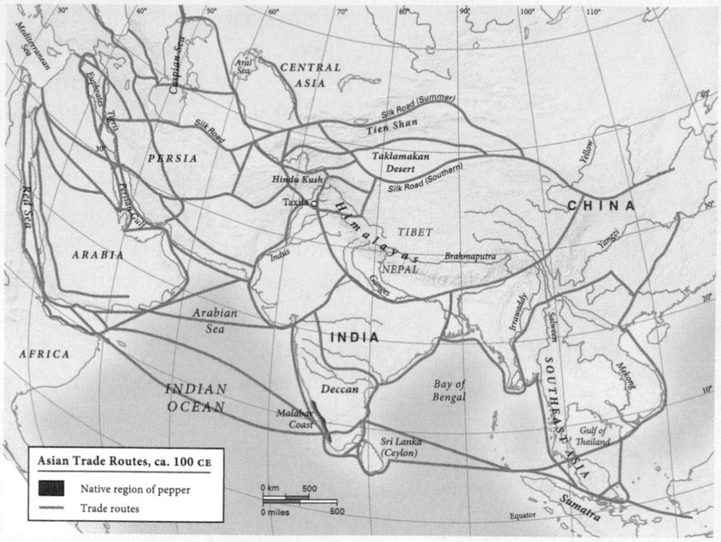

MAP 8.5 **Asian Trade Routes, ca. 100 CE.**

Questions

- How does the global trade in Indian pepper show the connectedness of Eurasia in this period in world history?
- What are the origins of the pepper trade? How did it change over time through interactions? What adaptations, if any, resulted from these interactions?

Jainism, Buddhism, and Caste Jainism and Buddhism had a considerable influence on the caste system as well. Although both religions accepted the theory of karma–samsara, their followers saw their own distinct practices as ways to break out of the cycle of death and rebirth. They thus represented powerful alternative traditions to the acceptance of *varna* and *jati*. Moreover, the potential for anyone, regardless of social position, to practice these methods undermined the hierarchical order of the caste system and made Jain and Buddhist practitioners equals in a society of believers. Their alternative institutions such as monasteries for men and women as well as their self-sufficiency, good works, and commercial expertise also gave them considerable material power in the larger community, particularly when patronized by nobles or monarchs.

Family Life and Hindu Culture As we saw in Chapter 3, the role of women both in the family and in Indian society was perhaps more complex than in any other agrarian-based culture. On the one hand, the idea of female "dependence" was central to the Hindu conception of the family. That is, a woman without the support and protection of a web of family relations was cast adrift in society, a kind of nonperson. Thus, to protect women was to safeguard the family and the social order. It followed from this that obedience and loyalty to senior female and male authority within the hierarchy of the family was the keystone of a woman's dharma, her duty according to her position. This fundamental duty was consistent regardless of her position in the caste system. In some regions, such loyalty found extreme expression in the act of *sati*. This controversial practice of a widow committing suicide by throwing herself on her husband's funeral pyre, however, remained largely confined to northern India and is legally prohibited today. During Britain's imperial period in India, attempts to suppress the practice were among the many cultural clashes that led to armed revolt in the late 1850s (see Chapter 26).

As in the strict division between men's and women's spheres in Confucian China we will see in Chapter 9, women's education and legal responsibilities in India were considerably narrower than those for men and tended to revolve around maintaining the home. Although in the Tamil areas of the south families remained matrilineal, property rights were limited. Yet wives customarily exercised the important responsibility of controlling the household accounts and supervising servants and hired help. For the more well-to-do, an appropriate knowledge of poetry, literature, and conversational skills was required, along with other attainments necessary for well-rounded, gracious living. And while men were somewhat less restricted in terms of marrying for love, the vast majority of men and women were united through marriages arranged by their families after careful negotiation and often betrothed before adolescence.

A number of texts were devoted to outlining the correct conduct of the "four stages of life" for men: student, householder, hermit, and wanderer. In the first stage, that of the student, boys of the "twice-born" upper castes were to be taken into the household of a *guru*, or teacher, for a minimum of 12 years. During this time, they were expected to study the works of the Vedic–Brahmanic–Upanishadic tradition. Upon entering into the second stage (householder), more mature men with sufficient savings should marry young women of good character and appropriate caste membership. In addition to providing for his household, servants, and relatives, a man should get up before dawn, offer the appropriate sacrifices throughout the day, and busy himself studying the Vedas, Puranas [poor-AHN-ahs] (genealogies and histories), and Itihasas [ee-tee-HAH-sahs] (legendary histories). As old age approaches, he enters the third stage (hermit) and should retreat to the forest, live on the roots and berries he can gather, and work to master the self in preparation for the end. In the final (wanderer) stage, he moves beyond desire for life or death, wandering without home or possessions. Caring not for anything of this world, he returns good for any evil done him and, ideally, attains moksha, or release from the cycle of death and rebirth at his journey's end.

Balancing Male and Female Roles Although women were, for the most part, treated as subservient members of a patriarchal society, as in China, they were also seen by men as complementary opposites, as symbols of harmony and balance, though also as real and imaginary temptations and impediments to their ultimate release (moksha). On the one hand, women in epic and popular literature, like Sita in the Ramayana, were often depicted as heroic and resourceful—Draupadi in the Mahabharata, for example, married five brothers in the Pandava family and aided all of them in their battles. Moreover, from the Gupta period on, a bewildering number of goddesses were increasingly appealed to by devotees for a variety of reasons. Fertility, sexuality, and growth, largely associated with femaleness, were all celebrated in Hindu literature, statuary, and religious symbolism. The lush depictions of frank sexuality in Hindu temples are among the most erotically charged artworks produced anywhere in the world. In contrast with this celebration of sexuality, on the other hand, was the perception of women as temptresses who anchored men to the sensual world. This in turn diverted them from the fundamental truth of the material world as transitory, thus potentially delaying their release from the karmic cycle through moksha.

The tensions growing from this duality and the difficulties of controlled enjoyment of the senses for both men and women as part of approved religious practice are graphically illustrated in Vatsyayana's [vaht-see-ai-AH-nah] famous *Kama Sutra,* or *Aphorisms of Love,* written perhaps sometime in the first or second century CE. Its frank handling of a multiplicity of sexual practices has created an aura of pornography about it for readers outside of India. Within a wider context, however, it should be seen more as a manual on the everyday worship of living. While the more sensational aspects of the arts of sexual love are certainly present, the majority of the text deals with how to become a well-rounded person of taste and culture. For women, no less than 64 separate skills are detailed, including singing, dancing, cooking, chemistry, first aid, metallurgy, architecture, and even driving horses and elephants. Here, at least, the "proper" sphere for women's activities was greatly expanded.

Gandharan Buddhas. One of the most stunning syntheses of artistic and religious traditions occurred in the wake of the decline of the Seleucid states and the invasion of the Kushans. In the area centered around Gandhara (in modern northeast Afghanistan and northwest Pakistan) Hellenistic artistic techniques of realistic human representation fused with the developing practices of Mahayana Buddhism to create sculptures like the head pictured here, from the second or third century CE, believed to be that of a bodhisattva, or perhaps of Siddhartha Gautama.

Strength in Numbers: Art, Literature, and Science

The vast number of artistic, literary, cultural, and scientific contributions arising from India makes it impossible to do more than hint at their richness here. One area worth noting in terms of its cross-cultural fertilization, however, is that of Gandharan art. During the time of the Kushan Empire, the powerful influences of the old empire of Alexander the Great were meeting the new religious movements arising within Buddhism to create a new "Gandharan" style of art.

Previous representations of the Buddha had not been anthropomorphic but were instead symbols associated with his life and lore: the "wheel of dharma," an empty throne, or a footprint. Around the beginning of the Common Era, perhaps coinciding with the development of Mahayana Buddhism, the distinctly realistic forms of Greek sculpture and the tradition of depicting the Greek gods as human merged with the new Buddhist sensibilities to create the first images of the Buddha, which looked remarkably like the Greek god Apollo. This synthetic Gandharan approach spread across northern India, and soon images of the Buddha were being turned out in great profusion. Over time, however, the more familiar, stylized, less realistic, and heavily symbolic representations became standard throughout the Mahayana religious sphere.

The Classical Age While relatively little art from the Mauryan era has survived, the Gupta period brought an explosion of art and literature from a multitude of

Philologist: A specialist in language study, particularly in the history and provenance of important terms.

artists patronized by the court and the upper classes. The "perfection" of Sanskrit as the medium of the sacred texts of Hinduism under the scholar and grammarian Panini and its systematic study under the **philologist** Patanjali several centuries later standardized the sacred language and caused it to be viewed and preserved as unchanging. As a classical language, Sanskrit was used in a staggering variety of works of poetry, prose, and drama, as well as in the *Puranas*—religious and secular historical genealogies. Other noteworthy works may include the poems and plays of "India's Shakespeare," Kalidasa (though some scholars place his life in the first century CE), such as the poignant romance *Shakuntala* and the poetic yearnings of *The Cloud Messenger*.

In addition to Sanskrit literature, scholarship of all types, including Buddhist works and scientific treatises, was undertaken at the great Buddhist monastery and university of Nalanda in northeastern India, founded in the fourth century CE.

Science and Mathematics In addition to Buddhism, the most profound intellectual influences from India on the surrounding regions were in science, especially mathematics. Despite the highly sophisticated speculative philosophy of the Upanishads, during the period from the second century BCE until the second century CE India was an importer of scientific and mathematical concepts from the Greco-Roman and Persian spheres. Greek geometry, for example, made its way into northern India during this time. In exchange, however, concepts of Indian health regimens—some involving yoga discipline—along with the vast body of Indian medicine, with its extensive knowledge of herbal remedies, also seem to have moved west. The second-century CE medical text *Charaka Samhita* for example, like its counterparts in the Mediterranean and later European world, taught a health regimen based on the balance of humors.

In the area of mathematics and astronomy an important synthesis of ideas took place from the time of the Mauryans through the twelfth and thirteenth centuries CE. Like the early Chinese methods of reckoning time, the first Indian calendars were based on the lunar months, though a year consisted of six seasons, and an intercalary period was inserted every 30 months to make up the difference with the solar year. During the Hellenistic period, Indians adopted the calendar of the eastern Mediterranean and southwest Asia, which had a 7-day week, a 24-hour day, and a 365-day solar year—along with the 12 zodiacal signs of the Greco-Roman world.

Indian thinkers refined these imported concepts to levels unsurpassed in the ancient world. The subtleties of some of the philosophical schools had already required intervals of time and numbers that still stagger the imagination today. For example, cycles of time marking eternity in some philosophical schools were measured in intervals larger than current estimates of the age of the universe; the shorter *kalpa*, reckoned at about 4 billion years, is only slightly less than current estimates of the age of the earth. Philosophical discussion on the nature of matter in infinitesimal space among some schools anticipated key arguments of modern physicists regarding the principle of indeterminacy.

The ability to conceive of mathematics on at once such a grand and such a tiny scale seems to have also helped Indian mathematicians and astronomers during the Gupta period to calculate a precise length of the solar year. Like the Chinese, they had already developed a decimal system; however, they now employed the first use of the zero, initially marked by a dot, as a placeholder, and developed a system of positive and negative numbers. Their work with the geometry of the Greeks enabled them to calculate pi to four decimal places as well as to develop methods for the solving of certain kinds of algebraic equations. By the eleventh and twelfth centuries CE, the acquisition of these techniques by the Arabs and their transmittal of them to the new universities of Christian Europe gave us the system we still use today, known by the somewhat erroneous name of "Arabic numerals."

Putting It All Together

interactive concept map

In roughly a millennium, a number of important patterns of world history emerged in India. The political, cultural, social, religious, and economic systems of the states along the Ganges River were diffused to all parts of the Indian subcontinent, where they were substantially—though by no means completely—received by the surrounding peoples. With the maturing of these patterns came the tendency to see the subcontinent as a unified entity in nearly every way except in politics. Here, despite the accomplishments of the Mauryans and Guptas, unity would prove elusive—in some respects even to the present day. This would prove particularly true, as we will see in later chapters, with the coming of Islam.

In terms of its regional influence and beyond, India's impact was disproportionately large. By at least the time of Ashoka, the population of the subcontinent was second only to that of China. Within it was contained the world's most active source of religious traditions, next to southwest Asia and the Mediterranean. The influence of one of these religions, Hinduism, spread to Indonesia and Southeast Asia; that of the other, Buddhism, could lay claim through this period to be the world's largest religious system as well as the first "universal" one.

Paradoxically, many of the factors that allowed for this tremendous richness of religious, cultural, and intellectual traditions also tended to abet the subcontinent's chronic political instability, particularly in the north. Here, continual migrations of outside peoples cross-fertilized the cultural resources of the region but also impeded political unification.

Review and Relate

Thinking Through Patterns

Examine the ways historians approach the big questions of this chapter.

Think about the reasons for the spread of Buddhism inside and outside of India. How have historians seen the decline of Buddhism in India?

An important historical pattern we examine in this part is that of individuals we call "visionaries"—people who, as the saying goes, "think outside the box" in their own societies. In this chapter, we place the Buddha in this category as a man who sought—and satisfied himself and his followers that he succeeded—to go beyond the Hindu bounds of death and rebirth. Like the other visionaries we examine, however, the Buddha's fundamental message of transcendence and enlightenment can be adapted to any belief system. As his message moves along the trade routes in India, central Asia, and, as we will see in later chapters, China, Korea, Japan, and Southeast Asia, it adapts to local customs by borrowing bits of indigenous religious mythology and belief to make it attractive to converts while keeping the fundamental message intact. Local people in turn adapt it to their own beliefs and make it their own. In the case of East Asia, this will receive a large boost from the translation of Buddhist scriptures into literary Chinese and the circulation of Buddhist practitioners, monks, merchants, and pilgrims throughout the Buddhist cultural sphere. Its decline in the place of its birth appears to be due in part to the shift of its cultural center to China and Japan and the official support of the Guptas for Hinduism.

» What do you consider to be the most influential patterns in Indian history to this point? Why?

How do historians establish criteria of "importance"? One measure of this is to assess the influence of certain patterns and practices on a culture or society over time. Change over time or the lack of it is an important indicator of the prevalence and kind of innovation taking place in a society. So some influential patterns in Indian history might include the permeation of religion into all aspects of Indian life, the search for transcendence of the material world, the caste system as the social fabric of the subcontinent, and the prominence of India as a crossroads astride the trade routes of the Indian Ocean and the great land routes across Eurasia.

» Do you think some of Ashoka's concepts could be implemented by governments today? Why or why not?

Ashoka's ideas seem quite modern in many ways, and his decrees regarding the protection of animals and ecological matters might certainly have some current application. His ideas of not taking life except in extreme circumstances and of giving prisoners time to repent also parallel modern concepts. Yet it must also be remembered that he is still far removed in time and culture from the modern world. His ideas of dharma as duty might not carry exactly the same import as today. Historians are routinely conscious of the pitfalls of identifying too closely with peoples in very different cultures in the remote past. "The past is a foreign country," it is often said. "They do things differently there."

Against the Grain

Consider this as a counterpoint to the main patterns examined in this chapter.

India's Ancient Republics

- What difficulties did all republics that sprang from agrarian–urban society face? Were they in the end insurmountable? Why?

As we have seen, in addition to numerous kingdoms, the ancient Gangetic states also counted republics (*ganas*) among them. Accustomed as we are to thinking of such political institutions as exclusive to the Mediterranean world, as with the Roman republic, representative forms of government have appeared at times in nearly all human societies. Yet until very recent times, as scientific–industrial society and the nation-state have come to dominate global politics and economics, republics had proved short-lived and problematic to sustain. In Greece and Rome, for example, popular-based governments seemed inevitably to descend into factionalism that in the end demanded a strong ruler to restore order.

- Do you think Indian republics were more vulnerable than those elsewhere to problems of disunity and factionalism? What role do you think religion played in sustaining or undermining them?

The early Indian republics of the late Vedic period were also seen by contemporaries to be models of power sharing in some respects, but were always vulnerable to the same weaknesses of internal dissention and factionalism as their counterparts elsewhere. For states moving toward a unified conception of concentrated power and religious unity—particularly when inheriting a tradition of rulers claiming divine sanction—the instability of power sharing seemed increasingly unattractive, even dangerous. Moreover, the requirements of economic stability in agrarian societies and the growing rigidity of caste also militated against the viability of republics.

And yet this form of social organization was discussed a number of times in the Mahabharata, in the accounts of Alexander's expeditions into India, and in a number of Buddhist accounts of northern Indian states as late as the second century CE. Detailed descriptions of their workings occur in the political treatises of Kautilya, and Arrian, the historian of Alexander, notes that republics such as Mallas offered the Greek armies some of the fiercest resistance they encountered. Perhaps here lies a clue to what contemporaries viewed as their true strengths and vulnerabilities: All commentators insist that no form of government works better when the people are unified and have a stake in the existing order; but factionalism and division are in the end fatal. As the Buddha himself notes in the Maha Nirvana Sutra, "So long as the Vajiyyans . . . so frequent the public meetings of their clan, so long they may be expected not to decline but to prosper." As Indian society as a whole became more complex and differentiated by religious tradition, economic station, and caste, the drive for political unity, so it was believed, would become that much stronger. With the creation of empires by the Mauryans and Guptas, the age of the republics in India was to pass—until 1947. Today, with its constitution and representative government, India prides itself on being the world's largest democracy.

Key Terms

audio flashcards

Altruism 227
Antimony 232
Atheistic 226
Devotional 222
Hinduism 221
Nexus 232
Philologist 238
Ritual pollution 233
Schism 225
Tariffs 232

For additional resources, please go to **www.oup.com/us/vonsivers.**
Please see the Further Resources section at the back of the book for additional readings and suggested websites.

PATTERNS OF EVIDENCE | Sources for Chapter 8

SOURCE 8.1 The Seven Pillar Edicts of King Ashoka

ca. 247–246 BCE

The third of the Mauryan kings, Ashoka ruled a vast empire throughout the Indian subcontinent in the period 273–231 BCE. His abrupt conversion to Buddhism in 260 led him to govern according to Buddhist principles—at least as he understood them. His new policies with respect to "righteous" governance were posted in a series of edicts that were engraved on rocks and pillars at strategic spots in his empire. A sample of these contains both very specific injunctions—imposed upon himself and upon his subordinates—and general principles, which could presumably be adapted to changing real-world circumstances.

1. Beloved-of-the-Gods speaks thus: This Dharma edict was written twenty-six years after my coronation. Happiness in this world and the next is difficult to obtain without much love for the Dharma, much self-examination, much respect, much fear (of evil), and much enthusiasm. But through my instruction this regard for Dharma and love of Dharma has grown day by day, and will continue to grow. And my officers of high, low and middle rank are practicing and conforming to Dharma, and are capable of inspiring others to do the same. Mahamatras in border areas are doing the same. And these are my instructions: to protect with Dharma, to make happiness through Dharma and to guard with Dharma.

. . .

4. Beloved-of-the-Gods speaks thus: This Dharma edict was written twenty-six years after my coronation. My Rajjukas are working among the people, among many hundreds of thousands of people. The hearing of petitions and the administration of justice has been left to them so that they can do their duties confidently and fearlessly and so that they can work for the welfare, happiness and benefit of the people in the country. But they should remember what causes happiness and sorrow, and being themselves devoted to Dharma, they should encourage the people in the country (to do the same), that they may attain happiness in this world and the next. These Rajjukas are eager to serve me. They also obey other officers who know my desires, who instruct

---

Source: Ven. S. Dhammika, trans. DharmaNet, 1994, http://www.cs.colostate.edu/~malaiya/ashoka.html#PILLAR.

the Rajjukas so that they can please me. Just as a person feels confident having entrusted his child to an expert nurse thinking: "The nurse will keep my child well," even so, the Rajjukas have been appointed by me for the welfare and happiness of the people in the country.

The hearing of petitions and the administration of justice have been left to the Rajjukas so that they can do their duties unperturbed, fearlessly and confidently. It is my desire that there should be uniformity in law and uniformity in sentencing. I even go this far, to grant a three-day stay for those in prison who have been tried and sentenced to death. During this time their relatives can make appeals to have the prisoners' lives spared. If there is none to appeal on their behalf, the prisoners can give gifts in order to make merit for the next world, or observe fasts. Indeed, it is my wish that in this way, even if a prisoner's time is limited, he can prepare for the next world, and that people's Dharma practice, self-control and generosity may grow.

7. Beloved-of-the-Gods, King Piyadasi, says: Along roads I have had banyan trees planted so that they can give shade to animals and men, and I have had mango groves planted. At intervals of eight **krosas**, I have had wells dug, rest-houses built, and in various places, I have had watering-places made for the use of animals and men. But these are but minor achievements. Such things to make the people happy have been done by former kings. I have done these things for this purpose, that the people might practice the Dharma.

Krosas: Unit of land measure.

Beloved-of-the-Gods, King Piyadasi, speaks thus: My Dharma Mahamatras too are occupied with various good works among the ascetics and householders of all religions. I have ordered that they should be occupied with the affairs of the Sangha. I have also ordered that they should be occupied with the affairs of the Brahmans and the Ajivikas. I have ordered that they be occupied with the Niganthas. In fact, I have ordered that different Mahamatras be occupied with the particular affairs of all different religions. And my Dharma Mahamatras likewise are occupied with these and other religions.

Beloved-of-the-Gods, King Piyadasi, speaks thus: These and other principal officers are occupied with the distribution of gifts, mine as well as those of the queens. In my women's quarters, they organize various charitable activities here and in the provinces. I have also ordered my sons and the sons of other queens to distribute gifts so that noble deeds of Dharma and the practice of Dharma may be promoted. And noble deeds of Dharma and the practice of Dharma consist of having kindness, generosity, truthfulness, purity, gentleness and goodness increase among the people.

Beloved-of-the-Gods, King Piyadasi, speaks thus: Whatever good deeds have been done by me, those the people accept and those they follow. Therefore they have progressed and will continue to progress by being respectful to mother and father, respectful to elders, by courtesy to the aged and proper behavior towards Brahmans and ascetics, towards the poor and distressed, and even towards servants and employees.

Beloved-of-the-Gods, King Piyadasi, speaks thus: This progress among the people through Dharma has been done by two means, by Dharma regulations and by persuasion. Of these, Dharma regulation is of little effect, while persuasion has much more effect. The Dharma regulations I have given are that various animals must be protected. And I have given many other Dharma regulations also. But it is by persuasion that progress among the people through Dharma has had a greater effect in respect of harmlessness to living beings and non-killing of living beings.

» Working with Sources

1. **To what extent did Ashoka claim to be occupying a paternal role in relationship to his people? Is it likely his specific instructions were actually carried out?**
2. **Are there indications here that Ashoka really aimed at creating what we might perceive as a kind of police state? In what respects?**

SOURCE 8.2

The Questions of King Milinda (The Milindapanha)

ca. 100 BCE

A series of Greek rulers attempted to maintain the Hellenizing goals of Alexander the Great in Bactria (modern Afghanistan), long after his death in 323 BCE. The most famous ruler in this line was Menander I (ca. 160–130 BCE), who achieved immortality in Buddhist literature by engaging in a debate with the Buddhist sage Nagasena. Their talks, set out as a series of dilemmas to be posed and (if possible) resolved, became an important exposition of Buddhist ideas and supposedly led to the conversion of Menander ("King Milinda") to Buddhism. In any event, *The Milindapanha* reflects the fusion of Greek and Indian traditions of philosophy, in the fascinating cauldron of world contact that existed in central and South Asia.

DILEMMA THE FORTY-SECOND. MODERATION IN FOOD.

4. 'Venerable Nâgasena, the Blessed One said:

"Be not remiss as to (the rules to be observed) when standing up (to beg for food). Be restrained in (matters relating to) the stomach."

But on the other hand he said:

"Now there were several days, Udâyin, on which I ate out of this bowl when it was full to the brim, and ate even more."

Source: T. W. Rhys Davids, trans., *The Questions of King Milinda*, vol. 2 (Oxford: Clarendon, 1894), 4–7 and 20–22.

"Now if the first rule be true, then the second statement must be false. But if the statement be true, then the rule first quoted must be wrong.

This too is a double-edged problem, now put to you, which you have to solve."

5. 'He who has no self-control as regards the stomach, O king, will destroy living creatures, will take possession of what has not been given to him, will be unchaste, will speak lies, will drink strong drink, will put his mother or his father to death, will slay an Arahat, will create a schism in the Order, will even with malice aforethought wound a Tathâgata. Was it not, O king, when without restraint as to his stomach, that Devadatta by breaking up the Order, heaped up for himself karma that would endure for a kalpa? It was on calling to mind this, O king, and many other things of the same kind, that the Blessed One declared:

"Be not remiss as to (the rules to be observed) when standing up (to beg for food). Be restrained in (matters relating to) the stomach."

6. 'And he who has self-control as regards the stomach gains a clear insight into the Four Truths, realizes the Four Fruits of the life of renunciation, and attains to mastery over the Four Discriminations, the Eight Attainments, and the Six Modes of Higher Knowledge, and fulfils all that goes to constitute the life of the recluse. Did not the parrot fledgling, O king, by self-restraint as to his stomach, cause the very heaven of the great Thirty-Three to shake, and bring down Sakka, the king of the gods, to wait upon him? It was on calling to mind this, O king, and many other things of a similar kind, that the Blessed One declared:

"Be not remiss as to (the rules to be observed) when standing up (to beg for food). Be restrained in (matters relating to) the stomach."

7. 'But when, O king, the Blessed One said: "Now there were several days, Udâyi, on which I ate out of this bowl when it was full to the brim, and ate even more," that was said by him who had completed his task, who had finished all that he had to do, who had accomplished the end he set before him, who had overcome every obstruction, by the self-dependent Tathâgata himself about himself.

Just, O king, as it is desirable that a sick man to whom an emetic, or a purge, or a clyster has been administered, should be treated with a tonic; just so, O king, should the man who is full of evil, and who has not perceived the Four Truths, adopt the practice of restraint in the matter of eating. But just, O king, as there is no necessity of polishing, and rubbing down, and purifying a diamond gem of great brilliancy, of the finest water, and of natural purity; just so, O king, is there no restraint as to what actions he should perform, on the Tathâgata, on him who hath attained to perfection in all that lies within the scope of a Buddha.'

'Very good, Nâgasena! That is so, and I accept it as you say.'

. . .

DILEMMA THE FORTY-SIXTH. THE MOCKING OF THE BUDDHA.

19. 'Venerable Nâgasena, it was said by the Blessed One of Six-tusks, the elephant king,

> "When he sought to slay him, and had reached him with his trunk,
> He perceived the yellow robe, the badge of a recluse,
> Then, though smarting with the pain, the thought possessed his heart,—
> 'He who wears the outward garb the Arahats wear
> Must be scatheless held, and sacred, by the good.'"

'But on the other hand it is said:

"When he was Gotipâla, the young Brahman, he reviled and abused Kassapa the Blessed One, the Arahat, the Buddha supreme, with vile and bitter words, calling him a shaveling and a good-for-nothing monk."

'Now if, Nâgasena, the Bodisat, even when he was an animal, respected the yellow robe, then the statement that as Gotipâla, a Brahman, he reviled and abused the Blessed One of that time, must be false. But if as a Brahman, he reviled and abused the Blessed One, the statement that when he was Six-tusks, the elephant king, he respected the yellow robe, must be false. If when the Bodisat was an animal, though he was suffering severe and cruel and bitter pain, he respected the yellow robe which the hunter had put on, how was it that when he was a man, a man arrived at discretion, with all his knowledge mature, he did not pay reverence, on seeing him, to Kassapa the Blessed One, the Arahat, the Buddha supreme, one endowed with the ten powers, the leader of the world, the highest of the high, round whom effulgence spread a fathom on every side, and who was clad in most excellent and precious and delicate Benares cloth made into yellow robes? This too is a double-edged problem, now put to you, which you have to solve.'

20. 'The verse you have quoted, O king, was spoken by the Blessed One. And Kassapa the Blessed One, the Arahat, the Buddha supreme, was abused and reviled by Gotipâla the young Brahman with vile and bitter words, with the epithets of shaveling and good-for-nothing monk. But that was owing to his birth and family surroundings. For Gotipâla, O king, was descended from a family of unbelievers, men void of faith. His mother and father, his sisters and brothers, the bondswomen and bondsmen, the hired servants and dependents in the house, were worshippers of Brahmâ, reverers of Brahmâ; and harboring the idea that Brahmans were the highest and most honorable among men, they reviled and loathed those others who had renounced the world. It was through hearing what they said that Gotipâla, when invited by Ghatîkâra the potter to visit the teacher, replied: "What's the good to you of visiting that shaveling, that good-for-nothing monk?"

21. 'Just, O king, as even nectar when mixed with poison will turn sour, just as the coolest water in contact with fire will become warm, so was it that

Gotipâla, the young Brahman, having been born and brought up in a family of unbelievers, men void of faith, thus reviled and abused the Tathâgata after the manner of his kind. And just, O king, as a flaming and burning mighty fire, if, even when at the height of its glory, it should come into contact with water, would cool down, with its splendor and glory spoilt, and turn to cinders, black as rotten blighted fruits—just so, O king, Gotipâla, full as he was of merit and faith, mighty as was the glory of his knowledge, yet when reborn into a family of unbelievers, of men void of faith, he became, as it were, blind, and reviled and abused the Tathâgata. But when he had gone to him, and had come to know the virtues of the Buddhas which he had, then did he become as his hired servant; and having renounced the world and entered the Order under the system of the Conqueror, he gained the fivefold power of insight, and the eightfold power of ecstatic meditation, and became assured of rebirth into the Brahmâ heaven.'

'Very good, Nâgasena! That is so, and I accept it as you say.'

» Working with Sources

1. To what extent does this dialogue reflect elements of the Greek philosophical tradition, explored in Chapter 7?

2. How do both speakers deploy real-world examples, in order to enhance their philosophical arguments?

SOURCE 8.3

Bamiyan Buddhas, Afghanistan

Late sixth century CE

A few months before the 9/11 terrorist attacks, in the spring of 2001, Taliban officials oversaw a series of explosions in the Bamiyan Valley, which deliberately detonated priceless elements of world heritage. Among the victims of this depredation were a set of enormous Buddha statues that had symbolized the unity of peoples in the region across religious lines. The two statues of Buddha (at 35 and 53 meters in height, one was the tallest Buddha in the world until its destruction) were rendered in a blended Hellenistic and South Asian style. Even after the collapse of the Taliban regime in Afghanistan, little has been done to restore the objects. (Next page, top: an 1880 drawing showing how they originally appeared; next page, bottom: what remained of the statues after their destruction.)

Source: ©SuperStock; ©Graciela Gonzalez Brigas.

Working with Sources

1. Why and under what circumstances would Buddhas have been carved into this mountainside in the first place?
2. Can any monotheistic system tolerate a fusion of cultural and religious values?

SOURCE 8.4

Seated Buddha, from the Gandhara culture, Afghanistan-Pakistan

second–third centuries CE

Gandhara became the center of a vibrant artistic tradition for several centuries. As Greek Bactrians merged their cultural values with Buddhists, Hellenistic artistic techniques fused with the practices of Mahayana Buddhism, yielding a renaissance of daring, boldly innovative sculpture. Among the products of this cultural synthesis was a seated Buddha which incorporates both Hellenistic and Indian aesthetic elements.

» Working with Sources

1. In what specific respects does this object reflect a conflation of Greek and Indian imagery, especially in the styles of clothing and hair?
2. Why is this object in the British Museum in London today?

SOURCE 8.5 Kalidasa, *The Cloud Messenger*

ca. fourth–fifth centuries CE

Sometimes described as the "Shakespeare of India," Kalidasa mastered various literary genres in his lifetime and continued to thrive, even in Western translations, into modern times. He composed three plays, two epic poems, and a series of shorter poems. Among these is *The Cloud Messenger*, in which a man asks a passing cloud to carry a message to his beloved wife, who is awaiting him in the Himalayas. Translated from the Sanskrit into English in the early nineteenth century, *The Cloud Messenger* served as the inspiration for composer Gustav Holst's 1910–1912 choral work *The Cloud Messenger*.

Yaksha: A demigod attendant to the god of wealth.

A certain **yaksha** who had been negligent in the execution of his own duties, on account of a curse from his master which was to be endured for a year and which was onerous as it separated him from his beloved, made his residence among the hermitages of Ramagiri, whose waters were blessed by the bathing of the daughter of Janaka and whose shade trees grew in profusion.

That lover, separated from his beloved, whose gold armlet had slipped from his bare forearm, having dwelt on that mountain for some months, on the first day of the month of Asadha, saw a cloud embracing the summit, which resembled a mature elephant playfully butting a bank.

Managing with difficulty to stand up in front of that cloud which was the cause of the renewal of his enthusiasm, that attendant of the king of kings, pondered while holding back his tears. Even the mind of a happy person is excited at the sight of a cloud. How much more so, when the one who longs to cling to his neck is far away?

As the month of Nabhas was close at hand, having as his goal the sustaining of the life of his beloved and wishing to cause the tidings of his own welfare to be carried by the cloud, the delighted being spoke kind words of welcome to the cloud to which offerings of fresh kutaja flowers had been made.

Owing to his impatience, not considering the incompatibility between a cloud consisting of vapor, light, water and wind and the contents of his message best delivered by a person of normal faculties, the yaksha made this request to the cloud, for among sentient and non-sentient things, those afflicted by desire are naturally miserable:

Without doubt, your path unimpeded, you will see your brother's wife, intent on counting the days, faithful and living on. The bond of hope generally

Source: http://allpoetry.com/poem/8526541-The-Cloud-Messenger---Part-01-by-Kalidasa

sustains the quickly sinking hearts of women who are alone, and which wilt like flowers.

Just as the favorable wind drives you slowly onward, this cataka cuckoo, your kinsman, calls sweetly on the left. Knowing the season for fertilization, cranes, like threaded garlands in the sky, lovely to the eye, will serve you.

Siddhas: Experts in spiritual matters.

Your steady passage observed by charming female **siddhas** who in trepidation wonder 'Has the summit been carried off the mountain by the wind?,' you who are heading north, fly up into the sky from this place where the nicula trees flourish, avoiding on the way the blows of the trunks of the elephants of the four quarters of the sky. . . .

Even though the route would be circuitous for one who, like you, is northward-bound, do not turn your back on the love on the palace roofs in Ujjayini. If you do not enjoy the eyes with flickering eyelids of the women startled by bolts of lightning there, then you have been deceived!

On the way, after you have ascended to the Nirvandhya River, whose girdles are flocks of birds calling on account of the turbulence of her waves, whose gliding motion is rendered delightful with stumbling steps, and whose exposed navel is her eddies, fill yourself with water, for amorous distraction is a woman's first expression of love for their beloved.

When you have passed that, you should duly adopt the means by which the Sindhu River may cast off her emaciation—she whose waters have become like a single braid of hair, whose complexion is made pale by the old leaves falling from the trees on her banks, and who shows you goodwill because she has been separated from you, O fortunate one.

. . .

Even if you arrive at Mahakala at some other time, O cloud, you should wait until the sun passes from the range of the eye. Playing the honorable role of drum at the evening offering to Shiva, you will receive the full reward for your deep thunder.

There, their girdles jingling to their footsteps, and their hands tired from the pretty waving of fly-whisks whose handles are brilliant with the sparkle of jewels, having received from you raindrops at the onset of the rainy season that soothe the scratches made by fingernails, the courtesans cast you lingering sidelong glances that resemble rows of honey-bees.

Then, settled above the forests whose trees are like uplifted arms, being round in shape, producing an evening light, red as a fresh China-rose, at the start of Shiva's dance, remove his desire for a fresh elephant skin—you whose devotion is beheld by Parvati, her agitation stilled and her gaze transfixed.

» Working with Sources

1. **How do the places seen by the cloud on its journey relate to the husband's feeling of longing for his wife?**
2. **How are the outer and inner worlds connected in this poem?**

Chapter 9 722 BCE–618 CE

China

IMPERIAL UNIFICATION AND PERFECTING THE MORAL ORDER

"Venerable sir, since you have not considered a thousand *li* too far to come, may I presume that you bring something that may profit my kingdom?" Even today one can sense the air of challenge, however polite, as the two men begin to take each other's measure. The speaker, King Hui of Liang, had seen his kingdom steadily eroded by the powerful surrounding states of Chu, Jin, and Qin, vying for supremacy at the height of China's Warring States period (403–221 BCE). Given the increasing desperation of his situation, perhaps he can be forgiven his somewhat sharp tone.

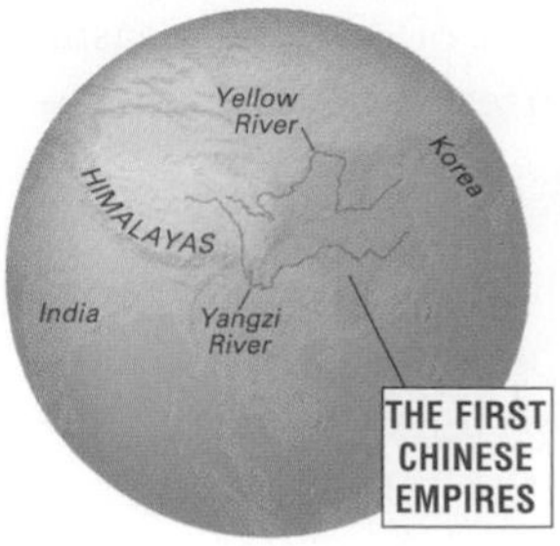

The "venerable sir" to whom he addressed his question, however, was in no mood to banter: "Why must Your Majesty use that word 'profit'? I bring only humanity and righteousness," he thundered. Warming to his topic, the Confucian sage Mencius now laid out his rebuttal:

> If Your Majesty says, "How may I profit my kingdom" the great officers will say, "How may we profit our families"; and the lesser officers and common people will say, "how may we profit ourselves." Superiors and inferiors will try to snatch this profit from each other and the kingdom will be endangered. . . [but] there never has been a humane man who neglected

***ABOVE:* One of the world's most recognizable structures, this section of the Great Wall near Beijing was upgraded in the early fifteenth century CE.**

his parents. There never has been a righteous man who made his ruler an afterthought.

—James Legge, trans., *The Works of Mencius* (New York: Dover Reprint, 1970, pp. 125–126)

Chastened by this confrontation, but also intrigued, King Hui now sought Mencius out for advice on a number of fronts. Through it all the sage refused to mince words with him about the extent of his misgovernment. Finally, both Hui and his son and successor, Xiang, said, "I wish quietly to receive your instructions."

This story from the opening pages of the fourth-century BCE *Mengzi*, known in English as the *Book of Mencius*, illustrates several important points not only about late Zhou China but also about the role of intellectual innovation, the ultimate direction of Chinese political thought, the way Chinese ideas would influence nearby peoples, and, more generally, the larger pattern of empires and states adopting the ideas of visionary thinkers. As we noted in Chapter 4, the Spring and Autumn and the Warring States periods in China during the final centuries of the Zhou era were socially and politically tumultuous. In spite, or perhaps because, of this, the period was also the most fertile one in China's long intellectual history. As we shall see, starting with Confucius—from whom Mencius drew his ideas—Chinese thinkers suggested ways of looking at the world, how to behave in it, and how to govern it that ranged from radically abstract to firmly practical, from collective to individualistic, and from an absence of active government to near totalitarianism.

From the time of the Han dynasty (202 BCE–220 CE) until the twentieth century, Confucianism, as interpreted by Mencius and adopted as a means of bureaucratic control, would be the governmental system of China. Moreover, as Chinese was adopted as the first written language by the Koreans, Japanese, and Vietnamese, Confucian concepts would be firmly planted in these lands as well. So in China, as in India, Persia, Rome, and eventually the Islamic world, the legacy of innovators we have identified as "visionaries" would be picked up and adopted by rulers as officially approved thought. As we will emphasize in this and the following chapters, an important pattern of world history emerges by the beginning of the Common Era: Large "world" empires utilize religions and systems of thought that have universal application and appeal.

Seeing Patterns

- **Was the First Emperor's ruthlessness justified by his accomplishments in his empire?**
- **How would you compare the values expressed by Confucius and Mencius to those of contemporary society?**
- **How have historians viewed the role of women in early imperial China?**

Visionaries and Empire

The period from the eighth century BCE until the first unification of China under the Qin in 221 BCE is universally regarded as China's most fertile period of intellectual exploration. The foundations of nearly every important school of Chinese

Chapter Outline

- Visionaries and Empire
- The Domestic Economy: Society, Family, and Gender
- Intellectual Trends, Aesthetics, Science, and Technology
- Putting It All Together

philosophy were laid during this era. By the time of the Confucian ethicist and political thinker Mencius in the fourth century BCE, so many competing systems of thought had emerged that Chinese chroniclers refer to them as the "hundred schools." Of these various systems, those that are best known and that had the greatest impact were Confucianism, Legalism, and Daoism.

Confucianism, Legalism, and Daoism

Like so many important figures in the world of ideas, the historical Confucius is an elusive figure. Contemporary researchers have widely differing views on his identity and his works. According to traditional accounts, he was born in 551 BCE to a family named Kong. Even today, the Kong family, some of whose members still live in the original family compound at Qufu [CHOO-foo] in modern Shandong Province, maintains what is claimed to be a continuous genealogy of the sage's descendants, who are now said to number in the millions.

In Confucian texts he is referred to as "the Master" (*zi* or *fuzi*) or "Master Kong" (*Kong fuzi*) [koong FOO-zuh]. European Roman Catholic missionaries in China during the seventeenth century rendered *Kong fuzi* into Latin, where it became "Confucius." As a member of the growing *shi* class of well-to-do, educated commoners and lower aristocracy (see Chapter 4), Confucius spent much of his early career seeking a position as political adviser to the courts of several of the Zhou states in northern China. Though tradition has him holding a minor position in his native state of Lu, his search for employment was largely unsuccessful. As with the visionaries we saw in the previous chapter in India, he ended up spending most of his life as an itinerant teacher, spreading his ideas about ethics and politics to a growing group of followers. Like the Buddha, however, it would be centuries before his ideas were applied on a large scale by a state.

selections from the *Analects*

Confucian Doctrine Confucius has been called "China's first great moralist." His teachings—as presented in the *Lunyu,* or *Analects,* the central Confucian text—have at their core a view of human beings as inclined toward ethical behavior and of human society as a perfectible moral order. According to Confucius, there are certain fundamental patterns that are manifestations of the *Dao* ("the Way") of the universal order.

One of these fundamental patterns is the relationship between parent and offspring. A child owes its life and body to its parents. Because of this, a child—even a grownup, who was, after all, once a child—dares not injure himself or herself or others. People develop their moral character to reflect well upon their parents and serve those in higher social or political stations as they serve their own parents. This example of human society as a kind of extended family applies at every level, from the peasant to the ruler—and even beyond: Drawing on the idea of the Mandate of Heaven (see Chapter 4), Confucius makes the ruler himself responsible to heaven for the state of his country. Indeed, emperors in later regimes would habitually refer to themselves as the "sons of heaven," to emphasize this filial duty.

Reciprocity: Mutual exchange of things, ideas, etc.

Though this view is avowedly hierarchical rather than egalitarian, the mutual obligations present at every level serve as checks for Confucius on the arbitrary exercise of power. Hence, when asked to sum up his thinking in one word, Confucius answered, "**Reciprocity**: Do not do unto others what you would not have them do to you." Confucius believed that individuals should strive for the qualities of *ren* (kindness or humaneness toward others) by faithfully following the practices of *li* (usually translated as "ritual": the observance of rules of decorum as guides to appropriate behavior toward others). People who did so would not only perfect their own character but also set an example for the rest of society.

Confucian Government Confucius lived during a time of great social and political disorder, and as a result many of his teachings center on ways to restore order and make government and society more humane. But because Confucian doctrine places great emphasis on personal responsibility, the structure of government is far less important than the ethical fitness of the ruler and the people. Good government, according to Confucius, begins with educated leaders and officials of strong moral character, like the Zhou kings Wen and Wu and the Duke of Zhou (see Chapter 4), who are often cited in the *Analects* as examples. To describe this ideal of behavior, Confucius introduced the concept of the **junzi** ("the superior man" or "gentleman").

Junzi: According to Confucius, the "superior man" or "gentleman" who behaves according to an ethical and moral ideal. A society run by *junzi* will foster social institutions that encourage proper behavior.

Those able to attain these ideals would comprise for Confucius a kind of aristocracy of merit, while rulers who possessed these qualities would set a sound example for their subjects to follow.

Just as the *junzi* cultivated his personal ethics and morals, a state run by *junzi* would spread these values to society by fostering ritual and social institutions that encouraged proper behavior among the people. In the same way that a musician's consistent practicing of scales eventually makes playing them correctly second nature, the consistent observance of *li* (ritual) would help make appropriate behavior routine among ordinary people. Not everyone would necessarily develop the high moral standards of the *junzi*, but at the very least, the majority of people would develop a sense of right and wrong and thus acquire a stake in the social order.

By the time Confucius died in 479 BCE, he had attracted a loyal following of adherents to his teachings. Two later students of Confucian doctrine, Mencius and Xunzi [SHWUN-zuh], continued to spread the teachings of the master, though with their own distinctive contributions. Despite challenges from a number of competing philosophical schools, Confucian ideals ultimately became the standard for Chinese politics and scholarship.

Mencius By Mencius's time, in the fourth century BCE, the intensity of the competition and continual warfare among the Zhou states had spawned most of the so-called hundred schools of thought as thinkers questioned fundamental assumptions about the private and social good. Not surprisingly, given the chaotic times, their

interactive timeline

722–481 BCE Spring and Autumn periods

403–221 BCE Warring States period

604 BCE Traditional date for birth of Laozi

551–479 BCE Traditional dates for life of Confucius

385–312 BCE Life of Mencius, champion of Confucianism

233 BCE Death of Han Fei, philosopher of legalism

221–206 BCE First Chinese Empire under Qin

202 BCE–8 CE Former Han dynasty

24–220 CE Later Han dynasty

220–589 CE Three Kingdoms, Six Dynasties, North and South Dynasties; rapid spread of Buddhism

589–618 CE Reunification of empire under the Sui

The Kong Family Mansion in Qufu. Though scholars have debated many aspects of the life and activities of the historical Confucius, his descendants have maintained the family genealogical records and compound over the centuries at Qufu in modern Shandong province. Since 1055 CE, Chinese emperors have bestowed on the eldest male family member in direct descent from the sage the title of "Duke Yansheng." The most recent holder of the title, Kung Te-cheng (Kong Dezheng), died in October 2008 in Taiwan at the age of 89. He was the seventy-seventh direct descendent of Confucius.

answers varied from radical individualism to universal love and altruism, with some, like Sun Zi (often spelled Sun Tzu) in *The Art of War,* examining the nature and practice of armed struggle.

Mencius (*Mengzi,* or Master Meng; ca. 385–312 BCE), like Confucius, believed that people were fundamentally good and that individuals must continually work to understand and refine this goodness in order to avoid being led astray by negative influences. Mencius used water, the nature of which is to flow downhill, as a familiar metaphor for human nature. It is possible, of course, to force water out of this natural tendency, said Mencius; but once such artificial means are removed, it reverts to its original course. Hence, he concluded, the way to proper behavior is through cultivating the Confucian virtues as a bulwark against forces pushing toward "unnatural" behavior.

Mencius traveled throughout China spreading Confucian ideals, especially as a basis for government practice. The *Mengzi,* or *Book of Mencius,* is written in more of a narrative form than the *Analects* and is supplemented by stories, parables, and debates with advocates of other schools of thought. Its most powerful sections deal with the obligations of rulers to their subjects. As the center of power and moral authority, a ruler's primary duty for Mencius is to maintain the "people's livelihood" and uphold the "righteousness" (*yi*—appropriate behavior by and toward all according to social rank) of the state. As an ideal way to maintain the people's livelihood, for example, Mencius advocated the "well-field" system (see Chapter 4) as a means of ensuring crop surpluses and equality among peasant cultivators.

As for the state, as Mencius said to King Hui of Liang in the chapter-opening vignette, "I bring only humanity [*ren*] and righteousness [*yi*]; why must Your Majesty use that word 'profit'?" Mencius argued that rulers who sought to profit from their states sowed the seeds of their own destruction by encouraging their subjects to profit only themselves. A state ruled by righteousness and humanity, on the other hand, ensured that the people would be prosperous and orderly, which automatically contributed to the "profit" of the ruler. A ruler who abused or neglected his subjects upset the social order and the natural tendency of people toward good. In such a case, the people had not only the right but also the obligation to invoke the Mandate of Heaven and depose him. In the end, said Mencius, anticipating a host of later Chinese thinkers, the people, not the ruler, are the foundation of the state.

Xunzi As states grew increasingly powerful, their armies larger, and warfare more deadly, Mencius's optimistic view of human nature seemed less and less practical to many thinkers. Like Mencius, Xunzi (trad. ca. 310–219? BCE) was also a student of Confucian philosophy but had a much darker view of human nature. Living during the apogee of the Warring States period, Xunzi came to believe that individuals were self-involved creatures with little interest in society as a whole and capable of regulating themselves only through immense effort. Only by enforcing the restraints of civilization, such as ritual, law, and the example of past model rulers, could individuals approach the Confucian ideals of virtue and humanity. Thus, by the end of the third century BCE, Confucian thinkers had come to radically opposed conclusions about their most fundamental premise: the nature of human beings. In the long run, the more moderate views of Confucius and Mencius won out. Xunzi's more pessimistic view of human nature, however, formed the basis of the Legalist school founded by two of his students, Han Fei and Li Si, that finally restored order and created the first Chinese empire.

Legalism The Legalist school is the most severe of the three major schools of philosophical thought that emerged during the Warring States period. For Legalists, building a strong state was of utmost importance. Out of Xunzi's view of human beings as inclined toward evil and drawing on the earlier practices of the Qin minister Lord Shang (d. 338 BCE), Han Fei (d. 233 BCE) and Li Si (d. 208 BCE) developed a system of uniform laws and practices based on the absolute will of the ruler. Order in a state, they claimed, could be implemented only through the institution of strict, detailed, and explicit laws diligently enforced and imposed on all subjects without regard to rank or class. Since Legalists believed that compliance on small matters led to compliance on larger ones, they imposed harsh punishments—forced labor, mutilation, in some cases death—for even the tiniest infractions. Although Legalism had many critics, it was its strict practices, not the more moderate ideals of Confucianism or Daoism that imposed order on China. The price it exacted for doing so, however, was considered by succeeding generations to have been intolerably high.

Han Fei, selections on Legalism

The Legalists argued that the state was all important; therefore, all subjects must serve the state through productive activities. Among these activities, agriculture and military service were the highest priorities. Individuals were encouraged to take up farming or military service as their livelihoods; any other occupation was discouraged. Idlers were put to work by force. Since dissent led to disorder, only government-approved history and literature were tolerated.

Daoism While most Chinese philosophical schools accepted the concept of the Dao as the ordering principle of the universe, they varied considerably as to the best means of achieving harmony with it. For Confucians, as we have seen, study and self-cultivation to the point of intuitive understanding put the individual in tune with the Dao. For followers of the Daoist tradition, attributed to Laozi (Lao Tzu), however, the Confucian path prevented genuine understanding of and harmony with the Dao.

The historical Laozi is even more obscure than Confucius. In fact, many scholars believe Laozi to be a mythical figure. Chinese tradition cites his birth date as 604 BCE and gives his name as Li Er. The honorific title "Laozi" is translated as either "the Old Master" or "the Old Child." The translation "Old Child" captures something of the Daoist belief that only a return to childlike simplicity would lead to union with the Dao.

For Daoists, in contrast to the Confucians, the Dao was not the ordering force *within* the universe but the transcendent first principle *beyond* the universe. The Confucian Dao, dealing with the particulars of this world, can be named; the Daoist Dao, like the relationship between atman and brahman we saw in Chapter 8, transcends all particulars and therefore cannot be named. The Dao is thus beyond all dualities and unifies them in a great oscillating whole.

In fact, the vocabulary Laozi used for this new measure of all phenomena is remarkably similar to that of other Eurasian visionaries discussed previously: Deutero-Isaiah, the Zoroastrian reformers, Anaximander, and the Buddha, as well as the

Upanishad writers. All were striving in their volatile kingdoms and empires, many of which worshipped large pantheons of gods, for one, single, unchangeable, and all-encompassing standard for morality and understanding.

Since the Dao transcended the world, including all such opposites as "good" and "evil," no single path of action would lead an individual to union with it. To choose the good, as the Confucians do, is therefore to follow only a limited part of the universal Dao. Instead, the Daoists taught that only through a life of quiet self-reflection and contemplation of opposites and paradoxes might an individual come to know the Dao. A classic tale that expresses this aspect of Daoist thought is the story of the philosopher Zhuang Zhou [JWONG joe], who lived in the fourth century BCE and awoke from a dream unsure of whether he had dreamed he was a butterfly or whether he was a butterfly dreaming he was Zhuang Zhou.

Daoism and Government Daoist political theory held that the best government was that which governed least. Here, the key idea is one from the most famous Daoist work, the *Daode Jing* (*The Classic of the Way and Virtue*, often spelled *Tao Te Ching*): "By non-action there is nothing that is not done." This is not to say that the ruler literally does nothing; rather, his role is to create the conditions that naturally lead to a society in which everyone spontaneously acts in accordance with the Dao. The ruler should not push specific policies but rather let all things take their natural course, for even as they run to extremes they will always reverse. The ruler's understanding of the flow of these universal cycles leads to union with the Dao and keeps the world in equilibrium.

These three schools of thought were all to play a role in the development of China's political and cultural life. Confucianism would provide the basis for the bureaucracy of China's empires and ideals of a perfectible moral order; Daoism would provide the mystical dimension of Chinese culture and a profound love and idealization of nature; finally, Legalism would provide the brute muscle of unifying the last of the warring states into a single structure under the Qin [chin].

The Qin Dynasty

As the period of the Warring States continued, the Qin state ultimately claimed victory over its opponents and established centralized rule throughout China. At first glance, Qin might seem unpromising as a candidate for empire. It was the smallest and poorest of the Zhou dependencies, located far to the west of most of the other Zhou states. However, Qin had several powerful advantages over its competitors. Its position on the fringe of the Zhou world meant that it was free to expand its economic base by promising land to peasant cultivators as the state seized territory on its western frontier.

Qin and Zhou The agricultural surplus that resulted from these land grants led to increased prosperity for the small but growing state. Qin's location was also a benefit when it came to military preparedness. Many of the warring states were in close proximity to each other, and the constant battles among them depleted their economic and military resources. Qin, on the other hand, did not have to fight off other states at its borders. Consequently, the Qin participated in limited military campaigns, mostly against nomadic groups, which strengthened their fighting skills but did not upset their economy or weaken their army. By 350 BCE, Qin rulers,

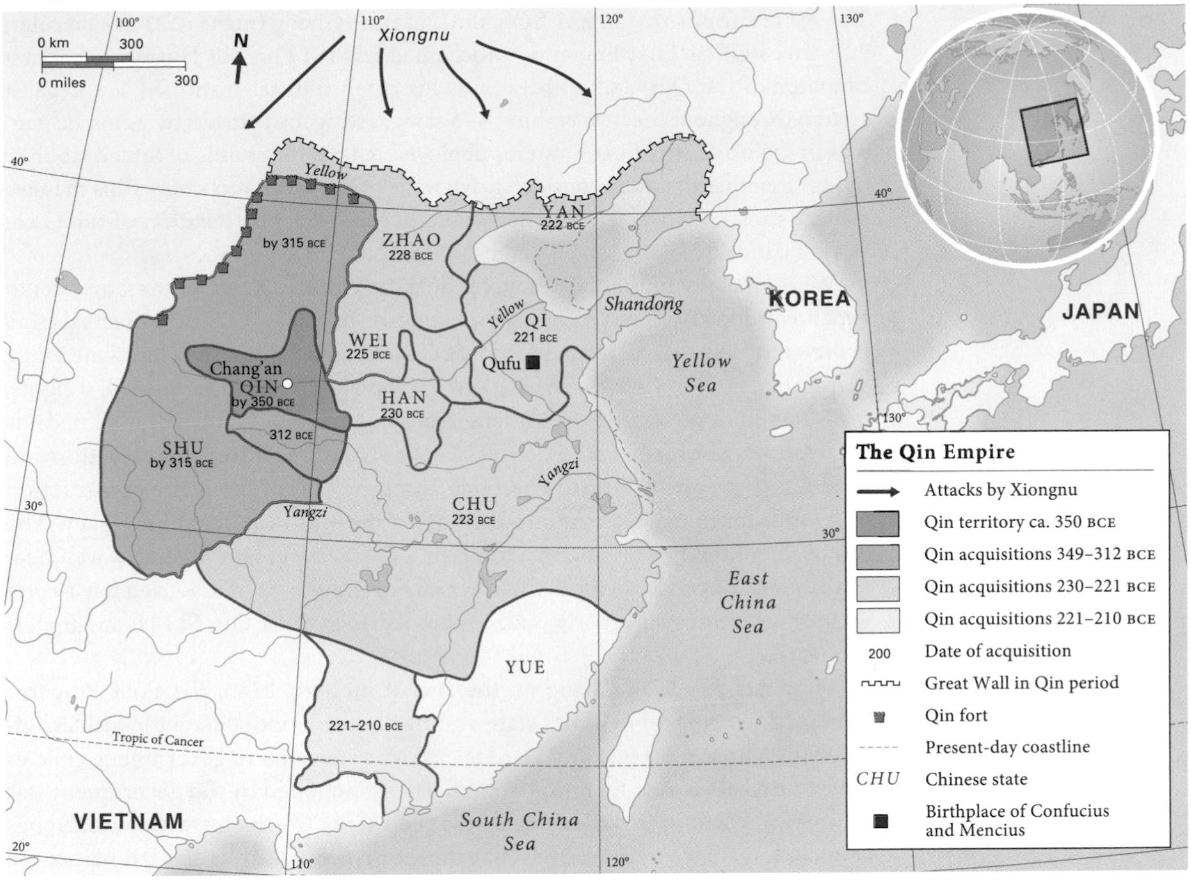

MAP 9.1 The Qin Empire.

particularly the famous Shang Yang, reorganized the state by eliminating the last of the old Zhou institutions and replacing them with a uniform, centralized system that anticipated a number of later Legalist principles. In 256 BCE, the Qin conquered Zhou itself and began the drive for empire in earnest (see Map 9.1).

With its strong economy, expert military, and the Legalist theorists Han Fei and Li Si advising the court, Qin took advantage of the collective exhaustion of the other northern Chinese states and conquered them at a pace reminiscent of Alexander the Great's campaigns of the previous century. With stunning swiftness, Qin armies, now swollen to hundreds of thousands of men, drove south and eliminated the opposition of the many tribal peoples below the state of Yue.

The Qin then continued into the northern part of modern Vietnam—thus beginning a long, and often bitterly contested, relationship with Southeast Asia. The Chinese would attempt to rule the area with limited success for over 1,000 years and claim it as a protectorate for nearly another thousand until they were ousted by the French in 1885. In the north and west, Qin armies fought a series of campaigns to drive nomadic peoples, especially the Xiongnu, or Huns, from newly established borders and secure the trade routes into central Asia. By the end of the 220s BCE, the Qin had subdued all of the states that would constitute what was about to become the first Chinese empire.

The First Emperor In 221 BCE, the Qin ruler Cheng (r. 246–221 as Qin ruler; 221–209 BCE as First Emperor) proclaimed himself Qin Shi Huangdi, the First Emperor of the Qin, and with Li Si as his chief minister instituted the Legalist system throughout the new empire. As a safeguard against attacks by nomadic peoples in the north, the First Emperor deployed tens of thousands of forced laborers to join together the numerous defensive walls of the old Zhou states. This massive project stretching over 1,400 miles would become the first iteration of the Great Wall of China.

With virtually unlimited resources and the ruthless drive of the Legalists to expand and fortify the state, the First Emperor began a series of projects during his reign of less than a dozen years that are still astonishing today in their scope and ambition. The Chinese writing system was standardized, as were all weights, measures, and coinage—even the length of axles on carts. Hundreds of thousands of conscript laborers worked on roads, canals, and a multitude of irrigation and water conservancy projects. The First Emperor also ordered the construction of a tomb for himself, a mammoth complex meant to celebrate his legacy. The discovery of the First Emperor's tomb in 1974 by a peasant digging a well near the modern city of Xi'an unearthed an army of thousands of life-sized terra-cotta warriors marching in orderly ranks, intended to protect Qin Shi Huangdi after his death.

From his palace in Chang'an, the site of modern Xi'an, the First Emperor tightened his control over the state and dealt with opponents with ruthless efficiency. Scholars, particularly Confucians, who objected to government policies were buried alive. Any literature not officially sanctioned by the government was destroyed. While it is difficult to assess the extent to which the book burnings actually took place, it is believed that a great many works that existed before the Qin were put to the torch. Writers of the following Han dynasty, emphasizing the horrors of the Qin, have left a number of accounts of mass executions of dissenting scholars.

image analysis

Terra-Cotta Warriors at the First Emperor's Tomb. One of the most important archaeological finds of the twentieth century, the Qin burial complex, was discovered in 1974 by a local farmer digging a well. Over 5,000 figures have been unearthed so far, all with individualized features. The dig has been enclosed and a museum built on site. Along with the Great Wall, it is one of China's most popular tourist destinations.

After a reign of about 12 years as emperor, Qin Shi Huangdi died. His strict laws, severe punishments, and huge construction projects had angered and exhausted the people, and soon after his death the empire erupted in rebellion. Ironically, the government's severe laws and punishments now worked against it as officials attempted to conceal the revolt's severity for fear of torture and execution. At the same time, Minister Li Si provoked additional discontent by conspiring to keep the First Emperor's death a secret in order to rule as regent for the monarch's son. He was captured attempting to flee the rebellion and executed in 208 BCE. In an attempt to make the punishment fit the crime, his captors lashed him to a board and slowly sawed him in half in accordance with Qin law. After a brief civil war, a general named Liu Bang put an end to the fighting and restored order to the region. He proclaimed himself emperor in 202 BCE and called his new dynasty the Han.

The Han Dynasty

If the Qin constructed the Chinese empire, the Han perfected it. Like the Roman Empire with which it is frequently compared, the Han developed over time a centralized political system of rule that blended the administrative structures of the Qin with more moderate Confucian ideals of government as a moral agent. This model of rule endured—with some interruptions and modifications—for over 2,000 years, by having its power tempered by a bureaucracy that saw its role as both carrying out the will of the court and acting as advocates for the people.

Unlike earlier rulers who came from aristocratic families, Liu Bang, who had taken the reign name Gaozu (r. 202–195 BCE), had been a peasant. Perhaps because of this background, he had little interest in restoring the decentralized system of the Zhou, which favored the aristocratic classes. Instead, he left intact the Qin structure of centralized ministries and regional **commanderies**. This structure seemed the only sensible way to keep such a large empire under control. To mollify advocates of returning to the old Zhou system, Han rulers offered them token distributions of land. They also reduced taxes and labor obligations and rescinded the most severe punishments imposed under the Qin. Han rulers altered the Qin system of leveling social classes by instituting uniform rules for different segments of society—aristocrats as well as commoners. Under the Han, the upper ranks of society were taxed at lighter rates and exempted from most forms of corporal punishment.

Commanderies: Districts under the control of a military commander.

As the Han Empire expanded—reaching a population recorded in 2 CE of just under 60 million—so did its bureaucracy. Within a century of Liu Bang's reign, the number of government officials had swollen to 130,000. Officials were divided into graded ranks ranging from the heads of imperial ministries to district magistrates. Below these officials were clan leaders and village **headmen**. Landowners were to collect and remit the taxes for themselves and their tenants, while the lower officials recorded the rates and amounts, kept track of the labor obligations of the district, and mobilized the people during emergencies.

Headmen: Local leaders; these are usually chosen by the people of the village, clan, district, etc., rather than appointed by the government.

Wudi, the Martial Emperor A high point of the Han dynasty came during the rule of the emperor Wudi, whose reign name means "Martial Emperor" (r. ca. 140–87 BCE). Like both his predecessors and successors, Wudi faced the complex problem of defending the empire's northern and western boundaries from diverse groups of nomadic peoples, especially the Xiongnu. He therefore extended the Great Wall begun by the Qin to provide greater protection. Hoping that a strong

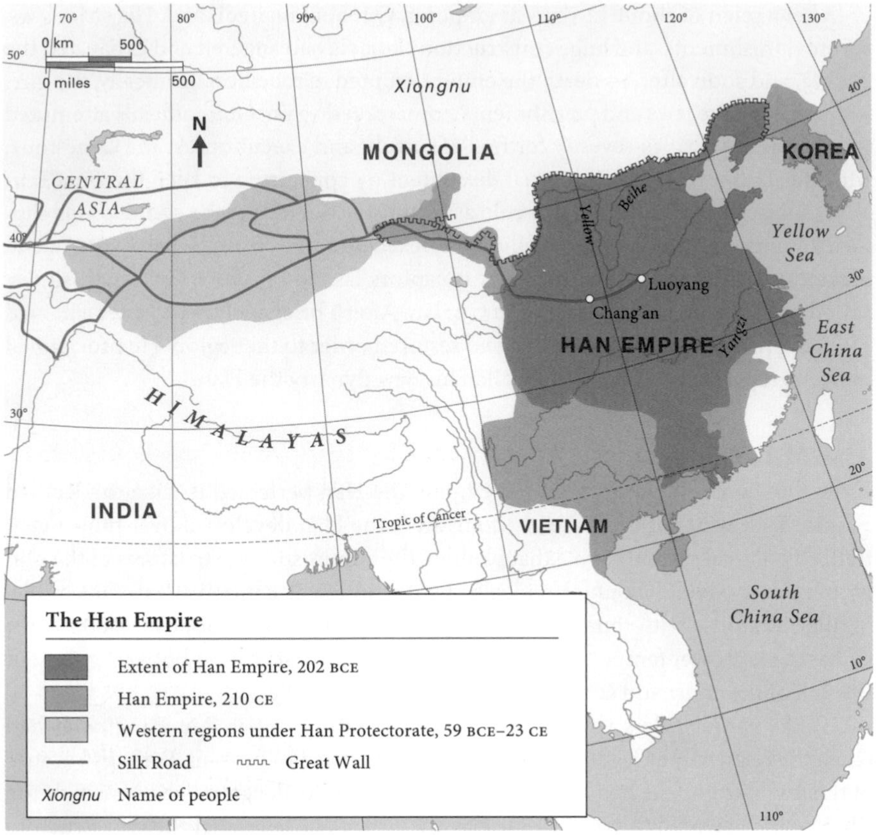

MAP 9.2 **The Han Empire.**

Sinicizing: The pattern by which newcomers to areas dominated by Chinese culture were encouraged to adopt that culture for themselves.

Chinese presence would discourage potential invasions, Wudi encouraged people to move to areas along the northern and western borders of the empire (see Map 9.2).

In addition to securing the empire, Wudi had to suppress Xiongnu raids on central Asian trade routes, especially the Silk Road. He made diplomatic efforts, offering the Xiongnu food and other necessary supplies, but when those efforts failed, he mounted military campaigns against them. Over the long term, the Han also adopted the practice of "**sinicizing**" the nomadic peoples, a process similar to that pursued by their contemporaries the Romans toward the peoples surrounding their empire. The practice of sinicizing involved encouraging nomadic peoples to assimilate themselves to Chinese culture and identity. Once they had been assimilated, the threat of nomadic invasion would be lessened. Wudi drove his armies into central Asia, where he established a lucrative trade with the peoples there, and again into northern Vietnam and Korea, extending Han rule into those areas. Along with the imposition of Han rule came the Chinese writing system and the infusion of Confucian ideology and practices.

Wang Mang and the Red Eyebrow Revolt Lasting more than 400 years, the Han era has traditionally been divided into the Former, or Western, Han (202 BCE–8 CE) and the Latter, or Eastern, Han (24–220 CE). During the brief interval between 8 and 24 CE, Han rule was temporarily interrupted when a relative of the royal family, Wang Mang (45 BCE–23 CE), seized power. Wang Mang attempted to introduce a number of reforms in land distribution in an effort to reduce the huge disparity between rich landowners and peasants, which had been inherited from the Warring States period. Wang Mang's proposed reforms provoked a revolt led by a Daoist secret society called the Red Eyebrows. The rebels killed Wang Mang and sacked the capital of Chang'an. An imperial relative restored the Han dynasty in 24 CE but moved the capital to Luoyang, where the empire continued in somewhat reduced size.

Wang Mang's attempts at land reform and the Red Eyebrow revolt hastened the collapse of the last of the old aristocratic landholdings. Together with the sense of renewal accompanying the restoration of the Han dynasty, these events helped to temporarily mask the empire's growing weakness.

Han Decline By the late second century CE the Han dynasty was showing signs of strain. Ambitious internal improvements ordered by Han emperors were carried out by *corvée* labor—labor required by the government as a form of taxation. These labor obligations made it increasingly difficult for peasants to tend their lands, and as a result agricultural productivity declined. Furthermore, the loss of some borderland territory reduced the tax base just when the empire required more taxes to maintain the Great Wall and far-flung military outposts also meant to protect the empire from nomadic invasions. Economic crises, however, were not the only threats to the empire. A series of internal battles within the royal family, aggravated by increasing regional power falling into the hands of Han generals and the rise of the Daoist Yellow Turban revolt after 184 CE, finally brought the Han dynasty to an end in 220 CE.

Between Empires Like the Romans of the late fourth century CE, who saw Germanic migrations as temporary disruptions rather than fatal blows to their empire, the Chinese expected that a new dynasty would shortly emerge after the collapse of the Han. Instead, China experienced its most chaotic postimperial political period. This interlude of turmoil is traditionally divided into the era of the Three Kingdoms (220–280 CE), the overlapping Six Dynasties period (222–589 CE), and the also overlapping period of the North and South Dynasties (317–589 CE).

From the initial Three Kingdoms period through the numerous small, weak, and short-lived "dynasties" that followed, the aim of reconstituting the empire was always present. As in so many other respects, the parallels with the problems besetting the Roman Empire at the same time were striking: The growing power of landed elites, the increasing weakness of the bureaucracy, the chronic defense problems of the north and west all continued and even multiplied. In the absence of effective centralized administration, the infrastructure fell into disrepair, the enormous internal economy grew more regionalized, external trade declined, and warfare, famine, and banditry haunted the land.

Unlike the Roman Empire, however, by the fifth century CE the rebuilding process had begun, when an eastern Mongolian people known as the Toba established the state of Northern Wei in northern China. Taking advantage of the possibilities of the new military tactics growing from the development of the stirrup, Northern Wei established itself as a dominant power in the region. By the beginning of the sixth century, the Toba had enacted a formal policy of assimilating into Chinese culture—taking

Patterns Up Close

The Stirrup

Given the long list of familiar Chinese pathbreaking technologies such as paper, the compass, printing, the horse collar, and, of course, gunpowder, it may seem strange that we would feature something as simple as the stirrup. Yet the stirrup's understated presence has long been recognized by historians as being of major importance. The reason is that it not only completely changed the way humans used horses but ushered in a new type of warfare that altered the structure of societies and dominated military strategy for 1,000 years.

Despite the fact that the horse had occupied a prominent place in Eurasian warfare for over 2,000 years, its utility had been limited to pulling chariots and supporting mounted archers and riders with light spears. The central problem of using horses in pitched battles was that the back of a horse was a precarious perch: It was difficult to mount a horse when one was weighed down with armor and weapons, but it was easy to be knocked from one, especially when one was engaged in close combat and swift maneuvering.

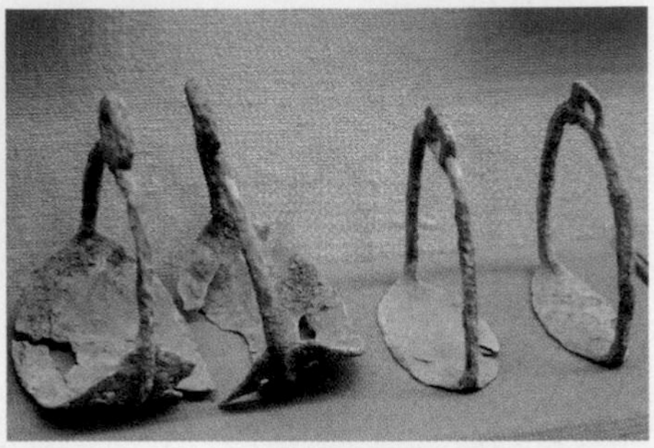

Jin Dynasty Iron Stirrups. Widespread use of the stirrup not only brought the use of cavalry back to the forefront of warfare, it led to a resurgence in power of Eurasian mounted nomadic peoples. The ornate stirrups pictured here helped the nomadic Jurchen people displace the Northern Song dynasty (see Chapter 12) and set up their own Jin dynasty, which lasted from 1127 to 1234. Their downfall was brought about by another mounted nomadic people—the Mongols—who not only displaced the Jurchens but went on to conquer the Southern Song in 1279 and incorporate their new Yuan dynasty into the short-lived Mongol super-empire spanning Eurasia in the late thirteenth and early fourteenth centuries.

Around the beginning of the Common Era the first attempts at saddles with straps for supporting a rider's feet began to appear in northern India. But these employed only a simple toe loop, and the saddle concentrated the rider's weight on a small area of the horse's back, tiring and hurting the animal. This basic idea for the stirrup, however, appears to have spread via the Silk Road, and by the early 300s CE a recognizably modern iron stirrup with a flat bottom and semicircular top began to be used in north and central China; the earliest remains discovered so far date to 302 CE. At about the same time, saddles with a rigid frame to distribute the rider's weight more evenly and better padding to cushion its effects on the horse began to be employed.

The effects of these changes were soon apparent in a China now dominated by feuding states and marauding nomads in the

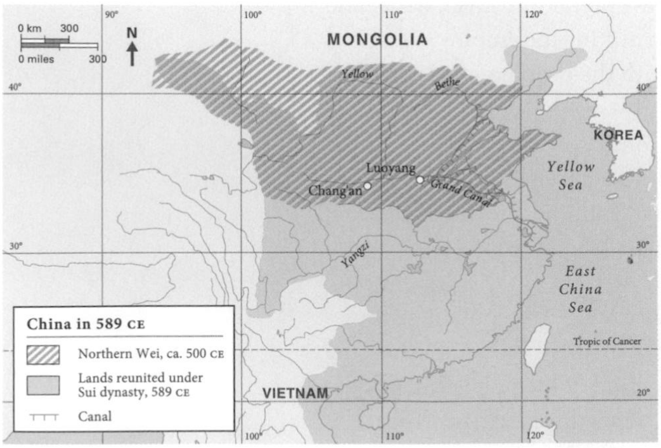

MAP 9.3 **China in 589 CE.**

Chinese names, marrying into leading families, reviving old imperial rites, and taking on the perennial problem of land reform. In organizing a program of land redistribution to the peasants, they helped pave the way for the return of centralized administration, military service, and tax collection. A Toba general named Yang Jian succeeded in uniting most of the old Han lands in 589 and called the reunified dynasty the Sui (see Map 9.3).

The Empire Reclaimed: The Sui Like the Qin before them, the forcefulness with which the Sui pursued empire building—particularly in an ill-conceived invasion of the Korean peninsula

post-Han era. With his legs secured to his mount and a high saddleback to cushion him in combat, a mounted warrior could use a long lance to charge directly into enemy formations without fear of being immediately unhorsed. Furthermore, he could wear a full complement of armor and armor his horse. The stirrup proved so effective that by the fifth century CE the armies of all the states in China had adopted and refined the technology. In China, it helped pave the way for the Sui reunification in 589.

It was in western Eurasia, however, that the new technology saw its greatest impact after its arrival in the seventh century CE. It has even been argued that the feudal society of Europe was ultimately derived from the stirrup. The ability of a heavy cavalry of armored warriors to break infantry formations and fight effectively at close quarters from horseback depended on refining armor and weapons, training warriors, and breeding bigger, faster, and stronger horses. The politically fractured eras of post-Roman and post-Carolingian Europe meant that local elites and regional strongmen had to mount their own defenses. The stirrup and the military innovations it spawned allowed them to do this without heavily equipped armies, while the expenses necessary to adopt the new technology ensured that it would remain a monopoly of the rich and powerful. Thus the relationships comprising feudalism matured as peasants placed themselves in the service of their mounted protectors. The rough parity and independence of this widely dispersed warrior elite proved a powerful obstacle to the patterns of centralized state formation and empire building. Ironically, it would be another Chinese invention that would ultimately end this way of warfare many centuries later: gunpowder.

Questions

- How does the stirrup show how a technological innovation can lead to cultural and societal adaptations across many regions and across time?
- Which environmental and geographical conditions facilitated the impact of the stirrup across Eurasia in a way that would not have been possible in the Americas?

after their ascension in 589 CE—prompted unrest among the people. The Sui used forced labor for several elaborate construction projects, including palatial palaces, roads, and perhaps the most ambitious project of all, the Grand Canal. Linking the Yangzi River with the Yellow River, the Grand Canal facilitated shipment of large quantities of rice and other food crops from the south directly to the refurbished capital at Chang'an. This was to prove a vitally important highway over the coming centuries as northern capitals increasingly depended on food supplies shipped from the south. The Grand Canal, still in operation today, would eventually be extended all the way to the Beihe River, which leads to Beijing.

The outbreak of rebellion following the death of the second Sui emperor, Yangdi, brought the precocious 16-year-old commander Li Shimin to power. Li had the Sui emperor killed, placed his own father on the throne, and announced the founding of the Tang dynasty in 618 CE. In less than a decade, he forced his father to abdicate and took power in his own right in 627 CE.

As we will see in the next part, the reconstitution of the Chinese empire under the Sui and its expansion and consolidation under the Tang not only marked a dramatic turning point in Chinese political history but also placed China among the world's regions marked by the ascendancy of religious civilizations. Like Christianity in the late Roman Empire, Buddhism made remarkable inroads in China during the period of fragmentation following the collapse of the Han. Indeed, through the work of Chinese monks it had also become firmly established in the Korean kingdoms and the Yamato state in Japan. The Tang would see the completion and high point of this process.

Buddhism and its institutions permeated Tang China to an extent never surpassed or even equaled in later dynasties. For a period in the late seventh and early eight centuries CE it even became the established Chinese state religion, under the remarkable empress Wu Zetian. In this regard, China became not only part of a giant regional religious and cultural sphere during the Tang but an important part of a new world pattern that would encompass Islamic civilization, orthodox Christianity in the eastern Roman (Byzantine) Empire and much of eastern Europe, and the Christian civilizations of Roman Catholicism and Protestantism.

The Domestic Economy: Society, Family, and Gender

Throughout Chinese history, various dynasties actively encouraged and supported agriculture as the basis of the domestic economy. Yet, from the Han dynasty on, China exported far more in luxury goods and technology than it imported. Unlike the various regimes in India, which actively sought to foster trade, the Confucian view of the pursuit of profit as corrupting meant that Chinese governments seldom encouraged merchants and generally preferred to adopt a passive, but controlling, role in trade. Although merchants were held in low esteem, the state recognized that trade was indispensable to the financial health of the empire and saw it as an expandable source of tax revenue.

Coal Mining. While the miners shore up a tunnel and gather coal into a basket lowered from above, a large bamboo pipe is thrust into the mine to draw off poisonous gases.

Industry and Commerce

Goods made in and distributed throughout the empire by the time of the Han included some of the best-known items of Chinese production. By the first century CE, Chinese manufacturers were making paper using a suspension of mashed plant fibers filtered through a fine-mesh screen and set aside to dry, a method still considered to produce the highest-quality product for painting or literary work.

Perhaps even more impressive, by this time artisans were also producing a kind of "proto-porcelain" that, with increasing refinement, would be known in the succeeding centuries to the outside world as "china." The earthenware produced during the Tang dynasty is among the most coveted in the world today. In other arts, the use of lacquer as a finish, as well as in artwork created by sculpting built-up layers of it, was also well established. By the second century CE, the Chinese had perfected silk production and had become world leaders in textile weaving. Both treadle- and water-powered looms were in widespread use, and bolts of silk with standardized designs were produced for export. The Chinese supply of silks could barely keep pace with demand, especially from Persia and Rome. But much of the most important domestic production centered on bulk strategic goods that sparked some of the world's first debates on the government's role in the economy.

Iron and Salt By the Han period, the Chinese were producing cast iron in huge foundries. According to one estimate, by 2 CE, there were no fewer than 48 major ironworks in north China, while the mining industry as a whole may have employed as many as 100,000 people. The foundries, which produced ingots of standardized sizes and weights, used sophisticated systems of forced-air control, including water-powered bellows. Salt mines employed complex gearing for lifting brine from deep wells, systems of bamboo piping for transferring it, and evaporators fired by natural gas for extracting the salt. Because of the enormous productivity of the iron-making and salt-mining industries, the government continually sought ways to regulate and control them.

Despite the increasing importance of industry and commerce to the imperial economy, the Han and succeeding dynasties continued to view merchants as a parasitic class, with no ties to the idealized relationships of agrarian life. Trade was thus a necessary evil. Nevertheless, government programs aimed at improving the empire's infrastructure facilitated commerce. The unpredictable flow of China's rivers required dikes, dredging, reservoirs, and especially canals to ease transportation. Along with roads, canals grew in importance as the empire relied more and more on the produce of the rich lands of the south to supply the capitals of the north. The Han emperor Wudi, as we have seen, began work on the Grand Canal that linked the Yangzi and the Yellow Rivers (see Map 9.4).

Land Reform By the time of the late Han, China's old aristocracy had largely died out, its place at the top of the social hierarchy assumed by the so-called *scholar-gentry*—the educated large landholders who constituted the Confucian bureaucracy. Despite the elimination of the old aristocracy, landlord holdings continued to expand. Since the upper ranks of the landowners and bureaucrats either were exempt from taxes or paid reduced amounts, the tax burden fell increasingly on tenants and owners of small parcels of land. Poor harvests or bad weather, particularly in the arid north and west, made the situation even worse for those already heavily taxed. Because the north, despite its elaborate irrigation works, was far less productive and more prone to crop failure than the south, it was also proportionally more heavily taxed.

Such problems made land reform and redistribution an ongoing concern. The Tang, for example, continued the policy of land redistribution begun during the brief Sui dynasty by allotting each peasant family a tract of 100 *mou*, one-fifth of which was inheritable, while the remainder reverted to the state for redistribution. Although the Tang land redistribution policy resulted in a relatively high level of prosperity, absentee landlordism, tenancy, and **usury** also rose again, particularly during times of economic stress. The continual problem of land tenure and attempts at reform and redistribution marked every dynasty and modern government down to the People's Republic—where it is even today a major concern.

Usury: The charging of interest on loans, usually on excessive ("usurious") terms.

Agricultural Productivity A number of technical and systemic innovations steadily increased agricultural productivity. In addition to such staples as wheat,

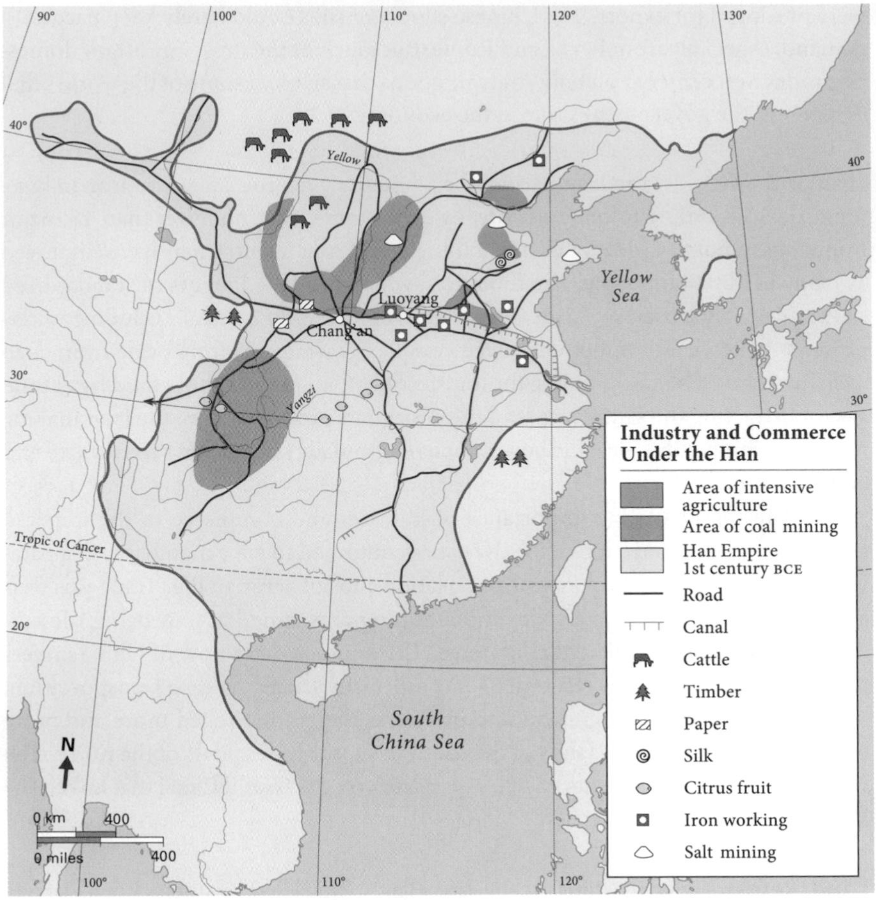

MAP 9.4 Industry and Commerce under the Han.

millet, and barley in the north and rice in the south, a wide variety of semitropical fruits and vegetables were cultivated within the empire. New strains of rice resulted in larger harvests on more marginal land. Trade with central Asia had introduced wine grapes, and the production of fermented grain beverages had become a substantial industry. New techniques of crop rotation, fertilization, and plowing were gradually introduced, as were the collar for draft animals and the wheelbarrow; oxen-drawn, iron-tipped plows; treadle hammers; undershot, overshot, and other types of waterwheels; the foot-powered "dragon" chain pump for irrigation; and the *fengche*—a hand-cranked winnowing machine with an internal fan to blow the chaff from the grain. With this basic, reliable technology, China led the world in agricultural productivity until the eighteenth century CE.

The Silk Road The dramatic expansion of maritime and caravan trade from the seventh century CE on, particularly within the huge Buddhist cultural sphere, spread Chinese technology abroad and brought new products into the Chinese empire. During the first millennium and a half of its history, China made numerous connections throughout the world and spread its influence in all directions. Early examples of silk appear to have reached the Mediterranean and North Africa through a long train of middlemen as early as the first millennium BCE. By the first century BCE, a variety of artifacts clearly identifiable as Chinese had turned up in Egypt; by the fourth and fifth centuries CE, Indian and Persian middlemen extended the Chinese trade to the African empires of Kush and Aksum.

The principal route connecting the Chinese to the various trading centers of central Asia, and ultimately to the Mediterranean and Rome, was known as the **Silk Road**. Along this route, the Chinese would forever be identified with silk; and though they tried to guard the secrets of its production, the demand was so high that many peoples along the caravan routes were soon engaged in making silk themselves. The techniques of raising silkworms and weaving silk reached the eastern Mediterranean between the third and fifth centuries CE. Competition among producers and merchants in western Eurasia became so keen that the Roman emperor Justinian allied with the African kingdom of Aksum in the sixth century CE to contest growing Persian dominance of the trade in fine silks. In the process, the Romans created their own silk monopoly to service the western trade.

Silk Road: Overland trade routes that connected eastern and western Eurasia, beginning at the end of the fourth century BCE.

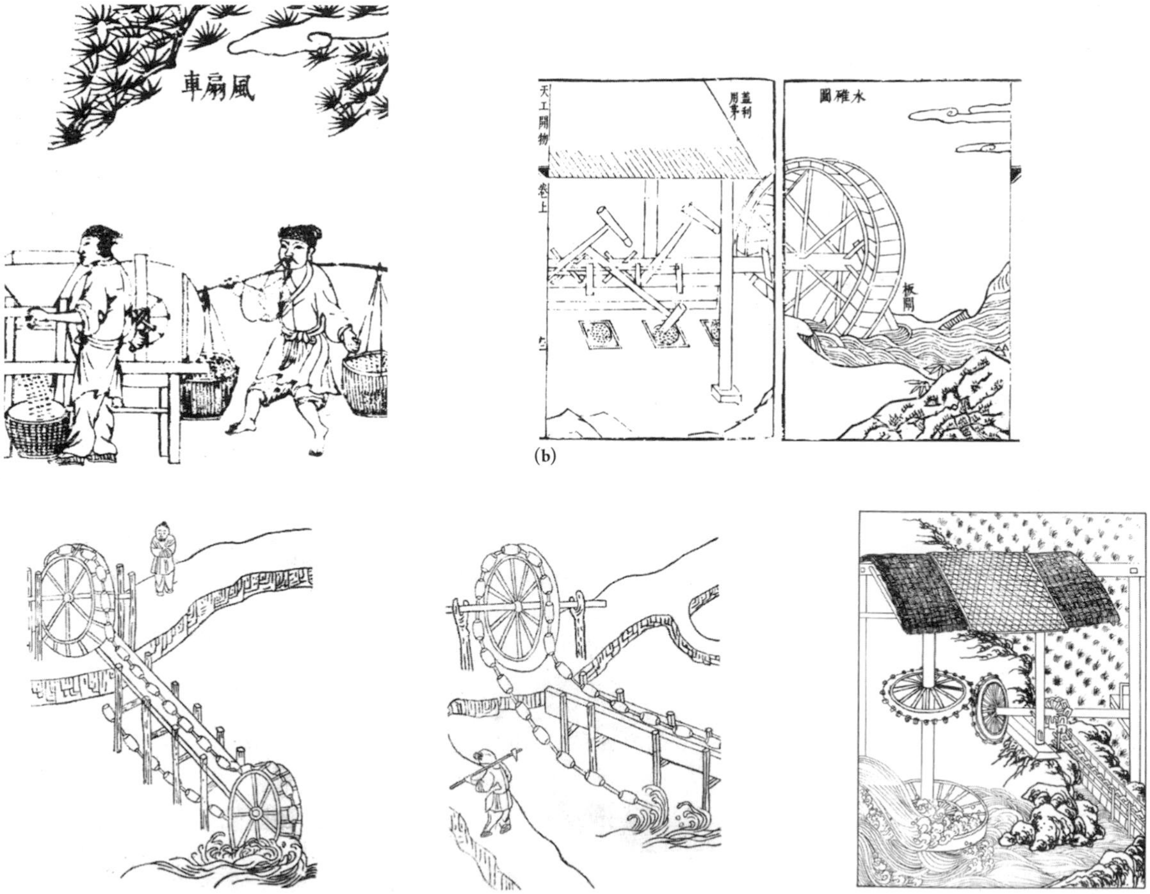

(a) (b) (c)

Han-Era Technology. By the first century CE, Chinese sophistication in crafts and labor-saving devices could be seen in a number of areas. While the illustrations here are from the famous seventeenth-century compendium of technology *Tiangong kaiwu (The Works of Nature and Man)*, all of them illustrate techniques in use during the Han period: fengche winnowing machine (*a*); undershot waterwheel driving hammers in a pounding mill (*b*); vertical and horizontal waterwheels driving chain-bucket "dragon pumps" for irrigation (*c*) .

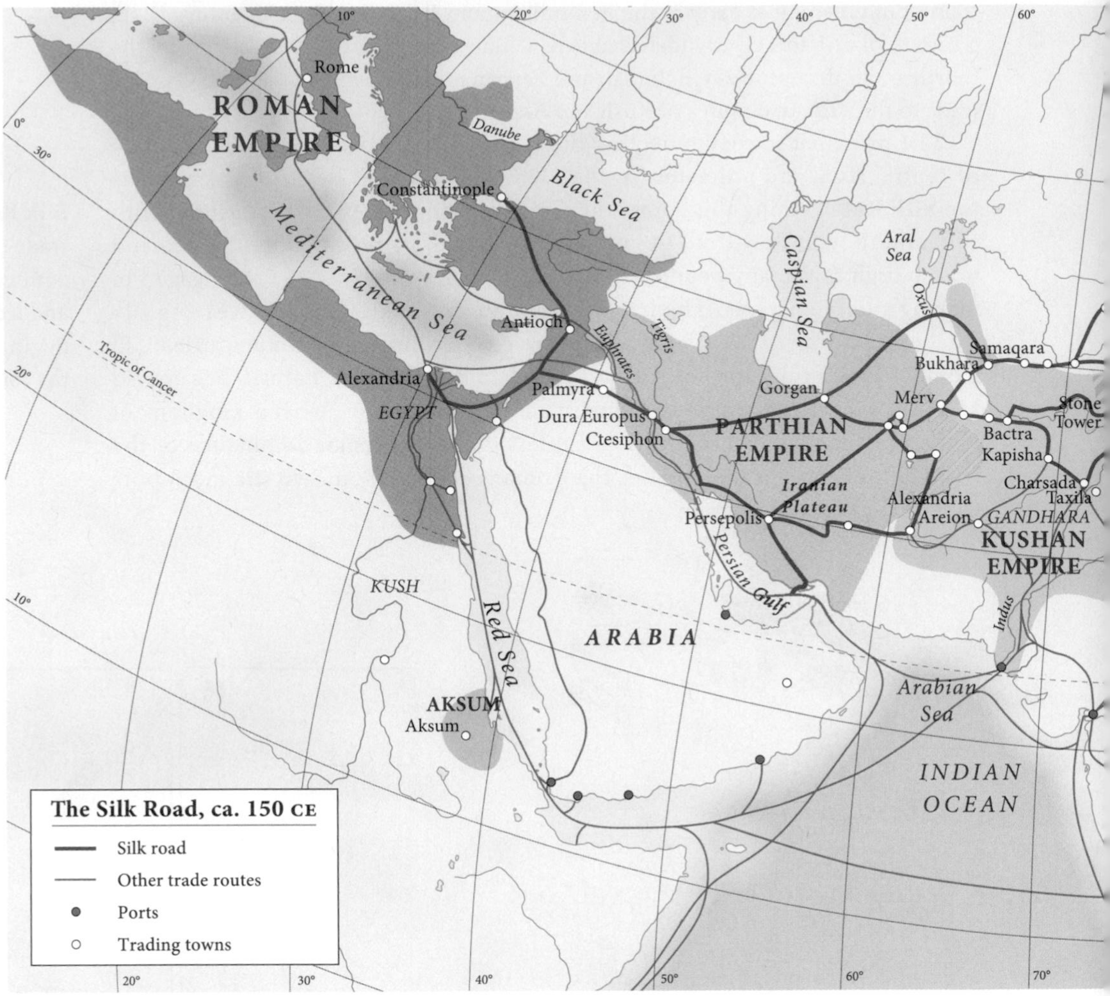

MAP 9.5 **The Silk Road, ca. 150 CE.**

Gender Roles

Women in imperial China, as in agrarian-based societies in general, were subordinate to men. Early Confucian works, while emphasizing reciprocal responsibilities within the family, were relatively flexible about the position of women. However, with the rise of the imperial bureaucracy during the Han and the increasing emphasis on filial piety within its new Confucian curriculum, a more rigidly hierarchical, patriarchal model of proper women's behavior gradually developed. At the same time, the emphasis on sons within the extended family as carriers of the ancestral line and their potential to win admission to official state service led to a gradual devaluing of daughters. In times of severe economic stress, when families had difficulty supporting several children, young girls were the first to suffer. Families, especially in rural areas, would sometimes sell their daughters into prostitution or kill female infants. By the Song era (960–1279 CE) problems relating to the treatment of young girls had become so acute that China's first foundling hospitals were opened in 1138.

Although some elite women achieved prominence in intellectual pursuits, like the historian Ban Zhao (48–116 CE), women's education centered primarily on

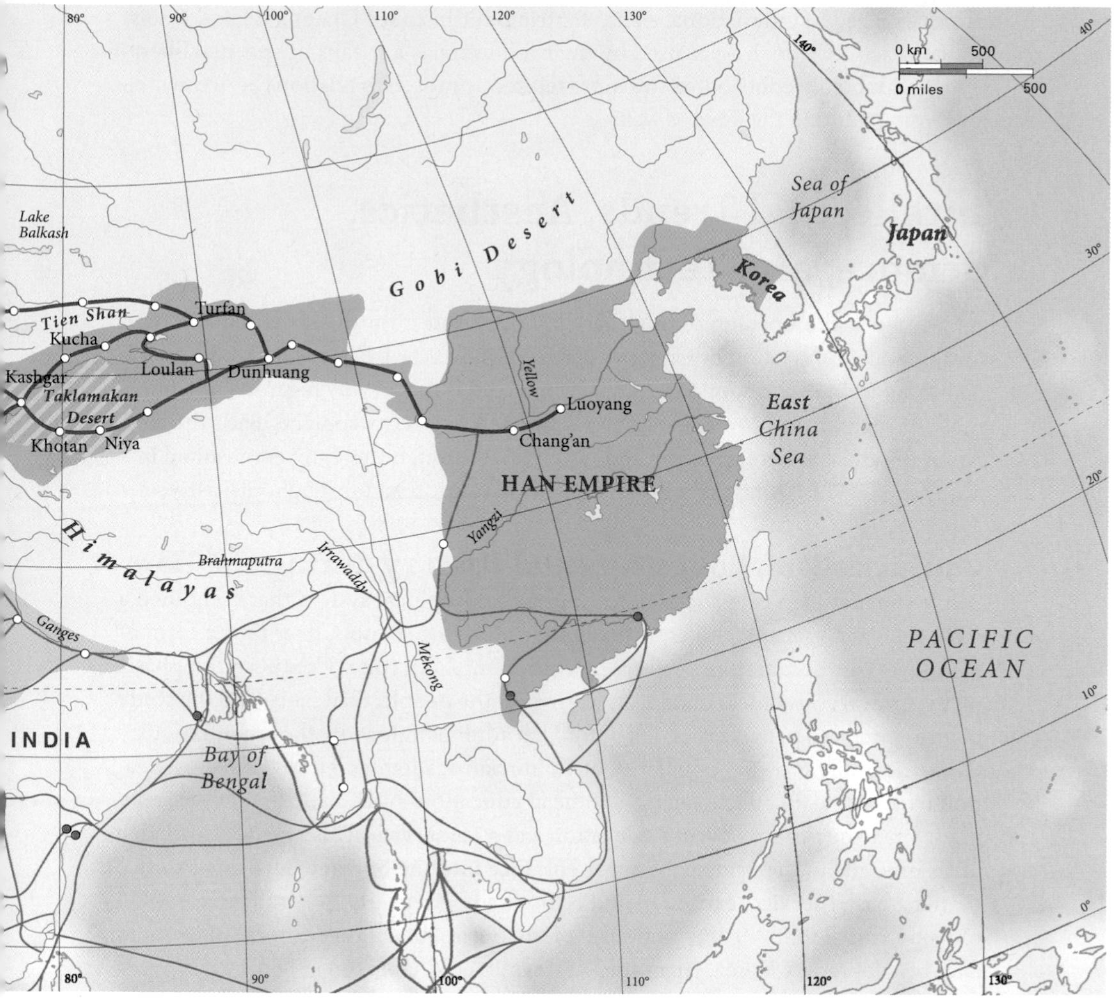

map analysis

cultivating the domestic virtues of devotion and obedience, as well as mastering crafts such as spinning and weaving. Daughters were expendable in the sense that they would marry or be placed with another family through adoption or servitude. Since these last options often brought advantages to the girl's family, daughters were frequently educated in singing, playing instruments, and chanting poetry, in order to make them desirable candidates for placement. Yet, in theory at least, there was always supposed to be an element of complementarity and reciprocity between men and women, especially husband and wife.

From the fifth century CE on, the popularity of monastic Buddhism created attractive alternatives for those fleeing family pressures, especially women. Those women enrolled in Buddhist schools that required extensive scriptural study became highly educated, and the communities themselves, like Christian monasteries in Europe, often owned large tracts of land and wielded considerable local influence. At the same time, the relative strictness of the practices regulating sexual and family life varied, particularly among high officials and the growing urban commercial classes. Foreign influences and fashions also affected behavior, particularly in Chang'an and places engaged in international trade. Tantric Buddhist (see Chapter 8) and Daoist sexual practices, which were used by their followers as a means of spiritual liberation, undoubtedly contributed to a more relaxed approach to relations between men and women during the Tang as well.

Intellectual Trends, Aesthetics, Science, and Technology

As we saw in the opening of this chapter, the period from the sixth century BCE until the first unification of China under the Qin in 221 BCE was marked by a dynamic collision of economic and social forces and is universally regarded as China's most fertile period of intellectual exploration. Long-term contacts with the East Asian Buddhist sphere from the end of the Han through the Tang era resulted in a number of new Buddhist schools being founded and spread throughout East Asia.

Confucianism, Education, and History during the Han

While the first Han rulers tended to favor a philosophical system that combined a more lenient Legalism with aspects of other surviving schools, over time a form of Confucianism became the preferred governmental doctrine. Confucian emphasis on the ethical correctness of officials, caring for the people, filial piety, and the study of history tended to make it a good fit for Han administrators. By the second century CE, the steadily growing popularity of Confucian academies led to their subsidization by the state, in effect placing all official education in the hands of these academies. Since the purpose of such education was state service, it also made knowledge of Confucianism the principal test for entrance into the bureaucracy. This practice of merit-based service, expanded and elaborated over nearly two millennia, would remain in force until the opening years of the twentieth century. A form of it would later be adopted by Korea, Japan, and Vietnam (see Chapter 13).

The Han Confucian Synthesis? Although Confucianism served as the foundation for the Han educational curriculum, Confucian doctrine had changed somewhat from the early teachings of Confucius and his disciples. During the Warring States period and the era of Qin rule, much Confucian thought—along with that of other philosophical schools—had been altered to suit the times, while a great many texts had been lost along the way. Thus, the Confucianism that finally received state approval included a number of elements reflecting the new realities of the Han dynasty. So many other elements from the fragments of philosophical tradition that had survived the Qin period went into government theory and practice that scholars have come to question the long-accepted perception of a straightforward "Han Synthesis."

This diverse blending of political, ethical, and cosmological thought is evident in the era's chief treatise on government, the *Huainan zi*. In this document, a number of Confucian ideals, rooted in humane, righteous, and filial behavior by the powerful, are linked with Daoist ideas of the ruler as divorced from day-to-day administration and Legalist notions on the role of officials. As the intermediary between heaven, humankind, and earth, the emperor occupied a position of cosmological significance by nourishing the people and holding all in balance. For continuity's sake, a dynasty had to be hereditary—in contradiction to Confucius's ideas. Hence, acceptance of a hereditary imperial line strengthened the emphasis on the notion of filial piety as a central virtue. Indeed, a short work that achieved widespread use as a first reader because of its basic ideas and limited vocabulary was the *Xiaojing*, the *Classic of Filial Piety*. At the same time the idea of dynastic cycles and the Mandate of Heaven became even stronger during this period as they were elaborated by the great Han historians.

Han Historians As we saw in Chapter 4, while there had been no shortage of history writing in the late Zhou period, much of it was seen even by contemporaries as overly partisan, fanciful, or tied to teaching moral lessons at the expense of accuracy. Mencius, for example, doubted the truthfulness of most of *The Book of History*. By the Han period, with the ideal of empire now encouraging a new sense of cultural unity, a series of court historians attempted to collate historical materials that had survived the Qin purges and to unify and systematize the writing of history.

For these men and women, the purpose of history writing, much as it was for the great Greek historians Herodotus (ca. 484–425 BCE) and Thucydides (ca. 460–ca. 395 BCE), was the accurate transmission of information—often with verbatim copies of important documents—and analysis of the events portrayed in terms of a larger vision of the direction and purpose of human history. For the Han historians, as for Chinese historians throughout the imperial era, history was cyclical: Human events, as manifestations of the great universal cycles of being, are a constant succession of birth, growth, decay, death, and rebirth, in which older ideas of the Mandate of Heaven, dynastic cycles, and yin and yang theory are imbedded. The moral lessons learned are therefore tied to actions taken at various stages of these cycles.

The basic format of long-term history was laid out by the father-and-son team of Sima Tan (d. 110 BCE) and Sima Qian (145–86 BCE). Their *Shiji* (*The Records of the Grand Historian*) attempts the first complete history of the Chinese people from the mythical Yellow Emperor to their own time. One particularly valuable section that became a staple of later histories was a survey of non-Chinese peoples encountered along with their habits, customs, religions, geography, and other significant traits. Hence, the Han records give us our first written accounts of Japan and other places on the Chinese periphery.

Like other Chinese officials, the historians took their role of "conscience" of the government seriously, sometimes at severe peril to themselves. As historian to the powerful Emperor Wudi, for example, Sima Qian offended the ruler by exonerating a general in his writings whom the emperor and court had accused of cowardice. Given the choice between execution and castration, Sima chose the latter; if he were dead, he explained, he could not finish his history, which he believed was his highest duty.

Several generations later, the Ban family comprised another dynasty of Han court historians. Writing after the Wang Mang interval, Ban Biao (3–54 CE) and his son Ban Gu (32–92 CE) pioneered the writing of dynastic history with their *Hanshu* (*The History of the Former Han*), which laid out the format followed by all subsequent dynastic histories. Ban Gu's daughters were also scholars and writers, and his sister Ban Zhao (48–116 CE) carried on the family tradition of history writing as well as a treatise on proper women's behavior, *Admonitions for Women*.

Interestingly, accounts of the historians' activities themselves may be found in the *Hou Hanshu* (*The History of the Latter Han*), written after the fall of the dynasty by Fan Ye (398–446 CE).

Buddhism in China

The growth of Buddhism as a universal missionary religion came, at least in part, from the adaptability of its doctrines to widely diverse peoples and belief systems. As we saw in Chapter 8, by the mid-first century CE, when it is first mentioned in Chinese accounts, Buddhism had already split into the major divisions of Theravada (Hinayana), which had established itself in southern India and Sri Lanka and was moving into Southeast Asia, and Mahayana, which would be established in China, Korea, Vietnam, and Japan.

Bodhisattva Guanyin, Sixth Century CE. Originally incorporating aspects of both genders, Guanyin (also spelled Kuan-yin) came to be depicted as female as Buddhism became firmly established in China. For Pure Land adherents, she was the bodhisattva invoked in times of extreme peril, and "the miracles of Guanyin" (*Kannon* in Japan) was a favorite theme of both Chinese and Japanese artists.

The introduction of Mahayana Buddhism into China presents a number of interesting parallels with that of Christianity into Rome, though there are important differences as well. Rather than focusing on the problems of practical government, both religions emphasized instead personal enlightenment or salvation. Both, to some extent, were initially seen as "foreign" systems and subjected to periodic persecution before emerging triumphant. Finally, while both challenged existing political and social hierarchies, the institutions of both were also adopted by rulers who wanted to strengthen or expand their power.

Language and Scripture The incompatibility of the Chinese written language with Sanskrit and Pali scriptures complicated the introduction of Buddhism to China. The earliest Buddhist missionaries had to rely heavily on transliterations, borrow extensively from Daoist terminology, and invent a new and diverse vocabulary of Chinese terms. Over the next several centuries, this eclecticism resulted in a proliferation of sects and a growing need on the part of Chinese and, later, Korean, Japanese, and Vietnamese converts to travel to India for study and guidance. The travel account of the Chinese monk and early pilgrim Fa Xian (see Chapter 8), who journeyed throughout central Asia and India from 399 to 414 CE in search of Pali copies of Buddhist works, contributed greatly to Chinese understanding of the growing Buddhist world. The most famous pilgrim, Xuan Zang (596–664 CE), went to India in 623 CE and brought back the extensive collection of scriptures still housed in the monastery he founded just outside Xi'an. His travels were later immortalized in the popular collection of fabulous tales called *A Journey to the West.*

Buddhist Schools The period between the dissolution of the Han and the ascendancy of the Tang was also marked by the founding of several of the most important schools of East Asian Buddhism. By the fifth century, the school of popular devotion to Amida, the Buddha of the Pure Land, was spreading rapidly in China. Like in the *bhakti* sects in India, no immersion in the texts is necessary for enlightenment for Pure Land followers; merely invoking Amida's name is sufficient for salvation. Even today, it remains the most popular Buddhist sect in both China and Japan. Amida is often pictured with the bodhisattva Guanyin—*Kannon* in Japan—the Goddess of Mercy who, like the Virgin Mary in Catholicism, is frequently invoked during times of peril.

Another influential Buddhist school was Tiantai, centered on the scripture of the *Lotus Sutra*. Tiantai emphasized contemplation of the sutras (Buddhist scriptures) as the vehicle to enlightenment and later inspired several schools of esoteric (see Chapter 8) paths to enlightenment. These schools exercised considerable influence over both the Tang and the Japanese court at Heian during the eighth and ninth centuries CE.

Finally, one school that later achieved fame, if not widespread popularity, was Chan Buddhism, better known by the name given it in Japan: Zen. As outlined in its central text, *The Platform of the Sixth Patriarch*, by Hui Neng (638–713 CE), enlightenment is transmitted not through scriptural study or personal devotion to a particular figure but rather through the discipline of meditation and the active example of a master. The intense give-and-take between master and pupil, the discipline involved in performing humble tasks, and the contemplation of paradoxical questions are all meant ultimately to generate an intuitive flash of enlightenment. While limited in its influence in China, the emphasis on discipline and obedience made Zen the preferred Buddhist school of Japan's warrior aristocracy after the twelfth century CE.

Intellectual Life

To a considerable degree, Chinese concepts of **aesthetics** that developed during the first millennium CE became the founding principles for the arts throughout East Asia. The most important developments during this period were the maturation of three disciplines: poetry, painting, and calligraphy. An important part of a well-rounded education even today, these three disciplines are considered to be closely interrelated and governed by the same overriding principles. Central to each discipline is the idea of spontaneous creation as a reflection of the inner state of the artist. The artist in each of these media seeks to connect with the Dao by indirectly suggesting some aspect of it in the work itself. For example, Chinese landscape paintings often feature misty mountains, lone pines, and tiny human figures, with the action and occasion implied rather than detailed, because too much detail would place limits on the illimitable.

Aesthetics: The study of the beautiful; the branches of learning dealing with categorizing and analyzing beauty.

The Sciences Because the imperial establishment relied on the prediction of comets, eclipses, and other omens to monitor the will of heaven, astronomy and mathematics were especially important disciplines. Chinese mathematicians had long used a decimal system and had worked out formulas and proofs to figure the areas of most standard geometric forms. They had also calculated pi to four places and were able to solve simultaneous algebraic equations. The astronomers Zhang Heng (78–139 CE) and Wang Chong (27–100) had each championed theories of a universe governed by comprehendible natural forces. Zhang built a water-powered *armillary sphere*—a hollow globe surrounded by bronze bands, representing the paths of the sun, stars, and planets—and, in 134 CE, devised what was perhaps the world's first practical earthquake detector.

Printing and Proto-Porcelain One of the signal innovations of Eurasia was printing. Believed to have their origins in the ancient practice of making rubbings on paper or silk of gravestone inscriptions, woodblock prints of popular Buddhist works had become available in major Chinese cities by the eighth century CE.

Earthquake Detector. One of the more ingenious pieces of high technology to come out of the Han period was a working earthquake detector created by Zhang Heng (78–139 CE) in 134 CE. In the model illustrated here, carefully balanced balls were placed inside the large, hollow vessel. A tremor coming from a particular direction would jar the ball closest to the direction of the quake loose and send it down a track where it would fly from from one of the ornate openings and fall into the yawning mouth of the frog underneath. Thus, anyone checking the device could tell at a glance that a quake had occurred and from what direction by seeing which frog held a ball.

By the end of the Tang and the beginning of the Song dynasties, presses employing both carved block and movable copper type were in regular use in China, Korea, and Japan. As it would later in Europe, the innovation of printing dramatically raised the literacy rates in all the areas it touched. By the beginning of the Song era, China had some of the highest preindustrial literacy rates achieved in human history—despite the difficulties of the written language.

The techniques involved in generating the extremely high temperatures required for casting iron were also transferable to porcelain production. Though there is debate about when the breakthroughs resulting in true porcelain first occurred, by the Tang period distinctive brown and green glazed figures, often depicting the vibrant parade of peoples and animals of the caravan trade, were widely exchanged. By the Song, delicate white, crackled glaze and sea-green celadon ware were produced and sought by connoisseurs as the height of aesthetic refinement. Today, such pieces are considered to be among the world's great art treasures.

Putting It All Together

interactive concept map

The political and social turmoil of the late Zhou era also marked an enormously innovative period in Chinese intellectual and cultural history. During this era the most important schools of Chinese thought and philosophy developed: Confucianism, Daoism, and Legalism. While Confucianism ultimately triumphed as the ideology of imperial China, it was the Legalist state of Qin that created the empire itself.

When the Qin dynasty fell in 206 BCE, much of the infrastructure of the early empire, including the Great Wall, was in place. The Han dynasty, from 202 BCE to 220 CE, retained the administrative structure of the Qin but softened the harsh laws and punishments of the Legalists. Eventually, the form of Confucianism practiced by the empire's administrators was taught in the imperial schools, becoming in effect the imperial ideology. By the end of the Han, China had created a solid alliance between the state and this all-encompassing ethical and legal system.

Perhaps more important than even the structures themselves, however, was that, like the Egyptians and Romans, the Chinese had become accustomed to what has been called the "habit of empire." As suggested in this chapter, 400 years of unity under the Qin and the Han had conditioned the Chinese to believe that empire was the natural goal of the patterns of political formation in China and that any interruptions in these patterns would be but brief interludes in the dynastic cycle. Thus, Chinese history has been marked by rhythms of inwardness and outwardness, inner renewal and usurpation of rule from the outside. Along with these rhythms came an inherited belief, reinforced by the theories of dynastic historians, that human society and the cosmos were knit together in a moral order, made perfectible by the power of the empire and the dedication of a bureaucracy selected for its understanding of ethics in human affairs. Throughout the imperial era—and even in our own time—the students and scholars of China have tried to keep faith with this heritage by guiding and remonstrating with those in power.

Review and Relate

Thinking Through Patterns

Examine the ways historians approach the big questions of this chapter.

» Was the First Emperor's ruthlessness justified by his accomplishments in his empire?

Addressing this question raises a very basic problem: Why do we study history? In ancient times, most people studied history for the moral lessons it offered and to avoid making the same mistakes their ancestors did. As we have also seen, some cultures, like the Chinese, studied it in hopes of grasping its basic patterns so as to understand the present and anticipate the future. Modern historians have generally taken their cue from Leopold von Ranke (1795–1886), who felt that scholars should rise above preconceived ideas and simply seek the past "as it really was." For most of the twentieth century, historians have sought to avoid making moral judgments about the past, to see their job as being detectives rather than judges. By that standard, the historian should empathetically enter the past and seek to understand it; to judge it by the standards of the present is to be "presentist." But how does one deal with such things as genocide, extreme cruelty, or slavery? Thus, one way out of this dilemma might be to weigh the actions of the First Emperor against the standards of morality current in *his* day. Yet here, too, we encounter a problem: There were so many new schools of thought emerging in China then that no single one dominated; moreover, the First Emperor himself created his own system of morality based on Legalism. Perhaps, then, the best that we can do at this point, aside from judging him privately by our personal standards, is to note that he set the fundamental pattern for Chinese imperial government for the next 2,000 years—but at considerable cost.

» How would you compare the values expressed by Confucius and Mencius to those of contemporary society?

Perhaps the biggest difference between Confucian society and modern American society is in the way both see the ideal forms of societal relations. Americans see the individual, the rule of law, democracy, and equality as fundamental to a good society. The purpose of government is to allow people to do as they wish while stipulating the limits within which they can do so. Confucian concepts of government and society put a premium on holism, hierarchy, and harmony. People are not seen as mere individuals but as part of larger patterns: family, clan, village, society, state. These are seen as part of a hierarchy that stretches from the poorest peasant to the emperor himself. Reciprocal rights and responsibilities are present at every level for protection of the weak, but equality is not seen as important. The role of government itself is seen in large part as being to provide a moral example to the people. If it teaches them well through regulations, customs, and ritual, then the people aspire to be good and will police themselves to a great extent.

How have historians viewed the role of women in early imperial China?

One of the most unattractive things about imperial China to the majority of us today is that it often appears that women were held in low regard, abused, denied basic human rights, and even tortured for fashion's sake, as with foot binding. The Confucian emphasis on hierarchy within society and the family tends to reinforce this impression. But scholars have in recent years begun to study the role of women at different times and in different regions of China, and the picture now appears much more complex than before. While scholars agree that in some respects, particularly foot binding from the Song period on, women's roles deteriorated, there were also times when the evidence suggests they exercised considerable freedom and influence, such as during the Tang and early Song periods. The pattern of "inner" and "outer" as it governed the traditional Chinese family is still discernible in many Chinese households today: While husbands go off to work, women definitely hold sway within the "inner" realm of the house.

Against the Grain

Consider this as a counterpoint to the main patterns examined in this chapter.

Yang Zhu and Mo Di

- The appearance of visionary thinkers appears to have been an extraordinarily widespread phenomenon. Why were the times of great turmoil in these societies such fertile ones for new ideas?
- What ideas in other cultures seem to be like those of Yang and Mo? How do they also differ? Do they spring from similar conditions?

The ideas that appeared during the period of the "hundred schools" of thought spread across an extraordinarily wide intellectual continuum, from the deceptively passive mysticism of the Daoists to the totalitarian ambitions of the Legalists. At its height, however, during the time of the Confucian thinker Mencius (385–312), the two schools of thought that he and his disciples considered most influential and dangerous were another exercise in extremes: the radical individualism of Yang Zhu and the advocacy of universal love of Mo Di (often spelled Mozi).

Yang Zhu taught that since life was short and death inevitable, people should take what enjoyment they can while they can. After all, he said, the four great sages (including Confucius) "during their life had not a single day's joy. Since their death they have had grand fame that will last through the ages. . . . Celebrate them—they do not know it; reward them—they do not know it. Their fame is no more to them than the trunk of a tree or a clod of earth." Moreover, the most infamous villains who enjoyed vast wealth and lusts and pleasures went smiling to their graves, caring not at all in death about their ill fame. So one should seize the day and take what enjoyment from it that one can.

Mo Di, on the other hand, taught that the only truly humane way to approach the world was to love all people equally. Everyone has a father and a mother; thus all should be regarded as one would regard one's own family. To do otherwise is to be overly partisan in one's duties to society. The followers of Mo put these ideas into action during the Warring States period by volunteering to help the inhabitants of besieged cities defend themselves.

For Mencius, the era was defined by "lords becom[ing] arbitrary and intemperate, and unemployed scholars [indulging] in uninhibited discussion. The words of Yang Zhu and Mo Di overflow the world; the world's words all go back if not to Yang then to Mo. Yang holds for egoism, which involves denial of one's sovereign; Mo holds for universal love, which entails denial of one's parents. To deny one's sovereign or one's parents is to be an animal."

In the end, the extremes of both systems would undoubtedly have made them unworkable, especially that of Yang, with its complete abandonment of altruism. That of Confucius, with its emphasis on family relationships and duties at the micro and macro levels, was ultimately more in harmony with Chinese society—so much so that it continues to shape that society at its deepest levels even today.

Key Terms

audio flashcards

Aesthetics 265
Commanderies 251
Headmen 251
Junzi 245
Reciprocity 244
Silk Road 259
Sinicizing 252
Usury 257

For additional resources, please go to **www.oup.com/us/vonsivers.**
Please see the Further Resources section at the back of the book for additional readings and suggested websites.

PATTERNS OF EVIDENCE |

Sources for Chapter 9

SOURCE 9.1 *Analects (Lunyu)* of Confucius

ca. 500–479 BCE

The details of Confucius's life are murky, especially given the chaos surrounding the declining Zhou period in the 490s and 480s BCE. It is important to take into account the impact of interstate conflict on Confucius's philosophical insights. A commoner who was effectively shut out of power by the three noble clans of Lu, Confucius was eventually driven out and forced to wander among the other states, because of the resentment of this traditional aristocracy. Despite the resistance of warring aristocrats, Confucius advocated a new approach to government, in which respect for the weak, poor, and defenseless would form the basis for civil society.

[12.7] Zigong asked about government. The Master [Confucius] said, "Sufficient food, sufficient arms, and popular trust [in the ruler]."

Zigong said, "If this were impossible, and we would have to dispense with one of these three, which should come first?"

[Confucius] said, "Dispense with arms."

Zigong said, "If this were impossible, and we would have to dispense with one of these two, which should come first?"

[Confucius] said, "Dispense with food. Since antiquity, there has always been death. But people without trust have no standing."

[12.11] Lord Jing of Qi asked Confucius about government. Confucius answered, "The lord acts as a lord, the minister as a minister, the father as a father, the son as a son."

The lord said, "Excellent! Surely, if the lord does not act as a lord, nor the minister as a minister, nor the father as a father, nor the son as a son, then although I might have grain, would I be able to eat it?"

[12.13] The Master said, "In hearing litigation, I am like other people. What is necessary is to cause there to be no litigation."

Source: Victor H. Mair, Nancy Shatzman Steinhardt, and Paul R. Goldin, eds., *Hawai'i Reader in Traditional Chinese Culture* (Honolulu: University of Hawai'i Press, 2005), 48–49.

[12.17] Ji Kangzi asked Confucius about government. Confucius answered, "To govern is to correct. If you lead with rectitude, who will dare not be correct?"

[12.18] Ji Kangzi was vexed at the thieving [in his state] and asked Confucius about it. Confucius answered, "If you, sir, were not covetous, then even if you were to reward them for it, they would not steal."

[13.3] Zilu said, "The Lord of Wei is waiting for you to effect government. What will you do first?"

The Master said, "What is necessary is to rectify names!"

Zilu said, "Is there such a thing? Master, you are wide of the mark. Why such rectification?"

The Master said, "You, you are uncouth. A noble man should appear more reserved about what he does not know. If names are not rectified, then speech does not flow properly. If speech does not flow properly, then affairs are not completed. If affairs are not completed, then ritual and music do not flourish. If ritual and music do not flourish, then punishments and penalties do not hit the mark. If punishments and penalties do not hit the mark, the people have no way to move hand or foot. Thus, for the noble man, names must be able to be spoken, and what he speaks must be able to be carried out. With regard to his speech, the noble man's [concern] is simply that there be nothing that is careless."

[13.10] The Master said, "If there were one [among the princes] who would make use of me, within no more than twelve months, [the government] would be acceptable. Within three years there would be success."

≫ Working with Sources

1. To what extent did Confucius expect to be consulted by the leaders of the various states?

2. What does he seem to have envisioned as the ultimate basis of proper government?

SOURCE 9.2 *Book of Mencius* (Mengzi)

ca. 310–289 BCE

A later student of Confucian doctrine, Master Meng (ca. 385–289 BCE) spread the teachings of the master, while also making his own distinctive contributions. Having traveled throughout China spreading Confucian

Source: Victor H. Mair, Nancy Shatzman Steinhardt, and Paul R. Goldin, eds., *Hawai'i Reader in Traditional Chinese Culture* (Honolulu: University of Hawai'i Press, 2005), 60–61.

ideals, particularly as a basis for governmental practice, Mencius composed a book that was in more of a narrative form than the *Analects* and was supplemented by stories, parables, and debates. He often used imagery drawn from the natural world and advocated the rulers' involvement in cultivating a "well-field" system, both literally and metaphorically.

[6A.2.] Master Gao said, "Human *xing* [nature] is like a torrent of water. If you clear a passage for it to the east, it will flow to the east; if you clear a passage for it to the west, it will flow to the west. Human *xing* is not divided into good or not good, just as water is not divided into east and west."

Mencius said, "Water is indeed not divided into east and west, but is it not divided into higher and lower? The goodness of human *xing* is like water's tendency to go downward. There is no person without goodness; there is no water that does not go downward. Now as for water, if you strike it and make it leap up, you can cause it to pass over your forehead; if you dam it and make it move [in a certain direction], you can cause it to stay on a mountain. Is this the *xing* of the water? Or is it force that makes it so? When people are caused to become bad, their *xing* is also like this."

[6A.8.] Mencius said, "The trees of Ox Mountain were once beautiful. Because it was in the suburbs of a great city, with axes and hatchets chopping at it, could it remain beautiful? With the respite that [the mountain] was afforded by the nights, and the moisture of the rain and dew, it was not without buds and sprouts that grew on it; but then the cattle and goats came to pasture there. That is why it is so bald. People see its baldness and suppose that it never had timber on it. Is this the *xing* of the mountain?

"Even what exists within human beings—are we without a mind of humanity and righteousness? The manner in which we let go of our good minds is like axes and hatchets with respect to trees. If [the trees] are chopped down every morning, can they remain beautiful? With the respite that we are afforded by the nights, and the [restorative influence] of the morning airs, our likes and dislikes are close to those of other people. [But the power of this restorative process] is slight, and it is fettered and destroyed by what takes place during the day. When this fettering is repeated again and again, the [restorative] nocturnal airs are insufficient to preserve [our goodness]. If the nocturnal airs are insufficient to preserve [our goodness], then we are not far from being disobedient beasts. People see our bestiality, and suppose that there was never any ability in us. Is this human *xing*?

"Thus, if it obtains its nourishment, no creature will fail to grow; if it loses its nourishment, no creature will fail to decay.

"Confucius said, 'It is to the mind alone that the following refers! If you grasp it, it will be preserved; if you discard it, it will be destroyed. There is no time to its comings and goings, and no one knows its province.'"

[6A.10.] Mencius said, "Fish is what I desire; bear's paw is also what I desire. Of the two, if I cannot have both, I will set aside fish and take bear's paw.

Life is what I desire; righteousness is also what I desire. Of the two, if I cannot have both, I will set aside life and take righteousness.

"Life is surely something I desire, but there are things I desire more than life, and thus I will not act improperly in order to retain [life]. Death is surely something I hate, but there are things I hate more than death, and thus there are troubles that I do not avoid.

"If one were to make people desire nothing more than life, then why would they not use every means by which they could retain their lives? If one were to make people hate nothing more than death, then why would they not do anything by which they could avoid trouble?

"There are cases where we do not use some means that would ensure our life, and there are cases where we do not do something that would ensure our avoidance of trouble.

"Therefore, there are things that we desire more than life, and there are things that we hate more than death—and it is not only a moral paragon who has such a mind. All people have it; the moral paragon is able to keep it from perishing."

» Working with Sources

1. **How does Mencius deploy naturalistic images to illustrate his points?**
2. **What does the parable of Ox Mountain indicate about the existence of evil people?**

SOURCE 9.3

Li Si, "Memorial on the Burning of Books," from the *Shiji*

ca. 100 BCE

Virtually no records have survived from the period between the unification of China in 221 BCE and the collapse of the Qin Empire 15 years later. Accordingly, historians are forced to rely on documents composed during the Han dynasty for relevant information. Nevertheless, one of the stories passed along, concerning the advice of Li Si to the emperor, is a stark reminder of how fragile learning can be, even in a temporarily successful polity. The *Records of the Grand Historian* (*Shiji*), a lengthy history of China compiled by Sima Qian (ca. 145–86 BCE), also includes a detailed biography of Li Si.

Source: *Shih chi* 87:6b–7a, in de Bary and Bloom, comps., *Sources of Chinese Tradition*, vol. 1 (New York: Columbia University Press, 1960), 140–141.

In earlier times the empire disintegrated and fell into disorder, and no one was capable of unifying it. Thereupon the various feudal lords rose to power. In their discourses they all praised the past in order to disparage the present and embellished empty words to confuse the truth. Everyone cherished his own favorite school of learning and criticized what had been instituted by the authorities. But at present Your Majesty possesses a unified empire, has regulated the distinctions of black and white, and has firmly established for yourself a position of sole supremacy. And yet these independent schools, joining with each other, criticize the codes of laws and instructions. Hearing of the promulgation of a decree, they criticize it, each from the standpoint of his own school. At home they disapprove of it in their hearts; going out they criticize it in the thoroughfare. They seek a reputation by discrediting their sovereign; they appear superior by expressing contrary views, and they lead the lowly multitude in the spreading of slander. If such license is not prohibited, the sovereign power will decline above and partisan factions will form below. It would be well to prohibit this.

Your servant suggests that all books in the imperial archives, save the memoirs of Qin, be burned. All persons in the empire, except members of the Academy of Learned Scholars, in possession of the *Book of Odes*, the *Book of History*, and discourses of the hundred philosophers should take them to the local governors and have them indiscriminately burned. Those who dare to talk to each other about the *Book of Odes* and the *Book of History* should be executed and their bodies exposed in the market place. Anyone referring to the past to criticize the present should, together with all the members of his family, be put to death. Officials who fail to report cases that have come under their attention are equally guilty. After thirty days from the time of issuing the decree, those who have not destroyed their books are to be branded and sent to build the Great Wall. Books not to be destroyed will be those on medicine and pharmacy, divination by the tortoise and milfoil, and agriculture and arboriculture. People wishing to pursue learning should take the officials as their teachers.

» Working with Sources

1. Li Si's advice may seem extreme, but is there a logical element to his reasoning?

2. Why was he advocating the destruction of these specific books?

SOURCE 9.4 *Han Shu (History of the Former Han Dynasty)*

ca. 100 CE

This dynastic history was a continuation of the *Records of the Grand Historian* (*Shiji*), originally compiled by Sima Qian (ca. 145–86 BCE), and it repeats many of the phrases and situations Sima Qian had described verbatim. However, these histories provide remarkable insights into the behavior of emperors and their families at court—while also suggesting developing notions of gender and education. This segment of the *Han Shu* covers the reign of Hsiao-Ai (Xiao Ai), in roughly 6–1 BCE.

The Annals of [Emperor Hsiao]-Ai

Emperor Hsiao-ai was the grandson of Emperor Yüan by a concubine and the son of King Kung of Ting-t'ao, [Liu K'ang(1a)]. His mother was the Concubine [née] Ting. When he was in his third year, he succeeded [his father] and was set up as King. When he grew up, he delighted in words and phrases and in the laws and statutes.

In [the period] Yüan-yen, the fourth year, he came [to Ch'ang-an] to pay court, followed by all [his high officials], his Tutor, his Chancellor, and his Commandant of the Capital. At that time the youngest brother of Emperor Ch'eng, King Hsiao of Chung-shan, [Liu Hsing], also came to pay court, followed [only] by his Tutor. The Emperor thought it strange, and asked [Liu Hsin(5), the future Emperor Ai], about it. The King of Ting-t'ao, replied, "According to the [imperial] ordinances, when vassal kings come to pay court, they are permitted to be accompanied by the [officials ranking at] two thousand piculs in their kingdoms. The Tutor, Chancellor, and Commandant of the Capital are all [officials ranking at] two thousand piculs in a kingdom, hence I am accompanied by them all." The Emperor ordered him to recite from the *Book of Odes*, and he understood and was versed in it, and was able to explain it.

On another day, [the Emperor] asked the King of Chung-shan, [Liu Hsing], in what law or ordinance [it was ordered that he should be] accompanied only by his tutor, and he was unable to reply. [The Emperor] ordered him to recite from the *Book of History*, and he broke off [in the middle of his recitation]. Moreover, [at an imperial feast], when he had been granted food in the presence of [the Emperor], he was the last to finish eating; when he arose, his stockings came down, [for] their ties had become loosened. Because of these [facts],

Source: *Han Shu*, Book 11 (Annals of the Emperor Hsiao-Ai), Chinese text and English translation: http://www2.iath.virginia.edu/saxon/servlet/SaxonServlet?source=xwomen/texts/hanshu.xml&style=xwomen/xsl/dynaxml.xsl&chunk.id=d2.49&toc.depth=1&toc.id=0&doc.lang=bilingual.

Emperor Ch'eng considered that he was incapable, and esteemed the King of Ting-t'ao, as capable, often exalting his abilities.

At this time the grandmother of the King, the Queen Dowager [of Ting-t'ao, née] Fu, had come with the King to pay court, and privately sent presents to the Brilliant Companion [née] Chao, whom the Emperor favored, and to the Emperor's maternal uncle, the General of Agile Cavalry and Marquis of Ch'ü-yang, Wang Ken. The Brilliant Companion [née Chao] and [Wang] Ken saw that the Emperor had no sons, and also wished beforehand to attach themselves [to the coming ruler] by a plan for the distant future, so both in turn praised the King of Ting-t'ao and urged the Emperor to make him his successor. Emperor Ch'eng of his own volition also exalted [Liu Hsin(5)'s] ability, and after having put the bonnet of virility upon him, sent him [back to his kingdom]. At that time he had [reached] his seventeenth year.

. . .

In [the period] Sui-ho, the second year, the third month, Emperor Ch'eng died, and in the fourth month, on [the day] *ping-wu*, the Heir-apparent took the imperial throne and presented himself in the Temple of [Emperor] Kao. He honored the Empress Dowager [née Wang] with the title, Grand August Empress Dowager, and the Empress [née Chao] with the title, Empress Dowager. He [granted] a general amnesty to the empire, granted one quadriga of horses to each king's son of the imperial house who was enregistered, to the officials and common people, noble ranks, to [each] hundred households, an ox and wine, and to the Thrice Venerable, the Filially Pious, the Fraternally Respectful, the [Diligent] Cultivators of the Fields, widowers, widows, orphans, and childless, silk.

The Grand Empress Dowager [née Wang] issued an imperial edict honoring King Kung of Ting-t'ao, [Liu K'ang], as Sovereign Kung [of Ting-t'ao]. In the fifth month, on [the day] *ping-hsü*, [the Emperor] established the Empress née Fu [as Empress]. An imperial edict said, "[According to the principle of] the *Spring and Autumn*, [in the *Kung-yang Commentary*] that 'a mother becomes honorable because of her son,' [We] honor the Queen Dowager [née Fu] of Ting-t'ao with the title, Empress Dowager Kung, and the Concubine [née] Ting [of Ting-t'ao with the title, Empress Kung, and establish for each an entourage, a Supervisor of the Household, and the income of an estate, like [the occupants of] the Ch'ang-hsin Palace and the Inner Palace. [We] posthumously honor the father of [the Empress Dowager née] Fu as the Marquis [through Whom the Emperor] Renders Homage to an Ancestor, and the father of [the Empress née] Ting as the Marquis in Recompense to his Virtue." The maternal uncle [of the Emperor], Ting Ming, had been made the Marquis of Yang-an, his maternal uncle's son, [Ting] Man, was made Marquis of Ping-chou, and [Ting] Man's father, [Ting] Chung, was posthumously [granted] the posthumous name, Marquis Huai of P'ing-chou. The Empress [née Fu's] father, [Fu(4)] Yen, had become the Marquis of K'ung-hsiang, and the younger brother of the Empress Dowager [née Chao], the Palace Attendant and Imperial Household Grandee Chao Ch'in(b), became the Marquis of Hsin-ch'eng.

In the sixth month, an imperial edict said, "'The melodies of Cheng are licentious' and bring disorder into music. They were banished by the Sage-kings. Let the Bureau of Music be abolished."

» Working with Sources

1. **What was thought to be the best course of education for the young Emperor?**
2. **What seems to have been the extent of the power of the Empress Dowager? Why?**

SOURCE 9.5 Ban Zhao, *Admonitions for Women (Nüjie)*

ca. 80 CE

Ban Zhao (45–ca. 116 CE) was by far the most educated woman of her day, and she trained many important male scholars. The *Han Shu* (the continuation of Sima Qian's *Shiji*) was originally undertaken by her father, Ban Biao (3–54 CE), and continued by her brother Ban Gu (32–92). Ban Zhao is credited with giving the Han Shu its present shape after the deaths of her father and brother, but she is most famous today for her advice book, directed toward young women.

I, the unworthy writer, am unsophisticated, unenlightened, and by nature unintelligent, but I am fortunate both to have received not a little favor from my scholarly Father, and to have had a cultured mother and instructresses upon whom to rely for a literary education as well as for training in good manners. More than forty years have passed since at the age of fourteen I took up the dustpan and the broom in the Cao family [the family into which she married]. During this time with trembling heart I feared constantly that I might disgrace my parents, and that I might multiply difficulties for both the women and the men of my husband's family. Day and night I was distressed in heart, but I labored without confessing weariness. Now and hereafter, however, I know how to escape from such fears.

Being careless, and by nature stupid, I taught and trained my children without system. Consequently I fear that my son Gu may bring disgrace upon the Imperial Dynasty by whose Holy Grace he has unprecedentedly received the extraordinary privilege of wearing the Gold and the Purple, a privilege for the attainment of which by my son, I a humble subject never even hoped. Nevertheless, now that he is a man and able to plan his own life, I need not again have concern for him. But I do grieve that you, my daughters, just now

Source: Nancy Lee Swann, *Pan Chao: Foremost Woman Scholar of China* (New York: London Century, 1932), 82–90.

at the age for marriage, have not at this time had gradual training and advice; that you still have not learned the proper customs for married women. I fear that by failure in good manners in other families you will humiliate both your ancestors and your clan. I am now seriously ill, life is uncertain. As I have thought of you all in so untrained a state, I have been uneasy many a time for you. At hours of leisure I have composed . . . these instructions under the title, "Lessons for Women." In order that you may have something wherewith to benefit your persons, I wish every one of you, my daughters each to write out a copy for yourself.

From this time on every one of you strive to practice these lessons.

HUMILITY

On the third day after the birth of a girl the ancients observed three customs: first to place the baby below the bed; second to give her a potsherd [a piece of broken pottery] with which to play; and third to announce her birth to her ancestors by an offering. Now to lay the baby below the bed plainly indicated that she is lowly and weak, and should regard it as her primary duty to humble herself before others. To give her potsherds with which to play indubitably signified that she should practice labor and consider it her primary duty to be industrious. To announce her birth before her ancestors clearly meant that she ought to esteem as her primary duty the continuation of the observance of worship in the home.

These three ancient customs epitomize woman's ordinary way of life and the teachings of the traditional ceremonial rites and regulations. Let a woman modestly yield to others; let her respect others; let her put others first, herself last. Should she do something good, let her not mention it; should she do something bad let her not deny it. Let her bear disgrace; let her even endure when others speak or do evil to her. Always let her seem to tremble and to fear. When a woman follows such maxims as these then she may be said to humble herself before others.

Let a woman retire late to bed, but rise early to duties; let her not dread tasks by day or by night. Let her not refuse to perform domestic duties whether easy or difficult. That which must be done, let her finish completely, tidily, and systematically. When a woman follows such rules as these, then she may be said to be industrious.

Let a woman be correct in manner and upright in character in order to serve her husband. Let her live in purity and quietness of spirit, and attend to her own affairs. Let her love not gossip and silly laughter. Let her cleanse and purify and arrange in order the wine and the food for the offerings to the ancestors. When a woman observes such principles as these, then she may be said to continue ancestral worship.

No woman who observes these three fundamentals of life has ever had a bad reputation or has fallen into disgrace. If a woman fail to observe them, how can her name be honored; how can she but bring disgrace upon herself?

. . .

IMPLICIT OBEDIENCE

Whenever the mother-in-law says, "Do not do that," and if what she says is right, unquestionably the daughter-in-law obeys. Whenever the mother-in-law says, "Do that," even if what she says is wrong, still the daughter-in-law submits unfailingly to the command. Let a woman not act contrary to the wishes and the opinions of parents-in-law about right and wrong; let her not dispute with them what is straight and what is crooked. Such docility may be called obedience which sacrifices personal opinion. Therefore the ancient book, "A Pattern for Women," says: "If a daughter-in-law who follows the wishes of her parents-in-law is like an echo and shadow, how could she not be praised?"

» Working with Sources

1. **What does Ban Zhao tell us about the status of daughters-in-law in her culture? Are these fates capable of being avoided?**
2. **What should be the central and perennial activities of a woman's life, in the opinion of Ban Zhao? Did she conduct her own life differently?**

PART THREE

The Formation of Religious Civilizations

600–1450 CE

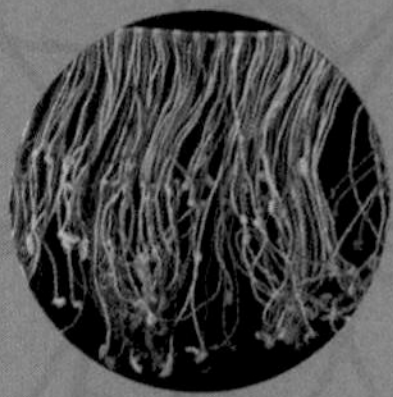

A vitally important pattern of world history during the period 600–1450 was the emergence and development of what may be called "religious civilizations." By this we mean the formation of religions and cultures in entire world regions, shared by the states and empires in these regions. In all cases, religious, philosophical, and/or ethical traditions based on monotheism or monism helped give legitimacy to the polities that adopted them. They helped unifiy individual states by providing them with a common set of cultural norms and bonds. Six religious civilizations emerged in a relatively short space of time in Eurasia and, to a lesser extent, in Africa during the second half of the first millennium. They were, from west to east, Western Christianity (from 476), Eastern Christianity (640), Islam (750), Hinduism (550), Buddhism (Korea 550, Japan 594, Vietnam 971), and Neo-Confucianism (China 960, Vietnam 1010). Each occupied a world region.

Uniqueness and Comparability

Uniqueness. The rise of religious civilizations on the continents of Asia, Europe, and Africa is a striking phenomenon that unifies the period 600–1450. In this respect, it may be considered as a continuation of the intellectual and institutional transformations that began with the emphasis on transcendence by the visionaries of the mid-first millennium BCE as a key aspect in understanding the world in which they lived.

Comparability. The religious civilizations were not monolithic and displayed many regional variations. Internal diversity notwithstanding, they shared a number of common characteristics:

- Religious civilizations formed in regions which were larger than any single state within them: They superseded empires as the largest units of human organization. They often consisted of commonwealths of competing states sharing common characteristics and even common cultures.

618–907 Tang dynasty in China

633–651 Arab conquest of Syria, Iraq, Egypt, and Iran

794–1185 Heian period, Japan

850–1000 Kingdom of Chichén Itzá in northern Yucatán Peninsula

918–1392 Koryo Kingdom, from which the name "Korea" is derived

960–1127 Neo-Confucian synthesis in China

ca. 1000 *Tale of Genji*, perhaps world's first novel, Japan

ca. 1000–1400 Kingdom of Ife in West African rain forest

1204 Sack of Constantinople by Crusaders

1206–1310 Mongol Conquests of Asia, eastern Europe, and the eastern Middle East

- The civilizations were *scriptural*—that is, based on bodies of texts inherited in most cases from earlier periods. In each religious civilization, followers were preoccupied with harmonizing the often conflicting texts into one coherent *canon:* a single, official interpretation adhered to by all.
- The guardians of the canon (clergy, scholars, sages) were members of educated elites who taught and interpreted it to laypeople.
- Despite hostilities among religious civilizations, merchants, missionaries, pilgrims, and travelers visited each other's areas in large numbers. They fostered a lively exchange of innovations from one end of Eurasia and Africa to the other.

Origins, Interactions, and Adaptations

The era of religious civilizations provides some striking examples of the processes of origins, interactions, and adaptations that we have emphasized in this book.

Internal Forces. The elements with which people built their religious civilizations came from the intellectual and institutional traditions of empires and kingdoms from the pre-600 period. These elements were for the most part found inside the territories of the evolving religious civilizations. Some exceptions include Korea, Japan, and Vietnam, which adopted Chinese Buddhist civilization more or less ready-made from the outside.

In the majority of religious civilizations, the scriptural canons were completed within two or three centuries. Thereafter, refinement within the confines set by the canons continued for many more centuries, in some cases even beyond 1450. Without outside challenges, however, these refinements slowed. Over time, scholars, thinkers, and artists tended to exhaust the possibilities which their civilizations offered them.

External Challenges. External intellectual challenges contributed to the reshaping of two religious civilizations during the period 600–1450: Neo-Confucian China and Western Christianity. China's intellectual foundation from the Han dynasty on was based on Daoism and Confucianism, harmonized with some difficulty during the early centuries of the millennium. Buddhism, coming from India, became a full-blown intellectual and institutional challenge by the 800s. In response, the Chinese reconfigured their canon from the mid-tenth century with the creation of Neo-Confucianism.

In Western Christianity, Latin Christians enlarged their canon twice, as a result of adapting to intellectual challenges coming from the outside: first around 1100–1250, after the arrival of Arabic and Greek texts, and second around 1400, after the arrival of another set of Greek and Hellenistic texts.

Thinking Like a World Historian

How was each religious civilization of the period 600–1450 unique? How were these civilizations comparable?

What impact did internal forces and external challenges have on the patterns of development in the religious civilizations of the period 600–1450?

Why do the civilizations of the Americas fall outside the patterns that characterize Eurasian and African civilizations during this period?

interactive timeline

1206–1526 Muslim Delhi Sultanate at height of power

1238–1492 Muslim kingdom of Granada

1240–1645 Empire of Mali in West Africa (rain forest, Sahel, and savanna)

1250–1505 Kingdom of Great Zimbabwe in southern Africa

1257–1287 Vietnamese repel three attempted Mongol invasions

1268 St. Thomas Aquinas' *Summa Theologica*

1336–1564 Dominance of Hindu state of Vijayanagar in southern India

1348–1352 Black Death in Middle East and Europe

1427–1521 Aztec Empire in Mesoamerica

1438–1533 Inca Empire in Andes

1453 Constantinople falls to Ottoman Empire

Chapter 10 600–1300 CE

Islamic Civilization and Byzantium

One cannot help but feel sympathy for Safra, a jilted wife whose husband left her for a more attractive woman in twelfth-century Cairo. Two letters by Safra to her estranged husband Khidr tell of her deep hurt and bitter anguish. She is offended that Khidr denigrates her as unattractive and reveals marriage secrets to his new lover, who is also married. In her words, his "repulsive, shameless talk" causes her deep suffering. Were she not a good Muslim, she says, she would curse him roundly and loudly, both privately and in public.

The letters also reveal that she was independently wealthy, while her husband was not. She freely admits that when they were married 3 years earlier, she did not realize that he was unreliable. Since he could not pay the obligatory portion of the "bride wealth" payable to her at the time of the wedding, she let it stand as a loan. Not only did he not make payments, but he did not even feed and clothe her or pay their rent. When he began his affair 2 years earlier, she went to the countryside to find distance and rest. But he tortured her with insistent demands to return and promised to leave his mistress. The moment she gave in and returned to Cairo, he went back to his lover. Like a ghost, he slipped into Safra's house at night for a few hours of sleep in his room, only to disappear the next morning. During his nightly visits he stole most of the household furnishings, so that in the end she found herself in an empty house.

BYZANTIUM AND THE ISLAMIC WORLD, ca. 1000 CE

ABOVE: **Detail of an early Quran (Surah 48: 27–28) written in Kufic script during the eighth or ninth century.**

Safra's reflections and actions provide an important glimpse into the legal side of Islamic civilization. Contrary to the widely held opinion in the contemporary West, Islamic law afforded women considerable protections. Safra was a woman of property, holding personal title to possessions as well as to debts payable to her. She could go to court, where she had standing as a complainant. She could initiate divorce proceedings, even if a wife's proceedings were more complicated than those of a husband. In short, even though Islamic civilization was as patriarchal as the other religious civilizations of the time, women exercised considerably more rights than in the Persian and Roman Empires.

The central patterns of Islamic civilization flowed from an empire that conquering Arabs from northern Arabia built during 628–750. These patterns would then develop across a 5,000-mile swath ranging from the Iberian Peninsula to Turkestan. The empire, ultimately ungovernable as a single unit, evolved into a **commonwealth** of smaller states. From 750 to 950 it underwent a formative period during which its inhabitants adapted to inherited Greco-Roman and Persian cultures. By the mid-tenth century, historians consider the empire "fully developed," meaning that it was subjected to few outside influences that changed it in substantive ways. After this time, Islamic civilization continued to be shaped by its patterns of characteristic religious, political, and cultural traditions and institutions. These patterns remained largely unchanged and unchallenged by new stimuli coming from the outside until well into the modern period around 1850. In this respect, Islamic civilization was similar to Byzantine Eastern Christian, Hindu Indian, Neo-Confucian Chinese, and Confucian–Buddhist Japanese civilizations. All of these, after their formation by the end of the first millennium, pursued a course more along their established internal patterns than as a result of innovation, interaction, and adaptation coming from the outside.

Seeing Patterns

» **Why can the period 600–1450 be described as the age of religious civilizations? How do Eastern Christian and Islamic civilizations fit this description?**

» **Which cultural traditions combined to form Islamic religious civilization during its formative period? What were the most characteristic patterns?**

» **How did Eastern Christian or Byzantine civilization evolve over time? On which institutions was this civilization based, and how did it evolve, wedged between Islamic and Western Christian civilizations?**

Commonwealth: An association of self-governing states sharing similar institutional and cultural traits.

The Formation of Islamic Religious Civilization

Arab conquests and the rise of the religion of Islam were foundational events during the period 600–900. In the 600s, the Arabs carved out a kingdom for themselves by exploiting the preoccupation of the eastern Roman and Sasanid Persian Empires with their destructive wars of conquest in 602–628. Two Arab dynasties, the Umayyads and then the Abbasids, built a vast empire stretching thousands of miles from east to west. Given the enormous distances, the Abbasids were forced to grant autonomy to many outlying provinces. In the process, their empire changed into a commonwealth of many states sharing a single Islamic religion. The pattern which Islamic religious civilization followed during its formative period was a variation of what happened in the other parts of Asia and Europe in the first millennium CE: Through conquest or peaceful expansion, regions of religious civilizations emerged which grew much larger than the political units within them, resulting in the appearance of commonwealths (Middle East, Europe, India) or periodic unity and disunity (China).

Chapter Outline

- The Formation of Islamic Religious Civilization
- Eastern Christian Civilization in Byzantium
- Islamic and Eastern Christian Civilizations at Their Height
- Religion, Sciences, and the Arts in Two Religious Civilizations
- Putting It All Together

The Beginnings of Islam

At the beginning of the 600s, the Sasanid Persian and Roman Empires battled each other in a lengthy war, which left their Arab subjects in Syria and Mesopotamia (which the Arabs subsequently called "Iraq") to their own devices. The Arabs had been nomadic inhabitants of the Syrian-Arabian desert since the use of the camel as a pack animal around 1000 BCE (domestication ca. 2500 BCE) and were founders of sedentary kingdoms and city-states around the rim of the desert on the Arabian Peninsula in the early centuries CE. By the early 600s, nearly all Arabs on the peninsula had been Christianized. In the mid-600s Arab leaders declared their rule over Roman Syria, conquered Sasanid Iraq, captured Egypt from the Romans, and destroyed the Sasanid Persian Empire. Through further conquests, the initial Arab realm became an empire, stretching by the mid-eighth century from Iberia (Spain and Portugal) in the west to the Indus River in the east.

The Final Roman–Persian War The long history of the Roman–Persian rivalry once more reached a climax during the first three decades of the 600s. In 602, King of Kings Khosrow II (r. 590–628) invaded the Roman Empire, using the pretext of a coup d'état in Constantinople that had brought to power a usurper. Within a little more than a decade his generals had conquered Syria, Egypt, and Anatolia, and the Romans were hard pressed to defend themselves in their capital. In the midst of its bleakest moment, the empire was saved by Heraclius (r. 610–641), the son of a governor from North Africa who seized power in Constantinople in 610. Borrowing huge sums, he reorganized the military and was able to drive the Sasanids back to Iraq. In 628 he achieved his greatest triumph when Khosrow was murdered by rivals and the Sasanids were forced to make peace.

After his victory, Heraclius restored the prewar administrative structures in the province of Syria. He subsidized Arab leaders and reintroduced locally recruited garrisons and bishops in cities. In order to pay back the war debt, he reduced the size of the army. To simplify the central administration, he replaced Latin with Greek as the language of the bureaucracy and the multiple Latin titles of the emperor (*imperator, caesar, augustus*) with the single Greek title of king (*basileus*), Christ's representative on earth. Thus, as many scholars of Byzantine history now emphasize, it was under Heraclius that the Roman Empire became the Byzantine Empire, or Byzantium.

The Arab Empire of the Umayyads The victory of Hercalius over the Sasanid Persians in 628 encouraged the eastern Arabs to begin incursions on their part from the north Arabian desert into Persian Iraq. After 602, when their viceroy was murdered by Khosrow II, they had retreated into the desert where they allied themselves with the western Arabs. In a series of revenge raids 628–631 they conquered Persian Iraq. The Persians, racked by a dynastic war in the wake of Khosrow II's defeat by Heraclius and his murder by a family member, found it difficult to stop the Arabs. The success of the eastern Arabs against the Persians encouraged the Arabs in the west to begin raids in 632 againt the Byzantines in Palestine. Heraclius had reestablished Byzantine rule in Syria and Palestine after 628, but the exorbitant costs of the war against the Sasanid Persians had led him to concentrate his limited military forces in the north on the Persian frontier. His inability to defend the south with full force cost him dearly: In a series of battles 634–638 he lost Palestine and Syria against the Arabs and was forced to retreat to Anatolia. Subsequently, the Arabs conquered

Byzantine Egypt (639–642) and ended the last resistance of the Sasanids in Persia in 651. An Arab empire rose in Palestine, Syria, Egypt, and Persia which the strongman Muawiya (r. 661–680) consolidated under the dynastic rule of the Umayyads.

Gold Coin of Abd al-Malik, ca. 696. This coin displays the characteristics of what were to become Islamic coins; that is, the avoidance of images and the use of religious phrases.

Umayyad Religious Developments Under the third Umayyad ruler, Abd al-Malik (685–705), early signs of a religious orientation in the Arab Empire became visible. Arabic inscriptions in and on the Dome of the Rock, dating to 691–692, refer to the prophet Muhammad and biblical predecessors, including Jesus the Messiah, as servants of God. Polemical verses oppose the Christian theology of Jesus as son of God, while other verses describe **Muslims** as believers in the "concordance" (*islam*) among all prophetic messages of the past. By implication this means that following God's commands in this concordance will bring salvation on the Day of Judgment.

The Dome of the Rock is a splendid, architecturally commanding structure on Jerusalem's Temple Mount which can be viewed as Abd al-Malik's counter monument to the Church of the Holy Sepulcher on the other side of Jerusalem, built on the site of Jesus' tomb. Presumably he saw himself as the true "representative of God" (*khalifa*, or **caliph**) vis-à-vis the Byzantine emperor. Similarly, the emerging Islamic faith of the One God, Allah, which he was shaping as the state religion of the Umayyad Empire, was offered as a faith superior to **Trinitarian** Byzantine Christianity. To buttress this anti-Byzantine state religion, Abd al-Malik created a strong central administration and army, with Arabic as the bureaucratic language and a reformed coinage which renounced any imagery, in contrast to Byzantine coins with their crosses and emperors. Abd al-Malik saw the Umayyad Empire as the true successor of a shrinking, perhaps even dying, Byzantine Empire.

Muslims: Initially: believer in the concordance among all prophetic messages from Abraham to Muhammad. Later on: believer who submits to the will of God (*Allah*).

Caliph: Representative of God, and later of Muhammad, on earth.

Trinitarian: Christianity based on the doctrine of God the Father, Son, and Holy Spirit.

Umayyad Conquests in West and East Abd al-Malik's successors continued the Umayyad efforts to take over Byzantium. Armies composed of Arabs and Berbers conquered Byzantine North Africa in 686–698, reducing Byzantium to parts of Italy, the Balkans, and Anatolia. Once North Africa was conquered, Abd al-Malik's successors became entangled in Western Christian politics. In 711, dissident Visigothic nobles called Berber and Arab troops into the Iberian Peninsula to help them in their bid to oust the reigning Visigothic king. After rising to dominance in the Visigothic kingdom, the Berbers, Arabs, and Visigothic allies divided Iberia among themselves. In the same year, the Umayyads expanded their rule into central Asia and the Indus Valley, creating an immense empire with copious amounts of booty and masses of enslaved war captives streaming to Syria.

interactive timeline

- **602–628** War between Sasanid Iran and Byzantium
- **628–651** Arab conquest of Syria, Iraq, Egypt, and Iran
- **661–750** Umayyad dynasty
- **711** Arab–Persian conquest of Indus Valley and Turkestan
- **726–787** First iconoclasm controversy in Eastern Christianity
- **750–1258** Abbasid dynasty
- **ca. 850** Emergence of Shiism as distinct branch of Islam
- **909–1171** Fatimid dynasty
- **971** Byzantine Empire defeats Bulgars
- **1040–1269** Almoravid and Almohad Berber dynasties in North Africa and Iberia
- **1056–1258** Seljuk Turkish sultans
- **ca. 1050** Muslim scholars integrate Sufism into Sunni Islam
- **1071** Battle of Manzikert: Seljuk defeat of Byzantium
- **1095–1099** First Crusade
- **1238–1492** Muslim kingdom of Granada
- **1099–1291** Crusader kingdom of Jerusalem
- **1204** Sack of Constantinople by crusaders
- **1250–1517** Mamluk sultanate of Egypt and Syria
- **1206–1286** Mongol conquests and rule in the Middle East

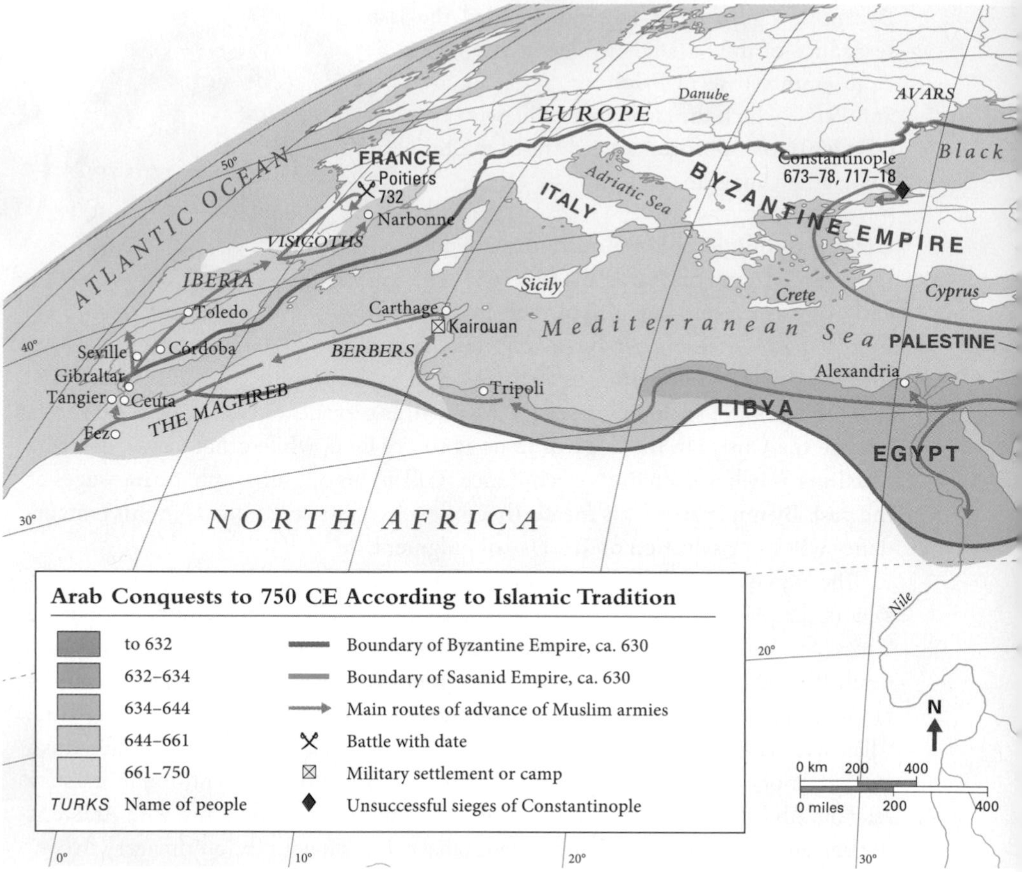

map analysis

MAP 10.1 Arab Conquests to 750.

Two decades later, the Iberian Berbers and Arabs pushed into France. One of these raids was commemorated in Western Christianity as the Battle of Tours in central France (732 or 733). Here, the founder of the Western Christian Carolingian Empire, Charles Martel (r. 714–741), beat back the invading raiders. Similarly, Arab campaigns in the Caucasus to take the Russian steppes failed around 740. From today's vantage point it looked as if the empire had reached its physical limits: It became evidently impossible to dispatch cavalry armies during summer campaigns from the capital of Damascus any farther than the Pyrenees, Hindu Kush, and Caucasus Mountains (see Map 10.1).

From the Umayyads to the Abbasids The end of expansion and the need to shift from conquest to consolidation created a profound religio-political crisis in several provinces of the empire. The one province where the crisis exploded into an uncontrollable revolution was Iran. Here, local Persian military lords and Arab settlers arose, expecting a "rightly guided" leader (*Mahdi*, or Messiah) to arrive and establish a realm of justice on earth at the end of time before God's Judgment. The revolutionaries overthrew the Umayyads in 750, but instead of the Mahdi and his realm of justice the new dynasty of the Abbasids emerged and displayed uncanny similarities to that of the overthrown Umayyads. After moving the capital of the empire to Baghdad in Iraq, the Abbasids built the same top-heavy central administration and army which had characterized the Umayyads.

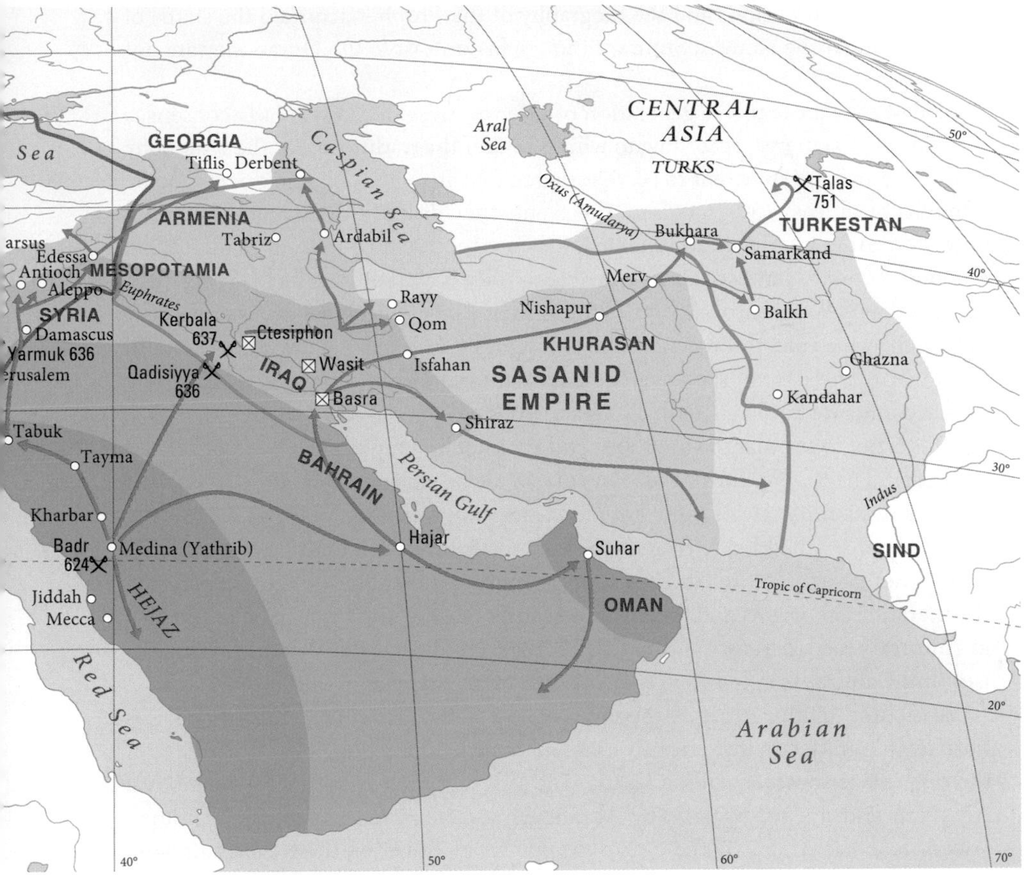

Islamic Theology, Law, and Politics

In Iraq, the Abbasids completed what the Umayyads had begun in Syria. They enlarged and systematized the state religion, built around the prophet Muhammad, God's commands, and salvation on the Day of Judgment. They sponsored the translation of scientific, philosophical, legal, and literary works from Syriac and Persian into Arabic. Schools and libraries spread from Baghdad to large and small cities everywhere in the region, from Iberia to northwest India. Many of these cities became cultural and political centers of their own, under autonomous dynasties that recognized the Abbasid caliphs in Baghdad but for all practical purposes were independent. By around 950, an Islamic religious civilization had come into being which was organized into a commonwealth of some two-dozen realms under ethnically diverse dynasties.

Shaping Islamic Theology In the 800s, scholars, judges, and bureaucrats in the Abbasid Empire completed the compilation of the Quran, the beginnings of which dated back to the mid-600s (see Source10.1). In contrast to the Christian New Testament, the Quran is like a lectionary that brings together small blocks of text summarizing biblical narratives or doctrinal statements. Since it is God's word, Muhammad himself appears only a few times in the Quran. Therefore, parallel to the compilation of the Quran, traditions (*ahadith*) about Muhammad's life were gathered and put into the form of encyclopedic collections as well as a biography (*sira*).

Sunna: The paradigmatic "path" of Muhammad's traditions which, if trodden by believers, will lead to salvation.

Together, these traditions and the biography of the Prophet acquired the status of scripture, under the name of **Sunna**, although in contrast to the Quran they are not revelations.

Today, after more than a generation of extensive research, a scholarly consensus is beginning to emerge, according to which neither the traditions nor the biography of Muhammad are sufficient to serve for a reliable history of Islamic origins. Being removed by at least 150 years from the events they describe as having taken place in western Arabian Mecca and Medina, they are too far away in time to be reliable accounts. Scholars have so far been unable to trace any traditions further back than ca. 720, that is, roughly to the time of the sons of Abd al-Malik, who was previously discussed as the ruler under whom the first signs of an emerging Islam appeared. In other words, there is no Islamic documentation for the events of the early 600s; the only accounts we have date to the 800s and 900s.

This is not to say that the traditions and Prophet biography are devoid of kernels of historical truth. Present-day scholars of Islamic origins merely argue that it is not possible to identify any of these kernels clearly and unambiguously as historically true. They are embedded in the religious preoccupations of the Abbasids and their scholars and are therefore theology more than history. Parallels to the gap between the literature on origins and the assumed earlier origins in Islam can be found also in Ancient Israel, Zoroastrianism, Christianity, Hinduism, Buddhism, Confucianism, and Daoism, as reflected in the corresponding chapters of this book.

According to the Abbasid theology of the 800s and 900s, Muhammad was born in 571 in Mecca, into a family that had once held the position of guardians of the pilgrimage sanctuary of the Kaaba. The sanctuary was founded by the biblical Abraham and his son Ismail (by Abraham's second wife Hagar), the founding ancestors of the Arabs. By the time of Muhammad, however, the Kaaba had deteriorated into a pagan temple. Muhammad himself grew up under the tutelage of one of his uncles, married the wealthy widow Khadija, and became a successful merchant buying and selling goods in Palestine and Syria. In the middle of his life (in ca. 610), during a meditative retreat, God sent his angel Gabriel and commanded Muhammad to preach the power as well as the mercy of the one invisible creator God to the pagan Meccans. The majority of the Meccans, however, did not want to give up their paganism and even threatened to kill Muhammad and his handful of followers. Muhammad saved himself and his followers by emigrating in 622 to Yathrib (renamed al-Madina) to the north. Here, Muhammad founded a community (***umma***) composed of his followers, Arab converts from among the Medinans, as well as Jewish inhabitants.

Umma: Community of all who believe in one God, with Muhammad as their prophet, and reject pagan idolatry (ignorance, *jahiliyya*) or associationism (*shirk*), such as the Christian doctrine of Trinity.

Muhammad now preached an enlarged message which assumed the size of what later became the divine book of the Quran. According to this message, there had been an entire series of prophets among the Israelites and Jews, all resisted by the people to whom God had sent them. They warned of the punishments of God if his commands would not be heeded. Muhammad was the final prophet, following Jesus the Messiah. God's Last Judgment was soon to follow. When the Jews rejected Muhammad as a prophet, however, he expelled them from Medina. And when the Meccans continued to resist his return to his birthplace, he battled against them, forcing them into a draw. In a final coup in 630, Muhammad arranged for a pilgrimage with his followers to the Kaaba, which he cleansed of all pagan divinities, rededicating it to the one God. He then returned to Medina and died in quiet meditation in 632. As with the prophets before him, God had finally granted him success: The Meccans converted to Islam.

The intention in this Abbasid theology of Islamic origins is clear: The caliphs and their scholars sought to further a new monotheistic religion that had left any Christian roots behind and centered on what one may call Islam's Triple Arabness: The Arab Muhammad preached an Arabic Quran to the Arabs of Arabia, thereby ending an assumed paganism on the peninsula. Instead of creating yet another Christian sect in the Middle East soon to be forgotten, as it had happened in previous centuries, the Abbasids turned Islam into its own separate religion. For this religion they claimed superiority: Thanks to their zeal of holy war (***jihad***) the Muslims had conquered the Persians and had reduced the Byzantines to Anatolia and the Balkans.

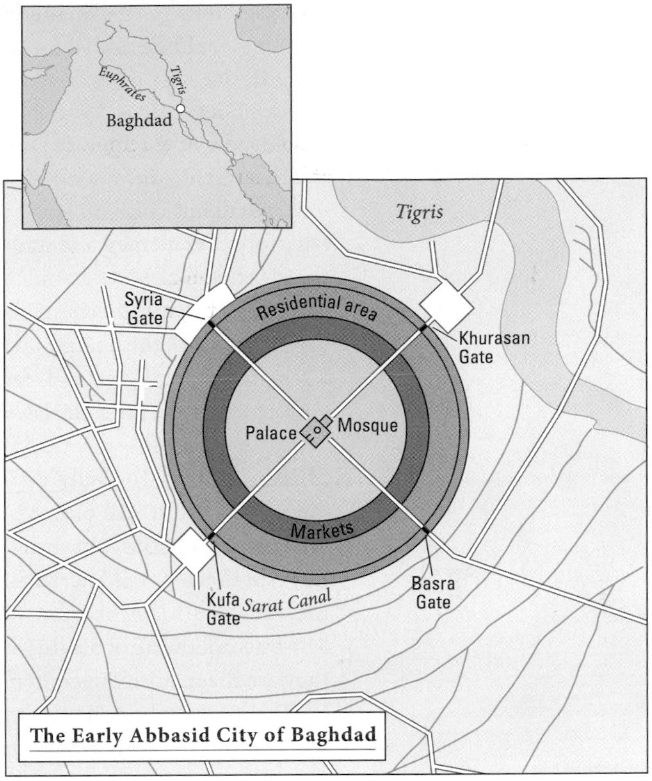

MAP 10.2 The Early Abbasid City of Baghdad.

The separateness of Islam is most pronounced in the five religious duties which identify a Muslim: the profession of faith, prayer, fasting, alms-giving, and pilgrimage to Mecca. The profession of faith is summed up in the formula "There is no God but God, and Muhammad is his messenger." The five-times-daily prayer requires the washing of hands and feet for ritual cleanliness and the performance of a sequence of bodily motions and prayers. On Fridays the noon prayer is to be performed in the congregational mosque. Fasting means a month-long abstinence during Ramadan from food, drink, and sex during the daylight hours. Alms-giving is a small (2.5 percent) donation or tax to the poor, and the pilgrimage is a journey made at least once in one's life to Mecca. These duties are very different from those defining Judaism and Christianity and make Islam not merely a denomination but a separate religion.

Jihad: Literally "struggle (for the path of God—*fi sabil Allah*)," that can range from personal struggle for faith to war in the name of Islam.

Creating Islamic Law The five religious duties form part of the much larger body of moral–legal duties, the **Sharia**. The Abbasids had inherited a judicial system from the Umayyads that was based on the disparate legal traditions of Roman Syria and Sasanid Persia. In the late 700s, the dynasty sponsored the translations of digests of the Justinian Roman law codex in order to create a unified legal system. Since Muslims were at the same time busy compiling the Quran and shaping Muhammadan traditions, it was not surprising that the creation of the Sharia became part and parcel of the same unification process. When it was completed in the mid-900s, the Sharia encompassed the legal verses of the Quran, the prophetic Sunna, and voluminous legal commentaries.

Sharia: The combined body of the legal verses of the Quran, the prophetic Sunna, and the legal commentaries of the 800s and 900s, covering law as well as morality.

The Separation of State and Religion The shaping of Islamic theology and law became a major matter of controversy toward the middle of the 800s. If all theology and law had to be based on the Quran and Sunna, sooner or later every possible moral or legal matter would be unchangeably grounded in God's authority. Nothing could be added to the Sharia or changed in it, and one could only interpret. To preserve their freedom to shape the Sharia, the caliphs instituted a loyalty oath (*mihna*) from 833 to 849 which required all judges, jurists, and jurisconsults employed by the administration or in the courts to support the policy of continued caliphal legislation.

A small but vocal minority refused the oath and found support among the ordinary folk of craftsmen and traders in Baghdad and other cities who were attracted to the idea that God's law should be above human manipulation. After riots the Abbasids gave in and enacted a compromise whereby the religious scholars (*ulama*) became the guardians of the Sharia and the caliphs its executors. This compromise resulted in a separation of religion and state, with the ulama responsible for the judicial system and the state executing the law according to its own often extrajudicial interests.

Shiite Islam The fully evolved Islam under the guardianship of the ulama, in place from about 950 onward, is known as **Sunni Islam**. It expresses the Sunna of the Prophet and the consensus of the religious community represented by the ulama and laid down in the Sharia. Sunni Islam always encompassed the large majority of Muslims and today amounts to about 90 percent of the totality. The minority of Muslims, followers of **Shiite** [SHEE-ite] **Islam**, make up about 10 percent, although they are the majority in contemporary Iran, Iraq, and Lebanon.

The historical origin of Shiite Islam can be dated to the end of the Umayyads, when revolutionaries proclaimed the imminent arrival of the Mahdi to usher in God's kingdom of justice on earth (see p. 276). Tradition places the Shiite beginnings in the period of the first four caliphs, when Caliph Ali lost his throne and Ali's grandson Husayn lost his bid for the caliphate against the Umayyads. According to tradition, Ali was a cousin of the Prophet; the husband of one of his daughters, Fatima; and the founder of the Alid family, where the eldest male in direct descent was entitled to the leadership of the Muslim community in place of the Umayyads.

The main differences between Sunnism and Shiism concern the roles of tradition and authority. The tradition of Husayn's martyrdom near Karbala in Iraq at the hands of the Sunni Umayyads is central for all Shiites and is commemorated during Ashura, the tenth day of the month Muharram. The authority of the Alid descendants in the past, and today of the leaders of the Shiite clergy, is absolute and infallible. Sunnis, by contrast, reject the Karbala tradition. For them the consensus of the community separate from rulers and the absence of a scholarly hierarchy among the ulama are supreme. In the history of Islamic civilization, Shiite–Sunni differences flared up repeatedly, and, unfortunately, they are acute again today, in the context of Iran's ambitions to play the role of a regional power.

When the Abbasids squashed the apocalyptical expectation of God's kingdom at the end of time, apocalypticism went underground. It resurfaced in 874 when the twelfth-generation descendant of Ali was reported to have disappeared without leaving a successor. A radical group formed in Syria around the doctrine that a descendant of the seventh-generation leader would appear soon as the Mahdi. A dispute concerning the legitimate successor in the seventh generation divided the Shiites. Those who accepted the twelfth-generation descendant remained nonrevolutionary.

The radical group of "Seveners" sent out emissaries who fomented armed rebellions around 900 in a number of outlying provinces of the Islamic commonwealth.

The most successful rebellion was that of the Fatimids in 909 in eastern Algeria and Tunisia. The Fatimids were Shiites who founded a counter caliphate to that of the Abbasids, extending from North Africa to Egypt, western Arabia, and parts of Syria, and were major players during the period of the Crusades. Until their end in 1171 they held up their claim of representing God's kingdom on earth through a higher form of justice than that of the Abbasids.

Abbasid Glory. Little is left of the Abbasid splendor during the 800s, since Iraq suffered several invasions in later history, in which palaces, mosques, and other structures were destroyed. This is the eighth-century Abbasid palace of Ukhaydir, southwest of Baghdad. The palace, built by a nephew of the first Abbasid caliph, included gardens, baths, residential suites, courtyards, and audience halls.

The Abbasids in Crisis In the second half of the 800s, right around the time when the Shiite underground began to reorganize itself, the Abbasids were hit by severe financial problems. The Sasanid Persian expansion of agriculture between the Euphrates and Tigris Rivers, continued by the Abbasids, had reached the limits of its potential. In many places, the soil was too salty because of poor drainage on the flat terrain of lower Iraq. Crop yields declined and agricultural tax revenue shrank. As a result, the administration found it difficult to maintain its lavish palace culture and massive bureaucracy. More acutely, it could no longer pay its palace guards, causing the officers to take over still fertile tax districts directly as personal assignments (sing. *iqta)* in place of salaries.

By the early eleventh century, a majority of the soldiers in the guards were Turks, recruited as slaves. Slave-raiding parties captured non-Muslim boys and girls during campaigns into Turkish central Asia. Merchants sold these youths to the caliphs in Baghdad, where they were converted to Islam and trained as soldiers. From 861 to 945, Turkish slave generals wielded power in Baghdad while retaining the caliphs as titular heads of the government. The main function of the generals was the control of political affairs in Iraq, but they also went on summer campaigns against Byzantium to continue the Umayyad holy war. The only other active jihad activity was the Muslim conquest of Byzantine Sicily by an autonomous dynasty in Tunisia, completed by the Fatimids (827-902). For all practical purposes the conquest period had ended.

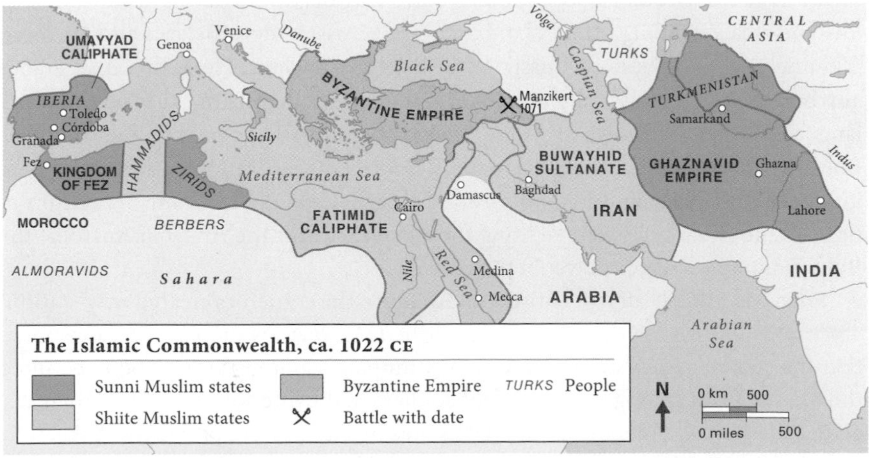

MAP 10.3 **The Islamic Commonwealth, ca. 1022 CE.**

Eastern Christian Civilization in Byzantium

Under siege by the Umayyads and Abbasids, the old eastern Roman Empire, now Byzantium, had retreated to Anatolia and parts of the Balkans. (In current scholarship, the transition from eastern Rome to Byzantium is usually dated to the loss of Palestine, Syria, and Egypt to the Arabs by ca. 640.) Byzantium survived because its emperors reconstituted the state on a new military and religious basis: locally organized border defenses and redefinition of Christian doctrine. Similar to the Abbasid Empire, Byzantium evolved into the center of a commonwealth of Eastern Christian states reaching deeply into Russia after the conversion of the principality of Kiev to Eastern Christianity in 988. Aided initially by the Crusades, later on the Byzantines became their victims. For a brief period, Byzantium was a Western Christian realm (1204–1261) before it recovered as a modest Eastern Christian realm (1261–1453).

Byzantium's Difficult Beginnings

While the Arabs created the new identity of Islamic religious civilization for themselves, the Roman transition to the Byzantine Eastern Christian civilization was more gradual. Nevertheless, the switch in emphasized title from emperor to king (*basileus*), the Umayyad military pressure, the organization of the Anatolian defense, and the interlude of iconoclasm collectively amounted also to the creation of a new civilizational identity. Once this new identity and the recovery from the Muslim (and, in the Balkans, Slavic) onslaughts were achieved, Byzantium followed a pattern similar to that of the Muslims. Eastern Christianity became a commonwealth, with autonomous Balkan and Ukrainian realms, and evolved into a top-heavy centralized state relying more and more on palace guards.

Survival Strategies Under constant Arab pressure in eastern Anatolia, northern Africa, and Sicily (636–863), the Byzantine Empire shrank to a small Anatolian–Balkan realm. Both the Umayyad and Abbasid caliphs either led or sent invasion forces a total of seven times between 653 and 838 by land and sea to attack Constantinople. The empire survived the attacks only by withdrawing from much of the Balkans. Around 580, southern Slavs had begun migrating from the large lowland area extending from Poland eastward across modern Belarus and northern Ukraine into northwestern Russia to settle in the Balkans. Here, the Slavs gradually became the linguistically dominant population, assimilating speakers of other languages, such as Turkish-speaking groups of Bulgars from eastern Russia. These Bulgars had migrated in the 500s to the Byzantine lower Danube, where they were influenced by Slavic culture and asserted their independence from Byzantium in 681. As the Byzantines were fighting for survival against the Arabs in Anatolia, the Bulgars became a major power in the Balkans.

Focusing initially almost entirely on Anatolia, the emperors created new, stationary troops known as "themes" (Greek *themata*). New research has demonstrated that the central administration in Constantinople, beginning around 660, recruited the themes from among volunteer foot soldiers in the interior Byzantine provinces, giving them small plots from imperial estates in the exposed provinces of Anatolia (and later also against the Slavs in the Balkans). In addition, it paid them small wages in cash and food provisions, which were collected as taxes from large landowner estates and free farmers. The themes' main task was to shadow and harass the invading Arabs, waiting for a lucky moment to strike back. One effect of these harassment tactics was an impoverishment of southern Anatolia, which suffered harshly from constant Arab raids. Provincial life in Anatolia became increasingly poor for its Christian inhabitants, and even Constantinople declined in wealth.

Iconoclasm Throughout this difficult period the Byzantine emperors continued to be active in the shaping of religious doctrine and law, similar to the caliphs in the Islamic empire. One religious dispute taken up by the emperors was **iconoclasm,** that is, the destruction of images in accordance with Exodus 20:40 in the Hebrew Bible (726–787 and 814–842; see Source 10.2). As the Christian Church had evolved in the first six centuries CE, church fathers and theologians who stressed the divinity of Jesus and the role of his mother Mary as the "God bearer" gained prominence, especially in Egypt and Syria. Churchmen who, by contrast, sought to hold on to the human status of Jesus and Mary, became marginal or were declared heretical. The rise of Islam, of course, reversed this trend, with its radical emphasis on all prophets, including Jesus, being mere humans. In the 720s, when Byzantium was no longer burdened with the Churches of Egypt and Syria, the return to a more even-handed view of Jesus as both divine and human became attractive again in the eyes of bishops and emperors.

Under orders by emperors, the destruction or plastering over of images gathered speed in the 750s, although it was by no means uniform or intense in all parts of the empire. Since the production of art was expensive and the state was strapped for resources at a time of still-dangerous Muslim incursions, the emperors were relieved to be able to reduce their patronage. But in the 800s, the Muslim danger abated and resistance in the ordinary population, still deeply committed to the trend of the previous centuries, made it increasingly difficult for the emperors to remain committed to iconoclasm. Monks, who were much closer to the population than bishops, patriarchs, and emperors, had a particular interest in images: Many monasteries contained the tombs of saints and their images, and both functioned for pilgrims in the same way as Jesus and Mary did; they were intercessors to God. By 842 the emperors gave up their support of iconoclasm and thereafter withdrew from imposing doctrines on the Church. Like the caliphs in the Abbasid Empire, the Byzantine emperors left religion to the religious institution. As we will see in Chapter 11, a similar disengagement between politics and religion occurred in Western Christianity after the investiture controversy

Iconoclasm: Removal of all religious images from churches and monasteries during a period in the Byzantine Empire (726–787, 814–842), under orders of the emperors.

image analysis

The Byzantine Commonwealth. Characteristic of eastern Christianity are the many churches dedicated to Hagia Sophia, "Holy Wisdom," which can be found throughout the Byzantine commonwealth, from the Balkans to the Caucasus. Though each region developed its own architectural style, they all organized sacred space in similar ways. A masterpiece of design and engineering based in part on the theories of the third-century BCE mathematician Archimedes, the Hagia Sophia in Constantinople was dedicated in 537 by the emperor Justinian on the foundations of an earlier structure (*a*). Its massive dome was often compared to the great dome of heaven itself, and the church would become the prototype for many others throughout the commonwealth in subsequent centuries, including the Cathedral of Saint Sophia in Kiev, whose foundations were laid early in the eleventh century (*b*). While it exhibits a distinctly Kievan style of church architecture, including over a dozen cupolas, the cathedral nonetheless embodies an unmistakable Byzantine tradition whose roots extend deep into the past.

two centuries later. In this respect, the religious civilizations of Islam, Byzantium, and Western Christianity followed similar patterns of development.

Transformation into a Commonwealth As the doctrinal quarrel over iconoclasm was being settled in the mid-800s, the strategy of using themes to defend Anatolia finally paid off. By exploiting the fiscal crisis of the Abbasids, theme commanders were able to go on the offensive after ca. 850 and raid Muslim settlements in eastern Anatolia and northern Iraq with increasing frequency. A century later, in 965, Byzantium had regained all of Anatolia and in 969 even retook the northern Syrian gateway of Antioch. The emperors were now able to turn their attention to the Balkans. Here, the Bulgars had converted to Eastern Christianity in 864 and, under their own emperors, had forced Byzantium to pay tributes in the early 900s. But in 971, the Byzantines crushed the Bulgars and reintegrated their realm into the empire. Toward the middle of the eleventh century, Byzantium again encompassed a respectably large territory, extending from Belgrade and the Balkans some 1,100 miles southeast to Antioch in northern Syria (see Map 10.4).

MAP 10.4 The Byzantine Empire, ca. 1025 CE.

The reintegration of the Balkans into the empire formed the background for the transformation of Byzantium into a commonwealth of Eastern Christianity. In the late 700s, Kiev in what is now the Ukraine was an outpost of the large, ethnically Turkish, and religiously mixed Jewish, Christian, and Muslim Khazar realm in southern Russia. The merchants in Kiev were "Rus" (from which the name "Russia" is derived), of Scandinavian origin. The Rus were active in Russia at the same time as their cousins, the Norsemen or Vikings in western Europe and the Atlantic. By the 800s, most Rus had intermarried with Slavs and had become culturally Slavic. The Rus traded furs from Scandinavia and the Urals and wine from western Europe for Indian spices and Chinese silk, traveling on the Dnieper and Volga Rivers and the Baltic Sea between the Abbasid and Carolingian Empires. In addition to trading, the Rus repeatedly raided Byzantium, thereby adding to the difficulties of the empire during the 800s and early 900s. By the mid-900s, Rus trading and raiding had made Kiev a regional power.

In 988, Grand Prince Vladimir I of Kiev (r. 980–1015) decreed the conversion of his subjects to Christianity. The conversion was part of a deal whereby Vladimir would convert and receive a Byzantine princess for marriage if he would assist the emperor with 6,000 Kievan troops against internal rebels. With this conversion of the Ukraine, Eastern Christianity expanded beyond the Byzantine Empire into the much larger region of Russia. An Eastern Christian commonwealth of states emerged in this region similar to that of Islamic Civilization in the Middle East and Mediterranean.

Military Changes The Kievan troops in the service of the Byzantine Empire, called the "Varangian Guard," formed the nucleus of foreign palace guards, recruited later also from among western Norsemen (including Normans—that is, Norsemen settled in France). The Varangian Guards fulfilled functions similar to those of the Turkish slave guards among the Abbasids. In Byzantium, they were added to balance older Armenian or indigenous regiments (*tegmata*) recruited from among the themes as special crack troops to protect the emperors from rivals for the throne. These rivals were often from provincial landowning families which had succeeded in monopolizing the position of commander (*strategos*) among the themes, responsible for the defense of the empire on the Arab–Muslim and Slavic–Balkan frontiers. The landowning families formed an aristocracy, which in many cases remained prominent until the end of Byzantium in 1453.

In the later 900s, when the empire had recovered, the emperors embarked on a recentralization of the empire. They began to reduce the themes in order to weaken the power of the aristocracy. In the mid-1000s, they demobilized entire themes, cutting the army by about a fifth. The effect of these changes in the military was a rising dependency of the emperors on palace guards and a serious weakening of the border defenses. The Byzantine Empire experienced the same—albeit milder—phenomenon of a top-heavy state and a power-hungry palace military that had already plagued the Abbasids for two centuries.

The first province where the beginning military weakness of Byzantium had consequences was southern Italy. In this restless place, the emperor had no choice in 1051 but to appoint a local lord to the governorship. Western Norsemen or Normans had entered the service of regional princes who combatted both the Byzantines and Muslim raiders from Sicily. Initially, Byzantium and the papacy in Rome cooperated against the Normans, even though the pope was at loggerheads with the patriarch of Constantinople over clerical jurisdiction in southern Italy. At one point, in 1053,

Byzantine Woman Defending Her Virtue. Conscious of their privileged status, the Varangian Guards often mistreated ordinary people in the population. Similar to the Turkish slave guards at the Abbasid court, they had the reputation of being thieves, murderers, and rapists. In this image, Ioannes Skylitzes (ca. 1040–1101), a historian and illustrator, delighted in depicting the story of a woman who not only defended her virtue successfully by killing her attacker but also had the stunned surviving Varangians turn over the clothes of their dead comrade to her.

the Normans achieved a military victory over the pope but since they submitted to his authority soon thereafter, the latter was now free to pursue his jurisdictional claims more forcefully. Striving for jurisdictional supremacy over both Western and Eastern Christianities, the pope dispatched an embassy to Constantinople to assert his claim.

Unfortuantely for the lead ambassador, the patriarch, Michael I Cerularius, was also a man of elevated views about his role. For him, the pope was at best a first among equals and he even viewed himself as the arbiter of the Byzantine imperial order, deciding among claimants to the imperial throne. He refused to meet with the ambassador for months even though the emperor still favored continued cooperation with the pope. The two Churches had not been in communication for about half a century, disagreeing over a variety of liturgical and monastic practices (among others, the *filioque* in the **Creed**, the bread of the **Eucharist**, and **celibacy**). The central dispute was about the jusrisdictional authority of the pope as laid down in the *Donation of Constantine*, a document forged in Rome in the 700s that gave the pope supremacy over the patriarchs of Constantinople, Alexandria, Antioch, and Jerusalem. Although taken at face value in the eleventh century, the *Donation* was interpreted differently in west and east. Only in the Renaissance, as explained in Chapter 17, did scholars unmask the document as a fake.

Eventually, in July 1054, the ambassador placed a letter on the altar of the Hagia Sophia, excommunicating Michael from the Church. Michael responded with an excommunication of the embassy. In order to pacify the popular unrest that was forming in the streets, both patriarch and emperor blamed the events on a conspiracy by the governor of southern Italy, alleged to be a secret Catholic, who had sent

Creed: "And in the Holy Spirit, the Lord, the giver of life, who proceeds from the Father (and the Son [*filioque*]),who with the Father and the Son is adored and glorified" (partial quote). The *filioque* was inserted into the Creed in Spain at the end of the 500s against Arianism which denied the divinity of Jesus, but it was never ratified in the east.

Eucharist: The partaking of bread and wine in commemoration of Jesus Christ's last supper. Byzantium accused Rome of serving the flat Middle Eastern bread which it denounced as "Jewish," in reference to Lev. 23:4–8.

Celibacy: Eastern Christianity allows clerical marriage and the wearing of beards.

a false embassy pretending to be from Rome. Thus, in 1054 the first formal step was taken to ratify what had been in existence already for several centuries, that is, the existence of two separate Christianities, an Eastern Orthodox Christianity and a Western Catholic Christianity.

The Seljuk Invasion and the Crusades

The decline of Byzantine power in Italy had an equally fatal parallel in the east of the Byzantine Empire, in Asia Minor or Anatolia. Islamized Seljuk [sel-JOOK] Turks had migrated in the early eleventh century southwestward from central Asia. They conquered the shrunken Abbasid realm outright and inflicted heavy land losses on the Byzantines in Anatolia. To beat back the Seljuks, the emperors called on the pope for help, the recent church split in 1054 notwithstanding. The pope responded by sending the First Crusaders, who conquered Jerusalem. The subsequent Crusade Kingdom of Jerusalem was of some help to Byzantium to regain land lost to the Seljuks in Anatolia, but it suffered a severe setback when Western Christians sacked Constantinople in the Fourth Crusade and established a Latin empire in Byzantium for nearly two generations (1204–1261). The Crusader kingdom survived for another century (1291), when the Muslim Mamluks of Egypt and Syria captured Jerusalem.

The Seljuk Invasion As discussed earlier, Turks formed part of the ethnic mix of Islamic civilization from the early 800s onwards. Technically, they had the status of military slaves (pl. *mamalik*) in the service of Arab and Persian dynasties as elite troops. Once converted to Islam and adult, however, they were free and as such some Turks even founded dynasties. To replenish the ranks of Turkish elite troops, the rulers sent raiding parties into the grazing grounds of central Asia inhabited by pagan nomadic Turkish clans and federations. Gradually, however, nomadic Turkish leaders benefiting from trade along the Volga and the Silk Road developed an interest in the benefits of urbanized Islamic civilization. This interest was similar to that of the Rus of Kiev seeking to adopt Eastern Christianity, as we already saw. It was in this context that the Seljuk Turks east of the Volga River, between the Caspian and Aral Seas, converted and began their migration into the Islamic commonwealth.

As newcomers to Islam, the Seljuk leaders made themselves champions of a renewal of jihad. In their eyes, Muslims had grown lax with their holy war against the Byzantines. Furthermore, they considered Shiism an abominable heresy. In Baghdad, freeborn nonrevolutionary "Twelver" Shiites had partially replaced the Turkish slaves in the palace guards. In Egypt and parts of Syria the revolutionary "Sevener" Fatimids still sought to overthrow the Abbasids in Iraq. Assuming the exalted title "sultan" (from Arabic for power), the Seljuk leaders devoted themselves wholeheartedly to jihad and began their first raids against the Byzantines in the 1040s. By 1059 they were in full control of Baghdad, as the springboard from which to conduct their double-pronged holy war against Byzantium and the Fatimids (see Map 10.5).

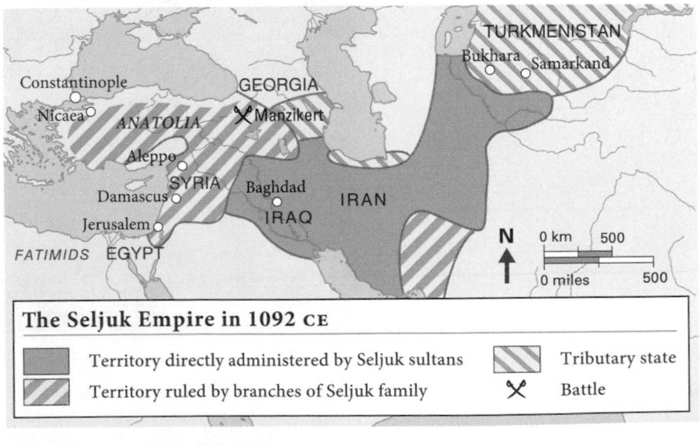

MAP 10.5 The Seljuk Empire in 1092 CE.

The Defeat of Manzikert Although cognizant of the Seljuk danger, the Byzantine emperors did not have sufficient time to rebuild a coherent army that could stop the Seljuks from full-fledged conquest. An effort in 1071 to drive the Seljuks from recently conquered eastern Anatolia failed miserably, in spite of the assembly of a huge army that was numerically superior to that of the Seljuks. The assortment of remaining theme soldiers and central regiments, as well as palace guards and other mercenaries, was unable to hold together for more than a few days of maneuver and battle at Manzikert in eastern Anatolia. In the end the emperor found himself a prisoner of the Seljuk sultan.

The consequences of the defeat were severe. In the following decade and a half the Seljuks occupied most of Anatolia, leaving the Byzantines in command of only a few coastal cities and islands. Normans in the mid-1000s carved out realms for themselves from Byzantine southern Italy and Greece. From here they invaded Greece and became a real threat for the empire in the second half of the eleventh century.

The situation improved only in 1092 when the reigning sultan died and the Seljuk Empire broke apart into a dozen or so competing successor states. By this time, a young, energetic, and reform-minded emperor, Alexius I Comnenus

Battle of Manzikert. The battle was not only a bitter defeat for the Byzantine army at the hands of the Seljuks; it was also a personal humiliation for Emperor Romanus IV who had done his best to prepare for battle. This humiliation had such repercussions even in western Christianity that Maître de Rohan, the artist of this miniature, in the early fifteenth century still found it worthy of commemoration. Rohan, in the service of members of the French aristocracy, was a major manuscript illustrator of his time.

(r. 1081–1118), had succeeded in driving out the Normans from Greece. He could now begin to turn his attention to his most dangerous Muslim neighbor, the Rum Sultanate of the Seljuks in Nicaea, just 60 miles from Constantinople. For dealing successfully with this neighbor he needed more troops than he was able to pay for in the Varangian Guard, his only reliable military force. Relations with Western Christianity had improved, and when Alexius sent an embassy in the spring of 1095 to Rome, he found a sympathetic ear.

The Crusades As it turned out, Alexius received more from the pope than he had bargained for. At the Council of Clermont in 1095, Pope Urban II (r. 1088–1099) issued a brilliantly crafted call for an armed pilgrimage to aid Byzantium and liberate the church from the "abominable" Seljuks, whom he accused of horrible crimes. Well-equipped knights with foot soldiers, as well as poorer folk with few supplies and weapons, responded enthusiastically by the tens of thousands (for more on the Crusades, see Chapter 11). For Alexius, the Crusade was an acute embarrassment. It included Normans who had battled him in Greece. Even if he were able to control them, how much land in Anatolia would the victorious crusaders turn over to him? And even if considerable territory were ceded, how would he be able to defend it by himself? At first, Alexius did indeed receive what he wanted: With the help of the Byzantine navy, the crusaders conquered Nicaea and grudgingly turned it over to him.

In the period thereafter, however, Alexius was under no illusion about the willingness of the crusaders to conquer Anatolia and Syria for him. Even though the emperor made efforts to support the crusaders during their difficult siege of Antioch (1097–1098), he did not receive the city after the crusaders' victory. Nor did he obtain Jerusalem, which the crusaders conquered from the Fatimids in 1099. Instead, in 1100 the crusaders made Jerusalem the capital of an independent crusader kingdom.

crusader Jerusalem

Muslim historians in the early 1100s were fully aware of the significance of the Crusades. (The term appeared after 1200 in French chronicles.) In their judgment, the Crusades were delayed Christian jihads in revenge for the great Arab expansion under the Umayyads. They dated the beginning of this revenge to the Norman invasion of Muslim Sicily in 1061 and the Castilian capture of Toledo in 1085. The fall of Jerusalem in 1099 was for them a logical continuation, exposing an alarming laxness of Muslim religious zeal.

The loss of Sicily, Toledo, and Jerusalem was indeed substantial. The agriculturally wealthy Emirate of Sicily had flourished for a century and a half. The Emirate of Toledo had been part of a nearly three-century-old brilliant Islamic culture in Iberia. In its heyday, this culture was even headed by its own caliphs reigning in Córdoba (Umayyad Andalus, 909–1031). The power of the caliphate rested on its gold trade with West Africa through the Sahara and on palace guards manned by Slavic slave soldiers who had been raided as boys by western European Christians in what was then still pagan eastern Europe. The losses of Sicily and Toledo effectively ended Muslim dominance in the Mediterranean.

Muslim Recovery and Byzantine–Crusader Cooperation Imad al-Din Zenki (r. 1127–1146) was a Turkish-descended leader from Upper Iraq who took the admonitions of the historians to heart. He sponsored religious scholars who revived the teaching of the law of jihad and poets who sang his praise as a holy warrior. He,

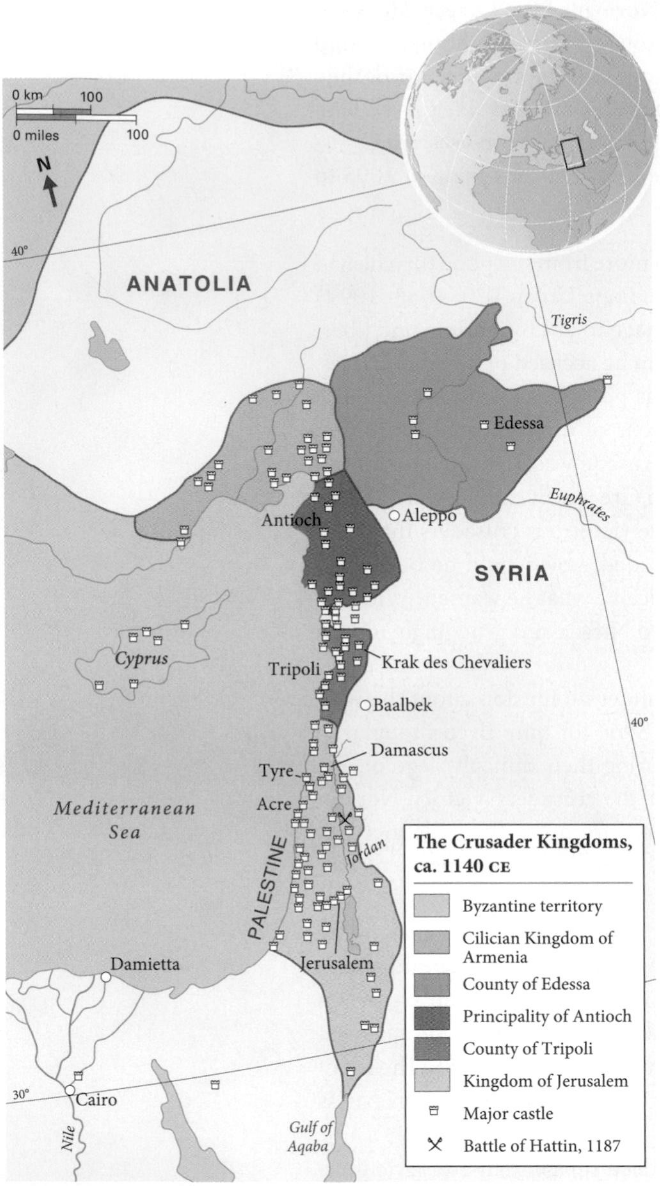

MAP 10.6 The Crusader Kingdoms, ca. 1140 CE.

and later his sons, made steady (although slow) progress against the Crusader Kingdom from his principality of Aleppo. He weathered the Second Crusade of 1147–1149, mounted in response to Zanki's sack of Edessa, but could not prevent the crusaders from repairing their strained relations with Byzantium. After submitting Antioch to Byzantine overlordship they received much-needed naval support in return. The king of Jerusalem took a Byzantine princess as his wife in 1158, and the emperor himself married a princess from Antioch in 1160. Constantinople and Jerusalem forged a powerful alliance.

The alliance paid off with a bold new initiative in 1169: A Byzantine fleet carried crusaders to agriculturally rich Fatimid Egypt for a full-fledged invasion. The Fatimids had never recovered from the loss of the Palestinian–Syrian coast after 1099 to the crusaders. A number of child caliphs in the 1160s signaled a serious dynastic enfeeblement. Unfortunately for the Byzantium–crusader alliance, however, the Muslims also eyed Egypt for its agricultural wealth. By 1171 Muslims had outfoxed the Christian alliance, ended the Fatimid dynasty, and joined Egypt to Aleppo and Damascus for the establishment of a formidable anticrusader realm (see Source 10.3).

Jerusalem and Constantinople Lost The Sunni Muslim conquest of Shiite Egypt was a turning point for both the crusaders and Byzantium. The Kurdish-descended emir Saladin (Salah al-Din Yusuf ibn Ayyub, r. 1174–1193), at the head of the new anticrusader realm, parlayed the agricultural wealth of Egypt into a formidable war machine that wore down the crusaders. In 1187 he succeeded in trapping the flower of crusader knighthood in the Battle of Hattin, near the Sea of Galilee. The battle enabled him to reconquer Jerusalem and nearly wipe out the kingdom.

The Third Crusade of 1189–1192, in response to the losses after Hattin, saved the rump kingdom from seemingly assured destruction. Its failure to regain Jerusalem, however, set the stage for the Fourth Crusade in 1204, planned as a mass campaign to take the holy city. But because of scheming among the participants, the Fourth Crusade became instead a conquest of Byzantium in 1204. This sack of Constantinople underlines how crucial the failure of gaining Egypt as a resource was. The concentrated urban wealth of Constantinople in Byzantium was too tempting as a substitute for Egypt to be resisted, even if Eastern Christians were brethren in the faith and Muslims the enemy.

Precarious Crusader Survival for Another Century Not surprisingly, once western Europeans had stripped Constantinople bare and established a precarious Latin regime (1204–1257), the idea of conquering Egypt became an obsession. Five more crusades were launched for the benefit of the Kingdom of Jerusalem (1191–1291), which now was a narrow coastal strip of land with Acre as it capital. Only one of these crusades landed in Acre; all others sailed to, or toward, Egypt without ever yielding significant material returns or leading to permanent conquest.

Beginning in the mid-1200s, however, it was only a question of time before the Crusader Kingdom would become the victim of new and powerful political forces arising in the Middle East. In 1250 the Mamluks—Turkish military slaves from the Russian steppes and dominant in the armies of Saladin's successors—established their own regime in Egypt (1250–1517). Barely in power, in 1260 the Mamluks had to face the pagan Mongols, who had emerged in the previous half-century under Genghis Khan (r. 1206–1227) and his descendants as a major power (see Chapter 13). The Mongols were conquerors of a giant but loosely organized cavalry-borne empire in central Asia, China, eastern Europe, and the eastern Middle East—so they were tough competition for the Mamluks (see Chapter 12).

The Mongols stormed into the Middle East in 1255, conquering Iran and Iraq, ending what remained of the Abbasid caliphate in Baghdad in 1258, and advancing into Syria. After conquering Baghdad, they tolerated the weak crusader kingdom, since their main target was the Mamluk Sultanate as the last remaining Islamic power in the Middle East. The Mamluks, however, defeated the Mongols in several battles between 1260 and 1303, thanks to their much heavier cavalry, and pushed them from Syria back into Iraq and Iran. Under the name of Ilkhanids, the Mongols converted to Islam and became linguistically Persian. Less concerned about the Mongol threat, the Mamluks terminated the crusader state in 1291 with the conquest of Acre.

Islamic and Eastern Christian Civilizations at Their Height

By 1300, the borders between Western and Eastern Christianity as well as Islam were again clearly drawn. The most important state was the Mamluk Sultanate in Egypt, Palestine, and Syria. It had been victorious against the crusaders and the Mongols and was the richest and most powerful state, enduring for nearly three centuries (1250–1517). It represented Middle Eastern Islamic civilization at its peak. Byzantium had been rebuilt as a small but culturally flourishing realm located mostly in the Balkans (1261–1453). Both were eventually succeeded by the Turkish Ottoman Empire (Chapter 16), the origins of which date to 1300, and which shifted the center of Islamic civilization from Egypt northward to Anatolia and the Balkans.

State and Society in Mamluk Egypt

Few in the Mamluk ruling class spoke Arabic or intermarried with the indigenous population of their realm in Egypt and Syria. The indigenous population in turn possessed its own autonomous institutions, such as judicial courts, Sufi (mystics') lodges, and religious endowments. Although the Mamluks provided military protection, especially during the time of the Mongol attacks, the indigenous population had to pay for it dearly with high taxes and often arbitrary rule.

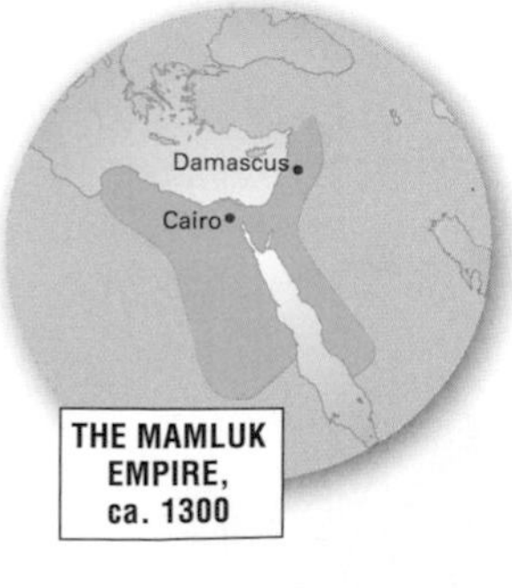

THE MAMLUK EMPIRE, ca. 1300

The Mamluk Ruling Class At the top of the ruling class was the sultan, who controlled the annual purchases of slaves and commanded the largest cavalry regiment. Raiding parties in the Mongol state of the Golden Horde (1241–1502) on the Russian steppes (and later the Caucasus) captured boys and girls from nomadic tribes and sold them to Genoese mariners, who shipped the slaves to Alexandria. The popes protested against the slave trade but to no avail.

The Mamluk sultan governed with a council of a dozen or so emirs at his side. Each commanded a cavalry regiment of his own. The lesser emirs in the council were stationed in the provincial cities of Egypt and Syria. Additional auxiliary troops, both infantry and light cavalry, consisted of sons of Mamluks, tribal nomadic contingents, and freeborn Turks. The sultans maintained a lavish court in Cairo, which included a splendid kitchen and some of the finest cooks of their time. A large civilian bureaucracy, composed of Muslim, Coptic Christian, and Jewish scribes and accountants, staffed the three main ministries—correspondence and archives, tax collection, and army administration. Other officials oversaw the construction and/or administration of granaries, oil presses, the mint, hospitals, the postal service (including pigeon courier), water supplies, sanitation, stud farms, horse stables, and the hippodrome (for polo games). The maintenance of a standing, well-supplied army ready for mobilization at any moment was of utmost concern.

Mamluk power was based on a large, state-centered economy. At the center was a rich, irrigated agriculture that did not suffer from the salinization that plagued Iraq. The annual Nile flood at the height of the summer rolled down at a steeper slope than that of the lower Euphrates and Tigris and therefore flushed waste water out into the sea more easily. In the countryside, the top tier of Mamluk officers held tax assignments (sing. *iqta*) in the form of village districts. They used the revenues

Mamluk Cavalry. Mamluk horsemen, protected by chain mail armor and wearing helmets with visors, wielded swords and lances similar to those of the crusaders. Stationed in barracks on Nile islands near Cairo, the Asian-born, originally pagan, Muslim-educated Mamluks formed a standing army of a dozen regiments that trained daily and could be mobilized within a short time. Their children were not slaves but freeborn Muslims, who were admitted only to auxiliary military units. The Mamluks were thus a one-generation ruling class replenished regularly from the outside.

from these assignments to pay the lower officers and regular soldiers of their regiments wages and food rations. Bureaucrats and managers recruited from the indigenous Arab population aided them in the collection of the taxes in grain and their sale on the market.

In the cities, the same top officers owned buildings and collected rents from residences, mills, ovens, workshops, inns, public baths, and bazaars. They hired large labor forces for the construction or repair of mosques, city walls, fortresses, and waterworks. Sultans and emirs even built entire city quarters. They usually paid regular wages to their workers but occasionally also used forced labor. The sultans had their own permanent labor force, which included prisoners and slaves. Their military campaigns were occasions for large numbers of craftspeople, traders, storytellers, entertainers, prostitutes, and other hangers-on to find additional employment. In short, nearly all economic activities in the villages as well as cities revolved around the demands of the sultans and emirs.

The Urban Working Population Below the Mamluk ruling class and the intermediate urban elite of judges and religious scholars were craftspeople, laborers, domestics, and farmers. Urban working people lived in city quarters, which were organized according to religious (Christian, Jewish), ethnic (Arab, Kurdish, Persian), and, in the case of the Sunni majority, family and clan ties. The city quarters were not closed communities, however, and always contained minorities.

City quarters, crafts clusters, and neighborhood mosques and Sufi lodges were autonomous structures in urban life. Although overseen by appointees of the market inspectors, the residents often engaged in acts of resistance and rebellion against the Mamluks in times of famine, overtaxation, or arbitrary rule. In addition, Syrian cities, such as Damascus and Aleppo, had a long tradition of rebellious youth gangs fomenting unrest in suburbs and adjacent villages outside the city walls. During times of peace these gangs collected protection money from owners of workshops and market stalls, inevitably coming into conflict with the market inspectors and their deputies whose turf they invaded. At times of economic or political distress they linked forces across city quarters and transformed themselves into formidable militias, holding down entire Mamluk regiments for days or weeks. The gangs provided a degree of protection for society from the state.

Gender Relations Islamic civilization followed the traditional Middle Eastern patriarchal family system. Within this system, as we saw at the beginning of the chapter, married women had definite rights and were no longer the chattel they had been in the Assyrian Empire. But the Syrian Muslim leader Usama ibn Munqidh (1095–1188) was shocked when he saw the behavior of the men and women in the Crusader Kingdom: Husbands allowed their wives to walk around alone in public and shake hands and converse with men to whom they were not married. The patriarchal order in Islamic civilization was clearly stricter than that in Western Christianity. Ibn Munqidh had only contempt for crusaders who had such a low sense of honor that they even went home alone when their wives wished to continue their chats (perhaps even flirtations) with other men. Evidently, a significant cultural difference existed between Western Christianity and Islamic civilization.

Divorce Court. Husband and wife arguing about a divorce before a judge; scene from al-Hariri, *Maqamat* (ms. dated 1222). Hariri's stories, among the most popular during the classical period, involve a poor but eloquent storyteller traveling from town to town in different disguises but being recognized each time by the fictional author. The stories include occurrences of everyday life, like this divorce.

Byzantine Provincial and Central Organization

The one-generational system defining the Mamluk ruling class was a unique form of governmental organization in the history of Islamic religious civilization. Just as unique was the theme organization in the Byzantine Empire. The crucial difference, of course, was the time disparity. The Mamluk Sultanate was a phenomenon at the height of Islamic civilization. The theme organization characterized the very beginning of the Byzantine Empire and was in the process of disappearing in 1204 when the empire was disrupted by the Fourth Crusade and subsequent Catholic regime in the Latin Empire (1204–1261). It was absent from the reconstituted Byzantine Empire in all but the name.

The Rise of the Landed Aristocracy In Egypt the requirements of irrigation favored social uniformity and administrative centralization. Byzantium with its rain-fed agriculture oscillated between free smallholder farms and big landlords on one hand and a large central administration on the other. This central administration could grow as large as it did by ca. 1100 under conditions of relative external peace because it was well protected by its maritime location and well connected with most provinces by easy sea and river communication.

When the themes were introduced around 660 the empire still possessed a functional urban system and money economy, in contrast to much of western Europe where Roman urban institutions had withered more dramatically. Granted, the emperors settled foot soldiers and horsemen on plots of land in partial payment for their services. But they also still possessed the means to collect taxes in money and distribute them in the form of stipends among the soldiers. Furthermore, although it is estimated that about a fifth of the Anatolian land was allocated to the themes, mostly from imperial estates, plenty of small freeholders as well as large landlords inherited from the late Roman period coexisted with them.

Anonymous, "The Farmer's Law" c. 700 CE

In the difficult years of defense, the emperor and his central administration were relatively weak. They could protect only the themes but not the small farmers and thereby were unable to prevent the rise of the landed aristocracy. From about the mid-700s, landlords typically began to gobble up small farms and reserve the positions of theme generals for their families: They became a hereditary aristocracy. Free farmers turned increasingly into tenant farmers of the aristocracy, and it is estimated that by 1200 the free farmers (by now also including demilitarized themes) had become a minority. Like the Mamluk emirs a little later, the aristocratic landlords had become the wealthiest segment of imperial society.

The Recentralization of the Empire Generals from the aristocracy were the main competitors for the office of emperor in Constantinople, from the beginning of the themes. But when the empire recovered and the central administration grew again from the 900s onward, high officials of the bureaucracy developed their own ambitions hostile to those of the aristocracy. An administrative handbook of 899 listed 59 high officials invited to the emperor's banquet table and some 500 additional officials invited to palace receptions. By 1187, as evidenced by a palace muster in that year, the size of the bureaucracy had doubled, mostly through title inflation and the sale of offices. The court of Constantinople resembled that of Versailles many centuries later.

In the eleventh and twelfth centuries the emperors were typically torn between the interests of the aristocracy and the central administration. They shared the interests of the aristocrats by wishing to preserve the themes so that the territorial integrity of the empire would be preserved. But they also sided with the central administration by not wishing to be pawns of the aristocrats, their potential rivals. In the eleventh century few emperors were up to the task of long-term reforms, such as ensuring regular theme training or exercises and prohibiting the acquisition of land by the aristocracy.

The easy way out was to hire mercenaries, beginning with the Varangian Guard. Competent emperors, as from the Komnenos dynasty (1081–1185), however, realized that the financial capacity of the state was insufficient to hire more than small numbers of mercenaries into these guards. They made extensive use of a hitherto seldom-used institution, the land assignment (*pronoia*), which allowed an assignee to collect all taxes from a parcel of land in return for military service. This institution, similar to that of the iqta used in Islamic countries (p. 281), became the backbone of a vast patronage system of family appointments and other leading families in Constantinople. Scholars have estimated that 90 percent of the upper military positions in the mid-1100s were occupied by members of the Komnenos family, with most paying themselves through assignments.

Of course, after the hiatus of 1204–1261, the court and its top families were largely gone. What were left were the aristocratic families in the reconstituted provinces. Their reluctance to submit permanently to the new Paleologus imperial family of post-1261 eventually doomed Byzantium when the Ottomans decided to end it in 1453.

Commercial Relations from the Atlantic to the South China Sea

The Persians and Romans had pioneered the trade of gold and silver for subtropical and tropical luxuries during the period 600 BCE–600 CE, as we discussed in Chapter 7. An enormous leap forward in this trade occurred during the Fatimid and Mamluk periods in Egypt. It was clearly facilitated by the existence of a cultural unity in the enormous expanse of Islamic civilization, even if this civilization was politically fragmented into a commonwealth of autonomous realms. In addition, Byzantium during its heyday (950–1050) and western Europe after the First Crusade (1099) were firmly integrated in this trade for luxuries. An Afro-Eurasian commercial world system, extending from West Africa to China and regularly connected by seasonal travel, linked the Islamic, Eastern Christian, and Western Christian civilizations to the Indian and Chinese civilizations (see Map 10.7).

Trade Routes and Commerce To understand the West Africa–China world trade, we begin with West Africa. Villagers mined gold in the rain forest on the upper Niger and Senegal Rivers and traded with African merchants from kingdoms located along the middle Niger. The kings sent raiding parties to other regions in the rain forest to capture slaves. Merchants and kings then sold the gold and surplus of slaves not employed in the kingdoms to visiting Muslim merchants from North Africa and Iberia.

The visitors from the north paid with North African and Iberian manufactures and with salt from mines in the Sahara. In the Mediterranean basin, Muslims, Jews, and Western and Eastern Christians shared the trade of West African gold (minted into coins) and European timber for Indian and Indonesian spices, dye stuffs, ointments, and cottons as well as Chinese silks, porcelain, and lacquerware. This sharing of the trade is known to us thanks to the rich trove of Jewish documents, the Geniza papyri, found at the end of the nineteenth century in the Cairo synagogue (see Source 10.4). The Mamluks allowed only Muslims and Jews to travel beyond the Mediterranean and thus Christians remained limited to the Mediterranean.

In addition to these main routes, there were three secondary trade routes. First, there was the overland Silk Road with its gold-for-luxuries trade that connected Iran with China via central Asia, active particularly during the Mongol period. Second, there was the maritime East African trade route, where merchants

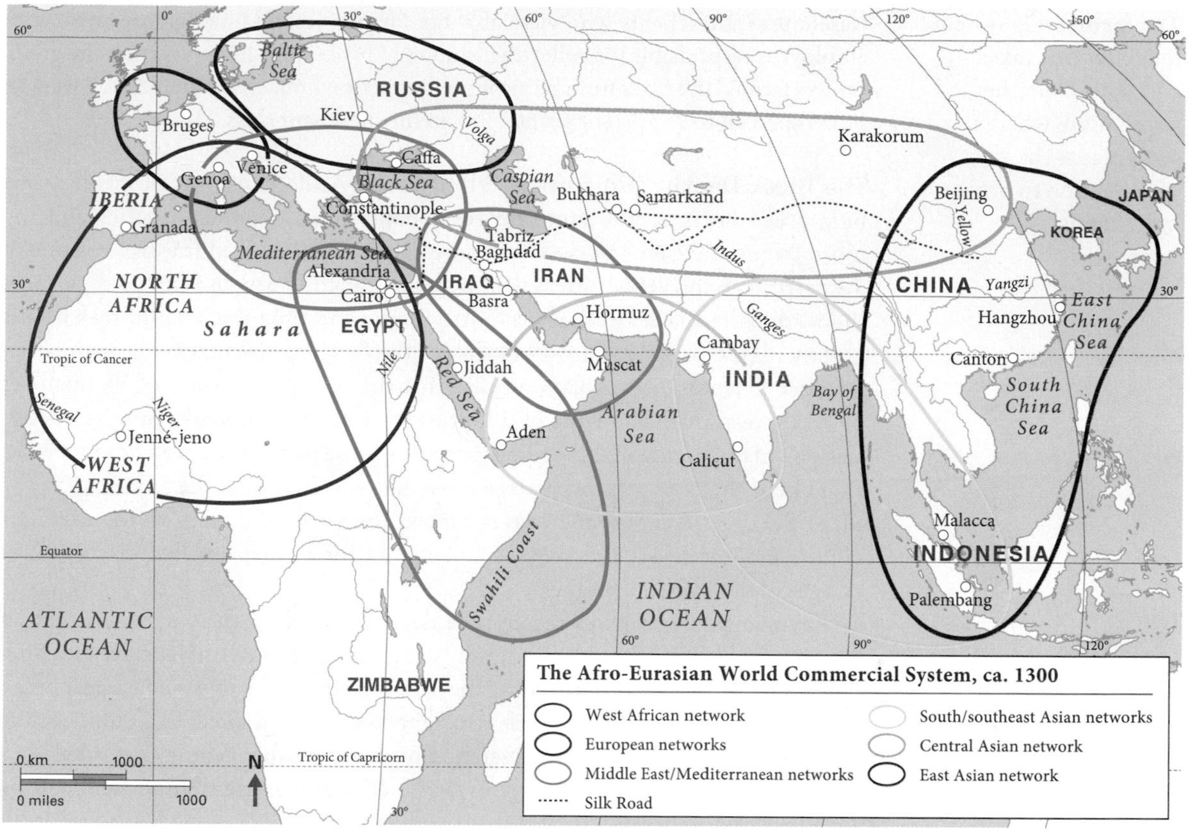

MAP 10.7 The Afro-Eurasian World Commercial System, ca. 1300.

exchanged manufactures for ivory, gold, and slaves. The latter route connected Egypt and Iraq with the Swahili Muslim city-states along the East African coast and the gold mines of Zimbabwe (see Chapter 14). And third, there was the Volga route, where Rus merchants traded gold, silver, spices, ivory, silk, wine, and fur, connecting the Middle East with western Europe. The Abbasid and Mamluk regiments were major consumers of the goods that flowed down from the Volga trade route, using Russian and Scandinavian furs for the designation of its ranks. Both primary and secondary trade routes yielded immense supplementary tax revenues, which added to the basic and highly dependable agricultural tax income of the Mamluks.

Nautical chart of the eastern Mediterranean, c. 1065 CE

Islamic and Jewish merchants in the Egyptian center of this network were for the most part wholesalers for whom the import and distribution of eastern luxuries formed only a part of their overall commercial activities. They also organized the regional production and distribution of raw materials, such as textile fibers (wool, flax, cotton, and silk), chemicals for dyeing and tanning, metal ingots for making utensils and jewelry, and pitch for caulking ships' planks. They contracted with craftspeople for the production of soap, glassware, candles, and perfume. Tailors, cobblers, and sugar mill owners delivered robes, slippers, and bags of refined sugar to the merchants. To provide their accountants, scribes, porters, and guards with daily food, these merchants had caterers deliver lunches and dinners to their residences and

Tax farmers: A system for collecting taxes and rents from the population, where the state grants the right of collection to private individuals.

warehouses. Merchants who were also **tax farmers** maintained grain stores, with employees responsible for collecting, shipping, brokering, and marketing the grain. Others farmed the taxes from ports or public auction houses. Diversification was the preferred path to consistent profitability in the merchant class.

The Black Death Extensive travel, however, yielded not only profits but also unforeseen horrors. The more densely people lived together in cities and the more frequently they traveled, the more often they incurred the risk of spreading terrifying and lethal diseases hitherto confined to small, isolated regions of the world. The Black Death of 1346 was the second time that an outbreak of this ghastly plague occurred in world history (the first was the Plague of Justinian in 541; see Chapter 7). Scholars surmise that the Mongol invasion of Vietnam set off the spread of this horrific mid-fourteenth-century pandemic. Southeast Asia was one of the permanent breeding grounds for the pandemic among rodent fleas. From here, the Mongols dispersed the bacillus via China and the Silk Road to the Black Sea area. Genoese merchants carried the virulent disease to the Mediterranean and northwest Europe (see Chapter 11 for a more detailed discussion of ravages of the bubonic plague).

Egyptian sources vividly recount the devastation which the plague wrought on the population. The plague was both sinister and incomprehensible to people at the time who had never experienced it. They possessed no effective medical resources, and thus found themselves powerless to fight it. Similarly difficult to fathom was the recurrence of the plague every generation or so for another century and a half, hitting rulers and subjects; rich and poor; and men, women, and children with equally appalling force. Not until the 1500s did Middle Eastern population levels recover to pre-1346 levels.

Religion, Sciences, and the Arts in Two Religious Civilizations

Despite the impact of the Black Death, Mamluk Egypt and reconstituted Byzantium during the 1300s and 1400s were highly active cultural centers. Although they sought or received little further cultural stimuli from outside their civilizations, scholars and artists developed their respective cultures further within traditional boundaries. In Islamic civilization, the most important new cultural phenomenon was mystical (Sufi) Islam, and in Eastern Christianity it was a revival of Platonism.

Islamic Culture: Intellectual and Scientific Expressions

Sufism: Meditative devotion to faith, expressed in the form of prayer, ecstasy, chanting, or dancing.

Like a number of other religions we have examined, Islam developed a devotional mystical tradition of its own. Mystical Islam, or **Sufism**, was an outgrowth of meditative thought and practices developed from the Christian, Zoroastrian, and Greek philosophical heritages interacting within the Muslim world. Around 1050 Muslim scholars integrated Sufism into the Sunni-dominated Islamic civilization, and around 1200 Sunni mystics adapted Sufism to popular practice in the form of congregational brotherhoods in lodges. Educated Muslims, in addition, were conversant in philosophy and the sciences, both of which experienced an important flowering in the period 1050–1300.

Sunni–Sufi Islam Sufism was a form of meditative practice that went beyond the prayers prescribed in Islam. A Sufi typically went step-by-step through stages to withdraw from sensory experience and arrive at the climax of pure ineffable consciousness. If pushed for words, Sufis identified this consciousness as their experience of the eternal and infinite divine. Since this experience took place within themselves, early Sufis in the 900s were often accused of violating the Islamic doctrine of God's transcendence. It was only in the second half of the eleventh century during the Seljuk-sponsored religious revival that a compromise was reached. The main figure representing this compromise was the Persian Abd al-Hamid al-Ghazali (1058–1111; see Source 10.5), who introduced a persuasive metaphor to illustrate the compromise: Believers, looking at a glass of red wine from a distance, are unable to decide whether they are not instead seeing an empty red glass. Ineffable experience cannot be expressed unambiguously.

Maritime Trade. This image, an illustration in Hariri's *Maqamat* (ms. dated 1236), depicts a stylized oceangoing sailboat used between Arabia and India.

In the 1200s, teachers of Sufism—often revered as saints—founded lodges in which they provided instruction and training in meditative practice for Muslims. With time, these lodges branched out, with hundreds of sublodges organized along the specific practices of its founder saints in urban centers as well as villages and even among nomadic tribes. Sunni Muslims of all walks of life joined, from legal scholars and judges to craftspeople, farmers, and nomads. By around 1450, Islamic civilization was a commonwealth not only of competing states but also of competing Sufi brotherhoods. The Sunni–Sufi compromise dominated in Islamic civilization until ca. 1900.

Philosophy and Sciences As in the case of Sufism, philosophers also encountered opposition from among the proponents of Sunnism and did so for the same reason of violating the transcendence doctrine. Greek philosophical writings were accessible in translation from Syriac since the 800s and had attracted Muslim thinkers well before the emergence of mature Sunnism. A central concern of the Muslim philosophers was the reconciliation of Platonic–Aristotelian thought with Islam. Leading philosophers, such as Ibn Sina (Avicenna, ca. 980–1037) and Ibn Rushd (Averroës, 1126–1198), achieved this reconciliation by viewing philosophy as the discipline of logical concepts and religion its equivalent in images. Philosophy, requiring literacy and extensive education, was practiced by the few, while religion, which relied on imagery, was accessible to the uneducated masses. Ibn Khaldun (1332–1406), a philosopher of history and political theorist, accepted this division between the few and the masses but sided with the latter, finding philosophy and speculative theology incompatible with religion. As in Western Christianity, thinkers struggled with the question of compatibility between thought and faith.

As in philosophy, scientific texts were also available in translation. Islamic scientists made major contributions early on, pushing beyond the discoveries of the Greeks. The Greeks had excelled in developing geometry into a mathematical science, but in the absence of a numbering system—they used letters as numbers—they had left algebra undeveloped until the Alexandrian period of Hellenism. The Persian Muhammad ibn Musa al-Khwarizmi (ca. 780–850) laid the foundations for the conversion of algebra into a science. In his textbooks, computation is based on a decimal system of "Arabic" numerals, from 0 to 9. He borrowed this system from

The Golden Age of Islam

India (where it had been developed 150 years earlier) and introduced algebraic equations for the determination of unknown quantities, expressed through letters, as is still done today.

After Khwarizmi, mathematicians developed decimal fractions, raised numbers to high powers, extracted roots from large numbers, and investigated the properties of complex equations with roots and higher-degree powers. Persian and Arab astronomers simplified the work of the Hellenistic astronomer Ptolemy (d. ca. 168 CE), whose trigonometry operated with a confusing variety of three centers for the planetary system. Physicists elaborated on Archimedes' investigations into the physics of balances and weights and developed the impetus theory of motion (force applied to thrown objects), adopted in Western Christian physics and much discussed there until the time of Galileo in the 1500s.

Medicine was based on comprehensive handbooks, with chapters on anatomy, bodily fluids ("humors"), diseases, diagnosis, surgery, therapy, and drugs. Specialized medical fields included ophthalmology (the treatment of eye diseases), obstetrics and pediatrics (which also dealt with sexual hygiene, birth, breast-feeding, childhood, and childhood diseases), as well as pharmacology, with descriptions of medicinal plants. The discovery in the 1200s of the pulmonary circulation system of the body anticipated similar European medical discoveries by several centuries, underlining the high degree of specialization which the sciences had reached in Islamic civilization. In general, prior to ca. 1500, the sciences in Islamic civilization were well ahead of those of the Western Christians. It was thanks to stimulation by the Muslims that the Christians eventually caught up.

Artistic Expressions in Islamic Civilization

During the formative period of Islamic civilization (800–950), secular poetry and prose flourished. As Sunni–Sufi Islam fully evolved (1050–1200), religion was interwoven with the telling of stories, the painting of miniatures, and the building of mosques and palaces. Persian artistic traditions reemerged from pre-Islamic times, and Turkish central Asian steppe traditions entered Islamic culture.

Islamic Literature The first extant poems in Arabic were odes celebrating the clan ethos of courage, trust, generosity, and hospitality in Arabia (800s). They follow the quest theme common to many folktales and myths, with its three distinct stages of loss, marginality, and reintegration that the hero has to experience to find peace. In the cosmopolitan culture of Baghdad, new forms of literature evolved which brought together highly literate secretaries and officials from a variety of non-Arab ethnic backgrounds. They cultivated poetry with urban themes, such as the pleasures of sensual abandonment, seduction, and homosexual love. Essays expressing refined taste, elegance, and wit circulated widely, on topics such as "The Art of Keeping One's Mouth Shut," "Against Civil Servants," "Arab Food," and "Levity and Seriousness." The most popular collection of short stories was the *Maqamat,* about an impersonator telling tall stories to gullible listeners, collecting money for his tales, and traveling from city to city in ever-new disguises. Another collection of stories, the *Arabian Nights,* was first written down in Mamluk Damascus during the 1300s. Even today, one admires the refined taste, elegance, and wit that people of cosmopolitan Islamic urbanity possessed.

The story of Ali Cogia, a merchant of Baghdad, from *The Arabian Nights*

Persian and Turkish Muslims preserved their pre-Islamic pasts in epics celebrating the heroic deeds of their ancestral leaders in central Asia. In the case of the Iranian *shahs*, the poet Firdosi (940–1020) spent a lifetime collecting the traditions of the Persians and rendering them into the 60,000 verses of the *Book of Kings* (*Shanameh*). The anonymous epic *Dede Korkut* originated among the central Asian Turks at the time of the Arab conquests and was written down in the 1300s. Both ethnic groups also produced outstanding poets, especially mystical poets, among whom the Afghanistan-born Jalal al-Din Rumi (1207–1273) acquired worldwide popularity. Similar to Ghazali, Rumi sought to illustrate the complexities of God's transcendence-cum-immanence through ambiguities and paradoxes. Although Arabic remained the basic literary language, Persian gained increasingly in popularity.

Painting and Architecture in Islam In the visual arts, Arabs and early Muslims continued to create paintings and sculptures in the hybrid realistic–hieratic style which had become common in the Mediterranean and Middle East during the 300s. The realism of the Greek sculptures and Roman frescoes was mixed with the hieratic figurative art of Sasanid reliefs. In the hieratic style, artists sought to capture the essence of their subjects, often neglecting the light-and-shadow as well as three-dimensional representational style typical of realism. Modern viewers have often described this hybrid style as less artistic and refined than that of Greco-Roman realism. But this description does not take into account the long tradition of Mesopotamian hieratic conventions which culminated with the Sasanid Persians. These conventions constitute an artistic style in its own right, even if it is perhaps less appealing to modern tastes.

Moreover, since Islamic law contains prohibitions against painting and sculpting, similar to Byzantine iconoclasm, the visual arts disappeared entirely from public spaces and retreated to the domestic sphere of the courts of rulers. The Umayyad and early Abbasid caliphs loved frescoes with hunting, drinking, and dancing scenes but confined them to the chambers of their palaces. The rulers of Granada in the 1400s enjoyed scenes of courtly love in their royal chambers. The Seljuk and Ilkhanid rulers were lavish sponsors of miniature painters. They delighted in richly illustrated biographies and histories, which played a role in their libraries similar to that of coffee-table books today.

By contrast, the architecture of mosques and palaces was intended for public use, often in commemoration of their state sponsors. Mosques followed the architectural style of the Arab open courtyard and covered prayer hall or Persian open courtyard with surrounding half domes and galleries, both with roots in the pre-Islamic past of the Middle East. Among the surviving palaces, the best preserved is the Alhambra of Granada (ca. 1350–1450), with its exquisite honeycomb-style decorations. Religious and palace architectures were perhaps the most direct forms in which the identity of Islamic culture was expressed. They are still admired today for their variation and richness.

Learning and the Arts in Byzantium

In contrast to Islamic civilization, the Eastern Christianity of Byzantium was a fully formed religious civilization from its beginning in 640, even if it underwent major doctrinal changes thereafter. The principal institutions of higher learning were the secular Magnaura and the theological Hagia Sophia, which offered the study of the liberal arts and theology. The liberal arts included the preparatory *trivium* (grammar, rhetoric, and dialectics), advanced *quadrivium* (arithmetic, geometry, music, and astronomy), and philosophy as the capstone. During its difficult struggle for survival against the Arabs, Slavs, Bulgars, and Rus, Constantinople declined in both wealth and sponsorship of knowledge and the arts. The copying of texts and teaching survived tenuously.

Patterns Up Close

Byzantine Icons and Islamic Miniatures

One prominent result of the interactions between the Mediterranean and the Middle East in the early centuries CE was a merging of their respective realistic and hieratic artistic styles, which led to a new hybrid pattern in the arts. In this pattern, artists focused on hieratic significance (that is, features essential for immediate recognition), neglecting realism in the execution of nonessential elements in the image. While the main subject or object remained realistic, symbolical features highlighted its significance. Background features appeared in schematic or generic (that is, nonrealistic) fashion, especially in miniature painting.

Of the many features characterizing the realistic–hieratic style, the halo serves as a useful example. The halo is a traditional Mesopotamian motif, dating back to the Sumerians, and was associated with gods, heroes, and kings, distinguishing these figures as standing out from (ordinary) mortals by a light of glory emanating from their heads. The three Persian dynasties (Achaemenids, Parthians, and Sasanids) adopted this Mesopotamian tradition, as did the imperial Romans. The first Roman ruler who chose the halo as his sign of glorious distinction was Emperor Theodosius I (r. 379–395).

Eventually, also in the fourth century, the halo was transferred from the gods, heroes, and kings to depictions of Jesus. Thus, the pagan symbol of glory ultimately became the sign of holiness in Christianity, figuring prominently in the Byzantine art of icons depicting Christ, the apostles, and saints. The halo similarly continued in Islamic miniatures where the Prophet Muhammad, prophets of the Hebrew Bible, and angels are surrounded by flaming halos, painted under Mongol-Chinese influence. In contrast to Western art, both Byzantine Christians and Muslims retained the halo for rulers. Muslims even applied it to ordinary humans to distinguish them from their schematic surroundings and thus emptied the halo of its original symbolic meaning.

Early icons were closely related to the realistic Hellenistic-Egyptian Fayyum funeral art. In Byzantium, icons became devotional paintings, predominantly on wooden panels, but also on other media, such as mosaics and textiles. They functioned as vehicles through which their owners transferred their veneration to the persons depicted. Icon painters also incorporated gold, silver, enamel, and gemstones on their icons, thereby giving them much greater value than that of the mass of ordinary icons. Portable or affixed to altars and walls, they became ubiquitous in Byzantium and later in Russia.

During the two periods of iconoclasm (726–787 and 814–842) when large numbers of icons were smashed, 12 particular icons survived because they were believed to show images miraculously generated without the action of human hands. Two of these icons depicted the image of a church father holding up the image of Christ imprinted on a towel (the Mandylion) and on a tile (the Keramion). It was on the basis of these imprints that the iconophiles were able to win the argument against the iconoclasts for the restoration of icons: If Christ created icons, humans were permitted to create them as well.

Accordingly, in the period of 900–1200 icons became not only increasingly important fixtures in churches and monasteries but also major elements in the church liturgy. Long rows of icons on church walls and templons (dividing screens between the nave and the apsis) marked the days of the church year. Priests and monks carried double-sided icons during processions inside and outside their buildings. Ironically, the largest production of icons for churches and monasteries occurred after the hiatus of the Latin Empire (1261–1453), during a time when Byzantium was a small and impoverished realm.

In contrast to the public role of church-commissioned icons in Byzantium, Islamic figurative art was private and entirely limited to the courts of rulers as the only patrons of artists. Scholars assume that the Muslims developed their aniconism (opposition to figurative images) parallel to the Byzantine periods of iconoclasm. This attitude is well represented in the literature of the Islamic tradition, where the Quranic warnings against idolatry (e.g., 21:57–59) are interpreted as prohibitions against figurative art. While the church hierarchy in Byzantium eventually overcame iconoclasm, however, there was no such hierarchy in Islam, and so aniconism remained in force.

The undiminished continuation of figurative art on palace walls or as miniatures in books nevertheless attests to the power of the Mesopotamian hieratic traditions over which the Islamic religious scholars had no influence. This art became increasingly wide ranging in its subjects as time progressed, leaving the production of strictly hieratic representations of rulers in their glory far behind. It began with the Umayyad, Abbasid, and Fatimid palace frescoes, reliefs, sculptures, ceramics, and metalwares of ca. 700–1200. Illustrations in the medical literature translated from Greek and Syriac into Arabic, dating to the 1110s, show great similarities with Byzantine icons. In the 1100s and early 1200s, courts in Iraq sponsored miniaturists for colored drawings of mechanical devices (al-Jazari, d. 1206) as well as urban and rural scenes in storybooks (al-Wasiti, fl. early 1200s; see the illustrations on pp. 248 and 249). After 1250, the Mamluk sultans commissioned miniaturists to illustrate their military exercise manuals (see the illustration on p. 292) and the kings of Granada hired painters to create frescoes with scenes of the court as well as courtly love. In later years miniature painting proliferated under the Ottoman, Safavid, and Mughal rulers (see Chapters 16 and 20), not to mention the many lesser rulers before them. Dozens of miniaturists acquired great fame for the illustration of the Persian and Indian classics or the glorious battles won by their benefactors. Similarly famous were the illustrated lives of the Prophet Muhammad and the prophets of the Muslim tradition—drawn and colored with often exquisite artistic refinement, as if aniconism had never existed in Islamic civilization.

Christ Pantocrator. This is the oldest Christ icon, dating to the sixth century. It is kept together with a large collection of icons at the Monastery of Saint Catherine on the Sinai Peninsula in Egypt. Like most icons in this collection it is encaustic—that is, painted with a mixture of heated beeswax and pigments. Later painters used egg yolk in the place of beeswax. The Greek word *pantocrator* means "Almighty" and refers to Jesus' majesty as the king of the kingdom to come. But Jesus was also the crucified human: The left side of his face is accordingly depicted—in a very subtle way—as more human than the right.

Questions

- Is it difficult to relate to the hieratic style in art—as exemplified by Byzantine icons—today? If yes, why?
- Why was representational art so important to Muslim rulers—so much so that they defied their religious scholars?

In the arts, Byzantine iconoclasm during the 700s and 800s caused the destruction of innumerable and irreplaceable icons and mosaics. It also disrupted the transmission of artistic techniques from masters to subsequent generations of artists. When the public display and veneration of images became the officially sanctioned doctrine again in the mid-800s, it took a while for the arts to recover. As artists were relearning their craft, they engaged in much initial experimentation.

Revival of Learning The subsequent mature period of ca. 950–1200 saw a veritable explosion in the production of icons, mosaics, and frescoes as well as the building of new churches and monasteries. Byzantine mosaic craftspeople and painters were also much sought after by the caliphs in Córdoba, who avoided hiring artists from their Abbasid and Fatimid rivals. Byzantine craftspeople were also popular with the princes of Kiev, who, after their conversion, carried the Byzantine arts into the commonwealth of Eastern Christian states, providing it with an immediately visible cultural unity.

Higher learning revived noticeably after 950. The state built a number of public schools of law and philosophy in the middle of the 1000s, followed by a church school for theology at the end of the century. Philosophers revived the tradition of commenting on Plato, Aristotle, and the Neo-Platonic synthesis inherited from Hellenistic antiquity. This revival aroused among churchmen the same suspicions as among the Muslim scholars and led to the condemnation of some philosophers. Two outstanding figures were Michael Psellos (ca. 1017–1078) and John Italos (fl. eleventh century). Both taught many students, but church or palace hostility forced them at points in their careers to cease teaching.

Byzantine Renaissance The disruption of 1204–1261 by the Fourth Crusade and Latin Empire saw a tremendous loss of Byzantine art as well as manuscripts, this time to Venetian pillage during the Fourth Crusade. When Byzantium was restored Plato scholars initiated a strong recovery of philosophy, which resulted in a return of Western Christians, this time peacefully, to that city in search of Platonic writings. The Academy of Florence, a leading institution of the Italian Renaissance (see Chapter 17), invited Byzantine Plato scholars to help in the recovery of the texts of this philosopher. Further scholars emigrated to Italy after the fall of Constantinople to the Ottomans in 1453. Thus, Western Christianity renewed its adaptation to stimuli from a neighboring civilization, in contrast to Eastern Christianity and Islamic civilization, which continued within their existing traditions.

Putting It All Together

interactive concept map

Both Islamic civilization and Eastern Christian civilization were based on a synthesis of religious revelation and Greek philosophy and science. This synthesis had begun in the Roman and Sasanid Persian Empires. Muslims accomplished their cultural synthesis after the period of Arab conquest, roughly during 800–950. Eastern Christians completed their synthesis in the period 950–1050, after their recovery from the Arab, Slav, Bulgar, and Rus onslaughts. Both refined their internal civilizational achievements to a high degree well into the 1400s. Thereafter, they did not absorb substantial new cultural stimuli from the outside until about 1700, when the Muslim Ottoman sultans invited western Europeans to reform their empire.

Islamic civilization was an outgrowth of the Arab conquests in the Middle East, central Asia, northern Africa, and Europe in the 600s and early 700s. It emerged as an adaptation of the Arabs to the heritages of the Jews, Christians, Greeks, Romans, and Persians. Its core was the monotheism of Allah, and its cultural adaptations were to Greek philosophy and science, Roman law, and Persian statecraft, as well as a variety of artistic and architectural traditions of the Middle East and Mediterranean. At its height, during 950–1450, a commonwealth of competing Islamic states represented Islamic civilization. This ethnically diverse commonwealth with Arab, Turkish, Persian, and Berber rulers and states shared a number of common characteristics, among which were the same canon of scriptures (the Quran and the Sunna), moral norms and laws (Sharia), and religious institutions (separate state and religious authorities as well as Sunni–Sufi brotherhoods). These characteristics endured to 1300 and beyond.

The Byzantine Empire succeeded the Roman Empire around 640 when the emperors, under attack by the Arabs, reorganized their military forces and redefined the inherited Christian theology. Byzantium recovered politically and culturally in the mid-900s, and the empire changed into a commonwealth when Russian Kievan Rus converted to Eastern Christianity. Unfortunately, the recovery lasted only a century. The Seljuk Muslim Turks conquered most Anatolian provinces of Byzantium (1071–1176), and the Venetians conquered Constantinople in the Fourth Crusade and established the Latin Empire (1204–1261). Byzantium recovered thereafter for another two and a half centuries and even flourished culturally, but after 1453 the center of Eastern Christian civilization shifted northward to Russia.

Review and Relate

Thinking Through Patterns

Examine the ways historians approach the big questions of this chapter.

The adoption of Christianity and Zoroastrianism as state or privileged monotheistic religions in the Roman and Sasanid Empires was late and ultimately did not prevent these empires from eventual collapse. But both empires helped launch the period of religious civilizations. New empires arose in this period, beginning around 600. Byzantium was Christian from its inception. The Arab Empire adopted Islam early on, initially under the Umayyads and fully in the Abbasid-led commonwealth of states. Eastern Christian and Islamic civilizations were characteristic of religious civilizations because both embraced basic religious scriptures, upheld a form of separation of state and religion, and adapted to inherited cultural traditions.

» Why can the period 600–1450 be described as the age of religious civilizations? How do Eastern Christian and Islamic civilizations fit this description?

Specifically, the pattern of Islamic civilization included revealed scripture, a religiously interpreted history, the separation of state and religion, the fusion of revealed religion and Greek philosophy, and the adaptation to the scientific and artistic heritage from Rome and Persia. The pattern was completed early, by about

» Which cultural traditions combined to form Islamic religious civilization? What

were the most characteristic patterns?

950 with the emergence of Sunni Islam, but continued to evolve internally, without further outside stimuli, through Sufi Islam and a myriad of Sufi brotherhood lodges. The result was an Islamic civilization around 1300 which was composed of many states and even more autonomous religious congregations existing alongside the mosques.

» How did Eastern Christian or Byzantine civilization evolve over time? On which institutions was this civilization based, and how did it evolve, wedged between Islamic and Western Christian civilizations?

The late Roman Empire achieved a close integration of Christianity, Greek-Hellenistic philosophy and science, and Roman law, but it was hard-pressed for survival by the conquering Arabs. When the Eastern Roman, or Byzantine, Empire recovered, it elevated Eastern Greek Orthodox Christianity to a supreme position. A powerful recentralization effort strengthened the empire, especially in the Balkans. But in the wake of the Seljuk invasions and Western Christian Crusades, the empire weakened again, surviving in a much diminished form until it was conquered by the Ottoman Muslims in 1453. Eastern Christianity survived as a state religion in Russia.

Against the Grain

Consider this as a counterpoint to the main patterns examined in this chapter.

Did Ibn Taymiyya "Have a Screw Loose"?

- Was Ibn Taymiyya right in standing up against the Muslims of his time and in preaching jihad against Mongols who had converted to Islam? If yes, for which reasons?
- Are contemporary Islamists correct in claiming that their present situation in Islamic countries closely resembles that of Ibn Taymiyya facing the Mongols? If yes, are rulers in contemporary Islamic countries similar to the Mongols?

Born in Harran, northern Iraq, Taqi al-Din ibn Taymiyya (1263–1328) became a refugee as a small child when his family of prominent religious scholars fled from the pagan Mongols, fulfilling their Sharia duty to live in a Muslim-governed country. Ibn Taymiyya grew up in Damascus, then ruled by the Egyptian Mamluks, and became a prominent religious scholar in the Hanbali legal school.

Among the four legal schools, the Hanbali school was the one most devoted to the study of the Quran and prophetic traditions. Ibn Taymiyya invoked these traditions when he dedicated his scholarly career to combating the form of popular brotherhood and saintly Islam dominant in the Islamic world at the time. In his view, Muslims engaged in popular brotherhood activities and devoted to Muslim saints were insufficiently committed to Islam. He did not condemn, however, Sunnis engaging in spiritual Sufi practices as individuals, engaging in retreat, prayer, and meditation—a point often overlooked by modern reformist Muslims, for whom he is a hero.

Most of Ibn Taymiyya's contemporaries would have shrugged off his rantings against brotherhood members practising music, dancing, and visiting saints' tombs for blessings, had he not shown exemplary courage during a time of continuing Mongol attacks. In 1260 the Mongols had tried to conquer Mamluk Egypt and thereafter they succeeded in occupying parts of Syria. At one point during the occupation, the Mamluks sent a mission of religious scholars, including Ibn Taymiyya, to the Mongols to implore their ruler Ghazan (r. 1295–1304) in the name of Islam to end his attacks. Ghazan had officially converted to Islam in 1295 but continued to adhere to Mongol law rather than the Islamic Sharia. Only Ibn Taymiyya had the courage to stand before the Mongol ruler and accuse him of being an infidel, lecturing him sternly on his Muslim duty of adherence to Islamic law and peace. This feat of courage earned Ibn Taymiyya both admiration and resentment from scholars of the other religious schools.

Ibn Taymiyya, a loner since his youth who never married or even had a concubine, apparently had both an aura of self-importance and a short temper—hence the unkind surmise by one contemporary scholar concerning his mental balance. (The rendering of this as "a screw loose" is by the Middle East scholar Donald P. Little.) It was this arrogance which Ibn Taymiyya's detractors confronted, attacking him on his own ground of legalism. They accused him of violating the Islamic unity doctrine in his teachings and misinterpreting the doctrine of fighting the infidels as a religious duty.

As a result of these accusations, the Mamluks imprisoned Ibn Taymiyya. In the end, Ibn Taymiyya died in jail, a lone dissenter during a time when the majority of Muslims adhered to the different form of saintly Islam. His teachings were revived, however, in the eighteenth century in Arabia by the Wahhabis and in the twentieth century when Islamists reclaimed him as the preacher of an Islamic revolution against their own "Mongol" rulers and Islamic laxity in general.

Key Terms

audio flashcards

Caliph 275
Celibacy 286
Commonwealth 273
Creed 286
Eucharist 286
Iconoclasm, 283
Jihad 279
Muslims 275
Sharia 279
Sufism 298
Sunna 278
Tax farmers 298
Trinitarian 275
Umma 278

For additional resources, please go to **www.oup.com/us/vonsivers.**
Please see the Further Resources section at the back of the book for additional readings and suggested websites.

PATTERNS OF EVIDENCE |

Sources for Chapter 10

SOURCE 10.1 Excerpts from the Quran, *Sura* 2, "The Cow"

ca. 650 CE

The name of the most holy book of Islam, the Quran, means "the recital." It contains, according to Islamic theology, the direct words of God (Allah), as told to his prophet Muhammad through the angel Gabriel. Muslims believe that the angel directed Muhammad to "recite" 114 *suras*, or books, beginning around 610 CE. After Muhammad's death in 632, an authorized text of these *suras* was compiled and publicized. The general arrangement of the Quran is according to the length of each document. It is important to note, therefore, that the Quran does not purport to be a continuous narrative, telling a series of stories, as is typical in other religious texts. This means that individual pronouncements can be taken out of context, and that various portions of the document can be quoted to different effects.

2:177
Righteousness is not that you turn your faces toward the east or the west, but [true] righteousness is [in] one who believes in Allah, the Last Day, the angels, the Book, and the prophets and gives wealth, in spite of love for it, to relatives, orphans, the needy, the traveler, those who ask [for help], and for freeing slaves; [and who] establishes prayer and gives *zakah* [charitable gifts]; [those who] fulfill their promise when they promise; and [those who] are patient in poverty and hardship and during battle. Those are the ones who have been true, and it is those who are the righteous.

2:178
O you who have believed, prescribed for you is legal retribution for those murdered—the free for the free, the slave for the slave, and the female for the female. But whoever overlooks from his brother anything, then there should be a suitable follow-up and payment to him with good conduct. This is an alleviation from your Lord and a mercy. But whoever transgresses after that will have a painful punishment.

2:179
And there is for you in legal retribution [saving of] life, O you [people] of understanding, that you may become righteous.

Source: Sahih International translation, available online at http://quran.com/4.

2:180
Prescribed for you when death approaches [any] one of you if he leaves wealth [is that he should make] a bequest for the parents and near relatives according to what is acceptable—a duty upon the righteous.

2:181
Then whoever alters the bequest after he has heard it—the sin is only upon those who have altered it. Indeed, Allah is Hearing and Knowing.

2:182
But if one fears from the bequeather [some] error or sin and corrects that which is between them, there is no sin upon him. Indeed, Allah is Forgiving and Merciful.

2:183
O you who have believed, decreed upon you is fasting as it was decreed upon those before you that you may become righteous.

2:184
[Fasting for] a limited number of days. So whoever among you is ill or on a journey [during them]—then an equal number of days [are to be made up]. And upon those who are able [to fast, but with hardship]—a ransom [as substitute] of feeding a poor person [each day]. And whoever volunteers excess—it is better for him. But to fast is best for you, if you only knew.

2:185
The month of Ramadhan [is that] in which was revealed the Qur'an, a guidance for the people and clear proofs of guidance and criterion. So whoever sights [the new moon of] the month, let him fast it; and whoever is ill or on a journey—then an equal number of other days. Allah intends for you ease and does not intend for you hardship and [wants] for you to complete the period and to glorify Allah for that [to] which He has guided you; and perhaps you will be grateful.

2:186
And when My servants ask you, [O Muhammad], concerning Me—indeed I am near. I respond to the invocation of the supplicant when he calls upon Me. So let them respond to Me [by obedience] and believe in Me that they may be [rightly] guided.

2:187
It has been made permissible for you the night preceding fasting to go to your wives [for sexual relations]. They are clothing for you and you are clothing for them. Allah knows that you used to deceive yourselves, so He accepted your repentance and forgave you. So now, have relations with them and seek that which Allah has decreed for you. And eat and drink until the white thread of dawn becomes distinct to you from the black thread [of night]. Then complete the fast until the sunset. And do not have relations with them as long as you are staying for worship in the mosques. These are the limits [set by] Allah, so do not approach them. Thus does Allah make clear His ordinances to the people that they may become righteous.

2:188
And do not consume one another's wealth unjustly or send it [in bribery] to the rulers in order that [they might aid] you [to] consume a portion of the wealth of the people in sin, while you know [it is unlawful].

2:189
They ask you, [O Muhammad], about the new moons. Say, "They are measurements of time for the people and for Hajj." And it is not righteousness to enter houses from the back, but righteousness is [in] one who fears Allah. And enter houses from their doors. And fear Allah that you may succeed.

2:190
Fight in the way of Allah those who fight you but do not transgress. Indeed Allah does not like transgressors.

2:191
And kill them wherever you overtake them and expel them from wherever they have expelled you, and fitnah [distress, civil strife, sedition] is worse than killing. And do not fight them at al-Masjid al-Haram until they fight you there. But if they fight you, then kill them. Such is the recompense of the disbelievers.

2:192
And if they cease, then indeed, Allah is Forgiving and Merciful.

2:193
Fight them until there is no [more] fitnah and [until] worship is [acknowledged to be] for Allah. But if they cease, then there is to be no aggression except against the oppressors.

2:194
[Fighting in] the sacred month is for [aggression committed in] the sacred month, and for [all] violations is legal retribution. So whoever has assaulted you, then assault him in the same way that he has assaulted you. And fear Allah and know that Allah is with those who fear Him.

2:195
And spend in the way of Allah and do not throw [yourselves] with your [own] hands into destruction [by refraining]. And do good; indeed, Allah loves the doers of good.

Working with Sources

1. **What are the requirements of believers, and what benefits and punishments are promised in response to their actions?**
2. **Why is it important to observe the rules regarding fasting and the pilgrimage?**

SOURCE 10.2 Documents related to the iconoclasm controversy

Seventh–ninth centuries CE

The Byzantine Empire was racked by a series of religious disputes that pulled in emperors as well as priests. One of the most significant of these was an ongoing difference of opinion concerning "graven images" of Jesus and other prominent figures in Christian narratives. Was it proper to create and display images of God, and, if so, should existing "icons" be destroyed in order to protect the faithful? These documents represent the two major perspectives on this debate, between the poles of the "iconodule" (pro-icon) position and the "iconoclastic" (anti-icon) position.

ICONODULE POSITION:

1. Quinsextum Council (in Trullo), 692 CE, ruling by Justinian II (685–695; 705–711):

"Now, in order that perfection be represented before the eyes of all people, even in paintings, we ordain that from now on Christ our God, the Lamb who took upon Himself the sins of the world, be set up, even in images according to His human character, instead of the ancient Lamb. Through this figure we realize the height of the humiliation of God the Word and are led to remember His life in the flesh, His suffering, and His saving death, and the redemption ensuing from it for the world."

2. John of Damascus (675–749), Oration (*Patrologia orientalis* 94, cols. 1258C-D):

"When we set up an image of Christ in any place, we appeal to the senses, and indeed we sanctify the sense of sight, which is the highest among the perceptive senses, just as by sacred speech we sanctify the sense of hearing. An image is, after all, a reminder; it is to the illiterate what a book is to the literate, and what the word is to the hearing, the image is to sight. We remember that God ordered that a vessel be made from wood that would not rot, gilded inside and out, and that the tables of the law should be placed in it and the staff and the golden vessel containing the manna—all this for a reminder of what had taken place, and a foreshadowing of what was to come. What was this but a visual image, more compelling than any sermon? And this sacred thing was not placed in some obscure corner of the tabernacle; it was displayed in full view of the people, so that whenever they looked at it they would give honor

Source: Excerpts from Anthony Bryer and Judith Herrin, eds., *Iconoclasm: Papers Given at the Ninth Spring Symposium of Byzantine Studies, University of Birmingham, March 1975* (Birmingham, UK: Centre for Byzantine Studies, University of Birmingham, 1977), available online at http://www.tulane.edu/~august/H303/readings/Iconoclasm.htm.

and worship to the God Who had through its contents made known His design to them. They were of course not worshipping the things themselves; they were being led through them to recall the wonderful works of God, and to adore Him Whose words they had witnessed."

3. *Horos* (Definition of Faith) at the Seventh Ecumenical Council, Nicaea, 787 CE:

"We define with accuracy and care that the venerable and holy icons be set up like the form of the venerable and life-giving Cross, inasmuch as the matter consisting of colors and pebbles and other matter is appropriate in the holy church of God, on sacred vessels and vestments, walls and panels, in houses and on the roads, as well as the images of our Lord and God and Savior Jesus Christ, of our undefiled Lady of the Holy Mother of God, of the angels worthy of honor, and of all the holy and pious men. For the more frequently they are seen by means of pictorial representation the more those who behold them are aroused to remember and desire the prototypes and to give them greeting and worship of honor—but not the true worship of our faith which befits only the divine nature—but to offer them both incense and candles, in the same way as to the form and the venerable and life-giving Cross and the holy Gospel and to the other sacred objects, as was the custom even of the ancients."

ICONOCLASTIC POSITION:

1. The *Horos* (Definition of Faith) at the Council of Hieria, 754 CE:

"The divine nature is completely uncircumscribable and cannot be depicted or represented in any medium whatsoever. The word Christ means both God and Man, and an icon of Christ would therefore have to be an image of God in the flesh of the Son of God. But this is impossible. The artist would fall either into the heresy which claims that the divine and human natures of Christ are separate or into that which holds that there is only one nature of Christ."

2. The *Horos* (Definition of Faith) at Iconoclastic Council of 815 CE:

"Wherefore, taking to heart the correct doctrine, we banish from the Catholic Church the unwarranted manufacture of the spurious icons that has been so audaciously proclaimed, impelled as we are by a judicious judgment; nay, by passing a righteous judgment upon the veneration of icons that has been injudiciously proclaimed by Tarasius [Patriarch, 784–802] and so refuting it, we declare his assembly [i.e., Seventh Ecumenical Council in 787] invalid in that it bestowed exaggerated honor to painting, namely, as has already been said, the lighting of candles and lamps and the offering of incense, these marks of veneration being those of worship. We gladly accept, on the other hand, the pious council that was held at Blachernae, in the church of the all-pure Virgin, under the pious Emperors Constantine V and Leo IV [in 754] that was fortified by the doctrine of the Fathers, and in preserving without alteration what was expressed by it, we decree that the manufacture of icons is unfit for veneration and useless. We refrain, however, from calling them idols since there is a distinction between different kinds of evil."

» Working with Sources

1. Do you find one of the positions in this theological debate more convincing than the other? Why?

2. Was it necessary for the Byzantine emperors to intervene in this controversy? Why or why not?

SOURCE 10.3 Memoirs of Usama Ibn Munqidh

ca. 1180s

A scholar, a gentleman, and a warrior, Usama (1095–1187) had ample opportunity to meet crusader forces in person on the battlefield and in civilian life. After a distinguished military career, he became a consultant and advisor to Saladin in 1174. Basking in Saladin's favor, Usama became the center of attention in Damascus. He began a memoir describing the various peoples whom he had encountered during his long and adventurous life. His observations are often humorous, sometimes baffling, but always imbued with curiosity about people whose customs are strange—and intriguing.

Among the Frankish [i.e., Crusaders, known to Arabs as "al-Ifranj"] captives who were carried into my father's home was an aged woman accompanied by her daughter—a young woman of great beauty—and a robust son. The son accepted Islam, and his conversion was genuine, judging by what he showed in the practice of prayer and fasting. He learned the art of working marble from a stonecutter who had paved the home of my father. After staying for a long time with us my father gave him as wife a woman who belonged to a pious family, and paid all necessary expenses for his wedding and home. His wife bore him two sons. The boys grew up. When they were five or six years old, their father, young Rā'ūl, who was very happy at having them, took them with their mother and everything that his house contained and on the second morning joined the Franks in Afāmiyah, where he and his children became Christians after having practiced Islam with its prayers and faith. May Allah, therefore, purify the world from such people!

Mysterious are the works of the Creator, the author of all things! When one comes to recount cases regarding the Franks, he cannot but glorify Allah

---

Source: Philip K. Hitti, trans., *An Arab-Syrian Gentleman and Warrior in the Period of the Crusades: Memoirs of Usāmah ibn-Munqidh* (Princeton, NJ: Princeton University Press, 1987), 160–161, 162–163, and 164–165.

(exalted is he!) and sanctify him, for he sees them as animals possessing the virtues of courage and fighting, but nothing else; just as animals have only the virtues of strength and carrying loads. I shall now give some instances of their doings and their curious mentality.

. . .

The king of the Franks [Fulk of Anjou, king of Jerusalem] had for treasurer a knight named Bernard, who (may Allah's curse be upon him!) was one of the most accursed and wicked among the Franks. A horse kicked him in the leg, which was subsequently infected and which opened in fourteen different places. Every time one of these cuts would close in one place, another would open in another place. All this happened while I was praying for his perdition. Then came to him a Frankish physician and removed from the leg all the ointments which were on it and began to wash it with very strong vinegar. By this treatment all the cuts were healed and the man became well again. He was up again like a devil.

Another case illustrating their curious medicine is the following:

In Shayzar we had an artisan named abu-al-Fath, who had a boy whose neck was afflicted with scrofula. Every time a part of it would close, another part would open. This man happened to go to Antioch on business of his, accompanied by his son. A Frank noticed the boy and asked his father about him, "Wilt thou swear by thy religion that if I prescribe to thee a medicine which will cure thy boy, thou wilt charge nobody fees for prescribing it thyself? In that case, I shall prescribe to thee a medicine which will cure the boy." The man took the oath and the Frank said:

"Take uncrushed leaves of glasswort, burn them, then soak the ashes in olive oil and sharp vinegar. Treat the scrofula with them until the spot on which it is growing is eaten up. Then take burnt lead, soak it in ghee butter and treat him with it. That will cure him."

The father treated the boy accordingly, and the boy was cured. The sores closed and the boy returned to his normal condition of health.

I have myself treated with this medicine many who were afflicted with such disease, and the treatment was successful in removing the cause of the complaint.

. . .

Here is an illustration which I myself witnessed:

When I used to visit Nāblus, I always took lodging with a man named Mu'izz, whose home was a lodging house for the Moslems. The house had windows which opened to the road, and there stood opposite to it on the other side of the road a house belonging to a Frank who sold wine for the merchants. He would take some wine in a bottle and go around announcing it by shouting, "So and so, the merchant, has just opened a cask full of this wine. He who wants to buy some of it will find it in such and such a place." The Frank's pay for the announcement made would be the wine in that bottle. One day this Frank went home and found a man with his wife in the same bed. He asked him, "What could have made thee enter into my wife's room?" The man replied, "I was tired, so I went in to rest." "But how," asked he, "didst thou get into my bed?" The other replied, "I found a bed that was spread, so I slept in it." "But," said he, "my wife was sleeping together with thee!" The other replied, "Well, the bed is hers. How could I therefore have prevented her from using her own bed?" "By the truth of my religion," said the husband, "if thou shouldst do it again, thou and I would have a quarrel." Such was for the Frank the entire expression of his disapproval and the limit of his jealousy.

» Working with Sources

1. **What proof does Usama offer of the uncivilized nature of the Christian invaders of the Middle East?**
2. **How does he demonstrate Islamic cultural, if not always military, superiority in his account?**

SOURCE 10.4 A Jewish engagement contract from Fustat (Old Cairo)

11 November 1146

A treasure trove of letters, contracts, legal instruments, etc., known as the Cairo Geniza, attests to the lives of both prominent and average Jewish people, especially in the eleventh and twelfth centuries. Due to their *dhimmi* status (that is, officially recognized religious minorities in a predominantly Muslim state), Jews experienced occasional persecution in the Middle East and North Africa (much less than in Europe). In the Fatimid Empire (909–1171), they engaged in normal business and personal activities, and these documents provide a welcome window into their daily life.

This is a copy of the engagement contract of Abū Mansūr Semah, son of Rabbānā Japheth [known as] the elder Abū ʿAlī, the perfumer, to Sitt al-Khāssa, the daughter of the elder Abu 'l-Barakāt Ibn al-Lebdī.

On Monday, the fifth day of the month of Kislev of the year 1458 of the era of the documents, in Fustat, Egypt, which is situated on the Nile River and which is under the jurisdiction of our lord Samuel, the great Nagrid—may his name be forever, M. Semah, the young man, son of M. and R. Japheth the elder, son of M. and R. Tiqvā, the elder, the Friend of the yeshiva—may he rest in Eden—concluded a match with Sitt al-Khāssa, his fiancée, a virgin, the daughter of M. and R. Berakhōt, the elder—may he rest in Eden.

His obligation is a first installment of 40 certified dinars, to be given as a gift at the time of the wedding, and a final installment of 100 certified dinars. Abū Mansūr Semah, the fiancé, presented the 40 dinars of the first installment, and the elder Abū'l-ʿAlā' Musallam, the perfumer, son of Sahl, received them from him. The wedding is set for the month of Kislev of the coming year—may we be destined for life in it—which is the coming year 1459 [1147].

Source: S. D. Goitein, *A Mediterranean Society: The Jewish Communities of the Arab World as Portrayed in the Documents of the Cairo Geniza*, vol. 4 (Berkeley: University of California Press, 1983), 317–319.

Semah assumed these obligations toward Sitt al-Khāssa: She will be regarded as trustworthy in all that concerns food and drink in the house, no suspicion may be cast upon her, nor can he demand from her an oath concerning any of these things, not even a supplementary oath. He may not marry another woman, nor retain a maidservant whom she dislikes. Should he do any of these things, the final installment is hers, and he must release her [from the marriage bond by divorce]. In the case that there are no children, half of what remains of the dowry returns to her family. She may choose the place and the domicile where she wishes to live. The rent of her properties is hers, she may spend it for whatever purpose she prefers; he has no say in the matter.

Should he nullify this engagement contract and not marry her during the said Kislev, she will receive 20 dinars. This is a debt and an obligation, binding [as from now]. We made the symbolic purchase from M. Semah, the young man, for Sitt al-Khāssa, the fiancée, according to all that is recorded above, a purchase which is definite and strict, made with the proper object for such a transaction.

We also made the symbolic purchase from Sitt al-Sāda, the daughter of the elder Abū Nasr, the physician, the mother of Sitt al-Khāssa, the fiancée, in the most rigorous terms, binding as from now: Should her daughter Sitt al-Khāssa nullify the engagement contract and refuse to marry the fiancé during the said month of Kislev, she would owe the fiancé 20 [dinars]. . . . This has taken place after the verification of her identity.

Signatures: Mevōrākh b. Solomon [of] b[lessed] m[emory]. Sadaqa b———.

Working with Sources

1. **Are the parties to this contract eager to demonstrate, particularly to Muslim officials, that they understand business affairs and can conduct them sensibly among themselves?**
2. **What differences are reflected in this document between the roles of women and men with respect to marriage?**

SOURCE 10.5 *The Alchemy of Happiness*, by Abd al-Hamid al-Ghazali

ca. 1095–1105

Born in 1058 to a family of spinners and sellers of wool in a small village in eastern Iran, Ghazali became one of the most prominent expounders of Islamic theology of his day. Traveling widely, from Persia to Baghdad to Damascus, he mastered a wide range of disciplines, and he energetically

Source: Abū Hāmid Muhammad al-Ghazzālī, *The Alchemy of Happiness*, trans. Claud Field (Armonk, NY: M. E. Sharpe, 1991), 6–7 and 11–13.

engaged in arguments with those he considered extremists. When he died in 1111, he left behind a series of treatises, many of them incorporating autobiographical material and personal reflections.

The first step to self-knowledge is to know that thou art composed of an outward shape, called the body, and an inward entity called the heart or soul. By "heart" I do not mean the piece of flesh situated in the left of our bodies, but that which uses all the other faculties as its instruments and servants. In truth it does not belong to the visible world, but to the invisible, and has come into this world as a traveler visits a foreign country for the sake of merchandise, and it will presently return to its native land. It is the knowledge of this entity and its attributes which is the key to the knowledge of God.

. . .

A mistake of an opposite kind is made by shallow people who, echoing some phrases which they have caught from Sufi teachers, go about decrying all knowledge. This is as if a person who was not an adept in alchemy were to go about saying, "Alchemy is better than gold," and were to refuse gold when it was offered to him. Alchemy is better than gold, but real alchemists are very rare, and so are real Sufis. He who has a mere smattering of Sufism is not superior to a learned man, any more than he who has tried a few experiments in alchemy has ground for despising a rich man.

Anyone who will look into the matter will see that happiness is necessarily linked with the knowledge of God. Each faculty of ours delights in that for which it was created: lust delights in accomplishing desire, anger in taking vengeance, the eye in seeing beautiful objects, and the ear in hearing harmonious sounds. The highest function of the soul of man is the perception of truth; in this accordingly it finds its special delight. Even in trifling matters, such as learning chess, this holds good, and the higher the subject-matter of the knowledge obtained, the greater the delight. A man would be pleased at being admitted into the confidence of a prime minister, but how much more if the king makes an intimate of him and discloses state secrets to him!

An astronomer who, by his knowledge, can map the stars and describe their courses, derives more pleasure from his knowledge than the chess-player from his. Seeing, then, that nothing is higher than God, how great must be the delight which springs from the true knowledge of Him!

. . .

Man has been truly termed a "microcosm," or little world in himself, and the structures of his body should be studied not only by those who wish to become doctors, but by those who wish to attain to a more intimate knowledge of God, just as close study of the niceties and shades of language in a great poem reveals to us more and more of the genius of its author.

» Working with Sources

1. **How does Ghazali demonstrate an understanding of "science," and which specific sciences does he reference?**
2. **Why is he angry at the Sufis? Is his analysis of the problems posed by some Sufis justified?**

Chapter 11 600–1450 CE

Innovation and Adaptation in the Western Christian World

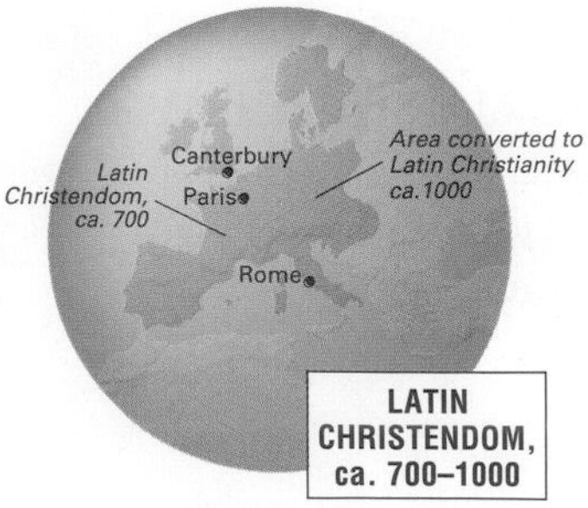

Around 575 a casual encounter took place in Rome that had enormous implications for the future of western Europe. While strolling through the forum, a young monk from the Monastery of St. Andrew came upon several boys for sale in the slave market. Struck by their fair skin and light hair, he asked about their ethnic origin. He was informed that the youths were from the far-off island of Britain and were called "Angles." The monk replied that because of their angelic appearance they should instead be called "angels." He then asked whether the inhabitants of this far-off land were Christians. When told that they still clung to pagan beliefs, he remarked that it was a pity that such beautiful young persons were not blessed with Christian faith.

In the year 596 the young monk, now elevated to the papacy as Pope Gregory I (r. 590–604), dispatched a group of monks to Britain, led by Augustine (later named the first archbishop of Canterbury), on a missionary campaign of conversion among the Anglo-Saxons of southern England. Throughout the seventh century Roman Christianity slowly spread northward into Anglo-Saxon England, eventually eclipsing the already established Celtic form of the faith brought over from Ireland in the fifth century.

ABOVE: **Detail of Bayeux Tapestry, an embroidered cloth dated ca. 1070 consisting of 75 scenes depicting events attending the Battle of Hastings, where William the Conqueror defeated Harold, Anglo-Saxon king of England. Here, the Latin title reads "King Harold is killed."**

During the first half of the eighth century English missionary monks, most notably St. Boniface (680–754), carried Christianity to the continent.

The papal reign of Gregory I represents the dawn of a new era in the history of western Europe. By encouraging the conversion of Germanic kings to Christianity in return for the sanction of the church, Gregory studiously advanced the role of the papacy in both ecclesiastical and secular affairs throughout Europe. Thus, Gregory was responsible for making the Roman papacy a significant power in the West. In the process, Gregory inaugurated new links between Rome and northwest Europe that went a long way toward the emergence of a new civilization distant from the Mediterranean. In addition, Gregory's efforts led to the eventual assertion of the independence of **Latin Christendom** from the Eastern Greek Church at Constantinople. Moreover, Gregory established an effective institutional structure and organized a hierarchy that provided the framework for a unified and well-regulated Christian civilization in emerging Europe that would endure until around 1450, when the Renaissance ushered in a new phase in European history.

The Formation of Christian Europe, 600–1000

During the fifth century, Roman provincial rule in the west collapsed and a new post-Roman period of cross-cultural interactions began, combining Greco-Roman and Germanic traditions, as well as Christian values. Even amid the chaos of the times, the Roman administrative practice of grouping provinces into dioceses formed the foundation of the diocesan system of the early church. Gradually, from these various ways of living emerged a distinctively Western Christian civilization. An important feature of this new civilization was the dominance of the church, whose alliance with Frankish kings—particularly Charlemagne—initiated a new church–state relationship in the West. This civilization nearly dissolved during the civil wars among Charlemagne's successors and the ninth-century invasions by non-Christians. During the tenth century, however, the slow process of restoring order was under way in post-Carolingian Europe. Despite the turbulence of the ninth and tenth centuries, a new cultural and religious cohesiveness provided a new sense of forward-looking optimism; Latin Christendom had survived.

Frankish Gaul and Latin Christianity

Amid the confusion caused by Germanic invasions and the breakdown of Roman rule during the fifth century, the first attempt to restore a semblance of political order appeared in Frankish Gaul. Although Merovingian kings relied on brute force to begin assembling a unified kingdom, they also recognized the importance of the church and its leaders as a unifying force. After a period of political turmoil a new line of Frankish kings, the Carolingians, emerged during the eighth century. At the same time, the Christian Church played an integral role in the shaping of Frankish Gaul and, in a larger sense, early medieval European civilization. It was during this period that the concept of *Christendom* as a common identity through the practice of Western Christianity began to take shape.

Seeing Patterns

» **How did the Merovingians and Carolingians construct a new Christian European civilization during the seventh and eighth centuries?**

» **What were key factors in the political, economic, and social recovery of Europe during the eleventh and twelfth centuries?**

» **What were some of the cultural and intellectual developments during the "twelfth-century renaissance," and how did they contribute to medieval civilization?**

» **How did the church influence political developments in Europe during the twelfth and thirteenth centuries?**

» **What events made fourteenth-century Europe so dismal? How did these combine to spell the gradual demise of medieval institutions and perspectives?**

Latin Christendom: Those countries professing Christian beliefs under the primacy of the pope.

Chapter Outline

- The Formation of Christian Europe, 600–1000
- Recovery, Reform, and Innovation, 1000–1300
- Crisis and Creativity, 1300–1415
- Putting It All Together

The Merovingians Unlike other Germanic tribes, the Franks did not invade the western Roman Empire but, rather, expanded from within the confines of its borders. The Franks, unlike most other Germans, became Western Christians. As a result, they were not rejected as heretics by native Gallo-Romans. For these reasons, Frankish Gaul was ideally suited to lay the foundation for the emergence of a Christian state in post-Roman Europe.

The first Frankish dynasty, the Merovingians [mer-oh-VIN-gee-anz], was established by the Frankish king Clovis (r. 481–511), who unified a number of northern Frankish tribes and defeated neighboring Germanic states. At some point in his reign, perhaps in 498, Clovis adopted Christianity, which gave him the backing of Christian bishops in Gaul. As a result, Clovis had powerful allies in his attempt to solidify his control over a unified Christian kingdom. However, because of the Merovingian practice of dividing inheritances among surviving heirs, soon after his death Clovis's kingdom was split up into Austrasia in the east, Neustria in the west, and Burgundy in the southeast.

The Carolingians During the eighth century one aristocratic family, the Carolingians, gradually rose to power in Austrasia and eventually took control of all of the Frankish lands. The power of the Carolingians was greatly enhanced during the eighth century by two outstanding leaders. Charles Martel ("the Hammer") (ca. 714–741) increased the authority of the Carolingians by promoting his ties with the church, such as his affiliation with the abbey church of St. Denis near Paris. His defeat of advancing Muslim armies at the Battle of Tours in 732 or 733 made him not only the most powerful man in Frankland but also the leader of the most powerful force in Latin Christendom.

Martel's son, Pepin III ("the Short") (751–768), succeeded his father as mayor of the palace in 741, and enhanced ties with the church in two ways. First, in 751 he was crowned by the reigning pope as the king of the Franks, thereby replacing the former Merovingian line of kings with a new Carolingian dynasty. Second, the **coronation** established a new Franco–papal alliance. One consequence of this was the establishment of a closer affinity between Rome and Frankish Gaul, an important factor in allowing Europe to develop independently of the Byzantine Empire in the East. In addition, the pope included the ceremony of **unction** (used earlier by the Visigoths) in the coronation ceremony, introducing into western European history the concept of sacred kingship, whereby kings now began to call themselves "kings by the grace of God."

Coronation: The act or ceremony of crowning a sovereign.

Unction: The act of anointing with oil as a rite of consecration.

The Early Medieval Church The church contributed greatly to the development of a new era in Western history during this period. The *secular clergy* (from the Latin *saeculum* [CY-cu-lum], or "world") included bishops—among them bishops of Rome, who later became popes—and urban priests. The *regular clergy* (from the Latin *regula*, or "rule") were monks who adopted a particular monastic rule and who lived in rural monasteries. Each of these monasteries made distinctive contributions to early medieval culture.

The Rule of St. Benedict

The model for monastic life was established by St. Benedict (ca. 480–543), whose *Holy Rule* governed such matters as the times for rising, praying, eating, and retiring, all supervised by an *abbot*, or head of the monastery. The daily lives of Benedictine monks were devoted to prayer and manual labor and were regulated by a series of "offices," or times of the day given over to specific tasks.

In economic terms, Benedictine monasteries helped to revitalize rural agricultural production because of their emphases upon economic self-sufficiency and manual labor as a form of prayer. Most monasteries had a watermill and a forge, and their large landholdings produced significant quantities of grain and wine. In addition, Benedictine monks expanded arable lands by draining swamps and clearing forests.

Above all else, monasteries preserved classical and early Christian culture in the midst of a mostly illiterate Germanic population. The limited education available during the early medieval period took place mostly in monasteries. It emphasized study of the Bible, church doctrine, and the "seven liberal arts"—consisting of the *trivium* (grammar, rhetoric, logic) and the *quadrivium* (arithmetic, geometry, music, astronomy). Monks copied and studied the works of the church fathers (such as Augustine, Jerome, and Ambrose), along with texts from the Bible and scattered papal decrees, thus laying the foundation for a new, Christian civilization for medieval Europe.

The Papacy While monks lived and worked in isolated rural monasteries, bishops of the church resided in urban centers. Although major cities throughout the Roman Empire had bishops, the bishop of Rome emerged as spiritual head of the Christian Church in western Europe. The most important of the early medieval popes, and indeed the pope usually credited with the foundation of the medieval papacy, was Gregory I.

In a wider sense, however, Gregory was responsible for making the Roman papacy a power in the West. His letters to Childebert II (r. 575–595), king of the Franks, laid the foundation for the Franco–papal alliance that came to fruition in the eighth century. Gregory also enhanced the prestige of the Roman papacy in Italy, which gave rise to the Papal States and the separation of the Roman and Eastern Roman Church. Finally, by encouraging the gradual mingling of Christian ideals and pagan rituals, Gregory facilitated the conversion of pagans to Christianity.

The Age of Charlemagne Following the death of Pepin III in 768, his son Charlemagne ("Charles the Great") (r. 768–814) inherited the Frankish crown. In his personal preferences and in his official policies, Charlemagne represents the first full synthesis of Roman, Germanic, and Christian elements to forge a unified Christian empire, establishing what many consider the "first Europe" (see Source 11.1). Because Charlemagne raised the status of western Europe to rival the civilizations of Byzantium and Islam, the Mediterranean was no longer the center of civilization in the West.

interactive timeline

- **590–604** Papacy of Gregory I ("the Great")
- **768–814** Reign of Charlemagne
- **987–1325** Capetian kings of France
- **1066–1327** Norman and Angevin kings of England
- **1095–1204** Crusades to the Holy Land
- **1200** Foundation charter of University of Paris
- **1215** *Magna Carta*, England
- **1268** St. Thomas Aquinas's *Summa Theologica*
- **1305–1378** Avignon Papacy
- **1337–1453** Hundred Years' War
- **1348–1352** Black Death
- **1415–1417** Council of Constance
- **1453** Constantinople falls to Ottoman Turks

Through extensive military campaigns and attention to effective rule, Charlemagne constructed and administered the largest empire in Europe since the collapse of Roman rule in 476 (see Map 11.1). An important step was the creation of a magnificent palace complex at Aachen [AH-ken] (Aix-la-Chapelle in French). From here Charlemagne ruled over a highly centralized empire—that is, a polity composed of many different ethnic and linguistic groups. Charlemagne also reformed legal practices by instituting the Frankish inquest, a forerunner of the jury system, which was carried to England at the time of the Norman Conquest.

Charlemagne's reign also resulted in significant intellectual contributions to medieval Europe. In an attempt to revive learning, especially among the aristocracy and the clergy, Charlemagne orchestrated a program of educational reform throughout his empire. Key to this effort was the appointment of Alcuin of York (ca. 735–804), the leading intellect of his age, as master of the palace school. Monks in several monastic schools were instructed to make copies of both Roman and Christian texts, including the Bible and the *Rule* of St. Benedict. This painstaking process produced around 50,000 books over the course of a century, preserving and disseminating many classical authors and texts.

Charlemagne's Throne. Charlemagne frequently traveled throughout his realm, and one place where he stopped several times was Ravenna on the Adriatic coast of Italy, where he would admire the magnificent sixth-century church of San Vitale. Inspired by its harmonious proportions and stunning mosaics, Charlemagne determined to build a replica at Aachen. The Palatine Chapel, the only surviving component of his palace, combines Byzantine and Carolingian architectural styles.

Like his forebears, Charlemagne also took an active interest in affairs of the church, often going beyond mere protection to outright interference. In the Capitulary for Saxony (775–790), for example, he ordered the forced conversion of Saxons to Christian practices. Not only did he promote the interests of Christianity throughout his kingdom, but he also intervened in papal affairs in Rome. In 774 Charlemagne journeyed to Rome to offer protection against the Lombards, and in 800 he gave assistance to Pope Leo III (r. 795–816), who was attacked by rivals. While attending Mass at St. Peter's on Christmas Day, Charlemagne was suddenly crowned "emperor of the Romans" by a grateful Leo III, an event Charlemagne later claimed was orchestrated by the pope without his prior knowledge.

The creation of a new Roman emperor in the West announced the independence of western Europe from the Byzantine East, and it signaled a shift in the center of power away from the Mediterranean and toward Europe north of the Alps. Charlemagne's new imperial status was recognized (reluctantly) not only by the Byzantine court but also by the Abbasid caliph in Baghdad, Harun al-Rashid (r. 786–809).

Post-Carolingian Europe Shortly after his death in 814, Charlemagne's empire was torn apart by internal wars and divisions. Charlemagne's eldest son, Louis the Pious (r. 814–840), followed the Frankish custom of dividing the empire among his three sons, who then squabbled over their respective shares. By the terms of the Treaty of Verdun in 843 the empire was divided into eastern, western, and central portions. At the same time, a series of devastating raids further disturbed the situation. From the north came the Norsemen, or Vikings, motivated by the quest for land and treasure. They sailed from Scandinavia into West Frankland and England in shallow-draft "long ships," causing terror and destruction wherever they landed along Europe's rivers. From the south, marauding bands of Muslim pirates created fear and destruction along the French coast of the Mediterranean and even penetrated inland

MAP 11.1 The Empire of Charlemagne.

as far as the Alps and to Rome itself in 846. Magyar horsemen from the plains of Hungary terrorized East Frankland in the same period, although they were more inclined to settle onto farmlands than to merely plunder (see Map 11.1).

Feudalism: An arrangement in which vassals were protected and maintained by their lords, usually through the granting of fiefs, and required to serve under them in war (see Source 11.2).

The Feudal Age The name traditionally given to the form of governance that arose in West Frankland during the ninth through the eleventh centuries is **feudalism**. But what, precisely, was feudalism? Historians have never fully agreed on a precise definition of the term, and some have suggested abandoning it altogether. Indeed, the term is often (and confusingly) used to describe similar arrangements that arose, in different periods, in Zhou China and Tokugawa Japan. It is true that feudalism was not a system *per se*; it was based on no theory, and it was nowhere uniform or consistent. Yet, amid the turmoil of the ninth and tenth centuries, feudalism provided security at the local level in the absence of central government.

Essentially, feudalism represented a new form of governance at the regional and local levels instead of from a centralized royal court. Feudalism consisted of powerful landed aristocrats (lords) who assembled small private armies consisting of dependents (vassals) in order to defend against the Norsemen, Muslims, and Magyars. Since wealth and power were now measured in terms of landholdings, vassals were rewarded for their services with grants of land, known as *fiefs*.

Lord–vassal relationships and institutions marked a turning point in European history that led to the later formation of centralized kingdoms. Most important was the concept of loyalty to someone higher in the feudal hierarchy. Even though in *practice* the local aristocratic lords were sometimes stronger than royal figures, in *theory* all land and power was possessed by kings, who stood at the apex of the feudal hierarchy. By using these and other elements of feudal relationships to his advantage, a royal figure could convert the feudal relationships to royal control of his realm.

Manorialism: The medieval European system of self-sustaining agricultural estates.

Whereas feudalism refers to the political and governmental aspects of life in the ninth and tenth centuries, **manorialism** refers to social and economic affairs of the time. Large manorial estates were established in rural areas and constituted self-sustaining agricultural communities. The manorial estate consisted of several buildings: the castle or manor house, the church, the barn, and the mill (see Figure 11.1).

Peasants lived in small cottages in a confined area of the estate. The typical cottage was windowless, constructed of mud and straw with an earthen floor. Cooking was done over a small stone hearth; a hole in the roof allowed smoke to escape. Interiors were very dark, and privacy was nonexistent. Surrounding all this were fields for crops, stands of timber for building and fuel, and a fishpond. The fields were arranged into long, narrow strips, some farmed by peasant families and others

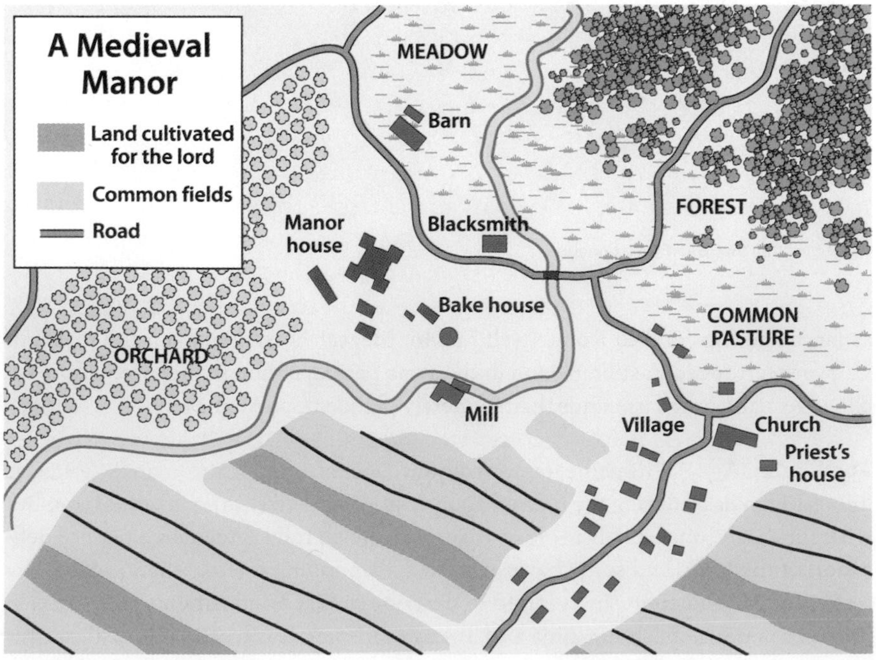

Figure 11.1 A Medieval Manor. This illustration shows the layout of a typical manor, with the manor and its satellite buildings next to a village surrounded by fields for planting and common (waste) land.

owned by the lord of the manor. Peasants had to provide free labor, called "boon work," on the lord's fields. The physical pattern of such manors may still be seen in many areas of France.

Recovery, Reform, and Innovation, 1000–1300

From about 1000 to 1300 Europe experienced a period of revitalization, expansion, and cultural creativity and innovation. The period began with the appearance of several competing, politically centralizing kingdoms and with advancements in agriculture, commerce, and trade. Reforms in the church provided an overarching framework that defined a unified western European Christian religious civilization, culminating in papal supremacy over Europe around the beginning of the thirteenth century. During the so-called twelfth-century renaissance, extending from ca. 1050 to 1250, a cultural revolution in universities produced new philosophical and scientific perspectives that, along with interaction with the Islamic world, came to distinguish western Europe from other world civilizations.

The Political Recovery of Europe

Europe in the middle of the ninth century was nearly everywhere in turmoil caused by internal civil wars and external invasions. As we have seen, all signs of central government had disappeared as a result of the collapse of the Carolingian Empire. In this turbulent setting most people were ruled by local lords. By around 1300, however, most of western Europe was governed by well-run centralized administrations headed by kings, who restored both political and fiscal health to their realms.

France and England The French nobility elected Hugh Capet (r. 987–996) as their king in 987 CE, beginning a long process of restoring centralized monarchy. This event marked the establishment of a new royal dynasty, the Capetians, in place of the former Carolingians. Although relatively weak in relation to powerful lords, the Capetians could claim several theoretical advantages. For one thing, the king's court served as the place where all disputes among his vassals were resolved, and the location of Hugh's royal **demesne** [deh-MAIN] in the lands around Paris meant that he was at the strategic and commercial center of France. Like the Carolingians, the Capetians enjoyed the support of the church. Not only did they have control over dozens of bishoprics and monasteries, they alone were anointed with holy oil (unction) as a part of the coronation ceremony, making their persons sacrosanct and safe from bodily injury.

Demesne: All territories within France controlled directly by the king.

Over the next 300 years, Capetian kings extended royal control in France. Success in petty wars against the nobles and arranged marriages between Capetian heirs and members of the nobility helped extend the domain and enhance Capetian power. Determined to make France the most powerful country in Europe, Philip IV (r. 1285–1314) established a representative assembly in France, the **Estates-General**, in order to raise needed revenues. Composed of the three social "estates"—the clergy, the nobility, and the townspeople—this body played an important role in later events leading up to the French Revolution.

Estates-General: The French representative assembly, composed of the three social "estates" in France, first convened by Philip IV.

Compared to the long and slow process of building a centralized monarchy in Capetian France, the establishment of centralized rule in England took place over a much shorter period of time. After the Norman duke William the Conqueror defeated an Anglo-Saxon army at the Battle of Hastings in 1066, he was proclaimed king of England as King William I (r. 1066–1087). William then seized control of all lands in the realm, distributing them to his followers. To secure his claim to the throne, he built castles throughout the country.

Baron: A term initiated by William I to designate feudal vassals who held lands in return for service and loyalty to the king.

Writ: A written order issued by a court, commanding the party to whom it is addressed to perform or cease performing a specified act.

Parliament: A representative assembly in England that, by the fourteenth century, was composed of great lords (both lay and ecclesiastical) and representatives from two other groups: shire knights and town burgesses.

William's successors continued his practice of centralizing authority. Henry II (r. 1154–1189), the first of the Plantagenet kings of England, reformed the judicial system by making royal courts the final courts of appeal, particularly in disputes over land, thereby overriding the authority of **baronial** courts. Moreover, Henry established a uniform code of justice (known as English common law) throughout the realm, which replaced the complex and frequently contradictory jurisdictions of baronial and local courts. Even more effective was Henry's reliance upon roving royal justices and the use of royal **writs** and the jury system, which provided justice for all disputants.

Henry's son John (r. 1199–1216), however, alienated the baronage of England, who forced the king to sign Magna Carta ("the Great Charter") in 1215. Magna Carta established several important principles: The king must rule in accordance with established feudal practices; he must consult with the barons before levying taxes; and all free men have the right to trial by jury if charged with a crime. Many of these concepts also contributed to the appearance of a new institution known as **Parliament**.

During the thirteenth century the English Parliament increased its power and scope. It also established certain principles that would be contested periodically by English monarchs over the next five centuries. In order to raise money for an anticipated French attack against England, Edward I (r. 1272–1307) found it expedient to convene in 1295 the so-called Model Parliament, composed of an upper house of nobles and a lower house of "knights of the shires and burgesses of the towns." This precedent established the origin of Parliament's House of Lords and House of Commons, which continues today.

Germany Events in East Frankland, or Germany, took a different turn. One setback to centralized rule was the division of the eastern portion of Charlemagne's realm into five regional groupings, or *duchies*, each under the control of a powerful duke. The result was that successive kings were chosen by the five regional dukes, making it difficult for kings to centralize royal authority.

Furthermore, imperial involvement in papal affairs in Italy provided another impediment to centralization. When Otto I of Saxony (r. 936–973) took power as king of the Germans, he extended Germanic influence in Italy in order to reestablish Charlemagne's protection of the papacy. In 962, Otto put down political disturbances and protests against the church. In gratitude, Pope John XII (r. 955–964) proclaimed Otto "emperor of the Romans," forming the basis of what has been termed the "Holy Roman Empire." Otto's successors continued the policy of interfering in papal affairs, with momentous results for both church and state.

In ensuing years Otto's successors continued efforts to extend German control south of the Alps into Italy. Through the tireless efforts of Frederick I (1152–1190), the first to bear the title Holy Roman Emperor, German holdings in Italy were greatly expanded in the north, and in 1155 he was named king of Italy. After his later defeat at the hands of a coalition of northern Italian cities in 1176, however, Frederick was forced to grant them quasi-independence, in return for their support against papal interests in the Italian peninsula. In his determination to encircle the Papal States, Frederick turned his attention to Sicily. Following the Norman liberation of Sicily from Muslim control in 1091, the Norman king Roger II (r. 1130–1154) established the Kingdom of Sicily, which included southern Italy as well as Sicily. By marrying his son, the future Henry VI (r. 1190–1197), to Constance of Sicily, daughter of Roger II, Frederick added the Kingdom of Sicily to the lands controlled by the Holy Roman Empire.

The Economic and Social Recovery of Europe

Yet another area of recovery for Europe around the year 1000 was the economy. At that time there was little manufacturing or commerce in Europe. Agriculture was still the mainstay of the economy, and there were few cities (and even these were underpopulated). Society was divided into three classes: those who worked, those who fought, and those who prayed. By 1300, however, the map of Europe was crisscrossed by scores of trade routes; trade and commerce were important features; urban life was humming; and a new social class of merchants had emerged in cities. How are we to explain this remarkable economic resurgence?

The Agricultural Revolution Developments in agriculture contributed to Europe's economic revival. In addition to land reclamation, as well as deep deposits of topsoil rich in nutrients, an important factor in the agricultural revolution was the heavy-wheeled plow, fitted with an iron blade and a *moldboard* (a curved iron blade to cut through the heavy sod of the region and lift and turn the newly dug soil). The use of new fertilizers and the transition from a two-field to a three-field system also provided a 33 percent increase in crop production. In the three-field system, one field was planted in the spring for a fall harvest, another was planted in the winter for a spring harvest, and the third remained fallow to enable its soil to regenerate nutrients.

It is important to note that the agricultural revolution in Europe was largely due to innovations from elsewhere in Eurasia (perhaps from China), which were transmitted to Europe through cross-cultural interactions (mostly via the Silk Road trade network). Among these innovations were the use of horses with collar harnesses (instead of slower-moving oxen), which provided a fivefold increase in traction, not to mention less injury to the animal; the use of iron horseshoes; the use of the tandem harness, allowing horses to work in pairs and further increasing production; the vertical waterwheel; and the single-wheeled barrow.

Moreover, new forms of mechanical energy—also of Asian origin—were introduced to Europe through interactions with the Islamic world. As early as 1050 watermills were in wide use, and although some historians attribute the watermill's origins to Rome, its design—particularly the incorporation of the trip-hammer—indicates Asian roots. Windmills, which were borrowed from Islamic Iran during the twelfth century, converted the power of water or wind into pounding and grinding motions used for the production of cloth goods, beer, and especially grain products; this in turn led to an increase in food production. Even the first deep-drilled water well, introduced in the twelfth century, was of Chinese origin. Finally, through Muslim Spain the Europeans benefited from several Islamic advances in agriculture, such as improvements in techniques of irrigation and drainage, and the introduction of new crops including rice, sugarcane, watermelons, and bananas.

These new crops and techniques meant an increase not only in the quantity of agricultural production but also, more important, in the quality and variety of food. Before the agricultural revolution, the European diet was based mainly on grains. Though rich in carbohydrates, it was low in protein. Peas and beans provided much-needed proteins and, when combined with chicken, fish, and eggs, resulted in a more balanced and nutritious diet. Improvements to the European diet resulted in an increase in population: In 1000, the population stood at about 36 million; by 1100 it had jumped to 44 million, and by 1200 to 58 million. By 1300 the European population reached about 80 million.

Commerce and Trade The revolution in agricultural production sparked in turn a rejuvenation of commerce and trade that spread throughout and beyond medieval Europe. As Europe's population grew, so did the demand for consumer goods, ranging from agricultural implements to household utensils, clothing and shoes, and numerous other commodities. The expansion of mercantile elites in thriving urban centers also provoked a brisk demand for luxury goods from beyond Europe, including silks, spices, and sugar.

One focal point of the revival of trade and commerce developed in northern Europe. Cloth goods, especially woolen products, had been a staple item in Flanders (along the coast of the North Sea in northeastern France) even before the Carolingian era. After the cessation of Viking raids, Flemish weavers began a flourishing exchange with wool-producing centers in England, particularly with monasteries in the north of the island, in the twelfth century. Another very productive source of the commercial trade revival in northern Europe was the importation of French wines into England beginning in the later eleventh century, occasioned by the Norman Conquest in 1066. German merchants established trade routes to London in the west and to Russian cities like Riga and Novgorod in the east.

Far more vital, however, was the remarkable revival of European commerce and trade across the Mediterranean. When Umayyad rulers were displaced by the Abbasids, who ruled from 750 to 1258, maritime contacts between Islamic and Christian merchants resumed. In addition, the Norman conquest of southern Italy and Sicily (1046–1091) afforded the northern Italian maritime cities of Pisa, Genoa, and Venice the opportunity to collaborate with Islamic merchants in Alexandria and the Levant. By the end of the eleventh century, Italian traders had established commercial ties with Constantinople, Syria, and Cairo and had begun the exchange of all manner of goods between Europe and Asia.

The most momentous change in European trade and commerce took place near the close of the thirteenth century. Around 1275, first Genoese and then Venetian maritime traders sailed westward across the Mediterranean, through the Strait of Gibraltar, and then out into the Atlantic. Then, Ferdinand IV (r. 1295–1312), king of Castile and León in Spain, claimed control of Gibraltar from the Muslims in 1309, ensuring full access to the waters of the Atlantic. Before these developments, trading patterns were primarily of a one-way nature: European merchants imported modest quantities of goods like *alum* (a mineral essential for dyeing cloth), spices, and silks from China and India. Thanks to economic advances in the West, however, European merchants now had products to export to the East: wool and tin from England, finished French and Flemish cloth goods, and manufactured items like iron agricultural and household implements (see Map 11.2).

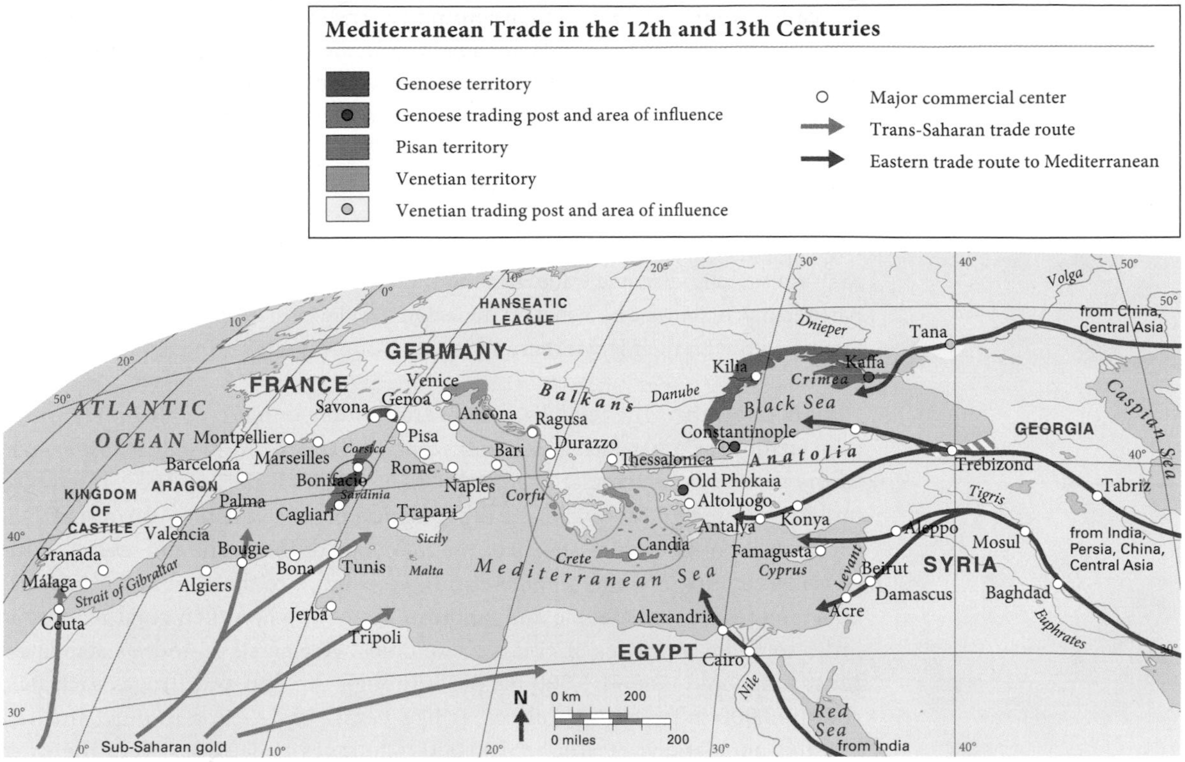

MAP **11.2** **Mediterranean Trade in the Twelfth and Thirteenth Centuries.**

Cross-Mediterranean trade and commerce were facilitated by several navigational innovations, some of which were assimilated as a result of interactions with Islamic and Byzantine merchants. Navigation was tremendously improved by advances in European ship design. Among the most important was the incorporation of the sternpost rudder. This concept was familiar to Chinese and Muslim sailors, but the European version—in use as early as 1180—was unique in that it used hinged iron plates firmly mounted to the ship's stern. The principal advantage of the stern-mounted rudder was that it allowed for the construction of larger ships, which in turn greatly increased the volume of transported goods. Another improvement was provided by the adoption from Muslim sailors of the *lateen sail,* a front-mounted triangular sail that allowed for tacking into the wind. It was largely owing to this navigational device that Italian ships were able to sail into the westerly winds that had previously prevented their sailing through the Strait of Gibraltar into the Atlantic. Most important was the introduction of the magnetic compass. Whether of independent invention or derived from China, where it was used on Chinese ships as early as around 1090, the magnetic (or mariner's) compass first appeared in Europe in 1190. Use of the compass greatly facilitated maritime travel beyond the sight of land, particularly across the Mediterranean.

Early Capitalism and a Cash Economy This renewed trans-Mediterranean commercial activity resulted in several innovations in commerce and monetary exchange that laid the foundation for the development of European **capitalism**.

Capitalism: An economic system characterized by private or corporate ownership of capital goods, by investments that are determined by private decision, and by prices, production, and the distribution of goods that are determined mainly by competition in a free market.

Increasing commercial transactions prompted a need for coined money in order to easily pay for exchanged goods. Meanwhile, medieval fairs gradually created new business procedures like record-keeping and accounting practices, along with bills of exchange (the forerunner of the modern bank check) to replace transport of large amounts of coins. These transactions were facilitated by the use of paper, invented in China during the Han dynasty (see Chapter 9), then adopted by Islamic merchants, and subsequently transmitted to Europe in the eleventh century through Muslim Spain. Several innovative financial and legal instruments were also devised to promote long-distance trade. Among these was the *commenda*, a legally binding partnership, first in use by Venetian traders in the eleventh century and borrowed via interactions with their Byzantine and Islamic counterparts.

Urban Growth The revitalization of trade and commerce contributed to the rejuvenation of urban life in eleventh-century Europe. Although many Roman towns survived the tribulations of the early medieval period, most resembled underpopulated ghost towns. The repopulation of these existing urban sites plus the creation of new cities attests to the influence of the economic revival of the eleventh century. Artisans and merchants were drawn to these vibrant urban centers, along with craftspeople and laborers, many of whom fled rural manors in order to begin new lives in cities. These cities were small by today's standards. Most numbered around 5,000 people, although London and Bruges each held about 40,000 inhabitants, while cities like Venice and Genoa in northern Italy boasted populations of around 100,000. Churches and castles were the most prominent urban buildings. Most urban areas were enclosed within stone walls and surrounded by agricultural fields.

Social Patterns Social patterns within the revitalized urban centers of the eleventh and twelfth centuries underwent change for several reasons. Of primary importance was the return of a money economy, which not only spelled the demise of feudalism—in that kings and nobles could now pay for armies with cash rather than with grants of land—but also resulted in the appearance of a new social class: the military. The effects of a new cash economy were especially noticeable in cities, which benefited from the cash contributions of wealthy businessmen in order to build cathedrals and large town halls. Finally, cities produced a new class of people, the **bourgeoisie** [boor-zhwa-ZEE]. Composed of merchants and artisans who lived in "burghs" (or cities) the bourgeoisie made their livings from producing and selling goods for commercial exchange. This new "middle class" of people was destined to exert an enormous influence on the development of medieval representative governments, primarily because their access to liquid cash made them attractive to European rulers.

Bourgeoisie: The urban-based middle class between the wealthy aristocracy and the working class.

Urban women worked in a variety of occupations, especially craft industries. Women were employed in a diverse array of crafts, as butchers, candle makers, metal crafters, silk weavers, and bookbinders. Nevertheless, women were rarely admitted as full members to craft **guilds**, and in the silk industry—the one area where women did predominate—there is no evidence of a guild. For the great majority of working women, better opportunities were available in what were known as "bye industries," or home-based enterprises, like spinning cloth and brewing ale. In some cases widows took over their late husband's trade and worked as single women.

Guilds: Associations of artisans and merchants intended to protect and promote affairs of common interest.

Jews occupied a distinct position in medieval towns and cities during the early years of the urban revival in the eleventh century. Comprising a small but distinct minority of the European population, Jews were spread in communities around the Mediterranean world. Through their travels and interactions with a wide variety of peoples, Jews developed both wide geographical knowledge and the command of multiple languages. For these reasons they sometimes served as diplomats, and they engaged in moneylending and banking.

As the eleventh century unfolded, however, tolerance toward Jews began to wane. Jews were increasingly vilified as murderers of Christ, a sentiment fanned by the First Crusade in 1096. In 1144 a full-scale assault against Jews was unleashed in the English town of Norwich. In many cases Jews were forced to live together in walled-off, gated ghettos in towns, which frequently held charters of liberty separate from those of the towns. Ghettos appeared as early as the thirteenth century in Spain, Portugal, Germany, and elsewhere. Several countries expelled Jews—England in 1290, France in 1306, and a number of continental cities in the early 1400s—resulting in their dispersal throughout eastern Europe.

The Virgin Mary Knitting. This fourteenth-century painting of the Virgin Mary knitting a garment for her unborn child is the earliest known representation of knitting, a medieval innovation. Knitwear was unknown in the ancient Mediterranean but was essential in the cold, damp climate of northern Europe.

Religious Reform and Expansion

During the period from 1000 to 1300 the clerical establishment of medieval Europe underwent dramatic reform as the church struggled to recover from nearly two centuries of decentralization and decline of learning. The reform movement in the church began in monasteries, then spread to the ecclesiastical hierarchy in cities, and eventually resulted in a new age of religious enthusiasm throughout Europe.

Monastic Reform The effort at monastic reform began in France in a monastery founded at Cluny in 910 by Duke William I (875–918) of Aquitaine. Cluny was established as a monastery totally free of obligations to either feudal lords or local ecclesiastical control, and committed to strict adherence to the Benedictine rule. The number of reformed monasteries increased during the eleventh and twelfth centuries. The most successful of new monastic orders was the Cistercians, founded in 1098 in a remote area of France at Citeaux. At its inception the order numbered only a handful of monastic houses, but by 1200 nearly 500 Cistercian monasteries were active throughout France. The appeal of the Cistercian order lay in its simple and austere way of life; Cistercians were enjoined to work and live in poverty and to devote their total beings to "God's work" (*opus Dei*).

Papal Reform and the Investiture Controversy As the monastic reform movement progressed, a similar reform effort took place in the papacy. One of the major concerns of the church was to establish its independence from secular influence, particularly the practice by which lay rulers appointed clergy, including the pope, to their offices. Popes, however, believed it was the exclusive right of the clergy to make such appointments. The creation of the College of Cardinals in 1150, followed by the Papal Election Decree in 1059, ensured that only the College of Cardinals was empowered to elect the pontiff of the Holy Catholic Church. The result was the elimination of the role of the Holy Roman (German) emperor in the appointment of popes.

This conflict came to a head in what is known as the "Investiture Controversy." Pope Gregory VII (r. 1073–1085), a staunch advocate of papal reform, insisted that appointment of the clergy was in future to be controlled solely by the church. When the German emperor Henry IV (1056–1106) openly challenged Gregory's proclamation, the pope excommunicated him. The struggle between popes and emperors dragged on for more than 40 years, until 1122 when an agreement known as the Concordat of Worms (named for the German city where the agreement was made) was reached. This agreement stipulated that German bishops must be elected by church officials.

The investiture controversy produced mixed results. On the one hand, Gregory's actions represented the enhanced power of the church and proved that popes could force emperors to acknowledge papal authority. On the other hand, Henry IV's struggle with the church proved disastrous for his successors. Later German emperors never fully recovered from the distraction of attempting to control matters in both Germany and Italy. Even such otherwise strong figures as Frederick I (r. 1152–1190) and Frederick II (r. 1215–1250) were unable to establish centralized rule in Germany. After Frederick's death, the five Germanic principalities reasserted their independence from royal control, and Germany remained disunited until the later nineteenth century.

Popular Piety and a Religious Society As early as the eleventh century Europe experienced a dramatic increase in popular piety, when ordinary people took a more active interest in religion. This movement was caused by several factors. One was the reform movement in the church, which resulted in both higher standards of conduct among regular and secular clergy and the increased visibility and temporal authority of the pope following the investiture controversy. Another factor was the construction of numerous shrines dedicated to Christian saints, whose *relics*—venerated items connected with their lives—were considered powerful aids in the quest for personal salvation.

Another factor that generated renewed enthusiasm for religion was new ways of depicting Jesus and Mary, the mother of Jesus. Whereas in the earliest years of the church the Crucifixion of Jesus was rarely shown—and then only in a stylized, unemotional manner—by the tenth century Christ was depicted as a compassionate figure, whose tragic death on the Cross was portrayed as a reminder of his sacrifice for the redemption of humanity's sins.

A further contribution of the popularization of Christian piety was the introduction of new concepts of time. One concept derives from the biblical book of Genesis, where the creation of the earth took 6 days, leaving the seventh day as a day of rest. Another concept, the numbering of years in accordance with the Christian era, was introduced in 532 by Dionysius Exiguus (ca. 470–544), a Roman monk.

(a)

(b)

Changing Views of Christ. The Crucifixion scene from the door of the basilica of Santa Sabina, Rome, ca. 430, is formal and stylized: Christ is remote (a). In contrast, the Crucifixion commissioned by the archbishop of Cologne, Germany, just before 1000 shows a suffering Christ—a human being in agony and sorrow, hanging from a cross (b).

For Dionysius historical time began with the birth of Christ, hence his designation of *Anno Domini* ("in the year of the Lord") to denote a new dating system. The new system was used by the eighth-century Anglo-Saxon scholar Bede (ca. 673–735) in his *Ecclesiastical History of the English People* and then popularized in Europe by Alcuin of York during the reign of Charlemagne.

These Christian influences on the perception of time had several implications for Europeans. For one thing, two crucial Christian feast days now became standard: The birth of Christ was celebrated on December 25 (Christmas) and his resurrection on a movable date called **Easter**. For another, saints' days, set aside for reflection and celebration, became major events around which Europeans' lives centered. Finally, the ringing of church and monastery bells announced the hours of the day, which provided for regulation of daily routines. Mechanical clocks, introduced into Europe in the early fourteenth century—and most likely derived from earlier Chinese models—later provided more precise measurement of time.

Easter: Christian celebration of the Resurrection of Christ; celebrated on the Sunday following the first full moon after the vernal equinox.

A less benign aspect of popular piety was an alarming trend toward the appearance of heretical movements within the church (see "Against the Grain," p. 340). In an effort to rechannel the devotion of the faithful, particularly in cities, Pope Innocent III (r. 1198–1216) licensed two new religious orders of friars ("brothers"), the Franciscans and the Dominicans. Founded by St. Francis of Assisi (1181/2–1226), the Franciscan order inspired a new dedication to Christianity in the form of living simply among the people, preaching repentance for sins, and aiding the poor and the sick. The Dominicans, founded by St. Dominic (1170–1221) in 1216, also lived among the people, but they were more interested in preaching and teaching, believing that the best way to combat heresy was to teach the doctrines of the church. The

Dominican order included many famous medieval theologians in its ranks, such as St. Thomas Aquinas (ca. 1225–1274).

The Crusades A movement that reflects both the growing appeal and power of the church as well as the renewed energy of a revitalized Europe centers on the Crusades. Like the reform movement of the church, the Crusades were in part inspired by the new wave of religious enthusiasm sweeping Europe during the period of recovery from the horrors of the ninth and tenth centuries. But there were other causal factors as well, chief among them the so-called *Reconquista*, or reconquest, of formerly Christian lands that had been taken over by Muslims.

Until the year 1000 Spanish Christians were forced to retreat into the far northwest of the Iberian Peninsula, while the Muslims controlled most of the lands from their capital in Córdoba. In 1031, however, internal squabbling among Muslim factions led to a loosening of Muslim control throughout Spain, which in turn prompted two kings of Christian territories to launch an offensive in order to reclaim land from the Muslims. The breakthrough occurred in 1085 when Toledo was liberated from Muslim control, resulting in almost half of Spain returning to Christian control.

A similar effort to retake Christian territory from Muslim control took place in southern Italy and Sicily. Beginning in 1061, a group of Norman knights began wresting Sicily from the Muslims, resulting in its eventual conquest in 1091. Across the twelfth century their successors established a strongly centralized Norman kingdom in Sicily. The Norman kings of Sicily allied themselves with the papacy. In return for their protection of the papacy, the kings were given the status of permanent papal legates, which in turn gave them total control over all the higher clergy in their realm.

These spectacular successes against the Muslims in the western Mediterranean occurred simultaneously with alarming developments in the eastern Mediterranean. As we have seen in Chapter 10, by the 1080s Seljuk Turks had seized control of substantial territories in the Middle East, prompting Pope Urban II to call for the launching of a crusade to the Holy Land during the Council of Clermont in France in 1095. Anxious not only to liberate the Holy Land but also to enhance papal prestige, Urban called on the great barons of Europe to assemble their feudal armies and march to the east to liberate Jerusalem from Muslim control. For their part, although they may have been partially driven by religious enthusiasm, Europe's feudal nobility most likely saw in this expedition the promise of new lands and a chance to use their military training for a good cause.

interactive map of the Crusades

In the summer of the following year the main force, consisting of approximately 7,000 mounted knights along with around 35,000 infantry and augmented by thousands of attendants, suppliers, and prostitutes, crossed over into Asia Minor and in 1097 took Nicaea from the Turks. Two years later, in the summer of 1099, Jerusalem was finally freed from Muslim control—but at a horrific cost in human life.

Other crusades followed throughout the twelfth century. In 1144 the fall of the crusader state of Edessa (in present-day Syria) to a resurgence of Islamic militancy caused renewed interest in a second crusade. Called for in a sermon by Bernard of Clairvaux, the crusade, led by King Louis VII of France and Holy Roman Emperor Conrad III, failed to reach Edessa. A surge of renewed interest in the crusading movement occurred in 1187, when Jerusalem was overrun by the renowned Muslim leader Saladin. Known as the "Crusade of the Three Kings," the Third Crusade was led by Frederick I of Germany, Philip II of France, and Richard I of England. The accidental drowning death of Frederick I removed the German contingent from the force, but the combined English and French forces managed to capture Acre from the Muslims in 1191. At that point, however, dissension between Philip II and Richard I resulted in Philip's hasty return to France.

Yet another crusading effort, the Fourth Crusade, was instigated by Pope Innocent III. Led by Baldwin IX, count of Flanders (r. 1194–1206), the crusade was launched in 1201. Consisting mainly of French knights, the crusading army contracted with the Venetians for passage by ship to the east. The crafty Venetians, who were quick to realize the advantage of transporting a crusading army, attacked the Adriatic port city of Zara, their commercial rival. Outraged by an attack on a Christian city, Innocent III excommunicated the crusaders, who ignored the papal ban. From Zara the Venetians transported the army to Constantinople in 1204, where they plundered the city, slaughtering innocent Christians in the process. In the long run the Fourth Crusade not only weakened the authority of subsequent Byzantine rulers but also deepened animosities between the Roman and Eastern Orthodox Churches.

Although the crusading movement ultimately failed to keep Jerusalem out of Muslim hands and resulted in cumulative casualties estimated in the millions, the Crusades produced some positive achievements for Europeans. The ability of popes to organize European knights into armies and to send them far afield in service of the church enhanced their prestige in both the west and the east. The Crusades also

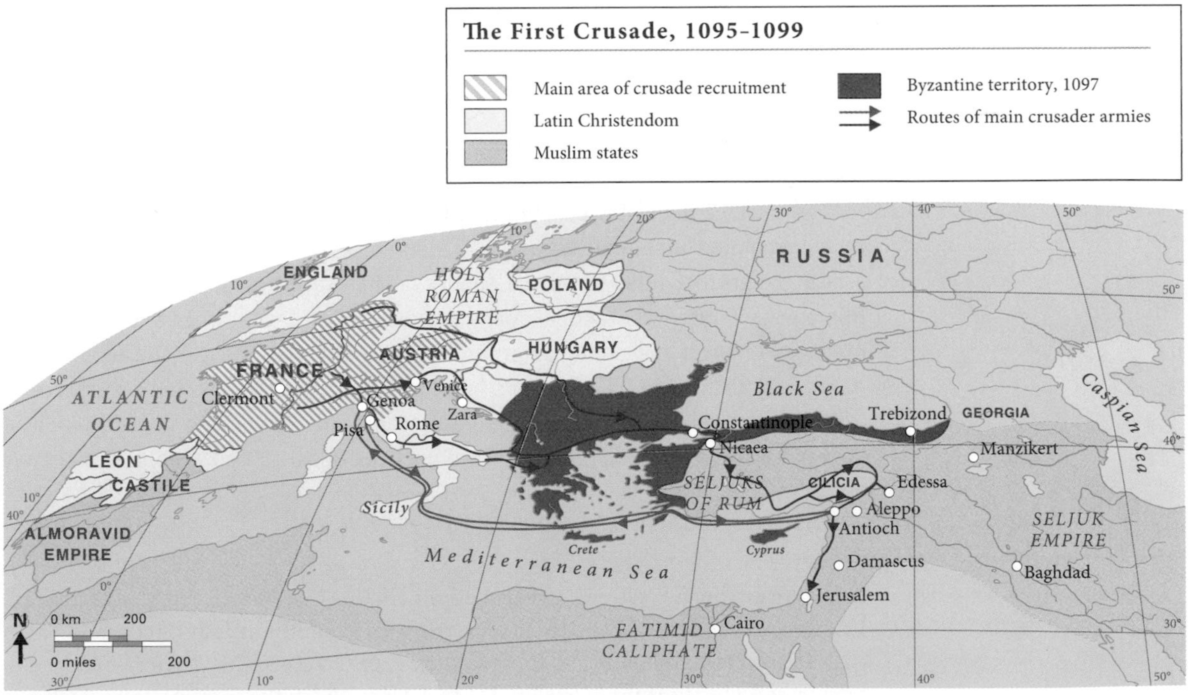

MAP **11.3 The First Crusade, 1095–1099.**

Patterns Up Close

The Gothic Cathedral

Although the Gothic cathedral is the iconic symbol of medieval European Christianity, its origins and evolution are less familiar.

Nave of the Abbey Church of St. Denis

The origin of the cathedral can be traced back to late imperial Rome. Following Constantine's Edict of Milan in 313, Christians no longer had to worship in secret, and church leaders sought a public building that could accommodate larger congregations. Many features of the Roman *basilica*, a civic hall traditionally used for public functions, rendered it ideal for early Christian worship. Its design was assimilated by the church and transformed from pagan to Christian usage. The basilica style featured a long central aisle (or nave), roofed over with timber, ending with an intersecting transept and an arched passage into a semicircular *apse* (or sanctuary) with a raised platform where the presiding magistrate sat in judgment.

During the post-Roman early medieval period, other earlier Roman and Christian architectural styles were adapted to European circumstances. The result was the Romanesque style of church architecture, which appeared in different guises from ca. 800 to 1000. A key feature of Romanesque architecture was the replacement of the basilica's low timber roofs with heavy stone barrel vaults, which required massive stone piers and exterior walls to support the weight and resulted in gloomy interiors. In addition, the apse was expanded beyond the transept by the addition of a circular walkway (the ambulatory) to allow crowds of pilgrims to view Christian relics. Finally, the focal point of the exterior was now the western façade, flanked by two towers. The spread of Benedictine monasteries as well as the emergence of powerful German emperors during the tenth and eleventh centuries prompted additional changes in Romanesque churches: the enlargement of interiors, the increased height of the nave—utilizing vaulting and groin arches—and the addition of a clerestory with rounded arches above the nave to admit more light into the interior.

The revitalization of urban life and lay piety in the eleventh and twelfth centuries prompted architects to assimilate some features of the Romanesque into a new design that reflected these changes. The first attempt to open up gloomy Romanesque interiors—and an early expression of the new Gothic style—was made in 1144 at the abbey church of St. Denis in Paris under the direction of Abbot Suger (1081–1151). Suger's intention was to enlarge the interior spaces of Romanesque churches, providing more light and increasing the upward reach of their exteriors. In order to realize these objectives Suger turned to solutions already

helped to establish Western Christian dominance of sea traffic in the Mediterranean. In addition, the retaking of Christian territories in southern Italy, Sicily, and Spain gave European scholars access to new sources of Greco-Arabic scientific advances, known collectively as the "New Logic," and it resulted in the transmission of Islamic architectural elements to western Europe (see "Patterns Up Close," above).

in practice in late Romanesque churches: the pointed arch, the ribbed vault, and flying buttresses.

Pointed arches allowed for higher vertical thrusts in weight distribution, resulting in soaring naves. The pointed arch, widely used as early as the eighth century in Islamic architecture, was most likely transmitted to Europe from Sicily. A likely scenario traces a route from Sicily to its first use in the construction of the porch of Monte Cassino in 1071. After the Norman conquest of Sicily in 1091 the concept of the pointed arch was transmitted to France, where it was used in the construction of the third church of Cluny (1088–1095). Abbot Suger visited Cluny in 1130 and would have been aware of the distinct advantages offered by the pointed arch.

Ribbed vaults were improvements over earlier Romanesque groin vaults in that they provided for elevated vaults while at the same time directing the vertical thrust downward through more slender columns, thus providing greater interior space. Ribbed vaults also allowed for thinner outer walls, which could accommodate large glass windows that allowed in more light. There is considerable conjecture over whether the technique of ribbed vaults may have originated in earlier Islamic architecture. For example, the great mosques at Córdoba in Spain and Tlemcen in Algeria utilized a form of crisscrossing webs in the construction of domes over the front aisle; this form may have found its way to European architects as a result of the fall of Toledo in 1085. It has been argued, however, that the earlier Islamic models were of a different sort than those of Christian Europe in that they were primarily used in domes instead of the nave, and in any event were designed for symbolic and decorative purposes, rather than for structural design. The consensus, then, is that the earliest example of a ribbed groin vault over a nave emanating from Romanesque architecture occurred at Durham Cathedral as early as 1093.

Another innovation at St. Denis was the incorporation of stained-glass panels (frequently depicting stories from the Bible) in the outer walls, which provided dazzling arrays of color and light in the interior. Flying buttresses—perhaps the most innovative feature of the Gothic style—were then used to support the thinner outer walls, distributing the thrust of the ribbed vaults and pointed arches away from the outer wall and down toward the ground.

Questions

- How does the Gothic cathedral demonstrate the origins–interactions–adaptations process in action?
- What types of cultural adaptations are evident in houses of worship built in modern times?

Intellectual and Cultural Developments

The High Middle Ages (ca. 1000–1300) saw a series of important new directions and institutions reflective of the intellectual and cultural expressions of Western Christian religious civilization. Perhaps the two most visible symbols of this civilization—the Gothic cathedral and the university—were born during the "twelfth-century renaissance." It was in the university that the study of Aristotle provoked a renewed interest in science and the natural world.

Universities As a result of the urban revolution of the eleventh century, monastic schools in rural areas began to lose ground to cathedral schools in urban centers, which offered more relevant instruction in reading and writing, mathematical reckoning, and logical reasoning—skills required by the commercial world of the twelfth century. Creative thinkers were now attracted to cathedral schools in the larger cities of Europe, where they in turn began to attract students. In time, larger groups of students and teachers formed the first universities at Salerno, Bologna, and Paris.

Particularly in Paris, the university curriculum began to focus on the philosophy of Aristotle, who had been all but ignored during the early Middle Ages. In large part this renewed focus was owing to the efforts of Gerbert of Aurillac (ca. 946–1003), described as "the most learned man of his century" and later named Pope Sylvester II (r. 999–1003). As a young man Gerbert had studied in Islamic Spain, where he pursued interests in mathematics, astronomy, and Aristotelian logic. Later, as deacon of the cathedral school at Reims, Gerbert introduced both the sciences and Aristotelian logic to his students, many of whom in turn helped spread the new learning throughout cathedral schools in Europe.

During the eleventh and twelfth centuries, two important developments in universities resulted from the growing popularity of Aristotelian logic. One of these was the emergence of a new method of pursuing philosophical and theological truth by use of Aristotelian logic, known as **scholasticism**. Adherents of this new methodology began to subject long-held doctrines of the church to rigorous scrutiny. The problem was that Aristotle posed a serious threat to church authority, since a better understanding of his ideas revealed just how incompatible his thinking was with religious doctrine. For example, Aristotle denied the creation of the world in favor of the world's eternity; he also denied the immortality of the individual soul.

Scholasticism: A medieval method of determining theological and philosophical truth by using Aristotelian logic.

What emerged was a fundamental disagreement between those who placed the truths of *faith* before the truths of *reason* in attempting to gain knowledge of God's existence and those who placed reason first. The most famous advocates of these opposing schools of thought were St. Anselm (ca. 1034–1109) and Peter Abelard (1079–1142). Anselm argued that faith must precede reason ("I believe in order that I might understand"). He further argued that proof of God's existence could be deduced by first accepting church doctrine on the basis of faith and then proceeding to support these notions by reasoned argument. Abelard, the most popular teacher at the cathedral school of Notre Dame in Paris during these years, disagreed, arguing, "I understand in order that I might believe." Abelard was particularly famous among twelfth-century scholars because of his tragic love affair with his student Heloise, niece of the canon of the cathedral school of Notre Dame, who became pregnant. The most sensational portion of Abelard's *Historia Calamitatum* (*The Story of My Misfortunes*) concerns his description of how Heloise's uncle took revenge when he discovered that, after their secret marriage, Abelard sent Heloise to a nunnery (see Source 11.3). As a result, Abelard's apparent favoring of reason over faith tipped the balance in favor of those who were inclined to question traditional Christian doctrine.

So popular was Aristotle by the middle of the thirteenth century that in addition to the earlier division between those who advocated either the truths of faith or reason, a third perspective was offered by those who took a middle path. It was to the latter camp that St. Thomas Aquinas (ca. 1224–1274) belonged. In his *Summa Theologica,* Aquinas argued that, instead of considering the truths of reason as being totally irreconcilable with the truths of faith, it was possible to consider a compromise, or a synthesis of the two, that would in the end lead to a knowledge of God's existence and, thus, to personal salvation. According to this construct, one could begin an upward journey to an understanding of God by first relying upon the truths of reason, but at a certain point one would have to abandon pure reason for the more enlightened approach afforded by faith, which would then allow an understanding of the mysteries of Christian doctrine and, thus, of God.

Law and Medicine In the twelfth century, universities began to offer training in two more disciplines critical to cosmopolitan urban life: law and medicine. By the early years of the century scholars at Bologna discovered the Roman legal tradition preserved in Justinian's celebrated *Corpus Iuris Civilis.* It was at Bologna around 1140 that the *Corpus* inspired a monk named Gratian to compile a compendium of ecclesiastical law known as the *Decretum.* Gratian's student Peter Lombard's *Book of Sentences,* produced in 1150, served along with the *Decretum* as the foundation for the development of **canon law**, utilized by the papacy in its struggles to contest secular power.

Canon law: The law of the church.

Medical studies were taught at Salerno in the late eleventh century. Located in Sicily, Salerno was able to assimilate Islamic and Byzantine medical advances. Serving as the nucleus of medical studies at Salerno were the works of the Roman physician Galen and the *Canon of Medicine* compiled by the Islamic scholar Ibn Sina (or Avicenna, 980–1037). These works formed the foundation of medical studies throughout medieval European universities.

Medieval Science Another consequence of the appeal of Aristotle was a corresponding fascination with scientific texts of the ancient Greeks. The initial impulse in this direction was provided not only by Gerbert of Aurillac but also by Christian advances into Spain and southern Italy during the waning years of the eleventh century. The Christian conquest of Toledo in 1085, followed by the retaking of Sicily in 1090, provided opportunities for scholars from all over Europe to gain access to Islamic treasure troves of scientific learning. Adelard of Bath (ca. 1080–1152) was one of the earliest Western scholars to translate Greek scientific texts from Arabic into Latin. As such, Adelard served as an important bridge between the Islamic and Western Christian worlds. It was largely owing to his efforts that a new sense of curiosity about natural science began to circulate in Western intellectual circles.

Adelard contributed to what is often referred to as the age of Latin translators. The most prolific of these translators was Gerard of Cremona (ca. 1114–1187), who provided Latin translations of over 70 Greek scientific texts, including Ptolemy's *Almagest* and most of Aristotle's works on physics, along with numerous mathematical treatises such as Euclid's *Elements* and al-Khwarizmi's *Algebra,* and several medical treatises such as Galen's texts and Avicenna's *Canon of Medicine.*

Merton College Library. Merton College was founded as a self-governing academic institution by Walter de Merton in 1264. During the fourteenth century scholars interested in mathematics and physics, known as the Merton (or Oxford) Calculators, produced significant advances that contributed to the European scientific revolution of the sixteenth and seventeenth centuries. In 1373 construction was begun on Merton College Library, but earlier records indicate that scholars at Merton began to build a collection of books as early as 1276.

Perhaps the most important of Adelard's successors in England was Robert Grosseteste (ca. 1175–1253). Grosseteste represented a rare combination of ecclesiastical and secular interests; he was for a time bishop of Lincoln but was also a dabbler in the new scientific studies of natural phenomena. Grosseteste made an important contribution to the advancement of science in that he recognized the value of mathematics. He was also among the earliest scholastics to question the scientific authority of Aristotle. Grosseteste's arguments were developed by his student Roger Bacon (ca. 1214–1294), whose principal contribution to the development of Western science was to emphasize the role of induction and experimentation.

During the early years of the fourteenth century another "school" of natural scientists, the so-called Oxford Calculators, advanced scientific studies. There were several influential members of this group, and all were associated with Merton College, Oxford. They were united by their interest in and pursuit of abstract mathematics combined with physics. Taken together, they investigated many of Aristotle's assumptions regarding natural science, including his denial of the existence of vacuum, his notion that objects of different weights fall to earth at different speeds (the heavier fall faster), and his theory of motion, which held that objects remain in motion only through the continuous application of an external force. Perhaps the best known of the Calculators' contributions is the mean speed theorem, which anticipates Galileo's law of falling bodies (two bodies, one falling and another moving at half the final speed of the first, cover the same distance).

Crisis and Creativity, 1300–1415

The fourteenth century marks the final phase of European Christian civilization and is often considered an age of transition to the European Renaissance. The early part of the century witnessed a series of economic reversals. Near mid-century a devastating plague originating in Southeast Asia ravaged Europe, killing as much as one-third of its population and generating further social upheaval. Centralized kingdoms developed a sense of national identity and consolidation; one result was a long, drawn-out period of war between England and France that began in 1337 and ended in 1453. In addition, the authority of the papacy was challenged from without by powerful European secular rulers and weakened from within by a series of internal problems and philosophical disputes. As bleak as things were, however, signs of new creative forces arising from the ashes of the fourteenth century appeared as early as the middle of the century.

The Calamitous Fourteenth Century

Fourteenth-century Europe experienced all manner of dearth, disease, death, and dissolution. The early part of the century witnessed a series of reversals in the economic and social realms, brought on initially by dramatic climatic change starting in the year 1315 that resulted in a prolonged period of poor harvests followed by famine. Near mid-century a disastrous plague added to the misery of daily life.

Famine During the early years of the fourteenth century Europe was hit by a disastrous combination of factors that produced a prolonged period of famine. One factor was a sudden disparity between an expanding population and its available food supply. From ca. 1000 to 1300 Europe's population had nearly doubled to a total of around 80 million, thanks to advances in agricultural technology. By 1300, however, no new advances were forthcoming. In addition, after centuries of expansion and clearing of lands, Europe suddenly ran out of new frontiers, resulting in a lack of land available for increased agricultural production. To make matters worse, the average annual temperature dropped during this period, which shortened the summer growing season. At the same time, an unusually prolonged series of rainy seasons in the spring and summer planting seasons, followed by a succession of harsh winters, resulted in a famine that extended from 1315 to 1322.

Plague Near mid-century, Europe's already weakened populations suffered a horrific outbreak of plague. The disease originated in Cambodia, Burma, and Vietnam; it was then transmitted across Asia in goods and wares transported by Mongol traders in the 1330s. From there it spread westward along trade routes to the Black Sea. The plague was introduced to the West when grain-carrying Genoese merchant ships, infested with rats, sailed from the Crimea to ports in Sicily and northern Italy in 1346–1347. Within a year, the plague had spread into northern Europe via trade routes, carried by infected rats and fleas, fanning out across Europe north of the Alps. Whereas this pestilence was originally considered to be a version of bubonic plague, recent research has shown that because of its rapid dissemination a more accurate designation is *pneumatic* plague. That is, people with infected lungs inadvertently spread the disease by close contact with others and by frequent coughing.

The disease took its name "Black Death" from the appearance of blackened body sores, called *buboes* (hence the name "bubonic plague"), especially near the lymph nodes, that announced the arrival of the disease. Once the dreaded black sores appeared, infected people suffered horribly with high fevers, swollen lymph nodes, and painfully aching joints and usually died within 3 days. The plague ravaged Europe from 1348 to 1352 and returned sporadically in the 1360s, 1370s, and 1390s.

The highly contagious disease was next to impossible to contain for a variety of reasons. For one thing, Europe's population was weakened as a consequence of the great famine. For another, overcrowded European cities, with their lack of sanitation, created ideal breeding conditions for the rapid spread of the disease. Moreover, medieval medicine was woefully backward when it came to the treatment of illnesses and diseases. John of Gaddesden (1280–1361), educated at Merton College, Oxford, whose *Rosa Anglica practica medicinae* was widely consulted by physicians (Chaucer lists the book as a staple in physicians' libraries), relies as much on charms and incantations as he does on rational practices for curing illnesses.

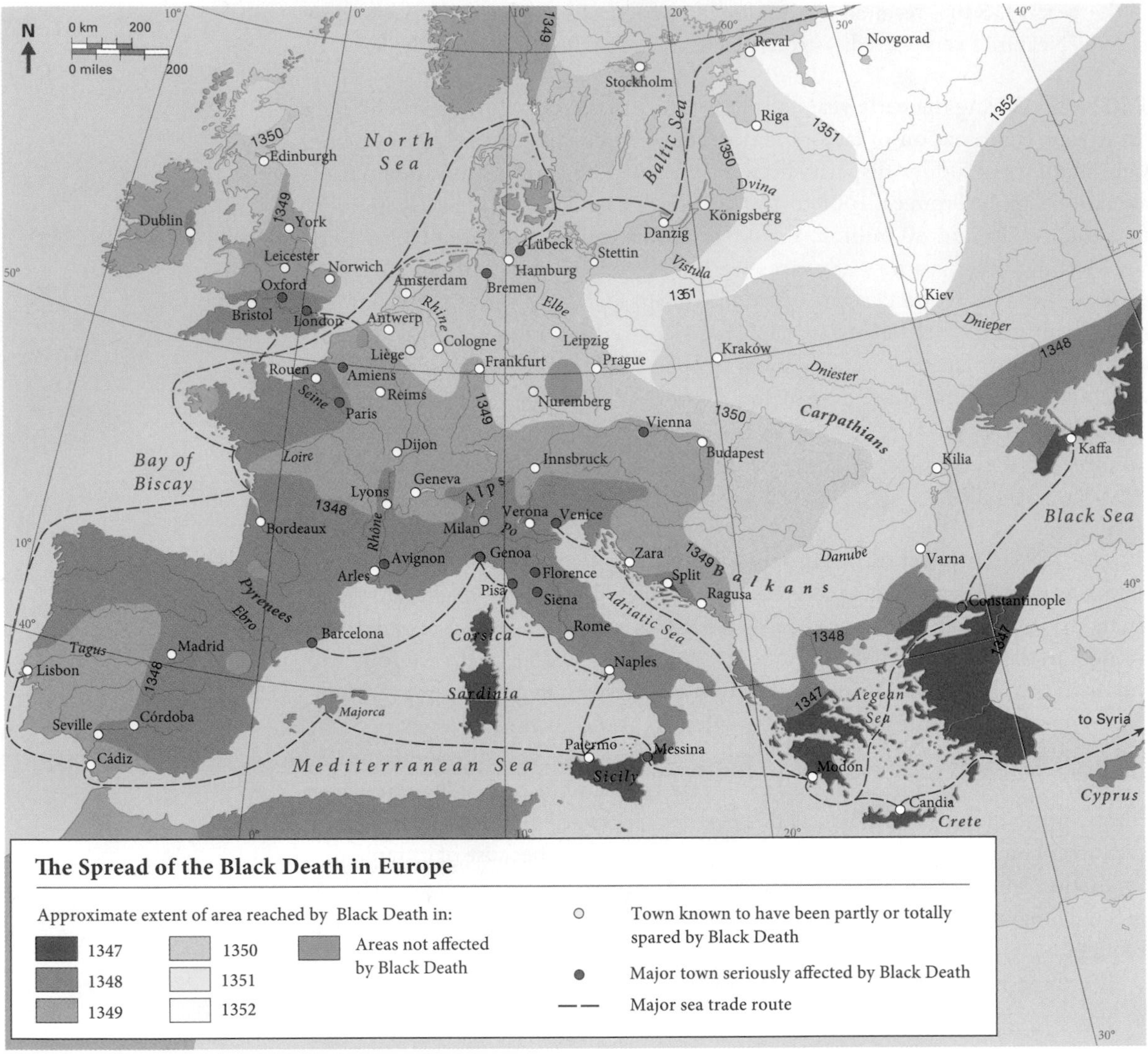

MAP 11.4 The Spread of the Black Death in Europe.

map analysis

It has been estimated that England alone may have lost nearly 1 million from a total population of around 4 million. Urban areas were the hardest hit; Florence suffered losses amounting to around 50,000 out of a total population of 85,000. A reasonable estimate of the number of people who died throughout Europe as a result of the first wave of the plague puts the total loss at about one-third of the entire population (see Map 11.4).

A series of economic and social consequences of the Black Death followed throughout Europe. It was widely believed that the plague was provoked by a wrathful God, who punished Christians for their sins (see Source 11.5). A more sinister response was another wave of anti-Semitism, seen earlier in the twelfth century. Considered heretics and "Christ killers," Jews were targeted as scapegoats and accused of poisoning wells, perhaps an ominous foreshadowing of the Inquisition (see Chapter 16). The falling off of Europe's population resulted in urban areas in

Burial of Plague Victims. With up to 50 percent of the people in some places in Europe dying of the plague, burial scenes, such as this one depicted in a Flemish manuscript, were common throughout the middle and late fourteenth century.

image analysis

less demand for goods and manufactured items, causing a downturn in commerce and trade, and in rural areas in a similar decline in demand for grain products. Another result of the overall decline in Europe's population was the reduction in the number of agricultural workers, whose labor was suddenly more sought after than before the plague. The result of these increasing tensions between the well-off and those less well-off was a series of social uprisings throughout Europe. In Paris a disturbance known as the Jacquerie broke out in 1358, and in Florence the Ciompi rebellion flared up in 1378. The most serious social revolt occurred in London in 1381. Known as the Peasants' Revolt, the uprising was more broadly based and included wealthy country residents as well as participants from the ranks of the urban working classes.

The Hundred Years' War From the mid-fourteenth to the mid-fifteenth century, Europe was embroiled in a disastrous conflict, dubbed the "Hundred Years' War" by nineteenth-century historians. At issue was a long-simmering dispute over English landholdings in France, the result of the Norman Conquest. More immediately, when the English king Edward III (r. 1327–1377) laid claim to the vacant French throne in 1328, his claim was rejected in favor of Charles IV (r. 1322–1328), the first of the Valois rulers. These issues came to a head in 1337 when Philip VI (r. 1328–1350) seized control of Gascony and fighting erupted in earnest between the two countries.

The conflict was fought in three phases. Early on, English forces racked up significant victories at the Battle of Crécy in 1346 and then again at the Battle of Poitiers in 1356, where English longbowmen handed smashing defeats to the mounted French knights. The same thing occurred later at the Battle of Agincourt in 1415, where Henry V (r. 1413–1422) led vastly outnumbered English forces (only 6,000 facing 20,000) to score a surprising victory while suffering relatively few casualties. Suddenly, however, when it seemed that English forces were on the verge of declaring victory, a 17-year-old peasant

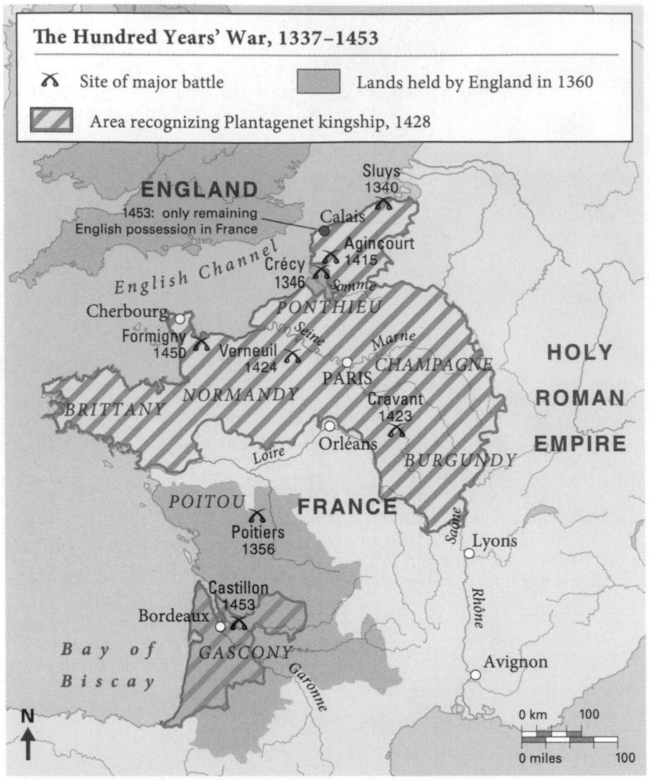

MAP 11.5 **The Hundred Years' War, 1337–1453.**

girl named Joan of Arc (ca. 1412–1431) encouraged the uncrowned Charles VII (r. 1422–1461) to relieve the siege of Orleans in 1429, where English forces were routed. The victory at Orleans inspired the French to one success after another. The conflict finally came to an end in 1453, when the English conceded a French victory in terms agreed to in the Treaty of Paris, leaving the English in possession of only the port of Calais (see Map 11.5).

The Hundred Years' War affected almost every aspect of European life. Like the plague, the war was a constant reminder of the omnipresence of death. The economic consequences of the war were equally serious. The war—fought entirely on French soil—destroyed both crops and small farms. In both England and France, financing the war meant new and increased taxes—and further woes for the peasantry, who bore the brunt of these increased financial obligations. The war even affected the religious realm. It prevented the resolution of the **Western Schism** as rival popes sought the support of contending French and English kings and their subjects.

Western Schism: The period 1378–1417, marked by divided papal allegiances in Latin Christendom.

Crises in the Church Troubles began during the papacy of Pope Boniface VIII (r. 1294–1303), whose stubborn personality clashed with the ambitious national interests of Philip IV (r. 1285–1314) of France. Philip, desperate for money in order to consolidate royal power, levied a tax on the French clergy. In response, Boniface excommunicated Philip; he retaliated by ordering the imprisonment of the pope in 1303, who subsequently died from the shock of this rude treatment. Boniface's successor, Clement V (r. 1305–1314), left Rome and took up residence in Avignon, on the French border. Clement appointed a number of French clergymen to the College of Cardinals. From 1305 to 1378 successive French popes continued to reside at Avignon, a period known as the *Avignon Papacy*.

In 1378 Pope Gregory XI (r. 1370–1378) returned to Rome, but he died shortly after his arrival there. Perhaps in response to pressure from a Roman mob to elect either a Roman or an Italian as the next pope, the predominantly French College of Cardinals elected an Italian archbishop, Urban VI (r. 1378–1389). Urban badly mistreated the cardinals and insisted on a series of outlandish reforms. The cardinals, regretting their selection of Urban, returned to Avignon and promptly elected a Frenchman as the new pope, Clement VII (r. 1378–1394). An attempt by the Council of Pisa in 1409 to resolve the conflict merely intensified the embarrassment. The council deposed both reigning popes and named a new one, Alexander V (r. 1409–1410). However, the two reigning popes refused to step down, with the result that the church had not one or two but *three* popes.

Adding to the church's problems were several outspoken critics of its doctrine. One of the earliest of these critics was John Wycliffe (ca. 1330–1384), an Oxford theologian. Wycliffe railed against the wealth and abuses of the higher clergy, denied the power of priests to act as intermediaries between believers and God, and disputed the validity of many **sacraments**, including the most central of Christian dogmas, the sacrament of the Eucharist (sometimes referred to as Communion or the Lord's Supper), which holds that Christ's presence is revealed in consecrated bread and wine. Wycliffe also oversaw the translation of the Bible into Middle English. Wycliffe's teachings reached Bohemia in central Europe when the English king Richard II (r. 1377–1399) married the princess Anne of Bohemia. John Huss (1370–1415), a radical religious reformer and preacher at Prague, enthusiastically supported Wycliffe's ideas, especially the English theologian's argument for the primacy of scripture as the basis for all Christian doctrine (see Map 11.6).

John Wycliffe. Educated at Oxford during the turbulent fourteenth century, Wycliffe attained the degree of doctor of divinity during the 1370s. In expressing dissident views regarding several doctrines of the church, including transubstantiation and the authority of the priesthood, Wycliffe went so far as to declare the pope an "antichrist." In 1382 Wycliffe completed his translation of the Bible into English. His radical teachings were carried throughout England by his followers, known as Lollards, and eventually to Germany, earning him the title "Morningstar of the Protestant Reformation."

Sacrament: An outward and physical sign of an inward and spiritual grace.

Signs of a New Era in the Fifteenth Century

All of the instances of doom and gloom we have mentioned signaled the waning of earlier medieval values, perspectives, and institutions. Yet, at the same time, dire situations in the fourteenth century prompted adaptations and subsequent transformations in the succeeding century that prefigured the transition to the Renaissance. We can observe these adjustments in political, economic, and cultural aspects of fifteenth-century Europe.

Political Reorganization in France and England Out of the ashes of the Hundred Years' War arose new conceptions of royal authority in both England and France that set the stage for the appearance of the "new monarchies" in the second half of the fifteenth century. In France, for example, fifteenth-century rulers utilized the pressures of warfare as rationales to centralize their authority. One expedient was to overhaul the royal bureaucracy in order to enhance its efficiency and power. Another was the raising of new taxes without consulting the Estates-General.

The state of politics in England was similarly affected by the course of the Hundred Years' War. Across the course of the war English monarchs were repeatedly forced to convene Parliament in order to gain quick access to much-needed funds to prosecute the war effort. Before granting monies to the crown, however, the House of Commons, consisting of merchants and lesser nobility, insisted on "redress of grievances before consent to taxation." As a result, the House of Commons eventually gained the right to introduce all important tax legislation in Parliament; it was granted its first speaker in 1376; and it was given the right to impeach irresponsible members of the king's government.

European Commerce and Trade Europe's fifteenth-century economic recovery was even more pronounced in commerce. When France regained control of Flanders during the course of the Hundred Years' War, England—then at war with the French—was forced to abandon its profitable wool trade with Flemish merchants.

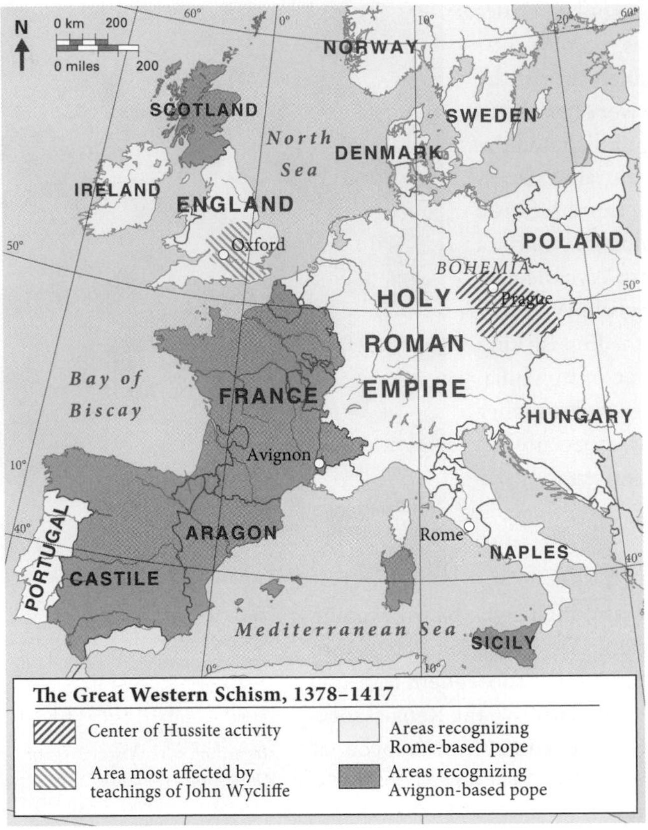

MAP 11.6 **The Great Western Schism, 1378–1417.**

Hanseatic League: A trade network of allied ports along the North Sea and Baltic coasts, founded in 1256.

As a result, England developed a far more lucrative trade in manufactured cloth products, of which by 1500 it had become a leading exporter.

When the Hundred Years' War disrupted trade in France, new lanes of commerce opened up across Europe. Germanic towns in northern Europe had formed a trading alliance, known as the **Hanseatic League** (from *Hansa*, meaning "company"), as early as the thirteenth century. The league reached its peak of influence during the later fourteenth and fifteenth centuries, with trading links from London in the west to Novgorod in Russia. A new commercial axis extended from the cities of the Hanseatic League in the north southward to the northern Italian cities of Venice and Genoa.

Of crucial importance for the future of European trade was the collapse of the so-called Pax Mongolica in 1368. Following the expansion of the Mongol Empire during the thirteenth and fourteenth centuries, travel and trade networks flourished between China and the West across the Silk Road. Thus, the Mongols facilitated the transfer of significant technological innovations from China to Europe. When, however, Mongol rule in China dissolved and was replaced by the Ming dynasty, which was less interested in ties with the West, travel on the Silk Road was no longer safe or profitable. Faced with the necessity of reaching the riches of the East by alternate means, European merchants were forced increasingly to rely on Muslim merchants on southern maritime routes, in use from the 750s onward.

Innovations in Business Techniques Several innovative economic practices contributed to a revitalization of Europe's economy during the fifteenth century. Smaller markets, shrunk by the economic crises of the fourteenth century, brought on increased competition among merchants, who sought evermore creative business methods in order to remain solvent. New accounting procedures, such as double-entry bookkeeping, increased the efficiency of record keeping. In addition, the introduction of maritime insurance, which protected investments in risky seaborne trade, fueled an increase in trans-Mediterranean trade and commerce, while at the same time increasing profits for individual investors.

New banking procedures also facilitated the expansion of Europe's economy by providing loans to merchants and manufacturers. Florence emerged as the center of huge banking partnerships such as the Medici Bank; the Medici family went on to dominate Florentine civic affairs by 1500.

Developments in the Church As a consequence of the disintegration of papal leadership during the fourteenth century, the church was controlled by councils of bishops in the early fifteenth century, a movement known as *conciliarism*. In order to resolve the crises of the fourteenth century, the Council of Constance (1414–1417) was convened by the Holy Roman emperor. Its first order of business was to depose the three reigning popes and to restore papal authority to a single pontiff, who took the name Martin V (r. 1417–1431). Second, to put an end to heretical movements, principally the teachings of John Wycliffe, the council convicted John Huss of heresy and burned him at the stake. The execution of Huss had momentous implications for the future of the church, especially in Germany. Huss's region of Bohemia emerged as a hotbed of heresy, and these anticlerical sentiments helped fuel Martin Luther's Protestant Reformation, which began in neighboring Saxony in the next century. Finally, to improve the management of the church, the council declared that henceforth councils of bishops would meet frequently in order to keep popes under their strict control.

The conciliar movement was an attempt by the bishops to wrest control of the church from popes. The popes resisted the conciliar movement but had to make concessions to secular rulers to gain their support. The result of these concessions was the further weakening of the Roman Church and the creation of national churches, independent of control from Rome.

Literature Significant and widespread changes in literary expression flourished, in large part due to the growing popularity of cultural expression in **vernacular** languages instead of Latin. Although writing in the vernacular first made its appearance in France in the later 1100s, education in the vernacular was especially popular in the city-states of northern Italy, where the emphasis was on educating students for productive careers in the secular world, rather than training them to become priests.

Vernacular: The native, common spoken language of a particular region.

A number of Italian authors chose to write in the vernacular rather than in Latin. A particularly noteworthy example is the poet Dante Alighieri (1265–1321), author of *The Divine Comedy*, a long epic poem written in Italian and completed in 1321. Two Italian authors of the next generation continued Dante's legacy. Francesco Petrarch (1304–1374), known as the "father of Renaissance humanism," turned to Roman authors and classical texts, whose values more closely resembled the secular, materialistic world of everyday life in Florence. Petrarch also wrote a series of love sonnets to his beloved Laura, in Tuscan Italian. The *Decameron* of Giovanni Boccaccio (1313–1375), written between 1352 and 1353, represents a further drift away from medieval literary conventions—and toward the Roman classical past—in that it draws its inspiration from the first-century Roman author Petronius and his scandalous *Satyricon* (see Source 11.4).

Canto XIX of Dante's *Inferno*

English and French writers of the fourteenth century also began to produce works in their native languages. *Piers Plowman*, composed in Middle English by William Langland (ca. 1332–1400), presents a series of complaints and laments about current abuses in late-fourteenth-century England, especially among the aristocracy and the clergy. Geoffrey Chaucer (ca. 1340–1400), a friend and contemporary of Langland's, also wrote in Middle English. Like Langland, Chaucer satirized abuses in contemporary society. His *Canterbury Tales* is a series of stories told by travelers making their annual pilgrimage from London to the shrine of St. Thomas Becket in Canterbury. Christine de Pizan (ca. 1364–1430) of France composed both poetry and prose; she was primarily concerned with advancing the status of women, and for her criticisms of male behaviors is often considered the first feminist writer. In

"The Wife of Bath's Tale" from *The Canterbury Tales*

her *Epistle to the God of Love*, for example, she criticizes the Roman poet Ovid for attributing "nasty ways" to women.

Philosophy Bold departures in the era's philosophy challenged basic medieval theological beliefs. In place of Aquinas's attempt to reconcile differences between the truths of faith and reason, the intellectuals of the time turned decidedly toward the latter, especially toward Aristotle. The earliest philosopher to take this approach was the Oxford Franciscan John Duns Scotus (ca. 1266–1308). Critical of Aquinas, Scotus argued for the strict separation of reason from theology. William of Ockham (ca. 1285–1349), another Oxford Franciscan, carried the assault on the Aquinas synthesis even further. He argued for extreme nominalism, arguing that only the truths of reason, vested in individual things, could be known for certain. Therefore, no metaphysical knowledge is possible; and, from this, it is impossible to have any sure knowledge of the existence of God. That being the case, only a personal, mystical association with God was available to the believer.

Putting It All Together

interactive concept map

Following the collapse of the united Mediterranean Roman Empire, a new postclassical, Christian religious civilization gradually developed in western Europe during the period ca. 600–1450. The Germanic invasions that brought down Roman rule in the western provinces destroyed imperial unity in the West and created in Europe a series of smaller political entities. After a brief period of centralized imperial rule during the reign of Charlemagne in the later eighth century, medieval Europe fell back in the ninth and tenth centuries into a pattern of decentralized political entities that provided for law and order at the local, instead of empire-wide, level. Feudalism, as this arrangement is known, prevented the reassertion of a centralized European empire and prepared Europe for the appearance of several highly centralized, competing kingdoms. One advantage of this "political pluralism" was the appearance of competition among the states of Europe, which in turn created a sense of vitality and progress in the West.

In terms of cultural developments, the Germanic invasions and subsequent destruction of Roman rule in the West were immensely disruptive, forcing the formation of a new, distinctly European, postclassical culture formed from a blending of three elements that had formerly been antagonistic to each other: Roman legacies, Germanic customs, and Christian institutions. Of these, the Christian Church would prove the most important in shaping a new European religious civilization. In much the same way that Buddhism, Hinduism, Confucianism, and Islam undergirded civilizations in Asia and Africa, Christianity served as the basic unifying force that held together the new European civilization.

During the fourteenth century Europe experienced several transforming events. The horrors of famine and plague, accompanied by over a century of warfare between England and France, cast a pall of gloom over European society, which in turn called into question traditional medieval values and perspectives. In addition, a series of internal problems in the church resulted in a lessening of its authority and prestige. At the same time, however, several developments—particularly in the cultural sphere—prepared Europe for the transition to Renaissance secularism and humanism.

Review and Relate

Thinking Through Patterns

Examine the ways historians approach the big questions of this chapter.

» How did the Merovingians and Carolingians construct a new Christian European civilization during the seventh and eighth centuries CE?

The Merovingians and Carolingians constructed a new Christian European civilization during the seventh and eighth centuries by utilizing the support of the Christian Church. Through their conversion to Christianity, as well as their support and encouragement of monastic expansion, they earned the support of bishops, priests, and monks in all regions of their kingdom. In addition, the creation of the Franco–papal alliance during the eighth century, followed by Charlemagne's personal involvement in church affairs, ensured the emergence of a new Christian foundation for Europe.

» What were key factors in the political, economic, and social recovery of Europe during the eleventh and twelfth centuries?

Some key factors in the political, economic, and social recovery of Europe during the eleventh and twelfth centuries included the emergence of centralized kingdoms in France and England, which replaced the decentralized cells of political authority during the ninth and tenth centuries. The expansion of agricultural advances and the development of commerce and trade produced a population surge, which in turn resulted in urbanization and the emergence of a new bourgeois middle class of merchants and traders.

» What were some cultural and intellectual developments during the "twelfth-century renaissance," and how did they contribute to medieval civilization?

During the "twelfth-century renaissance" urban-centered cathedral schools developed into universities in Europe. In order to serve the needs of an expanding urban and commercial economy, more practical disciplines like law and medicine were developed in revised curricula. The influx of Aristotelian logic and science, assimilated from contacts in Spain and Sicily between Latin scholars—known as the Latin translators—and their Muslim counterparts, resulted in a prolonged debate between the truths of reason and the truths of faith. Although temporarily resolved by Aquinas in the late thirteenth century, Aristotelian nominalism dominated philosophy and theology in the fourteenth century. Another result of the fascination with Aristotle was the development of natural science at Oxford and Paris, which during the later thirteenth and early fourteenth centuries began to uncover flaws in Aristotelian celestial and terrestrial scientific conceptions.

» How did the church influence political developments in Europe during the twelfth and thirteenth centuries?

As a result of a series of ecclesiastical reforms in both the monastic and episcopal arms of the church, a series of increasingly powerful popes began to assert papal primacy over secular rulers, and, indeed, over all European institutions. Pope Gregory VII humbled the German emperor Henry IV in the eleventh century, and Pope Innocent III did the same with King John of England in the beginning of the thirteenth century.

» What events made fourteenth-century Europe so dismal? How did these combine to spell the gradual demise of medieval institutions and perspectives?

The "calamitous fourteenth century" witnessed several unprecedented setbacks that, taken together, signaled the end of the medieval era and the early stages of the Renaissance era. Among these events were the Black Death, the Hundred Years' War, and the Avignon papacy followed by the Western Schism, which produced not one, not two, but eventually three popes. At the same time men of letters, philosophers as well as theologians, began to challenge earlier assertions of papal authority, resulting in the Council of Constance (1414–1417), which ultimately replaced papal control of the church with councils of bishops during the fifteenth century.

Against the Grain

Consider this as a counterpoint to the main patterns examined in this chapter.

The Cathar Heresy

- In what ways does Catharism represent a contrast to the patterns of development of medieval Europe?
- How does the Cathar heresy compare with other heresies in world religions?

In 1144, the dedication of the magnificent Gothic abbey church at St. Denis provided a physical manifestation of the power and glory of Roman Christianity in European Christendom. And yet, only one year earlier—in 1143—a heretical cult was identified as posing the most dangerous challenge to Catholic Christianity in its history.

Known as Cathars ("pure ones"), or Albigensians (from Albi, a region in southwestern France), this heretical movement reflected anticlerical sentiments emanating from mounting discontent among educated urbanites and rural laity alike, dismayed by the materialism, corruption, and increasing worldliness among the clerical establishment. It was derived from a combination of Christian Gnosticism and Manichaeism, dualistic faiths in which forces of good and light (represented by God and the spiritual world) struggle against forces of evil and darkness (represented by Satan) for dominance in the universe. Cathars believed that because Satan created the material world and imprisoned human souls within the physical body, the only way to end the cycle of reincarnation in the material world and to escape from Satan's grasp was to forego all material things of this world, including marriage, sex, and certain foods. And because Christ was of the material world, Cathars rejected elements of Catholic Christianity, including the Trinitarian doctrine, as well as many sacraments, including the Eucharist and baptism.

Alarmed at their growing influence, Pope Innocent III moved to suppress Catharism. His initial response was to try persuasion by enlisting the help of the recently licensed orders of Dominicans and Franciscans. When that failed, Innocent ordered the Albigensian crusade (1209–1229), which resulted in the brutal (even by medieval standards) suppression of the movement. When a force of French knights stormed the center of Cathar resistance at Béziers, they were ordered by the presiding bishop to slaughter all of its inhabitants, both Catholic and Cathar: "Kill them all. God will know His own." Further efforts to eliminate Catharism included the establishment of an Inquisition in 1234 and the final dissolution of the movement in 1329, when the last of the Cathars were burned at the stake.

Key Terms

audio flashcards

Baron 316
Bourgeoisie 320
Canon law 329
Capitalism 319
Coronation 310
Demesne 315
Easter 323
Estates-General 315
Feudalism 313
Guilds 320
Hanseatic League 336
Latin Christendom 309
Manorialism 314
Parliament 316
Sacrament 335
Scholasticism 328
Unction 310
Vernacular 337
Western Schism 334
Writ 316

For additional resources, please go to
www.oup.com/us/vonsivers.
Please see the Further Resources section at the back of the book for additional readings and suggested websites.

PATTERNS OF EVIDENCE |

Sources for Chapter 11

SOURCE 11.1 Einhard's *Life of Charlemagne*

ca. 830 CE

The model for Einhard's *Vita Caroli Magni* was Suetonius' biographies of the first 12 Roman emperors, and particularly of Augustus, composed in the second century CE. The biography is thus an example of the general attempt to revive interest in and appreciation for pre-Christian Roman antiquity in the midst of the "Carolingian Renaissance," of which Einhard was both a product and a driving force. Educated at the Palace School at Aachen (Charlemagne's capital), Einhard established a close personal and professional connection with the man himself. Due to his intimate knowledge of Charlemagne's behavior, habits, and outlook, Einhard was ideally placed to write his biography, which was composed after Charlemagne's death but contained pointed advice to the man's successors.

§24 . . . His main meal of the day was served in four courses, in addition to the roast meat which his hunters used to bring in on spits and which he enjoyed more than any other food. During his meal he would listen to a public reading or some other entertainment. Stories would be recited for him, or the doings of the ancients told again. He took great pleasure in the books of Saint Augustine and especially in those which are called *The City of God*.

. . .

§25 He spoke easily and fluently, and could express with great clarity whatever he had to say. He was not content with his own mother tongue, but took the trouble to learn foreign languages. He learnt Latin so well that he spoke it as fluently as his own tongue; but he understood Greek better than he could speak it. He was eloquent to the point of sometimes seeming almost garrulous.

He paid the greatest attention to the liberal arts; and he had great respect for men who taught them, bestowing high honours upon them. When he was learning the rules of grammar he received tuition from Peter the Deacon of Pisa, who by then was an old man, but for all other subjects he was taught by Alcuin, surnamed Albinus, another Deacon, a man of the Saxon race who came

---

Source: Einhard and Notker the Stammerer, *Two Lives of Charlemagne*, trans. Lewis Thorpe (Harmondsworth, UK: Penguin, 1969), 78–80.

from Britain and was the most learned man anywhere to be found. Under him the Emperor spent much time and effort in studying rhetoric, dialectic and especially astrology. He applied himself to mathematics and traced the course of the stars with great attention and care. He also tried to learn to write. With this object in view he used to keep writing-tablets and notebooks under the pillows on his bed, so that he could try his hand at forming letters during his leisure moments; but, although he tried very hard, he had begun too late in life and he made little progress.

§26 Charlemagne practised the Christian religion with great devotion and piety, for he had been brought up in this faith since earliest childhood. . . . He donated so many sacred vessels made of gold and silver, and so many priestly vestments, that when service time came even those who opened and closed the doors, surely the humblest of all church dignitaries, had no need to perform their duties in their everyday clothes. He made careful reforms in the way in which the psalms were chanted and the lessons read. He was himself quite an expert at both of these exercises, but he never read the lesson in public and he would sing only with the rest of the congregation and then in a low voice.

» Working with Sources

1. **How does this passage reflect the attempt to re-create the ancient past during the Carolingian Renaissance?**
2. **Did Charlemagne separate his private life from his public image? Why?**

SOURCE 11.2 Feudal contracts and the swearing of fealty

1127 and 1219

In the catastrophe brought on by the assaults on all their borders, some European Christians were forced to devise new means of self-protection. Into this vacuum of governmental authority came new "feudal" relationships between lords and vassals. Over time, these contractual relationships became increasingly regularized. The terms of these relationships can be reconstructed through documents describing the ceremonial and formulaic aspects of feudal obligations.

Source: James Harvey Robinson, *Readings in European History*, vol. 1 (Boston: Ginn & Company, 1904), 178–180.

How the Count of Flanders received the homage of his vassals (1127):

Enfeoffed: Invested with an estate, or "fief."

Through the whole remaining part of the day those who had been previously **enfeoffed** by the most pious Count Charles did homage to the [new] count, taking up now again their fiefs and offices and whatever they had before rightfully and legitimately obtained. On Thursday, the seventh of April, homages were again made to the count, being completed in the following order of faith and security.

First they did their homage thus. The count asked the vassal if he were willing to become completely his man, and the other replied, "I am willing"; and with hands clasped, placed between the hands of the count, they were bound together by a kiss. Secondly, he who had done homage gave his fealty to the representative of the count in these words, "I promise on my faith that I will in future be faithful to Count William, and will observe my homage to him completely against all persons, in good faith and without deceit." And, thirdly, he took his oath to this upon the relics of the saints. Afterward the count, with a little rod which he held in his hand, gave investitures to all who by this agreement had given their security and accompanying oath.

Pons of Mont-Saint-Jean becomes the man of the Countess of Champagne (1219):

I, Pons of Mont-Saint-Jean, make known to all, both present and future, that since I have long been the man of my beloved Lady Blanche, countess of Champagne, for twenty pounds assigned to the fair at Bar, and since later both the countess and my dear lord have added other twenty pounds assigned to the same fair and gave me three hundred pounds in cash,—I swore by the saints that I would in good faith aid them and their heirs with my people and fortifications. If necessary I will fight especially against Erard of Brienne and Philippa his wife, and against Adelaide, queen of Cyprus, and her heirs, and against all who would aid them; except that should the said countess or count or their people be against Milo of Noyers, my sister's husband, in his castle of Noyers or elsewhere in his lands, neither I nor my people shall be held to go thither. If, however, the said Milo or his people set upon the countess or the count or their people, we shall be held to defend them and their lands with all our might.

It is also to be known that my heir who shall hold Charniacum shall also have the fief above mentioned of forty pounds.

That all this shall be held valid, I corroborate what has here been written with the impression of my seal. Done in the year of grace 1219, in the month of June.

» Working with Sources

1. **Why are religious terms invoked so often in these documents in order to solidify the relationships between lords and vassals?**
2. **Did feudal contracts with women differ from those with men?**

SOURCE 11.3 Peter Abelard, *The Story of My Misfortunes*

ca. 1132

One of the most brilliant professors and theologians of the European Middle Ages, Peter Abelard (1079–1142) became a star performer in the academic art of "dialectic." His abilities also earned him many enemies. When he turned his attention to the thorny subject of the Trinity, one of the principal elements of Christian belief, Abelard incurred the wrath of powerful members of the institutional church, of which he, as a professor, was also a part. In his autobiography, *The Story of My Misfortunes*, Abelard detailed the episodes of envy, backbiting, and stupidity that dogged him throughout his life. He also recalled his affair with Heloise (d. 1163), his former pupil and intellectual equal. The letters they exchanged survive as some of the most passionate and beautiful documents of the period.

It so happened that at the outset I devoted myself to analysing the basis of our faith through illustrations based on human understanding, and I wrote for my students a certain tract on the unity and trinity of God. This I did because they were always seeking for rational and philosophical explanations, asking rather for reasons they could understand than for mere words, saying that it was futile to utter words which the intellect could not possibly follow, that nothing could be believed unless it could first be understood, and that it was absurd for any one to preach to others a thing which neither he himself nor those whom he sought to teach could comprehend. Our Lord Himself maintained this same thing when He said: "They are blind leaders of the blind" (Matthew, xv, 14).

Now, a great many people saw and read this tract, and it became exceedingly popular, its clearness appealing particularly to all who sought information on this subject. And since the questions involved are generally considered the most difficult of all, their complexity is taken as the measure of the subtlety of him who succeeds in answering them. As a result, my rivals became furiously angry, and summoned a council to take action against me, the chief instigators therein being my two intriguing enemies of former days, Alberic and Lotulphe.

. . .

On one occasion Alberic, accompanied by some of his students, came to me for the purpose of intimidating me, and, after a few bland words, said that he was amazed at something he had found in my book, to the effect that, although God had begotten God, I denied that God had begotten Himself, since there was only one God. I answered unhesitatingly: "I can give you an explanation of this if you wish it." "Nay," he replied, "I care nothing for human explanation or reasoning in such matters, but only for the words of authority." "Very well," I said; "turn the pages of my book and you will find the authority likewise." The

---

Source: Henry Adams Bellows, trans., *The Story of My Misfortunes: The Autobiography of Peter Abélard* (New York: Macmillan, 1922), 36–44.

book was at hand, for he had brought it with him. I turned to the passage I had in mind, which he had either not discovered or else passed over as containing nothing injurious to me. And it was God's will that I quickly found what I sought. This was the following sentence, under the heading "Augustine, On the Trinity, Book I": "Whosoever believes that it is within the power of God to beget Himself is sorely in error; this power is not in God, neither is it in any created thing, spiritual or corporeal. For there is nothing that can give birth to itself."

When those of his followers who were present heard this, they were amazed and much embarrassed.

. . .

Straightway upon my summons I went to the council, and there, without further examination or debate, did they compel me with my own hand to cast that memorable book of mine into the flames.

» Working with Sources

1. **Explain the positions of Abelard and Alberic concerning "logic" and "faith" in this regard.**
2. **How does Abelard turn the tables on Alberic in his line of reasoning?**

SOURCE 11.4 Giovanni Boccaccio, *The Decameron*, "Putting the Devil Back in Hell"

ca. 1350

A Latin scholar, poet, and biographer, Boccaccio (1313–1375) is most famous today as the author of the *Decameron*. This compilation of 100 tales, by turns serious, bawdy, and irreverent, purports to be a rendition of the stories told over the course of 10 days by 10 young men and women who had fled Florence to escape the Black Death. Many of the tales are based on older legends, and they frequently reflect the humor of the common people of the era, often at the expense of their spiritual and social betters. Religious authorities were frequent targets of this sort of satire, reflecting their ubiquitous presence in the lives of medieval Europeans, as well as, perhaps, a deep undercurrent of resentment regarding their privileges.

. . . And so, coming to the facts, I say that in the city of Gafsa in Tunisia there was once a very rich man who, among other children, had a beautiful and

---

Source: Giovanni Boccaccio, "Putting the Devil Back in Hell" (3.10), from *The Decameron: Selected Tales / Decameron: Novelle scelte*, trans. Stanley Appelbaum (Mineola, NY: Dover, 2000), 87–93.

genteel daughter named Alibec. She, not being a Christian, but hearing many Christians who lived in the city praising the Christian religion and the service of God, asked one of them one day how God could be served in the easiest way. This man replied that God was best served by those who fled worldly things, like those men who had gone into the lonely deserts of the Thebaid.

[Alibec goes into the desert, seeking out a willing hermit, and finally arrives at the door of a man who is willing to help her.]

. . . She reached the cell of a young hermit, a very devout and kind person named Rustico, and asked him the same thing she had asked the others.

. . .

First feeling his way with certain questions, he learned that she had never slept with a man and was just as naïve as she looked. And so he planned a way to have her submit to his pleasure under the pretext of serving God. First he told her at length that the devil was the enemy of God; then he gave her to understand that the service most pleasing to God was putting the devil back in hell, to which place God had condemned him.

The girl asked him how that was done, and Rustico replied: "You'll soon know; to make it happen, do what you see me doing." And he began to take off the few garments he was wearing until he was stark naked; and the girl did the same. Then he knelt down as if he were going to pray, and he made her do the same, facing him.

As they knelt there, Rustico's desire flared up more than ever at the sight of her great beauty, and there ensued the resurrection of the flesh. Seeing that and wondering at it, Alibec said: "Rustico, what's that thing I see on you sticking out like that? I don't have one."

"My daughter," said Rustico, "that's the devil I told you about. And now look: he's giving me terrible discomfort, so that I can hardly stand it."

Then the girl said: "Praised be God, for I see that I'm better off than you, because I don't have that devil!"

Rustico said: "It's true, but you have something else that I don't have, and you have it in place of this."

Alibec said: "What is it?"

Rustico replied: "You have hell, and, believe me, I think God has sent you here to save my soul, because, whenever this devil causes me this distress, if you want to take pity on me and let me put him back in hell, you will give me the greatest relief, and you're doing God the greatest pleasure and service—if you've really come to this area for that purpose, as you say."

The girl replied in good faith: "Oh, Father, since I have hell, let it be whenever you like."

Then Rustico said: "Bless you, daughter! Let's go put him back so he'll leave me in peace."

Saying that, he led the girl to one of their pallets and taught her how to position herself to imprison that being who was accursed of God.

. . .

After a fire destroys much of Gafsa, Alibec is the only surviving heir to her father's property, and she is married to a young man named Neerbal.

But, being asked by the ladies what she had done to serve God in the desert—this was before Neerbal had slept with her—she replied that she had served Him by putting the devil back in hell, and that Neerbal had committed a great sin by taking her away from that service. The ladies asked: "How is the devil put back in hell?"

Partly with words and partly with gestures, the girl showed them how. They laughed so loud at this that they're still laughing, and they said: "Don't fret, youngster, no, because that's done here, too; Neerbal and you will do God good service that way."

» Working with Sources

1. **Is Alibec's naïveté designed to convey a warning to the reader?**
2. **Does this tale reflect a mocking attitude toward *all* forms of religiosity?**

SOURCE 11.5 Flagellants attempt to ward off the Black Death in Germany and in England

1348 and 1349

Although flagellation (beating oneself with a whip) had been practiced as a means of spiritual discipline by monks long before, it did not emerge as a public group activity until the thirteenth century. While Europe was besieged by the Black Death (1348–1352), the Brotherhood of Flagellants (which also included women) resorted to ever more spectacular public flagellation. The movement probably originated in eastern Europe and took root most deeply in German-speaking areas, as the following account demonstrates. As we see from the subsequent report of Robert of Avesbury, however, they had also crossed into England, offering some sort of solution to the plague crisis.

In 1348 a race without a head aroused universal wonder by their sudden appearance in huge numbers. They suddenly sprang up in all parts of Germany, calling themselves cross bearers or flagellants.

. . .

They were called flagellants because of the whips [*flagella*] which they used in performing public penance. Each whip consisted of a stick with three knotted thongs hanging from the end. Two pieces of needle-sharp metal were run through the centre of the knots from both sides, forming a cross, the ends of

Source: "52. The Flagellants," from the *Chronicon Henrici de Hervordia and from the Concerning the Miraculous Deeds of King Edward III* by Robert of Avesbury, in Rosemary Horrox, *The Black Death* (Manchester, UK: Manchester University Press, 1994), 150–154.

which extended beyond the knots for the length of a grain of wheat or less. Using these whips they beat and whipped their bare skin until their bodies were bruised and swollen and blood rained down, spattering the walls nearby. I have seen, when they whipped themselves, how sometimes those bits of metal penetrated the flesh so deeply that it took more than two attempts to pull them out.

Flocking together from every region, perhaps even from every city, they overran the whole land. In open country they straggled along behind the cross in no particular order, but when they came to cities, towns and villages they formed themselves into a procession, with hoods or hats pulled down over their foreheads, and sad and downcast eyes, they went through the streets singing a sweet hymn. In this fashion they entered the church and shut themselves in while they stripped off their clothes and left them with a guard.

. . .

After this, one of them would strike the first with a whip, saying, "May God grant you remission of all your sins. Arise." And he would get up, and do the same to the second, and all the others in turn did the same. When they were all on their feet, and arranged two by two in procession, two of them in the middle of the column would begin singing a hymn in a high voice, with a sweet melody.

From Robert of Avesbury:

In that same year of 1349, about Michaelmas [29 September], more than 120 men, for the most part from Zeeland or Holland, arrived in London from Flanders. These went barefoot in procession twice a day in the sight of the people, sometimes in St Paul's church and sometimes elsewhere in the city, their bodies naked except for a linen cloth from loins to ankle. Each wore a hood painted with a red cross at front and back and carried in his right hand a whip with three thongs. Each thong had a knot in it, with something sharp, like a needle, stuck through the middle of the knot so that it stuck out on each side, and as they walked one after the other they struck themselves with these whips on their naked, bloody bodies; four of them singing in their own tongue and the rest answering in the manner of the Christian litany. Three times in each procession they would all prostrate themselves on the ground, with their arms outstretched in the shape of a cross. Still singing, and beginning with the man at the end, each in turn would step over the others, lashing the man beneath him once with his whip, until all of those lying down had gone through the same ritual. Then each one put on his usual clothes and, always with their hoods on their heads and carrying their whips, they departed to their lodgings. It was said that they performed a similar penance every night.

≫ Working with Sources

1. **What did the flagellants think was the source and cause of the plague?**
2. **How might their behavior have made matters worse for the observers?**

Chapter 12 **600–1600 CE**

Sultanates, Song, and the Mongol Super Empire

CONTRASTING PATTERNS IN INDIA, CHINA, AND INNER ASIA

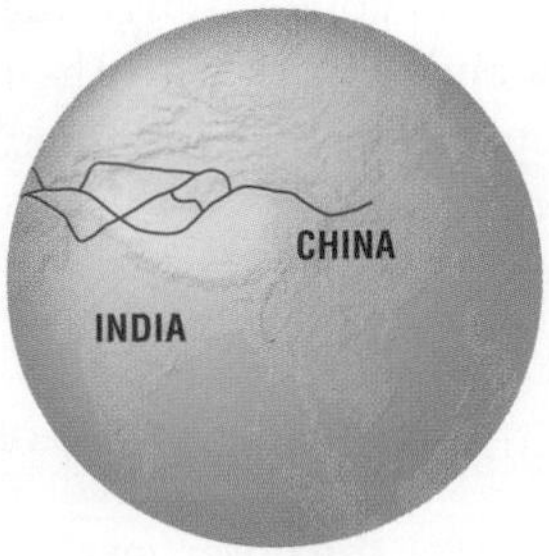

While Arab armies had worked their way through Sasanid Persia by the middle of the seventh century CE, their first reports on northwest India were not terribly encouraging. The land was described as desert waste, with few resources and a hostile populace. They made at least 10 attempts to invade the northwest Indian region of Sind, and all 10 times they were defeated by local rulers. According to the *Chachnama* (the history of the campaign written hundreds of years later, in the thirteenth century), following these failed attempts a more ambitious invasion was mounted by Muhammad Ibn Qasim, a cousin of the governor of Iraq who was responsible for the conquest of eastern lands.

Ibn Qasim's army pursued the move into India with brutal efficiency. Wearing coats of chain-mail armor and equipped with siege machinery for hurling projectiles and battering down walls, they decimated the major cities, executed most of the defenders, and extracted plunder and slaves before moving in to completely occupy the area in 711. Though Ibn Qasim's rule in the wake of his violent conquest was considered relatively moderate,

***ABOVE:* Completed in 1192, the Lugouqiao on the outskirts of modern Beijing acquired its Western association as Marco Polo Bridge because of a mention in Marco Polo's *Travels*. It was also the site of the incident that opened the Japanese invasion of China in 1937.**

the *Chachnama* claims that he met his death through a spectacular episode of duplicity concocted by his new subjects.

When the daughters of Dihar, the ruler of the conquered city of Dehal (Karachi in modern Pakistan), were taken back to the governor of Iraq as tribute, they accused Ibn Qasim of making sexual advances toward them. The governor immediately ordered his cousin Ibn Qasim to be sewn up in a stifling raw leather sheath and transported home. This torturous mode of transport was meant to inflict maximal suffering, and, indeed, the heat and lack of room for breathing soon did their work. Ibn Qasim died 2 days into the journey, and when his putrefied body was shown to the women who had accused him, they proudly admitted to their deception and revenge on their conqueror.

Seeing Patterns

» How did interactions between Muslims and Hindus in India lead to attempts at religious syncretism?

» What steps were taken by Hindus and Muslims to lessen the conflicts between the two rival religious traditions?

» How was the Tang dynasty in China different from its predecessors and successors?

» How effectively did the religious and philosophical traditions of Buddhism, Confucianism, and Daoism blend together in creating Neo-Confucianism? Where did they clash?

Though the reliability of the *Chachnama*'s account is questionable, it has come to symbolize the dramatic clash of cultural and religious outlooks that has marked the history of the Indian subcontinent ever since. In this contested area between radically different religious civilizations, the Hindu vision of Islam has remained one of ruthless conquest and purposeful disregard for long-established religious traditions. Muslims, on the other hand, have tended to view Hindus as despised infidels for whom no act of treachery is out of bounds. Such competing visions, despite periodic efforts to find compromise, have created over the centuries a pattern of fragile *syncretic* social and political formation (a pattern in which attempts are made to reconcile two different traditions with little or no common ground). In this case, the two cultures actually coexist with considerable hostility toward one another. Despite extensive interaction, neither side has adopted much from the other; in fact, the dominant pattern has been that each has used the differences of the other to define its own religious civilization more consciously and distinctly.

The case of China provides a useful contrast. Here, despite a pervasive belief among officials and scholars of the Song dynasty (960–1279) that the fall of the previous dynasty, the Tang, had come about in large part because of the influence of the "foreign" religion of Buddhism, there were no mass persecutions or forced conversions. While Song Confucian scholars tended to lecture their audiences about "unseemly" Buddhist "superstitions," they also borrowed from Buddhist cosmological perspectives and Daoist beliefs to create a pattern of *synthetic* social and political formation (a pattern in which the most durable opposing elements merge together into a compatible whole). The result was a coherent Chinese religious civilization for the next 1,000 years, based on Neo-Confucianism, incorporating the fused body of Daoist and Buddhist religious traditions, and Confucian ethics and theories of knowledge expanded to a cosmological scale.

India: The Clash of Cultures

As we saw in Chapter 8, the early centuries of the Common Era saw the maturing of two large divisions among the multiple varieties of religious and cultural experience of India. The first was the rise and spread of Buddhism out of northern India into

Chapter Outline

- India: The Clash of Cultures
- Interactions and Adaptations: From Buddhism to Neo-Confucian Synthesis in China
- Putting It All Together

central Asia via the Silk Road and on to China and ultimately to Korea, Japan, and Vietnam. Along the way, the main branches of the various Buddhist schools were created—Theravada and Mahayana—and their scriptural foundations solidified.

More important for the long term of Indian history, however, was that the efforts of the Guptas during India's "golden age" from the fourth to the sixth centuries CE helped in the maturation of the vast variety of religious practices that we know as "Hinduism." For it was Hinduism, rather than Buddhism, that would dominate Indian cultural and religious life until Islam ultimately established itself in the north. In the south and some areas of the north, however, Hinduism remained the dominant religious tradition down to the present day. Hence, India was transformed from a Hindu religious civilization into a frontier between the competing religious civilizations of Islam and Hinduism.

Following the collapse of India's "golden age" during the Gupta era, India experienced nearly 1,000 years of repeated attempts to establish unification of the subcontinent. None of these were effectual, however, owing not only to internal division and conflict among local rulers but also to different circumstances in the northern and southern parts of this vast region. Adding to the confusion were conflicting religious policies on the part of native Hindus and invading Muslims, which although producing a degree of grudging cooperation were never fully resolved.

Buddhist and Hindu India after the Guptas

By the 500s CE, the last Gupta monarchs were under increasing pressure from a branch of the central Asian Huns pressing on their borders. Following the old invasion routes through the Khyber Pass into northern India, the Huns established themselves in the Punjab and adjacent regions and soon settled there to create new states as the Gupta lands shrank and finally dissolved.

Harsha Vardhana One relatively stable regime that achieved a certain degree of power in the north following the Guptas was that of Harsha Vardhana (r. 606–647). Like Ashoka, Harsha is one of the few Indian monarchs about whom we know a good deal. The *Life of Harsha*, by the poet Bana, and the account of the famous Chinese Buddhist pilgrim Xuan Zang (see Chapter 9), who traveled throughout India from 630 to 644, offer a number of insights into Harsha's reign.

When Xuan Zang met Harsha in his capital at Kanauj on the Ganges River, he discovered that the ruler was a devout Buddhist. Xuan Zang's account notes the degree to which Buddhism had once permeated the land, despite the favoritism shown by the Guptas earlier toward Hinduism. It was also clear, however, that many Buddhist monasteries were now abandoned or in disrepair. Precipitated by the new devotional strains of Hinduism, the decline of Buddhism on the subcontinent as a whole was well advanced.

Still, Xuan Zang found Harsha's kingdom well run, wealthy, justly administered, and in many ways a model state. The state, however, barely outlived its ruler. The middle years of Harsha's reign

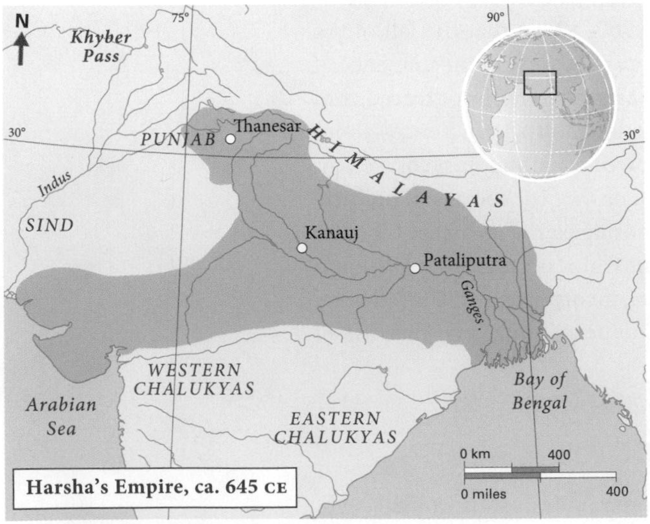

MAP 12.1 Harsha's Empire, ca. 645 CE.

saw the new power of the Arabs probing the borders of Sind, the arid plain to the east of the Indus River, in advance of their full conquest in 711. Meanwhile, following Harsha's reign, northern India was once again divided into regional kingdoms (see Map 12.1).

Rajarajeshwara Temple, Tanjore, India. This early eleventh-century Hindu temple is the largest in all of India and one of the most beautiful. It was richly endowed with spoils taken from Chola conquests.

The Hindu States of the South In the interim, the political center of the subcontinent had shifted south. By the latter part of the ninth century, a Chola [KO-luh] state based in Tanjore [tan-JO-ray] had concluded its long and bitter contest with the Pallavis. In 897 they captured Kanchipuram [kan-chih-POOR-um], advanced into the Pandya kingdom in the southern tip of the peninsula, and captured their capital at Madurai. In the next century, the Cholas conquered Kerala, invaded Sri Lanka, and launched campaigns aimed at expanding their control of the trade with Southeast Asia. The Cholas then advanced northward, allying themselves with the eastern Chalukyas in 1030. In the west, however, the revived western Chalukyas absorbed the Rashtakutras in 970 and repeatedly fought the Cholas to a standstill.

In the meantime, the development of the clove trade of the Molucca Islands (in what is now Indonesia) vastly increased the strategic value of that area, which the Indian-influenced Sumatran state of Srivijaya attempted to exploit in the tenth and eleventh centuries. In response to the exorbitant rates and threats of piracy Srivijaya posed, the Cholas sent a maritime expedition in 1025 that smashed its major ports and reduced its power for a time. In this context, the coming of the Arabs to northern India resulted in a broadening of the subcontinent's position in the world economy. Along the western ports of India, Arab merchants continued to peacefully ply their trade much as before. Despite the newfound religious antagonisms, caravan traffic also continued much as before, and India now became the bottom leg of a triangle of trade that spanned Eurasia (see Map 12.2).

Vijayanagar A new Hindu state emerged in 1336 with the founding of the city of Vijayanagar ("City of Victory"). The last in the two-millennium pattern of states ruled by god-kings, the new state was deemed fabulously wealthy by visitors to its capital, including the first Portuguese traders in the sixteenth century. From the City of Victory, the rulers presided over a political arrangement that, like the Gupta Empire, some scholars have described as feudal as it absorbed the remnants of the

interactive timeline

India

ca. 600–711 Reign of Harsha Vardhana, Buddhist king

ca. 600–1100 Prominence of Cholas and Pallavas in the south

ca. 750–1100 Muslim trading at Indian seaports

997–1030 Invasions of Mahmud of Ghazna

1206–1526 Muslim Delhi Sultanate

1336–1564 Dominance in the south of Hindu Vijayanagar

1398 Timur sacks Delhi

China

618–907 Tang dynasty, China's most cosmopolitan dynasty

960–1127 Northern Song dynasty

1127–1279 Southern Song dynasty

1280–1368 Yuan dynasty—China briefly part of a vast Mongol Empire

1368–1644 Ming dynasty

1405–1433 Zheng He's naval expeditions

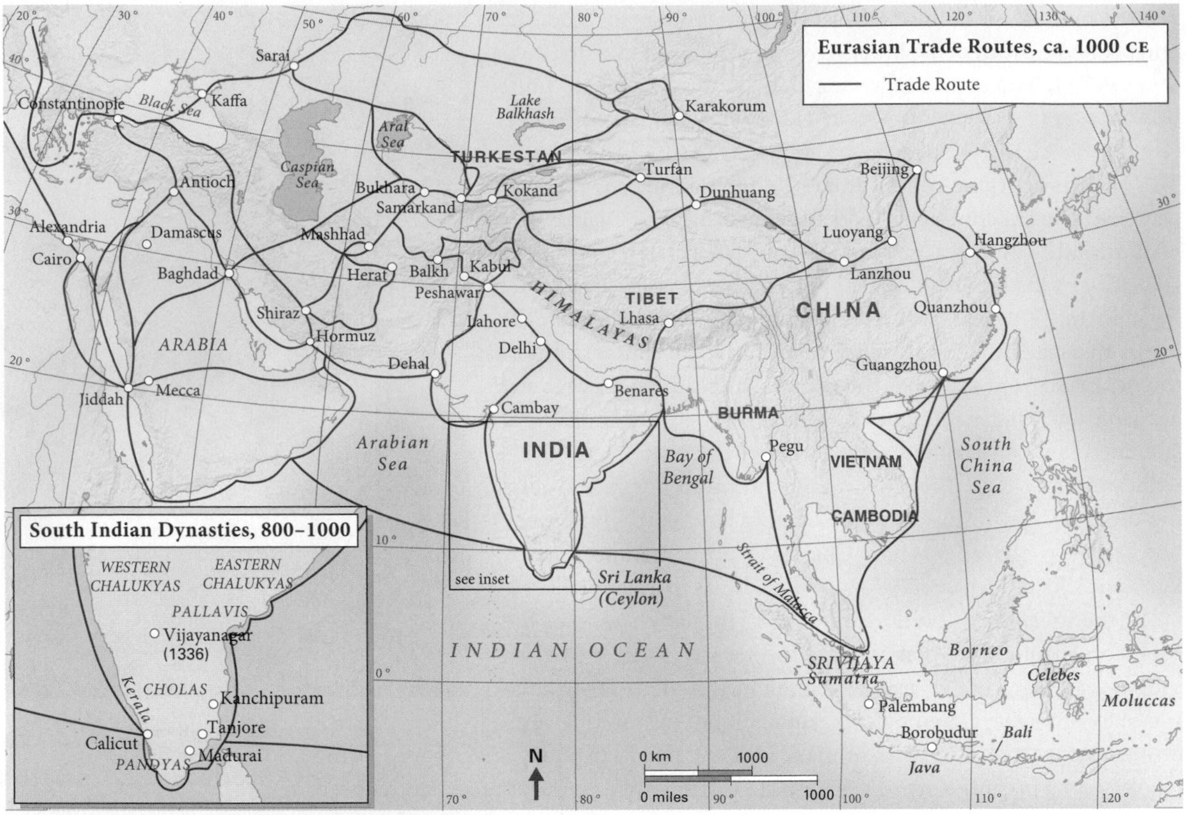

MAP 12.2 Eurasian Trade Routes, ca. 1000 CE.

older southern kingdoms. Local leaders collected taxes and provided men and provisions for the army, while retaining considerable autonomy within their own realms.

For more than 200 years the state of Vijayanagar withstood penetration by the various Islamic sultanates of the north. In 1564, however, their huge armies were decimated by a regional coalition of northern Muslim sultanates whose forces were equipped with the newest technologies—cannon and small arms. The city of Vijayanagar was abandoned, and for the next several centuries local leaders ruled independently in different areas of the peninsula.

Islam in India, 711–1398

Alberuni's observations of India, ca. 1030 CE

As we have seen in the opening vignette, conquering Arabs incorporated much of modern Afghanistan, Pakistan, and some parts of northwest India into their empire during the early 700s. But for several centuries the rest of India experienced contact with the religion of Islam more peacefully through maritime trade conducted by Muslim merchants. In central Asia, Arab armies moving eastward along the caravan routes advanced through conquest, settling in the cities of Turkestan and raiding into the territories of Turkic nomadic tribes. During 700–1000, first Arab governors and later Persian autonomous rulers supported a profitable slave trade.

The Career of Mahmud of Ghazna The Persian rulers in Iran and central Asia enrolled Turkic slaves (acquired as teenagers through raids, trained in cavalry warfare, and manumitted upon reaching adulthood) in their palace guards and converted them to Islam. The son of one of these slave officers was Sultan Mahmud of Ghazna, who declared himself independent of his Persian overlord and conquered the city of Ghazna in Afghanistan. In 997 Mahmud embarked on a career of expansion lasting three decades, until his death in 1030. His tactical brilliance and utter ruthlessness have left his name both revered and reviled in Muslim and Hindu circles ever since.

Early in his career, Mahmud conquered an immense territory comprising part of Iran as well as Afghanistan and Turkestan. The wealth he extracted from this empire turned Ghazna into an opulent city and left the door open for the next round of expeditions into the old Ganges River states.

Qutb Minar, Delhi. The sense of the northern Indian sultanates being a sanctuary for Muslims from other locales translated into efforts on the part of rulers to outperform their counterparts. The wealth of the area allowed them the resources with which to build a number of spectacular structures. The Qutb Minar, built next to Delhi's first mosque, is said to still be the world's largest minaret, requiring the efforts of two rulers before being finished by the Tughluq sultan Feroz Shah (d. 1388).

The Northern Sultanates Mahmud and his successors, the Ghaznavids, ruled for nearly two centuries. The provinces of their empire, however, were too disparate—ranging from the central Asian desert to the rain forests of northern India—to cohere. A Persian ruler subject to the Ghaznavids, Muhammad of Ghur, declared his independence and conquered most Ghaznavid lands. In 1192, he defeated the Rajputs, considered Hindu India's most ferocious warriors, allegedly killing 100,000 soldiers. Striking deep into northern India, Muhammad set up a Muslim state at Delhi. He subsequently lost his territories in the north, but the Indian state he had set up endured (1181–1526) under the name of the Sultanate of Delhi. The founders of this state were, like many state builders we have seen in Islamic history, Turkic generals of slave origin who seized power. Their successors were Turkic and Afghan dynasties who ruled until the invasion of Babur, the Mongol-descended founder of the Mughal Empire of India in 1526 (see Map 12.3).

The Delhi Sultanate successfully weathered an attempted invasion by Genghis Khan in 1222, whose military campaigns had so devastated the lands of southwest Asia and central Europe. Among the more colorful rulers of the Delhi Sultanate was the female sultan Raziya (r. 1236–1240), who seized the throne from her dissolute brother and, in an even more provocative move, dispensed with the veil required of Muslim women and wore male attire on the battlefield. During her short reign, she pressed south and east to Bengal and settled Muslim refugees from Mongol-controlled lands within her own domains.

The renewed Mongol expansion which led to the sack of Baghdad and the destruction of the Abbasid caliphate in 1258 was accompanied by raids along the Delhi Sultanate's borders. Out of this unsettled period came the long reign of Balban, who exercised power informally in Delhi for 20 years before ruling in his own right from 1266 through 1287. Balban's iron hand in suppressing potential rivals resulted in a succession struggle at his death, and a new set of sultans, the Khalijis, came to power in 1290. Like nearly all of their predecessors, the Khalijis soon expanded into southern India, where they acquired loot and established a short-lived overlordship.

image analysis

After a brief period of turmoil came the accession of the Tughluq rulers in 1320, who held power until 1413. Perhaps the most controversial ruler of the line was Muhammad ibn Tughluq (d. 1351), named by his detractors "Muhammad

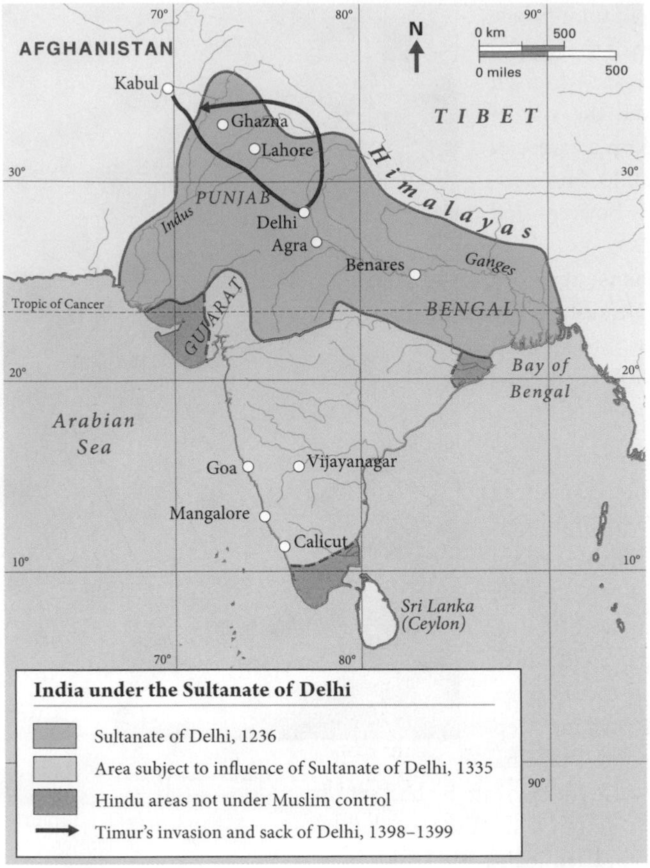

MAP 12.3 India under the Sultanate of Delhi.

the Bloody." Discontent over high taxes, debased coinage, famine, and ruthless atrocities against his enemies was prevalent during his reign. Such acts, however, seemed to contradict his considerably more peaceful personal attainments. By all accounts he was highly educated, a renowned poet and calligrapher, and humble and chaste in his behavior at court. Regardless of the ultimate effects of his rule, by the time of his death at mid-century, powerful forces were once again gathering to the north. Within a few decades they would bring about the end of Tughluq rule and alter the region's politics for generations to come.

Toward the Mughal Era, 1398–1450

In 1398, one of the last great invasions of central Asian nomads, that of Timur (r. 1370–1405) descended on northern India and southwest Asia (see Chapter 20). Though himself a Muslim, Timur did not spare the Muslim capital of Delhi. Though the wave of violence accompanying his conquests quickly subsided, his invasion had broken the power of the Tughluqs. Two smaller sultanates, those of the Sayyids (1414–1451) and the Lodis (1451–1526), held the area around Delhi. Once again, northern India had moved into a period of political disorder. The coming of the Mughals in 1526, however, would usher in another period of both stability and imperial aspirations.

Islamic India's Economy India's rich economy generated repeated political problems. It continually attracted invasions by outsiders eager to take advantage of its wealth. While scholars have long debated whether the first Arab and Turkic incursions into India were motivated primarily by religious or economic reasons or a combination of the two, the vast wealth accumulated as a result provided ample justification for continuing them. Like the constantly feuding southern states of the subcontinent, the turnover of goods acquired through raids and warfare helped finance the economies of the emerging northern Muslim sultanates. Even after these states became financially stable, the attraction of the wealth of the southern states resulted in frequent expeditions against them for financial gain.

The northern sultanates also supported their economies through heavy taxation. In addition to the *jizya* tax on nonbelievers, Ala-ud-din of the Tughluqs, for example, instituted a 50 percent land tax, taxes on the ownership of milk cows, and a household tax. Beyond this, he embarked on an ambitious campaign to institute wage and price controls on a dizzying array of occupations and commodities in order to keep food prices low and urban granaries full. In this, Ala-ud-din was surpassed in zeal by the notorious Muhammad "the Bloody" Tughluq, who had one tax offender flayed alive, his skin stuffed and mounted, and his remains served as a meal to his unfortunate relatives.

Muhammad also instituted price controls and attempted to stabilize the currency by minting new gold coins, debasing silver ones, and manufacturing bronze tokens for use as temporary currency, measures ultimately abandoned as disruptive to the economy. Despite the sultans' constant need for money, however, Muslim prohibitions against usury kept banking and capital firmly in the hands of Hindus, Buddhists, and *Parsees* (descendants of Zoroastrian emigrants from Persia).

Muslims and Caste The role of Islam in calling the faithful together as equals tended to appeal to those most discontented with the caste system. Islam's minority status in India, however, meant that it was never possible to carve out an Islamic state within the sultanates in the same fashion as had been the case in other parts of the Muslim sphere.

Over time, a certain amount of cross-cultural compromise was reluctantly granted by both sides. Nearly all Hindu and Muslim sects were eventually allowed to practice to some degree, with the dress and markings distinguishing different castes allowed to continue. Muslim repugnance toward Hindu nakedness—as in the case of devotees of certain gods and the working attire of some of the lower castes—as well as discomfort with Hindu concepts of religious sexuality, gradually became less overt. At the same time, Hindus in some areas adopted the Muslim practice of veiling women.

The Sikhs Despite their profoundly different worldviews, traditions, and practices, by the fifteenth century the unique position of the Muslim sultanates of northern India as havens for refugees from the ravages of the Mongols, as well as for Sufis (practitioners of Islamic mysticism) and Muslim dissidents, provided a rare opportunity for interchange between Muslim and Hindu sects. Starting with the poet Kabir (1440–1518), the commonalities of the ecstatic, mystical experience of communion with the absolute shared alike by Hindu and Muslim devotional sects was the subject of repeated attempts to find common ground between the two faiths.

The climax of this movement came with the guru ("teacher") Nanak (1469–1539), who founded the faith of **Sikhism**, *sikh* meaning "disciple," which also emphasized a direct emotional experience with the divine. Combining elements of Hinduism and Islam, the Sikhs, due to religious persecution in the seventeenth century, eventually became more of a fighting faith, a stance that, even to the present, has served to continually place them at odds with various Indian governments.

Sikhism: Indian religion founded by Guru Nanak that combines elements of Hindu and Muslim traditions.

While Sikhism at first appeared to be a step toward reconciliation between Islam and Hinduism, it in fact became the exception that proved the rule of their competition. Indeed, both Hindus and Muslims opposed the Sikhs, and they were persecuted a number of times under the Mughals. India thus remained a tenuously syncretic religious and cultural society among the world's religious civilizations. The experience of China, on the other hand, would be far less traumatic.

Interactions and Adaptations: From Buddhism to Neo-Confucian Synthesis in China

The Tang dynasty (618–907) marked the completion of the reconstitution of the Chinese empire begun under the Sui. At its height, the influence of Buddhism at the imperial court, especially with the famous Empress Wu, made China a Buddhist empire. Since the Han, China's ideology had been based on the ethics of Confucianism and some elements of Daoism combined with the imperial structure inherited from the Qin (see Chapter 9). By the mid-600s this ideology of statehood had fused with Mahayana Buddhism to give China for the first time an overtly religious civilization. China thus dramatically joined the ranks of Hindu India (soon to be split by Islam), the growing spread of the Islamic caliphates, the Christian eastern Roman Empire, and the developing states of Western Christian Europe as polities dominated by a universal religion. Such states would dominate world history until the European Enlightenment and Industrial Revolution created an entirely new type of society.

But the Tang, with their connections to the larger Buddhist cultural sphere, ultimately fell. The dynasty of their successors, the Song (960–1279), has often been seen as the beginning of China's early modern period, supported by the world's largest and most productive agrarian state. The political system that marked China from this period until the twentieth century, however, was in part derived from a departure from Buddhism, which was blamed for the downfall of the Tang. Instead, the new synthesis of official beliefs blended the ideas of three ethical–religious schools—Confucianism, Daoism, and Buddhism—to create a system called "Neo-Confucianism." Unlike India's competing religions, Neo-Confucianism in China had no real religious competitors inside or outside the empire, and its debates centered instead on interpretations and approaches to understanding its core teachings—not on the teachings themselves.

Creating a Religious Civilization under the Tang

As we saw at the end of Chapter 9, the installation by Li Shimin of his father on the throne in 618 saw the founding of the Tang. His dismissal of his father in 627 saw it begin in earnest. For the next 150 years, the dynasty expanded its reach deep into central Asia and made incursions into Korea and Vietnam until its shape resembled a dumbbell, bulging at both ends connected with the narrow territory adjacent to the Silk Road.

Expansion and Consolidation Determined to complete the consolidation begun under the Sui and expand the empire, the Tang led military expeditions into central Asia. The Tang reestablished rule in Korea and opened diplomatic relations with Japan, which in 645 announced the *Taika* (Great Reform)—a wholesale adoption of Tang imperial institutions, Buddhism, Confucian bureaucracy, record keeping, and even architecture. The Tang Empire's position as the eastern terminus of the Silk Road; its enhanced maritime trade with India, Japan, Southeast Asia, the Middle East, and even Africa; and its integration of Buddhist culture led to China's first extensive encounter with the major agrarian–urban societies to the west. During the seventh century, Muslim conquests in southwest Asia brought China into contact with the rapidly expanding Arab Empire. In 674, members of the Sasanian Persian royal house fled the advancing Arabs to the Tang capital at Chang'an, bringing in their wake communities of merchants who established a taste among the Tang elites for Arab, Persian, and central Asian goods and cultural forms.

Tang Taizong, "On Effective Government"

With the Tang Empire expanding, trade booming, and the bureaucracy well staffed and run, the Tang capital of Chang'an (the present city of Xi'an) grew into perhaps the largest city in the world, with its core comparable in size to Baghdad or Constantinople in the same era and as many as 2 million people living in its metropolitan area. Its streets, official buildings and residences, and south-facing imperial palace dominating the center became the model for urban planning throughout eastern Asia (see Map 12.4). The city included areas set aside for traders of many nationalities; even today one of Xi'an's attractions is its Muslim market.

The Examination System The Tang refined the bureaucratic structure pioneered by the Han into a form that, with only minor alterations, survived into the twentieth century. The most noteworthy aspect of the Tang bureaucratic structure was the introduction of an examination system for entry into government service. Because the exams were open to a relatively large portion of the male population, state service ensured a degree of social mobility based on merit rather than birth. The initial entry-level tests, based on knowledge of the Confucian classics and, for most of the Tang era, Buddhist and Daoist texts, were open to men of all classes except merchants, artisans, and convicted criminals. The few who passed the initial, district-level tests could sit for provincial exams and, if successful, would be eligible for minor posts. Individuals who passed the metropolitan tests, usually held every 3 years in the capital, were eligible for national service. Other reforms undertaken by the Tang included the creation of a board of censors to check arbitrary behavior among officials, the obligation of lower officials to report the infractions of those above them, and the practice of rotating official posts to prevent individuals from developing local power bases.

Camel with Musicians. Music played an important role in Tang China and was enjoyed privately as well as on public occasions. This brightly colored glazed earthenware sculpture, dated to 723 CE, shows three musicians riding a Bactrian (two-humped) camel. Their long coats, facial hair, and hats indicate that they are from central Asia; indeed, the lute held by one of the figures is an instrument that was introduced to China from central Asia in the second century CE.

Prosperity and Its Discontents As the prosperity of the Tang dynasty grew, many of the problems of uneven growth that had plagued the Han dynasty began to reassert themselves. For example, as the center of population continued to move south, the northern regions languished in relative poverty, while the capital grew economically isolated. The agriculturally productive subtropical areas south of the Yangzi now yielded about 90 percent of the empire's taxed grain and contained as much as 70 percent of the population. Moreover, as maritime trade grew and ports increased in size and number, the connecting infrastructure of roads, courier stations, and especially canals required ever more investment and attention. This was a particularly acute problem in the case of communication with the capital. As an administrative center and trade crossroads, the capital city of Chang'an had ballooned to a size that was now unsustainable without constant grain shipments from the south, while its isolation made it particularly vulnerable to attack. Thus, even before the Tang, work on the Grand Canal, connecting the Yangzi and Yellow Rivers, had been pushed forward to enhance water-based transport in the north.

Tang efforts to control military outposts along the Silk Road, with its lucrative trade and Buddhist shrines, brought the empire into conflict with Arab expansion by the early eighth century. Despite some early successes, Tang armies suffered a decisive defeat by Arab forces. That this loss followed a series of setbacks at the hands of the Tibetans from

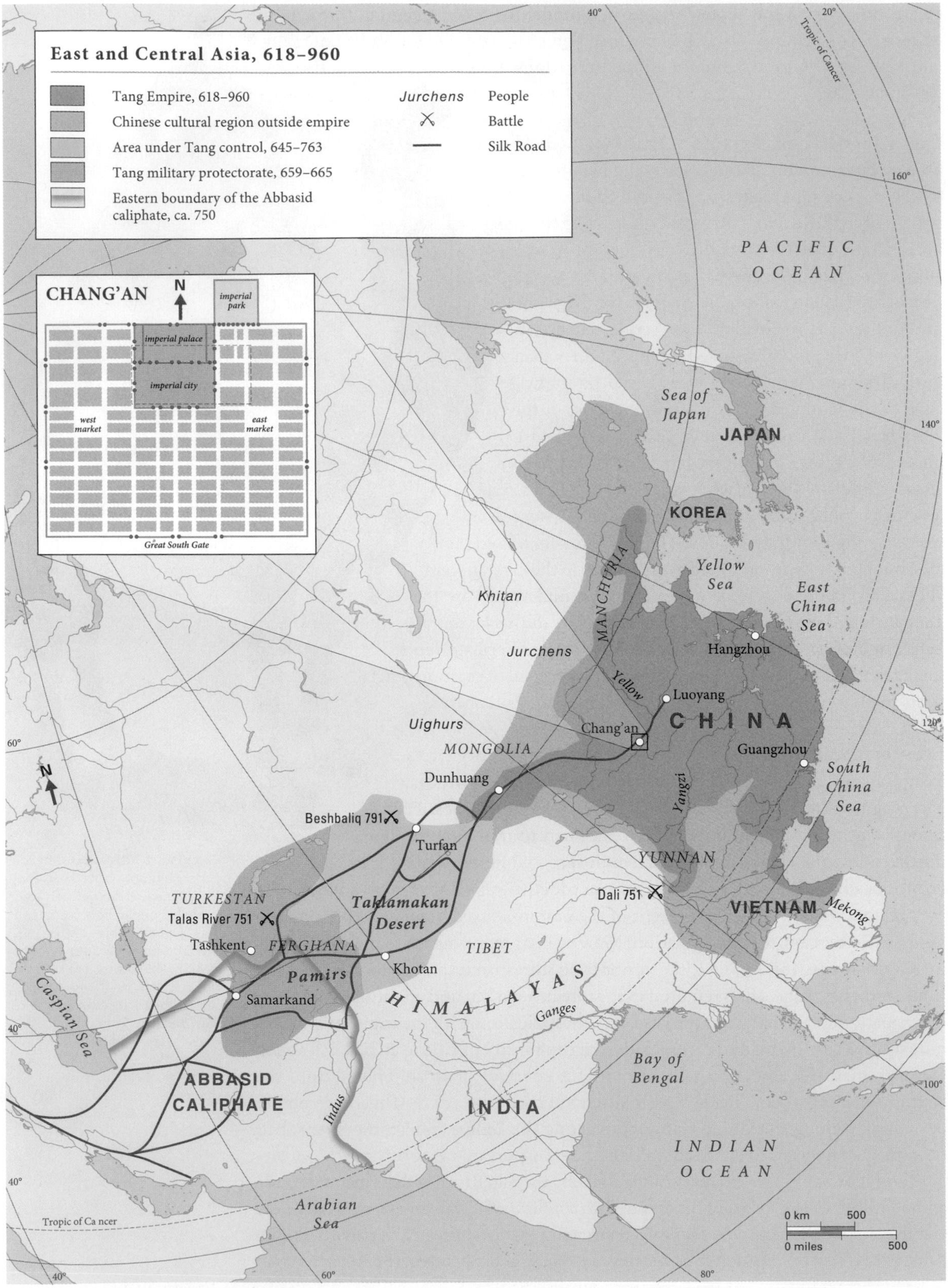

MAP 12.4 East and Central Asia, 618–960.

map analysis

745 to 750 and border uprisings in Manchuria, Korea, and the southern province of Yunnan helped spark a general revolt. From 755 to 762 a rebellion initiated by the Tang commander An Lushan (703–757) devastated large sections of the empire and resulted in heavy land taxes after its suppression. As with the later Han, the dynasty was now in a downward spiral, from which recovery would prove increasingly difficult.

For the next century and a half some economic and political recovery did in fact occur, but the problems of rebuilding and revenue loss persisted, accompanied by the questioning of a number of the premises of the regime, particularly by the Confucians. For example, Confucians criticized Buddhism for being patronized and subsidized by the Tang court. They were particularly critical of its "foreign" ideas and practices, such as monasticism, celibacy, and personal enlightenment, which contradicted the Confucian standards of filial piety, family life, and public service. At the same time, Buddhist monasteries, which paid no taxes, were tempting targets for an increasingly cash-strapped government. In 845, despite Tang sponsorship of Buddhism, the government forcibly seized all Buddhist holdings, although followers were allowed to continue their religious practices. Even with renewed campaigns against border peoples and other attempts at reinvigorating the empire, sporadic civil war continued for the remainder of the century, leading to the collapse of the Tang dynasty in 906. Following this collapse, China again entered a period of disunity as regional states battled for ultimate control. None of these states would be victorious until the emergence of the Song in 960.

Cosmopolitan Commerce From the capital in Chang'an, merchants, monks, pilgrims, diplomats, and travelers made their way along the Silk Road, while Chinese, Indian, and Arab ships plied the seas as far away as Africa. The compass, invented by Chinese fortune-tellers and adapted for use in keeping to a constant direction at sea, now guided ships throughout the Indian Ocean and Southeast Asia. In the Chinese versions of this instrument, however, the needle pointed south—the preferred direction of good fortune and architectural orientation. Drawn by lucrative opportunities, colonies of Chinese merchants could be found throughout the Indian Ocean and Southeast Asia.

Travel account of an Arab merchant who visited China in the 9th century CE.

Among the export items most coveted by foreign merchants were tea and silk. Initially brought to China from Southeast Asia, tea quickly established itself as the beverage of choice during the Tang and vied with silk for supremacy as a cash crop during the Song. Tea had a profound effect on the overall health of the population in China, Vietnam, Korea, Japan, and central Asia. The boiling of the water makes it potable, while the tea itself contains healthful properties. Moreover, its caffeine prompted alertness—an aid to monks in meditation. Tea production, particularly in the region near the city of Hangzhou, became a major industry and for hundreds of years remained China's most lucrative export item.

The influence of foreigners in art and artifact, fashion, taste, music, and dance marks a radical departure in many respects from the more demure Chinese styles that came before and after. For example, the Persian-influenced costumes of Tang dancers—with their daring and distinctive bare midriffs and transparent tops and trousers—were celebrated at the court in Chang'an but scandalized the more modest sensibilities of later centuries. Indeed, the period saw a number of controversial trends regarding the role and deportment of women. As exemplified in the person of the famous Empress Wu (r. 690–705), China's first **empress dowager**, women occasionally exercised considerable authority in political affairs during this period (see "Against the Grain").

Empress dowager: In monarchical or imperial systems in which succession is normally through the male line, the widow of the ruler.

Empress Wu. Mistress of Emperor Gaozong, Wu Zetian declared herself empress dowager after his death in 684 and founded a new Zhou dynasty in 690. She is the only woman in Chinese history until Empress Dowager Cixi at the turn of the twentieth century to exercise so much power.

Tang Poetry Tang poetry, especially the compressed "regulated verse" of eight five-character lines and the terse four-line "cut-off line" poems, attempts to suggest powerful emotions or themes in minimalist fashion. For example, the deep Confucian sensibilities of the Tang poet Du Fu (ca. 721–770) are often detectable in his emotionally charged poems such as "Mourning Chen Tao." Li Bai (or Li Bo, 701–762), his friend, was in many ways his opposite in both the way he lived his life and the emotions he sought to stir. Carefree, witty, a lover of wine and women—according to legend, Li Bai drowned after a drunken challenge to "embrace the moon" reflected in the water—his poetry evokes happier moments but frequently conveys them as fleeting and bittersweet. Wang Wei (ca. 699–759) was a third renowned Tang poet. Of him it was later said that "in every one of his poems is a painting, and in every painting a poem."

For all the accomplishments of the Tang, however, the role of Buddhism as a privileged religion left the dynasty open to severe criticism. With the coming of the Song, China would become a religious civilization in which its people reemphasized the indigenous traditions of Confucianism and Daoism, with elements of Buddhism on a more reduced level.

The Song and Yuan Dynasties, 960–1368

During the Song dynasty, China achieved in many ways its greatest degree of sophistication in terms of material culture, technology, ideas, economics, and the amenities of urban living. Its short-lived incorporation into the huge empire of the Mongols opened the country to renewed influence from neighboring peoples and helped to spread Chinese influence westward, most famously through the accounts of the travelers Marco Polo and Ibn Battuta. Finally, the new synthesis of Neo-Confucianism would carry China as a religious civilization into the twentieth century.

Reforms of Wang Anshi Like the Tang, the Song instituted a strong central government based on merit rather than heredity. The Song, however, broadened the eligibility of those seeking to take the civil service exams, and with increased opportunities to join the government service, a huge and increasingly unwieldy bureaucratic system emerged.

The need for administrative reform spurred the official Wang Anshi [wahng ahn-SHIR] (1021–1086) to propose a series of initiatives designed to increase state control over the economy and reduce the power of local interests. Wang proposed state licensing of both agricultural and commercial enterprises, the abolition of forced labor, and the creation of government pawnshops to loan money at reduced rates. He also urged cutting the number of bureaucratic positions in order to lessen the power of local officials and clan heads. Opposition to these proposed reforms, however, forced Wang from office in 1076.

In addition to internal problems, such as the financial strain of maintaining a huge bureaucracy, the Song faced external problems. Because the Tang had lost much of northern China, including the Silk Road, to nomadic groups, Song lands from the start were substantially smaller than those of the Tang. Although the Song spent a great deal of treasure and energy to maintain a professional army of more than 1.5 million as well as a formidable navy, this massive but ponderous force ultimately proved ineffective against the expert militaries of invading nomadic groups using swiftness to their advantage. The Song also tried careful diplomacy and bribery to maintain China's dominance. Such efforts, however, were unable to keep the northern part of the empire from falling to the nomadic Jurchens in 1127. Forced to abandon their capital at Kaifeng on the Grand Canal just south of the Yellow River, the Song created a new capital at Linan, the modern city of Hangzhou (see Map 12.5).

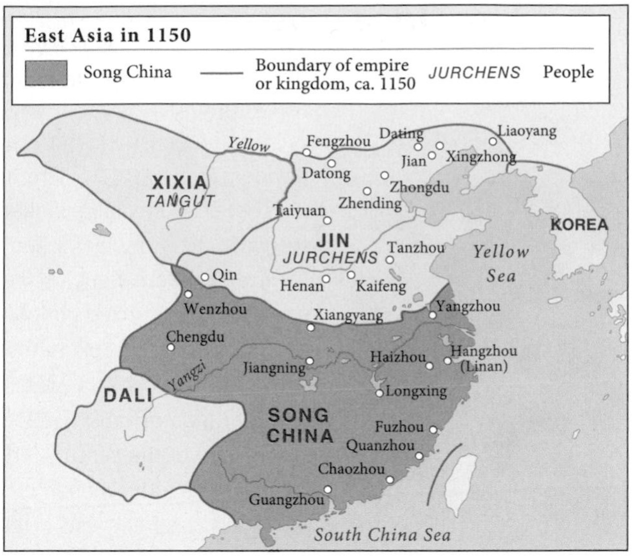

MAP 12.5 East Asia in 1150.

The decreased size of the Song Empire resulted in a more southern-oriented and urbanized economy. The new capital at Hangzhou [hahng-jo], described by Marco Polo as the most beautiful city in the world, may also have been the largest, with a population estimated at 1.5 million. Despite the bureaucracy's disdain for the merchant and artisan classes, the state had always recognized the potential of commerce to generate revenue through import, export, tariffs, and taxes. Thus, while attempting to bring the largest enterprises under state control, the government pursued measures to facilitate trade, such as printing the world's first paper notes, minting coins, and curbing usury. These practices, combined with an excellent system of roads and canals, fostered the development of an internal Chinese market. The Song conducted a lively overseas trade, and Chinese merchants established colonies in major ports throughout Southeast Asia and the Indian Ocean.

The Mongol Conquest Commercial success, however, could not save the Song from invasion by neighboring nomadic peoples. For centuries, disparate groups of nomadic Mongols had lived in tribes and clans in eastern central Asia. There was no real push to unite these groups until the rise to power of the Mongol leader Temujin (ca. 1162–1227). Combining military prowess with diplomatic strategy, Temujin united the various Mongol groups into one confederation in 1206. Temujin gave himself the title Genghis Khan ("Universal Ruler") of the united Mongol confederation.

▷ Genghis Khan

Following confederation, the Mongols launched a half-century of steady encroachment on northern China. The Mongols had several enormous advantages over the infantry-based armies of their opponents:

- their skill at horsemanship and archery
- their unsurpassed ability to fire arrows at pursuers while galloping away from them at full speed
- their repeatedly successful tactics of feigned retreat.

Genghis Khan's grandson Khubilai Khan [KOO-bleh con] (1215–1294) resumed the Mongol offensive in southern China after the Song unwisely attempted to enlist Mongol aid against the Jurchens. In 1267 he moved his capital from Karakorum to Khanbaligh, called by the Chinese "Dadu"—the future city of Beijing—and steadily ground down the Song remnant. Hangzhou fell to the Mongols in 1276; the death of the young Song emperor in 1279 as he attempted to flee by sea brought the dynasty to an end.

Patterns Up Close

Gunpowder

If fine porcelain, lacquerware, landscape painting, poetry, and calligraphy marked the refined side of Song life, the most momentous invention to emerge from the era was gunpowder. The substance was originally used as a medicine for skin irritations until its propensity to burn rapidly was established. The early Chinese term for gunpowder, *huoyao* (火药) "fire medicine," preserves this sense of its use.

Though it was long packed into bamboo tubes to create fireworks ignited during festivals, it is unclear when the first weapons employing gunpowder were used. By the Southern Song, however, the Chinese army and navy had a wide array of weapons that utilized gunpowder either as a propellant or as an explosive. The use of "fire arrows"—rockets mounted to arrow shafts—was recorded during a battle with the Mongols in 1232. The Song navy launched missiles and even employed ships with detachable sections filled with explosives with which to ram other ships. By the end of the century, primitive cannon were also employed as well as gunpowder satchels to blow open city gates and fortifications.

Korean Rocket Launcher. Adapting Mongol and Chinese military technology, the Koreans repelled a Japanese invasion in 1592 with hwacha, mobile rocket launchers that were used with great effect against both enemy land forces and ships.

The widespread use of gunpowder weapons by the Song against the Mongols was a powerful inducement to the invaders to adopt them for themselves. Indeed, toward the end of the war, the Mongols increasingly employed explosives in their siege operations against Chinese walled cities. They also used them in the 1270s and 1290s during their failed invasions of Japan. The need for these weapons pushed their dispersion throughout the Mongol holdings and beyond.

The Yuan Dynasty In 1280 Khubilai Khan proclaimed the Yuan dynasty, taking the reign name of Shizu. This short-lived dynasty pulled China into an empire spanning all of Eurasia from Korea to the interior of Poland and probing as far as Hungary, Java, and Japan. In a way, however, the acquisition of China also signaled a significant change in Mongol fortunes. On the one hand, many of the world's richest, most populous, and commercially vibrant areas were now under the control of what was nominally a unified empire. In terms of all the constituent khans encouraging trade, building infrastructure along land routes, and sponsoring and protecting caravans—including pioneering innovations in insuring them and in limiting liability for investors and traders— it did represent a prototype free trade zone. Politically, however, it became increasingly fragmented. By Khubilai's death in 1294 what had been one empire was now essentially four squabbling khanates: The Ilkhans in Persia and the Middle East, whose advance had been halted by the Mamluks of Egypt; the Golden Horde, occupying a vast stretch of territory in what is now Ukraine and Russia; the khanate of Chagatai, centered at Samarkand and occupying a pivotal position along the Silk Road in central Asia; and the Yuan dynasty of Khubilai Khan, stretching from Mongolia into Korea, through most of China and down into Tibet and Vietnam.

The necessity of adopting and inhabiting the institutions they now commanded required adaptation on an unprecedented scale in order to make them function in an orderly way. This was especially true for the Mongols because their tiny population of about a million had to rule as many as 100 times that number of people. Moreover, the brilliant governmental improvisations of Genghis Khan in conquering his empire now came up against institutions that in some cases had functioned for over a thousand years and were based on philosophical and ethical systems even older.

It is difficult to overestimate the importance of gunpowder in human affairs. The next round of empires, the Ottomans, Safavids, and Mughals, made its use in warfare so central to their efforts that historians often refer to them as "the gunpowder empires." Its use in sixteenth-century Japan was so important in battle that the Tokugawa Shogunate banned firearms for two centuries once peace had been established. But it was among the states of Europe that these weapons achieved their highest levels of development over the following centuries. Incessant warfare among the European states and against the Ottomans fueled the development of bigger and deadlier cannon and lighter and more accurate small arms. The use of these weapons helped speed the decline of the heavily armed and armored mounted knight and brought on the age of the infantry armed with muskets as "the queen of battles." By the end of the eighteenth century, even though muskets and artillery were technologically more or less the same the world over, a high degree of drill among bayonet-equipped grenadiers gave European armies an edge against the Ottomans, Mughals, and Africans.

Questions

- How do gunpowder's origins as a medicine complicate the way we typically view technological and cultural adaptations?
- What would have been the consequence for world history if the military uses of gunpowder had never been discovered?

Thus, the Mongols, like the Manchus who came after them, found themselves reluctantly adapting to Chinese culture to keep the existing systems in operation while struggling to maintain the culture, mores, and belief systems of the steppes.

Khubilai Khan as the First Yuan Emperor, Shizu (Shih-tzu).

In some ways this was an easier transition for Shizu than for those of Genghis Khan's generation. The grandson khans had come of age when their families were already fabulously wealthy and powerful, and in this respect it was hardly a leap for Khubilai to take on the trappings and dynastic rituals of a Chinese emperor. Moreover, the rigorous life of the steppe was now a distant memory, replaced with opulent ceremonial commemorations of those days. Even military campaigning was far less rigorous for the khans than in former times and so the skills so necessary to the Mongols' early successes were already eroding.

Mongol toleration of religious traditions now also left them free to experiment with foreign faiths. To a considerable extent, the fragmentation of the Mongol Empire broke down the idea of Genghis Khan that the leadership should not adopt any particular one of the existing systems of religious, cultural, and political traditions because none of them could be satisfactorily stretched to fit the needs of universal empire. Thus, the Ilkhans in southwest Asia now converted to Islam, married into the local population, and eventually disappeared as a distinct ethnicity. Likewise, the descendants of Chagatai converted to Islam and, though their line did not stay intact, attempted to maintain their genealogy. From this line the fourteenth-century conqueror Timur (Tamerlane) claimed Genghis Khan as his ancestor; Tamerlane's putative descendent, Babur, also claiming the legacy of Genghis Khan, became the progenitor of the Timurids (from Tamerlane), the dynasty in India called the Mughals (see Chapter 20). For their part, some of the Mongols in Yuan territories (as well as Han Chinese and members of other minority groups) also converted to Islam. Others converted to Buddhism, with the Tibetan varieties such as the Yellow Hat sect later headed by the Dalai Lama proving especially attractive.

In the Yuan territories, administrative needs ultimately trumped Mongol practices of circulating officials of different nationalities throughout the entire empire. Initially, a number of senior Chinese officials were purged and others resigned in protest to the new order. These changes even spawned a new genre of Chinese landscape painting, which featured a solitary figure in official's robes sitting in exile in his mountain fastness. The practice of bringing in officials and advisors from other regions in the empire had proved only partially successful and caused widespread consternation among the remaining Chinese officials and aspiring scholar-gentry. Ultimately, the examination system was reinstated in 1315 and continued until 1905.

While contemporary source material on the rise of the Mongols under Genghis Khan is scarce—the Persian accounts were written later and even the *Secret History of the Mongols* was composed around 1240, long after Genghis Khan had died—a number of accounts make their appearance from the second half of the thirteenth century on. Though the four large khanates competed for prestige and resisted Kubilai's claim to the title of Great Khan, the relative ease of travel and enhanced commerce continued. China was open on an unprecedented scale to a variety of foreign goods, ideas, and travelers, while Chinese goods like paper money, gunpowder, coal, the compass, and dozens of other innovations circulated in greater variety and profusion than ever before. Emissaries and missionaries from the developing states of Europe for the first time now traveled east to the capital city of Khanbaligh. The two most famous travel accounts of the era, those of the Venetian Marco Polo (1254–1324) and Ibn Battuta of Tangier (1304–1369), who lived and traveled throughout the Mongol Empire, are testaments to the powerful impact of Mongol rule in facilitating travel over such a vast area. Indeed, it was during the brief rule of the Mongols that the European image of China as a fairyland of exotica, fabulous wealth, and wondrous inventions was firmly set (see Map 12.6).

Selections from the *Travels of Marco Polo*

The End of the Khans The Yuan period is almost universally regarded by the Chinese as one of imperial China's darkest times. Although the Mongols quickly restored order and allowed a relative tolerance of religious practice and expression, the Yuan period was seen as an oppressive time of large standing armies, withdrawal from service of many Chinese officials, ineffective administration, forced labor, and heavy taxes. Compounding the intensity of the tensions between Mongols and their subjects was perhaps the single worst disaster of the fourteenth century, the bubonic plague—known in Europe as the Black Death. While scholars have only recently begun to examine Chinese mortality rates resulting from the plague, Chinese accounts suggest that they were in all likelihood similar to those of Europe in some areas, with perhaps one-third of the population of about 100 million being carried off from the 1340s until the end of the century. One thing that seems clear, however, was that by facilitating travel and commerce, the Mongol regimes unknowingly opened the door for the disease to go from being a regional disaster to a continent-wide pandemic.

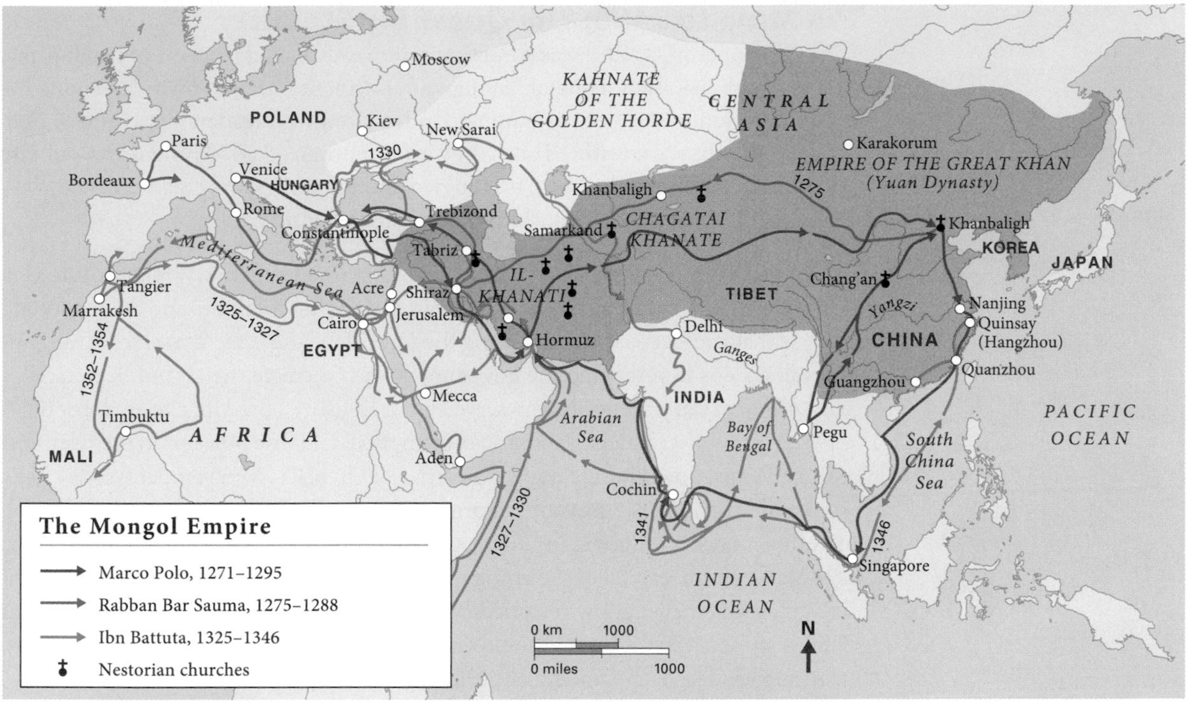

MAP 12.6 The Mongol Empire.

Over the following decades, the power of the Mongols continued to decline, both at the center and one by one in the peripheral states as well. Perhaps the first and most dramatic was the overthrow of the Yuan in China and the restoration of Chinese rule under the Ming dynasty. This was accompanied by an exodus of refugee officials and Mongol civilians, though many Mongols who had settled in China decided to take their chances and stay. As previously mentioned, many had also converted to Islam. By mid-century, all of these factors contributed to outbreaks of rebellion in China. In 1368, a coalition led by a soldier–Buddhist monk named Zhu Yuanzhang [JOO yuwen-JAHNG] (1328–1398) drove the Mongols from the capital at Khanbaligh and proclaimed a new dynastic line, the Ming.

How should we assess the Mongol era as a whole? Once considered a byword for barbarism on a stupendous scale, recent scholars have now recalibrated their views considerably. Mongol emphasis on destroying feudal aristocracies, elevating artisans and merchants, facilitating trade, and religious toleration have all been cited as paving the way for the early modern era. Some have gone so far as to claim that the Mongols in effect brought on the Renaissance in Europe. Most agree that the *Pax Mongolica* in creating a super-regional empire and trading sphere paved the way in some respects for the world systems to come. Yet it is undeniable that the creation of the empire and repeated wars among the later khans were accompanied by unprecedented death and destruction. Though we have no reliable figures for the region as a whole, rough estimates put the population of the areas touched by the Mongols at perhaps 150 million, of which perhaps 18 to 30 million may have died, excluding those killed during the bubonic plague. Thus, while many modern historians have come to see the Mongol era as a key, perhaps *the* key to the transition from the medieval to the early modern world, the cost was for many unacceptably high.

The Ming to 1450: The Quest for Stability

The "Pig Emperor," as Zhu was sometimes derisively called because of his ungainly features, took the reign name of "Hongwu" and spent much of his rule driving the remaining Mongols out of his empire. Under Hongwu's leadership, Chinese politics and customs were restored and a powerful centralized government was put into place. This new imperial state that Hongwu and his successors created would, with minor modifications, see China into the twentieth century.

The Grand Secretariat Hongwu sought to streamline this newly reconstituted bureaucracy by concentrating power and governmental functions around the emperor, a practice that had been common during the Qin, Han, and Tang dynasties. Thus, one of his first steps in reshaping the government was to create the Grand Secretariat, a select group of senior officials who served as an advisory board for the emperor on all imperial matters; it remained at the apex of imperial Chinese power into the twentieth century. With a powerful, centralized government in place, Ming emperors now had a base from which to take measures to protect the empire from incursions by Mongols and other nomadic groups in the north. One step to protect against invasion was taken in 1421, when the capital of the empire was moved from Nanjing in the south to the old site of Khanbaligh, now renamed Beijing ("Northern Capital"), so that a strong Chinese presence in the region would discourage invasion. Further safeguards against invasion included the upgrading of the fortifications along the Great Wall.

Population Recovery While the country fortified its borders and reinstated political systems that had been dismantled by the Mongols, it also had to contend with a sharp drop in population due to warfare and the lingering effects of the bubonic plague that ravaged the country in the 1340s. The population rebound, however, did not assume significant proportions until it was aided by the introduction of a number of new food crops in the sixteenth and seventeenth centuries, which boosted agricultural productivity.

pictorial map of the Yellow River, ca. 1370

With the coming of new food and cash crops from the Americas by way of Spanish and Portuguese merchants, including potatoes, sweet potatoes, maize (corn), peanuts, and tobacco, the country's population grew from a low of perhaps 60 million at the end of the Yuan period to an estimated 150 million in 1600. The efficiency of Chinese agriculture and the consequent growth of the empire's immense internal trade contributed to another doubling of the population, to perhaps 300 million by 1800.

The Interlude of Naval Power Thanks to the foundation laid by Hongwu [hoong-WOO], the dynasty's third emperor, Yongle [young-LUH], inherited a state in 1403 that was already on its way to recovering its economic dynamism. Taking advantage of this increasing prosperity, and fearful of potential usurpers, he ordered China's first and last great naval expeditions. These voyages, sent out from 1405 to 1433 under the command of his childhood friend and imperial eunuch Zheng He [jung huh] (1371–1435), were perhaps the most remarkable feats of their day.

The vast fleets that Zheng commanded were the largest amphibious forces the world would see until the twentieth century. With a length of over 400 feet, the largest of Zheng's "treasure ships," as they were called, was more than 4 times that of Columbus's *Santa Maria* and many times its bulk and was accompanied by a diverse array of smaller vessels that carried cargo, supplies, and troops. There were even tankers that carried fresh water for the fleet, while the larger ships grew fresh fruits and vegetables on their aft decks. Zheng's ships also carried a formidable arsenal of cannon, bombs, rockets, and other weaponry and a force of nearly 30,000 men. In addition, they featured such technological innovations as watertight compartments, sternpost rudders, magnetic compasses, and paper maps.

Chinese Treasure Ship Compared to Columbus's *Santa Maria*. Over 400 feet in length, the largest of Zheng He's treasure ships was nearly five times as long as the ships Columbus used to sail across the Atlantic.

The first voyages were expeditionary forces aimed largely at overawing any nearby foreign powers that might be harboring pretenders to Yongle's throne. As the realization set in that these foreign threats were nonexistent, the voyages became focused on trade and exploration and ranged farther and farther afield, ultimately covering the Indian Ocean, the Persian Gulf, and the East African coast. Along the way they planted or reestablished contact with Chinese merchants in south and Southeast Asia. Of particular interest were the first direct Chinese contacts with the Swahili-speaking states of East Africa. In one famous exchange of gifts, the king of Malindi (modern Kenya) sent Yongle a giraffe, which found the emperor among the awestruck admirers of the creature at the imperial court. Even today one can still see the stone markers left by the Chinese along the East African coast where their ships landed (see Map 12.7).

Although Zheng He's explorations firmly established Chinese predominance in naval technology and power, Yongle's successors put an end to the expeditions. The reasons for this abrupt turnabout were both political and strategic. By the 1430s the Mongols, having regrouped after their defeats, were again threatening the northern frontiers. The huge expense of the voyages and the realization that there were no significant naval rivals were convincing reasons to discontinue them in the face of the

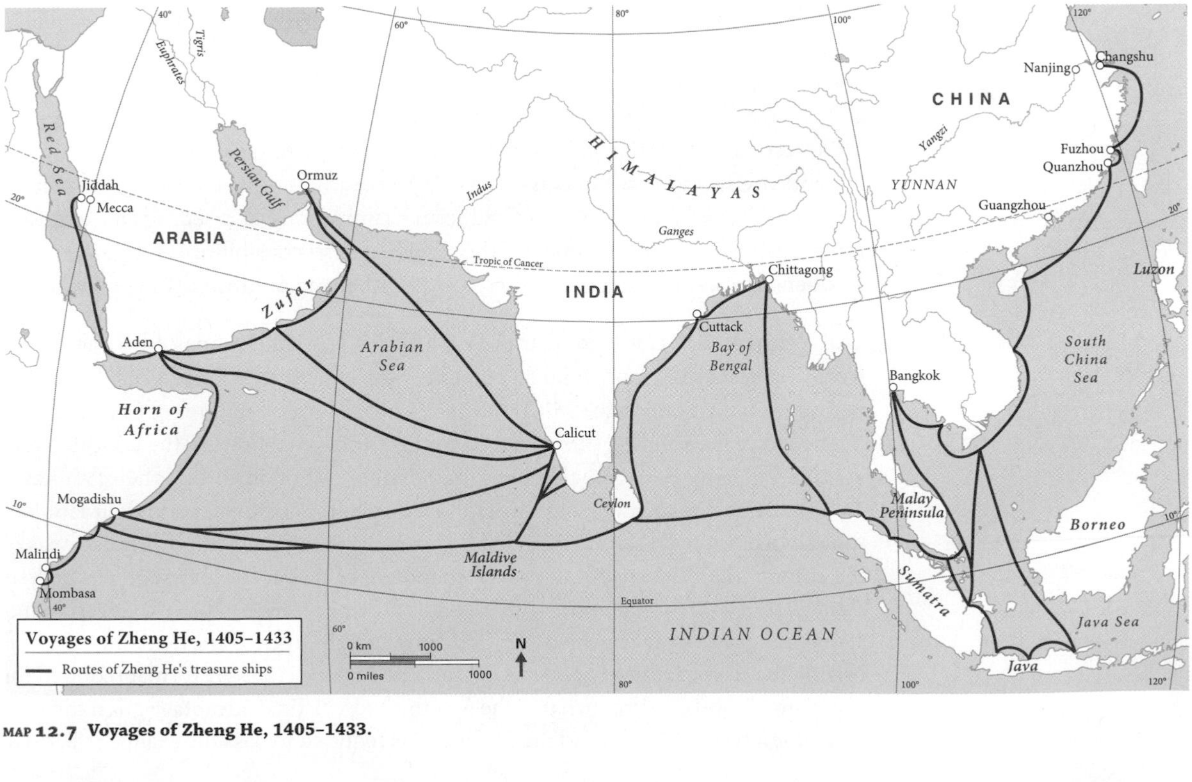

MAP 12.7 Voyages of Zheng He, 1405–1433.

Mongol threat. In addition, the Confucian officials, always suspicious of the profit motive, argued that maritime trade was not useful to the overall welfare of the empire.

Toward the Ming Decline The activist style of Hongwu and Yongle proved to be the exception rather than the rule during the nearly three centuries of Ming rule. As had so often been the case in Chinese history, a degree of weakness at the center of power encouraged probes of the frontier by nomadic peoples on the empire's periphery, a condition neatly summarized by the Chinese proverb "Disorder within, disaster without." A disconcerting foretaste of this occurred in 1449, when the emperor was taken prisoner by the Mongols following the defeat of his expeditionary force. Through most of the sixteenth century, a succession of weak emperors would erode the stability of the reformed Ming imperial system, which had been based on enhancing the emperor's power. To compensate for the chronic weakness at the center, power was increasingly diffused throughout the system. Over time, much of it was acquired by the grand secretaries and provincial governors, while at the village level magistrates and village headmen assumed the bulk of power and responsibility.

Society, Family, and Gender

With the refinement of the examination system and the elaboration of the bureaucracy during the Song, which was renewed during the Ming, the key point of intersection between the people and the government was the district magistrate. While magistrates occupied the lowest official rung of the bureaucracy, they wielded considerable power at the local level and constituted the entry-level position for the majority of those called to service. Some experience at the magistrate's level was considered essential for ambitious officials, and the wide-ranging skills developed during one's district tenure often proved indispensable for advancement to the higher levels of the bureaucracy.

The Magistrate The position of magistrate brought with it enormous responsibility. Even in rural areas, the magistrate might have charge of 100,000 people—and in urban areas perhaps 250,000. Assisted by a small group of clerks and secretaries, messengers, and constables, he supervised all aspects of local government: collecting taxes, policing and security, investigating and prosecuting crimes, settling legal disputes, sentencing and overseeing punishments—including executions—presiding over all official ceremonies, conducting the local Confucian examinations, and setting an exemplary moral example for his constituents. The magistrate's responsibilities and powers were so all-encompassing that he was referred to as "father and mother to the people."

The Scholar-Gentry and Rural Society While China boasted some of the world's largest cities, more than 85 percent of the country remained rural during the period from the Song to the Ming. At the top of the local structures of power and influence were the *scholar-gentry*. As a class, they were by definition the educated and included all ranks of degree holders, whether in or out of office, and their families.

Scholar-gentry membership was in theory open to most males and their families, though in practice it seldom exceeded 1–2 percent of the population in most areas of the empire. The chief qualification was attainment of at least the lowest official degree, *shengyuan* [SHUNG-yu-enn], which enabled the bearer to attend a government-sponsored academy for further study and draw a small stipend. The demands of memorizing the classical canon and learning to write in the rigid essay format required for the exams, however, were such that the wealthy had a distinct advantage given their leisure time, access to tutors, and the connections required to pass the exams. Still, there were enough poor boys who succeeded through hard work and the sacrifices of their families and neighbors to provide a surprising degree of mobility within the system.

Since prestige within the scholar-gentry derived from education even more than from wealth, it was not uncommon for individuals to purchase degrees, though technically they were barred from doing so in the upper three categories. Thus, there was considerable snobbery among the upper gentry of advanced degree holders and officials toward the lower gentry. This was reinforced by an array of **sumptuary laws** and a court-directed protocol of buttons worn on the hats of officials signifying to which of the nine official grades—each with an upper and a lower rank—they belonged.

Sumptuary laws: Regulations mandating or restricting the wearing of certain clothes or insignia among different classes of people.

In keeping with their role as the informal administrative apparatus of the magistrate, the scholar-gentry enjoyed a number of privileges as well as responsibilities. At the same time, their position as community leaders and their grounding in Confucian ethics frequently placed them in tension with the official bureaucracy, especially when local interests appeared at odds with regional or imperial ones. Along with the district magistrate, they presided over all ceremonies at temples, and those holding the highest ranks led all clan ceremonies. In addition, the scholar-gentry mingled with the official authorities more or less as social equals; in the case of those in between appointments to high office, they frequently outranked the local magistrate.

Local government relied to an extraordinary degree on the cooperation of the gentry and people with the magistrates, subprefects, and prefects in order to function. Because the presiding officials were moved so frequently, the gentry represented a consistent network of people to carry out the day-to-day work of government. They took very seriously the Confucian injunction to remonstrate with officials, especially when their complaints coincided with local interests. Thus, they could—and did—rally the people to subvert the policies of unpopular magistrates. Moreover, as influential men themselves—and often officials with national connections—they could force the resignation of officials and sometimes even bring about changes in regional or imperial policy.

Village and Family Life The tendency toward greater centralization under the Ming also reverberated within the structures of Chinese village life. While much of local custom and social relations among the peasants still revolved around family, clan, and lineage—with the scholar-gentry setting the pace—new institutions perfected under the Ming had a lasting impact into the twentieth century.

Originally conceived during the Song dynasty, the *baojia* system of village organization called for families to register all members and be grouped into clusters of 10. One family in each cluster was then assigned responsibility for the others. Each group of responsible families would then be grouped into 10, and a member would be selected from them to be responsible for the group of 100 households, and so on up to the 1,000-household level. The system was especially important in that it allowed the authorities to bypass potential gentry resistance to government directives and guaranteed a network of informers at all levels of rural life.

Peasant Women's Lives Despite China's technological prowess and the introduction of new strains of rice during the Song period that propelled a surge in population, the patterns of work and the overall rhythms of peasant life changed little from the Song through the Ming. The tools available to the vast majority of cultivators, as later depicted in the seventeenth-century technology manual *Tiangong Kaiwu* (*The Works of Nature and Man*), had remained fundamentally unchanged from their prototypes of the preceding centuries. The very simplicity and efficiency of such tools in such a labor-rich environment encouraged their continued use.

Tensions in the older patterns of village life continued to be magnified during times of stress in the lives of women and girls. The brief Mongol period of political domination had virtually no impact on Chinese social institutions. Mongol patterns of more egalitarian gender and class relations that had prevailed on the steppe thus remained limited to the Mongols themselves. For the Chinese, on the one hand, the education of upper-class women tended increasingly toward making them more marriageable. Study of proper Confucian etiquette (as outlined in Ban Zhao's *Admonitions for Women,* discussed in Chapter 9), light verse, and a heavy dose of filial piety occupied a large portion of their curriculum. The custom of painful **foot binding** originated during the Song, gained ground during the Ming, and continued until it was banned by the People's Republic of China after 1949. **Female infanticide** also rose markedly in rural areas during times of famine or other social stress. As in previous periods, rural girls were frequently sold into servitude or prostitution by financially pressed families.

Foot binding: The practice of tightly wrapping the feet of young girls in order to break and reset the bones to compress the feet to about one-third of their normal size. Mothers generally did this to their daughters to make them more marriageable, since tiny feet were considered the epitome of female beauty.

Female infanticide: The killing of girl babies.

Perceptions of Perfection: Intellectual, Scientific, and Cultural Life

The period from the Tang to the Ming was marked by unsurpassed technological prowess. Indeed, according to the leading scholar of China's record of innovation, Joseph Needham, China remained the world's leading producer of new inventions until roughly 1500. So striking is this record, and so suddenly does it subside after this time, that historians sometimes refer to the problem of why it took place as "the Needham question." One possible answer may be that the Chinese felt that they had achieved a degree of perfection in so many areas that, like their great naval expeditions, there was simply no pressing need to advance them further. Within a few hundred years, however, the momentum of technological innovation had shifted decisively to the small, feuding states of Europe.

The Neo-Confucian Synthesis The long period of the intermingling of Confucianism with Buddhist, Daoist, and other traditions of thought forced an extensive reformulation of its core concepts by the Song period. During the twelfth century, this reformulation matured into Neo-Confucianism, which combined the moral core of Confucian ethics with a new emphasis on speculative philosophy borrowed from Buddhist and Daoist thinkers. Though the impetus no doubt came in part from these other two systems, Neo-Confucian thinkers were careful to insist that all their key concepts could be found in the ideas of Confucius, Mencius, the Classics.

Neo-Confucianism holds that one cannot sit passively and wait for enlightenment, as the Buddhists were alleged to do, but must actively "seek truth through facts" in order to understand correctly the relationships of form and substance (*li*—not to be confused with ritual, which is also pronounced as "*li*") and *qi,* the dynamic force from which things and events are produced as they govern the constitution of the totality of the universe, or "supreme ultimate." Indeed, the ethical self and the epistemological self spring from the same source and are different manifestations of the same unity. Exploration of the physical universe undertaken in this spirit is thus the ultimate act of Confucian self-cultivation in that one apprehends the Way (*Dao*) on every level. Indeed, this method came to be called *daoxue,* "the study of the way (*dao*). This vision of Neo-Confucianism was propounded by the Cheng brothers, Hao (1032–1085) and Yi (1033–1107), and perfected by Zhu Xi [joo SHEE] (ca. 1129–1200), generally recognized as the leading Neo-Confucian thinker.

Zhu Xi's speculative Neo-Confucianism lost favor somewhat during a Buddhist revival of sorts during the Ming, in favor of the more direct ethical action favored by Wang Yangming [wahng yahn-MING] (1472–1529). For Wang, as for Zhu Xi, truth, whether in terms of epistemology or ethics, was unitary. He believed that all people carry within them an "original mind" in which rests an intuitive sense of the fundamental order of the universe. It is out of this instinct toward the right that one investigates the physical and moral universe in order to refine one's conclusions.

selections from the writings of Wang Yangming

Wang's other area of emphasis was the unity of knowledge and action. While everyone has the spark of intuition, he argued, true understanding is inseparable from active pursuit and cultivation of that spark. Moreover, the sage must act in the world as his knowledge becomes increasingly refined, both to be a moral example to others and to complete his own self-cultivation.

Technological Peaks In many respects, the notion of perfectibility woven through Song and Ming philosophy presented itself in the scientific and technical realms as well. A number of previous innovations were refined and, in some cases, brought to highly developed states. In a great many other cases, however, high points were achieved early on and continued substantially unchanged. For example, Zheng He's ships, with their dazzling array of innovative features in the fifteenth century, remained unsurpassed triumphs of Chinese naval architecture until the mid-nineteenth century, when the empire's first steamships were launched from Western-style dockyards. While new firearms were introduced in the seventeenth and eighteenth centuries, they came in part by way of Jesuit missionaries from Europe and remained essentially unchanged until the 1840s—yet another revealing pattern of core innovation (gunpowder weapons) reintroduced in improved form from the periphery.

From the Tang through the Southern Song, China was the site of an unprecedented number of technological innovations that would have a profound effect inside and outside the empire. The horse collar, moldboard plow, wheelbarrow, advanced iron casting, compass, gunpowder, porcelain, and paper diffused widely throughout Eurasia and the Indian Ocean basin. By the height of the Song period, tea, sugar, silk, porcelain, paper, and cotton cloth had all become major industries, and China dominated—in some cases, monopolized—production and distribution of all of them. An increasingly sophisticated infrastructure of commercial credit, printed paper money, and insurance for merchant houses and their agents supported and secured China's vast network of industry and trade.

early example of a printed map, Song Dynasty

Porcelain and Literature As we can see, many of the technical advances that took place revolved around luxury items. Most notable in this regard was the development of true porcelain. Following centuries of experimentation with kaolin clays, glazing mixes, and extremely high firing temperatures, Song craftspeople hit upon the formula for creating the world's most celebrated ceramics. Elegant white and celadon (a shade of green) porcelain vessels were manufactured in great numbers, and the surviving examples of Song wares today are among the world's most precious art treasures. Techniques for using distinctive blue cobalt oxide pigments were originally introduced from Iraq in the ninth century and were being utilized by Song and Ming potters to brighten their porcelain ware. Government-sponsored and government-run kilns, notably at the Jingdezhen works in Jiangxi Province, allowed for unprecedented volume and quality control.

Song Porcelain. Porcelain reached its full maturity during the Song dynasty, and objects from that period are highly coveted even today. This celadon (sea green, sometimes with a delicate crackle glaze) ewer with a double phoenix head and peony decorations dates from the Northern Song (960–1127).

The growing wealth, leisure, and literacy of the scholar-gentry and urban classes also created an increased demand for popular literature. The novel as a literary genre first made its appearance in China during the Yuan period but emerged as a form of mass entertainment only in the sixteenth century. Written in a rapidly evolving combination of classical and colloquial language, the swashbuckling adventures of the multiauthored *Water Margin* (or *All Men Are Brothers*) and the tale of family intrigue and woe of Cao Xueqin's [sow shew-eh-cheen] *The Dream of the Red Chamber* captured the imaginations of seventeenth- and eighteenth-century readers.

Putting It All Together

interactive concept map

The experiences of India and China during the period from the seventh through the fifteenth centuries provide us with several important areas of comparison. The first is in the realm of political continuity. India was subject to a succession of governments set up by invaders from the north and west, while the kingdoms to the south jockeyed for power among themselves and for power over the Indian-influenced states of Southeast Asia. While there was considerable cultural and religious continuity in the south, the north was alternately dominated by the Hinduism of the late Gupta period, the revived Buddhism of the seventh century, and ultimately by Islam. In the end, none of these claimed full dominance, though Islam remained the religion of the rulers after the twelfth century.

In the case of China, despite the Mongol invasion and political domination of China during the fourteenth century, the basic political structure changed relatively little and reemerged with greater centralization than ever during the Ming dynasty. Culturally, the Mongols' influence on China was negligible; moreover, the Mongols increasingly were compelled to make themselves culturally "Chinese" in order to rule, despite their concerted efforts to maintain their ethnic autonomy. Through it all, not only did Chinese leadership in technical innovation in so many fields keep up its former pace, but the brief incorporation into the Mongol Empire helped to greatly facilitate other cultures' interaction with and adaptation to Chinese advances.

The most dramatic difference, however, came in the realm of interaction with and adaptation to religion. India, from the time of Mahmud of Ghazna, never completely adapted itself to Islam—a situation that continues to the present day. Thus, northern India became an uneasily *syncretic* area—an area in which the worldviews of rival religious civilizations confronted each other but were not significantly adopted or adapted by the other. Instead, Hindus and Muslims attempted to coexist with each other. Even notable attempts to bridge the gulf between Hindus and Muslims, such as Sikhism, were not successful in attaining widespread acceptance.

In China, however, the dominant political structures of empire and the cultural assumptions of Confucianism not only resisted Mongol attempts to circumvent them but in the end were largely adopted by the conquerors. Unlike the Muslim conquerors in India, the Mongols did not adhere to a powerfully articulated universal religion. In fact, they proved receptive to several of the religious traditions they encountered in their conquests: Islam, Buddhism, and Nestorian Christianity all gained Mongol adherents. Even before this, however, in marked contrast to India's encounter with Islam, the very real tensions between Buddhism and Confucianism in China resulted not in persecution of the Buddhists but in Confucian thinkers borrowing their approaches to speculative philosophy and creating an expanded synthetic ideology, Neo-Confucianism.

Thus, until the nineteenth century, these religious and cultural trends would continue. India, dominated by the Muslim Mughals in the north and increasingly by the British from the eighteenth century on, would struggle to reconcile and balance the tensions of syncretism. The British, quick to sense these tensions, increasingly exploited them in their strategy of "divide and rule." The Chinese, firm in the belief that all outsiders could ultimately "become Chinese," continued to pursue this policy through the same period. Ultimately, both empires would be reduced by the British and their fellow European powers, whose centuries-long rise was shortly to begin.

Review and Relate

Thinking Through Patterns

Examine the ways historians approach the big questions of this chapter.

» How did interactions between Muslims and Hindus in India lead to religious syncretism?

In contemplating this question, we must consider what the fundamental beliefs of these two religious traditions were and what kinds of changes take place as religions move from one place to another and interact with other long-established beliefs. For Hindus, this is somewhat difficult, because Hinduism encompasses many different religious assumptions. Moreover, it has a long tradition of trying to fit newly arrived belief systems into its own traditions. This is where the clash with Islam is most evident. Islam teaches that there is no God but God (Allah); Hinduism would place Allah next to its other gods, which Muslims find intolerable. This fundamental clash of views makes any compromise difficult. But Muslim leaders find that they simply cannot coerce their Hindu subjects, who vastly outnumber them, to accept the new religion by force. They must therefore find ways to lessen its impact while holding true to the strictures of Islam. Thus, some leniency must be given, or rule becomes impossible, but each side keeps its distance from the other for fear of giving up core values. Thus, they coexist, albeit very uneasily.

» What steps were taken by Hindus and Muslims to lessen the conflicts between the two rival religious traditions?

Some compromises were made along the way to lessen conflict between the major traditions. Muslim rulers routinely had to suspend their insistence on governing by strict Islamic law and let the Hindu majority govern itself according to its own traditions. In some cases, Hindu women even adopted the veil, like their Muslim counterparts. The most spectacular steps were the founding of new religious traditions incorporating both Hindu and Muslim elements—Sikhism, for example, and, as we will see in Chapter 20, the Mughal ruler Akbar's attempt at a synthetic religion.

» How was the Tang dynasty in China different from its predecessors and successors?

As we saw, the Tang was China's most cosmopolitan dynasty, and this alone made it quite different from its predecessors. But why was it so cosmopolitan? Here, a large part of the answer must be seen in the widespread practice of Buddhism. China was now integrated into a Buddhist cultural sphere that allowed a greatly enhanced circulation of ideas and goods. Thus, China's rulers knew a good deal more about their neighbors than ever before and through Buddhism shared a community of religious interest with them. The reaction to Buddhism as a "foreign" faith in the Song period made China turn more inward; consequently, its larger ties with the Buddhist world deteriorated, never to reach Tang-level connections again.

» How effectively did the religious and philosophical traditions of Buddhism, Confucianism, and Daoism blend together in creating Neo-Confucianism? Where did they clash?

The longevity and diversity of Neo-Confucianism over time suggest that the blending was quite effective. It represented a synthesis in which ethics and epistemology—Confucian, humanist-based morality coupled with the speculative ventures of Daoists and Buddhists—created a complete, self-sustaining system. In this, it parallels attempts by contemporary Christian and Muslim thinkers to marry faith and reason into an all-encompassing system designed to provide a means to answer both concrete and speculative questions.

Against the Grain

Consider this as a counterpoint to the main patterns examined in this chapter.

Empress Wu

- In what ways does Empress Wu appear as a classic nonconformist?

The Tang ruler Wu Zetian, or Empress Wu (r. 690–705), exemplified her era's contradictory trends toward both greater restrictiveness and wider latitude in personal behavior, particularly in the case of women. The daughter of a public works official, she spent a brief period at court as a servant to the empress. Disillusioned by life in the capital and drawn to the austerities of Buddhism, she joined a women's monastery, only to return to the palace when her beauty piqued the interest of an imperial prince. Seeing the opportunities this opening presented, she exploited them ably.

- In what ways does Empress Wu resemble other ambitious women in history?

As in the case of Cleopatra in Egypt, hostile chroniclers in subsequent dynasties attributed much of her success to her sexual exploits, though the records also note that she was well educated, shrewd in her dealings with ministers, and a polished hand at employing imperial spectacle. In 684, after the death of her husband, who had become the emperor, she ruled as empress dowager and as regent for her son. In reality, however, she held all the actual power. A devout Buddhist, she declared Buddhism the state religion. She maneuvered to rule in her own right, and in 690, she inaugurated the new Zhou dynasty. The final step came in 693, when she took the Buddhist title Divine Empress Who Rules the Universe.

Though she was an able ruler according to the Tang official histories, the act of creating her own dynasty and new titles for herself—including an insistence on the "male" title of "emperor"—was considered usurpation by many of her subjects, and a resistance soon followed. In the eyes of many influential Tang leaders, Wu's blatant empowering of Buddhists and Daoists over Confucians was deplorable. As a result, scurrilous accusations were laid against her, including allegations of sexual depravity, executing and torturing of her opponents; and even the murder of her own child in her quest to achieve political power. Unlike many other Chinese rulers, however, she was able to stifle revolts and to preserve the continuity of the dynasty, only succumbing to natural causes in 705.

Following the Confucian backlash of the Song era, no woman in imperial China would wield this kind of power again until the reign of the empress dowager Cixi in the late nineteenth and early twentieth centuries. Even today, however, Wu remains a controversial figure; while she is widely celebrated in China as an early feminist role model, she is also seen as an ambitious, cruel, and self-serving schemer.

Key Terms

audio flashcards

Empress dowager 353
Female infanticide 364
Foot binding 364
Sikhism 349
Sumptuary laws 363

For additional resources, please go to **www.oup.com/us/vonsivers.**
Please see the Further Resources section at the back of the book for additional readings and suggested websites.

PATTERNS OF EVIDENCE |

Sources for Chapter 12

SOURCE 12.1 The *Chachnamah*

ca. 1200

Composed in Arabic and translated into Persian in the twelfth and thirteenth centuries, the *Chachnamah* details the Arab conquest of the Sind (a province corresponding to northwest India and Pakistan) in the eighth century. The work details the campaign led by Muhammad Ibn Qasim, which was the most successful of the many attempts by Muslims to conquer the region. In this history of the campaign, Ibn Qasim is both a conquering hero and a defender of Islam, subduing non-Muslims and imposing new religious values in his wake.

A description of the battle.

Hazlí states that, in that army of the Arabs there was a brave soldier by name Háris son of Marrah. He was at the head of a column of one thousand fully armed warriors. He had three brave slaves with him, one of whom he retained to bear his arms, and the other two he appointed as officers in the army, each being made the leader of 500 men. When they arrived at Makrán the news was carried to Kíkánán, where the people prepared for battle and commenced fighting. They were about 20,000 men.

[Nevertheless] the army of Islám attacked them and overpowered them, and seeing no other help, the natives retreated to the gates of the town. But when the Arab army left the battle-field and marched after the residents of Kíkánán, the latter came down to obstruct their progress. The Arab army made an onset, with their war cry of "Alláhu Akbar" [God is great] and from the left and the right the cliffs echoed the cry of "Alláhu Akbar." When the infidels of Kíkánán heard those cries they were much frightened, and some of them surrendered and accepted Islám and the rest fled away, and from that time up to our day, on the anniversary of that battle, cries of "Alláhu Akbar" are heard from the mountain.

They had already completed this victory when they received the sad news of the martyrdom of His Highness the Commander of the Faithful, Alí son of Abí Tálib, (on whom be peace). They, therefore, turned back, and when they arrived at Makrán, they learnt that Muáwiyeh son of Abísafiyán had become the Khalífah.

. . .

Source: *The Chachnamah: An Ancient History of Sind*, trans. Mirza Kalichbeg Fredunbeg, available online at http://persian.packhum.org/persian/main?url=pf%3Ffile%3D12701030%26ct%3D0.

A tradition.

It is related by Abul Hasan, who heard it from Hazlí, and Hazlí from Muslim son of Muhárib son of Muslim son of Ziyád, that when Muáwiyeh despatched the expedition of 4,000 men under Abdulláh son of Sawád, no one had to kindle fire in his camp, as they had carried abundant provisions for the journey, ready made for use. It was only on a single night that fire-light was perceived in the camp, and, on enquiry being made, it was found that a pregnant woman had been confined and fire was urgently required. Abdulláh gave her permission and she gave a merry banquet, and for three days continually entertained the whole army (with fresh-cooked food).

When Abdulláh arrived at Kíkánán, the enemy made an assault on him, but the army of Islám routed them, and secured plenty of booty. The people of Kíkánán assembled in large numbers, and occupied the mountain passes. The battle now raged furiously and Abdulláh son of Sawád found it necessary to keep his men in their ranks, by making a stand himself with a party of selected men, fully armed; and he appealed to the hearts of others in the following words: "O children of the Prophet's companions, do not turn your faces from the infidels, so that your faith may remain free from any flaw and you acquire the honour of martyrdom." Hearing these words his men assembled round the standard of Abdulláh, and one of these men, who belonged to the family of Abdul Kais, came out with a challenge to a single fight. Instantly the chief of the enemy's forces engaged with him. The example of this hero was followed by another Yásar son of Sawád. The chief was killed, but the army of Kíkánán made a general assault, by which the army of Islám was ultimately put to flight. The whole mountainous region now became alive with fighting men and the Musalmans beat a (hasty) retreat, and came back to Makrán.

A tradition.

Abul Hasan relates that he heard Hátim son of Kutai-bíah Sahlí say: "That day I myself was in the army when the son of Sawád fought with his youthful adversary, and his friends advanced in the same manner, and killed many men of the enemy's side. After a hard fight they at last fell martyrs and I stripped the dead bodies of the enemy, and found a hundred signet rings."

. . .

Safyán son of U'r dí appointed to carry on the religious war in Hind.

It is related by Hazlí who heard it from Tibuí son of Músá, who again heard it from his father, that on Abdulláh son of Sawád being martyred, he appointed Sinán son of Salmah as his successor. Soon afterwards Muáwiyeh wrote to Ziyád, (the then governor of Irák) to select a proper person for the holy wars in Hind. When he received the letter, Ziyád nominated Ahnaf son of Kais, who was liked by all, and was the pride of the Faithful. Ahnaf forthwith went to Makrán, where he remained for a period of two years, and after two years and one month he was removed from that post.

» Working with Sources

1. **To what extent is this conflict envisioned as a "religious war"?**
2. **Why does the document concern itself with successions of political power?**

SOURCE 12.2

Harsha Vardhana, *The Lady of the Jewel Necklace*

ca. 640 CE

Harsha Vardhana, one of the better-known monarchs of India, controlled a wide swath of territory in the northern subcontinent between 606 and 647. Harsha was visited during his reign by the Chinese Buddhist pilgrim Xuan Zang, who described his court and government, and the poet Bana wrote a biography of the king called the *Harshacarita*. However, Harsha himself also wrote at least three plays, two of which were dedicated to the Hindu god Shiva and incorporated actual incidents from his court. While the plays are ostensibly fictional, the scene below draws on a real event, reported by Xuan Zang, in which Harsha saved an image of Buddha from a fire that had broken out in his palace. His plays reflect the cosmopolitan and religiously eclectic nature of his court, as well as his view of the status of the advisors and women in his orbit.

KING: (*arising in haste*) What? A fire in the women's quarters? Oh no! What if Queen Vásava·datta has been burnt! Oh, my dear Vásava·datta!

VÁSAVA·DATTA: Help, my husband, help!

KING: Oh! Why, in my extreme haste and confusion, I didn't notice the queen even though she was standing right here beside me. Courage, my queen, courage!

VÁSAVA·DATTA: My husband, I didn't speak for my own sake. But Ságarika may die, for in my cruelty I had her chained up here. Save her, please, my husband.

KING: What? Ságarika may die, my queen? I will go!

VASU·BHUTI: Your majesty, why should you go the way of a moth for no real reason?

BABHRÁVYA: Your majesty, what Vasu·bhuti said is right.

JESTER: (*grabbing the King by his shirt*) My friend, don't do anything so rash!

KING: (*freeing his shirt*) You idiot! Ságarika may die! Why is the breath of life still in me even now? (*He mimes rushing into the fire and being overcome by smoke.*)

Source: Harsha Vardhana, *The Lady of the Jewel Necklace*, trans. Wendy Doniger (New York: NYU Press, 2006), 259–265.

Stop, fire, stop! Give up
this unbroken wave of smoke!
Why do you brandish on high
this circling mass of flames?
If I wasn't burnt up by the fire
of separation from my dear one,
that blazed like the doomsday
fire, what can you do to me?

VÁSAVA·DATTA: Since my husband has unhesitatingly done this because of what I said—miserably unlucky woman that I am—I, too, will follow my husband.

JESTER: (*walking around and standing in front of her*) I, too, ma'am, will be your pathfinder.

VASU·BHUTI: Why, the king of Vatsa has already entered the fire! Then it is proper that I, too, who saw the princess die, should offer myself as an oblation into the fire here.

BABHRÁVYA: Your majesty, why jeopardize the race descended from Bharata for no good reason? But what's the use of idle talk? I too will act in accordance with my devotion.

All mime entering the fire.

Enter Ságarika, *in chains.*

SÁGARIKA: (*looking in all directions*) Oh no! The fire is blazing up on all sides! (*thinking, with satisfaction*) Fortunately, the fire, carrier of oblations, will put an end to my suffering today.

KING: Ságarika is here near the fire! I'll help her right away. (*approaching her in haste*) My dear, how can you remain so self-possessed even now in this haste and confusion?

SÁGARIKA: (*seeing the King, to herself*) Why, it's my husband! When I see him, my love of life comes back again. (*aloud*) Save me, your majesty! Save me!

KING: Don't be afraid, my timid one:

. . .

Clearly the fire does not really burn you,
even though it has caught you,
for your touch now, darling,
takes away
even my burning anguish.

. . .

VÁSAVA·DATTA: (*touching the* KING*'s body, with joy*) Thank goodness, my husband's body is unhurt.

KING: This is Babhrávya—

BABHRÁVYA: We've been brought back to life, your majesty.

KING: —and this Vasu·bhuti!—

VASU·BHUTI: Total victory to the great king!

Working with Sources

1. **What does the play suggest about Harsha's vision of the ideal relationship between a king and his courtiers?**
2. **Why was Harsha so careful with stage directions? Did he intend the work to be performed, and how?**

SOURCE 12.3

Poetry of the Tang Dynasty

ca. 750 CE

The Tang period (618–907) witnessed a renaissance of poetry, oftentimes compressing vivid natural imagery and poignant emotion into short pieces of only a few verses. The poetry of Li Bo (or Li Bai, 701–762) was particularly influential in the West when his verses on drinking and the pleasures of life were rendered in translation. However, there is also a strong undercurrent of pacifism, drawing on Confucian philosophy, in Tang poetry, and the poems below address war and its consequences. A poem by Du Fu (ca. 721–770), who was also Li Bo's friend, reflects the same sentiment.

Du Fu, "A Drawing of a Horse by General Cao at Secretary Wei Feng's House"

Throughout this dynasty no one had painted horses
Like the master-spirit, Prince Jiangdu—
And then to General Cao through his thirty years of fame
The world's gaze turned, for royal steeds.
He painted the late Emperor's luminous white horse.
For ten days the thunder flew over Dragon Lake,
And a pink-agate plate was sent him from the palace—

Source: "A Drawing of a Horse by General Cao at Secretary Wei Feng's House" adapted from http://www.shigeku.com/xlib/lingshidao/hanshi/dufu.htm, Li Bo poem adapted from *Bright Moon, White Clouds: Selected Poems of Li Po*, ed. and trans. J. P. Seaton (Boston: Shambhala, 2012), 113–115.

The talk of the court-ladies, the marvel of all eyes.
The General danced, receiving it in his honoured home
After this rare gift, followed rapidly fine silks
From many of the nobles, requesting that his art
Lend a new lustre to their screens.
. . . First came the curly-maned horse of Emperor Taizong,
Then, for the Guos, a lion-spotted horse. . . .
But now in this painting I see two horses,
A sobering sight for whosoever knew them.
They are war-horses. Either could face ten thousand.
They make the white silk stretch away into a vast desert.
And the seven others with them are almost as noble
Mist and snow are moving across a cold sky,
And hoofs are cleaving snow-drifts under great trees-
With here a group of officers and there a group of servants.
See how these nine horses all vie with one another—
The high clear glance, the deep firm breath.
. . . Who understands distinction? Who really cares for art?
You, Wei Feng, have followed Cao; Zhidun preceded him.
. . . I remember when the late Emperor came toward his Summer Palace,
The procession, in green-feathered rows, swept from the eastern sky—
Thirty thousand horses, prancing, galloping,
Fashioned, every one of them, like the horses in this picture. . . .
But now the Imperial Ghost receives secret jade from the River God,
For the Emperor hunts crocodiles no longer by the streams.
Where you see his Great Gold Tomb, you may hear among the pines
A bird grieving in the wind that the Emperor's horses are gone.

Li Bo, from *Bright Moon, White Clouds*

Moon over the Pass
Bright moon suddenly up from beyond Heaven Mountain,
where it had lain hid in the dark, endless sea of clouds.
The long winds came down tens of thousands of miles,
from the north to blow through Jade Gate Pass.
Here Han troops climbed the road to Paideng Mountain,
because the barbarians wanted our Great Dark Sea in the desert.
Of all who stood upon that ancient field,
I've never heard one returned.
Armed sojourners, they gazed hopelessly

homeward over barren ground,
their hearts gone home: read the bitter faces.
In home's many mansions, facing this same moon:
the wives and loved ones also
sigh and see clear, in the mind's eye, yet can't let go.

War South of the Wall
Last year, war:
at the Sang-gan's source.
This year, war:
along the Tsung-ho Road
Our whole army washed weapons in the Tiao-chih Sea,
and set horse to graze on the grass that grew in patches
underneath the snows of the T'ian Shan Range.
Three thousand miles of battles,
three armies exhausted, withering away, grown old . . .
The Huns farm these battlefields for bones:
since the time of the Ancients, nothing to see
but bleached bones on yellow sands, their fields.
Ch'in built the Wall to keep them out.
Han fed the beacon fires to burn unceasing,
yet the War went on:
war, wasteland: men dying there.
The horses of the conquered neighing skyward, mourning.
Vultures feed on man guts.
With flesh in their beaks they fly up,
fly up to hang those guts in the withered branches.
Soldiers die, blood splashes brush and grass.
Generals?
Is all this done in vain? You know that soldiers
are the direst of instruments. The wise make use of them
only when there is no other way.

➤ Working with Sources

1. **What does this poetry suggest about the Confucian and Daoist conceptions of war and its consequences?**
2. **How do the poems reflect on the preservation of historical memory in monuments and paintings?**

SOURCE 12.4

Marco Polo, "Khubilai Khan at War"

ca. 1290

Marco Polo (1254–1324) was a member of a clan of Venetian merchants who had been active in trade in the Middle East for some decades. Polo claims to have accompanied his father and uncle on an extensive trade and diplomatic excursion to China in 1271, and in this account he describes the voyage as well as the people and places he has seen. He further claims to have lived 17 years in China and to have met with, and even served as an official for, Khubilai Khan (1215–1294), Genghis Khan's grandson. While some historians have suggested that the account may not be reliable, it demonstrates, at the very least, Western curiosity about Asia and the catalyst of trade in driving some Europeans into hitherto unknown parts of the world.

When the Great Khan had mustered the mere handful of men of which I have spoken, he consulted his astrologers to learn whether he would defeat his enemies and bring his affairs to a happy issue. They assured him that he would deal with his enemies as he pleased. Thereupon he set out with all his forces and went on until after twenty days they came to a great plain where Nayan lay with all his forces, who were not less than 400,000 horsemen. They arrived early in the morning and caught the enemy completely unawares; the Great Khan had had all the roads so carefully watched that no one could come or go without being intercepted, and had thus ensured that the enemy had no suspicion of their approach. Indeed, when they arrived Nayan was in his tent, dallying in bed with his wife, to whom he was greatly attached.

What more shall I say? When the day of battle dawned, the Great Khan suddenly appeared on a mound that rose from the plain where Nayan's forces were bivouacked. They were quite at their ease, like men who had not the faintest suspicion that anyone was approaching with hostile intent. Indeed they felt so secure that they had posted no sentries round their camp and sent out no patrols to van or rear. And suddenly there was the Great Khan on the hill I have mentioned. He stood on the top of a wooden tower, full of crossbowmen and archers, which was carried by four elephants wearing stout leather armour draped with cloths of silk and gold. Above his head flew his banner with the emblem of the sun and moon, so high that it could be clearly seen on every side.

. . .

When Nayan and his men saw the troops of the Great Khan surrounding their camp, they were utterly taken aback. They rushed to arms, arrayed themselves in haste, and formed their ranks in due order.

. . .

Source: Marco Polo, *The Travels of Marco Polo*, trans. Ronald Latham (Harmondsworth, UK: Penguin, 1958), 115–118.

So loud was the shouting and the clash of armies that you could not have heard the thunder of heaven. You must know that Nayan was a baptized Christian and in this battle he had the cross of Christ on his standard.

What need to make a long story of it? Enough that this was the most hazardous fight and the most fiercely contested that ever was seen. Never in our time were so many men engaged on one battlefield, especially so many horsemen. So many died on either side that it was a marvel to behold. The battle raged from daybreak till noon, and for a long time its issue hung in the balance; Nayan's followers were so devoted to him, for he was an open-handed master, that they were ready to die rather than turn their backs. But in the end the victory fell to the Great Khan. When Nayan and his men saw that they could hold out no longer, they took to flight. But this availed them nothing; for Nayan was taken prisoner, and all his barons and his men surrendered to the Great Khan.

When the Great Khan learnt that Nayan was a prisoner, he commanded that he should be put to death. And this was how it was done. He was wrapped up tightly in a carpet and then dragged about so violently, this way and that, that he died. Their object in choosing this mode of death was so that the blood of the imperial lineage might not be spilt upon the earth, and that sun and air might not witness it.

» Working with Sources

1. **How did the Great Khan employ elements of "psychological warfare" on the battlefield?**
2. **Does Marco Polo seem to have felt sympathy for the defeat of a fellow Christian by the non-Christian Khan? Why not?**

SOURCE 12.5

Model of a Ming ship in the flotilla of Zheng He

ca. 1420

Between 1405 and 1433, a series of naval expeditions were sent out by Yongle, the third emperor of the Ming dynasty, under the command of the remarkable Zheng He (1371–1435). The largest of Zheng's ships were over 400 feet long and were thus more than four times the length of Christopher Columbus's *Santa Maria*. His voyages took Zheng to the coasts of Southeast Asia, Indonesia, India, Arabia, and East Africa. In 2010, marine archaeologists attempted to find remains of one of Zheng's ships off the coast of Kenya, near Malindi, a site Zheng visited in 1418. This photograph shows a model of one of Zheng's ships, compared with a model of the *Santa Maria*. The model is displayed in a shopping mall in Dubai, United Arab Emirates.

Source: © Liu Liqun/Chinastock.

» Working with Sources

1. What does the greater size of Zheng He's ships compared to the ones Columbus used say about the imperial ambitions of Ming China in the fifteenth century?
2. Why might this ship be of interest to shoppers in Dubai?

Chapter 13 550–1500 CE

Religious Civilizations Interacting

KOREA, JAPAN, AND VIETNAM

Syllabary: A system of written symbols representing the sounds of syllables, rather than individual consonants and vowels.

The brushstrokes flowed across the fine rice paper, as they had thousands of times since she began carefully practicing them as a young girl. For Murasaki Shikibu (ca. 973–1025), the daughter of a minor noble in the court at Heian-Kyo in central Japan, the words that now came so effortlessly had become her refuge from the rigid routine of palace life, where a woman's every move was carefully prescribed. The court women of Heian Japan (794–1185 CE), in their thick, stiff winter kimonos, their teeth blackened and faces powdered white to enhance their beauty, were carefully monitored by palace chamberlains and commented on by court gossips. Some of the women, like Murasaki's older contemporary Sei Shonagon, responded to this restricted life with savage wit and scathing commentary, skewering its pretentions in her scandalous *Pillow Book*.

Murasaki's literary interests, however, took a somewhat different turn. Though trained in *kanji*, the literary Chinese that functioned as Japan's first written language, her private writings, as were those of the handful of other literate Japanese women, were written in the simpler *kana* script based on a **syllabary** of sounds in the Japanese spoken language. Like Sei's, her work also centered on court life. But her subject was the adventures, loves, trials, and triumphs of a fictional prince named Genji. When

***ABOVE:* Detail from twelfth-century Japanese scroll depicting *The Tale of Genji*.**

it was finished, she had created in her *Genji Monagatari, The Tale of Genji* (ca. 1000), what scholars have since recognized as the world's first novel. It remains even today Japan's most popular work of fiction and one of the world's great literary masterpieces.

The story of Murasaki, the court women of Heian-Kyo—the city we know today as Kyoto—and eleventh-century Japan more generally all help to illustrate the patterns of world history featured in this book.

In the sixth century CE, Chinese writing, culture, thought, and Buddhism arrived simultaneously in Japan and were swiftly adopted by the ambitious Japanese state of Yamato. Sensing that power and prestige would grow from adapting China's centralized imperial institutions to Japanese conditions, Yamato leaders thoroughly remade their state along these lines over the next two centuries. But in many ways, as we shall see, the suitability of these institutions to Japan's clan-based society was at best uneven.

The tensions in state formation, both large and small, created by this situation were noticeable as well in Korea and Vietnam, also in the process of interaction and adaptation to Chinese institutions. Like the Japanese, the Koreans and Vietnamese would go on to create their own writing systems while retaining Chinese as a literary language. They would also struggle, like the Japanese and Chinese, to balance the differing traditions of Buddhism with the practical elements of Confucian government. The dynamism within these tensions would allow each to ultimately make imported Chinese culture their own as they followed distinct courses of state formation: Korea and Vietnam, often struggling under China's political shadow, and Japan, clinging fiercely to its independence and protected by the intervening Sea of Japan.

Seeing Patterns

» **How was the history of Korea affected by its relations with China? With Japan?**

» **Which important elements of Chinese culture were adapted by the Japanese for their own purposes? What advantages did Japan have over Korea and Vietnam in this regard?**

» **Which Japanese adaptations of Chinese institutions did not work well in Japan? Why?**

» **In what ways was the experience of Vietnam similar to that of Japan and Korea? How was it different?**

Korea to 1450: Innovation from Above

Like the influence of the Greek-Hellenistic and Roman worlds, that of imperial China became widespread throughout east, northeast, and southeast Asia. Chinese writing, literature, law, government, and thought, as well as imported religions such as Buddhism, shaped local social, cultural, and religious customs and practices. But as these imports were often imposed from the top down, they met frequent resistance at the village and clan levels. Thus, tensions between elites and locals continually played out in the assorted Korean kingdoms against a backdrop of invasion and collaboration. From the beginning these societies asserted their political independence from the Chinese. However, their position on or near the Chinese border, the role of the Korean kingdoms as havens for refugees, and the continual pressures of potential invasion provided a conduit for the spread of Chinese innovations—even to the islands of Japan. For the Koreans themselves, shifting relations with China provided both unity and disarray in the struggles of different kingdoms for dominance.

People and Place: The Korean Environment

The terrain of the Korean peninsula resembles in many ways that of the adjacent region of Manchuria. The north is mountainous, marked by the Nangnim and

Chapter Outline

- Korea to 1450: Innovation from Above
- Japan to 1450: Selective Interaction and Adaptation
- Vietnam: Human Agency and State Building
- Putting It All Together

Hamyong ranges running northeast to southwest, with the Taebaek chain running north and south along the coast facing the Sea of Japan. The Amnokkang, better known as the Yalu River, and the Kangnam Mountains form the present dividing line with Manchuria, but Korean kingdoms have at times extended far beyond them into modern China's northeast. The areas south of the modern city of Seoul are somewhat flatter, but the entire peninsula is generally hilly, and agriculture has historically been concentrated in the river floodplains and coastal alluvial flats.

Climate and Agriculture The climate of Korea is continental in the north but influenced by the monsoon system in the south. As in northern China, summer and winter temperatures tend to be extreme, with distinct rainy (summer) and dry (winter) seasons. Because of the configuration of the mountains and the peninsula's position along the northern perimeter of the monsoon, annual rainfall amounts differ widely: from average lows of 30 inches in the northeast to 60–70 inches in the southwest. Like the western side of the Japanese islands, however, Korea is largely blocked by Japanese mountain ranges from the moderating effects of the Japan Current.

The difficulties of the terrain and the ever-present possibility of drought have rendered the challenges of the region similar to those facing agriculturalists in northern China, with crops such as millet and wheat dominating and rice farming catching on only much later in the south, where rainfall and the terracing of hillsides made it feasible (see Map 13.1).

Ethnic Origins The ethnic origins of the Koreans are still obscure, though the slim archaeological and linguistic evidence seems to point to a central Asian homeland and links to the **Altaic**-speaking peoples. In this way, the modern Korean language may be distantly related to such languages as Mongolian, Manchu, and possibly Japanese. East and northeast Asia, as we have seen, was home to some of the world's first pottery, though the potter's wheel did not arrive in the area for millennia. In the case of the Korean peninsula, potsherds dating from 4000 BCE have been uncovered in **striated** styles not unlike the Jomon wares of Japan, which some scholars have suggested points to an early period of interaction or perhaps even a common ancestry.

Altaic: In linguistics, the family of languages descended from that spoken by inhabitants of the region of the Altai Mountains in central Asia. Examples include the Turkish languages, Mongolian, and Manchu.

Striated: Having thin lines or bands.

Conquest and Competition: History and Politics to 1450

Though developments in northern China have long had a bearing on events on the Korean peninsula, the first Korean state predated any such influence. Zhou Chinese annals contain apparent references to the kingdom of Choson—"The Land of the Morning Calm." Choson seems to have extended deep into southern Manchuria, with its capital located on the site of the modern city of Pyongyang. It is believed to have been founded sometime after 1000 BCE. In the absence of a written Korean language, however, no indigenous records exist of its early years.

The "Three Kingdoms" Such Chinese cultural influences as the use of written language appear to have been present in the region even before the first attempt at invasion under the Qin (221–206 BCE). By 108 BCE, their successors, the Han, briefly succeeded in bringing much of the peninsula under their sway. It is from this period that the first written records of exchanges with such outlying peoples as the Koreans, Japanese, and Vietnamese find their way into Han histories. As related in Sima Qian's *Records of the Grand Historian,* the Han quest to pursue the conquest of "Chaoxian" (Choson) was rife with chaos and mismanagement.

Long before this, however, Chinese agricultural techniques and implements, methods of bronze and iron smelting, and a wide variety of other technologies found their way to Choson and beyond. Early contacts between Choson and the Zhou Chinese states from the ninth century BCE on saw the arrival of bronze tools, coins, and weapons. By the fifth century BCE, the technology of iron smelting was also firmly established on the Korean peninsula.

Following the Han conquests, a more systematic Chinese transformation was attempted. The Han incorporated approximately two-thirds of the peninsula into their empire and took over Pyongyang as their regional capital. They also encouraged Chinese settlement in the newly acquired territories in order to help ensure loyalty. One of the indirect effects of the conquest was a steady stream of refugees into the unoccupied regions of the south and to the small tribal societies of Japan. This constant traffic back and forth across the narrow, 100-mile strait separating the Japanese islands from the mainland created a

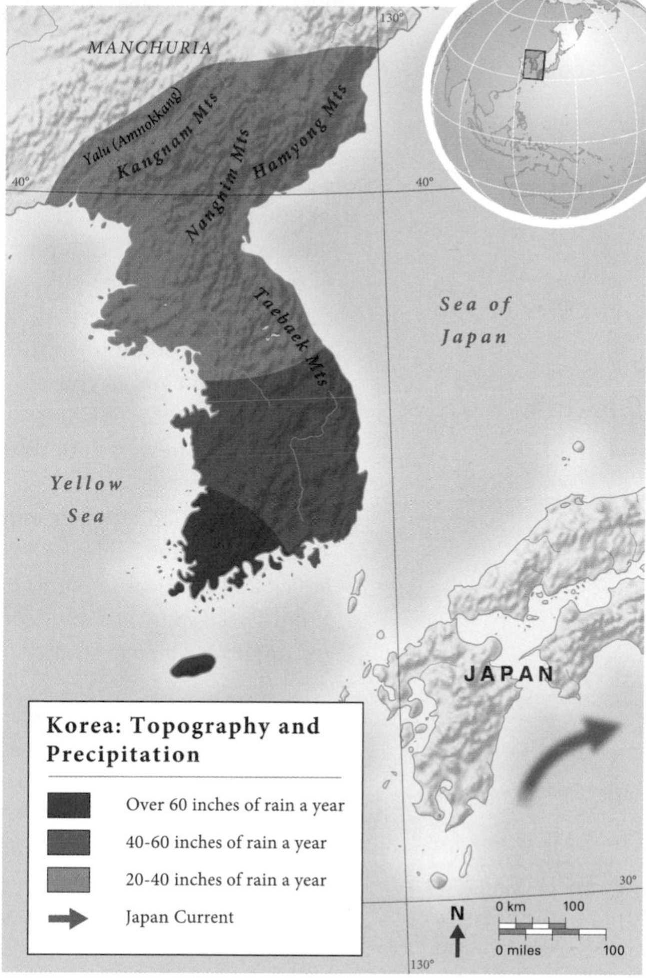

MAP 13.1 **Korea: Topography and Precipitation.**

Korea

- **108 BCE** Northern Korea occupied by Han China
- **57 BCE–935 CE** Era of the Three Kingdoms and Kaya
- **589–735** Sui and Tang Chinese invasions of Korea
- **618–935** Parhae kingdom in northern Korea and southern Manchuria
- **918–1392** Koryo kingdom
- **1392–1910** Yi dynasty forms second state of Choson
- **1443** King Sejong promulgates *han-gul* phonetic writing system

interactive timeline

Japan

- **300 BCE–ca. 250 CE** Yayoi period
- **250–710 CE** Yamato period
- **794–1185** Heian period
- **ca. 1000** *The Tale of Genji,* considered to be the world's first novel, by Murasaki Shikibu
- **1185–1333** Kamakura shogunate
- **1337–1467** Ashikaga shogunate

Vietnam

- **ca. 200 BCE** Theravada Buddhism arrives in Southeast Asia from Ceylon (Sri Lanka)
- **221 BCE** China's first empire, the Qin, pushes into northern Vietnam
- **39 CE** Revolt of the Trung sisters
- **968** Dinh Bo Linh creates a unified Vietnamese dynasty
- **1010–1225** Li (Le) dynasty adopts Chinese forms and Song Neo-Confucianism
- **1225–1400** Tran dynasty
- **1257–1287** Vietnamese repulse three attempted Mongol invasions
- **1428–1789** New Le dynasty of Le Loi

transient population of colonists in both places and greatly facilitated cultural exchanges. Koreans became established as important actors in early Japanese history, and with the founding of the small Japanese holding of *Kaya* (Gaya) in 42 CE, Japanese territorial claims were established on the peninsula.

At the same time, the foundations had been laid for the so-called Three Kingdoms of Korea: *Koguryo* [go-GUR-yo] (37 BCE–668 CE), *Paekche* [BAAK-chih] (18 BCE–660 CE), and *Silla* [Si-lah] (57 BCE–935 CE). By the fourth century CE, the dissolution of the Han Empire encouraged the Koreans to push the Chinese out of the peninsula. In the wake of their retreat, the three rival kingdoms began a process of intrigue and intermittent war among themselves for dominance. Koguryo, in the extreme north, formed the largest state as the Chinese evacuated, moving into southern Manchuria in the absence of any strong rivals. In the south, the areas that had never been under Chinese control had a history of close ties to the developing Japanese clan powers and, consequently, tended to be more outward looking (see Map 13.2).

In 372 the Chinese state of Jin began sending Buddhist missionaries to Koguryo. With them came Chinese writing and literature—and, significantly, Confucian ethics and political thought. In 427, Koguryo remade itself along Chinese lines. From Pyongyang a central Confucian bureaucracy was set up, examinations were instituted, and a reconstituted land tax and conscription system were installed.

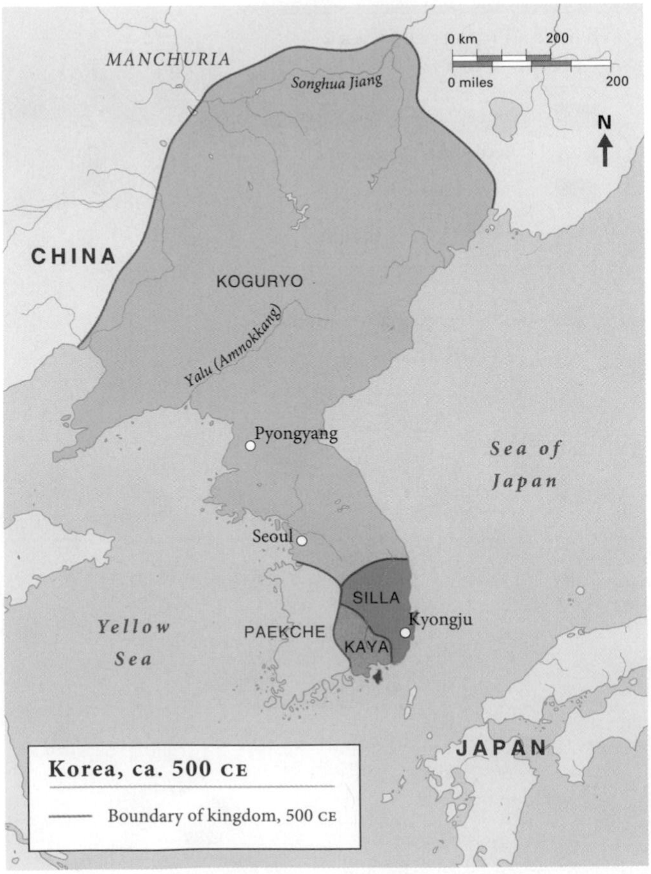

MAP 13.2 Korea, ca. 500 CE.

Meanwhile, the two southern kingdoms fought continually to stave off domination by their northern rival. Paekche's maritime contacts with south China aided the spread of Buddhism there, as did, to some degree, its wars with Koguryo from 364 to 371. Buddhism had also come to Silla, but Chinese political institutions did not take the same form there as elsewhere. A clan-based, autocratic monarchy, Silla adopted a Chinese-style bureaucracy but retained its system of hereditary ranks, leaving power largely in the hands of warrior aristocrats.

The power struggle among the peninsular states was long and bitter and from time to time also involved China. In 550, Silla allied with Paekche against the renewed expansionist aims of Koguryo, in the course of which Kaya was eliminated in 562. The reunification of China under the short-lived Sui dynasty in 589 soon resulted in another invasion of the north. After several Tang campaigns were repulsed, the Chinese decided on a new strategy and concluded an alliance with Silla in 660, spelling the immediate end of Paekche. Threatened along two fronts, Koguryo itself finally submitted in 668. Silla was ultimately recognized by the Chinese as a client state controlling all of Korea south of Pyongyang in 735.

Pulguksa Temple. Buddhism put down strong roots in Silla after its introduction in the fourth century. The Pulguksa temple was first built in Kyongjiu, the Silla capital, in 535 as part of the state Buddhist school. The stone pagodas were built in the ninth century under the auspices of the new Son school, better known by its Japanese name, Zen.

Korea to the Mid-Fifteenth Century By the middle of the eighth century, Silla was in decline. In 780 the king was assassinated, and revolts led by various pretenders threatened to leave the country unstable for some time to come. Among the most restive members of Silla society were the merchants, who, like their counterparts in China, were aware of their growing economic power, though sensitive to the fear and contempt in which they were held by the Confucian-influenced aristocracy and bureaucrats.

One such merchant, Wong Kon (d. 943), subdued the crumbling kingdom and reconstituted it as Koryo—from which comes the name "Korea." The Chinese imperial model of state formation proved attractive to Wong, who, after the practice of Chinese emperors, was accorded a posthumous reign name, Taejo. He moved the capital to Kaesong, where he laid out a city in the grid pattern of the Tang capital of Chang'an and adopted Chinese-style bureaucratic and tax systems, with military and labor conscription. Koryo even built its own version of the Great Wall near the Yalu River as a barrier to the nomadic peoples to the north (see Map 13.3).

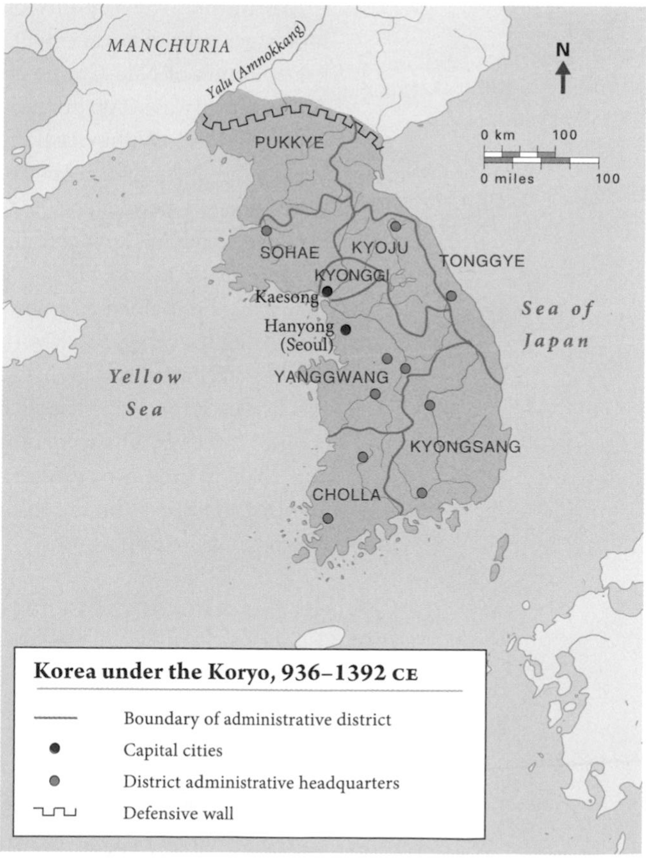

MAP 13.3 Korea under the Koryo, 936–1392.

By the middle of the thirteenth century, Koryo, like much of the rest of Asia, had begun to feel the power of Mongol expansion. In 1231, with rockets, bombs, and assorted other new military items acquired from their wars with the Chinese and the Jurchen state of Jin, Mongol forces laid siege to Kaesong. The fall of the city inaugurated four decades of irregular warfare against the occupiers and forced the withdrawal of the government to the south. The Mongols' imperial ambitions prompted the deportation of perhaps 250,000 Koreans as slave laborers to other parts of the Mongol Empire, beginning in 1254. After the Koryo court finally capitulated in 1259, the Mongols intermarried and assimilated to Korean culture. As in most of the occupied areas of Eurasia, the advantages brought by Mongol unity in terms of easier travel and transport and increased public works were eclipsed in Korea by the cruelty of the conquest itself, the widespread perception of misrule, and oppressive taxation.

In 1368, the Mongol Yuan dynasty in China was overthrown by the forces of the soldier–monk Zhu Yuanzhang, who inaugurated the Ming dynasty (1368–1644). As had nearly every previous dynasty, the Ming laid plans to invade Korea. In 1388 the Korean leader Yi Song-gye made the strategic decision not to resist the Ming but moved against the Korean court instead, founding the Yi Dynasty in 1392 and resurrecting the name of Choson for the new state. The Yi proved to be Korea's final imperial dynasty, ruling until the peninsula was annexed by Japan in 1910. The Yi concluded a diplomatic–commercial agreement with China that formed the heart of what is often, though somewhat erroneously, referred to as the Ming "tribute system" (see Chapter 21).

Meanwhile, the Yi polity once again adapted to Chinese-style institutions. The highly centralized governmental structure of the Ming was echoed in Choson, and the adoption of Neo-Confucianism slowly began to drive out older local customs. A new capital was set up on the site of present-day Seoul, and the state was divided into eight provinces. Within each of these, the Chinese model of prefectures and districts was followed. A uniform law code was later promulgated in 1485, calling for, among other things, a permanent hereditary class structure. The Confucian exam structure was also broadened to include a two-tiered official class, the *yongban* and *chungin*.

Yet, for all the advantages created by the new class structure, old cleavages in many cases remained and new unanticipated ones soon developed. As a means of stabilizing the *yongban* class (and, so it was assumed, society as a whole), the Yi rulers made large land grants to the great officials of the kingdom. These landholders, however, tended to use such grants to amass more and more local power. Unlike Chinese officials, who were moved from place to place to avoid just this, they tended to remain in their own territories, where they could use a host of informal controls to resist attempts from the throne to rein in their excesses. Over time, many became like regional rulers.

Economy, Society, and Family

Like their counterparts in China, rulers and government officials in the various Korean kingdoms tended to be preoccupied with recurrent problems of landlordism and tenancy, land reform, and maintenance of local infrastructures—especially in wet rice-producing areas—and alleviating want during times of shortage.

Land Reform At various times, therefore, those under Chinese influence proposed schemes of land redistribution based on the Chinese "well-field" model (see Chapter 4). More ambitious was the *chongjon* system of Silla, begun in 722. Following a combination of Buddhist and Confucian precepts and with an eye to local custom, the *chongjon* system mandated a government-sponsored distribution of land, with taxes paid in kind. Additionally, peasants were instructed to develop specialized cash crops or engage in small-craft manufacture. A prime example was the planting of mulberry trees as food for silkworms and the development of sericulture.

Under the Yi dynasty of Choson, the implanting of Neo-Confucian values in the countryside as well as among elites became a prime consideration. For example, a new system of land tenure was made part of a more general stabilizing of all classes. Peasant rents were fixed at half the crop, and a hierarchy of village headmen, bureaucrats, and magistrates similar to that of the Chinese system was set up to collect taxes, settle disputes, and dispense justice.

As noted previously, the institution of Chinese systems in Korea tended to attract the elites more than the peasant and artisan classes. Their spotty success in taking root tended in many ways to aggravate societal tensions, despite the governmental efficiencies they created. One factor in this was a repeated attempt on the part of the bureaucracy to enhance its power at the expense of the merchant and artisan classes. In the countryside, power remained in the hands of the landholder aristocracy, which tended to ensure that the peasants would be bound to them in a fashion not unlike the serfdom of their European contemporaries.

Neo-Confucian Influence Particularly in the cities, the high level of Song Chinese–influenced material culture was increasingly evident by the eleventh and twelfth centuries. Interregional trade was brisk, and Korea's position at the center of the East Asian Buddhist world made it a trade and pilgrimage crossroads. Korean artisans became highly proficient in the new technologies of porcelain making and book printing; many of the oldest Chinese, Korean, and Japanese works extant were printed by Korean publishers.

Under the Yi, the Confucian exams became more open, though the new social arrangements called for two official classes, the *yongban*, or scholar-gentry, drawn from high civil and military officials, and the *chungin*, or minor officials. Below these were the *yangmin*, commoners of different professions as well as peasants and serfs, while the lowest group, the *chonmin*, consisted of bond slaves, laborers, and prostitutes.

Though approximating the class structure in China, the new system was more like the composite one created in Heian Japan. As in Japan, it proved a troublesome fit, particularly in remote rural areas. Though the Confucian exams theoretically allowed for some degree of social mobility, they tended to be monopolized by the *yongban*. The institution of hereditary classes, intended to create a stable and harmonious social structure, instead concentrated wealth in the hands of the rural gentry, who often lacked a proper Confucian sense of the official responsibilities of their positions. In many places, the older patterns of aristocratic local power simply continued with only cosmetic changes. Thus, by the end of the fifteenth century, the divide between the wealthy, educated, sophisticated capital and large provincial cities and the tradition-bound countryside was steadily increasing.

Women and Society Until the arrival of Confucian institutions in the Korean countryside, local village life, as in Vietnam and Japan, tended toward more egalitarian structures, especially between men and women, than would later be the case.

In Korea, this egalitarianism retained a remarkable vitality in the face of Neo-Confucian precepts. Even today, there is far less of the traditional emphasis on filial piety and patriarchal custom than in China. Until the sixteenth and seventeenth centuries, for example, bilateral and matrilocal marriage patterns tended to be the norm. As in Japan and Vietnam, the communal and meticulous nature of rice agriculture tended to lessen the division between "male" and "female" work roles and made women and girls more equal partners in local rural society. Women's property and inheritance rights, far more expansive than in Confucian China, also reflected this.

Under the Neo-Confucian reforms of the Yi, however, some of these practices began to change. The idea of strictly delineated gender roles, of men dominating in the "outer" world and women being preeminent in the "inner" world of the home—long a staple among the urban elites and official classes—now became a cornerstone of moral training in rural academies and in the home.

Religion, Culture, and Intellectual Life

A Korean Foundation Myth

As with many peoples of north and central Asia, early Korean religion appears to have been nature-spiritual. One could appeal to the spirits through shamans or animals believed to have certain powers. Like Shinto in Japan, these beliefs continued at the local level for many hundreds of years after the introduction of more formalized systems. The invasion of the Han brought the Chinese concepts of heaven, earth, and humankind along with the imperial rituals associated with them. Of more long-term importance, however, was the introduction of Buddhism to the Three Kingdoms during the fourth century CE.

Korean woodblock printing of the *Tripitaka*, 1251 CE

Buddhism, Printing, and Literacy All the Korean kings seized to varying degrees on the combination of Buddhism, Han Confucian political and moral philosophy, and their supporting institutions as a way to enhance the material and ethical foundation of their states. In Silla, for example, the court pursued a course of striving for Buddhist "perfection." It patronized a popular Buddhist–Confucian society, Hwarang—the "Flower of Youth Corps"—that helped to build the 210-foot Hwang Nyonsu Temple in 645. Others sponsored mammoth publication projects of Buddhist works: Koryo produced a version of the *Tripitaka* printed on 80,000 hand-carved woodblocks as an act of piety and supplication during the war with the Mongols. All of this tended to expand the relatively high level of functional literacy in written Chinese among Korean elites. As a result, twelfth-century Korea developed into one of the world's handful of centers of printing and publishing due in large part to the demand for Buddhist works. By the 1100s as well, publishers were employing what may have been the world's first movable, cast-metal type (see "Patterns Up Close: Printing").

Han-gul: Korean phonetic script, introduced in the middle of the fifteenth century.

Korea's leading role in world literacy in the preindustrial era received a further boost during the reign of King Sejong (r. 1418–1450). Here, the development of the Korean phonetic script ***han-gul***, like the use of *kana* in Japan, made the introduction of writing much simpler and closer to the vernacular than literary Chinese. Yet, like *kana* in Japan, it also tended to create a two-tiered system of literacy: Chinese tended to remain the written medium of choice among the highly educated and largely male elites, while *han-gul* became the written language of the commoners and, increasingly, women. One of the best examples of this is the anonymous, autobiographical *Memoirs of Lady Hyegong,* written in the eighteenth century.

Such divisions notwithstanding, however, the explosion of vernacular literature—satires on *yongban* manners, social criticism, fiction, advice manuals for a variety of tasks—all contributed to Korea attaining, with Japan, some of the highest levels of functional literacy in the preindustrial world.

Consonants \ Vowels	ㅏ (a)	ㅑ (ya)	ㅓ (ŏ)	ㅕ (yŏ)	ㅗ (o)	ㅛ (yo)	ㅜ (u)	ㅠ (yu)	ㅡ (ŭ)	ㅣ (i)
ㄱ (k,g)	가	갸	거	겨	고	교	구	규	그	기
ㄴ (n)	나	냐	너	녀	노	뇨	누	뉴	느	니
ㄷ (t,d)	다	댜	더	뎌	도	됴	두	듀	드	디
ㄹ (r,l)	라	랴	러	려	로	료	루	류	르	리
ㅁ (m)	마	먀	머	며	모	묘	무	뮤	므	미
ㅂ (p,b)	바	뱌	버	벼	보	뵤	부	뷰	브	비
ㅅ[1] (s,sh)	사	샤	서	셔	소	쇼	수	슈	스	시
ㅇ[2]	아	야	어	여	오	요	우	유	으	이
ㅈ (ch,j)	자	쟈	저	져	조	죠	주	쥬	즈	지
ㅊ (ch')	차	챠	처	쳐	초	쵸	추	츄	츠	치
ㅋ (k')	카	캬	커	켜	코	쿄	쿠	큐	크	키
ㅌ (t')	타	탸	터	텨	토	툐	투	튜	트	티
ㅍ (p')	파	퍄	퍼	펴	포	표	푸	퓨	프	피
ㅎ (h)	하	햐	허	혀	호	효	후	휴	흐	히

The Conventions and Alphabet of *Han-gul*. As originally given by King Sejong in his 1446 *Hunmin chong-um* ("Proper Sounds to Instruct the People"), *han-gul* contained 28 syllables. These have now been reduced to 24, with five double consonants and the additional vowels shown. The ease of learning the system is such that Korea has one of the highest levels of literacy in the world.

Japan to 1450: Selective Interaction and Adaptation

Of all the places we have examined in East and South Asia thus far, Japan raises the most exciting questions about the effects of relative isolation. Like Britain, Japan's geographical position allowed it to selectively interact with and adapt to continental innovations, experimenting, refining, and occasionally abandoning them as needed. Indeed, having never experienced a successful invasion, Japan's acculturation was almost completely voluntary, a characteristic unique among the societies of Eurasia.

The Island Refuge

Japan's four main islands, Honshu, Hokkaido, Kyushu, and Shikoku, are varied in climate. The northernmost island of Hokkaido has cold, snowy winters and relatively cool summers; the central island of Honshu, bisected roughly north to south by substantial mountain ranges, has a temperate to subtropical climate on the eastern side—where it is moderated by the Japan Current—and a colder, more continental climate to the west of the mountains on the side facing Korea and northeastern China. The small southern island of Shikoku and the southernmost island of Kyushu have an abundance of warm, moist weather and are largely governed by the Pacific monsoon system (see Map 13.4).

The Limitations of the Land The formation of Japan's islands from volcanic activity means that only about one-fifth of the territory has historically been arable. In the narrow plains and valleys, however, the majority of which are on the temperate Pacific side of the mountains, the soil is mineral rich and the rainfall abundant. But the islanders from early on have also had to face the limitations of the land in supporting a steadily growing population. Like the Korean peninsula, the ruggedness of the land tended to force its people to live in politically isolated, culturally united communities. Thus, communication by water was often the most convenient method, both among the Japanese home islands and across the 100-mile strait to southern Korea.

Adaptation at Arm's Length: History and Politics

Like those of the first peoples to inhabit the Korean peninsula, the origins of the Japanese are obscure. Two distinct groups appear to have migrated to the islands from the Asian mainland via Ice Age land bridges, perhaps 10,000–20,000 years ago. Their descendants, the Utari, are today regarded as Japan's aboriginal peoples and referred to by the Japanese as *Ainu,* the "hairy ones," or in early imperial times as *Emishi.* Their physical features, tribal hunting society, and language mark them as

Patterns Up Close

Printing

The Korean Printing Industry. Because of its position as the northern crossroads of the Buddhist and Chinese literary world, Korea was a major center of printing. Printing with carved wooden blocks had been developed during the eighth century, and large publishers and academies kept great numbers of them on hand. The most famous was this storehouse, which still preserves the 80,000 blocks of the Tripitaka, carved between 1237 and 1257.

While the invention of the printing press and movable type is widely recognized as having revolutionized the intellectual life of early modern Europe, it is equally true that these developments seven centuries earlier in East Asia had a similar effect. Yet, in many respects, the consequences of these innovations were different because of the requirements of the languages and the technical media with which printers in China, Korea, Japan, and Vietnam worked. As in other places, the cultural patterns of handwriting and calligraphy as artistic skills necessary for elites to cultivate in order to complete their aesthetic and moral development also hampered the spread of printing to some degree. Yet, for all these differences, by the fourteenth century the societies of East Asia still achieved the highest preindustrial literacy rates in the world. These would be unmatched in Europe until centuries after the use of printing had become widespread there.

By the fall of the Han dynasty in 220 CE, we have the earliest remnant examples of wood-block printing. Printers carved single- or double-page blocks of text on book-sized boards, inked them, and pressed the cloth or paper pages on them to get their copies. The boards could then be shaved down and carved again as needed. By the eighth century the Chinese had also begun to experiment with copper movable type inserted vertically into standardized rows in a system very much like the one Gutenberg devised centuries later. But, ironically, these presses remained more curiosities than practical devices for printing a variety of documents. Here, the chief problem was the nature of the Chinese written language—and, at this time, the written languages of Korea, Japan, and Vietnam as well.

distinct from the later arrivals. Details of their religious practices and recent DNA typing have led some anthropologists to link them to the peoples of central Asia, Siberia, and the Americas.

The later inhabitants may have originally come from the peoples who migrated into Southeast Asia, Indonesia, and eventually the central Pacific. They may also have been descended from later Polynesian travelers and later migrants from the Asian mainland. Linguistic evidence suggests a very tenuous connection to Korean and even to the Altaic language family. Japan's long linguistic isolation, however, renders its ultimate origins obscure at the present time.

Microlith: A very small blade made of flaked stone and used as a tool, especially in the Mesolithic era.

Matriarchal: A social system in which the mother is head of the family.

Matrilineal: Relating to, based on, or tracing ancestral descent through the maternal line.

Jomon and Yayoi Japan's prehistory, which lasted from ca. 10,000 BCE down to 300 BCE, has been designated by archaeologists as the Jomon period. While pottery fragments at some sites have been dated to as early as 14,500 BCE, the most distinctive artifacts are of somewhat more recent vintage: lightly fired clay vessels marked with a unique horizontal herringbone pattern and often fanciful decorations, clay female figurines called *dogu,* and phallic symbols called *bo.* Others include a wide assortment of **microlith** items: arrowheads, spear points, tools made of bone and antler, and nets and fishhooks. **Matriarchal** and **matrilineal** clans appear to have dominated society, clustered mostly near the sea or slightly inland. Because game was increasingly limited on the islands, fishing and harvesting seaweed were the major forms of subsistence. As among the American peoples of the Pacific Northwest, the

Unlike the English alphabet with its 26 letters, literary Chinese has thousands of different characters. It was simply impractical for typesetters to cast adequate supplies of even the most common characters, organize them, and sort through them to compose the text to be copied. It was far less work to just carve the text blocks from scratch, especially of popular works that would be widely copied and circulated.

In this case, one of the chief catalysts for printing was the growing popularity of Buddhism throughout East Asia. As would be the case centuries later with the spread of religious tracts during the Protestant Reformation, the desire of Buddhists to read scriptures and the openness of the various schools to all classes proved a stimulus to literacy, though in practical terms only those with considerable leisure could master the literary Chinese of the scriptures. Still, by the fourteenth century, the pattern of woodblock printing as a major industry in East Asia, with printing centers in the major cities of China, Japan, and Korea, has been seen by a variety of scholars as one of the hallmarks of early modernity centuries before that term is applied to Europe.

Questions

- How did the innovation of wood-block printing facilitate the spread of Buddhism throughout East Asia?
- What does the use of *han-gul* script in Korea say about the relationship between literacy and state formation?

bounty of the sea and forests enabled substantial settled village life to develop in the absence of an early agricultural revolution.

During the final half-millennium before the Common Era, increased intercommunication among Japanese, Koreans, and some members of the Late Zhou Chinese coastal states laid the groundwork not only for the introduction of agriculture to the Japanese islands but for an almost simultaneous Bronze Age as well. During the last centuries of the Jomon period, it appears that some of the grain crops of northern Asia (such as millet) found their way to the islands. During a 600-year period designated Yayoi (300 BCE–300 CE), imported and domestically manufactured bronze and iron articles appeared. The fertile plains of southern Honshu and Kyushu also saw the cultivation of northern Eurasian vegetables and fruits and, most significantly, rice. The swiftness of these changes was in part because of the dislocations resulting from the creation of China's first empire in 221 BCE and the influx of Korean refugees in the wake of the initial Chinese invasion of Korea.

Jomon Jar and Yamato Sharinseki Disk. The distinctive herringbone pattern and flared top mark this pottery as Middle Jomon, perhaps 5,000–6,000 years old. The disk made of finely worked steatite was taken from a third-century CE *kofun* burial mound in central Japan. It may be related as a religious object to similar kinds of ornaments found in China.

As it had in other areas of Asia, the rice revolution not only allowed the development of larger populations in Japan but also demanded them for efficient cultivation. The movement away from fishing and gathering combined with the efficiency of metal tools and weapons also fostered state formation among the larger and more

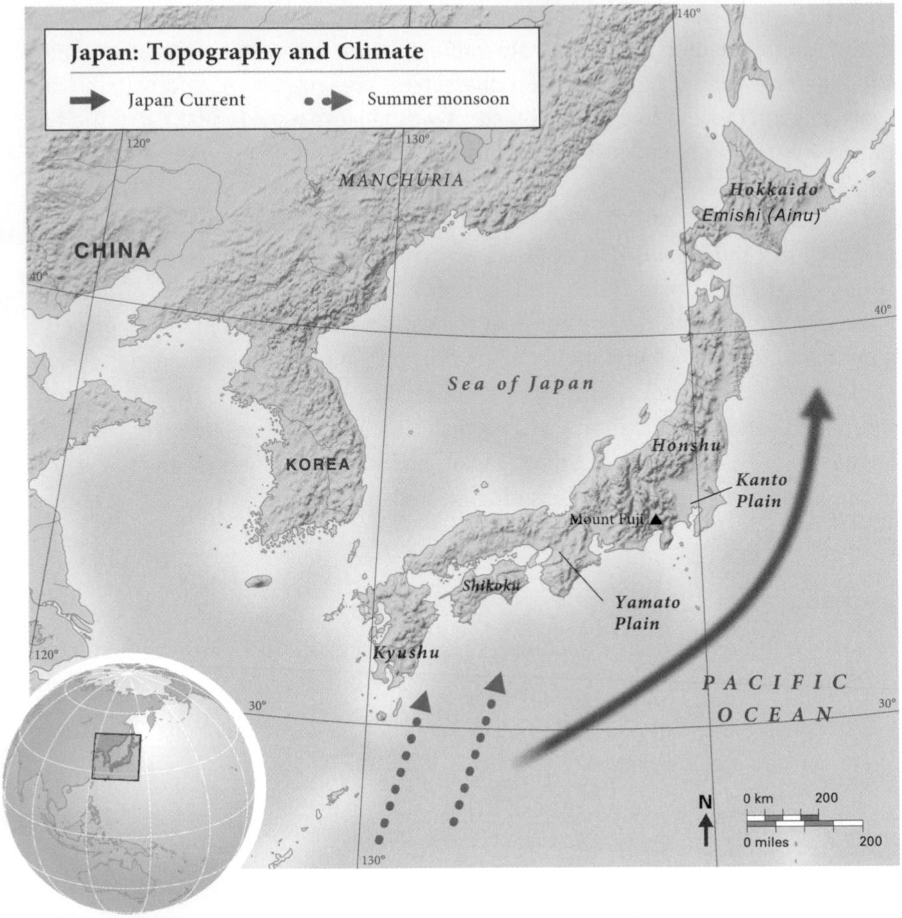

map analysis

MAP 13.4 Japan: Topography and climate.

powerful clans, or *uji*. The role of the new technologies is witnessed by the items included even now in the imperial regalia at the Shrine of Ise in southern Honshu: a jewel, a bronze mirror, and an iron sword, all of which date from about 260 CE. Thus, sometime after 250 CE, Japan's first fully evolved state, Yamato, centered on the Kanto Plain near modern Tokyo, emerged and quickly expanded, absorbing its weaker rivals on Honshu. Japan's first monumental architecture, enormous burial mounds called *kofun,* date from this period.

Toward the Imperial Order While the nature of rulership in Japan is still obscured by myth, the earliest written records describing the islands were composed by Chinese chroniclers in 57 CE. In 297 CE, we have the first mention of the Yamato state, though, characteristically, the writers considered their subjects scarcely civilized.

Although there had been steady diplomatic and cultural contact back and forth across the Sea of Japan from the first century CE, a particularly high level was reached during the later sixth century CE. In 552, tradition has it that Buddhism was introduced to the islands from Paekche. With it came the Chinese writing system and written works of every description. A decade later, in 562, the Korean kingdom of Silla eliminated the Japanese colony of Kaya on the peninsula, precipitating a new flow of refugees to Japan. As we have seen, the years from 589 into the early seventh century saw the rise of the Sui and Tang dynasties in China, resulting in yet more Chinese attempts to dominate the Korean kingdoms, and pushing the level of emigration to new levels.

The impact of these events on Yamato cannot be overstated. The growing power of China and Silla helped prompt the Soga *uji*'s Empress Suiko (r. 592–628) and her nephew, Prince Shotoku (ca. 573–621), to connect Yamato more firmly to the mainland and its conceptions of politics, culture, literature, and, ultimately, the imperial system itself. A few signposts along the way include the adoption of Buddhism as a state religion (594), the adoption of the Chinese lunar calendar for state record-keeping (604), and the adoption of the prince's 17-article constitution modeled on Confucian and Buddhist precepts (604).

But perhaps the most far-reaching changes came later in the century, with the *Taika*, or Great Reform, of 645. The systematic remaking of the Yamato regime along Chinese lines in the wake of the *Taika* marks the beginning of the imperial Japanese state—that is, of a kingdom bent on expansion over multiple political groups and clans. Among other things, Soga clan control of the court was overturned, and Fujiwara No-Kamatari, who emerged as adviser to the new emperor, Tenchi, ushered in a connection between his family and the imperial court that continued into the twentieth century. In less than a century the first Chinese-style imperial histories, the *Kojiki* (712) and *Nihongi* (720), were composed; the concept of the Mandate of Heaven was adopted to justify the overthrow of the Sogas; the emperor as the center of a hierarchical system of government run through a rigorously selected bureaucracy was institutionalized; and a census, uniform taxation on land and produce, and systems of conscription and labor service were enacted. The edicts mandating these changes were promulgated as the Taiho Code of 702, which remained the basis of Japanese law until the late nineteenth century.

selections from the *Taika*

Yamato's spiritual roots in Shinto, with its connection to the rhythms of nature and renewal, had dictated that the seat of the state be frequently moved. Even today, the sacred shrine at Ise is disassembled and rebuilt every 20 years. Because of the requirements of a far larger and more sophisticated system of government, however, it was decided that a permanent capital be built. The first site selected, at Nara, saw the creation in 710 of a close replica of the Tang capital at Chang'an, down to the axial boulevards, grids of streets, and propitious placement of temples and government buildings. In 794, a larger capital was completed nearby along the same lines called Heian-kyo, the future city of Kyoto. The era of imperial rule from this capital, which lasted until 1185, is thus often referred to as the "Heian" period (see Map 13.5).

Heian Japan As the imperial order penetrated all the Japanese home islands except Hokkaido and the widespread adoption of Buddhist culture connected Japan to an enormous, interconnected economic and cultural Asian sphere, Heian Japan increasingly became a land of contrasts, with local rumblings of discontent never far below the surface. For the elites of the capital and provincial administrative centers, life was not unlike that of their counterparts in Korea, Vietnam, or even China itself. The spread of literacy at the top and the common currency of Confucianism, Chinese literature, and the various Buddhist schools helped these elites see themselves as part of a cosmopolitan world, as did frequent travel for trade and pilgrimage. The latest fashions in poetry, literature, fine arts, calligraphy, music, and (to a lesser extent) clothing all found their way to court and beyond.

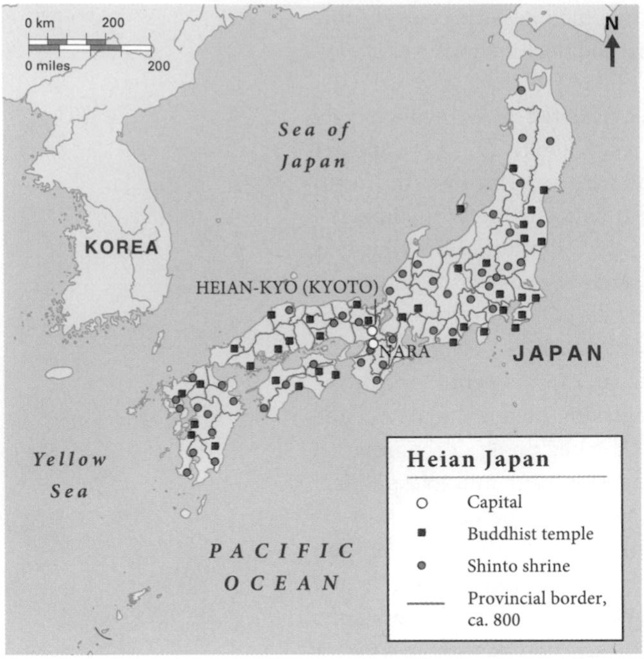

MAP 13.5 Heian Japan.

For the members of the new classes into which the vast majority of Japan's people had now been placed (peasants, artisans, and merchants—with Buddhist monks occupying an increasingly significant position in the hierarchy), many of the changes had been disruptive at best. Perhaps most tellingly, power, and soon military strength, was diffusing from the court and capital out into the countryside. This was particularly true in more remote regions where the most aggressive *uji* had assembled forces in support of their battles with the Eishi. The bureaucracy, a tenuous institution at best during the Heian period, became weaker as the local *uji* began to reassert power. This was given a considerable push in the wake of a virulent smallpox epidemic (735–737), during which the population may have been reduced by as much as one-third.

Despite court attempts to create a Chinese-style "well-field" system, tenancy became a chronic problem. In many cases, the *shoen*, or clan estates, were given tax-exempt status because of their military contributions. The estates of Buddhist monasteries were similarly exempt and provided social services and refuge for outcasts, in effect becoming shadow societies of their own. By the late eleventh century, perhaps half of the land in the empire had become exempt from taxes. As the countryside became more self-sufficient, the capital became more isolated—and more reliant on local military cooperation.

Japanese rice field survey, eighth century CE

In addition, the court itself was often divided by factional disputes, spurred by the practice of emperors abdicating but staying on as regents or advisers. Three decades of civil war between factions supporting the claims of the Taira clan and those pledged to the Minamoto, or Genji, finally ended in 1185 with the defeat of the Taira. Shortly thereafter, Minamoto Yoritomo was given the title Sei-i-tai **Shogun** (the "Great Barbarian-Suppressing General"), and the period of the **Shogunates** was inaugurated, lasting until 1867.

Shogun: The chief military official of Japan. The office was hereditary under the Tokugawa family from 1603 until 1867.

Shogunate: The government, rule, or office of a shogun.

Japan under the Shoguns Though the emperor at Kyoto theoretically remained in charge with the shogun as his deputy, the arrangement in fact hastened the drain of power from the capital. Because of its parallels to the political and social order in Europe at the time, the term "feudal" has sometimes been applied to this period. As we saw with the *fengjian* system in Zhou China, however, such similarities should not be pushed too far. In order to restore order in the hotbed of Taira opposition, Yoritomo set up his headquarters at Kamakura in 1192, several hundred miles from Kyoto near present-day Tokyo, beginning an interval known as the Kamakura shogunate, officially lasting from 1185 until 1333. The court itself remained the center of religious and ceremonial life as well as a forum for intrigue, but the real center of power now resided at the shogun's headquarters. Meanwhile, in 1274, the Mongols launched the first of two major attempts to invade Japan. Their first armada was defeated handily, while in 1281 a much larger second fleet was

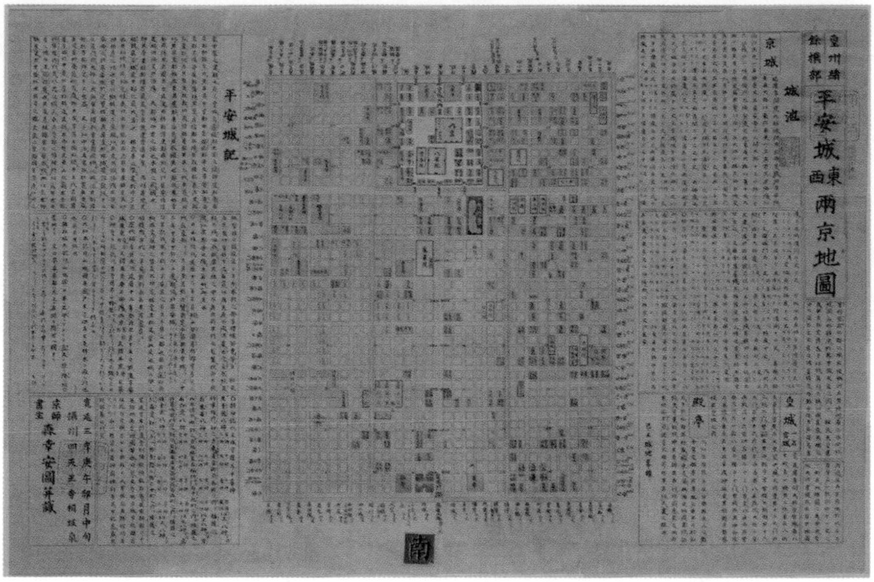

Plan of the Capital at Heian-kyo (Kyoto). The desire to copy the grandeur of Tang institutions extended even to city planning for the eighth-century Japanese court. The capital city at Heian was a faithful copy of the plan of the Tang capital of Chang'an, at the time one of the world's largest cities. The city grid was strictly laid out on a north–south axis, with the most important structures like the imperial palace placed in the northern section and their courtyards and main gates all facing south, the most propitious direction, indicated by the Chinese character highlighted in red at the bottom of the page, meaning "south." The placement of gardens and outlying structures was also carefully calculated according to Chinese notions of *feng shui* geomancy regarding trees, hills, and water.

smashed by a typhoon, known ever after by the Japanese as *kamikaze,* the "divine wind." Though the country was briefly roused to common action in the face of this threat, the dissipation of imperial power for the most part continued unabated.

Court life became even more ossified and formalized, while emperors very occasionally led unsuccessful attempts to reassert their own power. The most ambitious of these was the revolt by Emperor Go-Daigo in 1333. Securing the support of the powerful leader Ashikaga Takauji [ah-shee-KAH-gah tah-kah-OO-jee], Go-Daigo's faction was crippled when the opportunistic Ashikaga switched sides twice during the conflict. Ashikaga finally placed his own candidate on the throne, drove Go-Daigo into exile, and moved his headquarters to the Muromachi [moo-roe-MA-chee] district in northern Kyoto. For the first time in nearly 200 years, the seats of political and cultural influence were reunited in the same city (see Map 13.6). Even more important for the future of Japanese aesthetics and cultural institutions, the refinements of court life were now available to the warrior classes. There thus was born the union of *bu* and *bun,* the "dual way" of the sword and writing brush. The patronage of the *daimyo,* or regional lords, and their retainers, the **samurai**, ensured steady development of the Chinese-inspired arts of painting, poetry, and calligraphy, while the introduction of Zen and tea in the twelfth century forged an armature of discipline in both the martial and courtly arts that helped to foster the preservation of both for centuries to come.

Samurai: A Japanese warrior who was a member of the feudal military aristocracy.

While the aesthetic refinement of the warrior classes proceeded, the size and scope of warfare itself grew larger and ever more deadly. As with the codes of chivalry current in Europe at this time, *daimyo* and samurai prided themselves on acting according to a strict system of loyalty and honor, *bushido,* the "Way of the Warrior." A samurai was expected to be not just expert with sword and writing brush but unswervingly loyal to his *daimyo* to the point of death. Indeed, the tradition of *seppuku* or *hara-kiri*—ritual suicide—developed originally as a way to show one's "sincerity" and disdain for death and capture on the battlefield. One was also expected to show honor and respect to one's opponents, and tales abound from the period of warriors perfuming their helmets and decorating themselves so that whoever killed them

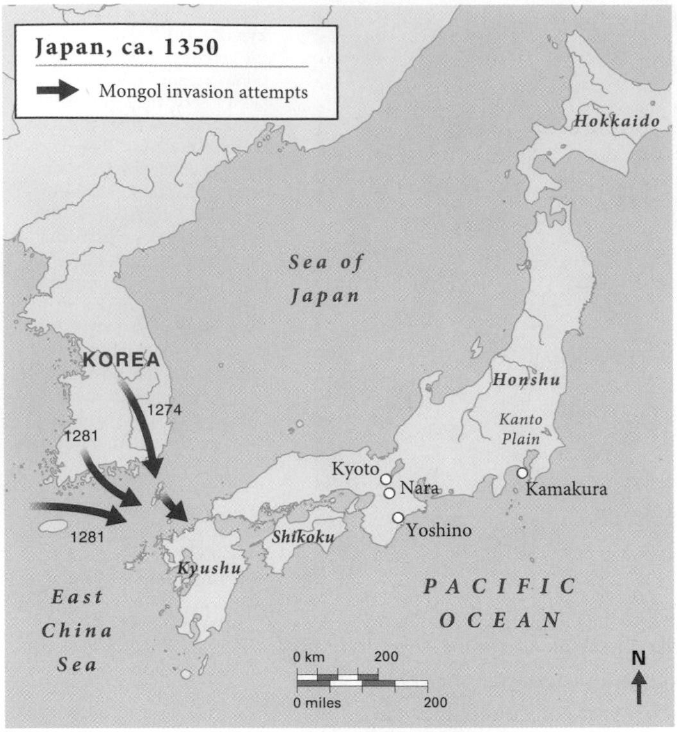

MAP 13.6 Japan, ca. 1350.

would have a tolerable aesthetic experience amidst the gore of the battlefield.

By the fifteenth century, however, these personal touches were giving way to armies increasingly dominated by massed ranks of infantry, in some cases ballooning into the hundreds of thousands of men. By the middle of the following century, the adoption of firearms and accompanying advances in fortification made Japan perhaps the most heavily armed country on earth. The fluidity of the military situation had major social consequences as well, and by the middle of the sixteenth century it was increasingly possible for commoners to rise through the ranks and become commanders and even *daimyo*.

One important reason for these conditions was the chronic instability of the Ashikaga shogunate. The position was never intended to be hereditary and was always the subject of *daimyo* intrigue both in Kyoto, where manipulation of the emperor was vital in order to achieve favor, and in the countryside, where power had become increasingly concentrated. In 1467, factional struggles would finally erupt into all-out war for 10 years, the effects of which would last more than a century.

Economy, Society, and Family

The real beginning of the diversification of Japan's economy came with the Yayoi period, beginning around 300 BCE. As the early Japanese communities adopted wet rice and vegetable agriculture they gained the ability to sustain a sedentary population, which would prove crucial for assimilating new technologies and allowing the concentration of power for state formation. The limited amount of arable land also meant that the populations of the few large open areas like the Kanto Plain were in an advantageous position to subdue their less numerous neighbors. In addition, they were better able to adopt technologies like bronze and iron making, silk weaving, and so forth that required an increasingly complex infrastructure. By the high point of the Yamato period, therefore, one finds Chinese accounts describing an economy that seems to resemble that of the Chinese or Korean countryside, with the majority of inhabitants engaged in agriculture and identifiable merchant and artisan classes coming into view.

The New Economy The introduction of Chinese writing, concepts of law, and Buddhism during the sixth century allow historians to view in far greater detail the workings of the Japanese economy. By this point, nearly every domesticated plant and animal from the mainland suitable to the environment had been introduced to Japan, and the productivity of the island's agriculture would soon approach levels comparable to those in China and Korea. Like its counterparts on the mainland, the

Yamato court and its successors at Nara and Heian-kyo attempted to regulate economic activity in the form of land and produce taxes, taxes on trade, monopolies on strategic commodities, and requisitions of labor for infrastructural projects.

Yet almost from the beginning, as we noted earlier, these efforts at centralization were only partially effective. The larger *uji*, whose power had theoretically been cut by the creation of a state bureaucracy, got around the problem by supplying many of the officials for the new body. They took advantage of government incentives to reclaim land from the wilderness and the Ainu. By such means the large *shoen* holdings and monastery estates with their tax exemptions tended to acquire regional political and military power.

Such multiple centers also produced an increase in and decentralization of trade. The period from 1250 to 1450 saw cycles of expansion in overseas commerce, with colonies of Japanese merchants—and often Japanese pirates—operating in the Philippines, Java, and Malacca as well as Korea and China. Through their wares, the *daimyo* and samurai became increasingly sophisticated connoisseurs of luxury goods such as silks, jade, porcelain, lacquerware, rare woods, and books and paper. As the early ports, market towns, regional capitals, and, by the sixteenth century, castle towns, grew, Japanese craftspeople became adept at imitating and refining Chinese crafts, in some cases surpassing the quality of the originals. Moreover, a growing and increasingly diverse middle class of merchants, artisans, actors, dancers, **sake** brewers, shipbuilders, and others organized into trade guilds (*za*) all partook of such luxury items. The increased demand for capital among them spurred a monetization of the economy and the beginnings of banking and credit systems.

Japanese *Daimyo* Armor. This extraordinarily well-preserved torso armor and helmet is believed to date from the fourteenth century and may have belonged to the shogun Ashikaga Takauji (r. 1338–1358). The helmet is bronzed iron, while the cuirass is made of thousands of overlapping iron and lacquered leather scales held together in horizontal rows by means of rivets. The combination made for effective protection against swords and arrows while allowing considerable freedom of movement.

Sake: Traditional alcoholic drink brewed from rice.

Advances in Agriculture Most of this would not have been possible without dramatic increases in food production. The period from 1250 to 1600 saw a vast increase in both intensive cultivation of Japan's limited arable land and the introduction of a host of new crops to multiply its productivity. As it had throughout East Asia, the widespread use of fast-ripening Champa rice strains from Southeast Asia in southern Honshu, Kyushu, and Shikoku vastly enhanced stocks of this staple. In Kyushu it allowed three crops a year; in other areas, the wet paddy fields it required allowed dry raised beds for vegetables to be made from the soil taken out of the paddies. At the same time the introduction of the Chinese "dragon pump" (see Chapter 9) allowed for easy, small-scale irrigation. Finally, a triple-cropping system consisting of buckwheat in winter, wheat in spring, and rice during the monsoon, with vegetables grown on the raised beds in between fields, allowed an average family to sustain itself on only a few acres of land.

If one factors in the use of terracing and dry rice cultivation in more marginal areas and the introduction of oranges, grapes, and tea, the leaps in population seem almost inevitable. From an estimated population of about 5 million in 1100 a doubling occurred, perhaps as early as 1300; by 1450 it was on its way to doubling again.

Family Structure As in Korea, the earliest social structures of Japan appear to have been matrilocal and, most likely, matriarchal. *Uji* before the sixth century were organized around female lineages, and the first Chinese accounts mention semi-mythical figures such as Queen Pimiko. With the coming of Chinese institutions, however, this changed radically at the uppermost levels and more gradually below. As we have seen, during the early importation of Chinese influences in the sixth and seventh centuries, women at the top could still wield considerable political power, as witnessed by Empress Suiko of the Soga clan. By the height of the power of the Heian court, Confucian patriarchal institutions had made a great deal of headway in Japan but were moderated somewhat by the pervasive influence of Buddhism and Shinto. Thus, aristocratic women controlled property, though they increasingly tended to wield political power through men. They were sequestered at court and forced into a highly refined and regulated ritual life, yet they created their own highly influential cultural world. Women like Murasaki Shikibu and Sei Shonagon (ca. 965–1025) set the standards for literary and aesthetic appreciation for generations to come in *The Tale of Genji* and *The Pillow Book*, respectively.

Outside the court, the moderating institution for commoners, and particularly women, was the Buddhist monastery. As in China and Korea, the monasteries provided havens for women and men who did not marry or had fled bad marriages. They provided enough education to allow reading the sutras, thus helping to increase literacy. They also provided important avenues of political power as large landholders, innkeepers, peacekeepers, and advisers.

As in China and Korea, however, the family life of commoners was mostly governed by a mix of Confucian filial piety, local clan relations, and the desire to improve the family's position through marriage. As in China, girls came to be considered expendable because they would move in with their husband's family. Arranged marriages were the norm, and by way of forcing such issues, rape, kidnapping, and family vendettas were all too common. A woman who would not consent to such a marriage, for example, could evade it only if she fled to a monastery before the groom's relatives caught up with her. Failure to escape could result in a beating or even murder. Such informal sanctions eventually gave way under the Tokugawa shogunate to strictly regulated Neo-Confucian family codes enforced by the shogun's local officials.

Religion, Culture, and Intellectual Life

The foundations of Japan's original religion, Shinto, go far back into remote antiquity. Some scholars have used the word "vitalism"—akin to African spiritual practices and shamanism in Siberia and the Americas—to describe its common features: a deep-seated belief in the power of *kami*—spirits of divinities, beings living and departed, nature as a whole, and even inanimate objects like mountains and streams. Reverence for these forces extended early on to fertility and earthly vitality.

The importance of vitality was reinforced by a tremendous emphasis on ritual purity—as Chinese observers recorded nearly 2,000 years ago, the Japanese seemed to bathe constantly—and waterfalls were enormously popular as places of ritual ablution and even miracle working. On the other hand, death and corruption were things to be separated from as much as possible—hence the practice of distancing shrines from burial mounds.

The Way of the Gods Shinto means "the way of the gods," and Japanese mythology recognized a staggering array of deities. Chief among these were Izanagi and Izanami, whose initial sexual act created the Japanese home islands, as well as Amaterasu, the sun goddess, considered the ancestor of Japan's emperors, purportedly starting with Jimmu in 660 BCE. Until the emperor Hirohito officially renounced his divinity at the end of World War II, every Japanese emperor was considered a god in the Shinto pantheon by believers.

Although it had undoubtedly arrived some time before, the customary dating of the introduction of Buddhism to Japan is 552 CE, when the king of Paekche sent a collection of Buddhist scriptures as a present to Yamato. The new religion soon became well established among Japanese elites, and after four decades of struggle with the Shinto establishment at court, Buddhism had become the state religion of Yamato in 594. Both religious traditions, however, were ultimately able to coexist and, to some extent, fuse. The ability of Buddhism to adapt the cosmologies of other traditions to its core beliefs, along with its reverence for nature, emphasis on the transcendental, and lack of a priestly hierarchy, made it an easy fit for Shinto. For their part, Shinto believers could add the bodhisattvas and other Buddhist entities to the list of *kami*. Coupled with an already great admiration for things Chinese in Japan, such accommodations facilitated the spread of the religion.

Most of the schools of Buddhism established in Japan had first become popular in China. The first to establish itself at Nara was the Hosso school, based on the newly recovered texts brought back by the Chinese monk Xuan Zang from India. This was shortly displaced by the highly influential Tendai (from the Chinese Tiantai) school and the Shingon sect, which dominated the imperial court for most of the Heian period.

As noted in Chapter 9, for Tendai followers, the most important scripture was the Lotus Sutra, which includes the key revelation that all beings possess a "Buddha nature" and, hence, the potential for salvation. Esoteric Buddhism, on the other hand, placed more emphasis on scriptural study and aesthetics. For both, the degree to which one can grasp the central truth varies according to the capacity of the individual to study and contemplate it, but it is in theory open to all at some level. The popular devotional schools of Buddhism also came to Japan during the eighth and ninth centuries. Their simplicity and optimism—simply bowing repeatedly and calling on Amida Buddha with a sincere heart in order to be saved (*nembutsu*)—and the hope for a place in the Pure Land, or Western Paradise, ensured widespread adherence. Even today, as in China, it remains the most popular of the Japanese Buddhist schools.

excerpt from *The Tale of the Heike*

Though neither achieved widespread popularity, two other Buddhist schools deserve mention because of their influence. The first is a wholly Japanese development. Nichiren (1222–1282) advocated a Japan-centered, patriotic form of Buddhism. Japan, he believed, because of its unique history and centrality in the Buddhist world, had become the repository of "true" Buddhism in the present decadent age and must be defended at all cost, a view that he believed was confirmed by the miraculous Japanese deliverance from the Mongols.

Perhaps more influential was the practice of Zen. Again, the Chinese origins of this movement, known as *chan*, were introduced in Chapter 12. Arriving in Japan in the twelfth century, it spread among the *daimyo* and samurai, who had the discipline to pursue its rigors. Zen seeks to achieve *satori*, a flash of enlightenment signaling the recovery of one's Buddha nature. Everyone's path to this is different, so one must follow the instructions of an experienced master rather than engage in prolonged scriptural study. Zen practitioners seek to open themselves to enlightenment by lowly, repetitive tasks, contemplating paradoxes (koans) and, in some schools, sitting in meditation (*zazen*).

All of these practices can be useful to a warrior. Endless drilling with bow and arrow or sword to the point that the use of each weapon becomes instinctive certainly refines one's martial talents. Such an approach is equally useful in painting, poetry, and calligraphy, where a distinct Zen style of spontaneous, minimalist art

The Miracles of Kannon. Amida Buddhism was the most popular school throughout East Asia, and the most popular figure of the many bodhisattvas was Kannon (Guanyin in China). On this long-hand scroll dated to 1257, Kannon saves her followers from assorted tribulations: Here, she appears to two men set upon by soldiers or brigands.

suggesting the true inner nature of subject and artist is still a vital area of Japanese aesthetics today.

One final area in which Zen permeated the life of the warrior classes was in the use of tea. Introduced from China by the Zen monk Eisai (1141–1215), tea drinking in Japan became widely adopted as an aid to discipline and meditation among monks in the twelfth century. Soon, however, it became quite popular among the upper classes, and its presentation was ultimately refined into the ritual of the tea ceremony. Here, inside the teahouse where all were equal, under the movements prescribed by the sixteenth-century tea master Sen-no Rikyu (1522–1591), host and guest were to approach their encounter as if they were sharing their last moments together on earth. Since the ceremony was a popular preparation for battle among *daimyo* and samurai, this was often the case.

Forging a Japanese Culture With the importation of Chinese political theory to Japan came an understanding of the importance of histories and record-keeping. Thus, the first Chinese-influenced Japanese histories, the *Nihongi* (*Chronicles of Japan*) and *Kojiki* (*Records of Ancient Matters*), made their appearance during the early eighth century. At about the same time, the first collection of Japanese poetry published in Chinese, the *Man'yoshu* (*The Ten Thousand Leaves*) appeared in 760. This work, however, also illustrated the problems inherent in using Chinese characters as a method of rendering Japanese sounds.

The *Man'yoshu* uses one-syllable Chinese characters picked for their similarity to Japanese sounds and strings them together into Japanese words. If one can follow the *sounds* of the words, one can grasp the meaning of the poems; if, however, one attempts to read them based on the *meaning* of the characters, they become gibberish. This fundamental problem was solved by devising the *kana* syllabary, a system of 50 symbols that form the building blocks of Japanese words. By the late ninth century, a kind of social divide had arisen—as it did later with *han-gul* in Korea—between predominantly male, Buddhist, elite users of literary Chinese and literate women and members of the lower elites who favored the convenience of the *kana* system. As in China and Korea, the technology of printing greatly spurred the circulation of these works and over the centuries helped push functional literacy to some of the highest premodern levels in the world.

In addition to the development of the 31-syllable *tanka* poetry form, perhaps the most important literary developments to come from the use of *kana* were the novel and the prose diary. The former, as we have seen, is credited to Murasaki Shikibu, whose *Tale of Genji* is often considered the world's first novel. A skilled diarist as well, Murasaki was a tutor to the powerful courtier Fujiwara Michinaga, and she put all of her acute observations of the subtleties of court life into *Genji*. Seclusion for court women fostered a considerable amount of self-analysis, and one sees in Murasaki's writing a tension between Buddhist ideas and the requirements of place, name, reputation, and hierarchy at court.

Vietnam: Human Agency and State Building

For much of the twentieth century, the history of Southeast Asia was written according to the cultural divisions separating the areas influenced by China from those influenced by India. In the 1960s, however, this concept of a derivative "Indo-Chinese" history was challenged by scholars, who emphasized the similarities of the lived experience of the common people on both sides of the cultural divide. Of equal importance in this new approach was the *agency* of the people in question: their taking of the initiative in deciding matters of acculturation, political systems, and so forth. Our focus on the patterns of interactions and adaptations here is to explore the agency of people in their acceptance and rejection of certain influences and innovations.

The Setting and Neolithic Cultures

The topography of Southeast Asia as a whole is similar, from the borders of Assam in India to the Mekong delta in the south of what is now Vietnam. Divided by several major river systems—the Irawaddy, Salween, and Mekong—running roughly north to south, and by the Red River, running northwest to southeast through Hanoi and meeting the Gulf of Tonkin at Haiphong, the region is divided into watersheds separated by low to medium mountain ranges running generally parallel to them. Even today much of the region is heavily forested, with abundant rainfall supplied by the summer monsoon, which acts as the region's principal climatic regulator. The river valleys and coastal plains are believed to have supplied the wild ancestors of the first rice plants, as well as some of the world's first domesticated fowl sometime after 8000 BCE (see Map 13.7).

The Neolithic revolution appears to have taken place in Southeast Asia at about the same time as it did in southwest Asia. This *Hoabinhian culture* was characterized by the cultivation of root crops, millet, and rice and by about 6000 BCE saw the domestication of pigs and chickens. By 4500 BCE, the *Dongsan cultures* had emerged, marked shortly after by some of humankind's earliest bronze artifacts. The origins of these peoples are still obscure, with contemporary speculation centering on a homeland perhaps in southern China. Out of the fertile subtropical and tropical regions in which they settled, it is believed that the basics of wet rice agriculture and the domestication of chickens and pigs may well have diffused north into China and perhaps west to northern India.

Bride-price: Amount negotiated between the family of the groom and the family of the bride to be paid by the former to the latter in some marriage traditions, as compensation for the loss of her labor.

Village Society and Buddhism The earliest records of the peoples and states in the region are likewise fragmentary. Late Zhou Chinese references frequently mention the state of Yue, but its southern borders appear to have been fluid and probably included parts of the modern provinces of Guangdong and Guangxi and perhaps the northern part of Vietnam. Once more, the social structure suggests a village-based agricultural system in which women enjoyed far more equality than would later be the case. Villages and clans were often bilateral or matrilineal and matrilocal. Men paid a **bride-price** to the families of their wives, and divorce for either spouse appears to have been relatively easy. As in other places in East Asia during the first millennium BCE, women occupied roles as officials, diplomats, merchants, and small-business operators. The area also became one of the first outposts of Theravada Buddhism outside India through the efforts of missionaries from Ceylon (Sri Lanka) in the second century BCE. It would come to be the majority religion in the region for the next 2,000 years.

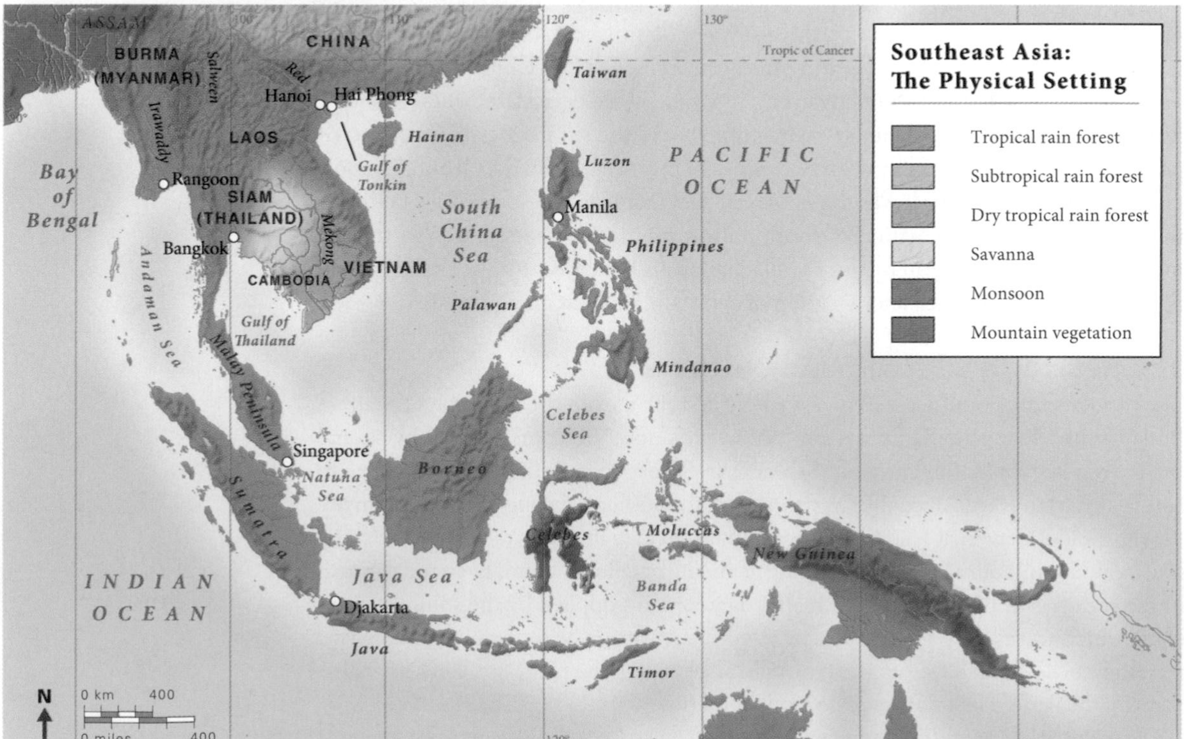

MAP 13.7 Southeast Asia: The Physical Setting.

The "Far South": History and Politics to 1450 With the unification of China under the Qin in 221 BCE, Yue was incorporated into the First Emperor's new state. Thus began a prolonged period of Chinese occupation and local resistance in the area, ultimately lasting over 1,000 years. As in Korea, the occupation brought with it a cultural invasion, including the full spectrum of Chinese writing, political ideas, and cultural preferences. Like their counterparts in Korea and Japan as well, the new Vietnamese literate elites were incorporated into the increasingly far-flung world of Chinese civilization and the Buddhist cultural and religious sphere. Southeast Asia's geographical position in the center of the maritime portion of this economic and cultural sphere encouraged a considerable openness to outside influences.

Sinicization and Resistance On the other hand, the repeated invasions from the north also encouraged a Vietnamese ethnic identity. The collapse of the Qin in the period 206–202 BCE encouraged a rebellion against the local Chinese officials of "Nam Viet"—the Vietnamese name for the Chinese *Nanyue* ("Far South"), as the Qin had called their new southern province. The Han emperor Wudi reoccupied northern Vietnam in 111 BCE, however, and swiftly reimposed Chinese institutions on the region.

Han attempts at sinicization raised tensions between the new Chinese-influenced elites and those who thus far had managed to retain their cultural independence. The situation was sufficiently volatile that in 39 BCE another rebellion began that to this day is commemorated as helping to form the modern Vietnamese national identity. Trung Trac, the widow of a local leader executed by the Chinese, and her sister Trung Nhi (both ca. 12–43) led their local militia and defeated the Han garrison, sparking a general revolt. The Chinese shortly regrouped, however, and overpowered the forces of the Trung sisters, who drowned themselves rather than be taken alive. For the next millennium, northern Vietnam would be firmly within the imperial Chinese orbit.

In the three and a half centuries following the breakup of the Han Empire in 220 CE, the region was able to gain a degree of political autonomy, but the power of Vietnam's sinicized elites continued to ensure their cultural loyalty to China. The growing regional power of the north allowed it to expand into the more Indian-influenced Buddhist kingdoms to the south. With the reunification of China under the Sui and Tang, the drive for Chinese political control of the region was taken up again—as with Korea—and the north was soon fully reincorporated into imperial China. During the political chaos following the fall of the Tang, however, the long-awaited opportunity for independence arrived again.

Independence Dinh Bo Linh, the first emperor of Vietnam, solidified his control of the region in 968. Though politically independent of China, Vietnam's new Li dynasty (1010–1225), long immersed in Chinese notions of Confucianism and statecraft, swiftly instituted Song-style institutions and created its own bureaucracy. Continuing what by now was a long-established pattern of expansion, the Li systematically pushed south during their two centuries of control.

With the fall of the Li dynasty, the Tran dynasty (1225–1400) soon faced the potent threat of the Mongols, who in 1280 subdued the Southern Song in China and formed the Yuan dynasty. The first Mongol attempt at invasion, in 1257, was mounted as the Mongols were busily reducing the last strongholds of the Southern Song. Once this was accomplished, the attempt was renewed in 1285 and again in 1287. The unsuitability of Mongol strategy and tactics and the stubborn resistance of the Vietnamese ultimately prevented further Mongol expansion and allowed the Tran to keep the dynasty intact.

Cultural and Political Conflict Even during the height of the Mongol threat, the Tran continued to push southward. Much of this drive was aimed at the state of Champa—the home of the fast-growing rice strains that would do so much to increase East Asian populations. Champa itself had ambitions to achieve regional dominance. Centuries before, in the complex interplay of political and cultural rivalries marking the region, the Vietnamese had expanded at the expense of Champa. Champa and the Khmers, heavily influenced by India, had briefly united to subdue another Indian-influenced state, the trading kingdom of Funan, in the 600s. A reconstituted Champa now represented not just a strong political threat but, as a Sanskrit, Hindu, and Theravada Buddhist state, a cultural rival as well. In the resulting war, the new Le dynasty of Dai Viet ("Great Viet"), founded in 1428 by Le Loi, decisively broke the power of the Chams in 1471. The remnants of their state were incorporated into Vietnam in 1720 (see Map 13.8).

Economy, Society, and Family

Since the Neolithic domestication of rice, Vietnam has been one of the world centers of wet rice cultivation. Perhaps 300 strains of rice were cultivated in northern Vietnam by the mid-fifteenth century, with yields running as high as 25 bushels per acre. Roughly 90 percent of the people were engaged in agriculture, a figure consistent with other East Asian agrarian-based societies. Like them, too, the rhythms of the agricultural year were governed by the monsoon cycle. During the long rainy season of the summer, rice, vegetables, and commercial crops such as hemp would be cultivated.

As in southern China and Japan, families could be sustained on relatively small amounts of land and required few complex tools beyond the treadle-powered "dragon pump" or a hand-cranked winnowing machine (see Chapter 9). Along with draft animals like water buffalo, these would often be held communally by clans within the *xa*, or village. Villages commonly consisted of raised, thatch-roofed dwellings, surrounded by a bamboo fence and centered on a shrine to the ancestral spirits.

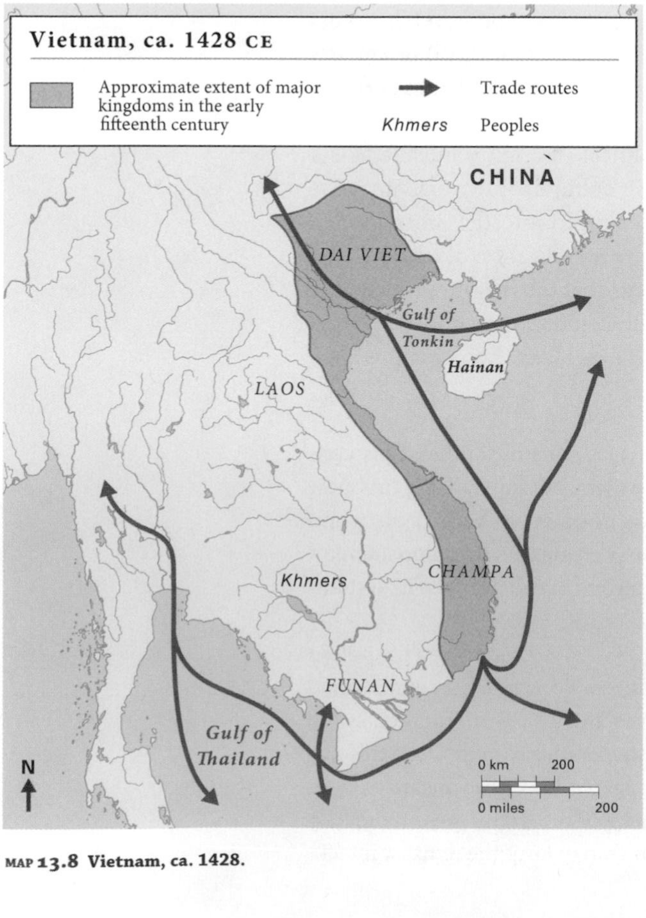

MAP 13.8 Vietnam, ca. 1428.

Politics, Labor, and Trade Two key political institutions kept order and acted as checks upon each other. The village headman, the *xa troung*, was elected but had to be approved by the imperial court, which, like its Chinese counterpart, ruled through a Confucian bureaucracy of provincial governors, prefects, and magistrates. The magistrate and his staff were the last official layer above the *xa troung*, so the headman had considerable power and responsibility at the local level. He collected the taxes and dues and sat with a council of notables. His powers, however, were checked by the council itself, which consisted of members of a scholar-gentry class much like that in China and who had to share in all major decisions, especially those regarding the use of communal land, about 20 percent of the total by the end of the sixteenth century. Thus, there was a balanced tension between the power of the central government and local interests. As in both China and Korea, however, the power of the local council often resulted in periods of increased landlordism and tenancy.

One legacy of the long period of Chinese occupation was the use of conscription and corvée labor by Vietnamese dynasties. Peasants were required to serve in the army 4 months per year—indefinitely during national emergencies. They could also be sentenced to slave labor for various offenses. In many cases, they would be sent to open up virgin land for agriculture, which would be theirs to keep upon the expiration of their sentences.

Changing Position of Women One pattern of history the Vietnamese shared with the other societies we have examined in this chapter is that of changes in the status of women over time. The nature of the agricultural work undertaken was communal, and men and women tended to work in the fields together. As in Korea and Japan, kinship lines were bilateral—traced through either spouse—or matrilineal. Here again, the long period of Chinese influence and Neo-Confucian emphasis on filial piety, hierarchy, and sharply separate roles for men and women eroded this equality somewhat, though much less markedly than in Korea or Japan. In the villages, or in the ports and market cities, women commonly exercised prominent roles as merchants, entrepreneurs, and craftspeople. This was reinforced by the prominence of the different Mahayana schools of Buddhism. Once more, as in China, Korea, and Japan, the role of the monastery for both men and women allowed a place for, and gave an education to, those who for whatever reason were on society's fringes. Buddhist nuns and abbesses thus wielded considerable power, though their positions were often at odds with the Confucian precepts of the elites. Still, women's rights to divorce and property ownership were upheld in the Neo-Confucian law code of 1460.

Religion, Culture, and Intellectual Life

Just as the Vietnamese struggled to maintain their political independence, they continually labored to develop their own cultural distinctiveness. While the porous border region with southern China and geographical and ethnic ties to other Southeast Asian peoples ensured a constant flow of influences, not all were readily absorbed, and some were played against each other.

Mahayana Buddhism Among the most important of these influences was that of religion. Whether the practice of ancestor veneration arrived with the Chinese or whether it was present before is as yet unsettled. Nearly all villages even into the twentieth century, however, had a shrine for a founding ancestor or famous headman where periodic ceremonies honoring him would take place. As in Korea, the coming of the Han emperor Wudi's armies in the second century BCE brought the imperial system of the Son of Heaven as intermediary between heaven and earth. At about the same time, however, Theravada was being established in the Indianized ports of Southeast Asia and became the first branch of Buddhism to be established there. Thus, as the Han retreat from the north allowed some political breathing space, the barest beginnings of Mahayana began to come into the area as well. For several hundred years, though, Indian-influenced Theravada dominated the religious and cultural life of Vietnam. Buddhist stupas were erected, and the austere, mendicant, saffron-robed monks held sway in northern Vietnam, as they still do in much of Southeast Asia.

Temple of Literature, Hanoi. The independent Vietnamese states, beginning with Dai Viet in 939, instituted Chinese-style examinations for their civil service. The Temple of Literature was the first national academy for Confucian training, founded in 1076. This building was the examination hall for those testing for the equivalent of the Chinese *jinshi*, or metropolitan degrees. The large Chinese characters, read right to left, carry the motto "A Pattern for Emulation Through the Ages."

The Tang occupation brought a large infusion of Mahayana influence with its vibrant art motifs, temples, and monasteries as well as the entire spectrum of Confucian and Daoist ideas. While Mahayana became the dominant division from this time on, the Vietnamese at the local level tended to pursue a synthesis of all of these systems in their beliefs. As in China, this collection was often referred to as *tam giao*, after the Chinese *san jiao*—"the three religions."

Similarly, the Vietnamese court sought to reconcile the differences among the systems by promulgating edicts on their compatibility. Indeed, some emperors sought to take a leading role in developing a unique strain of Vietnamese Buddhism. The later emperor Minh Mang (r. 1820–1841), for example, advocated combining the opposites of "abstention" from the world and "participation" in it.

Chu Nom During the fifteenth-century consolidation of Dai Viet, the Le dynasty undertook a thoroughgoing sinicization of the country, in much the same way as under the Yi in Korea. Chinese law codes and even dress were adopted. As in Korea and Japan, Chinese-style histories were also compiled and court-sponsored literary projects of various sorts commissioned. Yet here again, the literary language favored by the court for such projects continued to be the Chinese of the elites who had the time and means to undertake its study. As in Korea and Japan as well, an attempt was made to develop a vernacular writing system, in this case sometime during the tenth century. Called *chu nom* ("southern characters"), the new script combined existing Chinese characters picked for the similarity of their sounds to Vietnamese words with newly invented Chinese-style characters for meaning. It was similar in this respect to the formation of many complex Chinese characters but would in theory be easier to use as a tool for literacy. However, it never had the widespread circulation of *han-gul* or *kana* in Korea or Japan.

Putting It All Together

interactive concept map

While there are a great many commonalities among the patterns of state formation and religious interaction among the states along the outer ring of Chinese influence, each responded to that influence in its own way. From the beginning, each state sought to maintain its political independence, though all acculturated to some degree to Chinese models. Yet here it should be stressed that the relative attractiveness of those models was largely related to their usefulness in state building. That is, while the Koreans and Vietnamese struggled to throw off the Chinese political yoke, the systems and values of the invaders also gave powerful tools to the invaded, allowing them to organize their new regimes after they had won independence. In a sense, the invaders had provided a ready-made package of laws, moral codes, and social organization for the new states but also came with moderating institutions like Mahayana Buddhism. They were therefore equipped with a wide range of options to adopt or discard as the situation demanded. In that sense, the cultural intrusion was far more successful than the political one.

In the case of Japan, since the early Yamato state did not have Chinese traditions imposed on it from the outside, its leaders could afford to be more selective in what to adopt. However, the wholesale adoption of Chinese institutions proceeded even more quickly in Japan than on the mainland. Part of this may be attributed to the growing sense of the power that such institutions could provide to a government; part of it may also have been a growing sense on the part of the Japanese that states on the mainland based on these institutions were a potential threat. In essence, they felt they had to join them to avoid being beaten by them.

By the end of the fifteenth century, all three of these states were in the process of consolidating civilizations based to varying degrees on Chinese models and prominently including Neo-Confucianism and Buddhism among their governing traditions. They may therefore be considered part of the dominant trend toward the formation of religious civilizations, a pattern we have emphasized in Part 3 of this volume. However, given the specific adaptations to local conditions, the three states were quite different from each other and from China. For example, the Japanese role of *daimyo* as feudal lords and samurai as retainers would have been unthinkable in China, Vietnam, or Korea. Yet all four of these countries, faced with varying degrees of dislocation, foreign intrusion, or rebellion, would seek similar solutions to solve these problems.

Review and Relate

Thinking Through Patterns

Examine the ways historians approach the big questions of this chapter.

How was the history of Korea affected by its relations with China? With Japan?

The most obvious and dramatic way the various Korean kingdoms were affected by China was through conquest. Chinese culture and institutions were firmly planted in Korea during the Qin, Han, Sui, and Tang eras. In many respects this also prompted the Korean kingdoms to assert their political independence and to be discriminating about which Chinese institutions to adopt. Thus, Neo-Confucianism was adopted because of its use as a state-supporting ideology. Chinese writing, though quite useful as the means of acquiring the literature of China, ultimately yielded to the *han-gul* system as more convenient and user-friendly.

In the case of Japan, Korea's position was as a cultural intermediary and as a mainland target for conquest. Thus, during certain periods, Korea's status as a buffer between the two regional powers made its position precarious.

» Which important elements of Chinese culture were adapted by the Japanese for their own purposes? What advantages did Vietnam have over Korea and Japan in this regard?

In addition to the Bronze Age elements of wet rice cultivation and bronze implements—which moved Japan ultimately toward agrarian–urban society—the cultural elements, beginning with the Chinese writing system, were the most influential. With the writing system came ideas of government, ethics, philosophy, literature, and, of course, Buddhism. Unlike Korea and Vietnam, Japan acquired all of these more or less voluntarily and had the leisure to adopt them according to its own needs, rather than have them imposed by conquest.

» Which Japanese adaptations of Chinese institutions did not work well in Japan? Why?

While the Chinese writing system gave Japan a ready-made literature, the language itself was not well suited to the Japanese vernacular. Thus, by the 800–900s it had to be supplemented with the *kana* systems. But more serious was the less-than-perfect fit of the Chinese governmental structures with Japan's still clan-based society. Here, the cleavages developing during the Heian period would cause the social breakdown that resulted in the era of the shoguns, lasting until 1867.

» In what ways was the experience of Vietnam similar to that of Japan and Korea? How was it different?

Like Japan and Korea, much of Vietnam was influenced by the importation of Chinese culture, including Buddhism, the imperial system, and Confucianism. Like Korea, and unlike Japan, Vietnam suffered centuries of Chinese invasion and occupation. But Vietnam, positioned on the border with the Indianized states of Southeast Asia, also was influenced by Indian culture in its southern and western areas, causing interactions and adaptations that did not take place in the other states inside the Chinese sphere of cultural and political influence.

Against the Grain

Consider this as a counterpoint to the main patterns examined in this chapter.

Zen and Bushido

One seemingly counterintuitive development in the political and religious history of Japan is the marriage of a sect of Buddhism—an avowedly pacifistic belief system—to the warrior nobility of Japan, the *daimyo*, and their retainers, the samurai. As we have seen, there were in fact two sects, Zen and Nichiren Buddhism, that had martial associations.

But Nichiren Buddhism was centered on a kind of "Japanism" peculiar to Nichiren himself, and had its greatest influence during the time of grave national crisis precipitated by the Mongol invasions. Zen exercised a much deeper and longer-lasting effect, becoming the central religious practice of the warrior classes. The adoption by warriors of a pacifistic creed is not unique to Japan—one need only consider the history of Christianity to see some broad parallels. But Christianity, as the state religion of Rome and its successor empires and kingdoms, was the only approved religion for all classes. Zen was one of many competing variants of Buddhism available to Japanese warriors. So how does one account for its appeal?

Perhaps we may view it this way: While the overall tenets of Buddhism teach respect for all sentient beings, the duties of a warrior might induce one to extend the ideal of "nonattachment" to a state of indifference toward one's own life or death—and by extension to that of others. Moreover, the rigors of Zen training and practice are not unlike that of military training in some important respects: breaking down the ego by performing endless humbling tasks, being remade by strict discipline and constant repetition, and finally achieving a new "self" as a result of the long and rigorous training process. There is also an invaluable element of elitism in becoming one of the few who achieve the highest levels, though those who do reach them are expected to be extraordinarily humble in their bearing. Zen thus provides a carefully balanced harmony of opposites—the strict discipline to fight without regard for one's own safety on the battlefield, and in the process to transcend the self, reaching a state in which one is able to apprehend through extreme "mindfulness" the ultimate insights that bring the flash of enlightenment—*satori*. This condition of disciplined mindfulness extended to the aesthetic arts of poetry, painting, and calligraphy, providing the basis for yet another unity of opposites: the dual way of the sword and the writing brush unique to Japan.

- Are there other religions in Japan (such as Shinto) that might work equally well for warriors? Why?
- Is Japan unique in adapting a pacifistic religion for use by warrior classes? Can you think of ways that, for example, Christian warriors adapted their beliefs to support their profession?

Key Terms

audio flashcards

Altaic 372
Bride-price 392
Han-gul 378
Matriarchal 380
Matrilineal 380
Microlith 380
Samurai 385
Sake 387
Shogun 384
Shogunate 384
Striated 372
Syllabary 370

For additional resources, please go to **www.oup.com/us/vonsivers.**
Please see the Further Resources section at the back of the book for additional readings and suggested websites.

PATTERNS OF EVIDENCE |

Sources for Chapter 13

SOURCE 13.1 Murasaki Shikibu, *The Tale of Genji*

ca. 1000

The daughter of a minor noble in the court at Heian-Kyo in central Japan, Murasaki Shikibu (ca. 973–1025) created Japan's most popular work of fiction and one of the world's great literary masterpieces. *The Tale of Genji* (*Genji Monagatari*) is composed of acute observations of the subtleties of court life, and Murasaki focused particularly on the lives of women at court. Although the tale is ostensibly fictional, it reflects the era in which it was written, as the novelist strove to make the action in it plausible to the reader. In the process, she also crafted a compelling and compulsively readable story.

When he [Genji] returned to His Excellency's residence, sleep eluded him. Images of her [the Rokujō Haven, his love interest] as he had known her down the years ran through his mind, and he wondered in vain regret why she had taken such offense at each of his casual diversions, undertaken while he complacently assumed that she would eventually change her mind about him, and why she had persisted to the end in disliking him so. It seemed like a dream now to be wearing gray, and the thought that her gray would have been still darker if she had outlived him prompted,

> I may do no more, and the mourning I now wear is a shallow gray,
> but my tears upon my sleeves have gathered in deep pools.

Lord Fugen: A bodhisattva closely associated with the Lotus Sutra.

He went on to call the Buddha's Name, looking more beautiful than ever, and his discreet chanting of the scripture passage, "O **Lord Fugen** who seest all the manifest universe," outdid the most practiced monk's. The sight of his little son would start fresh tears for "the grasses of remembering" and yet without this reminder of her. . . . The thought gave him some comfort.

. . .

He now held the world and its ways, so distasteful already, in unqualified aversion, and he thought that without this fresh tie he would certainly assume the guise to which he aspired, except that every time his mind took this turn, he would straightaway start thinking how much his young lady in the west

---

Source: Murasaki Shikibu, *The Tale of Genji*, trans. Royall Tyler (Harmondsworth, UK: Penguin, 2001), "Heart-to-Heart" (Aoi), 178–179.

wing must miss him. He still felt a void beside him, however closely his women might gather around him while he lay at night alone in his curtained bed. Often he lay wakeful, murmuring, "Is autumn the time to lose one's love?" and listening, sick at heart, to the priests, whom he had chosen for their voices, calling the name of the Buddha Amida.

Oh, how sadly the wind moans as autumn passes! he thought as for once he lay alone and sleepless into a foggy dawn, but then a letter arrived on deep blue-gray paper, tied to chrysanthemums just now beginning to open and placed beside him by a messenger who left without a word. The delightful effect pleased him, and he noted that the writing was the Haven's.

> "Have you understood my silence? The sad news I hear, that a life can pass so soon, brings tears to my eyes, but my thoughts go first of all to the sleeves of the bereaved. My heart is so full, you know, beneath this sky."

Her writing is more beautiful than ever! He could hardly put it down, but her pretense of innocence repelled him. Still, he had not the heart to withhold an answer, and he hated to imagine the damage to her name if he should do so. Perhaps the lady he had lost had indeed been destined somehow to meet this end, but why should he have seen and heard the cause so clearly? Yes, he was bitter, and despite himself he did not think that he could ever feel the same about the Haven again.

After long hesitation, since the Ise Priestess's purification might well present another difficulty, he decided that it would be cruel not to answer a letter so pointedly sent, and he wrote on mauve-gray paper, "My own silence has indeed lasted too long, but although I have thought of you, I knew that in this time of mourning you would understand."

» Working with Sources

1. **What view of Japanese court life in the Heian period is revealed in this passage? How do the requirements of place, name, reputation, and hierarchy create tension for Genji?**
2. **What does the passage suggest about the religious beliefs and syncretism of Japanese society in this period?**

SOURCE 13.2 *Haedong kosŭng chŏn*, on Buddhism in Korea

ca. 1215

The *Lives of Eminent Korean Monks* is a compilation of biographies of Buddhist monks from the Three Kingdoms period of Korean history (first century BCE through the tenth century CE). It promotes Buddhist piety by

Source: "Pŭpkong Declares Buddhism the National Faith," in Peter H. Lee, ed. *Sourcebook of Korean Civilization*, vol. 1, From Early Times to the Sixteenth Century (New York: Columbia University Press, 1993), 75–77.

stressing the (often supernatural) deeds of these monks, and it is also a valuable source for Korean history. In spite of its importance, the work was long thought lost until portions of it were found at a Buddhist temple in the early twentieth century. This passage of the *Lives* deals with the introduction of Buddhism as the national faith of the Silla Kingdom in 527 CE, under King Pŏpkong.

The monk Pŏpkong was the twenty-third king of Silla, Pŏphŭng [514–540]. His secular name was Wŏnjong; he was the first son of King Chijŭng [500–514] and Lady Yŏnje. He was seven feet tall. Generous, he loved the people, and they in turn regarded him as a saint or a sage. Millions of people, therefore, placed confidence in him. In the third year [516] a dragon appeared in the Willow Well. In the fourth year [517] the Ministry of War was established, and in the seventh year [520] laws and statutes were promulgated together with the official vestments. After his enthronement, whenever the king attempted to spread Buddhism his ministers opposed him with much dispute. He felt frustrated, but, remembering Ado's devout vow, he summoned all his officials and said to them: "Our august ancestor, King Mich'u, together with Ado, propagated Buddhism, but he died before great merits were accumulated. That the knowledge of the wonderful transformation of Śākyamuni should be prevented from spreading makes me very sad. We think we ought to erect monasteries and recast images to continue our ancestor's fervor. What do you think?" Minister Kongal and others remonstrated with the king, saying, "In recent years the crops have been scarce, and the people are restless. Besides, because of frequent border raids from the neighboring state, our soldiers are still engaged in battle. How can we exhort our people to erect a useless building at this time?" The king, depressed at the lack of faith among his subordinates, sighed, saying, "We, lacking moral power, are unworthy of succeeding to the throne. The yin and the yang are disharmonious and the people ill at ease; therefore you opposed my idea and did not want to follow. Who can enlighten the strayed people by the wonderful dharma?" For some time no one answered.

In the fourteenth year [527] the Grand Secretary Pak Yŏmch'ok (Ich'adon or Kŏch'adon), then twenty-six years old, was an upright man. With a heart that was sincere and deep, he advanced resolutely for the righteous cause. Out of willingness to help the king fulfill his noble vow, he secretly memorialized the throne: "If Your Majesty desires to establish Buddhism, may I ask Your Majesty to pass a false decree to this officer that the king desires to initiate Buddhist activities? Once the ministers learn of this, they will undoubtedly remonstrate. Your Majesty, declaring that no such decree has been given, will then ask who has forged the royal order. They will ask Your Majesty to punish my crime, and if their request is granted, they will submit to Your Majesty's will."

The king said, "Since they are bigoted and haughty, we fear they will not be satisfied even with your execution." Yŏmch'ok replied, "Even the deities venerate the religion of the Great Sage. If an officer as unworthy as myself is killed for its cause, miracles must happen between heaven and earth. If so, who then will dare to remain bigoted and haughty?" The king answered, "Our basic wish is to further the advantageous and remove the disadvantageous. But now we have to injure a loyal subject. Is this not sorrowful?" Yŏmch'ok replied, "Sacrificing his life in order to accomplish goodness is the great principle of the official. Moreover, if it means the eternal brightness of the Buddha Sun and the perpetual solidarity of the kingdom, the day of my death will be the year of my birth." The king, greatly moved, praised Yŏmch'ok and said, "Though you are a commoner, your mind harbors thoughts worthy of brocaded and embroidered robes." Thereupon the king and Yŏmch'ok vowed to be true to each other.

Afterward a royal decree was issued, ordering the erection of a monastery in the Forest of the Heavenly Mirror, and officials in charge began construction. The court officials, as expected, denounced it and expostulated with the king. The king remarked, "We did not issue such an order." Thereupon Yŏmch'ok spoke out, "Indeed, I did this purposely, for if we practice Buddhism the whole country will become prosperous and peaceful. As long as it is good for the administration of the realm, what wrong can there be in forging a decree?" Thereupon, the king called a meeting and asked the opinion of the officials. All of them remarked, "These days monks bare their heads and wear strange garments. Their discourses are wrong and in violation of the Norm. If we unthinkingly follow their proposals, there may be cause for regret. We dare not obey Your Majesty's order, even if we are threatened with death." Yŏmch'ok spoke with indignation, saying, "All of you are wrong, for there must be an unusual personage before there can be an unusual undertaking. I have heard that the teaching of Buddhism is profound and arcane. We must practice it. How can a sparrow know the great ambition of a swan?" The king said, "The will of the majority is firm and unalterable. You are the only one who takes a different view. I cannot follow two recommendations at the same time." He then ordered the execution of Yŏmch'ok.

» Working with Sources

1. **What does Yŏmch'ok's plan reveal about resistance to Buddhism in Korea in the sixth century—and about the role of an advisor to the Korean king in the period?**
2. **What seems to have been the role of self-sacrifice in the establishment of Buddhism in Korea?**

SOURCE 13.3 *Nihongi (Chronicles of Japan)*

ca. 720 CE

The *Nihongi* (*Nihon Shoki*) is the first official history of Japan. It draws on numerous sources, including Chinese histories, clan histories, and the accounts of religious authorities. While it parallels the *Kojiki* in describing

Source: "The Empress and Her Brother Prince Sahobiko," from *Traditional Japanese Literature: An Anthology, Beginnings to 1600*, ed. Haruo Shirane (New York: Columbia University Press, 2007), 47–49.

the ancient and mythological origins of Japan, it continues the narrative far beyond the *Kojiki* into the recent past, specifically the reign of the empress Jitō (686–697). This particular story concerns the eleventh emperor of Japan, Suinin, but it differs from the *Kojiki* in certain key details, and probably reflects the values of the eighth century rather than its ostensible setting (the first century CE).

Fourth year, autumn, Ninth Month, twenty-third day. The empress's elder maternal brother, Prince Sahobiko, plotted treason and tried to endanger the state. He watched for an occasion when the empress was enjoying her leisure and addressed her as follows: "Whom do you love best—your elder brother or your husband?"

At this, the empress, ignorant of his object in making this inquiry, immediately answered, saying: "I love my elder brother." Then he enticed the empress by saying: "If one serves a man by beauty, when the beauty fades, his affection will cease. . . . I beg you, therefore, to slay the emperor for me." So he took a dagger and, giving it to the empress, said: "Put on this dagger with your garments, and when the emperor goes to sleep, stab him in the neck and kill him."

. . .

Fifth year, winter, Tenth Month, first day. The emperor proceeded to Kume, where he dwelled in Takamiya. Now the emperor took his noon-day nap with the empress's knees as his pillow. Up to this time the empress had done nothing but thought vainly to herself: "This would be the time to do what the prince, my elder brother, plotted." And she wept tears which fell on the emperor's face.

The emperor woke and addressed the empress, saying: "Today we have had a dream. A small brocade-color snake coiled itself around our neck and a great rain arose from Saho, which coming here wet our faces. What does this portend?" At this the empress, knowing that she could not conceal the plot, in fear and awe bowed to the earth and informed the emperor fully of the circumstances of the prince's, her elder brother's, treason.

. . .

Then the emperor addressed the empress, saying: "This is not your crime," and raising a force from the neighboring district, he commanded Yatsunada, the remote ancestor of the Kimi of Kōzuke, to slay Sahobiko. Now Sahobiko withstood him with an army, and, hastily piling up rice stalks, made a castle, which was so solid that it could not be breached. This is what was called a "rice castle." A month passed, and yet it did not surrender.

The empress grieved at this, saying: "Even though I am empress, with what countenance can I preside over the empire, after bringing to ruin the prince, my elder brother?" Accordingly, she took in her arms the imperial prince Homutsu-wake and entered the rice castle of the prince, her elder brother. The emperor increased his army still more and, having surrounded the castle on all sides, proclaimed to those inside, saying: "Send forth quickly the empress and the imperial prince." But they would not send them out. So General Yatsunada set fire to the castle. Then the empress, taking in her bosom the imperial child, crossed the castle and came out.

Immediately she sought the emperor saying: "The reason why your handmaiden at first fled into her elder brother's castle was in the hope that her elder brother might be absolved from guilt for the sake of her and her child. But now he has not been absolved, and I know that I am guilty. Shall I have my hands tied behind my back? There is nothing left but for me to strangle myself. But even though I, your handmaiden, die, I cannot bear to forget the favor shown me by the emperor. I pray, therefore, that the empress's palace, which I had charge of, may be granted to consorts for you. In the land of Tanba there are five ladies, all of virtuous minds, the daughters of the prince, who is Michi no Ushi of Tanba. Let them be placed in the side courts to complete the number of the consort chambers." To this the emperor agreed. Then the fire blazed up, and the castle was destroyed. All the troops ran away, and Sahobiko and his younger sister died together inside the castle. Thereupon the emperor commended the good service of General Yatsunada and granted him the name of Yamato-hi-muke-hiko Yatsunada.

» Working with Sources

1. **Contrast the emperor's reactions to his wife in the two episodes. What do these differences reveal about Japanese culture?**
2. **What does the document suggest about women's familial roles and expectations for their behavior?**

SOURCE 13.4 P'i Jih-hsiu, "Three Poems of Shame"

ca. 865 CE

Because there are very few sources of information on the history of Vietnam before the Li dynasty (1010–1225), Chinese dynastic histories and Chinese poetry are indispensable sources. They are valuable even when, as in this case, they were composed by those on the other side of conflict with Vietnamese insurgents. P'i Jih-hsiu was a prominent Tang poet of the late ninth century, and he was particularly drawn to the Mencian notion that the people have the right to revolt if their country is being mismanaged. While traveling through the country in 865, he stopped in the city of Hsü, from which 2,000 men had been drafted for the Tang army and sent to fight Nan-chao in Vietnam. These soldiers were probably lost when Nan-chao defeated the Chinese forces in Vietnam in early 863, and news of their defeat apparently reached Hsü while Jih-hsiu was there.

Source: Keith Weller Taylor, *The Birth of Vietnam* (Berkeley: University of California Press, 1983), 345–346.

The south was neglected, officials were not selected,
Causing the overthrow of our Giao-chi,
Which, for three or four successive years,
Has drifted away, bringing disgrace to the empire.
The timid yield readily in battle;
The warlike revel in their weapons.
Soldiers fill the empire,
Battle leaders accumulate treasure;
Exactions reduce the common people to misery,
In order to distribute the wages of valiant men.
Brave Hsü-ch'ang warriors,
Their loyalty and daring brought honor to their families;
They went with the wind of myriad galloping horses,
They ceased in a river of flesh.
Yesterday morning the defeated troops returned;
There is weeping at a thousand gates and ten thousand hearths.
The sound of wailing echoes through the village streets;
Resentment spreads over the mountains and valleys.
Who can listen to wardrums in the daytime,
And not suffer the sight of metal arrowheads?
I have a plan for victory,
Though irregular and considered worthless by others.
I store it in my mind and heart;
I am ashamed to see the families of the Hsü warriors.
I lament those thoughtless ones,
Who simply follow the steps of their ancestors.
My family does not produce grain for the army;
I am not familiar with military affairs.
Yet I wear the same kind of clothing as the Hsü warriors,
And I eat the same kind of food as the Hsü warriors.
Now I know that the teachings of the Ancients
Are already enough to shelter me.
To whose shame is this song sung?
The Ying River flows far and green.

» Working with Sources

1. **Can this poem be compared with other T'ang poetry regarding pacifism and war?**
2. **What does the poem indicate about the growth of a national identity and culture in Vietnam?**

SOURCE 13.5 Copper head of Bodhisattva Avalokiteshvara, Vietnam

eighth–ninth century CE

This head, crafted from copper alloy, is all that remains of an impressive image found in central Vietnam. It depicts the Avalokiteshvara, the embodiment of Buddhist compassion, and the Amitabha Buddha is perched on the crown. It points to the emergence of a pan–Southeast Asian bodhisattva type in the eighth and ninth centuries, as well as to the superb metal-casting skills of artisans in the Cham territories of Vietnam.

» Working with Sources

1. **How does the image reveal the phenomenon of "religious civilizations interacting" and the emergence of an international Buddhist culture in Southeast Asia?**
2. **What does the head suggest about the social structure of Vietnam in this period?**

Source: Thierry Ollivier. © RMN-Grand Palais/Art Resource, NY.

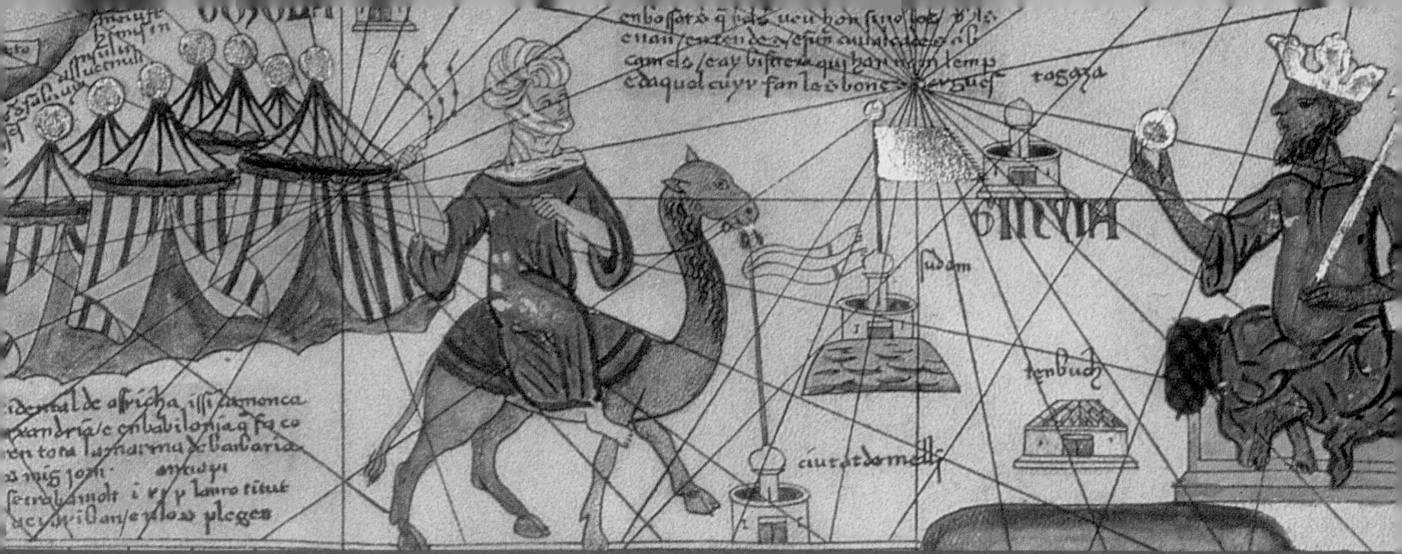

Chapter 14 600–1450 CE

Patterns of State Formation in Africa

According to local tradition, the founder of the gold-trading kingdom of ancient Ghana (ca. 400–1200) in West Africa was Dinga. He was a descendant of Bilal, the Ethiopian whom, according to tradition, the Prophet Muhammad chose as the first *muezzin*, or crier who calls the Muslim faithful to prayer. When Dinga arrived from Arabia to the Sahel, the east–west belt of steppe south of the Sahara Desert in West Africa, he asked a many-headed snake at a well for water. The snake refused, and Dinga subdued her through magic to receive his drink. After marrying the snake's three daughters, he fathered three sons, the eldest of whom was a half-human, half-serpent being who went to live underground. The two younger sons were still growing when their father left to return to Arabia.

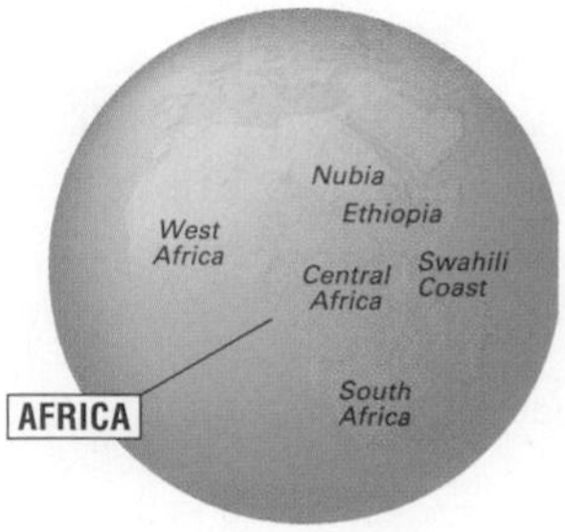

The second son grew into an inconsiderate man who mistreated his father's old servant. The third son turned into a much kinder person, giving the same servant his leftover meals. Years later, Dinga, nearly blind, felt his end coming and summoned his two sons to give them their respective heritages. The elderly servant, who had never forgotten the kindness of the younger son, persuaded the youngest son to go first, disguised as his older brother, to receive the lion's share of Dinga's estate. Indeed, the father bestowed his power of magic as well as the kingdom on the youngest son, while the older son received the more modest power of rainmaking.

ABOVE: **Detail from the Catalan Atlas (1375), showing Mansa Musa, the king of Mali, on his throne.**

The two sons struck a deal whereby Ghana would receive enough rain and gold as long as its people would sacrifice a virgin and a colt every year. After many years of human and animal sacrifices, a Wagadu man and admirer of a virgin about to be sacrificed slew the snake brother. As he was dying, the snake brother cursed the people of Wagadu, which lost its abundance of rain and gold. A parched and impoverished Ghana fell to its enemies.

This story gives us a glimpse of a main pattern underlying the history of sub-Saharan Africa between 600 and 1450: adaptation of African spirituality to Islam. The pattern played itself out particularly in West and East Africa, whose rulers converted to Islam and incorporated Islamic beliefs and practices into their traditional **African spirituality**.

Seeing Patterns

» **What patterns of adaptation did the Christian kingdoms of northeast Africa demonstrate in their interactions with the civilizations of the Middle East and eastern Mediterranean?**

» **What were the responses of Africans to Muslim merchants who connected them with the trading zone of the Indian Ocean and Mediterranean? As these Africans adapted to Islam, which forms of political organization did they adopt?**

» **In what ways did the economic and political transformations on the East African coast and in West Africa affect developments in the interior?**

While the Eurasian and North African pattern during 600–1450 was that of the formation of religious civilizations that contained commonwealths of states, the pattern of sub-Saharan Africa in the same period was that of religious kingdom and empire formation. In the northeast of sub-Saharan Africa, kingdoms had already adapted to Christianity prior to 600, and the new kingdoms of Nubia and Ethiopia continued the Christian heritage, with Ethiopia assuming imperial dimensions. In West Africa, Mali, the successor of ancient Ghana, adapted to Islamic imperial traditions and became a multilinguistic, multiethnic, and multireligious empire. On Africa's east coast, a set of small Islamic merchant states emerged, the Swahili port cities, under either kings or councils of notables. Finally, in the interior of central and southern Africa, indigenous kingdoms rose on the basis of the African tradition of magic-empowered authority, descended from the naturalist spiritual heritage.

Christians and Muslims in the Northeast

During 600–1250, Nubia was a Christian kingdom along the middle Nile in the Sahara and sub-Saharan steppe, built on agriculture and trade between tropical Africa and the Middle East. Ethiopia, Nubia's neighbor in the highlands to the southeast, was similarly Christian but, unlike Nubia, was initially a collection of decentralized chiefdoms. When one of the chiefs eventually centralized rule in 1137, the new kingdom of Ethiopia unified the highlands, sent missionaries to the southern provinces to convert non-Christian Africans, and battled the Muslims in the lowlands on the Red Sea coast in the name of a Christian crusade. Both Nubia and Ethiopia were fascinating cases of sub-Saharan polities adopting patterns of state formation from the Middle East into their African heritage: They adapted to Middle Eastern plow agriculture and Christianity, while long retaining African traditions of decentralization.

African spirituality: The experience of and/or belief in the presence of a life substance or spirit shared by all living beings and things in nature. People or ancestors, therefore, could influence each other positively or negatively. A human or animal mask allowed a person to assume a different identity.

Nubia in the Middle Nile Valley

About a century after the end of the kingdom of Meroë, sometime around 350 (see Chapter 6), small Nubian successor states dominated the middle Nile valley

Chapter Outline

- Christians and Muslims in the Northeast
- Adaptation to Islam: City-States and Kingdoms in East and South Africa
- Cultural Encounters: West African Traditions and Islam
- Putting It All Together

from north to south. In the course of the mid-500s, these states converted to Coptic Christianity and subsequently united into a single kingdom. Open to trade with the then rising empire of the Arab Umayyads, Nubia experienced a gradual ascendancy of Arab merchants to dominance in Nubian commerce. Eventually, the enhanced position of these merchants led to Muslim political control: In 1276, the Egyptian Mamluks defeated the Christian king of Nubia and installed a puppet regime. By around 1450 Christianity in Nubia had largely given way to Islam.

The Rise of Christian Kingdoms in Nubia Meroë's power ended likely as a result of deforestation near the capital and nomadic attacks against its northern provinces. The nomads had adapted to the use of the camel in the early centuries of the Common Era, which allowed them to carry out swift long-distance raids over vast tracts of inhospitable territory. Indeed, the use of the camel created a transportation revolution in the Sahara in general and opened up new routes for commerce and invasion. One immediate result of this was that a new ruling class of Nubians arose in the middle Nile valley during the 400s. Nubian chiefs and their followers established three small kingdoms along the middle Nile that prospered in large part as the result of the rapid spread of the animal-driven waterwheel invented in Egypt in the first century CE. Water could now be lifted into channels all year round, even at some distance from the river, for the purpose of planting two annual grain crops. Archaeological evidence points to a substantial increase in the number of villages in the region as a result of this innovation.

Coptic Christianity: A branch of Christianity centered in Egypt that emphasizes the single, divine nature of Jesus, into which his human nature was *incorporated*, in contrast to Catholic Western and Orthodox Eastern Christianities, in which Jesus is believed to have been endowed with both a divine and human, albeit unified, nature.

In the 500s, Egyptian missionaries converted the Nubians to **Coptic Christianity**. Pagan temples became churches, and new churches and monasteries were built, ultimately in nearly every village. Kings and members of the ruling class sponsored these Christian institutions. As did their contemporaries in the Mediterranean and Middle East, the Nubian rulers appreciated the unifying effect of a single state religion over the multiplicity of local temple cults.

Barely Christianized, Nubia now had to withstand an invasion of Arabs from Egypt. After the establishment of the Arab emirate of Syria, Iraq, and Egypt (see Chapter 10), the new governors in Egypt organized military campaigns into neighboring countries. In 652, one of these campaigns penetrated deep into Nubia. The Arab military used siege engines and caused considerable damage to one of the Nubian capitals. But an army of Nubian archers, long famous for their skills with bow and arrow, defeated the Arabs, forcing them to retreat. In a subsequent agreement, the two sides formally recognized each other, made a pact, and drew up a schedule of future friendly exchanges among their respective rulers. Later Muslim historians reinterpreted this pact, ignoring the defeat and presenting it as a treaty of submission to Islamic hegemony. Such differing interpretations notwithstanding, the pact endured and blocked the advance of Islam into East Africa for 600 years.

Royal Power and Governance At the turn of the 700s, a "great king" emerged who unified the three Nubian kingdoms. Power remained largely decentralized, however, with a dozen vassal rulers and an appointed—later hereditary—official called an "eparch." This official governed the northern subkingdom and was responsible for its defense against Egypt. The Coptic patriarch of Alexandria appointed the bishops, who, therefore, were independent from the kings, in marked contrast to Catholic Europe in the contemporary early Middle Ages, where the kings appointed church officials (see Chapter 11).

In terms of financial administration, archaeologists have so far discovered no evidence of a kingdom-wide taxation system. The dozen vassal rulers were probably powerful landlords who might have sent presents to the great king as tokens of their position. As in Europe, abbots of monasteries were also landlords, endowed with royal grants of villages, where peasant farmers paid rent. Monasteries, however, were not numerous, given the limited fertile land on the Nile banks, in contrast to Ethiopia, western Europe, and Byzantium. Most likely, in the vicinity of the great king's residence some basic fiscal mechanisms existed whereby village headmen delivered taxes in kind. Another, perhaps even the principal, source of income for the kings and eparchs was long-distance trade, which they controlled. In this respect, the Christian great kings of Nubia were similar to their Islamic counterparts in East and West Africa.

Agriculture The farmland of the Nubian villages consisted of small strips of arable land on the up-to-2-mile-wide fertile banks of the Nile. The annual summer floods between June and September inundated these strips, leaving them covered with rich sediment. In a few places, a wider valley or low-level islands in the river allowed for the farming of additional fields. Palm orchards helped to anchor the silt, and stone walls and jetties built into the Nile captured additional amounts of alluvial soil. As the floods receded in fall, villagers grew sorghum, millet, barley, wheat, and cotton with the help of plows pulled by oxen.

Higher fields away from the banks, which required waterwheels for irrigation, were planted during the winter with pulses, okra, melons, and other garden crops for spring harvesting. In the spring, farmers planted second crops on both the banks and higher elevations. Vineyards became more important as the kingdoms evolved, and wine was consumed by villagers in taverns as well as by priests and monks in daily religious services. Farmers also planted limited amounts of alfalfa for the feeding of cattle and donkeys. Sheep and goats fed on the stubble of grain fields and on scrubland, while pigs ate household remnants. Arabic written sources report the necessity of occasional food transports during local famines on the Nile, but generally the Nubian villages were self-supporting.

Long-Distance Trade The pact of 652 between the Arabs and Nubia included clauses concerning the trade of Egyptian cloth, pottery, iron utensils, leather goods,

interactive timeline

ca. 450–1450
Kingdom(s) of Nubia on Middle Nile

ca. 650–1137
Kingdom of Aksum in northeast Africa

ca. 750–nineteenth century
Swahili city-states in coastal East Africa

ca. 750–1240
Kingdom of ancient Ghana in West Africa

ca. 1000–1400
Kingdom of Ife in West African rain forest

1070–1300
Kingdom of Mapungubwe in southern Africa

1137–1270
Kingdom of Ethiopia under the Zagwe

ca. 1217–1255
Mansa Sundiata of Mali

1250–1505
Kingdom of Great Zimbabwe in southern Africa

1235–1645
Empire of Mali in West Africa

1270–1974
Kingdom of Ethiopia, Solomonid dynasty

ca. 1300–1885
Kingdom of Luba in central Africa

and wine for ivory and slaves. The latter two items came from the tropical territories on the White Nile, though nothing is known about how Nubian merchants and slave-raiding troops operated in these territories. Whatever the specifics of the Nubian activities along the White Nile, the kings taxed the merchant caravans at various resting places along the way.

In the period between 800 and 1200, the long-distance trade attracted Muslim merchants and craftspeople from beyond Aswan to the northern province of the Nubian kingdom, where they settled in a number of villages and possibly built mosques. A ruling in the mid-800s by an Egyptian Muslim judge (recognized by Nubia) allowed the Muslims in Nubia to acquire private property. A money economy then emerged, based on Islamic gold dinars. Muslim merchants also settled along the Red Sea coast, especially once the North African Fatimid caliphs had conquered Egypt in 969. To compete with the Iraqi Abbasid caliphs on the Persian Gulf, the Fatimids developed maritime trade with India through the Red Sea. Both of these trade avenues would bolster the commerce of the entire Mediterranean region and even reach to far-off western Europe (see Map 14.1).

From Christian to Islamic Nubia In the mid-1000s, to secure their hold on the Red Sea, Egyptian rulers resettled nomadic migrants from Arabia to Upper Egypt. Unfortunately for Nubia, these migrants and their neighbors began raiding the kingdom in the early 1100s. The local rulers in northern Nubia, principal defenders against the raids, gained in power vis-à-vis the Nubian kings. Perhaps as a

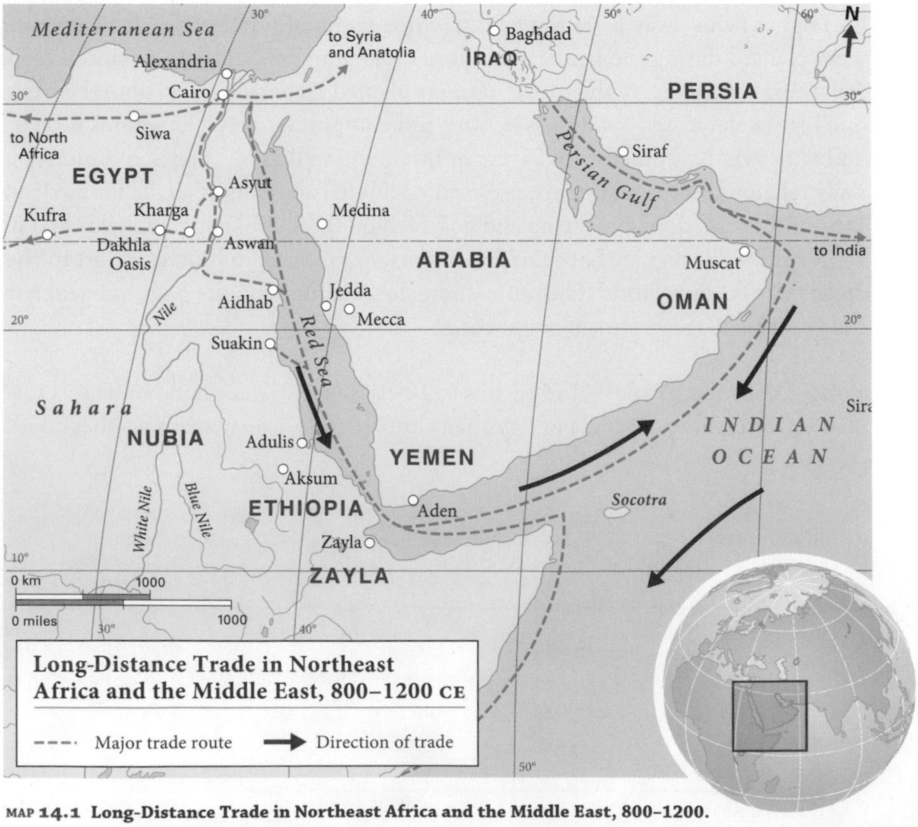

MAP **14.1 Long-Distance Trade in Northeast Africa and the Middle East, 800–1200.**

consequence, dynastic rivalries broke out, and in the 1200s both usurpers and pretenders to the throne appealed to Egypt for support. The Mamluks, who governed Egypt at this time (1250–1517, see Chapter 17), responded to the appeals with enthusiasm, including Nubia in their anti-Christian holy war efforts. They propagated the reinterpreted pact of 652 as a treaty requiring regular tributes, particularly the delivery of slaves, from Nubia. In 1276, they conquered Nubia, installed a Christian vassal king, and levied the *jizya* head tax, which non-Muslims in Islamic lands had to pay. In due time, the Christian dynasty gave way to Muslim rulers; and in 1365, after a new wave of Arab nomadic incursions, the Nubian kingdom ceased to exist altogether.

Viewed in retrospect, through interaction with the Roman Empire Nubia adapted itself to the Christian institutions of sacred kingship. A specifically Nubian pattern of political formation emerged that resembled the feudal practices (see Chapter 11) of many other places around the world. In this pattern, kings acted as representatives of God on earth but lacked the resources to govern with the help of centralized institutions. Instead, they relied on the support of federated chiefs, who functioned much like vassals.

The kings were also not strong enough to incorporate the clerical hierarchy into their states, so the patriarch of Alexandria never lost control over the appointment of Nubian bishops—unlike the pope in his struggles during the high Middle Ages with the Holy Roman emperors over lay investiture. Nubian churches were outposts of the Egyptian Coptic Church rather than indigenous institutions with their own hierarchy intertwined with the Nubian royal dynasty. Had the Nubian Church been a "national church" like those we will examine in Europe (see Chapter 17), it might have been in a better position to resist Islamization once Muslim rulers took over.

Ethiopia in the Eastern Highlands

After the Christian kingdom of Aksum had lost Yemen to the Sasanid Persians in 570 and had exhausted the timber resources around its capital in the 600s, it shriveled to a chiefdom. However, in cooperation with the Coptic Church, Aksum continued to represent the church's mission to convert the southern highland Africans. Eventually, new dynasties arose and renewed the mission, among which the Solomonids and their Christian Crusades were the most successful. In Ethiopia, the adaptation to Christianity was more thorough than in Nubia. The Ethiopians embarked on a pattern of forming an African Christian civilization, including the Judeo-Christian symbolism of Zion and Christian law.

Christianity in the Highlands The kings of Aksum and the patriarch of the Coptic Church abandoned the capital perhaps as early as the mid-600s and reestablished themselves in a modest chiefdom with better agrarian resources farther south. They continued to trade ivory, ostrich feathers, musk, and myrrh for linen and cotton textiles as well as spices on the Red Sea but no longer issued coins. When Muslim rulers in Egypt in the late 800s occupied ports on the west coast of the Red Sea and expanded trade with India and East Africa, Aksum became a partner in this trade. In addition to these goods, it sold slaves captured in raids in the lowlands to the south. The main effort of the small Aksum kings was directed toward campaigning southward, taking priests and settlers with them to convert and pacify the defeated highland Africans. A monastery, founded in the late 800s some 200 miles southwest of Aksum, became the main center for sending out missionaries to the south. Reduced as it was, Aksum continued to be a factor in highland politics.

Quite dramatically, however, in the 970s the Africans subjected to conversion struck back. A mysterious queen, Gudit (Judith), led several destructive campaigns in which churches and monasteries were burned, towns destroyed, and thousands of people killed or enslaved. The situation was so chaotic that the patriarch of Alexandria refused to appoint the customary metropolitan bishop from Egypt to the country. Scholars, scouring the scant evidence to identify the area of this queen's origin, have determined that she might have been from the recently Christianized parts of the southern highlands. After her reign of terror of a purported 40 years, a remnant of the Aksumite kingdom recovered and survived modestly for another century, but little is known about its kings and nothing about the extent of their rule.

State and Church under the Zagwe Kings Political stability eventually returned to the highlands with the foundation of the Zagwe dynasty (1137–1270), centered on a Christianized province some 300 miles south of Aksum. To its neighbors, the Zagwe kingdom was known as Ethiopia or Abyssinia, names rooted in the Hebrew and Christian Bibles. The Zagwe kings laid the foundation for a return to dominant royal power and continued the Aksumite tradition of church sponsorship and missionary work in the south.

A first step toward reunification was the request of an early king in the mid-twelfth century to his metropolitan bishop to appoint seven additional bishops. The idea was that this nucleus of an Ethiopian episcopate would later grow to the 10 members required for a vote of independence from the patriarch of Alexandria. The king, however, did not get far with his attempt to create an independent Ethiopian Church. After lengthy negotiations with the patriarchs of Egypt and Syria and the

image analysis

Church of St. George, Lalibela, Ethiopia. Stonemasons cut this church and its interior from the surrounding rock formation. This and 10 other churches, built in the early 1200s, are part of a pilgrimage center created in the image of the Holy Land in Palestine.

Muslim ruler of Egypt, the Egyptian sultan refused the split. The Muslims were not about to relinquish the indirect leverage they possessed in Ethiopia through their political control over the patriarchs in Egypt. Had Ethiopia succeeded, the significant development of a "national church" would have occurred—just the opposite of the situation in Europe at that time, where the pope wrested control of the church from the kings during the investiture controversy (see Chapter 11).

Church sponsorship expressed itself in the construction of 11 remarkably innovative structures carved out from subterranean rock during the early 1200s, called the Lalibela churches. The kings arranged the churches in two groups, separated by a stream named the Yordanos, after the biblical Jordan River. The policy of the Zagwe dynasty was the re-creation of Zion, perhaps in succession to Jerusalem, which the Muslims reconquered in 1187 from the western European crusaders. Accordingly, the dynasty used these churches for elaborate annual masses and processions during Holy Week. The Lalibela monoliths are unique in the history of Christian church construction and have no parallels elsewhere.

Under the Zagwe kings, the conversion of the peoples in the central and southern highlands to Christianity resumed. In addition, the kings encouraged the colonization of the land with Christian settlers from the north. These settlers introduced the plow and cereal agriculture, adding them to the existing hoe and tuber crops (ensete, taro, and yam). The central and southern highlands were geographically much larger than those in the north and offered ample opportunities for the establishment of new villages, fields, and pastures. With its fertile volcanic soil, southern Ethiopia became one of the most productive agricultural regions of sub-Saharan Africa.

The political system that emerged in the center and south was an extension of what Aksum had pioneered in the north. Under a king ruling by divine right, Ethiopia was a confederation of provincial lords, some of whom also used royal titles. These lords lived in villages among their farmers and collected rents, consisting of grain, pulses, and cattle. Legally, ownership of the land was vested in families and had the status of inalienable property, with the family lords holding the right to collect rents.

The Solomonid Dynasty Once Christians from the north had settled as farmers in the central highlands and had converted the locals to Christianity, they shifted the focus of their missionary efforts southward. In 1270, a new dynasty of kings, the Solomonids, emerged some 300 miles south of Aksum, in the region of today's capital of Ethiopia, Addis Ababa. These new kings claimed descent from the Aksumite kings and sponsored the composition of an elaborate foundation narrative, the *Kebra Negast*, which legitimized the Solomonid dynasty until its fall in 1974.

According to this narrative, the kings of Aksum were not only the descendants of a union between the queen of Sheba and the Israelite king Solomon but also the heirs to the Israelite Ark of the Covenant after the destruction of the First Temple by the Neo-Babylonians. The Ethiopians thus appropriated the biblical heritage more thoroughly than any eastern or western European Christian peoples did. The religious heritage of the Solomonids still lives on in Ethiopia. Outside Africa, this heritage has been embraced by the *Rastafarians*—Afrocentric Christians who form a small minority in Jamaica and who have found many admirers, some perhaps

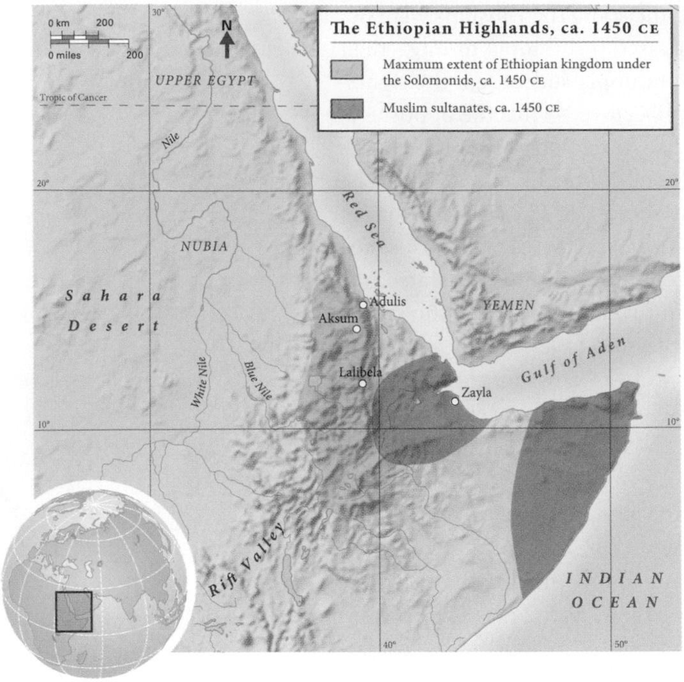

MAP 14.2 The Ethiopian Highlands, ca. 1450.

more because of the popular reggae music of Bob Marley (1945–1981) than its doctrines.

Ethiopian Christians and Coastal Muslims

During the 1300s and most of the 1400s, Ethiopia was a powerful kingdom. The kings continued to depend on the collaboration of their provincial lords, but they also commanded a sizable mercenary army of their own. With this army, they extended their authority over small principalities of Christians, traditional Africans, and Muslims in the southern highlands and Rift Valley, as well as Muslim sultanates along the Red Sea coast.

This extension began with the conquests of King Amda Seyon (r. 1314–1344), who in effect doubled the kingdom's territory. An unknown priest accompanied the king on his campaigns, which he related to posterity in vivid prose and with great detail in *The Glorious Victories of Amda Seyon*, one of the earliest written histories in sub-Saharan Africa. A century after the Mamluks had eradicated the Crusader Kingdom of Jerusalem in the Middle East (1291), Solomonid Ethiopia was carrying on the Christian holy war in sub-Saharan Africa (see Map 14.2).

selection from *The Glorious Victories of Amda Seyon*

The Muslim sultanates along the Red Sea coast relied principally on trade, linking East Africa via the Rift Valley with the India–Mediterranean sea lane. Only the sultanate of Zayla, near modern Djibouti, and a few other places along the coast had sufficient water from wells to allow for a modest garden agriculture. The steppe lowlands farther away from the coast were too dry to support more than widely dispersed populations of camel nomads, who supplied animals and guides to the trade caravans and soldiers to the wars of the sultans against Ethiopia. Urban dwellers, nomads, and pastoralists astride the trade route through the Rift Valley had converted to Islam gradually in the centuries after 800 when autonomous Muslim rulers in Egypt began the expansion of trade via the Red Sea with India and East Africa.

Initially, the Ethiopian kings were ruthless in their efforts to subdue the sultans. But the kings' crusading image notwithstanding, they were also pragmatic enough to exempt Muslim merchants and pastoralists from the church's missionary efforts in the south of the kingdoms. Similarly, in the end, the kings had little choice but to tolerate the sultans as Muslim vassals. Ethiopia became de facto a multiethnic, multilinguistic, and multireligious empire in which the kings limited the church's conversion efforts.

Legally, however, the kings continued to emphasize their Christian identity, adopting in the mid-1400s a Christianized version of Roman law, *The Law of the Kings* (*Fetha Nagast*), from the Egyptian Copts. The law brought with it an intriguing history. According to Islamic law, Christians in Islamic civilization were entitled to self-rule, and for this purpose, the Coptic Church in Egypt adopted portions of Justinian's code and resolutions of church councils for its governance. In the mid-1300s, an Egyptian Copt compiled these law books and resolutions into a single codex governing church affairs, civil law, and criminal law, translated from Greek into Arabic. The Ethiopian translator added a section on kingship, and, as such, *The Law of the Kings* remained the law of the land until 1930, when the Ethiopian emperor Haile Selassie issued the first modern constitution (see Source 14.1).

The reinvigorated Ethiopian kingdom of the Solomonids was keenly interested in establishing contacts with Western Christianity, wishing especially for the dispatch of craftspeople (and receiving a few). A first embassy of 30 members traveled in 1297–1312 to visit the popes. A churchman in Genoa reported on these visitors, identifying their king for the first time with the mythical Prester John, a great Christian ruler in the "east" expected to come to the aid of the crusaders in recovering Jerusalem and the Holy Land. Previously, Prester John had been considered to be an Indian priest-king, commander of a huge army; but now after the loss of the Holy Land in 1291, Ethiopia appeared as a better hope for an ally than the more distant India.

Adaptation to Islam: City-States and Kingdoms in East and Southern Africa

During the period 600–1450, the Swahili people emerged as an indigenous African population of Muslims. They formed a society with common features but were divided into dozens of city-states along a 2,000-mile stretch of the African east coast, from today's Somalia in the north to Mozambique in the south. The Swahilis' most common feature was the function of their merchants as middlemen between the interior of East Africa and the Middle East as well as India. In the interior, increasing agricultural resources and trade with the Swahilis encouraged the expansion of chiefdoms but not yet the rise of kingdoms, except in the far south, in the middle Limpopo valley, and on the Zimbabwean plateau, where local people mined gold. Here, beginning around 1075, towns, cities, and kingdoms arose, the best known of which was Great Zimbabwe (ca. 1250–1505).

The Swahili City-States on the East African Coast

Dissenting Arabs, driven by the centralizing caliphs to the margins of the Arab Empire in the Middle East, were the first to establish trade contacts in the 700s with Bantu-speaking villagers in coastal East Africa. In the following centuries, these villagers adapted themselves to long-distance trade and Islamic civilization. They evolved into an urban society of kings, **patricians**, religious scholars, sailors, fishermen, and farmers based in small port cities. The kings and patricians were consumers of luxury goods brought to them by Middle Eastern and Indian merchants. As sellers of goods manufactured in their cities to the populations of the interior, the patricians acquired goods from the interior, which the Muslim merchants from overseas took back home. Thus, the Swahilis were brokers in a complex system of exchanges among the people around the Indian Ocean.

Patrician: Term used in this chapter to denote Muslims in Swahili society claiming Middle Eastern descent and, by virtue of profiting from long-distance trade with the countries around the Indian Ocean, either ascending to the throne of their cities as kings or governing their cities in councils, together with other patricians.

Swahili Beginnings The East African coast follows a fairly straight line from the northeast to the southwest, with few bays and natural harbors. For the most part, the coast is low, in most places rising only gradually. Many small rivers open into the Indian Ocean, and their estuaries provide some room for anchorage. Only the Zambezi River in the south was large enough to allow longer-range river traffic and the building of inland towns. Islands, reefs, and mangrove swamps were numerous and favored the construction and use of small vessels among the Swahilis for communication along the coast. Under the influence of the monsoons blowing from the southwest from April to September, the northern half of the East African coast—from today's northern Tanzania to southern Somalia—receives most of its annual rain during the summer. These monsoon winds supported sailing with the wind to the Middle East and India. The opposite direction of the winter monsoons facilitated the return voyages. The southern half of the coast, from northern Tanzania to Mozambique, has rainy winters and no reliable seasonal winds, making sailing conditions less predictable. Accordingly, the southern half was less settled than the northern part.

The main ethnic group in the interior of sub-Saharan Africa was that of the Bantus, who had migrated to central, eastern, and southern Africa from roughly 600 BCE to 600 CE (see Chapter 6). The Bantus possessed a diversified agriculture and a wide variety of iron implements. In the mid-700s CE, a cultural differentiation between the Bantus of the interior and the east coast began to emerge. Archaeological remnants from Shanga, near today's Somali–Kenyan border, indicate the existence of a small wooden Islamic congregation hall, holding perhaps 25 people, and Muslim burials with an orientation toward Mecca. Small silver coins with Islamic inscriptions similar to Yemeni coins of the same period but minted in Shanga have also been found. The coastal population thus adapted to Islam, while the hinterland remained wedded to traditional African spirituality.

The earliest Muslim merchants in East Africa were Khariji dissidents from the Middle East. These Muslims were sectarians who opposed the emergence of a centralized empire, whose caliphs were actively shaping the emergent Islamic state religion. The caliphs pursued them relentlessly, pushing them into political insignificance in faraway provinces, such as Oman at the mouth of the Persian Gulf and oases in the North African Sahara. Given the agricultural limitations in these regions, the Kharijis took to trade, in both East and West Africa.

Early on, the Kharijis were mostly interested in slaves, who were in great demand in the Islamic empire. Merchants in Basra, the main port for the Indian Ocean trade, invested their profits in the purchase of marshland around the mouth of the Tigris–Euphrates Rivers and in the acquisition of slaves from East Africa to clear this land for the planting of rice and sugarcane. From 868 to 883, a revolt among these slaves disrupted the Abbasid Empire's entire trade through the Persian Gulf with India, East Africa, and China. When the caliphs finally succeeded in suppressing the revolt, large-scale agricultural slavery in the region ended. Black slave imports from East as well as West Africa continued on a smaller scale, however, primarily for domestic purposes.

Adapting to Islam When the Kharijis lost their edge in the trade after the slave revolt, mainstream Muslim merchants from the heartland of the Islamic empire traveled with textiles, glazed pottery, and glassware to East Africa to purchase luxury goods, such as ivory, hardwoods, and skins. One of the heartland cities was Shiraz, the capital of the Shiite dynasty of the Buyids (945–1055) in Iran. Their prestige appears to have surpassed that of the Kharijis, since wealthy Swahili merchant families associated themselves with them, claiming Shirazi descent. Members of these families migrated from the northern Swahili city of Shanga southward and founded new trading centers as far away as the Comoros Islands.

After 1050, mainstream Islam, with its mixture of Sunnism and mysticism, rose in prestige. *Sharifian* descent—that is, the possession of a genealogy going back to the Prophet Muhammad—began to rival Shirazi descent among the coastal elites. Leading Islamic families claiming Shirazi or Sharifian descent thus assumed dominant positions in the Swahili cities, from Mogadishu in the north to Chibuene (in Mozambique) in the south.

Urbanism Swahili urbanism along the East African coast encompassed several hundred towns and about two-dozen city-states of up to 10,000 inhabitants, either on the mainland or on islands off the coast (see Map 14.3). The mark of many cities was the central open space containing the Friday mosque for the congregational noon prayer, the main city well, and tombs of Islamic saints. Around the mosque and usually facing the sea were the densely built inner cities of the patricians. In the less densely settled outskirts, nonpatricians from overseas or the interior and manumitted slaves earned their living as craftspeople. On the perimeter were cemeteries, pastures, brushland, and mangrove swamps.

Separate commoner towns housed fishermen, boatbuilders, and sailors. Their families grew vegetables and fruits in their gardens and sold the surplus in the nearby patrician cities. Further inland lived various non-Muslim client populations who traded meat and food staples, primarily sorghum, to the cities. Cities, towns, and inland people thus formed loosely organized city-states under the leadership of the patricians.

selection from The Swahili saga of Liyongo Fumo

Governance In the period 600–1450, the Swahili city-states were governed by kings and/or councils of patrician elders. Mainland cities, such as Mogadishu, Gede, and Malindi, were more vulnerable to occasionally hostile hinterland people and, therefore, more dependent on inland alliances than cities located on islands, such as Lamu, Paté, Pemba, or Zanzibar. Both hinterland and inland populations were trade partners whom the Swahili patrician merchants or their agents—usually slaves—visited but among whom they did not settle. The merchants did not establish mosques in the interior, and the interior population did not convert to Islam, nor did holy men venture into non-Islamic territories to establish retreats or pilgrimage centers.

In the absence of Islam as a common bond, the office of chieftainship as the traditional African institution binding lineage federations together served to express the communality of the cities and surrounding rural peoples. The mainland kings were Muslims from leading Shirazi or Sharifian patrician families, but in the dealings with their non-Muslim allies they acted more like traditional chiefs. By contrast, the patrician councils in the island cities—often clusters of several cities, commoner towns, and villages—had no inland allies and at times even dispensed with kings.

The Swahili city-states or port states were considerably smaller than the Christian or Islamic kingdoms of Nubia, Ethiopia, and southern, central, and western Africa. Nevertheless, the patricians' regalia clearly expressed the same royal aspirations. The Moroccan Muslim traveler Ibn Battuta (1304–1369) visited Mogadishu in 1331 and left a detailed description of the African-spiritual and Islamic royal customs as

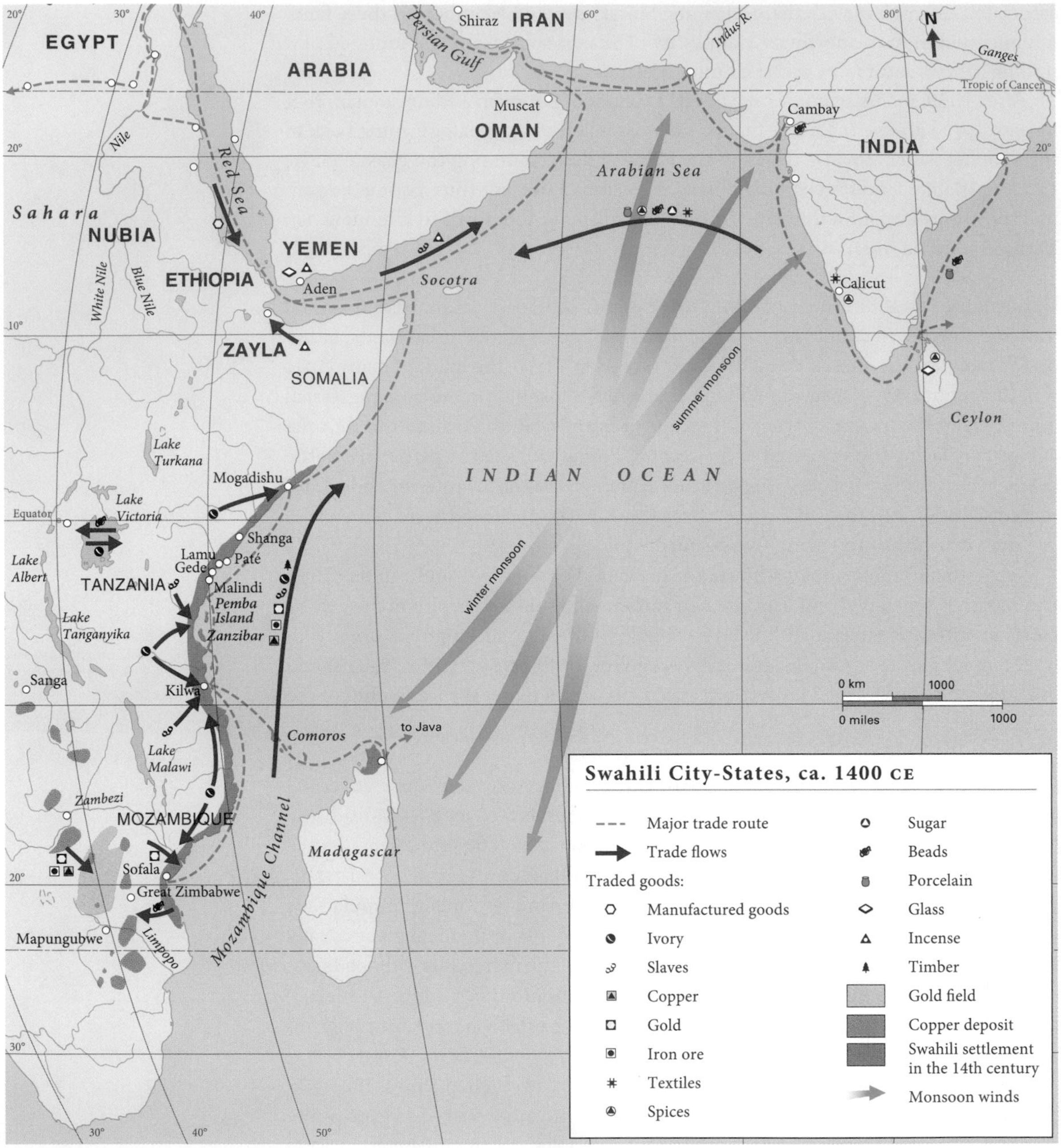

MAP **14.3 Swahili City-States, ca. 1400.**

displayed by Sheikh Abu Bakr, who claimed Yemeni Sharifian descent. Every Friday, so Ibn Battuta writes, the king attended the noon prayer in his enclosed space in the mosque. Afterward, in a procession led by royal musicians (playing large drums, trumpets, and wind instruments), the king, judge, officials, and military commanders walked through town to the audience hall of the palace. The most important royal prerogative was the minting of coins, made of copper or gold. Given, however, that power on the Swahili coast was based on commercial, and not landed, wealth from which to collect taxes, in administrative practice the kings were never more than firsts among equals in the patriciate.

Another prominent visitor was Zheng He, the admiral whom the Ming emperors entrusted with an Indian Ocean expedition and who in 1405 explored among other areas the Swahili coast (see Chapter 12). Wherever he landed along the coast, he presented his hosts with gold, silver, porcelain, and silk. In return, the Swahili rulers and merchants presented the visitors with the exotic tropical animals (as seen in the following image) they often bought from their contacts in the African interior. Zheng He followed maritime routes well traveled in previous centuries, and even though his journey was more for the purpose of displaying Ming power after the Mongol interlude, it can be seen as falling within the pattern of routine merchant journeys across the Indian Ocean and the South China Sea.

Traditional Kingdoms in Southern and Central Africa

The first region in the interior where a pattern of increasing wealth and population density became visible during the period 600–1505 was southern Africa, on and around the Zimbabwean plateau. Here, the original foragers of the vast grasslands were in the process of adapting to the Bantu culture arriving from the north, which included the influx of herders and farmers discussed in Chapter 6. Chiefs became powerful on the basis of large herds of cattle. Later, by trading first ivory and then also gold to coastal Swahili merchants, the chiefs initiated a pattern of political formation, building cities and kingdoms, such as Mapungubwe and Great

Gift of a Lion by a Swahili Merchant. This painting, which dates from the Ming Dynasty (1368–1648), depicts the exchanges between East Africa and the Ming court in China.

Zimbabwe. Adapting their new economic power to indigenous traditions, these kings assumed the same exalted status which we encountered in the cases of Christian Nubia and Ethiopia.

The Kingdom of Mapungubwe In the course of the 700s, hunters increasingly went after elephants for their ivory. Khariji Swahili merchants from the north had founded the coastal town of Chibuene for the purpose of buying ivory, in return for textiles, glass beads, glazed pottery, and glass bottles. These items, being storable goods, added to the wealth accumulated by chiefs. Thus, the ivory trade marked the beginning of the southern African hinterland being incorporated into Swahili long-distance trade.

When chiefs acquired cattle and imported goods from the coast, the first towns arose in the interior. Larger towns with around 1,500 inhabitants followed during the next few centuries, culminating with Mapungubwe [mah-poon-GOOB-way], the capital of the first full-fledged kingdom (1070–1300), with some 5,000 inhabitants. In the early 900s, villagers to the north, on the Zimbabwean plateau, began to mine gold, which for the next four centuries was the major export item from Swahili cities to the Middle East and India. Workshops for the manufacture of ivory and gold figurines in the Limpopo towns testify to the emergence of an indigenous demand for the products of specialized craftspeople. When Mapungubwe arose as an urban-centered kingdom, the southern African interior not only was integrated into the Swahili Indian Ocean trade but also developed the crucial urban and royal mark of an urban craftspeople class who did not practice agriculture and cattle herding.

Excavations in Mapungubwe and ethnographic studies have yielded important insights into the institution of southern African kingship. The king resided on a hill that had previously been used chiefly for rainmaking ceremonies. He and his family were in ritual seclusion from the commoners, who lived in the town at the foot of the hill. The hill also contained residences for a few senior wives. Many female members of the royal family resided in villages outside Mapungubwe, where they were married to allies and clients of the kings. The graves of the royal cemetery contained large numbers of gold and glass beads, a bowl made of gold leaf, and shards of Chinese dishes. Seclusion and an elaborate set of regalia thus marked the king of Mapungubwe (see Source 14.3).

Golden Rhinoceros. This golden rhinoceros was found among the items of the royal dynasty of Mapungubwe, signifying the power and magic of the kings. The kingdom was organized around the mining and trading of gold with the Swahili cities and, from there, with the Islamic Middle East.

Court rituals emphasized the exalted position of the king. The king was in charge of rainmaking ceremonies and harvest feasts, but the actual rituals were conducted by the diviner. Of forager descent and often itinerant, diviners were experts in spirituality, experienced in dealing with the realm of the benevolent and evil spirits. Although royal power was associated with spiritual authority, there was an institutional division between the king's power over life and death and the diviner's authority to summon the spirits. Thus, African kingship shared the pattern of rulership development encountered also in Eurasia and the Americas: Royal power was legitimate only if combined with spiritual or divine authority.

The Kingdom of Great Zimbabwe The kingdom of Great Zimbabwe (1250–1505) represents the culmination of the southern African kingdoms (see Map 14.4). Initially a tributary state of Mapungubwe, Great Zimbabwe emerged as a kingdom in its own right when the cooling and drying trend in the climate, which in Eurasia signaled the end of the early medieval agricultural expansion, made agriculture in the relatively dry Limpopo valley more difficult. Inhabitants abandoned Mapungubwe in the second half of the 1200s, with evidence of some royalty migrating north to Great Zimbabwe, which was more humid.

Great Zimbabwe, Passageway. The man, visible at the end of the curve, provides an idea of the massive urban structures erected under the kings. The stonemasons were highly specialized craftspeople, who constructed walls that have outlasted the demise of the Zimbabwe kingdom in the middle of the fifteenth century.

Great Zimbabwe was located at the southern end of the arc of rock surfaces on the Zimbabwean plateau where gold was found. Granite for the construction of stone walls could be quarried easily, using heat from fires to split off layers of rock. Regular building blocks from these layers could be dressed with less effort than in Mapungubwe. At its height, the capital encompassed 18,000 inhabitants and was the seat of a kingdom extending northward across the Zimbabwean plateau. Most settlements in the kingdom were dedicated to gold mining and trading, but a few practiced different trades, such as iron mining and salt panning. The primary sources of income, however, were cattle and grain.

Today, three main archaeological complexes remain of the capital. The first is a hill with a walled palace, accessible through a staircase. Two other complexes at a distance of half a mile to the south are the Western and Central Valley Walled Enclosures. The best-known structure is the so-called Great Enclosure within the Western Enclosure complex, an imposing 36-foot-high circular wall built of closely fitting blocks of granite. The royal palace precinct contained buildings similar to those in Mapungubwe. In the enclosures, some of the better-preserved ruins indicate that they once were buildings with solid stone walls, with plastered and perhaps even painted surfaces inside. Some residences were connected with walls which formed courtyards or narrow passageways. All enclosures were once densely packed with houses, presumably occupied by the kings and/or the ruling classes. Commoners lived in the space between the hill and the two enclosures, occupying simple thatched huts built with timber and plastered with clay.

The kingdom of Great Zimbabwe ended around 1505 when Swahili merchants replaced the initial southern Limpopo trade route with the shorter northern Zambezi route. A Chinese porcelain dish bearing this date was found in a burned and collapsed structure in the compound, though it appears that portions of Great Zimbabwe were still inhabited for some time. Thus, there was some overlap between the decline of Zimbabwe and the rise of the new trade route.

Central African Chiefdoms and Kingdoms

The central African rain forest and savanna, although more sparsely settled than most other parts of Africa during 600–1450, nevertheless participated in the general pattern of increased agricultural production and population expansion. In a number of places, especially the Congo Basin, relatively favorable agricultural conditions

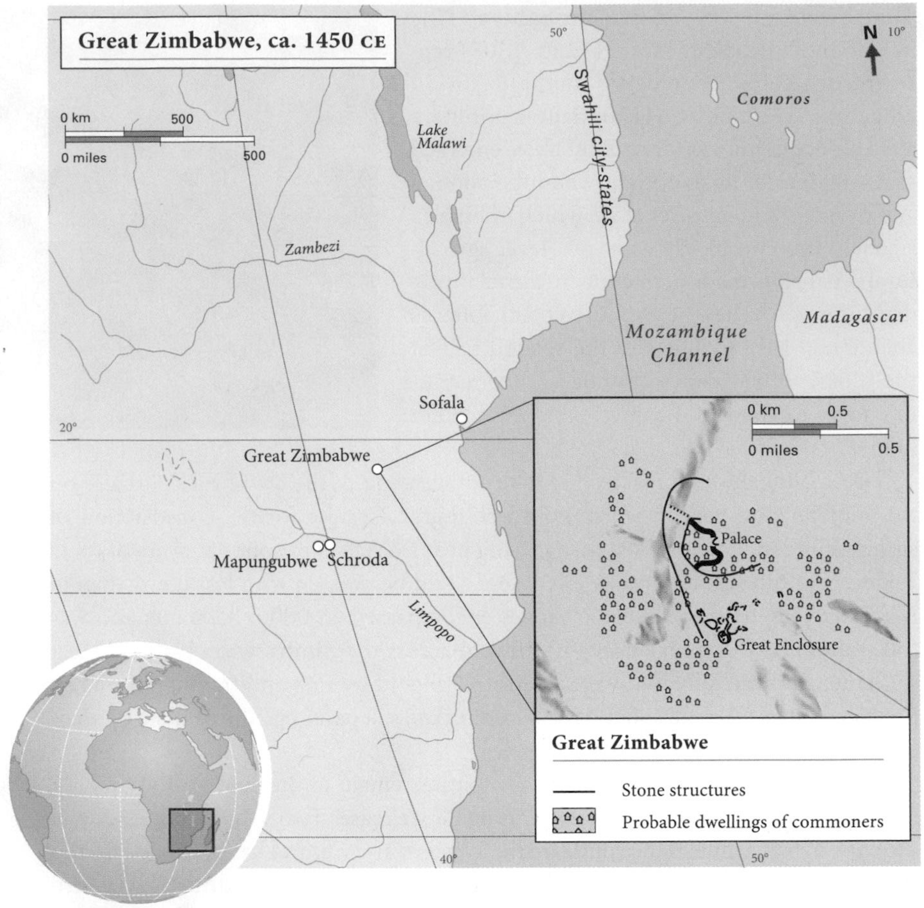

MAP 14.4 Great Zimbabwe, ca. 1450.

supported the formation of chiefdoms which evolved into kingdoms. One savanna site, the Lake Upemba depression in the south of today's Democratic Republic of the Congo, was the home of the Luba people, who founded a kingdom based on a diversified agriculture and regional trade sometime in the period between 1000 and 1300 (see Map 14.5).

Luba Origins Archaeologists date the earliest evidence for the existence of permanent agricultural and fishing settlements around Lake Upemba to the period around 800. They found these settlements between the lakes, marshes, and rivers of one of the tributaries of the Congo River. Apart from fish, the villagers also relied on sorghum, millet, chickens, goats, and sheep for their sustenance. Locally produced iron and salt added to the resources. Hunting groups cut across the village lineages and formed the nucleus, around 1000, for the emergence of chiefs who were recognizable in their graves through copper ornaments. Copper had to be acquired through regional trade with the west, and its value made it the metal preferred for jewelry, as in many other parts of Africa.

Luba oral tradition reaches back to the period between 1000 and 1300. The founding myth appears to refer to a process whereby two chiefs, each claiming his own source of legitimacy, were competing for the unification of the villages. As in many other African foundation stories, the true founder is conceived of as a suffering, disadvantaged hero who has to go against multiple enemies before becoming a successful founder king. In the traditions of Africa, as in those of many other parts of the world, exalted kingship was unacceptable unless rooted in humble beginnings.

Similar to the kings of Mapungubwe and Zimbabwe, Luba kings possessed magic powers, which entitled only the descendants from their bloodline to succeed to the throne. The chieftains of other clans, although holding court offices and meeting in council to assist in the administration, were excluded from the succession. The royal clan maintained a small military force, sufficient to collect tributes from outlying villages but not large enough to destroy any of the chieftainships. A stable balance was established between the king and the chieftains, making Luba the model for subsequent kingdoms in the savanna of central Africa. The Luba kingdom itself survived until the beginning of Belgian colonialism at the end of the nineteenth century.

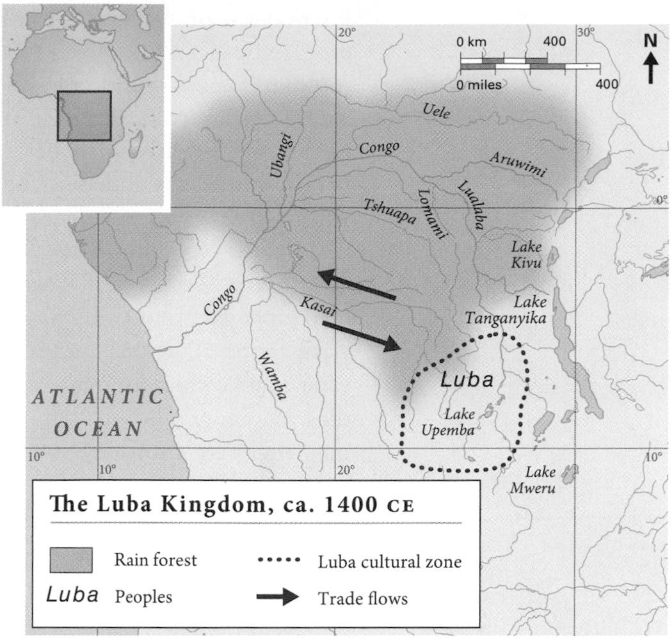

MAP 14.5 The Luba Kingdom, ca. 1400.

Cultural Encounters: West African Traditions and Islam

A pattern of regional trade, urbanization, and chiefdom formation was also characteristic for the Sahel and savanna of West Africa from the middle of the first millennium CE onward. Around 600, chiefs became kings when they unified their clans, conquered some neighbors from whom they collected tributes, and arranged alliances with others. Like their later African colleagues in the eastern half of Africa, they claimed to possess magic powers and adopted royal customs of seclusion. Two kingdoms, ancient Ghana and Mali, followed each other in the period 600–1450. Their royal–military ruling clans benefited from trans-Saharan trade with Islamic civilization and gradually converted to Islam, while the general population of herders, farmers, miners, smiths, and other craftspeople remained faithful to their African religious traditions.

The Kingdom of Ancient Ghana

Ancient Ghana emerged in the 600s as the strongest group of chiefdoms in the Sahel and savanna between the Niger inland delta in the east and the Senegal valley in the west. It advanced to the status of a kingdom after 750, when it became the center for trade across the Sahara with the North African Islamic states. Thanks to this trade, the kingdom was dominant in the Sahel for half a millennium. In the 1100s, however, drought and provincial unrest weakened Ghana. The kingdom gave way in 1240 to Mali, an empire which began its rise in the upper Niger rain forest and savanna.

Formation of Ancient Ghana As discussed in Chapter 6, a long period of progressive desertification (3000–300 BCE) had driven the inhabitants of the southern Sahara southward into what became the Sahel, a belt of steppe, grassland, and marginal agriculture. They had domesticated millet and bred cattle herds in Saharan villages shortly before the desiccation began. During the period 600 BCE–600 CE, the climate stabilized, and millet agriculture, cattle herding, and village formation expanded across the Sahel and northern savanna from Lake Chad in the east to the Senegal valley in the west. In some places, as in the inland delta of the Niger, where irrigation was possible, villages were clustering. Jenné-jeno emerged around 300 as a city surrounded by a cluster of villages. The city was a center of regional trade for iron and gold from the upper Niger and Senegal valleys and copper from the Sahara, in return for urban manufactures, such as textiles, leather goods, metal implements, and utensils. The people who populated the Sahel were ethnically Soninke, speaking a Niger-Congo language, as the majority of West Africans did.

After 300, the regional trade became a long-distance trade. Thanks to the arrival of the Arabian camel among the Berbers of North Africa and the northern Sahara, it became possible to travel through the desert. Long-distance merchants from the cities of Roman North Africa made contact with Soninke merchants in the Sahel, some 3 months away by camel caravan. They exchanged Roman manufactures, such as glassware, cloth, and ceramics, plus Saharan copper and salt for gold. Berber miners in the central Sahara quarried salt from deposits left by dried-up prehistoric lakes. Cowrie shells, imported by Rome from the Indian Ocean and exported to West Africa, attest to trade connections even farther than the Mediterranean.

It took some time, however, for the initially infrequent trans-Saharan exchanges to intensify and become regular. Only after the loss of their gold mines in northwestern Iberia to Germanic migrants did the Romans regularize the trans-Saharan trade, beginning in the mid-500s. The regularization had a profound effect in the Sahel. In the 600s, Soninke chiefs on the western outskirts of the inland Niger delta, enriched by the profits from the Saharan trade, equipped their followers with arms, such as swords and lances. Riding on small West African horses immune to the diseases carried by the tsetse fly (see Chapter 6), they subjugated more distantly related Soninke groups in the Sahel between the Niger and Senegal valleys. In the mid-700s, one of the chiefs proclaimed himself king in Wagadu, a city in the Sahel northwest of the inland delta, and founded the kingdom of ancient Ghana (as distinguished from the modern state of Ghana).

As told in the founding myth at the beginning of this chapter, Dinga was the first mythical king. His kingdom, so it was foretold, was destined to rule the Sahel, dominate the gold trade, and benefit from abundant rain as long as its subjects sacrificed a virgin and a colt every year to its well-dwelling patron snake. Modern scholars would say that ancient Ghana lasted through the wet period of the first millennium (300–1100) and eventually succumbed to the successor state of Mali, when it could not adapt in the Sahel to the emerging dry period (1100–1500) (see Source 14.4).

From Roman to Islamic Trade Ancient Ghana received its gold from Bambuk, a region in the rain forest at the western edge of the kingdom. Villagers on a left-bank tributary of the middle Senegal River panned and mined the metal during the dry season, and Soninke merchants transported it by donkey and bullock some 500 miles east to Wagadu. The Bambuk gold fields occupied a no-man's-land between the kingdom of ancient Ghana and the chiefdom of Takrur on the lower Senegal. The two polities left the villagers to their own devices, since neither possessed the technical and administrative means to organize or even control the panning and mining operations. Soninke merchants went no farther than nearby towns, from which they conducted their trading activities with the villagers.

Romanized Berbers gave way to Islamized Berbers in the trans-Saharan trade after about 750. As was the case in Swahili East Africa, Khariji merchants, pushed by the emerging Islamic empire into the outer provinces, were the first Muslims to travel to the African interior. According to an eleventh-century Arabic source, Wagadu was a twin city, with its merchant and royal halves several miles apart. If Wagadu can be identified with the partially excavated ruins of Koumbi-Saleh on the southern border of today's Mauritania—an identification still disputed among scholars—the merchant city had a dozen mosques, a marketplace, and residences. Several thousand inhabitants called it their home.

The royal city consisted of a domed palace and other domed buildings, including a courthouse and the homes of the king's treasurer, translator, and other ministers. A grove surrounded the palace area, containing the royal prison and the dwellings of the priests and diviners, as well as the tombs of ancestral kings. In contrast to their Swahili colleagues, the kings of Ghana avoided a combination of traditional kingship with Islam. Even though they benefited from including Muslims in their administration, they were not about to surrender their exalted, magical royal authority over life and death to the supremacy of Islamic law.

From African Spirituality to Islam in the Ruling Class While the kings of Ghana had reasons to hold on to traditional African spirituality, the Soninke merchants gradually converted to Islam. Business with the North African and Middle Eastern merchants was easier to transact if everyone adhered to the same ethics and laws. By the early 1000s, the merchants in the trading towns near the Bambuk villages were Muslims, and the adjacent state of Takrur had also become Islamic. The sectarian Khariji Islam gave way to mainstream Sunnism. In North Africa, the proponents of Sunnism were the Almoravids, southern Moroccan Berbers who spearheaded a movement that evolved into a short-lived empire in Morocco, the western Sahara, and Islamic Spain.

Perhaps under the pressure of the Almoravids, in the early 1100s the kings of Ghana followed their merchants by also converting to Islam. The Sahel and savanna villagers, however, remained wedded to their African spirituality. As a result, Ghana now resembled the states on the Swahili coast and their hinterlands, where only the rulers and merchants were Muslim. In addition to the villagers, a number of allied Soninke chiefs remained faithful to traditional spirituality; and during the second half of the 1100s the cohesion of the kingdom began to soften. In 1180, the founding clan of ancient Ghana ceded power to another clan, which established a new dynasty in Wagadu and adopted a policy of conquest of the southern savanna. For the next half-century Ghana was an imperial power, trading gold not only from the Senegal River in the west but also from newly developed fields in the rain forest on the upper Niger and Black Volta Rivers (see Map 14.6).

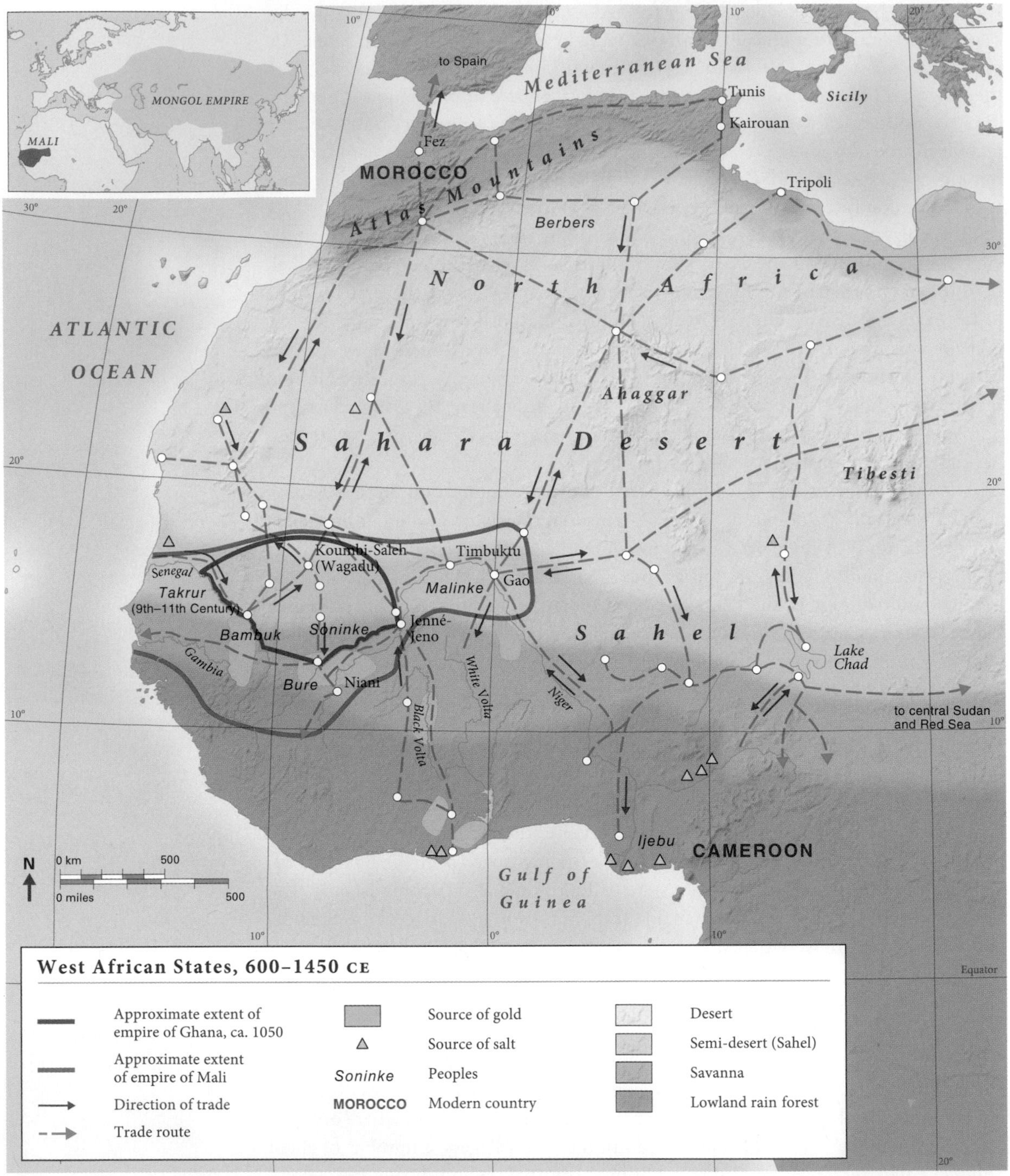

MAP 14.6 West African States, 600–1450.

map analysis

The Empire of Mali

The opening of new gold fields in the rain forest exposed hitherto marginal peoples to the influence of long-distance trade, royal rule, and Islam. One of these peoples, the Malinke (variant terms Manden, Mandinka), followed the by-now-familiar pattern of rallying around an inspiring chief who, as a conqueror, laid the foundations for an expanding polity. By uniting both savanna and Sahel peoples, the Malinke built the empire of Mali, a polity of many ethnic, linguistic, and religious groups. At its height, Mali stretched from the Atlantic to the Niger bend and from the Sahara to the rain forest.

Increased Trade Mali was the beneficiary of a significantly increased demand for gold in the Islamic realm on the other side of the Sahara. In addition to the existing Islamic mints, Christian mints began to stamp gold coins. The king of Castile in Spain was the first, in 1173, and by the mid-1200s Italian city-states had followed suit. In response to this increased demand, merchants encouraged the aforementioned opening of new gold fields in the savanna and rain forest of the upper Niger and its tributaries.

The people in this region were Malinke villagers who spoke a language related to that of the Soninke in the north but who were ethnically distinct. In the course of the 1000s, these villagers had acculturated to ancient Ghana, which they recognized as overlord. Living in dozens of chiefdoms, the Malinke also encompassed hunter groups, apart from the chiefdoms, which formed the basis for ambitious leaders seeking to unify the Malinke. When the new dynasty of Ghana conquered much of the Malinke lands at the end of the 1100s, resistance led by the hunters against the new rulers rose quickly. In a rebellion in 1230–1235, the Malinke not only liberated themselves but went on to conquer ancient Ghana.

The leader of the conquest was the inspiring hero Sundiata (also spelled Sunjata or Sundjata, ca. 1217–1255). He and his adventures were at the center of an **oral tradition**, with traveling bards telling stories which they handed down from generation to generation and told and retold publicly in villages. In the nineteenth and twentieth centuries, anthropologists recorded these traditions and made them available in translation. According to this tradition, at the head of a cavalry force borrowed from a chiefdom in the Sahel, Sundiata defeated ancient Ghana in 1235 and founded the empire of Mali, with its capital, Niani, on an upper Niger tributary in modern Guinea.

Oral traditions: Myths, tales, and stories (e.g., the foundation myth of Wagadu) handed down from generation to generation. In the absence of other sources, oral traditions should not be equated with documented history.

The Malian Empire Mali was the first enduring empire in sub-Saharan Africa, lasting officially for over four centuries (1235–1645). At its height in the early 1300s, Mali encompassed most of the West African Sahel, large parts of the savanna, and the gold fields in the rain forest—a territory surpassed only by that of the contemporary Mongol Empire. At the core of the empire were privileged Malinke clans whose kings and chiefs formed an alliance and met in an assembly (Malinke *gbara*), under the emperors who assumed the title of *mansa*. We do not know how frequently or long this assembly met. Oral tradition records the laws, customs, and traditions of which the assembly was the guardian and according to which the empire was governed. As in Mesopotamia, Vedic India, Greece, and Rome, Mali preserved traditions of chiefly assemblies from preroyal forms of social organization.

The Epic of Sundiata

Similar to that of ancient Ghana, Mali's power rested on a large, horseborne army recruited from the Soninke clans that could move swiftly and overwhelm its opponents with surprise attacks. From the 1300s onward Mali began to import tall Middle Eastern and North African horses in larger numbers and formed cavalry units equipped with chain mail, lances, and swords. But this cavalry was probably not large enough to become the elite force characteristic of the Middle East and

Patterns Up Close

The Sculptures of Ife

Guardian Figure, Bakota Area, Gabon, Nineteenth–Twentieth Century (*a*). The abstract Bakota figure, with its generic geometric elements, represents the collective lineage spirit; the much more realistic Nigerian figure on the next page represents royalty who wished to be remembered individually.

Sculptures, figures, and figurines in Africa followed a pattern that was shared early on with Eurasia and, during the periods of 600 BCE–600 CE and 600–1450 CE, also with Australia, the Pacific, and parts of the Americas. Broadly speaking, forager, village, and pastoral societies developing in the direction of chiefdoms, but not yet kingdoms, preserved traditional ancestor cults within their African spirituality.

As lineages evolved, the memory of the generations between the founder and living people blurred so that the in-between ancestors became an anonymous collective. The spirits of the ancestors in the invisible world, therefore, were conceived as being collectively present, to be consulted, nourished through sacrifices, or cajoled. One could "trap" them in sculptures, figures, and figurines, which emphasized the head, believed to be the seat of the spirit, at the expense of the torso and limbs, which were indicated in rudimentary fashion. Even the heads were generally fashioned in abstract, geometrically simplified ways, corresponding to the collective nature of the ancestors. These artifacts, therefore, were not "primitive," even though they are still today often described as such. Their style was generic because the collective of the ancestors was generic.

When societies reached levels of wealth and complexity that led to the emergence of kingdoms, kings became exceptional persons, endowed with ancestral magic or a divine mandate to exercise power, not merely chiefly authority. Generic ancestor "traps" would not do: Artists had to apply the techniques of naturalistic

Europe prior to the introduction of firearms. Infantry, using bow and arrow and moving about on small horses, continued to form the backbone of the military.

Also like their royal predecessors in ancient Ghana, the Malian emperors relied on a small central administration primarily concerned with finances and justice and run by Muslims as well as by slaves. The empire financed itself with tributes from vassal kingdoms in the Sahel and river chiefdoms with villagers and fishermen, as well as taxes on the commerce of gold, iron, copper, salt, textiles (both local and foreign), leather goods, and other manufactures. Since the new gold fields and the capital of Niani were located on a tributary of the Niger, the rulers relied on water transport downriver to the cities of Jenné-jeno, Timbuktu (founded in 1100), and Gao. In the mid-1300s, these three cities replaced Wagadu as the main transshipment centers of goods for the Saharan caravans. With the rise of Mali, the trans-Saharan trade shifted eastward.

Mansa Musa, from the Catalan Atlas

In 1324, the most famous ruler of Mali, Mansa Musa (r. ca. 1312–1337), annexed the city of Timbuktu from its Touareg Berber founders. There he founded a college (Arabic *madrasa*) and library, part of the Sankoré Mosque. Timbuktu became a center of learning, focused on Islamic law but also offering geometry, algebra, geography, and astronomy as ancillary fields of study, which judges and independent scholars were required to know. The independent scholars were often well-off members of merchant families. Many kept private libraries in their residences, where they and their descendants accumulated masses of manuscripts over the centuries, estimated today to number in the hundreds of thousands. In the mid-1400s, with some

representation so that the kings would recognize themselves in them. Of course, after a while sculptures turned into generic likenesses again, as they did in Mesopotamia and Egypt, since kingship evolved into an ordinary institution with undistinguished kings not worth remembering (*a*).

The Ife terra-cotta, copper, and bronze royal heads stem from that short, experimental, and highly innovative time period of about 200 years (1100–1300) when kingship was new in Ife. The naturalism of these figures is striking, especially when one takes into consideration that Christian and Muslim figurative art during the same period was still nonrepresentative, in the sense of being hieratic—that is, it typically represented standardized ideas about how biblical and prophetic figures should look so that their God-pleasing nature was immediately recognizable. The stripes on the faces of some Ife figures (*b*) are believed to represent *scarifications*, or scars marking the passage from youth to adulthood or distinguishing one lineage from another, as practiced in parts of Africa.

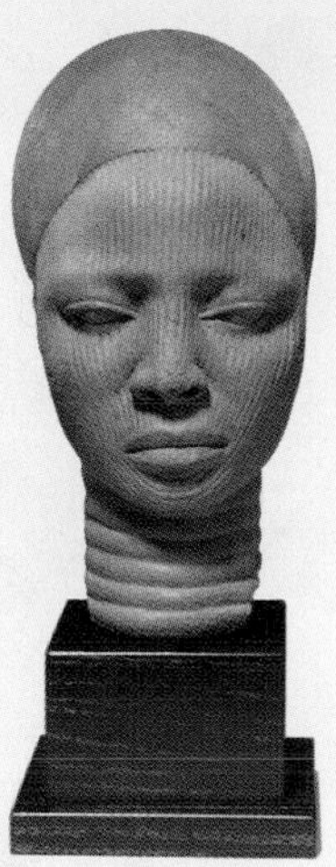

Ife Shrine Head, Terra-Cotta, Nigeria, ca. 1200 (*b*).

Questions

- How does the history of African sculpture, such as those from Ife, provide evidence for studying the patterns of state building in this period?
- Why does material culture represent such an important dimension in understanding the African past?

100,000 inhabitants, the commercial and scholarly hub of Timbuktu was one of the larger cities in the world (see Source 14.2).

The Decentralization of Mali Timbuktu flourished even while its imperial overlord, Mali, became more loosely organized in the later 1300s. Weak rulers arrived on the throne and dynastic disputes broke out. Outside groups that had adapted to Malian influences—rain-forest groups with newly acquired horses and Touareg nomads from the desert—attacked from the south and north. As a result, some of the subjugated provinces in the Sahel began to break away and established independent kingdoms. More generally, even though Mali had exploited the weakening of ancient Ghana at the onset of the dry period after 1100, the deepening of the drought conditions eventually caught up with Mali as well. By 1450, Mali had shrunk to a kingdom in the savanna.

Rain-Forest Kingdoms

As discussed in earlier chapters, the West African rain forest was a 200-mile-wide strip of tropical vegetation stretching from modern Guinea above the southwestern corner of West Africa to Cameroon on the bend to central Africa, where it transitions to the Congo rain forest. In the earlier period of 600 BCE to 600 CE, savanna peoples with iron implements had entered the rain forest and founded villages in clearings, farming oil palms, yams, and bananas. As elsewhere in Africa, the result was a pattern of political formation which included village clusters, chiefdoms, and kingdoms with urban centers and sophisticated crafts, such as bronze casting in Nigeria.

The Sankoré Mosque of Timbuktu, Mali. The mosque evolved in the fourteenth century into a large university with a library housing hundreds of thousands of manuscripts. A preservation program under UN auspices seeks to restore and preserve these manuscripts today.

The Kingdom of Ife The earliest village cluster to urbanize was that of Ife [EE-fay], west of the Niger delta, in 500 CE, the spiritual center of the Yoruba ethnic group and its oral traditions. By 1000 it was a kingdom with a walled capital, which enclosed a palace, groves, shrines, stone-built residences, and craft workshops for pottery, textiles, and glassware (especially beads). Courtyards and passageways in the city were paved with terra-cotta, to remain passable during the rainy season. One highly developed art was sculpting, in terra-cotta, copper, or bronze, documenting Ife's urban achievements.

Sungbo's Eredo Ife set the example for several further chiefdoms to advance to the threshold of kingdoms between 1000 and 1450. One of them toward the north was Oyo, which (thanks to the adoption of a cavalry force) expanded from the rain forest northward toward the edge of the savanna. It arose as a trade center for the exchange of palm oil kernels and kola nuts (a mild narcotic containing caffeine) in return for Mediterranean manufactures and Sahel horses, through first Ghanaian and then Malian merchants. In the other chiefdoms, leaders mobilized villagers for the construction of earthworks, including Sungbo's Eredo, which astound even today with their size and scope. One of these chiefdoms, Ijebu, encompassed a capital and villages on a territory of 22 square miles, surrounded by a combined moat and rampart up to 70 feet deep/high and 100 miles long. In nearby Benin, smaller earthworks around villages collectively added up to 10,000 miles and became the nucleus for an important kingdom in 1440. In both Ijebu and Benin, the moats and ramparts cut through the hard, iron-saturated soil, rivers, and swamps, requiring centuries of hard labor with nothing more than iron shovels.

Scholars are still undecided over the purpose of these constructions: Did they protect against enemies and elephants, were they boundary markers for ancestral lands and their spirits, or did they facilitate the collection of tolls? Perhaps they were intended to do all three. Equally difficult is the explanation for the phenomenon of collective labor: How were chiefs able to motivate workers to contribute their voluntary efforts? Evidently they were, as they were also in the Americas and Pacific, where followers built huge temples or rolled heavy stone sculptures across distances. Authority without power, buttressed by ancestral pedigree and spirituality, can thus be seen as a powerful motivator to take on great tasks and validate the institutions it represents (see Source 14.5).

Putting It All Together

interactive concept map

Africa in the period 600–1450 displayed patterns of political and cultural development that included the creative adaptation of African spirituality to the monotheisms of Christianity and Islam and indigenous kingdom formation. Depending on regional conditions and the degree of integration into Eurasian long-distance trade, peoples in the different parts of sub-Saharan Africa mixed the two cultural heritages of Christianity and Islam in a variety of ways. The Nile valley and northeastern highlands, long adapted to the Mediterranean prior to 600, incorporated Christianity into their local traditions. They adopted the Christian institutional division between kingship and church, in which kingship was a sacred office but subject to Christian law and ethics. The church, for its part, was an autonomous, hierarchical body. As in post-1000 Christian western Europe, the Nubian and Ethiopian churches were subject to a distant religious authority.

Coastal East and West Africa adopted Islam, which arrived through merchants, not soldiers or missionaries. In East Africa, Islam took root among the coastal people and did not penetrate inland. In West Africa, only merchants and kings converted but did so across the interior. Thus, Africans adapted to Christianity and Islam during 600–1450 in very different ways.

In the same period, African kingship was a new institution with roots in the traditions of chieftainship in villages and village clusters. The kings emphasized their royal powers over life and death but also continued to claim the traditional chiefly powers of spirituality and magic. As Christians or Muslims, they paid at least lip service to the divine laws to which they were subject. In southern and central Africa, kingship arose from its African context without modification by Christian or Islamic law, and it is important to emphasize that Africa needed neither Christianity nor Islam to embark on its own distinctive pattern of kingdom formation.

During 600–1450, however, this pattern clearly remained an exception amid the sub-Saharan population, the majority of which remained "stateless," to use an expression in common use among historians of Africa. This population, organized in farming villages or herder camps, possessed chiefs, often with slave retinues, but did not grow into larger polities or trade farther away than regionally for locally unavailable metals and salt. It also had specialized craftspeople forming villages, such as smiths or leather workers. The silent presence of this unrecorded majority of stateless Africans should always be kept in mind, alongside the kingdoms and empires, in seeking to understand Africa's significance in world history during this period.

Review and Relate

Thinking Through Patterns

Examine the ways historians approach the big questions of this chapter.

In the period 600–1450, the northeast of sub-Saharan Africa was firmly drawn into the orbit of eastern Christian and Islamic civilizations, without, however, fully adopting their formative patterns. Perhaps the most extensive adaptation occurred in the sphere of trade, where the Christian kingdoms became the providers of luxury goods, such as ivory, skins, and hardwoods from tropical Africa to the Middle East and eastern Mediterranean, in return for manufactures, Indian spices, and Chinese silks. Beginning in 1250 in the Nilotic kingdom of Nubia, the expansionist regime of the Muslim Mamluks in Egypt put the African Christians on the defensive. By 1450 the middle Nile region was Islamized. In contrast, an expansionist Christian Ethiopia put Muslims on the coast of the Red Sea on the defensive and Christianized the pagan southern highlands.

» What patterns of adaptation did the Christian kingdoms of northeast Africa demonstrate in their interactions with the civilizations of the Middle East and eastern Mediterranean?

What were the responses of Africans to Muslim merchants who connected them with the trading zone of the Indian Ocean and Mediterranean? As these Africans adapted to Islam, which forms of political organization did they adopt?

The inclusion of the East African coast and sub-Saharan West Africa into the Muslim Indian Ocean and Mediterranean trading zone resulted in the rise of small coastal Swahili states and two large West African polities: the kingdom of ancient Ghana and the empire of Mali. Muslim mariners and merchants interacted with Islamized local African rulers and merchants to exchange Middle Eastern textiles, leather goods, and metal wares for ivory, gold, slaves, skins, and hardwoods. African rulers and merchants obtained their African goods from pagan miners and hunters in the African interior outside their states. Adaptation to Islamic religious civilization was a phenomenon limited to the ruling classes and associated merchant circles.

In what ways did the economic and political transformations on the East African coast and in West Africa affect developments in the interior?

The adaptation of coastal East Africa to Islamic religious civilization had an indirect effect on the interior in the region of southern Africa. Here, chiefs in Zimbabwe attached themselves to the Swahili trade network and used the wealth from this trade for the transformation of their chiefdoms into kingdoms. Impressive masonry constructions serving as centers for incipient administrative structures testify to the ability of kings to transform chiefly authority into royal military power. The East and West African expansion of trade under the impact of Islam may have also indirectly led to a population increase in the interior of Africa. Such an increase became noticeable toward the 1300s, especially in the Congo Basin, where the Luba kingdom was the first to emerge.

Against the Grain

Consider this as a counterpoint to the main patterns examined in this chapter.

Sundiata's Rise to Power

- What are the similarities and differences between the epics of Sundiata and Homer (Chapter 7)?
- Compare the messages of the Epic of Sundiata and Machiavelli's *The Prince* (Chapter 17). In what ways are they comparable, even if separated by time and region?

The Sundiata epic is the story of a disadvantaged hero who rises in spite of the most hostile environment imaginable. It begins with a king's sister: Insulted by not receiving her fair share of a meal during a royal feast, she turns herself into a forest buffalo and devastates the fields of the kingdom's villages. Hunters from the neighboring kingdom of the Malinke slay her. As forest people, they know how to deal with the dangerous spirits of the wilderness (such as buffaloes). The king rewards them with an ugly hunchback woman, heir of the buffalo spirit's forest powers. The reward is in fulfillment of a prophecy according to which the Malinke king has to find an ugly hunchback to give him a successor. But a jealous co-wife casts a spell, and Sundiata, the successor, is born a cripple, walking on all fours. During puberty, thanks to the inheritance of his mother's forest powers, Sundiata stands up, uproots a tree, and becomes a physically superior man—a true hunter.

But the king's co-wife does not give up and forces Sundiata into exile. Her son, succeeding to the throne, is unable to withstand conquest by another neighboring king. As a former blacksmith, this king is endowed with forest powers. He uses them for malevolent purposes, tyrannizing the Malinke. In despair, the Malinke recall Sundiata from exile. The tyrant king and Sundiata fight each other in titanic battles. In the end, Sundiata prevails because his beautiful sister sacrifices her honor. During a one-night stand in the tyrant's chamber she discovers his dark secret: A cock's spur attached to an arrow can break his invulnerability. Shooting one such arrow, Sundiata achieves his final victory and creates the empire of Mali.

Traditional West African spirituality is built on the conceptualization of a world created by a remote god, in which civilization and nature mingle. Accordingly, existence is embedded in pairs of opposing but complementary elements, such as village/forest, civilization/wilderness, order/chaos, safety/danger, village farmer/forest hunter or blacksmith, man/woman, beauty/ugliness, invisible (masked) village spirits/visible forest spirits, etc. These pairs are skillfully woven into the epic, suggesting that figures marginal to village life, such as hunters or blacksmiths, can cut across the established social order with its jealousies and intrigues and tap into the wild, creative, benevolent (or evil) forces of nature, and found new kingdoms and empires.

Key Terms

audio flashcards

African spirituality 401
Coptic Christianity 402
Oral traditions 421
Patrician 409

For additional resources, please go to **www.oup.com/us/vonsivers.**
Please see the Further Resources section at the back of the book for additional readings and suggested websites.

PATTERNS OF EVIDENCE |

Sources for Chapter 14

SOURCE 14.1 *The Fetha Nagast,* Ethiopia

Fifteenth century

In the classical period Ethiopia was a multiethnic, multilingual, and multireligious state in which the kings limited the Church's conversion efforts. Nevertheless, the kings continued to emphasize their Christian identity, and this factor is reflected in their adoption and endorsement of the Fetha Nagast, or Law of the Kings, in the mid-fifteenth century. This legal code had originally been written in Arabic by a Coptic Christian in Egypt, probably in the mid-thirteenth century. While living under Muslim rule, the Copts were allowed to adopt portions of Justinian's law code and the resolutions of church councils for their own governance. Translated from Greek, and with many biblical passages added, the code connected Egyptian Christians to their Byzantine, Roman, and Judeo-Christian heritage, founding the basis of law squarely in that tradition. The Ethiopian monarchs had the Arabic source translated into Ge'ez (the state language of Ethiopia at the time), and the translator added a section on kingship, a portion of which is subsequently offered. The Law of the Kings remained the law in Ethiopia until 1930, when Emperor Haile Selassie I issued the country's first modern constitution.

CHAPTER XLIV

KINGS

Section I.

TH. The king you appoint must be one of your brethren. It is not proper for you to appoint over yourself an alien and an infidel, lest he multiply horses, women, gold and silver [to himself]. And when he sits on the throne of his kingdom, some priests shall write for him the Divine Book, so that he may keep it by his side and read it throughout his life, in order to learn the fear of God, his Creator, to observe his commandments, and to practice them, lest his heart become proud [and feel contempt] for his brethren. He must never swerve either to the right or to the left from what has been laid down in the Law, so that his days and his sons' days may be prolonged in his kingdom [Deuteronomy 17:15f], and his faith in God may be perfect. **EB 9.** Because of faith the walls of Jericho were

Source: Excerpt from *The Fetha Nagast*, trans. Paulos Tzadua, ed. Peter L. Strauss (Durham, NC: Carolina Academic Press, 2009), 271–273.

pulled down, when the sons of Israel marched around them for seven days. Because of faith, Gideon and Barak and Samson and Jephtha and David defeated the kings, served the cause of justice, found what they hoped for, were victors in war, and defeated the army of the enemy [Hebrews 11:30, 32f]. **RSTA 54**. And if the king becomes a heretic, from that moment he is no longer a king, but a rebel.

Section II.

Our Lord said in the Gospel: "Give to the king what is the king's and to God what is God's [Matthew 22:21]." And Apostle Paul said in his letter to the Romans: "Every one of you must be submissive to the authority of your ruler, since a ruler is appointed only by God. And God has appointed all these rulers. . . ." [Romans 13:1f].

St. John Chrysostom, in his explanation of this passage, has said: The Apostle had already shown [this] in his other letters, commanding the [lesser] chiefs to give due obedience to the higher chiefs, as the servant must obey the master. This the Apostle did, showing that Our Lord did not abrogate all the laws by His precepts, but confirmed them. And his saying: "Every soul" is because every man must conform himself to this; and his saying: "A ruler is appointed only by God," means that God has provided for the appointment of judges and rulers to take place, so that the world may become beautifully calm. And for that reason He has established the ruler, since equality of forces causes many wars. And God in His wisdom has established many kinds of authority, such as that of a man in respect to woman, the father in respect to the son, the old in respect to the young, the master in respect to the slave, the teacher in respect to the disciple, and, more so, the chief in respect to the one who is placed under him. The Lord acted in the same manner with the body, [creating] the head and placing the other parts under it; he also did thus with other animals, such as bees, **raza**, ants, antelopes, eagles, buffaloes, and all kinds of fish—every one has its chief, and when there is no authority there is confusion and lack of order. And his words: "Since he is God's minister calling thee to good and beautiful things," mean that he will lead you daily in your obedience to God. His punishments will be directed against those who rebel against God, murderers, fornicators, thieves, and wrong-doers; but his favors go to the obedient, who obey the Highest—Whose name be praised!—to those who despite the world and to those who do works of perfection and are righteous.

Raza: A type of bird.

. . .

Section III.

MAK 37. Let the king give honor to the order of the clergy, as Constantine, elected, faithful, and righteous king, and those who were after him did. Let him give from his wealth to each of them, according to their rank. First of all he shall give to the bishops, then to the priests, next, to the deacons, and then to those who are below them. He shall exempt them from tribute, presents, and the other things to be given to the rulers. Let him assign something to the churches for the maintenance of widows, orphans, and the poor, so that they may entreat God to strengthen the true faith with belief in the Holy Trinity, so that the day of the Christians' king may be long.

. . .

Section IV.

The king shall judge with equity in the middle of his people. He shall not be partial, either toward himself or toward the others, toward his son, his relatives, his friends, or the alien in any way which brings about injustice. And it is written in reference to kings: "The honored king loves justice, but the unjust king loves evil and injustice, to the ruin of his soul." And Solomon the wise has said: "To increase justice and save the oppressed is better than the offering and sacrifices" [Proverbs 21:3].

Do not take the wealth of anyone by violence; do not buy from him by force, either openly or by trick, in order not to be afflicted by God in this world and in the future. In this world, as befell the King Ahab and his wife Jezebel, when Naboth refused to sell him his vineyard and Jezebel schemed to kill him and took the vineyard; God smote Ahab and made his race perish; and next to him he smote Jezebel, and the dogs ate her in the aforesaid vineyard [2 Kings 21]. As for the future world, the Apostle said: "Wrong-doers and apostates shall not inherit God's Kingdom" [1 Corinthians 6:9].

» Working with Sources

1. **How does the author of this portion of *The Fetha Nagast* use biblical passages and historical comparisons to accentuate his points? Why?**
2. **What is the king's primary obligation to his people? Under what conditions could he lose his power?**

SOURCE 14.2 Ibn Battuta on Mali, from the *Rihla*

ca. 1354

One of the great world travelers of all time, Ibn Battuta was an educated Moroccan who journeyed throughout Africa, the Middle East, Persia, and Asia. In 1354, at age 50, Ibn Battuta dictated an account of his travels, the *Rihla* (the *Journey*), to Ibn Juzayy, a court secretary in Morocco. Both men therefore had a role to play in shaping the narrative.

I set out on the 1st Muharram of the year seven hundred and fifty-three (18 February, 1352 CE) with a caravan including amongst others a number of the merchants of Sijilmasa [present-day Morocco/Algerian frontier region]. After twenty-five days we reached Taghaza, an unattractive village, with the curious feature that its houses and mosques are built of blocks of salt, roofed with camel skins. There are no trees there, nothing but sand. In the sand is a

Source: Ibn Battuta, "Mali," from *Travels in Asia and Africa, 1325–1354*, trans. and ed. H. A. R. Gibb (New York: Robert M. McBride, 1929), 323–327, 329–330.

salt mine; they dig for the salt, and find it in thick slabs, lying one on top of the other, as though they had been tool-squared and laid under the surface of the earth. A camel will carry two of these slabs. No one lives at Taghaza except the slaves of the Masufa tribe, who dig for the salt; they subsist on dates imported from Dara and Sijilmasa, camel's flesh, and millet imported from the Negrolands. The Negroes come up from their country and take away the salt from there. At Walata a load of salt brings eight to ten mithqals; in the town of Mali it sells for twenty to thirty, and sometimes as much as forty. The Negroes use salt as a medium of exchange, just as gold and silver is used elsewhere; they cut it up into pieces and buy and sell with it. The business done at Taghaza, for all its meanness, amounts to an enormous figure in terms of hundredweights of gold dust. . . .

Thus we reached the town of Walata after a journey of two months to a day. Walata is the northern most province of the Negroes, and the Sultan's representative there was one Farba Husayn, Farba meaning deputy (in their language). . . .

It was an excessively hot place, and boasts a few small date-palms, in the shade of which they sow watermelons. Its water comes from underground water beds at that point, and there is plenty of mutton to be had. The garments of the inhabitants, most of whom belong to the Masufa tribe, are of fine Egyptian fabrics. Their women are of surpassing beauty, and are shown more respect than the men. The state of affairs amongst these people is indeed extraordinary. Their men show no sign of jealousy whatever; no one claims descent from his father, but on the contrary from his mother's brother. A person's heirs are his sister's sons, not his own sons. This is a thing which I have seen nowhere in the world except among the Indians of Malabar. But those are heathens; these people are Muslims, punctilious in observing the hours of prayer, studying books of law, and memorizing the Koran. Yet their women show no bashfulness before men and do not veil themselves, though they are assiduous in attending prayers. Any man who wishes to marry one of them may do so, they do not travel with their husbands. . . .

The women have their "friends" and "companions" amongst the men outside their own families, and the men in the same way have "companions" amongst the women of other families. A man may go into his house and find his wife entertaining her "companion," but he takes not objection to it. One day at Walata I went into the ***qadi's*** house, after asking his permission to enter, and found him with a young woman of remarkable beauty. When I saw her I was shocked and turned to go out, but she laughed at me, instead of being overcome by shame, and the qadi said to me, "Why are you going out? She is my companion." I was amazed at their conduct, for he was a theologian and a pilgrim to boot. I was told that he had asked the sultan's permission to make the pilgrimage that year with his "companion" (whether this one or not I cannot say) but the sultan would not grant it.

***Qadi*:** A Muslim judge.

. . . On feast-days, after Dugha [interpreter] has finished his display, the poets come in. Each of them is inside a figure resembling a thrush, made of feathers, and provided with a wooden head with a red beak, to look like a thrush's head. They stand in front of the sultan in this ridiculous make-up and recite their poems. I was told that their poetry is a kind of sermonizing in which they say to the sultan: "This pempi [throne] which you occupy was that whereon sat this king and that king, and such were this one's noble actions and such and such the other's. So do you too do good deeds whose memory will outlive you." After that the chief of the poets mounts the steps of the pempi and lays his head on the sultan's lap, then climbs to the top of the pempi and lays his head first on the sultan's right shoulder and then on his left, speaking all the while in their tongue, and finally he comes down again. I was told that this practice is a very old custom amongst them prior to the introduction of Islam, and they have kept it up.

. . . The Negroes possess some admirable qualities. They are seldom unjust, and have a greater abhorrence of injustice than any other people. The sultan shows no mercy to anyone who is guilty of the least act of it. There is a complete security in their country. Neither traveler nor inhabitant in it has anything to fear from robbers or men of violence. They do not confiscate the property of any white man [Arab trader] who dies in their country, even if it be accounted wealth. On the contrary, they give it into the charge of some trustworthy person among the whites, until the rightful heir takes possession of it. They are careful to observe the hours of prayer, and assiduous in attending them in congregations, and in bringing up their children to them. On Fridays, if a man does not go early to the mosque, he cannot find a corner to pray in, on account of the crowd. It is a custom of theirs to send each man his boy (to the mosque) with his prayer-mat; the boy spreads it out for his master in a place befitting him and remains on it (until his master comes to the mosque). The pray-mats are made of the leaves of a tree resembling a date-palm, but without fruit.

Another of their good qualities is their habit of wearing clean white garments on Fridays. Even if a man has nothing but an old worn shirt, he washes it and cleans it, and wears it at the Friday service. Yet another is their zeal for learning the Koran by heart. They put their children in chains if they show any backwardness in memorizing it, and they are not set free until they have it by heart. I visited the qadi in his house on the day of the festival. His children were chained up, so I said to him, "Will you not let them loose?" He replied, "I shall not do so until they learn the Koran by heart." Among their bad qualities are the following. The women servants, slave-girls, and young girls go about in front of everyone naked, without a stitch of clothing on them. Women go into the sultan's presence naked and without coverings, and his daughters also go about naked. Then there is the custom of their putting dust and ashes on their heads as a mark of respect, and the grotesque ceremonies we have described when the poets recite their verses.

» Working with Sources

1. **Why does Ibn Battuta remark so often on the lack of generosity on the part of the sultan of Mali?**
2. **Ibn Battuta offers many details about the material culture of Mali. What does his description reveal about the interactions between Mali and other cultures? How do they interact?**

SOURCE 14.3 Golden Bracelets from the "Lost City" of Mapungubwe, South Africa

Thirteenth century

The archaeological site of Mapungubwe, first discovered and excavated in the 1930s, spans the borders of present-day South Africa, Zimbabwe, and Botswana. It was one of the most powerful African Iron Age states, dominating southern Africa from 1070 to 1300 and establishing trade contacts with the Middle East and India. The source of its influence was the gold mined in the territory, fashioned into objects, and then exported far beyond the borders of the kingdom.

» Working with Sources

1. **How do these items crafted from gold illustrate the sophistication of Mapungubwe culture, as well as its desire to display wealth?**
2. **Might these particular items have been related to the social structure of Mapungubwe, and particularly to the role of royal wives?**

SOURCE 14.4 'Abd al-'Azīz al-Bakrī, *Description of West Africa*

1068

Al-Bakrī was born in Spain, and it appears that he never left that country. However, he collected information from people he met who had traveled to the Sahara and the Sudan, and he published his findings in a work called

---

Source: 14.3: University of Pretoria Museums, South Africa, Mapungubwe Collection, copyright University of Pretoria. 14.4: 'Abd al-'Azīz al-Bakrī, "Ghāna and the Customs of Its Inhabitants," trans. J. F. P. Hopkins, in N. Levtzion and J. F. P. Hopkins, *Corpus of Early Arabic Sources for West African History* (Cambridge, UK: Cambridge University Press, 1981), 79–81.

The Book of Routes and Realms (*Kitab al-masālik wa-'l-mamālik*). Al-Bakrī, who died in 1094, was famous for his curiosity about the geography, languages, and natural landscape of places he had not himself visited. The greater part of his major book is still unpublished, but the following section provides insight into the changing religious landscape in Ghana in the early eleventh century.

GHĀNA AND THE CUSTOMS OF ITS INHABITANTS

Ghāna is a title given to their kings; the name of the region is Awkār, and their king today, namely in the year 460/ 1067–8, is Tunkā Manīn. He ascended the throne in 455/ 1063. The name of his predecessor was Basī and he became their ruler at the age of 85. He led a praiseworthy life on account of his love of justice and friendship for the Muslims. At the end of his life he became blind, but he concealed this from his subjects and pretended that he could see. When something was put before him he said: "This is good" or "This is bad." His ministers deceived the people by indicating to the king in cryptic words what he should say, so that the commoners could not understand.

. . .

The city of Ghāna consists of two towns situated on a plain. One of these towns, which is inhabited by Muslims, is large and possesses twelve mosques, in one of which they assemble for the Friday prayer. There are salaried imams and muezzins, as well as jurists and scholars. In the environs are wells with sweet water, from which they drink and with which they grow vegetables. The king's town is six miles distant from this one and bears the name of Al-Ghāba. Between these two towns there are continuous habitations. The houses of the inhabitants are of stone and acacia (*sunṭ*) wood. The king has a palace and a number of domed dwellings all surrounded with an enclosure like a city wall (*sūr*). In the king's town, and not far from his court of justice, is a mosque where the Muslims who arrive at his court (*yafid 'alayh*) pray. Around the king's town are domed buildings and groves and thickets where the sorcerers of these people, men in charge of the religious cult, live. In them too are their idols and the tombs of their kings. These woods are guarded and none may enter them and know what is there. In them also are the king's prisons. If somebody is imprisoned there no news of him is ever heard. The king's interpreters, the official in charge of his treasury and the majority of his ministers are Muslims. Among the people who follow the king's religion only he and his heir apparent (who is the son of his sister) may wear sewn clothes. All other people wear robes of cotton, silk, or brocade, according to their means. All of them shave their beards, and women shave their heads.

. . .

When the people who profess the same religion as the king approach him they fall on their knees and sprinkle dust on their heads, for this is their way of greeting him. As for the Muslims, they greet him only by clapping their hands.

Their religion is paganism and the worship of idols (*dakākīr*). When their king dies they construct over the place where his tomb will be an enormous dome of *sāj* [acacia?] wood. Then they bring him on a bed covered with a few carpets and cushions and place him beside the dome. At his side they place his ornaments, his weapons, and the vessels from which he used to eat and drink, filled with various kinds of food and beverages. They place there too the men who used to serve his meals. They close the door of the dome and cover it with mats and furnishings. Then the people assemble, who heap earth upon it until it becomes like a big hillock and dig a ditch around it until the mound can be reached at only one place.

» Working with Sources

1. **Is there anything surprising, at least in al-Bakrī's description, in the reinforcement of royal authority in Ghana?**
2. **How was the religious balance between Muslims and non-Muslims maintained in this kingdom, and why?**

SOURCE 14.5

Walls and moats at Sungbo's Eredo, Nigeria

ca. 1000–1450

The chiefdom of Ijebu encompassed a capital and villages on a territory of 22 square miles, surrounded by a deep moat and towering rampart almost 100 miles long. The iron-saturated soil would have made the construction process very difficult, especially since the labor was achieved with nothing more than iron shovels. This drawing illustrates what archaeologists believe to have been the arrangement of a typical cross section of this structure. It is named for Bilikisu Sungbo, a mythical priestess-queen who was credited with ordering the construction of the moat and rampart.

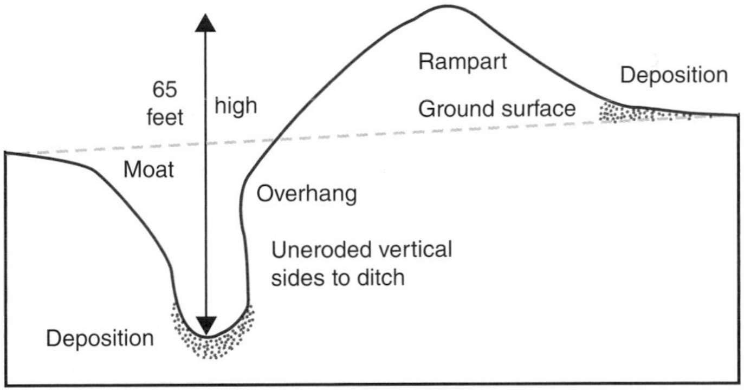

» Working with Sources

1. **Was this moat and rampart constructed for defensive purposes, or for some other reason? How do the size and extent of walls and moats of Ijebu compare with defensive structures created by other civilizations in the period before 1500 CE?**
2. **What does the existence of this edifice reveal about the use of collective labor in Ijebu in this period?**

Source: P.J. Darling, "Sungbo's Eredo, Southern Nigeria," *Nyame Akuma*, 48 (1998), 55–61.

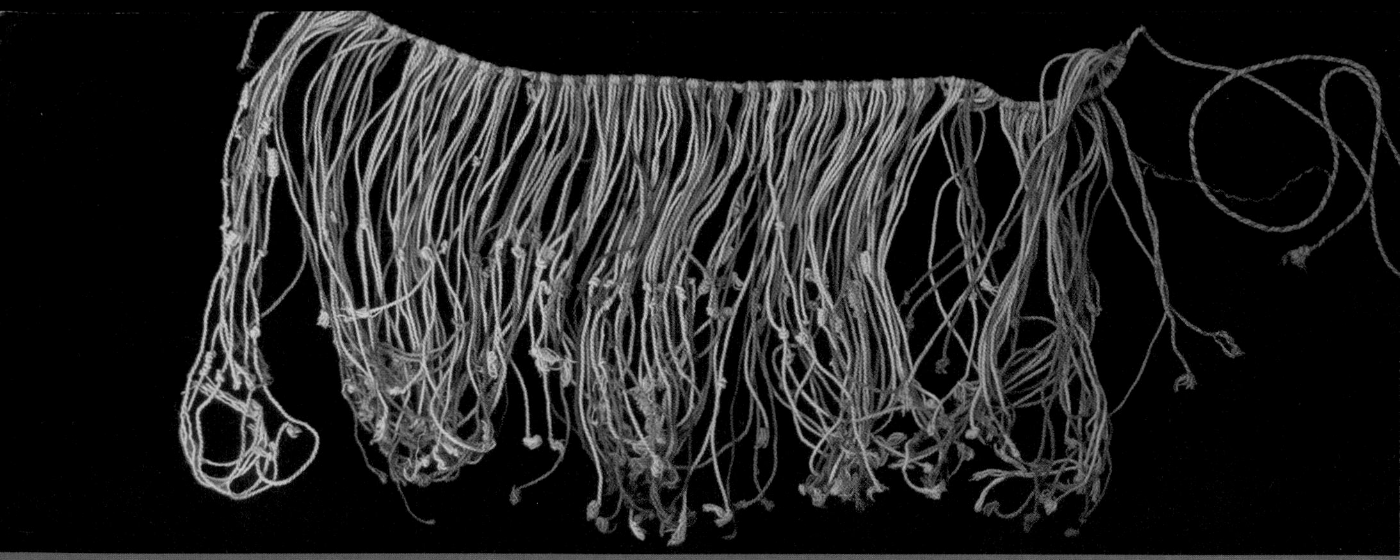

Chapter 15 **600–1550 CE**

The Rise of Empires in the Americas

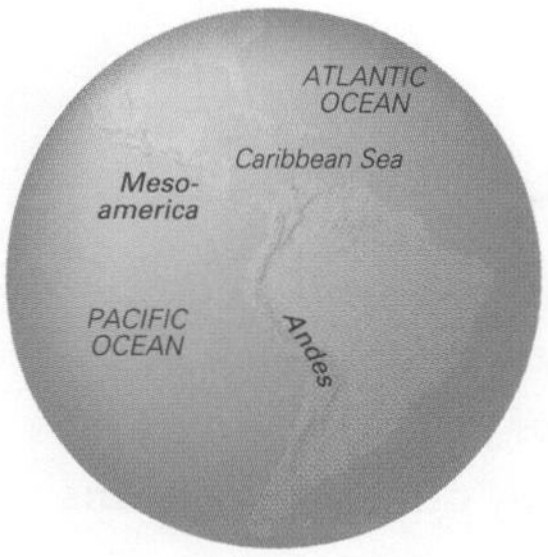

Just outside Lima, in a sandy and dry ravine 3 miles to the east of the city, is the shantytown of Túpac Amaru, named after the last Inca ruler, who died in 1572. People fleeing the Maoist Shining Path guerillas in the highlands southeast of Lima settled here during the 1980s. Archaeologists had known for years that the site was an ancient burial place called Puruchuco (Quechua "Feathered Helmet") but could not prevent the influx of settlers. By the late 1990s, the temporary shantytown had become an established settlement with masonry houses, streets, and a school. Dwellers were anxious to acquire title to their properties, introduce urban services and utilities, and clean up the ground contaminated in many places by raw sewage. However, residents realized that archaeologists had to be called in before the shantytown could be officially recognized. Túpac Amaru was facing an increasingly familiar dilemma in the developing world, pitting modern needs against the wish to know the past through discovering and (if possible) preserving its last traces.

During emergency excavations from 1999 to 2001, the archaeologist Guillermo Cock, together with Túpac Amaru residents hired as field assistants, unearthed one of the most astounding treasures in the history of American archaeology. The team discovered some 2,200 mummies, most of them bundled up in blankets and perfectly preserved with their hair, skin, eyes, and genitals intact. Many bundles also contained rich burial

***ABOVE:* This kind of knotted string assembly (a *quipu*) was used in the Andes from ca. 2500 BCE onward for the recording of taxes, population figures, calendar dates, troop numbers, and other data.**

gifts, including jewelry, corn, potatoes, peanuts, peppers, and coca leaves. Forty bundles had false heads made of cotton cloth, some topped with wigs, making the bundles look like oversized persons.

Scholars hope that in a few years, when all of the mummies have been unwrapped, answers can be given as to the social characteristics of the buried people. Were they members of an Inca colony planted into one of the empire's provinces? Or were they locals under their own lord, recognizing Inca overlordship? Were they specialized laborers, such as weavers, who produced cloth tributes for the Incas? Were children and women sacrificed to accompany the cotton king in his journey to the afterlife? Had assimilation between the conquerors and conquered begun? These questions are difficult to answer as so much about the Inca Empire that ruled the Andes from 1438 to 1533 remains unknown. Yet the questions are exciting precisely because they could not have been posed prior to the discovery of these mummies.

Seeing Patterns

» **Within the patterns of state formation basic to the Americas, which types of states emerged in Mesoamerica and the Andes during the period 600–1550? What characterized these states?**

» **Why did the Tiwanaku and Wari states have ruling classes but no dynasties and central bureaucracies? How were these patterns expressed in the territorial organization of these states?**

» **What patterns of urban life characterized the cities of Tenochtitlán and Cuzco, the capitals of the Aztec and Inca Empires? In which ways were these cities similar to those of Eurasia and Africa?**

The Inca Empire and its contemporary the Aztec Empire (1427–1521) grew out of political, economic, and cultural patterns that began to form around 600 CE in Mesoamerica and the Andes (see Chapter 5). At that time, kingdoms had emerged out of polities in two small areas of Mesoamerica, the southern Yucatán Peninsula and the Mexican Basin. After 600, kingdom formation became more general across Mesoamerica and arose for the first time in the Andes. These kingdoms were states with military ruling classes that used new types of weapons and could conquer larger territories than was possible prior to the 600s. Military competition prepared the way for the origin of empires—multireligious, multilinguistic, and multiethnic states encompassing many thousands of square miles. Even though empires arrived later in the Americas than in Eurasia, they demonstrate that humans, once they had adopted agriculture, followed remarkably similar patterns of social and political formation across the world.

The Legacy of Teotihuacán and the Toltecs in Mesoamerica

As discussed in Chapter 5, the city-state of Teotihuacán had dominated northern Mesoamerica from 200 BCE to the late 500s CE. It fell into ruin probably as the result of an internal uprising against an overbearing ruling class. After its collapse, the surrounding towns and villages, as well as half a dozen other cities in and around the Mexican Basin, perpetuated the cultural legacy of Teotihuacán for centuries. Employing this legacy, the conquering state of the Toltecs unified a major part of the region for a short period from 900 to 1180. At the same time, after an internal crisis, the southern Maya kingdoms on the Yucatán Peninsula reached their late flowering, together with the northern state of Chichén Itzá.

Chapter Outline

- The Legacy of Teotihuacán and the Toltecs in Mesoamerica
- The Legacy of Tiwanaku and Wari in the Andes
- American Empires: Aztec and Inca Origins and Dominance
- Imperial Society and Culture
- Putting It All Together

Militarism in the Mexican Basin

After the ruling class of Teotihuacán disintegrated at the end of the sixth century, the newly independent local lords and their supporters in the small successor states of Mesoamerica continued Teotihuacán's cultural heritage. This heritage was defined by Teotihuacán's temple style, ceramics, textiles, and religious customs, especially the cult of the feathered serpent god Quetzalcoatl [ket-sal-COA]. The Toltecs, migrants from the north, militarized the Teotihuacán legacy and transformed it into a program of conquest.

Ceremonial Centers and Chiefdoms In the three centuries after the end of the city-state of Teotihuacán, the local population declined from some 200,000 to about 30,000. Although largely ruined, the ceremonial center continued to attract pilgrims, but other places around the Mexican Basin and beyond rose in importance. The semiarid region to the northwest of the valley had an extensive mining industry, with many mine shafts extending a mile or more into the mountains. The region produced a variety of gemstones. Independent after 600, inhabitants built ceremonial centers and small states of their own, trading their gemstones to their neighbors in all directions.

To the north were the Pueblo cultures in today's southwestern United States. These cultures were based on sophisticated irrigated farming systems and are known for their distinctive painted pottery styles. They flourished between 700 and 1500 in the canyons of what are today the states of New Mexico, Arizona, southwestern Colorado, and southeastern Utah. In turn, these cultures might have been in contact with the Mississippi cultures, among which the ceremonial center and city of Cahokia (650–1400) near modern St. Louis is the best-known site. An obsidian scraper from the Pachuca region north of the Mexican Basin found in Spiro Mounds, Oklahoma, attests to at least occasional contacts between Mesoamerica and the Mississippi culture (see Map 15.1).

To the south, in western Mesoamerica, ceremonial centers and chiefdoms flourished on the basis of metallurgy, which arrived through Ecuadoran seaborne merchants ca. 600–800. The Ecuadorans received their copper from Peru, in return for seashells found in the warm waters off the coast of Ecuador as well as farther north. Copper, too soft for agricultural implements or military weapons, served mostly in households and as jewelry for the rich. A number of small, fortified hilltop states also flourished in the south. Their inhabitants built moats and ramparts to protect these states. More than in other Mesoamerican states, the ruling classes were embroiled in fierce wars during 600–900, images of which are depicted in stone reliefs of gruesome battle scenes.

The Toltec Conquering State Early after the collapse of Teotihuacán, craftspeople and farmers migrated some 60 miles north to Tula, a place on a ridge in the highlands watered by two tributaries of a river flowing into the Gulf of Mexico. They founded a small ceremonial center and town with workshops known for the high quality of the scrapers, knives, and spear points fabricated from the local Pachuca obsidian. Around 900, new migrants arrived from northwest Mexico as well as from the Gulf Coast. The northerners spoke Nahuatl [NA-hua], the language of the later Aztecs, and after taking possession of Tula, they made it their ancestral city.

The integration of the new arrivals was apparently not peaceful, since it resulted in the abandonment of the temple and the departure of a defeated party of Tulans.

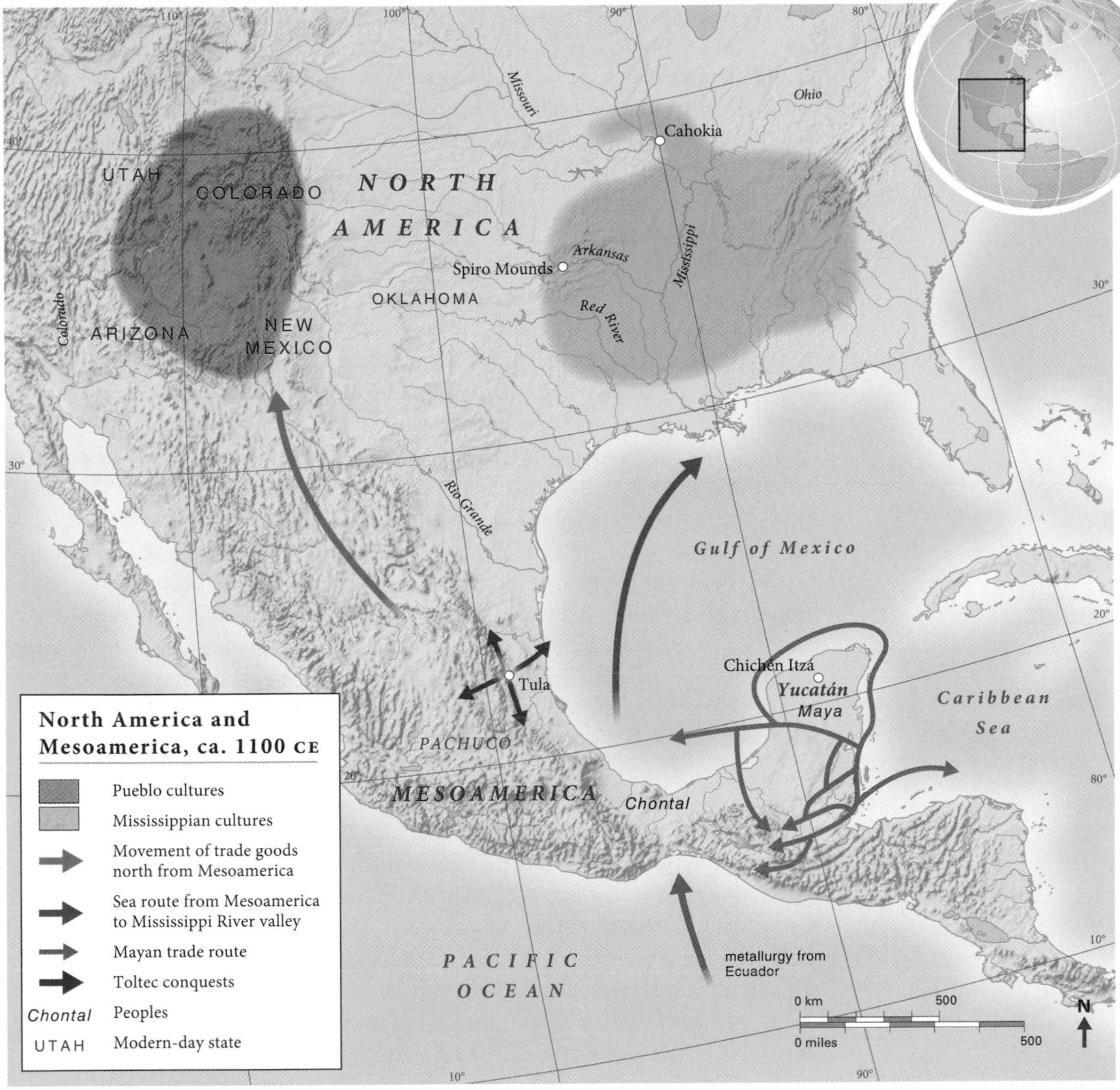

MAP 15.1 North America and Mesoamerica, ca. 1100.

This abandonment may well have been enshrined in the myth of Tolpiltzin, a priest-king of the feathered serpent god Quetzalcoatl, who after his departure to the east would one day return to restore the cult to its rightful center. Later, Spaniards used the myth to justify their rule in the Americas (see Chapter 18).

interactive timeline

- **600** End of city-state of Teotihuacán in Mexican Basin
- **600–1100** Conquering state of Tiwanaku in Andes (southern Peru/Bolivia)
- **600–900** Late Maya kingdoms in Yucatán Peninsula
- **700–1000** Conquering state of Wari in Andes (central Bolivia)
- **850–1000** City-state of Chichén Itzá in northern Yucatán Peninsula
- **900–1170** Toltec conquering state, north of Mexican Basin
- **1427–1521** Aztec Empire in Mesoamerica
- **1438–1533** Inca Empire in Andes

The new Tula of 900 developed quickly into a large city with a new temple, 60,000 urban dwellers, and perhaps another 60,000 farmers on surrounding lands. It was the first city-centered state to give pictorial prominence to the sacrifice of captured warriors. As it evolved, Tula became the capital of the conquering state of the Toltecs, which imprinted its warrior culture on large parts of Mesoamerica from around 900 to 1180 (see Map 15.1).

The Toltecs introduced two innovations in weaponry that improved the effectiveness of hand-to-hand combat. First, there was the new weapon of a short (1.5-foot) sword made of hardwood with inlaid obsidian edges, which could slash as well as crush, in contrast to the obsidian-spiked clubs that had been the primary weapons in earlier times. Second, warriors wore obsidian daggers with wooden handles inside a band on the left arm, replacing simpler obsidian blades, which were difficult to use as they had no handles. Traditional dart throwers and slings for stone projectiles completed the offensive armament of the warriors.

The Toltec army of 13,000–26,000 soldiers was sufficiently large to engage in battles of conquest within an area of 4 days' march (roughly 40 miles) away from Tula. Any target beyond this range was beyond their capabilities, given the logistics of armor, weapons, food rations, narrow dirt roads, and uneven terrain—and, of course, Toltecs did not have the benefit of wheeled vehicles. Thus, the only way of projecting power beyond the range of 40 miles was to establish colonies and to have troops accompany traders, each of which could then supply themselves by foraging or through trade along the way. As a result, the Toltec state projected its power through the prestige of its large military, rather than through a full-scale administrative scheme with the imposition of governors, tributes, and taxes.

Trade Apart from demonstrating military might, the Toltecs pursued the establishment of a large trade network. Merchants parlayed Tula's obsidian production into a trade network that radiated southward into the cacao, vanilla, and bird-feather production centers of Chiapas and Guatemala; to the north into gemstone mining regions; and westward into centers of metal mining. Metallurgy advanced around 1200 with the development of the technology of bronze casting. Bronze axes were stronger and more useful for working with wood than copper axes. Bronze bells produced a greater variety of sounds than those of copper. As ornamental objects, both were trade goods highly prized by the elites in Tula.

The Late Toltec Era Toltec military power declined in the course of the twelfth century when the taxable grain yield around the city diminished, because of either prolonged droughts or a depletion of the topsoil on the terraces, or a combination of the two. Sometime around 1180, a new wave of foraging peoples from the northwest invaded, attacking with bows and arrows and using hit-and-run tactics against Toltec communication lines. The disruptions caused an internal revolt, which brought down the ceremonial center and its palaces. By 1200, Tula was a city with a burned-out center, like Teotihuacán six centuries earlier, and Mesoamerica relapsed into a period of small-state coexistence like that of the pre-600 period.

Late Maya States in Yucatán

Teotihuacán's demise at the end of the sixth century was paralleled by a realignment of the balance of power among the Maya kingdoms in the southern Yucatán lowlands of Mesoamerica. This realignment, accompanied by extensive warfare, was resolved by around 650. A period of late flowering spanned the next two centuries, followed by a shift of power from the southern to the northern part of the peninsula.

The Southern Kingdoms At its height during the fourth and fifth centuries, Teotihuacán in the Mexican Basin had interjected itself into the delicate balance of power existing among the Maya kingdoms of southern Yucatán. Alliances among the states shifted, and prolonged wars of conquest racked the lowlands, destroying several older states. A dozen new kingdoms emerged and established a new balance of power among themselves. After a lengthy hiatus, Maya culture entered its final period (650–900).

Mayan ceremonial ball game scene, Late Classic Period

The most striking phenomenon of the final period in the southern, rain-forest–covered lowlands and adjacent highlands were massive new programs of agricultural expansion and ceremonial monument construction. Agriculture was expanded again through cutting down the rain forest on hillsides and terracing the hills for soil retention. The largest kingdoms grew to 50,000–60,000 inhabitants and reached astounding rural population densities of about 1,000 persons per square mile. (In comparison, England's most densely populated counties just prior to its agricultural expansion after 1700 were Middlesex and Surrey, with 221 and 207 persons per square mile, respectively.) Although the late Maya states were geographically small, they were administratively the most centralized polities ever created in indigenous American history.

The late Maya states did not last long. In spite of all efforts, the usually torrential downpours of the rainy season gradually washed the topsoil from the newly built hillside terraces. The topsoil, accumulating as alluvium in the flatlands, was initially quite fertile, but from around 800 onward it became more and more depleted of nutrients. In addition, in many wetlands, farmers found it difficult to prevent clay from forming over the alluvium and hardening in the process. Malnutrition resulting from the shrinking agricultural surface began to reduce the labor force. Ruling classes had to make do with fewer workers and smaller agricultural surpluses. In the end, even the ruling classes suffered, with members killing each other for what remained of these surpluses. By about 900, the Maya kingdoms in southern Yucatán had shriveled to the size of chiefdoms with small towns and villages.

Mayan city-state of Palenque

Chichén Itzá in the North A few small Maya states on the periphery survived. The most prominent among them was Chichén Itzá [chee-CHEN eat-SA] in the northern lowlands, which flourished from about 850 to 1000. At first glance the region would appear to be less than hospitable to a successful state. The climate in the north was much drier than that in the south. The surface was rocky or covered with thin topsoil, supporting mostly grass, scrub vegetation, and isolated forests. In many places, where the soil was too saline, agriculture was impossible, and the production of salt was the only source of income. There were no rivers, but many sinkholes in the porous limestone underneath the soil held water. Countless cisterns to hold additional amounts of water for year-round use were cut into the limestone and plastered to prevent seepage. This water, carried in jars to the surface, supported an intensive garden agriculture, productive enough to sustain entire towns and city-states.

Chichén Itzá was founded during the phase of renewed urbanization in 650. It was built near two major sinkholes and several salt flats. The population was composed

Chacmool (Offering Table) at the Entrance to the Temple of Warriors, Chichén Itzá. Chacmools originated here and spread to numerous places in Mesoamerica, as far north as Tenochtitlán and Tula. Offerings to the gods included food, tobacco, feathers, and incense. Offerings might have included also human sacrifices. The table in the form of a prostrate human figure is in itself symbolic of sacrifice.

of local Maya as well as the Maya-speaking Chontal from the Gulf Coast farther west. Groups among these people engaged in long-distance trade, both overland and in boats along the coast. Since trade in the most lucrative goods (such as cacao, vanilla, jade, copper, bronze, turquoise, and obsidian) required contact with people well outside even the farthest political reach of either Teotihuacán or Tula, merchants (*pochtecas* [potsh-TAY-cas]) traveled in armed caravans. These merchant groups enjoyed considerable freedom and even sponsorship by the ruling classes of the states of Mesoamerica.

Chontal traders adopted Toltec culture, and when they based themselves in Chichén Itzá around 850 they superimposed their adopted culture over that of the original Maya. How the city was ruled is only vaguely understood, but there is some evidence that there were two partially integrated ruling factions, possibly descended from the Chontal and local Maya, sharing in the governance of the city. At the very end of the period of Teotihuacán, Maya, and Toltec cultural expansion, the three cultures finally merged on the Yucatán Peninsula, albeit in only one geographically marginal place. This merger did not last long: Already around 1000 the ruling-class factions left the city-state for unknown reasons. As a result, the city-state diminished in size and power to town level.

The Legacy of Tiwanaku and Wari in the Andes

Mesoamerica and the Andes, from the time of chiefdom formation in 2500 BCE in Caral-Supé onward, shared the tradition of regional temple pilgrimages. In the Andes, the chiefdoms remained mostly coastal, with some inland extensions along valleys of the Andes. Around 600 CE, the two conquering states of Tiwanaku in the highlands of what are today southern Peru and Bolivia and Wari in central Peru emerged. Both states encompassed tens of thousands of inhabitants and represented a major step in the formation of larger, militarily organized polities.

The Expanding State of Tiwanaku

Tiwanaku was a political and cultural power center in the south-central Andes during the period 600–1100. It began as a ceremonial center with surrounding villages and gradually developed into a state dominating the region around Lake Titicaca. At its apogee it was an expanding state, planting colonies in regions far from the lake and conveying its culture through trade to peoples even beyond the colonies.

Agriculture on the High Plain The Andes consist of two parallel mountain chains stretching along the west coast of South America. For the most part, these chains are close together, divided by small plains, valleys, and lower mountains. In southeastern Peru and western Bolivia an intermountain plain, 12,500 feet above sea level, extends as wide as 125 miles. At its northern end lies Lake Titicaca, subdivided into a larger and deeper northern basin and a smaller, shallower, swampy, and reed-covered southern basin. Five major and 20 smaller rivers coming from the eastern Andes chain feed Lake Titicaca, which has one outlet at its southern end, a river flowing into Lake Poopó [po-POH], a salt lake 150 miles south. The Lake Titicaca region, located above the tree line, receives winter rains sufficient for agriculture and grazing, whereas the southern plain around Lake Poopó is too dry to sustain more than steppes.

Tiwanaku, Kalassaya Gate. Within the Temple of the Sun, this gate is aligned with the sun's equinoxes and was used for festive rituals. Note the precise stone work, which the Incas later developed further.

In spite of its elevation, the region around Lake Titicaca offered nearly everything necessary for an advanced urbanization process. The lake's freshwater supported fish and resources such as reeds from the swamps, which served for the construction of boats and roofs. Corn flourished only in the lower elevations of the Andes and had to be imported, together with the corn-derived *chicha,* a beer-like drink. Instead of corn, the food staples were potatoes and quinoa. The grasslands of the upper hills served as pastures for llama and alpaca herds. Llamas were used as transportation animals, and alpacas provided wool. The meat of both animals—preserved for winter through drying—was a major protein source. Although frost was an ever-present danger in Tiwanaku, nutrition was quite diversified.

Farmers grew their crops on hillside terraces, where runoff water could be channeled, or on raised fields close to the lake. The raised-field system, which farmers had adopted through interaction with the peoples of the Maya lowlands, consisted of a grid of narrow strips of earth, separated from each other by channels. Mud from the channels, heaped onto the strips, replenished their fertility. A wooden foot plow, perhaps with a bronze blade, seems to have been the main farming implement, although hard archaeological proof is still elusive. By 500, the combined sustenance from fishing, hunting, farming, and herding supported dozens of villages and, by 700, the city of Tiwanaku and its 20,000 inhabitants.

Coordinated with the calendar as well as life-cycle events (such as initiation rituals), ceremonial feasts brought together elite lineages and clients, or ordinary craftspeople and villagers. Elites and clients cohered through **reciprocity**—that is, communal labor for the construction of the ceremonial centers and elaborate feasting, in which elite wealth was expended for the ceremonial leveling of status differences. Until shortly before the end of the state, it does not appear that this reciprocity gave way to more forcible ways of allocating labor through conscription or taxation.

Reciprocity: In its basic form, an informal agreement among people according to which a gift or an invitation has to be returned after a reasonable amount of time; in the pre-Columbian Americas, an arrangement of feasts instead of taxes shared by ruling classes and subjects in a state.

Expansion and Colonization Like Tiwanaku, the core region around the southern basin of Lake Titicaca housed a set of related but competing elite–client hierarchies. Ruling clans with intermediate leaders and ordinary farmers in the villages comprised a state capable of imposing military power beyond the center. But counterbalancing clans at the head of similar hierarchies prevented the rise of dynasties that would command permanent, unified central administrations and military forces.

The projection of power over the northern lake, therefore, was not primarily of a military nature: The prevalent form of Tiwanaku authority was the outstanding prestige of its ceremonial center. This center attracted pilgrims not merely from the northern lake but also from more distant regions. Pilgrims partaking in Tiwanaku feasting ceremonies can be considered extensions of the reciprocity and clientage system of the ruling classes and, hence, of Tiwanaku power.

But there were also armed trading caravans and the foundation of colonies in the western valleys of the Andes, where military force played a role. Merchants accompanied by warriors and llama drivers crossed multiple polities in order to exchange textiles and ceramics for basalt cores in the south, metal ingots and obsidian cores in the north, and coca leaves and other psychotropic substances in the east, often hundreds of miles away. Settler colonies were additional forms of power projection, especially those established in the Moquegua [mow-KAY-gah] valley 200 miles, or 10–12 days of walking, to the west. Here, at some 2,800 feet above sea level, Tiwanaku emigrants established villages, which sent some of their corn or beer to the capital in return for salt, as well as stone and obsidian tools. Although overall less militarily inclined than the Mesoamerican states of the same time period, Tiwanaku wielded a visible influence over southern Peru (see Map 15.2).

The Expanding City-State of Wari

Little is known about early settlements in central Peru, some 450 miles, or 3–4 weeks of foot travel, north from Tiwanaku. The state of Wari emerged around 600 from a number of small polities organized around ceremonial centers. Expansion to the south put Wari into direct contact with Tiwanaku. The two states came to some form of mutual accommodation, and it appears that neither embarked on an outright conquest of the other. Their military postures remained limited to their regional spheres of influence.

Origins and Expansion Wari was centered on the Ayacucho valley, a narrow plain in the highlands of northern Peru. Here, the land between the two chains of the Andes is mountainous, interspersed with valleys and rivers flowing to the Pacific or the Amazon. The elevation of 8,000 feet in the Ayacucho valley allowed for the cultivation of potatoes as well as corn and cotton. In the course of the seventh century, Wari grew into a city of 30,000 inhabitants and brought a number of neighboring cities under its control. It also pushed for an enlargement of the agricultural base through the expansion of terrace farming. Like Tiwanaku, Wari eventually became the center of a developed urbanism and a diversified agriculture.

In addition to maintaining control over the cities in its vicinity, Wari employed architects who constructed new towns. These planned centers included plazas, housing for laborers, and halls for feasting. Outside the core area, Wari elites established colonies between 100 and 450 miles away. It appears that Wari exercised much stronger political control over the chiefs of its core region than Tiwanaku and was more active in founding colonies.

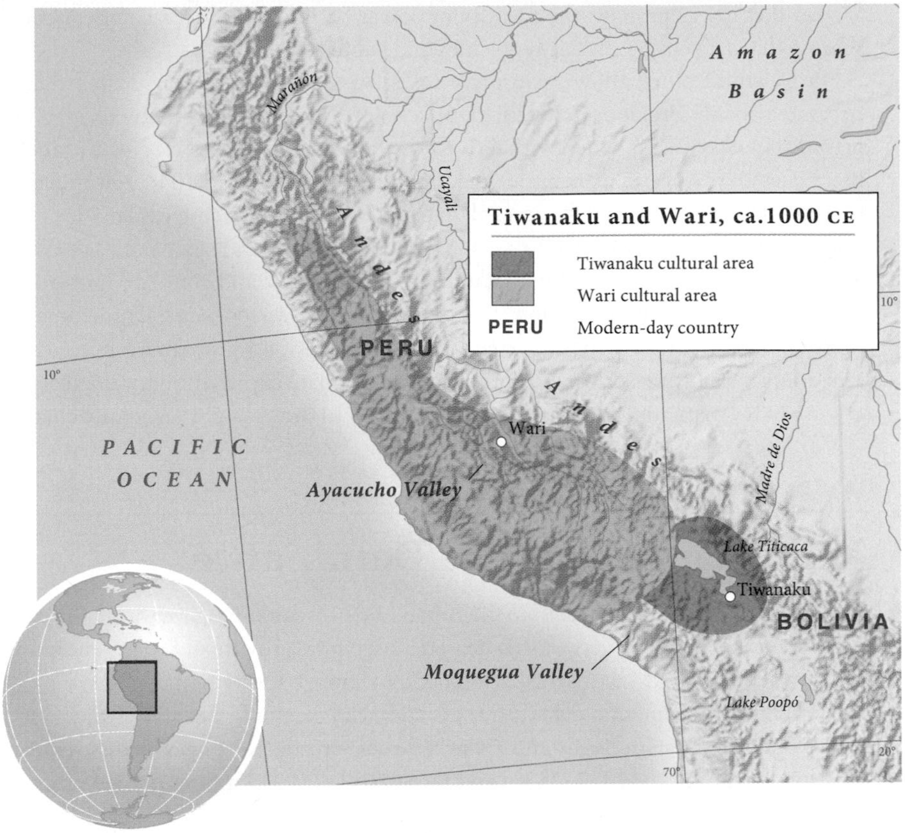

MAP **15.2** **Tiwanaku and Wari, ca. 1000.**

The Wari–Tiwanaku Frontier Early on, Wari established a colony upstream in the Moquegua valley near southern Peru's west coast, some 100 miles southeast. The settlers built extensive terraces and canals together with protective walls and settlements on mountain peaks. This building activity coincided with the establishment by Tiwanaku of downstream farming colonies. It is possible that there was considerable tension with Tiwanaku during the initial period (650–800) over the division of water between the two colonies. But during 800–1000 the two agricultural communities developed closer ties, with indications that the two local elites engaged in a peaceful sharing of the water resources and common feasting activities. Very likely, the Moquegua valley was politically so far on the periphery of both states that neither had the means to impose itself on the other.

In its evolution, Wari was an expanding state very similar to Tiwanaku. Both were governed by elite clans under leaders who derived their strength from reciprocal patron–client organizations binding leaders to farmers and craftspeople. Extensive feasts strengthened the bond. Something must have happened to erode this bond, however, since there is evidence of increased internal tension after 950 in the two states. Groups arose which defaced sculptures, destroyed portals, and burned down edifices. Somehow, crowds previously happy to uphold elite control in return for participation in the lavish feasts must have become angry at these elites, their ceremonies, and the temple sculptures (which show traces of breakage). Scholars have argued that it was perhaps the fragility of power based on an increasingly unequal sharing that caused the rift between elites and subjects.

Why would elites allow reciprocity to be weakened to such a degree that it became a sham? Previous generations of scholars argued that climatic change deprived the elites of the wherewithal to throw large feasts. In the case of Tiwanaku there is evidence that a drought hit the high plain beginning in 1040, but this date is clearly a century too late for an explanation. A more convincing explanation suggests environmental degradation as the result of agricultural expansion. Land that was only marginally suitable for agriculture was exhausted and could no longer sustain a vastly increased population, as with the late Maya kingdoms. Unfortunately, there is still too little evidence to extend the environmental argument from the Maya kingdoms to the Andes highland and sierra. An ultimate explanation for the disintegration of the expanding states of Tiwanaku and Wari thus remains currently elusive.

American Empires: Aztec and Inca Origins and Dominance

Expanding and conquering states in the Andes and Mesoamerica gave way in the early fifteenth century to empires. At this time, demographic growth and the evolution of militarism in the Americas reached a point of transition to the pattern of imperial political formation. Conquering states had been cities with ceremonial centers, which dominated agricultural hinterlands and projected their prestige or power across regions. By contrast, the Aztec (1427–1521) and Inca (1438–1533) Empires in Mesoamerica and the Andes were states with capitals and ceremonial centers, vastly larger tributary hinterlands, and armies capable of engaging in campaigns at distances twice (or more) as far as previous states could. As in Eurasia, they were centralized multireligious, multiethnic, and multilinguistic polities: empires in every sense of the word.

The Aztec Empire of Mesoamerica

Forming part of the Uto-Aztecan–speaking group of Native Americans in the Great Basin of the American Southwest, the ancestors of the Aztecs left Tula and arrived at the Mexican Basin at an unknown time and they did so probably as migrants in search of a better life. They found this life eventually as conquerors of the Basin, the site of today's Mexico City (after the drainage of most of the valley). In the course of the fifteenth century they conquered an empire that eventually encompassed Mesoamerica from the Pacific to the Gulf of Mexico and from the middle of modern northern Mexico to the Isthmus of Panama.

Settlement in the Mexican Valley Once arrived in the Mexican Basin, the Aztecs traced their beginnings to a founding myth. According to this myth, the first Aztec was one of seven brothers born on an island in a lake or in a mountain cave 150 leagues (450 miles) northwest of the Mexican Basin. The distance, recorded by Spaniards in the sixteenth century, can be interpreted as corresponding to a mountain in the modern state of Guanajuato [goo-wa-na-hoo-WA-to]. This Aztec ancestor and his descendants migrated south as foragers dressed in skins and lacking agriculture and urban civilization. Their hunter–warrior patron god Huitzilpochtli [hoo-it-zil-POSHT-lee] guided them to a promised land of plenty.

The Founding of Tenochtitlán

After settling for a while in Tula (claimed later as a place of heritage), their god urged the foragers to move on to the Mexican Basin. Here, an eagle perched on a cactus commanded the Aztecs to settle and build a temple to their god. In this temple, they were to nourish him with the sacrificial blood of humans captured in war. Like many peoples in Eurasia as well as the contemporary Incas, the Aztecs contrasted their later empire and its glory with a myth of humble beginnings and long periods of wandering toward an eventual promised land.

The historical record in the Mexican Basin becomes clearer in the fourteenth century. In the course of this period, the Aztecs appeared as clients of two Toltec-descended overlords in city-states on the southwestern shore. Here, they created two islands, founded a city with a ceremonial center, engaged in farming, and rendered military service to their overlords. Thanks to successes on the battlefield, Aztec leaders were able to marry into the elites of the neighboring city-states and gained the right to have their own ruler presiding over a council of leading members of the elite and priests. Toward the end of the fourteenth century, an emerging Aztec elite was firmly integrated with the ruling classes of many of the two dozen or so city-states in and around the valley.

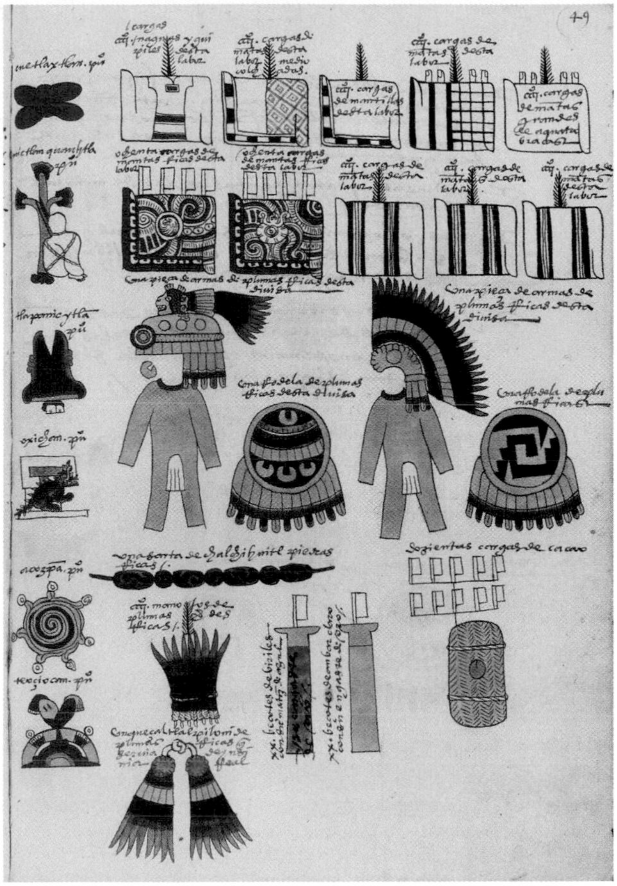

List of Tributes Owed to the Aztecs. The list includes quantities of cotton and wool textiles, clothes, headgear with feathers, and basketry. The Aztecs did not continue the complex syllabic script of the Maya but used instead images, including persons with speech bubbles, for communication. Spanish administrators and monks who copied the Aztec manuscripts added their own explanations to keep track of Native American tributes.

image analysis

The Rise of the Empire After the successful rebellion in 1428 of a triple alliance among the Aztec city-state and two other vassal states against the reigning city-state in the Mexican Basin the Aztec leader Itzcóatl [its-CO-aw] (r. 1428–1440) emerged as the dominant figure. Itzcóatl and his three successors, together with the rulers of the two allied states, expanded their city-states on the two islands and the shore through conquests into a full-fledged empire. Tenochtitlán, the Aztec city on one of the islands, became the capital of what became an empire that consisted of a set of six "inner provinces" in the Mexican Basin. Local elites were left in place, but they were required to attend ceremonies in Tenochtitlán, bring and receive gifts, leave their sons as hostages, and intermarry with the elites of the triple alliance. Commoner farmers on the periphery of the cities had to provide tributes in the form of foodstuffs and labor services, making the imperial core self-sufficient.

After the middle of the fifteenth century, the triple alliance conquered a set of 55 city-states outside the valley as "outer provinces." It created an imperial polity from the Pacific to the Gulf, from Tarasco, 200 miles to the northwest, to Oaxaca, over 500 miles to the south (see Map 15.3). This state was now far more centralized than the preceding Teotihuacán and Toltec city-states. In this empire, local ruling families with their ceremonial centers and gods were generally left in place, but commoners had to produce tributes in the form of raw materials or lightweight processed and manufactured goods.

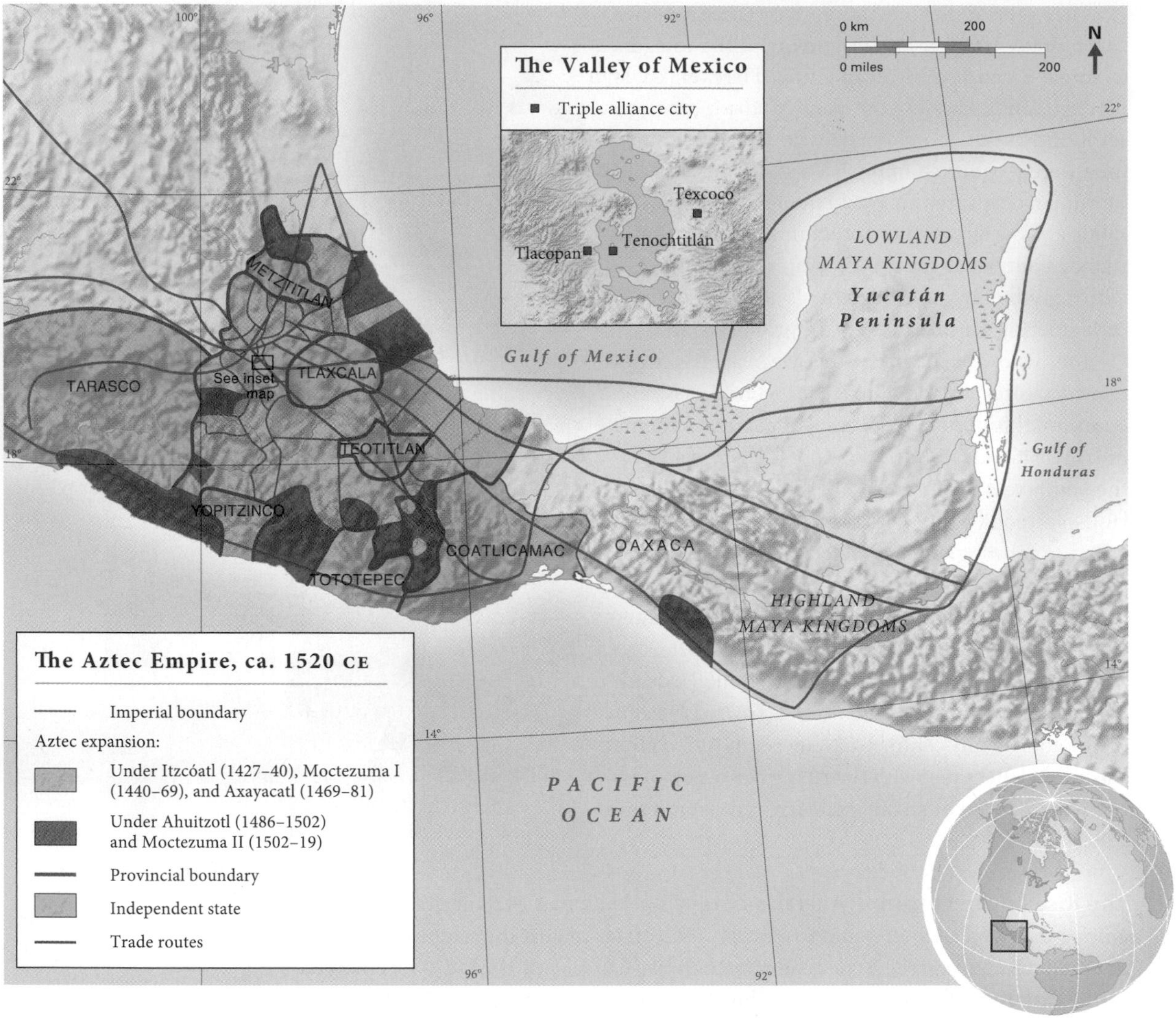

MAP 15.3 The Aztec Empire, ca. 1520.

In some provinces, Aztec governors replaced the rulers; in most others, Aztec tribute collectors (supported by troops) held local rulers in check and supervised the transportation of the tributes by porters to the valley. Reciprocity, once of central importance in Mesoamerica, continued on a grand scale but was now clearly subordinate to military considerations.

The resulting multiethnic, multireligious, and multilinguistic empire of eventually some 19 million inhabitants was still a work in progress in the early sixteenth century when the Spanish arrived. Right in the middle of the empire, just 50 miles east of the Mexican Basin, the large state of Tlaxcala [tlash-KAH-lah], Nahuatl-speaking like the Aztecs, held out in opposition, together with a number of enemy states on the periphery. Although the ruling elites of the triple alliance did everything to expand, even inviting enemy rulers to their festivities in order to secure their loyalty through gestures of reciprocity, pockets of anti-Aztec states survived and eventually became crucial allies of the Spanish, providing the latter's tiny military forces with a critical mass of fighters.

Some outer provinces possessed strategic importance, with Aztec colonies implanted to prepare for eventual conquest of remaining enemies of the empire. The most relentlessly pursued policy of continued expansion of Aztec central control was the threat of warfare, for the purpose of capturing rebels or enemies as prisoners of war to be sacrificed to the gods in the ceremonial centers. This fear-inducing tactic—or "power propaganda"—was an integral innovation in the imperialism of the Aztecs.

Aztec Weapons. Aztec weapons were well-crafted hardwood implements with serrated obsidian edges, capable of cutting through metal, including iron. As slashing weapons they were highly effective in close combat.

The Military Forces The triple alliance ruled a Nahuatl-speaking population of some 1.5 million inhabitants in the core provinces of the Mexican Basin. This number yielded a maximum of a quarter of a million potential soldiers, taking into consideration that most soldiers were farmers with agricultural obligations. From this large number of adult males, the Aztecs assembled units of 8,000 troops each, which they increased as the need arose. Initially, the army was recruited from among the elite of the Aztecs and their allies. But toward the middle of the fifteenth century, Aztec rulers set up a military school system for the sons of the elite plus those commoners who were to become priests. A parallel school system for the sons of commoners, aged 15–20 years, also included military training. After graduation, recruits began as porters, carrying supplies for the combat troops—an Aztec innovation which considerably enlarged the marching range of armies on campaign. Soldiers rose in the army hierarchy on the basis of merit, particularly as demonstrated by their success in the capture of enemies for future sacrifice.

The Aztecs inherited the weaponry and armor of the Toltecs but also made some important innovations. The bow and arrow, which arrived from northwest Mexico at the end of Toltec rule, became a standard weapon in Aztec armies. In addition, perhaps as late as the fifteenth century, the Aztecs developed the 3-foot obsidian-spiked broadsword, derived from the Toltec short sword, in order to enhance the latter's slashing force. As a result, clubs, maces, and axes declined in importance in the Aztec arsenal. Thrusting spears, dart throwers, and slings continued to be used as standard weapons. Body armor, consisting of quilted, sleeveless cotton shirts, thick cotton helmets, and round wooden or cane shields, was adopted from the Toltecs. With the arrival of the Aztecs, the Americas had acquired the heaviest infantry weaponry in their history, reflective of the intensity of militarism in their society—a militarism which was also typical of the earlier empires of the beginning Iron Age in the Middle East.

The Inca Empire of the Andes

After the disintegration of Tiwanaku and Wari around 1100, the central Andes returned to the traditional politics of local chiefdoms in small city-states with ceremonial centers and agricultural hinterlands. The best-known city-state was Chimú on the Peruvian coast, with its capital of Chan Chan numbering 30,000 inhabitants. Tiwanaku cultural traditions, however, remained dominant and were expressed in religious ceremonies, textile motifs, and ceramic styles.

Given the fierce competition among the ceremonial centers for pilgrims, insecurity was rampant during the period 1100–1400. Occasional charismatic military leaders projected military force and pacified the land. After a gestation period during the fourteenth century, the southern Peruvian city-state of Cuzco with its Inca elite emerged in the early fifteenth century at the head of a highly militaristic conquering polity. Within another century, the Incas had established an empire, called Tawantinsuyu [ta-wan-tin-SOO-yuh] (Quechua "Four Regions"), symbolizing its geographical expanse. It stretched from Ecuador in the north to central Chile in the south, with extensions into the tropical upper Amazon region and western Argentinean steppes (see Map 15.4).

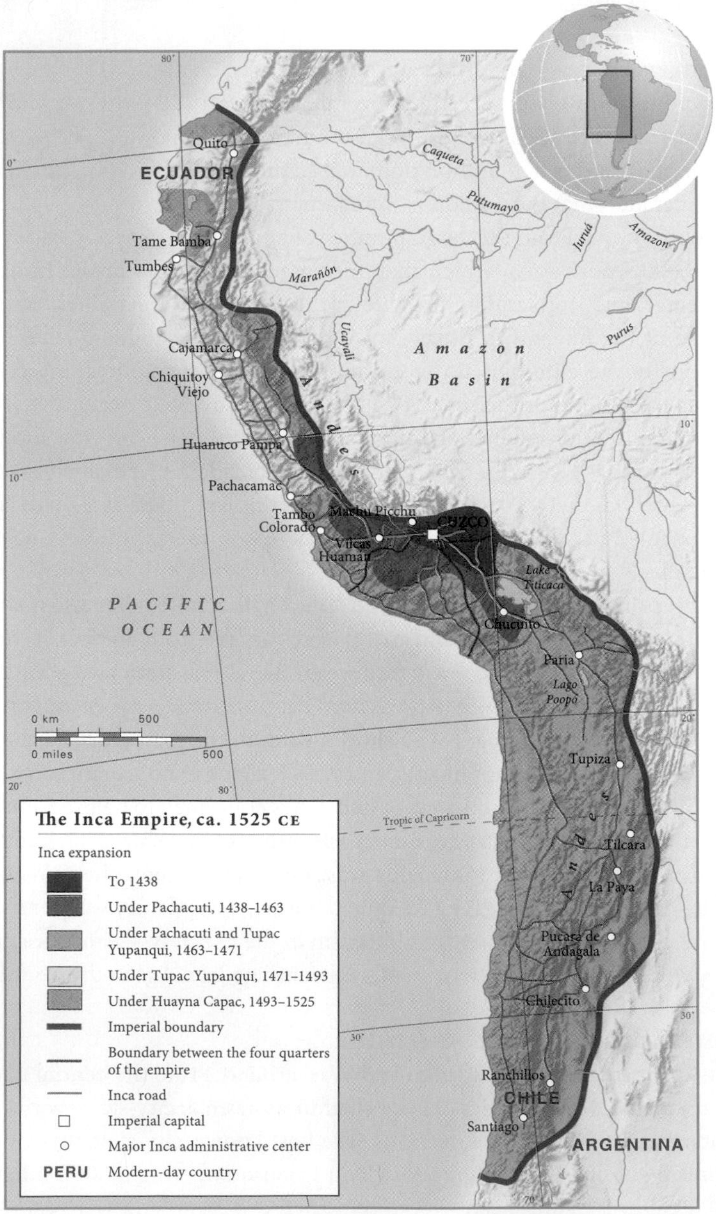

MAP 15.4 The Inca Empire, ca. 1525.

map analysis

As in the case of the Aztecs, the founding myth of the Incas involves a cave, an island, and a promised land of rich agriculture. In one version, the creator god Viracocha [vee-rah-KO-chah] summoned four brothers and four sisters from caves 7 leagues (21 miles) from Cuzco to the south, pairing them as couples and promising them a land of plenty. They would find this land when a golden rod, to be used on their wanderings, would get stuck in the soil. Alternatively, the sun god Inti [IN-tee] did the pairing of the couples on an island in Lake Titicaca and thereby bestowed the glory of Tiwanaku on them, before sending them with the golden rod to their promised land. Cuzco, where the rod plunged into the fertile soil, was settled land, however, and a war ensued in which the Incas drove out the existing farmers.

In the fourteenth century, Cuzco became a serious contender in the city-state competition. Like Wari, Cuzco was located at a highland elevation of 11,300 feet between the two Andes chains of southern Peru, roughly one-third of the way from Lake Titicaca north to Wari. Eight rulers (*curacas* [koo-RA-kas]) are said to have succeeded each other in the consolidation of Cuzco as a regional power. Although their names are recorded, events are hazy and dates are missing altogether. Firm historical terrain is reached with the ninth ruler, Pachacuti (r. 1438–1471). The history of the Incas from 1438 onward is known much better, primarily because of the memories of the grandchildren of the fifteenth-century Inca conquerors, recorded by the Spanish who defeated them in their conquest.

Imperial Expansion The system of reciprocity that characterized earlier Mesoamerican and Andean history continued under the Incas but was also, as in the case of Aztecs, decisively cast in the mold of power-enforced unilateralism. *Ayllu* [AY-yoo], the Quechua term for a household with an ancestral lineage, implied mutual obligations among groups of households, neighborhoods, villages, and city-states. To negotiate these obligations, Inca society—from households to provinces—was divided into two halves with roughly equal reciprocities. At the elite level, there were two sets of reciprocities, the first within two main branches of the elite and the second between the two branches of the elite and the subjects. The most important social expression of reciprocity remained the feast. In the Incan Empire, the state collected considerably more from the subject *ayllus* than Tiwanaku and Wari had done, but whether it returned comparable amounts through feasts and celebrations was a matter of contention, often leading to armed rebellion.

The earliest conquests under Pachacuti were toward the near south around Lake Titicaca, as well as the agriculturally rich lands north of the former Wari state. Thereafter, in the later fifteenth century, the Incas expanded 1,300 miles northward to southern Ecuador and 1,500 miles southward to Chile. The final provinces, added in the early sixteenth century, were in northern Ecuador as well as on the eastern slopes of the Andes, from the upper Amazon to western Argentina. The capital, Cuzco, which counted some 100,000 inhabitants in the early sixteenth century, was laid out in a cross-shaped grid of four streets leading out into the suburbs. Symbolically, as indicated by the empire's Quechua name, the capital reached out to the four regions of the empire—coast, north, south, and Amazon rain forest.

Administration Ethnic Inca governors administered the four regions, which were subdivided into a total of some 80 provinces, each again with an Inca

***Mit'a*:** Innovation of the Incas in which subjects were obligated to deliver a portion of their harvests, animal products, and domestically produced goods to nearby storehouses for use by Inca officials and troops. The *mit'a* also provided laborers for construction projects as well as workers on state farms or mines.

***Quipu*:** Knotted string assembly, used in the Andes from ca. 2500 BCE onward for the recording of taxes, population figures, calendar dates, troop numbers, and other data.

subgovernor. Most provinces were composites of former city-states, which remained under their local elites but had to accept a unique decimal system of population organization imposed by the Inca rulers. According to this system, members of the local elites commanded 10,000, 1,000, 100, and 10 household heads for the purpose of recruiting the manpower for the ***mit'a*** [MIT-ah] ("to take a turn," in reference to service obligations rotating among the subjects). The services, which subjects owed the empire as a form of taxes, were in farming, herding, manufacturing, military service, and portage. In its structure it was not unlike the Ming and Qing Chinese systems of local organization called *baojia* (see Chapter 12).

The *mit'a* was perhaps the single most important innovation the Incas contributed to the history of the Americas. In contrast to the Aztecs, who shipped taxes in kind to their capital by boat, the Incas had no efficient means of transportation for long distances. The only way to make use of the taxes in kind was to store them locally. The Incas built tens of thousands of storehouses everywhere in their empire, requiring subjects to deliver a portion of their harvests, animal products, and domestically produced goods under *mit'a* obligations to the nearest storehouse in their vicinity. These supplies were available to officials and troops and enabled the Incas to conduct military campaigns far from Cuzco without the need for foraging among local farmers. In addition, it was through the *mit'a* that quotas of laborers were raised for the construction of inns, roads, ceremonial centers, palaces, terraces, and irrigation canals, often far away from the urban center. Finally, the *mit'a* provided laborers for mines, quarries, state and temple farms, and colonies. No form of labor or service went untaxed.

To keep track of *mit'a* obligations, officials passed bundles of knotted cord (***quipu***, or *khipu* [KEE-poo], "knot") upward from level to level in the imperial administration. The numbers of knots on each cord in the bundles contained information on population figures and service obligations. As discussed in Chapter 5, the use of *quipus* was widespread in the Andes long before the Inca and can be considered as the Andean equivalent of a communication system. The only innovation contributed by the Incas seems to have been the massive scale on which these cord bundles were generated and employed. Some 700 have been preserved. Unfortunately, all modern attempts to decipher them have so far failed, and thus it is impossible to accurately outline the full picture of Inca service allocations.

Military Organization Perhaps the most important *mit'a* obligation which subject households owed to the Inca in the conquest phase of the empire was the service of young, able-bodied men in the military. Married men 25–30 years old were foot soldiers, often accompanied by wives and children; unmarried men 18–25 years of age served as porters or messengers. As in the Aztec Empire, administrators made sure that enough laborers remained in the villages to take care of their other obligations of farming, herding, transporting, and manufacturing. Sources report armies in the range of 35,000–140,000. Intermediate commanders came from the local and regional elites, and the top commanders were members of the two upper and lower Inca ruling elites.

Inca weaponry was comparable to that of the Aztecs, consisting of bows and arrows, dart throwers, slings, clubs with spiked bronze heads, wooden broadswords, bronze axes, and bronze-tipped javelins. Using Bolivian tin, Inca smiths were able to make a much harder and more useful bronze than was possible with earlier techniques. The Incas lacked the Aztec obsidian-serrated swords but used a snare (which

Inca Roads. Inca roads were paths reserved for runners and the military. They were built on beds of rocks and rubble and connected strategic points in the most direct line possible.

the Aztecs did not possess) with attached stone or bronze weights to entangle the enemy's legs. Protective armor consisted of quilted cotton shirts, copper breastplates, cane helmets, and shields. Of course, these types of weapons and armor were also widely found among the enemies of the Incas. The advantage enjoyed by the Incas, however, resulted from the sheer massiveness of their weapons and supplies, procured from craftspeople through the *mit'a* and stored in strategically located armories.

During the second half of the fifteenth century the Incas turned from conquest to consolidation. Faced at that time with a number of rebellions, they deemphasized the decimal draft and recruited longer-serving troops from among a smaller number of select, trusted peoples. These troops garrisoned the forts distributed throughout the empire. They also were part of the settler colonies implanted in rebellious provinces and in border regions. The fiercest resistance came from the people of the former Tiwanaku state and from the northeast Peruvian provinces, areas with long state traditions of their own. Since elite infighting also became more pronounced toward the end of the fifteenth century, personal guards recruited from non-Inca populations and numbering up to 7,000 soldiers accompanied many leading ruling-class members. The professionalization of the Inca army, however, lagged behind that of the Aztecs, since the Incas did not have military academies open to their subjects.

Communications Although they lacked the military professionalization of the Aztecs, the Incas created an imperial communication and logistics structure that was unparalleled in the Americas. Early on, the Incas systematically improved on the road network that they inherited from Tiwanaku, Wari, and other states. Two parallel trunk roads extended from Cuzco nearly the entire length of the empire in both southerly and northerly directions. One followed the coast and western slopes of the western Andes chain; the other led through the mountain lands, valleys, and high plains between the western and eastern Andes chains. In numerous places, additional highways connected the two trunk roads. Suspension bridges made of thick ropes crossed gorges, while rafts were used for crossing rivers. The roads, 3–12 feet wide, crossed the terrain as directly as possible, often requiring extensive grounding, paving, staircasing, and tunneling. In many places, the 25,000-mile road network still exists today, attesting to the engineering prowess of the Incas.

The roads were reserved for troops, officials, and runners carrying messages. For their convenience, every 15 miles, or at the end of a slow 1-day journey, an inn provided accommodation. Larger armies stopped at barracks-like constructions or pitched tents on select campgrounds. Like the Romans, and despite the fact that they did not have wheeled transport, the Incas were well aware of how crucial paved and well-supplied roads were for infantry soldiers.

Aqueduct from the Western Hills to Tenochtitlán. This aqueduct, still standing today, provided fresh water to the palace and mansions of the center of the island, to be used as drinking water and for washing.

Imperial Society and Culture

As Mesoamerica and the Andes entered their imperial age, cosmopolitan capitals with monumental ceremonial centers and palaces emerged. The sizes of both capitals and monuments were visual expressions of the exalted power that the rulers claimed. Almost daily ceremonies and rituals, accompanied by feasts, further underscored the authority of rulers. These ceremonies and rituals expressed the American spiritual and polytheistic heritage but were modified to impress on enemies and subjects alike the irresistible might of the empires.

Imperial Capitals: Tenochtitlán and Cuzco

In the fifteenth century, the Aztec and Inca capitals were among the largest cities of the world, encompassing between 100,000 and 200,000 inhabitants. Both cities maintained their high degree of urbanism through a complex command system of labor, services, and goods. Although their monumental architecture followed different artistic traditions, both emphasized platforms and sanctuaries atop large pyramid-like structures as symbols of elevated power as well as closeness to the astral gods, especially those associated with the sun and Venus.

Tenochtitlán as an Urban Metropolis More than half of the approximately 1.5 million people living during the fifteenth century in the Mexican Basin were urban dwellers, including elites, priests, administrators, military officers, merchants, traders, craftspeople, messengers, servants, and laborers. Such an extraordinary concentration of urban citizens was unique in the agrarian world prior to the industrialization of Europe (beginning around 1800), when cities usually held no more than 10 percent of the total population (see Map 15.5).

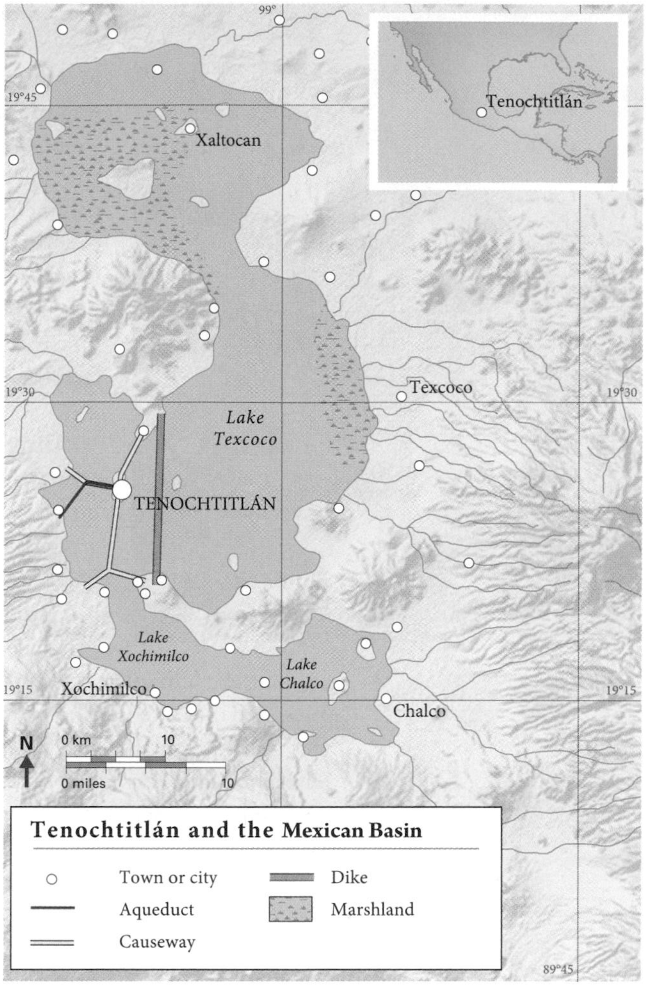

MAP 15.5 Tenochtitlán and the Valley of Mexico.

The center of Tenochtitlán, on the southern island, was a large platform where the Aztec settlers had driven pilings into marshy ground and heaped rocks and rubble. In an enclosure on this platform were the main pyramid, with temples to the Aztec gods on top, and a series of smaller ceremonial centers. Adjacent to these centers on the platform were a food market and a series of palaces of the ruling elite, which included guest quarters, administrative offices, storage facilities for tributes, kitchens, the high court for the elite and the court of appeals for commoners, the low court for civil cases, workshops for craftspeople, the prison, and councils for teachers and the military. Large numbers of Aztecs and visitors assembled each day to pay respect to the ruler and to trade in the market in preparation for assemblies and feasts.

In 1473, the southern island was merged with the northern island to form a single unit. At the center of the northern island was a platform that contained the principal market of the combined islands. This daily market attracted as many as 40,000 farmers, craftspeople, traders, porters, and laborers. The sophistication of the market was comparable to that of any market in Eurasia during the fifteenth century.

A number of causeways crossed the capital and linked it with the lakeshore. People also traveled inside the city on a number of main and branch canals. Dikes with sluices on the east side regulated both the water level and the salinity of the

Cuzco Stone Masonry. Inspired by the masonry of the people of Tiwanaku, the Inca built imposing structures with much larger blocks of limestone or granite. To cut the blocks, masons used copper and bronze chisels, making use of natural fissures in the stone.

lake around the islands. The runoff during the summer rainy season from the southwestern mountains provided fresh water to dilute the lake's salinity, and the eastern dikes kept out salt water from the rest of the lake. Potable water arrived from the shore via an aqueduct on one of the western causeways. This aqueduct served mostly the ceremonial center and palace precinct, but branches brought potable water to a number of elite residences nearby as well. Professional water carriers took fresh water from the aqueduct to commoners in the various quarters of the city; professional waste removers collected human waste from urban residences and took it to farmers for fertilizer. In short, Tenochtitlán possessed a fully developed urban infrastructure.

The two city centers—the pyramid and palaces in the south and the market in the north—were surrounded by dozens of residential city quarters. Built on a layer of firm ground, many of these quarters were inhabited by craftspeople of a shared profession, who practiced their crafts in their residences. As discussed earlier in this chapter, merchants occupied a privileged position between the elite and the commoners. As militarily trained organizers of large caravans of porters, the merchants also provided the Aztec capital with luxury goods. Depending on their social rank, craftspeople occupied residences of larger or smaller size, usually grouped into compounds of related families. The rooms of the houses surrounded a central patio on which most of the household activities took place—an architectural preference common to Mesoamerica and the Andes, as well as the Middle East and Mediterranean.

Residents of quarters farther away from the center were farmers. In these quarters, making up nearly two-thirds of Tenochtitlán's surface, families engaged in intensive farming. Here, a grid of canals encased small, rectangular islands devoted to housing compounds and/or farming. People moved within these barrios by boat. Since the Mexican Basin received year-round rains that were often insufficient for dry farming, a raised-field system prevailed, whereby farmers dredged the canals, heaped the fertile mud on top of the rectangular islands, called ***chinampas,*** and added water from the canals and waste from their households or brought by boat from the urban neighborhoods. In contrast to the luxurious palaces of the elite, housing for farmers consisted of plastered huts made of cane, wood, and reeds. As in all agrarian societies, farmers—subject to high taxes or rents—were among the poorest folk.

Chinampas: Mesoamerican agricultural practice by which farmers grew crops on small, human-made islands in Lake Texcoco.

On the surface of the *chinampas,* farmers grew corn, beans, squash, amaranth, and peppers. These seed plants were supplemented by *maguey* [mag-AY], a large succulent agave. This evergreen plant grew in poor soils; had a large root system, which helped in stabilizing the ground; and produced fiber useful for weaving and pulp useful for making *pulque* [POOL-kay], a fermented drink. To plant these crops in the soft soil, a digging stick, slightly broadened at one end, was sufficient. Regular watering made multicropping of seed plants possible. Trees, planted at the edges, protected the *chinampas* against water erosion.

Ownership of the *chinampas* was vested in clans, which, under neighborhood leaders, were responsible for the allocation of land and adjudication of disputes as well as the payment of taxes in kind to the elite. But there were also members of the elite who, as absentee owners, possessed estates and employed managers to collect rents from the farmers. Whether there was a trend from taxes to rents (that is, from a central tax authority to a decentralized landowner class) is unknown. Given the high productivity of raised-field farming, which was similar to that of the Eurasian agrarian–urban centers, such a trend would not have been surprising.

Cuzco as a Ceremonial–Administrative City The site of the Inca city of Cuzco was an elongated triangle formed by the confluence of two rivers. At one end, opposite the confluence, was a hill with a number of structures, including the imperial armory and a temple dedicated to the sun god. Enormous, zigzagging walls followed the contours of the hill. The walls were built with stone blocks weighing up to 100 tons and cut so precisely that no mortar was needed, a technique which the Incas adopted from Tiwanaku.

Below, on the plain leading to the confluence, the city was laid out in a grid pattern. The residents of the city, all belonging to the upper and lower Inca ruling class, lived in adobe houses arranged in a block-and-courtyard pattern similar to that of Wari. Several squares and temples within the city served as ceremonial centers. One plaza contained a platform, with the imperial throne and a pillar placed symbolically atop what the Incas considered the earth's center or navel. The Coricancha [co-ri-CAN-tsha], the city's main temple, stood near the confluence of the rivers. This temple was a walled compound comprising six buildings set around a courtyard. Chambers in these buildings contained the Inca gods and goddesses as well as the divine statues or sacred objects confiscated from the provinces. Each year priests of the empire's ceremonial centers sent one such sacred object to the Coricancha, to demonstrate their obedience to the central Inca temple (see Map 15.6).

Across the rivers, in separate suburbs, were settlements for commoners with markets and storehouses. They were surrounded by fields, terraces, and irrigation canals. In the fields, interspersed stone pillars and shrines were aligned on sight lines radiating from the Coricancha, tying the countryside closely to the urban center. These alignments were reminiscent of the Nazca lines drawn half a millennium earlier in southern Peru (Chapter 9). Farther away were imperial estates with unfree laborers from outside the *mit'a* system and its reciprocal feasting. In contrast to the Aztec elite, which allowed meritorious generals to rise in the hierarchy, the Inca elite remained exclusionary, allowing no commoners to reside in Cuzco.

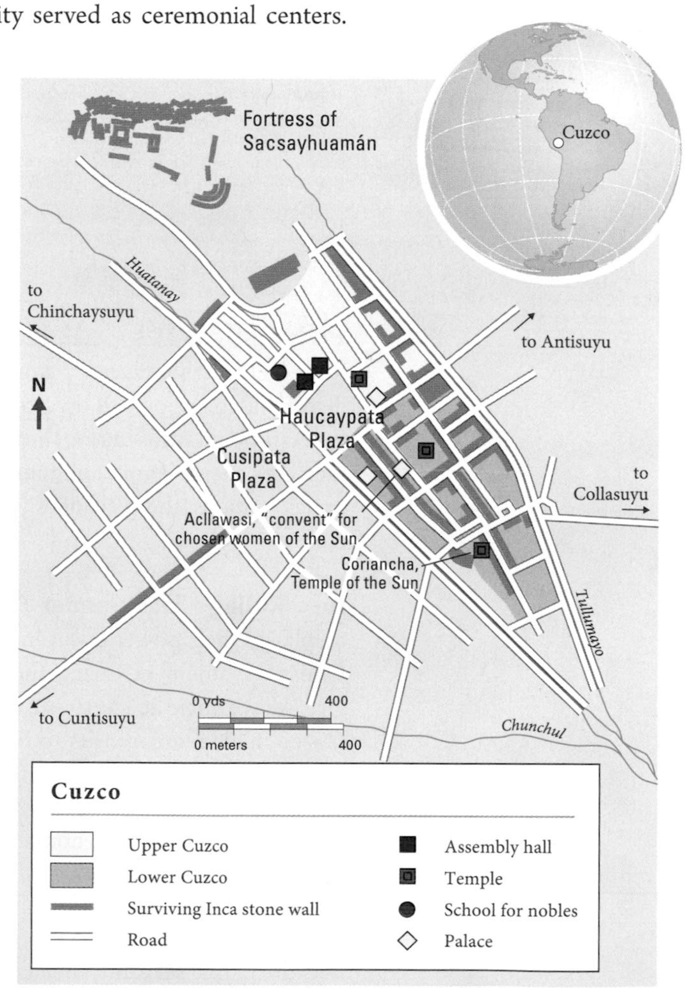

MAP 15.6 **Cuzco.**

Patterns Up Close

Human Sacrifice and Propaganda

In the first millennium CE, Mesoamerica and the Andes evolved from their early religious spirituality to polytheism. The spiritual heritage, however, remained a strong undercurrent. Both American regions engaged in human as well as animal and agricultural sacrifices. Rulers appeased the gods also through self-sacrifice—that is, the piercing of tongue and penis, as was the case among the Olmecs (1400–400 BCE) and Mayas (600 BCE–900 CE). The feathered serpent god Quetzalcoatl was the Mesoamerican deity of self-sacrifice, revered in the city-states of Teotihuacán (200 BCE–570 CE) and Tula (ca. 900 CE). Under the Toltecs and the Aztecs, this god receded into the background, in favor of warrior gods such as Tezcatlipoca and Huitzilpochtli. The survival of traditional blood rituals within polytheism was a pattern that distinguished the early American empires from their Eurasian counterparts.

Whether human sacrifices were prolific under Aztec and Inca imperialism is questionable. About the same number of human victims were excavated at the Feathered Serpent Temple of Teotihuacán and at the Templo Mayor of Tenochtitlán: 137 versus 126 skeletons. These numbers are minuscule in comparison to the

Human Sacrifice. Human sacrifice among the pre-Columbian Mesoamericans and Andeans was based on the concept of a shared life spirit or mind, symbolized by the life substance of blood. In the American spiritual-polytheistic conceptualization, the gods sacrificed their blood, or themselves altogether, during creation; rulers pierced their earlobes, tongues, or penises for blood sacrifices; and war captives lost their lives when their hearts were sacrificed.

Power and Its Cultural Expressions

Ruling elites, as repeatedly emphasized in this chapter, put a strong emphasis on displaying their power during the period 600–1500. This was particularly true with the Aztecs and Incas during the fifteenth century. Among these displays were human sacrifices, mausoleums, and mummy burials. Although all three involved changes in social relations, these changes were accommodated in the existing overall religious culture.

Inca Ruling-Class Gender Relations The ruling classes in the Inca Empire displayed their power in several ways. Among the examples were the "Houses of Chosen Women" in Cuzco and provincial colonies. The greatest honor for Inca girls was to enter at age 10–12 into the service of these houses. An inspector from Cuzco made regular visits to the villages of the empire to select attractive young girls for the service. The girls were marched to the capital or the colonies, where they were divided according to beauty, skills, and social standing. These houses had female instructors who provided the girls with a 4-year education in cooking, beer making, weaving, and officiating in the rituals and ceremonies of the Inca religion. After their graduation, the young women became virgin temple priestesses, were given in marriage to non-Incas honored for service to the ruler, or became palace servants, musicians, or concubines of the Inca elite. The collection of this girl tribute was separate from the reciprocity system. As such, it was an impression created by the Spanish conquerors and encourage doubts about the magnitude of human sacrifices in temple ceremonies. It appears that even though the Aztec and Inca ruling classes were focused on war, the ritual of human sacrifice was not as pervasive as has been widely assumed.

Could it be that there was no significant increase in human sacrifice under the Aztecs and Incas, as the self-serving Spanish conquerors alleged? Were there perhaps, instead, imperial propaganda machines in the Aztec and Inca Empires, employed in the service of conquest and consolidation—similar to those of the Assyrians and Mongols in Eurasia—who sought to intimidate their enemies? In this case, the Aztec and Inca Empires would not be exceptional barbaric aberrations in world history. Instead, they would be but two typical examples of the general world-historical pattern of competitive militaristic states during the early agrarian era using propaganda to further their imperial power.

Questions

- In examining the question of whether empires such as the Inca and the Aztec employed human sacrifice for propaganda purposes, can this practice be considered an adaptation that evolved out of earlier rituals, such as royal bloodletting?
- If the Aztec and the Inca did indeed employ human sacrifice for propaganda purposes, what does this say about the ability of these two empires to use cultural and religious practices to consolidate their power?

act of assigning gender roles in an emerging social hierarchy defined by power inequalities.

Traditionally, gender roles were less strictly divided than in Eurasia. The horticultural form of agriculture in Mesoamerica and the Andes gave males fewer opportunities to accumulate wealth and power than plow agriculture did in Eurasia. Hoes and foot plows distinguished men and women from each other less than plows and teams of oxen or horses did. Nevertheless, it comes as no surprise that the gradual agrarian–urban diversification of society, even if it was slower in the Americas than in Eurasia, proceeded along similar paths of increasing male power concentration in villages, ceremonial centers, temple cities, conquering states, and empires. Emphasizing gender differences, therefore, should be viewed as a characteristic phenomenon arising in imperial contexts.

Inca Mummy Veneration Other houses in Cuzco were ghostly residences in which scores of attendants and servants catered to what were believed to be the earthly needs of deceased, mummified Inca emperors and their principal wives. During the mummification process attendants removed the cadaver's internal organs, placed them in special containers, and desiccated the bodies until they were completely mummified. Servants dressed the mummies (*mallquis* [MAY-kees]) in their finest clothing and placed them back into their residences amid their possessions, as if they had never died. The mummies received daily meals and were carried around by their retinues for visits to their mummified relatives. On special occasions, mummies were lined up according to rank on Cuzco's main plaza to participate in ceremonies and processions. In this way, they remained fully integrated into the daily life of the elite.

"Ghost residences" with mummies can be considered an outgrowth of the old Andean custom of mummification. This custom was widely practiced among the elites of the ceremonial centers, who, however, generally placed their ancestors in temple tombs, shrines, or caves. Mummies were also buried in cemeteries, sometimes collectively in bundles with false heads made of cotton. Preserving the living spaces of the deceased obviously required considerable wealth—wealth provided only by imperial regimes for their elites.

As a general phenomenon in Andean society, of course, mummies were a crucial ingredient in the religious heritage, in which strong spiritual elements survived underneath the polytheistic overlay of astral gods. In the spiritual tradition, body and spirit cohabit more or less loosely. In a trance, a diviner's mind can travel, enter the minds of other people and animals, or make room for other people's minds. Similarly, in death a person's spirit, while no longer in the body, remains nearby and therefore still needs daily nourishment in order not to be driven away. Hence, even though non-Incan Andean societies removed the dead from their daily living spaces, descendants had to visit tombs regularly with food and beer or provide buried mummies with ample victuals.

The expenses for the upkeep of the mummy households were the responsibility of the deceased emperor's bloodline, headed by a surviving brother. As heirs of the emperor's estate, the members of the bloodline formed a powerful clan within the ruling class. The new emperor was excluded from this estate and had to acquire his own new one in the course of his rule, a mechanism evidently designed to intensify his imperial ambitions for conquest. In the early sixteenth century, however, when it became logistically difficult to expand much beyond the enormous territory already accumulated in the Andes, this ingenious mechanism of keeping the upper and lower rungs of the ruling class united became counterproductive. Emperors lacking resources had to contend with brothers richly endowed with inherited wealth and ready to engage in dynastic warfare—as actually occurred shortly before the arrival of the Spanish (1529–1532).

Putting It All Together

interactive concept map

During the short time of their existence, the Aztec and Inca Empires unleashed extraordinary creative energies. Sculptors, painters, and (after the arrival of the Spanish) writers recorded the traditions as well as the innovations of the fifteenth century. Aztec painters produced codices, or illustrated manuscripts, that present the divine pantheons, myths, calendars, ceremonial activities, chants, poetry, and administrative activities of their societies in exquisite and colorful detail. They fashioned these codices using bark paper, smoothing it with plaster, and connecting the pages accordion-style. Today, a handful of these codices survive, preserved in Mexican and European libraries.

The Aztec and Inca Empires were polities that illustrate how humans not in contact with the rest of the world and living within an environment that was different from that of Eurasia and Africa in many respects developed patterns of innovation that were remarkably similar. On the basis of an agriculture that produced ample surpluses, humans made the same choices as their cousins in Eurasia and Africa. Specifically, in the period 600–1500, they created temple-centered city-states, just like their Sumerian and Hindu counterparts. Their military states were not unlike the Chinese warring states. And, finally, their empires—although just beginning to flourish in the Bronze Age—were comparable to those of the New Kingdom Egyptians or Assyrians. The Americas had their own unique variations of these larger historical patterns, to be sure; but they nevertheless displayed the same humanity as found elsewhere.

Review and Relate

Thinking Through Patterns

Examine the ways historians approach the big questions of this chapter.

The basic pattern of state formation in the Americas was similar to that of Eurasia and Africa. Historically, it began with the transition from foraging to agriculture and settled village life. As the population increased, villages under elders became chiefdoms, which in turn became city-states with temples. As in Eurasia and Africa, American city-states often became conquering states, beginning with the Maya kingdoms and Teotihuacán. Both, however, remained small. Military states, in which ruling classes sought to expand territories, such as Tula and, to a lesser degree, Tiwanaku and Wari, were characteristic for the early part of the period 600–1550. The successors of these—the Aztec and Inca Empires—were multiethnic, multilinguistic, and multireligious polities that dominated Mesoamerica and the Andes for about a century, before the Spanish conquest brought them to a premature end.

» Within the patterns of state formation basic to the Americas, which types of states emerged in Mesoamerica and the Andes during the period 600–1550? What characterized these states?

The states of Tiwanaku and Wari had more or less cohesive ruling classes but no dynasties of rulers and centralized bureaucracies. These ruling classes and their subjects—corn and potato farmers—were integrated with each other through systems of reciprocity—that is, military protection in return for foodstuffs. They customarily renewed the bonds of reciprocity in common feasts. After one or two centuries, however, tensions arose, either between stronger and weaker branches of the ruling classes or between rulers and subjects over questions of obligations and justice. When these tensions erupted into internal warfare, the states disintegrated, often in conjunction with environmental degradation and climate change.

» Why did the Tiwanaku and Wari states have ruling classes but no dynasties and central bureaucracies? How were these patterns expressed in the territorial organization of these states?

Tenochtitlán and Cuzco, the capitals of the Aztec and Inca Empires, were two urban centers organized around temples and associated residences of the ruling dynasties and their priestly classes. They also contained large city quarters inhabited

» What patterns of urban life characterized the cities of

Tenochtitlán and Cuzco, the capitals of the Aztec and Inca Empires? In which ways were these cities similar to those of Eurasia and Africa?

by craftspeople specializing in the production of woven textiles, pottery, leather goods, and weapons. Large central markets provided for the exchange of foodstuffs, crafts, and imported luxury goods. Armed caravans of merchants and porters transported the luxury goods, such as cacao, feathers, obsidian, and turquoise, across hundreds of miles. Tenochtitlán had an aqueduct for the supply of drinking water, and Cuzco was traversed by a river. Both capitals had agricultural suburbs in which farmers used irrigation for the production of the basic food staples.

Against the Grain

Consider this as a counterpoint to the main patterns examined in this chapter.

Amazon Rain-Forest Civilizations

- Which is more important: to save the rain forest or uncover its archaeological past? Can the two objectives be combined?
- Compare the Amazonian earthworks to those of Benin in Africa during the same period (Chapter 14). Which similarities and differences can you discover?

For many years, prevailing scholarly opinion held that the vast Amazonian river basin, covered by dense rain forest, was too inhospitable to allow for more than small numbers of widely dispersed foragers to subsist. Even farmers, living in more densely populated villages, could not possibly have founded complex, stratified societies. Slash-and-burn agriculture, the common form of farming on poor tropical soils even today, by definition prevented the advance of urban life: After exhausting the soil in a given area, whole villages had to pack up and move.

Beginning in the 1990s, however, a few scholars realized that this belief was erroneous. Modern farmers, increasingly encroaching on the rain forest, made these scholars aware of two hitherto neglected features. First, these farmers often advanced into stretches of forest and savanna on top of what is called in Portuguese *terra preta*—black soil so fertile that it did not require fertilizers for years. Second, as they slashed and burned the rain forest and savanna with their modern tools, the farmers exposed monumental earthworks that had previously escaped attention under the cover of vegetation. The two features were actually connected. *Terra preta* was the result of centuries of patient soil enrichment by indigenous people who were also the builders of the earthworks. Instead of slashing and burning, these people had engaged in "slashing and charring"—that is, turning the trees into longer-lasting nutrient-rich charcoal rather than less fertile and quickly depleted ash.

Since the early 2000s, scholars have documented large-scale settlements in areas along the southern tributaries to the Amazon, describing large village clusters with central plazas, fortification walls, bridges, causeways, and waterworks. One such cluster is located on the upper Xingu, a tributary of the lower Amazon. A set of two clusters is situated near the upper reaches of the Purus, a tributary of the upper Amazon. One occupies a fertile floodplain, the other the less fertile highlands farther away from the river. In the Purus region, researchers employing aerial photography revealed a huge area home to perhaps 60,000 inhabitants during a period around the late thirteenth century. This area is adjacent to the farthest northeastern extension of the Inca Empire into the Amazon, with fortresses being excavated by Finnish teams. Thus, when the Incas expanded into the rain forest, they clearly did so to incorporate flourishing, advanced societies into their empire. Thanks to scholars who challenged the orthodoxy of the "empty rain forest," we are rediscovering the Amazonian past.

Key Terms

audio flashcards

Chinampas 448
Reciprocity 435
Mit'a 444
Quipu 444

For additional resources, please go to
www.oup.com/us/vonsivers.
Please see the Further Resources section at the back of the book for additional readings and suggested websites.

PATTERNS OF EVIDENCE |

Sources for Chapter 15

SOURCE 15.1 The Temple of the Jaguars, Chichén Itzá

ca. 850–1000 CE

Chichén Itzá was founded during a period of renewed urbanization in the Mayan states around 650, and a remarkable state flourished in its vicinity between 850 and 1000. The population was composed of local Maya, as well as Maya-speaking peoples from the Gulf of Mexico coast. It owed its prosperity to long-distance trade, both overland and in boats along the coast. Around 1000, the ruling-class factions abandoned Chichén Itzá for unknown reasons, and the city-state dwindled in size to the level of a town.

Source: Dreamstime/©Alexandre Fagundes De Fagundes (top); Shutterstock/Danilo Ascione (bottom).

» Working with Sources

1. What does the construction of this monument suggest about the social structure of Chichén Itzá at its height?
2. What might have been the significance of the jaguars? Why would the temple have been decorated in such an elaborate fashion?

SOURCE 15.2

Skeletons in a Wari royal tomb site, El Castillo de Huarmey, Peru

ca. 600–1000 CE

In 2013, 63 skeletons were discovered in a tomb at El Castillo de Huarmey, about 175 miles north of Lima, in what would seem to be the first imperial tomb of the Wari culture discovered in modern times. Most of the bodies were female, and wrapped in bundles in a seated position typical of Wari burials. Three of the women appear to have been Wari queens, as they were buried with gold and silver jewelry and brilliantly painted ceramics. However, six of the skeletons were not wrapped in the textiles, but instead positioned on top of the burials. Archaeologists have concluded that these people may have been sacrificed for the benefit of the others.

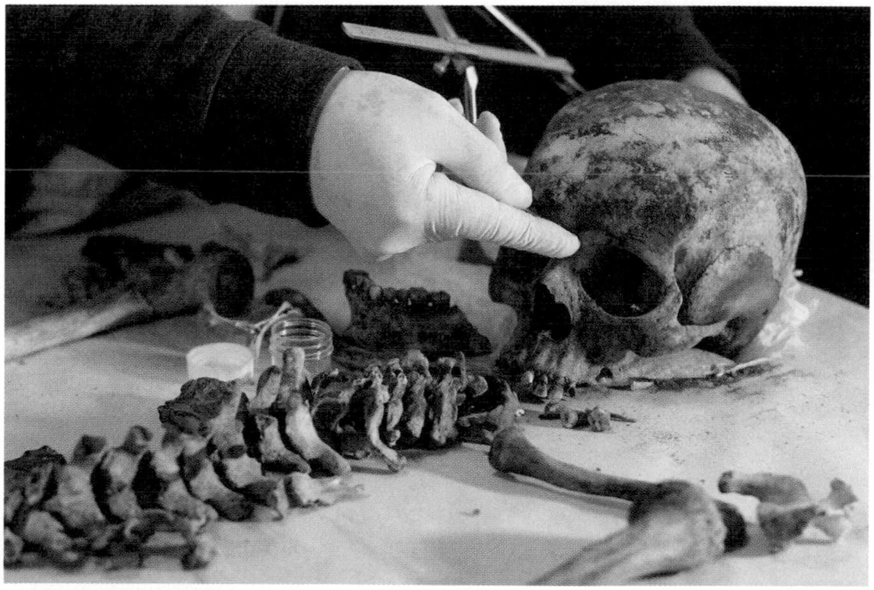

Source: REUTERS/Enrique Castro-Mendivil.

» Working with Sources

1. **How do the burial practices of Wari culture compare with those of other civilizations in Mesoamerica and the Andes?**
2. **What might this tomb suggest about the roles and expectations of women in Wari culture?**

SOURCE 15.3 Bernal Díaz, *The Conquest of New Spain*

ca. 1568

In the course of the fifteenth century, the Aztecs established an empire centered in the Mexican Basin (surrounding present-day Mexico City, after the drainage of most of the valley) but encompassing Mesoamerica from the Pacific to the Gulf of Mexico. The resulting state, far more centralized than the preceding Teotihuacán and Toltec city-states, commanded a large extent of territory and thrived on the trade in raw materials that were brought in from both coasts of their empire. Bernal Díaz, born in 1492 in Spain, would join the Spaniards in the "conquest" of Mexico, but he also left behind vivid eyewitness accounts of occupied Aztec society in the sixteenth century. Among them is this description of the market in Tlatelolco, one of the central cities at the heart of Aztec imperial power.

Caciques: Nobles.

Our Captain and those of us who had horses went to Tlatelolco mounted, and the majority of our men were fully equipped. On reaching the market-place, escorted by the many ***Caciques*** whom Montezuma had assigned to us, we were astounded at the great number of people and the quantities of merchandise, and at the orderliness and good arrangements that prevailed, for we had never seen such a thing before. The chieftains who accompanied us pointed everything out. Every kind of merchandise was kept separate and had its fixed place marked for it.

Let us begin with the dealers in gold, silver, and precious stones, feathers, cloaks, and embroidered goods, and male and female slaves who are also sold there. They bring as many slaves to be sold in that market as the Portuguese bring Negroes from Guinea. Some are brought there attached to long poles by means of collars round their necks to prevent them from escaping, but others are left loose. Next there were those who sold coarser cloth, and cotton goods and fabrics made of twisted thread, and there were chocolate merchants with their chocolate. In this way you could see every kind of merchandise to be

---

Source: Bernal Díaz del Castillo, *The Conquest of New Spain*, trans. J. M. Cohen (Baltimore: Penguin, 1963), 232–234.

found anywhere in New Spain, laid out in the same way as goods are laid out in my own district of Medina del Campo, a centre for fairs, where each line of stalls has its own particular sort. So it was in this great market. There were those who sold sisal cloth and ropes and the sandals they wear on their feet, which are made from the same plant. All these were kept in one part of the market, in the place assigned to them, and in another part were skins of tigers and lions, otters, jackals, and deer, badgers, mountain cats, and other wild animals, some tanned and some untanned, and other classes of merchandise.

. . .

Then there were the sellers of pitch-pine for torches, and other things of that kind, and I must also mention, with all apologies, that they sold many canoe-loads of human excrement, which they keep in the creeks near the market. This was for the manufacture of salt and the curing of skins, which they say cannot be done without it. I know that many gentlemen will laugh at this, but I assure them it is true. I may add that on all the roads they have shelters made of reeds or straw or grass so that they can retire when they wish to do so, and purge their bowels unseen by passers-by, and also in order that their excrement shall not be lost.

But why waste so many words on the goods in their great market? If I describe everything in detail I shall never be done. Paper, which in Mexico they call *amal*, and some reeds that smell of liquid amber, and are full of tobacco, and yellow ointments and other such things, are sold in a separate part. Much cochineal is for sale too, under the arcades of that market, and there are many sellers of herbs and other such things. They have a building there also in which three judges sit, and there are officials like constables who examine the merchandise. I am forgetting the sellers of salt and the makers of flint knives, and how they split them off the stone itself, and the fisherwomen and the men who sell small cakes made from a sort of weed which they get out of the great lake, which curdles and forms a kind of bread which tastes rather like cheese. They sell axes too, made of bronze and copper and tin, and gourds and brightly painted wooden jars.

Cue: Temple.

We went on to the great ***cue***, and as we approached its wide courts, before leaving the market-place itself, we saw many more merchants who, so I was told, brought gold to sell in grains, just as they extract it from the mines. This gold is placed in the thin quills of the large geese of that country, which are so white as to be transparent. They used to reckon their accounts with one another by the length and thickness of these little quills, how much so many cloaks or so many gourds of chocolate or so many slaves were worth, or anything else they were bartering.

≫ Working with Sources

1. **How and why does Díaz use comparisons from other markets while describing the one in Tlatelolco?**
2. **What do the specific elements of this market suggest about the importance of trade and commerce in pre-Columbian Mexico?**

SOURCE 15.4 Pedro Cieza de León on Incan roads

1541–1547

The Incas created an imperial communications and logistics infrastructure that was unparalleled in the Americas, with two highways extending to the north and south from Cuzco nearly the entire length of the empire. The roads, which were up to 12 feet wide, crossed the terrain as directly as possible, which clearly required a tremendous labor force to create. In many places, even today, the 25,000-mile road network still exists. Pedro Cieza de León was born in Spain in 1520 and undoubtedly traveled along the extensive, and still-functional, Roman road system of his native land as a child. When he arrived in the New World at the age of 13, he was captivated and impressed by the civilizations that the Spanish were supplanting. In 1541, he began writing his account of the Incas, tracing their heritage and government for the benefit of those who would never see the territory he did—or travel the roads that made his observations possible.

CHAPTER 42 (ii.xv)

Of how the buildings for the Lord-Incas were constructed, and the highways to travel through the kingdom [of Peru].

One of the things that most took my attention when I was observing and setting down the things of this kingdom was how and in what way the great, splendid highways we see throughout it could be built, and the number of men that must have been required, and what tools and instruments they used to level the mountains and cut through the rock to make them as broad and good as they are. For it seems to me that if the Emperor were to desire another highway built like the one from Quito to Cuzco, or that which goes from Cuzco to Chile, truly I do not believe he could do it, with all his power and the men at his disposal, unless he followed the method the Incas employed. For if it were a question of a road fifty leagues long, or a hundred, or two hundred, we can assume that, however rough the land, it would not be too difficult, working hard, to do it. But there were so long, one of them more than 1100 leagues, over mountains so rough and dismaying that in certain places one could not see bottom, and some of the sierras so sheer and barren that the road had to be cut through the living rock to keep it level and the right width. All this they did with fire and picks.

. . .

When a Lord-Inca had decided on the building of one of these famous highways, no great provisioning or levies or anything else was needed except for the Lord-Inca to say, let this be done. The inspectors then went through

---

Source: Pedro Cieza de León, *The Incas*, trans. Harriet de Onis, ed. Victor Wolfgang von Hagen (Norman: University of Oklahoma Press, 1959), 135–137.

the provinces, laying out the route and assigning Indians from one end to the other to the building of the road. In this way, from one boundary of the province to the other, at its expense and with its Indians, it was built as laid out, in a short time; and the others did the same, and, if necessary, a great stretch of the road was built at the same time, or all of it. When they came to the barren places, the Indians of the lands nearest by came with victuals and tools to do the work, and all was done with little effort and joyfully, because they were not oppressed in any way, nor did the Incas put overseers to watch them.

Aside from these, great fine highways were built, like that which runs through the valley of Xaquixahuana, and comes out of the city of Cuzco and goes by the town of Muhina. There were many of these highways all over the kingdom, both in the highlands and the plains. Of all, four are considered the main highways, and they are those which start from the city of Cuzco, at the square, like a crossroads, and go to the different provinces of the kingdom. As these monarchs held such a high opinion of themselves, when they set out on one of these roads, the royal person with the necessary guard took one [road], and the rest of the people another. So great was their pride that when one of them died, his heir, if he had to travel to a distant place, built his road larger and broader than that of his predecessor, but this was only if this Lord-Inca set out on some conquest, or [performed] some act so noteworthy that it could be said the road built for him was longer.

» Working with Sources

1. How were the Incas' roads a manifestation of royal power, at least in Cieza de León's estimation?

2. What technical challenges faced the Incan road builders, and how did they overcome them?

SOURCE 15.5 Garcilaso de la Vega, "The Walls and Gates of Cuzco"

1609–1616

The Incan city of Cuzco was an elongated triangle formed by the confluence of two rivers. At one end, enormous, zigzagging walls followed the contours of a steep hill. The walls were built with stone blocks weighing up to 100 tons and cut so precisely that no mortar was needed. The ruins of the walls were still visible after the Spanish siege of 1536 (as they are today), and they were a marvel to Garcilaso de la Vega, when he viewed them in the mid-sixteenth century. Garcilaso was born in 1539, the decade of the conquest of Peru, to a Spanish conqueror and a Native American princess,

---

Source: Garcilaso de la Vega, *Royal Commentaries of the Incas and General History of Peru*, trans. Harold V. Livermore, vol.1 (Austin: University of Texas Press, 1966), 463–468.

a second cousin of the last two Inca rulers. As a young man, Garcilaso left his native Peru, never to return. Toward the end of his life he retired to a secluded Spanish village, where he wrote his general history of the Incas. He was particularly proud of the monumental achievements of his Incan relatives and of the power that their construction projects represented.

CHAPTER XXVII

The fortress of Cuzco; the size of its stones.

The Inca kings of Peru made marvelous buildings, fortresses, temples, royal palaces, gardens, storehouses, roads, and other constructions of great excellence, as can be seen even today from their remaining ruins, though the whole building can scarcely be judged from the mere foundations.

The greatest and most splendid building erected to show the power and majesty of the Incas was the fortress of Cuzco, the grandeur of which would be incredible to anyone who had not seen it, and even those who have seen it and considered it with attention imagine, and even believe, that it was made by enchantment, the handiwork of demons, rather than of men. Indeed the multiplicity of stones, large and small, of which the three **circumvallations** are composed (and they are more like rocks than stones) makes one wonder how they could have been quarried, for the Indians had neither iron nor steel to work them with. And the question of how they were conveyed to the site is no less difficult a problem, since they had no oxen and could not make wagons: nor would oxen and wagons have sufficed to carry them. They were in fact heaved by main force with the aid of thick cables. The roads by which they were brought were not flat, but rough mountainsides with steep slopes, up and down which the rocks were dragged by human effort alone.

Circumvallations: Walls built around the city.

. . .

CHAPTER XXVIII

The three circumvallations, the most remarkable part of the work.

On the other side, opposite this wall, there is a large level space. From this direction the ascent to the top of the hill is a gradual one up which an enemy could advance in order of battle. The Incas therefore made three concentric walls on the slopes, each of which would be more than two hundred fathoms long. They are in the shape of a half moon, for they close together at the ends to meet the other wall of smooth masonry on the side facing the city. The first of these three walls best exhibits the might of the Incas, for although all three are of the same workmanship, it is the most impressive and has the largest stones, making the whole construction seem incredible to anyone who has not seen it, and giving an impression of awe to the careful observer who ponders on the size and number of the stones and the limited resources of the natives for cutting and working them and setting them in their places.

. . .

Almost in the middle of each wall there was a gate, and these gates were each shut with a stone as high and as thick as the wall itself which could be raised and lowered. The first of these was called Tiupuncu, "gate of sand," since the plain is rather sandy or gravelly at this point: *tiu* is "sand," or "a sandy place," and *puncu*, "gate, door." The second is called Acahuana Puncu, after the master mason, whose name was Acahuana, the syllable *ca* being pronounced deep down in the throat. The third is Viracocha Puncu, dedicated to the god Viracocha, the phantom we have referred to at length, who appeared to Prince Viracocha Inca and forewarned him of the rising of the Chancas, as a result of which he was regarded as the defender and second founder of Cuzco, and therefore given this gate with the request that he should guard it and defend the fortress as he had guarded the city and the whole empire in the past.

≫ Working with Sources

1. **Why did the Incas feel the need to fortify Cuzco so heavily, and would these preparations have been successful in typical battle situations?**
2. **What aspect of the city's walls most arouses Garcilaso's admiration and wonder, and why?**

PART FOUR

Interactions across the Globe

1450–1750

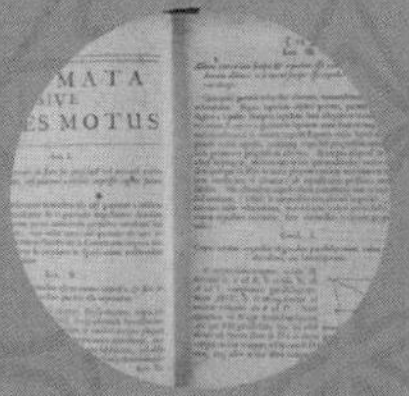

Starting around 1450, important changes can be detected in the patterns of world history. The religious civilizations that had emerged in the period after 600 CE continued to evolve, but the competing states that constituted these civilizations began to give way to new empires, such as those of the Mughals, the Ottomans, the Safavids, and the Habsburgs. China, historically an empire, had already reconstituted itself under the Ming after the collapse of the Mongol super-empire that had straddled Eurasia. Finally, on the Atlantic coast, smaller European countries, such as Portugal, Spain, the Netherlands, England, and France, were creating the first global seaborne empires. Large or small, land based or maritime, however, all of these empires employed the vitally important innovation of firearms. In addition, many reorganized themselves as centralized polities based on money economies, large bureaucracies, and professional armies. Locked into far-flung competition for resources, markets, and ideological influence, they interacted with each other with increasing intensity.

While this renewal of the drive for empire among these civilizations was a significant turning point in world history, two new phenomena appeared during the three centuries in question that would have further far-reaching implications. Indeed, they would ultimately provide the basis on which our modern society was to be built: the New Sciences (or Scientific Revolution) and the Enlightenment. Attempts to found an understanding of the universe on mathematics and experimentation would lead to science as the chief mode of interpreting the physical realm. Attempts to apply principles of science to understanding and improving human societies would lead to the concepts of individual rights, natural law, and popular sovereignty that would become the modern legacy of the Enlightenment. The combination of these two trends created the foundations of the *scientific–industrial society* that now dominates our modern global culture.

The process by which this formation of *scientific–industrial society* took place was, of course, extremely complex, and it is impossible for us to do more than suggest some of the larger patterns of it here. Moreover, because of the long-standing argument in Western historiography for European "exceptionalism"—that there was something unique in the European historical experience that preordained it to rise to

1440–1897 Benin kingdom, West Africa

1453 Ottoman capture of Constantinople

1492 Spanish conquest of Granada, expulsion of Jews, and discovery of the Americas

1498 Vasco da Gama's circumnavigation of Africa and journey to India

ca. 1500 Beginning of Columbian Exchange

1511 First African slaves taken to Caribbean

1514 Nicolaus Copernicus formulates the heliocentric model

1517 Martin Luther publishes his 95 theses; beginning of Protestant Reformation

dominance—we must be careful to explore the various aspects of this process without sliding into easy assumptions about their inevitability. For example, one question that suggests itself is "To what extent did the societies of western Europe (what we have termed the 'religious civilization' of Western Christianity) part ways with the other religious civilizations of the world?" Here, aspects of the question are tantalizingly complex and, thus, have recently been the subject of considerable debate:

- On one hand, there appears to have been no movement comparable to that of the European Renaissance or Reformation arising during this time in the other parts of the world to create a new culture similar to that of Europe. The Middle East, India, and China for the most part continued ongoing cultural patterns, although often on considerably higher levels of refinement and sophistication. Recent scholarship on neglected cultural developments in these areas from 1450 to 1750 has provided ample proof for the continuing vitality of Islamic, Hindu, Buddhist, Confucian, and Daoist cultural traditions. Thus, former assumptions of stagnation or decline no longer seem supportable.
- On the other hand, Europe, like much of the rest of the world, remained rooted in agrarian–urban patterns until the effects of the Industrial Revolution began to be felt sometime after 1800. The centuries-old patterns in which the majority of the population was employed in agriculture and did not live in cities continued unchanged. Furthermore, through nearly this entire period, China and India were more populous and at least as wealthy and diversified in their economies and social structures as their European counterpart. The "great divergence," as scholars currently call it, happened only *after* the Western constitutional and industrial revolutions. Nonetheless, the overall wealth of European countries involved in the conquest and exploitation of the resources of the Americas and the development of global trading systems advanced immensely—as did knowledge of the globe as a whole. Thus, while India and China had long possessed immense and varied resources, Europeans were now acquiring and utilizing similar ones at an accelerating rate. This wealth and the patterns of its acquisition and distribution would eventually have far-reaching consequences.

It is important to emphasize that those developments we deem crucial today were not immediately apparent to the people living at the time. Indeed, for the great majority of people, even in 1750, much seemed to go on as before. Everywhere in the world empires continued to grow and decline, religious tensions continued to erupt into warfare, and rulers continued to ground their authority not in their peoples but in the divine. Thus, for a full understanding of world history during 1450–1750, one has to carefully balance cultural, political, social, and economic factors and constantly keep in mind that although change was certainly occurring, it was often too imperceptible for contemporaries to detect.

Thinking Like a World Historian

- **What new and different patterns characterized the development of states and empires in the period 1450–1750?**
- **How did the emergence of centralizing states lead to more intensive and frequent interactions among empires in the period 1450–1750?**
- **How did the New Sciences and the Enlightenment lay the foundation for the scientific–industrial society that dominates our global culture today?**
- **To what extent did the societies of western Europe diverge from other civilizations in the period 1450–1750? Why is the notion of "exceptionalism" problematic in examining this question?**

interactive timeline

1521, 1533 Spanish conquest of the Aztec and Inca Empires

1542–1605 Akbar, the most innovative of the Mughal rulers (India)

1577 Matteo Ricci, first Jesuit missionary to arrive in China

1604 Galileo Galilei formulates the mathematical law of falling bodies

1607 Founding of Jamestown, Virginia

1687 Isaac Newton unifies physics and astronomy

1720 Edo, capital of Japan, world's largest city

1736–1795 Reign of Qianlong emperor, China

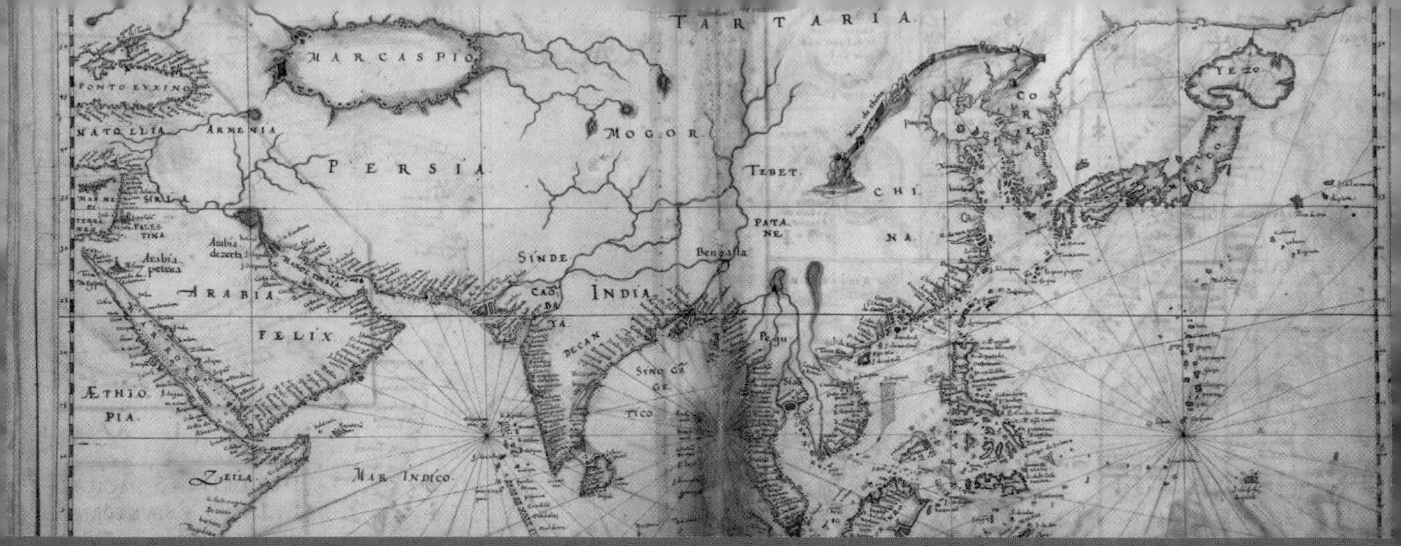

> Chapter 16 1450–1650

Western European Expansion and the Ottoman–Habsburg Struggle

Al-Hasan Ibn Muhammad al-Wazzan (ca. 1494–1550) was born into a family of bureaucrats in Muslim Granada soon after the Christian conquest of this kingdom in southern Iberia in 1492. Unwilling to convert to Christianity, Hasan's family emigrated to Muslim Morocco around 1499–1500 and settled in the city of Fez. Here, Hasan received a good education in religion, law, logic, and the sciences. After completing his studies, he entered the administration of the Moroccan sultan, traveling to sub-Saharan Africa and the Middle East on diplomatic missions.

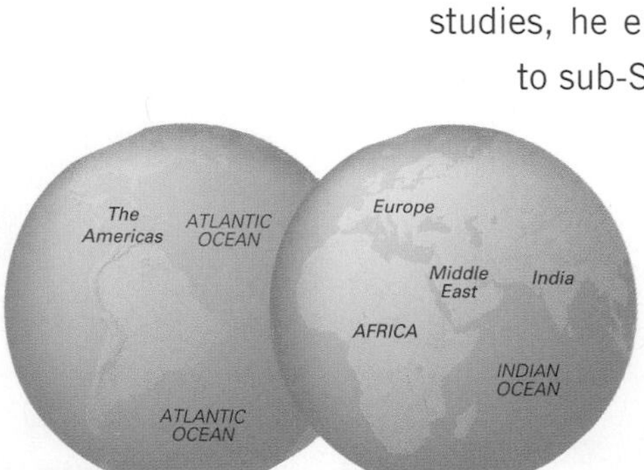

In 1517, as he was returning home from a mission to Istanbul, Christian **corsairs** kidnapped him from his ship. Like their Muslim counterparts, these corsairs roamed the Mediterranean to capture unsuspecting travelers, whom they then held for ransom or sold into slavery. For a handsome sum of money, they turned the cultivated Hasan over to Pope Leo X (1513–1521), who ordered Hasan to convert to Christianity and baptized him with his own family name, Giovanni Leone di Medici. Hasan became known in Rome as Leo Africanus ("Leo the African"), in reference to his travels in sub-Saharan Africa. He stayed

***ABOVE:* This 1630 map by João Teixeira Albernaz the Elder (late 1500s–ca. 1662), member of a prominent family of Portuguese mapmakers, shows Arabia, India, and China.**

for 10 years in Italy, initially at the papal court and later as an independent scholar in Rome. During this time, he taught Arabic to Roman clergymen, compiled an Arabic–Hebrew–Latin dictionary, and wrote an essay on famous Arabs. His most memorable and enduring work was a travelogue, first composed in Arabic and later translated into Italian, *Description of Africa*, which was for many years the sole source of information about sub-Saharan Africa in the Western Christian world.

After 1527, however, life became difficult in Rome. In this year, Charles V (r. 1516–1558), king of Spain and emperor of the Holy Roman Empire of Germany, invaded Italy and sacked the city. Hasan survived the sack of Rome but departed for Tunis sometime after 1531, seeking a better life in Muslim North Africa. Unfortunately, all traces of Hasan after his departure from Rome are lost. It is possible that he perished in 1535 when Charles V attacked and occupied Tunis (1535–1574), although it is generally assumed that he lived there until around 1550.

The world in which Hasan lived and traveled was a Muslim–Christian world composed of the Middle East, North Africa, and Europe. Muslims on the Iberian Peninsula and in the Balkans bracketed this world, with the Western Christians in the center. Although Muslims and Christians traveled in much of this world more or less freely—as merchants, mapmakers, adventurers, mercenaries, or corsairs—the two religious civilizations were locked in a pattern of fierce competition. During 800–1050, the Muslims justified their conquests as holy wars (*jihads*), and during 1050–1300 the Christians retaliated with their Crusades and the *Reconquista* of Iberia.

By the fifteenth century, the Christians saw their liberation of Iberia and North Africa from Muslim rule and circumnavigation of the Muslims in the Mediterranean as steppingstones toward rebuilding the crusader kingdom of Jerusalem, which had been lost to the Muslims in 1291. Searching for a route that would take them around Africa, they hoped to defeat the Muslims in Jerusalem with an attack from the east. Driven at least in part by this search, the Christians discovered the continents of the Americas. For their part, the Muslims sought to conquer eastern and central Europe while simultaneously shoring up their defense of North Africa and driving the Portuguese out of the Indian Ocean. After a hiatus of several centuries—when commonwealths of states had characterized Western Christian and Islamic civilizations—imperial polities reemerged, in the form of the Ottoman and Habsburg Empires vying for world rule.

The Muslim–Christian Competition in the East and West, 1450–1600

After a long period during which the Christian kings in Iberia found tributes by the Muslim emirs more profitable than war, in the second half of the fifteenth century the kings resumed the *Reconquista*. During the same time period, the small principality

Seeing Patterns

» What patterns characterized Christian and Muslim competition in the period 1300–1600? Which elements distinguished them from each other, and which elements were similar? How did the pattern change over time?

» How did centralizing states in the Middle East and Europe function in the period 1450–1600? How did economics, military power, and imperial objectives interact to create the centralizing state?

» Which patterns did cultural expressions follow in the Habsburg and Ottoman Empires? Why did the ruling classes of these empires sponsor these expressions?

Corsairs: In the context of this chapter, Muslim or Christian pirates who boarded ships, confiscated the cargoes, and held the crews and travelers for ransom; they were nominally under the authority of the Ottoman sultan or the pope in Rome but operated independently.

Chapter Outline

- The Muslim–Christian Competition in the East and West, 1450–1600
- The Centralizing State: Origins and Interactions
- Imperial Courts, Urban Festivities, and the Arts
- Putting It All Together

of the Ottomans took advantage of Mongol and Byzantine weakness to conquer lands in both Anatolia and the Balkans. After the Muslim conquest of Constantinople in 1453 and the Western Christian conquest of Granada in 1492, the path was open for the emergence of the Ottoman and Habsburg Empires.

Iberian Christian Expansion, 1415–1498

During a revival of anti-Muslim crusade passions in the fourteenth century, Portugal resumed its *Reconquista* policies by expanding to North Africa in 1415. Looking for a way to circumnavigate the Muslims, collect West African gold, and reach the Indian spice coast, Portuguese sailors and traders established fortified harbors along the African coastline. Castile and Aragon, not to be left behind, conquered Granada in 1492, occupied ports in North Africa, and sent Columbus to discover an alternate route to what the Portuguese were seeking. Although Columbus's discovery of America did not yield Indian spices, he delivered the prospects of a new continent to the rulers of Castile and Aragon (see Map 16.1).

Maritime Explorations Portugal's resumption of the *Reconquista* had its roots in its mastery of Atlantic seafaring. In 1277–1281, mariners of the Italian city-state of Genoa pioneered commerce by sea between the Mediterranean and northwestern Europe. One port on the route was Lisbon, where Portuguese shipwrights and their Genoese teachers teamed up to develop new ships suited for the stormy Atlantic seas. In the early fifteenth century they developed the *caravel*, a small ship with high, upward-extending fore and aft sides, a stern rudder, and square as well as triangular lateen sails. With their new ships, the Portuguese became important traders between England and the Mediterranean countries.

The sea trade stimulated an exploration of the eastern Atlantic. By the early fifteenth century, the Portuguese had discovered the uninhabited islands of the Azores and Madeira, while the Castilians, building their own caravels, began a century-long conquest of the Canary Islands. Here, the indigenous, still Neolithic Berber inhabitants, the Guanches, put up a fierce resistance. But settlers, with the backing of Venetian investors, carved out colonies on conquered parcels of land, on which they enslaved the Guanches to work in sugarcane plantations. They thus adopted the sugarcane plantation system from the eastern Mediterranean, where it had Byzantine and crusader roots on the island of Cyprus, as discussed in greater detail in Chapter 18, and made it an Atlantic one.

Military orders: Ever since the early 1100s, the papacy encouraged the formation of monastic fighting orders, such as the Hospitalers and Templars, to combat the Muslims in the crusader kingdom of Jerusalem; similar *Reconquista* orders, such as the Order of Santiago and the Order of Christ, emerged in Iberia to eliminate Muslim rule.

Apocalyptic Expectations Parallel with the Atlantic explorations, Iberian Christians began to rethink their relationship with the Muslims on the peninsula. The loss of the crusader kingdom in Palestine to the Muslim Mamluks in 1291 was an event that stirred deep feelings of guilt among the Western Christians. Efforts to dispatch military expeditions to reconquer Jerusalem failed, however, mostly because rulers in Europe—busy centralizing their realms—were now more interested in warring against each other for territorial gain. The failure did not dampen spiritual revivals, however, especially in the Franciscan and **military orders** of Iberia. These monks, often well connected with the Iberian royal courts as confessors, preachers, and educators, were believers in Revelation (Greek *Apokalypsis*)—that is, the imminent end of the world, the calamities of this end, and the Second Coming of Christ.

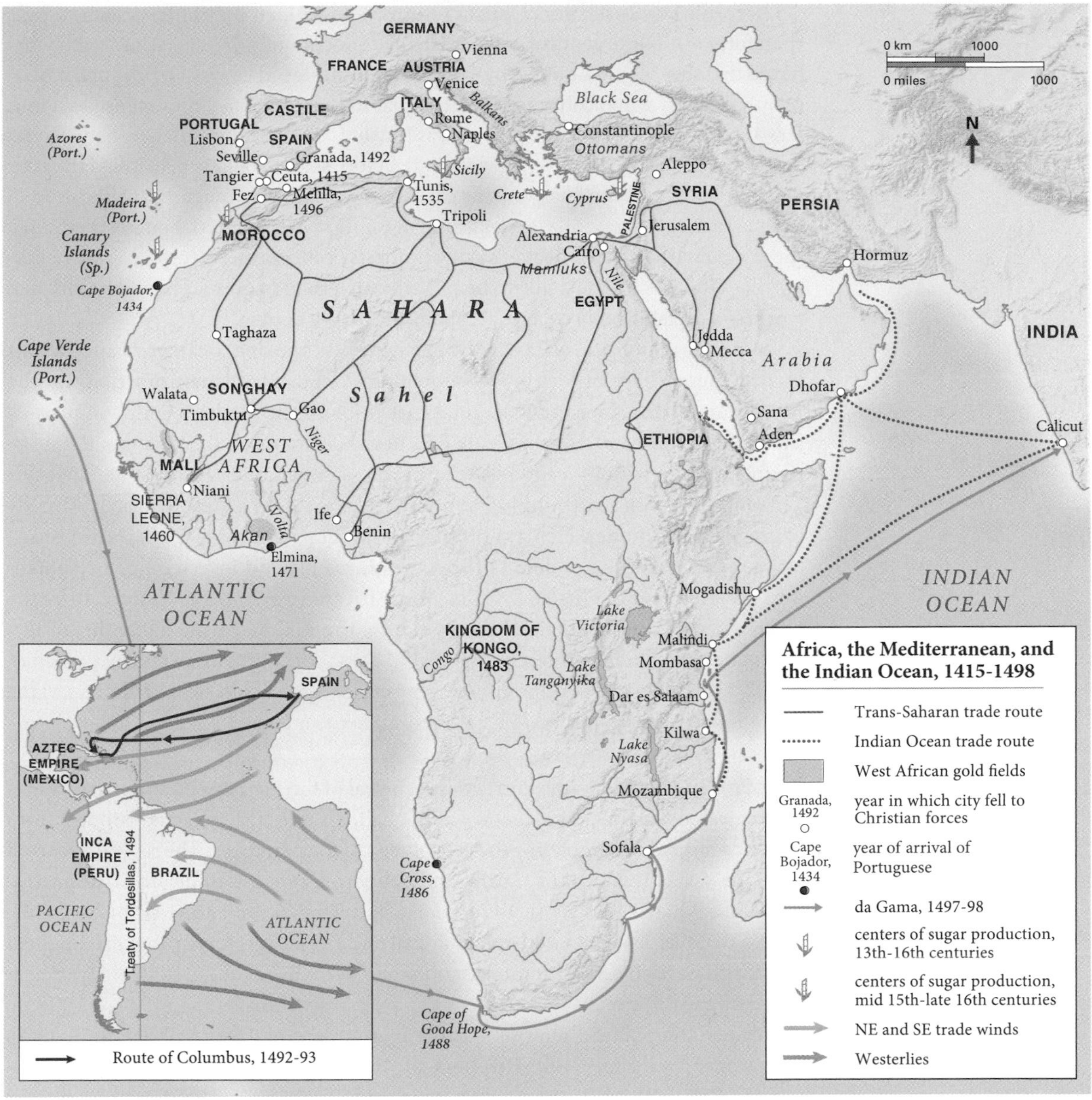

MAP 16.1 Africa, the Mediterranean, and the Indian Ocean, 1415–1498.

interactive timeline

1415 Portuguese conquest of Ceuta in North Africa

1453 Ottoman capture of Constantinople

1479 Union of Aragon and Castile

1481 Beginning of Spanish Inquisition

1492 Spanish conquest of Granada, expulsion of Jews, and sponsorship of Columbus's voyage to America

1494 Treaty of Tordesillas dividing South America between Spain and Portugal

1498 Vasco da Gama's circumnavigation of Africa and journey to India

1529 First Ottoman siege of Vienna

1561 Construction of El Escorial Palace for Philip II of Spain

1571 Naval battle at Lepanto, Habsburg victory over Ottomans

1606 Peace treaty between Ottomans and Austrian Habsburgs

1609 Expulsion of Muslims from Spain

According to Revelation, Christ's return could happen only in Jerusalem, which, therefore, made it urgent for the Christians to reconquer the city. They widely believed that they would be aided by Prester John, an alleged Christian ruler at the head of an immense army from India or Ethiopia. In the context of the intense religious fervor of the period, Christians as well as Muslims saw no contradiction between religion and military conquest. A providential God, so they believed, justified the conquest of lands and the enslavement of the conquered. The religious justification of military action, therefore, was not a pretext for more base material interests (though these would be a likely effect of such conquests) but a proud declaration by believers that God was on their side to help them convert and conquer the non-Christian world—a declaration no longer acceptable today, of course.

In Portugal, political claims in the guise of end-time or apocalyptic expectations guided the military orders in "reconquering" Ceuta, a northern port city of the Moroccan sultans. The orders argued that prior to the Berber–Arab conquest of the early eighth century CE, Ceuta had been Christian and that it was therefore lawful to undertake its capture. Accordingly, a fleet under Henry the Navigator (1394–1460) took Ceuta in 1415, capturing a huge stock of West African gold ready to be minted as money. Henry, a brother of the ruling Portuguese king, saw himself as a precursor in the unfolding of apocalyptic events and invested huge resources into the search for the *Rio de Oro*, the West African "river of gold," thought to be the place where Muslims obtained their gold. By the middle of the fifteenth century, Portuguese mariners had reached the "gold coast" of West Africa (today's Ghana), where local rulers imported gold from the interior Akan fields, near a tributary of the Niger River—the "gold river" of the Muslim merchants.

map of the known world by Martellus, ca. 1489

Reforms in Castile The Portuguese renewal of the *Reconquista* stimulated a similar revival in Castile. For a century and a half, Castile had collected tributes from Granada instead of completing the reconquest of the peninsula. The revival occurred after the dynastic union of Castile and Aragon–Catalonia under their respective monarchs, Queen Isabella (r. 1474–1504) and King Ferdinand II (r. 1479–1516). The two monarchs embarked on a political and religious reform program designed to strengthen their central administrations and used the reconquest ideology to help speed up the reforms.

Among the political reforms was the recruitment of urban militias and judges, both under royal supervision, to check the military and judicial powers of the aristocracy. Religious reform focused on improved education for the clergy and stricter enforcement of Christian doctrine among the population at large. The new institution entrusted with the enforcement of doctrine was the Spanish Inquisition, a body of clergy first appointed by Isabella and Ferdinand in 1481 to ferret out any people whose beliefs and practices were deemed to violate Christian theology and church law. With their religious innovations, the monarchs regained the initiative from the popes and laid the foundations for increased state power.

The Conquest of Granada The *Reconquista* culminated in a 10-year campaign (1482–1492), now fought with cannons on both sides. In the end, Granada fell into Christian hands because the Ottomans, still consolidating their power in the Balkans, sent only a naval commander who stationed himself in North Africa and harassed Iberian ships. The Mamluks of Egypt, less powerful than the Ottomans, sent an embassy to Granada that made a feeble threat of retribution against Christians in Egypt and Syria. Abandoned by the Muslim powers, the last emir of Granada negotiated terms for an honorable surrender. According to these terms, Muslims who chose to stay as subjects of the Castilian crown were permitted to do so, practicing their faith in their own mosques.

The treaty did not apply to the Jews of Granada, however, who were forced either to convert to Christianity or emigrate. In the 1300s, anti-Jewish preaching by the Catholic clergy and riots by Christians against Jews in Seville had substantially reduced the Jewish population of some 300,000 at its peak (ca. 1050) to a mere 80,000 in 1492. Of this remainder, a majority emigrated in 1492 to Portugal and the Ottoman Empire, strengthening the urban population of the latter with their commercial and crafts skills. Portugal adopted its own expulsion decree in 1497. Thus, the nearly millennium-and-a-half-long Jewish presence in Sefarad, as Spain was called in Hebrew, ended, with an expulsion designed to strengthen the Christian unity of Iberia.

After the expulsion of the Jews, it did not take long for the Christians to violate the Muslim treaty of surrender. The church engaged in forced conversions, the burning of Arabic books, and transformations of mosques into churches, triggering an uprising of Muslims in Granada (1499–1500). Christian troops crushed the uprising, and Isabella and Ferdinand used it as an excuse to abrogate the treaty of surrender. In one province after another during the early sixteenth century, Muslims were forced to convert, disperse to other provinces, or emigrate.

Columbus's Journey to the Caribbean At the peak of their royal power in early 1492, Isabella and Ferdinand seized a golden opportunity to catch up quickly with the Portuguese in the Atlantic. They authorized the seasoned mariner Christopher Columbus (1451–1506) to build two caravels and a larger carrack and sail westward across the Atlantic. Columbus promised to reach India ahead of the Portuguese, who were attempting to find a route to India by sailing around Africa. The two monarchs pledged money for the construction of ships from Castilian and Aragonese crusade levies collected from the Muslims.

In September, Columbus and his mariners departed from the Castilian Canary Islands, catching the favorable South Atlantic easterlies. After a voyage of a little over a month, Columbus landed on one of the Bahaman islands. From there he explored a number of Caribbean islands, mistakenly assuming that he was close to the Indian subcontinent. After a stay of 3 months, he left a small colony of settlers behind and returned to Iberia with seven captured Caribbean islanders and a small quantity of gold.

Columbus was a self-educated explorer. Through voracious but indiscriminate reading, he had accumulated substantial knowledge of such diverse subjects as geography, cartography, the Crusades, and the Apocalypse. On the basis of this reading (and his own faulty calculations), he insisted that the ocean stretching between western Europe and eastern Asia was relatively narrow. Furthermore, he fervently believed that God had made him the forerunner of an Iberian apocalyptic world ruler who would recapture Jerusalem from the Muslims just prior to the Second Coming of Christ (see Source 16.1).

For many years, Columbus had peddled his idea about reaching India (and subsequently Jerusalem) from the east at the Portuguese court. The Portuguese, however, while sharing Columbus's apocalyptic fervor, dismissed his Atlantic Ocean calculations as fantasies. Even in Castile, where Columbus went after his rejection in Portugal, it took several years and the victory over Granada before Queen Isabella finally listened to him. Significantly, it was at the height of their success at Granada in 1492 that Isabella and Ferdinand seized their chance to beat the Portuguese to Asia. Although disappointed by the meager returns of Columbus's first and subsequent voyages, Isabella and Ferdinand were delighted to have acquired new islands in the Caribbean, in addition to the Canaries. In one blow they had drawn even with Portugal.

Vasco da Gama's Journey to India Portugal redoubled its efforts after 1492 to discover the way to India around Africa. In 1498, the king appointed an important court official and member of the crusading Order of Santiago, Vasco da Gama (ca. 1469–1524), to command four caravels for the journey to India. Da Gama, an experienced mariner, made good use of the accumulated Portuguese knowledge of seafaring in the Atlantic and guidance by Arab sailors in the Indian Ocean. After a journey of 6 months, the ships arrived in Calicut, the main spice trade center on the Indian west coast.

The first Portuguese mariner sent ashore by da Gama in Calicut encountered two North African Muslims, who addressed him in Castilian Spanish and Genoese Italian: "The Devil take you! What brought you here?" The mariner replied: "We came to seek Christians and spices." When da Gama went inland to see the ruler of Calicut, he was optimistic that he had indeed found what he had come for. Ignorant of Hinduism, he mistook the Indian religion for the Christianity of Prester John. Similarly ignorant of the conventions of the India trade, he offered woolen textiles and metal goods in exchange for pepper, cinnamon, and cloves. The Muslim and Hindu merchants were uninterested in these goods designed for the African market and demanded gold or silver, which the Portuguese had only in small amounts. Rumors spread about the Muslims plotting with the Hindus against the apparently penniless Christian intruders. Prudently, da Gama lifted anchor and returned home with small quantities of spices.

Pedro Reinel's map of East Africa and the Indian Ocean, c. 1507

After these modest beginnings, however, within a short time Portugal had mastered the India trade. The Portuguese crown organized regular journeys around Africa, and when Portuguese mariners on one such journey—taking a far western route in the Atlantic—landed in northeast Brazil they claimed it for their expanding commercial network. During the early sixteenth century, the Portuguese India fleets brought considerable amounts of spices from India back to Portugal, threatening the profits of the Egyptian and Venetian merchants who had hitherto dominated the trade. Prester John, of course, was never found, and the project of retaking Jerusalem receded into the background.

Rise of the Ottomans and Struggle with the Habsburgs for Dominance, 1300–1609

While Muslim rule disappeared in the late fifteenth century from the Iberian Peninsula, the opposite was happening in the Balkans. Here, the Ottoman Turks spearheaded the expansion of Islamic rule over Christians. By the late sixteenth century, when the East–West conflict between the Habsburgs and Ottomans reached its peak, entire generations of Croats, Germans, and Italians lived in mortal fear of the "terrible Turk" who might conquer all of Christian Europe.

Late Byzantium and Ottoman Origins The rise of the Ottomans was closely related to the decline of Byzantium. The emperors of Byzantium had been able to reclaim their "empire" in 1261 from its Latin rulers and Venetian troops by allying themselves with the Genoese. This empire, which during the early fourteenth century included Greece and a few domains in western Anatolia, was no more than a midsize kingdom with modest agricultural resources. But it was still a valuable trading hub, thanks to Constantinople's strategic position as a market linking the Mediterranean with Slavic kingdoms in the Balkans and the Ukrainian–Russian principality of Kiev. Thanks to its commercial wealth, Byzantium experienced a cultural revival, which at its height featured the lively scholarly debate over Plato and Aristotle that exerted a profound influence on the western Renaissance in Italy (see Chapter 10).

Inevitably, however, both Balkan Slavs and Anatolian Turks appropriated Byzantine provinces in the late thirteenth century, further reducing the empire. One of the lost provinces was Bithynia, across the Bosporus in Anatolia. Here, in 1299, the Turkish warlord Osman (r. 1299–1326) gathered his clan and a motley assembly of Islamic holy warriors (Turkish *gazis*, including a local saint and his followers), as well as adventurers (including renegade Byzantines), and declared himself an independent ruler. Osman and a number of other Turkish lords in the region were nominally subject to the Seljuks, the Turkish dynasty which had conquered Anatolia from the Byzantines two centuries earlier but by the early 1300s was disintegrating.

During the first half of the fourteenth century, Osman and his successors emerged as the most powerful emirs by conquering further Anatolian provinces from Byzantium. The Moroccan Abu Abdallah Ibn Battuta (1304–1369), famous for his journeys through the Islamic world, Africa, and China, passed through western Anatolia and Constantinople during the 1330s, visiting several Turkish principalities. He was duly impressed by the rising power of the Ottomans, noting approvingly that they manned nearly 100 forts and castles and maintained pressure on the Eastern Christian infidels. In 1354, the Ottomans gained their first European foothold on a peninsula about 100 miles southwest of Constantinople. Thereafter, it seemed only a matter of time before the Ottomans would conquer Constantinople.

Through a skillful mixture of military defense, tribute payments, and dynastic marriages of princesses with Osman's descendants, however, the Byzantine emperors salvaged their rule for another century. They were also helped by Timur the Great (r. 1370–1405), a Turkish-descended ruler from central Asia who sought to rebuild the Mongol Empire. He surprised the Ottomans, who were distracted by their ongoing conquests in the Balkans, and defeated them decisively in 1402. Timur and his successors were unsuccessful with their dream of Neo-Mongol world rule, but the Ottomans needed nearly two decades (1402–1421) to recover from their collapse and reconstitute their empire in the Balkans and Anatolia. Under Mehmet II, "the Conqueror" (r. 1451–1481), they finally assembled all their resources to lay siege to the Byzantine capital.

Patterns Up Close | Shipbuilding

With the appearance of empires during the Iron Age, four regional but interconnected shipbuilding traditions—Mediterranean, North Sea, Indian Ocean, and China Sea—emerged.

In the Mediterranean, around 500 BCE, shipwrights began to use nailed planks for their war galleys as well as cargo transports, as evidenced by shipwrecks of the period. In the Roman Empire (ca. 200 BCE–500 CE), nailed planking allowed the development of the roundship (image *a*), a large transport 120 feet in length with a capacity of 400 tons of cargo transporting grain from Egypt to Italy. The roundship and its variations had double planking, multiple masts, and multiple square sails. After 100 BCE, the triangular (lateen) sail allowed for tacking (zigzagging) against the wind, greatly expanding shipping during a summer sailing season.

The Celtic North Sea tradition adapted to the Mediterranean patterns of the Romans. When the Roman Empire receded during the 300s CE, shipwrights in Celtic regions continued with their own innovations, shifting to frame-first construction for small boats in the 300s. At the same time, Norsemen, or Vikings, innovated by introducing overlapping (clinkered) plank joining for their eminently seagoing boats. The North Sea innovations, arriving as they did at the end of the western Roman Empire, remained local for nearly half a millennium.

The evolution of China into an empire resulted in major Chinese contributions to ship construction. In the Han period (206 BCE–220 CE) there is evidence from clay models of riverboats for the use of nailed planks. One model, dating to the first century CE, shows a central steering rudder at the end of the boat. At the same time, similar stern rudders appeared in the Roman Empire. Who adopted what from whom, if at all, is still an unanswered question.

Patterns of Shipbuilding. Left to right: Hellenistic-Roman roundship (*a*), Chinese junk (*b*) Indian Ocean dhow (*c*).

From Istanbul to the Adriatic Sea Similar to Isabella and Ferdinand's siege of Granada, Mehmet's siege and conquest of Constantinople (April 5–May 29, 1453) is one of the stirring events of world history. The Byzantines were severely undermanned and short of gunpowder, unable to defend the full length of the imposing land walls that protected the city. Although they had some help from Genoese, papal, and Aragonese forces, it was not nearly enough to make a difference. Using their superiority in troop strength of 11 to 1 for a tight siege, the Ottomans

Shipbuilding innovations continued after 600 CE. In Tang China, junks with multiple bulkheads (watertight compartments) and multiple layers of planks appeared. The average junk was 140 feet long, had a cargo capacity of 600 tons, and could carry on its three or four decks several hundred mariners and passengers (see image *b*). Junks had multiple masts and trapezoidal (lug) and square sails made of matted fibers and strengthened (battened) with poles sewed to the surface. The less innovative Middle Eastern, eastern African, and Indian dhow was built with sewed or nailed planks and sailed with lateen and square sails, traveling as far as southern China (see image *c*).

(d)

In western Europe, the patterns of Mediterranean and North Sea shipbuilding merged during the thirteenth century. At that time, northern shipwrights developed the cog as the main transport for Baltic grain to ports around the North Sea. The cog was a ship of some 60 feet in length and 30 tons in cargo capacity, with square sails and flush planking below and clinkered planking above the waterline. Northern European crusaders traveled during 1150–1300 on cogs via the Atlantic to the Mediterranean. Builders adapted the cog's clinker technique to the roundship tradition that Muslims as well as Eastern and Western Christians had modified in the previous centuries. Genoese clinkered roundships pioneered the Mediterranean–North Sea trade in the early fourteenth century (see image *d*).

Lisbon shipwrights in Portugal, learning from Genoese masters, borrowed from local shipbuilding traditions and Genoese roundship construction patterns for the development of the caravel around 1430. The caravel was a small and slender 60-foot-long ship with a 50-ton freight capacity, a stern rudder, square and lateen sails, and a magnetic compass (of Chinese origin). The caravel and, after 1500, the similarly built but much larger galleon were the main vessels the Portuguese, Spanish, Dutch, and English used during their oceanic voyages from the mid-fifteenth to mid-eighteenth centuries (see image *e*).

(e)

Patterns of Shipbuilding (*Continued*). From top: Baltic cog (*d*), Iberian caravel (*e*). These ships illustrate the varieties of shipbuilding traditions that developed over thousands of years.

Questions

- How does the history of shipbuilding demonstrate the ways in which innovations spread from one place to another?
- Do the adaptations in shipbuilding that flowed between cultures that were nominally in conflict with each other provide a different perspective on the way these cultures interacted?

bombarded Constantinople's walls with heavy cannons. A weak section was on the northeastern side, along the harbor in the Golden Horn, where the walls were low. Here, the Byzantines had blocked off the entrance to the Golden Horn with a huge chain. In a brilliant tactical move, Mehmet circumvented the chain. He had troops drag ships on rollers over a hillside into the harbor. The soldiers massed on these ships were ready to disembark and assault the walls with the help of ladders. On the first sign of cracks in the northeastern walls, the Ottoman besiegers stormed the city.

Siege of Constantinople, 1453. Note the soldiers on the left pulling boats on rollers and wheels over the Galata hillside. With this maneuver, Sultan Mehmet II was able to circumvent the chain stretched across the entrance to the Golden Horn (in place of the anachronistic bridge in the image). This allowed him to speed up his conquest of Constantinople by forcing the defenders to spread their forces thinly over the entire length of the walls.

The last Byzantine emperor, Constantine XI, perished in the general massacre and pillage which followed the Ottoman occupation of the city (see Source 16.2).

Mehmet quickly repopulated Constantinople ("Istanbul" in Turkish, from Greek "to the city," *istin polin*) and appointed a new patriarch at the head of the Eastern Christians, to whom he promised full protection as his subjects. In quick succession, he ordered the construction of the Topkapı Palace (1459), the transfer of the administration from Edirne (which had been the capital since 1365) to Istanbul, and the resumption of expansion in the Balkans, where he succeeded in forcing the majority of rulers into submitting to vassal status. One of the Balkan lords resisting the sultan was Vlad III Dracul of Wallachia, who according to tradition in 1461–1462 impaled a contingent of Ottoman troops sent against him on sharpened tree trunks. Mehmet replaced Vlad with his more compliant brother, but the memory of the impalements lived on to inspire vampire folktales and, eventually, in 1897, the famous Gothic horror novel *Dracula*.

Mehmet's ongoing conquests eventually brought him to the Adriatic Sea, where one of his generals occupied Otranto on the heel of the Italian peninsula. The Ottomans were poised to launch a full-scale invasion of Italy from Otranto, when the sultan died unexpectedly. His successor evacuated Otranto, preferring to consolidate the Ottoman Empire in the Middle East, North Africa, and the Balkans before reconsidering an invasion of central and western Europe.

Imperial Apogee Between 1500 and 1600 the Ottoman sultans succeeded magnificently in the consolidation of their empire. In 1514, with superior cavalry and infantry forces, cannons, and muskets, the Ottomans defeated the Persian Safavids in Iran, who had risen in 1501 to form a rival Shiite empire in opposition to the Sunni Ottomans. In the southern Middle East, intermittent tensions between the Ottomans and the Mamluk Turks in Egypt, Syria, and eastern Arabia gave way to open war in 1517. The Ottomans, again due to superior firepower, defeated the Mamluks and took control of western Arabia, including the holy pilgrimage city of Mecca. A year later, in 1518, Sultan Süleyman I, "the Magnificent" (r. 1520–1566), appointed a naval commander to drive the Spanish from a series of fortifications and cities in North Africa, which the latter had conquered in the name of the *Reconquista* in the 1490s and early 1500s.

In the Balkans, the Ottomans completed their conquests of Serbia and Hungary with the annexation of Belgrade and Buda (now part of Budapest) as well as a brief siege of Vienna in 1529, begun too late in the year and eventually stopped by the approaching winter. By the second half of the sixteenth century, when the submission of most of Hungary had been secured, the Ottoman Empire was a vast multiethnic and multireligious state of some 15 million inhabitants extending from Algeria in the Maghreb to Yemen in Arabia and from Upper Egypt to the Balkans and the northern shores of the Black Sea (see Map 16.2).

Morocco and Persia In the period of 1450–1600, the two large empires of the Ottomans and Indian Mughals dominated Islamic civilization. Two smaller and more short-lived realms existed in Morocco and Persia, ruled by the Saadid

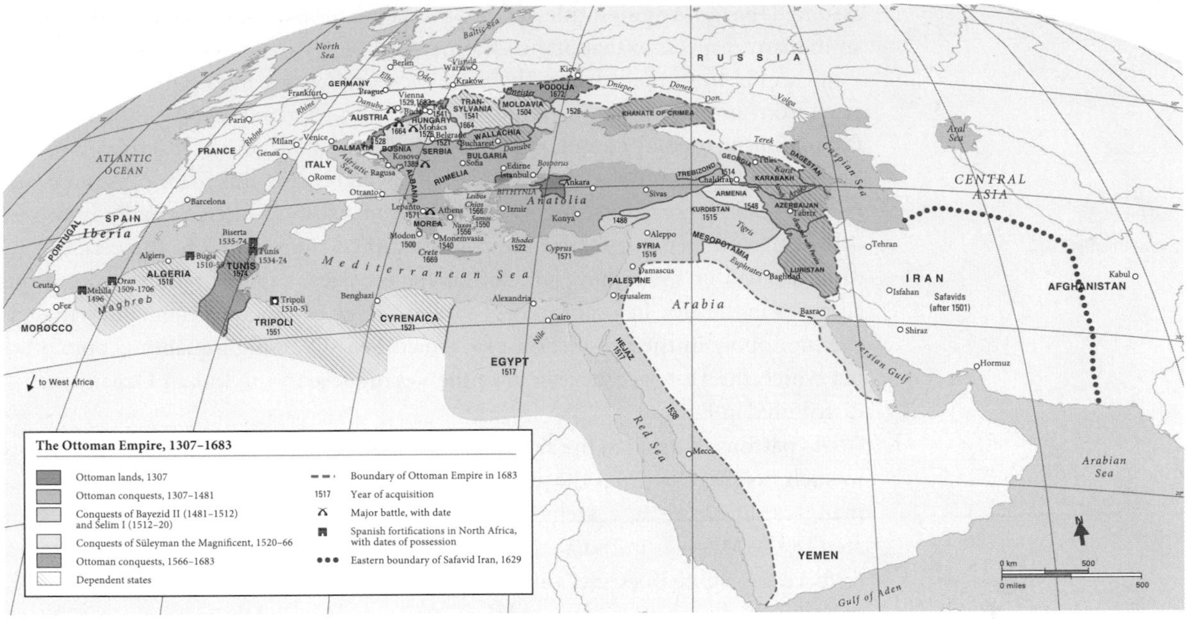

MAP 16.2 The Ottoman Empire, 1307–1683.

map analysis

(1509–1659) and Safavid (1501–1722) dynasties, respectively. The Saadid sultans defended themselves successfully against the Ottoman expansion and liberated themselves from the Portuguese occupation of Morocco's Atlantic ports which had followed the conquest of Ceuta in 1415. In 1591, after their liberation, the Saadids sent a firearm-equipped army to West Africa in order to revive the gold trade, which had dwindled to a trickle after the Portuguese arrival in Ghana. The army succeeded in destroying the West African empire of Songhay but failed to revive the gold trade. Moroccan army officers assumed power in Timbuktu, and their descendants, the Ruma, became provincial lords independent of Morocco. The Saadids, unable to improve their finances, split into provincial realms. The still-reigning Alaouite dynasty of Moroccan kings replaced them in 1659.

The Safavids grew in the mid-1400s from a mixed Kurdish–Turkish mystical brotherhood in northwestern Iran into a Shiite warrior organization (similar to the Sunni one participating in the early Ottoman expansion) that carried out raids against Christians in the Caucasus. In 1501, the leadership of the brotherhood put forward the 14-year-old Ismail as the Hidden Twelfth Imam. According to Shiite doctrine, the Hidden Imam, or Messiah, was expected to arrive and establish a Muslim apocalyptic realm of justice at the end of time, before God's Last Judgment. This realm would replace the "unjust" Sunni Ottoman Empire. The Ottomans countered the Safavid challenge in 1514 with the Battle of Chaldiran, where they crushed the underprepared Safavids with their superior cannon and musket firepower. After his humiliating defeat, Ismail dropped his claim to messianic status, and his successors

Vlad Dracul next to Impaled Ottoman Soldiers. The woodcut depicts the alleged impalement of 1,000 Ottoman soldiers sent against Vlad Dracul, prior to Sultan Mehmet II leading a victorious campaign into Wallachia and removing Dracul from power. Dracul's cannibalism, suggested in the image, is not confirmed by historical sources.

assumed the more modest title of king (Persian *shah*) as the head of state, quite similar in many respects to that of the Ottomans.

Learning from their defeat, the Safavids recruited a standing firearm-equipped army from among young Christians on lands conquered in the Caucasus. They held fast to Shiism, thereby continuing their opposition to the Sunni Ottomans, and supported the formation of a clerical hierarchy, which made this form of Islam dominant in Iran. As sponsors of construction projects, the Safavids greatly improved urbanism in the country. After moving the capital from Tabriz to the centrally located Isfahan in 1590, they built an imposing palace, administration, and mosque complex in the city. In a suburb they settled a large colony of Armenians, who held the monopoly in the production of Caspian Sea silk, a high-quality export product which the Dutch—successors of the Portuguese in the Indian Ocean trade—distributed in Europe.

a Safavid battle tunic

As patrons of the arts, the shahs revived the ancient traditions of Persian culture to such heights that even the archrival Ottomans felt compelled to adopt Persian manners, literature, and architectural styles. Persian royal culture similarly radiated to the Mughals in India. Not everyone accepted Shiism, however. An attempt to force the Shiite doctrines on the Afghanis backfired badly when enraged Sunni tribes formed a coalition, defeated the Safavids, and ended their regime in 1722.

Rise of the Habsburgs Parallel to the rise and development of the Ottomans and Safavids, Castile–Aragon on the Iberian Peninsula evolved into the center of a vast empire of its own. A daughter of Isabella and Ferdinand married a member of the Habsburg dynastic family, which ruled Flanders, Burgundy, Naples, Sicily, and Austria, as well as Germany (the "Holy Roman Empire of the German Nation," as this collection of principalities was called). Their son, Charles V (r. 1516–1558), not only inherited Castile–Aragon, now merged and called "Spain," and the Habsburg territories but also became the ruler of the Aztec and Inca Empires in the Americas, which Spanish adventurers had conquered in his name between 1521 and 1536 (see Chapter 18). In both Austria and the western Mediterranean the Habsburgs were direct neighbors of the Ottomans (see Map 16.3).

After a victorious battle against France in 1519, Charles V also won the title of emperor from the pope, which made him the overlord of all German principalities and supreme among the monarchs of Western Christianity. Although this title did not mean much in terms of power and financial gain in either the German principalities or Western Christianity as a whole, it made him the titular political head of Western Christianity and thereby the direct counterpart of Sultan Süleyman in the struggle for dominance in the Christian–Muslim world of Europe, the Middle East, and northern Africa. Both the Habsburgs and the Ottomans renewed the traditional Islamic–Christian imperialism which had characterized the period 600–950 and which had been replaced by the Muslim and Christian commonwealths of 950–1450.

Habsburg Distractions Charles V faced a daunting task in his effort to prevent the Ottomans from advancing against the Christians in the Balkans and Mediterranean. Multiple problems in his European territories diverted his attention and forced him to spend far less time than he wanted on what Christians in most parts of Europe perceived as a pervasive Ottoman–Muslim threat. During the first three decades of

MAP 16.3 Europe and the Mediterranean, ca. 1560.

the sixteenth century, revolts in Iberia, the Protestant Reformation in the German states, and renewed war with France for control of Burgundy and Italy commanded Charles's attention.

The emperor's distractions increased further in 1534 when, in an attempt to drive the Habsburgs out of Italy, France forged an alliance with the Ottomans. This alliance horrified western Europe. It demonstrated, however, that the Ottomans, on account of their military advances against the Christians in eastern Europe and the western Mediterranean, had become crucial players in European politics. As fierce as the struggle between Muslims and Christians for dominance was, when the French king found himself squeezed on both sides of his kingdom by his archrival, Charles V, the Ottomans became his natural allies.

Habsburg and Ottoman Losses All these diversions seriously strained Habsburg resources against the Ottomans, who pressed relentlessly ahead on the two fronts of the Balkans and North Africa. Although Charles V deputized his younger brother Ferdinand I to the duchy of Austria in 1521 to shore up the Balkan defenses, he was able to send him significant numbers of troops only once. After a series of dramatic defeats, Austria had to pay the Ottomans tribute and, eventually, even sign a humiliating truce (1562). On the western Mediterranean front, the Habsburgs did not do well either. Even though Charles V campaigned several times in person, most garrisons on the coast of Algeria, Tunisia, and Tripoli were too exposed to withstand the Ottoman onslaught by sea and by land. In 1556, at the end of Charles V's reign, only two of eight Habsburg garrisons had survived.

A third frontier of the Muslim–Christian struggle for dominance was the Indian Ocean. After Vasco da Gama had returned from India in 1498, the Portuguese kings invested major resources into breaking into the Muslim-dominated Indian Ocean trade. In response, the Ottomans made great efforts to protect existing Muslim commercial interests in the Indian Ocean. They blocked Portuguese military support for Ethiopia and strengthened their ally and main pepper supplier, the sultan of Aceh on the Indonesian island of Sumatra, by providing him with troops and weapons. War on land and on sea, directly and by proxy, raged in the Indian Ocean through most of the sixteenth century.

Portuguese trading posts in the Indian Ocean, 1630

In the long run, the Portuguese were successful in destroying the Ottoman fleets sent against them, but smaller convoys of Ottoman galleys continued to harass Portuguese shipping interests. As new research on the Ottoman "age of exploration" in the Indian Ocean has demonstrated, by 1570 the Muslims traded again as much via the Red Sea route to the Mediterranean as the Portuguese did by circumnavigating Africa. In addition, the Ottomans benefited from the trade of a new commodity—coffee, produced in Ethiopia and Yemen. Portugal (under Spanish rule 1580–1640) reduced its unsustainably large military presence in the Indian Ocean, followed by the Ottomans, which allowed the Netherlands in the early seventeenth century to overtake both Portugal and the Ottoman Empire in the Indian Ocean spice trade (see Map 16.4).

Habsburg–Ottoman Balance In the 1550s, Charles V despaired of being able to ever master the many challenges posed by the Ottomans as well as by France and the Protestants. He decided that the only way to ensure the continuation of Habsburg power would be a division of his western and eastern territories. Accordingly, he bestowed Spain, Naples, the Netherlands, and the Americas on his son Philip II (r. 1556–1598). The Habsburg possessions of Austria, Bohemia, and the remnant of Hungary not lost to the Ottomans, as well as the Holy Roman Empire (Germany), went to his brother Ferdinand I (r. 1558–1564). Charles hoped that his son and brother would cooperate and help each other militarily against the Ottomans.

Moriscos: From Greek *maurus* ("dark"); Castilian term referring to North Africans and to Muslims under Spanish rule.

When Philip took over the Spanish throne, he realized, to his concern, that most of the Habsburg military was stationed outside Spain, leaving that country vulnerable to attack. As the Ottomans had recently conquered most Spanish strongholds in North Africa, a Muslim invasion of Spain was a distinct possibility. Fearful of **morisco** support for an Ottoman invasion of Spain, Philip's administration and the Inquisition renewed their decrees of conversion which had lain dormant for half a century.

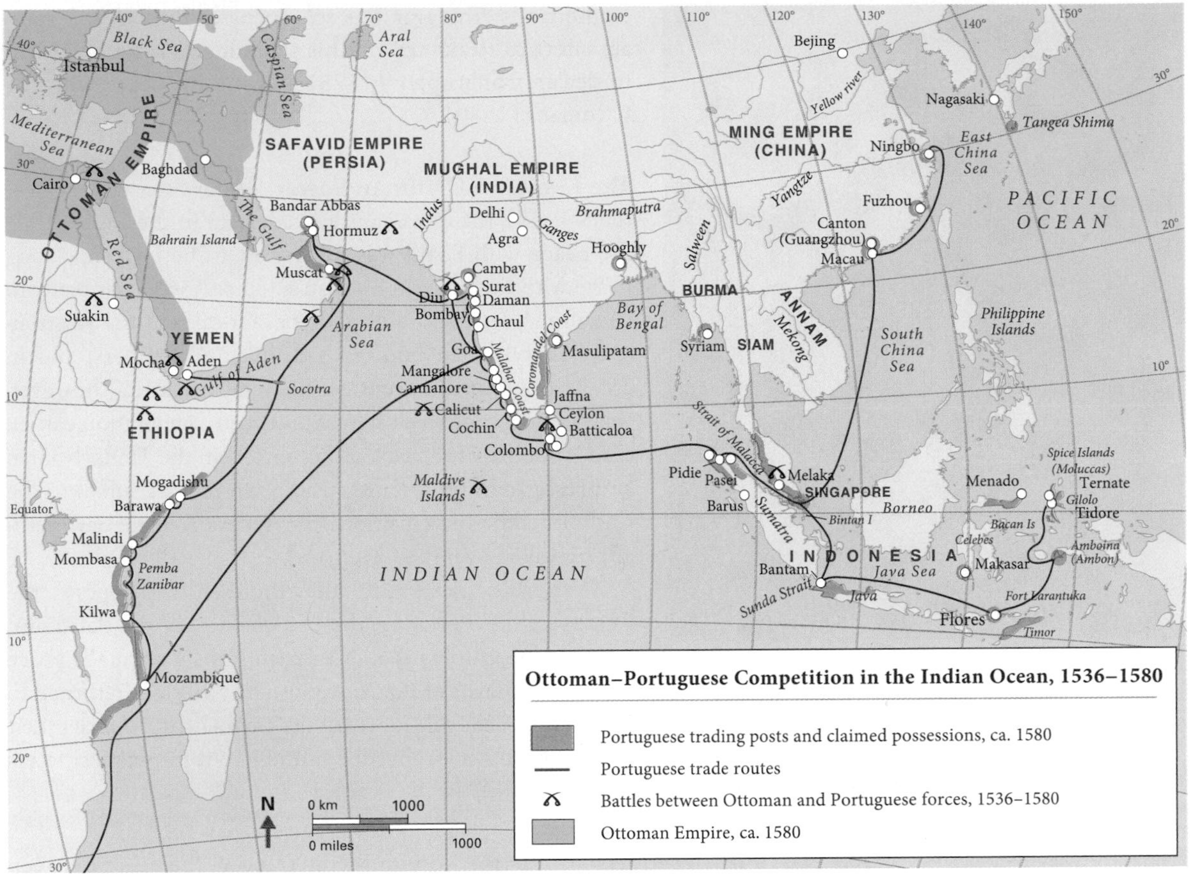

MAP 16.4 Ottoman–Portuguese Competition in the Indian Ocean, 1536–1580.

This sparked a massive revolt among the moriscos of Granada in 1568–1570, supported by Ottoman soldiers and Moroccan arms. Philip was able to suppress the revolt only after recourse to troops and firearms from Italy. To break up the dangerously large concentrations of Granadan moriscos in the south of Spain, Philip ordered them to be dispersed throughout the peninsula. At the same time, to alleviate the Ottoman naval threat, Philip, the pope, Venice, and Genoa formed a Holy Christian League. Its task was the construction of a fleet which was to destroy Ottoman sea power in the eastern Mediterranean. The fleet succeeded in 1571 in bottling up the entire Ottoman navy at Lepanto, in Ottoman Greece, destroying it in the ensuing firefight.

The Ottomans, however, had enough resources not only to rebuild their navy but also to capture the strategic port city of Tunis in 1574 from the Spaniards. With this evening of the scores, the two sides decided to phase out their unsustainable naval war in the Mediterranean. After this date, Venice was the only (but formidable) naval enemy of the Ottomans, at various times in control of Aegean islands and southern Greece. The Ottomans, for their part, turned their attention eastward, to the rival Safavid Empire, where they exploited a period of dynastic instability for the conquest of territories in the Caucasus (1578–1590). The staunch Catholic Philip II, for his part, was faced with the Protestant war of independence in the

Paolo Veronese, *Battle of Lepanto*, altar painting with four saints beseeching the Virgin Mary to grant victory to the Christians (ca. 1572). In the sixteenth century, the entire Mediterranean, from Gibraltar to Cyprus, was a naval battleground between Christians and Muslims. The Christians won the Battle of Lepanto thanks to superior naval tactics. At the end of the battle "the sea was entirely covered, not just with masts, spars, oars, and broken wood, but with an innumerable quantity of blood that turned the water as red as blood."

Netherlands. This war was so expensive that, in a desperate effort to straighten out his state finances, Philip II had to declare bankruptcy (1575) and sue for peace with the Ottomans (1580).

The Limits of Ottoman Power After their victory over the Safavids, the Ottomans looked again to the west. While the peace with Spain was too recent to be broken, a long peace with Ferdinand I in Austria (since 1562) was ready to collapse. A series of raids and counter-raids at the Austrian and Transylvanian borders had inflamed tempers, and in 1593 the Ottomans went on the attack. Austria, however, was no longer the weak state it had been a generation earlier. Had it not been for a lack of support from the Transylvanian and Hungarian Protestants, who preferred the sultan to the Catholic emperor as overlord, the Austrians might have actually prevailed over the Ottomans.

Eventually, thanks to the Protestants' support, the Ottomans drew even on the battlefield with the Austrians. In 1606, the Ottomans and Austrian Habsburgs made peace again. With minor modifications in favor of the Austrians, the two sides returned to their earlier borders. The Austrians made one more tribute payment and then let their obligation lapse. Officially, the Ottomans conceded nothing, but in practical terms Austria was no longer a vassal state.

Expulsion of the Moriscos In the western Mediterranean, the peace between the Ottomans and Spanish Habsburgs held. But Philip and his successors remained aware of the possibility of renewed Ottoman aid to the Iberian Muslims. Even though they had been scattered across the peninsula after 1570, the moriscos continued to resist conversion. Among Castilians, an intense debate began about the apparent impossibility of assimilating them to Catholicism in order to create a religiously unified state. The church advocated the expulsion of the moriscos, arguing that the allegedly high Muslim birthrate in a population of 7.5 million (mostly rural) Spaniards was a serious threat.

Fierce resistance against the proposed expulsion, however, rose among the Christian landowners in the southeastern province of Valencia. These landowners benefited greatly from the farming skills of the estimated 250,000 morisco tenant farmers who worked their irrigated rice and sugarcane estates. Weighing the potential Ottoman threat against the possibility of economic damage, the government decided in 1580 in favor of expulsion. Clearly, they valued Christian unity against the Ottomans more than the prosperity of a few hundred landowners in Valencia.

It took until 1609, however, before a compensation deal with the landowners in Valencia was worked out. In the following 5 years, some 300,000 moriscos were forcibly expelled from Spain, under often appalling circumstances: They had to leave all their possessions behind, including money and jewelry, taking only whatever clothes and household utensils they could carry. As in the case of the Jews a century earlier, Spain's loss was the Ottoman Empire's gain, this time mostly in the form of skilled irrigation farmers.

Expulsion of the Moriscos (secret Muslims) from Spain, 1609–1614. The moriscos had to leave all their valuables behind, carrying only their barest belongings. They were watched closely by Spanish soldiers, as seen in this etching.

The Centralizing State: Origins and Interactions

The major technological change that occurred in the Middle East and Europe during 1250–1350 was the growing use of firearms. It took until the mid-1400s, however, before cannons and muskets were technically effective and reliable enough to make a difference in warfare. At this time, a pattern emerged whereby rulers created centralized states to finance their strategic shift to firearm-bearing infantries. They resumed the policy of conquest and imperialism, which had lain dormant during the preceding period, when the religious civilizations of Islam and Christianity had evolved into commonwealths of many competing realms. Both the Ottomans and the Habsburgs raised immense amounts of cash in silver and gold to spend on cannons, muskets, and ships for achieving world rule.

State Transformation, Money, and Firearms

In the early stages of their realms, the kings of Iberia (1150–1400) and the Ottoman sultans (1300–1400), with little cash on hand, compensated military commanders for their service in battle with parcels of conquered land, or land grants. That land, farmed by villagers, generated rental income in kind for the officers. Once the Iberian and Ottoman rulers had conquered cities and gained control over long-distance trade, however, patterns changed. Rulers began collecting taxes in cash, with which they paid regiments of personal guards to supplement the army of land-grant officers and their retainers. They created the centralizing state, forerunner of the absolutist state of the early seventeenth century.

The Land-Grant System When the Ottoman *beys*, or military lords, embarked on their conquests in the early 1300s, they created personal domains on the choice lands they had conquered. Here, they took rents in kind from the resident villagers to finance their small dynastic households. Their comrades in arms, such as members of their clan or adherents (many of whom were holy warriors and/or adventurers), received other conquered lands, from which they collected rents for themselves. As the Ottomans conquered Byzantine cities, first in Anatolia and then, in the second half of the 1300s, in the Balkans, they gained access to the **money economy**. They collected taxes in coins from the markets and tollbooths at city gates where foods and crafts goods were exchanged, as well as from the Christians and Jews subject to the head tax. The taxes helped in adding luxuries to the households of the Ottoman beys and enabling them to build palaces.

Money economy: Form of economic organization in which mutual obligations are settled through monetary exchanges; in contrast, a system of land grants, with its rents from peasants, obliges the landholders to provide military service, without payment, to the grantee (sultan or king).

Janissaries: Infantry soldiers recruited among the Christian population of the Ottoman Empire and paid from the central treasury.

Devşirme: The levy on boys in the Ottoman Empire; that is, the obligation of the Christian population to contribute adolescent males to the military and administrative classes.

As a consequence of the full conquest of the southern Balkans by the Ottoman Empire in the fifteenth and sixteenth centuries, both the land-grant system and the money economy expanded exponentially. An entire military ruling class of grant holders emerged, forming the backbone of the early Ottoman army and administration. The grant holders were cavalrymen who lived with their households of retainers in the villages and towns of the interior of Anatolia and the Balkans. Most of the time, they were away on campaign with the sultans, leaving managers in charge of the collection of rents from the villagers on their lands. At the conclusion of the period of rapid growth of the Ottoman Empire in the early years of the sixteenth century, the landed ruling class of cavalrymen numbered some 80,000, constituting a vast reserve of warriors for the mobilization of troops each summer.

The Janissaries An early indicator of the significance of the money economy in the Ottoman Empire was the military institution of the **Janissaries**—troops which received salaries from the central treasury. This institution probably appeared during the second half of the fourteenth century and is first documented in 1395. It was based on a practice (called ***devşirme*** [dev-SHIR-me]) of conscripting young boys, which palace officers carried out irregularly every few years among the empire's Christian population. For this purpose, the palace officers traveled to Christian villages, towns, and cities in the Balkans, Greece, and Anatolia. At each occasion, they selected boys between the ages of 6 and 16 and marched them off to Istanbul, where they were converted to Islam and trained as future soldiers and administrators. The boys and young men then entered the central system of palace slaves under the direct orders of the sultan and his viziers or ministers.

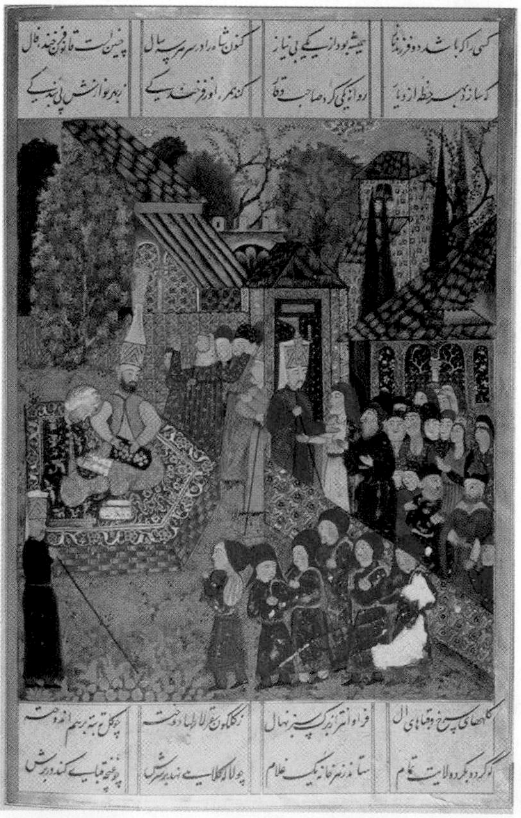

Boy Levy (*devşirme*) in a Christian Village. This miniature graphically depicts the trauma of conscription, including the wailing of the village women and the assembly of boys waiting to be taken away by implacable representatives of the sultan.

The *devşirme* contradicted Islamic law, which forbade the enslavement of "peoples of the Book" (Jews, Christians, and Zoroastrians). Its existence, therefore, documents the extent to which the sultans reasserted the Roman–Sasanid–Arab imperial traditions of the ruler making doctrine and law. Ruling by divine grace, the Ottomans were makers of their own law, called *kanun* (from Greek *kanon*). Muslim religious scholars, who had assumed the role of guardians of law and doctrine during the preceding commonwealth period of Islamic civilization (950–1300), had no choice but to accept sultanic imperialism and seek to adapt it to the Sharia as best they could.

Toward the first half of the fifteenth century, the sultans equipped their Janissaries with cannons and matchlock muskets. According to reports in Arabic chronicles, firearms first appeared around 1250 in the Middle East, probably coming from China. When the Janissaries received them, firearms had therefore undergone some 150 years of experimentation and development in the Middle East and North Africa. Even though the cannons and muskets were still far from being decisive in battle, they had become sophisticated enough to make a difference. By the mid-1400s, gigantic siege cannons and slow but reliable matchlock muskets were the standard equipment of Ottoman and other armies. The sultans relied on large numbers of indigenous, rather than European, gunsmiths, as new research in Ottoman archives has revealed (see Source 16.5).

Ottoman Siege of a Christian Fortress. By the middle of the fifteenth century, cannons had revolutionized warfare. Niccolò Machiavelli, ever attuned to new developments, noted in 1519 that "no wall exists, however thick, that artillery cannot destroy in a few days." Machiavelli could have been commenting on the Ottomans, who were masters of siege warfare. Sultan Mehmet II, the conqueror of Constantinople in 1453, founded the Imperial Cannon Foundry shortly thereafter; it would go on to make some of the biggest cannons of the period.

Revenues and Money The maintenance of a salaried standing army of infantry soldiers and a central administration to provide the fiscal foundation would have been impossible without precious metals. Therefore, the Ottoman imperial expansion was driven by the need to acquire mineral deposits. During the fifteenth century the Ottomans captured the rich silver, lead, and iron mines of Serbia and Bosnia. Together with Anatolian copper, iron, and silver mines conquered earlier, the Balkan mines made the Ottomans the owners of the largest precious metal production centers prior to the Habsburg acquisition of the Mexican and Andean mines in the mid-1500s.

The sultans left the Balkan mining and smelting operations in the hands of preconquest Christian entrepreneurs from the autonomous Adriatic coastal city-state of Ragusa or Dubrovnik. These entrepreneurs were integrated into the Ottoman imperial money economy as tax farmers obliged to buy their right of operation from the government in return for reimbursing themselves from the mining and smelting profits. **Tax farming** was the preferred method of producing cash revenues for the central administration. The holders of tax farms delivered the profits from the production of metals, salt, saltpeter, and other minerals to the state, minus the commission they were entitled to subtract for themselves. They also collected the head tax—payable in money—from the Jews and Christians and the profits from the sale of the agricultural dues from state domains. Thus, tax farmers were crucial members of the ruling class, responsible for the cash flow in the state.

The right to mint silver into the basic coin of the empire was similarly part of the tax-farm regime, as were the market, city gate, and port duties. The tax-farm regime, of course, was crucially dependent on a strong sultan or chief minister, the grand vizier. Without close supervision, this regime could easily deteriorate into a state of decentralization, something which indeed eventually happened in the Ottoman Empire on a large scale, although not before the eighteenth century.

Tax farming: Governmental auction of the right to collect taxes in a district, market, or mine. The tax farmer advanced these taxes to the treasury and retained a commission.

Süleyman's Central State The centralizing state of the Ottomans reached its apogee under Sultan Süleyman I, "the Magnificent." At the beginning of the sultan's reign, the amount of money available for expenditures was twice that of half a century earlier. By the end of his reign, this amount had again doubled. With this money, the sultan financed a massive expansion of the military and bureaucracy. Palace, military, and bureaucracy formed a centralized state, the purpose of which was to project power and cultural splendor toward its predominantly rural subjects in the interior as well as Christian enemies outside the empire.

The bureaucrats were recruited from two population groups. Most top ministers and officers in the fifteenth and sixteenth centuries came from the *devşirme* among the Christians. The conscripted boys learned Turkish, received an Islamic education, and underwent intensive firearm and (for some) horsemanship training, in preparation for salaried service in the Janissary army or administration.

The empire's other recruits came from colleges in Istanbul and provincial cities to which the Muslim population of the empire had access. Colleges were institutions through which ambitious villagers far from major urban centers could gain upward mobility. Graduates with law degrees found employment in the bureaucracy or as judges in the villages, towns, and cities. Muslims of Christian parentage made up the top layer of the elite, while Muslims of Islamic descent occupied the middle ranks.

Under Süleyman, the Janissaries comprised about 18,000 soldiers, divided into 11,000 musket-equipped troopers, a cavalry of 5,000, and 2,000 gunners who formed the artillery regiments. Most were stationed in barracks in and near the Topkapı Palace in Istanbul, ready to go on campaign at the sultan's command. Other Janissaries provided service in provincial cities and border fortresses. For his campaigns, the sultan added levies from among the cavalry troops in the towns and villages of the empire.

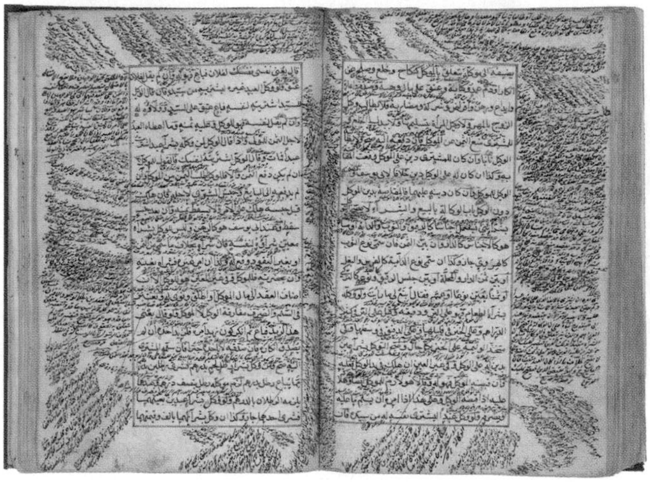

Ottoman Law Book. Covering the entire range of human activity—from spiritual matters, family relations, and inheritances to business transactions and crimes—the *Multaqa al-abhur* (*The Confluence of the Currents*) was completed in 1517 and remained for hundreds of years the authoritative source for many of the laws in the Ottoman Empire. It was written in Arabic by the legal scholar Ibrahim al-Halabi; later commentators added annotations in the margins and within the body of the text itself.

Typical campaigns involved 70,000 soldiers and required sophisticated logistics. All wages, gunpowder, and weapons and the majority of the foodstuffs were carried on wagons and barges, since soldiers were not permitted to provision themselves from the belongings of the villagers, whether friend or foe. Although the state collected heavy taxes, it had a strong interest in not destroying the productivity of the villagers (see Source 16.4).

Charles V's Centralizing State The centralizing state began in Iberia with the political and fiscal reforms of Isabella and Ferdinand and reached its mature phase under Charles V. From the late fifteenth century onward, Castile and Aragon shared many fiscal characteristics with those of the Ottomans. The Spanish monarchs derived cash advances from tax farmers, who organized the production and sale of minerals and salt. From other tax farmers, they received advances on the taxes collected in money from the movement of goods in and out of ports, cities, and markets, as well as on taxes collected in kind from independent farmers and converted through sale on urban markets. In addition, Muslims paid head taxes in cash. Most of the money taxes were also enforced in Flanders, Burgundy, Naples, Sicily, and Austria, after Iberia's incorporation into the Habsburg domain in 1516. Together, these taxes were more substantial than those of Spain, especially in highly urbanized Flanders, where the percentage of the urban population was about twice that of Spain.

From 1521 to 1536, the Spanish crown enlarged its money income by the one-fifth share to which it was entitled from looted Aztec and Inca gold and silver treasures. Charles V used these treasures to finance his expedition against Tunis. Thereafter, he collected a one-quarter share from the silver mines in the Americas that were brought into production beginning in 1545. Full production in the mines was not reached until the second half of the sixteenth century, but already under Charles V Habsburg imperial revenues doubled, reaching about the same level as those of the Ottomans. Thus, at the height of their struggle for dominance in the Muslim–Christian world, the Habsburgs and the Ottomans expended roughly the same amounts of resources to hurl against each other in the form of troops, cannons, muskets, and war galleys.

In one significant respect, however, the two empires differed. The cavalry ruling class of the Ottoman Empire was nonhereditary. Although land-grant holdings went in practice from father to son and then grandson, their holders had no recourse to the law if the sultans decided to replace them. By contrast, ever since the first half of the thirteenth century, when the Iberian kings were still lacking appreciable monetary resources, their landholders possessed a legal right to inheritance. The landholders met more or less regularly in parliaments (Spanish *cortes*), where they could enforce their property rights against the kings through majority decisions. When Isabella and Ferdinand embarked on state centralization, they had to wrestle with a powerful, landed aristocracy that had taken over royal jurisdiction and tax prerogatives (especially market taxes) on their often vast lands, including cities as well as towns and villages. The two monarchs took back much of the jurisdiction but were unable to do much about the taxes, thus failing in one crucial respect in their centralization effort. Although Habsburg Spain relied on precious metals as heavily as the Ottoman Empire did, it was in the end less centralized than that of the Ottomans.

The Habsburgs sought to overcome their lack of power over the aristocracy and the weakness of their Spanish tax base by squeezing as much as they could out of the Italian and Flemish cities and the American colonies. But in the long run their finances remained precarious, plentiful in some years but sparse in others. Relatively few Spanish aristocrats bothered to fulfill their traditional obligation to unpaid military service. Others who did serve forced the kings to pay them like mercenaries. As a result, in the administration and especially in the military, the kings hired as many Italians, Flemings, and Germans as possible. At times, they even had to deploy these mercenaries to Spain in order to maintain peace there. Most of these foreigners were foot soldiers, equipped with muskets.

The Ottoman and Habsburg patterns of centralized state formation bore similarities to patterns in the Roman and Arab Empires half a millennium earlier. At that time, however, the scale was more modest, given that the precious metals from West Africa and the Americas were not yet part of the trade network. In addition, earlier empires did not yet possess firearms, requiring an expensive infrastructure of charcoal and metal production, gunsmithing, saltpeter mining, and gunpowder manufacture. Thanks to firearms, the centralizing states of the period after 1450 were much more potent enterprises. They were established polities, evolving into absolutist and eventually national states.

Imperial Courts, Urban Festivities, and the Arts

Ottoman and Habsburg rulers set aside a portion of revenues to project the splendor and glory of their states to subjects at home as well as enemies abroad. They commissioned the building of palaces, mosques, and churches and sponsored public festivities. Since the administrators, nobility, tax farmers, and merchants had considerable funds, they also patronized writers, artists, and architects. Although Christian and Muslim artists and artisans belonged to different religious and cultural traditions and expressed themselves through different media, their artistic achievements were inspired by the same impulse: to glorify their states through religious expression.

The Ottoman Empire: Palaces, Festivities, and the Arts

The Ottomans built palaces and celebrated public feasts to demonstrate their imperial power and wealth. In Ottoman Islamic civilization, however, there were no traditions of official public art. The exception was architecture, where a veritable explosion of mosque construction occurred during the sixteenth century. Refined pictorial artistry, in the form of portraits, book illustrations, and miniatures, was found only inside the privacy of the Ottoman palace and wealthy administrative households. As in Habsburg Spain, theater and music enjoyed much support on the popular level, in defiance of official religious restrictions against these forms of entertainment.

The Topkapı Palace When the Ottoman sultans conquered the Byzantine capital Constantinople in 1453, they acquired one of the great cities of the world. Although richly endowed with Roman monuments and churches, it was dilapidated and depopulated when the Ottomans took over. The sultans initiated large construction projects, such as covered markets, and populated the city with craftspeople and traders drawn from both the Asian and European sides of their empire. By 1600 Istanbul was again an imposing metropolis with close to half a million inhabitants, easily the largest city in Europe at that time.

One of the construction projects was a new palace for the sultans, the Topkapı Sarayı, or "Palace of the Gun Gate," begun in 1459. The Topkapı was a veritable minicity, with three courtyards, formal gardens, and forested hunting grounds. It also included the main administrative school for the training of imperial bureaucrats, barracks for the standing troops of the Janissaries, an armory, a hospital, and—most important—the living quarters, or harem, for the ruling family. Subjects were permitted access only through the first courtyard—reserved for imperial festivities—to submit their petitions to the sultan's council of ministers.

The institution of the harem rose to prominence toward the end of the reign of Süleyman. At that time, sultans no longer pursued marriage alliances with neighboring Islamic rulers. Instead, they chose slave concubines for the procreation of children, preferably boys. Concubines were usually from the Caucasus or other frontier regions, often Christian, and, since they were slaves, deprived of family attachments.

A concubine who bore a son to the reigning sultan acquired privileges, such as influence on decisions made by the central administration.

The head eunuch of the harem guard evolved into a powerful intermediary for all manner of small and large diplomatic and military decisions between the sultan's mother, who was confined to the harem, and the ministers or generals she sought to influence. In addition, the sultan's mother arranged marriages of her daughters to members of the council of ministers and other high-ranking officials. In the strong patriarchal order of the Ottoman Empire, it might come as a surprise to see women exercise such power, but this power evidently had its roots in the tutelage exercised by mothers over sons who were potential future sultans.

Imperial Hall, Topkapı Palace. The Ottomans never forgot their nomadic roots. Topkapı Palace, completed in 1479 and expanded and redecorated several times, resembles in many ways a vast encampment, with a series of enclosed courtyards. At the center of the palace complex were the harem and the private apartments of the sultan, which included the Imperial Hall, where the sultan would receive members of his family and closest advisors.

image analysis

Public Festivities As in Habsburg Spain, feasts and celebrations were events that displayed the state's largesse and benevolence. Typical festivities were the Feast of Breaking the Fast, which came at the end of the fasting month of Ramadan, and the Feast of Sacrifice, which took place a month and a half later at the end of the Meccan pilgrimage. Festive processions and fairs welcomed the return of the Meccan pilgrimage caravan. Other feasts were connected with the birthday of the Prophet Muhammad and his journey to heaven and hell. Muslims believed that the Prophet's birth was accompanied by miracles and that the angel Gabriel accompanied him on his journey, showing him the joys of heaven and the horrors of hell. Processions with banners, music, and communal meals commemorated the birthdays of local Muslim saints in many cities and towns. As in Christian Spain, these feasts attracted large crowds.

Wrestlers, ram handlers, and horsemen performed in the Hippodrome, the stadium for public festivities. Elimination matches in wrestling determined the eventual champion. Ram handlers spurred their animals to gore one another with their horns. Horsemen stood upright on horses, galloping toward a mound, which they had to hit with a javelin. At the harbor of the Golden Horn, tightrope artists stood high above the water, balancing themselves on cables stretched between the masts of ships, as they performed juggling feats. Fireworks—featuring a variety of effects, noises, and colors—completed the circumcision festival in the evening. Court painters recorded the procession and performance scenes in picture albums. The sultans incorporated these albums into their libraries, together with history books recording in word and image their military victories against the Habsburgs (see Source 16.3).

Popular Theater The evenings of the fasting month of Ramadan were filled with festive meals and a special form of entertainment, the Karagöz ("Black Eye") shadow theater. This form of theater came from Egypt, although it probably had Javanese–Chinese roots. The actors in the Karagöz theater used figures cut from thin, transparent leather, painted in primary colors, and fashioned with movable jaws and limbs. With brightly burning lamps behind them, actors manipulated

Ottoman Festivities, 1720. The sultan watches from a kiosk on the shore of the Golden Horn as artists perform high-wire acts, musicians and dancers perform from rowboats offshore, and high officials and foreign dignitaries view the festivities from a galleon.

the figures against a cloth screen. The audience was seated on the other side of the screen, following the plays with rapt attention (or not).

Among boys, a performance of the Karagöz theater accompanied the ritual of circumcision, a rite of passage from the ancient Near East adopted in Islamic civilization. The custom called for boys between the ages of 6 and 12 to be circumcised. Circumcision signified the passage from the nurturing care of the mother to the educational discipline of the father. Groups of newly circumcised boys were placed in beds from which they watched the Karagöz plays.

Mosque Architecture During the sixteenth century, the extraordinarily prolific architect Sinan (ca. 1492–1588) filled Istanbul and the earlier Ottoman capital Edirne with a number of imperial mosques, defined by their characteristic slender minarets. According to his autobiography, Sinan designed more than 300 religious and secular buildings, from mosques, colleges, and hospitals to aqueducts and bridges. Sultan Süleyman, wealthy officials, and private donors provided the funds. Sinan was able to hire as many as 25,000 laborers, enabling him to build each of his mosques in six years or less.

Sinan described the Shehzade and Süleymaniye mosques in Istanbul and the Selimiye mosque in Edirne as his apprentice, journeyman, and master achievements. All three followed the central dome-over-a-square concept of the Hagia Sophia, which in turn is built in the tradition

Selimiye and Hagia Sophia. The architect Sinan elegantly melded the eight, comparatively thin, columns inside the mosque (*a*) with the surrounding walls and allowed for a maximum of light to enter the building. In addition, light enters through the dome (*b*). Compare this mosque with the much more heavily built, late-Roman-founded Hagia Sophia (*c*).

of Persian and Roman dome architecture. His primary, and most original, contribution to the history of architecture was the replacement of the highly visible and massive four exterior buttresses, which marked the square ground plan of the Hagia Sophia, with up to eight slender pillars as hidden internal supports of the dome. His intention with each of these mosques was not massive monumentality but elegant spaciousness, giving the skylines of Istanbul and Edirne their unmistakable identity.

The Spanish Habsburg Empire: Popular Festivities and the Arts

The centrality of Catholicism gave the culture of the Habsburg Empire a strongly religious coloration. Both state-sponsored spectacles and popular festivities displayed devotion to the Catholic faith. More secular tendencies, however, began to appear as well, if only because new forms of literature and theater emerged outside the religious sphere as a result of the Renaissance. Originating in Italy and the Netherlands, Renaissance aesthetics emphasized pre-Christian Greek and Roman heritages, which had not been available to medieval Christian artists.

Capital and Palace The Habsburgs focused relatively late on creating the typical symbols of state power and splendor—that is, a capital city and a palace. Most Spaniards lived in the northern third and along the southern and eastern rims of the Iberian Peninsula, leaving the inhospitable central high plateau, the Meseta, thinly inhabited. Catholicism was the majority religion by the sixteenth century and a powerful unifying force, but there were strong linguistic differences among the provinces of the Iberian Peninsula. Charles V resided for a while in a palace in Granada next door to the formerly Muslim Alhambra palace. Built in an Italian Renaissance–derived style and appearing overwhelming and bombastic in comparison to the outwardly unprepossessing Alhambra, Granada was too Moorish and, geographically, too far away in the south for more than a few Spanish subjects to be properly awed.

Only a few places in the river valleys traversing the Meseta were suited for the location of a central palace and administration. Philip II eventually found such a place near the city of Madrid (built on Roman–Visigothic foundations), which in the early sixteenth century had some 12,000 inhabitants. There, he had his royal architect in chief and sculptor Juan Bautista de Toledo (ca. 1515–1567), a student of Michelangelo, build the imposing Renaissance-style palace and monastery complex of El Escorial (1563–1584).

As a result, Madrid became the seat of the administration and later of the court. A large central square and broad avenue were cut across the narrow alleys of the old city, which had once been a Muslim provincial capital. People of all classes gathered in the square and avenue, to participate in public festivities and learn the latest news "about the intentions of the Grand Turk, revolutions in the Netherlands, the state of things in Italy, and the latest discoveries made in the Indies," as the writer Antonio de Liñán y Verdugo remarked in a work published in 1620.

Like its Italian paradigm, the architecture of the Spanish Renaissance emphasized the Roman imperial style—itself derived from the Greeks—with long friezes, round arches, freestanding columns, and rotunda-based domes. With this style, Spanish architects departed from the preceding Gothic, stressing horizontal extension rather than height and plain rather than relief or ornament-filled surfaces.

Christian State Festivities Given the close association between the state and the church, the Spanish crown expressed its glory through the observance of feast days of the Christian calendar. Christmas, Easter, Pentecost, Trinity Sunday, Corpus Christi, and the birthdays of numerous saints were the occasion for processions and/or **passion plays**, during which urban residents affirmed the purity of their Catholic faith. Throngs lined the streets or marched in procession, praying, singing, weeping, and exclaiming. During Holy Week, the week preceding Easter, Catholics—wearing white robes, tall white or black pointed hats, and veils over their faces—marched through the streets, carrying heavy crosses or shouldering wooden platforms with statues of Jesus and Mary. A variety of religious lay groups or confraternities competed to build the most elaborately decorated platforms. Members of flagellant confraternities whipped themselves. The physical rigors of the Holy Week processions were collective reenactments of Jesus' suffering on the Cross.

Passion play: Dramatic representation of the trial, suffering, and death of Jesus Christ; passion plays are still an integral part of Holy Week in many Catholic countries today.

By contrast, the Corpus Christi (Latin, meaning "body of Christ") processions that took place on the Sunday after Trinity Sunday (several weeks after Easter) were joyous celebrations. Central to these processions was a platform with a canopy covering the consecrated host (bread believed to have been transfigured into the body of Jesus). Marchers dressed as giants, serpents, dragons, devils, angels, patriarchs, and saints participated in jostling and pushing contests. Others wore masks, played music, performed dances, and enacted scenes from the Bible. Being part of the crowd in the Corpus Christi processions meant partaking in a joyful anticipation of salvation.

The Auto-da-Fé The investigation or proceeding of faith (Portuguese *auto-da-fé*, "act of faith") was a show trial in which the state, through the Spanish Inquisition, judged a person's commitment to Catholicism. Inquisitional trials were intended to display the all-important unity and purity of the Catholic Reformation. The Inquisition employed thousands of state-appointed church officials to investigate anonymous denunciations of individuals failing to conform to the prescribed doctrines and liturgy of the Catholic faith.

Suspected offenders, such as Jewish or Muslim converts to Catholicism or perceived deviants from Catholicism, had to appear before one of the 15 tribunals distributed throughout the country. In secret trials, officials determined the degree of the offense and the appropriate punishment. These trials often employed torture, such as stretching the accused on the rack, suspending them with weights, crushing hands and feet in an apparatus called "the boot," and burning them with firebrands. In contrast to the wide perception of the Inquisition as marked by pervasive cruelties, however, scholarship has emphasized that in the great majority of cases the punishments were minor, or the investigations did not lead to convictions.

Popular Festivities *Jousts* (mock combats between contestants mounted on horseback) were secular, primarily aristocratic events, also frequently connected with dynastic occurrences. The contestants, colorfully costumed as Muslims, Turks, and Christians, rode their horses into the city square accompanied by trumpets and drums and led their horses through a precise and complex series of movements. At the height of the spectacle, contestants divided into groups of three or four at each end of the square. At a signal, they galloped at full speed past each other, hurling their javelins at one another while protecting themselves with their shields. The joust evolved eventually into exhibitions of dressage ("training"), cultivated by the Austrian Habsburgs, who in 1572 founded the Spanish Court Riding School in Vienna.

Bullfights, also fought on horseback, often followed the jousts. Fighting wild animals, including bulls, in spectacles was originally a Roman custom that had evolved from older bovine sacrifices in temples around the Mediterranean. During the Middle Ages, bullfights were aristocratic pastimes that drew spectators from local estates. Bullfighters, armed with detachable metal points on 3-foot-long spears, tackled several bulls in a town square, together with footmen who sought to distract the bulls by waving red capes at them. The bullfighter who stuck the largest number of points into the shoulders of the bull was the winner.

Theater and Literature The dramatic enactments of biblical scenes in the passion plays and Corpus Christi processions were the origin of a new phenomenon in Italy and Spain, the secular theater. During earlier centuries, traveling troupes had often performed on wagons after processions. Stationary theaters with stages, main floors, balconies, and boxes appeared in the main cities of Spain during the sixteenth century. A performance typically began with a musical prelude and a prologue describing the piece, followed by the three acts of a drama or comedy. Brief sketches, humorous or earnest, filled the breaks. Plays dealt with betrayed or unrequited love, honor, justice, or peasant–nobility conflicts. Many were hugely successful, enjoying the attendance or even sponsorship of courtiers, magistrates, and merchants.

The Auto-da-Fé This detail from an 1683 painting by the Italian-born painter Francisco Rizi shows a huge assembly in the Plaza Mayor of Madrid. It captures the solemn spectacle of the trial: In the center, below a raised platform, the accused stand in the docket waiting for their convictions to be pronounced; ecclesisatical and civil authorities follow the proceedings from grandstands. On the left, an altar is visible: The celebration of mass was a common feature of the auto-da-fé.

El Greco, *View of Toledo*, ca. 1610–1614. The painting, now in the Metropolitan Museum of Art in New York City, illustrates El Greco's predilection for color contrasts and dramatic motion. Baroque and Mannerist painters rarely depicted landscapes, and this particular landscape is represented in eerie green, gray, and blue colors, giving the impression of a city enveloped in a mysterious natural or perhaps spiritual force.

An important writer of the period was Miguel de Cervantes (1547–1616), who wrote his masterpiece, *Don Quixote*, in the new literary form of the novel. *Don Quixote* describes the adventures of a poverty-stricken knight and his attendant, the peasant Sancho Panza, as they wander around Spain searching for the life of bygone *Reconquista* chivalry. Their journey includes many hilarious escapades during which they run into the reality of the early modern centralizing state dominated by monetary concerns. Cervantes confronts the vanished virtues of knighthood with the novel values of the life with money.

Painters The outstanding painter of Spain during Philip II's reign was El Greco (Domenikos Theotokopoulos, ca. 1546–1614), a native of the island of Crete. After early training in Crete as a painter of Eastern Christian icons, El Greco went to Venice for further studies. In 1577, the Catholic hierarchy hired him to paint the altarpieces of a church in Toledo, the city in central Spain that was one of the residences of the kings prior to the construction of El Escorial in Madrid. El Greco's works reflect the spirit of Spanish Catholicism, with its emphasis on strict obedience to traditional faith and fervent personal piety. His characteristic style features elongated, pale figures surrounded by vibrant colors and represents a variation of the so-called mannerist style (with its perspective exaggerations), which succeeded the Renaissance style in Venice during the later sixteenth century.

Putting It All Together

interactive concept map

The Ottoman–Habsburg struggle can be seen as another chapter in the long history of competition that began when the Achaemenid Persian Empire expanded into the Mediterranean and was resisted by the Greeks in the middle of the first millennium BCE. Although India and China were frequently subjected to incursions from central Asia, neither of the two had to compete for long with any of its neighbors. Sooner or later the central Asians either retreated or were absorbed by their victims. The Ottomans' brief experience with Timur was on the same order. But the Middle East and Europe were always connected, and this chapter, once more, draws attention to this connectedness.

There were obvious religious and cultural differences between the Islamic and Western Christian civilizations as they encountered each other during the Ottoman–Habsburg period. But their commonalities are equally, if not more, interesting. Most important, both Ottomans and Habsburgs were representatives of the return to imperialism, and in the pursuit of their imperial goals, both adopted the policy of the centralizing state with its firearm infantries and pervasive urban money economy. Both found it crucial to their existence to project their glory to the population at large and to sponsor artistic expression. In the long run, however, the imperial ambitions of the Ottomans and Habsburgs exceeded their ability to raise cash. Although firearms and a monetized urban economy made them different from previous empires, they were as unstable as all their imperial predecessors. Eventually, around 1600, they reached the limits of their conquests.

Review and Relate

Thinking Through Patterns

Examine the ways historians approach the big questions of this chapter.

In 1300, the Ottomans renewed the Arab-Islamic tradition of jihad against the Eastern Christian empire of Byzantium, conquering the Balkans and eventually defeating the empire with the conquest of Constantinople in 1453. They also carried the war into the western Mediterranean and Indian Ocean. In Western Christian Iberia, the rekindling of the reconquest after the lull of the thirteenth and fourteenth centuries was more successful. Invigorated by a merging of the concepts of the Crusade and the *Reconquista*, the Iberians expanded overseas to circumvent the Muslims and trade for Indian spices directly. The so-called Age of Exploration, during which Western Christians traveled to and settled in overseas lands, is deeply rooted in the Western traditions of war against Islamic civilization.

» What patterns characterized the Christian and Muslim imperial competition in the period 1300–1600? Which elements distinguished them from each other, and which elements were similar? How did the pattern change over time?

In the mid-1400s, the Middle East and Europe returned to the pattern of imperial state formation after a lull of several centuries, during which states had competed against each other within their respective commonwealths. The element which fueled this return was gunpowder weaponry. The use of cannons and handheld firearms became widespread during this time but required major financial outlays on the part of the states. The Ottomans and Habsburgs were the states with the most resources, and the Ottomans even assembled the first standing armies. To pay the musket-equipped soldiers, huge amounts of silver were necessary. The two empires became states based on a money economy: Bureaucracies maintained centralized departments that regulated the collection of taxes and the payroll of soldiers.

» How did the centralizing state in the Middle East and Europe function in the period 1450–1600? How did economics, military power, and imperial objectives interact to create the centralizing state?

The rulers of these empires were concerned to portray themselves, their military, and their bureaucracies as highly successful and just. The state had to be as visible and benevolent as possible. Rulers, therefore, were builders of palaces, churches, or mosques. They celebrated religious and secular festivities with great pomp and

» Which patterns did cultural expressions follow in the

Habsburg and Ottoman Empires? Why did the ruling classes of these empires sponsor these expressions?

encouraged ministers and the nobility to do likewise. In the imperial capitals, they patronized architects, artists, and writers, resulting in a veritable explosion of intellectual and artistic creativity. In this regard, the Ottomans and the Habsburgs followed similar patterns of cultural expression.

Against the Grain

Consider this as a counterpoint to the main patterns examined in this chapter.

Tilting at Windmills

- What explains the lasting literary success of *Don Quixote*?
- Why has the phrase "tilting at windmills" undergone a change of meaning from the original "fighting imaginary foes" to "taking on a situation against all seeming evidence" in our own time?

Cervantes's *The Ingenious Gentleman Don Quixote of La Mancha* was an instant hit in the Spanish-speaking literary world of the early 1600s and contributed to the rise of the novel as a characteristic European form of literary expression. As stated in his preface, Cervantes composed his novel in opposition to the dominant literary conventions of his time, to "ridicule the absurdity of those books of chivalry, which have, as it were, fascinated the eyes and judgement of the world, and in particular of the vulgar."

Every episode in this novel, from the literary frame to its most famous story, Don Quixote's joust against windmills he believes to be fantastic giants, is cast in the forms of gentle, hilarious, or biting parodies of one or another absurdity in society. The frame is provided by the fictional figure of Cide Hamete Benengeli, a purportedly perfidious Muslim and historian who might or might not have been lying when he chronicled the lives of the knight Don Quixote and his squire Sancho Panza in the 74 episodes of the novel. Don Quixote's joust, or "tilting," against windmills has become a powerful metaphor for rebelling against the often overpowering conventions of society.

Don Quixote is today acclaimed as the second most printed text after the Bible. Over the past four centuries, each generation has interpreted the text anew. Revolutionary France saw Don Quixote as a doomed visionary; German Romantics, as a hero destined to fail; Communists, as an anti-capitalist rebel before his time; and secular progressives, as an unconventional hero at the dawn of modern free society. For Karl Marx, Don Quixote was the hidalgo who yearned for a return to the feudal aristocracy of the past which in his time was becoming a pleasure aristocracy, enjoying its useless life at the royal court and imitated later by the bourgeoisie. Sigmund Freud enjoyed reading and rereading *Don Quixote* throughout his life, looking at the knight-errant as "tragic in his helplessness while the plot is unraveled." In our own time, Don Quixote became the quintessential postmodern figure; in the words of Michel Foucault, his "truth is not in the relation of the words to the world but in that slender and constant relation woven between themselves as verbal signs. The hollow fiction of epic exploits has become the representative power of language. Words have swallowed up their own nature as signs." As a tragic or comic figure, Don Quixote continues to be the irresistible symbol of opposition.

Key Terms

audio flashcards

Corsairs 459
Devşirme 476
Janissaries 476
Military orders 460
Money economy 475
Moriscos 472
Passion play 484
Tax farming 477

For additional resources, please go to **www.oup.com/us/vonsivers.**
Please see the Further Resources section at the back of the book for additional readings and suggested websites.

PATTERNS OF EVIDENCE |

Sources for Chapter 16

SOURCE 16.1

Christopher Columbus, *The Book of Prophecies*

1501–1502

Although he is more famous for his voyages—and for the richly detailed accounts he made of them—Columbus (1451–1506) also composed a book of prophetic revelations toward the end of his life, entitled *El Libro de las Profecias*. Written after his third voyage to the Americas, the book traces the development of God's plans for the end of the world, which could be hastened along, particularly by a swift and decisive move to reclaim Jerusalem from Muslim control. When Jerusalem was once more restored to Christian sovereignty, Columbus predicted, Jesus could return to earth, and all of the events foreseen in the Book of Revelation (and in various medieval revelations, as well) could unfold. It is helpful to place the plans for Columbus's original voyage in 1492 against the backdrop of his religious beliefs, as he encourages Ferdinand and Isabella to take their rightful place in God's mystical plan—as well as in Columbus's own cartographic charts.

Letter from the Admiral to the King and Queen [Ferdinand and Isabella]

. . .

Most exalted rulers: At a very early age I began sailing the sea and have continued until now. This profession creates a curiosity about the secrets of the world. I have been a sailor for forty years, and I have personally sailed to all the known regions. I have had commerce and conversation with knowledgeable people of the clergy and the laity. Latins and Greeks, Jews and Moors, and with many others of different religions. Our Lord has favored my occupation and has given me an intelligent mind. He has endowed me with a great talent for seamanship; sufficient ability in astrology, geometry, and arithmetic; and the mental and physical dexterity required to draw spherical maps of cities, rivers and mountains, islands and ports, with everything in its proper place.

During this time I have studied all kinds of texts: cosmography, histories, chronicles, philosophy, and other disciplines. Through these writings, the hand of Our Lord opened my mind to the possibility of sailing to the Indies and gave

---

Source: Christopher Columbus, *The Book of Prophecies*, ed. Roberto Rusconi, trans. Blair Sullivan, vol. 3 (Berkeley: University of California Press, 1997), 67–69, 75–77.

me the will to attempt the voyage. With this burning ambition I came to your Highnesses. Everyone who heard about my enterprise rejected it with laughter and ridicule. Neither all the sciences that I mentioned previously nor citations drawn from them were of any help to me. Only Your Highnesses had faith and perseverance. Who could doubt that this flash of understanding was the work of the Holy Spirit, as well as my own? The Holy Spirit illuminated his holy and sacred Scripture, encouraging me in a very strong and clear voice from the forty-four books of the Old Testament, the four evangelists, and twenty-three epistles from the blessed apostles, urging me to proceed. Continually, without ceasing a moment, they insisted that I go on. Our Lord wished to make something clearly miraculous of this voyage to the Indies in order to encourage me and others about the holy temple.

. . .

Most of the prophecies of holy Scripture have already been fulfilled. The Scriptures say this and the Holy Church loudly and unceasingly is saying it, and no other witness is necessary. I will, however, speak of one prophecy in particular because it bears on my argument and gives me support and happiness whenever I think about it.

I have greatly sinned. Yet, every time that I have asked, I have been covered by the mercy and compassion of Our Lord. I have found the sweetest consolation in throwing off all my cares in order to contemplate his marvelous presence.

I have already said that for the voyage to the Indies neither intelligence nor mathematics nor world maps were of any use to me; it was the fulfillment of Isaiah's prophecy. This is what I want to record here in order to remind Your Highnesses and so that you can take pleasure from the things I am going to tell you about Jerusalem on the basis of the same authority. If you have faith in this enterprise, you will certainly have the victory.

. . .

I said above that much that has been prophesied remains to be fulfilled, and I say that these are the world's great events, and I say that a sign of this is the acceleration of Our Lord's activities in this world. I know this from the recent preaching of the gospel in so many lands.

The Calabrian abbot Joachim said that whoever was to rebuild the temple on Mount Zion would come from Spain.

The cardinal Pierre d'Ailly wrote at length about the end of the religion of Mohammed and the coming of the Antichrist in his treatise *De concordia astronomicae veritatis et narrationis historicae* [*On the agreement between astronomical truth and historical narrative*]; he discusses, particularly in the last nine chapters, what many astronomers have said about the ten revolutions of Saturn.

» Working with Sources

1. **How does Columbus appeal to the "crusading" goals of Ferdinand and Isabella, and why?**
2. **Would this appeal have found favor with the monarchs, given their other actions in Spain in 1492?**

SOURCE 16.2 Thomas the Eparch and Joshua Diplovatatzes, "The Fall of Constantinople"

1453

The siege and conquest of Constantinople by the Ottoman Turks under Mehmet II (r. 1451–1481) was one of the turning points of world history. Unfolding over two months between April 5 and May 29, 1453, the siege exposed the inability of the Byzantine emperor Constantine XI to withstand a sustained and massive attack. Outnumbering the defenders 11 to 1, the Ottomans battered Constantinople's walls with heavy cannons and took advantage of the natural weaknesses of the city's geography. This account, told by two survivors and (self-proclaimed) eyewitnesses to the siege and its aftermath, details some of the specific stages of the defeat—and the suffering for Christians that came as a result.

When the Turk then drew near to Pera in the fortified zone, he seized all the boats he could find and bound them to each other so as to form a bridge which permitted the combatants to fight on the water just as they did on land. The Turks had with them thousands of ladders which they placed against the walls, right at the place which they had fired [their cannon] and breached the wall, just as they did at the cemetery of St. Sebold. The Genoese handled this breach; they wanted to protect it with their ships because they had so many. In the army of the Turk the order had been given fifteen days before the attack that each soldier would carry a ladder, whether he was fighting on land or sea. There also arrived galleys full of armed men: it seemed that they were Genoese and that they had come to aid the besieged, but in fact they were Turks and they were slipping into the gates. Just as this was becoming less worrisome and the city seemed secure, there arrived under the flag of the Genoese several ships which repelled the Turks with great losses.

At dawn on Monday, 29 May, they began an attack that lasted all night until Tuesday evening and they conquered the city. The commander of the Genoese, who was leading the defense of the breach, pretended to be wounded and abandoned his battle station, taking with him all his people. When the Turks realized this, they slipped in through the breach. When the emperor of the Greeks saw this, he exclaimed in a loud voice: "My God, I have been betrayed!" and he suddenly appeared with his people, exhorting the others to stand firm and defend themselves. But then the gate was opened and the crush of people became such that the emperor himself and his [men] were killed by the Turks and the traitors.

Then the Turks ran to the Hagia Sophia, and all those whom they had imprisoned there, they killed in the first heat of rage. Those whom they found later, they bound with a cord around their neck and their hands tied behind

---

Source: trans. William L. North from the Italian version in A. Pertusi, ed., *La Caduta di Constantinopoli: Le testimonianze dei contemporanei* (Milan: Mondadori, 1976), 234–239, available online at https://apps.carleton.edu/curricular/mars/assets/Thomas_the_Eparch_and_Joshua_Diplovatatzes_for_MARS_website.pdf.

their backs and led them out of the city. When the Turk learned that the emperor had been killed in Constantinople, he captured the Grand Duke who was governing in the emperor's stead and had the Grand Duke's son beheaded and then the Grand Duke himself. Then he seized one of the Grand Duke's daughters who was quite beautiful and made her lie on the great altar of Hagia Sophia with a crucifix under her head and then raped her. Then the most brutish of the Turks seized the finest noble women, virgins, and nuns of the city and violated them in the presence of the Greeks and in sacrilege of Christianity. Then they destroyed all the sacred objects and the bodies of the saints and burned everything they found, save for the cross, the nail, and the clothing of Christ: no one knows where these relics ended up, no one has found them. They also wanted to desecrate the image of the Virgin of St. Luke by stabbing six hundred people in front of it, one after another, like madmen. Then they took prisoner those who fell into their hands, tied them with a rope around the neck and calculated the value of each one. Women had to redeem themselves with their own bodies, men by fornicating with their hands or some other means. Whoever was able to pay the assessed amount could remain in his faith and whoever refused had to die. The Turk who had become governor of Constantinople, named Suleiman in German, occupied the temple of Hagia Sophia to practice his faith there. For three days the Turks sacked and pillaged the city, and each kept whatever he found—people and goods—and did with them whatever he wished.

. . .

All this was made known by Thomas the Eparch, a count of Constantinople, and Joshua Diplovatatzes. Thutros of Constantinople translated their Greek into "welisch" and Dumita Exswinnilwacz and Matheus Hack of Utrecht translated their welisch into German.

» Working with Sources

1. **What does this account suggest about the preparedness of the Turks for the sack of Constantinople—and the lack of preparation on the part of the Byzantine defenders?**
2. **What details indicate that the taking of Constantinople was seen as a "religious" war on the Ottoman side?**

SOURCE 16.3

Evliya Çelebi, "A Procession of Artisans at Istanbul"

ca. 1638

Born on the Golden Horn and raised in the sultan's palace in Istanbul, Çelebi traveled throughout Ottoman domains between 1640 and 1680. He published an account of his travels and experiences as the *Seyahatname*, or *Book of Travels*. In the first of his 10 books in the document, Çelebi

Source: Robert Dankoff, *An Ottoman Mentality: The World of Evliya Çelebi*, 2nd ed. (Leiden, the Netherlands: Brill, 2006), 86–89.

provides a lengthy description of Istanbul around the year 1638, including a panoramic view of 1,100 artisan and craft guilds. The numbers and diversity of trades represented underscore the extent of Ottoman commerce—as well as the pride of place each of the city's working people claimed as their due.

The numbers in brackets refer to the order of listing in this chapter.

I: Ship-captains [7] vs. Saddlers [30]

Following the bakers [6], the saddlers wished to pass, but the ship-captains and sea-merchants raised a great fuss. When Sultan Murad got wind of the matter, he consulted with the ulema and the guild shaikhs. They all agreed that it made sense for the ship-captains to proceed after the bakers, because it was they who transported the wheat, and the bakers were dependent on them, and also because Noah was their patron saint.

Comment: the saddlers do not reappear until much later, between the tanners [29] and the shoemakers [31].

. . .

III: Egyptian Merchants [9] vs. Butchers [10]

Following the procession of these Mediterranean Sea captains, the butchers were supposed to pass, according to imperial decree. But all the great Egyptian merchants, including the dealers in rice, hemp, Egyptian reed mats, coffee and sugar gathered together and began quarreling with the butchers. Finally they went before the sultan and said: "My padishah, our galleons are charged with transporting rice, lentils, coffee and hemp. They cannot do without us, nor we without them. Why should these bloody and tricky butchers come between us? Plagues have arisen from cities where they shed their blood, and for fear of this their stalls and shambles in other countries are outside of the city walls. They are a bloody and filthy band of ill-omen. We, on the other hand, always make Istanbul plentiful and cheap with grains of all sorts."

Now the butchers' eyes went bloodshot. "My padishah," they said, "Our patron saint is Butcher Cömerd and our occupation is with sheep, an animal which the Creator has made the object of mercy, and whose flesh He has made lawful food for the strengthening of His servants' bodies. Bread and meat are mentioned as the foremost of God's gifts to mankind: with a small portion of meat, a poor man can subsist for five or six days. We make our living with such a lawful trade, and are known for our generosity (*cömerdlik*). It is we who make Istanbul plentiful and cheap. As for these merchants and dealers and profiteers: concerning them the Koran says (2:275), 'God has made selling lawful and profiteering unlawful'. They are such a despised group that after bringing their goods from Egypt they store it in magazines in order to create a shortage, thus causing public harm through their hoarding.

. . .

"Egyptian sugar? But in the Koran the rivers of paradise are praised as being made 'of pure honey' (47:15). Now we have honey from Turkey, Athens,

Wallachia, Moldavia, each with seventy distinct qualities. Furthermore, if my padishah wished, thousands of quintals of sugar could be produced in Alanya, Antalya, Silifke, Tarsus, Adana, Payas, Antakya, Aleppo, Damascus, Sidon, Beyrut, Tripoli and other such provinces—enough to make it plentiful and cheap throughout the world—so why do we need your sugar?

"As for coffee: it is an innovation; it prevents sleep; it dulls the generative powers; and coffee houses are dens of sedition. When roasted it is burnt; and in the legal compilations known as *Bezzaziye* and *Tatarhaniye* we have the dictum that 'Whatever is carbonized is absolutely forbidden'—this holds even for burnt bread. Spiced sherbet, pure milk, tea, fennel, salep, and almond-cream—all these are more wholesome than coffee."

. . .

To these objections of the butchers, the Egyptian merchants replied:

. . . "It is true that Turkey has no need of sugar and hemp, and that European sugar is also very fine. But tell us this, O band of butchers: what benefit and return do you offer to the public treasury?"

The butchers had nothing to say to this, and the Egyptian merchants continued: "My padishah, the goods arriving in our galleons provide the public treasury an annual revenue of 11,000 purses from customs dues. As a matter of justice (*'adalet ederseñiz*) we ought to have precedence in the Muhammadan procession, and the butchers ought to come after us." The *şeyhülislam* Yahya Efendi and Mu'id Ahmed Efendi cited the hadith, "The best of men is he who is useful to mankind," and the sultan gave the Egyptian merchants a noble rescript authorizing them to go first, and the butchers to go second.

» Working with Sources

1. **Why did the order in which they appeared in the procession matter so much to these particular groups?**
2. **How did appeals to the Quran accentuate or diminish their case to be placed ahead in the procession?**

SOURCE 16.4 Ogier Ghiselin de Busbecq, "The Court of Suleiman the Magnificent"

1581

Ghiselin (1522–1592) was a Flemish ambassador who represented the Austrian Habsburgs at the court of Suleiman the Magnificent (1520–1566) in Istanbul. In 1581, he published an account of his time among the Ottomans as *Itinera Constantinopolitanum et Amasianum* (*Travels in*

Source: Wayne S. Vucinich, *The Ottoman Empire: Its Record and Legacy* (Princeton, NJ: Van Nostrand, 1965), 127–129.

Constantinople and Asia Minor). In this segment of his travel narrative, he draws attention to the personal habits and behaviors of a contemporary emperor—one who saw himself as the heir to the Romans as well as to the other monarchs who had held Constantinople/Istanbul.

The Sultan was seated on a very low ottoman, not more than a foot from the ground, which was covered with a quantity of costly rugs and cushions of exquisite workmanship; near him lay his bow and arrows. His air, as I said, was by no means gracious, and his face wore a stern, though dignified, expression. On entering we were separately conducted into the royal presence by the chamberlains, who grasped our arms. . . . After having gone through a pretense of kissing his hand, we were conducted backwards to the wall opposite his seat, care being taken that we should never turn our backs on him. The Sultan then listened to what I had to say; but the language I held was not at all to his taste, for the demands of his Majesty breathed a spirit of independence and dignity . . . and so he made no answer beyond saying in a tetchy way, "Giusel, giusel," i.e. well, well . . .

. . .

I was greatly struck with the silence and order that prevailed in this great crowd. There were no cries, no hum of voices, the usual accompaniments of a motley gathering, neither was there any jostling; without the slightest disturbance each man took his proper place according to his rank. The Agas, as they call their chiefs, were seated, to wit, generals, colonels (*bimbashi*), and captains (*soubashi*). Men of a lower position stood. The most interesting sight in this assembly was a body of several thousand Janissaries, who were drawn up in a long line apart from the rest; their array was so steady and motionless that, being at a little distance, it was some time before I could make up my mind as to whether they were human beings or statues; at last I received a hint to salute them, and saw all their heads bending at the same moment to return my bow.

. . .

When the cavalry had ridden past, they were followed by a long procession of Janissaries, but few of whom carried any arms except their regular weapon, the musket. They were dressed in uniforms of almost the same shape and colour, so that you might recognize them to be the slaves. . . . There is only one thing in which they are extravagant, viz., plumes, head-dresses, etc., and veterans who formed the rear guard were specially distinguished by ornaments of this kind. The plumes which they insert in their frontlets might well be mistaken for a walking forest.

» Working with Sources

1. **Why were order and discipline apparently so important at Suleiman's court?**
2. **Why might Ghiselin have found the Janissaries so particularly impressive?**

SOURCE 16.5 Janissary Musket

ca. 1750–1800

The Janissaries constitute the most famous and centralized of the Ottomans' military institutions. A feared and respected military force, the Janissaries were Christian-born males who had been seized from their homes as boys, converted to Islam, and then trained as future soldiers and administrators for the Turks. Under the direct orders of the sultan and his viziers, the Janissaries were equipped with the latest military innovations. These units received cannons and matchlock (later flintlock, below) muskets. The muskets continued their evolution in the Janissaries' hands, becoming standard equipment for Ottoman and other armies.

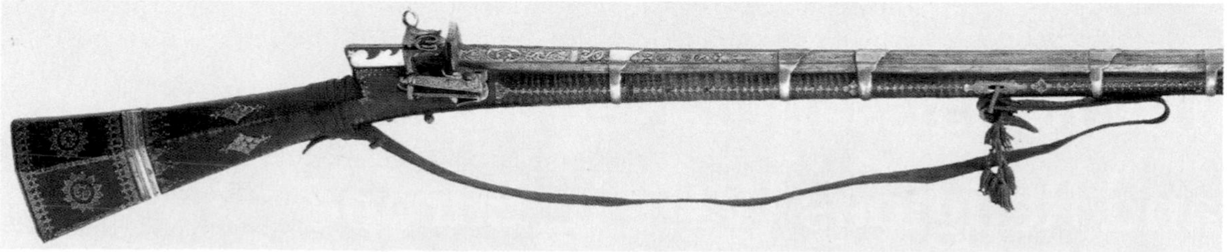

» Working with Sources

1. **What does the elaborate decoration of this musket suggest about its psychological as well as its practical effects?**
2. **Was this firearm likely to have been produced by indigenous, rather than European, gunsmiths? Why or why not?**

5 Source: © INTERFOTO/Alamy.

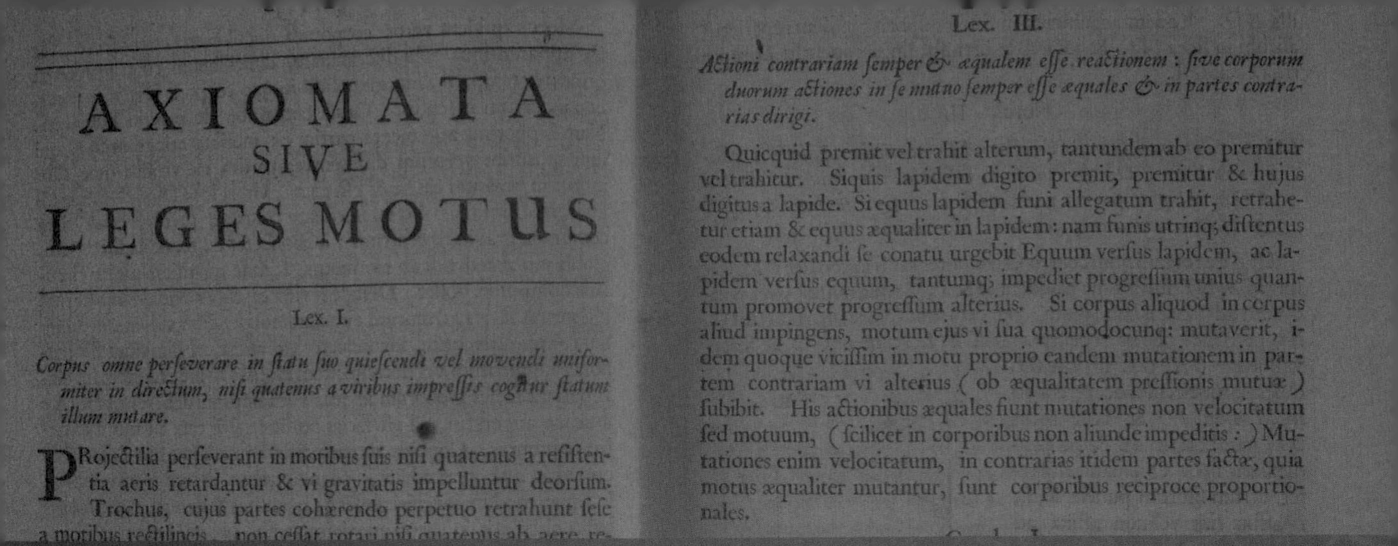

AXIOMATA
SIVE
LEGES MOTUS

Lex. I.

Corpus omne perseverare in statu suo quiescendi vel movendi uniformiter in directum, nisi quatenus a viribus impressis cogitur statum illum mutare.

Projectilia perseverant in motibus suis nisi quatenus a resistentia aeris retardantur & vi gravitatis impelluntur deorsum. Trochus, cujus partes cohærendo perpetuo retrahunt sese a motibus rectilineis, non cessat rotari nisi quatenus ab aere re-

Lex. III.

Actioni contrariam semper & æqualem esse reactionem: sive corporum duorum actiones in se mutuo semper esse æquales & in partes contrarias dirigi.

Quicquid premit vel trahit alterum, tantundem ab eo premitur vel trahitur. Siquis lapidem digito premit, premitur & hujus digitus a lapide. Si equus lapidem funi allegatum trahit, retrahetur etiam & equus æqualiter in lapidem: nam funis utrinq; distentus eodem relaxandi se conatu urgebit Equum versus lapidem, ac lapidem versus equum, tantumq; impediet progressum unius quantum promovet progressum alterius. Si corpus aliquod in corpus aliud impingens, motum ejus vi sua quomodocunq; mutaverit, idem quoque vicissim in motu proprio eandem mutationem in partem contrariam vi alterius (ob æqualitatem pressionis mutuæ) subibit. His actionibus æquales fiunt mutationes non velocitatum sed motuum, (scilicet in corporibus non aliunde impeditis:) Mutationes enim velocitatum, in contrarias itidem partes factæ, quia motus æqualiter mutantur, sunt corporibus reciproce proportionales.

Chapter 17 1450–1750

The Renaissance, New Sciences, and Religious Wars in Europe

Though less celebrated than many of her male contemporaries, one of the most remarkable scientific minds of the seventeenth century was Maria Cunitz (ca. 1607–1664). Under the tutorship of her father, a physician, she became accomplished in six languages (Hebrew, Greek, Latin, Italian, French, and Polish), the humanities, and the sciences. For a number of years, while the Thirty Years' War (1618–1648) raged in Germany and her home province of Silesia, Cunitz and her Protestant family sought refuge in a Cistercian monastery in neighboring Catholic Poland. There, under difficult living conditions, she wrote *Urania propitia* (*Companion to Urania*), in praise of the Greek muse and patron of astronomy. When the family returned to Silesia after the war, Cunitz lost her scientific papers and instruments in a fire, but she continued to devote her life to science through her careful astronomical observations.

Cunitz's book is a popularization of the astronomical tables of Johannes Kepler (1571–1630), the major scientific innovator remembered today for his discovery of the elliptical trajectories of the planets. Cunitz's book makes corrections in Kepler's tables and offers simplified calculations of star positions. Writing in both Latin and German, she published it privately

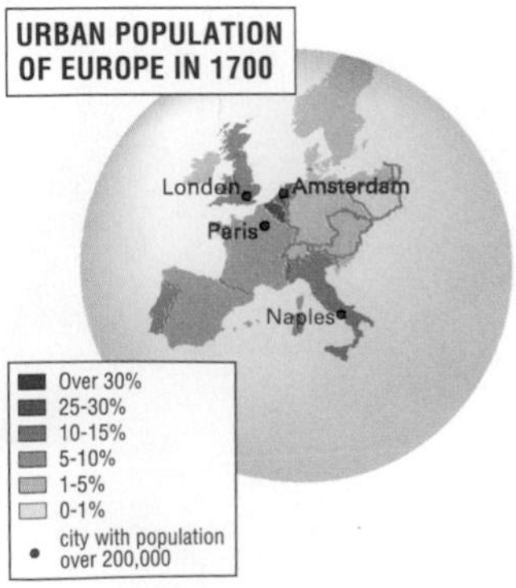

ABOVE: **In his *Principia Mathematica*, first published in 1687, Isaac Newton (1643–1727) unified physics and astronomy into a single mathematic system.**

in 1650. It was generally well received, although there were a few detractors who found it hard to believe that a woman could succeed in the sciences. Whatever injustice was done to her during her lifetime, today the scientific community has made amends. A crater on Venus has been named after her, and a statue of her stands in the town where she grew up.

Cunitz lived in a time when Western Christianity had entered the age of early global interaction, from 1450 until 1750. During most of this time, Europe remained institutionally similar to the other parts of the world, especially the Middle East, India, China, and Japan. Rulers throughout Eurasia governed by divine grace. All large states followed patterns of political centralization. Their urban populations were nowhere more than 20 percent, and their economies depended on the productivity of agriculture. As research on China, the Middle East, and India during 1450–1750 has shown, there was no "great divergence" in the patterns of political organization, social formation, and economic production between Western Christianity and the other religious civilizations until around 1750.

Culturally, however, northwestern Europe began to move in a different direction from Islamic, Hindu, Neo-Confucian, and Buddhist civilizations after 1500. New developments in the sciences and philosophy in England, France, the Netherlands, and parts of Germany initiated new cultural patterns for which there was no equivalent in the other parts of Eurasia, including southern Europe. As significant as these patterns were, for almost the entire span of time between 1500 and 1750 the new mathematized sciences remained limited to a few hundred and later to a few thousand educated persons, largely outside the ruling classes. Their ideas and outlooks diverged substantially from those represented by the Catholic and Protestant ruling classes and resulted frequently in tensions or, in a few cases, even repression of scientists by the authorities. The new scientific and intellectual culture broadened into a mass movement only after 1750. The subsequent Industrial Revolution of modernity was rooted in this movement.

Seeing Patterns

» What were the reasons for the cultural change that began in Europe with the Renaissance around 1400? In which ways were the subsequent patterns of cultural change different from those in the other religious civilizations of Eurasia?

» When and how did the mathematization of the sciences begin, and how did it gain popularity in northwestern Europe? Why is the popularization of the sciences important for understanding the period 1500–1750?

» What were the patterns of centralized state formation and transformation in the period 1400–1750? How did the Protestant Reformation and religious wars modify these patterns?

The European Renaissance, Baroque, and New Sciences formed a cultural sequence that broke with much that had been inherited from medieval times. It began with the appropriation of the Greek and Roman cultural heritage, allegedly absent from the Middle Ages, by a small educated elite. In their enthusiasm for all things Greek and Roman, however, the members of this elite overestimated the extent of their break from the Middle Ages. In today's view from a greater distance, we think of this break as far less radical, with much in culture remaining unchanged. Many centuries were needed before the new cultural pattern initiated by Renaissance, Baroque, and the New Sciences became a general phenomenon.

Chapter Outline

- Cultural Transformations: Renaissance, Baroque, and New Sciences
- Centralizing States and Religious Upheavals
- Putting It All Together

Similarly, the political and social changes of the period 1400–1750 have to be balanced against the inherited continuities. The rise of firearm-equipped armies of foot soldiers was a new phenomenon, but the use of these infantries by rulers to further increase their centralizing powers was an inheritance from the Middle Ages. The idea of a religious return to the roots of Christianity, pursued by the leaders of the Protestant Reformation, can also be traced back to the Middle Ages. When rulers used the Reformation for their centralizing ambitions, however, the ensuing religious wars became a new phenomenon. Overall, the seeds of an eventual departure of Western Christianity from the general patterns of agrarian–urban society were planted around 1500. But for a long time thereafter these seeds remained largely underground, and the "great divergence" from the agrarian–urban patterns of Islamic, Hindu, and Chinese civilizations began only after 1750.

Cultural Transformations: Renaissance, Baroque, and New Sciences

Renaissance: "Rebirth" of culture based on new publications and translations of Greek, Hellenistic, and Roman authors whose writings were previously unknown in Western Christianity.

New Sciences: Mathematized sciences, such as physics, introduced in the 1500s.

The **Renaissance** was a period of cultural transformation which in the fifteenth century followed the scholastic Middle Ages in Western Christianity. In many ways, the Renaissance was an outgrowth of scholasticism, but its thinkers and artists saw themselves as having broken away from scholastic precepts. They considered their period a time of "rebirth" (which is the literal meaning of "renaissance" in French). During this period they were powerfully influenced by the writings of Greek and Hellenistic-Roman authors who had been unknown during the scholastic age. In the sixteenth century, the Renaissance gave way to the Baroque in the arts and the **New Sciences**. Thus, the Renaissance was just the first of a sequence of periods of cultural transformation following each other in rapid succession.

The Renaissance and Baroque Arts

Beginning around 1400 in Italy and spreading later through northwestern Europe, an outpouring of learning, scholarship, and art came from theologians, philosophers, writers, painters, architects, and musical composers. These thinkers and artists benefited from Greek and Hellenistic-Roman texts which scholars had discovered recently in mostly Eastern Christian archives in Byzantium. In addition, in the early fifteenth century Byzantine scholars from Constantinople arrived in Italy with further newly rediscovered texts, which had a profound impact. The emerging cultures of the Renaissance and Baroque were creative adaptations of those Greek and Hellenistic-Roman writings to the cultural heritage of Western Christianity. Out of this vibrant mixture arose the overarching movement of **humanism**.

Humanism: Intellectual movement focusing on human culture, in such fields as philosophy, philology, and literature, and based on the corpus of Greek and Roman texts.

New Manuscripts and Printing Eastern Christian Byzantium experienced a cultural revival between its recovery in 1261 from the Latin interlude and its collapse in 1453 when the Muslim Ottomans conquered Constantinople. During this revival, scholars engaged in a vigorous debate about the compatibility of Plato and Aristotle with each other. The debate made Italian scholars fully aware of how much of Greek literature was still absent from Western Christianity. For example, at the time they possessed just two of Plato's 44 dialogues. Italians invited about a dozen Eastern Christian scholars, who brought manuscripts to Florence, Rome, and Venice to translate and teach. Their students became fluent in Greek and translated Hesiod and Homer, some Greek tragedies and comedies, Plato and the Neo-Platonists, the remaining works of Aristotle, Hellenistic scientific texts, and the Greek church fathers. Western Christianity had finally absorbed the ancient heritage.

The work of translation was helped by the development of a more rounded, simplified Latin script, which replaced the angled, dense Gothic script used since the 1150s. In addition, the costly vellum (scraped leather) writing material on which many manuscripts had been laboriously written was replaced by cheaper paper, which had been introduced from Islamic Spain in the early twelfth century and had become common in the rest of Europe by 1400. Experimentation in the 1430s with movable metal typeface resulted in the innovation of the printing press. A half-century later, with more than 1,000 printers all over Europe and more than 8 million books in the hands of readers, a veritable printing revolution had taken place in Europe.

Bookseller. By 1600, the increase in literacy levels combined with widespread printing of books, pamphlets, and tracts had made people like this itinerant bookseller in Italy a commonplace sight throughout much of Europe.

Philology and Political Theory The flood of new manuscripts and the renewed examination of existing manuscripts in libraries encouraged the study of Greek, Latin, and Hebrew philology. Scholars trained in these languages edited critical texts based on multiple manuscripts. The best known among these philologists was the Dutchman Desiderius Erasmus (1466–1536), who published an edition of the Greek and Latin New Testaments in 1516. Critical textual research, which became central to subsequent scholarship, can trace its foundations to the Renaissance.

Another type of critical stance emerged as a central element in political thought. In *The Prince*, Niccolò Machiavelli (1469–1527) reflected on the ruthless political competition among the princes of Europe for dominance over his hopelessly disunited native Italy. What Italy needed in his own generation, Machiavelli argued, was a unifier who possessed what Aristotle discussed in Book 5 of his *Politics*, namely a person of intuitive strength, valor, or indomitable spirit (Italian, *virtù*) to take the proper steps—subtle or brutal—when political success was to be achieved. Many Renaissance scholars preferred Plato, but Machiavelli remained faithful to Aristotle, the superior political realist—an Aristotle held in high esteem centuries later by the American founding fathers.

interactive timeline

- **1506–1558** Reign of King Charles V of Spain
- **1514** First formulation of the heliocentric solar system by Nicolaus Copernicus
- **1517** Martin Luther posts his 95 theses; beginning of Protestant Reformation
- **1524–1525** German Peasants' War
- **1545** Beginning of Catholic Reformation
- **1562–1598** French war of religion
- **1565–1620** Dutch Protestant war of liberation from Spain
- **1571–1630** Johannes Kepler, discoverer of the elliptical paths of the planets
- **1589–1610** Reign of King Henry IV of France

- **1556–1598** Reign of King Philip II of Spain, the Netherlands, and the Americas
- **1604** Galileo Galilei's first formulation of the mathematical law of falling bodies
- **1618–1648** Thirty Years' War in Germany
- **1639–1660** Religious wars and aftermath in England, Scotland, and Ireland
- **1643–1715** King Louis XIV of France
- **1687** Isaac Newton unifies physics and astronomy
- **1688** "Glorious Revolution" in England
- **1690** Denis Papin's first steam engine
- **1740–1786** Frederick II, builder of the centralizing state of Prussia

Albrecht Dürer, *The Fall of Man (Adam and Eve)*, 1504

The Renaissance Arts In Italy, the reception of the new texts of the fifteenth century was paralleled by a new artistic way of looking at the Roman past and the natural world. The first artists to adopt this perspective were the sculptor Donatello (ca. 1386–1466) and the architect Filippo Brunelleschi (1377–1446), who received their inspiration from Roman imperial statues and ruins. The artistic triumvirate of the high Italian Renaissance was composed of Leonardo da Vinci (1452–1519), Michelangelo (1475–1564), and Raphael (1483–1520). Inspired by the Italian creative outburst, the Renaissance flourished also in Germany, the Netherlands, and France, making it a Europe-wide phenomenon (see Source 17.4).

The earliest musical composers of the Renaissance in the first half of the fifteenth century were Platonists, who considered music a part of a well-rounded education. The difficulty, however, was that the music of the Greeks or Romans was completely unknown. A partial solution for this difficulty was found through emphasizing the relationship between the word—that is, rhetoric—and music. In the sixteenth century this emphasis coincided with the Protestant and Catholic demand for liturgical music, such as hymns, masses, and *madrigals* (verses sung by unaccompanied voices). A pioneer of this music was the Italian composer Giovanni Pierluigi da Palestrina (ca. 1525–1594), who represented Renaissance music at its most exquisite.

The theater was a relatively late expression of the Renaissance. The popular mystery, passion, and morality plays from the centuries prior to 1400 continued in Catholic countries. In Italy, in the course of the fifteenth century, the *commedia dell'arte* (a secular popular theater) emerged, often using masked actors in plays of forbidden love, jealousy, and adultery. In England during the sixteenth century the popular traveling theater troupes became stationary and professional, attracting playwrights who composed more elaborate plays. Sponsored by the aristocracy and the Elizabethan court, playwrights wrote hundreds of scripts—some 600 are still extant—beginning in the 1580s. The best known among these playwrights was William Shakespeare (1564–1616), who also acted in his tragedies and comedies.

The Baroque Arts The Renaissance gave way around 1600 to the Baroque, which dominated the arts until about 1750. Two factors influenced its emergence. First, the Protestant Reformation, Catholic Reformation, and religious wars changed the nature of patronage, on which architects, painters, and musicians depended. Many Protestant churches, opposed to imagery as incompatible with their view of early Christianity, did not sponsor artists for the adornment of their buildings with religious art. Wealthy urban merchants, often Protestant, stepped into the breach but avoided paintings with religious themes, preferring instead secular portraits, still lifes, village scenes, and landscapes.

Second, the predilection for Renaissance measurement, balance, and restraint gave way in both Catholic and Protestant regions to greater spontaneity and dramatic effect. Even more pronounced was the parallel shift in church and palace architecture to a "baroque" voluptuousness of forms and decorations, exemplified by Bavarian and Austrian Catholic churches, the Versailles Palace, and St. Paul's Cathedral in London, all completed between 1670 and 1750. Baroque music, benefitting from ample church and palace patronage and exemplified by the Italian Antonio Vivaldi (1678–1741) and the German Johann Sebastian Bach (1685–1750), experienced a veritable explosion of unrestrained exploration.

Renaissance Art. Brunelleschi's cupola for the cathedral of Florence, completed in 1436, was one of the greatest achievements of the early Renaissance (*a*). Raphael's *School of Athens* (1509–1510) depicts some 50 philosophers and scientists, with Plato (in red tunic) and Aristotle (blue) in the center of the painting (*b*). Peter Brueghel's *The Harvesters* (1565) shows peasants taking a lunch break (*c*).

image analysis

The New Sciences

Eastern Christian scholars invited from Byzantium to Florence in Italy during the first half of the fifteenth century brought with them Hellenistic scientific treatises, which aroused great interest among Italian Renaissance scholars. Battle lines were drawn between those scholars who continued to adhere to the Aristotelian-scholastic scientific method, even though this method had undergone significant changes during the 1300s, and scholars (such as Copernicus) who were more interested in newly translated mathematical, astronomical, and geographical texts. Eventually, in the 1600s, two scientific pioneers—Galileo and Newton—abandoned much of the *qualitative* scientific method of Aristotelian scholasticism in favor of the quantitative, *mathematized* science of physics. In the eighteenth century, Newton's unified astronomical-physical-based science of a mechanical, deterministic universe became the foundation for the development of modern scientific–industrial society.

Copernicus's Incipient New Science According to Aristotle, nature was composed of the four elements of (in ascending order of lightness) earth, water, air, and fire. In astronomical terms, he thought that these elements formed distinct layers, together shaping the world. In geographical terms, however, it was obvious to Aristotle that not all earth was submerged by water. He knew that Europe, Asia, and Africa formed a contiguous land mass of continents above water. Aristotle did not resolve the contradiction in his writings, but subsequent medieval scholars sought to find a resolution. They developed the theory of the "floating apple," whereby they assumed that most of earth was submerged, and a minimal protruding amount—the three continents—was surrounded everywhere by water.

During the Renaissance, the *Geography*, written by the Hellenistic cosmographer Ptolemy (see Chapter 5), became available from Constantinople. This important work proposed the geographical concept of a globe composed of a single sphere of intermingled earth and water. When Nicolaus Copernicus (1473–1543) appeared on the scene, scholars were still grappling with these competing theories of the floating apple and the intermingled earth–water spheres.

Copernicus was born in Torun, a German-founded city which had come under Polish rule a few years before his birth. He began his studies at the University of Kraków, the only eastern European school to offer courses in astronomy. During the years 1495–1504, he continued his studies—of canon law, medicine, geography, cosmography, and astrology—at Italian universities. In 1500 he briefly taught mathematics in Rome and perhaps read Greek astronomical texts translated from Arabic in the library of the Vatican. Eventually, Copernicus graduated with a degree in canon law and took up an administrative position at the cathedral of Torun, which allowed him time to pursue astronomical research.

Sometime between 1507 and 1514 Copernicus realized that the discovery of the Americas in 1492 provided a decisive empirical proof for the theory of the world as a single earth–water sphere. During this time, it is likely that he saw the new world map by the German cartographer Martin Waldseemüller (ca. 1470–1520), which made him aware of the existence of the Americas as hitherto unknown inhabited lands on the other side of the world. Much more land protruded from the water and was not limited to the interconnected land mass of Eurasia–Africa, than had been previously assumed in the floating-apple theory.

As a result, this theory became questionable. Copernicus firmly espoused the Ptolemaic theory of the single intermingled water–earth sphere with mountainous protrusions. A globe with well-distributed water and land masses is a perfect body that moves in perfect circular paths, so he argued further, and formulated his hypothesis, according to which the earth is a body that has the same appearance and performs the same motions as the other bodies in the planetary system. The discovery of the Americas, therefore, can be considered as the empirical trigger that convinced Copernicus of the correctness of his trigonometric calculations, which removed the earth from the center of the planetary system and made it revolve around the sun.

Copernicus's heliocentric universe

Galileo's Mathematical Physics During the near century between the births of Copernicus and Galileo Galilei (1564–1642), mathematics—with its two branches of Greek geometry and Arabic algebra—improved considerably. Euclid's *Elements*, badly translated from Arabic in the late twelfth century, with a garbled definition of proportions, was retranslated correctly from the original Greek in 1543. Shortly thereafter, the new translation in 1544 of a text on floating and descending bodies by the Hellenistic scholar Archimedes (287–212 BCE) attracted intense scholarly attention. The text, unknown to the Muslims, had been translated from the Greek in the thirteenth century but subsequently remained unappreciated, on account of its incompatibility with the then-prevailing Aristotelian scholasticism.

What was required for a scholar critical of scholastic traditions was to combine geometry, algebra, and Archimedean physics. In 1604, that scholar appeared in the person of Galileo, when he formulated his famous mathematical "law of falling bodies." It is true that this law had been foreshadowed by the reflections of scholastic scholars at the University of Oxford's Merton College and the University of Paris in

Waldseemüller's 1507 World Map. The German mapmaker Martin Waldseemüller was the first western Christian to draw a world map which included the newly discovered Americas. He gave them the name "America" after the Italian explorer Amerigo Vespucci (1454–1512), who was the first to state that the Americas were a separate land mass, unconnected to Asia. The single copy of Waldseemüller's map still extant is among the holdings of the US Library of Congress.

image analysis

the 1300s. But these earlier scholars reflected on the logical and/or geometric properties of motion only "according to imagination." Galileo was the scholar who systematically combined imagination with empirical research and experimentation and thereby became the founder of what we now call the (mathematized) New Sciences.

Running Afoul of the Church Galileo was not only a physicist but also a first-rate astronomer, one of the first to use a telescope, which had been recently invented in Flanders. On the basis of his astronomical work, in 1610 he received a richly endowed appointment as chief mathematician and philosopher at the court of the Medici, the ruling family of Florence. But his increasing fame also attracted the enmity of the Catholic Church.

As a proponent of Copernican heliocentrism, Galileo seemed to contradict the passage in the Hebrew Bible where God recognized the motion of the sun around the earth. (In Joshua 10:12–13, God stopped the sun's revolution for a day, in order to allow the Israelites to win a critical battle against the Amorites.) In contrast to the more tolerant pope at the time of Copernicus, the Roman Inquisition favored a strictly literal interpretation of this passage, which implied that God had halted the sun's motion around the earth. In 1632 Galileo found himself condemned to house arrest and forced to make a public repudiation of heliocentrism (see Source 17.5).

Galileo's views of the moon

The condemnation of Galileo had a chilling effect on scientists in the southern European countries where the Catholic Reformation was dominant (see p. 499). Prudent patrons reduced their stipends to scientists, and scientific research subsequently declined. During the seventeenth century, interest in the New Sciences shifted increasingly to France, Germany, the Netherlands, and England. In these countries, no single church authority, of either the Catholic or the Protestant variety, was sufficiently dominant until the end of the seventeenth century to enforce the literal understanding of scripture. As a result, these countries produced numerous mathematicians, astronomers, physicists, and inventors, Catholic as well as Protestant. The New Scientists in northern Europe had a certain liberty that their southern colleagues lacked. It was this relative intellectual freedom, not any great sympathy on the part of religious authorities for the New Sciences, which allowed the latter to flourish, especially in the Netherlands and England.

Iberian Natural Sciences The shift of New Sciences research to northwestern Europe notwithstanding, southern European countries such as Spain were well situated to make substantial scientific contributions, even if not in the New Sciences. Hundreds of botanists, geographers, ethnographers, physicians, and metallurgists fanned out across the new colonies to take advantage of what their northern colleagues in the New Sciences could not do: They researched the new plants, diseases, peoples, and mineral resources of the New World, Africa, and Asia with the traditional descriptive and qualitative methods of the natural sciences and accumulated a voluminous amount of knowledge. For long periods, the Habsburg monarch kept the manuscripts with this knowledge under wraps, fearful that his colonial competitors would benefit from them—hence it was only through recent research efforts that the Iberian contributions to the sciences in the 1500s and 1600s have become more widely known.

Isaac Newton's Mechanics In the middle of the English struggles between the Protestants and the Catholic/Catholicizing Stuart monarchs, Isaac Newton (1643–1727) brought the New Sciences of Copernicus and Galileo to their culmination. As a professor at the University of Cambridge, he worked in the fields of mathematics, optics, astronomy, physics, alchemy, and theology. His primary early contribution was calculus, a new field in mathematics, which he developed at the same time as the German philosopher Gottfried Wilhelm Leibniz (1646–1716). Later in his career, Newton unified the fields of physics and astronomy, establishing the so-called Newtonian synthesis. His *Mathematical Principles of Natural Philosophy,* published in 1687, was the towering achievement of the New Sciences. It established a deterministic universe following mathematical rules and formed the basis of science until the early twentieth century, when Albert Einstein's relativity theory superseded Newtonianism.

The New Sciences and Their Social Impact

Scientists in the seventeenth century were in close communication with each other. They met in scientific societies or residential salons. Popularizers introduced an increasingly large public to the New Sciences. Scientists carried out experiments with constantly improved scientific instruments, such as telescopes, microscopes, thermometers, and barometers. Experience with barometers led technically versatile scientists and engineers to experiment with vacuum chambers and cylinders operating with condensing steam. Experimentation culminated with the invention of the steam engine in England in 1712.

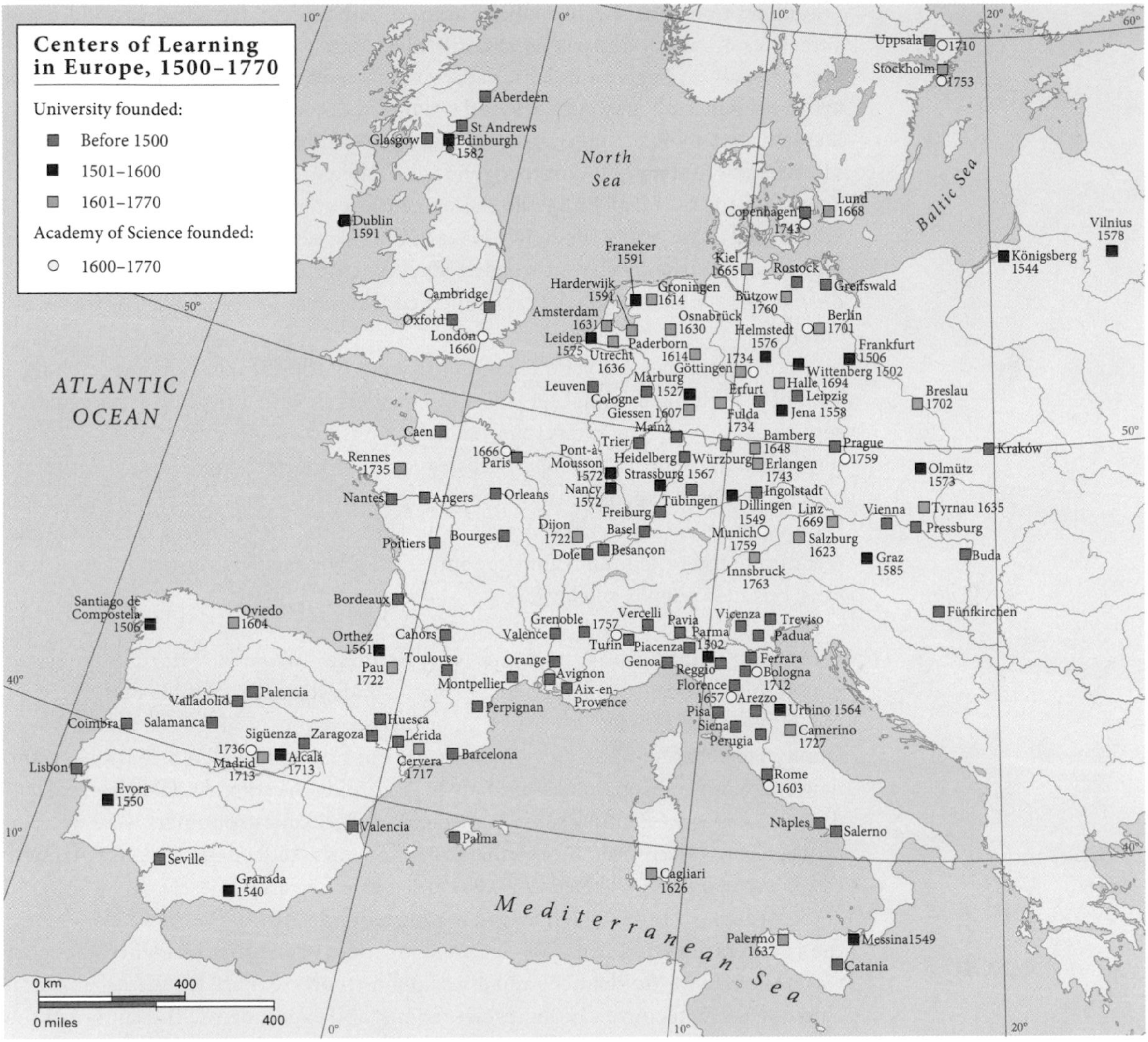

MAP **17.1** **Centers of Learning in Europe, 1500–1770.**

map analysis

New Science Societies When the Catholic Reformation drove the New Sciences to northwestern Europe, the Italian-style academies gave way to chartered scientific societies, such as the Royal Society of London (1660) and the Paris Academy of Sciences (1666). Other countries, like Prussia, Russia, and Sweden, soon followed suit. These societies employed staffs of administrators, co-opted scientists as fellows, held regular discussion meetings, challenged their fellows to answer scientific questions, awarded prizes, and organized field trips and expeditions. They also published transactions, correspondences, and monographs. Many societies attracted thousands of members—famous pioneers, obscure amateurs, technically proficient tinkerers, theoretical mathematicians, daring experimenters, and flighty dreamers—representing an important cross section of seventeenth-century urban society in northwest Europe (see Map 17.1).

Other popularizers were textbook authors and itinerant lecturers who addressed audiences of middle-class amateurs, instrument makers, and specialized craftspeople, especially in England and the Netherlands. Many lecturers toured coffeehouses, urban residences, country estates, and provincial schools. Coffeehouses allowed the literate urban public to meet, read the daily newspapers (first appearing in the early seventeenth century), and exchange ideas. Coffee, introduced from Ethiopia and Yemen via the Ottoman Empire in the sixteenth century, was the preferred nonalcoholic social drink before the arrival of tea in the later eighteenth century. Male urban literacy is estimated to have exceeded 50 percent in England and the Netherlands during this period, although it remained considerably lower in France, Germany, and Italy.

Some lecturers were veritable entrepreneurs of the speaking circuit, teaching a kind of "Newtonianism lite" for ladies and gentlemen with little time or patience for serious study. Other lecturers set up subscriptions for month-long courses. Wealthy businessmen endowed public lectures and supported increasingly elaborate experiments and expensive laboratory equipment. In the first half of the eighteenth century, the New Science triumphed in northwestern Europe in a scientifically and technically interested public of experimenters, engineers, instrument makers, artisans, business people, and lay folk.

Women, Social Salons, and the New Science Women formed a significant part of this public. In the fields of mathematics and astronomy, Sophie Brahe (1556–1643), sister of the Danish astronomer Tycho Brahe (1546–1601), and Maria Cunitz (see chapter-opening vignette) were the first to make contributions to the new astronomy of Copernicus and Kepler. According to estimates, in the second half of the seventeenth century some 14 percent of German astronomers were women. A dozen particularly prominent female astronomers practiced their science privately in Germany, Poland, the Netherlands, France, and England.

Another institution which helped in the popularization of the New Sciences was the salon. As the well-furnished, elegant living room of an urban residence, the salon was both a domestic chamber and a semipublic meeting place for the urban social elite to engage in conversations, presentations, and experiments. The culture of the salon emerged first in Paris sometime after the closure of the court-centered Palace Academy in the 1580s. Since the Catholic French universities remained committed to Aristotelian scholasticism, the emerging stratum of educated urban aristocrats and middle-class professionals turned to the salons as places to inform themselves about new scientific developments. Furthermore, French universities as well as scientific academies refused to admit women, in contrast to Italian and German institutions. The French salon, therefore, became a bastion of well-placed and respected female scholars.

One outstanding example of French salon science was Gabrielle-Emilie du Châtelet (1706–1749). In her youth, Châtelet fulfilled her marital duties to her husband, the Marquis of Châtelet. She had three children before turning to the sciences. In one of the Paris salons she met François Marie Arouet, known as Voltaire (1694–1778), the eighteenth-century Enlightenment writer, skeptic, satirist, and amateur Newtonian. Châtelet and Voltaire became intimate companions under the benevolent eyes of the marquis at the family estate in Lorraine in northeastern France. Although Voltaire published prolifically, Châtelet eventually outstripped him both in research and scientific understanding. Her lasting achievement was the translation of Newton's *Mathematical Principles* into French, published in 1759.

New Scientist. Maria Cunitz is honored today with a sculpture in Świdnica, Poland, where she grew up.

Discovery of the Vacuum Among the important scientific instruments of the day were telescopes, microscopes, and thermometers. It was the barometer, however, that was the crucial instrument for the exploration of the properties of the vacuum and condensing steam, eventually leading to the invention of the steam engine. The scientist laying the groundwork for the construction of the barometer was Evangelista Torricelli (1608–1647), a mathematician and assistant of Galileo. In collaboration with Florentine engineers, he experimented with mercury-filled glass tubes, demonstrating the existence of atmospheric pressure by the air and of vacuums in the tubes.

A few years later, the French mathematician and philosopher Blaise Pascal (1623–1662) had his brother-in-law haul a mercury barometer up a mountain to demonstrate lower air pressures at higher altitudes. Soon thereafter, scientists discovered the connection between changing atmospheric pressures and the weather, laying the foundations for weather forecasting. The discovery of the vacuum, the existence of which Aristotle had held to be impossible, made a deep impression on the scientific community in the seventeenth century and was an important step toward the practical application of the New Sciences to mechanical engineering in the eighteenth century.

The Steam Engine The French Huguenot scientist and engineer Denis Papin (ca. 1647–1712) took the first crucial step from the vacuum chamber to the steam engine. In 1690, when he was a court engineer and professor in Germany, Papin constructed a cylinder with a piston. Weights, via a cord and two pulleys, held the piston at the top of the cylinder. When heated, water in the bottom of the cylinder turned into steam. When subsequently cooled through the injection of water, the steam condensed, forcing the piston down and lifting the weights up. Papin spent his last years (1707–1712) in London, where the Royal Society of London held discussions of his papers, thereby alerting engineers, craftspeople, and entrepreneurs in England to the steam engine as a labor-saving machine. In 1712, the mechanic Thomas Newcomen built the first steam engine to pump water from coal mine shafts.

Altogether, it took a little over a century, from 1604 (Galileo) to 1712 (Newcomen), for Europeans to apply the New Sciences to engineering—that is, the construction of the steam engine. Had it not been for the New Sciences, this engine—based on contracting steam—would not have been invented. (Hero of Alexandria, who invented steam-driven machines in the first century CE, made use of the expanding force of steam.) Prior to 1600, mechanical inventions—such as the

Vacuum Power. In 1672, the mayor of Magdeburg, the New Scientist Otto von Guericke, demonstrated the experiment that made him a pioneer in the understanding of the physical properties of the vacuum. In the presence of German Emperor Ferdinand III, two teams of horses were unable to pull the two sealed hemispheres apart. Guericke had created a vacuum by pumping out the air from the two sealed copper spheres.

wheel, the compass, the stern rudder, and the firearm—were constructed by anonymous tinkerers with a good commonsense understanding of nature. In 1700, engineers had to have at least a basic understanding of mathematics and such abstract physical phenomena as inertia, gravity, vacuums, and condensing steam if they wanted to build a steam engine or other complex machinery.

The New Sciences: Philosophical Interpretations

The New Sciences engendered a pattern of radically new intellectual, religious, and political thinking, which evolved in the course of the seventeenth and early eighteenth centuries. This thought was largely incompatible with the inherited medieval scholasticism. It eventually evolved into a powerful instrument of critique of Christian doctrine and the constitutional order of the absolutist states. Initially, the new philosophical interpretations were confined to a few thinkers, but through the new concept of the social contract in the course of the 1700s they became a potent political force.

Descartes's New Philosophy After the replacement of qualitative with mathematical physics, brought about by Galileo with his law of descending bodies, the question arose whether Aristotelian philosophy and Catholic theology were still adequate for the understanding of reality. New Scientists perceived the need to start philosophizing and theologizing from scratch. The first major New Scientist who, in his own judgment, started a radical reconsideration of philosophy from the ground up was the Frenchman René Descartes (1596–1650). He earned a degree in law, traveling widely after graduation. In the service of the Dutch and Bavarian courts, he bore witness to the beginning of the Thirty Years' War and its atrocities committed in the name of religious doctrines. During the war, he spent two decades in the Netherlands, studying and teaching the New Sciences. His principal innovation in mathematics was the discovery that geometry could be converted through algebra into analytic geometry.

Descartes was shocked by the condemnation of Galileo and decided to abandon all traditional propositions and doctrines of the church as well as Aristotelianism.

Realizing that his common sense (that is, the five senses of seeing, hearing, touching, smelling, and tasting) was unreliable, he determined that the only reliable body of knowledge was thought, especially mathematical thought. As a person capable of thought, he concluded—bypassing his unreliable senses—that he existed: "I think, therefore I am" (*cogito ergo sum*). A further conclusion from this argument was that he was composed of two radically different substances, a material substance consisting of his body (that is, his senses) and another, immaterial substance consisting of his thinking mind. According to Descartes, body and mind, although joined through consciousness, belonged to two profoundly different realms of reality.

Descartes, selections from *A Discourse on Method* (1637)

Variations on Descartes's New Philosophy Descartes's radical distinction between body and mind stimulated a lively debate among a growing circle of philosophers of the New Sciences. Was this distinction only conceptual while reality was experienced as a unified whole? If the dualism was real as well as conceptual, which substance was more fundamental, sensual bodily experience or mental activity, as the creator of the concepts of experience? The answers of three philosophers—Baruch Spinoza, Thomas Hobbes, and John Locke—stood out in the 1600s. They set the course for two major directions of philosophy during the so-called Enlightenment of the 1700s (see Chapter 23), one Continental European and the other Anglo-American.

For Baruch Spinoza (1632–1677), Descartes's distinction between body and mind was to be understood only in a conceptual sense. In our daily experience we do not encounter either bodies or minds but persons endowed with both together. He therefore abandoned Descartes's distinction and developed a complicated philosophical system that sought to integrate Galilean nature with the ideas of God, the Good in ethics, and the Just in politics into a unified whole. The Jewish community of Amsterdam, into which he had been born, excommunicated him for heresy, since he seemed to make God immanent to the world. But he enjoyed a high esteem among fellow philosophers on the continent who appreciated his effort to moderate Descartes's radical mind–body distinction.

Both Thomas Hobbes (1588–1679) and John Locke (1632–1704) not only accepted Descartes's radical distinction; they furthermore made the body the fundamental reality and the mind a dependent function. Consequently, they focused on the bodily passions, not reason, as the principal human character trait. For Hobbes, the violent passions of aggression and fear were constitutive of human nature. He speculated that individuals in the primordial state of nature were engaged in a "war of all against all." To survive, they forged a social contract in which they transferred all power to a sovereign. Hobbes's famous book *Leviathan* (1651) can be read as a political theory of absolute rule, but his ideas of a social contract and transfer of power nevertheless imply a sprinkling of constitutionalism.

frontispiece to *Leviathan*

Locke, who lived through the less violent phases of the English religious wars, focused on the more benign bodily passion of acquisitiveness. Primordial individuals, so he argued, engaged as equals in a social contract for the purpose of erecting a government that protected their properties and, more generally, established a civil society governed by law. With Hobbes and Locke a line of new thought came to its conclusion, leading from Galileo's mathematized physics and Descartes's two substances to the ideas of absolutism as well as democratic constitutionalism.

Locke, *An Essay Concerning Human Understanding* (1690)

Patterns Up Close | Mapping the World

The world—its shape, its size, its orientation—has been rendered so thoroughly knowable by modern technology that we fail to appreciate how long it took to map the planet scientifically.

In 1400, no accurate map of the world existed anywhere on the planet. Prior to the first Portuguese sailing expeditions down the west coast of Africa in the 1420s and 1430s, mariners all over the world relied on local knowledge of winds, waves, and stars to navigate. The Portuguese were the first to use science to sail, adapting highly sophisticated scholarship in trigonometry, astronomy, and solar timekeeping developed in previous centuries by Jewish and Muslim scientists in Iberia.

Crucial to this novel approach was latitude. Mathematically challenging, fixing exact latitude required precise calculations of the daily changes in the path of the sun relative to the earth and determination of the exact height of the sun. The invention of the nautical astrolabe in 1497 by the Jewish scientist Abraham Zacuto aided this process tremendously. Determining longitude was also important, and Jewish scientists in Portugal adapted a method based on the pioneering work of the Islamic astronomer al-Biruni (973–1048).

Although primarily resting on achievements in astronomical observation and measurement in the Jewish and Islamic scientific traditions, the new maps of the fifteenth century also drew on an innovation from another part of the world: the compass. Originating in China, the compass was first widely used as a navigational

Centralizing States and Religious Upheavals

The pattern of the centralizing state transforming the institutional structures of society was characteristic not only of the Ottoman and Habsburg Empires during 1450–1750, as we have seen in Chapter 16, but also of other countries of Europe, the Middle East, and India. The financial requirements for sustaining such a state required everywhere a reorganization of the relationship among rulers, ruling classes, and regional as well as local forces. The Protestant Reformation and religious wars slowed the pattern of central state formation, but once the religious fervor died down, two types of states emerged: the French, Russian, and Prussian landed centralizing state and the Dutch and English naval centralizing state.

The Rise of Centralized Kingdoms

The shift from feudal mounted and armored knights to firearm-equipped professional infantries led to the emergence of states whose rulers sought to strengthen the power of their administrations. Rulers sought to centralize state power, collect higher taxes to subsidize their infantries, and curb the decentralizing forces of the nobility, cities, and other local institutions. Not all autonomous units (such as city-states, city-leagues, and religious orders dating to the previous period, 600–1450) were able to survive the race to centralization. A winnowing process occurred during 1450–1550, which left only a few territorially coherent kingdoms in control of European politics.

instrument by Muslim sailors during the twelfth century. In the thirteenth century, mapmakers in the Mediterranean began to include compasses on portolans, or nautical charts, enabling sailors to follow their direction on a map.

With an accurate science for fixing latitude and improved knowledge for longitude (determining precise longitude would not be achieved until 1774 with the invention of the marine chronometer), the science of cartography was transformed in the fifteenth and sixteenth centuries. Any place on earth could be mapped mathematically in relation to any other place, and the direction in which one place lay in relation to another could be plotted using compass lines. By 1500 mapmakers could locate any newly discovered place in the world on a map, no matter how remote.

Portolan by Pedro Reinel. Drawn in 1504 by the great Portuguese cartographer Pedro Reinel (ca. 1462–ca. 1542), this nautical chart (portolan) shows compass lines and is the earliest known map to include lines of latitude.

Questions

- How were adaptations from various cultural traditions essential to the transformation of cartography in the fifteenth and sixteenth centuries?
- How are developments in cartography in this time period an example of the shift from descriptive science to mathematical science?

The Demographic Curve Following the demographic disaster of the Black Death in 1348 and its many subsequent cycles, the population of the European states expanded again after 1470. It reached its pre-1348 levels around 1550, with some 85 million inhabitants (not counting the Spanish Habsburg and Ottoman Empires). The population continued to grow until about 1600 (90 million), when it entered a half-century of stagnation during the coldest and wettest period in recorded history, the Little Ice Age (1550–1750).

During 1650–1750, the population rose slowly at a moderate rate from 105 to 140 million. In 1750, France (28 million) and Russia (21 million) were the most populous countries, followed by Germany (18 million), Italy (15 million), Poland (13 million), England (7 million), and the Netherlands and Sweden (2 million each). While the population figures of the individual countries for the most part bore little resemblance to their political importance during 1450–1750, as we shall see, the overall figures for Europe demonstrate that Western Christianity had risen by 1750 to the status of demographic equivalence to the two leading religious civilizations of India (155 million) and China (225 million).

A Heritage of Decentralization Bracketed between the two empires of the Ottomans and Habsburgs at either geographical end, Western Christian Europe during the second half of the fifteenth century was a quilt of numerous independent or autonomous units, including the nascent centralizing kingdoms of France and England, the Hanseatic League of trading cities, the territory ruled by the Catholic crusading order of Teutonic Knights, and the small kingdoms of Denmark, Sweden,

Norway, Poland–Lithuania, Bohemia, and Hungary. It furthermore comprised the principalities and cities of Germany, the duchy of Burgundy, the Alpine republic of Switzerland, and the city-states of Italy. At the northeastern periphery was the Grand Duchy of Moscow, representing Eastern Christianity after the fall of Byzantium to the Ottomans in 1453. In this quilt, the majority of units competed vigorously with each other, seeking either to exploit the new possibilities which armies of mercenaries with firearms gave them or to survive as best as possible with just a handful of mercenaries.

TABLE 17.1 Victims of State Centralization in Europe, 1450–1600.

• Duchy of Burgundy, absorbed by France, 1477
• City-states Milan, Naples, taken by France 1499–1501
• Rest of Italy, except Venice, taken by Spain, 1550s
• Kingdoms of Bohemia and rump Hungary taken by Austrian Habsburgs, 1526; majority of Hungary to the Ottoman Empire
• Calais, last toehold of England on continent, to France, 1558
• Hanseatic League of ports in northern Europe, centered on the Free Cities of Lübeck and Hamburg, de facto dissolved 1669
• Duchy of Prussia lost by Teutonic Order to the kingdom of Poland, 1525; Prussia as fief of the kingdom of Poland, under its own dynasty of the Hohenzollern
• Prussia united with Brandenburg, 1618; Hohenzollerns as Polish vassals in Prussia and Habsburg vassals in Brandenburg
• Sweden independent from Denmark, 1523

Military and Administrative Capacities In the course of the sixteenth century, some kingdoms turned their mercenary troops into standing armies and stationed them in star-shaped forts. These forts were a fifteenth-century Italian innovation that made walls more resistant to artillery fire and trapped attackers in cross fires. Habsburg imperial as well as Dutch troops introduced the line infantry in the course of the sixteenth century. In this formation, three- to six-deep lines of musketeers advanced on a broad front toward the enemy, with the front line firing, stepping back to reload, and making room for the next line to step forward and repeat the actions. Since the line formation required extensive peacetime drills and maneuvers, the regimental system came into use. Soldiers formed permanent regiments and wore standardized, multicolored uniforms.

The French-invented flintlock gradually replaced the matchlock musket during 1620–1630, the advantage being that the flint produced a spark more quickly than the wick fuse. Similarly, during 1660–1700 the French introduced and gradually improved the bayonet—a sharp knife fixed to the end of the muzzle. With the appearance of the bayonet, pikemen, equipped with thrusting spears-cum-battle-axes for the protection of musketeers in hand-to-hand combat, were phased out. By 1750, armies in the larger European countries were both more uniform in their armaments and larger, increasing from a few thousand to tens of thousands of soldiers (see Map 17.2).

The military forces devoured copious amounts of tax money. Accordingly, taxes expanded substantially during the period 1450–1550. But rulers could not raise land, head, and commerce taxes without the formal (in assemblies) or informal (based on customs and traditions) assent of the ruling classes and cities. Similarly, villagers voted with their feet when taxes became too oppressive. The taxation limits were reached in most European countries in the mid-sixteenth century, and for the next two centuries rulers could raise additional finances only to the detriment of

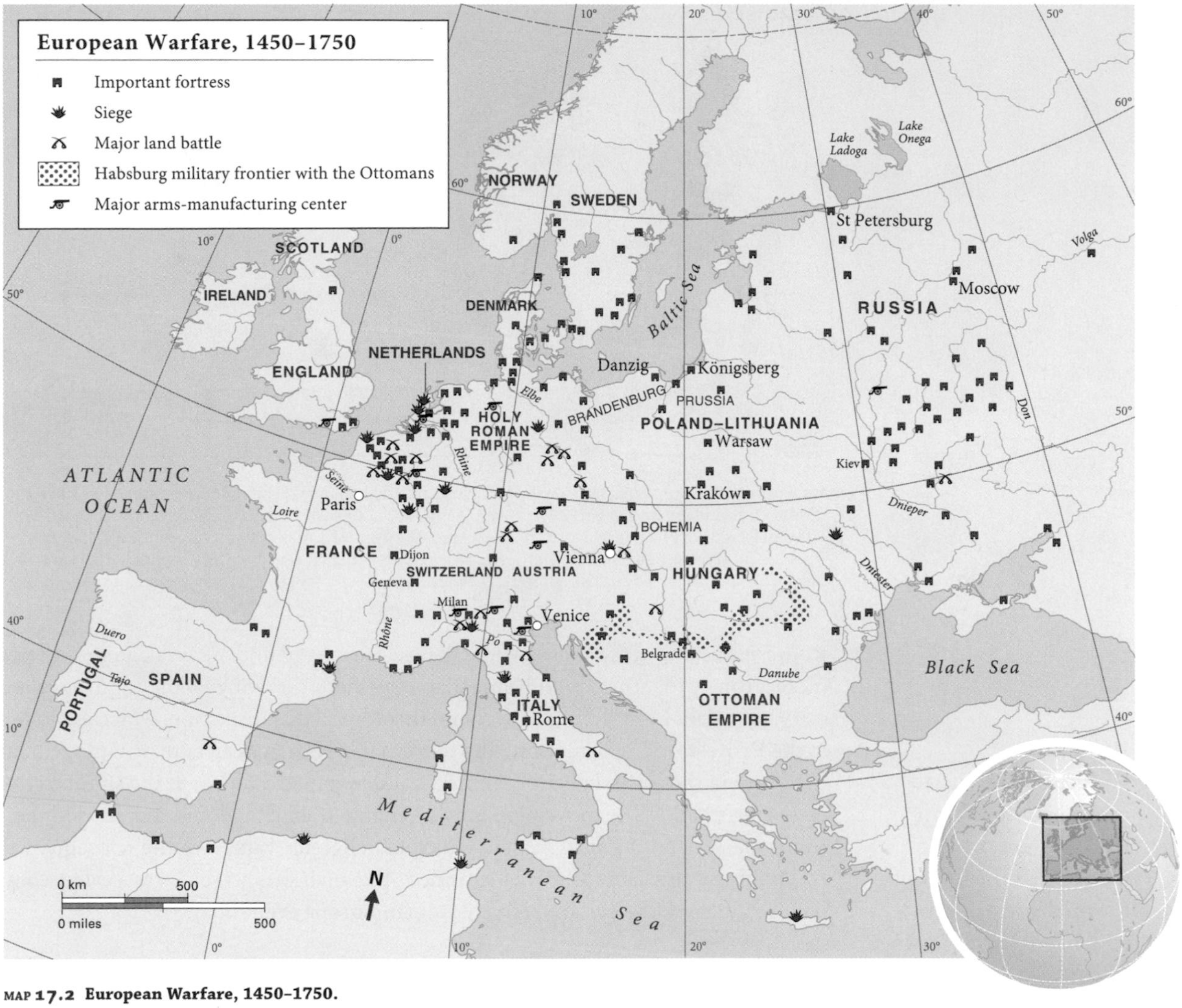

MAP 17.2 **European Warfare, 1450–1750.**

their previously acquired central powers, such as by borrowing from merchants and selling offices. The Netherlands was an exception. Only there did the urban population rise from 10 to 40 percent, willing to pay higher taxes on expanded urban manufactures and commercial suburban farming. The Dutch government also derived substantial revenues from charters granted to armed overseas trading companies. Given the severe limits on revenue-raising measures in most of Europe, the eighteenth century saw a general deterioration of state finances, which eventually became major contributing factors to the American and French Revolutions.

The Protestant Reformation, State Churches, and Independent Congregations

Parallel to the growing centralism of the kings, the popes restored the central role of the Vatican in the church hierarchy, after the devastating Great Schism of competing papal lines (1305–1415). Outwardly, the popes displayed this restoration through expensive Vatican construction projects that aroused considerable criticism outside

Musketeers. These pictures from an English illustrated drill manual demonstrate the steps by which a seventeenth-century musketeer "makes ready" his weapon, typically in less than 30 seconds. In battle, a sergeant would stand alongside each company of musketeers, organizing its movements and volley fire. Once a rank of musketeers had discharged its weapons, it would move out of the way for another rank to fire. If combat was joined at close quarters, the musketeers would use their rifle butts as clubs.

Rome, especially in Germany, where the leading clergy under a weak emperor were more strongly identified with Rome than elsewhere. Growing literacy and lay religiosity helped in the growth of a profound theological dissatisfaction, which exploded in the **Protestant Reformation**. The Reformation began as an antipapal movement of reform in the early sixteenth century that demanded a return to the simplicity of early Christianity. The movement quickly engulfed the kingdoms and divided their ruling classes and populations alike. Vicious religious wars were the consequence. Although these wars eventually subsided, the divisions were never healed completely and mark the culture of many areas in Europe even today.

Protestant Reformation: Broad movement to reform the Roman Catholic Church, the beginnings of which are usually associated with Martin Luther.

Background to the Reformation Several religious and political changes in the fifteenth century led to the Protestant Reformation. One important religious shift was the growth of popular theology, a consequence of the introduction of the printing press (1454–1455) and the distribution of printed materials. A flood of devotional tracts, often read aloud to congregations of illiterate believers, catered to the spiritual interests of ordinary people. Many Christians attended Mass daily, confessed, and did penance for their sins. Wealthy Christians endowed saint cults, charitable institutions, or confraternities devoted to the organization of processions and passion plays. Poor people formed lay groups or studied scripture on their own and devoted themselves to the simple life of the early Christians. More Europeans than in previous centuries had a basic, though mostly literal, understanding of Christianity.

An important political change in the fifteenth century was an increasing inability for the popes, powerful in Rome, to appoint archbishops and bishops outside Italy. The kings of France, Spain, England, and Sweden were busy transforming their kingdoms into centralized states, in which they reduced the influence of the popes. Only in Germany, where the powers of the emperor and the rulers in the various principalities canceled each other out, was the influence of the popes still strong. What remained to the popes was the right to collect a variety of dues in the kingdoms of Europe. They used these dues to finance their expensive and, in the eyes of many,

Erasmus, *Julius Excluded from Heaven* (1514)

luxuriously worldly administration and court in Rome, from which they engaged in European politics. One of the dues was the sale of **indulgences**, which, in popular understanding, were tickets to heaven. Many contemporary observers found the discrepancy between declining papal power and the remaining financial privileges disturbing and demanded reforms.

Indulgence: Partial remission of sins after payment of a fine or presentation of a donation. Remission would mean the forgiveness of sins by the Church, but the sinner still remained responsible for his or her sins before God.

Luther's Reformation One such observer was Martin Luther (1483–1546), an Augustinian monk, ordained priest, and New Testament professor in northeastern Germany. Luther was imbued with deep personal piety and confessed his sins daily, doing extensive penance. After a particularly egregious sale of indulgences in his area, in 1517 he wrote his archbishop a letter with 95 theses in which he condemned the indulgences and other matters as contrary to scripture. Friends translated the theses from Latin into German and made them public. What was to become the Protestant Reformation had begun.

News of Luther's public protest traveled quickly across Europe. Sales of indulgences fell off sharply. In a series of writings, Luther spelled out the details of the church reform he envisaged. One reform proposal was the elevation of original New Testament scripture over tradition—that is, over canon law and papal decisions. Salvation was to be by faith alone; good works were irrelevant. Another reform was the declaration of the priesthood of all Christians, doing away with the privileged position of the clergy as mediators between God and believers who could forgive sins. A third reform was a call to German princes to begin church reform in their own lands through their power over clerical appointments, even if the Habsburg emperor was opposed. Finally, by translating the Bible into German, Luther made the full sacred text available to all who, by reading or listening, wanted to rely solely on scripture as the source of their faith. Luther's Bible was a monument of the emerging literary German language. A forceful and clear writer in his translation and own publications, Luther fully explicated the basics of Protestantism.

Reaction to Luther's Demands Both emperor and pope failed in their efforts to arrest Luther and suppress his call for church reform. The duke of Saxony was successful in protecting the reformer from seizure. Emperor Charles V, a devout Catholic, considered Castile's successful church reform of half a century earlier to be fully sufficient. In his mind, Luther's demands for church reform were to be resisted. Two other pressing concerns, however, diverted the emperor's attention. First, the Ottoman-led Islamic threat, in eastern Europe and the western Mediterranean, had to be met with decisive action. Second, his rivalry with the French king precluded the formation of a common Catholic front against Luther. Enthusiastic villagers and townspeople in Germany exploited Charles's divided attention and abandoned both Catholicism and secular obedience. A savage civil war, called the Peasants' War, engulfed Germany from 1524 to 1525, killing perhaps as many as 100,000 people.

Luther and other prominent reformers were horrified by the carnage. They drew up church ordinances that regulated preaching, church services, administrative councils, education, charity, and consistories for handling disciplinary matters. In Saxony, the duke endorsed this order in 1528. He thereby created the model of Lutheran Protestantism as a state religion, in which the rulers were protectors and supervisors of the churches in their territories. A decade later, Saxony was fully Lutheran.

A minority of about half a dozen German princes and the kings of Denmark and Sweden followed suit. In England, Protestants gained strength in the wake of

Anti-Catholic Propaganda. This anonymous woodcut of 1520 by a German satirist depicts the devil (complete with wings and clawed feet) sitting on a letter of indulgence and holding a money collection box. The devil's mouth is filled with sinners who presumably bought letters of indulgence in good faith, thinking they had been absolved of their sins.

the break with Rome by Henry VIII (r. 1509–1547) and his assumption of church leadership in his kingdom. Although remaining Catholic, he surrounded himself with religious reformers and proclaimed an Anglican state church whose creed and rites combined elements of Catholicism and Protestantism. In Switzerland, several cantons adopted the religious reforms of Huldrych Zwingli (1484–1531). In Scotland, the reforms of John Knox (1514–1572) became the foundation for the state church. Thus, most of northern Europe followed a pattern of alliances between Protestant reformers and the state (see Map 17.3).

Calvinism in Geneva and France In France, as in England, the king controlled all church appointments. King Francis I, however, did not take the final step toward the creation of an independent state church. Since he competed with Charles V of the Habsburg Empire for dominance over the papacy in Italy, he had to appear especially loyal and devout. When a few Protestants in France went public with their demands for church reform, Francis I gave them the stark choice of exile or burning at the stake.

One reformer who chose exile was the French lawyer John Calvin (Jean Cauvin, 1509–1564). During his exile, he passed at one point through Geneva, where a French friend of his beseeched him to help him in preaching the faith. Calvin relented and began a stormy and at one point interrupted career as the city's religious reformer. Geneva—not yet part of Switzerland and under the nominal rule of the duke of Savoy (himself under the nominal rule of the Habsburgs)—was unsure about which path of reform to embrace. It took Calvin well into the 1550s before his form of Protestantism prevailed in the city.

As expressed in Calvin's central work, *Institutes of the Christian Religion* (1536), and numerous other writings, a crucial doctrine of Calvin's was *predestination*. According to this doctrine, God has "predestined" each human prior to birth for heaven or hell. Believers could only hope, through faith alone, that sometime during a life of moral living they would receive a glimpse of their fate. In contrast to Luther, however, Calvin made the enforcement of morality through a formal code, administered by local authorities, part of his version of Protestantism.

Interestingly, this code did not prohibit the taking of interest on loans. While Luther as well as the Catholic Church, in accordance with scripture, condemned all interest as usury, Calvin considered a few percentage points to be entirely justifiable. The strong condemnation of interest on loans in the Hebrew Bible was rooted in the precariousness of Mediterranean rain-fed agriculture: Several years of drought could drive farmers into total dependence on landlords if the latter demanded interest on loans. By placing moneylending into the increasingly urban context of the 1500s, Calvin displayed a greater sense of economic reality than Luther. Acquiring wealth with the help of money and thereby perhaps gaining a glimpse of one's fate became one of the hallmarks of Calvinism. Wealth began to become respectable in Christian society.

Calvin died in his Genevan exile, but Geneva-trained Calvinist preachers went to France and the Netherlands in the mid-1500s. Under the protection of local

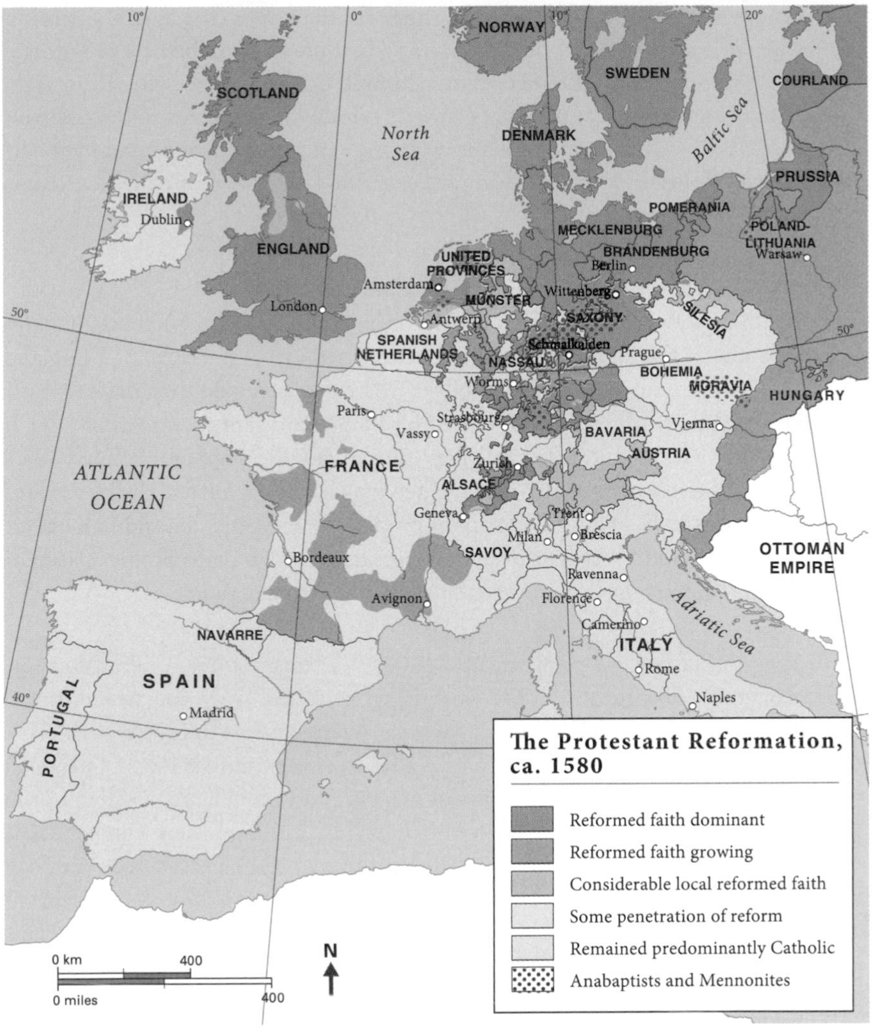

MAP **17.3** **The Protestant Reformation, ca. 1580.**

magistrates, they organized the first clandestine independent Calvinist congregations. Calvinist religious self-organization by independent congregations thus became a viable alternative to Lutheran state religion (see Source 17.2).

The Catholic Reformation The rivalry between Spain and France made it initially difficult for the popes to tackle the problem of Catholic reforms in order to meet the Protestant challenge. When they finally called together the Council of Trent (1545–1563), they abolished payment for indulgences and phased out other church practices considered to be corrupt. These actions launched the **Catholic Reformation**, an effort to gain back dissenting Catholics. Supported by the kings of Spain and France, however, the popes made no changes to the traditional doctrines of faith together with good works, priestly mediation between believer and God, and monasticism. They even tightened church control through the revival of the papal Inquisition and a new Index of Prohibited Books.

Catholic Reformation: Also Counter-Reformation. Reaffirmation of Catholic papal supremacy and the doctrine of faith together with works as preparatory to salvation; such practices as absenteeism (bishops in Rome instead of in their bishoprics) and pluralism (bishops and abbots holding multiple appointments) were abolished.

To counterbalance these punitive institutions, the popes furthered the work of the Basque priest Ignatius Loyola (1491–1556). At the head of the new order of the Society of Jesus, or Jesuits, Loyola devoted himself tirelessly to the education of the clergy, establishment of a network of Catholic schools and colleges, and conversion of Protestants as well as non-Christians by missionaries to the Americas and eastern Asia. Thanks to Jesuit discipline, Catholics regained a semblance of self-assurance against the Protestants.

Religious Wars and Political Restoration

The growth of Calvinism led to a civil war in France and a war of liberation from Spanish Catholic rule in the Netherlands in the later sixteenth century. In England, the slow pace of reform in the Anglican Church, with which neither Calvinists nor Catholics could identify, erupted in the early seventeenth century into a civil war. In Germany, the Catholic–Protestant struggle turned into the devastating Thirty Years' War (1618–1648), which France and Sweden won at the expense of the Habsburgs. On the religious level, Western Christians grudgingly accepted denominational toleration; on the political level, the centralizing states evolved into polities based on absolutism, tempered by provincial and local administrative practices.

Civil War in France During the mid-1500s, Calvinism in France grew to about 1,200 congregations, mostly in the western cities of the kingdom, where literate merchants and craftspeople catering to trade overseas were receptive to Protestant publications. Calvinism was essentially an urban denomination; and peasants, rooted more deeply in traditional ways of life, did not join in large numbers. Some 2 million, or 10 percent of the total population of 18.5 million, were Huguenots, as the Protestants were called in France. They continued to be persecuted, but given their numbers, it was impossible for the government to imprison and execute them all. In 1571, they even met in a kingdom-wide synod, where they ratified their congregational church order. They posed a formidable challenge to French Catholicism.

In many cities, relations between Huguenots and Catholics were uneasy. From time to time, groups of agitators crashed each other's church services. Hostilities escalated after 1560 when the government weakened under a child king and was unable to deal with the increasingly powerful Huguenots. In four western cities the Huguenots achieved self-government and full freedom of religious practice from the crown. Concerned to find a compromise, in 1572 the now reigning king married his sister to the leader of the Huguenots, King Henry III of Navarre (later King Henry IV of France, 1589–1610), a Protestant of the Bourbon family in southwestern France. Henry detested the fanaticism that surrounded him.

Only 6 days after the wedding, on St. Bartholomew's Day (August 24, 1572), outraged members of the Catholic aristocracy perpetrated a wholesale slaughter of thousands of Huguenots. This massacre, in response to the assassination of a French admiral, occurred with the apparent connivance of the court. For over a decade and a half, civil war raged, in which Spain aided the Catholics and Henry enrolled German and Swiss Protestant mercenaries. A turning point came only in 1589 when Henry of Navarre became King Henry IV of France. Surviving nearly three-dozen plots against his life, the new king needed 9 years and two conversions to Catholicism—"Paris is well worth a Mass," he is supposed to have quipped—before he was able to calm the religious fanaticism among the majority of French people.

With the Edict of Nantes in 1598, he decreed freedom of religion for Protestants. A number of staunch Catholic adherents were deeply offended by the edict as well as the alleged antipapal policies of Henry IV. The king fell victim to an assassin in 1610. Catholic resentment continued until 1685, when King Louis XIV revoked the edict and triggered a large-scale emigration of Huguenots to the Netherlands, Germany, England, and North America. At last, France was Catholic again.

The Dutch War of Independence In the Netherlands, the Spanish overlords were even more determined to keep the country Catholic than the French monarchs. When Charles V resigned in 1556 (effective 1558), his son Philip II (r. 1556–1598) became king of Spain and the Netherlands, consisting of the French-speaking regions of Wallonia in the south and the Dutch-speaking regions of Flanders and Holland in the north. Like his father, Philip was a staunch supporter of the Catholic Reformation. He asked the Jesuits and the Inquisition to aggressively persecute the Calvinists. For better effect, Philip subdivided the bishoprics into smaller units and recruited clergymen in place of members of the nobility.

In response, in 1565 the nobility and Calvinist congregations rose in revolt. They dismantled the bishoprics and cleansed the churches of images and sculptures, thereby triggering what was to become a Protestant war of Dutch liberation from Catholic Spanish overlordship (1565–1621). Philip retaliated by sending in an army that succeeded in suppressing the liberation movement. He reimposed Catholicism, and executed thousands of rebels, many of them members of the Dutch aristocracy.

Remnants of the rebellion struggled on and, in 1579, renewed the war of liberation in three of the 17 northern provinces making up the Netherlands. Later joined by four more provinces, the people in these breakaway regions called themselves members of the "United Provinces of the Dutch Republic." Spain refused to recognize the republic and kept fighting until acute Spanish financial difficulties prompted the truce of 1609–1621. Although drawn into fighting again during the Thirty Years' War, the Netherlands gained its full independence eventually in 1648.

first Dutch national atlas, 1622

Civil War in England As in the Netherlands, the prevalent form of Protestantism in England was Calvinism. During the sixteenth century, the Calvinists numbered about 10 percent in a kingdom of some 7 million in which the Anglican Church encompassed the vast majority of subjects. English Catholics numbered 3 percent, but contrary to the Calvinists they refused to recognize the king as the head of the Anglican church. The percentage of Calvinists was the same as in France before 1685, but the partially reformed Anglican Church under the tolerant queen Elizabeth I (1533–1603) was able to hold them in check.

The Calvinists were, furthermore, a fractious group, encompassing moderate and radical tendencies that neutralized each other. Among the radicals were the Puritans, who demanded the abolition of the Anglican clerical hierarchy and a new church order of independent congregations. When Anglican Church reform slowed with the arrival of the Stuart monarchs on the throne of England (1603–1685), unfortunately the balance among the religious tendencies unraveled. As rulers of England, the Stuarts were officially heads of the Anglican state church, but except for the first king, the three successors were either Catholics or Catholic sympathizers. Since they were furthermore rulers of what was called the England of the Three Kingdoms they found it impossible to maneuver among the demands of the English

Puritans, Scottish Presbyterians (self-governing regional Calvinists), and Catholic Irish. The issue of how little or how far the Anglican Church had been reformed away from Catholicism and how dominant it should be in the three realms became more and more divisive (see Source 17.1).

In addition, the Stuarts were intent on building their version of the centralized state. They collected taxes without the approval of Parliament. Many members resented being bypassed since Parliament was the constitutional co-sovereign of the kingdom. A slight majority in the House of Commons was Puritan, and what they considered the stalled church reform added to their resentment. Eventually, when all tax resources were exhausted, the king had to call Parliament back together. The two sides were unable, however, to come to an agreement and civil war broke out. Since this war was also a conflict among the Three Kingdoms, it had both religious and regional aspects (1639–1651).

The war was generally less vicious than that in France. Nevertheless, because of widespread pillage and destruction of crops and houses, the indirect effects of the war for the population of thousands of villages were severe. The New Model Army, a professional body of 22,000 troops raised by the Puritan-dominated English Parliament against the royal forces, caused further upheavals by cleansing villages of their "frivolous" seasonal festivals, deeply rooted in local traditions. In the end, the monarchy was replaced with a republican theocracy, the "Commonwealth of England."

Republic, Restoration, and Revolution The ruler of this theocracy, Oliver Cromwell (r. 1649–1658), was a Puritan member of the lower nobility (the gentry) and a commander in the New Model Army. After dissolving Parliament, Cromwell handpicked a new Parliament but ruled for the most part without its consent. Since both Scotland and Ireland were opposed to the English Puritans, Cromwell waged a savage war of submission against the two. The Dutch and Spanish, also opponents of the Puritans, were defeated in naval wars that substantially increased English shipping power in the Atlantic. But fear among the gentry in Parliament of a permanent centralized state led to a refusal of further financial subsidies for the military. After Cromwell's death in 1658, it took just 3 years to restore the Stuart monarchy and the Anglican state church to their previous places.

The recalled Stuart kings, however, resumed the policies of centralization. As before, the kings called Parliament together only sparingly and raised funds without its authorization. But their standing army of 30,000, partially stationed near London, was intended more to intimidate the parliamentarians than to subjugate them. In 1687, the king, James II (r. 1685–1688), even espoused a major plan of reform, as new research has shown. In the "Glorious Revolution" of 1688, a defiant Parliament deposed the king and made his daughter Mary and her Dutch husband William the new co-regents.

The Thirty Years' War in Germany As religious tensions were mounting in England during the early seventeenth century, similar tensions erupted into a full-blown war in Germany, bringing about the second such conflagration in a century, the Thirty Years' War. As we saw earlier, even though the rulers of the German principalities had made either Catholicism or Protestantism their state religion, minorities were tolerated or even admitted to offices. The Jesuit-educated Ferdinand II (r. 1619–1637), ruler of the Holy Roman Empire, however, refused to appoint Protestants in majority-Protestant Bohemia, of which the Habsburgs were kings since 1526. In response, Protestant leaders in 1618 renounced Ferdinand's authority and made the Calvinist prince of the Palatinate in the Rhineland their new king. With these events in Protestant Bohemia, open hostilities between the religious denominations began in Germany.

In a first round of war (1619–1630), Ferdinand and the Catholic princes suppressed the Bohemian rebellion and slowly advanced toward northern Germany, capturing Lutheran territories for reconversion to Catholicism and defeating Denmark. In 1630, however, the Lutheran king Gustavus II Adolphus (r. 1611–1632) of Sweden intervened. The king's main goal was the creation of a Swedish-Lutheran centralized state around the Baltic Sea, a project already begun before the Thirty Years' War.

Centralizing States at War. German imperial troops besiege Swedish troops in the northern German city of Stralsund in 1628. The etching shows typical features of the centralizing state, from top to bottom: galleon-style warships (successors of the caravel); a star-shaped fort (an Italian innovation) designed to withstand artillery barrages; the medieval walls of the city; musket-equipped infantry troops; field cannons; and the colorful Baroque uniforms worn by the musketeers of the period.

By aiding the German Lutherans, he hoped to consolidate or even increase his predominance in the region. Louis XIII (r. 1610–1643) of France granted Sweden financial subsidies, since he was concerned that Ferdinand's victories would further strengthen the Habsburg Spanish–Flemish–Austrian–German–Italian grip around France. With the politically motivated alliance between Sweden and France, the German Catholic–Protestant war turned into a war for state dominance in Europe.

The Swedes were initially successful but withdrew when Gustavus II Adolphus fell unexpectedly in battle. Ferdinand decided to compromise with the Protestant princes of Germany, by reestablishing the prewar divisions, in order to keep the French out of the war. But Louis XIII entered anyway, and during the next 13 years, French armies sought to cut the Habsburg supply lines from Italy to the Netherlands by occupying Habsburg Alsace. Swedish armies, exploiting the French successes against the Habsburgs, fought their way back into Germany. In the end, the Austrian–German Habsburgs, pressured on two sides and exhausted from the war, agreed in October 1648 to the Peace of Westphalia.

The agreement provided for religious freedom in Germany and ceded Habsburg territories in Alsace to France and the southern side of the Baltic Sea to Sweden. It granted territorial integrity to all European powers. The Spanish Habsburgs continued their war against France until 1659, when they also bowed to superior French strength, giving up parts of Flanders and northeastern Spain. In the Caribbean, Spain lost territories to France, the Netherlands, and England, accelerating the decline of Spain's overseas power. France emerged as the strongest country in Europe, and the Spanish-dominated Caribbean became an area of open power rivalry (see Map 17.4).

Absolutism in France? During its period of greatest political dominance, France came under the rule of its longest-reigning monarch, King Louis XIV (1643–1715). He was of small stature—for which he compensated with high-heeled shoes—but his hardy constitution and strong self-discipline helped him to dominate even the most grueling meetings with his advisors. He enjoyed pomp and circumstance and built Versailles—his gigantic palace and gardens near Paris, populated with 10,000 courtiers, attendants, and servants—into a site of almost continuous feasting, entertainment, and intrigue. It was here that Louis, the "Sun King," beamed benevolently with his "absolute" divine mandate upon his aristocracy and commoners alike (see Source 17.3).

Versailles played an important role in Louis' efforts to undercut the power of the nobility. Anyone with any aspirations of attracting the king's attention had to come to the palace to attend him. He kept both friends and potential enemies close by, forcing them to spend themselves lavishly into ruin to keep up with the fashions inspired by the king. Like the Tokugawa shoguns in Edo, Japan, he bypassed them administratively and ruled through central bureaucratic institutions (see Chapter 21).

Absolutism: Theory of the state in which the unlimited power of the king, ruling under God's divine mandate, was emphasized. In practice, it was neutralized by the nobility and provincial and local communities.

In practice, the French **absolutism** of Louis XIV and his eighteenth-century successors, as well as absolutism in other European countries, was a complex mixture of centralized and decentralized forces. On one hand, after the end of the religious wars in 1648, mercenary armies under autonomous dukes and counts disappeared from the European scene, replaced by permanent armies or navies under the central command of royal relatives or favorites. The kings also no longer called their assemblies of nobles and notables together to have new taxes approved (in France from 1614 to 1789), and thus many of the nobility's tax privileges disappeared.

On the other hand, the kings of the seventeenth century were acutely aware that true absolutism was possible only if the taxes were collected by centrally salaried

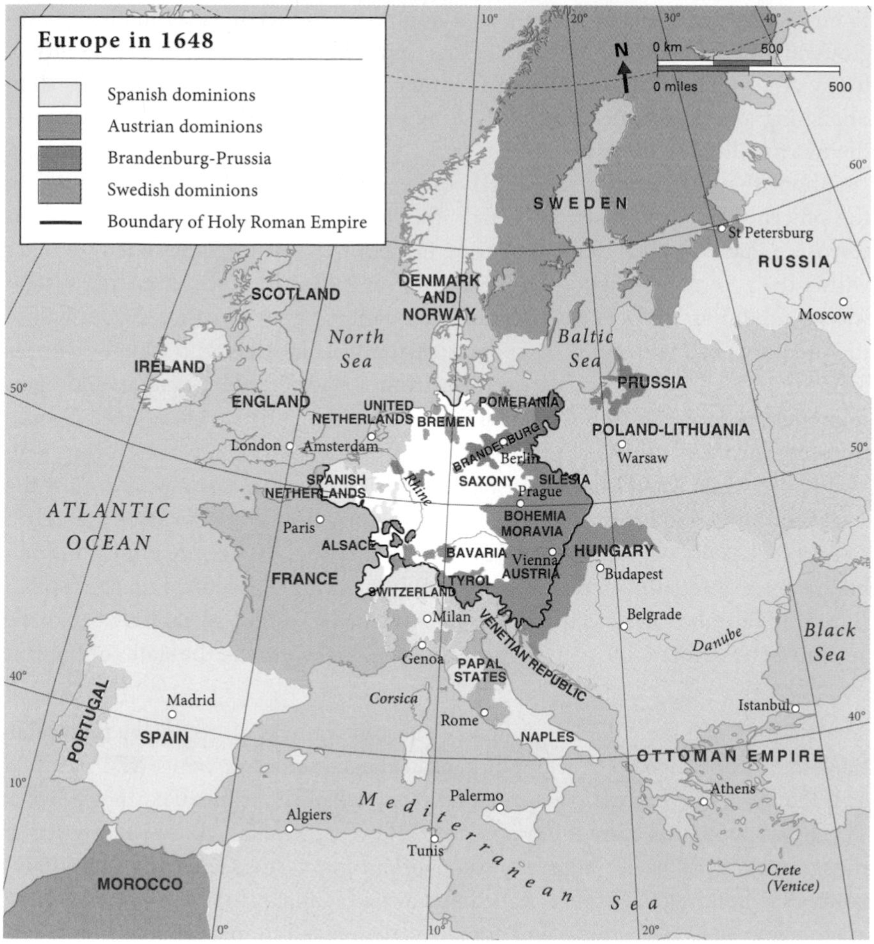

MAP 17.4 Europe in 1648.

employees. It was physically impossible, however, to transport tax revenues, in the form of silver money and grain, from the provinces to the capital, pay the central bureaucrats, and then cart the remaining money back to the provinces to pay salaried tax collectors there. A centrally paid bureaucracy would have required a central bank with provincial branches, using a credit and debit system. The failed experiment with such a bank in Paris from 1714 to 1720 demonstrates one such effort to find a solution to the central salarization problem. The bank's short life demonstrates that absolute central control was beyond the powers of the kings.

Instead, the kings had to rely on subcontracting out most offices and the collection of most taxes to the highest bidders, who then helped themselves to the collection of their incomes. Under Louis XIV, a total of 46,000 administrative jobs were available for purchase in Paris and the provinces. Anyone who had money or borrowed it from financiers was encouraged to buy an office—from the old aristocracy receiving rents from the farmers on their rural estates to ordinary merchants' sons with law degrees borrowing money from their fathers.

Once in office, these officers were often forced by the government to grant additional loans to the crown. To retain their loyalty, the government rewarded them with first picks for retaining their offices within the family. They were also privileged to buy landed estates or acquire titles of nobility to the secondary (and less prestigious) tier of the "nobility of the robe" (as opposed to the old first-tier "nobility of the sword," which by the seventeenth century was demilitarized). With this system of offering offices and titles for sale, the king sought to bind the financial interests of the two nobilities to those of his own.

About the only way for Louis XIV to keep a semblance of a watchful eye on the officeholders was to send salaried, itinerant *intendants* around the provinces to ensure that collecting taxes, rendering justice, and policing functioned properly within the allowable limits of the "venality of office," as the subcontracting system was called. Louis XIV had roughly one intendant for each province. About half of the provinces had *parlements*—appointed assemblies for the ratification of decrees from Paris—whose officeholders, drawn from the local noble, clerical, and commoner classes, frequently resisted the intendants. The Paris *parlement* even refused to accept royal writs carried by the intendants.

In later years, when Louis XIV was less successful in his many wars against the rival Habsburgs and Protestant Dutch than previously, the crown overspent and had to borrow heavily with little regard for the future. Louis' successors in the second half of the eighteenth century were saddled with crippling debts. French-inspired European "absolutism" was thus in practice a careful (or not so careful) balancing act between the forces of centralization and decentralization in the states of Europe.

The Rise of Russia Although France's absolutism was more theory than practice, its glorious ideological embodiment in the Versailles of Louis XIV spawned adaptations across Europe. These adaptations were most visible in eastern Europe, which was populated more thinly and had far fewer towns and cities. Since rulers in those areas did not have a large reservoir of urban commoners to aid them as administrators in building the centralized state, they had to make do with the landowning aristocracy. As a result, rulers and aristocracy connived to finance state centralization through an increased exploitation of the farmers in the villages: In the 1600s, their legal status deteriorated, their tax liabilities increased, and they became serfs.

Tsar (or Czar): Derived from "Caesar," title used by the Russian rulers to emphasize their imperial ambitions.

In Russia, **Tsar** Peter I, "the Great" (r. 1682–1725), of the Eastern Christian Romanov dynasty, was a towering figure who singlehandedly sought to establish the French-type centralized state during his lifetime. At nearly 7 feet tall, Peter was an imposing, energetic ruler, controllable only by his second wife (and former mistress) Catherine, a warmhearted woman and beloved tsarina. Peter invited western European soldiers, mariners, administrators, craftspeople, scholars, and artists into his service and succeeded within just a few years in building a disciplined army and imposing navy. He built ports on the Baltic Sea and established the new capital of St. Petersburg, distinguished by many very beautiful palaces and official buildings.

Peter the Great, "Decree on the Invitation to Foreigners" (1702)

A typical example among the thousands invited to Russia by the tsar was Peter von Sivers, a Danish mariner (and ancestor of one of the coauthors of this book) who rose to the position of admiral in the Baltic fleet that broke Swedish dominance in northern Europe. Since the tsar was not able to pay these advisors salaries (any more than Louis XIV could pay salaries to advisors to the French court), he gave many western officers estates with serfs in the Baltic provinces and Finland, conquered from Sweden, and made them aristocrats in his retinue.

The Russian military was completely reorganized by the tsar. After an early rebellion, Peter savagely decimated the inherited firearm regiments and made them part

A World Turned Upside Down. In this popular satirical woodcut of 1766, based on a similar woodcut from the early 1700s, the mice are capturing and burying the cat: In other words, Peter the Great has turned the world upside down with his reforms.

of a new army recruited from the traditional Russian landed nobility. Both classes of soldiers received education at military schools and academies and were required to provide lifelong service. In order to make his soldiers look more urban, Peter decreed that they shave their traditional beards and wear European uniforms or clothes. Every twentieth peasant household had to deliver one foot soldier to conscription. A census was taken to facilitate the shift from the inherited household tax on the villagers to a new capitation tax collected by military officers. In the process, the remaining free farmers outside the estate system of the aristocracy found themselves classified and taxed as serfs, unfree to leave their villages. The result of Peter's reforms was a powerful, expansionary centralizing state that played an increasingly important role among European kingdoms during the eighteenth century (see Map 17.5).

The Rise of Prussia Similar to Russia, the principality of Prussia-Brandenburg was underurbanized. It had furthermore suffered destruction and depopulation during the Thirty Years' War. When the Lutheran Hohenzollern rulers embarked on the construction of a centralized state in the later seventeenth century, they first broke the tax privileges of the landowning aristocracy in the Estates General and raised taxes themselves through agents. As in Russia, farmers who worked on estates held by landlords were serfs. Since there were few urban middle-class merchants and professionals, the kings enrolled members of the landlord aristocracy in the army and civilian administration.

Elevated by the Habsburg Holy Roman emperor from the status of dukes to that of kings in 1701, the Hohenzollern monarchs systematically enlarged the army, employing it during peacetime for drainage and canal projects as well as palace construction in Berlin, the capital. Under Frederick II, "the Great" (1740–1786), Prussia pursued an aggressive foreign policy, capturing Silesia from the Habsburgs in a military campaign. Frederick also expended major efforts to attracting immigrants, intensifying agriculture, and establishing manufacturing enterprises. Prussia emerged as a serious competitor of the Habsburgs in the Holy Roman Empire of Germany.

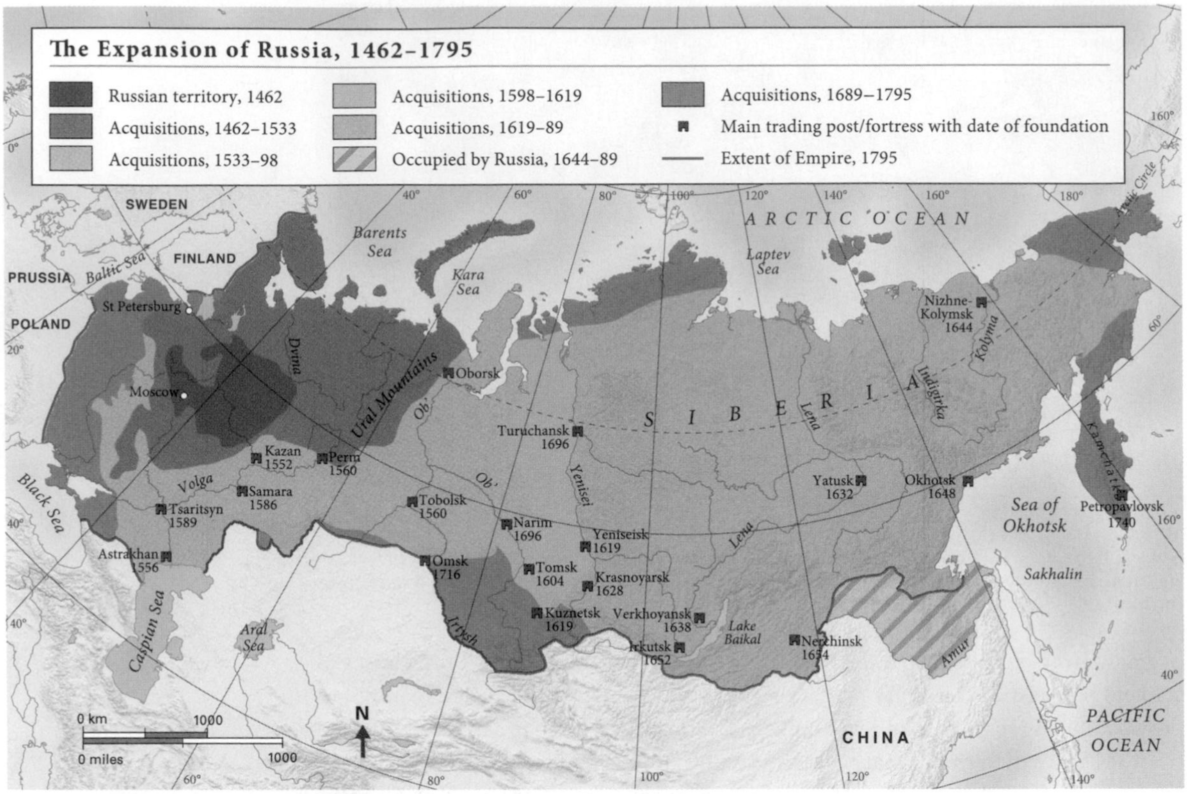

MAP 17.5 **The Expansion of Russia, 1462–1795.**

English Constitutionalism In contrast to Prussia, France, Spain, Austria, and other European states, England had since 1450 a political system ruled by a king or a queen, with a Parliament composed of the aristocracy as well as representatives of towns and cities. Only in England did the interests of the nobility and the urban merchants gradually converge: Younger sons, unable to inherit the family estate, sought their fortunes in London. Rulers on the European continent financed their early centralizing states through raising indirect taxes on sales, commerce, imports, and exports, affecting cities more than noble estates. In England, the cities allied with the aristocracy in resisting indirect tax increases and forcing the throne to use the less ample revenues of its royal estates to pay soldiers. Efforts of the Stuart kings to create a centralized land-based state based on firearm infantries failed. Instead, the ruling class preferred to build a centralized naval state. After the Glorious Revolution of 1688, England became the dominant power on the world's oceans.

After its victory over the Stuart kings, Parliament consolidated its financial powers through the creation of the Bank of England in 1694, two decades before a similar but ill-fated attempt in France. When Mary and William died without children, England continued in 1714 with a king from the principality of Hannover in Germany distantly related to the previous royals. Around the same time, England and Scotland united, creating the United Kingdom. Parliament collected higher taxes than France and, through its bank, was able to keep its debt service low during the early 1700s. The navy grew twice as large as that of France and was staffed by a well-salaried, disciplined military, while the few land troops, deemed superfluous, were mostly low-paid Hessian-German mercenaries. A rudimentary two-party system of

Prussian Military Discipline. The Prussian line infantry made full use in the mid-1700s of flintlock muskets, bayonets, and drilling.

two aristocracy–merchant alliances came into being. The two parties were known as the Tories and the Whigs, the former more royalist and the latter more parliamentarian, with the Whigs in power for most of the first half of the eighteenth century.

Putting It All Together

interactive concept map

Prior to 1500, all religious civilizations possessed sophisticated mathematics and practiced variations of qualitative sciences, such as astrology, geography, alchemy, and medicine. The one exception was trigonometry-based astronomy in Islamic, Hindu, and Christian religious civilizations, pioneered by the Hellenistic scholar Ptolemy (Chapter 5). Physics became the second mathematical science in the early 1500s, but only in Western Christianity. This transformation of the sciences, however, had no practical (that is, engineering) consequences prior to the invention of the steam engine in the 1700s and the subsequent industrialization of England in the 1800s. Furthermore, the mathematization of physics did little to influence the continued prevalence of qualitative description as the methodology of the other sciences. Astrology, alchemy, and medicine continued with what we regard today as outmoded qualitative theories well into the nineteenth century.

Most important, the rise of the New Sciences should not be confused with the vast political, social, economic, and cultural changes, called "modernity" after 1800, which propelled the West on its trajectory of world dominance. Although the West began to acquire its specific scientific and philosophical identity with the introduction of the mathematical sciences in the century between Copernicus and Galileo (1514-1604), the impact of these sciences on the world was felt only after 1800 when they were applied to industry. Once this application gathered momentum, in the nineteenth century, Asia and Africa had no choice but to adapt to modern science and industrialization.

Review and Relate

Thinking Through Patterns

Examine the ways historians approach the big questions of this chapter.

» What were the reasons for the cultural changes that began in Europe around 1450? In which ways were the patterns of cultural changes during 1450–1750 different from those in the other religious civilizations of Eurasia?

Located far from the traditional agrarian–urban centers of Eurasia, Western Christianity repeatedly adapted its culture (particularly theological, philosophical, scientific, and artistic forms of expression) in response to outside stimuli coming from Islamic and Eastern Christian civilizations. Without these stimuli, the Renaissance, Baroque, New Science, and Enlightenment would not have developed. In contrast, the Middle East, Byzantium, India, and China, originating firmly within the traditional agrarian–urban centers, received far fewer outside stimuli prior to the scientific–industrial age. Scholars and thinkers in these religious civilizations did not feel the same pressure to change their cultural heritage and adapt as their colleagues in Western Christianity did.

» When and how did the New Sciences begin, and how did they gain popularity in northwestern European society? Why is the popularization of the New Sciences important for understanding the period 1450–1750?

The discovery of the two new continents of the Americas prompted Nicolaus Copernicus to reject Aristotle's astronomical theory of spheres and to posit a sun-centered planetary system. Copernicus's new approach to science continued with Galileo Galilei's discovery of the mathematical law of falling bodies in physics and was completed when Isaac Newton unified physics and astronomy. The New Sciences became popular in educated urban circles in northwestern Europe, where Catholic and Protestant Church authorities were largely divided. In southern Europe, where the Catholic Reformation was powerful and rejected Galileo, the adoption of the New Sciences occurred more slowly. As scientists in northwestern Europe discovered, the New Sciences possessed practical applicability: After studying the properties of condensing steam and the vacuum, scientists and mechanics began experimenting with steam engines, which served as the principal catalysts for the launching of the scientific–industrial age.

» What were the patterns of centralized state formation and transformation in the period 1450–1750? How did the Protestant Reformation and religious wars modify these patterns?

European kingdoms, such as France, Sweden, and Prussia, expanded their powers of taxation to the detriment of the nobility. With the accumulated funds, they hired and salaried mercenary infantries equipped with firearms, using them to conquer land from their neighbors. The religious wars of the 1500s and 1600s strengthened centralization efforts and hastened the demise of the nobility as an obstacle to the centralized state. In England, Parliament blocked the Stuart kings from building a landed central state and instead pursued the construction of a naval state, which succeeded a similar one built by the Netherlands in 1688.

Against the Grain

Consider this as a counterpoint to the main patterns examined in this chapter.

The Digger Movement

In April 1649, toward the end of the English Civil War and just 3 months after the execution of King Charles I, a group of 70, mostly landless, farmers and day laborers occupied "common" (public) land near Walton, Surrey (about 25 miles south of London), to establish a colony. As the farmers and laborers dug up the soil and sowed the ground with parsnips, carrots, and beans, they came to be called the "Diggers."

Driven off by enraged small landowners who benefited greatly from the use of common land for grazing sheep and cutting timber, a much-reduced group of colonists moved on to common land in nearby Cobham in August 1649. After some delay, this time it was the gentry with their manor rights to the common land who destroyed the Diggers' cottages and fields in the winter of 1650. The Diggers, although ultimately unsuccessful, made a much-publicized statement that public land was "the treasure of all people" and should not be reserved for the benefit of anyone, be they gentry or even small property owners—a bold demand which ran counter to the rapidly increasing privatization of land and commercialization of agriculture.

The leader of the group was Gerrard Winstanley (1609–1670), an embittered former cloth merchant in London who had to abandon his trade in 1643 after he became insolvent. He struggled to regain his solvency in the countryside of Surrey, at one point working as a grazier of cattle. Parts of Surrey had suffered substantial hardship during the Civil War, having been forced to provision and quarter troops. In a flurry of pamphlets between 1648 and 1650 Winstanley explained the motives and goals of the Diggers most eloquently, displaying a remarkable familiarity with local affairs. In addition, he had a superb ability to make these affairs relevant, in the religious idiom of Protestantism, for England as a whole. He was the first to clearly identify the problem of the rising numbers of rural landless laborers victimized by the increasing commercialization of agriculture in England—a labor force that continued to increase until the industrializing cities of the later 1700s eventually absorbed them.

- Was Winstanley hopelessly utopian in his efforts to establish farmer communities on common land in England?
- How have other figures in world history sympathized with the lot of poor and landless farmers and attempted reform (or revolution) on their behalf?

Key Terms

audio flashcards

Absolutism 516
Catholic Reformation 511
Humanism 492
Indulgence 509
New Sciences 492
Protestant Reformation 508
Renaissance 492
Tsar (or Czar) 518

For additional resources, please go to **www.oup.com/us/vonsivers.**
Please see the Further Resources section at the back of the book for additional readings and suggested websites.

PATTERNS OF EVIDENCE |

Sources for Chapter 17

SOURCE 17.1 Examination of Lady Jane Grey, London

1554

Jane Grey, the granddaughter of Henry VIII's sister Mary, was born in 1537, the same year as Edward VI, the only surviving son of the king who had sought a male heir so desperately. Jane, who like Edward was raised in the Protestant religion Henry had introduced to England, proved a diligent and intellectually gifted teenager. In spite of her youth and gender, Jane corresponded with Protestant authorities on the Continent, but fast-moving events in England precluded further study. When Edward died without an heir in 1553, the throne passed, by prearranged agreement, to his fiercely Catholic half-sister Mary.

However, in order to forestall a Catholic successor—and the dramatic rollback of the Protestant reforms instituted by Henry's and Edward's Church of England—Jane's relatives proclaimed her queen. Her rule lasted a mere nine days. She was imprisoned in the Tower of London by Mary, who was then forced to consider whether Jane's execution was warranted. Shortly before Jane's death, at age 16, Queen Mary sent her own chaplain, Master Feckenham (sometimes rendered as "Fecknam") to try to reconcile Jane to the Catholic faith. The results of this attempt were triumphantly recorded in John Foxe's *Acts and Monuments*, published after the Protestant Queen Elizabeth had triumphed over Mary and the Catholics. Although the conversation recorded here is not a trial transcript—and is a highly partisan account—it does distill some of the central issues that divided Catholics and Protestants in an extremely chaotic and violent period.

FECKNAM: "I am here come to you at this present, sent from the queen [Mary] and her council, to instruct you in the true doctrine of the right faith: although I have so great confidence in you, that I shall have, I trust, little need to travail with you much therein."

JANE: "Forsooth, I heartily thank the queen's highness, which is not unmindful of her humble subject: and I hope, likewise, that you no less will do your duty therein both truly and faithfully, according to that you were sent for."

. . .

Source: "The Examination of Lady Jane Grey (1554)," from Denis R. Janz, ed., *A Reformation Reader: Primary Texts with Introductions*, 2nd ed. (Minneapolis, MN: Fortress, 2008), 360–362, taken from *The Acts and Monuments of John Foxe* (London: Seeleys, 1859), 415–417.

FECKNAM: "How many sacraments are there?"

JANE: "Two: the one the sacrament of baptism, and the other the sacrament of the Lord's Supper."

FECKNAM: "No, there are seven."

JANE: "By what Scripture find you that?"

FECKNAM: "Well, we will talk of that hereafter. But what is signified by your two sacraments?"

JANE: "By the sacrament of baptism I am washed with water and regenerated by the Spirit, and that washing is a token to me that I am the child of God. The sacrament of the Lord's Supper, offered unto me, is a sure seal and testimony that I am, by the blood of Christ, which he shed for me on the cross, made partaker of the everlasting kingdom."

FECKNAM: "Why? What do you receive in that sacrament? Do you not receive the very body and blood of Christ?"

JANE: "No, surely, I do not so believe. I think that at the supper I neither receive flesh nor blood, but bread and wine: which bread when it is broken, and the wine when it is drunken, put me in remembrance how that for my sins the body of Christ was broken, and his blood shed on the cross; and with that bread and wine I receive the benefits that come by the breaking of his body, and shedding of his blood, for our sins on the cross."

FECKNAM: "Why, doth not Christ speak these words, 'Take, eat, this is my body?' Require you any plainer words? Doth he not say, it is his body?"

JANE: "I grant, he saith so; and so he saith, 'I am the vine, I am the door'; but he is never the more for that, the door or the vine. Doth not St. Paul say, 'He calleth things that are not, as though they were?' God forbid that I should say, that I eat the very natural body and blood of Christ: for then either I should pluck away my redemption, or else there were two bodies, or two Christs. One body was tormented on the cross, and if they did eat another body, then had he two bodies: or if his body were eaten, then was it not broken upon the cross; or if it were broken upon the cross, it was not eaten of his disciples."

. . .

With these and like such persuasions he would have had her lean to the [Catholic] church, but it would not be. There were many more things whereof they reasoned, but these were the chiefest.

After this, Fecknam took his leave, saying, that he was sorry for her: "For I am sure," quoth he, "that we two shall never meet."

JANE: "True it is," said she, "that we shall never meet, except God turn your heart; for I am assured, unless you repent and turn to God, you are in an evil case. And I pray God, in the bowels of his mercy, to send you his Holy Spirit; for he hath given you his great gift of utterance, if it please him also to open the eyes of your heart."

» Working with Sources

1. What does this source reveal about the religious education of young people in the extended royal household during the final years of Henry VIII and the reign of Edward VI?

2. How does the literal interpretation of the Bible enter into this discussion, and why?

SOURCE 17.2 Sebastian Castellio, *Concerning Whether Heretics Should Be Persecuted*

1554

In October 1553, the extraordinarily gifted Spanish scientist Michael Servetus was executed with the approval and the strong support of John Calvin and his followers in Geneva. The charge was heresy, specifically for denying the existence of the Trinity and the divinity of Christ, and the method of execution—burning at the stake—elicited commentary and protest from across Europe. One of the fullest and most sophisticated protests against this execution was issued by Sebastian Castellio, a professor of Greek language and New Testament theology in the Swiss city of Basel. His book *De Haereticis* is a collection of opinions, drawn from Christian writers, from both before and after the Protestant Reformation and across 15 centuries. It is more than an academic exercise, however, as this dedication of the Latin work to a German noble demonstrates.

Turks: Muslims.

From the Dedication of the book to Duke Christoph of Württemberg:

. . . And just as the **Turks** disagree with the Christians as to the person of Christ, and the Jews with both the Turks and the Christians, and the one condemns the other and holds him for a heretic, so Christians disagree with Christians on many points with regard to the teaching of Christ, and condemn one another and hold each other for heretics. Great controversies and debates occur as to baptism, the Lord's Supper, the invocation of the saints, justification, free will, and other obscure questions, so that Catholics, Lutherans, Zwinglians, Anabaptists, monks, and others condemn and persecute one another more cruelly than the Turks do the Christians. These dissensions arise solely from ignorance of the truth, for if these matters were so obvious and evident as that there is but one God, all Christians would agree among themselves on these points as readily as all nations confess that God is one.

Source: Sebastian Castellio, *Concerning Heretics, Whether They Are to Be Persecuted and How They Are to Be Treated, A Collection of the Opinions of Learned Men Both Ancient and Modern*, trans. Roland H. Bainton, (New York: Octagon, 1965), 132–134.

What, then is to be done in such great contentions? We should follow the counsel of Paul, "Let not him that eateth despise him that eateth not . . . To his own master he standeth or falleth" [Romans 14:3–4]. Let not the Jews or Turks condemn the Christians, nor let the Christians condemn the Jews or Turks, but rather teach and win them by true religion and justice, and let us, who are Christians, not condemn one another, but, if we are wiser than they, let us also be better and more merciful. This is certain that the better a man knows the truth, the less is he inclined to condemn, as appears in the case of Christ and the apostles. But he who lightly condemns others shows thereby that he knows nothing precisely, because he cannot bear others, for to know is to know how to put into practice. He who does not know how to act mercifully and kindly does not know the nature of mercy and kindness, just as he who cannot blush does not know the nature of shame.

If we were to conduct ourselves in this fashion we should be able to dwell together in concord. Even though in some matters we disagreed, yet should we consent together and forbear one another in love, which is the bond of peace, until we arrive at the unity of the faith [Ephesians 4:2–3]. But now, when we strive with hate and persecutions we go from bad to worse. Nor are we mindful of our office, since we are wholly taken up with condemnation, and the Gospel because of us is made a reproach unto the heathen [Ezekiel 22:4], for when they see us attacking one another with the fury of beasts, and the weak oppressed by the strong, these heathen feel horror and detestation for the Gospel, as if it made men such, and they abominate even Christ himself, as if he commanded men to do such things. We rather degenerate into Turks and Jews than convert them into Christians. Who would wish to be a Christian, when he saw that those who confessed the name of Christ were destroyed by Christians themselves with fire, water, and the sword without mercy and more cruelly treated than brigands and murderers? Who would not think Christ a **Moloch**, or some such god, if he wished that men should be immolated to him and burned alive? Who would wish to serve Christ on condition that a difference of opinion on a controversial point with those in authority would be punished by burning alive at the command of Christ himself more cruelly than in the bull of **Phalaris**, even though from the midst of the flames he should call with a loud voice upon Christ, and should cry out that he believed in Him? Imagine Christ, the judge of all, present. Imagine Him pronouncing the sentence and applying the torch. Who would not hold Christ for a Satan? What more could Satan do than burn those who call upon the name of Christ?

Moloch: A Phoenician deity who, according to the Bible, demanded the sacrifice of human children.

Phalaris: Tyrant in pre-Christian Sicily who burned victims alive in a giant bronze bull.

» Working with Sources

1. **Was Castellio minimizing the significant theological disputes that had arisen as a result of the Reformation? Were his objections directly applicable to the Servetus case?**
2. **What did Castellio see as the practical, as well as the theological, consequences of burning those perceived to be "heretics"? Is he convincing on this point?**

SOURCE 17.3 Duc de Saint-Simon, "The Daily Habits of Louis XIV at Versailles"

ca. 1715

A noble at Louis XIV's court at Versailles, Louis de Rouvroy, the duc de Saint-Simon (1675–1755), would achieve lasting fame after his death with the publication of his copious, frank, and witty observations of the court. While resident at Versailles for brief periods after 1702 until the king's death in 1715, Saint-Simon paid particular attention to the maneuverings of his fellow aristocrats. He managed to garner the resentment of many of them, especially the king's illegitimate children, "the Bastards," who held a prominent place at court. His accounts of the daily routine of life at Versailles, and the central position of the king who had famously declared, "L'état, c'est moi!," are often applied today to spectacles that can also be described as at once grand and a little absurd.

At eight o'clock the chief valet de chambre on duty, who alone had slept in the royal chamber, and who had dressed himself, awoke the King. The chief physician, the chief surgeon, and the nurse (as long as she lived), entered at the same time. The latter kissed the King; the others rubbed and often changed his shirt, because he was in the habit of sweating a great deal. At the quarter [hour], the grand chamberlain was called (or, in his absence, the first gentleman of the chamber), and those who had, what was called the *grandes entrées*. The chamberlain (or chief gentleman) drew back the curtains which had been closed again, and presented the holy water from the vase, at the head of the bed. These gentlemen stayed but a moment, and that was the time to speak to the King, if any one had anything to ask of him; in which case the rest stood aside. When, contrary to custom, nobody had aught to say, they were there but for a few moments. He who had opened the curtains and presented the holy water, presented also a prayer-book. Then all passed into the cabinet of the council. A very short religious service being over, the King called, they re-entered. The same officer gave him his dressing-gown; immediately after, other privileged courtiers entered, and then everybody, in time to find the King putting on his shoes and stockings, for he did almost everything himself and with address and grace. Every other day we saw him shave himself; and he had a little short wig in which he always appeared, even in bed, and on medicine days. He often spoke of the chase, and sometimes said a word to somebody. No toilette table was near him; he had simply a mirror held before him.

As soon as he was dressed, he prayed to God, at the side of his bed, where all the clergy present knelt, the cardinals without cushions, all the laity remaining standing; and the captain of the guards came to the balustrade during the prayer, after which the King passed into his cabinet.

Source: *Memoirs of the Duc de Saint-Simon*, trans. Bayle St. John, ed. W. H. Lewis (New York: Macmillan, 1964), 140–141, 144–145.

He found there, or was followed by all who had the entrée, a very numerous company, for it included everybody in any office. He gave orders to each for the day; thus within half a quarter of an hour it was known what he meant to do; and then all this crowd left directly. The bastards, a few favourites, and the valets alone were left. It was then a good opportunity for talking with the King; for example, about plans of gardens and buildings; and conversation lasted more or less according to the person engaged in it.

. . .

At ten o'clock his supper was served. The captain of the guard announced this to him. A quarter of an hour after the King came to supper, and from the antechamber of Madame de Maintenon [his principal mistress] to the table again, any one spoke to him who wished. This supper was always on a grand scale, the royal household (that is, the sons and daughters of France), at table, and a large number of courtiers and ladies present, sitting or standing, and on the evening before the journey to Marly all those ladies who wished to take part in it. That was called presenting yourself for Marly. Men asked in the morning, simply saying to the King, "Sire, Marly." In later years, the King grew tired of this, and a valet wrote up in the gallery the names of those who asked. The ladies continued to present themselves.

. . .

***Ruelle*:** The "little path" between a bed and the wall.

The King, wishing to retire, went and fed his dogs; then said good night, passed into his chamber to the ***ruelle*** of his bed, where he said his prayers, as in the morning, then undressed. He said good night with an inclination of the head, and whilst everybody was leaving the room stood at the corner of the mantelpiece, where he gave the order to the colonel of the guards alone. Then commenced what was called the *petit coucher*, at which only the specially privileged remained. That was short. They did not leave until he got into bed. It was a moment to speak to him.

» Working with Sources

1. **Why does Saint-Simon pay particular attention to moments of the day during which a courtier could speak directly with the king?**
2. **What does the combination of religious and secular pursuits in the king's daily habits suggest about life at his court?**

SOURCE 17.4 Giorgio Vasari, *The Life of Michelangelo Buonarroti*

1550

Trained as a painter, architect, and goldsmith, Giorgio Vasari (1511–1574) practiced various artistic trades, but is most renowned today as the first art historian. His *Lives of the Most Eminent Painters, Sculptors,*

Source: Giorgio Vasari, *The Lives of the Artists*, trans. Julia Conaway Bondanella and Peter Bondanella (New York: Oxford University Press, 1998), 418–420; 427–428.

and Architects, first published in 1550, is the principal source of information about the most prominent artists of the European Renaissance. Having studied under the great artist Michelangelo Buonarroti (1475–1564), Vasari was particularly keen to tell this story. In these scenes from his biography of Michelangelo, Vasari draws attention to his master's early training, as well as the prominent roles Lorenzo il Magnifico de' Medici and ancient sculpture played in his artistic development.

In those days Lorenzo de' Medici the Magnificent kept Bertoldo the sculptor in his garden near Piazza San Marco, not so much as the custodian or guardian of the many beautiful antiquities he had collected and assembled there at great expense, but rather because he wished above all else to create a school for excellent painters and sculptors . . . Thus, Domenico [Ghirlandaio] gave him some of his best young men, including among others Michelangelo and Francesco Granacci; and when they went to the garden, they found that Torrigiani, a young man of the Torrigiani family, was there working on some clay figures in the round that Bertoldo had given him to do.

After Michelangelo saw these figures, he made some himself to rival those of Torrigiani, so that Lorenzo, seeing his high spirit, always had great expectations for him, and, encouraged after only a few days, Michelangelo began copying with a piece of marble the antique head of an old and wrinkled faun with a damaged nose and a laughing mouth, which he found there. Although Michelangelo had never before touched marble or chisels, the imitation turned out so well that Lorenzo was astonished, and when Lorenzo saw that Michelangelo, following his own fantasy rather than the antique head, had carved its mouth open to give it a tongue and to make all its teeth visible, this lord, laughing with pleasure as was his custom, said to him: "But you should have known that old men never have all their teeth and that some of them are always missing." In that simplicity of his, it seemed to Michelangelo, who loved and feared this lord, that Lorenzo was correct; and as soon as Lorenzo left, he immediately broke a tooth on the head and dug out the gum in such a way that it seemed the tooth had fallen out, and anxiously awaited Lorenzo's return, who, after coming back and seeing Michelangelo's simplicity and excellence, laughed about it on more than one occasion, recounting it to his friends as if it were miraculous. . . .

. . .

Around this time it happened that Piero Soderini saw the statue [the *David*, finished in 1504], and it pleased him greatly, but while Michelangelo was giving it the finishing touches, he told Michelangelo that he thought the nose of the figure was too large. Michelangelo, realizing that the Gonfaloniere [a civic official in Florence] was standing under the giant and that his viewpoint did not allow him to see it properly, climbed up the scaffolding to satisfy Soderini (who was behind him nearby), and having quickly grabbed the chisel in his left hand along with a little marble dust that he found on the planks in the scaffolding, Michelangelo began to tap lightly with the chisel, allowing the dust to fall little by little without retouching the nose from the way it was. Then, looking down at the Gonfaloniere who stood there watching, he ordered:

"Look at it now."

"I like it better," replied the Gonfaloniere: "you've made it come alive."

Thus Michelangelo climbed down, and, having contented this lord, he laughed to himself, feeling compassion for those who, in order to make it appear that they understand, do not realize what they are saying; and when the statue was finished and set in its foundation, he uncovered it, and to tell the truth, this work eclipsed all other statues, both modern and ancient, whether Greek or Roman; and it can be said that neither the Marforio in Rome, nor the Tiber and the Nile of the Belvedere, nor the colossal statues of Monte Cavallo can be compared to this David, which Michelangelo completed with so much measure and beauty, and so much skill.

› Working with Sources

1. **How do these anecdotes illustrate the relationship between artists and their patrons (and funders) during the Renaissance?**
2. **How did Michelangelo deal with the legacy of artists from Greco-Roman antiquity?**

SOURCE 17.5 Galileo Galilei, Letter to the Grand Duchess Christina de' Medici

1615

This famous letter is often cited as an early sign of Galileo's inevitable conflict with church authorities over the Copernican system of planetary motion—and the theory's theological, as well as its scientific, ramifications. Galileo (1564–1642) would be condemned to house arrest in 1632 and forced to make a public repudiation of the heliocentric theory first advanced by Copernicus in the sixteenth century. However, Galileo's connection to the renowned Medici family of Florence was also cause for comment—and caution—from 1610, when he received an appointment and their implicit endorsement.

Constructing a telescope in 1609 (which he proudly claimed could "magnify objects more than 60 times"), Galileo trained it on the moons of Jupiter, which he tracked over several days in 1610. Having named these objects for the Medici family, he rushed these and many other astronomical observations into print in the *Sidereus Nuncius* (*The Starry Messenger*). Inviting other scientists to "apply themselves to examine and determine" these planetary motions, Galileo demonstrated a preference

---

Source: Galileo Galilei, *The Essential Galileo*, ed. and trans. Maurice A. Finocchiaro (Indianapolis: Hackett, 2008), §4.2.5—4.2.6, 140–144.

for the Copernican theory and elicited sharp responses, particularly from church officials. In 1615, the dowager Grand Duchess Christina, mother of his patron, Cosimo II, expressed her own reservations about the implications of the Copernican theory for a passage in the Old Testament. Galileo's response attempts, or seems to attempt, to reconcile experimental science and received religion.

Thus let these people apply themselves to refuting the arguments of Copernicus and of the others, and let them leave its condemnation as erroneous and heretical to the proper authorities; but let them not hope that the very cautious and very wise Fathers and the Infallible One with his absolute wisdom are about to make rash decisions like those into which they would be rushed by their special interests and feelings. For in regard to these and other similar propositions which do not directly involve the faith, no one can doubt that the Supreme Pontiff always has the absolute power of permitting or condemning them; however, no creature has the power of making them be true or false, contrary to what they happen to be by nature and de facto. So it seems more advisable to first become sure about the necessary and immutable truth of the matter, over which no one has control, than to condemn one side when such certainty is lacking; this would imply a loss of freedom of decision and of choice insofar as it would give necessity to things which are presently indifferent, free, and dependent on the will of the supreme authority. In short, if it is inconceivable that a proposition should be declared heretical when one thinks that it may be true, it should be futile for someone to try to bring about the condemnation of the earth's motion and sun's rest unless he first shows it to be impossible and false.

There remains one last thing for us to examine: to what extent it is true that the Joshua passage [Joshua 10:12–13] can be taken without altering the literal meaning of the words, and how it can be that, when the sun obeyed Joshua's order to stop, from this it followed that the day was prolonged by a large amount.

. . .

I think therefore, if I am not mistaken, that one can clearly see that, given the Ptolemaic system, it is necessary to interpret the words in a way different from their literal meaning. Guided by St. Augustine's very useful prescriptions, I should say that the best nonliteral interpretation is not necessarily this, if anyone can find another which is perhaps better and more suitable. So now I want to examine whether the same miracle could be understood in a way more in accordance with what we read in Joshua, if to the Copernican system we add another discovery which I recently made about the solar body. However, I continue to speak with the same reservations—to the effect that I am not so enamored with my own opinions as to want to place them ahead of those of others; nor do I believe it is impossible to put forth interpretations which are better and more in accordance with the Holy Writ.

Let us first assume in accordance with the opinion of the above-mentioned authors, that in the Joshua miracle the whole system of heavenly motions was stopped, so that the stopping of only one would not introduce unnecessarily universal confusion and great turmoil in the whole order of nature.

. . .

Furthermore, what deserves special appreciation, if I am not mistaken, is that with the Copernican system one can very clearly and very easily give a literal meaning to another detail which one reads about the same miracle; that is, that the sun stopped in the middle of heaven. Serious theologians have raised a difficulty about this passage: it seems very probable that, when Joshua asked for the prolongation of the day, the sun was close to setting and not at the meridian; for it was then about the time of the summer solstice, and consequently the days were very long, so that if the sun had been at the meridian then it does not seem likely that it would have been necessary to pray for a lengthening of the day in order to win a battle, since the still remaining time of seven hours or more could very well have been sufficient.

. . .

We can remove this and every other implausibility, if I am not mistaken, by placing the sun, as the Copernican system does and as it is most necessary to do, in the middle, namely, at the center of the heavenly orbs and of the planetary revolutions; for at any hour of the day, whether at noon or in the afternoon, the day would not have been lengthened and all heavenly turnings stopped by the sun stopping in the middle of the heavens, namely, at the center of the heavens, where it is located. Furthermore, this interpretation agrees all the more with the literal meaning inasmuch as, if one wanted to claim that the sun's stopping occurred at the noon hour, then the proper expression to use would have been to say that it "stood still at the meridian point," or "at the meridian circle," and not "in the middle of the heaven"; in fact, for a spherical body such as heaven, the middle is really and only the center.

» Working with Sources

1. **How does Galileo deal with the apparently irreconcilable conclusions of science and the Bible?**
2. **How would you characterize Galileo's tone in his analysis of the verses from the Book of Joshua?**

Chapter 18 1500–1800

New Patterns in New Worlds

COLONIALISM AND INDIGENOUS RESPONSES IN THE AMERICAS

Alonso Ortíz was a deadbeat. He fled from his creditors in Zafra, Estremadura, in southwestern Spain, in the early 1770s to find a new life in the Americas. In Mexico City, with the help of borrowed money, he set up shop as a tanner. His business flourished, and, with a partner, Ortíz expanded into two rented buildings. Eight Native American employees, whom he had trained, did the actual labor of stomping the hides in the vats filled with tanning acids. A black slave, belonging to his partner, was the supervisor. Happy that he no longer had to take his shoes off to work, Ortíz concentrated on giving instructions and hustling up business.

Ortíz's situation in Mexico City was not entirely legal, however. He had left his wife, Eleanor González, and children alone in Zafra, though the law required that families should be united. The authorities rarely enforced this law, but that was no guarantee for Ortíz. Furthermore, he had not yet sent his family any remittances, leaving Eleanor to rely on the largesse of her two brothers back home in Estremadura for survival. And then there was still the debt. Ortíz had reasons to be afraid of the law.

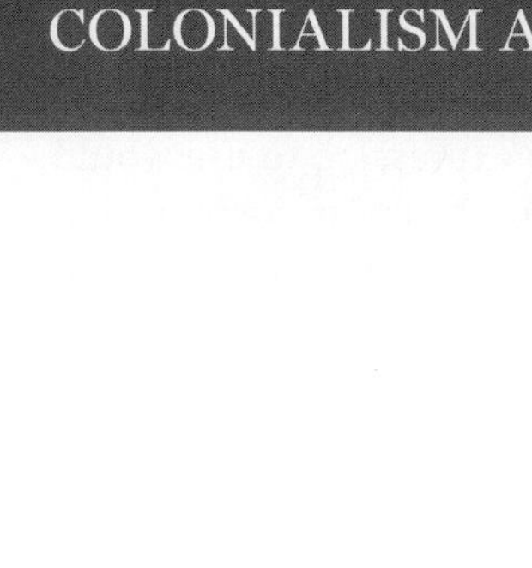

To avoid prosecution, Ortíz wrote a letter to Eleanor. In this letter, he proudly described the comfortable position he had achieved. He announced that his kind business partner was sending her a sum of money sufficient

ABOVE: **In his monumental *Historia de la conquista de México*, written more than 150 years after the events described, Antonio de Solís (1610–1686) depicted the meeting of Moctezuma and Cortés .**

to begin preparations for her departure from Spain. To his creditors, Ortíz promised to send 100 tanned hides within a year. "Your arrival would bring me great joy," he wrote to Eleanor, reneging on an original promise to have already returned home to Spain. Evidently aware of her reluctance to join him in Mexico, Ortíz closed his letter with a request to grant him 4 more years abroad and to do so with a notarized document from her hand. Unfortunately, we do not know her answer.

The Ortíz family drama gives a human face to European colonialism and emigration to the "New World" of the Americas. Like Alonso Ortíz, some 300,000 other Spaniards left the "Old World" (Europe, contiguous with Asia and Africa) between 1500 and 1800. They came alone or with family, temporarily or for good, and either failed or succeeded in their new lives. A few hundred letters by emigrants exist, giving us glimpses of their lives in Mexico, Peru, and other parts of the Americas conquered by the Spanish and Portuguese in the sixteenth century. As these relatively privileged immigrants settled, they hoped to build successful enterprises using the labor of Native Americans as well as that of black slaves imported from Africa. The example of Ortíz shows that even in the socially not very prestigious craft of tanning a man could achieve a measure of comfort by having people of even lower status working for him.

Seeing Patterns

- What is the significance of western Europeans acquiring the Americas as a warm-weather extension of their northern continent?
- What was the main pattern of social development in colonial America during the period 1500–1800?
- Why and how did European settlers in South and North America strive for self-government, and how successful were they in achieving their goals?

Beginning in the sixteenth century, the Americas became an extension of Europe. European settlers extracted mineral and agricultural resources from these new lands. In Europe these resources had become increasingly expensive and impractical to produce (if they could be produced at all). A pattern emerged in which gold and silver, as well as agricultural products that could not be grown in Europe's cooler climate, were intensively exploited. In their role as supplementary subtropical and tropical extensions of Europe, the Americas became a crucial factor in Europe's changing position in the world. First, Europe acquired large quantities of precious metals, which its two largest competitors, India and China, lacked. Second, with its new access to warm-weather agricultural products, Europe rose to a position of agrarian autonomy similar to that of India and China. In terms of resources, compared with the principal religious civilizations of India and China, Europe grew between 1550 and 1800 from a position of inferiority to one of near parity.

The Colonial Americas: Europe's Warm-Weather Extension

The European extension into the subtropical and tropical Americas followed Columbus's pursuit of a sea route to India and its spices that would circumvent the Mediterranean and its dominance by Muslim traders. The Spaniards justified the conquest of these new continents and their Native American inhabitants with

Chapter Outline

- **The Colonial Americas: Europe's Warm-Weather Extension**
- **The Making of American Societies: Origins and Transformations**
- **Putting It All Together**

Christ's command to convert the heathen in the Spanish Habsburg World Empire, the glorious final empire before Christ's return. They financed their imperial expansion as well as their wars against Ottoman and European rivals with American gold and silver, leaving little for domestic investment in productive enterprises. A pattern evolved in which Iberian settlers transformed the Americas into mineral-extracting and agrarian colonies based on either cheap or forced labor.

The Conquest of Mexico and Peru

The Spanish conquerors of the Aztec and Inca Empires, although few in number, succeeded by exploiting internal weaknesses in the empires. They swiftly eliminated the top of the power structures, paralyzing the decision-making apparatuses long enough for their conquests to succeed. Soon after the conquests, the Old World disease of smallpox—to which New World inhabitants had never been exposed and therefore had never developed immunity—ravaged the Native American population and dramatically reduced the indigenous labor force. To make up for this reduction, colonial authorities imported black slaves from Africa for employment in mines and in agriculture. Black Africans, who had long been in contact with Eurasia, were, like Europeans, less susceptible to smallpox. A three-tiered society of European immigrants, Native Americans, and black slaves emerged in the Spanish and Portuguese Americas.

From Trading Posts to Conquest Columbus had discovered the Caribbean islands under a royal commission, which entitled him to build fortified posts and to trade with the indigenous Taínos. Friendly trade relations with the Taínos, however, quickly deteriorated into outright exploitation, with the Spaniards usurping the traditional entitlements of the Taíno chiefs to the labor of their fellow men, who panned gold in rivers or mined it in shallow shafts. With the help of **land-labor grants** (Spanish *encomiendas*), the Spanish took over from the Taíno chiefs and, through forced labor, amassed sizable quantities of gold. What had begun as tradepost settlement turned into full-blown conquest of land.

Land-labor grant (*encomienda*): Land grant by the government to an entrepreneur entitling him to use forced indigenous or imported slave labor on that land for the exploitation of agricultural and mineral resources.

The Spaniards conquered the Caribbean islands not only through force. Much more severe in its consequences was the indirect conquest through disease. The Old World disease of smallpox quickly wiped out an estimated 250,000 to 1 million Taínos on the larger northern islands as well as the less numerous Caribs on the smaller southern islands. Isolated since the Ice Age from the rest of humankind, Native Americans possessed no immunity against smallpox and were similarly ravaged by other introduced diseases.

Protests, mostly among members of the clergy, arose against both the brutal labor exploitation by the conquerors and the helplessness of the Taínos against disease. Unfortunately, the protesters remained a small minority, even within the clergy. One notable protestor was Bartolomé de las Casas (1474–1566), from a family of merchants in Seville. Las Casas had practiced law before emigrating to Hispaniola, where he received an *encomienda*. After becoming a priest in 1510 and later a Dominican monk, however, he became a bitter opponent of the land-labor grant system, which finally came to an end after 1542 with the introduction of the *repartimiento* system (see p. 534).

Bartolomé de las Casas, from *A Short Account of the Destruction of the Indies* (1542)

First Mainland Conquests Another early settler on Hispaniola was Hernán Cortés (1485–1547). His father was a lower-level nobleman in Estremadura, a rough, formerly Islamic frontier region in southwestern Iberia. Chosen by his parents for a career in law, Cortés learned Latin but left the university before graduation. After his arrival in the New World in 1504, he advanced quickly from governmental scribe in Hispaniola to mayor of Santiago in Cuba. Thanks to several labor grants, he became rich. When the Cuban governor asked him in the fall of 1518 to equip and lead a small preparatory expedition for trade and exploration to the Yucatán Peninsula in southeastern Mexico, Cortés enthusiastically agreed. Within a month he assembled 300 men, considerably exceeding his contract. The governor tried to stop him, but Cortés departed quickly for the American mainland.

Cultural Intermediary. The Tabascans gave Malinche, or Doña Marina, to Hernán Cortés as a form of tribute after they were defeated by the Spanish. Malinche served Cortés as a translator and mistress, playing a central role in Cortés's eventual victory over the Aztecs. She was in many respects the principal face of the Spanish and is always depicted center stage in Native American visual accounts of the conquest.

As the Cuban governor had feared, Cortés did not bother with trading posts in Yucatán. The Spanish had previously learned of the existence of the Aztec Empire, with its immense silver and gold treasures. In a first encounter, Cortés's motley force—numbering by now about 530 Spanish men—defeated a much larger indigenous force at Tabasco. The Spaniards' steel weapons and armor proved superior in hand-to-hand combat to the obsidian-spiked lances and wooden swords, as well as quilted cotton vests of the defenders.

Among the gifts of submission presented by the defeated Native Americans in Tabasco was Malinche, a Nahuatl [NA-hua]-speaking woman. Her widowed Aztec mother had sold her into slavery to the Tabascans after her remarriage. Malinche quickly learned Spanish and became the consort of Cortés, teaching him about the subtleties of Aztec culture. In her role as translator, Malinche was nearly as decisive as Cortés in shaping events. Indeed, Aztecs often used the name of Malinche when addressing Cortés, forgetting that her voice was not that of Cortés. With Tabasco conquered, Cortés quickly moved on; he was afraid that the Cuban governor, who was in pursuit, would otherwise force him to return to Cuba.

Conquest of the Aztec Empire On the southeast coast of Mexico, Cortés founded the city of Veracruz as a base from which to move inland. In the city, he had his followers elect a town council, which made Cortés their head and chief justice, allowing Cortés to claim legitimacy for his march inland. To prevent opponents in his camp from notifying the Cuban governor of his usurpation of authority, Cortés

interactive timeline

1492
Christopher Columbus lands in the Caribbean

1500
Pedro Álvares Cabral claims Brazil for Portugal

1516–1556
Reign of Charles V, Habsburg king of Spain and the Americas

1519–1521
Reign of Cuauhtémoc, last ruler of the Aztec Empire

1521
Spanish conquest of the Aztec Empire in Mexico

1532–1533
Reign of Atahualpa, last ruler of the Inca Empire

1533
Spanish conquest of the Inca Empire in Peru

1545
Founding of silver mine of Potosí

1607
Jamestown, Virginia, first permanent English settlement

1608
Quebec City, first permanent French settlement

1690
Gold discovered in Brazil

Cortés and the conquest of the Aztec Empire

had all ships stripped of their gear and the hulls sunk. Marching inland, the Spaniards ran into resistance from indigenous people, suffering their first losses of horses and men. Although bloodied, they continued their march with thousands of Native American allies, most notably the Tlaxcalans, traditional enemies of the Aztecs. The support from these indigenous peoples made a crucial difference when Cortés and his army reached the court of the Aztecs.

When Cortés arrived at the city of Tenochtitlán on November 2, 1519, the emperor Moctezuma II (r. 1502–1519) was in a quandary over how to react to these invaders whose depredations neither his tributaries nor his enemies had been able to stop. To gain time, Moctezuma greeted the Spaniard in person on one of the causeways leading to the city and invited him to his palace. Cortés and his company, now numbering some 600 Spaniards, took up quarters in the palace precincts. After a week of gradually deteriorating discussions, Cortés suddenly put the incredulous emperor under house arrest and made him swear allegiance to Charles V.

Before being able to contemplate his next move, however, Cortés was diverted by the need to march back east, where troops from Cuba had arrived to arrest him. After defeating those troops, he pressed the remnants into his own service and returned to Tenochtitlán. During his absence, the Spaniards who had remained in Moctezuma's palace had massacred a number of unarmed Aztec nobles participating in a religious ceremony. An infuriated crowd of Tenochtitlán's inhabitants invaded the palace. In the melee, Moctezuma and some 200 Spaniards died. The rest of the Spanish fled for their lives, retreating east to their Tlaxcalan allies, who, fortunately, remained loyal. Here, after his return, Cortés devised a new plan for capturing Tenochtitlán.

"The Capture of Tenochtitlán"

After 10 months of preparations, the Spaniards returned to the Aztec capital. In command now of about 2,000 Spanish soldiers and assisted by some 50,000 Native American troops, Cortés laid siege to the city, bombarding it from ships he had built in the lake and razing buildings during forays onto land. After nearly 3 months, much of the city was in ruins, fresh water and food became scarce, and smallpox began to decimate the population of some 3–4 million inhabitants in the Mexican Basin and 25 million throughout the Aztec Empire. On August 21, 1521, the Spaniards and their allies stormed the city and looted its gold treasury. They captured the fiercely resisting last emperor, Cuauhtémoc [cu-aw-TAY-moc], a few days later and executed him in 1525, thus ending the Aztec Empire (see Map 18.1 and Source 18.1).

Conquest of the Inca Empire At about the same time, a relative of Cortés, Francisco Pizarro (ca. 1475–1541), conceived a plan to conquer the Andean empire of the Incas (which, in 1492, comprised some 9–12 million inhabitants). Pizarro, like Cortés born in Estremadura, was an illegitimate and uneducated son of an infantry captain from the lower nobility. Arriving in Hispaniola as part of an expedition in 1513 that went on to discover Panama and the Pacific, he became mayor of Panama City, acquired some wealth, and began to hear rumors about an empire of gold and silver to the south. After a failed initial expedition, he and 13 followers captured some precious metal from an oceangoing Inca sailing raft. Receiving a permit to establish a trading post from Charles V, Pizarro departed with a host of 183 men in late December 1530.

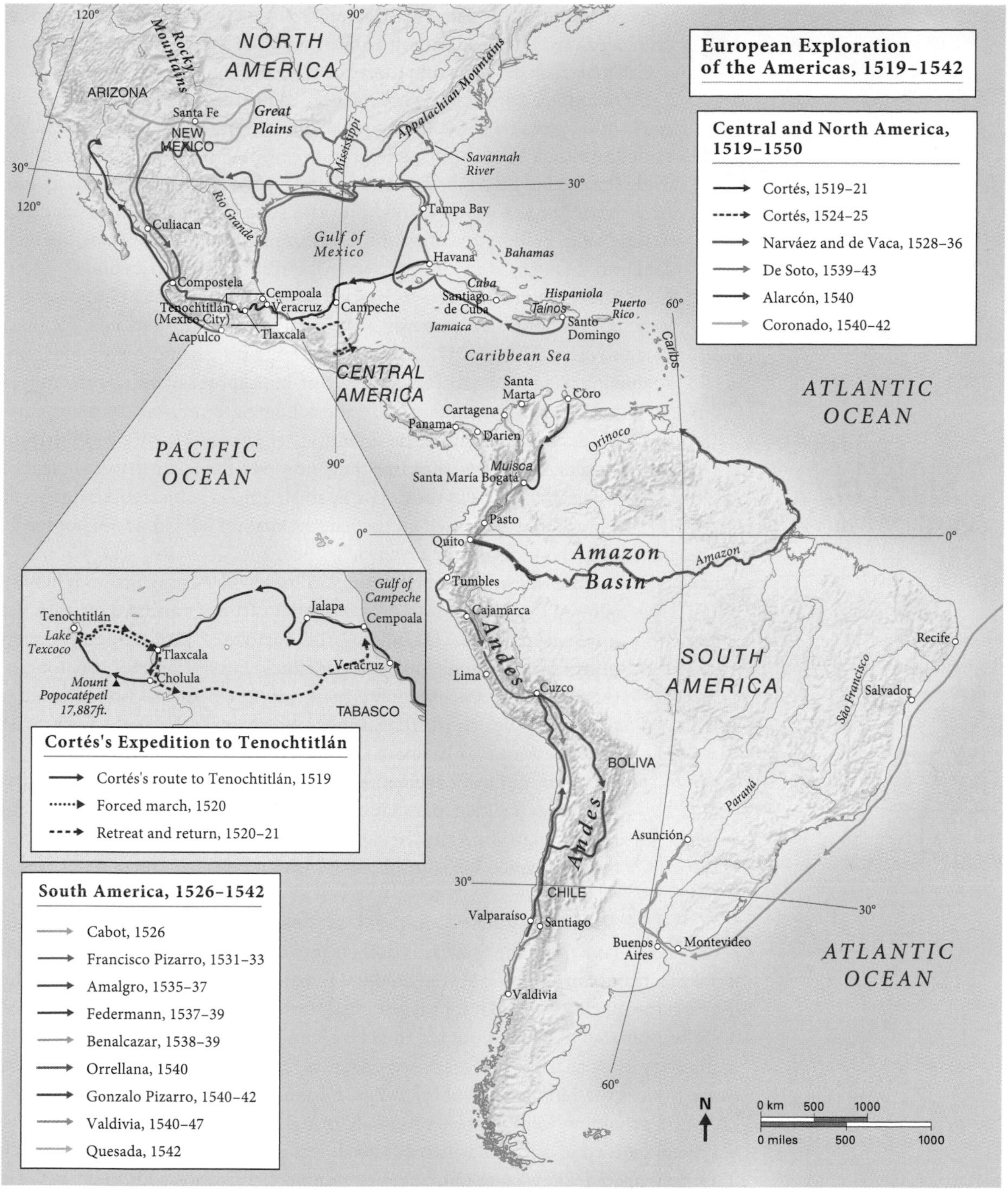

MAP 18.1 The European Exploration of the Americas, 1519–1542.

In a grimly fortuitous bit of luck for Pizarro, smallpox had preceded him in his expedition. In the later 1520s, the disease had ravaged the Inca Empire, killing the emperor and his heir apparent and leading to a protracted war of succession between two surviving sons. Atahualpa, in the north, sent his army south to the capital, Cuzco, where

Conquest by Surprise. The Spanish conqueror Francisco Pizarro captured Emperor Atahualpa (*top*) in an ambush. Atahualpa promised a roomful of gold in return for his release, but the Spaniards collected the gold and murdered Atahualpa (*bottom*) before generals of the Inca army could organize an armed resistance.

it defeated his half-brother, Huáscar. When Pizarro entered the Inca Empire, Atahualpa was encamped with an army of 40,000 men near the northern town of Cajamarca, on his way south to Cuzco to install himself as emperor.

Arriving at Cajamarca, Pizarro succeeded in arranging an unarmed audience with Atahualpa in the town square. On November 16, 1532, Atahualpa came to this audience, surrounded by several thousand unarmed retainers, while Pizarro hid his soldiers in and behind the buildings around the square. At a signal, these soldiers rushed into the square. Some soldiers captured Atahualpa to hold him hostage. In the ensuing bloodbath, not one Spanish soldier was killed. The whole massacre was over in less than an hour.

With his ambush, Pizarro succeeded in paralyzing the Inca Empire at the very top. Without their emperor, Atahualpa, none of the generals in Cuzco dared to seize the initiative. Instead of ordering his generals to liberate him, Atahualpa sought to satisfy the greed of his captors with a room full of gold and silver as ransom. In the following 2 months, Inca administrators delivered immense quantities of precious metals to Pizarro in Cajamarca. During the same time, however, the Spanish were in fear of being attacked from the north. Spanish officers subjected Atahualpa to a mock trial and executed the hapless king on July 26, 1533, hoping to keep the Incas disorganized.

And indeed, the northern forces broke off their march and thereby allowed the Spaniards to take the capital. The Spaniards did so against minimal resistance, massacring the inhabitants and stripping Cuzco of its immense gold and silver treasures. Pizarro did not stay long in the now worthless, isolated city in the Andes. In 1535 he founded a new capital, Lima, which was more conveniently located on the coast and about halfway between Cajamarca and Cuzco. At this time, Incas in the south finally overcame their paralysis. Learning from past mistakes, they avoided mass battles, focused on deadly guerilla strikes, and rebuilt a kingdom that held out until 1572. It was only then that the Spanish gained full control of the Inca Empire.

The Portuguese Conquest of Brazil The Portuguese were not far behind the Spaniards in their pursuit of conquest. Navigators from both Spain and Portugal had first sighted the Brazilian coast in 1499–1500, and the Portuguese quickly claimed it for themselves. Brazil's indigenous population at that time is estimated to have amounted to nearly 5 million. The great majority lived in temporary or permanent villages based on agriculture, fishing, and hunting. Only a small minority in remote areas of the Amazon were pure foragers.

The Portuguese were interested initially in trade with the villagers, mostly for a type of hardwood called brazilwood, which was used as a red dye. When French traders appeared, ignoring the Portuguese commercial treaties with the tribes, the Portuguese crown shifted from simple trade agreements to trading-post settlements. This involved giving land grants to commoners and lower noblemen with the obligation to build fortified coastal villages for settlers and to engage in agriculture and friendly trade. By the mid-sixteenth century, a handful of these villages became successful, their inhabitants intermarrying with the surrounding indigenous chieftain families and establishing sugarcane plantations.

Brazil in 1519. The early map is fairly accurate for the northern coast but increasingly less accurate as one moves south. First explorations of the south by both Portuguese and Spanish mariners date to 1513–1516. Ferdinand Magellan passed through several places along the southern coast on his journey around the world in 1520–1521. The scenes on the map depict Native Americans cutting and collecting brazilwood, the source of a red dye much in demand by the Portuguese during the early period of colonization.

Explanations for the Spanish Success The slow progression of the Portuguese in Brazil is readily understood. But the stupendous victories of handfuls of Spaniards over huge empires with millions of inhabitants and large cities defy easy explanation. Five factors invite consideration.

First, and most important, the conquistadors went straight to the top of the imperial pyramid. The emperors and their courts expected diplomatic deference from inferiors, among whom they included the minuscule band of Spaniards. Confronted, instead, with a calculated combination of arrogance and brutality, the emperors and courts were thrown off balance by the Spaniards, who ruthlessly exploited their opportunity. As the emperors were removed from the top level, the administration immediately below them fell into paralysis, unable to seize the initiative and respond in a timely fashion.

Second, both the Aztec and Inca Empires were relatively recent creations in which there were individuals and groups who contested the hierarchical power structure. The conquistadors either found allies among the subject populations or encountered a divided leadership. In either case, they were able to exploit divisions in the empires.

Third, European-introduced diseases, traveling with or ahead of the conquerors, took a devastating toll. In both empires, smallpox hit at critical moments during or right before the Spanish invasions, causing major disruptions.

Fourth, thanks to horses and superior European steel weapons and armor, primarily pikes, swords, and breastplates, small numbers of Spaniards were able to hold large numbers of attacking Aztecs and Incas at bay in hand-to-hand combat. Contrary to widespread belief, cannons and matchlock muskets were less important, since they were useless in close encounters. Firearms were still too slow and inaccurate to be decisive.

A fifth factor, indigenous religion, was probably of least significance. According to some now-outdated interpretations, Moctezuma was immobilized by his belief in a prophecy that he would have to relinquish his power to the savior Quetzalcoatl returning from his mythical city of Tlapallan on the east coast (see Chapter 15). Modern scholarship provides convincing reasons, however, to declare this prophecy a postconquest legend, circulated by Cortés both to flatter Charles V and to aggrandize himself as the predicted savior figure bringing Christianity.

The Establishment of Colonial Institutions

The Spanish crown established administrative hierarchies in the Americas, similar to those of the Aztecs and Incas, with governors at the top of the hierarchy and descending through lower ranks of functionaries. A small degree of settler autonomy

Spanish Steel. The *Lienzo de Tlaxcala*, from the middle part of the sixteenth century, is our best visual source for the conquest of Mexico. In this scene, Malinche, protected by a shield, directs the battle on the causeway leading to Tenochtitlán. The two Spanish soldiers behind her, one fully armored, brandish steel swords, which were more effective than the obsidian blades carried by the Aztec defenders (one of whom is dressed in leopard skins), shown on the left.

Creoles: American-born descendants of European, primarily Spanish, immigrants.

was permitted through town and city councils, but the crown was determined to make the Americas a territorial extension of the European pattern of centralized state formation. Several hundred thousand settlers (including Alonso Ortíz) found a new life in the Americas, mostly as urban craftspeople, administrators, and professionals. By the early seventeenth century, a powerful elite of Spanish who had been born in America, called **Creoles** (Spanish *criollos*) was in place, first to assist and later to replace most of the administrators sent from Spain in the governance of the Americas (see Map 18.2).

From Conquest to Colonialism The unimaginable riches of Cortés and Pizarro inspired numerous further expeditions. Adventurers struck out with small bands of followers into Central and North America, Chile, and the Amazon. Their expeditions, however, yielded only modest amounts of gold and earned more from selling captured Native Americans into slavery. In the north, expeditions penetrated as far as Arizona, New Mexico, Texas, Oklahoma, Kansas, and Florida but encountered only villagers and the relatively poor Pueblo towns. No new golden kingdoms (the mythical El Dorado, or "golden city") beyond the Aztec and Inca Empires were discovered in the Americas.

In the mid-sixteenth century, easy looting was replaced by a search for the mines from where the precious metals came. In northern Mexico, Native Americans led a group of soldiers and missionaries in 1547 to a number of rich silver mines. In addition, explorers discovered silver in Bolivia (1545) and northern Mexico (1556), gold in Chile (1552), and mercury in Peru (1563). The conquistadors shifted from looting to the exploitation of Native American labor in mines and in agriculture.

In a small number of areas, indigenous peoples resisted incorporation into the Spanish colonies. Notably, in southern Chile the Mapuche repulsed all attempts by the Spanish to subdue them. They had already prevented the Incas from expanding their empire to the southern tip of the continent. Initially, in 1550–1553 the Spanish succeeded in establishing a number of forts and opening a gold mine. But in campaign after campaign they failed to gain more than a border strip with an adjacent no-man's-land. In 1612 they agreed to a temporary peace which left the majority of the Mapuche independent.

Another Native American people who successfully resisted the Spanish conquest were the Asháninka in the Peruvian rain forest. Located along the Eno River, one of the headwater tributaries of the Amazon, they were the first standing in the way of the Spanish attempts to extend their dominance from Peru eastward. The Asháninka exploited hillside salt veins in their region and were traders of goods between the Andes and the rain forest. Although Jesuits and later Franciscans established missions among the Asháninka in the 1600s, they failed to make many converts. It was only in 1737 that the Spanish finally built a fort in the region—a first step toward projecting colonial power into the rain forest.

Bureaucratic Efficiency During the first two generations after the conquest, Spain maintained an efficient colonial administration, which delivered between 50

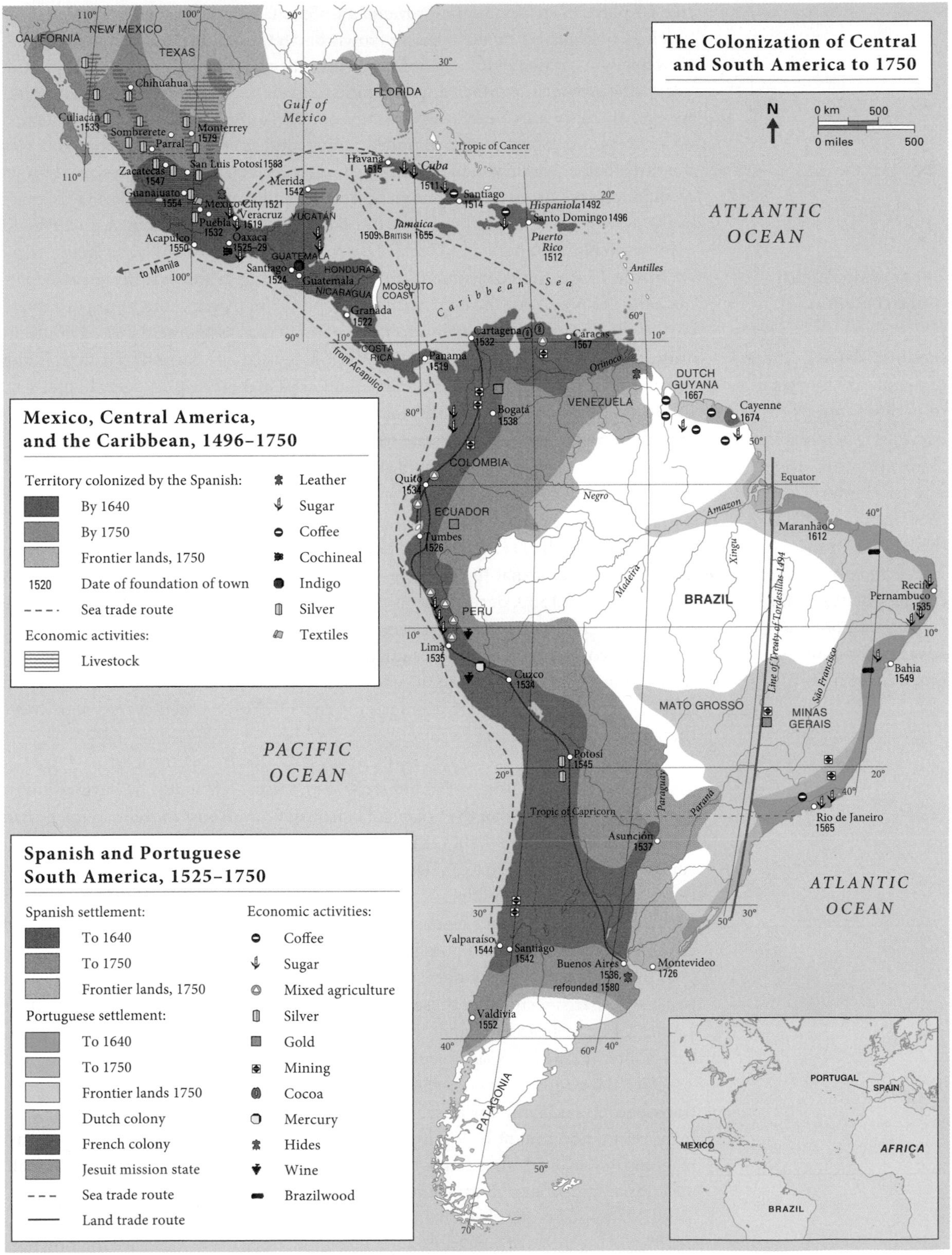

MAP 18.2 The Colonization of Central and South America to 1750.

map analysis

and 60 percent of the colonies' revenues to Spain. These revenues contributed as much as one-quarter of the Spanish crown budget. In addition, the viceroyalty of New Spain in Mexico remitted another 25 percent of its revenues to the Philippines, the Pacific province for which it was administratively responsible from 1571 onward. As in Spain, settlers in New Spain had to pay up to 40 different taxes and dues, levied on imports and exports, internal trade, mining, and sales. The only income tax was the tithe to the church, which the administration collected and, at times, used for its own budgetary purposes. Altogether, however, for the settlers the tax level was lower in the New World than in Spain, and the same was true for the English and French colonies in North America.

Labor assignment (*repartimiento*): Obligation by villagers to send stipulated numbers of people as laborers to a contractor, who had the right to exploit a mine or other labor-intensive enterprise; the contractors paid the laborers minimal wages and bound them through debt peonage (repayment of money advances) to their businesses.

In the 1540s the government introduced rotating **labor assignments** (*repartimientos*) to phase out the *encomiendas* that powerful owners sought to perpetuate within their families. This institution of rotating labor assignments was a continuation of the *mit'a* system, which the Incas had devised as a form of taxation, in the absence of money and easy transportation of crops in their empire (see Chapter 15). Rotating labor assignments meant that for fixed times a certain percentage of villagers had to provide labor to the state for road building, drainage, transportation, and mining. Private entrepreneurs could also contract for indigenous labor assignments, especially in mining regions.

In Mexico the *repartimiento* fell out of use in the first half of the seventeenth century due to the toll of recurring smallpox epidemics on the Native American population. It is estimated that the indigenous population in the Americas, from a height of 54 million in 1550, declined to 10 million by 1700 before recovering again. The replacement for the lost workers was wage labor. In highland Peru, where the indigenous population was less densely settled and the effects of smallpox were less severe, the assignment system lasted to the end of the colonial period. Wage labor expanded there as well. Wages for Native Americans and blacks remained everywhere lower than for those for Creoles.

The Rise of the Creoles Administrative and fiscal efficiency, however, did not last very long. The wars of the Spanish Habsburg Empire cost more than the crown was able to collect in revenues. King Philip II (r. 1556–1598) had to declare bankruptcy four times between 1557 and 1596. In order to make up the financial deficit, the crown began to sell offices in the Americas to the highest bidders. The first offices put on the block were elective positions in the municipal councils. By the end of the century, Creoles had purchased life appointments in city councils as well as positions as scribes, local judges, police chiefs, directors of processions and festivities, and other sinecures. In these positions, they collected fees and rents for their services. Local oligarchies emerged, effectively ending whatever elective, participatory politics existed in Spanish colonial America.

Over the course of the seventeenth century a majority of administrative positions became available for purchase. The effects of the change from recruitment by merit to recruitment by wealth on the functioning of the bureaucracy were far-reaching. Creoles advanced on a broad front in the administrative positions, while fewer Spaniards found it attractive to buy their American positions from overseas. The only opportunities which European Spaniards still found enticing were the nearly 300 positions of governors and inspectors, since these jobs gave their owners the right to subject the Native Americans to forced purchases of goods, yielding huge profits. For the most part, wealthy Spanish merchants delegated junior partners to these highly lucrative activities. By 1700, the consequences of the Spanish crown selling most of its American administrative offices were a decline in the competence of office holders, the emergence of a Creole elite able to bend the Spanish administration increasingly to its will, and a decentralization of the decision-making processes.

Northwest European Interference As Spain's administrative grip on the Americas weakened during the seventeenth century, the need to defend the continents militarily against European interlopers arose. At the beginning, there were European privateers, holding royal charters, who harassed Spanish silver shipments and ports in the Caribbean. In the early seventeenth century, the French, English, and Dutch governments sent ships to occupy the smaller Caribbean islands not claimed by Spain. Privateer and contraband traders stationed on these islands engaged in further raiding and pillaging, severely damaging Spain's monopoly of shipping between Europe and the Caribbean.

engraving showing English attack on the Spanish settlement of St. Augustine, Florida, 1589

Conquests of Spanish islands followed in the second half of the century. England captured Jamaica in 1655, and France colonized western Hispaniola (Saint-Domingue) in 1665, making it one of their most profitable sugar-producing colonies. Along the Pacific coast, depredations continued into the middle of the eighteenth century. Here, the galleons of the annual Acapulco–Manila fleet carrying silver from Mexico to China and returning with Chinese silks, porcelain, and lacquerware were the targets of English privateers. Over the course of the seventeenth century, Spain allocated one-half to two-thirds of its American revenues to the increasingly difficult defense of its annual treasure fleets and Caribbean possessions.

Bourbon Reforms After the death of the last, childless Habsburg king of Spain in 1700, the new French-descended dynasty of the Bourbons made major efforts to regain control over their American possessions. They had to begin from a discouragingly weak position as nearly 90 percent of all goods traded from Europe to the Americas were of non-Spanish origin. Fortunately, population increases among the settlers as well as the Native Americans (after having overcome their horrific losses to disease) offered opportunities to Spanish manufacturers and merchants. After several false starts, in the middle of the eighteenth century the Bourbon reform program began to show results.

The reforms aimed at improved naval connections and administrative control between the mother country and the colonies. The monopolistic annual armed silver fleet was greatly reduced. Instead, the government authorized more frequent single sailings at different times of the year. Newly formed Spanish companies, receiving exclusive rights at specific ports, succeeded in reducing contraband trade. Elections took place again for municipal councils. Spanish-born salaried officials replaced scores of Creole tax and office farmers. The original two viceroyalties were subdivided into four, to improve administrative control. The sale of tobacco and brandy became state monopolies. Silver mining and cotton textile manufacturing were expanded. By the second half of the eighteenth century, Spain had regained a measure of control over its colonies.

As a result, government revenues rose substantially. Tax receipts increased more than twofold, even taking into account the inflation of the late eighteenth century.

In the end, however, the reforms remained incomplete. Since the Spanish economy was not also reformed, in terms of expanding crafts production and urbanization, the changes did not diminish the English and French dominance of the import market by much. Spain failed to produce textiles, metalwares, and household goods at competitive prices for the colonies; thus the level of English and French exports to the Americas remained high.

Early Portuguese Colonialism In contrast to the Spanish Americas, the Portuguese overseas province of Brazil remained initially confined to a broad coastal strip, which developed only slowly during the sixteenth century. The first governor-general arrived in 1549. He and his successors (after 1640 called "viceroys," as in the Spanish colonies) were members of the high aristocracy, but their positions were salaried and subject to term limits. As the colony grew, the crown created a council in the capital of Lisbon for all Brazilian appointments and established a high court for all judicial affairs in Bahia in northern Brazil. Commoners with law degrees filled the nonmilitary colonial positions. In the early seventeenth century, however, offices became as open to purchase as in the Spanish colonies, although not on the city council level, where a complex indirect electoral process survived.

Jesuits converted the Native Americans, whom they transported to Jesuit-administered villages. Colonial cities and Jesuits repeatedly clashed over the slave raids of the "pioneers" (*bandeirantes*) in village territories. The bandeirantes came mostly from São Paulo in the south and roamed the interior in search of human prey. Native American slaves were in demand on the wheat farms and cattle ranches of São Paulo as well as on the sugar plantations of the northeast. Although the Portuguese crown and church had, like the Spanish, forbidden the enslavement of Native Americans, the bandeirantes exploited a loophole. The law was interpreted as allowing the enslavement of Native Americans who resisted conversion to Christianity. For a long time, Lisbon and the Jesuits were powerless against this flagrantly self-interested interpretation.

Expansion into the Interior In the middle of the seventeenth century, the Jesuits and Native Americans finally succeeded in pushing many bandeirantes west and north, where they switched from slave raiding to prospecting for gold. In the far north, however, the raids continued until 1680, when the Portuguese administration finally prevailed and ended Native American slavery, almost a century and a half after Spain. Ironically, it was mostly thanks to the "pioneer" raids for slaves that Brazil expanded westward, to assume the borders it has today.

As a result of gold discoveries in Minas Gerais in 1690 by bandeirantes, the European immigrant population increased rapidly, from 1 to 2 million during the 1700s. Minas Gerais, located north of Rio de Janeiro, was the first inland region of the colony to attract settlers. By contrast, as a result of smallpox epidemics beginning in the 1650s in the Brazilian interior, the Native American population declined massively, not to expand again until the end of the eighteenth century. To replace the lost labor, Brazilians imported slaves from Africa, at first to work in the sugar plantations and, after 1690, in the mines, where their numbers increased to two-thirds of the labor force. In contrast to Spanish mines, Brazilian mines were surface operations requiring only minimal equipment outlays. Most blacks worked with pickaxes and shovels. The peak of the gold boom came in the 1750s, when the importance of gold was second only to that of sugar among Brazilian exports to Europe.

Early in the gold boom, the crown created the new Ministry of the Navy and Overseas Territories, which greatly expanded the administrative structure in Brazil. It established 14 regions and a second high court in Rio de Janeiro, which replaced Bahia as the capital in 1736. The ministry in Lisbon ended the sale of offices, increased the efficiency of tax collection, and encouraged Brazilian textile manufacturing to render the province more independent from English imports. By the mid-1700s, Brazil was a flourishing overseas colony of Portugal, producing brazilwood, sugar, gold, tobacco, cacao, and vanilla for export.

Mine Workers. The discovery of gold and diamonds in Minas Gerais led to a boom, but did little to contribute to the long-term health of the Brazilian economy. With the Native American population decimated by disease, African slaves performed the backbreaking work.

North American Settlements Efforts at settlement in the less hospitable North America in the sixteenth century were unsuccessful. Only in the early part of the seventeenth century did French, English, and Dutch merchant investors succeed in establishing small communities of settlers on the coast, who grew their own food on land purchased from the local Native American villagers. These settlements were Jamestown (founded in 1607 in today's Virginia), Quebec (1608, Canada), Plymouth and Boston (1620 and 1630, respectively, in today's Massachusetts), and New Amsterdam (1625, today's New York). Subsistence agriculture and fur, however, were meager ingredients if the settlements were to prosper. The settlements struggled through the seventeenth century, sustained either by Catholic missionary efforts or by the Protestant enthusiasm of the Puritans who had escaped persecution in England. Southern places like Jamestown survived because they adopted tobacco, a warm-weather plant, as a cash crop for export to Europe. In contrast to Mexico and Peru, the North American settlements were not followed—at least not at first—by territorial conquests (see Map 18.3).

Samuel de Champlain's map of the northeast coast of North America, ca. 1607

Native Americans European arrivals in North America soon began supplementing agriculture with trade. They exchanged metal and glass wares, beads, and seashells for furs, especially beaver pelts, with the Native American groups of the interior. The more these groups came into contact with the European traders, however, the more dramatic the demographic impact of the trade on them was: Smallpox, already a menace during the 1500s in North America, became devastating as contacts intensified. In New England, for example, of the approximately 144,000 estimated Native Americans in 1600, fewer than 15,000 remained in 1620.

The introduction of guns contributed an additional lethal factor to trading arrangements, as English, French, and Dutch traders provided their favorite Native

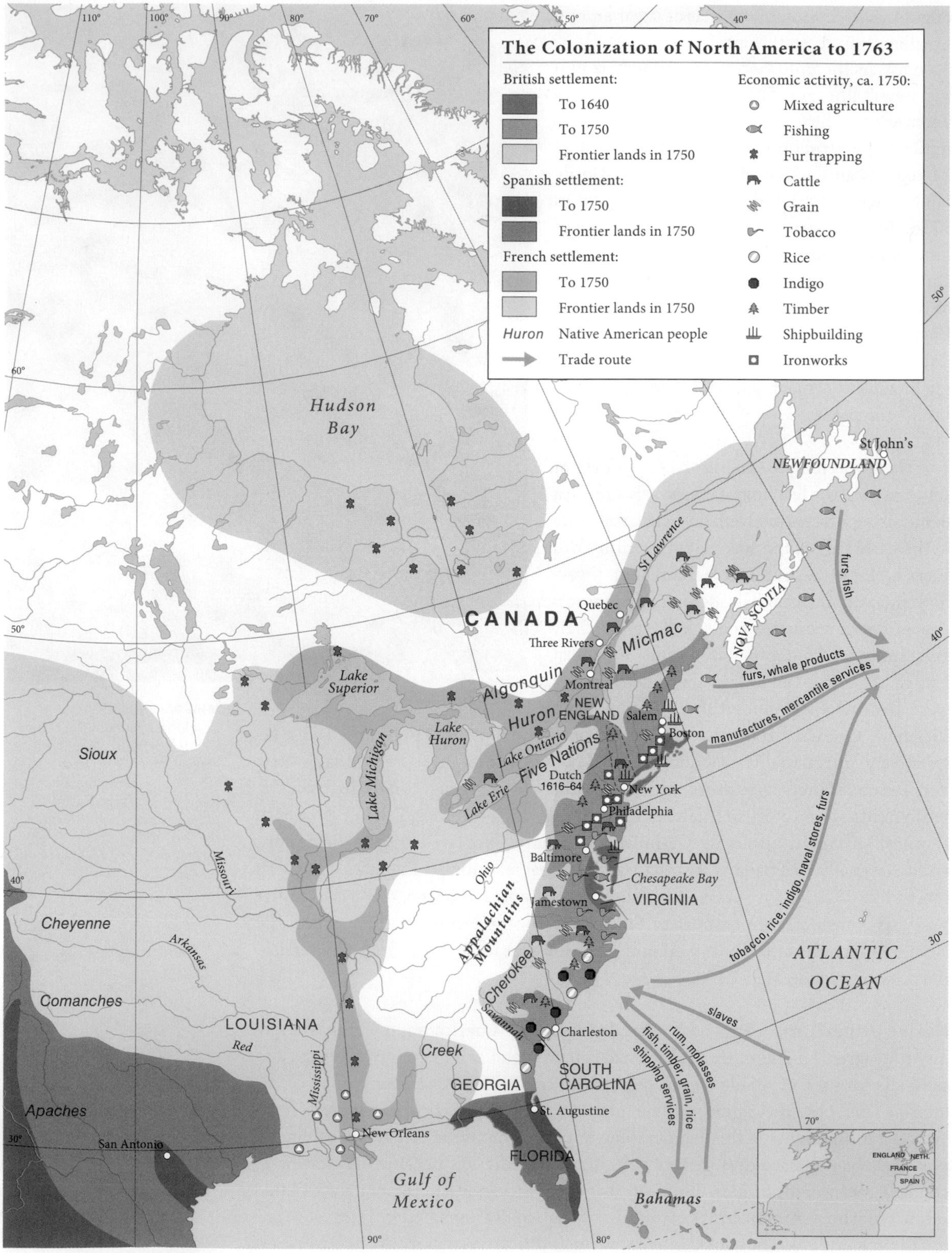

MAP 18.3 **The Colonization of North America to 1763.**

American trading partners with flintlocks in order to increase the yield of furs. As a result, in the course of the 1600s the Iroquois in the northeast were able to organize themselves into a heavily armed and independent-minded federation, capable of inflicting heavy losses on rival groups as well as on European traders and settlers.

Farther south, in Virginia, the Jamestown settlers encountered the Powhatan confederacy. These Native Americans, living in some 200 well-fortified, palisaded villages, dominated the region between the Chesapeake Bay and the Appalachian Mountains. Initially, the Powhatan supplied Jamestown with foodstuffs and sought to integrate the settlement into their confederation. When this attempt at integration failed, however, benevolence turned to hostility, and the confederacy raided Jamestown twice in an attempt to rid their region of foreign settlers. But the latter were able to turn the tables and defeat the Powhatan in 1646, thereafter occupying their lands and reducing them to small scattered remnants. Pocahontas, the daughter of the Powhatan chief at the time of the foundation of Jamestown, was captured during one of the raids, converted to Christianity, and lived in England for a number of years as the wife of a returning settler. The decline of the Powhatan in the later 1600s allowed English settlers to move westward, in contrast to New England in the north, where the Iroquois, although allied with the English against the French, blocked any western expansion.

John Smith, excerpt from *The Generall Historie of Virginia* (1624)

The Iroquois were fiercely determined to maintain their dominance of the fur trade and wrought havoc among the Native American groups living between New England and the Great Lakes. In the course of the second half of the 1600s they drove many smaller groups westward into the Great Lakes region and Mississippi plains, where these groups settled as refugees. French officials and Jesuit missionaries sought to create some sort of alliance with the refugee peoples, to counterbalance the powerful Iroquois to the east. Many Native Americans converted to Christianity, creating a Creole Christianity similar to that of the Africans of Kongo and the Mexicans after the Spanish conquest of the Aztecs.

Major population movements also occurred farther west on the Great Plains, where the Apaches arrived from the Great Basin in the Rockies. They had captured horses which had escaped during the Pueblo uprising of 1680–1695 against Spain. The Comanches, who arrived at the same time also from the west and on horses, had, in addition, acquired firearms and around 1725 began their expansion at the expense of the Apaches. The Sioux from the northern forests and the Cheyenne from the Great Basin added to the mix of federations on the Great Plains in the early 1700s. At this time, the great transformation of the Native Americans in the center of North America into horse breeders and horsemen warriors began. Smallpox epidemics did not reach the Plains until the mid-1700s while in the east the ravages of this epidemic had weakened the Iroquois so much that they concluded a peace with the French in 1701.

Land Sale. Signatures of the leaders of the Iroquois federation on a treaty with Thomas and Richard Penn in 1736. By the terms of this treaty the Iroquois sold lands west of the Susquehanna River to the sons of the founders of the English colony of Pennsylvania. The leaders of the six nations that made up the Iroquois federation (Mohawk, Oneida, Onondaga, Cayuga, Seneca, and Tuscarora) signed with their pictograms. Their names were added later.

French Canada The involvement of the French in the Great Lakes region with refugees fleeing from the Iroquois was part of a program of expansion into the center of North America, begun in 1663 (see Source 18.4). The governor of Quebec had dispatched explorers, fur traders, and missionaries not only into the Great Lakes region but also into the Mississippi valley. The French government then sent farmers, craftspeople, and young single women from France with government-issued agricultural implements and livestock to establish settlements. The most successful settlement was in the subtropical district at the mouth of the Mississippi, called "La Louisiane," where some 300 settlers with 4,000 African slaves founded sugar plantations. Immigration was restricted to French subjects and excluded Protestants. Given these restrictions, Louisiana received only some 30,000 settlers by 1750, in contrast to English North America, with nearly 1.2 million settlers by the same time.

Colonial Assemblies As immigration to New England picked up, the merchant companies in Europe, which had financed the journeys of the settlers, were initially responsible for the administration of about a dozen settlement colonies. The first settlers to demand participation in the colonial administration were Virginian tobacco growers with interests in the European trade. In 1619 they deputized delegates from their villages to meet as the House of Burgesses. They thereby created an early popular assembly in North America, assisting their governor in running the colony. The other English colonies soon followed suit, creating their own assemblies. In contrast to Spain and Portugal, England—racked by its internal Anglican–Puritan conflict—was initially uninvolved in the governance of the overseas territories.

When England eventually stepped in and took the governance of the colonies away from the charter merchants and companies in the second half of the seventeenth century, it faced entrenched settler assemblies, especially in New England. Only in New Amsterdam, conquered from the Dutch in 1664–1674 and renamed "New York," did the governor initially rule without an assembly. Many governors were deputies of wealthy aristocrats who never traveled to America but stayed in London. These governors were powerless to prevent the assemblies from appropriating rights to levy taxes and making appointments. The assemblies thus modeled themselves after Parliament in London. As in England, these assemblies were highly select bodies that excluded poorer settlers, who did not meet the property requirements to vote or stand for elections.

Territorial Expansion Steady immigration, also from the European mainland, encouraged land speculators in the British colonies to cast their sights beyond the Appalachian Mountains. (According to historical convention, the English are called "British" after the English–Scottish union in 1707.) In 1749, the Ohio Company of Virginia received a royal permit to develop land, together with a protective fort, south of the Ohio River. The French, however, also claimed the Ohio valley, considering it a part of their Canada–Mississippi–Louisiana territory. A few years later, tensions over the valley erupted into open hostility. Initially, the local encounters went badly for the Virginian militia and British army. In 1755, however, the British and French broadened their clash into a worldwide war for dominance in the colonies and Europe, the Seven Years' War of 1756–1763.

powder horn, ca. 1757

The Seven Years' War Both France and Great Britain borrowed heavily to pour resources into the war. England had the superior navy and France the superior army. Since the British navy succeeded in choking off French supplies to its increasingly isolated land troops, Britain won the war overseas. In Europe, Britain's failure to supply the troops of its ally Prussia against the Austrian–French alliance caused the war on that front to end in a draw. Overseas, the British gained most of the French holdings in India, several islands in the Caribbean, all of Canada, and all the land east of the Mississippi. The war costs and land swaps, however, proved to be unmanageable for both the vanquished and the victor. The unpaid debts became the root cause of the American, French, and Haitian constitutional revolutions that began 13 years later. Those revolutions, along with the emerging industrialization of Great Britain, signaled the beginning of the modern scientific–industrial age in world history.

The Making of American Societies: Origins and Transformations

The patterns which made the Americas an extension of Europe emerged gradually and displayed characteristics specific to each region. On one hand, there was the slow transfer of the plants and animals native to each continent, called the **Columbian Exchange** (see "Patterns Up Close"). On the other hand, Spain and Portugal adopted different strategies of mineral and agricultural exploitation. In spite of these different strategies, however, the settler societies of the two countries in the end displayed similar characteristics.

Columbian Exchange: Exchange of plants, animals, and diseases between the Americas and the rest of the world.

Exploitation of Mineral and Tropical Resources

The pattern of European expansion into subtropical and tropical lands began with the Spanish colonization of the Caribbean islands. When the Spanish crown ran out of gold in the Caribbean, it exported silver from Mexico and Peru in great quantities to finance a centralizing state that could compete with the Ottomans and European kings. By contrast, Portugal's colony of Brazil did not at first mine for precious metals, and consequently the Portuguese crown pioneered the growing of sugar on plantations. Mining would be developed later. The North American colonies of England and France had, in comparison, little native industry at first. By moving farther south, however, they adopted the plantation system for indigo and rice and thus joined their Spanish and Portuguese predecessors in exploiting the subtropical–tropical agricultural potential of the Americas.

Silver Mines When the interest of the Spaniards turned from looting to the exploitation of mineral resources, two main mining centers emerged: Potosí in southeastern Peru (today Bolivia) and Zacatecas and Guanajuato in northern Mexico. For the first 200 years after its founding in 1545, Potosí produced over half of the silver of Spanish America. In the eighteenth century, Zacatecas and Guanajuato jumped ahead of Potosí, churning out almost three times as much of the precious metal. During the same century, gold mining in Colombia and Chile rose to importance as well, making the mining of precious metals the most important economic activity in the Americas.

Patterns Up Close

The Columbian Exchange

Few of us can imagine an Italian kitchen without tomatoes or an Irish meal without potatoes or Chinese or Indian cuisine without the piquant presence of chilies, but until fairly recently each of these foods was unknown to the Old World. Likewise, the expression "As American as apple pie" obscures the fact that for millennia apples, as well as many other frequently consumed fruits, such as peaches, pears, plums, cherries, bananas, oranges, and lemons, were absent from the New World. It was not until the sixteenth century, when plants, animals, and microbes began to flow from one end of the planet to another, that new patterns of ecology and biology changed the course of millions of years of divergent evolution.

When historians catalog the long list of life forms that moved across the oceans in the Columbian Exchange, pride of place is usually reserved for the bigger, better-known migrants like cattle, sheep, pigs, and horses. However, the impact of European weeds and grasses on American grasslands, which made it possible for the North American prairie and the South American pampas to support livestock, should not be overlooked. By binding the soil together with their long, tough roots, these "empires of the dandelion" provided the conditions for the grazing of sheep, cattle, and horses, as well as the planting of crops like wheat.

The other silent invader that accompanied the conquistadors was, of course, disease. Thousands of years of mutual isolation between the Americas and Afro-Eurasia rendered the immune systems of Native Americans vulnerable to the scourges that European colonists unwittingly brought with them. Smallpox, influenza, diphtheria, whooping cough, typhoid, chickenpox, measles, and meningitis wiped out millions of Native Americans—by some estimates, the native populations of Mesoamerica and the Andes plummeted by 90 percent in the period 1500–1700. In comparison, the contagions the New World was able to reciprocate upon the Old World—syphilis and tuberculosis—did not unleash nearly the same devastation, and the New World origin of these diseases is still debated.

It is therefore obvious that the big winner in the Columbian Exchange was western Europe, though the effects of the New World bounty took centuries to be fully discerned. While Asia and Africa also benefited from the Columbian Exchange in the forms of new foods that enriched diets, the Europeans got a continent endowed with a warm climate in which they could create new and improved versions of their homelands. The Native Americans were nearly wiped out by disease, their lands

Innovations, such as the "patio" method, which facilitated the extraction process through the use of mercury, and the unrestrained exploitation of indigenous labor made American silver highly competitive in the world market. Conditions among the Native Americans and blacks employed as labor were truly abominable. Few laborers lasted through more than two forced recruitment (*repartimiento*) cycles before they were incapacitated or dead.

Given gaps in bookkeeping and high levels of smuggling, scholars have found it extremely difficult to estimate the total production of the American mines from 1550 to 1750. The best current estimate is that Spanish America produced 150,000

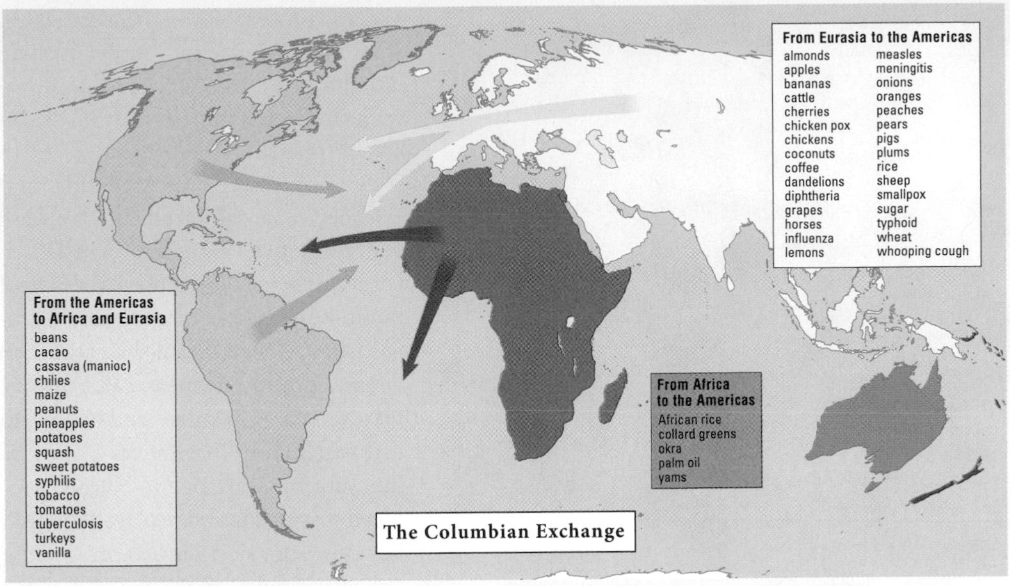

MAP 18.4 The Columbian Exchange.

appropriated, and the survivors either enslaved or marginalized. The precipitous drop in the population of Native Americans, combined with the tropical and semi-tropical climate of much of the Americas, created the necessary conditions for the Atlantic slave trade. The population losses from this trade were monumental, although the Columbian Exchange, which brought manioc and corn to Africa, balanced these losses to a degree.

Questions

- Can the Columbian Exchange be considered one of the origins of the modern world? How? Why? How does the Columbian Exchange demonstrate the origins, interactions, and adaptations model that is used throughout this book?
- Weigh the positive and negative outcomes of the Columbian Exchange. Is it possible to determine whether the overall effects of the Columbian Exchange on human society and the natural environment were for the better or for the worse?

tons of silver (including gold converted into silver weight). This quantity corresponded to roughly 85 percent of world production. The figures underline the extraordinary role of American silver for the money economies of Europe, the Middle East, and Asia, especially China.

Since the exploitation of the mines was of such central importance, for the first century and a half of New World colonization the Spanish crown organized its other provinces around the needs of the mining centers. Hispaniola and Cuba in the Caribbean were islands which had produced foodstuffs, sugar, and tobacco from the time of Columbus but only in small quantities. Their main function was to

The Silver Mountain of Potosí. Note the patios in the left foreground and the water-driven crushing mill in the center, which ground the silver-bearing ore into a fine sand that then was moistened, caked, amalgamated with mercury, and dried on the patio. The mine workers' insect-like shapes reinforce the dehumanizing effects of their labor.

feed and protect Havana, the collection point for Mexican and Peruvian silver and the port from where the annual Spanish fleet shipped the American silver across the Atlantic.

A second region, Argentina and Paraguay, was colonized as a bulwark to prevent the Portuguese and Dutch from cutting across the southern end of the continent and accessing Peruvian silver. Once established, the two colonies produced wheat, cattle, mules, horses, cotton, textiles, and tallow to feed and supply the miners in Potosí. The subtropical crop of cotton, produced by small farmers, played a role in Europe's extension into warm-weather agriculture only toward the end of the colonial period.

A third colonial region, Venezuela, began as a grain and cattle supply base for Cartagena, the port for the shipment of Colombian gold, and Panama and Portobelo, ports for the transshipment of Peruvian silver from the Pacific to Havana. Its cocoa and tobacco exports flourished only after the Dutch established themselves in 1624 in the southern Caribbean and provided the shipping. Thus, three major regions of the Spanish overseas empire in the Americas were mostly peripheral as agricultural producers during the sixteenth century. Only after the middle of the century did they begin to specialize in tropical agricultural goods, and they were exporters only in the eighteenth century. By that time, the Dutch and English provided more and more shipping in the place of the Spanish.

Wheat Farming and Cattle Ranching To support the mining centers and administrative cities, the Spanish colonial government encouraged the development of agricultural estates (*haciendas*). These estates first emerged when conquistadors used their *encomienda* rights to round up Native American labor to produce subsistence crops. Native American tenant farmers were forced to grow wheat and raise cattle, pigs, sheep, and goats for the conquerors, who were now agricultural entrepreneurs. In the latter part of the sixteenth century, the land grants gave way to rotating forced labor as well as wage labor. Owners established their residences and built dwellings for tenant farmers on their estates. A landowner class emerged.

map of Mexican town drawn by indigenous artists, 1579

Like the conquistadors before, a majority of landowners produced wheat and animals for sale to urban and mining centers. Cities purchased wheat and maintained granaries in order to provide for urban dwellers in times of harvest failure. Entrepreneurs received commissions to provide slaughterhouses with regular supplies of animals. As the Native American population declined in the seventeenth century and the church helped in consolidating the remaining population in large villages, additional land became available for the establishment of estates. From 1631 onward, authorities granted Spanish settler families the right to maintain their estates undivided from generation to generation. Through donations, the church also acquired considerable agricultural lands. Secular and clerical landowning interests supported a powerful upper social stratum of Creoles from the eighteenth century onward.

Plantations and Gold Mining in Brazil Brazil's economic activities began with brazilwood, followed by sugar plantations, before gold mining rose to prominence in the eighteenth century. A crisis hit sugar production in 1680–1700, mostly as a result of the Dutch beginning production of sugar in the Antilles. It was at that time that the gold of Minas Gerais, in the interior of Brazil, was discovered.

Gold-mining operations in Brazil during the eighteenth century were considerably less capital-intensive than the silver mines in Spanish America. Most miners were relatively small operators with sieves, pickaxes, and a few black slaves as unskilled laborers. Many entrepreneurs were indebted for their slaves to absentee capitalists, with whom they shared the profits. Since prospecting took place on the land of Native Americans, bloody encounters were frequent. Most entrepreneurs were ruthless frontiersmen who exploited their slaves and took no chances with the indigenous people. Brazil produced a total of 1,000 tons of gold in the eighteenth century, a welcome bonanza for Portugal at a time of low agricultural prices. Overall, minerals were just as valuable for the Portuguese as they were for the Spanish.

Plantations in Spanish and English America The expansion of plantation farming in the Spanish colonies was a result of the Bourbon reforms. Although sugar, tobacco, and rice had been introduced early into the Caribbean and southern Mexico, it was only in the expanded plantation system of the eighteenth century that these crops (plus indigo, cacao, and cactuses as host plants for cochineal) were produced on a large scale for export to Europe. The owners of plantations did not need expensive machinery and invested instead in African slave labor, with the result that the slave trade hit full stride, beginning around 1750.

English Northeast American settlements in Virginia and Carolina exported tobacco and rice beginning in the 1660s. Georgia was the thirteenth British colony, founded in 1733 as a bulwark against Spanish Florida and a haven for poor Europeans. In 1750 it joined southern Carolina as a major plantation colony and rice and indigo producer. In the eighteenth century, even New England finally had its own export crop, in the form of timber for shipbuilding and charcoal production in Great Britain, at the amazing rate of 250 million board-feet per year by the start of the nineteenth century. These timber exports illustrate an important new factor appearing in the Americas in the eighteenth century. Apart from the cheap production of precious metals and warm-weather crops, the American extension of Europe became increasingly important as a replacement for dwindling fuel resources across much of northern Europe. Altogether, it was thanks to the Americas that mostly cold and rainy Europe rose successfully into the ranks of the wealthy, climatically balanced, and populated Indian and Chinese empires.

Social Strata, Castes, and Ethnic Groups

The population of settlers in the New World consisted primarily of Europeans who came from a continent that had barely emerged from its population losses to the Black Death. Although population numbers were rising again in the sixteenth century, Europe did not have masses of emigrants to the Americas to spare. Given the small settler population of the Americas, the temptation to develop a system of forced labor in agriculture and mining was irresistible. Since the Native Americans and African slaves pressed into labor were ethnically so completely different from the Europeans, however, a social system evolved in which the latter two not only were economically underprivileged but also made up the ethnically nonintegrated lowest rungs of the social ladder. A pattern of legal and customary discrimination evolved which, even though partially vitiated by the rise of ethnically mixed groups, prevented the integration of American ethnicities into settler society.

The Social Elite The heirs of the Spanish conquistadors and estate owners—farmers, ranchers, and planters—maintained city residences and employed managers on their agricultural properties. In Brazil, cities emerged more slowly, and for a long time estate owners maintained their manor houses as small urban islands. Estate owners mixed with the Madrid- and Lisbon-appointed administrators and, during the seventeenth century, intermarried with them, creating the top tier of settler society known as Creoles, some 4 percent of the population. In a wider sense, the tier included also merchants, professionals, clerks, militia officers, and the clergy. They formed a relatively closed society in which descent, intermarriage, landed property, and a government position counted more than money and education.

In the seventeenth and eighteenth centuries, the estate owners farmed predominantly with Native American forced labor. They produced grain and/or cattle, legumes, sheep, and pigs for local urban markets or mining towns. In contrast to the black slave plantation estates of the Caribbean and coastal regions of Spanish and Portuguese America, these farming estates did not export their goods to Europe. From the beginning of colonialism, furthermore, Madrid and Lisbon discouraged estate owners, as well as farmers in general, from producing cash crops, such as olive oil, wine, or silk, to protect their home production.

As local producers with little competition, farming and ranching estate owners did not feel market pressures. Since they lived for the most part in the cities, they exploited their estates with minimal investments and usually drew profits of less than 5 percent of annual revenues. They were often heavily indebted, and as a result there was often more glitter than substance among the landowning Creoles.

Lower Creoles The second tier of Creole society consisted of people like Alonzo Ortíz, the tanner introduced at the beginning of this chapter. Even though of second rank, they were privileged European settlers who, as craftspeople and traders, theoretically worked with their hands. In practice, many of them were owner-operators who employed Native Americans and/or black slaves as apprentices and journeymen. Many invested in small plots of land in the vicinity of their cities, striving to rise into the ranks of the landowning Creoles.

Wealthy weavers ran textile manufactures mostly concentrated in the cities of Mexico, Peru, Paraguay, and Argentina. In some of these manufactures, up to 300 Native American and black workers produced cheap, coarse woolens and a variety of cottons on dozens of looms. Men were the weavers and women the spinners—in contrast to the pre-Columbian period, when textile manufacture was entirely a woman's job. On a smaller scale, manufactures also existed for pottery and leather goods. On the whole, the urban manufacturing activities of the popular people, serving the

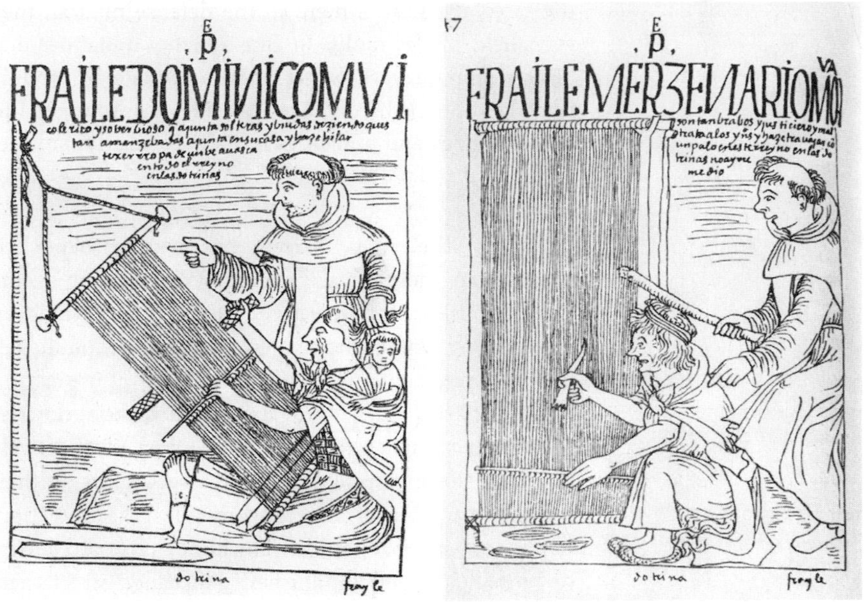

Textile Production. Immigrants from Spain (like Alonso Ortíz, discussed at the beginning of the chapter), maintained workshops (*obrajes*) as tanners, weavers, carpenters, or wheelwrights. As craftspeople producing simple but affordable goods for the poor, they remained competitive throughout the colonial period, in spite of increasingly large textile, utensil, and furniture imports from Europe. At the same time, indigenous textile production by native women continued as in the preconquest period, albeit under the constraints of labor services imposed by officials or clergy, as shown in these examples.

poor in local markets, remained vibrant until well into the nineteenth century, in spite of massive European imports. Prior to the arrival of railroads, the transportation of imports into the interior of the Americas was prohibitively expensive.

Mestizos and Mulattoes The mixed European–Native American and European–African populations had the collective name of "caste" (*casta*), or ethnic group. The term originated in the desire of the Iberian and Creole settlers to draw distinctions among degrees of mixture in order to counterbalance as much as possible the masses of Native Americans and Africans, especially from the eighteenth century onward. The two most important castes were the *mestizos* (Spanish) or *mestiços* (Portuguese) who had Iberian fathers and Native American mothers, and *mulatos,* who had Iberian fathers and black mothers. By 1800 the castas as a whole formed the third largest population category in Latin America (20 percent), after Native Americans (40 percent) and Creoles (30 percent). In Brazil, black freedmen and mulattoes were numerically even with Creoles (28 percent each), after black slaves (38 percent) and before Native Americans (6 percent in the settled provinces outside Amazonia). In both Spanish and Portuguese America, there were also a small percentage of people descended from Native American and black unions. Thus, most of the intermediate population groups were sizable, playing important neutralizing roles in colonial society, as they had one foot in both the Creole and subordinate social strata (see Figure 18.1).

As such neutralizing elements, mestizos and mulattoes filled lower levels of the bureaucracy and the lay hierarchy in the church. They held skilled and supervisory positions in mines and on estates. In addition, in the armed forces mulattoes dominated

Race, Class, and Gender in Colonial Mexico. An outraged black woman defends herself against an aggressive Creole man, with a fearful mulatta child clinging to the woman's skirt.

the ranks of enlisted men; in the defense militias, they even held officer ranks. In Brazil, many mulattoes and black freedmen were farmers. Much of the craft production was in their hands. A wide array of laws existed to keep mestizos and mulattoes in their peculiarly intermediate social and political positions.

Women The roles played by women depended strongly on their social position. Well-appointed elite Creole households followed the Mediterranean tradition of secluding women from men. Within the confines of the household, elite women were persons of means and influence. They were the owners of substantial dowries and legally stipulated grooms' gifts. Often, they actively managed the investment of their assets. Outside their confines, however, even elite women lost all protection. Crimes of passion, committed by honor-obsessed fathers or husbands, went unpunished. Husbands and fathers who did not resort to violence nevertheless did not need witnesses to obtain court judgments to banish daughters or wives to convents for alleged lapses in chastity. Thus, even elite women were bound by definite limits set by a patriarchal society.

On the lower rungs of society, be it popular Creole, mestizo, mulatto, or Native American, gender separation was much less prevalent. After all, everyone in the family had to work in order to make ends meet. Men, women, and children shared labor in the fields and workshops. Girls or wives took in clothes to wash or went out to work as domestics in wealthy households. Older women dominated retail in market stalls. As in elite society, wives tended to outlive husbands. In addition, working families with few assets suffered abandonment by males. Women headed one-third of all households in Mexico City, according to an 1811 census. Among black slaves in the region of São Paulo, 70 percent of women were without formal ties to the men who fathered their children. Thus, the most pronounced division in colonial society was that of a patriarchy among the Creoles and a slave society dominated by women, with frequently absent men—an unbridgeable division that persists still today.

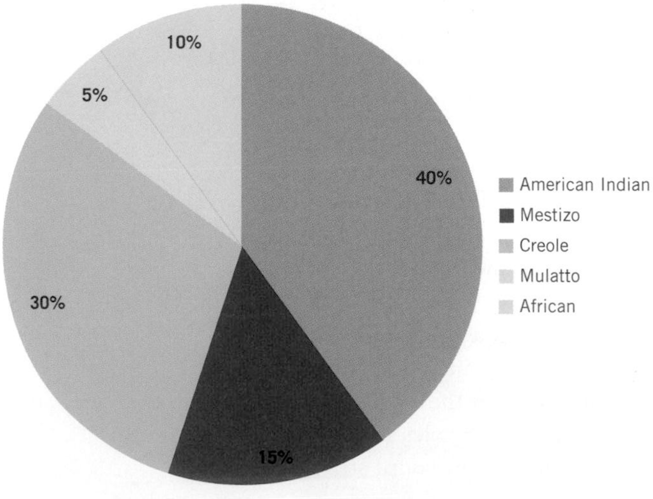

Figure 18.1 Ethnic Composition of Latin America, ca. 1800.

Native Americans In the immediate aftermath of the conquest, Native Americans could be found at all levels of the social scale. Some were completely marginalized in remote corners of the American continents. Others acculturated into the ranks of the working poor in the silver mines or textile manufactures. A few even formed an educated Aztec or Inca propertied upper class, exercising administrative functions

Illustration from an Indian Land Record. The Spaniards almost completely wiped out the Aztec archives after the conquest of Mexico; surviving examples of Indian manuscripts are thus extremely rare. Although the example shown here, made from the bark of a fig tree, claims to date from the early 1500s, it is part of the so-called Techialoyan land records created in the seventeenth century to substantiate native land claims. These "títulos primordiales," as they were called, were essentially municipal histories that documented in text and pictures local accounts of important events and territorial boundaries.

in Spanish civil service. Social distinctions, however, disappeared rapidly during the first 150 years of Spanish colonialism. Smallpox reduced the Native American population by nearly 80 percent. Diseases were more virulent in humid, tropical parts of the continent than in deserts, and the epidemics took a far greater toll on dense, settled populations than they did on dispersed forager bands in dry regions. In the Caribbean and on the Brazilian coast, Native Americans disappeared almost completely; in central and southern Mexico, their population shrank by two-thirds. It was only in the twentieth century that population figures reached the preconquest level again in most parts of Latin America.

Apart from European diseases, the native forager and agrarian Native Americans in the Amazon, Orinoco, and Maracaibo rain forests were the least affected by European colonials during the period 1500–1800. Not only were their lands economically the least promising, but they also defended those lands successfully with blowguns, poison darts, and bow and arrow. In many cold and hot arid or semiarid regions, such as Patagonia, southern Chile, the Argentine grasslands (*pampas*), the Paraguayan salt marshes and deserts, and northern Mexican mountains and steppes, the situation was similar. In these lands, the seminomadic Native Americans quickly adopted the European horse and became highly mobile warrior peoples in defense of their mostly independent territories.

The villagers of Mexico, Yucatán, Guatemala, Colombia, Ecuador, and Peru had fewer choices. When smallpox reduced their numbers in the second half of the sixteenth century, state and church authorities razed many villages and concentrated the survivors in *pueblos de indios*. Initially, the Native Americans put up strong resistance against these resettlements by repeatedly returning to their destroyed old settlements. From the middle of the seventeenth century, however, the pueblos were fully functional, self-administering units, with councils (*cabildos*), churches, schools, communal lands, and family parcels.

The councils were important institutions of legal training and social mobility for ordinary Native Americans. Initially, the traditional "noble" chiefly families descending from the preconquest Aztec and Inca ruling classes were in control as administrators. The many village functions, however, for which the *cabildos* were responsible allowed commoners to move up into auxiliary roles. In some of these roles, they had opportunities to learn the system and acquire modest wealth. Settlers constantly complained about insubordinate Native Americans pursuing lawsuits in the courts. Native American villages were closed to settlers, and the only outsiders admitted were Catholic priests. Contact with the Spanish world remained minimal, and acculturation went little beyond official conversion to Catholicism. Village notaries and scribes were instrumental in preserving Nahuatl in Mexico and Quechua in Peru, making them into functional, written languages. Thus, even in the heartlands of Spanish America, Native American adaptation to the rulers remained limited.

Unfortunately, however, tremendous demographic losses made the Native Americans in the pueblos vulnerable to the loss of their land. Estate owners expanded their holdings, legally and illegally, in spite of the heroic litigation efforts of the villages opposed to this expansion (see Source 18.3). When the population rebounded, many estates had grown to immense sizes. Villages began to run out of land for their inhabitants. Increasing numbers of Native Americans had to rent land from estate owners or find work on estates as farmhands. They became estranged from their villages, fell into debt peonage, and entered the ranks of the working poor in the countryside or city, bearing the full brunt of colonial inequities.

New England Society For a long time in the early modern period, the small family farm, where everyone had to work to eke out a precarious living, remained the norm for the majority of New England's population. Family members specializing in construction, carpentry, spinning, weaving, or ironworks continued to be restricted to small perimeters around their villages and towns. An acute lack of money and cheap means of transportation hampered the development of market networks in the interior well into the 1770s. The situation was better in the agriculturally more favored colonies in the Mid-Atlantic, especially in Pennsylvania. Here, farmers were able to produce marketable quantities of wheat and legumes for urban markets. The number of plantations in the south rose steadily, demanding a substantial increase in numbers of slaves (from 28,000 in 1700 to 575,000 in 1776), although world market fluctuations left planters vulnerable. Except for boom periods in the plantation sector, the rural areas remained largely poor.

Real changes occurred during the early eighteenth century in the urban regions. Large port cities emerged which shipped in textiles and ironwares from Europe in return for timber at relatively cheap rates. The most important were Philadelphia (28,000 inhabitants), New York (25,000), Boston (16,000), and Newport, Rhode Island (11,000). A wealthy merchant class formed, spawning urban strata of professionals (such as lawyers, teachers, and newspaper journalists). Primary school education was provided by municipal public schools as well as some churches, and evening schools for craftspeople existed in some measure. By the middle of the eighteenth century a majority of men could read and write, although female literacy was minimal. Finally, in contrast to Latin America, social ranks in New England were less elaborate.

The Adaptation of the Americas to European Culture

European settlers brought two distinct cultures to the Americas. In the Mid-Atlantic, Caribbean, and Central and South America, they brought with them the Catholic Reformation, a culture and perspective that resisted the New Science of Galileo and the Enlightenment thought of Locke until the late eighteenth century. In the northeast, colonists implanted dissident Protestantism as well as the Anglicanism of Great Britain and the Presbyterianism of Scotland. The rising number of adherents of the New Science and Enlightenment in northwestern Europe had also a parallel in North America. In general, settlers and their locally born offspring were proud of their respective cultures, which, even though provincial, were dominant in what they prejudicially viewed as a less civilized, if not barbaric, Native American environment.

Catholic Missionary Work From the beginning, Spanish and Portuguese monarchs relied heavily on the Catholic Church for their rule in the new American provinces. The pope granted them patronage over the organization and all appointments on the new continents. A strong motive driving many in the church as well as society at large was the belief in the imminent Second Coming of Jesus. This belief was one inspiration for the original Atlantic expansion (see Chapter 16). When the Aztec and Inca Empires fell, members of the Franciscan order, the main proponents of the belief in the imminence of the Second Coming, interpreted it as a sign of the urgent duty to convert the Native Americans to Christianity. If Jesus's kingdom was soon to come, according to this interpretation, all humans in the Americas should be Christians.

Jesuit missionaries, from the Church of San Pedro in Lima, Peru, ca. 1700

Thousands of Franciscan, Dominican, and other preaching monks, later followed by the Jesuits, fanned out among the Native Americans. They baptized them, introduced the sacraments (Eucharist, baptism, confession, confirmation, marriage, last rites, and priesthood), and taught them basic theological concepts of Christianity. The missionaries learned native languages, translated the catechism and New Testament into those languages, and taught the children of the ruling native families how to read and write. Thanks to their genuine efforts to understand the Native Americans on their own terms, a good deal of preconquest Native American culture was recorded without too much distortion.

The role and function of saints as mediators between humans and God formed one element of Catholic Christianity to which Native Americans acculturated early. Good works as God-pleasing human efforts to gain salvation in the afterlife formed another. The veneration of images of the Virgin Mary and pilgrimages to the chapels and churches where they were kept constituted a third element. The best-known example of the last element is Our Lady of Guadalupe, near Mexico City, who in 1531 appeared in a vision to a Native American in the place where the native goddess Tonantzin used to be venerated. On the other hand, the Spanish Inquisition also operated in the Spanish and Portuguese colonies, seeking to limit the degree to which Catholicism and traditional religion mingled (see Source 18.2). The church treaded a fine line between enforcement of doctrine and leniency toward what it determined were lax or heretical believers.

Earliest representation of the Madonna and Child created by Indians in the New World (1531)

Education and the Arts The Catholic Reformation expressed itself also in the organization of education. The Franciscans and Dominicans had offered general education to the children of settlers early on and, in colleges, trained graduates for

Spanish Cruelty to Incas. Felipe Guamán Poma de Ayala, a Peruvian claiming noble Inca descent, was a colonial administrator, well educated and an ardent Christian. He is remembered today as a biting critic of the colonial administration and the clergy, whom he accused of mistreating and exploiting the Andean population, as in this colored wood print.

illustration from Willem Piso's *Natural History of Brazil* (1637)

missionary work. The first New World universities, such as Santo Domingo (1538), Mexico City, and Lima (both 1553), taught theology, church law, and Native American languages. Under the impact of the Jesuits, universities broadened the curriculum, offering degrees also in secular law, Aristotelian philosophy, the natural sciences, and medicine. Although the universities did not admit the New Sciences and Enlightenment of northwestern Europe into their curriculum, there was nevertheless considerable scientific research on tropical diseases, plants, and animals as a counterbalance. The vast extent of this research, long kept secret by the Spanish and Portuguese monarchs from their European competitors, is becoming gradually known only now.

Furthermore, missionary monks collected and recorded Native American manuscripts and oral traditions, such as the Aztec *Anales de Tula* and the Maya *Popol Vuh*. Others wrote histories and ethnographies of the Taíno, Aztec, Maya, Inca, and Tupí peoples. Bartolomé de las Casas, Toribio Motolonía de Benavente, Bernardino de Sahagún, Diego de Landa, Bernabé Cobo, and Manuel da Nóbrega are merely a handful of noteworthy authors who wrote about the Native Americans. Many labored for years, worked with legions of informers, and produced monumental tomes.

A number of Native American and mestizo chroniclers, historians, and commentators on the early modern state and society are similarly noteworthy. Muñoz Camargo was a Tlaxcaltecan; Fernando de Alva Ixtlixóchitl and Fernando Alvarado Tezózomoc were Mexican mestizos; and Juan de Santa Cruz Pachacuti Yamqui and Felipe Inca Garcilaso de la Vega were Peruvian mestizos, all writing on their native regions. Felipe Guamán Poma de Ayala (ca. 1535–1616), a native Peruvian, is of particular interest. He accompanied his 800-page manuscript, entitled (in English translation) *The First New Chronicle and Good Government*, with some 400 drawings of daily-life activities in the Peruvian villages. These drawings provide us with invaluable cultural details, which would be difficult to render in writing. Unfortunately, King Philip II of Spain, a relentless proponent of the Catholic Reformation, took a dim view of authors writing on Native American society and history. In 1577 he forbade the publication of all manuscripts dealing with what he called idolatry and superstition. Many manuscripts lay hidden in archives and did not see the light of day until modern times.

Protestantism in New England From the start, religious diversity was a defining cultural trait of English settlements in North America. The spectrum of Christian denominations ranged from a host of English and continental European versions of Protestantism to Anglicanism and a minority of Catholics. As if this spectrum had not been sufficiently broad, dissenters frequently split from the existing denominations, moved into new territory, and founded new settlements. Religiosity was a major characteristic of the early settlers.

An early example of religious splintering was the rise of an antinomian ("antilaw") group within Puritan-dominated Massachusetts. The Puritans dominant in this colony generally recognized the authority of the Anglican Church but strove to move it toward Protestantism from within. The preachers and settlers represented in the General Court, as their assembly was called, were committed to the Calvinist balance between "inner" personal grace obtained from God and "outer" works according to the law. The antinomian group, however, digging deep into early traditions in Christianity, advocated an exclusive commitment to inner grace through spiritual perfection.

Their leader was Anne Hutchinson, an early and tireless proponent of women's rights and an inspiring preacher. She was accused of arguing that she could recognize those believers in Calvinist Protestantism who were predestined for salvation and that these believers would be saved even if they had sinned. After a power struggle with the deeply misogynistic magistrates opposed to influential women, the General Court prevailed and forced the antinomians to move to Rhode Island in 1638.

The New Sciences in the New World. This painting by Samuel Collings, *The Magnetic Dispensary* (1790), shows how men and women, of lay background, participated in scientific experiments in the English colonies of North America, similar to educated middle-class people in western Europe at the same time.

The example of Hutchinson is noteworthy because it led to the founding of Harvard College in 1636 by the General Court. Harvard was the first institution of higher learning in North America, devoted to teaching the "correct" balanced Calvinist Protestantism. Later, the college functioned as the main center for training the colony's ministers in Puritan theology and morality, although it was not affiliated with any specific denomination.

New Sciences Research As discussed in Chapter 17, the New Sciences had found their most hospitable home in northwestern Europe by default. The rivalry between Protestantism and Catholicism had left enough of an authority-free space for the New Sciences to flourish. Under similar circumstances—intense rivalry among denominations—English North America also proved hospitable to the New Sciences. An early practitioner was Benjamin Franklin (1706–1790), who began his career as a printer, journalist, and newspaper editor. Franklin founded the University of Pennsylvania (1740), the first secular university in North America, and the American Philosophical Society (1743), the first scientific society. This hospitality for the New Sciences in North America was quite in contrast to Latin America, where a uniform Catholic Reformation prevented its rise.

Witch Hunts In the last decade of the seventeenth century, a high level of religious intensity and rivalry was at the root of a witchcraft frenzy which seized New England. The belief in witchcraft was the survival on the popular level of the ancient concept of a shared mind or spirit that allows people to influence each other, either positively or negatively. Witches, male and female, were persons exerting a negative influence, or black magic, on their victims. In medieval Europe, the church had kept witchcraft out of sight, but in the wake of Protestantism and the many challenges to church authority it had become more visible. In the North American colonies, with no overarching religious authority, the visibility of witchcraft was particularly high.

The one case where this sensitivity erupted into hysteria was that of Salem, Massachusetts. Here, the excitement erupted in 1692 with Tituba, a Native American slave from Barbados who worked in the household of a pastor. Tituba practiced voodoo, the West African–originated, part-African and part-Christian religious practice of influencing others. When a young daughter and niece in the pastor's household suffered from convulsions, mass hysteria broke out, in which 20 women accused of being witches were executed, although Tituba, ironically, survived. A new governor finally calmed the passions and restored order (see Source 18.5).

Witch Trial. In the course of the 1600s, in the relatively autonomous English colonies of Northeast America, more persons were accused, tried, and convicted of witchcraft than anywhere else. Of the 140 persons coming to trial between 1620 and 1725, 86 percent were women. Three witch panics are recorded: Bermuda, 1651; Hartford, Connecticut, 1652–1665; and Salem, Massachusetts, 1692–1693. This anonymous American woodcut of the early 1600s shows one method to try someone for witchcraft: swim or float if guilty, or sink if innocent.

Revivalism Religious fervor expressed itself also in periodic Protestant renewal movements, among which the "Great Awakening" of the 1730s and 1740s was the most important. The main impulse for this revivalist movement came from the brothers John and Charles Wesley, two Methodist preachers in England who toured Georgia in 1735. Preachers from other denominations joined, all exhorting Protestants to literally "start anew" in their relationship with God. Fire-and-brimstone sermons rained down on the pews, reminding the faithful of the absolute sovereignty of God, the depravity of humans, predestination to hell and heaven, the inner experience of election, and salvation by God's grace alone. Thus, revivalism, recurring with great regularity to the present, became a potent force in Protestant America, at opposing purposes with secular founding-father constitutionalism.

Putting It All Together

interactive concept map

During the period 1500–1800 the contours of a new pattern in which the Americas formed a resource-rich and warm-weather extension of Europe took shape. During this time, China and India continued to be the most populous and wealthiest agrarian–urban regions of the world. Scholars have estimated China's share of the world economy during this period as comprising 40 percent. India probably did not lag far behind. In 1500, Europe was barely an upstart, forced to defend itself against the push of the Ottoman Empire into eastern Europe and the western Mediterranean. But its successful conquest of Iberia from the Muslims led to the discovery of the Americas. Possession of the Americas made Europe similar to China and India in that it now encompassed, in addition to its northerly cold climates, subtropical and tropical regions which produced rich cash crops as well as precious metals. Over the course of 300 years, with the help of its American extension, Europe narrowed the gap between itself and China and India, although it was only after the beginning of industrialization, around 1800, that it eventually was able to close this gap.

Narrowing the gap, of course, was not a conscious policy in Europe. Quite the contrary, because of fierce competition both with the Ottoman Empire and internally, much of the wealth Europe gained in the Americas, especially silver, was wasted on warfare. The centralizing state, created in part to support war, ran into insurmountable budgetary barriers, which forced Spain into several state bankruptcies. Even mercantilism, a logical extension of the centralizing state, had limited effects. Its centerpiece, state support for the export of manufactures to the American colonies, functioned unevenly. The Spanish and Portuguese governments, with weak urban infrastructures and low manufacturing capabilities, especially in textiles, were unable to enforce this state-supported trade until the eighteenth century and even then only in very limited ways. France and especially England practiced mercantilism more successfully but were able to do so in the Americas only from the late seventeenth century onward, when their plantation systems began to take shape. Although the American extension of Europe had the potential of making Europe self-sufficient, this potential was realized only partially during the colonial period.

A fierce debate has raged over the question of the degree of wealth the Americas added to Europe. On one hand, considerable quantitative research has established that the British slave trade for sugar plantations added at best 1 percent to the British gross domestic product (GDP). The profits from the production of sugar on the English island of Jamaica may have added another 4 percent to the British GDP. Without doubt, private slave-trading and sugar-producing enterprises were at times immensely profitable to individuals and groups, not to mention the mining of silver through forced labor. In the larger picture, however, these profits were considerably smaller if one takes into account the immense waste of revenues on military ventures—hence the doubts raised by scholars today about large gains made by Europe through its American colonial acquisitions.

On the other hand, the European extension to the Americas was clearly a momentous event in world history. It might have produced dubious overall profits for Europe, but it definitely encouraged the parting of ways between Europe on one hand and Asia and Africa on the other, once a new scientific–industrial society began to emerge around 1800.

Review and Relate

Thinking Through Patterns

Examine the ways historians approach the big questions of this chapter.

» What is the significance of western Europeans acquiring the Americas as a warm-weather extension of their northern continent?

In their role as supplementary subtropical and tropical extensions of Europe, the Americas had a considerable impact on Europe's changing position in the world. First, Europe acquired large quantities of precious metals, which its two largest competitors, India and China, lacked. Second, with its new access to warm-weather agricultural products, Europe rose to a position of agrarian autonomy similar to that of India and China. In terms of resources, compared with the principal religious civilizations of India and China, Europe grew between 1550 and 1800 from a position of inferiority to one of near parity.

» What was the main pattern of social development in colonial America during the period 1500–1800?

Because the numbers of Europeans who emigrated to the Americas was low for most of the colonial period—just 300,000 Spaniards left for the New World between 1500 and 1800—they never exceeded the numbers of Native Americans or African slaves. The result was a highly privileged settler society that held superior positions on the top rung of the social hierarchy. In principle, given an initially large indigenous population, labor was cheap and should have become more expensive as diseases reduced the Native Americans. In fact, labor always remained cheap, in part because of the politically supported institution of forced labor and in part because of racial prejudice.

» Why and how did European settlers in South and North America strive for self-government, and how successful were they in achieving their goals?

Two contrasting patterns characterized the way in which European colonies were governed. The Spanish and Portuguese crowns, primarily interested in extracting minerals and warm-weather products from the colonies, had a strong interest in exercising as much centralized control over their possessions in the Americas as they could. In contrast, the British crown granted self-government to the northeast American colonies from the start, in part because the colonies were initially far less important economically and in part because of a long tradition of self-rule at home. Nevertheless, even though Latin American settlers achieved only partial self-rule in their towns and cities, they destroyed central rule indirectly through the purchase of offices. After financial reforms, Spain and Portugal reestablished a degree of central rule through the appointment of officers from the home countries.

Against the Grain

Consider this as a counterpoint to the main patterns examined in this chapter.

Juana Inés de la Cruz

In the wake of the Protestant and Catholic Reformations of the 1500s, it was no longer unusual for European women to pursue higher education. In the considerably more conservative Latin American colonies of Spain, Juana Inés de la Cruz (1651–1695) was less fortunate, even though her fame as the intellectually most brilliant figure of the seventeenth century in the colonies endured.

De la Cruz was the illegitimate child of a Spanish immigrant father and a Creole mother. She grew up on the hacienda of her maternal grandfather, in whose library she secretly studied Latin, Greek, and Nahuatl, and also composed her first poems. Unable as a woman to be admitted to the university in Mexico City, de la Cruz nevertheless was fortunate to receive further education from the wife of the vice regent of New Spain. In order to continue her studies and eschewing married life in the ruling class, in 1668 she entered a convent. Here, she continued to study and write hundreds of poems, comedies, religious dramas, and theological texts. Her seminars with courtiers and scholarly visitors were a major attraction in Mexico City.

In 1688, however, she lost her protection at court with the departure of her viceregal supporters for Spain. Her superior, the archbishop of Mexico, was an open misogynist, and even though her confessor and the bishop of Puebla were admirers, their admiration had limits. A crisis came in 1690 when the bishop of Puebla published de la Cruz's critique of a famous sermon of 1650 by the Portuguese Jesuit António Vieira on Jesus's act of washing his disciples' feet, together with his own critique of de la Cruz. The complex theological arguments addressed the question of whether the foot washing was an inversion of the master–slave (Vieira) or master–servant (de la Cruz) relationship—a theological question unresolved in the Gospels, as well as among the Christian churches in the subsequent centuries. De la Cruz viewed Vieira's interpretation as more hierarchical–male and her own interpretation as more humble–female.

A year later, in 1691, de la Cruz wrote a highly spirited, lengthy riposte to the bishop's apparently well-meaning advice to her in his critique to be more conscious of her status as a woman. Her message was clear: Even though women had to be silent in church, as St. Paul had taught, neither study nor writing were prohibited for women. Before the church could censor her, in 1693 Juana Inés de la Cruz stopped writing. She died two years later.

- Why were the Latin American colonies more socially conservative than Europe?
- Was de la Cruz right to stop her correspondence with the Mexican clergy in 1693?

Key Terms

audio flashcards

Columbian Exchange 541
Creoles 532
Labor assignment (*repartimiento*) 534
Land-labor grant (*encomienda*) 526

For additional resources, please go to **www.oup.com/us/vonsivers.**
Please see the Further Resources section at the back of the book for additional readings and suggested websites.

» PATTERNS OF EVIDENCE |

Sources for Chapter 18

SOURCE 18.1

Hernán Cortés, *Second Letter from Mexico to Emperor Charles V*

1522

With a handful of untrained and poorly equipped soldiers, Hernán Cortés overthrew the powerful Aztec civilization between 1519 and 1521. Born in Spain around 1485, Cortés decided to inform the king of Spain (and Holy Roman emperor) Charles V of his achievements, in a series of written updates. Despite their ostensible purpose, these "letters" were designed for more than the edification and delight of the emperor. Like Julius Caesar's dispatches from the Gallic Wars of the 50s BCE—in which at least one million Gauls were purportedly killed and another million enslaved—these accounts were designed for broad public consumption. Each letter was sent to Spain as soon as it was ready, and it seems likely that Cortés's father, Martín, arranged for their immediate publication. Over the course of these five published letters, although Cortés developed a persona for himself as a conquering hero and agent of imperial power, he also exposed the ruthlessness and brutality of his "conquest" of Mexico.

From henceforth they offered themselves as vassals of Your Sacred Majesty and swore to remain so always and to serve and assist in all things that Your Highness commanded them. A notary set all this down through the interpreters which I had. Still I determined to go with them; on the one hand, so as not to show weakness and, on the other, because I hoped to conduct my business with Mutezuma from that city because it bordered on his territory, as I have said, and on the road between the two there is free travel and no frontier restrictions.

When the people of Tascalteca saw my determination it distressed them considerably, and they told me many times that I was mistaken, but since they were vassals of Your Sacred Majesty and my friends they would go with me to assist me in whatever might happen. Although I opposed this and asked them not to come, as it was unnecessary, they followed me with some 100,000 men, all well armed for war, and came within two leagues of the city. After much

---

Source: Hernán Cortés, *Letters from Mexico*, ed. and trans. Anthony Pagden (New Haven, CT: Yale University Press, 1986), 72–74.

persuasion on my part they returned, though there remained in my company some five or six thousand of them. That night I slept in a ditch, hoping to divest myself of these people in case they caused trouble in the city, and because it was already late enough and I did not want to enter too late. The following morning, they came out of the city to greet me with many trumpets and drums, including many persons whom they regard as priests in their temples, dressed in traditional vestments and singing after their fashion, as they do in the temples. With such ceremony they led us into the city and gave us very good quarters, where all those in my company were most comfortable. There they brought us food, though not sufficient.

. . .

During the three days I remained in that city they fed us worse each day, and the lords and principal persons of the city came only rarely to see and speak with me. And being somewhat disturbed by this, my interpreter, who is an Indian woman from Putunchan, which is the great river of which I spoke to Your Majesty in the first letter, was told by another Indian woman and a native of this city that very close by many of Mutezuma's men were gathered, and that the people of the city had sent away their women and children and all their belongings, and were about to fall on us and kill us all; and that if she wished to escape she should go with her and she would shelter her. All this she told to Gerónimo de Aguilar, an interpreter whom I acquired in Yucatán, of whom I have also written to Your Highness; and he informed me. I then seized one of the natives of this city who was passing by and took him aside secretly and questioned him; and he confirmed what the woman and the natives of Tascalteca had told me. Because of this and because of the signs I had observed, I decided to forestall an attack, and I sent for some of the chiefs of the city, saying that I wished to speak with them. I put them in a room and meanwhile warned our men to be prepared, when a harquebus was fired, to fall on the many Indians who were outside our quarters and on those who were inside. And so it was done, that after I had put the chiefs in the room, I left them bound up and rode away and had the harquebus fired, and we fought so hard that in two hours more than three thousand men were killed.

. . .

After fifteen or twenty days which I remained there the city and the land were so pacified and full of people that it seemed as if no one were missing from it, and their markets and trade were carried on as before. I then restored the friendly relations between this city of Curultecal and Tascalteca, which had existed in the recent past, before Mutezuma had attracted them to his friendship with gifts and made them enemies of the others.

» Working with Sources

1. **Does Cortés offer a justification for his treatment of the people of Tascalteca? Why or why not?**
2. **What were the risks associated with Cortés's reliance on translators as he conquered the natives of Mexico?**

SOURCE 18.2

Marina de San Miguel's Confessions before the Inquisition, Mexico City

1598–1599

The Inquisition was well established in Spain at the time of Cortés's conquest in the 1520s. A tribunal of the Holy Office of the Inquisition came in the conquistadors' wake, ultimately established at Mexico City in 1571 with authority to regulate Catholic morality throughout "New Spain." Most of the Inquisition trials concerned petty breaches of religious conduct, but others dealt with the much more serious crime of heresy. In November 1598, the Inquisition became alarmed about the rise of a group who believed that the Day of Judgment was at hand. Among the group denounced to the Holy Office was Marina de San Miguel, a Spanish-born woman who held a high status due to her mystical visions. Her confessions reveal the degree to which admissions of "deviance" could be extorted from a victim. In March 1601, Marina was stripped naked to the waist and paraded upon a mule. Forced to confess her errors, she was sentenced to 100 lashes with a whip. Confined to a plague hospital, she died some time later.

First Confession

In the city of Mexico, Friday, November 20, 1598. The Lord Inquisitor *licenciado* don Alonso de Peralta in his morning audience ordered that a woman be brought before him from one of the secret prisons of this Holy Office. Being present, she swore an oath *en forma devida de derecho* under which she promised to tell the truth here in this audience and in all the others that might be held until the determination of her case, and to keep secret everything that she might see or believe or that might be talked about with her or that might happen concerning this her case.

. . .

She was asked if she knows, presumes, or suspects the cause for her arrest and imprisonment in the prisons of the Holy Office. . . . The inquisitor said that with her illness she must have imagined it. And she says that she wants to go over her memory so that she can tell the truth about everything that she might remember.

With this the audience ceased, because it was past eleven. The above was read and she approved it and signed it. And she was ordered to return to her cell, very admonished to examine her memory as she was offered to do.

. . .

Source: Jacqueline Holler, "The Spiritual and Physical Ecstasies of a Sixteenth-Century Beata: Marina de San Miguel Confesses Before the Mexican Inquisition," in Richard Boyer and Geoffrey Spurling, eds., *Colonial Lives: Documents on Latin American History, 1550–1850* (New York: Oxford University Press, 2000), 79–98.

Third Confession

In the city of Mexico, Tuesday, November 24, 1598. . . .

She said that what she has remembered is that in the course of her life some spiritual things have happened to her, which she has talked about to some people. And she believes that they have been the cause of her imprisonment, because they were scandalized by what she told them.

. . .

And then she opened her eyes and began to shake and get up from the bench on which she was seated, saying, "My love, help me God, how strongly you have given me this." And among these words she said to the Lord Inquisitor that when she is given these trances, she should be shaken vigorously to awaken her from her deep dream. Then she returned to being as though sleeping. The inquisitor called her by her name and she did not respond, nor the second time. And the third time she opened her eyes and made faces, and made signs with her hands to her mouth.

. . .

Sixth Confession

In the city of Mexico, Monday, January 25, 1599. . . .

She said that it's like this. . . . She has been condemned to hell, because for fifteen years she has had a sensual temptation of the flesh, which makes her perform dishonest acts with her own hands on her shameful parts. She came to pollution [orgasm] saying dishonest words that provoke lust, calling by their dishonest names many dirty and lascivious things. She was tempted to this by the devil, who appeared to her internally in the form of an Angel of Light, who told her that she should do these things, because they were no sin. This was to make her abandon her scruples. And the devil appeared to her in the form of Christ our Redeemer, in such a way that she might uncover her breasts and have carnal union with him. And thus, for fifteen years, she has had carnal union occasionally from month to month, or every two months. And if it had been more she would accuse herself of that too, because she is only trying to save her soul, with no regard to honor or the world. And the carnal act that the devil as Angel of Light and in the form of Christ had with her was the same as if she had had it with a man. And he kissed her, and she enjoyed it, and she felt a great ardor in her whole body, with particular delight and pleasure.

. . .

Eighth Confession

In the city of Mexico, Wednesday, January 27, 1599. . . .

But all the times she had the copulation with the devil in the form of Christ she doubted whether it was the devil or not, from which doubts one can infer that she did not believe as firmly as she ought to have that such things could not possibly be from Christ. In this she should urgently discharge her conscience. . . .

. . .

[After the *Ninth Confession*:]

In the city of Mexico, Tuesday, Day of the Purification of our Lady, February 2, 1599, the Lord Inquisitor in his afternoon audience ordered Marina de San Miguel brought before him. And once present she was told that if she has remembered anything in her case she should say it, and the truth, under the oath that she has made.

She said no. . . .

Working with Sources

1. **What does this document indicate about the working methods of the Inquisition (and their "successes") in Mexico in the 1590s?**
2. **Does the Inquisition seem to have been more concerned about Marina's sexuality than her mystical experiences?**

SOURCE 18.3 Nahuatl Land Sale Documents, Mexico

ca. 1610

After the conquest of the Aztec imperial capital of Tenochtitlán, Spaniards turned their attention to the productive farmland in the surrounding countryside, which was inhabited by Nahuatl-speaking native people. By the late sixteenth century, Spaniards began to expand rapidly into this territory. They acquired estates in a variety of ways, from royal grants to open seizure of property. Nevertheless, the purchase of plots of land from individual Nahuas was also common—although sometimes the sellers came to regret the transaction and petitioned higher authorities for redress of their grievances.

***Altepetl*:** City-state.

***Teopixqui*:** Priest, in Nahuatl.

***Tlaxilacalli*:** Subunit of an *altepetl*.

Here in the ***altepetl*** Santo Domingo Mixcoac, Marquesado del Valle, on the first day of July of the year 1612, I, Joaquín de San Francisco, and my wife, Juana Feliciana, citizens here in the *altepetl* of Santa María Purificación Tlilhuacan, sell to Dr. Diego de León Plaza, ***teopixqui***, one field and house that we have in the ***tlaxilacalli*** Tlilhuacan next to the house of Juan Bautista, Spaniard. Where we are is right in the middle of [in between] their houses. And now we receive [the money] in person. The reason we sell it is that we have no children to whom it might belong. For there is another land and house, but [the land] here we can no longer [work] because it is really in the middle of [land belonging to] Spaniards. [The land] is not *tributario*, for my father, named Juan Altamirano, and my mother, María Catalina, really left it to me. And now I give it to [the doctor] very voluntarily. And now he is personally giving me 130 pesos. Both my wife and I receive it in person before the witnesses. And the

Source: Rebecca Horn, "Spaniards in the Nahua Countryside: Dr. Diego de León Plaza and Nahuatl Land Sale Documents (Mexico, Early Seventeenth Century)," in Richard Boyer and Geoffrey Spurling, eds., *Colonial Lives: Documents on Latin American History, 1550–1850* (New York: Oxford University Press, 2000), 102–103, 108–109.

tribute will be remedied with [the price]; it will pay it. The land [upon which tribute is owed] is at Colonanco. It is adjacent to the land of Miguel de Santiago and Lucas Pérez. And the witnesses [are] Antonio de Fuentes and señora Inés de Vera and Juana de Vera, Spanish women (and the Nahuas) Juan Josef, Gabriel Francisco, María, Mariana, and Sebastián Juan. And because we do not know how to write, I, Joaquín [de San] Francisco, and my wife asked a witness to set down [a signature] on our behalf [along with the notary?] Juan Vázquez, Spaniard. Witnesses, Antonio de Fuentes, [etc.] Before me, Matías Valeriano, notary. And both of them, he and his wife [Joaquín de San Francisco and Juana Feliciana], received the 140 pesos each three months, [presumably paid in installments?] before the witnesses who were mentioned. Before me, Matías Valeriano, notary.

. . .

[Letter of complaint to the authorities of Santo Domino Mixcoac, on the behalf of a group of Nahuas, undated:]

We are citizens here in Santo Domingo Mixcoac. We state that we found out that Paula and Juana and María and Catalina and Inés and Anastacia complain about the ***teniente*** before you [the *corregidor, gobernador, regidores,* etc.]. It is Antonio de Fuentes whom they are accusing because they say he mistreats them. [They say] he robs [people's land].

***Teniente*:** Lieutenant.

. . .

And now [the] Spaniard Napolles disputes with the *teniente*. And Napolles goes around to each house exerting pressure on, forcing many people [to say "get rid of the *teniente*"]. [He says:] "Let there be no officer of the justice. I will help you expel the *teniente* because we will be happy if there is no officer of the law on your land." Napolles, Spaniard, keeps a woman at his house and he is forcing her. For this reason [the authorities] arrested him for concubinage. They gave him a fine about which he became very angry and they arrested him. He stole four pigs, the property of a person named Francisco Hernández, Spaniard, and because of that they arrested him. He was scorched [burned] for their relatives accuse them.

. . .

And so now with great concern and with bowing down we implore you [the *corregidor, gobernador,* and *regidores,* etc.] and we ask for justice. Everyone knows how [the blacks and *mestizos*] mistreat us. They don't go to confession. They are already a little afraid and are already living a little better. And we ask for justice. Let them be punished. We who ask it are Juan Joseph, Francisco de San Juan, and Francisco Juan.

❯ Working with Sources

1. **Why do the documents incorporate Nahuatl terms at some times but not at others?**
2. **How do the documents illustrate the various levels of justice available to native people and to "Spaniards"?**

SOURCE 18.4 *The Jesuit Relations*, French North America

1649

The Jesuit Relations are the most important documents attesting to the encounter between Europeans and native North Americans in the seventeenth century. These annual reports of French missionaries from the Society of Jesus document the conversions—or attempted conversions—of the various indigenous peoples in what is today the St. Lawrence River basin and the Great Lakes region. When they arrived on the banks of the St. Lawrence in 1625, French Jesuits were entering a continent still very much under control of First Nations peoples, who were divided by their own ethnic and linguistic differences. Even the catchall terms "Huron" and "Iroquois" masked their nature as confederacies, composed of several distinct nations, who had joined together prior to the arrival of Europeans.

When the Jesuits made headway with one group, they usually lost initiative with the group's rivals—and sometimes found themselves in the midst of a conflict that they could barely understand or appreciate. This section of the *Relations* concerns the torture and murder of Jean Brébeuf, who had lived among the Hurons at various points from the 1620s through the 1640s, observing their culture and systematically attempting to convert them to Catholicism. However, when an Iroquois raiding party invaded his settlement, the depth of the Hurons' Christian commitment—and his own—would be tested.

The sixteenth day of March in the present year, 1649, marked the beginning of our misfortunes—if an event, which no doubt has been the salvation of many of God's elect, can be called a misfortune.

The Iroquois, enemies of the Hurons, arrived by night at the frontier of this country. They numbered about a thousand men, well furnished with weapons, most of them carrying firearms obtained from their allies, the Dutch. We had no knowledge of their approach, although they had started from their country in the autumn, hunting in the forests throughout the winter, and had made a difficult journey of nearly two hundred leagues over the snow in order to take us by surprise. By night, they reconnoitered the condition of the first place upon which they had designs. It was surrounded by a pine stockade fifteen or sixteen feet in height, and a deep ditch with which nature had strongly fortified this place on three sides. There remained only a small space that was weaker than the others.

It was at this weak point that the enemy made a breach at daybreak, but so secretly and promptly that he was master of the place before anyone could mount a defense. All were then sleeping deeply, and they had no time to recognize the danger. Thus this village was taken, almost without striking a blow and with only ten Iroquois killed. Part of the Hurons—men, women, and

---

Source: Paul Ragueneau, "Relation of 1648–49," in Allan Greer, ed., *The Jesuit Relations: Natives and Missionaries in Seventeenth-Century North America* (Boston: Bedford/St. Martin's, 2000), 112–115.

children—were massacred then and there, while the others were made captives and were reserved for cruelties more terrible than death.

. . .

The enemy did not stop there, but followed up his victory, and before sunrise he appeared in arms to attack the town of St. Louis, which was fortified with a fairly good stockade. Most of the women and the children had just gone from it upon hearing the news which had arrived regarding the approach of the Iroquois. The people of greatest courage, about eighty persons, being resolved to defend themselves well, courageously repulsed the first and the second assaults, killing about thirty of the enemy's boldest men, in addition to many wounded. But finally, the larger number prevailed, as the Iroquois used their hatchets to undermine the palisade of stakes and opened a passage for themselves through some considerable breaches.

About nine o'clock in the morning, we perceived from our house at St. Marie the fire which was consuming the cabins of that town, where the enemy, after entering victoriously, had reduced everything to desolation. They cast into the flames the old, the sick, the children who had not been able to escape, and all those who, being too severely wounded, could not have followed them into captivity. At the sight of those flames, and by the color of the smoke which issued from them, we understood sufficiently what was happening, for this town of St. Louis was no more than a league distant from us. Two Christians who escaped the fire arrived about this time and confirmed this.

In this town of St. Louis were at that time two of our fathers, Father Jean de Brébeuf and Father Gabriel Lalemant, who had charge of a cluster of five towns. These formed but one of the eleven missions of which we have spoken above, and we call it the mission of St. Ignace.

Some Christians had begged the fathers to preserve their lives for the glory of God, which would have been as easy for them as for the more than five hundred persons who went away at the first alarm, for there was more than enough time to reach a place of safety. But their zeal could not permit such a thing, and the salvation of their flock was dearer to them than the love of their own lives. They employed the moments left to them as the most previous which they had ever had in the world, and through the heat of the battle their hearts were on fire for the salvation of souls. One was at the breach, baptizing the **catechumens**, and the other was giving absolution to the **neophytes**. Both of them urged the Christians to die in the sentiments of piety with which they consoled them in their miseries. Never was their faith more alive, nor their love for their good fathers and pastors more keenly felt.

Catechumens: Native converts who had not yet been baptized.

Neophytes: Recently baptized Christians.

An infidel, seeing the desperate situation, spoke of taking flight, but a Christian named Etienne Annaotaha, the most esteemed in the country for his courage and his exploits against the enemy, would never allow it. "What!" he said. "Could we ever abandon these two good fathers, who have exposed their lives for us? Their love for our salvation will be the cause of their death, for there is no longer time for them to flee across the snows. Let us then die with them, and we shall go together to heaven." This man had made a general confession a few days previously, having had a presentiment of the danger awaiting him and saying that he wished that death should find him disposed for Heaven. And indeed he, as well as many other Christians, had abandoned themselves to fervor in a manner so extraordinary that we shall never be sufficiently able to bless the guidance of God over so many predestinated souls. His divine providence continues lovingly to guide them in death as in life.

» Working with Sources

1. **How well do the Jesuits seem to have understood the conflicts among native peoples in this region?**
2. **How was Ragueneau's reporting of the battle designed to highlight the "success" of the mission, despite an apparent setback?**

SOURCE 18.5 The Salem Witch Trials, British North America

1692

The witch hunt that took place in Salem, Massachusetts, in 1692 has been frequently (if sensationally) depicted in modern films and plays. But a reading of the extant documents used in the trial of the supposed witches provides a more nuanced insight into the process of denunciation, conviction, and execution that unfolded in this persecution, which was among the last in the Western world. Although the Salem witch hunt resulted in the conviction of 30 and the execution of 19, the total number of persons who had been formally accused reached 164. Doubts about the guilt of those executed eventually led to a reconsideration of the procedures used in the trial, and the governor of the colony abruptly suspended the trials in the autumn of 1692. In spite of the admission by some of the Salem jurors that they had been mistaken, the judgments passed on seven of the convicted were not reversed until 2001.

Samuel Gray of Salem, aged about 42 years, testifieth and saith that about fourteen years ago, he going to bed well one [a.m.] one Lord's Day at night, and after he had been asleep some time, he awakened and looking up, saw the house light as if a candle or candles were lighted in it and the door locked, and that little fire there was raked up. He did then see a woman standing between the cradle in the room and the bedside and seemed to look upon him. So he did rise up in his bed and it vanished or disappeared. Then he went to the door and found it locked, and unlocking and opening the door, he went to the entry door and looked out and then again did see the same woman he had a little before seen in the room and in the same garb she was in before. Then he said to her, "What in the name of God do you come for?" Then she vanished away, so he locked the door again and went to bed, and between sleeping and waking he felt something come to his mouth or lips cold, and thereupon started and looked up again and did see the same woman with some thing between both her hands holding before his mouth upon which she moved. And the child in the cradle gave a great screech out as if it was greatly hurt and she disappeared, and taking the child up could not quiet it in some hours from which time the

Source: Brian P. Levack, ed., *The Witchcraft Sourcebook* (New York: Routledge, 2004), 225–226, 228–229.

child that was before a very lively, thriving child did pine away and was never well, although it lived some months after, yet in a sad condition and so died. Some time after within a week or less he did see the same woman in the same garb and clothes that appeared to him as aforesaid, and although he knew not her nor her name before, yet both by the countenance and garb doth testify that it was the same woman that they now call Bridget Bishop, alias Oliver, of Salem. Sworn Salem, May 30th 1692.

. . .

The deposition of Joseph Ring at Salisbury, aged 27 years, being sworn, saith that about the latter end of September last, being in the wood with his brother Jarvis Ring hewing of timber, his brother went home with his team and left this deponent alone to finish the hewing of the piece for him for his brother to carry when he came again. But as soon as his brother was gone there came to this deponent the appearance of Thomas Hardy of the great island of Puscataway, and by some impulse he was forced to follow him to the house of Benovy Tucker, which was deserted and about a half a mile from the place he was at work in, and in that house did appear Susannah Martin of Amesbury and the aforesaid Hardy and another female person which the deponent did not know. There they had a good fire and drink—it seemed to be cider. There continued most part of the night, [the] said Martin being then in her natural shape and talking as if she used to. But towards the morning the said Martin went from the fire, made a noise, and turned into the shape of a black hog and went away, and so did the other. Two persons go away, and this deponent was strangely carried away also, and the first place he knew was by Samuel Woods' house in Amesbury.

. . .

The deposition of Thomas Putnam, aged 40 years and [Edward Putnam] aged 38 years, who testify and say that we have been conversant with the afflicted persons or the most of them, as namely Mary Walcott, Mercy Lewes, Elizabeth Hubbard, Abigail Williams, Sarah Bibber and Ann Putnam junior and have often heard the aforementioned persons complain of Susannah Martin of Amesbery [sic] torturing them, and we have seen the marks of several bites and pinches which they say Susannah Martin did hurt them with, and also on the second day of May 1692, being the day of the examination of Susannah Martin, the aforenamed persons were most grievously tortured during the time of her examination, for upon a glance of her eyes they were struck down or almost choked and upon the motion of her finger we took notes they were afflicted, and if she did but clench her hands or hold her head aside the afflicted persons aforementioned were most grievously tortured, complaining of Susannah Martin for hurting them.

» Working with Sources

1. **What do these documents suggest about the (supposed) powers of witches, especially in terms of acting at a distance upon their victims?**
2. **Although all of the witnesses in this set of documents were men, do they reveal something about the connection between witchcraft accusations and gender?**

Further Resources

Chapter 1

Burroughs, William J. *Climate Change in Prehistory: The End of the Reign of Chaos.* Cambridge: Cambridge University Press, 2005. Very well-researched and up-to-date discussion of climate and human evolution.

Finlayson, Clive. *The Humans Who Went Extinct: Why Neanderthals Died Out and We Survived.* Oxford and New York: Oxford University Press, 2010. A comprehensive history of human evolution in the context of geological and climatic changes, by the excavator of the last Neanderthal traces in Europe.

Flood, Josephine. *Archaeology of the Dreamtime: The Story of Prehistoric Australia and Its People.* New Haven, CT.: Yale University Press, 1989. Overview of the Australian archaeological record; short on discussion of Aboriginal Dreamtime and myths.

Johanson, Donald, and Kate Wong. *Lucy: The Quest for Human Origins.* New York: Three Rivers, 2009.

Lawson, Andrew J. *Painted Caves: Palaeololithic Rock Art in Western Europe.* Oxford and New York: Oxford University Press, 2012. Presents an extensive overview ("gazetteer") of the various sites and analyzes the rock art phenomenon in great detail.

McBrearty, Sally, and Allison S. Brooks. "The Revolution that Wasn't: A New Interpretation of the Origin of Modern Human Behavior." *Journal of Human Evolution* 39 (2000): 453–463. Crucial, pioneering article in which the authors grounded anatomically and intellectually modern *H. sapiens* in Africa.

Pääbo, Svante. *Neanderthal Man: In Search of the Lost Genomes.* New York: Basic Books, 2014. Pääbo is the first palaeogeneticist to sequence the full genome of a Neanderthal fossil as well as that of a new species of hominin, Dinoseva, discovered in Siberia in 2010.

Pauketat, Timothy, ed. *The Oxford North American Handbook of Archaeology.* Oxford and New York: Oxford University Press, 2012. Very detailed coverage of Paleo-Indian migrations and settlements. Needs to be supplemented with the March 2014 article in *Science* by Dennis O'Rourke, John Hoffecker, and Scott Elias on humans being trapped for 10,000 years on the habitable south coast of Beringia.

Tattersall, Ian. *Masters of the Planet: The Search for Human Origins.* New York: Palgrave Macmillan, 2012. A scholarly well-founded overview for the general reader, by one of the leading senior paleoanthropologists.

WEBSITES

Bradshaw Foundation, http://www.bradshawfoundation.com/. The Bradshaw Foundation has a large website on human evolution and rock art, with many images, and a link to Stephen Oppenheimer's website Journey of Mankind: The Peopling of the World, an important overview of *Homo sapiens'* migrations.

Institute of Human Origins, Arizona State University, http://iho.asu.edu/. Arizona State University's Institute of Human Origins runs the popular but scholarly well-founded website Becoming Human (http://www.becominghuman.org/).

Chapter 2

Alcock, Susan E., John Bodel, and Richard J. A. Talbert, eds. *Highways, Byways, and Road Systems in the Pre-Modern World.* Chichester: John Wiley & Sons, 2012. Fascinating global survey of methods of transport and communication.

Assmann, Jan. *The Search for God in Ancient Egypt.* Ithaca, N.Y.: Cornell University Press, 2001. Reflective investigation of the dimensions of Egyptian polytheism by a leading Egyptologist.

Bottéro, Jean. *Mesopotamia: Writing, Reasoning, and the Gods.* Chicago: University of Chicago Press, 1992. Classic intellectual history of ancient Mesopotamia.

Drews, Robert. *The End of the Bronze Age: Changes in Warfare and the Catastrophe ca. 1200 B.C.* Princeton, N.J.: Princeton University Press, 1993. Closely argued essay on the destruction of Mycenaean culture and its consequences for the eastern Mediterranean.

Finkelstein, Israel. *The Archaeology of the Israelite Settlement.* Jerusalem: Israel Exploration Society, 1988. Authoritative presentation of the archaeology of the earliest period of Israelite social formation.

Kramer, Samuel Noah. *The Sumerians: Their History, Culture, and Character.* Chicago: University of Chicago Press, 2010. An expanded version of Kramer's earlier work, *History Begins at Sumer* (1988), this is a fascinating presentation of the many "firsts" originating in the world's earliest urban civilization, written by a leading Sumerologist.

Mithen, Steven. *After the Ice: A Global Human History, 20,000–5000 B.C.* Cambridge, Mass.: Harvard University Press, 2003. Engagingly written story of humans settling, becoming farmers, and founding villages and towns, as seen through the eyes of a modern time traveler.

Podany, Amanda H. *The Ancient Near East: A Very Short Introduction.* Oxford and New York: Oxford University Press, 2014. Readable survey of the origin and development of Near Eastern civilizations.

Van de Mieroop, Marc. *The Ancient Mesopotamian City.* Oxford: Clarendon, 1997. Full examination of Mesopotamian urban institutions, including city assemblies.

WEBSITES

British Museum. Ancient Egypt, http://www.ancientegypt.co.uk/menu.html. Pictorial introduction, with short texts.

Livius.org. "Mesopotamia," http://www.livius.org/babylonia.html. A large collection of translated texts and references to philological articles, with portals on Mesopotamia, Egypt, Anatolia, and Greece.

Oriental Institute, University of Chicago. Ancient Mesopotamia, http://mesopotamia.lib.uchicago.edu/. A user-friendly portal to the world-renowned Mesopotamia collection of the Oriental Institute.

Chapter 3

Bryant, Edwin. *The Quest for the Origins of Vedic Culture: The Indo-Aryan Migration Debate.* Oxford and New York: Oxford University Press, 2001. A scholarly yet readable attempt to address the linguistic and archaeological evidence surrounding the thesis of Aryan migration versus the more recent theory of indigenous Vedic development.

Embree, Ainslee T., ed. *Sources of Indian Tradition*, vol. 1, 2nd ed. New York: Columbia University Press, 1988. Though the language is dated in places, this is still the most comprehensive sourcebook of Indian thought available. Recent additions on women and gender make it even more so. Sophisticated yet readable introductions, glosses, and commentary.

Eraly, Abraham. *Gem in the Lotus: The Seeding of Indian Civilization*. London: Weidenfeld & Nicholson, 2004. Readable, comprehensive survey of recent scholarship from prehistory to the reign of Ashoka during the Mauryan dynasty of the fourth and third centuries BCE. Emphasis on transitional period of sixth-century religious innovations, particularly Buddhism.

Kenoyer, Jonathan Mark. *Ancient Cities of the Indus Valley Civilization*. Oxford and New York: Oxford University Press, 1998. Comprehensive work by team leader of Harappan Research Project. Particularly good on Lothal.

Klostermaier, Klaus. *A Survey of Hinduism*, 3rd ed. Albany, NY: SUNY Press, 2007. Comprehensive thematic treatment of major themes of Hinduism from the Vedas to Hinduism's relationship to modern science.

Possehl, Gregory L., ed. *Harappan Civilization: A Recent Perspective*, 2nd ed. New Delhi: Oxford University Press, 1993. Sound and extensive treatment of recent work and issues in Indus valley archaeology by one of the leading on-site researchers and a former student of Fairservis. Used to best advantage by experienced students.

Singh, Upinder. *A History of Ancient and Early Medieval India: From the Stone Age to the 12th Century*. New Delhi: Pearson, 2008. Sweeping text by a longtime instructor of Indian history at the University of Delhi. Suitable for undergraduates and current on the latest debates on ancient origins.

Trautmann, Thomas. *India: Brief History of a Civilization*. Oxford and New York: Oxford University Press, 2011. A succinct and lucid account of 4,000 years of Indian history, with particular emphasis on early developments.

Wolpert, Stanley. *A New History of India*, 5th ed. Oxford and New York: Oxford University Press, 2004. Another extremely useful, readable, one-volume history from Neolithic times to the present. Excellent first work for serious students.

WEBSITES

Columbia University Libraries. South and Southeast Asian Studies, www.columbia.edu/cu/lweb/indiv/southasia/cuvl/history.html. Run by Columbia University, this site contains links to "WWW.Virtual Library: Indian History"; "Regnal Chronologies"; "Internet Indian History Sourcebook"; and "Medical History of British India."

Harappa, http://www.harappa.com. Contains a wealth of images of artifacts and other archaeological treasures from the Indus Valley.

Chapter 4

Chang, Kwang-chih. *The Archaeology of Ancient China*, 4th ed. New Haven, CT.: Yale University Press, 1986. Sophisticated treatment of archaeology of Shang China. Prime exponent of the view of overlapping periods and territories for the Sandai period. Erudite, yet accessible for experienced students.

Ebrey, Patricia Buckley, ed. *Chinese Civilization: A Sourcebook*, 2nd ed. New York: Free Press, 1993. Wonderful supplement to the preceding volume. Some different classical sources and considerable material on women and social history. Time frame of this work extends to the modern era.

Keightly, David N., ed. *The Origins of Chinese Civilization*. Berkeley and Los Angeles: University of California Press, 1983. Symposium volume on a variety of Sandai topics by leading scholars. Some exposure to early Chinese history and archaeology is necessary in order to best appreciate these essays.

Linduff, Katheryn M., and Yan Sun, eds. *Gender and Chinese Archaeology*. Walnut Creek, CA: Altamira, 2004. Reexamines the role of gender in ancient China in the context of a critique of the general lack of gendered research in archaeology as a whole.

Liu, Xiang. *Exemplary Women of Early China: The Lienu zhuan of Liu Xiang*. Edited and translated by Anne Behnke Kinney. New York: Columbia University Press, 2014. One of the few accounts we have of the lives of women during the Three Dynasties period; covers 120 short biographies of Zhou women.

Lowe, Michael, and Edward L. Shaughnessy, eds. *The Cambridge History of Ancient China: From the Origins of Civilization to 221 B.C.* Cambridge, UK: Cambridge University Press, 1999. The opening volume of the Cambridge History of China series, this is the most complete multiessay collection on all aspects of recent Chinese ancient historical and archaeological work. The place to start for the serious student contemplating in-depth research.

Thorp, Robert L. *China in the Early Bronze Age: Shang Civilization*. Philadelphia: University of Pennsylvania Press, 2006. Comprehensive yet accessible survey of recent archaeological work on the period 2070–1046 BCE, including traditional Xia and Shang periods under the heading of China's "bronze age."

Wang, Aihe. *Cosmology and Political Culture in Early China*. Cambridge: Cambridge University Press, 2000. Part of the Cambridge Studies in Chinese History, Literature, and Institutions series. Wang argues that control of *cosmology*—how the world and universe operate—was a vital key to the wielding of power by the Shang and Zhou rulers. Recommended for serious students.

Wang, Robin. *Images of Women in Chinese Thought and Culture: Writings from the Pre-Qin Period Through the Song Dynasty*. Indianapolis, IN: Hackett Publishing, 2003. Excerpts from classical and more obscure texts on the role and treatment of women in early China. A large and useful section on pre-Confucian texts.

Watson, Burton, trans. *The Tso Chuan: Selections from China's Oldest Narrative History*. New York: Columbia University Press, 1989. Elegant translation by one of the most prolific of scholars working today. Excellent introduction to Zhou period and politics. Appropriate for beginning students, though more useful for those with some prior introduction to the period.

WEBSITES

http://lucian.uchicago.edu/blogs/earlychina/ssec/. This is the site of the journal *Early China*, published by the Society for the Study of Early China.

British Museum. Ancient China, http://www.ancientchina.co.uk. This site provides access to the British Museum's ancient Chinese collections and is highly useful for students seeking illustrations of assorted artifacts in a user-friendly environment.

Chapter 5

The Americas

Bellwood, Peter. *First Migrants: Ancient Migration in Global Perspective.* Chichester, UK: John Wiley & Sons, 2013. An intriguing study of prehistoric migration and its role in shaping the emergence of civilization.

Benson, Sonia, and Deborah J. Baker. *Early Civilizations in the Americas Reference Library*, 3 vols. Farmington Hills, MI: Gale UXL, 2009. Extensive three-volume encyclopedia available as a download or in hard copy. Contains an almanac of historical information and one of biographies and primary sources. Recommended for beginning and experienced students.

Bruhns, Karen Olsen, and Karen E. Stothert. *Women in Ancient America.* Norman: University of Oklahoma Press, 1999. A comprehensive account of women's roles in daily life, religion, politics, and war in foraging and farming as well as urban societies in the Americas.

Fiedel, Stuart J. *Prehistory of the Americas*, 2nd ed. Cambridge, UK: Cambridge University Press, 1992. Accessible, detailed survey of the archaeology of the Americas by a leading American scholar.

Solis, Ruth Shady, Haas, Jonathan, and Creamer, Winifred. "Dating Caral, a Preceramic Site in the Supe Valley on the Central Coast of Peru," *Science* 292:5517(2001): 723-726. Pathbreaking early report of early scientific work on Caral Supe and the oldest American cities.

Thomas, David Hurst. *Exploring Native North America.* Oxford and New York: Oxford University Press, 2000. Selected chapters are useful on the major early North American sites, particularly Adena and Hopewell.

Trigger, Bruce G., Wilcomb E. Washburn, Richard E. W. Adams, Murdo J. MacLeod, Frank Salomon, and Stuart B. Schwartz, eds. *Cambridge History of the Native Peoples of the Americas*, 3 vols. Cambridge, UK: Cambridge University Press, 1996–2000. As with all of the Cambridge histories, this is a highly useful set for beginner and accomplished scholar alike. Useful bibliographies with the article entries.

von Hagen, Adriana, and Craig Morris. *The Cities of the Ancient Andes.* New York: Thames & Hudson, 1999. While more geared to later periods, still a useful overview, with illustrations, by specialists on Andean cultures.

Oceania

Carson, Mike T., *First Settlement of Remote Oceania: Earliest Sites in the Mariana Islands.* Heidelberg: Springer-Verlag, 2014. Study based on new archaeological research by a specialist on Pacific research.

Kirch, Patrick V. *The Lapita Peoples: Ancestors of the Oceanic World.* Cambridge, MA: Blackwell, 1997. Basic introduction by one of the pioneers of Polynesian research.

Matsuda, Matt K.. *Pacific Worlds: A History of Seas, Peoples, and Cultures.* Cambridge, UK: Cambridge University Press, 2012. General history of the Pacific with an emphasis on the early modern period.

Vlchek, Andre. *Oceania: Neocolonialism, Nukes and Bones.* Auckland, New Zealand: Atuanui, 2013. Analysis and discussion of the harmful effects of colonialism and neocolonialism on the development of Oceania.

WEBSITES

Foundation for the Advancement of Mesoamerican Studies (FAMSI), http://www.famsi.org/. Home page for the foundation, which has recently begun collaboration with the Los Angeles County Museum of Art and runs a wide range of scholarly, funding, and educational outreach programs aimed at advancing studies of Mesoamerica.

http://www.britannica.com/EBchecked/topic/468832/Polynesian-culture. Good link leading to an 8,000-word essay on leading topics concerning Polynesia and Oceania. In order to access the complete essay the reader must apply for a free trial of the online *Encyclopedia Britannica.*

Chapter 6

Sub-Saharan Africa

Chami, Félix. *The Unity of African Ancient History: 3000 BC to 500 AD.* Dar es Salaam: E&D, 2006. General overview by one of the leading archaeologists of East Africa.

McIntosh, Roderick J. *Ancient Middle Niger: Urbanism and the Self-Organizing Landscape.* Cambridge, UK: Cambridge University Press, 2005. Important revisionist work on the origins of urbanism and kingship in West Africa.

Mitchell, Peter, and Paul Lane. *The Oxford Handbook of African Archaeology.* Oxford: Oxford University Press, 2013. A total of 70 essays by specialists on all aspects of human culture in Africa, with an emphasis on foragers, agriculturalists, and early urbanists.

Vansina, Jan. *Paths in the Rainforests: Toward a History of Political Tradition in Equatorial Africa.* Madison: University of Wisconsin Press, 1990. Magisterial presentation of the Bantu dispersal and village life in the rain forest.

Mesoamerica and the Andes

Aveni, Anthony F. *Skywatchers*, rev. ed. Austin: University of Texas Press, 2001. Classic study on astronomy and calendars of pre-Columbian Americans, including a discussion of the Nazca lines.

Braswell, Geoffrey E., ed. *The Ancient Maya of Mexico: Reinterpreting the Past of the Northern Lowlands.* Milton Park, UK, and New York: Routledge, 2014. Contains articles on the origins of the ballgame and the Mayan "collapse."

Evans, Susan Tobey. *Ancient Mexico and Central America: Archaeology and Culture History.* London: Thames & Hudson, 2004. Densely but clearly written and detailed, with many sidebars on special topics.

Grube, Nikolai, ed. *Maya: Divine Kings of the Rain Forest.* Cologne, Germany: Könemann, 2001. Lavishly illustrated book with short contributions by many hands.

Schele, Linda, and David Freidel. *A Forest of Kings: The Untold Story of the Ancient Maya.* New York: Quill-William Morrow, 1990. Classic study summarizing the results of the decipherment of Maya glyphs, by two pioneers.

Stuart, David. *The Order of Days: Unlocking the Secrets of the Ancient Maya.* New York: Three Rivers Press, 2011. Magisterial summary of our current knowledge of Maya culture.

WEBSITES

Museum of Native American History. http://www.monah.us/precolumbian: Basic but fairly comprehensive website on pre-Columbian peoples and civilizations.

Stanford University Libraries. Africa South of the Sahara, http://www-sul.stanford.edu/depts/ssrg/africa/history.html. A large, resource-filled website based at Stanford University.

Chapter 7

Boatwright, Mary, Daniel J. Gargola, and Richard J. A. Talbert. *The Romans: From Village to Empire*. New York: Oxford University Press, 2004. Clearly written, comprehensive introduction to Roman history.

Boyce, Mary. *A History of Zoroastrianism*. Vol. 1, *The Early Period*, rev. ed. Handbuch der Orientalistik. Leiden, the Netherlands: E. J. Brill, 1989. Standard work by the leading scholar on the subject.

Briant, Pierre. *From Cyrus to Alexander: A History of the Persian Empire*. Winona Lake, IN: Eisenbrauns, 2000. Monumental work; the most detailed and authoritative study of the topic to date.

Cameron, Averil. *The Mediterranean World in Late Antiquity, AD 395–600*. London: Routledge, 1993. New perspective on the strengths and weaknesses of the late Roman empire.

Dignas, Beate, and Engelbert Winter. *Rome and Persia in Late Antiquity: Neighbours and Rivals*. Cambridge, UK: Cambridge University Press, 2007. Detailed historical investigation of the rivalry between Rome and Persia.

Freeman, Phillip. *Alexander the Great*. New York: Simon & Schuster, 2011. Illuminating study of Alexander the Great intended for a general audience.

Hubbard, Thomas K., ed. *A Companion to Greek and Roman Sexualities*. Chichester, UK: John Wiley & Sons, 2014. Far-ranging and informative collection of essays on all aspects of sexuality in ancient Greece and Rome.

Lehoux, Daryn. *What Did the Romans Know? An Inquiry into Science and Worldmaking*. Chicago: University of Chicago Press, 2012. Sophisticated analysis of Roman science in both its derivative and unique aspects.

Mathisen, Ralph. *Ancient Mediterranean Civilizations: From Prehistory to 640 CE*, 2nd ed. Oxford and New York: Oxford University Press, 2014. Revised overview with special emphasis on ethnicity, gender, and slavery.

Shaked, Shaul. *Dualism in Transformation: Varieties of Religion in Sasanian Iran*. London: School of Oriental and African Studies, 1994. Short history of the different religions in Sasanid Persia.

Smith, Mark S. *The Early History of God: Yahweh and the Other Deities in Ancient Israel*. San Francisco: Harper & Row, 1990. Very readable introduction to the problem of early monotheism among Israelites.

WEBSITES

British Museum. Ancient Greece, http://www.ancientgreece.co.uk/menu.html. Open the door to the compelling world of Ancient Greece. The British Museum has compiled a collection of images and information on various aspects of Greek history such as the Acropolis, Athens, daily life, festivals and games, Sparta, war, and gods.

Harvard University. Digital Atlas of Roman and Medieval Civilizations, http://darmc.harvard.edu/icb/icb.do?keyword=k40248&pageid=icb.page188868. Harvard University allows students to tailor searches in order to access specific geopolitical and spatial cartographical representations of the Roman and medieval worlds.

Perseus Digital Library, http://www.perseus.tufts.edu/hopper/. Probably the largest website on Greece and Rome, with immense resources, hosted by Tufts University.

Chapter 8

Auboyer, Jeannine. *Daily Life in Ancient India*. London: Phoenix, 2002. Overview consisting of sections on social structures/religious principles; individual/collective existence; and royal and administrative existence. Multidisciplinary approach appropriate for most undergraduates.

Carter, John Ross, and Mahinda Palihawadana, trans. *The Dhammapada*. Oxford and New York: Oxford University Press, 1987. Erudite but accessible translation of one of the key texts in the Buddhist corpus. Students with some exposure to the introductory ideas of Buddhism will find it very useful in its step-by-step elucidation of a number of central concepts.

Chakravarti, Uma. *The Social Dimensions of Early Buddhism*. New Delhi: Oxford University Press, 1987. Thorough analysis, with extensive glossary, of the influence of the north Indian economic transition to peasant market farming on the social milieu of early Buddhism.

Diem-Lane, Andrea. *Ahimsa: A Brief Guide to Jainism*. Walnut, CA: MSAC Philosophy Group, 2016. Short, student-friendly guide to Jain concepts, history, and Jainism today.

Doniger, Wendy. *The Hindus: An Alternative History*. New York: Penguin, 2009. Vivid but controversial new interpretation of the history of Hinduism by one of the leading scholars of Indian history. The book's portrayals of Hindu history, particularly in the area between myth and history, have prompted a lawsuit in India, which resulted in the withdrawal of the book there by the publisher in early 2014.

Embree, Ainslee T. *Sources of Indian Tradition*, 2 vols, 2nd ed. New York: Columbia University Press, 1988. The latest edition contains a number of new selections useful for the study of social relations in addition to the older religious material. As with all of the works in this series, the level of writing is sophisticated, though accessible; the overviews are masterly; and the works are ably translated.

Keay, John. *India: A History*. New York: Grove, 2000. Lively, highly detailed narrative history, with a number of useful charts and genealogies of ruling houses. Sympathetic treatment of controversial matters.

Knott, Kim. *Hinduism: A Very Short Introduction*. Oxford and New York: Oxford University Press, 1998. Sound, brief discussion of modern Hinduism and its formative influences. Asks provocative questions such as "What is a religion?" and "Is Hinduism something more than the Western conception of religion?"

Nikam, N. A., and Richard McKeon, eds. and trans. *The Edicts of Asoka*. Chicago: University of Chicago Press, 1959. Slim but useful volume for those interested in reading the entire collection of Ashoka's Pillar, Cave, and Rock Edicts. Short, accessible introduction.

Willis, Michael. *The Archaeology of Hindu Ritual*. Cambridge, UK: Cambridge University Press, 2009. Best utilized by experienced students, this book uses site archaeology, Sanskrit documents, and studies of ancient astronomy to plot the development of Hinduism under the Guptas and their use of it in statecraft as they created their vision of a universal empire.

Wolpert, Stanley. *A New History of India*, 6th ed. Oxford and New York: Oxford University Press, 2000. The standard introductory work to the long sweep of Indian history. Evenly divided between the period up to and including the Mughals and the modern era. Good coverage of geography and environment, as well as social and gender issues. Good select bibliography arranged by chapter; highly useful glossary of Indian terms.

WEBSITE

Digital Library of India, http://www.dli.ernet.in. This online resource, hosted by the Indian Institute of Science, Bangalore, contains primary and secondary sources not only for history but also for culture, economics, literature, and a host of other subjects.

Chapter 9

Henricks, Robert C., trans. *Lao-Tzu, Te-Tao Ching. A New Translation Based on the Recently Discovered Ma-wang-tui Texts.* New York: Ballantine Books, 1989. Some of the intitial work done on the earliest extant Daoist texts, reinterpreting our understanding of philosophical Daoism.

Hinsch, Bret. *Women in Early Imperial China.* Lanham, MD: Rowman & Littlefield, 2002. Broad examination of the place of women, and transition of the place of women, during the crucial early Chinese dynasties.

Huang, Ray. *China: A Macro History.* Armonk, NY: M. E. Sharpe, 1997. Readable, entertaining, and highly useful one-volume history. Particularly good on the complex politics of the post-Han and Song–Yuan periods.

Keay, John. *China: A History.* New York: Basic Books, 2009. Adventurous and well-written general history of China from prehistory to the present. Especially good for students with some previous grounding in the essentials of Chinese history.

Lewis, Mark Edward. *The Early Chinese Empires: Qin and Han.* Cambridge, MA: Harvard University Press, 2007. Detailed exploration of the rise and adaptations of China's initial empires. Better for advanced students.

Qian, Sima. *Records of the Grand Historian.* Translated by Burton Watson. 3 vols., rev. ed. New York: Columbia University Press, 1993. Powerful translation of China's supreme historical work by one of its best interpreters. Includes material from the Qin and Han dynasties. Invaluable source for serious students.

Snow, Philip. *The Star Raft: China's Encounter with Africa.* Ithaca, NY: Cornell University Press, 1988. Important, accessible study of the little-known area of China's maritime trade with Africa from Han times to the epic fifteenth-century voyages of Zheng He and beyond.

Yao Xinzhong. *An Introduction to Confucianism.* Cambridge, UK: Cambridge University Press, 2000. Overview of the tradition of the *ru* as it evolved and its status today.

WEBSITES

Asian Topics for Asian Educators. "Defining 'Daoism': A Complex History," http://afe.easia.columbia.edu/cosmos/ort/daoism.htm. Looks at Daoism as a term, its use, and its practice in terms of morality, society, nature, and the self.

http://bulldog2.redlands.edu/Dept/AsianStudiesDept/index.html. *East and Southeast Asia: An Annotated Directory of Internet Resources.* One of the most complete guides to websites dealing with all manner of Chinese and East Asian history and society.

Chapter 10

The Arabian Nights. Translated by Husain Haddawy. New York: Norton, 1990. Translation of the critical edition by Muhsin Mahdi, which reconstitutes the original thirteenth-century text.

Barry, Michael. *Figurative Art in Medieval Islam and the Riddle of Bihazâd of Herât (1465–1535).* Paris: Flammarion, 2004.

Chaudhuri, K. N. *Trade and Civilization in the Indian Ocean.* Cambridge, UK: Cambridge University Press, 1985. Discusses the historical evolution of the trade and its various aspects (sea route, ships, commodities, and capital investments).

Fryde, Edmund. *The Early Palaeologan Renaissance (1261–c. 1360).* Leiden, the Netherlands: E. J. Brill, 2000. Detailed presentation of the main philosophical and scientific figures of Byzantium after the recovery from the Latin interruption.

Herrin, Judith. *Unrivalled Influence: Women and Empire in Byzantium.* Princeton, NJ: Princeton University Press, 2013. Detailed investigation by a leading Byzantine historian and engagegd feminist.

Hoyland, Robert. *In God's Path: The Arab Conquests and the Creation of an Islamic Empire.* Oxford and New York: Oxford University Press, 2014. A new history of Islamic origins, seeking to combine Christian and Islamic sources.

Khalili, Jim al-. *The House of Wisdom: How Arabic Science Saved Ancient Knowledge and Gave Us the Renaissance.* New York: Penguin, 2010. In spite of the somewhat overwrought title, an expertly written introduction to the golden age of Arabic science by a scientist.

Laiou, Angeliki E., and Cécile Morrisson. *The Byzantine Economy.* Cambridge, UK: Cambridge University Press, 2007. Comprehensive and well-researched study of ups and downs in the demography, productive capacity, and long-distance trade of Byzantium.

Lapidus, Ira. *Muslim Cities in the Later Middle Ages.* Cambridge, UK: Cambridge University Press, 1984. Seminal work and still the only study of Muslim urban society, although it should be supplemented by Shlomo D. Goitein's monumental study of Jews, *A Mediterranean Society* (1967–1993).

Rippin, Andrew. *Muslims: Their Religious Beliefs and Practices*, 2nd ed. London: Routledge, 2001. One of the best and most accessible introductions to the basic beliefs and practices of Islam, based on the reevaluation of Islamic origins also presented in this chapter.

Tyerman, Christopher. *God's War: A New History of the Crusades.* Cambridge, MA: Belknap, 2006. Persuasive revisionist history by a leading Crusade historian.

Whittow, Mark. *The Making of Byzantium, 600–1025.* Berkeley and Los Angeles: University of California Press, 1996. Revisionist study of the Byzantine struggle for survival in the early years.

WEBSITES

BBC—Religion: Islam. http://www.bbc.co.uk/religion/religions/islam/. A very basic overview of Islamic Civilization. Most websites on Islam and Islamic civilization are apologetic (pro-Muslim or pro-Christian), and earlier scholarly websites are no longer available.

Islamic Awareness. http://www.islamic-awareness.org/. This website, even though Islam-apologetic, is a fountain of early documents relevant for Islamic history.

Chapter 11

Bartlett, Robert. *The Making of Europe: Conquest, Colonization, and Cultural Change, 950–1350*. Princeton, NJ: Princeton University Press, 1993. Analyzes the expansion of Europe from a cultural perspective.

Berend, Norma, Przemyslaw Urbanczlyk, and Przemyslaw Wiszewski. *Central Europe in the High Middle Ages: Bohemia, Hungary and Poland, ca. 900–ca. 1300*. New York: Cambridge University Press, 2013. Learned and insightful study that explores frequently overlooked aspects of medieval Europe.

Brown, Peter. *The Rise of Western Christendom: Triumph and Diversity, A.D. 200–1000*, 2nd ed. Oxford, UK: Wiley-Blackwell, 2003. Traces the development of Christian Europe from the perspective of the church.

Grant, Edward. *The Foundation of Modern Science in the Middle Ages*. Cambridge, UK: Cambridge University Press, 1996. Seminal study of the contributions of medieval science to the scientific revolution of the seventeenth century.

Lawrence, C. H. *Medieval Monasticism: Forms of Religious Life in Western Europe in the Middle Ages*, 2nd ed. New York: Longman, 1984. Thorough survey of the development of the Western monastic tradition.

McKitterick, Rosamond. *Charlemagne: The Formation of a European Identity*. Cambridge, UK: Cambridge University Press, 2008. An examination of how Charlemagne's policies contributed to the idea of Europe.

Platt, Colin. *King Death: The Black Death and Its Aftermath in Late-Medieval England*. Toronto: University of Toronto Press, 1997. Riveting analysis of the effects of the Black Death on all aspects of society.

Riley-Smith, Jonathan, ed. *The Oxford Illustrated History of the Crusades*. Oxford and New York: Oxford University Press, 1995. A very useful and readable history of the crusading movement.

Turner, Denys. *Thomas Aquinas: A Portrait*. New Haven, CT: Yale University Press, 2013. Up-to-date biography of one of the greatest figures in medieval philosophy.

Wickham, Chris. *Medieval Europe*. New Haven, CT: Yale University Press, 2016. A scintillating and innovative study that presents new interpretations of important turning points in the development of medieval European civilization.

WEBSITES

British Library. Treasures in Full: Magna Carta, http://www.bl.uk/treasures/magnacarta/virtual_curator/vc9.html. An excellent website that makes available a digitized version of Magna Carta. Audio files answer many FAQs about the manuscript and its significance.

Howe, Jeffery. A Digital Archive of Architecture, http://www.bc.edu/bc_org/avp/cas/fnart/arch/gothic_arch.html. Jeffery Howe's Digital Archive of Architecture has a quick index reference guide, which links to images of both early and high Gothic architecture.

Chapter 12

Asif, Manan Ahmed. *A Book of Conquest: The Chachnama and Muslim Origins in South Asia*. Cambridge, MA: Harvard University Press, 2016. Comprehensive study of the pivotal story of deceit and conquest and the contentious legacy surrounding the initial Muslim forays into India.

Bulag, Uradyn Erden. *The Mongols at China's Edge: History and the Politics of National Unity*. Lanham, MD: Rowman & Littlefield, 2002. New historical overview of the Mongols through historical and anthropological lenses that seeks to demythologize their experience and interactions with China and central Asian peoples.

Chiu-Duke, Josephine. *To Rebuild the Empire: Lu Chih's Confucian Pragmatist Approach to the Mid-Tang Predicament*. Albany, NY: SUNY Press, 2000. Political and philosophical study of one of the Tang era's most important prime ministers and his attempts to retrieve Tang fortunes and actions in the beginning of the period's Confucian revival.

De Bary, William T., and Irene Bloom, eds. *Sources of Chinese Tradition*, 2nd ed., vol. 1. New York: Columbia University Press, 1999. Excellent introduction to major Chinese philosophical schools. Extensive coverage of Buddhism and Neo-Confucianism with accessible, highly informative introductions to the documents themselves.

Ebrey, Patricia Buckley, ed. *The Inner Quarters*. Berkeley and Los Angeles: University of California Press, 1993. Perhaps the best scholarly exploration of the roles of women in Song China.

Hansen, Valerie. *The Open Empire: A History of China to 1600*. New York: W. W. Norton, 2000. A fresh and accessible synthesis of pre-modern Chinese history.

Levathes, Louise. *When China Ruled the Seas: The Treasure Fleet of the Dragon Throne 1405–1433*. New York: Simon & Schuster, 1994. Delightful coverage of the voyages of Zheng He from 1405 to 1433. Particularly good on the aftermath of the voyages.

Robinson, Francis. *Islam and Muslim History in South Asia*. Oxford and New York: Oxford University Press, 2004. Compendium of essays and reviews by the author on a variety of subjects concerning the history and status of Islam in the subcontinent. Of particular interest is his response to Samuel Huntington's famous "clash of civilizations" thesis.

Singh, Patwant. *The Sikhs*. London: John Murray, 1999. Readable popular history of the Sikh experience to the present by an adherent. Especially useful on the years from Guru Nanak to the changes of the early eighteenth century and the transition to a more militant faith.

WEBSITES

Asian Topics in World History. "The Mongols in World History," http://afe.easia.columbia.edu/mongols/. With a timeline spanning 1000–1500, "The Mongols in World History" delivers a concise and colorful history of the Mongols' impact on global history.

Fordham University. Internet Indian History Sourcebook, http://www.fordham.edu/halsall/india/indiasbook.asp. One of the series of online "sourcebooks" by Fordham containing links to important documents, secondary literature, and assorted other web resources.

Fordham University. Internet East Asian History Sourcebook, http://www.fordham.edu/halsall/eastasia/eastasiasbook.asp. As with its counterpart above, this is one in the series of useful online sources and links put together by Fordham, in this case about East Asia, with particular emphasis on the role of China as a center of cultural diffusion.

Chapter 13

General

Holcombe, Charles. *A History of East Asia, From the Origins of Civilization to the Twenty-First Century.* Cambridge, UK: Cambridge University Press, 2011. A top one-volume history of China, Korea, and Japan, with an emphasis on the region's shared past.

Mann, Susan. *East Asia (China, Korea, Japan).* Washington, DC: American Historical Association, 1999. The second volume in the Women's and Gender History in Global Perspective series. Short, informative work with historiographic overviews and cross-cultural comparisons among the three countries named in the title. Critical annotated bibliographies on the use of standard texts in integrating women and gender into Asian studies.

Neuman, W. Lawrence. *East Asian Societies.* Ann Arbor, MI: Association For Asian Studies, 2014. Part of the AAS's "Key Issues in Asian Studies," this provides a short, accessible introduction to the region for beginning students.

Ramusack, Barbara N., and Sharon Sievers. *Women in Asia.* Bloomington: Indiana University Press, 1999. Part of the series Restoring Women to History. Far-ranging book divided into two parts, "Women in South and Southeast Asia" and "Women in East Asia." Coverage of individual countries, extensive chronologies, valuable bibliographies. Most useful for advanced undergraduates.

Korea

De Bary, William T., ed. *Sources of Korean Tradition*, vol. 1. Introduction to Asian Civilizations. New York: Columbia University Press, 1997. Part of the renowned Columbia series on the great traditions of East Asia. Perhaps the most complete body of accessible sources for undergraduates.

Korean Overseas Information Service. *A Handbook of Korea.* Seoul: KOIS, 1993. Wonderfully complete history, geography, guidebook, and sociology text. Excellent source, but students should keep in mind its provenance and treat some of its historical claims to uniqueness accordingly.

Seth, Michael J. *A Concise History of Korea.* 2nd ed. Lanham, MD: Rowman and Littlefield, 2016. Well-researched and comprehensive history of the Korean peninsula from Neolithic times to 2016. Covers both North and South Korea, though the South comes in for the most detailed treatment.

Japan

De Bary, William T., ed. *Sources of Japanese Tradition*, vol. 1. Introduction to Asian Civilizations. 2nd ed. New York: Columbia University Press, 2002. Like the volume above on Korea and the others in this series on India and China, the sources are well selected, the glossaries are sound, and the overviews of the material are masterful. As with the other East Asia volumes, the complexities of the various Buddhist schools are especially well drawn. Students with some previous experience will derive the most benefit from this excellent volume.

Murasaki Shikibu. *The Diary of Lady Murasaki.* Richard Bowring, trans. New York: Penguin, 1996. Capable translation of the court diary of the author of *The Tale of Genji* and an intimate glimpse into lives of the elite of Heian Japan.

Totman, Conrad. *A History of Japan.* Oxford, UK: Blackwell, 2000. Part of Blackwell's History of the World series. A large, well-balanced, and comprehensive history. More than half of the material is on the pre-1867 period, with extensive coverage of social history and demographics.

Vietnam

Steinberg, Joel David, ed. *In Search of Southeast Asia*, rev. ed. Honolulu: University of Hawaii Press, 1987. Extensive coverage of Vietnam within the context of an area study of Southeast Asia. Though weighted toward the modern period, very good coverage of agricultural and religious life in the opening chapters.

Taylor, Keith W. *The Birth of Vietnam.* Berkeley and Los Angeles: University of California Press, 1983. Comprehensive, magisterial volume on early Vietnamese history and historical identity amid the long Chinese occupation. Best for students with some background in Southeast Asian and Chinese history.

WEBSITES

Department of Prints and Drawings, British Museum, http://www.britishmuseum.org/the_museum/departments/prints_and_drawings.aspx. A comprehensive source for all manner of interests related to Asian studies.

Public Broadcasting Service, Hidden Korea, http://www.pbs.org/hiddenkorea/history.htm. Sound introduction to the geography, people, history and culture of Korea, with links to additional source material.

Cambridge Journals Online, Journal of Southeast Asian Studies, http://journals.cambridge.org/action/displayJournal?jid=SEA. Online version of the scholarly publication of the same name, features articles on the history, sociology, cultural studies, and literature of the region. It aims for scholarly but accessible presentations. Recommended for advanced students.

Chapter 14

Birmingham, David, and Phyllis M. Martin, eds. *History of Central Africa*, vol. 1. London: Longman, 1983. The first chapter, by Birmingham, provides an excellent summary of the history of Luba prior to 1450.

Collins, Robert O., and James M. Burns. *A History of Subsaharan Africa*, 2nd ed. Cambridge: Cambridge University Press, 2014. Authoritative history by two well-known Africanists, updated by James Burns after the death of Robert Collins.

Crummey, David. *Land and Society in the Christian Kingdom of Ethiopia: From the Thirteenth to the Twentieth Century.* Urbana: University of Illinois Press, 2000. The first book in which the rich land records of the church have been used for a reconstruction of agriculture and land tenure.

Horton, Mark, and John Middleton. *The Swahili: The Social Landscape of a Mercantile Society.* Oxford, UK: Blackwell, 2000. A study that gives full attention to the larger context of East Africa in which the Swahilis flourished. Middleton is the author of another important study, *The World of the*

Swahili: An African Mercantile Civilization (Yale University Press, 1992).

Huffman, Thomas N. *Mapungubwe: Ancient African Civilization on the Limpopo*. Johannesburg: Witwatersrand University Press, 2005. Short but illuminating summary of the archaeological record by a leading South African expert, although his interpretation of Zimbabwe in an earlier work (*Snakes and Crocodiles*, Witwatersrand University Press, 1996) is controversial.

Levtzion, Nehemia. *Ancient Ghana and Mali*. New York: Africana, 1980. Originally published London: Methuen, 1973. Standard history of ancient Ghana, Mali, and Songhay based on a thorough knowledge of the Arabic sources; a revision by David Conrad, Paulo Farias, Roderick J. McIntosh, and Susan McIntosh has been announced but has yet to appear.

Robinson, David. *Muslim Societies in African History*. Cambridge, UK: Cambridge University Press, 2004. Advertised as part of a series of new approaches, this book nevertheless presents a conventional view of Islam, albeit in its African context.

Trigger, Bruce. *History and Settlement in Lower Nubia*. Yale University Publications in Anthropology 69. New Haven, CT: Yale University Press, 1965. Chapter 9 is still the best overview of Nubian history, by a scholar with a broad understanding of early civilizations.

WEBSITES

Heilbrunn Timeline of Art History. "Ife (from ca. 350 B.C.)," http://www.metmuseum.org/toah/hd/ife/hd_ife.htm. An excellent introductory website hosted by the Metropolitan Museum of Art. It contains many links and presents clear overviews.

For a website by Patrick Darling, the principal archaeological investigator of the Nigerian earthworks, see http://cohesion.rice.edu/CentersAndInst/SAFA/emplibrary/49_ch09.pdf for a copy of a 1998 article.

Chapter 15

Bruhns, Karen Olsen, and Karen E. Stothert. *Women in Ancient America*. Norman: University of Oklahoma Press, 1999. Comprehensive account of women's role in daily life, religion, politics, and war in forager and agrarian–urban societies.

Brumfield, Elizabeth M., and Gary F. Feinman, eds. *The Aztec World*. New York: Abrams, 2008. Collection of expert short chapters on a variety of topics, richly illustrated.

Carrasco, Davíd. *The Aztecs: A Very Short Introduction*. Oxford and New York: Oxford University Press, 2012. Clear, compressed account by a specialist, containing all essential information.

D'Altroy, Terence. *The Incas*. 2nd ed., Hoboken, NJ: John Wiley and Sons, 2014. Well-organized, comprehensive, and up-to-date overview.

Hassig, Ross. *War and Society in Ancient Mesoamerica*. Berkeley and Los Angeles: University of California Press, 1992. Best study of the rising importance of militarism in Mesoamerican city-states, up to the Aztec Empire.

Julien, Catherine. *Reading Inca History*. Iowa City: University of Iowa Press, 2000. Ambitious "reading" of "genres" of memory in the available, mostly Spanish sources.

Malpass, Michael A. *Daily Life in the Inca Empire*, 2nd ed. Westport, CT: Greenwood, 2009. Clear, straightforward, and readable account of ordinary people's lives by a specialist.

Smith, Michael E., *The Aztecs*, 3rd ed. Hoboken, NJ: Wiley, 2013. Up-to-date, extensive account of all aspects of Inca history and civilization.

WEBSITE

Aztec History, http://www.aztec-history.com/. Introductory website, easily navigable, with links.

Chapter 16

Ágoston, Gábor. *Guns for the Sultan: Military Power and the Weapons Industry in the Ottoman Empire*. Cambridge, UK: Cambridge University Press, 2005. Thorough study, which is based on newly accessible Ottoman archival materials and emphasizes the technological prowess of Ottoman gunsmiths.

Casale, Giancarlo. *The Ottoman Age of Exploration*. Oxford and New York: Oxford University Press, 2010. Detailed correction, based on Ottoman and Portuguese archives, of the traditional characterization of the Ottoman Empire as a land-oriented power.

Casey, James. *Early Modern Spain: A Social History*. London: Routledge, 1999. Detailed, well-documented analysis of rural–urban and king–nobility tensions.

Elliott, John Huxtable. *Spain, Europe, and the Wider World: 1500–1800*. New Haven, CT: Yale University Press, 2009. A comprehensive overview, particularly strong on culture during the 1500s.

Glete, Jan. *War and the State in Early Modern Europe: Spain, the Dutch Republic, and Sweden as Fiscal–Military States, 1500–1660*. London: Routledge, 2002. A complex but persuasive construction of the forerunner to the absolute state. Unfortunately leaves out the Ottoman Empire.

Murphey, Rhoads. *Ottoman Warfare, 1500–1700*. New Brunswick, NJ: Rutgers University Press, 1999. Author presents a vivid picture of the Janissaries, their discipline, organization, campaigns, and voracious demands for salary increases.

Pamuk, Sevket. *A Monetary History of the Ottoman Empire*. Cambridge, UK: Cambridge University Press, 2000. Superb analysis of Ottoman archival resources on the role and function of American silver in the money economy of the Ottomans.

Ruiz, Teofilo R. *Spanish Society, 1400–1600*. London: Longman, 2001. Richly detailed social studies rewarding anyone interested in changing class structures, rural–urban movement, and extension of the money market into the countryside.

Subrahmanyam, Sanjay. *The Career and Legend of Vasco da Gama*. Cambridge, UK: Cambridge University Press, 1997. Focuses on the religious motivations of Vasco da Gama and the commercial impact of his journey to India.

WEBSITES

Frontline, "Apocalypse! The Evolution of Apocalyptic Belief and How It Shaped the Western World," PBS, 1995, http://www.pbs.org/wgbh/pages/frontline/shows/apocalypse/. The contribution by Bernard McGinn, University of Chicago, under the heading of "Apocalypticism Explained: Joachim of Fiore," is of particular relevance for the understanding of Christopher Columbus viewing himself as a precursor of Christ's Second Coming.

Islam: Empire of Faith: Timeline, http://www.pbs.org/empires/islam/timeline.html. Comprehensive and informative, this

PBS website on the Ottoman Empire examines the various facets of this Islamic culture such as scientific innovations, faith and its leaders.

Chapter 17

Biro, Jacquelin. *On Earth as in Heaven: Cosmography and the Shape of the Earth from Copernicus to Descartes*. Saarbrücken, Germany: VDM Verlag Dr. Müller, 2009. Short study establishing the connection between geography and cosmology in Copernicus. Uses the pathbreaking articles by Thomas Goldberg.

Black, Jeremy. *Kings, Nobles, and Commoners: States and Societies in Early Modern Europe—A Revisionist History*. London: I.B. Tauris, 2004. Available also electronically on ebrary; persuasive thesis, largely accepted by scholars, of a continuity of institutional practices in Europe across the sixteenth and seventeenth centuries, casting doubt on absolutism as being more than a theory.

Cañizares-Esguerra, Jorge. *Nature, Empire, and Nation: Explorations of the History of Science in the Iberian World*. Stanford, CA: Stanford University Press, 2006. A collection of essays that provides new perspectives on the history of science in early modern Iberia.

Geanakoplos, Deno John. *Constantinople and the West: Essays on the Late Byzantine (Palaeologan) and Italian Renaissances and the Byzantine and Roman Churches*. Madison: University of Wisconsin Press, 1989. Fundamental discussion of the extensive transfer of texts and scholars during the 1400s.

Jacob, Margaret C. *Scientific Culture and the Making of the Industrial West*. Oxford and New York: Oxford University Press, 1997. Widely cited short book emphasizing the connections among New Science, scientific societies, and the steam engine.

Margolis, Howard. *It Started with Copernicus: How Turning the World Inside Out Led to the Scientific Revolution*. New York: McGraw-Hill, 2002. Important scholarly study of the connection between the discovery of the Americas and Copernicus's formulation of a sun-centered planetary system.

Nexon, Daniel H. *The Struggle for Power in Early Modern Europe: Religious Conflict, Dynastic Empires and International Change*. Princeton, NJ: Princeton University Press, 2009. Charles Tilly–inspired reevaluation of the changes occurring in sixteenth- and seventeenth-century Europe.

Park, Katharine, and Lorraine Daston, eds. *The Cambridge History of Science*. Vol. 3, *Early Modern Science*. Cambridge, UK: Cambridge University Press, 2006. Voluminous coverage of all aspects of science, under the currently paradigmatic thesis that there was no dramatic scientific revolution in Western Christian civilization.

Rublack, Ulinka. *Reformation Europe*. Cambridge, UK: Cambridge University Press, 2006. Cultural history approach to the effects of Luther and Calvin on western Christians.

Schiebinger, Londa. *The Mind Has No Sex? Women in the Origins of Modern Science*. Cambridge, MA: Harvard University Press, 1989. A pioneering study presenting biographies and summaries of scientific contributions made by women. Discusses the importance of Marie Cunitz.

Wiesner-Hanks, Merry E. *Early Modern Europe, 1450-1789*. 2nd ed. Cambridge, UK: Cambridge University Press, 2013. Textbook in the Cambridge History of Europe series with a braod coverage of topics.

WEBSITES

Ames Research Center. "Johannes Kepler: His Life, His Laws and Times," http://kepler.nasa.gov/Mission/JohannesKepler/. This NASA website looks at the life and views of Johannes Kepler. It examines his discoveries, his contemporaries, and the events that shaped modern science.

Howard, Sharon. "Early Modern Resources," http://sharonhoward.org/earlymodern.html. Website with many links on the full range of institutional and cultural change.

Chapter 18

Alchon, Suzanne A. *A Pest in the Land: New World Epidemics in a Global Perspective*. Albuquerque: University of New Mexico Press, 2003. A broad overview, making medical history comprehensible.

Behringer, Wolfgang. *Witches and Witch-Hunts: A Global History*. Cambridge, UK: Polity, 2004. A well-grounded overview of the phenomenon of the fear of witches, summarizing the scholarship of the past decades.

Bulmer-Thomas, Victor, John S. Coatsworth, and Roberto Cortés Conde, eds. *The Cambridge Economic History of Latin America*. Vol. 1, *The Colonial Era and the Short Nineteenth Century*. Cambridge, UK: Cambridge University Press, 2006. Collection of specialized summary articles on aspects of Iberian colonialism.

Burkholder, Mark A., and Lyman L. Johnson. *Colonial Latin America*, 6th ed. Oxford and New York: Oxford University Press, 2008. A well-established text, updated multiple times.

Eastman, Scott, *Preaching Spanish Nationalism across the Hispanic Atlantic, 1759–1823*. Baton Rouge: Louisiana State University Press, 2012. Close look at the national reform debates in the Iberian Atlantic world at the close of colonialism.

Ekberg, Carl J. *French Roots in the Illinois Country: The Mississippi Frontier in Colonial Times*. Urbana: University of Illinois Press, 1998. Detailed, deeply researched historical account.

Peloso, Vincent. *Race and Ethnicity in Latin America*. Milton Park and New York: Routledge, 2014. Excellent presentation of the publicly enshrined, complex racial and ethnic identities-during colonialism and since independence.

Socolow, Susan M. *The Women of Latin America*. Cambridge, UK: Cambridge University Press, 2000. Surveys the patriarchal order and the function of women within it.

Stein, Stanley J., and Barbara H. Stein. *Silver, Trade, and War: Spain and America in the Making of Early Modern Europe*. Baltimore: Johns Hopkins University Press, 2000. Covers the significance of American silver reaching as far as China.

Taylor, Alan. *American Colonies*. London: Penguin, 2001. History of the English colonies in New England, written from a broad Atlantic perspective.

Wood, Michael. *Conquistadors*. Berkeley and Los Angeles: University of California Press, 2000. Accessible, richly illustrated history of the conquest period.

WEBSITE

Conquistadors, http://www.pbs.org/conquistadors/. Wonderful interactive website that allows you to track the journeys made by the Conquistadors such as Cortés, Pizarro, Orellana, and Cabeza de Vaca. Learn more about their conquests in the Americas and the legacy they left behind them.

Chapter 19

Berlin, Ira. *Many Thousands Gone: The First Two Centuries of Slavery in North America.* Cambridge, MA: Harvard University Press, 1998. One of the most authoritative studies of antebellum chattel slavery by one of the era's leading historians.

Carney, Judith A. *Black Rice: The African Origins of Rice Cultivation in the Americas.* Cambridge, MA: Harvard University Press, 2001. Study which goes a long way toward correcting the stereotype that black slaves were unskilled laborers, and carefully documents the transfer of rice-growing culture from West Africa to the Americas.

Dubois, Laurent, and Julius S. Scott, eds. *Origins of the Black Atlantic: Rewriting Histories.* New York: Routledge, 2010. Book that focuses on African slaves in the Americas as they had to arrange themselves in their new lives.

Gray, Richard, and David Birmingham, eds. *Pre-Colonial African Trade.* London and New York: Oxford University Press, 1970. Collective work in which contributors emphasize the growth and intensification of trade in the centuries of 1500–1800.

Hall, Gwendolyn Midlo. *Slavery and African Ethnicities in the Americas: Restoring the Links.* Chapel Hill: University of North Carolina Press, 2005. Study that focuses on slaves in the Americas according to their regions of origin in Africa.

Heywood, Linda M., and John K. Thornton. *Central Africans, Atlantic Creoles, and the Foundation of the Americas.* Cambridge, UK: Cambridge University Press, 2007. Pathbreaking investigation of the creation and role of Creole culture in Africa and the Americas.

Iliffe, John. *Africans: The History of a Continent, 2nd ed.* Cambridge, UK: Cambridge University Press, 2007. Standard historical summary by an established African historian.

Kriger, Colleen E. *Cloth in West African History.* Lanham, MD Altamira, 2006. Detailed investigation of the sophisticated indigenous West African cloth industry.

LaGamma, Alisa. *Kongo: Power and Majesty.* New York: Metropolitan Museum of Art, 2015. Superbly illustrated exhibition catalogue, with articles by leading Africanists.

Oliver, Roland, and Anthony Atmore. *Medieval Africa, 1250–1800.* Cambridge, UK: Cambridge University Press, 2001. Revised and updated historical overview, divided into regions and providing detailed regional histories on the emerging kingdoms.

Stapleton, Timothy J. *A Military History of Africa.* Vol. 1, *The Precolonial Period: From Ancient Egypt to the Zulu Kingdom (Earliest Times to ca. 1870).* Santa Barbara, CA: Praeger, 2013. Summary of the historical evolution of West, East, Central, and South Africa.

Thornton, John. *The Kongolese Saint Anthony: Dona Beatriz Kimpa Vita and the Antonian Movement, 1684–1706.* Cambridge, UK: Cambridge University Press, 1998. Detailed biography of Dona Beatriz, from which the vignette at the beginning of the chapter is borrowed; includes a general overview of the history of Kongo during the civil war.

WEBSITES

British Museum. "Benin: An African Kingdom," www.britishmuseum.org/PDF/british_museum_benin_art.pdf. In addition to offering a brief historical backdrop to the art of the Benin kingdom, the British Museum's PDF also depicts various artifacts taken by the British from the Royal Palace.

Voyages: The Atlantic Slave Trade Database, http://www.slavevoyages.org/tast/index.faces. A large electronic website based at Emory University and sponsored by a number of American universities, presenting up-to-date demographic tables.

Chapter 20

Bernier, François. *Travels in the Mogul Empire, A.D. 1656–1668.* Translated by Archibald Constable. Delhi: S. Chand, 1968. One of many fascinating travel accounts by European diplomats, merchants, and missionaries.

Eaton, Richard M. *Essays on Islam and Indian History.* Oxford and New York: Oxford University Press, 2002. A compendium of the new scholarly consensus on, among other things, the differences between the clerical view of Islamic observance and its actual impact in rural India. Contains both historiography and material on civilizational and cultural issues.

Gommans, J. J. L. *Mughal Warfare: Indian Frontiers and Highroads to Empire 1500–1700.* New York: Routledge, 2002. Sound examination of the Mughal Empire as a centralizing state increasingly reliant on a strong military for border defense and extending its sway. Examination of the structure of Mughal forces and the organization and weapons of the military.

Hunt, Margaret R., and Philip J. Stern, eds. *The English East India Company at the Height of Mughal Expansion: A Soldier's Diary of the 1689 Siege of Bombay with Related Documents.* Boston and New York: Bedford/St. Martin's, 2016. Illuminating look at the interplay of Mughal and European actors during the reign of Aurangzeb through the eyes of James Hilton, an English East India Company soldier, whose diary had previously been unpublished.

Kearney, Milo. *The Indian Ocean in World History.* New York: Routledge, 2003. Long view of the history of Indian Ocean trade from ancient times. Particularly relevant in examining the vital period in which the Portuguese and later East Indian Companies come to dominate the trade.

Nizami, Khaliq A. *Akbar and Religion.* Delhi: IAD, 1989. Extensive treatment of Akbar's evolving move toward devising his din-i ilahi movement, by a leading scholar of Indian religious and intellectual history.

Richards, John F. *The Mughal Empire.* Cambridge, UK: Cambridge University Press, 1993. Comprehensive volume in the New Cambridge History of India series. Sophisticated treatment; best suited to advanced students. Extensive glossary and useful bibliographic essay.

Schimmel, Annemarie. *The Empire of the Great Mughals: History, Art, and Culture.* London: Reaktion, 2004. Revised edition of a volume published in German in 2000. Lavish illustrations, wonderfully drawn portraits of key individuals, and extensive treatment of social, family, and gender relations at the Mughal court.

Srivastava, M. P. *The Mughal Administration.* Delhi: Chugh, 1995. Solid overview and analysis of the development and workings of the Mughal bureaucracy. Best utilized by advanced students.

WEBSITES

Association for Asian Studies http://www. asian-studies.org/ As with other Asian topics, one of the most reliable websites is sponsored by the Association for Asian Studies, the largest professional organization for scholars of Asia.

BBC: Religions. "Mughal Empire (1500s, 1600s)" http://www.bbc.co.uk/religion/religions/islam/history/mughalempire_1.shtml. The Mughal Empire ruled most of India and Pakistan in the sixteenth and seventeenth centuries. Learn more about the religious divides and governance of Muslim Mughals in a country with a majority of Hindu populace.

Chapter 21

China

Crossley, Pamela K. *A Translucent Mirror: History and Identity in Qing Imperial Ideology.* Los Angeles: University of California Press, 1999. Pioneering study of the transformation of Qing self-image to one of leading a universal, multicultural empire.

De Bary, William T., and Irene Bloom, comps. *Sources of Chinese Tradition,* 2 vols., 2nd ed. New York: Columbia University Press, 1999. Thoroughgoing update of the classic sourcebook for Chinese literature and philosophy, with a considerable amount of social, family, and women's works now included.

Mungello, D. E. *The Great Encounter of China and West.* Lanham, MD: Rowman & Littlefield, 1999. Sound historical overview of the period marking the first European maritime expeditions into East Asia and extending to the height of the Canton trade and the beginnings of the opium era.

Pomeranz, Kenneth. *The Great Divergence: China, Europe, and the Making of the Modern World Economy.* Princeton, NJ: Princeton University Press, 2001. Pathbreaking work mounting the strongest argument yet in favor of the balance of economic power remaining in East Asia until the Industrial Revolution was well under way.

Shuo Wang. "Manchu Women in Transition: Gender Relations and Sexuality," in Stephen A. Wadley and Carsten Naeher, eds. *Proceedings of the First North American Conference on Manchu Studies.* Wiesbaden, Germany: Otto Harrassowitz Verlag, 2006: 105–130. Pathbreaking study of the role of Manchu women in Qing China in resistance to assimilation and preserving cultural identity.

Spence, Jonathan. *The Memory Palace of Matteo Ricci.* New York: Penguin, 1984. Highly original treatment of Ricci and the beginning of the Jesuit interlude in late Ming and early Qing China. Attempts to penetrate Ricci's world through the missionary's own memory techniques.

Japan

De Bary, William T., ed. *Sources of Japanese Tradition,* 2 vols. New York: Columbia University Press, 1964. The Tokugawa era spans volumes 1 and 2, with its inception and political and philosophical foundations thoroughly covered in volume 1 and the Shinto revival of national learning, the later Mito school, and various partisans of national unity in the face of foreign intrusion covered in the beginning of volume 2.

Duus, Peter. *Feudalism in Japan,* 3rd ed. New York: McGraw-Hill, 1993. Updated version of a short, handy volume spanning all of Japanese history to 1867, with special emphasis on the shogunates. Good introduction on the uses and limitations of the term "feudalism" with reference to Japan within a comparative framework.

Gordon, Andrew. *A Modern History of Japan from Tokugawa Times to the Present.* Oxford and New York: Oxford University Press, 2009. One of the few treatments of Japanese history that spans both the Tokugawa and the modern eras, rather than making the usual break in either 1853 or 1867/1868. Both the continuity of the past and the novelty of the new era are therefore juxtaposed and highlighted. Most useful for students with a background at least equivalent to that supplied by this text.

WEBSITE

National Geographic. China's Great Armada, http://ngm.nationalgeographic.com/ngm/0507/feature2/map.html. Track the voyages made by Zheng He to Southeast Asia, India, Arabia, and Africa.

Chapter 22

Herb, Guntram H. *Nations and Nationalism: A Global Historical Overview.* Santa Barbara, CA: ABC-Clio, 2008. Contains a large number of articles on the varieties of ethnic nationalism and culture and the proliferation of nationalism in Europe and Latin America.

Israel, Jonathan I. *A Revolution of the Mind: Radical Enlightenment and the Origins of Modern Democracy.* Princeton, NJ: Princeton University Press, 2010. Israel is a pioneer of the contemporary renewal of intellectual history, and his investigations of the Enlightenment tradition are pathbreaking.

Kaiser, Thomas E., and Dale K. Van Kley, eds. *From Deficit to Deluge: The Origins of the French Revolution.* Stanford, CA: Stanford University Press, 2011. Thoughtful reevaluation of the scholarly field that takes into account the latest interpretations.

Kitchen, Martin. *A History of Modern Germany: 1800 to the Present.* Hoboken, NJ: Wiley-Blackwell, 2011. A broadly conceived historical overview, ranging from politics and economics to culture.

Osterhammel, Jürgen. *The Transformation of the World: A Global History of the Nineteenth Century.* Princeton, NJ: 2015. Celebrated evaluation of the myriads of changes and transformations characterizing the nineteenth century.

Rakove, Jack. *Revolutionaries: A New History of the Invention of America.* Boston: Houghton Mifflin, 2010. A new narrative history focusing on the principal figures in the revolution.

Riall, Lucy. *Risorgimento: The History of Italy from Napoleon to Nation-State.* New York: Palgrave Macmillan, 2009. Historical summary, incorporating the research of the past half-century, presented in a clear overview.

West, Elliott. *The Last Indian War: The Nez Perce Story.* Oxford and New York: Oxford University Press, 2009. Vivid story of the end of the US wars for the subjugation of the Native Americans.

Wood, Gordon S. *The American Revolution: A History.* New York: Modern Library, 2002. A short, readable summary reflective of many decades of revisionism in the discussion of the American Revolution.

WEBSITES

Liberty, Equality, Fraternity: Exploring the French Revolution, http://chnm.gmu.edu/revolution/. This website boasts 250 images, 350 text documents, 13 songs, 13 maps, and a timeline all focused on the French Revolution.

Nationalism Project, http://www.nationalismproject.org/. A large website with links to bibliographies, essays, new books, and book reviews.

Chapter 23

Adelman, Jeremy. *Sovereignty and Revolution in the Iberian Atlantic*, Princeton, NJ: Princeton University Press, 2006. A leading study in a group of recent works on the transatlantic character of colonial and postcolonial Latin America.

Brown, Matthew. *The Struggle for Power in Post-Independence Colombia and Venezuela*. New York: Palgrave Macmillan, 2012. Detailed history of the forces pulling for democracy as well as authoritarianism on the north coast of South America.

Bulmer-Thomas, Victor. *The Economic History of Latin America since Independence*, 2nd ed. Cambridge, UK: Cambridge University Press, 2003. A highly analytical and sympathetic investigation of the Latin American export and self-sufficiency economies, calling into question the long-dominant dependency theories of Latin America.

Burkholder, Mark, and Lyman Johnson. *Colonial Latin America*, 6th ed. New York: Oxford University Press, 2008. Overview, with focus on social and cultural history.

Dawson, Alexander. *Latin America since Independence: A History with Primary Sources*. New York: Routledge, 2011. Selection of topics with documentary base; for the nineteenth century covers the topics of the nation-state, caudillo politics, race, and the policy of growth through commodity exports.

Drake, Paul W. *Between Tyranny and Anarchy: A History of Democracy in Latin America*. Stanford, CA: Stanford University Press, 2009. The author traces the concepts of constitutionalism, autocracy, and voting rights since independence in clear and persuasive strokes.

Girard, Philippe, *The Slaves Who Defeated Napoléon: Toussaint Louverture and the Haitian War of Independence, 1801–1804*. Tuscaloosa: University of Alabama Press, 2011. Thoroughly researched study of the leader of the revolution, with a number of revisionist conclusions.

Hämäläinen, Pekka. *The Comanche Empire*. New Haven, CT: Yale University Press, 2008. A revisionist account that puts the extraordinary importance of the Comanche empire for the history of Mexico and the United States in the 19th century into the proper perspective.

Moya, Jose C., ed. *The Oxford Handbook of Latin American History*. Oxford and New York: Oxford University Press, 2011. Important collection of political, social, economic, and cultural essays by leading specialists on nineteenth-century Latin America.

Popkin, Jeremy D. *The Haitian Revolution and the Abolition of Slavery*. Cambridge, UK: Cambridge University Press, 2010.

Sanders, James E. *Vanguard of the Atlantic World: Creating Modernity, Nation, and Democracy in Nineteenth-Century Latin America*. Durham, NC: Duke University Press, 2014. Ambitious effort to evaluate the Latin American contributions to the creation of the modern state.

Sater, William F. *Andean Tragedy: Fighting the War of the Pacific, 1879–1884*. Lincoln: University of Nebraska Press, 2007. Close examination of this destructive war on the South American west coast.

Skidmore, Thomas. *Brazil: Five Centuries of Change*, 2nd ed. Oxford and New York: Oxford University Press, 2010. Short but magisterial text on the history of Brazil, with a detailed chapter on Brazil's path toward independence in the nineteenth century.

Wasserman, Mark, and Cheryl English Martin. *Latin America and Its People*, 2nd ed. New York: Pearson Longman, 2007. Thematic approach, drawing general conclusions by comparing and contrasting the individual countries of Latin America.

WEBSITE

Casahistoria. "19th Century Latin America," http://www.casahistoria.net/latin_american_history19.html. Website on nineteenth-century Latin America, for students.

Chapter 24

China

Cohen, Paul. *Discovering History in China*. New York: Columbia University Press, 1984. Pivotal work on the historiography of American writers on China. Critiques their collective ethnocentrism in attempting to fit Chinese history into Western perspectives and approaches.

Fairbank, John K., and Su-yu Teng. *China's Response to the West*. Cambridge, MA: Harvard University Press, 1954. Though dated in approach, still a vitally important collection of sources in translation for the period from the late eighteenth century till 1923.

Kang, David C. *East Asia before the West: Five Centuries of Trade and Tribute*. New York: Columbia University Press, 2010. An excellent companion piece to D. E. Mungello's work covering the period from 1500 to 1800. Especially good on the Ming era.

Meyer-Fong, Tobie. *What Remains: Coming to Terms With Civil War in 19th Century China*. Stanford, CA: Stanford University Press, 2013. Extensive treatment of individual experiences during the world's bloodiest civil war, the Taiping movement.

Platt, Stephen R. *Autumn in the Heavenly Kingdom*. New York: Knopf, 2012. Reinterpretation of the Taiping era as global political and economic phenomena involving the curtailing of US cotton exports during its civil war, their effects on the British textile industry, and the loss of Chinese markets during the Taiping Rebellion.

Spence, Jonathan D. *The Search for Modern China*. New York: Norton, 1990. Extensive, far-reaching interpretation of the period from China's nineteenth-century decline in the face of Western imperialism, through its revolutionary era, and finally to its recent bid for global preeminence.

Japan

Keene, Donald. *Emperor of Japan: Meiji and His World, 1852–1912*. New York: Columbia University Press, 2002. Masterly treatment of Japan's modernizing emperor and his vast influence on Japan and Asia, by one of the twentieth century's finest translators and scholars of Japan.

Reischauer, Edwin O., and Albert M. Craig. *Japan: Tradition and Transformation*. Boston: Houghton Mifflin, 1989. Somewhat dated but still highly useful introductory text by two of the twentieth century's leading scholars of Japanese history.

Totman, Conrad. *Politics in the Tokugawa Bakufu, 1600–1843*. Berkeley: University of California Press, 1988. (Paperback edition with new preface and enhanced bibliography). Updated edition of Totman's breakthrough 1967 work. It remains one of the few highly detailed and deeply sourced monographs on the inner workings of the Tokugawa shogunate.

Walthall, Anne, and M. William Steele, *Politics and Society in Japan's Meiji Restoration: A Brief History with Documents*. New York: Bedford/St. Martin's, 2016. As with others in this series, a sound introduction for students with little or no background in the subject, accompanied by well-chosen documents.

WEBSITES

Association for Asian Studies, http://www.asian-studies.org/. This website of the Association for Asian Studies has links to sources more suited to advanced term papers and seminar projects.

Education about Asia, http://www.asian-studies.org/eaa/. This site provides the best online sources for modern Chinese and Japanese history.

Sino-Japanese War 1894–5, http://sinojapanesewar.com/. Packed with maps, photographs and movies depicting the conflict between Japan and China at the end of the nineteenth century, students can learn more about causes and consequences of the Sino–Japanese War.

Chapter 25

Gaudin, Corinne. *Ruling Peasants: Village and State in Later Imperial Russia*. DeKalb: Northern Illinois University Press, 2007. A close and sympathetic analysis of rural Russia.

Inalcik, Halil, and Donald Quataert, eds. *An Economic and Social History of the Ottoman Empire*. Vol. 2, *1600–1914*. Cambridge, UK: Cambridge University Press, 1994. A pioneering work with contributions by leading Ottoman historians on rural structures, monetary developments, and industrialization efforts.

Kasaba, Resat, ed. *The Cambridge History of Turkey*. Vol. 5, *Turkey in the Modern World*. Cambridge, UK: Cambridge University Press, 2008. An ambitious effort to assemble the leading authorities on the Ottoman Empire and provide a comprehensive overview.

Lieven, Dominic. *Empire: The Russian Empire and Its Rivals*. New Haven, CT: Yale University Press, 2002. Broad, comparative history of the Russian Empire, in the context of the Habsburg, Ottoman, and British Empires.

Massie, Robert K. *Catherine the Great: Portrait of a Woman*. New York: Random House, 2012. A comprehensive and insightful biography of one of the most fascinating women in history, whose policies, reforms, and personal life changed the course of Russian history.

Nikitenko, Aleksandr. *Up from Serfdom: My Childhood and Youth in Russia, 1804–1824*. Translated by Helen Saltz Jacobson. New Haven, CT: Yale University Press, 2001. Touching autobiography summarized at the beginning of the chapter.

Poe, Marshall T. *Russia's Moment in World History*. Princeton, NJ: Princeton University Press, 2003. A superb scholarly overview of Russian history, written from a broad perspective and taking into account a good number of Western stereotypes about Russia, especially in the nineteenth century.

Quataert, Donald. *Manufacturing in the Ottoman Empire and Turkey, 1500–1950*. Albany, NY: State University of New York Press, 1994. The author is still the leading American historian on workers and the early industrialization of the Ottoman Empire.

Riasanovsky, Nicholas, and Mark Steinberg. *A History of Russia*, 8th ed., 2 vols. Oxford and New York: Oxford University Press, 2011. A comprehensive, fully revised history, ranging from politics and economics to literature and the arts.

Uyar, Mesut, and Edward J. Erickson. *A Military History of the Ottomans: From Osman to Atatürk*. Santa Barbara, CA: Praeger Security International, 2009. A detailed, well-documented history of the Ottoman Empire from the perspective of its imperial designs and military forces, by two military officers in academic positions.

Zurcher, Erik J. *The Young Turk Legacy and Nation Building: From the Ottoman Empire to Atatürk's Turkey*. London: I. B. Tauris, 2010. Detailed yet readable account of how the Young Turk movement laid the foundation for Kemal Atatürk's Republic of Turkey.

WEBSITE

Russian Legacy. "Russian Empire (1689–1825)," http://www.russianlegacy.com/en/go_to/history/russian_empire.htm. Russian Legacy, a website devoted to the Russian Empire, organized as a timeline with links.

Chapter 26

Allen, Robert C. *The British Industrial Revolution in Global Perspective*. Cambridge, UK: Cambridge University Press, 2009. An in-depth analysis, well supported by economic data, not only of why the Industrial Revolution occurred first in Britain but also of how new British technologies carried industrialism around the world.

Dublin, Thomas, ed. *Farm to Factory: Women's Letters, 1830–1860*. New York: Columbia University Press, 1981. A fascinating collection of correspondence written by women who describe their experiences in moving from rural areas of New England to urban centers in search of work in textile factories.

Griffin, Emma. *Liberty's Dawn: A People's History of the Industrial Revolution*. New Haven, CT: Yale University Press, 2013. Riveting study of the impact of the Industrial Revolution on the lives of working men and women in Britain, as told in autobiographies and memoirs.

Headrick, Daniel R. *The Tools of Empire: Technology and European Imperialism in the Nineteenth Century*. Oxford and New York: Oxford University Press, 1981. A fascinating and clearly written analysis of the connections between the development of new technologies and their role in European imperialism.

Hobsbawm, Eric. *The Age of Revolution: 1789–1848*. London: Vintage, 1996. A sophisticated analysis of the Industrial Revolution (one element of the "twin revolution," the other being the French Revolution) that examines the effects of industrialism on social and cultural developments from a Marxist perspective.

More, Charles. *Understanding the Industrial Revolution*. London: Routledge, 2000. A comprehensive explanation of how theories of economic growth account for the development of the industrial movement in Britain.

Rosen, William. *The Most Powerful Idea in the World: A Story of Steam, Industry, and Innovation*. Chicago: University of Chicago Press, 2012. Absorbing history of the importance of steam technologies in the development of industrialism.

Roudinesco, Elisabeth, and Catherine Porter. *Freud: In His Time and Ours*. Cambridge, MA: Harvard University Press, 2016. A bold, comprehensive, and innovative analysis of one of the most influential—and complex—figures at the turn of the twentieth century.

Sperber, Jonathan. *Karl Marx: A Nineteenth-Century Life*. New York: W. W. Norton, 2013. A carefully researched biography that contextualizes Marx vis-à-vis the age of early industrialism and in comparison with other luminaries in the turbulent nineteenth century.

WEBSITES

Claude Monet: Life and Paintings, http://www.monetpainting.net/. A visually beautiful website which reproduces many of Monet's masterpieces; this site also includes an extensive biographical account of the famous painter's life and works. It also includes information about his wife Camille, his gardens at Giverny, and a chronology.

Darwin Online, http://darwin-online.org.uk/. This website has reproduced, in full, the works of Charles Darwin. In addition to providing digitized facsimiles of his works, private papers, and manuscripts, it has also added a concise biographical account and numerous images of Darwin throughout his life.

Einstein Archives Online, http://www.alberteinstein.info/. Fantastic and informative website that houses digitized manuscripts of Einstein's work. Also includes a gallery of images.

ThomasEdison.org, http://www.thomasedison.org/. Remarkable website that explores Thomas Edison's impact on modernity through his innovations and inventions. This site also reproduces all of Edison's scientific sketches, which are available to download as PDF files.

Chapter 27

Belich, James. *Replenishing the Earth: The Settler Revolution and the Rise of the Anglo-World, 1783–1939*. Oxford and New York: Oxford University Press, 2009. Important study by an Australian historian, focusing on the British settler colonies.

Chamberlain, M. E. *The Scramble for Africa*. New York: Routledge, 2013. Insightful account of the European colonization of Africa during the period 1870 to 1914.

Ferguson, Niall. *Empire: The Rise and Demise of the British World Order and the Lessons for Global Power*. New York: Perseus, 2002. Controversial but widely acknowledged analysis of the question of whether imperialism deserves its negative reputation or not.

Hobsbawm, Eric. *The Age of Empire, 1875–1914*. New York: Vintage, 1989. Immensely well-informed investigation of the climactic period of the new imperialism at the end of the nineteenth century.

Hochschild, Adam. *King Leopold's Ghost: A Story of Greed, Terror, and Heroism in Colonial Africa*. New York: Houghton Mifflin, 1998. A gripping exposé of Leopold II's brutal tactics in seizing territory and exploiting African labor in the Congo.

Jefferies, Matthew. *Contesting the German Empire, 1871–1918*. Malden, MA: Blackwell, 2008. Up-to-date summary of the German historical debate on the colonial period.

Münkler, Herfried. *Empires:The Logic of World Domination from Ancient Rome to the United States*. Cambridge, UK: Polity Press, 2007. Short but wide-ranging and historically well-informed analysis of the phenomena of empire and imperial hegemony in world history.

Vickers, Adrian. *A History of Modern Indonesia*, 2nd ed. Cambridge, UK: Cambridge University Press, 2013. Well-written account of Indonesia growing from heteregenous Dutch colonial islands into a modern nation state.

Singer, Barnett, and John Langdon. *Cultured Force: Makers and Defenders of the French Colonial Empire*. Madison: University of Wisconsin Press, 2004. Study of the principal (military) figures who helped create the French nineteenth-century empire.

Streets-Salter, Heather, and Trevor R. Getz, *Empires and Colonies in the World: A Global Perspective*. Oxford and New York: Oxford University Press, 2015. Particularly illuminative chapters on the new imperialism in the nineteenth century.

WEBSITES

The Colonization of Africa, http://exhibitions.nypl.org/africanaage/essay-colonization-of-africa.html. An academically based summary with further essays on African topics, as well as multimedia functions.

South Asian History—*Colonial* India, http://www.lib.berkeley.edu/SSEAL/SouthAsia/india_colonial.html. Very detailed website with primary documents and subtopics of nineteenth-century British India.

Chapter 28

Berend, Ivan T. *An Economic History of Twentieth-Century Europe: Economic Regimes from Laissez-Faire to Globalization*. Cambridge, UK: Cambridge University Press, 2006. Includes Europe-wide, comparative chapters on laissez-faire and state-directed economies, including deficit spending.

Bose, Sugata, and Ayesha Jalal. *Modern South Asia: History, Culture, Political Economy*. New York: Routledge, 2004. Well-informed analyses by two of the foremost South Asia specialists.

Clark, Christopher. *The Sleepwalkers: How Europe Went to War in 1914*. New York: HarperPerennial, 2014. One of a slew of new investigations into the origins of the war published to mark its centennial; emphasizes the Austrian–Serbian roots of the war.

Cohen, Adam. *Imbeciles: The Supreme Court, American Eugenics, and the Sterilization of Carrie Buck*. New York: Penguin, 2016.

Fritzsche, Peter. *Life and Death in the Third Reich*. Cambridge, MA: Harvard University Press, 2008. Book that seeks to understand the German nation's choice of arranging itself to Nazi rule.

Gelvin, James L. *The Modern Middle East: A History*, 4th ed. Oxford and New York: Oxford University Press, 2015. Contains chapters on Arab nationalism, British and French colonialism, and Turkey and Iran in the interwar period.

Gordon, Andrew. *A Modern History of Japan: From Tokugawa Times to the Present*, 2nd ed. Oxford and New York: Oxford University Press, 2009. Detailed overview of Japan's interwar period in the middle chapters.

Grasso, June M., J. P. Corrin, and Michael Kort. *Modernization and Revolution in Modern China: From the Opium Wars to the Olympics*, 4th ed. Armonk, NY: M. E. Sharpe, 2009. General overview with a focus on modernization in relation to the strong survival of tradition.

Martel, Gordon, ed. *A Companion to Europe 1900–1945*. Malden, MA: Wiley-Blackwell, 2010. Collective work covering a large variety of cultural, social, and political European topics in the interwar period.

Meade, Teresa A. *A History of Modern Latin America: 1800 to the Present*. Malden, MA: Wiley-Routledge, 2010. Topical discussion of the major issues in Latin American history, with chapters on the first half of the twentieth century.

Neiberg, Michael S. *The Treaty of Versailles: A Concise Study*. Oxford and New York: Oxford University Press, 2017. An assessment of the complexities attending the settlement of World War I, along with the consequences of its many flaws and failures.

Snyder, Timothy. *Bloodlands: Europe between Hitler and Stalin*. New York: Basic Books, 2010. Book that chronicles the horrific destruction left behind by these two dictators.

Wilson, Mark R. *Destructive Creation: American Business and the Winning of World War II*. Philadelphia: University of Pennsylvania Press, 2016. A thoroughly researched revisionist interpretation of the strained relationship between big business and the federal government as America mobilized for, and engaged in, World War II.

WEBSITES

BBC. World War One, http://www.bbc.co.uk/ww1, and World War Two, http://www.bbc.co.uk/history/worldwars/wwtwo/. The BBC's treatment of the causes, course, and consequences of both WWI and WWII from an Allied position.

Marxists Internet Archive. "The Bolsheviks," http://www.marxists.org/subject/bolsheviks/index.htm. A complete review of the Bolshevik party members, including biographies and links to archives which contain their works.

1937 Nanking Massacre, http://www.nanking-massacre.com/Home.html. A disturbing collection of pictures and articles tell the gruesome history of the Rape of Nanjing.

United States Holocaust Memorial Museum. Holocaust Encyclopedia, http://www.ushmm.org/wlc/en/article.php?ModuleId=10005151. The US Holocaust Memorial Museum looks back on one of the darkest times in Western history.

U.S. History, http://www.ushistory.org/us/. Maintained by Independence Hall Association in Philadelphia, this website contains many links to topics discussed in this chapter.

Chapter 29

Baret, Roby Carol. *The Greater Middle East and the Cold War: US Foreign Policy under Eisenhower and Kennedy*. London: I.B. Tauris, 2007. Thoroughly researched analysis of American policies in the Middle East, North Africa, and South Asia.

Birmingham, David. *Kwame Nkrumah: Father of African Nationalism*. Athens: University of Ohio Press, 1998. Short biography by a leading modern African historian.

Conniff, Michael L. *Populism in Latin America*. Tuscaloosa: University of Alabama Press, 1999. The author is a well-published scholar on modern Latin America.

Damrosch, David, David Lawrence Pike, Djelal Kadir, and Ursula K. Heise, eds. *The Longman Anthology of World Literature*. Vol. F, *The Twentieth Century*. New York: Longman/Pearson, 2008. A rich, diverse selection of texts. Alternatively, Norton published a similar, somewhat larger anthology of world literature in 2003.

De Witte, Ludo. *The Assassination of Lumumba*. Translated by Ann Wright and Renée Fenby. London: Verso, 2002. An admirably researched study of the machinations of the Belgian government in protecting its mining interests, with the connivance of CIA director Allen Dulles and President Dwight D. Eisenhower.

Goscha, Christopher E., and Christian F. Ostermann. *Connecting Histories: Decolonization and the Cold War in Southeast Asia, 1945–1962*. Stanford, CA: Stanford University Press, 2009.

Guha, Ramachandra. *India after Gandhi: A History of the World's Largest Democracy*. New York: Harper Collins, 2007. Highly readable, popular history with well-sketched biographical treatments of leading individuals, more obscure cultural figures, and ordinary people. Accessible to even beginning students.

Hasegawa, Tsuyoshi. *The Cold War in East Asia, 1945–1991*. Stanford, CA: Stanford University Press, 2011. A new summary, based on archival research by a leading Japanese historian teaching in the United States. New insights on the Soviet entry into World War II against Japan.

Herman, Arthur. *Joseph McCarthy: Reexamining the Life and Legacy of America's Most Hated Senator*. New York: Free Press, 2000. A fascinating study of the Wisconsin senator whose virulent campaign against communism launched decades of fear and reprisals in America during the Cold War era.

Jansen, Jan C., and Jürgen Osterhammel. *Decolonization: A Short History*. Princeton, NJ: Princeton University Press, 2017. Superb, analytical well-grounded summary of the decolonization process and its aftermath in the second half of the twentieth century.

Meredith, Martin. *The Fate of Africa: A History of the Continent since Independence*. Philadelphia: Perseus, 2011. A revised and up-to-date study of a fundamental analysis of Africa during the modern era.

WEBSITES

Economist. "The Suez Crisis: An Affair to Remember," http://www.economist.com/node/7218678. The *Economist* magazine looks back on the Suez Crisis.

NASA. "Yuri Gagarin: First Man in Space," http://www.nasa.gov/mission_pages/shuttle/sts1/gagarin_anniversary.html. In addition to information and video footage regarding Yuri Gagarin's orbit of the earth, students will also find information on America's space history.

Newseum. The Berlin Wall, http://www.newseum.org/berlinwall/. The Newseum's interactive website looks at what life was like on both sides of the Berlin Wall.

Chapter 30

Ash, Timothy Garton. *The Magic Lantern: The Revolution of '89 Witnessed in Warsaw, Budapest, Berlin, and Prague*. New York: Random House, 1999. A gripping first-hand account of the wave of anticommunist revolutions that rocked Eastern Europe after 1989.

Duara, Prasenjit, ed. *Decolonization: Perspectives from Now and Then*. London: Routledge, 2004. A leading scholar of China and postcolonial studies edits essays in this offering in the Rewriting Histories series on the fall of the colonial empires by scholars such as Michael Adas and John Voll and activists and leaders such as Frantz Fanon and Kwame Nkrumah.

Fanon, Frantz. *The Wretched of the Earth*. New York: Grove, 1961. One of the most provocative and influential treatments of theoretical and practical issues surrounding decolonization. Fanon champions violence as an essential part of the decolonization process and advocates a modified Marxist approach that takes into consideration the nuances of race and the legacies of colonialism.

Frieden, Jeffrey. *Global Capitalism: Its Fall and Rise in the Twentieth Century*. New York: W. W. Norton, 2006. Despite the title, a comprehensive history of global networks from the days of mercantilism to the twenty-first century. Predominant emphasis on twentieth century; highly readable, though the material is best suited for the nonbeginning student.

Gaddis, John Lewis. *The Cold War: A New History*. New York: Penguin, 2005. Though criticized by some scholars for his pro-American positions, America's foremost historian of the Cold War produces here a vivid, at times counterintuitive, view of the Cold War and its global impact. Readable even for beginning students.

Gitlin, Todd. *The Sixties: Years of Hope, Days of Rage*, rev. ed. New York: Bantam, 1993. Lively, provocative account of this pivotal decade by the former radical, now a sociologist. Especially effective at depicting the personalities of the pivotal period 1967–1969.

Goodwin, Doris Kearns. *Lyndon Johnson and the American Dream*. New York: St. Martin's Press, 1991. Insightful and probing study of President Johnson's character and personality, from its formation in his early years through his extensive political career.

Harmer, Tanya. *Allende's Chile and the Inter-American Cold War. Chapel Hill: University of North Carolina Press,* 2014. A reinterpretation of American determination to overturn Allende's leftist government and its subsequent results.

Liang Heng, and Judith Shapiro. *After the Nightmare: A Survivor of the Cultural Revolution Reports on China Today*. New York: Knopf, 1986. Highly readable, poignant, first-person accounts of people's experiences during the trauma of China's Cultural Revolution by a former husband-and-wife team. Especially interesting because China was at the beginning of its Four Modernizations when this was written, and the wounds of the Cultural Revolution were still fresh.

Raleigh, Donald J. *Soviet Baby Boomers: An Oral History of Russia's Cold War Generation*. Oxford and New York: Oxford University Press, 2012. A revealing and entertaining account of new social and cultural trends among Russia's youth, as told in a series of interviews.

Smith, Bonnie, ed. *Global Feminisms since 1945*. London: Routledge, 2000. Part of the Rewriting Histories series, this work brings together under the editorship of Smith a host of essays by writers such as Sara Evans, Mary Ann Tetreault, and Miriam Ching Yoon Louie on feminism in Asia, Africa, and Latin America, as well as Europe and the United States. Sections are thematically arranged under such headings as "Nation-Building," "Sources of Activism," "Women's Liberation," and "New Waves in the 1980s and 1990s." Comprehensive and readable, though some background in women's history is recommended.

WEBSITES

Cold War International History Project, http://www.wilsoncenter.org/program/cold-war-international-history-project. Run by the Woodrow Wilson International Center for Scholars. Rich archival materials including collections on the end of the Cold War, Soviet invasion of Afghanistan, Cuban Missile Crisis, and Chinese foreign policy documents.

College of DuPage Library, http:codlibrary.org. Entering "Research guide to 1960s websites" in the search box yields a wide-ranging set of relevant topics.

Chapter 31

Chau, Adam Yuet, ed. *Religion in Contemporary China*. New York: Routledge, 2011. Collection of fascinating chapters on the revival of Daoist, Confucian, and Buddhist traditions and their adaption to middle-class modernity, with their proponents operating often in a gray zone between official recognition and suppression.

Daniels, Robert V. *The Rise and Fall of Communism in the Soviet Union*. New Haven, CT: Yale University Press, 2010. A magisterial summary of the communist period by a specialist.

Dillon, Michael. *Contemporary China: An Introduction*. New York: Routledge, 2009. Concise yet quite specific overview of the economy, society, and politics of the country.

Eichengreen, Barry. *Exorbitant Privilege: The Rise and Fall of the Dollar and the Future of the Monetary System*. Oxford and New York: Oxford University Press, 2011. The author is an academic specialist on US monetary policies, writing in an accessible style and presenting a fascinating picture of the role of something as prosaic as greenbacks.

Faust, Aaron M. *The Ba'thification of Iraq: Saddam Hussein's Totalitarianism*. Austin: University of Texas Press, 2015. Based on meticulous research among Ba'th Party documents, this study reveals how Saddam Hussein developed a totalitarian regime in Iraq, and why his dictatorship succeeded in gaining the loyalty of millions of Iraquis for nearly 25 years.

Gelvin, James L. *The Arab Uprisings: What Everyone Needs to Know*. Oxford and New York: Oxford University Press, 2012. Concise overview of the Arab Spring events with carefully selected background information.

Houghton, John. *Global Warming: The Complete Briefing*. 5th ed. Cambridge, UK: Cambridge University Press, 2015. One of the most authoritative summaries of all aspects of global warming.

Jacka, Tamara, Andrew Kipnis, and Sally Sargeson. *Contemporary China: Society and Social Change*. Cambridge, UK: Cambridge University Press, 2013. Ambitious sociological–historical study focusing on the many differences within Chinese society and the forces that drive change in contemporary China.

Meade, Teresa A. *A History of Modern Latin America: 1800 to the Present*. 2nd ed. Malden, MA: Wiley-Blackwell, 2016. The book is an excellent, comprehensive analysis and has a strong final chapter on recent Latin America.

Saxonberg, Steven. *The Fall: A Comparative Study of the End of Communism in Czechoslovakia, East Germany, Hungary, and Poland*. Amsterdam, The Netherlands: Harwood Academic, 2001. A well-informed overview of the different trajectories by an academic teaching in Prague.

Swanimathan, Jayshankar M. *Indian Economic Superpower: Fact or Fiction?* Singapore: World Scientific Publishing, 2009. A thoughtful evaluation of the pros and cons of economic growth in India, in concise overviews.

WEBSITES

BBC. Nelson Mandela's Life and Times, http://www.bbc.co.uk/news/world-africa-12305154. The BBC News looks back at the life and career of Nelson Mandela.

Environmental Protection Agency. Climate Change, http://www.epa.gov/climatechange/. The US Environmental Protection Agency's website on climate change reviews the threat to the world's climate and the implications of consistent abuse. The site also looks at various initiatives to help reverse some of the damage already done.

Sierra Club, http://sierraclub.org/. Balanced and informative environmental websites.

Credits

Chapter 1: Reprinted by permission from Macmillan Publishers Ltd: Nature 521, 310–315 (21 May 2015), copyright 2015, p. 6; Bettman/Getty Images, p.7; (top left) akg-images / CDA/Guillemot; p. 12 (top right) akg-images /CDA/Guillemot; p. 12 (bottom) National Museum of Tanzania, Dar es Salaam, (c) 1985 David L. Brill, p. 9; © Kenneth Garrett Photography, p. 13; CC-by-SA-2.0 Bradshaw Art, TimJN1 via Wikicommons, p. 17; (top) INTERFOTO/Alamy Stock Photo; (bottom) Foto: Hilde Jensen, copyright University Tübingen, p. 18; Walter Geiersperger/Getty Images, p. 19; Philippe Psaila/Science Source, p. 20; DEA/C. SAPPA/Getty Images, p. 22; James Chatters/ASSOCIATED PRESS, p. 27.

Chapter 2: The Trustees of The British Museum/Art Resource, NY, p. 30; DEA PICTURE LIBRARY/Getty Images, p. 37; Erich Lessing/Art Resource, N.Y, p. 39; Réunion des Musées Nationaux-Grand Palais/Art Resource, NY, p. 43; (top) © Copyright Alfred Molon, p. 44; (bottom) pius99/iStock Photo, p. 44; Werner Forman/Art Resource, NY, p. 49; SOTK2011/ Alamy Stock Photo, p. 50; Ivy Close Images/Alamy Stock Photo, p. 57; (right) akg-images/John Hios. (left, nude) Egyptian Museum, Cairo, p. 59.

Chapter 3: © DeA Picture Library/Art Resource, NY, p. 64; Photo courtesy of National Museum of Pakistan, Karachi, p. 71; © Doranne Jacobson/International Images, p. 73; Firmin Didot, ~ 1810, Copyright: ImagesofAsia.com, p. 77; bpk, Bildagenteur/Museum fuer Asiatische Kunst, Staatliche Museen /Iris Papadopoulos/ Art Resource, NY, p. 81; © Doranne Jacobson/International Images, p. 85; © Doranne Jacobson/International Images, p. 86.

Chapter 4: Xiaoyang Liu/Getty Images, p. 90; (top and middle) © by Liu Liquin/ChinaStock, p. 95; Martha Avery/Getty Images, p. 96; V&A Images, London/Art Resource, NY, p. 100; © Gary Lee Todd, p. 101; Lowell Georgia/Getty Images, p. 111; joannawnuk/Shutterstock Photo, p. 112; Martha Avery/Getty Images, p. 114.

Chapter 5: ERNESTO BENAVIDES/AFP/Getty Images, p. 118; The Witte Museum, p. 126; H. John Maier Jr./The LIFE Images Collection/Getty Images, p. 127; Adapted from Greger Larson and Dorian Fuller/The Evolution of Animal Domestication/The Annual Review of Ecology, Evolution and Systematics, 45:115–36, 2014, p. 128; © Sean Sprague/The Image Works, p. 130; Insights/UIG via Getty Images, p. 133; akg/Bildarchiv Steffens AKG603103, p. 134; "From MA. DEL CARMEN RODRÍGUEZ MARTÍNEZ, PONCIANO ORTÍZ CEBALLOS, MICHAEL D. COE, RICHARD A. DIEHL, STEPHEN D. HOUSTON, KARL A. TAUBE, ALFREDO DELGADO CALDERÓN "THE OLDEST WRITING IN THE WORD" SCIENCE, 15 SEPT. 2006 : 1610–1614. Reprinted with permission from AAAS, p. 137; © Caroline Penn/Alamy Stock Photo, p. 141; Keystone/Getty Images, p. 142.

Chapter 6: Kazuyoshi Nomachi/Getty Images, p. 148; Werner Forman/Art Resource, NY, p. 155; The Metropolitan Museum of Art, New York. Purchase, Buckeye Trust and Mr. and Mrs. Milton F. Rosenthal Gifts, Joseph Pulitzer Bequest and Harris Brisbane Dick and Rogers Funds, 1981, p. 156; Werner Forman/Art Resource, NY, p. 160; Gardel Bertrand/Hemis/Alamy Stock Photo, p. 163; bpk, Bildagentur/Ethnologisches Museum, Staatliche Museen/Art Resource, NY, p. 167; Photograph K2803© Justin Kerr, p. 168; DEA/G. DAGLI Orti/Getty Images, p. 171; DEA/G. DAGLI ORTI/De Agostini/Getty Images, p. 172; Keren Su/Getty Images, p. 173.

Chapter 7: Vanni Archive/Art Resource, NY, p. 178; SEF/Art Resource, NY, p. 182; 205 Louis and Nancy Hatch Dupree Collection, Williams Afghan Media Project Archive, p. 186; Vanni Archive/Art Resource, NY, p. 189; © Vanni Archive/Art Resource, NY, p. 190; Wolfgang Kaehler/Getty Images, p. 199; © Zev Radovan/Bridgeman Images, p. 203; akg-images/Gerard Degeorge, p. 206; Image copyright © The Metropolitan Museum of Art. Image source: Art Resource, NY, p. 208; (top) MS Vat. lat. 3867 (Romanus), folio 106 recto (5th c CE), p. 209; (bottom) Erich Lessing/Art Resource, NY, p. 209.

Chapter 8: Courtesy of the Library of Congress, p. 214; Borromeo/Art Resource, NY, p. 220; Coins of the Northwest, Second Century BCE and Late First Century CE, p. 222; JeremyRichards/iStock Photo, p. 223; R. u. S. Michaud/akg-images, p. 226; akg-images/A.F.Kersting, p. 228; © The Trustees of the British Museum, p. 234; Image copyright © The Metropolitan Museum of Art/Art Resource, NY, p. 237.

Chapter 9: © The Trustees of the British Museum/Art Resource, NY, p. 242; © Glow Asia RF/Alamy, p. 246; akg-images/Laurent Lecat, p. 250; photo by Gary Lee Todd, p. 254; Researched by Liu Liqin/ChinaStock, 256; Courtesy of ChinaStock, p. 259; Photograph © 2014 Museum of Fine Arts, Boston, p. 264; SSPL/Getty Images, p. 266.

Chapter 10: Courtesy of the Library of Congress, p. 272; The Trustees of the British Museum/Art Resource, NY, p. 275; ALIMDI.NET/Fabian von Poser, p. 281; John Hicks/Getty Images, p. 283; Album/Art Resource, NY, p. 286; Paris, Bibliotheque Nat., p. 288; © British Library Board. All Rights Reserved./Bridgeman Images, p. 292; Scala/White Images/Art Resource, NY, p. 294; bpk, Bildagentur/Bibliotheque Nationale /Gérard Le Gall/Art Resource, NY, p. 299.

Chapter 11: World History Archive/Alamy Stock Photo, p. 308; bpk, Bildagentur/Cathedral (Palatine Chapel), Aachen, Germany/Stefan Diller/Art Resource, NY, p. 312; bpk, Bildagentur/Hamburger Kunsthalle /Elke Walford/Art Resource, NY, p. 321; (a) © Santa Sabina, Rome Italy, Alinari/Bridgeman Images, p. 323; (b) akg-images/Henning Bock, p. 323; Peter Willi/Bridgeman Images, p. 326; Jorge Royan/Alamy Stock Photo, 330; akg-images/VISIOARS, p. 333; Georgios Kollidas /ShutterStock Photo, 335.

Chapter 12: Henry Westheim Photography/Alamy Stock Photo, p. 342; Ivan Vdovin/Alamy Stock Photo, p. 345; akg-images/Gerard Degeorge, p. 347; Martha Avery/Getty Images, 351; © British Library Board/Robana/Art Resource, NY, p. 354; Granger Historical Picture Archive/Alamy Stock Photo, p. 357; Jan Adkins/http://www.southchinasea.org, p. 361; © RMN-Grand Palais/Art Resource, NY, p. 366.

Chapter 13: Photo © AISA/Bridgeman Images, p. 370; Atlantide Phototravel/Getty Images, p. 380; Image copyright © The Metropolitan Museum of Art/Art Resource, NY, p. 381; Plan of Heiankyo. Transcribed by Mori Koan in 1750. National Archives of Japan, p. 385; Image copyright © The Metropolitan Museum of Art. Image source: Art Resource, NY, p. 387; Image copyright © The Metropolitan Museum of Art. Image source: Art Resource, NY, p. 390; John S. Lander, p. 396.

Chapter 14: © Bibliotheque Nationale, Paris, France/Bridgeman Images, p. 400; infocusphotos.com/Alamy Stock Photo, p. 406; Werner Forman/Art Resource, NY, 413; Courtesy of the University of Pretoria Museums: Mapungubwe collection, University of Pretoria, p. 414; Desmond Kwande/Getty Images, p. 415; akg-images/André Held, p. 422; Image courtesy of The Minneapolis Institute of Arts, p. 423; Werner Forman/Art Resource, NY, 424.

Chapter 15: Granger Historical Picture Archive/Alamy Stock Photo Detail, p. 428; Album/Art Resource, NY, 434; DEA/M. Seemuller, 435; bpk/Ibero-Amerikanisches Institut, Stiftung Pressischer Kulturbesitz, Berlin, Germany, p. 439; © Gianni Dagli Orti/The Art Archive at Art Resource, NY, p. 441; (top) Joerg Steber/Shutterstock.com, p. 445; © RICKEY ROGERS/Reuters/Corbis, p. 445; © Ellisphotos/Alamy Stock Photo, p. 446; DEA/G. DAGLI Orti/Getty Images, p. 448; Bettmann/ Getty Images, p. 450.

Chapter 16: Courtesy of the Library of Congress, p. 458; (a) © DeA Picture Library/Art Resource, NY; (b) ART Collection/Alamy Stock Photo; c) John Warburton-Lee Photography/Alamy Stock Photo, p. 466; (a) AP Photo/Thomas Haentzschel; (b) North Wind Picture Archives/Alamy Stock Photo, p. 467; © The Granger Collection, New York, p. 468; ullstein—Archiv Gerstenberg/akg, p. 469; Cameraphoto Arte, Venice/Art Resource, NY, p. 474; World History Archive/Alamy Stock Photo, p. 475; Topkapi Palace Museum, Istanbul, Turkey/ Bridgeman Images, p. 476; Bridgeman-Giraudon/Art Resource, NY, p. 477; Courtesy of the Library of Congress, p. 478; Kerry Whitworth/Alamy Stock Photo, p. 481; Gianni Dagli Orti/Topkapi Museum Istanbul/The Art Archive/Art Resource, NY, p. 482; (a) Art Resource, NY; (b) Vanni/Art Resource, NY; (c) Aliaksandr Mažurkevich/Alamy Stock Photo, p. 482; Erich Lessing/Art Resource, NY, p. 485; Images copyright © The Metropolitan Museum of Art. Image source: Art Resource, NY, p. 486.

Chapter 17: Courtesy of the Library of Congress, p. 490; Courtesy of the Library of Congress, p. 493; (a) Alinari/Art Resource NY; (b) Reunion des Musees Nationaux/Art Resource NY; (c) Image copyright © The Metropolitan Museum of Art. Image source: Art Resource, NY, p. 495; Courtesy of the Library of Congress, p. 497; Witold Skrypczak/Lonely Planet Images/Getty Images, p. 501; akg-images/Guericke/Magdeburg Hemispheres, p. 502; Wikimedia Commons, p. 505; Peter Newark Military Pictures/Bridgeman Images, p.508; ©DHM/Bridgeman Images, p. 510; Wikimedia Commons, p. 515; akg-images/Sputnik, p. 519; akg-images, p.521.

Chapter 18: Courtesy of the Library of Congress, p. 524; Archives Charmet/Bridgeman Images, p. 527, (a) bpk, Berlin/Ethnologisches Museum /Dietrich Graf/Art Resource NY, (b) INTERFOTO/Alamy Stock Photo, p. 530; Scala/White Images/Art Resource NY, p. 531; DEA/G. DAGLI ORTI/Getty Images, p. 537; Ivy Close Images/Alamy Stock Photo, p. 539; Courtesy of The Hispanic Society of America, New York, p. 544; Snark/Art Resource, NY, p. 547; Museo de America, Madrid, Spain/Bridgeman Images, p. 548; Courtesy of the Library of Congress, p. 549; Granger Historical Picture Archive/Alamy Stock Photo, p. 552; The Library Company of Philadelphia, p. 553; © The Stapleton Collection/Bridgeman Images, p. 554.

Chapter 19: Erich Lessing/Art Resource, NY, p. 566; (a) akg-images/De Agostini Picture Library/G. Dagli Orti,(b) Werner Forman/Art Resource, NY, p. 567; Werner Forman/Art Resource, NY, p. 568; Image copyright © The Metropolitan Museum of Art. Image source: Art Resource, NY, p. 570; Art Resource/Art Resource, NY, p. 571; HIP/Art Resource, NY, p. 575; Art Resource/Art Resource, NY, p. 579; © Michael Graham-Stewart/Bridgeman Images, p. 582; Robert Holmes/CORBIS/VCG/Getty Images, p. 584; Collection of Herbert M. and Shelley Cole. Photo by Don Cole, p. 585; Abby Aldrich Rockefeller Fold Art Museum, The colonial Williamsburg Foundation, Williamsburg, VA, p. 586; Archives Charmet/Bridgeman Images, p. 587.

Chapter 20: © travelib prime/Alamy Stock Photo, p. 592; V&A Images/The Art Archive at Art Resource, NY, p. 596;

© British Library Board/Robana /Art Resource, NY, p. 597; © The Metropolitan Museum of Art. Image source: Art Resource, NY, p. 598; Joana Kruse/Alamy Stock Photo, p. 599; Akbar and the Jesuits, The Book of Akbar (In 03.263), © The Trustees of the Chester Beatty Library, Dublin, p. 602; FineArt/Alamy Stock Photo, p. 605; Digital Image ©2009 Museum Associates/LACMA . Licensed by Art Resource, NY, p. 610; Erich Lessing/Art Resource, NY, p. 615.

Chapter 21: John C. Weber Collection. Photo: John Bigelow Taylor, p. 620; Metropolitan Museum of Art, Rogers Fund, 1917, p. 626; Image copyright © The Metropolitan Museum of Art. Image source: Art Resource, NY, p. 627; © by Qi Wen/ChinaStock, p. 629; Bettmann/Getty Images, p. 631; Roy Miles Fine Paintings/Bridgeman Images, p. 632; © Chinese Commercial Enterprises, p. 634; Courtesy of the Library of Congress, p. 635; Réunion des Musées Nationaux-Grand Palais/Art Resource, NY, p. 637; © The Granger Collection, New York, p. 639; Courtesy of the Library of Congress, p. 642; University of British Columbia Library, Rare Books and Special Collections, p.643; akg-images, p. 646; V&A Images, London/Art Resource, NY, p. 648.

Chapter 22: HIP/Art Resource, NY, p. 654; (a) (top left) © Bettmann/Getty Images, (b) (bottom left) Classic Image/Alamy Stock Photo, (c) (right) Niday Picture Library/Alamy Stock Photo, p. 661; Print Collector/Getty Images, p. 662; © RMN-Grand Palais/Art Resource, NY, p. 664; Wellcome Images/Science Source, p. 669; bpk, Bildagentur/Art Resource, NY, p. 670; Culture Club/Getty Images, p. 673; Artokoloro Quint Lox Limited/Alamy Stock Photo, p. 679; (a) National Gallery, London/Art Resource, NY, (b) Erich Lessing/Art Resource, NY, p. 683; Hulton-Deutsch Collection/Getty Images, p. 684.

Chapter 23: Courtesy of the Library of Congress, p. 688; Library of Congress Reproduction Number: LC-USZ62-99485, p. 692; The Granger Collection, New York, p. 696; Gianni Dagli Orti/Topkapi Museum Istanbul/The Art Archive/Art Resource, NY, p. 698; Schalkwijk/Art Resource, NY. © 2017 Banco de Mexico Diego Rivera Frida Kahlo Museums Trust, Mexico, D.F./Artists Rights Society (ARS), New York, p. 701; Library of Congress/Getty Images, p. 702; Library of Congress reproduction number LC-USZ62-125988, p. 702; Erich Lessing/Art Resource, NY, p. 705; Library of Congress reproduction number LC-USZ62-73425, p. 707; Courtesy of the Library of Congress, LC-USZ62-26047, p. 714.

Chapter 24: Collection of Museum of Fine Arts, Boston via Wikipedia Commons, p. 722; The Art Archive at Art Resource, NY, p. 727; Courtesy of the Library of Congress, p. 727; Hirarchivum Press/Alamy Stock Photo, p. 728; (a) National Palace Museum, (b) The Print Collector/Print Collector/Getty Images, p.731; (a) akg-images/British Library, (b) © Peter NEWark Pictures/Bridgeman Images, p. 732; (a) © Philadelphia Museum of Art, (b) British Library via Wikicommons, p. 735; Heritage Images/Getty Images, p.736; Private Collection/Bridgeman Images, p. 737; IAM /akg/NA, p. 739; John Thomson, (1874). Illustrations of China and Its People, Vol 4. MIT Libraries, p. 743; Courtesy of the Library of Congress, p. 747.

Chapter 25: Bettmann/Getty Images, p. 761; Bettmann/Getty Images, p. 763; SEF/Art Resource, NY, p. 766; Michael Kappeler/AP Photo, p. 768; Print Collector/Getty Images, p. 773; North Wind Picture Archives/Alamy Stock Photo, p. 775; RussiaSputnik/Bridgeman Images, p. 780.

Chapter 26: SSPL/Science Museum/Art Resource, NY, p. 784; Science & Society Picture Library/Getty Images, p. 792; Robert Hunt Library/Chronicle/Alamy Stock Photo, p. 796; The Print Collector/Alamy Stock Photo, p. 801; The Stapleton Collection/Bridgeman Images, p. 802; Bettmann/Getty Images, p. 803; Archives Charmet/Bridgeman Images, p. 804; © Peter NEWark Pictures/Bridgeman Images, p.807; Natural History Museum, London, UK/Bridgeman Images, p. 810.

Chapter 27: Chronicle/Alamy Stock Photo, p. 816; (a) Peter Horree/Alamy Stock Photo, (b) Granger Historical Picture Archive/Alamy Stock Photo, p. 819; Bettman Images/Getty Images, p. 822; Réunion des Musées Nationaux-Grand Palais/Art Resource, NY, p. 826; Archives Charmet/Bridgeman Images, p. 827; Hulton-Deutsch Collection/Getty Images, p. 830; Timewatch Images/Alamy Stock Photo, p. 835; Panos Pictures ASL00010DRC, p. 836; Courtesy of the Library of Congress, p. 841.

Chapter 28: Courtesy of the Library of Congress, p. 850; Hulton-Deutsch/Getty Images, p. 852; Photograph, World War One, Western Front, (1914–1918), 1916. Imperial War Museum, UK, p. 855; Courtesy of the Library of Congress, p. 858; Hulton Archives/Getty Images, p. 859; Library of Congress LC-USW3-001543-D, p. 860; Kurt Hutton/Getty Images, p. 863; Fotosearch/Getty Images, p. 866; Bettman Images /Getty Images, p. 867; Heritage Image Partnership Ltd/Alamy Stock Photo, p. 870; World History Archive/Alamy Stock Photo, p. 873; Courtesy of the Library of Congress, p. 877; Hulton Archives/Getty Images, p. 880; Bettman/Getty Images, p. 882.

Chapter 29: Keystone/Getty Images, p. 888; Alfred Eisenstaedt/Getty Images, p. 890; Associated Press, p. 893; Bettmann/Getty Images, p. 896; Rykoff Collection/Getty Images, p. 898; Library of Congress/Getty Images, p. 900; (a) © The Museum of Modern Art/Licensed by SCALA/Art Resource, NY. With permission of the Renate, Hans & Maria Hoffman Trust/Artists Rights Society (ARS), New York, (b) © 2009 Museum Associates/LACMA/Art Resource, NY. © 2017

The Willem de Kooning Foundation/Artists Rights Society (ARS), New York, p. 901; Courtesy of the Library of Congress, p. 906; Lisa Larsen/Getty Images, p. 915; Courtesy of the Library of Congress, p. 916.

Chapter 30: Alain DeJean/Sygma/Getty Images, p. 924; Historical/Getty Images, p. 927; MARKKU VUORELA/AFP/Getty Images, p. 929; Bettmann/Getty Images, p. 933; lev radin/Shutterstock.com, p. 935; Henry Diltz/Getty Images, p. 936; The India Today Group/Getty Images, p. 939; Bettmann/Getty Images, p. 941; Bettman/Getty Images, p. 944; CHAUVEL/Getty Images, p. 946; Courtesy of the Library of Congress, p. 953.

Chapter 31: Associated Press/Sputnik, p. 960; dpa picture alliance/Alamy Stock Photo, p. 967; (a) Associated Press/str, (b) Associated Press/Xinhua, Liu Weibing, p. 972; Ali Atmaca/Anadolu Agency/Getty Images, p. 979; Fathi Belaid/APF/Getty Images, p. 980; Associated Press/Manish Swarup, p. 983; AP Photo/Muzaffar Salman, p. 984; Louise Gubb/Getty Images, p. 987; Peter Parks/Getty Images, p. 989.

Source Index

Page numbers of the form S8-7–S8-8 indicate, in this case, a source document in chapter 8 on pages 7–8 in the source documents at the end of chapter 8. If the page number for the source document is followed by (d) this indicates a text source document. If the page number for the source document is followed by (v) this indicates a visual source document.

Admonitions for Women (Nüjie) (Ban Zhao), S9-9–S9-11 (d)
Afghanistan: Bamiyan Buddhas, S8-7–S8-8 (v)
Afghanistan-Pakistan: Seated Buddha, Gandhara culture, S8-9 (v)
Alchemy of Happiness, The (al-Ghazali), S10-10–S10-11 (d)
Alexander II (Russia), abolition of serfdom, S25-8–S25-10 (d)
Alexandria, Egypt: Murder of the Philosopher Hypatia (Socrates Scholasticus), S7-9–S7-11 (d)
Analects (Lunyu) (Confucius), S9-2–S9-3 (d)
Azamgarh Proclamation, S27-2–S27-3 (d)

Baburnama, The (Babur), S20-2–S20-3 (d)
Babylonian Poem of the Righteous Sufferer, S2-4–S2-5 (d)
Bahia, Brazil: Amulet containing passages from the Quran worn by Muslim slaves, S23-9–S23-10 (d)
Bhagavadgita, The (with the Sanatsugatiya and the Anugita), S3-3–S3-6 (d)
Book of Lord Shang, The (Shangjun Shu), S4-4–S4-5 (d)
Book of Mencius (Mengzi), S9-3–S9-5 (d)
Book of Odes, The (Shi Jing), S4-3–S4-4 (d)
Book of Prophecies, The (Columbus), S16-2–S16-3 (d)
Botswana: Rhino Cave, python-shaped ornamented rock, S1-3 (v)
Boxer Rebel and a British Family Killed during the Boxer Rebellion, S24-6–S24-7 (v)
Brihadaranyaka Upanishad, The, S3-6–S3-8 (d)
British North America: Salem Witch Trials, The, S18-10–S18-11 (d)
Burial Mound at L'Anse Amour, Labrador, Canada, S5-4 (v)

Calico textile, S20-9 (v)
Canon of Shun, The, S4-6–S4-7 (d)
"Capitalism: A Ghost Story" (Roy), S31-10–S31-13 (d)
Çelebi, Evliya, S16-5–S16-7 (d)
Chachnama, The: An Ancient History of Sind, S12-2–S12-4
Chavín de Huántar, Peru: Textile fragment, S5-3 (v)
Chichén Itzá: Temple of the Jaguars, S15-2–S15-3 (v)
China: Lin Zexu's letter to Queen Victoria of Great Britain, S24-2–S24-3 (d)
China in the Sixteenth Century (Ricci), S21-4–S21-6 (d)
Cloud Messenger, The (Kalidasa), S8-10–S8-11 (d)
Code of Manu, The (*The Law of Manu*, in *The Sacred Books of the East*, vol. 25, 1886), S3-8–S3-10 (d)
Concerning Whether Heretics Should Be Persecuted (Castellio), S17-4–S17-5 (d)
Conquest of New Spain, The (Díaz), S15-4–S15-5 (d)
Cosmas Indicopleustes (Cosmas the India-Voyager), S6-3–S6-4 (d)
"Court of Suleiman the Magnificent, The" (Ghiselin de Busbecq), S16-7–S16- (d)
Crimea region: Address to the Duma concerning the annexation of Crimea (Putin), S31-4–S31-7 (d)
Cuban Missile Crisis: Letters between Fidel Castro and Nikita Khrushchev, S29-7–S29-31
Cyrus Cylinder, The, S7-2–S7-3 (d)

"Daily Habits of Louis XIV at Versailles, The" (Saint-Simon), S17-6–S17-7 (d)
Death of William Huskisson, First Casualty of a Railroad Accident, The, S26-3–S26-4 (d)
Decameron, The, "Putting the Devil Back in Hell" (Boccaccio), S11-6–S11-8 (d)
Declaration of the Rights of Man and the Citizen, S22-2–S22-3 (d)
Declaration of the Rights of Woman, The (de Gouges), S22-4–S22-6 (d)
"Declaration of War against the Americans Occupying the Land of the Two Holy Places" (bin Laden), S31-2–S31-4 (d)
Deogarh, India: Image of Draupadi and the Pandava, from the Dashavatara Temple, S3-10–S3-11 (v)
Description of West Africa (Bakri), S14-7–S14-9 (d)
Diplovatatzes, Joshua, S16-4–S16-5 (d)

Edicts of Aurangzeb, S20-5–S20-7 (d)
Egypt, Middle, Kingdom, Twelfth Dynasty: Advice from a royal scribe to his apprentice, S2-6–S2-7 (d)
El Castillo de Huarmey, Peru: Wari royal tomb skeletons, S15-3–S15-4 (v)
Emperor Qianlong's Imperial Edict to King George III, S21-6–S21-9 (d)
Eredo, Nigeria: Sungbo's walls and moats, S14-9 (v)
Ethiopia: *Fetha Nagast*, S14-2–S14-4 (d)

"Fall of Constantinople, The" (Diplovatatzes and Thomas the Eparch), S16-4–S16-5 (d)
Feudal contracts and the swearing of fealty, S11-3–S11-4 (d)
Five Jewels, The (Ghwath Gwaliori), S20-7–S20-9 (d)
Formosa: Treaty between Koxinga and the Dutch government, S21-2–S21-3 (d)
"Foundations and Doctrine of Fascism" (Mussolini and Gentile), S28-6–S28-8 (d)
French North America: *Jesuit Relations, The*, S18-9–S18-10 (d)
Fustat (Old Cairo): Jewish engagement contract, S10-9–S10-10 (d)

Gallipoli: ANZAC troops at Gallipoli, S28-2–S28-4 (d)
Germany and England: Flagellants attempt to ward off the Black Death, S11-8–S11-9 (d)
Ghiselin de Busbecq, Ogier, S16-7–S16-8 (d)
Goban Taiheiki (Chikamatsu), S21-9–S21-11 (d)
Great Hymn to the Aten, The, S2-8–S2-9 (d)
Grotte des Pigeons, Taforalt, Morocco: Shell bead jewelry, S1-2 (v)

Hard Times (Dickens), S26-2–S26-3 (d)
Histories (Herodotus), S7-3–S7-4 (d)
History of the Former Han Dynasty (Han Shu), S9-7–S9-9 (d)
Hymns to Agni *(Rig-Veda)*, S3-2–S3-3 (d)

Iconoclasm controversy, related documents, S10-5–S10-7 (d)
"I Have a Dream" speech (King, Jr.), S30-4–S30-6 (d)
Imperial Edict of the Rose Garden, S25-4–S25-6 (d)
Incan roads (de León), S15-6–S15-7 (d)
Interesting Narrative of the Life of Olaudah Equiano (Equiano), S19-8–S19-10 (d)
Iron Curtain speech (Churchill), S29-5–S29-6 (d)
Iron sword with jade handle (Western Zhou), S4-7 (v)

"Jamaica Letter, The" (Bolívar), S23-4–S23-6 (d)
Janissary Musket, S16-9 (v)
Japan: Meiji Constitution, S24-7–S24-9 (d)
Jenné-jeno, Mali: The Market, S6-4–S6-5 (v)
Jesuit Relations, The (French North America), S18-8–S18-10 (d)

"Khubilai Khan at War" (Polo), S12-8–S12-10 (d)
Knossos, Minoan Crete: sketch of the palace complex, S2-7–S2-8 (v)
Kokoro (Soseki), S24-9–S24-11 (d)
Kongo: Letter of Nzinga Mbemba (Afonso I) to the King of Portugal, S19-3–S19-5 (d)
Korea, Buddhism in (Haedong kosŭng chŏn), S13-3–S13-5 (d)

Lady of the Jewel Necklace, The (Vardhana), S12-4–12-6 (d)
"Last Words to the Nation" (Allende), S30-11–S30-12 (d)
Law Code of Hammurabi, S2-2–S2-3 (d)
Lessons for Women (Nüjie) (Ban Zhao), S9-9–S9-11 (d)
Letters from the Levant (Montagu), S25-2–S25-4 (d)

"Letter to the Grand Duchess Christina de' Medici" (Galilei), S17-9–S17-11 (d)
Liberia: Independence Day Address (Blyden), S27-5–S27-7
Life of Charlemagne (Einhard), 11-2–11-3 (d)
Life of Michelangelo Buonarroti, The (Vasari), S17-7–S17-9 (d)
Life of the Sudanese Mahdi (Ibn Abd al-Qadir), S27-4–S27-5 (d)
London, England: "Examination of Lady Jane Grey, The," S17-2–S17-4 (d)

1 Maccabees, S7-5–S7-7 (d)
Mali: Ibn Battuta, on *(Rihla)*, S14-4–S14-6 (d)
Mapungubwe, South Africa: "Lost City" golden bracelets, S14-7 (v)
Mein Kampf (Hitler), S28-9–S28-11 (d)
Memoirs of General Antonio López de Santa Anna (Santa Anna), S23-2–S23-4 (d)
Memoirs of Usama Ibn Munqidh (Ibn Munqidh), S10-7–S10-9 (d)
Meroë, Sudan: relief sculpture, S6-2 (v)
Mexico: Casta paintings, S19-10–S19-11 (v)
Mexico: Nahuatl Land Sale Documents, S18-6–S18-7 (d)
Mexico City: Marina San Miguel's Confessions before the Inquisition, S18-4–S18-6 (d)
Ming Dynasty, ship model, flotilla of Zheng He, S12-10-S11 (v)
Mingling of Two Oceans, The (Dara Shikuh), S20-4–S20-5 (d)

Narrative of the ship *Nemesis* during the First Opium War, S24-4–S24-6 (d)
Nihon Shoki (Chronicles of Japan), S13-5–S13-7 (d)

Origin of Species, The (Darwin), S26-9–S26-11 (d)

Palenque: Limestone panel from a Mayan temple, S6-5 (v)
Paris: United Nations Framework Convention on Climate Change, S31-13–S31-15 (d)
"Path Which Led Me to Leninism, The" (Ho Chi Minh), S29-10–S29-11 (d)
Perestroika: New Thinking for Our Country and the World (Gorbachev), S30-2–S30-4 (d)
Peru, Caral-Supe culture: Quipu, S5-2 (v)
Peru: Photograph of a Chinese coolie, S23-11 (d)
Pompeii: Graffiti from the walls, S7-7–S7-9 (d)
"Procession of Artisans at Istanbul, A" (Çelebi), S16-5–16-7(d)

Questions of King Milinda, The (The Milindapanha), S8-4–S87 (d)
Quran, Sura 2, "The Cow," S10-2–10-4 (d) (excerpt)

Reflections on the Revolution in France (Burke), S22-7–S22-9 (d)
Republic of Georgia: Flax fibers found at the Dzudzuana Cave, S1-5 (v)
Rhode Island: Documents concerning the slave ship, *Sally*, S19-5–S19-8 (d)
Rights of Man (Paine), S-22–S-24
Rig Veda. See Hymns to Agni
Roosevelt, Franklin D.: Undelivered Jefferson Day address, S28-11–S28-13 (d)
Russia: Abolition of serfdom by Tsar Alexander, S25-8–S25-10 (d)

Saint-Simon, Duc de, S17-6–S17-7 (d)
Salem Witch Trials, The (British North America), S18-10–S18-11 (d)
Santillana del Mar, Spain: paintings in the Cave of Altamira, S1-4 (v)
Scholars of Timbuktu (al-Saadi), S19-2–S19-3 (d)
Second Letter from Mexico to Emperor Charles V (Cortés), S18-2–S18-3 (d)
Second Sex, The (de Beauvoir), S30-6–S30-8 (d)
"Secret Plan for Managing the Country" (Toshiaki), S21-11–S21-13 (d)
Seven Pillar Edicts of King Ashoka, The, S8-2–S8-4 (d)
Shiji: Memorial on the Burning of Books (Li Si), S9-5–S9-6 (d)
Socrates Scholasticus. *See* Alexandria, Egypt: Murder of the Philosopher Hypatia
Story of My Misfortunes, The (Abelard), S11-5–S11-6 (d)
Tale of Genji, The (Shikibu), S13-2–S13-3 (d)
Tang Dynasty: Poetry, S12-6–12-8 (d)
Testament of Youth (Brittain), S28-4–S28-6
Thomas the Eparch, S16-4–S16-5 (d)
"Three Poems of Shame" (P'i Jih-hsiu), S13-7–S13-8
Tiananmen Square protests, coverage of, S30-8–S30-10 (d)
"Torture," from *Philosophical Dictionary* (Voltaire), S22-6–S22-7 (d)
"To the Person Sitting in Darkness" (Twain), S27-9–S27-11 (d)
Travels in the United States in 1847 (Sarmiento), S23-7–S23-8 (d)
Tunisia: Arab Spring triggered by Mohammed Bouazizi, S31-7–S31-10 (d)

Universal Declaration of Human Rights, S29-2–S29-5 (d)
Upanishads. *See Brihadaranyaka Upanishad, The*

Vanuatu, Western Pacific: Lapita pot shards, S5-5 (v)
Vasari, Giorgio, S17-7–S17-9 (d)
Vietnam: Copper head of Bodhisattva Avalokiteshvara, S13-9 (v)

"Wage Labour and Capital" (Marx), S26-7–S26-9 (d)
"Walls and Gates of Cuzco, The" (Garcilaso de la Vega), S15-7–S15-9 (d)
West Africa, Description of (Bakri), S14-7–S14-9 (d)
"What Educated Women Can Do" (Gandhi), S29-11–S29-13 (d)
What Is to Be Done? (Chernyshevsky), S25-11–S25-13 (d)
"White Man's Burden, The" (Kipling), S27-7–S27-9 (d)
Writings of Bahá'u'lláh, S25-6–S25-8 (d)

Young Miner's Testify to the Ashley Commission, S26-5–S26-7 (d)

Zuo Commentary, The (Zuozhuan), S4-2–S4-3 (d)

Subject Index

Page numbers followed by f denote a figure or illustration. Page numbers followed by m denote a map.

Aachen palace, 312
Abbasid Dynasty: apocalyptic beliefs, 280; Baghdad city map, 279m; Byzantine raids on Muslims, 284; emergence of, 276; empire building by, 273; and Fatimid Dynasty, 280–1; financial crisis, 281; granting of autonomy by, 273; Mongol conquests, 347; Quran compilation by, 277; Roman law codex adopted by, 195, 279; theology of, 278–9; timeline placement, 275f; trade activities, 285; Umayyad comparison with, 276
Abd al-Malik, 275, 278
Abdülhamit II (Ottoman Sultan) 763–5
Abhidhamma doctrines (Buddhism), 227
Abolition of slavery: in Brazil, 653f, 691f; in China, 354, 821; in Great Britain, 582f, 694; international desires for, 589; in the U.S., 587
Aboriginals (Australia): described, 15; Dreamtime ritual, 16–17, 28; marriage customs, 16; rock art, 17; social structures, cultural expressions, 16
Abortive Russian Revolution (1905), 757f, 769, 779–80
Absolutism, 503, 516–18, 605, 671, 879
Abu Bakr (Swahili Sheikh), 412–13
Academy of Florence, 304
Academy of Medicine (France), 663
Academy of Plato, 204
Academy of Sciences (Paris, France), 499
Aceh War (1873–1903), 839m
Achaemenid Persian Empire: administration of, 181–3; Alexander's conquests of, 178, 186; conquests of, 179, 180; dates of, 146f, 182f; divine and heroic myths in, 205; empire building by, 146; military losses to Greece, 185; origins of, 146f, 180–3; scope of, 181, 181m; Zoroastrianism in, 199. *See also* Sasanid Persian Empire
Acheulian tool technology, 9, 9f
Adena culture, North America, 123f, 137, 138m
Admonitions for Women (Ban Zhao), 263
Adowa, Battle of (1896; East Africa), 836
Advanced Research Projects Agency (ARPA), 984
Aegean Sea, 31
Aeschylus (Greek writer), 207
Aethiopica (Heliodorus of Emesa), 153
Affordable Care Act (ACA), 974
Afghanistan: Alexander's victory in, 186; Cold War proxy war in, 849; Cyrus II the Great conquests, 180; geographic features, 33; Kushan Empire expansion in, 220; Mahmud of Ghazna's conquests in, 347; Sher Khan Sur, Afghan leader, 597; Soviet invasion of, 849f, 924–5, 929; Timur's activities in, 594; trade activities, 72; U.S. invasion of, 967
Africa: African National Congress, 953–4; agricultural development, 3, 119; Americas comparison with, 160–1; Americas kingship comparison, 414; atrocities and genocides, 835–6; Bantu people, 151f, 155, 157–8, 410, 413, 953; Benin Kingdom, 424; Bunyoro Kingdom, 561f, 564; central Africa chieftains, kingdoms, 415–17; central African rain forests, 20; China's expansion into, 629–30; Christianity in, 401–2, 560, 584, 832–4, 834m; "civilizing mission" in, 832–4; climate, 124; Congo's independence struggles, 919–20; Da Gama's circumnavigation of, 456f, 461f, 565, 566; as the "Dark Continent," 832; decline of Second German Empire, 849; decolonization in, 848f, 908m, 917–18; Democratic Republic of the Congo, 416; early cities in, 119; eastern sahel and savanna, 563; Enlightenment era interests in, 832–3; European imperialism in, 832–7, 833m; food crops trade, 622; German Southwest Africa, 835–6; Hausa Kingdoms, 561, 563, 951; Hutu genocide, 564; Ice Age and, 20–1; independence of most colonies, 891f; intellectual link with Meroë, 153; Iron Age rituals in, 159; iron working skills, 152; Islam and Christianity map, 834m; Khoisan-family languages, 158–9; kingdom development pattern, 160–1; malaria, yellow fever in, 833; map (1415-1498), 461m; material technology, 2; migrations from, 2, 5, 13, 14m, 120; Namoratunga observatory, Kenya, 148; National Congolese Movement, 919; Ndongo Kingdom, 561f, 569–70, 580, 583; Nigerian civil war, 951; origins of humanity, 4–29; origins of modern humans, 2; "out of Africa" theory, 10, 14m; Paleolithic weaponry inventions, 150; political transformations in, 985–7; Prestor John, Christian ruler in, 461, 464, 566; Rastafarianism in, 407–8; religion, spirituality of, 159; revolution in Zimbabwe, 951–2; rise of religious civilizations, 270; Sanusiyya Brotherhood, 837; Scramble for Africa, 832–7; sculptures, figures, figurines, 421–2; settler resistance to independence in Kenya, 919; slave trade of, 560–71, 575, 576, 834; South Central Africa, 563–4, 832; state formation in, 215; "superstitious" religion in, 834; Swahili Muslim city-states, 297; Tang maritime trade with, 350; taxation in, 403, 412–13, 422, 569; Tichitt-Oualata villages, 150–1; tool development, 2; U.S. training of dissidents in, 897–8; weapons introduced to, 125; Zheng He's voyages to, 623f. *See also* Aksum Kingdom; Central Africa; East Africa; Ghana Kingdom; North Africa; Northeast Africa; Nubian Kingdom; South Africa; Sub-Saharan Africa; West Africa
African Americans: civil rights movements and, 933–4, 936–8; early colonial America population, 578, 586f; fundamentalist's intolerance of, 860; GI Bill for, 900f; Harlem Renaissance, 859, 860–1; impact of the 2001-2003 financial crisis, 973; limited opportunities for women, 858; lynching of, 677–8, 859f, 860; voting rights issues, 677, 936
African Christian spirituality, 558
African Diaspora, 560, 583–5, 860–1
African National Congress (ANC), 953–4, 958–9
African slave trade, 456f
Afro-Eurasian continent, 14
Afro-Eurasian global commercial system, 296–8
Agincourt, Battle of, 333
Agrarian-urban society: in Africa, 149; in the Americas, 3; in China, 3, 350, 554; Christianity and, 492; decline of, 784; defined, 30, 33; in Egypt, 35, 179; in Eurasia, 3, 162, 449, 451, 457, 522; in Europe, 457; Fertile Crescent origins, 2, 3, 31–46; foraging transition to, 27; of the Harappans, 72–3; in India, 2, 3, 72–3, 83, 88–9, 215, 240, 554, 633; in Japan, 398, 650; in Mayan Kingdoms, 169; in the Middle East, 3, 30, 38, 40; modernity's impact on, 652, 653; patriarchy connection with, 12, 40; in sub-Saharan Africa, 149
Agriculture: in Africa, 3; in the Americas, 2, 3; in Caral-Supe valley, Peru, 129; in China, 2, 3, 107, 257–8, 351, 622, 634; corn domestication, cultivation, 118, 130–1; in Cuzco city-state, 443; in East Asia, 3; Eurasian innovations, 317; European revolution in, 317–18; Fertile Crescent origins, 33–48; in Japan, 387; in Latin America, 712, 715–16; in Mayan Kingdoms, 161, 162–3, 165, 433; in Meroë Kingdom, Africa, 150; in the Middle East, 2, 3; monsoon system influences, 66–7; in Mughal Empire, India, 607–8; in Nubian Kingdom, 403; origins of centers of, 2, 3; rice domestication, 70, 78–9, 82; in Sasanid Persian Empire, 281; slash-and-burn cultivation methods, 156, 165; in South America, 697; in the Soviet Union, 853f; Soviet Union's collectivization of, 870–1; Tenochtitlán *chinampas* practice, 448–9; in Tiwanaku state, 435; in Wari city-state, 443; in West Africa, 3156
Aguinaldo, Emilio, 842
Ahimsa doctrine (nonviolence), 219, 225–6

Ahmadinejad, Mahmoud, 978
Ahuramazda (god of the Zoroastrians), 181, 199, 205
AIDS/HIV, 971, 985–6
Ainu culture (Japan), 27, 27f
Airplanes, early, 787f
Akbar, Jalal ud-Din (Mughal ruler), 457f, 595f; abhorrence of religious violence, 597; ascendancy of, 597; Ashoka's similarity to, 603; Aurangzeb's repudiation of, 603; city-building skills, 598–9; control of Silk Road network, 599; map of empire under, 598m; marriage to Hindu princess, 598–9; military campaigns of, 597–600, 598m; move to Lahore, 599; Mughal India under, 598m; religious synthesis attempt, 368, 602–3; religious tolerance during reign, 601, 609; revenue gains during reign of, 608; revolt of sons of, 599–600; timeline placement, 457f, 595f
Akbar Shah II (Mughal Emperor), 819f
Akhenaten the Transgressor (Egypt), 62
Akkadian Kingdom, 33f, 39–40, 40m, 44, 51
Aksum Kingdom (Africa), 146; Coptic Christianity in, 154; flourishing of, 149, 153–4; imperialism and crisis in, 154–5; map, 152m; political system, 407; Sasanid Persian invasion of, 155, 405; splendor of, 154; timeline placement, 147f, 151f, 403f; trade activities, 155, 405
Ala-ud-Din, 348
Alaska: Beringia land bridge, 24
Albania, 898
Al-Biruni (Islamic astronomer), 504
Alcium of York, 312
Alexander I (Russian Tsar), 772
Alexander II (Russian Tsar), 774, 776, 777, 780–1, 783, 788, 869
Alexander III (Russian Tsar), 776, 783
Alexander the Great: avenging nature of, 179; Chandragupta's meetings with, 215, 217; Cleitus's conflicts with, 178–9; conquest in Afghanistan, 186; conquests in Persia, 178, 185–6; dates of life, 182f; death of, 186; imperial pattern adoption, 146; India campaigns, 186, 214–15; northern India campaigns, 217f; role in India's Mauryan Empire, 217; scope of empire, 187m; successors of, 185–7, 187m, 201; unification of Greece by, 179, 210–11
Alexander V (Pope), 334
Alexandria (Egypt): Coptic Christianity in, 402–3, 405–6; papal supremacy in, 286; sciences library, 204–5; slave trade in, 292; trade activities, 318
Alexis I Comnenus, 288–9
Algebra (al-Khwarizmi), 329
Algeria: business privatization in, 976; Fatimid rebellion in, 281; French conquest of, 817, 819f, 829, 843; Hussein's rule in, 816; Islamic civilization in, 468; mosques in, 327; Ottoman losses in, 472; quest for independence, 917
Al-Hajj Umar (Islamic reformer), 834–5
Al-Hasan Ibn Muhammad al-Wazzan. *See* Leo Africanus
Allegory (defined), 593
Almagest (Ptolemy), 329
Almoravid Dynasty, 275f, 419
Alpern, Stanley, 152–3
Al-Qaeda terrorist group, 849f, 925, 963f, 967, 976–7, 982, 985
Altaic-speaking peoples, 594
Alt-Right (U.S.), 974
Al-Wazzan. *See* Leo Africanus
Amazonian peoples, South America, 137–8
Amazon rain-forest civilizations, 454–5
Amazon River, 121
Amda Seyon (Ethiopian Emperor), 408
Amenhotep III (Egyptian Pharaoh), 46, 62
Amenhotep IV (Egyptian Pharaoh), 62. *See also* Akhenaten the Transgressor
American Civil War, 677
American Federation of Labor (AFL), 859
American Indian Movement (AIM), 934
American Revolution, 652f, 656–8, 657f, 667
Americas (North, Central, South): adaptation to European culture, 551–4; Africa's comparison with, 160–1, 419; agricultural developments in, 2, 3, 118; Amazonian culture, 137–8; animal, plant domestication, 127–8; archaeological discoveries, 118, 136, 428; archaeological findings, 118, 136; artistic achievements in, 134; Austronesian cultural family, 139; burial sites and customs, 128, 135–6; Caral-Supe city, 3f, 118–19, 123f, 129–31; Catholic missionary work in, 551; cattle ranching, 544–5; Chavin de Huántar city, 123f, 132–4; Columbus's voyage to, 460, 461f, 565; cordilleras, mountain ranges, 121; corn cultivation, 130–1, 132; development of settlements, 125–6; early ceremonial life, 126; early evidence of humans, 2; early human settlements, 5; environment of, 121, 122m, 123–4; European colonialism in, 525–41; Europe's exploration of, 529m; food crops trade, 622; fossil discoveries, 24–5; human migrations, 20–7, 26m, 123f, 124–6; hunters and foragers, 120–6, 123f; hunting technology, 124–5; interest in China's Ming porcelain, 627; land-labor grants (Spanish *encomiendas*), 526; migrations to, 20–7, 26m; music in, 126, 130, 133; Neolithic settlements, 127–8; as the "New World," 524; ocean currents, hurricanes, El Niño, 123–4; origins of urban life, 118, 129–34; plantation slavery in, 572–6; precious metals mining in, 532, 541–3; *quipu* record keeping method, 119; sculptures, figures, figurines, 422; shamanism in, 126; slave revolts, 561f, 586–7, 588m; smallpox epidemics, 144, 526, 528–9, 531, 534, 536–7, 539, 542, 549, 574; Spain's discovery of, 456f; Spanish administrative hierarchies in, 531–40, 533m, 538m; sub-Saharan Africa comparison, 149, 150; weaponry advances, 120; wheat farming, 544–5; writing developments, 137f. *See also* Andes culture; Caribbean Islands; Colonial North America; New World; North America; South America
Analects (Lunyu) (Confucius), 244, 245, 246
Anatolia: Achaemenid expansion into, 180; appropriation of Byzantine provinces, 465; Armenian minority in, 764; city-states in, 183; conquests of Byzantine provinces, 465; Crusades and, 289; farming settlements, 31–2, 46; flooding, 35; Göbekli Tepe sanctuary in, 56; grassroots resistance groups, 866; ironworking craft, 54, 77; Judaism in, 198; migrations to Syria, 53; military recruits from, 180; Neo-Assyrian dominance of, 207; Ottoman conquest in, 460, 475; Persia's conquests in, 274; spread of agriculture to, 46; Timur's activities in, 594; trade activity, 46, 50, 52, 54
Anaximander (Greek philosopher), 182f, 200
Ancestor spirits, 159
Andes culture: agrarian transition, 123f, 128; Army of the Andes, 691; ceremonial centers, 132, 134, 169, 170, 171, 441, 446, 452; Chavin de Huántar city, 123f, 132–4, 133f, 161, 170; cultural regions, 173m; El Paraíso villages, 131–2; fishing, 128; geographic features, 435; imperial age of, 446; Moche chiefdom, 147f, 151f, 171–2; Moche culture, 171–2; Paracas chiefdom, 172; pottery making, 128; road-building, 128; urban centers, 129m. *See also* Tiwanaku state; Wari city-state
Anglican Church, 510, 512–14, 552
Anglo-American nation-state building: buffalo herds, destruction of, 679; Great Britain, 680–1; Native Americans, 678–9; reform measures, 679–80; United States, 677–8, 678m
Anglo-Saxons, 308
Angola: Christianity in, 560; independence of, 952
Animal domestication, 127–8, 128f
Anthony of Padua, Saint, 558, 559, 570f
Antigonid Greece, 154, 186, 187m, 189
Antonian-African Christianity, 459
Anzick-1 fossil, 25
Apartheid in South Africa, 952–3; defined, 952–3; ending of, 849f, 953–4, 963f; origins, 571, 918
Apocalypticism, 280
Apollo 11 Cave, Namibia, 13f
April 6 Youth Movement (Facebook group), 985
Arab Empire: Caucasus military campaigns, 276; conquests in France, 278; conquests of, 270f, 273, 275m, 276m; incursions into India, 348; Nubia invaded by, 402; Ottoman conflicts with, 468; push into France, 278; trading pact with Nubia, 403–4; victory against Tang Dynasty, 351. *See also* Abbasid Dynasty; Umayyad Dynasty
Arab-Israeli War (1948), 848f, 891f
Arab-Israeli War (1967; Six-Day War), 927f, 946–8, 946f, 947m
Arab-Israeli War (1973: Yom Kippur/Ramadan War), 927f, 937, 947m, 948
Arab Spring (2011), 849f, 961, 963f, 976–7, 980–2, 984, 991
Arafat, Yasir, 946f, 947, 949, 977
Aragon Dynasty (Spain), 461f, 462
Archaeological discoveries: in the Americas, 118, 136, 168, 428; Bactria-Margiana Archaeological Complex, 71; in Brazil, 25; Buddhist sites, 64; Caral-Supe valley, Peru, 118, 119; in Central Africa, 416; in Chile, 25; in Dhar Tichitt and Dhar

Oualata villages, 151; in Great Zimbabwe Kingdom, 415; Harappa, 64–5, 71; hominins, 4; in Mapungubwe, 414; in Nubia, 150; in Peru, 428; in Teotihuacán, 166–8; in West Africa, 156–7; Xia Dynasty, China, 98
Archimedes (Greek mathematician), 205
Architectural achievements: in Chavin de Huántar, 133; India, 592m, 593, 595, 595f, 601, 613, 615–16; Islamic civilization, 301; monumental architecture, 71, 89, 118–19, 210, 382, 447, 616; Muslims, 301; in Ottoman Empire, 482–3; in Roman Empire, 210; in Sasanid Persia, 206
Ardi *(Ardipithecus ramidus)*, 7, 27
Argentina: beef production in, 712; demographic growth in, 692–3; independence gained from Spain, 690–1; migrations to, 692; Mothers of Plaza de Mayo, 955; political instability in, 691–2; populist regime in, 904; Radical Party in, 692; railroads in, 692; San Martín's liberation of, 690–1; slow state formation in, 691–2; Socialist Party in, 692; trade activities, 690
Arianism, 286
Aristotle/Aristotelianism, 213, 304, 328–30, 338, 339, 465, 492–3, 493f, 495, 502–3
Armies of the Green Standard (China), 628, 727
Arms. *See* Weaponry
Army of the Andes, 691
Arouet, François Marie (Voltaire), 500–1
Arthashastra (Hindu sacred text), 222
Artillery innovations, 795–6
Artistic achievements: abstract expressionism, 901f; Africa, 421–2; the Americas, 422; Andean cultures, 128; Baroque era, 492, 494; Buddhist art, 72; cave paintings, 20, 22, 28; Chavín de Huántar, 133, 134; China, 95–6, 256, 623, 626–7; Europe, rock art, 17, 18–19, 20f; Greece, 58–9, 206, 207–8; Habsburg Empire, 486; hieratic style of art, 210; Ice Age art, 21f; impressionist art movement, 811–12; India, 237–8, 614–15; industrialism era (1750–1914), 811–12; Islamic civilization, 300–1; Italy, 208–10, 209f, 494; Japan, 385, 647; Jenné-jeno, West Africa, 156f; Latin America, 718; Mayan Kingdoms, 164; Mexico, pottery making, 128; Muslims, 301; Olmecs, jade mask, 134f; Ottoman Empire, 480–3; Pedra Furada rock wall paintings, 126, 127f; Peru, 119; post-WW II, 900–1, 901f; Renaissance era, 494–5; rock art, 2, 13, 17–20, 20f; Romanticism era, 681–2, 883f; U.S. post-WW I, 858–9
Art of War, The (Sun Zi), 80, 246, 881
Aryans (Indo-Europeans): inconclusive knowledge about, 74; Indo-Aryans division, 76; name derivation, 74; religious rituals, 77
Asceticism path (India), 85, 85f, 225
Ashikaga Shogunate (Japan), 373f, 638–9
Ashoka (Indian ruler): Akbar's similarity to, 603; conflict with Kalinga Kingdom, 218; dharma path followed by, 219, 233; Harsha Vardhana comparison, 344; Mauryan Empire leadership, 218m; moral order creation, 219–20; protection of animal species, 219; timeline placement, 217f; unification of commercial law, 219
Asia: agrarian development in, 2, 3; decline of Second German Empire, 849; East and Central Asia (618-960), 352m; mechanical energy inventions, 317; migrations to Australia, 14–17; Mongol conquests, 270f; post-Black Death population recovery, 756; rice revolution, 381; rise of religious civilizations, 270, 273; Timur's activities in, 594
Asian Tigers, 964–5
Assad, Bashar al- (Syrian President), 977
Assemblies, in Mesopotamia, 36
Assembly line, 807f
Assyrian Empire: empire building, 50–1; gender relations, 293; law code, 43; map, 51m; military setbacks, 50; origins, 33f, 50–1; role in unifying Middle East, 51, 150. *See also* Neo-Assyrian Empire
Assyrian Empire in Fars, 180
Astronomy, 265, 490; Copernican revolution in, 652; Galileo's discoveries, 497; in India, 611–12; Kepler's discoveries, 493f; Mughal innovations, 611–12; Newton's discoveries, 493f
Atahualpa (Inca Empire ruler), 527f, 529–30
Athens, Greek city-state, 53, 55, 183–5; forts in, 53, 55; "golden age" of democracy in, 184; independent rule of, 183; political reforms in, 55; rivalry with Sparta, 184; trading activities, 184; women in, 212–13
Atlantic slave trade: African diaspora and, 583; coastal Africa and, 566–71; conditions leading to, 543; economic patterns of, 580–3; growth of, 560–1, 566–7; middle passage, 581–3; passage from Africa, 573m, 577m; Portugal's role in, 567–8; rum and gun running, 581; slave ship layout, 582f; timeline placement, 561f. *See also* Slavery; Slave trade
Atlantic system, 580m, 581
Atomic bomb, 884
Augustine, St. (Church Father), 203
Augustus (Roman Emperor), 190–1, 190f
Aurangzeb (Mughal ruler): anti-Sikh actions, 604; ascendancy of, 601–4; carrot-and-stick strategy, 604; championing of Quranic law, 601; destruction of Hindu temples, 603–4; Islamification efforts, 603; Maratha wars, 602, 604, 616, 618; religious suppression during reign, 609, 613, 619; revenue gains during reign of, 608; strict Sunni Islam policies, 617–18; taxation on nonbelievers, 609, 613; timeline placement, 595f
Austen, Jane, 682
Australia: Aboriginal rock art in, 17, 17f; British colonialism in, 825–7; British convicts shipped to, 819f; Catholic churches, 494; decline in boom years, 826–7; early human settlements, 5; El Niño weather phenomenon, 825, 826; European emigration to, 798; gold-rush immigration waves, 825, 826–7; *H. sapiens* migration to, 14f, 15, 25; Ice Age and, 20–1; South Asian migrations to, 14–17; white settlement in, 825
Australopiths *(Australopithecus)*, 7, 8, 29
Austria: alliance against Napoleon, 662; Austro-Prussian War, 675; Ottoman sieges of Vienna, 461f, 468, 757f; restoration of monarchy, 829; role in Seven Years' War, 826; uprisings in, 674
Austria-Hungary, 763, 764, 851–4
Austrian-Habsburgs. *See* Habsburg Empire
Austronesian cultural family, 139, 159
Automobiles, early, 787f, 794
Avatars and alvars (in Hinduism), 230
"Avenue of the Dead" buildings (Teotihuacán), 168
Avicenna (Ibn Sina), 299, 329
Avignon papacy, 311f, 334
Aztec Empire: beliefs/gods of, 438–9; conquests of, 441; Cortés' conquests in, 527–8; Cuauhtémoc, Aztec,ruler, 527f; expansion of, 440m; governance, 439–40; Itzcóatl's leadership, 439; list of tributes owed to, 439f; map, 440m; Mexican Valley settlement, 438; military forces, 429, 440–1, 446; origins, 429, 438–41; reciprocity agreements in, 440–1; rise of, 439; Spain's conquest of, 457, 526, 527–8; timeline placement, 271f, 431f; triple alliance of, 439, 441; weaponry innovations, 441; writing development, 136. *See also* Tenochtitlán
Azurduy de Padilla, Juana, 688–9, 698

Baader-Meinhof Gang (West Germany), 937
Baath Party, 966, 982
Babur (Zahir Ud-din Muhammad Babur): administrative challenges of, 596; conquests of, 347, 595–6, 596m; forced governing style, 606; Indian Timurid line foundedby, 595–6; relation to Tamerlane, 358, 596; rise to power, 610; timeline placement, 595f
Babylonian Kingdom: Cyrus II the Great's campaign against, 180; kingship of Hammurabi, 40; law codes, 40, 42–3; Minoan palace-state, 33; Old Babylonian period, 59; Urukagina of Lagash, 42. *See also* Neo-Babylonians
Bach, Johann Sebastian, 494
Bacon, Roger, 330
Bactria-Margiana Archaeological Complex (BMAC), 71, 73
Baghdad, Mongol conquest of, 347
Al-Baghdadi, Abu Bakr, 982–3
Bahadur Shah Zafar (Mughal Emperor), 821
Bahrain, Arab Spring protests, 960–1, 981
Baldwin IX (Count of Flanders), 325
Balfour Declaration (1917), 865
Balkans: Cold War and, 893; empires and nations in, 852–3; mass exodus of refugees, 975
Balkan Slavs, 460, 462, 476
Balkan Wars, First and Second, 756, 764
Balmaceda, José, 705, 720–1
Baluchistan (Neolithic Baluchistan), 68
Banana phytoliths, 157
Ban Biao (Chinese historian), 263
Bandaranaike, Sirimavo, 888–9, 910, 915
Ban Gu (Chinese historian), 263
Bank of England, 786
Banner system, Qing Dynasty, 625, 628–9

Banpo Village (China), 92, 93m, 94–5, 116
Bantu people, 151f, 155, 157–8, 410, 413, 953
Ban Zhao (Chinese historian), 260–1, 263–4
Baojia local organization system (Ming, Qing dynasties, China), 363, 444, 633
Baronial courts, England, 316
Baroque arts, 492, 494
Bartholdi, Frederic A., 792
Battle of Agincourt, 333
Battle of Chaldiran (Ottomans vs. Safavids), 469–70
Battle of Crécy, 333
Battle of Gwalfor, 217f
Battle of Manzikert, 275f
Battle of Omdurman (1898), 796f
Battle of Tours and Poitiers, 276, 333
Bay of Pigs invasion (1961), 898
Beat Generation (Beats), 923
Beatles, 4, 923.936
Becquerel, Antoine, 808
Bede (Anglo-Saxon scholar), 323
Beethoven, Ludwig van, 657f, 681
Belgium: early industrialism in, 789; imperialism by, 828m; independence of, 838–9; Leopold II's leadership in, 835, 836, 846
Bell, Alexander Graham, 795, 804
Ben Ali, Zine El Abidine, 981
Benedict, Saint, 310–11
Benedictine monasteries, 310–11
Benin Kingdom (West Africa), 424, 456f; Christianity in, 560; slave trade, 568–9; timeline placement, 561f
Benz, Karl, 794
Berber dynasties (North Africa), 275f, 276, 305, 418–19, 460,564–5
Beringia land bridge, 24–5, 26, 26m, 27, 28
Berlin Airlift, 893
Berlin Conference (1884 -1885), 819, 832, 836
Berlin Wall, 849f, 891f, 898, 926, 927f
Berlioz, Hector, 681
Bernard of Clairvaux, 324
Beyond Good and Evil (Nietzsche), 811
Bhagavad Gita (Indian sacred text), 81, 82
Bharatiya Janata Party (India), 983
Bhutto, Benazir, 889
Bin Laden, Osama, 967
Birth of Tragedy, The (Nietzsche), 811
Bismarck, Otto von (Chancellor of Germany), 675–6, 832
Black Death (bubonic plague): in China, 358, 359, 360, 622; demographic consequences, 505; in Europe, 271f, 331, 332m; historical background, 298; in Middle East, 271f; Mongols and, 298; population recovery, post-plague, 756
Black Man's Burden, The (Morel), 846
Blake, William, 801
Blanc, Louis, 802
Boccaccio, Giovanni, 337
Bodhisattva concept (Buddhism), 228
Bohemia: anticlerical sentiments in, 337; Habsburg rule in, 472; Thirty Years' War and, 514–15; as victim of state centralization, 506t; Wycliffe's teachings in, 335
Bolívar, Simón, 688–9, 697, 699
Bolivia, 690, 700, 902
Bolshevik Party (Russia), 779, 854, 868, 869
Bolshevik Revolution (Russia), 848f, 853f, 880, 890
Bolsheviks, 779
Bonaparte, Louis-Napoleon (Napoleon III), 675–6, 698, 704, 761–2, 805, 843
Bonaparte, Napoleon: conquests in Europe, 671; defeat in Russia, 662; domestic reforms, 662–3; Egypt invasions by, 652f, 661, 755, 757f; ending of empire of, 662; failures in Egypt, Europe, 828; French empire rebuilding efforts, 665–6; invasion of Russia, 755; occupation of Egypt, 652f, 661, 755, 757f; occupation of Iberia, 689–90, 693; role in ending French Revolution, 661, 671; sale of Louisiana to U.S., 665–6
Boniface VIII (Pope), 334
Book of History (Chinese text), 109
Book of Mencius, 243
Book of Sentences (Lombard), 329
Book of Songs (China), 114, 117
Book of the Dead (Egypt), 33
Boomerang invention, 24
Borana calendar, 148, 159
Bosnia, 763
Bosnia-Herzegovina, 763, 764, 853, 975–6
Boston Tea Party (1773), 658
Bouazizi, Mohamed, 980f, 981
Bourbon monarchy (France), 512, 535–6, 545, 673, 690, 816
Bourgeoisie social class (Europe), 320, 798
Boxer Rebellion (China), 653f, 725f, 736–7, 760, 879
Brahe, Sophie, 500
Brahe, Tycho, 500
Brazil: African slaves in, 536–7, 561, 572, 663; antimonarchy agitation in, 695; archaeological discoveries, 25; Cabral's landing in, 527f, 561f; *capoeira* martial arts system of slaves, 587; cave paintings in, 126; coffee production in, 695–6, 712, 713; Creoles in, 693; diamond mining in, 537; economic miracle in, 955–6; end of slavery in, 653f, 691f, 694; extreme inequality in, 663–4; federalist interlude in, 694; gold mining in, 527f, 536–7, 545; growth of cities in, 546; import-substitution industrialization in, 696; music of, 584; Pedro I's authoritarianism, 693–4; plantations in, 578; plantation slavery in, 576, 712; political instability in, 691–2; populist regime in, 904; Portuguese conquest of, 464, 530–1, 536; railroads in, 694, 695, 697; revolt against Pedro I, 694; slave revolts, ending of slavery in, 694–5, 696–7; sugar empire, 576; trade activities, 530, 695; union with Portugal, 691f, 693
Brazilian Shield (geographic region), 123
Brest-Litovsk Treaty (Germany), 854
Brexit (United Kingdom), 974
Brezhnev, Leonid, 926, 928–9
Brezhnev Doctrine, 928
Bride-price (Vietnam), 392
British Coercive Acts, 658
British East India Company: Chinese operations, 632, 633, 725–6; dismantling of, 822; evolutionary role of, 818; expanding role in India, 632, 818, 819f, 838; exploitation of Mughal Dynasty, 817; founding timeline, 819f; India's First War of Independence, 821–2; international trade competition, 608–9; nabobs (local magnates), 818–19; near-bankruptcy of, 657; reform perils, 819–21; role in dynastic wars, 838; role in Seven Years' War, 618, 818; use of iron-hulled steamers, 789; victory of, 605
British North America. *See* Colonial North America
British North America map, 657m
Brontë, Anne, 682
Brontë, Charlotte, 682
Brontë, Emily, 682
Bronze Age: in China, 115; collapse of, 33, 49, 50, 51–2; historical background, 38, 40; spread of crafts, technologies, 75, 78; usefulness of bronze, 38
Brown v. Board of Education (1954), 933
Brueghel, Peter, 495f
Brunelleschi, Filippo (architect), 494, 495f
Bubonic plague (Plague of Justinian), 194–5. *See also* Black Death
Buddha, 217f, 226, 235, 398–9
Buddhism: ahimsa doctrine, 219, 225–6; Ashoka's conversion to, 218, 219; *bodhisattva* concept, 228; Buddhist schools, 264–5; challenges presented by, 271; in China, 256, 262, 264–5, 343, 349–50; Confucians' criticisms of, 353; continuing vitality of, 457; cosmological perspectives, 343; early works among Bactrian Greeks, 217f; eightfold path, 226–7; Four Noble Truths, 226–7; global reach of, 214m, 219, 220, 229m; as Gupta privileged religion, 222; in India, 64, 65, 72, 87; influence on Confucianism, Daoism, 147; Islam and, 278; in Japan, 270, 343, 382–3, 386, 388–90; Kanishka's adoption of, 217f, 220; in Korea, 270, 343, 374, 375f, 378–9; Mahayana branch, 228–9, 237f, 264, 350, 395–6; Menander's adoption of, 220; monastic Buddhism alternative, 261; Nichiren Buddhism in, 389, 398–9; nirvana, 226–7; origins, 217f, 224, 226, 270; texts, 227–8; Theraveda branch, 227–9, 228–9, 264, 344, 373f, 392, 394, 395–6, 889; *Tripitaka* texts, 227, 378; in Vietnam, 270, 344, 373f, 392, 395–6; Zen Buddhism, 375f, 385, 389–90, 398–9
Buddhist-Confucian society (Hwarang), 378
Buddhist missionaries, 374
Buddhist schools, 264–5
Bulgaria: Eastern Bloc country, 898; ethnic uprisings, 763; First Balkan War participation, 764; independence gained by, 757f
Bulgars, Byzantine defeat of, 275f
Bunyoro Kingdom (Africa), 561f, 564
Burial sites and customs: of the Americas, 128, 135–6; China, Qin Dynasty, 250f; of China, 92, 99, 101; of Harappa, 72–3; of India, 592; of Natufians, 33; in Neolithic Americas, 128; of Peru, 428; Puruchuco burial place, 428
Burma, 331, 911
Bush, George W., 966–7
Bushido (Way of the Warrior), 385, 398–9
Buyid Shiite Dynasty (Iran and Iraq), 410, 766

Byzantine Empire (Byzantium): Anatolia's conquests in, 465; *Codex* adopted by, 195, 279; conquests of Ottomans, 475; Crusaders cooperation with, 289–90; cultural revival, 492; defeat of Bulgars, 275f; defenselessness of, 466; difficult beginnings, 282–7; Eastern Christian civilization in, 273, 282–91; iconoclasm controversy, 275, 283–4; icons, 302–3; influence on Ottoman Empire, 755; influence on Russia, 755; Islamic civilization comparison, 273; landed aristocracy in, 295; Latin empire in, 287; learning and the arts, 301; map of empire, 272m, 284m; military changes in, 285–7; Muslim conquests of, 281; origins, 465; plantation slavery roots in, 571–2; provincial, central organization, 294–6; recentralization of, 295–6; rise of Ottomans, decline of, 464; Roman Empire transition to, 274; scientific achievements, 495; Seljuk conquests of, 275f, 287–9; survival strategies, 282–3; transformation into commonwealth, 284–5; war with Sasanid Iran, 275f

Cabral, Pedro Álvares, 527f, 561f
Caesar, Julius, 190
Calendars: and African spirituality, 159; of agrarian peoples, 612; in the Americas, 435; Borana, 159; Christian calendars, 484; in eastern Mediterranean region, 238; in Genesis, 199; in India, 238; of indigenous cultures, 584; Julian calendar, 854; of Kenyan Kushite nomads, 174; Mayan, 164–5; in Americas, 148–9; of Romans, 189; San Lorenzo religious cycle, 135
Calico Acts (1700, 1720, Great Britain), 786
Calligraphy, in China, 112–13
Calvin, John
Calvinism, 510–11, 510–12
Cambodia: Black Death origination, 331; Buddhism in, 232; Khmer Rouge revolutionary group, 946; location (description), 232; map location, 945m; new imperialism in, 837; origin of, 917; Roman/Greek coins found in, 232; war, communist rule in, 945
Camp David peace process, 948, 978
Canada: European emigration to, 798; geographic regions, 121; railroad development, 716
Canon law, 329
Canon of Medicine (Avicenna), 329, 330
Canterbury Tales (Chaucer), 337
Canton trade, China, 631–3
Cao Xueqin, 744
Capetian kings (France), 311f
Capitalism: in Australia, 988; in Canada, 988; "carpetbagger" capitalism, 930; cash economy and, 319–20; China's experiment with, 940, 942; "crony" capitalism, 960, 981; defined, 319; demise of, 803; in Europe, 319–20; industrial society and, 719, 745, 785, 789–99; in Japan, 745, 746; Lenin's comment on, 844; market capitalism, 863; Marxism and, 779, 940; middle-class capitalism vs. mercantilism, 815; Morel on, 846; Soviet adoption of, 956; state capitalism, 862, 866, 982; technology and, 965; in the U.S., 988
Capitalist democracy: attractiveness of, 961, 992; Britain's advocacy of, 885; Cold War and, 889, 915, 925, 956; communism and, 851, 889–901, 911, 920–1; defined, 848, 849; in Eastern Bloc countries, 975–6; France's advocacy of, 885; global movement for, 925; and the Great Depression, 862, 871; Great Depression and, 851; and modernity, 871, 920, 962–88, 991; supremacist nationalism and, 871, 899, 920; U.S. advocacy of, 885
Capitulary for Saxony (Charlemagne), 312
Capoeira martial arts system, of slaves, 587
Caral-Supe valley, Peru: agriculture in, 129; archaeological findings, 118, 119, 149; growth of, 129–31; origins of, 3f, 123f; trading networks, 129
Caribbean Islands: African cloth, 567; geography and climate, 121, 123–4; Columbus arriving, 527f; coolies, 715; diseases, 549; economy (1900), 709m, European colonization, 533m; European interlopers, 535, 544; forager settlements, 138–9; mercantilism in, 574–6; new nation states (1831), 703m; plantation system, 545–6, 573–4, 578–9, 589; population growth in, 903m; Santería, 584-5; Seven-Years' War, 541,529m; shamanism, 139; slavery and slave revolts, 561f, 576–7,586–7, 588m; Spanish colonization in, 541–4; Spanish conquests in, 526; Taíno chiefdom society, 138–9; trade activities, 659; triangular trade, 580m, 581; urbanization in, 903m warm-weather crops, 541, 543, 576, 578, 581
Carnegie, Andrew, 679, 806–7
Carnegie Endowment, 861
Carolina colonies (North and South Carolina): establishment of, 561f; indentured laborers in, 578; Native American slaves in, 578; production of plantation commodities in, 578–89; slave culture in, 586f
Carolingian Empire, 276, 285, 309, 310
Carranza, Venustiano, 707–8
Cartagena, Spain, 697–8
Carter, Jimmy, 929, 948, 950, 955
Cartography (mapmaking), 496, 497f
Caste system (India), 67f, 76–7, 82–6, 88, 230, 231, 233–6, 349, 754
Castile Kingdom (Spain), 318, 421, 460, 462, 464, 470, 509
Castro, Fidel, 891, 897–8
Cataphracts, 180, 189
Categorical imperative (Kant), 668–9
Cathar Heresy, 340–1
Catherine II of Russia (Catherine the Great), 757f, 770
Catholicism: in Africa, 570, 583; Buddhism comparison, 264; in Castile, 474, 475f; Charles V and, 509; in China, 631; in colonial America, 550; Creoles and, 711, 717; in Europe, 403; in France, 512; French Catholicism, 512; French Revolution and, 660; in Germany, 514–15; Jewish, Muslim converts to, 484; in the Kingdom of Kongo, 570, 583; Lateran Accords, in Italy, 872; in Mexico, 701; missionaries in China, 244, 256, 631; missionaries in the Americas, 551; in the Netherlands, 513; New Sciences and, 553; in the Philippines, 840; Renaissance and, 494; in Spain, 485, 486; in Switzerland, 510
Catholic Reformation, 493f, 497–9, 511–12, 551–2
Caudillo authoritarian regimes (Latin America), 693, 697, 699–700, 702, 705, 710, 719
Cave paintings, 20, 22, 28
Cavour, Count Camillo di, 674–5
Ceauşescu, Elena, 931
Ceauşescu, Nicolae, 931
Celibacy, 286
Cell phones, global numbers of, 963f
Central Africa: chieftains and kingdoms, 415–17; Creoles, 583; Luba Kingdom, 403f, 416–17, 417m, 426; rain forests, 20; rise of indigenous kingdoms, 401
Central America: agricultural developments in, 2, 121; authoritarian regimes in, 954; European explorations, 529m; geographic regions, 121, 123; indigo production in, 579; Mayan Kingdom in, 147f. *See also* individual countries
Central Asia: agriculture in, 3, 46–7; early human settlements, 18, 22; horse domestication, 47, 75; horses and chariots from, 47; Hun invasions from, 182f; Indo-European migrants from, 75; map, 352m; migrations to, 217f; monsoon system, 66; Sayyid sultanate, 348; Scythian culture, 108–9; trade activities, 71–2, 108–9; trade network, 147
Central Intelligence Agency (CIA), 891f, 893–4, 894m, 897, 904, 919, 954–5
Centralization of government: in China, 108, 116; demographic curve, 505; in Egypt, 42; in England, 505, 508; European victims (1450-1600), 506t; in France, 505, 508; in Habsburg Empire, 479; in India, 79; in Oceania, 143; in Ottoman Empire, 477–8, 504; in Polynesia, 141; Protestant Reformation's influence, 504; in Sweden, 508
Ceremonial centers: in Americas, 132, 134, 169, 430, 446; in Andean culture, 132, 169, 170, 171, 441, 446, 452; of the Aztecs, 438, 439, 444; in Cuzco, 449; of the Incas, 441–2; in La Venta settlement, 136; in Morocco, 172; of Nazca chiefdoms, 172; in Peru, 171, 172; in Teotihuacán Kingdom, 169, 170, 430–1, 439, 447; in Tiwanaku, 435, 436; in Toltec city-states, 430, 439; in Wari, 436
Césaire, Aimé, 861
Ceylon: Bandaranaike's leadership, 888–9, 910, 914; gaining of independence, 911; political turbulence era in, 889; Tamil civil disobedience campaign, 889; Theraveda Buddhism origins, 373f, 392
Chachnama, 342–3
Chaldiran, Battle of, 469–70
Chalukya Kingdom (Southern India), 217f, 345
Chamberlain, Neville, 876
Chandragupta I (Gupta Empire ruler), 220

Chandragupta Maurya (Indian ruler): Alexander's meeting with, 215; background of, 215, 217; building of Mauryan Empire, 217; Jain monk phase, 217–18; political practices of, 217. *See also* Ashoka; Mauryan Empire
Chariots: in central Asia, 47; in China, 78, 93f, 101, 101f; in eastern Mediterranean region, 47; in Hittite Empire, 47
Charlemagne (Charles the Great): Capitulary for Saxony, 312; church role and interests, 312; educational reforms, 312; empire map, 313m; papacy protected by, 312; reign of, 311f
Charles IV (King of France), 333
Charles V (King of Spain, Holy Roman Emperor): alliance with Ottomans, 471; central state formation, 478–9; efforts against the Ottomans, 470–1; ending of reign, 472; invasion of Italy, 459; occupation of Tunis, 459; Protestant Reformation and, 471, 509; rule of Western Christianity, 470; timeline placement, 493f, 527f
Charles X (French Bourbon King), 816–17
Charter of the United Nations, 669, 889, 915
Chartism reform movement (Great Britain), 802
Châtelet, Gabrielle-Emilie du, 500–1
Chaucer, Geoffrey, 337
Chavin de Huántar city (Andes): architecture, 133; artistic achievements, 133, 134; ceremonial center, 132–3, 170; decline of, 133–4; geographic features, 132; human sacrifices, 133; origin, 123f; textile making in, 133
Chemical manufacturing industry, 793–4
Chernobyl nuclear accident (Ukraine), 930
Chernyshevsky, Nikolai, 782–3
Chiang K'ai-shek, 880, 881, 884, 905
Chicago Field Museum, 118
Chichén Itzá Kingdom (Maya): flourishing of, 433; origins, 433–4; timeline placement, 270f, 431f; trade activities, 434
Chiefdoms: defined, 149; Jenné-jeno, West Africa, 151f, 156; Mexican Basin, 430; Moche chiefdom, northern Peru, 147f, 151f; Paracas chiefdom, southern Peru, 151f; Polynesia, kinship-based, 141; Saharan chiefdoms, 150; Taíno chiefdom, Hispaniola, 139; Teotihuacán Kingdom, 169, 170, 430–1
Childebert II, (Merovingian King), 311
Chikamatsu, Monzaemon, 623f, 647
Child labor, 784–5, 801
Children's and Household Stories (Grimm Brothers), 670f
Chile: archaeological discoveries, 25; Balmaceda's leadership, 705; early industrialization in, 720–1; migrations to, 26m; populist regime in, 904; San Martín's liberation of, 690; territorial conflicts, 700; War of the Pacific victory, 720
China, 242–69; and Africa, 629–30; agrarian-urban society, 3, 350, 554; agricultural development in, 3, 257–8, 622; aid in spreading Buddhism in Korea, 374; anti-Manchu elements in, 730; armies of the Green Standard, 628, 727; artisan pottery, 95–6, 256, 265–6, 623; Banpo Village, 92, 93m, 94–5, 116; between empires period, 253–4; Black Death in, 358, 359, 360, 622; Boxer Rebellion, 653f, 725f, 736–7, 760, 879; as brief part of Mongol Empire, 345f; British East India Company in, 632; Bronze Age, 115; Buddhism in, 256, 264–5, 349–50; burial sites and customs, 92, 99, 101; campaigns against Xiongnu, 220; Canton trade system, 631–3, 632f; chariots in, 78, 93f, 101, 101f; Chiang K'ai-shek's leadership in, 880, 881, 884, 905; Chinese Nationalist Party, 879; Christianity in, 730; commercial enterprises, 622–4, 634f; concentration of power in, 605–6; conflicts with Great Britain, 727–8; Confucianism in, 244–6, 350, 722; Cultural Revolution, 848f, 849f, 853f, 926, 940–2; Daoism in, 350; Dapenkeng culture, 96; Deng Xiaoping's leadership, 906, 907, 927f, 940, 942, 957; Eastern Zhou Dynasty, 93f, 104–5; economic boom, 971–2; 1800-1900, share of world manufacturing output, 821f; elite Shang Dynasty women, 109–10; Emperor Qin Shi Huangdi, 92; empire consolidation in, 146; Empress Wu (Wu Zeitan), 256, 349–51, 353, 354f, 356, 368–70; encyclopedia projects, 636; era of "culture heroes" and "sage kings," 93f; Erlitou culture, 93f, 98–9, 102; as Eurasian economic engine, 819; evolution as an empire, 466; family adaptation in, 105–10; First Opium War, 724, 725f, 727, 728, 738; 589 CE, empire map, 254m; Four Modernizations, 849f, 942–3; gender roles,109–10, 260–2, 635; geography and climate, 92, 93m, 94; Grand Secretariat of, 360, 621, 623f; Great Leap Forward, 849f, 891f, 907; Han Dynasty invention of paper, 320; Hideyoshi's dreams of conquering, 621, 625; high level equilibrium trap in, 622; Huangdi ("Yellow Emperor"), 97; Hundred Days of Reform, 725f, 736; Hundred Flowers campaign, 906; Ice Age influence, 20; imperialism of, 724–37, 734; import, export activities, 624; import substitution industrialization in, 964–5; industry and commerce, 256–60; intellectual life, 265–6; interaction, adaptation in, 732f; invasion of Tibet, 940; iron and salt production, 257; Japan's rule of, 905; Jesuit missionaries in, 457f; King Wu Ding, 90–1, 100, 102, 109, 111; land reforms in, 257, 905–6; legalism philosophy, 244, 245f, 247, 248, 262, 266, 267; *lijia* tax system for households, 633; Lin Zexu's destruction of opium, 726–7, 733; literary achievements, 102–3, 105, 109–10, 114; literary works, 98, 102–3; Liu Shaoqi's leadership, 907, 940; local customs, religion, 637–8; Longshan culture, 95–6; Macartney's Beijing mission, 724, 725f; Manchus occupation of Beijing, 625; Mandate of Heaven, 103–4, 116, 244, 246, 263, 383; Mao Zedong's leadership, 880–1, 884, 905–6, 937, 940–2; map (1600), 623m; maritime trade, 319, 350, 351, 362, 625, 632f, 649–50, 724–7, 726m; market economics experiment, 930; "Marxism-Leninism-Mao Zedong Thought," 942; Marxist principles in, 905; Meiji Constitution, 791; Mencius's spreading of Confucianism, 245–6; migrations to, 13; missionaries in, 244, 457f, 623f, 631; Mongol conquests in, 345f, 354, 355; monsoons in, 32, 66; mythological background, 97–9; Neo-Confucianism in, 270f, 271, 343, 350, 354, 364, 376, 397, 607, 624, 636–7, 636m, 732–3, 739; Neolithic settlements, 91–2, 93f, 96, 128; 1960–1966, technological, military advances, 940; North and South dynasties period, 253; Northern Song Dynasty, 254f, 345f, 366f; occupation of Vietnam, 373f, 393, 940, 946; opium trade, 724–30, 732–3, 738, 741, 751, 819; Opium Wars, 635, 724, 725f, 726–31, 726m, 738, 744, 760; oracle bones, early writing, 91, 93f, 103, 109, 110–13, 115; patriarchy in, 106, 116–17; People's Liberation Army, 905, 941; periodic unity/disunity in, 273; political and cultural life options, 65, 248; post-WW I ideology of, 851; printing developments, 265–6; Protestantism in, 730; push into Vietnam, 373f; Qi Dynasty, 105; Qin era, 103, 105, 111; Rape of Nanjing, 853f, 881–2; reemergence of nationalism, 880–1; religion, spirituality in, 110–14, 244–8; religion in, 110–14; "Resist America, Aid Korea" campaign, 905–6; resources of, 457; reunification under the Sui, 245f, 256; Revolutionary Alliance of 1905, 879; Ricci's missionary work in, 457f, 623f, 631f; rice cultivation in, 2, 3f, 78–9, 93f, 94, 96–7, 107, 111; scholar-gentry, 257, 358, 362–3, 366, 377, 394–5, 633–5, 730; Second Opium War, 762, 773, 821; Self-Strengthening Movement, 722, 725f, 731f, 732–4; Shimonoseki Treaty with Japan, 722–3, 735, 736; shipbuilding innovations, 466–7, 466f; *Shujing* (historical text), 97, 98, 99, 103–4; silk production, 256–7; Silk Road, 260f; single-whip tax edicts, 623f, 633; Sino-Japanese War, 722–3, 722m, 725f, 734–6, 740, 750, 778; Sino-Soviet split, 940; Six Dynasties period, 253; Soviet's border dispute with, 926; Spain's trade with, 840; Spring and Autumn periods, 93f, 103, 105, 110, 115, 243, 245f; steam power origins in, 728f; student demonstrations, 936; Sui Dynasty, 245f, 254–6, 350; survival of communism in, 971; Taiping Rebellion, 628, 635, 725f, 729–30, 731m, 751; taxation in, 107–8, 251, 253, 257, 353, 355, 358, 377; technical innovations, 363, 731; textile trade, 780; Third Communist International, 880; Three Kingdoms period, 253; "three Rs" (reaction, reform, revolution) in, 731; Tiananmen Square demonstrations, massacre, 849f, 927f, 944; Tibetan Stupa and Temple, Beijing, 228f, 629f; trade imbalances, 724–5; treatment of young girls, 260; Treaty of

Nanjing with Britain, 728, 730; treaty ports, 727–34, 729f, 735f; unification under the Qin, 243; visionaries in, 243–56; Warring States period, 103, 105, 242, 243, 245f, 246–8, 253, 262, 269; weapon innovations, 476, 611, 731f; "well-field" tenancy system, 384; Western science, Eastern ethics in, 732–3; Western Zhou Dynasty, 93f, 104, 114; writing developments, 91, 93f, 103, 109, 110–13, 115, 250, 264, 371, 381, 386; in WW I, 848f, 853f; WW II campaigns, 848f; Xia Dynasty, chariot origins, 78; Yangshao culture, 93f, 94–5, 98; Yellow River cultures, 68, 91–9; Zhou treatises, 80. *See also* Confucianism; Daoism; Han Dynasty; Manchus; Ming Dynasty; Neo-Confucianism; Qianlong Emperor; Qi Dynasty; Qin Dynasty; Qing Dynasty; Shang Dynasty; Song Dynasty; Sui Dynasty; Xia Dynasty; Yellow River cultures; Yuan Dynasty; Zhou Dynasty
"China's sorrow," 94
Chinese Nationalist Party (Guomindang, GMD), 879
Chinese Republican Revolution, 879
Cholas state (India), 345, 345f
Christian Arabs, 982
Christian Church, 203–4; African Christian churches, 584; architectural style, 326; bishop of Rome as head of, 311; Church Fathers and, 203–4, 283; early medieval church, 310–11; Eastern Christian Church, 584; fifteenth century developments, 336–7; Great Western Schism, 334, 336m; Lalibela monoliths, 407; Nicene Creed and, 193; regular and secular clergy, 310; role in shaping Frankish Gaul, 309; shaping of European religious civilization, 338; Western Schism, 334, 336m; Zoroastrianism comparison, 200. *See also* Jesus (Jesus of Nazareth, Jesus Christ, Jesus the Messiah)
Christian Europe: Carolingians role in, 310; Cathar Heresy, 340–1; early medieval church, 310–11; famine (14th century), 331; feudalism in, 313–15; formation of, 309–15; 14th century crises, 330–5; Merovingians role in, 310; the papacy in, 311; plague, 331; post-Carolingian Europe, 312–13; reign of Charlemagne, 311–12; universities in, 239; Western Christian Europe, 350
Christianity: in Africa, 401–2; African Christian spirituality, 558; in Aksum Kingdom, 153, 154; Antonian-African Christianity, 459; apocalyptic expectations in Portugal, 460, 462; in Benin Kingdom, West Africa, 560; in China, 730; Church Fathers, 203–4, 283, 311, 493; Clovis's adoption of, 310; Columbus's apocalyptic beliefs, 463–4; conquest of Granada, 460; conversions, 526; Coptic Christianity, 154; Dominican religious order, 323–4, 340, 551–2, 631; Eastern Christianity, 275f, 280; Eastern Orthodox Christianity, 755; in Ethiopia; face-off vs. Zoroastrianism, 179; Franciscan religious order, 323, 340, 532, 551–2, 631; in Iberia, 462–4; Iberian apocalyptic explorations, 460, 462; Islam's origins and, 278; Jewish founding of, 147; Latin Christendom, 271, 309, 310, 334; Muslim competition with, 459–75, 566; Native American conversions, 405–9, 532, 536, 551; New Testament, 202–3, 277, 493, 509, 551, 559; Nicene Creed, 193; in Nubian Kingdom, 401–2; origins of, 147, 202–3; Qing China's ban on Christian proselytizing, 730; Roman adoption of, 154, 182f, 193, 195–6, 264; Sasanid protection of, 193; Tokugawa intolerance of, 643–4; Trinitarian Byzantine Christianity, 275; unction ceremony, 310; war with Muslims, 566; Western Christianity, 270; in Zagwe Dynasty, 406. *See also* Jesus (Jesus of Nazareth, Jesus Christ, Jesus the Messiah)
Christian missionaries, 406; in Africa, 832–4; in China, 457f, 623f, 630–1; in India, 821; in Indochina, 842–3
Church Fathers, 203–4, 283, 311, 493
Churchill, Winston, 846, 876, 891, 891f
Church of England, 680
CIA. *See* Central Intelligence Agency
Cistercians, 321
City of God, The (St. Augustine), 203
City-states (*polis*): administration of, 54; in Americas, 161; in Anatolia, 183; Athens, 55; characteristics, 54; defined, 37; Greece, 3, 33f, 52, 54, 55, 59, 183; in Italy, 183; Mesopotamia, 52, 57; Mycenae, 59; patriarchal society in, 42; Phoenician Kingdom, 52; soldiering in, 54–5; Sparta, 55; Syria, 51–2; Uruk, 33f, 37–8; warring among, 40
Civilizing mission, in Africa, 832–4
Civil Rights Act (1964), 934
Civil rights movements (U.S.), 933–7; and African Americans, 933–4, 936–8; gay rights movement, 935; global youth movement, 935–6; Great Society programs, 934; "hippies" movement, 936; Montgomery, Alabama bus boycott, 933f; and Native Americans, 934; student demonstrations, 936–7; women's rights, sexual revolution, 934–5
Civil service system: in China, 354, 641; in India, 822–5, 912; in Spain, 548–9; in Vietnam, 396f, 641
Civil War, United States, 677, 704–5, 790
Clay tablets, in Mesopotamia, 44, 46
Clement VII (Pope), 334
Clement V (Pope), 334
Clinton, Bill, 965–6
Clinton, Hillary, 961, 974
Clive, Robert, 818, 819f
Clovis I (Frankish King), 310
Clovis points (spearhead flutes), 125
Clovis spear-point people, 24–5
"Coal and colonies" theory (about Britain), 786
Cock, Guillermo, 428
Code of Hammurabi. *See* Law Code of Hammurabi
Code of Manu treatise, 233
Codex Justinianus, Roman Empire, 195, 279
Coercive Acts ("Intolerable Acts"), Colonial North America, 658
Coffee: in Brazil, 695–6, 712, 713; Ethiopia's introduction of, 500; in Latin America, 712
Cold War era (1945–1991): Balkans and, 893; Berlin Wall, 849f, 891f, 898, 926; Central Intelligence Agency (CIA), 893–4; civil rights movements and, 933–4; communism in Cuba, 897–8; communist-controlled countries, 892m; Cuban Missile Crisis, 849, 849f, 890, 891f, 899m, 926, 944; defined, 890; Eastern Bloc countries, 898–9; Eastern Europe and, 891, 895–7; ending of, 927f; erection of Berlin Wall, 891; "hot" phase (1945–1962), 890–9; ICBMs and Sputniks, 848f, 891f, 897, 898f; import substitution industrialization, 964; Korean War, 894–5; map, 892m; McCarthyism in the U.S., 895; 1947–1949 confrontations, 891, 893; 1945–1962 period, 890–9; nonaligned countries, 892m; Non-Aligned Movement and, 888; nuclear-capable countries, 892m; origins, 890–1; postwar Eastern Europe, 898–9; proxy wars, 849; revolt in East Germany, 895–6; revolts in Poland and Hungary, 896–7; Soviet invasion of Afghanistan, 849f, 924–5; Stalin's ratcheting up of, 894
College of Cardinals, 322
Colombia, 689, 711, 712, 903
Colonialism: in Africa, 834–5; in the Americas, 532; of Belgium, 417; defined, 817; of Europe, 525–41, 684; of Great Britain, 817, 819f, 829, 831; in India, 819f; in Latin America, 699; in the Middle East, 831; of Portugal, 464, 530–1, 536; in Southeast Asia, 818, 837–44; of Spain, 531–41, 699; of Uruguay, 690
Colonial North America: African slaves in, 540, 561f; Boston settlement, 537; Boston Tea Party, 658; British North American map, 657m; British settlements, 538m, 540; British slavery in, 576–9; Carolina colonies, 561f, 578–9, 586f; Carolina colony, 561f; Coercive Acts ("Intolerable Acts"), 658; conditions leading to revolution in, 656–8; Continental Association (1774–1776), 658; French Settlement, 538m, 540; growth of democracy, economy, 656; House of Burgesses, 540; Jamestown, Virginia, settlement, 457f, 527f, 537, 539, 577–8; Native Americans in, 537–9, 656; New Amsterdam (New York) settlement, 537; New England assemblies, 540; New England colonies, 540, 552–4; New Sciences research, 553; Plymouth, Massachusetts, settlement, 537; Quebec City settlement, 527f, 537, 540; religious revivalism, 554; "sot weed" enterprise, 577–8; Spanish settlement, 538m; sugar, rice, indigo, crop production, 579, 581; territorial expansion in, 540; Thirteen Colonies, 657m; witch hunts, 553–4
Columbian Exchange, 128, 456f, 541, 542–3, 622
Columbus, Christopher: apocalyptic beliefs of, 463–4; Caribbean journey, 235, 463–4, 463–5, 526, 527f; India sea route pursuit, 525; ship size comparison, 360, 361f; voyage to Americas, 460, 461f, 565

Comanches (Native Americans), 539, 702, 704
Commentaries of Mr. Zuo, The (Zuo Zhuan), 102–3, 105
Committee of Public Safety (France), 661
Committee of Union and Progress (CUP), 764
Communication revolution, 794–5
Communism: capitalist democracy and, 889–901; collapse in Eastern Europe, 849f, 932–3, 932m, 961; in Cuba, 897–8; Marx's founding of, 869; in the Soviet Union, 848, 869
Communist Eastern Europe map, 928m
Communist Manifesto, The (Marx and Engels), 652f, 787f
Communist Party, 803; in Czechoslovakia, 928; in France, 864; Stalin's building of, 868; takeover in Russia, 849
Companion to Urania (Cunitz), 490
Concert of Europe, 755, 763, 829
Confederate States of America, 677
Confessions (St. Augustine), 203
Confucianism: *Analects (Lunyu),* 244, 245, 246; Buddhist influences on, 147; in China, 244–6, 350, 722; continuing vitality of, 457; criticisms of Buddhism, 353; doctrine, 244–5; global reach of, 262; Han-Confucian synthesis, 262–3; *Huainan zi* document, 262; influence on government, 244–6; Islam and, 278; junzi (description), 245; Mencius's spreading of, 245–6; on position on women, 260; in Song China, 343; Xunzi's interpretation of, 246–7. *See also* Neo-Confucianism
Confucius, 146f, 244–5, 245f
Congo, Democratic Republic of, 416Congo Reform Association, 846
Congress of Vienna, 652f, 657f, 671–2
Conrad III (Holy Roman Emperor), 324
Constantine I, the Great (Roman Emperor), 193, 326
Constantine XI (Byzantine Emperor), 468
Constantinople: alliance with Jerusalem, 290; crusaders conquest of, 270f, 275f; Eastern Greek Church, 309; Latin regime in, 291; Mehmet II's siege, conquest of, 466–7; Muslim conquest of, 460; North Africa power grab in, 274; Ottoman conquest of, 271f, 311f, 456f, 461f; Russia's goal of conquering, 755
Constitutionalism: American, French, Haitian revolutions and, 670; ethnic nationalism vs., 670; in France, 670, 671; in Germany, 674; in Great Britain, 520–1, 652–3, 670, 680–1; in Latin America, 710–11; in Mexico, 707; opposition to serfdom, 755; in Prussia, 675
Constitutional Revolution (1906; Iran), 769
Constitutions: of Argentina, 691–2; of Australia, 827; of China, 383; of Ethiopia, 409; of France, 516, 654, 661, 665, 666; of Germany, 670, 674, 685; of Gran Columbia, 696; of India, 230, 233, 241, 911; of Japan, 739, 746–8, 791; of Mexico, 706; of the Ottomans, 761–2; of Pakistan, 912; of Portugal, 693; of Rome, 189; of the Soviet Union, 869; of the U.S., 658
Containment policy, Great Britain, 829–30
Continental Association, Colonial North America, 658
Cook, James, 825
Copernicus, Nicolaus, 205, 456f, 493f, 495–6, 652
Copper (Chalcolithic) Age, 37
Coptic Christianity: in Aksum Kingdom, 154; in Egypt, 154, 408–9; in Ethiopia, 565; in Nubian Kingdom, 402–3, 405–6
Cordilleras (mountain ranges), 121
Corn origins and cultivation, 130–1, 131f
Coronation (defined), 310
Corpus Iuris Civilis (Justinian), 329
Cortés, Hernán, 526–8, 529m, 531, 532
Costa Rica: coffee growing in, 712; democracy in, 903; independence gained by, 701; populist regime in, 904
Cottage industries, 786
Council for Mutual Economic Assistance (COMECON), 893
Council of Clermont (France), 289, 324
Council of Constance, 311f, 337
Council of Nicaea (Rome), 193
Creamer, Winifred, 118
Crécy, Battle of, 333
Creoles: African Creole culture, 570; in Brazil, 693; in Buenos Aires, 690; central African Creoles, 583; Christian Creoles, 583; conflict with San Martín, 691; defined, 532; early Atlantic world, 583–7; ethnic groups, mixes, 547; First Republic of Cartagena, 698; in Latin America, 710; lower tier of, 546–7; in Mexico, 706, 708; music and food, 584–5; Muslim Creoles, 583; New Granada Creoles, 689–90, 697–8; in northern South America, 697–8; patriarchy among, 548; plantation life and resistance, 585–7; political domination by, 692; rebellion against, 697; rise of, 534–5; roles of women, 548; in South America, 698–9; in top tier of settler society, 546
Crimea, Russia's annexation of, 963f
Crimean War (1853–1856), 692, 755, 757f, 762, 773, 774, 777, 791, 830
Critique of Practical Reason (Kant), 668
Critique of Pure Reason (Kant), 668
Crô-Magnon humans, 18
Cromwell, Oliver, 514
Crony capitalism, 960, 981
Crowther, Samuel Adjai, 834, 835f
Crusades (to the Holy Land): conquest of Constantinople, 270f, 275f; cooperation with Byzantines, 289–90; First Crusade, 275f, 287, 296, 321, 325m; Fourth Crusade, 287, 290, 294, 304, 305; historical significance of, 289, 324; kingdoms of, 275f, 290m; Second Crusade, 290; Seljuk invasion and, 289; Third Crusade, 290; timeline placement, 311f
Cuauhtémoc (Aztec Empire ruler), 527f, 528
Cuba: Bay of Pigs incident, 898; Castro's rise to power, 891; communism in, 897–8; land reforms in, 902; plantation slavery in, 712; slave revolts in, 696–7; student demonstrations, 936; survival of communism in, 971; Yoruba confraternity *(cabilde)* in, 697
Cuban Missile Crisis, 849, 849f, 890, 891f, 899m, 926, 944
Cultivation system, in Indonesia, 839
Cultural nationalism: in Germany, 670–1
Cultural Revolution (China), 848f, 849f, 853f, 926, 940–2
Cuneiform writing, development of, 38, 39f, 52, 53–4
Cunitz, Maria, 490–1, 500, 501f
Cunningham, Alexander, 64–5
Curie, Marie, 808
Cuzco (Peru): agriculture, 443; as ceremonial-administrative city, 449; grid-pattern layout, 443; "House of Chosen Women" in, 450; map, 449m; military force, 442; mummy veneration in, 451–2; road networks, 446; stone masonry, 448f; urban life patterns in, 429, 453–4
Cyprus, 763
Cyrus II, the Great (Achaemenid Persian King), 180
Czechoslovakia: Communist Party in, 928; as Eastern Bloc country, 898; Husák's leadership, 928, 931; independence gained by, 931; Prague Spring in, 927–8; Soviet's dismantling of reforms in, 928; uprisings in, 674

Da Gama, Vasco, 456f, 461f, 461m, 464, 472, 565, 604
Daimler, Gottlieb, 794
Dalai Lama, 940
Damascus Spring, 982
Dante Alighieri, 337
Daoguang Emperor (China), 726
Daoism: Buddhism influenced by, 584; in China, 350; Confucianism and, 637; continuing vitality of, 457; description, 247–8; government influenced by, 248; influences in China, 248, 271; Islam and, 278; Neo-Confucianism and, 343; popular culture influenced by, 637–8
Dapenkeng culture (China), 96
Darfur crisis, 963f
Dark Continent. *See* Africa
Darwin, Charles, 787f, 809; *Descent of Man, The,* 787f, 809; *On the Origin of Species by Means of Natural Selection,* 787f, 809
Daughters of Liberty, 657
Da Vinci, Leonardo, 494
De Beauvoir, Simone, 934
Decameron (Boccaccio), 337
Decembrist Revolt (1825; Russia), 771
Declaration of Independence (U.S.), 653, 658, 761
Declaration of the Rights of Man and of the Citizen (France), 653, 660, 661
De Iturbide, Agustín, 701
De Klerk, Frederik Willem, 963–4
Delacroix, Eugène, 683f
Delhi Sultanate (India), 271f, 345f, 347, 348m
Democracy: defined, 55; in Europe, 902–3; in Latin America, 903–4; in North America, 902–3; in Romania, 931. *See also* Capitalist democracy
Deng Xiaoping, 906, 907, 927f, 940, 942, 957
De Piérola, Nicolás, 700
Descartes, René, 502–3, 667, 668
Descent of Man, The (Darwin), 787f, 809
Dessalines, Jean-Jacques, 666
Détente, between the U.S. and Soviet Union, 849, 925, 926–7, 927f
Deutero-Isaiah (Second Isaiah), 198–9

Deval, Pierre, 816
Devşirme practice (conscription of young boys), 476
Dewey, John, 866
Dharma, 81, 82–4, 86
Dialectical materialism (of Marx), 803
Díaz, Porfirio, 705–6
Dickens, Charles, 682
Diderot, Denis, 667–8
Digests, 195
Digger Movement (England), 923
Ding Ling (Chinese feminist author), 939
Dinh Bo Linh, 373f
Diocletian (Roman Emperor), 192
Dionysiac cult (Greece), 207
Dirty War (Latin America), 955
Divine Comedy, The (Dante), 337
DNA, 5, 18, 22–5, 27, 68
Dome of the Rock, 275
Dominic, Saint, 323
Dominican religious order, 323–4, 340, 551–2, 631
Dona Beatriz, 558–60
Donatello (sculptor), 494
The Dream of the Red Chamber (Cao Xueqin), 744
Dreamtime ritual (Aboriginals), 16–17, 28
Dubček, Alexander, 928
DuBois, W. E. B., 861
Du Fu (Tang poet), 354
Duke of Zhou (Zhou Dynasty), 245
Dulles, Allen, 897
Dutch Cape Colony, South Africa, 561f
Dutch (United) East India Company (VOC), 605f, 608–9, 819f, 838, 845
Dutch war of independence, 513
Dutch West India Company, 570
Dylan, Bob, 923
Dynamite (TNT), invention of, 793–4, 796

Early Classic Period (Maya), 163
Early Dynastic period (Egypt), 42–3
Early medieval church, 310–11
Earth orbit, by Gagarin, 891f, 897
East Africa: Bantus in, 151f; Battle of Adowa, 836; China's Ming porcelain in, 627; climatic conditions, 32, 35; conquest and resistance in, 835; fossil discoveries, 7; genocide in, 564, 835–6; German colonialism in, 835; hominins in, 6, 7; *Homo erectus* in, 10; *Homo sapiens* in, 7, 10, 11, 13; incipient urbanism in, 159–60; Indonesia contact with, 159; Kushite herders of, 148; Maji Maji rebellion against Germany, 835–6; migrations from, 7, 28; Nile source, 35; Omani Arab colonialism in, 835; Portugal's imperialism in, 8335; rain-forest, 7; Sasanid imperialism in, 155; Swahili city-states, 410–13, 412m; Swahili city-states in, 403f; trade activities, 155, 159–60, 405, 835; village life in, 157–60; Zheng He's visit, 413. *See also* Swahili city-states
East Asia: agricultural developments, 3; challenges of modernity, 722–53; *Homo erectus* in, 10; interest in Sino-Japanese War, 723; map, 352m; migrations to, 18; modernity in, 817; origins of agriculture, 2
Eastern Bloc countries: Cold War era revolt in, 929–30; collapse of communism, 849f, 932–3, 932m, 961, 963f; Stalin and, 895; struggles for independence, 921; student demonstrations in, 936; suppression of anticommunist unrest in, 897; transformations in, 925, 931–3; Warsaw Pact and, 893, 928m
Eastern Christianity: in Byzantium, 275f, 282–91; emergence of, 270; height of, 291–8; Church, 584; iconoclasm controversy, 275, 283–4; Islamic civilization comparison, 273; Orthodox Christians, 286, 309, 755–6, 761, 772
Eastern Europe: Christianity in, 256, 289, 471; Cold War and, 891, 896–9; collapse of communism, 849f, 932m, 961; communism map, 928m; Communist Eastern Europe map, 928m; dispersal of Germans in, 670, 852; emigrations to Great Britain, 868975; emigrations to Mexico, 868; fall of communism, 849f, 932–3, 932m; German-held territories in, 891; Hitler's conquests in, 874–5; *Homo erectus* fossil discoveries, 10; Hungarian uprisings, 927–8; Jews in, 321, 865; Mongol conquests, 270f, 291; Ottomans in, 756; post-WW II in, 898–9; Prague Spring, Czechoslovakia, 927–8; Russian Empire and, 769, 828; Solidarity labor union in Poland, 928–9; Soviet Union and, 890–1; Stalin's policy in, 890
Eastern Mediterranean region: Bronze Age collapse, 49; development of chariots and composite bow, 47; environment of, 31–3; farming and settlements, 31–4, 32m, 47, 60; fifth millennium BCE climate changes, 35; foraging lifestyle, 31–4; geographic scope of, 31; Hittite Empire in, 48, 48m; map, 48m; monsoons in, 32; Mycenaean palace-states, 52–4; Ottomans in, 594; political traditions, 55; rise of Iron Age, 49; Seljuks in, 594; settlements of foragers, 31–4; Timur's activities in, 594; bronze in, 38; warfare developments, 46
Eastern Zhou Dynasty (China), 93f, 104–5
East Germany, 895, 896, 898, 931
East India companies: British East India Company, 605, 608–9, 618, 632; Clive's leadership, 818; competition among, 608–9; Dutch United East India Company, 605f, 608–9, 838, 845; expansion into India, 818; founding of, 605–5; French East India Company, 605, 608–9; growing power of, 593; near bankruptcies of, 657. *See also* specific East India companies
East India Railway, 64
Ebert, Friedrich, 872
Ecclesiastical History of the English People (Bede), 323
Economy: Brazil's economic miracle, 955–6; of China, 725, 930, 971–2; dollar regime, U.S., 964; dual economic recessions, U.S., 973; in Enlightenment era, Europe, 669; global financial crisis, 849f, 963f; globalization and, 965–6; Great Depression, U.S., 848f, 849, 853f; in Habsburg Empire, 479; in India, 231–3, 348–9; innovations in Europe, 336; of Japan, 386–7, 644–7; of Latin America, 711–12; of Mughal Empire, 607–9; New Conservatism, 973; 1970s, 1980s, 937; in Nubian Kingdom, 403; in Ottoman Empire, 477, 765; Qing Dynasty, China, 725, 741–2; Russia's crisis, recovery, 970; stagflation (1970s), 837; stock market crash, U.S., 848f, 853f; 2012, global distribution of wealth, 963m; 2001-2003 financial crisis, 973; of Vietnam, 394–5; Zhou Dynasty, China, 107–9
Ecuador, 689, 711, 902, 904
Edict of Milan, 326
Edict of Nantes (France), 513
Edison, Thomas, 787f, 805
Edo, Japan, 457f
Edward III (King of England), 333
Edwin Smith Papyrus, 60
Egypt: agrarian-urban society, 35, 179; Arab conquest of, 275f; Arab Spring protests, 960–1, 981; *Book of the Dead,* 33; British occupation of, 819f, 830–1; British–French garnishment of tax revenues, 830–1; bureaucratic system, 44; clash with Hittites, 49; colonization of Nubia, 150; control of Palestinian towns, 52; Coptic Christianity in, 154, 408–9; creation myth of, 58; defeat of Syria, 52; Early Dynastic period, 42–3; early towns, 35–6; Euphrates/Nile floods, 35; Fatimid defeat of, 404; first written records, 150; hieroglyphic writing, 44, 44f, 52, 136; kingdoms in, 42–4, 57; liberation of Napata Kingdom from, 150; Library of Alexandria, 204–5; Middle Kingdom, 46, 62; military, 45; military coup d'état in, 963f; military slaves' power grab, 760; Muhammad Ali's leadership, 761, 830; Muslim Brotherhood, 909, 947; Napoleon's occupation of, 652f, 661, 755, 757f; Nasser's leadership, 889, 891f, 909–11, 915, 947, 950; New Kingdom Egypt, 41, 49, 57f, 59; Nile River valley agriculture, 31, 150; 1973 surprise attack on Israel, 927; Old Kingdom Egypt, 44, 44f, 45m, 62; origins, 402; ouster of Mubarak, 981, 985; patriarchal society in, 40–1, 42; Persia's conquests in, 274; post-WW II officer coup, 909–11; Ptolemaic Egypt, 154, 186, 187–8, 187m, 204, 234; pyramids, 44–5, 44f, 119; religion, spirituality in, 57, 154; rivalry with Kerma, 150; Roman rule of, 190; science and math beginnings in, 59–60; sculpture and paintings, 58–9, 59f; seasonal celebrations, 207; Sphinx, 44f; spread of agriculture from, 46; taxation in, 53; temples in, 33f, 36, 37, 37f; as "the gift of the Nile," 68; trade activities, 46, 65; unification of, 33, 57, 65; urban centers origins, 35–8, 36m; Wafd Party, 866
Egyptian New Kingdom (1550–1070 BCE), 41, 49, 57f, 59
Eiffel, Alexandre Gustave, 805–6
Einstein, Albert, 787f, 809
Eisai (Zen monk), 390
Eisenhower, Dwight D., 895, 897, 933
Elamite-Dravidian language (India), 68

Electricity, technical advances, 794–5
Elements (Euclid), 329
Eliot, George (Mary Ann Evans), 682
El Niño weather phenomenon, 123–4, 125, 825, 826, 831, 832
Empire State Building (New York), 806
Empress Suiko (Japan), 383
Encyclopédie (Diderot), 667–8
Engels, Friedrich, 652f, 787f, 801. *See also Communist Manifesto, The*
England: agricultural expansion, 433; Angevin and Norman kings, 311f; Anglican Church in, 513–14; Anglo-Saxons in, 308; Augustus's rule of, 190; Bank of England, 786; baronial courts, 316; Black Death in, 194; call for industrialism reforms, 803; Calvinism in, 513; centralization of government in, 505, 508; chartism reform movement, 802; Christian conversions in, 308; civil war in, 513–14; claims in France, 333; Constantine's fight with Rome, 193; constitutionalism in, 520; Digger Movement, 923; female scientists in, 500; 15th century political reorganization, 335; Glorious Revolution, 493f, 653, 786; Ice Age influence, 20; Industrial Revolution, 652; interest in China's Ming porcelain, 627; Jews expelled from, 321; legal system in, 312; *Magna Carta,* 311f; male urban literacy rates, 500; Married Woman's Property Act, 805; New Model Army, 514; New Science in, 667; Obscene Publications Bill, 800; opening of passenger railroad, 787f; political recovery of, 315–16, 335; population growth, 797; post-Black Death population recovery, 505; Protestantism in, 509–10, 513; Puritans in, 513–14; racket sports, 806; religious wars, 493f; rise of naval power, 580–1; Royal Society of London, 499, 501; scientific, philosophical developments, 330, 491, 498, 500–1; seizure of Jamaica from Spain, 561f; trade activities, 460; trade unions, 802; traveling theater troupes, 494; wool-production, 318
Enlightenment era, 667–71; advances leading to, 456; American, French, Haitian Revolutions and, 667; categorical imperative, 668–9; defined, 667; economic liberalism, 669; *Encyclopédie* (Diderot), 667–8; explorations of Africa, 832–3; guillotine executions, 661–2; Herder-inspired ethnic version, 671; ideology of progress as legacy of, 785; in Latin America, 689; literature and music, 669; morality, 668; philosophy, 667, 668–9, 670; social contract expansion, 667; timelines placement, 657f
Enmebaragesi of Kish (Mesoptamian King), 39
Entente Cordiale, between Britain and France, 837
Enuma Elish creation myth (Mesopotamia), 33f, 57, 58
Environment: of the Americas, 121, 122m, 123–4; of ancient Middle East, Mediterranean region, 31–3; Chernobyl nuclear accident, 930; climate change performance map, 990f; El Niño phenomenon, 123–4, 825, 826; of Eurasia, 121; greenhouse gases, 963f; Kyoto Protocol agreement, 990–1; limits of modernity, 989–91; of Pacific Islands, 139, 140–1; ritual pollution, 233–4; scientific and political debate, 990–1; sustainability and global warming, 989–90, 993; UN Conferences, 990–1
Epic of Gilgamesh, 57–8
Epistle to the God of Love (Pizan), 337–8
Equal Employment Opportunity Law (Japan), 939
Erasmus, Desiderius, 493
Erdoğan, Recep Tayyip, 979–80
Erligang, capital city (China, Shang period), 106, 113
Erlitou city and palace complex (China), 93f, 98, 99, 102
Erlitou culture (China), 93f, 98–9, 102
Eroica (Beethoven), 657f
Ethiopia: agriculture, 153–4; Amda Seyon, Ethiopian Emperor, 408; animal breeding, 154; Christianity in, 401, 405–9, 565; coastal Muslims, 408–9; fossil discoveries, 4–5, 7, 7f; highlands, 146, 153–4; introduction of coffee, 500; Italy's conquest of, 872; monasteries in, 406; Muslim political control in, 407; Portuguese support vs. Ottomans, 561f, 566; Solomonid Dynasty, 403f, 407–8; state and church in, 406–7; Swahili city-states comparison, 411; timeline placement, 403f; trade activities, 153; Zagwe Dynasty, 403f, 406–7. *See also* Aksum Kingdom; Meroë Kingdom
Ethnic cleansing. *See* Genocide
Ethnic nationalism: Bosnia-Herzegovina issue, 853; in Great Britain, 680–1; in Italy, 674–5; in Serbia, 853; unresolved issues of, 853
Eubanks, Mary, 131
Eucharist, 286
Eugenics (defined), 860–1
Eurasia: Afro-Eurasian global commercial system, 296–8; agrarian-urban patterns, 3, 162, 449, 451, 457, 522; agricultural innovations, 317; China's economic role in, 627, 819; Clovis points (spearhead flutes), 125; early cities in, 119; early human settlements, 5; empire formation in, 149; *H. sapiens* migration to, 94; hominins in, 6; *Homo neanderthalensis* in, 22; Ice Age influence, 20, 21; India's economic role in, 819; intellectual link with Meroë, 153; interactions with sub-Saharan Africa, 147; migrations to, 10–12, 123f; monotheism/monism religion, 147; Neolithic settlements, 75; premodern world ambitions of, 561; religious civilizations in, 270; rise of firearm-equipped infantries, 826; rule by divine grace in, 491; ruling class, 165; similarity to Mali Empire, 561; trade activities, 346m, 724; trade routes, 346m; visionaries of reality in, 147
Euripides (Greek writer), 207
Europe: agricultural revolution, 317–18; anti-globalization movement, 974; Asian migrations to, 18–20; attraction of artisans, merchants, 320; Black Death spread in, 271f, 331–3, 332m; boomerang invention, 24; bourgeoisie social class, 320, 798; bubonic plague in, 194; canon law and medicine, 329; Catholicism in, 403; centers of learning, 499m; challenges of slavery in, 755; China's Ming porcelain in, 627; colonialism of, 525–41; commerce and trade, 318–19, 319m, 335–6, 624; commonwealths, 273; Communist Eastern Europe, 928m; Concert of Europe, 755, 763, 829; Congress of Vienna, 652f, 657f, 671–2; the Crusades, 324–6; early capitalism, cash economy, 319–20; economic innovations, 336; edge gained by using gunpowder, 357; 1800-1900, share of world manufacturing output, 821f; 1871 map, 676m; emigration from, 797–8; exceptionalism, 456–7; exploration of the Americas, 529m; factory towns, 801; 15th century reorganization, 335–8; fossil discoveries in, 17; 14th century crises, 330–5; guilds, growth of, 320; Hundred Years' War, 311f, 333–4, 334m; Ice Age influence, 20, 21; imperialism in Africa, 832–7, 833m; industrial advances (1750–1870), 785–90, 788m; industrial advances (1871–1914), 790–6, 791m; influence on Japan, 723; intellectual, cultural developments, 327–30; Japan's studies of commerce in, 745–6; Jews expelled from, 321; literary achievements, 337–8; management style advances, 807; map (1648), 517m; map (ca. 1560), 471m; maritime empires, 653; Marxism in, 692; medieval science, 329; middle class society, 800; migrations to, 13, 17, 18; Napoleon's failures in, 828; Neanderthal, in Germany, 18, 22, 23; 1914, 1923 map, 857m; 1936 empire map, 865m; nomadic steppe peoples in, 3; onset of "scientific-industrial society," 785; origins of humans in, 7; papal reforms, 321–2; philosophical challenges, 338; political, economic revolts, 657f; political-industrial revolutions in, 653; political recovery of, 315–17; popularization of Christian piety, 322; population movements (1750–1914), 800m; post-Black Death population recovery, 756; post-Carolingian era, 312–13; refugee crisis in, 963f; religious reform, expansion, 321–6; resistance to adaptation, 653; rise of religious civilizations, 270, 273; rising income disparities, 974; rock art in, 17, 17f, 18–20; scientific, philosophical developments, 491; Socialism in, 692; social patterns, 320–1; student demonstrations, 936; technological change in, 475; trading posts in India, 609m; trading posts in Southeast Asia, 609m; uniqueness of, among global civilizations, 786; universities and scholasticism, 328–9; upper class society, 799; uprisings (1750–1815), 674; urban growth, 320; urbanization in, 797; victims of state centralization (1450–1600), 506t; warfare (1450–1750), 507m; working class society, 800–1; in WW II,

848f. *See also* Christian Europe; Crusades (to the Holy Land); Renaissance (European Renaissance); individual countries; specific countries
European-Native American mix, 547
European Union (EU), 962, 963f, 971, 974–5, 986, 990–1
Evans, Mary Ann (George Eliot), 682
Evolutionary theory, 787f, 809
"The Exaltation of Inanna" poem (Enheduanna), 30
Existentialism (defined), 900
Extraterritoriality (defined), 728
Ezana (King of Aksum), 154

Facebook, 961, 984–5
"Facebook Revolution," 985
Factory Act (1833), 803
Factory system developments (1700–1800), 787–8, 789, 801, 803–4
Fan Ye (Chinese historian), 264
Faraday, Michael, 794
Far from the Madding Crowd (Hardy), 811
Fascism, 851, 871–2, 899, 902, 956
Fatimid Dynasty: commercial development, 296–8; defeat of Egypt, 404; maritime trade with India, 404; rebellion vs. Abbasids, 280–1; timeline placement, 275f
Faust (Goethe), 669
Fa Xian (Buddhist monk), 217f
February Revolution (Russia), 854
Federal Reserve Act (1913, U.S.), 680
Federal Trade Commission Act (1914, U.S.), 680
Female infanticide, 364
Feminist movement: de Pizan's literary contribution, 337; emergence of, 12; Empress Wu's contribution, 369; first-wave, second-wave feminism, 937; Pankhurt's contribution, 805; sexual revolution and, 934; third-wave feminism, 937–8; women's liberation movement, 927f, 938–9
Fengjian system (Zhou Dynasty, China), 104, 384
Ferdinand I (King of Spain), 472
Ferdinand II (King of Aragon), 462, 463–4
Ferdinand II (Holy Roman Emperor), 514–15
Ferdinand IV (Spanish King), 318
Fernando VII (King of Spain), 690, 698
Fertile Crescent: agrarian origins in, 2, 3, 31–46; agricultural pioneering in, 30–1; geographic features, 31–2; Natufian culture, 33–4; Ubaid culture, 35, 56
Fertility religion (Harappa), 72
Feudalism: defined, 104, 313–14; manorialism comparison, 314; in post-Carolingian Europe, 255, 314; in Tokugawa Japan, 313; in Zhou China, 104–5, 313
Fichte, Johann Gottlieb, 670
Fieldhouse, David K., 844
Final Solution against Jews (by Nazis), 848f, 853f, 876–7
First Balkan War, 764
First Crusade (to the Holy Land), 275f, 287, 296, 321, 325m
First Emperors Tomb, terra-cotta warriors (China), 250f, 252f
First Opium War (China), 724, 725f, 727, 728, 738
First Ottoman-Russian War, 757f
First Republic of Cartagena, 698
First War of Independence (India), 819f, 821–2, 822f
First-wave feminism, 937–8
Five Treatises (Panchatantra), fables, 205–6
Flaubert, Gustave, 682, 684
Flying shuttle (invention), 787
Foot binding, 364
Foragers (hunters and gatherers): agricultural pioneering by, 30–1; in the Americas, 120–6; Australian Aborigines, 14, 16; in the Caribbean Islands, 138–9; in the eastern Mediterranean region, 31–4; the Inuit, 136; livelihood of, 18; in the Middle East, 31–4; migration from Middle East, 3; Paleolithic foragers, 12; shift to agrarian-urban society, 27, 86, 149; social formation developments, 2, 11, 16; sub-Saharan Africa transition from, 149
Ford, Henry, 861
Fortunate Edict, The (Ottoman Empire), 762
Fossil discoveries: in the Americas, 24–5; Anzick-1 fossil, 25; australopiths, 7; Baltic amber, 24; *H. erectus,* 10; *H. neanderthalensis,* 18, 22; *H. sapiens,* 10, 22, 23, 24, 27; Hadar AL 288-1 ("Lucy"), 4–5, 7; hominins, 2, 7; *Homo floresiensis,* 29; Kaddaba teeth, 7; Kennewick Man, 25; Lucy (Hadar AL 288-1), 4–5, 7, 7f; in North America, 7; in northern Beringia, 24; Orrorin femurs, 7; Paleolithic humans, 18; "Spirit Cave mummy" fossil, 7, 28–9; Toumaï, 2, 6, 7
Fourier, Charles, 802
Four Modernizations (China), 849f, 942–3
Fourth Crusade, 287, 290, 294, 304, 305
France: absolutism in, 516–18; Academy of Medicine, 663; Academy of Sciences, 499; alliance with Ottomans, 471, 762; anti-globalization movement, 974; Arabs, Berbers Iberian conquests, 278; Battle of Tours, 276; Bourbon monarchy, 512, 535–6, 545, 673, 690, 816; Calvinism in, 510–12; Capetian kings, 311f; capitalist democracy in, 848; Catholicism in, 512; centralization of government in, 505, 508; China's treaty port opened with, 729m; Civil Code, legal system, 662; civil war in, 512–13; colonialism, imperialism in Southeast Asia, 839m, 842–4; colonial North America settlements, 538m; colonization of Hispaniola, 535; Committee of Public Safety, 661; Communist Party, 864; conquest of Algeria, 819f, 829, 843; conquest of Vietnam, 819f, 842–4; constitutionalism in, 670, 671; Council of Clermont, 289, 324; Crimean War, 692, 755, 757f, 762, 773, 774, 777, 791, 830; Declaration of the Rights of Man and of the Citizen, 653, 660, 661, 761; defeat of Mamluks, 826f; demesne of, 315; early industrialism in, 789, 791m; Edict of Nantes, 513; Eiffel Tower, 805–6; English claims in, 333; Enlightenment era economic liberalism, 669; *Entente Cordiale* with Britain, 837; Estates-General, National Assembly, 660; female scientists in, 500; 15th century political reorganization, 335; Franco-Prussian War, 675, 790; garnishment of Egyptian tax revenues, 830–1; Haitian Revolution and, 663–5; imperialism in Africa, 836–7; interest in China's Ming porcelain, 627; Latin American exports to, 713; leisure and sports activities, 806; literary achievements, 682, 684; loss of West African trade forts, 834; male urban literacy rates, 500; military forces in Mexico, 704; military loss to Habsburgs, 470; modernity in, 817; monastic reforms, 321; National Assembly, 660, 662; Négritude cultural movement, 861; New Science in, 667; observation of American Revolution, 659; occupation of Morocco, 837; Old Regime, 660; Paris Academy of Sciences, 499; Paris Exposition, 806; Paris Global Climate Agreement, 963f; political recovery of, 315–16, 335; Popular Front coalition, 864; positivism ideology in, 695; post-Black Death population recovery, 505; post-French Revolution revolutions, 673; post-WW I colonialism, 848–9; post-WW I recovery, 863–4; protectorate of Tunisia, 831–2; Renaissance in, 494; restoration of monarchy, 829; rock art discoveries in, 19, 20f; role in Suez Canal construction, 830; scientific, philosophical developments, 491; Seven Years' War, 540, 541, 657f, 658, 659, 826; Sino-Japanese War and, 735; Socialist Party, 864; Society of the Friends of Blacks, 654; Suez War vs. Egypt, 891f; Third Republic, 676, 686–7, 803, 843; Tour de France, bicycle race, 806; treaty of mutual support with Soviets, 875; Triple Intervention against Japan, 723; University of Paris, 311f; victory at Battle of the Pyramids, 826f; war of religion, 493f; weaponry innovations, 506; in World War I, 853–4; in World War II, 875–6; WW I losses, 863
Franciscan religious order, 323, 340, 532, 551–2, 631
Francis of Assisi, Saint, 323
Franco, Francisco, 875
Franco-papal alliance, 310
Franco-Prussian War (1870), 675, 790, 853
Frankish dynasties. *See* Merovingians, Carolingian Empire
Frankish Gaul, 309–10
Frederick I (Holy Roman Emperor), 316, 322, 325
Frederick II (King of Prussia), 316, 322, 493f
French Canada, 540
French East India Company, 605, 608–9
French League of Women's Rights, 805
French Revolution, 652, 652f; Catholic Church and, 660; conditions leading to, 315, 658–9, 667; constitutional monarchy phase, 660; influence on Russia, 772; military consolidation phase, 660, 661; Napoleon's role in ending, 661, 671; National Assembly, 660, 662, 664; Ogé, Vincent, and, 654–5, 664; radical republicanism phase, 660–1; Reign of Terror, 661, 662; storming of the Bastille, 660, 661f; three phases of, 660–1; timeline placement, 657f; use of guillotine, 661–2

Freud, Sigmund, 787f, 809–10
Fugitive Slave Act (U.S.), 587
Fukuyama, Francis, 956
Fulton, Robert, 789

Gagarin, Yuri, 891f, 897
Galilei, Galileo, 457f, 493f, 496–8
Gandhi, Indira, 619, 889
Gandhi, Mohandas K., 823, 825, 867, 912, 952, 961
Ganges valley (India), 79–80, 87, 88, 215, 217f, 224, 233
Gaozu (Han Dynasty ruler), 251
Garibaldi, Giuseppe, 675, 694
Garvey, Marcus, 861
Gatling gun, 796
Gautama (the Buddha or Enlightened One), 224, 226–7, 237f
Gay Liberation Front (GLF), 935
Gay rights movement, 935, 935f
Gender roles and divisions: Assyrian Empire, 293; in China, 109–10, 260–2, 635; in Creole culture, 548; in early human society, 11, 12, 15, 27; in early Middle East society, 40–1; in forager/agrarian-urban society, 12; in the Inca Empire, 450–1; in India, 83–4, 236–7, 609–10; in Latin America, 718; in Mamluk Egypt, 293; in Mayan Kingdoms, 165; of Native Americans, 548; in Paleolithic era, 40; in Timur Empire, 610. *See also* Feminist movement
Genghis Khan, 291, 347, 355–8, 594–6
Genocide: in Africa, 564, 835–6; Final Solution against Jews, 848f, 853f, 876–7; in former Yugoslavia, 849f; Germany vs. the Herero and Nama people, 836; Rape of Nanjing, 853f, 881–2; in Rwanda, 564, 963f; in Yugoslavia, 963f
Geography (Ptolemy), 495
Gerard of Cremona, 329
German Democratic Republic (GDR, East Germany), 895, 898, 931
German Southwest Africa (Namibia), 835–6
Germany: Berlin Conference, 819, 832, 836; Berlin Wall, 849f, 891f, 898, 926, 927f; Bismarck-Wilhelm I's coalition, 675–6; Boxer Rebellion and, 736–7; Brest-Litovsk Treaty, 854; budget-cutting, public savings policies, 974–5; China's treaty port opened with, 729m; Cold War era revolt in East Germany, 895–6; colonialism in East Africa, 835; constitutional assembly, 674; cultural nationalism in, 670–1; early human fossil discoveries, 19; early industrialism in, 789; East Germany, 895, 896, 898, 931; erection of Berlin Wall, 891; expansionist aspirations, 852; fear of the Ottomans, 465; female scientists in, 500; Frederick I, reign of, 325; genocide of Herero and Nama people, 836; imperialism in Southeast Asia, 839m; imperial rivalry with Britain, 763; Latin American exports to, 713; Maji Maji rebellion, East Africa, 835–6; male urban literacy rates, 500; Marshall Plan and, 893; Nazism ideology in, 851; New Science in, 667; papal influence in, 508; Peasants' War, 493f; political recovery of, 316–17; post-Black Death population recovery, 505; post-WW I supremacist nationalism, 849; pre-WW I rise to power, 837; quest for *Lebensraum* (living space), 854, 874, 875; Renaissance in, 494; rock art in, 18–19; Schlieffen Plan, 853; scientific, philosophical developments, 491; Second German Empire, 676; Thirty Years' War, 490, 514–16; Treaty of Brest-Litovsk, 854; Triple Intervention against Japan, 723; unification of, 657f, 849f, 927f; Union of German Women's Organizations, 805; uprisings in, 674; Versailles Treaty and, 856; Weimar Republic, 872–3; WW II participation, 872–7; WW I participation, 837, 853–4; WW I reparations, 863. *See also* German Democratic Republic (GDR, East Germany); Hitler, Adolf; Nazi Germany
Ghana Kingdom: conversions to Islam, 419; origins of, 151, 417, 418; quest for independence, 918–19; trade activities, 418–19; traditional African spirituality in, 419
Ghaznavid Sultanate, India, 346–7
Gilded Age, United States, 679
Gimbutas, Marija, 12
Ginsberg, Allen, 922–3
Giza pyramids (Egypt), 44, 44f
Glasnost policy (Soviet Union), 849f, 927f, 928–31
Global expansion (1990s), 962–71; global financial crisis and recovery, 970; globalization and poor countries, 971; Russia's crisis and recovery, 970–1; 2012, global distribution of wealth, 963m
Globalization: anti-globalization movements, 974; criticism of, 966; defined, 965; Israel's technological, scientific developments, 977; Middle East rejection of, 976; and poor countries, 971; U.S. technological renewal and, 965–6
Global shifts (21st century): African transformations, 985–7; Arab Spring, 849f, 961, 963f, 976–7, 980–2, 984, 991; ascent of Turkey, 979–80; growth of Hezbollah, 977; Iranian ambitions, 982; Israel and Gaza, 977–8; Latin American expansion, 987–8; Middle East/Islamism, 961, 976, 986; rise of India's middle class, 983–5; social networking, 984–5; Western unease, 973–5; Yugoslavian civil war, 975–6
Global warming, 989–90, 993
Glorious Revolution (England), 493f, 653, 786
Glorious Victories of Amda Seyon, The (Seyon, Ethiopian Emperor), 408
Glyphic alphabet, Mayans, 151f, 163, 165–6, 167f
Göbekli Tepe sanctuary (Anatolia), 56
Go-Daigo (Japanese Emperor), 385
Goethe, Johann Wolfgang von, 669
Goodyear, Charles, 794
Gorbachev, Mikhail, 928, 929–33
Gothic cathedrals, 326–7
Government of India Act (Britain), 867
Granada Kingdom: Christian conquest of, 460; forced Jewish conversions, 463; Mamluk embassy in, 462–3; morisco revolt in, 473; Spain's conquest of, 456f, 461f, 462–3; timeline placement, 271f
Gran Chaco (geographic region), 123
Grand National Consolidated Trades Union, 802
Gray, Tom, 4
Great Britain: alliance against Napoleon, 662; alliance with Ottomans, 762; American Revolution, 652f, 656–8, 667; antiforeign activism in, 975; Berlin Airlift with U.S., 893; Brexit decision to leave the EU, 963f; British North America map, 657m; Calico Acts, 786; capital investments in Latin America, 719; capitalist democracy in, 848; chartism, reform movement, 802; China's treaty ports opened, 729m; "coal and colonies" theory about, 786; Coercive Acts, 658; colonialism in Australia, 825–7; colonialism in India, 818–25, 819f, 820m, 823m; colonial North American settlements, 538m, 540; conflicts with China, 727–8; constitutionalism in, 520–1, 652–3, 670, 676–7, 680–1; containment policy, 829–30; control of South Africa, 823; Corn Laws, repeal of, 680; Crimean War participation, 692, 755, 757f, 762, 773, 774, 777, 791, 830; direct rule of India, 822–5; dismantling of East India Company, 822; "divide and rule" tactics in India, 823–5; early industrialism in, 785–9, 788m, 790; as Eastern Hemisphere colonial power, 817; Enlightenment era economic liberalism, 669; *Entente Cordiale* with France, 837; ethnic nationalism in, 680–1; extraterritoriality imposed on China, 728; Factory Act, 803; factory system in, 787–8; Glorious Revolution, England, 493f, 653, 786; Government of India Act, 867; Great Game against Russia in Asia, 829–30; Great Reform Bill, 680; House of Commons, 316, 335, 514, 590, 786; House of Lords, 316, 748; imperialism in Africa, 836–7; imperialism in Egypt, 830–1; imperialism in Southeast Asia, 839m; imperialism in Sudan, 831; imperial rivalry with Germany, 763; Indian Army of Great Britain, 823; industrialism (1750–1870), 785–9, 788m; Industrial Revolution, 624, 652, 653; Japan's alliance with, 725f; Latin American exports to, 713; leisure and sports activities, 806–7; maritime trade of, 609; Middle East role, 18th-early 19th centuries, 827–8; military advisory role for Ottomans, 827–8; military forces in Mexico, 704; Mines Act of 1842, 803; nation-state building, 680–1; Newcomen steam engines in, 792; new technologies, power sources, 787; nontariff autonomy of China, 728; occupation of Egypt, 819f; onset of "scientific–industrial society," 785; and opium trade with China, 727, 819; opium wars with China, 725f, 821; post-WW I colonialism, 848; post-WW I recovery, 863–4; promise of Palestine to Arabs, 853f, 864–5; promise of Palestine to Jews, 853f, 864–5; railroads, 789; rising influence in India, 595f; Second

Reform Act, 680–1; Seven Years' War, 540, 541, 657f, 658, 659, 826; shipping of convicts to Australia, 819f; Sino-Japanese War and, 735; 1600-1700 population growth data, 786; social, cultural capital of, 786–7; social contract theory, 652–3; steel manufacturing in, 790; Suez War vs. Egypt, 891f; tax system reforms, 659; Ten Hours Act, 803; Thatcher's leadership, 973; trade activities, 690, 789, 834; Treaty of Nanjing with China, 728, 730; Welsh nationalism in, 680; in WW I, 853–4. *See also* England

Great Depression (U.S.), 837, 848f, 849, 851, 853f, 861–2, 970

Great Leap Forward (China), 849f, 891f, 907

Great Proletarian Cultural Revolution (China), 941–2

Great Rebellion (India), 819f, 821–2

Great Reform Bill (1832, Great Britain), 680

Great Reform *(Taika)* in Japan, 383

Great Western Schism (Latin Christendom), 334, 336m

Great Zimbabwe Kingdom (South Africa), 271f, 403f, 409, 415, 416m, 564

Greco-Roman tradition, 309

Greece: Alexander's quest for unification, 179, 210–11; alphabet invention, 53f, 54; Antigonid Greece, 154, 186, 189; aristocrats-tyrants conflicts, 54–5; artistic achievements, 58–9, 206, 207–8; Athens, city-state, 53, 55, 183–5; chiefly assemblies tradition, 421; city-states in, 3, 183; constitutional rule in, 184–5; Cyrus II the Great conquests, 180; divine and heroic myths in, 205; emigrations to Middle East, 186; First Balkan War participation, 764; Greek theater, 207; Hellenistic period, 186; independence from the Ottomans, 652f, 757f, 761; literary achievements, 207; maritime commercial wealth of, 185; mathematics advances, 238–9; military victories against Achaemenids, 185; Mycenaean palace-states in, 33f; Olympic Games, 1896, 806; oracles in, 183; Persian Empire's interactions with, 179–86; *phalanx* military tactic, 55; philosophical schools in, 204; raid of Mycenaean palace-states, 54; repulsion of Persian invasions, 185; rise of artistic creativity, 206; Russian role as coreligionist, protector, 829; sixth century BCE political reforms, 55; sixth century map, 183m; Sparta, city-state, 53, 55, 183–5; spread of agriculture to, 46; trade activities, 54; women in democratic Athens, 212–13

Greek philosophy, 200, 204

Greenhouse gases, 963f

Gregorian Calendar, 164

Gregory I (Pope), 308, 309, 311, 311f

Gregory VII (Pope), 322

Gregory XI (Pope), 334

Grimm, Jakob, 670f

Grimm, Wilhelm, 670f

Gromyko, Andrei, 927f

Grosseteste, Robert, 330

Guanajuato silver mine, Mexico, 541

Guatemala, 711, 902, 904

Guericke, Otto von, 502f

Guerrero, Vicente, 701–2

Guevara, Ernesto "Che," 937

Guilds, growth of, in Europe, 320

Guillotin, Joseph Ignace, 662–3

Guillotine ("decapitation machine"), 661–2

Gulag system, Russia, 898–9

Gülen, Fethullah, 980

Gunpowder, 356–7

Gunpowder empires, 357, 611

Gun running, British North America, 581

Gupta Empire (India), 220–2; artistic, literary achievements, 237–8; Chandragupta II's leadership, 221; Chandragupta I's leadership, 220; court and culture in, 221; decline of, 217f, 222; Huns invasion of, 194; map, 221m; marriage of state and religion in, 216; origins of, 220; reunification of India, 147f, 217f; rule during "golden age," 344; Samudragupta's leadership, 220–1

Gustavus II Adolphus (King of Sweden), 515

Gu Yanwu (Qing philosopher), 637

Gwalfor, Battle of, 217f

Haas, Jonathan, 118

Habsburg Empire: artistic achievements, 486; Austrian Habsburgs, 461f; *auto-da-fé* ("act of faith") in, 484; Catherine II's dismantling of, 770; centralized state formation, 479, 504; Christian conversions in, 526; Christian state festivities, 484; conflicts with Ottomans, 756; distractions of, 470–1; gold financing of imperial expansion, 526; losses in conflicts, 472; military overextensions of, 756–7; military spending, 475; money economy in, 479; opposition to Russian expansionism, 852; origins, 456, 460; peace treaty with Ottomans, 461f; popular festivities, 484–5; possession of Austria, Bohemia, Hungary, 472; public festivities, 481; rise of, 470; theatre and literature, 485–6; victory against France, 470; victory over Ottomans, 461f

Hadar AL 288-1 fossil ("Lucy"), 4–5, 6f, 7–8

Hagia Sophia ("Holy Wisdom"), 195–6

Haiti: belief in equal rights, 653; colonization, 139; Ogé's imprisonment and torture, 654–5; slave revolt, 664–5

Haitian Revolution, 652, 652f, 663–4, 665m, 667, 689, 691f

Halifax Gibbet (guillotine), 661

Hamas, Islamic guerilla organization, 963f, 976, 977–8

Hammurabi (Babylonian King), 40, 42–3. *See also* Law Code of Hammurabi

Han Dynasty (China), 190; "Armies of the Green Standard" in, 628; bureaucratic, political structure, 251; civilian administration, 191; Confucianism in, 350; conquests of, 373; decline of, 253, 374; "dynastic cycle," 104; Former, 245f, 252–3; government system, 243; Han-Confucian synthesis, 262–3; headmen in, 251; history writing during, 263–4; invention of paper, 320; Latter, 245f, 252–3; map, 252m; metropolitan growth, 168, 190; naming of, 251; North Korea occupied by, 373; printing advancements, 380; religion, spirituality in, 271; shipbuilding in, 466; Silk Road trading link, 232; sinicizing of nomadic peoples, 252; technological developments, 259f; uneven growth in, 351; Wang Mang, Red Eyebrow Revolt, 252–3, 263; Wudi, the Martial Emperor, 188, 251–4, 253–4, 259, 265

Han Fei (Chinese legalism theorist), 245f, 247, 249

Han-gul phonetic writing system (Korea), 373f, 378

Hanseatic League, 336, 505

Hanshu (The History of the Former Han) (Ban Gu and Ban Biao), 263

Hara-kiri (ritual suicide), 385

Harappa: archaeological discoveries, 64–5, 71; architectural uniformity in, 69–70; burial rituals, 72–3; cesspits (toilets), 70; civilization timeline, 67f, 69m; collapse of cities, 73–4; comparison to Mesopotamia, 68; culture of, 3; decimal system development, 70–1; diet, 70; domestication of animals, 74; geographic features, 66; government, 78–9; language groups, 70–1; Lothal seaport, 70, 72, 73f; religion, 71f, 72–3; trade networks, 65, 71–2; vanished origins of, 65–74; writing system, 65

Hardy, Thomas, 811

Harlem Renaissance (U.S.), 860–1

Harold (Saxon King of England), 308m

Harsha Vardhana regime (India), 344–5, 344m, 345f

Harvesters, The (Brueghel), 495f

Hasan ibn Muhammad al-Wazzan al-. *See* Leo Africanus

Hasmonean (Maccabean) Kingdom, 182f

Hatshepsut (female "Pharaoh" in New Kingdom Egypt), 41

Hausa Kingdoms (Africa), 561, 563, 951

Haussmann, Georges, 805

Havel, Vaclav, 931

Hay, John, 735–6

Hebrew Bible (Old Testament), 53, 58

Hegel, Georg Wilhelm Friedrich, 803

Hegemony system (defined), 105

Heian period (Japan), 270f, 370, 373f, 377, 383–4, 384m, 387–9

Heliocentric theory (Copernicus), 493f

Hellenistic period, Greece, 186

Hendrix, Jimi, 936f

Henry III (King of Navarre), 512

Henry IV (King of France), 493f, 512–13

Henry the Navigator, 564–5

Henry VIII (King of England), 510

Heraclitus (Greek philosopher), 200, 274

Herder, Johann Gottfried, 670–1

Herodotus (Greek historian), 263

Hertz, Heinrich Rudolf, 795

Herzegovina, 763

Herzl, Theodor, 865

Hesiod (Greek writer), 207

Hezbollah terrorist organization, 976, 977, 978, 982

Hideyoshi, Toyotomi: Battle of Sekigahara, 639–40; dreams of conquering China, 621; military campaigns of, 620–1, 625, 638, 639, 640m; withdrawal to Japan, 621

Hieratic style of art, 210
Hieroglyphic writing, Egypt, 44, 44f, 52
Hindenburg, Paul von, 874
Hinduism: Aurangzeb's destruction of temples, 603–4; avatars and alvars, 230; Classical period, 84; description, 221; devotional branches, 222; dominance in India, 222, 344, 821; family life and, 235–6; Ganges River bathing ritual, 86f; Islam's origins and, 278; Muslim problems with nakedness in, 349; origins, 65, 72–3, 221, 270; permeation in India, 88; persecution of Sikhs, 349; sacred texts of, 74, 76, 77–8, 88, 222; Shakti and tantra, 230–1; temple carvings, 71f; term derivation, 84
Hindu-Muslim interactions, 345
Hindu Rajputs, 347, 596–8, 618, 824
Hindustan (northern India), 594, 597–8
"Hippies" movement (1960s), 936
Hiroshige, Ando, 648
Hispaniola: African slaves in, 561f; colonization, 139; Cortés's settling on, 526–7; French colonization in, 535; Las Casas's emigration to, 526; trade activities, 543–4
Hitler, Adolf, 74; eugenics and, 861; failed invasion of Soviet Union, 876; Final Solution against Jews, 848f, 853f, 876–7; invasion of Soviet Union, 876; *Mein Kampf* autobiography, 873–4, 876; Munich Agreement, 875; Mussolini's association with, 872; occupation of Sudetenland, 875; quest for *Lebensraum*, 854, 874, 875; rise to power, 853f, 861, 873–5. *See also* Nazi Germany
Hittite Empire: clash with Egypt, 49; collapse of, 52; empire building, 47–9; geographic reach of, 47, 48m; "great kings" self-labeling, 47–8; iron making mastery in, 47, 49, 152; map, 48m; military preparedness, 47, 48; origins, 33f; use of chariots, 47
Hoabinhian culture, 391–2
Hobbes, Thomas, 503, 667
Hobsbawm, Eric, 652
Ho Chi Minh (Vietnamese leader), 916, 917, 925, 937
Hofmann, Hans, 901f
Hokusai, Katsushika, 648
Holocaust of World War II, 876–7, 877f, 886, 889
Homer (Greek writer), 207
Hominins: archaeological discoveries, 4; Ardi *(Ardipithecus ramidus)*, 7, 27; australopiths, 7, 8, 29; bipedalism of, 7; defined, 6; dietary patterns, 9; discovery of Lucy (Hadar AL 288-1), 4–5, 7, 7f; *Homo erectus*, 6, 7, 7f, 8–11, 14f, 19, 30, 31; hunting patterns, 11; livelihood of, 11; Toumaï, 2
Homo erectus (Upright Human), 6, 7, 7f, 8–11, 14f, 19, 30, 31
Homo floresiensis, 29
Homo neanderthalensis (Neanderthals), 18, 21–3, 28
Homo sapiens: anatomical modernity of, 13; boomerang invention, 24; cave paintings of, 22; cultural creativity of, 18–19; cultural foundations of, 13; dietary patterns, 11; dwellings of, 11; emergence in East Africa, 2; environmental adaptability of, 13, 18, 22, 24; hunting skills, 23; interbreeding with Neanderthals, 23, 28; mental life development, 12–13; migration patterns, 14f, 15, 17, 18, 25, 94, 120; Neanderthal comparisons with, 18, 23; origins, 2, 7, 10, 11, 13, 94; relation to *H. erectus*, 9, 10; Siberian *H. sapiens*, 25; symbols created by, 12–13; toolmaking skills, 11, 12, 13, 28; tools and toolmaking, 11, 12, 13, 18, 28; weaponry development, 22
Hongwu Emperor (Japan), 621
Hoover, Herbert, 862
Hopewell culture, North America, 137, 138m
Hoplites (foot soldiers), 180
Hospitalers (monastic fighting order), 460
Hou Hanshu (The History of the Latter Han), 264
House Committee on Un-American Activities, 895, 922
Household slavery, 567
House of Burgesses (colonial America), 540
House of Commons (Britain), 316, 335, 514, 590, 786
House of Lords (Great Britain), 316, 748
Howl and Other Poems (Ginsberg), 922–3
Huainan zi (Confucian document), 262
Huangdi (China's "Yellow Emperor"), 97
Huang Zongxi (Qing philosopher), 637
Hughes, Langston, 860–1
Huguenots (Protestants), 512
Humanism, 492
Human origins, 2–29; African origins, 2, 5; bipedalism of, 7; Crô-Magnon humans, 18; DNA and, 5, 18, 22–5, 27; empires, 2, 3; environmental adaptability, 6, 7–8, 13; *Homo erectus*, 6, 7, 9, 14f; *Homo floresiensis*, 29; Ice Age crisis, 20–1, 21m; Kennewick Men, 7, 25–6, 27, 124; migrations from Africa, 2, 5, 7, 13, 14m; migrations to Australia, 14–17; migrations to Beringia, 25; migrations to Europe, 13, 18–20, 19; migrations to the Americas, 20–7, 26m; Neanderthals, 18, 21, 22–3, 28. *See also* Fossil discoveries; Hominins; *Homo sapiens;* Paleolithic (Old Stone Age) era
Human sacrifices: Aztecs, 441, 450-1; Chavin de Huántar, 133; Ince, 429; Mayan Kingdoms, 169, 434; Moche chiefdom, 171; Tula, 432; Xia and Shang dynasties, 113
Humayan (Mughal Sultan), 596–7, 600, 612, 614, 619
Hunas (White Huns), 222
Hundred Days of Reform (China), 725f, 736
Hundred Flowers campaign (China), 906
Hundred Years' War, 311f, 333–4, 334m
Hungary: Cold War era revolt, 896–7; as Eastern Bloc country, 898; Kádár's reforms, 928; nationalists rise to power, 975; Ottoman conquests in, 468; uprisings in, 674, 927–8
Huns: development as raiding, fighting forces, 594; India invaded by, 194; migrations to northern India, 217f; Sasanid Empire invaded by, 194
Hunting technology, in the Americas, 124–5
Hurrians, 48
Hurston, Zora Neale, 860–1
Husák, Gustáv, 928, 931
Huss, John, 337
Hussein, Saddam, 950, 966–7
Hussein (Algerian ruler), 816
Hutchinson, Anne, 553
Hutu genocide, 564

Iberia: Christian apocalyptic explorations, 460, 462; Christian expansion, 460, 462–4; fight against Muslim rule, 460; Franciscan and military orders of, 460; land grants for military leaders, 475; Napoleon's occupation of, 689–90, 693; natural sciences, 498; Second Coming of Christ preparations, 460, 462
Ibn Abdallah, Muhammad Ahmad, 831
Ibn Abd al-Wahhab, Muhammad, 760
Ibn Battuta, Abu Abdallah, 354, 358, 359m, 411–12, 465
Ibn Khaldun, Abd al-Rahman, 299
Ibn Munqidh, Usama, 293
Ibn Musa al-Khwarizmi, Muhammad, 458
Ibn Qasim, Muhammad, 342–3
Ibn Rushd (Averroës), 299
Ibn Sina. *See* Avicenna
Ibn Taymiyya, Taqi al-Din, 306–7
Ibn Tughluq, Muhammad ("Muhammad the Bloody"), 347–9
Ibrahim Lodi (Sultan), 595
ICBMs (intercontinental ballistic missiles), 897, 925
Ice Age: art, 21f; Beringia land bridge, 24–5, 26m, 27; crisis, 20–1, 21m; death of large mammals, 127–8; ending of, 2, 23, 27, 32, 33, 150; land bridge connections, 15, 24; living conditions, 24; map, 21m; origins, 2f; post-Ice Age thaw, 27
Ieyasu, Tokugawa, 639, 640–1
Ife Kingdom (West African rain forest), 270f, 403f, 422–3, 424
Imperialism: by the Aksum Kingdom, 154; by the Aztecs, 441, 450; by China, 724–37, 734, 750, 751; by Egypt, 48, 49, 179; by France, 763–4; by Great Britain, 681, 763–4; by the Incas, 450; by Japan, 750, 751; Lenin's comment on, 844; Marxism on, 940; in the Mediterranean, 146; in the Middle East, 146, 470, 475; 1914, global competitive imperialism, 828m; by the Ottomans, 470, 475, 756–9; by Persia, 185; by the Roman Empire, 182f. *See also* New Imperialism
Import-substitution industrialization (defined), 696
Impression, Sunrise (Monet), 787f, 811
Impressionist art movement, 811–12
Inca Empire (Andes): adobe houses for ruling class, 449; Atahualpa's rule of, 527f, 529–30; ceremonial centers, 442; communications structure, 446; consolidation, 445–6; founding myth of, 443; government administration, 443–4; imperial expansion, 443; map, 442m; military organization, 429, 442, 444–6; mummy veneration, 451–2; origins, 429; road networks, 445f, 446; ruling class, gender relations, 450–1; smallpox epidemic, 529; Spain's conquests in, 526, 527f, 528–30; timeline placement, 431f;

use of *quipu* communication system, 131; weaponry of, 444–5
India, 214–41; agrarian-urban society, 2, 3, 72–3, 83, 88–9, 215, 240, 554, 633; ahimsa doctrine, 219, 225–6; Alexander's invasion of, 186, 210-11, 214–15; ancient republics of, 240–1; Arab incursions into, 348; architectural achievements, 592m, 593, 595f, 601, 613, 615–16; artistic achievements, 614–15; Battle of Plassey, 819f; *bhakti* sects, 264; Bharatiya Janata Party, 983; Britain's rising influence in, 595f; British "divide and rule" tactics, 823–5; British "new imperialism" in, 818–25, 820m, 823m; Buddhist archaeological sites, 64; burial sites and customs, 592–3; caste system, 67f, 76–7, 82–6, 88, 230, 231, 233–6, 754; Christian missionaries in, 821; civil service system, 822–5; collapse of cities in, 73–4; collapse of "golden age," 344; commonwealths, 273; Congress Party, 823; conquests of Babur, 347, 595–6; cultural interactions, 84–6; culture clashes within, 343–9; Da Gama's journey to, 456f, 461f, 464, 472, 604; Dalai Lama's flight to, 940; Delhi Sultanate, 271f, 345f, 347, 348m; dharma and social class, 82–3; direct British rule of, 822–5; East India Company expansion, 818; East India Railway, 64; economics in Islamic India, 348–9; economy, 231–3; 1800-1900, share of world manufacturing output, 821f; empire consolidation in, 146; as Eurasian economic engine, 819; European trading posts, 609m; family life in, 81–4, 235–6, 609–10; First War of Independence, 819f, 821–2, 822f; Gandhi's push for self-rule, 823, 825, 867; Ganges valley states, 79–80, 82, 87, 88, 215, 217f, 224, 233; gender roles and divisions, 83–4, 236–7, 609–10; geographic features, 66–8, 67m; Ghaznavid Sultanate, 346–7; gods and priests, 84–5; Harappan culture in, 3; Harsha Vardhana regime, 344–5, 344m, 345f; Hinduism in, 67f, 85, 87, 222, 344; Hindu-Muslim interactions, 345; Hindu Rajputs, 347, 596–8, 618, 824; Hindustan, 594, 597–8; Huns invasion of, 194; independence gained by, 848f, 866–7, 891f, 911–13; Indira Gandhi's leadership, 619, 889; Indo-European migration to, 67f; innovators, visionaries in, 243; invasion patterns, 65; Islam in, 346–8; Islam religion in, 344; Kosala, state, 216, 220; literary achievements, 237–8, 613–14; Lodi Sultans, 595–6; Maghada, state, 214, 216–17, 220, 231; Maratha wars, 602, 604, 616, 618; maritime trade, 219, 232, 346, 404, 789; maritime trade with Fatimids, 404; mathematical innovations in, 204, 238–9, 611–12; Mehrgarh Neolithic culture, 67f, 68; migration patterns, 65; military of, 594–5, 597, 599–601, 604, 606, 617; Mohenjo-Daro culture, 65, 68–70, 70m, 71f, 73; monsoon cycle in, 66–8, 67m; Muslim trading, 345f; nabobs, 818–19; National Congress, 822–3; Nehru's leadership, 889, 912–13; new middle class, 983–5; Northern India interactions, 74–81; Pallava Kingdom, 217f, 220, 222, 345, 345f; Punjab state, 215, 224, 233; Rajputanas Kingdom, 222; Rajputs of India, 347, 596, 618, 824; Rashtakutra state, 345; regional struggles, 223; religion, 65, 84–6; resources of, 457; reunification under Gupta Empire, 147f, 217f; rice domestication, 70, 78–9, 82, 92, 608; rulership ideology, 80–1; sacred texts, 65, 67f, 85, 87; Sanskrit language, 67f; Sasanid imperialism in, 155; science in, 238–9, 611–12; Sepoy Mutiny, 653f, 819f, 821–2, 827; shipbuilding in, 466f; *smriti* law codes, 83; society and family in, 81–4; southern India states, 345; South India dynasties, 217f, 222–3, 345, 346m; spice trade of, 566; state formation patterns, 215–23; stone tool discoveries, 10; subalterns in, 824–5; Sufism in, 349; Tang maritime trade with, 350; taxation in, 79, 217, 219, 231–2, 345–6, 348, 818; temple complexes, 222–3; textile trade, 610, 780; Timur's activities in, 594; topography of, 66; trade activities, 71; trade and expansion, 217, 219, 222, 225, 228, 231–5; Tughluq Dynasty, 348; unification of, 216; urbanization in, 225; Vajjian Confederacy, 79–80; Vedic religion in, 57, 67f, 74–8, 80–1, 83–8; Vijayanagar ("City of Victory") state, 271f, 345–6; Zheng He's voyages to, 623f. *See also* Aryans; Gupta Empire; Harappa; Hinduism; Indus Valley; Jainism; Mauryan Empire; Mohenjo-Daro; Mughal Empire; Northern India; Sikhs and Sikhism; Vedas; Vedic society
Indian Army of Great Britain, 823
Indian National Congress, 825
Indian Ocean trade route, 461m
Indian Removal Act (1830, U.S.), 679
Indian sacred texts: Bhagavad Gita, 81, 82; Puranas, 81; *Rig-Veda*, 74, 76–8, 88; Upanishads, 67f, 85–6
Indochina, 753, 842–3, 916
Indonesia: contacts with Africa, 159; Dutch colonialism in, 819f, 837–40; Dutch cultivation system in, 839; *H. floresiensis* in, 29; *H. sapiens* in, 25; independence gained by, 911; land bridges connections, 15, 24; migrations to, 13, 139, 159, 380, 571; monsoon system, 66; Sukarno's leadership, 889; trade activities, 141, 159–60, 345, 571, 623–4, 845; volcanic eruptions in, 194
Indulgences, religious (defined), 509
Industrialism (1750–1914), in Belgium, 789; calls for reforms, 803, factory system, 787–8; in France, 789; in Germany, 789; global commerce, 789; in Great Britain, 785–9, 788m; power sources, 787; preconditions for, 786; social and economic impact, 797–807; child labor, 801; criticism of, 801–3; demographic changes, 797–8; electricity, sanitation improvements, 805–6; European migrations, 800m; factory towns, 801; improved standards of living, 803–5; improved urban living, 805–6; industrial society, 798–801; inquiries and reforms, 803; intellectual, cultural responses to, 808–10; large firms, growth of, 806–7; leisure time and sports, 806; literature and the arts, 811–12; management style advances, 807; middle class society, 801; philosophy and religion, 810–11; population growth, 797; scientific developments, 808–10; socialists' criticism of, 802–3; technological advances, 787; trade unions, 802; transportation, 789; upper class society, 799; urbanization, 797; women's suffrage movement, 804–5; working class society, 801–2
Industrialism (1871–1914), 790–7; chemical manufacturing, 793–4; communication revolution, 795; electricity, development and applications, 794–5; excavation projects, 793–4; "hygiene revolution," 794; in Japan, 791; in Russia, 791; steel manufacturing, 790–2; weaponry advances, 795–6; world population growth, 798–9m
Industrial Revolution, 457, 491, 624, 652, 653
Indus Valley: Arab-Persian conquest of, 275f; archaeological discoveries, 64–6, 71, 74; cultural interactions, 84; flourishing period, 65; geographic features, 67, 73–4; Mehrgarh culture in, 68; religion in, 72, 73; social system, 84; trade activities, 71; transition to agrarian center, 86, 89; urban life adaptations, 68–73
Information technology (IT), 965
Innocent III (Pope), 325
Inquiry into the Nature of Causes of the Wealth of Nations (Smith), 669
Institutes of the Christian Religion (Calvin), 510
Institutional Revolutionary Party (Partido Revolucionario Institucional, PRI), 868
Institutions (instructional textbook), Roman Empire, 195
Intercontinental ballistic missiles (ICBMs), 897, 925
Internet, 795, 965–6, 981, 984–5
Interpretation of Dreams, The (Freud), 787f, 809
Inuit culture, 123f, 135–6
Investiture Controversy (Papacy), 321–2
Ionia, 54, 55, 181
Iran: aborted Constitutional Revolution, 769; Ahmadinejad's presidency, 978; Arab conquest of, 275f; Buyid Shiite Dynasty, 410, 766; CIA-inspired coup, 891f; geographic features, 33; Islamic Revolution in, 949–50; Judaism in, 198; overthrow of Shah of Iran, 849f, 927f; Parthian victory in, 188; Persian palaces in, 182; Qajar Dynasty, 765, 768–9, 780; Rouhani's presidency, 978; Safavid Persian rule in, 765, 766, 768–9; Timur's activities in, 594; U.S. nuclear agreement with, 963f; Western challenge, 765, 768–9. *See also* Safavid Persian Empire; Sasanid Persian Empire
Iraq: Arab conquest of, 275f; early agricultural settlements, 31; ISIS jihadist movement in, 963f; maritime trade, 404; military slaves' rise to power 760; origins, 402; UN weapons inspections, 967; U.S. invasion of, 963f, 966–7. *See also* Abbasid Dynasty; Sasanid Persian Empire

Ireland, 308–9, 493f, 514, 680, 797, 827
Iron Age, 3, 49, 159
Isabella (Queen of Castille), 462, 463–4
ISIS (Islamic State in Iraq and al-Sham) jihadist movement, 963f, 982–3
Islamic civilization: adaptations to, 409–18; architectural achievements, 301; artistic expressions, 300–1; commonwealth period, 273, 281m, 476; continuing vitality of, 457; heights of, 291–8; Ibn Battuta's travels in, 465; in India, 346–8; influence on Ottoman Empire, 755; intellectual, scientific expressions, 298–300; Iranian-Islamic revolution, 949–50; literary achievements, 300–1; Mughal domination of, 468–70; in Mughal Empire, India, 613; in Nubia, 404–5; origins of, 274–6; Ottoman domination of, 468–70; prohibition of enslavement, 476; Ramadan observance, 279, 481–2, 816, 927, 937; religious civilization formation, 273–81; scientific achievements, 299–300; Sharia law, 279–80, 305, 306–7, 476, 603, 761, 948, 986; Shiite Islam, 280; state-religion separation, 279–80; Sunni Islam, 275f, 280, 305–6; in West Africa, 401; writing paper introduction, 493. *See also* Byzantine Empire; Fatimid Dynasty; Islam religion; Mamluk Egypt; Seljuk Empire
Islamic Sufi brotherhood, 831
Islamism, 961, 976, 986
Islamist terrorism, 967
Islam religion: in Africa, 834m; al-Hajj Umar's rejuvenation of, 834–5; in India, 344; Mongol conversions to, 357; Mukhtar, Umar (Quran teacher), 836–7; in Nubian Kingdom, 402; origins, 270, 277–9; Ramadan observance, 279, 481–2, 816, 927, 937; Sunni-Sufi Islam, 299, 300; theology and origins, 277–9; umma community, 278. *See also* Muhammad (Prophet of Islam); Quran; Shiite Islam; Sunni Islam
Israel: Arab-Israeli War (1948), 848f, 891f; Arab-Israeli War (1967), 848f, 891f, 927f, 946–8, 946f, 947m; Arab-Israeli War (1973), 927f, 947m; Balfour Declaration, 865; founding of, 848f, 891f; invasion of Gaza and, 977–8; 1947-1949 conflict with Palestine, 908–9; Suez War vs. Egypt, 891f; technological, scientific developments, 977; war against Hamas, 963f. *See also* Jews and Judaism
Israelite Ark of the Covenant, 407
Israelites, 33f, 52, 53
Isthmus Declaration (Rome), 189
Italian Combat Squad (of Mussolini), 871
Italy: artistic achievements, 494; Charles V's invasion of, 459; city-states in, 183; conquests of, 872; Copernicus's studies in, 496; depression in, 872; early industrialism in, 791m; ethnic nationalism in, 674–5; fascist ideology in, 851, 871–2; fear of the Ottomans, 465, 468; imperialism in East Africa, 836; invasion of Tripolitania, 764; Lateran Accords, 872; male urban literacy rates, 500; Mussolini's march on Rome, 853f; Norman conquest of, 318; post-Black Death population recovery, 505; post-WW I supremacist nationalism, 849; revolt against Roman imperialism, 189–90; unification of, 182f, 657f, 674; uprisings in, 674; violent revolutionary organizations, 937
Ito Hirobumi, 722–3, 746

Jainism: atheistic element of, 226; egalitarian influence of, 230; in Gupta Empire, 222; influences on caste system, 231, 235; origins, 65, 217f, 224, 225; religious practices, 225–6
Jamaica, 407–8, 535, 555, 561f, 575, 587, 663
James, Henry, 684
Jamestown, Virginia, settlement (North America), 457f, 527f, 537, 539, 577–8
Janissaries (military troops), 476, 478, 480, 757, 760–1, 765, 826
Japan: adoption of written Chinese, 243; agrarian-urban society, 398, 650; agricultural advances, 387; Ainu culture, 27, 27f; alliance with Great Britain, 725f; annexation of Manchuria, 853f; artistic achievements, 385, 647; Ashikaga shogunate, 373f, 638–9; atomic bombing by U.S., 889, 890f; Boxer Rebellion and, 736; Buddhism in, 270, 343, 374, 375f, 382–3, 386, 388–90; *bushido* (Way of the Warrior), 385, 398–9; capitalism in, 745, 746; China's treaty port opened with, 729m; Chinese sophisticates opinion of, 601; concentration of power in, 605–6; Confucianism in, 262; cultural developments, 390–1, 750; early industrialism in, 851; early settlements, 16; economic growth, stagnation, 644–7; economy of, 386–7; Edo, capital of Japan, 457f, 623f; empire creation, 740–1, 740m; Empress Suiko, 383; Equal Employment Opportunity Law, 939; Euro-American influences in, 723; evolving social structure, 384; expulsion of Phan Boi Chau, 844; family structure, 387–8; feudalism in Tokugawa, 313; Gekokujo period, 639; gender equality in, 377–8; geographic position, 379; *hara-kiri, seppuku* (ritual suicide), 385; Heian period, 270f, 370, 373f, 377, 383–4, 384m, 387–9; Hideyoshi's withdrawal to, 621; Hongwu Emperor, 621; imperial order in, 382–3; import, export activities, 624; import substitution industrialization in, 964; industrialism in, 791; interaction, adaptation in, 732f; invasion, occupation of Manchuria, 723; islands making up, 379; Jomon period, 372, 380–1; Kamakura shogunate, 373f, 384; *kamikaze* ("divine wind"), 385; *kokutai* (national polity/essence), 748, 851, 878; Korea intercommunication with, 381; land bridge connections, 13; land limitations, 379; liberalism and military assertion, 878–9; literary achievements, 270f, 370–1, 373, 388, 391; Mandate of Heaven, 383; Marco Polo Bridge Incident, 882; matriarchal, matrilineal clans, 380–1, 387; Meiji era, 737–41; microlith artifacts in, 380; militaristic expansion, 879; military, 386; missionary work in, 631; modernization (to 1910), 747m; Mongol's defeated by, 621; nation-state creation, 739–40; Neo-Confucianism in, 607, 621, 641, 650, 732–3; Nicheren Buddhism in, 389, 398–9; occupation of Korea, 722; origins, 379–80; patriarchal institutions, 388; Peace Preservation Law, 878; Perry's diplomatic, trade missions, 652f; Perry's trade missions, 636, 652f, 725f, 738–9, 745, 749, 791; phallic symbols in, 380; population, food, commerce, 645; population growth, 623f; Portuguese merchants, missionaries in, 639; post-WW I supremacist nationalism, 849, 851; pre-WW I global influence, 724; Rape of Nanjing, 853f, 881–2; Restoration War, 725f; rice cultivation, 381–2, 386, 387; rice in, 381–2, 386, 387; rise of power in, 621; rule of China, 905; rural transformations, 645–6; Russo-Japanese War, 653f, 723, 757f, 778, 779; sake brewing, 387; *sakoku* (closed country) policy, 649, 650–1; sakoku seclusion policies, 650; samurai warriors, 39–399, 385, 387, 389–90, 640–3, 645–7; Seiyukai Party, 725f, 748; Shimabara rebellion, 623f, 643; Shimonoseki Treaty with China, 722–3, 735, 736; Shinto religion in, 378, 383, 388–90, 399; Shogunates period, 384–96, 639; Sino-Japanese War, 722–3, 722m, 725f, 734–6, 740, 750; smallpox epidemic, 384; Spanish merchants, missionaries in, 639; spread of literacy, 383; student demonstrations, 936; *Taika* (Great Reform of 645), 383; "Taisho Democracy," 878; Tang maritime trade with, 350; tea drinking, 385, 387, 390; technical innovations, 363, 731; tenancy issues, 384; theater traditions, 647–8; Tokugawa shoguns, 606; topography and climate, 382m; trade activities, 387; transport routes (ca. 1800), 644m; Treaty of Shimonoseki, 723; "tribute missions" to China, 625; Triple Intervention against, 723, 741, 778; urbanization in, 644; urban population (ca. 1800), 644m; Yamato period, 371, 373f, 382–3, 386–7, 389, 397; Yayoi period, 373f, 380–1, 386; Zen Buddhism in, 375f, 385, 389–90, 398–9. *See also* Hideyoshi, Toyotomi; Meiji (Japanese Emperor) era; Tokugawa Shogunate
Jefferson, Thomas, 658
Jenné-jeno city-state, West Africa, 151f, 153f, 155–6, 157–8, 160, 418, 422, 561
Jerusalem: alliance with Constantinople, 290; as Crusader Kingdom, 287, 289; fall of, 289; First Crusaders defeat of, 287; Mamluk's capture of, 287, 408; papal supremacy over, 286; preparations for Christ's return, 462; Saladin's capture of, 325; Temple Mount, 275
Jesuits, 512
Jesus (Jesus of Nazareth, Jesus Christ, Jesus the Messiah), 193, 202–4, 275, 278, 283, 460, 462
Jewish National Fund, 865

Jews and Judaism: Zoroastrianism, Greek philosophy, 147; in Aksum Kingdom, 154–5; deportation from Neo-Babylon, 198; Deutero-Isaiah and, 198–9; emigration to Ottoman Empire, 463; England's expulsion of, 321; forced conversions in Granada, 463; founding of Christianity, 147; Hitler's Final Solution against, 848f, 853f, 876–7; Kabbala traditions, 614; origins of Judaism, 198–9; in Palestine, 201–2, 201m; in Persian Empire, 193; promise of Palestine homeland, 853f, 864–5; rebuilding of temple in Jerusalem, 180; scientific discoveries in Portugal, 504; Spain's expulsion of, 456f, 461f; taxation by Ottomans, 475, 477; WW II genocide against, 853f
Jihad (holy war), 279
Joan of Arc, 333–4
Johanson, Donald, 4
John Paul I (Pope), 928
Johnson, Ellen, 986
Johnson, James Weldon, 860–1
Johnson, Lyndon B., 927f, 934, 945–6
John XII (Pope), 316
Jomon period (Japan), 372, 380–1
Junzi doctrine (Confucianism), 245
Justinian, Plague of, 194–5, 194m, 196m
Justinian I, the Great, (Roman Emperor), 194–6, 329
Justinian Roman law codex, 195, 279

Kabbala traditions, 614
Kádár, János, 928
Kaddaba fossils, 7
Kadesh, Treaty of, 49
Kahun Papyrus, 60
Kailasantha Temple (southern India), 222–3, 223f
Kalakmul city-state (Maya), 161, 163
Kalidasa (Indian poet), 217f
Kalinga Kingdom, 218
Kamakura shogunate (Japan), 373f, 384
Kama Sutra, 84, 222
Kanchipuram state (India), 345
Kanem-Bornu caliphate (Africa), 561f, 563
Kangxi Emperor (Qing Dynasty, China), 623f, 628–9, 631–2, 636, 637f
Kang Youwei (Chinese official), 736
Kanishka (Kushan Empire ruler), 217f, 220
Kant, Immanuel, 681; categorical imperative, 668–9; *Critique of Practical Reason,* 668; *Critique of Pure Reason,* 668; *Perpetual Peace,* 668–9
Kanun law (Ottoman Empire), 476
Karadžić, Radovan, 976
Karman, Tawakkol, 961–2
Keman, Mustafa, 866
Kennan, George F., 891
Kennedy, John F., 898, 899, 917, 926, 934
Kennedy, Robert, 937
Kennewick Man, 7, 25–6, 27, 124
Kepler, Johannes, 490, 493f
Kerala state (India), 345
Kerma, 150
Kerouac Jack, 923
Khafre pyramid, Egypt, 44f
Khmer Rouge (Cambodian revolutionary group), 946
Khoisan-family languages (Africa), 158–9
Khomeini, Ayatollah Ruhollah, 767, 949
Khosrow I (Sasanid Persian King), 196
Khosrow II (Sasanid Persian King), 274
Khrushchev, Nikita, 890, 896, 897–8, 905, 926, 927f, 940
Khubilai Kan, Yuan Emperor, 356, 357f
Khufu pyramid (Egypt), 44
Kikuchi, Baron Takeo, 850
Kim Jong-un (Supreme Leader, North Korea), 994
King, Martin Luther, Jr., 933, 934, 936–7, 961
King Leopold's Role in Africa (Morel), 846
King List (2125 BCE), 39
Kipling, Rudyard, 846
Knox, John, 510
Koguryo Kingdom (Korea), 374
Kokutai (national polity/essence), Japan, 748, 851, 878
Kong family (China), 244, 246
Kongo Kingdom (Africa): African Christian spirituality in, 564–5; African Creole culture in, 570; Christianity in, 560, 569–70; rule of Pedro IV, 559–60; slave trade, 570; timeline placement, 561f; trade with Portugal, 569
Kooning, Willem de, 901f
Korea, 371–9; adoption of Confucian exam structure, 376; adoption of written Chinese, 243; agriculture, 372; border uprisings in Manchuria, 353; Buddhism in, 270, 343, 374, 375f, 378–9; China's imperialism in, 734; Chinese style bureaucracy in, 374; class structure, 376, 377; climate, 372; Confucianism in, 262; egalitarian social structure in, 378; ethnic origins, 372; foreshadowing of conflict with, 620–1; geography, environment, 371–2; Han China occupation, 373; *han-gul* phonetic writing system, 373f, 378–9; Hideyoshi's attempted invasion, 625; Japan's intercommunication with, 381; Japan's occupation of, 722; Koguryo Kingdom, 374; Koryo Kingdom, 270f, 375–6, 375m, 378; land reforms, 376–7; map, 500 CE, 374m; mobile rocket launchers of, 356f; Mongol expansion into, 375–6; name derivation, 270f; Neo-Confucian influences, 377, 378, 607; Paekche Kingdom, 374, 382, 389; Parhae Kingdom in, 373f; printing advances, 378; rice in, 372, 376, 378; Silla Kingdom, 374–7, 378, 382–3; Sun and Tang invasions, 373f; Tang rule in, 350; Three Kingdoms era, 372–4, 373f, 378; topography, precipitation, 373m; trade activities, 243; "tribute missions" to China, 625; women and society, 377–8; writing developments, 373f, 378–9; Yi Dynasty, 373f, 376–8, 396; Zhou China's references to, 372. *See also* Koryo Kingdom
Korean War (1950–1953), 848f, 891f, 895
Koryo Kingdom (Korea), 270f, 375–6, 375m, 378
Kosala (Indian state), 216, 220
Ku Klux Klan, 859f, 860
Kushan Empire (northern India), 217f, 220–1, 237f
Kush Kingdom, 149
Kuwait, 963f, 966
Kwantung Army (Japan), 879
Kyoto Protocol agreement (1997), 990–1

Labor assignments (*repartimiento* system), 526, 534, 542
Labor unions, 708, 779, 808, 859, 865, 872, 878, 904, 910, 928, 937, 943, 954
Lalibela monoliths, 407
Land Code (1858; Ottomans), 762
Land-grants system, 475–6
Land-labor grants (Spanish *encomiendas*), 526, 534
Langland, William, 337
Laozi, 245f, 247
Lapita cultural complex (Western Pacific), 3, 123f, 139, 140–1, 143
Las Casas, Bartolomé de, 526
Lateran Accords (1926–1929, Italy), 872
Latin America: agricultural self-sufficiency, 712, 715–16; authoritarian Dirty War in, 955; authoritarian rule in, 867–8; Azuduy's leadership in, 688–9; Bolívar as liberation hero, 689, 698; British, U.S. capital investments in, 719; capitalist democracy in parts of, 848; caudillo authoritarian regimes, 693, 697, 699–700, 702, 705, 710, 719; constitutionalism in, 710–11; Creoles in, 710; disappearances of citizens, 955; economy, economic recovery, 709m, 711–12; eighteenth-century Enlightenment in, 689; expansion in, 987–8; export-led growth, 712; factories, 716–17; family relations, 717–18; independence from Spain, 709–10; independence movements, 719; inequalities in, 902; labeling as "banana republic," 718; labor and immigrants, 714–15, 715m; Mothers of Plaza de Mayo organization, 955; new nation states (1831), 703m; political divisions in, 710–11; population growth in, 903m; populist wave, 903–4; post-independence struggles, 709–10; post-WW II, rural and urban society, 902; pre-WW I development, 715; proxy wars, 954–6; railroads in, 714–16; raw materials, cash crops, 712; reconstruction era, 708–12; rise of living standards, 713; role of the church, 717; split over church-state relations, 711; trade activities, 711–12, 713; urbanization in, 903m; U.S. training of dissidents in, 897–8; visual and literary arts, 718. *See also* Central America; Creoles; Haiti; Mexico; South America; specific countries
Latin Christendom, 271, 309, 310, 334
La Venta settlement (Olmec culture), 123f, 136, 137–8
Law Code of Hammurabi, 41, 42–3
Law of the Kings, The (Fetha Nagast) (Ethiopia), 408, 409
Lawrence, T. E. ("Lawrence of Arabia"), 864–5
League of Nations, 848f, 856, 889
Lebanese civil war, 948–9
Le Dynasty. *See* Li Dynasty
Legalism philosophy (ancient China), 244, 245f, 246, 247, 247f, 248, 249, 250, 262, 264, 266, 267, 269, 271

Legal systems: Assyrian Empire, 43; of France, 662; Justinian's *Codex*, 195, 279; Law Code of Hammurabi, 41, 42–3; of Sharia law, 279–80, 305, 306–7, 476, 603, 761, 948, 986; Sumerian law code, 43
Legge, James, 242
Legionaries (foot soldiers), of Rome, 189, 191
Leibniz, Gottfried Wilhelm, 498
Lejju, B. Julius, 157
Lenin, Vladimir Ilyich, 779, 782–3, 844; adaptation of Marxism, 869; Bolshevik Party leadership, 854, 869; *What Is to Be Done?*, 779, 783. *See also* Bolshevik Party
Lennon, John, 923
Leo Africanus ("Leo the African"), 458–9
Leo II (Pope), 312
Leo III (Pope), 312
Leopold II (King of Belgium), 835, 836, 846
Leo X (Pope), 458
Lepanto, Battle of, 461f
Lesbian, gay, bisexual, and transgender (LGBT) people, 935
Levallois toolmaking, 8f, 11
Leviathan (Hobbes), 503
Lewis-Williams, J. David, 20
Liang Qichao (Chinese political theorist), 736
Li Bai (Tang poet), 354Library of Alexandria (Egypt), 204–5
Libya: Arab Spring protests, 960–1, 981; Italy's conquest of, 872; toppling of Qaddafi, 981
Li Dynasty (Vietnam), 373f, 393
Life leases, 757
Life of Harsha (Bana), 344
Lightbulb, incandescent (Edison), 787f
Li Hongzhang, 722, 731f, 737–8
Lin Biao, 941
Lincoln, Abraham, 677, 685
Linear A and B script, 46, 53–4
Lin Zexu (Chinese official), 726–7, 727f
Li Si (Chinese Legalist theorist), 247, 249, 251
Literary achievements: of China, 102–3, 105, 109–10, 114, 354, 366, 744; encyclopedia projects, China, 636; Enlightenment era, 669; of Europe, 337–8; of France, 682, 684; of Greece, 207; of the Habsburg Empire, 485–6; of India, 237–8, 613–14; industrialism era (1750–1914), 811–12; Islamic civilization, 300–1; of Japan, 270f, 370–1, 373, 388, 391, 623f; of Kipling, Rudyard, 846; of Latin America, 718; of Leo the African, 458; of the Persian Empire, 205; realism, in prose literature, 682, 684; in the Romanticism era, 682; of Rome, 208
Liu Bang (Chinese general), 251
Liu Shaoqi (Chinese leader), 907, 940
Livingstone, David, 832
Locke, John, 503, 658, 667
Lodi Sultans (India), 595–6
Lombard, Peter, 329
London Working Men's Association (England), 802
Long Count Calendar (Mayas), 164
Longshan culture (China), 95–6
Lorentz, Hendrik, 808
Lothal seaport (Harappa), 70, 72, 73f
Louisiana Purchase, 665, 678, 691f
Louis the Pious (son of Charlemagne), 312
Louis VII (King of France), 324
Louis XIII (King of France), 516
Louis XIV (King of France), 493f, 516–17, 659
Loyola, Ignatius, 512
Luba Kingdom (central Africa), 403f, 416–17, 417m, 426
Lucy (Hadar AL 288-1), 4–5, 7, 7f
Lumumba, Patrice, 919–20, 951
Luther, Martin, 337, 456f, 493f, 509–10, 559. *See also* Protestant Reformation
Lydian Kingdom, 180
Lynchings, of African Americans, 677–8, 859f, 860

MacArthur, Douglas, 895
Macartney, Lord George, 724, 725f
Macauley, Thomas B., 821
Maccabean Kingdom. *See* Hasmonean Kingdom
Macedonian Empire, 146, 179
Machiavelli, Niccolò, 493
Madame Bovary (Flaubert), 684
Madero, Francisco, 706–7
Magellan, Ferdinand, 840
Maghada (Indian state), 214, 216–17, 220, 231
Magic Flute, The (Mozart), 669
Magna Carta (England), 311, 311f
Mahabharata (Hindu poem), 80–1
Mahavira (founder of Jainism), 217f
Mahayana Buddhism, 228–9, 237f, 264, 350, 395–6
Mahendra Vikruma Varman I (Pallava ruler), 222
Mahmud of Ghazna, 345f, 346–8
Maji Maji rebellion (East Africa), 835–6
Malaria in Africa, 833
Malaysia, 13, 24, 25, 911
Mali Empire (West Africa): armed revolts (2012, 2013), 986; chieftains in, 420–1, 561; decentralization of, 423; Islamic imperial traditions in, 401; military power of, 421–2; minting of gold coins in, 421; oral tradition in, 421; relation to Songhay, 561; rule of Mansa Sundiata, 403f, 421, 426–7; scholarly activities in, 422–3; similarity to Eurasia, 561; social organization in, 421; timeline placement, 271f, 403f; trade activities, 421, 563
Mamluk Egypt: capture of Jerusalem, 287, 408; commercial development, 296–8; conquests in Nubian Kingdom, 402, 405; economy, 292–3; embassy in Granada, 462–3; establishment in Egypt, 291; gender relations, 293; loss to France at Battle of the Pyramids, 826f; military, 292f; Ottoman conflicts with, 468; ruling class, 292–3; state and society in, 291–3; sultanate, 275f; timeline placement, 275f; urban working population, 293; victories against Mongols, 291
Manchuria: border uprisings in, 353; China's move into, 374; Choson Kingdom in, 372; establishment of borders, 632; geographic features, 371–2; Japanese invasion, occupation of, 723, 879; Japan's annexation of, 853f; nomadic, pastoral people in, 102; Parhae Kingdom in, 373f; soybean agriculture, 107
Manchus (Chinese ruling minority): adaptations to Chinese culture, 357; administrative responsibilities, 628; banner system of, 625, 628; consolidation of rule by, 628; foot binding by, 743; as hereditary warrior class, 628; occupation of Beijing, 625; as patrons of the arts, 636; rebellion against, 730; rise of, 621–2, 625
Mandate of Heaven (China), 103–4, 116, 244, 246, 263, 383
Mandate of Heaven (Japan), 383
Mandela, Nelson, 849f, 954, 961, 963f, 987f
Manet, Édouard, 705f
Manorialism, in medieval Europe, 314–15, 315f
Mansa Musa (Mali ruler), 422
Manumission (defined), 578
Manzikert, Battle of, 275f
Mao Zedong, 880–1, 884, 895, 905–6, 937, 940–2
Mapungubwe Kingdom (South Africa), 403f, 414, 415, 417
Maratha wars (India), 602, 604, 616, 618
Marconi, Guglielmo, 787f, 795
Marcus, Siegfried, 787f, 794
Marie-Antoinette (Queen of France), 660–1
Maritime trade: of China, 350, 351, 362, 625, 632f, 649–50, 724–7, 726m; of the Dutch, 609; of Fatimids, 404; of Genoa and Vienna, 318; of Great Britain, 609; of Harappa, 72; of India, 219, 232, 346, 404, 789; of Sparta, 184
Marley, Bob, 407–8
Marne, Battle of (1914), 853
Married Woman's Property Act (1882; England), 805
Marshall Plan, 891, 893, 900, 904
Martel, Charles ("the Hammer"), 276, 310
Martin V (Pope), 337
Marx, Karl, 488, 801; background information, 802–3; *Communist Manifesto*, 652f, 787f, 802–3; dialectical materialism of, 803; Engel's collaboration with, 801; founding of communism, 869; quote on history repeating itself, 676
Marxism: appeal to Westerners, 897; on capitalism, imperialism, 940; Colombian guerilla warfare and, 988; in Europe, 692; Lenin's adaptions of, 869; Lenin's adherence to, 779; Mao and, 881, 905; Mussolini's disillusionment with, 871; North Korea's abandonment of, 993; Russian Revolution and, 780; in the Soviet Union, 869; U.S. opposition to, 954
"Marxism-Leninism-Mao-Zedong Thought" (China), 942
Mass consumption culture, post-World War II, 900
Mathematical innovations: calendars and, 164–5; Diophantus's contributions, 204; Euclid's contributions, 204; Galileo's law of falling bodies, 457f, 493f; Hypatia's contributions, 204; in India, 204, 238–9, 611–12; Islamic civilization, 300; *Principia Mathematica* (Newton), 490, 498; Scientific Revolution and, 456
Mathematical Principles of Natural Philosophy (Newton), 498
Matriarchal/matrilinear clans, in Japan, 38–381
Matter, quest for understanding, 808
Mauryan Empire (India), 216–20; advocacy for dharma path, 233; Ashoka's reign, 217f, 218m, 219–20, 233, 344; ending of, 220; origins, 147f; reunification of India, 217f

Maxim, Hiram, 787f, 796, 796f
Maximilian (Austrian prince), 704–5
Maxwell, James Clerk, 795
Mayaland, Yucatán Peninsula, 161–2
Mayan Calendar Round, 164
Mayan Kingdoms, 161–6; agricultural developments, 161, 162–3, 165, 433; alliances of, 433; artistic achievements, 164; calendar development, 164–5; Chichén Itzá, 270f, 431f, 433–4; civilization map, 162m; classic period, dates, 147f; commoners, 165; crises in, 166; cultural expansion, 434; decline of, 433; early kingdoms, 162–3; gender roles and divisions, 165; glyphic alphabet, writing, 151f, 163, 165–6, 167f; human sacrifices, 169; influence on Taíno chiefs, 139; Kalakmul city-state, 161, 163; Mayaland, Yucatán Peninsula, 161–2; realignment of power, 432–3; ruling classes, 164–5; social stratification in, 165; spirituality, polytheism, 164; team ball game, 168–9; Tikal city-state, 161, 163; timeline placement, 431f; trade activities, 431m; village transitions to towns, 162
McCarthy, Joseph: McCarthyism, 895
McKay, Claude, 860–1
Mecca, 278–9, 410, 468, 481, 601
Medici, Giovanni Leone di. *See* Leo Africanus
Medicine: Avicenna's contributions, 329; in China, 97, 820; Copernicus's studies, 496; in early China, 97; in Egypt, 60; French Academy of Medicine, 663; Galen's contributions, 329; in India, 238; Industrial Revolution and, 797; in Islamic civilization, 300; in Japan, 749; Pasteur's contributions, 810; in Rome, 195, 329; in sub-Saharan Africa, 918; in twelfth century Rome, 329; use of gunpowder as, 356
Medina, 278–9
Mehmet II, the Conqueror (Ottoman Sultan), 465–8, 466–7, 468
Mehrgarh Neolithic culture (India), 67f, 68, 70
Meiji Constitution (1868), 791
Meiji (Japanese Emperor) era, 725f, 737–41; acceptance of Christianity, 643; commerce and cartels, 745–9; constitution and political life, 746–8; cooperation and capitalism, 746; economy and society, 724, 745–50; political parties, 748; portrait of, 739f; progressive measures, 739; social experiments, 748–9; timeline placement, 653f, 725f; transportation, communications revolutions, 746
Mein Kampf (My Struggle) (Hitler), 873–4, 876
Menander (northern Indian ruler), 220
Mencius (Chinese philosopher), 242–3, 242–6, 245–6, 245f, 263, 267, 268–9
Mensheviks, 779
Mercantilism: in the Caribbean, 574–6; in Europe, 624; in Latin America, 712
Meroë Kingdom (Africa): agricultural production, 151–2; conflicts with Rome, 153; cultural achievements, 153; decline of, 153, 401; description, 146; flourishing of, 149; iron production, 152–3; map, 152m; Nubian-Egyptian heritage, 153; origins of, 151; timeline, 151f; trade activities, 151–2, 1650; weaponry production, 152
Meroitic pyramids (Sudan), 148m, 153
Merovingians, 310, 339
Merton, Walter de, 330
Mesoamerica: agrarian villages, 123f, 127-8, 134, 151f, 448; animal and plant domestication, 127–8; architecture, 132–3; ball game, 168–9; calendars, 148–9; climate and geography, 121–3; corn, 130-1; cultural specificity, 143; economy, 429, 431m; human sacrifice, 450–1; imperial age, 446; kingdom formation, 146, 161–70; militarism, 430; patterns, 453; religion, 446; *See also* Mexico and Central America; Central America; Aztecs, Maya; Toltec culture
Mesopotamia: Akkadian Kingdom, 33f, 39–40, 40m, 44, 51; assemblies in, 36; chiefly assemblies tradition, 421; clay tablets, 44, 46; comparison to Harappa, 68; conflicts and wars in, 39; cuneiform writing development, 38, 39f; Cyrus II the Great's campaign, 180; early towns, 6; *Enuma Elish* creation myth, 33f, 57, 58; *Epic of Gilgamesh,* 57–8; Euphrates/Nile floods, 35; gender roles, 41–2; geographic features, location, 32, 33; hierarchical social structures, 41; Judaism in, 198; King List, 39; kingship in, 39; literature of, 59; Parthian victory in, 188, 190; patriarchal society in, 40–1; Peace/Banquet scene, 30f; Persian palaces in, 182; roles of women in, 41; rule by Sargon of Akkad, 30, 39–45, 65; scientific beginnings in, 59–60; sculpture and paintings, 58–9, 59f; seasonal celebrations, 207; sharecroppers in, 36; spread of agriculture from, 46; temples in, 33f, 36, 37, 37f; trade activities, 37; Ubaid culture, 35, 56; urban centers origins, 35–8, 36m; Uruk, city-state, 33f, 37–8; writing system development, 46. *See also* Aztec Empire
Mestizos, 547–8, 552, 689–90, 697, 700–1, 710. *See also* Mulattoes
Metternich, Klemens von (Chancellor of Austrian Habsburg Empire), 671–2, 674, 680
Mexican-American War (1846–1848), 738
Mexican Basin, 167
Mexican Revolution (1910–1917), 691f, 700, 702f, 706–8, 716
Mexican War of Liberation (1810–1821), 691f
Mexico and Central America: agrarian villages, 123f, 127, 128; agricultural adaptation, 127, 160–1; animal and plant domestication, 127–8; ball game, 168–9; architecture, 133; calendars in, 148–9; Carranza's leadership, 707–8; centralist rule in, 702; ceremonial centers, 132, 134, 169, 430, 446; climate, 123; Comanche's in northern Mexico, 702; constitutionalism in, 707; corn cultivation, 127, 130–1; Creole landowners in, 706, 708; cultural patterns, 429; cultural prowess of, 148; depression years, 868; Díaz's leadership, 705–6; economic inequality in, 902; economic patterns, 429; empire in 19th century, 701; environment of, 121; European forces in, 704; first settlements, 121, 129, 134–6; geographic features, 121, 123; Guerrero's leadership, 701–2; imperial age of, 446; Iturbe's leadership, 701; kingdom formation, 146; Maximilian, Emperor, 704; Mexican-American War, 738; nature-spiritual and polytheistic heritage, 446; pottery making, 128; political patterns, 429; Pueblo cultures, 430, 431m; railroads in, 706, 712; Reform War in, 704; *repartimiento* system, 526, 534, 542; republic status gained by, 701–2; Revolution, 706–8; silver mines in, 541; smallpox epidemic in, 549; *soldaderas* (revolutionary women), 702f; Spanish conquests in, 526–30; state-church issues in, 711; state formation in, 215; Teotihuacán's domination of, 429; Texas's independence from, 691f; textile factories, 716f; timeline of events, 151f; trade activities, 431m; uprising in New Spain, 700–1; urbanization in, 868; U.S. citizens emigration to, 702–3; U.S.–Mexico War, 703–4; villages, settlements, 151f.; War of Independence, 701–2. *See also* Aztec Empire; Mayan Kingdoms; Mexican Basin; Olmec culture; Teotihuacán Kingdom; Toltec culture
Microlith artifacts, in Japan, 380
Middens (defined), 126
Middle East: Achaemenid Persian conquest of, 179; agrarian-urban society, 3, 30, 38, 40; agricultural developments, 150, 151; Alexander's quest for unification, 210–11; Arab-Israeli conflicts, 848f, 891f, 927f, 937, 946, 946f, 947m; Arab Spring uprisings, 849f, 961, 963f, 976–7, 980–2, 984, 991; Assyria's role in unification of, 51, 150; astronomy studies, 205; British role, 18th, early 19th centuries, 827–8; bubonic plague in, 194; commonwealths, 273; cultural diversity in, 179; Cyrus II the Great's conquests, 180; early farming and settlements, 31–4, 32m, 47, 60; early forms of writing, 38; emergence of warring kingdoms, 12; empire developments, 3; fear of Islamism in, 976–7; firearm development, 476; foraging lifestyle, 31–4; gender roles and divisions, 40–1; Greek emigrations to, 186; interactions with Saharan Africans, 149; Iranian Islamic Revolution, 949–50; iron working skills, 152; Lebanese civil war, 948–9; Mongol conquests, 270f; monotheism in, 57, 197–204; monsoons in, 32; 1914, 1923 map, 857m; oil discovery, 848f; Ottoman imperialism in, 756; patriarchal society in, 40–1; polytheist belief, 192–3; post-Black Death population recovery, 756; Roman expansion into, 146; Sasanid Persian transmission of Indian texts to, 205–6; Seljuk victories in, 324; shipbuilding innovations, 467; slavery in, 12; Sunni-Shiite conflict, 961–2; Tang maritime trade with, 350; technological change in, 475; trade routes, 404m; U.S. training of dissidents in, 897–8; usefulness of bronze in, 38; warfare developments, 46. *See also* Arab-Israeli War entries; Neo-Assyrian Empire; individual countries

Middle Kingdom, Egypt, 46, 62
Middlemarch (Eliot), 682
Middle Nile Valley, 401–2
Migrations (human migrations): from Africa, 2, 5, 7, 13, 14m, 120; to the Americas, 20–7, 26m, 123f, 124–6; from Asia to Europe, 18–20; to Beringia, 25; to Eurasia, 123f; to India, 67f; from the Middle East, 3; of Olmecs, 162; from Russian steppes to Europe, 19; from South Asia to Australia, 14–17; from South Asia to Europe, 13; from Taiwan, 123f
Military (militarism): in the Americas, 429–30, 438; artillery innovation, 795–6; of the Aztecs, 429, 440–1; of the Incas, 429, 442, 444–6; of India, 594–5, 597, 599–601, 604, 606, 617; in the Mexican Basin, 430–2, 439; in Ming Dynasty China, 636; of Nubia, 150; of the Qing Dynasty, 629; of Tenochtitlán, 447–8; of the Toltecs, 432; of Wari, 434, 436. *See also* Weaponry innovations
Millet cultivation (China), 94
Ming Dynasty (China): administrative restructuring, 633; agricultural developments, 634; *baojia* local organization system, 363, 444, 633; ceramic and porcelain artistry, 626–7; Confucian bureaucracy in, 621; decline of, 362, 621, 625; dynastic cycle pattern in, 621; female infanticide, 364; foot binding, 364; founding of, 623f; global commercial revolution a, 622–4; Grand Secretariat of, 360, 621, 623f, 628; loyalists flight to Taiwan, 625; magistrate system, 362; map (1600), 623m; military superpower status, 636; missionaries in, 631; naval power, 360–2; origin of, 621; overthrow of Yuan Dynasty, 376; peace and stability in, 624; peasant women's lives, 363–4; population recovery, growth, 360, 622; rural life in, 633–4; rural society, 362–3; scholar gentry, 362–3; science and literature, 636; social stability during, 648; technological innovations, 361; technological prowess, 364, 365; timeline placement, 345; Timur's contemplated invasion of, 595; urbanism in, 622; village and family life, 363, 633–5; weaponry of, 636; weaponry used by, 611; Yongzheng, Emperor, 628; Zheng He's visit to East Africa, 413; Zhu Yuanzhang's inauguration of, 376
Minoan Kingdom (palace-state), 33f, 46, 54, 136
Minobe, Tatsukichi, 850–1
Mississippian cultures, 431m
Mithridates II, "the Great" (Persian ruler), 188
Mladić, Ratko, 976
Moche chiefdom (northern Peru), 147f, 151f, 171–2
Moctezuma II (Aztec Emperor), 528
Modernism (defined), 900
Mohenjo-Daro (Indus civilization), 65, 68–70, 70m, 71f, 73
Monasteries and monasticism: in Africa, 406; Benedictine, 326; in Byzantine Empire, 283, 286, 302–3; in China, 261, 264, 353; and early medieval church, 310–11; in England, 315, 318; in Ethiopia, 406; French monastic reforms, 321; in India, 218, 226, 233, 235, 238, 344; in Japan, 384, 387, 388; military monastic order, 460; in Nubia, 402; of Saint Andrew, Rome, 308; St. Benedict model, 310–11
Monastic fighting orders, 460
Monet, Claude, 787f, 811
Money economy (defined), 475
Mongol Empire: Abbasids conquest by, 347; adapting to Chinese culture, 357; Asian conquests, 270f; Baghdad conquest by, 347; Black Death in, 298; China conquests, 345f, 354, 355; conversions to Islam, 357; decline of, 594; eastern Europe conquests, 270f; expansion into Korea, 375–6; fragmentation of, 357; incursions into China, 345f, 354; invasions of Japan, 384–5; Japan's conquest of, 621; Mamluk's victories against, 291; map, 359m; Middle East conquests, 270f; Song Dynasty conquest by, 355; thirteenth century expansion, 375–6; Vietnam's repulsion of invasions, 271f. *See also* Yuan Dynasty
Mongols of the Golden Horde, 770
Monotheism (and monism): Akhenaten's approach to, 62; Eurasian formulations, 146, 147; Middle East adaptations to, 57, 197–204; Persian adoption of, 192; polytheism's move to, 200; Roman adoption of, 192; 600 CE dominance of, 147; in sub-Saharan Africa, 147. *See also* Christianity; Jews and Judaism; Zoroastrianism
Monroe Doctrine (U.S.), 704
Monsoon system: in China, 32, 92; in East Africa, 32; in the eastern Mediterranean, 32, 35; in India, 66–8, 67m, 92; in Middle East, 32, 35
Montenegro, 653, 757f, 763, 764, 775–6
Montgomery, Alabama bus boycott, 933f
Monumental architecture, 71, 89, 118–19, 210, 382, 447, 616
Monzaemon. *See* Chikamatsu
Morel, Edward D., 846
Moriscos, 472–5, 475f
Morocco: ceremonial centers, 172; early toolmaking, 12; feminism in, 939; France's occupation of, 837; independence gained by, 891f; invasion of Africa, 560; Portuguese occupation of ports, 565; Saadid rule in, 468–9; trade activities, 52, 561; victories against Portugal, 563
Morrison, Jim, 923
Morse, Samuel F. B., 795
Mothers of Plaza de Mayo (Argentina), 955
Mozambique, independence of, 952
Mozart, Wolfgang Amadeus, 669
Mubarak, Hosni, 981, 985
Mughal Empire (India), 598–625; administrative personnel, 606–7; agricultural and rural life, 607–8; Akbar Shah II's leadership, 819f; Akbar's leadership, 457f, 597–9; architectural achievements, 593, 595, 601, 613, 615–16; artistic achievements, 614–15; astronomy innovations, 611–12; Bahadur Shah Zafar's leadership, 821; caste, clan, and village ties, 609; changing fortunes of, 599–605; consolidation and expansion, 597–8; decline of, 595f, 817, 818, 819; domination of Islamic civilization, 468–70; early modern economy, 607–9; "extraction state" status of, 593–4; family and gender, 609–10; as gunpowder empire, 611; history and political life of, 593–605; insoluble problems of, 606; international trade, 608–9; Islamic developments in, 613; literary achievements, 613–14; loss and recovery of, 596–7; mathematical innovations, 611–12; military victories, 597; Muslim elites assimilated in, 610; non-Muslims in, 612–13; origins, 348, 456; political structure, 606; religious politics, new directions, 601; war state, renewed expansion of, 600–1; wealth of, 606; weaponry innovation, 611. *See also* Akbar, Jalal ud-Din; Aurangzeb; Babur (Zahir Ud-din Muhammad Babur); Shah Jahan; Timur (Timur-i Lang)/Timur Empire
Muhammad Ali (Egyptian ruler), 761, 830
Muhammad (Prophet of Islam), 275, 277–9, 302–3, 400
Muhammad the Bloody. *See* Ibn Tughluq, Muhammad
Mukhtar, Umar (Libyan resistance leader), 836–7
Mulattoes, 547–8, 654–5, 663–4, 665, 690. *See also* Mestizos
Munich Agreement, 875
Murasaki Shikibu, 270f, 370, 371, 373, 373f, 388, 391
Music: in Africa, 584–5; in the Americas, 126, 130, 133, 584; in Baroque era, 492; of Brazil, 584; in Byzantium, 301; in Caral-Supe valley, Peru, 130; in China, 126, 351f, 353; of Creole culture, 584–5; in early agricultural centers, 20; in the Enlightenment era, 669, 681; in Ethiopia, 407–8; and global youth movement, 935–6; in Great Britain, 680; in Habsburg Spain, 481; in Incan culture, 450; industrialism era (1750–1914), 811–12; and information technology, 965; in Japan, 383; in the Kongo Kingdom, 570; modernism in, 812; in Ottoman culture, 480, 482f, 485; in postwar Eastern Europe, 898; Rastafarians and, 407; in the Renaissance, 494; in Renaissance era, 494; in the Romanticism era, 681
Muslim Brotherhood (Egypt), 909, 947
Muslim League, 867, 911
Muslims: Abbasid raids on, 284; artistic achievements, 301; Battle of Tours defeat, 310; beliefs of, 275; Carolingian defeat of, 310; caste and, 349; Christian competition with, 459–75, 566; coastal Muslims, Ethiopia, 408–9; compiling of the Quran by, 279; conquest of Byzantine Sicily, 281; conquest of Constantinople, 460; conquests in Southeast Asia, 350; Crusades and, 289; cultural synthesis of, 304; Delhi Sultanate, India, 271f, 345f, 347, 348m; expulsion from Spain, 461f; French coast attacks by, 312–13; Hindu-Muslim interactions, 345; icons, Islamic miniatures, 302–3; Indian Ocean

trade activities, 222; invasion of West Africa, 560; jihad (holy wars) of, 279, 287; maritime knowledge, 319; mathematics achievements, 204–5; persecution of Sikhs, 349; Persian Muslims, 300–1; philosophical concerns of, 299; political control of Ethiopia, 407; practice of veiling women, 349; Ramadan observance, 279, 481–2, 816, 927, 937; recovery and Byzantine-Crusader cooperation, 289–90; repugnance toward Hindu nakedness, 349; revival of learning, 304; Shiite Islam faith, 280; Sicily's liberation from control by, 317; Spanish Muslims, 317, 320; Sufism-Sunni integration, 275f, 298; Sunni Islam faith, 280, 766–7, 768, 950, 976; Swahili Muslim city-states, 297; trade activities, 296; trading at Indian seaports, 345f; Turkish Muslims, 300–1; usury prohibition of, 349. *See also* Abbasid Dynasty; Delhi Sultanate; Granada Kingdom; Islam religion; Mamluk Egypt; Ottoman Empire; Seljuk Empire; Timur (Timur-i Lang)/Timur Empire
Mussolini, Benito, 853f, 871–2
Mycenaeans, 33f, 52, 53, 54, 59

Nabobs (in India), 818–19
Namoratunga observatory (Kenya), 148
Nanak (Sikh guru), 349
Nanjing, Treaty of, 728, 730
Napata Kingdom (Africa), 150
Nasser, Gamel Abdel, 889, 891f, 909–11, 915, 947–8, 950
National Association for the Advancement of Colored People (NAACP), 861
National Commission on the Disappearance of Persons (CONADEP), 955
National Congolese Movement, 919
National Organization for Women (NOW), 937–8
National Rifle Association (NRA), 974
National Security Strategy of 2002 (Bush), 966
National Socialist German Worker's Party (NSDAP, Nazi Party), 873
National Society for Women's Suffrage, 805
Nation-state building in Anglo-America (1783–1900), 676–81; buffalo herds, destruction of, 679; Great Britain, 680–1; Native Americans, 678–9; reform measures, 679–80; United States, 677–8, 678m
Nation-states, growth of (1815–1871): Congress of Vienna, 652f, 657f, 671–2; ethnic nationalism in Italy, 674–5; restoration monarchies, 671–6; revolutions in France, 673; uprisings across Europe, 674
Nation-states, origins (1750–1815), 655–67; Congress of Vienna, 652f, 657f; early United States, 658–9; French Revolution, conditions for, 315, 658–9, 667; Haitian Revolution, conditions for, 663–5; uprisings across Europe, 674
Native Americans: American Indian Movement, 934; arrival in North America, 537, 539, 548–9; bloody battles with, 545; Bourbon reforms and, 535; Christian conversions of, 532, 536, 551; civil rights for, 934; in colonial North America, 537–9, 656; Comanches, 539, 702, 704; in Creole society, 546–7; DNA ancestry identification, 24, 27; enslavement of, 532, 578; European-Native American mix, 547; exploitation of, 532; federal land rights of, 25, 27; forced labor by, 542, 544, 546; forced moves to reservations, 679; forced resettlements, 548–50; gender separation, 548; geoglyphs used by, 173; Indian Removal Act, 679; Kennewick Man fossil, 7, 25–6, 27, 124; limited role in wars of independence, 689; manuscripts, oral traditions of, 552; nation-state building and, 678–9; in Peru, 690; Powhatan Confederacy, 539; resettlements of, 549–50; role in conquests in the Americas, 528, 532, 536; smallpox decimation of, 526, 534, 536, 542–3, 549, 556; southern states discrimination against, 679; Spanish conquests of, 525–6; trading in North American settlements, 537–9; "Trail of Tears," 679; tributes given to Aztecs, 439f; unification goal, defeat of, 678; Uto-Aztecan-speaking group, 438; Wounded Knee Creek massacre, 679, 934
Natufian culture, Fertile Crescent, 33–4
Naturalism, 55
Nature spirits, 159
Nazca chiefdom (Peru), 151f, 172–3, 176, 449
Nazca geoglyphs, 172–3, 176
Nazi Germany, 72, 74; Enabling Act, 874; eugenics and, 861; Final Solution against Jews, 848f, 853f, 876–7; Franco's support of, 875; Hitler's rise to power, 861, 873–5; occupation of Sudetenland, 875; repudiation of peace settlements, 875; resistance of Yugoslavia, 891
Ndongo Kingdom (Africa), 561f, 569–70, 580, 583
Neanderthals. *See Homo neanderthalensis*
Négritude cultural movement (France), 861
Nehru, Jawaharlal, 889, 912–13
Neo-Assyrian Empire, 3, 50, 146, 207
Neo-Babylonians, 53, 180, 198
Neo-Confucianism: in China, 271, 343, 350, 354, 364, 376, 397, 607, 624, 636–7, 636m, 732–3, 739; description, 350, 364, 367; exploitation of, 636–7; in Japan, 607, 621, 641, 650, 732–3; in Korea, 377, 378, 607; longevity, diversity of, 368; Song Neo-Confucianism, 373f; in Vietnam, 607; of Zhu Xi, 365
Neolithic cultures: in the Americas, 127–8; animal domestication, 34, 61, 70, 127–8; Banpo Village, China, 92, 93m, 94–5, 116; in China, 91–2, 93f, 96, 128; Dapenkeng culture, China, 96; in Egypt, 35; grain cultivation, 34, 61, 70, 78; in India, 67f, 68, 75; Longshan villages, China, 95–6; Neolithic Berbers in Canary Islands, 460; origins, 34, 94–7; plant domestication, 127–8; rise of agriculture, 40, 56; stone tools, 37; in Vietnam, 391–4; Yangzi River basin, China, 96
Nestorian Christianity, 359m
Netherlands: colonialism in Southeast Asia, 838–40, 839m; Dutch Cape Colony, South Africa, 561f, 570–1; female scientists in, 500; imperialism in Indonesia, 837–40; interest in China's Ming porcelain, 627; male urban literacy rates, 500; post-Black Death population recovery, 505; Protestant war of independence, 473–4; Renaissance in, 494; scientific, philosophical developments, 491, 499; trade forts of, 838; war of independence, 513
New Amsterdam (New York) settlement, 537
Newcomen, Thomas, 792–3
New Conservatism, 973
New Deal (U.S.), 853f, 862
New England (colonial North America): assemblies, 540; emigration to, 540; export crops, 545, 581; Native Americans in, 537, 539; Protestantism in, 552–3; society in, 550; witch hunts, 553–4
New Granada Creoles, 689–90, 697–8
New Imperialism (19th century): in Africa and the Middle East, 827–37; in Australia, 825–7; defined, 817; in India, 818–25; and military transformations, 826–7; in Southeast Asia, 837–44
New Kingdom Egypt, 41, 49, 57f, 59
New Model Army (England), 514
New Sciences (Scientific Revolution), 495–8; Archimedean physics, 496; astronomy, 265, 490, 493f, 497; astronomy-physics unification, 490; cartography (mapmaking), 496, 497f; Catholic Reformation and, 497–8, 499; Copernicus's contributions, 205, 456f, 493f, 495–6, 652; Darwin's evolutionary theory, 787f, 809; defined, 492; Descartes's new philosophy, 502–3; Diderot's *Encyclopédie* and, 667–8; Enlightenment era, 667; Galileo's contributions, 457f, 493f, 496–7; Iberian natural sciences, 498; Jefferson's education in, 658; Kepler's astronomic tables, 490–1; new science societies, 499–500; Newton's contributions, 457f, 490, 493f, 495, 498, 501, 522; philosophical interpretations, 502–3; relativity theory, 787f, 809; research in colonial North America, 553; social impact of, 498–502; steam engine invention, 501–2; theoretical physics, 808; vacuum, discovery of, 501, 502f; women scientists, 500–1; X-ray technology, 808
Newspapers, 500, 656, 667, 735f, 744, 750, 762, 773, 871
New Stone Age (Neolithic), 37
New Testament, 202–3, 277, 493, 509, 551, 559
Newton, Isaac, 457f, 490, 493, 493f, 495, 498, 501, 522
New World: African slaves in, 572; Americas as, 524; Cortés's arrival in, 527; diseases in, 144, 526, 542; European colonization in, 534, 543, 556; New Sciences in, 498, 553f; precious metals mining in, 532, 541–3; slave religions in, 584–5; social groups, castes, ethnic groups in, 545–50. *See also* Americas (North, Central, South)
New Zealand, women's voting rights, 819f
Nguyen Van Thieu (Vietnamese President), 944

Nicaragua: authoritarian government in, 988; independence gained by, 701; railroads in, 719; revolution in, 954
Nicene Creed, 193, 286
Nichiren Buddhism (Japan), 389, 398–9
Nicholas II (Russian Tsar), 776–7
Nicholas I (Russian Tsar), 771
Nietzsche, Friedrich, 811
Nigantha Nataputta (Jain founder), 225
Nigerian civil war, 951
Nikiteno, Aleksandr, 754–5, 772
Nilo-Saharan chiefdom (Sudan), 150
Nineteenth Amendment (U.S. Constitution), 858
Nobel, Alfred Bernhard, 793–4
Nobunaga, Oda, 620, 638, 639
Nomads, 3, 36, 48, 86, 92, 151, 153, 157–9, 180, 188, 193, 222, 254–5, 299, 348, 402
Non-Aligned Movement (NAM), 888, 910–11, 913, 914–15, 916f, 921
Nontariff autonomy (defined), 728
Norsemen, 285, 312, 314, 466
North Africa: Arab Spring protests, 960–1; Berber dynasties, 275f, 276, 305, 418–19, 460.564–5; 1914, 1923 map, 857m; Ottoman conquest of, 472, 756; Portugal's conquest of Ceuta, 461f; seizure of Constantinople, 274; weaponry innovations, 476
North America: Adena culture, 123f, 137, 138m; agricultural developments in, 2; Beringia land bridge, 24; British North America map, 657; British settlements, 538m; climate, 123–4; Clovis points (spearhead flutes), 125; conditions for revolution, 656–8; constitutional revolution in, 652; corn cultivation, 130–1; early migrations to, 118–19; environment of, 121; European emigration to, 798; European explorations, 529m; fossil discoveries, 7, 24; French settlements, 538m; geographic regions, 121; Hopewell culture, 137, 138m; Inuit migrations, 123f, 137; Jamestown, Virginia, settlement, 457f, 527f; migration to, 13, 16, 24–5; mountain systems, 121; Native Americans in, 537, 539; ocean currents, hurricanes, El Niño, 123–4; Spanish settlements, 538m. *See also* Colonial North America
North and South Dynasties period (China), 253
North Atlantic Treaty Organization (NATO), 891f, 892m, 893, 971
Northeast Africa: Aksum Kingdom in, 403f; Christian Kingdoms in, 401; Prester John legend and, 566f; trade routes, 234, 404m
Northern India: agrarian-urban centers in, 215; Alexander's conquests in, 214, 216–17, 217f; Bactrian Greek rulers in, 220; Hindustan, 594, 597–8; Huns migrations to, 217f; interactions (1500–600 BCE), 74–81; Kushan Empire, 217f, 220–1, 237f; Maghada state, 214, 216–17, 220, 231; map, 216m; nomadic kingdoms, 220; Vedic world, 75–9. *See also* Mauryan Empire
Northern Song Dynasty (China), 254f, 345f, 366f
North Korea: abandonment of Marxism, 993; Han China occupation of, 373; Kim Jong-un's leadership, 994; and Korean War, 848f, 891f, 894–5; nuclear ambitions, 978, 994; socialism, self-sufficiency, isolation, militarism ideology, 971
Norwegian Nobel Committee, 961
Nubian Kingdom, 32; agricultural activities, 403; agricultural settlements, 34; Arab invasions, 402; archaeological discoveries, 150; climate, 150; Coptic Christianity in, 401–2; economic administration, 403; Egypt's colonization of, 150; flourishing of, 149; Islamic rule in, 404–5; Islam religion in, 402; Mamluk Egypt conquests in, 402, 405; middle Nile valley domination, 401–2; military prowess, 45, 49, 150; origins/growth of, 149, 150; Roman Empire interactions, 405; royal power and governance, 402–3; Swahili city-states comparison, 411; timeline placement, 403f; trade activities, 37, 402, 403–4
Nuclear Test Ban Treaty (1963), 849f, 899, 925, 927f
Nzinga (Ndongo Queen), 570, 571f

Obama, Barack, 966, 973–4
Obregón, Álvaro, 707
Obscene Publications Bill (England), 800
Oceania, 120, 123f, 139, 142, 143–5
October Manifesto, 779
October War. *See* Yom Kippur/Ramadan War
Oda Nobunaga, 620
Odyssey (Homer), 207
Office of Strategic Services (OSS), 894
Ogé, Vincent, 654–5, 664
Oglethorpe, James, 579, 590–1
Old Babylonian period, 59
Old Kingdom Egypt, 44, 44f, 45m, 62
Oldowan tools, 8–9
Old Regime, France, 660
Old Testament (Hebrew Bible), 53, 58
Olmec culture: jade mask, 134f; La Venta settlement, 123f, 137–8; map, 135m; migrations, 162; origins, 123f, 134; religion, spirituality, 135; San Lorenzo settlement, 123f, 134; Tres Zapotes settlement, 136; writing developments, 136, 137f, 143
Omani Arab expeditionary force, 835
Omdurman, Battle of (1898; Sudan), 796f, 831
On the Genealogy of Morals (Nietzsche), 811
On the Origin of Species by Means of Natural Selection (Darwin), 787f, 809
On the Origins of Language (Herder), 671
On the Road (Kerouac), 923
Opium Wars (China), 635, 726–31, 726m, 738, 744, 760; First Opium War, 724, 725f, 727, 728, 738; Second Opium War, 762, 773, 821
Oracle bones (Ancient China), 91, 93f, 103, 109, 110–13, 115
Oracles, in Greek city-states, 183
Order of Christ (monastic fighting order), 460
Order of Santiago (monastic fighting order), 460
Organization of the Petroleum Exporting Countries (OPEC), 927, 937, 964, 966
Organization of Work, The (Blanc), 802
Origen of Alexandria, 203
Orrorin fossils, 7
Orthodox Christianity. *See* Eastern Christianity
Ortiz, Alonso, 524–5
Osman (founder of Ottoman Empire), 465
Otto I of Saxony (Holy Roman Emperor), 316
Ottoman Empire: Abdülhamit II's leadership, 763–4; alliance with Britain, 471, 762; alliance with France, 471, 762; artistic achievements, 480–3; autocratic rule, 762–4; Battle of Chaldiran, 469–70; battle with Portuguese forces, 473m; British advisory rule for, 827–8; Byzantine traditions in, 755; capture of Constantinople, 271f, 311f, 456f, 461f, 492; capture of Tunis, 473; centralized state formation, 477–8, 504; Committee of Union and Progress, 764; conflicts with Habsburgs, 461f, 526, 756; conquest of Anatolia, 460, 475; conquest of Balkans, 476; conquest of North Africa, 472; conquest of the Balkans, 460, 462; constitution and war, 762–3; Crimean War participation, 692, 755, 757f, 762, 773, 774, 777, 791, 830; decentralization in, 758–60, 768; decline of (1683–1923), 758–9m, 764–5, 849; destabilizing humiliations, 760; *devşirme* practice, 476; domination of Islamic civilization, 468–70; early industrialism in, 851; in eastern Mediterranean region, 594; economic development, 765; empire consolidation, 468; ethnic-nationalist demands in, 852; First Balkan War, 764; First Ottoman-Russian War, 757f; French imperialism in, 764; Greece's independence from, 652f, 757f, 761; as gunpowder empire, 611; imperialism, 1600s and 1700s, 756–9; Indian Ocean competition with Portugal, 473m; invasion of Spain, 472; Islamic traditions in, 755; Janissary military troops, 757, 760–1, 765, 826; Jewish emigration to, 463; *kanun* law, 476; Land Code, 762; land-grants system, 475–6; life, honor, and property, 761; life leases, 757; limits to power of, 474; liquidation of, 849; losses in conflicts, 472; map (1307–1683), 469m; massacre of Armenians, 853f; military overextensions of, 756–7; military spending, 475; modernity in, 817; money economy in, 477; moriscos, 474–5; mosque architecture, 482; Napoleon's invasion of, 755, 826; origins, 456, 460, 465; palaces, 480–1; peace treaty with Austrian Habsburgs, 461f, 475f; Portugal and Ethiopia, 561f, 566; public festivities, 481; reform efforts, 757–8, 761–2; rise of, 464–75; rivalry with Russia, 756; Rose Garden Edict, 761; Russo-Ottoman War, 763; and Safavid Empire, 473; scope of, 468; Second Balkan War, 756; sieges of Vienna, 461f, 468, 757f; slavery/ending of slavery in, 754–5; Sunni Ottomans, 765; Tanzimat Reforms, 652f, 757f, 761; Tatar-Ottoman alliance, 770; taxation of Jews, 475, 477; theater, 481–2; Timur's encounters with, 486; Versailles Treaty

and, 856; victories over Safavids, 468, 473, 474; weaponry used by, 611; Western Challenges, 759–65; Young Ottomans, 653f, 757f, 762–4, 769
Ottoman-Portuguese Indian Ocean competition, 473m
Out-of-Africa theory, 10
Owen, Robert, 802

Pacific Island migrations: colonization map, 140m; Lapita cultural complex, 3, 123, 139, 140–1, 143; Oceania, 120, 123f, 139, 142, 143–5; origins of, 139–42; Polynesia, 96, 123f, 139, 141–2, 145
Paekche Kingdom (Korea), 374, 382, 389
Pahlavi, Shah Muhammad, 949–50
Pakistan, 220, 848f, 889, 891f, 911–12
Palace-state (defined), 46
Paleolithic (Old Stone Age) era: early forms of writing, 38; forager period, 12; gender functions in, 40; invention of ceramics, 19; Neanderthal fossil discoveries, 18; population growth, 27; religious artifacts, 20; spiritual preoccupations, 56; time frame of, 9, 20
Palestine: Arab-Jewish conflict, 865, 908–9, 909m; Arab rule in, 274–5; Christianity in, 202, 773; geographic features, 31–2; Judaism in, 198, 201–2, 853, 865; Mamluk Sultanate in, 291, 460; nationalist movement, 947–8; New Kingdom conquest of, 49; 1947-1949 conflict with Israel, 908–9; promise as Jewish homeland, 853f, 864–5
Palestine Liberation Organization (PLO), 947, 948, 949, 977–8
Palestinian-Arab nationalist uprisings, 865
Palestrina, Pierluigi da, Giovanni, 494*Pali Canon* (Buddhist text), 227
Pallava Kingdom (Southern India), 217f, 220, 222, 345, 345f
Panama, 689
Panama Canal, 700, 794
Pandya Kingdom (India), 345
Pankhurst, Emmeline, 805
Papacy: Alexander V, 334; Avignon Papacy period, 311f, 324; Boniface VIII, 334; canon law utilized by, 329; Charlemagne's protection of, 312; Clement V, 334; Clement VII, 334; College of Cardinals, 322; encouragement of monastic fighting orders, 460; European reforms, 321–2; Franco-papal alliance, 310; Gregory I, 308, 309, 311, 311f; Gregory VII, 322; Gregory XI, 334; influence in Germany, 508; Innocent III, 325; Investiture Controversy, 321–2; John Paul I, 928; John XII, 316; Leo II, 312; Leo III, 312; Leo X, 458; Martin V, 337; Sylvester II, 328; Urban II, 324; Urban VI, 334
Papal Election Decree (1059), 322
Papin, Denis, 493f, 501–2, 792
Papyrus, 44, 182
Paracas chiefdom (Peru), 151f, 172
Paraguay, 690; political instability in, 691–2; War of Paraguay, 696
Paraguayan War, 692
Pardos settlements, in South America, 697–8
Parhae Kingdom (Korea), 373f
Paris, Treaty of (1453), 234
Paris Academy of Sciences, 499
Paris Exposition (1889), 806
Paris Global Climate Agreement, 963f
Parmenides (Greek philosopher), 200
Parthian Persian Empire, 179, 182f, 187–8, 190
Pascal, Blaise, 501
Pastoral Symphony (Beethoven), 681
Patagonian Shield (geographic region), 123
Patriarchal society: in Alexandria, 405–6; in China, 106, 116–17, 238, 260, 265, 388; in Constantinople, 203, 285; of Creoles, 548; in Egypt, 42, 406; gender and, 40; in India, 77–8, 939; in Islamic civilization, 273, 283, 293; in Korea, 378; in Latin America, 717; in Mesopotamia, 41; in Middle Eastern cultures, 40; in Nubia, 402–3; origins, 12; in Rome, 208, 213; in Syria, 406; in Western Europe, 652
Patterns Up Close: the "age of steam," 792–3; Akbar's attempt at religious synthesis, 602–3; Babylonian law codes, 42–3; Bandung/origins of non-aligned movement, 914–15; Byzantine icons and Islamic miniatures, 302–3; the caste system, 76–7; the "China" trade, 626–7; disappearance of Neanderthals, 22–3; global trade of Indian pepper, 234–5; gothic cathedrals, 326–7; the guillotine, 662–3; gunpowder, 356–7; Harlem Renaissance, African Diaspora, 860–1; human sacrifice and propaganda, 450–1; mapping the world, 504–5; Mayan ball game, 168–9; military transformations, new imperialism, 826–7; origin of corn, 130–1; Plague of Justinian, 194–5, 194m; printing, 379–80; sculptures of Ife, 422–3; self-strengthening, Western science, Eastern Ethics, 732–3; shipbuilding, 466–7; slave rebellions in Cuba and Brazil, 696–7; social networking, 984–5; the stirrup, 254–5; Sunni and Shiite Islam, 766–7; voodoo and other New World slave religions, 584–5; from women's liberation to feminism, 938–9
Paul, Mary, 784–5, 802
Peace of Westphalia, 516
Peace Preservation Law (Japan), 878
Pearl River system (China), 92
Peasants' War (Germany), 493f
Pedra Furada rock paintings (Brazil), 126, 127f
Pedro II (Emperor of Brazil), 694
Pedro I (Emperor of Brazil), 693–4
Pedro IV (King of Kongo), 559–60
Pelesets (Philistines), 49, 52–3
People's Liberation Army (China), 905, 941
Pepin III ("the Short") (Carolingian mayor), 310
Pepper trade, of India, 234–5
Perestroika policy (Soviet Union), 849f, 927f, 928–31
Perón, Eva Duarte, 904
Perón, Juan, 904
Perpetual Peace (Kant), 668–9
Perry, Mathew C., 636, 652f, 725f, 738–9, 745, 749, 791
Persian Empire: administration of, 181–3; Alexander's conquests in, 178, 185–6; bubonic plague in, 194; components of, 181; conquests of, 180; divine and heroic myths in, 205; failed invasions in Greece, 185–6; final Persian-Roman war, 274; Greece's interactions with, 179–86; as gunpowder empire, 611; Hun invasions, 182f; imperial recovery in, 182f; innovators, visionaries in, 243; Jews and Judaism in, 193; Khosrow I, 196; Khosrow II, 274; legal system, 181; military prowess of, 180–1; Mithridates II renewal of, 188; monotheism, adoption of, 192; palaces in Iran, Mesopotamia, 182; rejuvenation of, 192; religion, spirituality, 181; Roman Empire interactions with, 186–97; satraps (provincial governors), 181; shahinshahs ("king of kings"), 181–2, 193, 204; trade activities, 182, 296; tributes and taxes, 181; weaponry used by, 611; writing developments, 182; Zoroastrianism adopted by, 193. *See also* Achaemenid Persian Empire; Parthian Persian Empire; Sasanid Persian Empire
Persians, The (Aeschylus), 207
Peru: archaeological findings, 118, 119; Caral-Supe city, 3f, 118, 119, 123f; ceramic achievements, 119; ceremonial centers, 171, 172; copper mining, 430; economic inequality in, 902; El Paraíso structures, 131–2; independence gained by, 689; Moche chiefdom, 147f, 151f, 171–2; Native Americans in, 690; Nazca chiefdom, 151f, 172–3, 176, 449; Paracas chiefdom, 151f, 172; populist regime in, 904; Puruchuco burial place, 428; San Martin's liberation of, 690; silver mining, 541, 690; Spanish conquests in, 526–30; territorial conflicts, 700; Túpac Amaru burial site, 428–9. *See also* Wari city-state
Peter the Great (Russian Tsar), 769–70
Petrarch, Francesco, 337
Phallic stones, 72–3, 84
Phan Boi Chau (Vietnamese leader), 844
Philip II (King of France), 325
Philip II (King of Spain), 461f, 493f
Philippine-American War, 842
Philippines: defeat of Spain, 842; Spanish colonialism in, 840–2; trade activities, 387; U.S. conquest of, 819f
Philistines (Pelesets), 33f
Phillip II (King of Macedonia), 185–6, 188
Phillip II (King of Spain), 840
Philology, in the Renaissance era, 493
Phoenician Kingdom, 181; city-states in, 52; construction of galleys for Persian navy, 181; founding of ports, 52; letter alphabet invention, 52, 53f, 54; origins, 33f, 51–2; trade activities, 52, 54
Phytoliths (banana phytoliths), 156–7
Picasso, Pablo, 812
Piers Plowman (Langland), 337
Pillow Book (Sei Shonagon), 370
Pizan, Christine de, 337–8
Pizarro, Francisco, 528–30, 532
Planck, Max, 808
Plantation slavery, in the Americas: Brazil's sugar empire, 576; Byzantium roots, 571–2; Caribbean plantations, 573; Carolina plantations, 578–9; chattel slavery, 572–4; defined, 572; indentured laborers, 576, 578; mercantilism in the Caribbean, 574–6; numbers of slaves, 572; serfdom comparison, 754–5

Plassey, Battle of (1757), 819f
Plato, 146f, 182f, 492, 493
Platonic-Aristotelian thought, 299
Platonists, 494
Plessy v. Ferguson (1896), 933
Plow and wheel, introduction of, 33
Plymouth, Massachusetts, settlement, 537
Poe, Edgar Allan, 682
Poetry Classic (Book of Odes), 109–10, 114
Poitiers, Battle of, 333
Poland: Catherine II's dismantling of, 770; Cold War era revolt in, 896–7, 929–30; as Eastern Bloc country, 898; female scientists in, 500; Havel's interim presidency, 931; independence gained by, 931; nationalists rise to power, 975; post-Black Death population recovery, 505; Solidarity labor union, 928–9; Velvet Revolution in, 931; Walesa's leadership, 931; in World War II, 875–6
Political theory, in the Renaissance era, 493
Politics (Aristotle), 493
Polo, Marco, 355, 359m
Pol Pot (Khmer Rouge leader), 946
Polynesia, 96, 123f, 139, 141–2, 145
Polytheism: challenges to, 198–200; defined, 56; kingship origins, 57; in Mayan Kingdoms, 164; in Middle East, Mediterranean, 192–3; move to monotheism, 199–200; naturalism transition toward, 55; writing's connection to, 56–7
Pomeranz, Kenneth, 624
Popular Front coalition (France), 864
Portugal: apocalyptic expectations, 460, 462; astronomical discoveries, 504; Atlantic slave trade of, 567–8; battle with Ottoman forces, 473m; Cabral's claim of Brazil for, 527f; Catholicism in, 551; China's treaty port opened with, 729m; colonialism of, 464, 530–1, 536; conquest of Brazil, 464, 530–1, 536; conquest of Ceuta, North Africa, 461f; early industrialism in, 791m; Ethiopian support against Ottomans, 561f; fossil discoveries, 23; Ice Age influence, 20; imperialism in Africa, 835, 836; imperialism in Southeast Asia, 838; Indian Ocean competition with Ottomans, 473m; interest in China's Ming porcelain, 627; maritime explorations, 460, 464; Moroccan victories in, 563; post-WW I ideology of, 851; raids against West Africa, 567–8; *Reconquista* policies, 460, 462, 564; Saint Anthony of Padua, 558, 559, 570f; Sebastião's leadership, 570; shipbuilding innovations, 467; slave trade, 570; territorial imperialism by, 817; trade activities, 473m, 530; trade fort monopoly of, 580; trade forts of, 838; Treaty of Tordesillas with Spain, 461f; union with Brazil, 691f, 693; West Africa explorations, 561f, 564–5
Positivism, 695
Postcolonialism, 962
Postmodernism, 488, 962
Potosí silver mines, Peru, 527f, 541
Potsdam Conference (1945), 891f
Power loom (invention), 787
Powhatan Confederacy, Native Americans, 539
"Prague Spring" (Czechoslovakia), 927–8
Predestination doctrine, in Calvinism, 510
Presentism, 573
Prestor John (mythical Christian ruler), 461, 464, 566
Prince, The (Machiavelli), 493
Principia Mathematica (Newton), 490
Printing developments: in China, 380–1; in Japan, 380–1; in Korea, 377, 378, 380–1; in Renaissance Europe, 492–3; in Vietnam, 380–1
Progressive era, United States, 679
Progressive Organization for Women (POW), 939
Protestantism: in Bulgaria, 474; in China, 730; in England, 509–10, 513; in Hungary, 474; Netherlands war of independence from, 473–4; in New England, 552–3; in northeast colonies, 551; Renaissance and, 494
Protestant Reformation: Baroque arts and, 494; Bohemia's role in fueling, 337; central state formation and, 504; Charles V and, 471, 509; influence on central state formation, 504; map, 511m; origins, 456f, 493f, 508–9; spread of religious tracts during, 381, 508; Wycliffe and, 335f
Proto-Indo-Europeans, 47
Prussia: alliance against Napoleon, 662; Catherine II's dismantling of, 770; constitutionalism in, 675; Franco-Prussian War, 675, 790; Frederick II, reign of, 493f; restoration of monarchy, 829; rise of, 519; role in Seven Years' War, 826; scientific societies in, 499; as victim of state centralization, 318
Prussian-Austrian War (1866), 675
Ptolemaic Egypt, 154, 186, 187–8, 187m, 204, 234
Ptolemy, Claudius, 205, 329, 495
Pueblo cultures, 430, 431m
Pueblo Revolt (1680), 702
Punjab state (India), 215, 224, 233
Pure Food and Drug and Meat Inspection Acts (1906, U.S.), 680
Puritans, 513–14, 537
Puruchuco burial place (Peru), 428
Putin, Vladimir, 970–1
Pyramids, Battle of (1798), 826f
Pyramids of Egypt, 44–5, 44f, 119

Qaddafi, Muammar el-, 981
Qajar Dynasty (Iran), 765, 768–9, 780
Qianlong Emperor (China): Castiglione's artistic influence, 637; China during the reign of, 630m; interaction with Macartney, 725; military campaigns of, 629; as patron of the arts, 629, 636, 637; political tensions, economic stresses, 634; reign of, 457f, 623f, 628; timeline placement, 725f
Qi Dynasty (China), 103, 105
Qin Dynasty (China), 103, 105, 111; battles against nomadic peoples, 249; burial customs, 250f; Chinese character development, 111; conflict in (modern) Vietnam, 249; Confucianism during, 262; conquest of Zhou, 248–9; empire map, 249m; first Chinese emperor in, 245f; Legalism in, 248, 249; origin, 103; power struggles, 242; role in China's unification, 105, 243, 248; Shang Yang, ruler, 249; timeline placement, 147f
Qing Dynasty (China): administrative restructuring, 633; agricultural developments, 634; anti-Qing rebellions, 736–7; banner system expansion, 625, 628–9; ban on Christian proselytizing, 730; *baojia* local organization system, 444, 633; brink of collapsing of, 722; "carrot and stick" border safeguard strategy, 629; culture, arts, and science, 743–5; dispute resolution with Tibetan Buddhism, 629; economy, 725, 741–2; fall of, 629, 848f, 853f, 879; global commercial revolution a, 622–4; Grand Council advisory group, 628; hair styles (queues) for men, 628; Kangxi Emperor, 623f, 628–9, 631–2, 636, 637f; limited resistance to foreign demands, 729; military strength of, 629; modernity, new economic order in, 741–5; opium trade and, 727; origin of, 621–2, 623f, 625; philosophy in, 637; poetry, travel accounts, newspapers, 744; retention of Ming Grand Secretariat, 628; Revolt of the Three Feudatories, 629; rural economics and society, 742; rural life in, 633–4; science and literature, 636; self-strengthening by, 741–2; social stability during, 648; social trends, 742–3; technology in, 744–5; village and family life, 633–5; weaponry of, 629, 636; Yongzheng Emperor, 628, 636
Qin Shi Huangdi (First Emperor of China), 92, 250–1, 250f
Quebec City, French settlement (Canada), 527f, 537, 540
Quetzalcóatl, Temple of the Feathered Serpent God, 169
Qufu compound (Shandong Province, China), 244
Quipu coded communication system (Americas), 119, 130–1
Quotations from Chairman Mao Zedong, 941
Quran (Islam holy scripture), 277–9, 303, 305, 306, 593, 599f, 601

Radical republicanism, 666
Radiocarbon dating, 118, 120
Railroads: in Argentina, 692; in Brazil, 694, 695, 697; in Canada, 716; in England, 787f; in Great Britain, 789; in Latin America, 714–16; in Mexico, 706, 712; in Nicaragua, 719; Trans-Siberian Railroad, 778; in the U.S., 787f, 790; in Venezuela, 700
Rain-forest settlements: in Africa, 6, 7, 150, 155–7;of early hominins, 8; of La Venta, 135; of Olmecs, 134; West Africa, 156
Rajputanas Kingdom (Gujarat), 222
Rajputs of India, 347, 596, 618, 824
Ramadan observance, 279, 481–2, 816, 927, 937
Ramayana (Hindu sacred text), 80–1, 83
Ranke, Leopold von, 267
Rapa Nui monoliths (Oceania), 141, 142, 145
Rape of Nanjing, 853f, 881–2
Rashtakutra state (India), 345

Rastafarians, 407–8
Raziya (female Sultan), 347
Reagan, Ronald, 929, 937, 954, 973
Realism, in prose literature, 682, 684
Reciprocity agreements (Early Americas), 435–6, 438
Reciprocity doctrine (in Confucianism), 244–5
Reconquista: defined, 324; fall of Granada, as culmination, 462–3; of Iberia, 459; North Africa and, 564; Portugal's policies, 460, 462, 564; West Africa and, 564–5
Records of the Grand Historian (Shiji) (Sima Qian), 103, 373
Red Brigades (West Germany), 937
Red Eyebrow Revolt (Han Dynasty, China), 252–3
Red Rubber (Morel), 846
Reform War (Mexico), 704
Reign of Terror (French Revolution), 661, 662
Relativity theory (Einstein), 787f, 809
Religion/spirituality: in Africa, 159; in Andes culture, 133–4; Catholic missionaries in China, 244; in China, 110–14, 244–8, 350–4; Dreamtime ritual, 16–17, 28; in Eurasia, 147, 270; European reforms, 321–6; in Harappa, 72–3; in India, 57, 65, 67f, 84–7; in Mayan Kingdoms, 164; naturalism transition to polytheism, 55–6; in New Kingdom Egypt, 57; New World slave religions, 584–5; of Olmecs, 135; Paleolithic era, 56; in Persian Empire, 181; in sub-Saharan Africa, 147; symbols, 2; in Ubaid Mesopotamia, 56. *See also* Religious civilizations; specific religions
Religious civilizations: of Asia, 256, 270, 273; Christian Rome's foundation, 216; disappearance of polytheism, 200; emergence and development (600-1450), 270; of Europe, 273; external challenges, 271; Hinduism's evolution, 233; internal forces in, 271; in Islamic, 273–81; monotheism, monism foundations of, 146; roles of followers, 271
Renaissance (European Renaissance): Baroque arts and, 492, 494; Catholicism and, 494; cultural transformations, 491, 492; description, 492; music, sculpture, theater, 494; origins, 457; philology and political theory, 493; printing and new manuscripts, 492–3; Protestantism and, 494
Republicanism: Bolívar's preference for, 699; defined, 55; France and, 660, 673, 685, 772; U.S. and, 685
Restoration War (Japan), 725f
Revelation (Greek *Apokalypsis*), 460, 462
Revolt of the Three Feudatories (Qing Dynasty), 629
Revolutionary Alliance of 1905 (China), 879
Rhind Mathematical Papyrus (early Egyptian mathematics textbook), 59–60
Rhodes, Cecil, 837
Ricci, Matteo, 457f, 623f, 631f
Rice: in China, 2, 3f, 78–9, 93f, 94, 96–7, 107, 111; in India, 78, 79, 82, 92, 608; in Japan, 381–2, 386, 387; in Korea, 372, 376, 378; in Neolithic cultures, 70, 78–9; in Vietnam, 391–2, 394
Richard I (King of England), 325
Richard II (King of England), 335
Rig-Veda (Hindu text), 74, 76, 77–8, 88
Ritual pollution, 233–4
Rivera, Diego, 701f
Roaring Twenties (U.S.), 858, 861–2
Rock art/paintings: in the Americas,126f, 127f; in Australia, 17; in Brazil, 126; emergence of humans and, 2, 5; in Europe, 17, 18–19, 20f; by *H. sapiens,* 18–20; in South Africa, 13
Rockefeller, John D., 679
Roentgen, Wilhelm, 808
Roe v. Wade (1973), 934
Roman Catholicism, 256
Roman Empire: Academy of Plato, 204; Arab conquests, 273; architectural style, 326; architecture of, 210; artistic achievements, 208–10, 209f; Augustan age, 190–1, 190f; barbarian migrations into, 196m; bubonic plague in, 194–5; chiefly asslemblies tradition, 421; Christianity adopted by, 154, 182f, 193, 195–6, 308; conflicts with Meroë, 153; dates of early empire, 147f; decline of, 320; defeat of Antigonids, 189; empire building, 146, 189–90; end of, 147f; expansion into Middle East, 146; final Roman-Persian war, 274; Hun invasions, 182f; imperialism of, 182f; innovators, visionaries in, 243; Isthmus Declaration, 189; Italian peninsula unification, 182f; Justinian I's reconstruction of, 194–6; late period dates, 182f; legal system, 195; legionaries (foot soldiers) of, 189, 191; literary achievements, 208; medicine, 329; monotheism, adoption of, 192; nomadic invasions, 196m; Nubian Kingdom interactions, 405; in 100 CE, 191m; origins, 189; Parthian contact with, 188; Persian Empire interactions with, 186–97; political and economic crisis, 192; republican origins of, 188–9; Sasanid war with, 146; shipbuilding in, 466; taxation of, 191; trade activities, 296; unification efforts, 189; western empire, ending of, 182f
Romania, 757f, 898, 931
Romanov Dynasty (Russia), 769–70
Roman Peace *(pax romana),* 191
Roman-Persian War, 274
Romanticism era, 681–2
Rommel, Erwin ("the Desert Fox"), 877
Roosevelt, Franklin, 853f, 862. *See also* New Deal
Roosevelt, Theodore, 679–80, 700
Rose Garden Edict (Ottoman Empire), 761
Rouhani, Hasan, 978
Rousseau, Jean-Jacques, 660, 668–9
Royal Society of London (England), 499, 501
Rum running, British North America, 581
Rum Sultanate (Seljuk Empire), 289
Russia: Alexander I's leadership, 772; Alexander II's leadership, 774, 776, 777, 780–1, 783, 788, 869; Alexander III's leadership, 776; alliance against Napoleon, 662; annexation of Crimea, 963f; Arab campaigns against, 276; Bolshevik Party, 854, 869; Bolshevik Revolution, 848f, 853f, 880, 890; Boxer Rebellion and, 736; Britain's Great Game against, 829–30; Byzantine Christian civilization in, 755; Catherine II's reforms, 757f, 770; civil war and reconstruction, 869; communism ideology in, 851; Communist Party takeover, 849; country name derivation, 285; Crimean War, 692, 755, 757f, 762, 773, 774, 777, 783–4, 791, 830; Decembrist Revolt, 771; early industrialism in, 851; early 19th century, 771–4; Eastern Orthodox Christianity, 755; economic crisis, recovery, 970; emancipation of serfs, 757f; ending of serfdom in, 755; ethnic nationalism organizing ideology of, 829; expansion of, 520m; February Revolution, 854; First Ottoman-Russian War, 757f; French Revolution's influence, 772; gulag system, 898–9; Habsburg opposition to expansion by, 852; Ice Age influence, 21; imperialism against Qajars, 768; industrialism and society, 777–8; industrialism in, 791; industrialization in, 777; intervention in Syria, 963f; losses in WW I, 781, 863; "matristic" society in, 12; migration from, 19, 22; military slaves, 291; Napoleon's invasion of, 755; Nicholas I's leadership, 771; Nicholas II's leadership, 776–7; nomadic invasions, 193; Peter the Great's leadership, 769–70; post-Black Death population recovery, 505; Pugachev's Cossack revolt, 770; Putin's presidency, 970–1; Qing, Meiji, Ottomans comparison, 769; restoration of monarchy, 829; revolution of 1905, 757f, 769, 779–80; rise of, 518–19; rivalry with Ottomans, 756; role as Greece's coreligionist, protector, 829; role in Seven Years' War, 826; Romanov Dynasty, 769–70; Russo-Japanese War, 723, 757f; Russo-Ottoman War, 763; scientific societies in, 499; serfdom in, 754; Sino-Japanese War and, 735; Slavs emigrations to, 282; Social Democratic Labor Party, 779; support for Serb ethnic nationalism, 853; territorial expansion (1795–1914), 771m; Triple Intervention against Japan, 723; westernization in, 769–70; in WW I, 853–4. *See also* Lenin, Vladimir Ilyich; Russo-Japanese War; Siberia
Russian Revolution, 757f
Russo-Japanese War (1904–1905), 653f, 723, 757f, 778, 779
Russo-Ottoman War, 763
Rutherford, Ernest, 808
Rwanda, 963f

Saadid Empire, 468–9
Sacco, Ferdinando Nicola, 860
Safavid Persian Empire: Battle of Chaldiran, 469–70; growth into Shiite warrior organization, 469–70; military vulnerability of, 768; origins, 456; Ottoman victories over, 468, 473, 474; raids against Christians, 469; rule in Iran, 765, 768–9; rule in Morocco, 469
Saharan chiefdoms and kingdoms, 150
Sahel (steppe), sub-Saharan Africa, 155, 156
Saint-Simon, Henri de, 802

Sake brewing (Japan), 387
Sakoku (closed country) policy, Japan, 649, 650–1
Salah al-Din (Saladin) Ibn Ayyub, 290
Salim Chishti (Sufi mystic), 598–9, 601
Samarkand, 356, 594–6
Samudragupta (ruler of Gupta Empire), 220–1
Samurai warriors (Japan), 385, 387, 389–90, 397, 398–9, 646–7
Sandinista National Liberation Front (FSLN), 954
Sandrokoptros, 214–15
San Lorenzo settlement (Olmec culture), 123f, 134
San Martin, José de, 690–1, 698–9; meeting with Bolívar, 698–9
Santa Anna, Antonio Lopez de, 702, 703–4, 705
Sanusiyya Brotherhood (North Africa), 837
Sarasvati River (India), 215
Sargon of Akkad, 30, 39–40, 39–45, 65
Sasanid Persian Empire: agricultural expansion, 281; Arab conquests, 273; Arab exploitation of, 273; architecture, 206; Christianity adopted by, 193; consolidation of rule, 192; Heraclitus's conquests in, 274; Hun invasions of, 194; imperialism of, 155; Indian texts transmitted by, 205–6; invasion of Aksum Kingdom, 155, 405; Khosrow I, 196–7; Khosrow II, 210–11; map, 197m; rivalries in, 179; Roman competition with, 146; timeline of, 182f; war of succession, 210–11; war with Byzantium, 275f; Zoroastrianism in, 182f, 193
Satraps (provincial governors), in Persia, 181
Savery, Thomas, 792
Sayyid Sultanate, 348
Schall von Bell, Adam, 631
Schlieffen Plan (Germany), 853
Schoenberg, Arnold, 812
Scholar-gentry, of China, 257, 358, 362–3, 366, 377, 394–5, 633–5, 730
School of Athens (Raphael), 495f
Scientific achievements: in Byzantium, 495; in China, 265; in India, 238–9; Islamic civilization, 299–300; at the Library of Alexandria, 204–5; medieval Europe, 329. *See also* New Sciences
Scientific-industrial society, 456
Scotland: ethnolinguistic sense of identity, 680; New Lanark community, 802; religious wars, 493f; trade activities, 789
Scottish Maiden (guillotine), 662
Scotus, John Duns, 338
Scramble for Africa, 832–7
Scythian culture (central Asia), 108–9
Sea Peoples, 49, 52
Sea trade networks, 460
Sebastião I (King of Portugal), 570
Second Balkan War (1913), 756
Second Coming of Christ, 460, 463
Second Crusade (to the Holy Land), 290
Second German Empire, 676, 849
Second Opium War (China), 762, 773, 821
Second Reform Act (1867, Great Britain), 680–1
Second Sex, The (de Beauvoir), 934
Second-wave feminism, 937–8
Securities and Exchange Commission (SEC), 862
Sei Shonagon, 388
Seiyukai (Constitutional Government Party; Japan), 725f
Seiyukai Party (Japan), 725f, 748
Sejong (Korean King), 373f
Sekigahara, Battle of, 639–41
Seleucid Kingdom (Southeast Asia), 186–8, 187m, 324. *See also* Parthian Persian Empire
Seleucus Nikator, 80, 215, 217
Self-Help (Smiles), 800
Self-Strengthening Movement (China), 722, 725f, 731f, 732–4, 741–2
Seljuk Empire: conquests of Byzantines, 275f, 287–9; Crusades and, 289; defeat of Manzikert, 288; invasions, 287; map, 287m; move to eastern Mediterranean region, 594; Rum Sultanate, 289; timeline placement, 275f
Senghor, Léopold, 861
Sepoy Mutiny (India), 653f, 819f, 821–2, 827
Seppuku (ritual suicide), 385
September 11, 2001, terrorist attack, 967
Serbia: ethnic nationalism of, 853; First Balkan War participation, 764; independence gained by, 757f; Ottoman conquests in, 468
Serfdom: defined, 754; end of, in Russia, 755; Enlightenment constitutionalism opposition to, 755; in Russia, 754
Seven Years' War (1756-1763), 663–4; causes, 540–1, 618, 656, 826; France, 659, 834; Great Britain, 656; Louisiana Purchase and, 665; role of British East India Company, 618, 818; role of Russia, 826; timeline placement, 657f
Sexual revolution, 934–5
Shahinshahs (Persian Empire), 181–2, 193, 204
Shah Jahan (Mughal Emperor): building of Taj Mahal, 592m, 593, 595f, 601, 613, 615–16; depressed state of mind of, 592; legalistic traditions of, 601; timeline placement, 595f
Shah of Iran, overthrow of, 849f
Shakespeare, William, 494
Shakti and tantra (in Hinduism), 230–1
Shamans/shamanism: in the Americas, 126, 132–3, 135; Australian Dreamtime, 16; in Caribbean cultures, 139; ceremonial caves, 20; Dreamtime ritual, 16–17, 28; in Korea, 378; in Peru, 172, 173
Shang Dynasty (China), 92; armies and expansions, 100; bronze articles and weapons, 90, 96, 98–102, 101, 111; chariot introduction in, 101, 101f; decline of, 104; elite women of, 109–10; Erligang, capital city, 106, 113; historical background, 99–102; horses, 78;human sacrifices, 113; interactions with other states, 102; King Wu Ding, 90–1, 100, 102, 109, 111; Longshan culture absorbed by, 95; map, 100m; mythology, 98; Neolithic Yellow River settlements, 91; origins of, 3, 3f, 93f; politics and foreign relations, 102; religion, 111–13; social class and labor, 106; society of, 106; weaponry, 100f; writing developments, 110–13; writing scripts, 136
Shapur II (Persian ruler), 193
Sharecroppers, in Mesopotamia, 36
Sharia law, 279–80, 305, 306–7, 476, 603, 761, 948, 986
Shaw, George Bernard, 811
Shen Nong, 97
Sher Khan Sur (Afghan leader), 597
Shia Islam, 597
Shiite Islam (Shiism): in Africa, 400; in Baghdad, 287; in Egypt, 290; in India, 613; in Iran, 469, 765; origins, 275f, 280–1; Sunni Islam rivalry, 46, 470, 600, 765, 766–7; "Twelver" Shiites, 287
Shiji (The Records of the Grand Historian) (Sima Tan and Sima Qian), 263
Shimabara rebellion (Japan), 623f, 643
Shimonoseki Treaty (China-Japan), 722–3, 735, 736
Shinto religion (Japan), 378, 383, 388–9, 399
Shipbuilding traditions, 465–6
Shirazi, Fathullah (Indian scientist, philosopher), 611
Shogunates period (Japan), 384–96
Shujing (Chinese historical text), 97, 98, 99, 103–4
Siberia: Beringia land bridge, 24; early human evidence, 7; fossil discoveries, 18, 25; Ice Age influence, 20, 24; migrations from, 13, 27; migrations to, 13
Siberian *H. sapiens,* 25
Sieyès, Emmanuel-Joseph, 660
Sikhs and Sikhism: Aurangzeb's stance against, 604; Hindu/Muslim persecution of, 349; origins, 349
Silk production (China), 256–7
Silk Road trade network: Akbar's control of, 599; Black Death transmission, 298; China's passage through, 92, 188, 232, 252, 258–9, 260m; cross-cultural interactions, 317; description, 258–9; map, 260m; nomadic migrations using, 1193; origin, 109, 188; places to stay along, 233; raids on, 252; regions covered by, 92, 147, 232, 259; spread of Buddhism and, 343; stirrup idea spread on, 254; Tang Dynasty and, 351–3, 354. *See also* Trade activities
Silkworm cultivation, 97
Silla Kingdom (Korea), 374–7, 378, 382–3
Silver flows, global (1650–1750), 626m
Sima Qian (Chinese historian), 263, 373
Sima Tan (Chinese historian), 263
Single-whip tax edicts (China), 623f, 633
Sinicization/sinicizing, 252, 393
Sino-Japanese War, 722–3, 722m, 725f, 734–6, 740, 750, 778
Sino-Soviet split, 940
Sioux, Native Americans, 539, 679
Six Day War (Arab-Israeli War, 1967), 927f, 946f, 947–8, 947m
Six Dynasties period (China), 253
Slash-and-burn agricultural method, 156, 165
Slater, Samuel, 790
Slave revolts: in the Americas, Caribbean Islands, 561f, 586–7, 588m; in Brazil, 694, 696–7; in Cuba, 696–7; in Haiti, 664–5, 665m
Slavery: in Abbasid court, 286f; in Alexandria (Egypt), 292; in the Americas, 572–6; in Brazil, 536–7, 561, 572, 663; in British North America, 576–9; in Byzantium, 285; in Central Asia, 281; in East Africa,

410, 411; ending of, in Brazil, 653f, 691f, 694; in Hispaniola, 561f; household slavery, 567; Islamic prohibition, 476; in Mamluk Empire, 292, 293; in the Middle East, 12; of Native Americans, 532; in the New World, 572; in Nubian Kingdom, 404; in the Ottoman Empire, 754–5; revolts in Americas and Caribbean Islands, 561f; by the Seljuks, 287; Slavic slave soldiers, 289; in Syria, 275; trading of, 296–7; Turkish military slaves, 291. *See also* Abolition of slavery; Atlantic slave trade; Plantation slavery, in the Americas; Slave trade
Slave trade: African, 560–71, 834; Atlantic, 124, 543, 560–1, 561f, 566–71, 580–3; Benin, 568–9; British, 555; Kongo Kingdom, 570; Mediterranean, 560; middle passage, 581–3; Persian Empire, 346; plantation slavery and, 545, 571–6, 579; Portugal, 570; protest by popes against, 292; sub-Saharan Africa, 568. *See also* Atlantic slave trade; Plantation slavery, in the Americas
Smail, Daniel Lord, 6
Smallpox epidemics: in the Americas, 144, 526, 528–9, 531, 534, 536–7, 539, 542, 549, 574; in Eurasia, 144; in Japan, 384
Smiles, Samuel, 800
Smith, Adam, 669, 674–5
Smoot-Hawley Tariff (U.S.), 862
Smriti law codes (India), 83
Snowden, Edward, 963f
Social Contract (Rousseau), 668
Social contract theory (Locke), 652
Social Darwinism, 809, 846
Social Democratic Labor Party (Russia), 779
Social Democratic Party (Germany, SPD), 872
Socialist Party (France), 864
Social networking sites (SNSs), 961, 984–5. *See also* Facebook; Twitter
Social Security Act (U.S.), 862
Society of Jesus, 512
Society of the Friends of Blacks (France), 654
Society of the Harmonious Fists (China), 736
Solano López, Francisco, Jr., 692
Solidarity labor union, Poland, 928–9
Solis, Ruth Shady, 118
Soldaderas (revolutionary women), in Mexico, 702f
Solomonid Dynasty (Ethiopia), 403f, 407–9
Somoza Garcia, Anastasio, 954
Song Dynasty (China): artistic achievements, 365, 366f; beliefs about Tang Dynasty, 343; ceramics artistry, 626–7; Confucianism in, 343; creation of Hangzhou capital, 355; economy and commerce, 355; literary achievement, 366; military ineffectiveness, 354–5; Mongol conquest of, 355; Northen Song Dynasty, 345f; Northern Song Dynasty, 254f, 345f, 366f; as origins of early modern period, 350; rhythm of peasant life in, 363; roads and canals, 355; Southern Song Dynasty, 345f; technological achievements, 354, 365; timeline placement, 345f; Wang Anshi's reforms, 354–5; young girls, issues with treatment of, 260
Songhay Empire (West Africa): attacks on Hausa Kingdoms, 563; decline of, 562–3; gold trade, 561–2; origins, rise of, 561–2, 562m; Saadids's conquest in, 469; timeline placement, 561f; varieties of servitude in, 568
Sons of Liberty, 657
Sophocles (Greek writer), 207
"Sot weed" enterprise (colonial North America), 577–8
South Africa: African National Congress, 953–4; apartheid, 571, 918, 952–3; apartheid, ending of, 953–4; bow and arrow development, 15; British control of, 823; ceremonial rituals, 159; Dutch Cape Colony in, 561f, 570–1; end of apartheid, 849f, 963f; fossil discoveries, 7, 9, 13, 20; Great Zimbabwe Kingdom, 271f, 403f, 409, 415, 416m, 564; Mapungubwe Kingdom, 403f, 414, 415, 417; rise of indigenous kingdoms, 401; Swahili city-states comparison, 411; village life in, 157–60. *See also* Mandela, Nelson
South Africa for Indian Rights, 952
South America: agricultural developments in, 2, 697; Amazonian peoples, 137–8; Bolívar as liberation hero, 689, 697, 698, 699–700; climate, 123; Creole settlements, 697–8; de Piérola's political stability, 700; early migrations to, 118–19; environment of, 121; European emigration to, 798; European explorations, 529m; first settlements, 121; geographic regions, 121, 123; independence from Spain, 691f; mass immigration to, 691f; mountain systems, 121; Pardos settlements, 697–8; student demonstrations, 936; territorial conflicts in, 700. *See also* specific countries
South Central Africa, 563–4, 832
Southeast Asia: China's imperialism in, 734; *Dongsan* cultures, 392; Dutch colonialism in, 838–40, 839m; European trading posts in, 609m; French colonialism, imperialism in, 842–4; *Hoabinhian* culture, 391–2; import substitution industrialization in, 964; Muslim conquests in, 350; origins of agriculture, 3; physical setting map, 392m; Portuguese imperialism in, 838; post-World War II, 916–17; Tang maritime trade with, 350; Western imperialism in, 837–44, 839m; Zheng He's voyages to, 623f. *See also* Vietnam
Southern Cone, 690–2. *See also* Argentina; Brazil; Paraguay; Uruguay
Southern Song Dynasty (China), 345f
South India dynasties, 217f, 222–3, 345, 346m
Soviet Union: boycott of OPEC, 927; Brezhnev's leadership, 926, 928–9; China's border dispute with, 926; collapse of communism, 849f, 932–3, 932m; collapse of communism in, 849f, 932m; collapse of détente with Soviet Union, 929; collectivization of agriculture, 853f, 870–1; collectivization of industrialization, 870–1; communism in, 848, 869; Communist Eastern Europe map, 928m; declining power of, 926–33; dismantling of Czechoslovakia's reforms, 928; Eastern Bloc transformations, 931–3; Eisenhower's fear of, 897; era of détente with U.S., 849, 925, 926–7, 927f; founding of, 848f, 849; glasnost policy, 849f, 927f, 928–32; Gorbachev's leadership, 928, 929–33; Hitler's failed invasion of, 876; invasion of Afghanistan, 849f, 924–5, 929; invasion of Balkans, 891; Khrushchev's leadership, 890, 905; Nuclear Test Ban Treaty, 849f, 899, 925, 927f; perestroika and glasnost, 849f; perestroika policy, 849f, 927f, 928–31; post-Stalinist period industrialization, 899; Sino-Soviet split, 940; socialism in, 848; space race with U.S., 897; Sputnik satellite launch, 848f, 891f, 897, 898f; support of Arabs against Israel, 925; support of Cuba, 897–8; treaty of mutual support with France, 875; U.S. containment policy versus, 891; Yeltsin's leadership, 932–3. *See also* Lenin, Vladimir Ilyich; Stalin, Joseph
Spain: administrative hierarchies in Americas, 531–40, 533m, 538m; Americas discovered by, 456f; Argentina's independence from, 690–1; bureaucratic efficiency of, 532, 534; Castile, 318, 421, 460, 462, 464, 470, 509; Catholicism in, 551; cave paintings, 18; centralization of government in, 508; colonialism of, 531–41, 538m, 840–2; conflicts with Ottomans, 472, 756; conquest of Aztec Empire, 457, 526, 527–8, 527f; conquest of Granada, 456f, 461f, 462–3; conquest of Inca Empire, 526, 527f, 528–30; conquests in the Caribbean Islands, 526, 541–4; conquests of Native Americans, 525–6; construction of El Escorial Palace, 461f; Dutch Protestant war of liberation from, 493f; early industrialism in, 791m; England's seizure of Jamaica from, 561f; entrance into Seven Years' War, 659; expulsion of moriscos, 474–5, 475f; fossil discoveries, 18; Ice Age influence, 20; interest in China's Ming porcelain, 627; Jews expelled from, 456f, 461f; land-labor grants *(encomiendas)*, 526, 534; Latin America's independence from, 709–10; military forces in Mexico, 704–5; money economy in, 479; Muslims expelled from, 461f; Neanderthal era, 23; origins of, 470; Ottoman's invasion of, 472; Philippine victory against, 842; post-WW I ideology of, 851; Pueblo Revolt (1680), 702; reasons for successes of, 531; separation from Viceroyalty of Peru, 690; territorial imperialism by, 817; trade activities, 840; Treaty of Tordesillas with Portugal, 461f; union of Aragon and Castile dynasties, 461f. *See also* Habsburg Empire
Spanish-American War, 842, 846
Spanish Civil War (1936–1939), 853f, 875
Spanish Inquisition, 461f
Sparta, Greek city-state: agriculture in, 184; forts in, 53; independent rule of, 183; maritime trade, 184; military service in, 184; political reforms in, 55; rivalry with Athens, 184
Spartacus, 189–90
Sphinx, Egypt, 44f
Spinning jenny, 787
Spinning mule, 787

Spinoza, Baruch, 503, 667
Spring and Autumn Chronicles (Chunqiu), 103, 105
Spring and Autumn periods (China), 93f, 103, 105, 110, 115, 243, 245f
Sputnik satellite (Soviet Union), 848f, 891f, 897, 898f
Stagflation (1970s), 837
Stalin, Joseph: actions in World War II, 868, 875; blessing for Korean War, 894; building of Communist Party, 868, 870; Churchill's secret deal with, 891; collectivization of agriculture, industrialization, 870–1; leadership of East Germany, 898; prewar "socialism in one country" policy, 890
Stamp Act (U.S.), 656
Stanley, Henry Morton, 832, 835
State formation patterns, in India, 215–23
Statue of Liberty, 792
Steam engine: Newcomen's advances on, 792–3; Papin's invention of, 493f, 501–2, 652, 792; Watt's perfection of, 652f, 787f, 792
Steam-powered factories, 789
Steam-powered riverboats, 789
Steel manufacturing industry, 790–2
Stirrup, development in China, 254–5
Stock market crash (U.S.), 848f, 853f
Strategic Arms Limitation Talks (SALT), I and II, 929
Strategic Defense Initiative (SDI) ("Star Wars"), 929
Student demonstrations, global (1960s), 936–7
Subaltern relationship (defined), 824–5
Sub-Saharan Africa: Americas comparison with, 149; Bantu people, 151f, 155, 157–8, 410, 413, 953; cultural prowess of, 148; Ghana's quest for independence, 918–19; interactions with Eurasia, 14, 147; iron smelting in, 146f, 151f, 152; kingdom formation in, 146; Leo Africanus's travels in, 458–9; monotheism, monism religion, 147; patterns of development, 401; people and kingdoms (1450–1750), 562m; religion, spirituality in, 147; Sahel (steppe), 155, 156; slave trade in, 568; spread of villages in, 155–60, 158m; trade activities, 147. *See also* Aksum kingdom; Meroë kingdom; West Africa
Sudan: Battle of Omdurman, 796f, 831; British imperialism in, 831; Meroitic pyramids, 148m, 150m, 153; Nilo-Saharan chiefdom in, 150
Suez Canal, 787f, 830, 866
Suffragettes, Suffrage movement, 804–5, 819f
Sufi Brotherhood, 831
Sufi Islam (Sufism): in India, 349; integration into Sunni Islam, 275f; origins of, 298, 299; Salim Chishti (Sufi mystic), 599
Suicide bombings, 967, 977
Sui Dynasty (ancient China): empire building, 254–5; internal power rebellion, 255; Korea invaded by, 373f; reunification of China under, 245f, 256, 350; rise of, 383
Sukarno, 889
Süleyman I, the Magnificent (Ottoman Sultan), 468
Sumerian law code, 43
Summa Theologica (St. Thomas Aquinas), 271f, 311f
Summer of love (U.S., 1967), 936
Sundiata (Mali ruler), 403f, 421, 426–7
Sunna (Muhammad's traditions), 278
Sunni Arabs, 982
Sunni Islam (Sunnism), 766–7; Aurangzeb's strict policies, 617–18; evolution, emergence of, 28, 305–6; integration with Sufism, 275f; in the Ottoman Empire, 469; Shiite Islam rivalry, 46, 470, 600, 765, 766–7
Sunni Kurds, 982
Sunni Muslims, 299, 597
Sunni Ottomans, 765
Sunni-Shiite conflict, 961–2
Sunni-Sufi Islam, 299, 300, 305
Sun Yat-Sen, 879–80
Sun Zi (Sun Tzu), 80, 246, 881
Supreme Court rulings: *Brown v. Board of Education*, 933; on the New Deal, 862; *Plessy v. Ferguson*, 933; *Roe v. Wade*, 934
Sustainability, 989–90, 993
Swahili city-states (East African coast): adapting to Islam, 410–11; map, 412m; origin, 409–10; slavery in, 410, 411; timeline placement, 403f; trade activities, 413; urbanism in, 411; Zheng He's visit, 413
Sweden: centralization of government in, 508; post-Black Death population recovery, 505; scientific societies in, 499
Switzerland, 510–11
Sylvester II (Pope), 328
Symphonie phantastique (Berlioz), 681
Syria: Arab conquest of, 275f; Arab Spring protests, 960–1, 981; Assad's presidency, 977; Crusades and, 289; Damascus Spring, 982; early agricultural settlements, 31–2; Egypt's defeat of, withdrawal from, 52–3; Heraclitus's restoration of administrative structures, 274; ISIS jihadist movement in, 963f; mass exodus of refugees, 975; military slaves' power grab, 760; Neo-Assyrian dominance of, 207; 1973 surprise attack on Israel, 927; origins, 402; Ottoman conflicts with, 468; Pelesets overthrow of, 53; Persia's conquests in, 274; Roman rule of, 190; Russian intervention in, 963f; spread of agriculture from, 46

Tailor's Rebellion, 697
Taíno (chiefdom society Caribbean), 139, 526, 552, 667
Taiping Rebellion (China), 628, 635, 725f, 729–30, 731m, 751
Taiwan: annexation of, 723; early migrations from, 123f; import substitution industrialization in, 964; opium trade, 724
Taj Mahal ("Crown Palace"), 592m, 593, 595f, 601, 613, 615–16
Tale of Genji (Murasaki Shikibu), 270f, 371, 373, 388, 391
Taliban regime, 967, 976, 985
Tamil Tiger liberation war (Ceylon), 889
Tang Dynasty (China): agriculture in, 351; Arab conquests in, 351; Buddhist culture in, 256, 262, 265, 350; cosmopolitan character of, 345f; cosmopolitan commerce, 353; decline of, 343, 350, 353; earthenware production, 256; Empress's Wu's rule, 256, 350–1, 353, 354f, 368–9; examination, testing system, 351; expansion and consolidation, 350–1; Korea invaded by, 373f; land distribution policies, 257; losses in northern China, 354; map location, 352m; origin, 255, 264, 270f, 345f; poetry accomplishments, 354; printing presses in, 266; prosperity and growth issues, 351, 353; religious influences in, 350–4; rise of, 383; role in China's reconstitution, 256, 349–50; rule in Korea by, 350; Silk Road and, 351–3; Song Dynasty's beliefs about, 343; technological prowess, 364, 365; trade activities, 232
Tanzimat Reforms (Ottoman Empire), 652f, 757f, 761
Tao Te Ching (Daoist literature), 248
Tatar-Ottoman alliance, 770
Taxation: in Africa, 403, 412–13, 422, 569; in Americas, 163, 165, 444, 448; in Anatolia, 282–3; in Andes culture, 435; in Aztec Empire, 444; in China, 107–8, 251, 253, 257, 353, 355, 358, 377, 563, 633; in Egypt, 43, 53, 291, 293, 298; in England, 316, 335, 514; in France, 316, 335, 516–18; in Iberia, 475; in India, 79, 217, 219, 231–2, 345–6, 348, 818; in Japan, 384, 387; in Middle East, 478–9, 504, 506–7, 758; in New Spain, 534; in Nubia, 403; in Persia, 181–2, 196; in Prussia, 519; in Roman Empire, 191; in Tenochtitlán, 448–9; in Toltec Empire, 432; in Vietnam, 394
Taylor, Frederick W., 806
Taylorism, 807
Tea drinking (Japan), 385, 387, 390
Tea Party movement (U.S.), 973–4
Technological advances: automobiles, 794; communication revolution, 794–5; electricity, 794; internal combustion engine, 794; 1700-1800 period, 787; transcontinental airplane, 795. *See also* Steam engine
Tecumseh (Native American leader), 678
Telegraph, electric, 795
Telephone, 795, 804
Templars (monastic fighting order), 460
Temple at Eridu (Egypt), 37f
Temple complexes: in southern India, 222–3
Temple Mount (Jerusalem), 275
Tennessee Valley Authority, 862
Tenochtitlán (Aztec capital): aqueduct, 446f; as capital of the "inner provinces," 439; causeways and canals, 447–8; *chinampas* agricultural practice, 448–9; Cortés's expedition to, 528, 529m; geographic features, 447, 447m; military of, 447–8; pyramids and palaces, 448; urban life patterns in, 429, 447–9, 453–4
Tenskwatawa (Native American leader), 678
Teotihuacán Kingdom, Mexican Basin: agriculture, 166–7; archaeological discoveries, 166–8; building projects, 168; canal system, 167; ceremonial centers, 169, 170, 430–1, 439, 447; city-state development, 168; climate, 166; cultural expansion, 434; decline of, 432–3; diversified urban culture in, 161;

predominance, 429; ending of, 169–70, 431f; legacy of, 429–34; militarism in, 430–2; religion, spirituality, 169; timeline placement, 151f; writing developments, 167–8
Tereshkova, Valentina, 897
Tesla, Nikola, 794
Thackeray, William Makepeace, 682
Thales (Greek philosopher), 200
Thatcher, Margaret, 973
Theater: in Greece, 207; in Japan, 647–8; in the Renaissance, 494; in Spain, 480–3, 485
Theogony (Hesiod), 207
Theory of Harmony (Schoenberg), 812
Theory of relativity (Einstein), 787f, 809
Theravada Buddhism, 227–9, 264, 344, 373f, 392, 394, 395–6, 889
Third Communist International (Comintern) (China), 880
Third Crusade, 290
Third Republic (France), 676, 686–7, 803, 843
Third-wave feminism, 937–8
Thirteen Colonies (Colonial North America), 657m
Thirty Years' War (Germany), 490, 514–16
Thomas Aquinas, Saint, 271f, 311f, 338
Three Kingdoms era (Korea), 372–4, 373f, 378
Three Kingdoms period (China), 253
Thucydides (Greek historian), 263
Tiananmen Square demonstrations, massacre (China), 849f, 927f, 944
Tibet, 940
Tibetan Buddhism, 629
Tichitt-Oualata villages (Africa), 150–1
Tigris-Euphrates river valley, 31
Tikal city-state (Maya), 161, 163
Timur (Timur-i Lang)/Timur Empire: administration challenges, 596, 606–7; areas subjugated by, 594–5, 595m; Babur's relation to, 358, 596; claimed relation to Genghis Khan, 357–8, 594; claim of special destiny, 465, 595; governing style, 606; encounters with Ottomans, 465, 486; gender roles and divisions, 610; India invaded by, 345f, 348; institutionalization challenges, 597; Mongolian Empire, rebuilding efforts, 465; political challenges, 606; rule by Humayan, 596–7, 600, 612, 614, 619; timeline placement, 595f; trading activities, 594–5
Tito, Josip (Yugoslavian President), 975
Tiwanaku state: agriculture, 435; ceremonial center, 436; disintegration of, 441; expansion, colonization, 436; governmental authority in, 436; map, 437m; reciprocity agreements, 435–6; ruling class of, 429; timeline placement, 431f; Wari comparison, 437; Wari-Tiwanaku frontier, 437–8
Tokugawa Shogunate (Japan): arrival of the "black ships," 738–9; artistic achievements, 648; *bakufu* ("tent government"), 641; banning of firearms by, 357, 642; Battle of Sekigahara victory, 639; central administrative system challenges, 606; commercial enterprise development, 745; decline of seclusion of, 738; engagement of Western science, 749–50; establishment of, 623f; feudalism in, 313; intolerance of Christianity, 643–4; limitations on foreigners, 632, 642–3, 649; long rule by, 621; Neo-Confucianism and, 388, 640; pottery production during, 627; rural transformations, 645–6; samurai warriors, 646–7; view of foreign influence, 624–5; warrior bureaucracy of, 739
Tokugawa shoguns (Japan), 606
Toltec culture: ceremonial centers, 430, 439; conquests of, 431m; cultural expansion, 430, 434; decline of, 432; military, 432; origins, 430–1, 431m; timeline placement, 431f; trade activities, 432; Tula, capital, 432; weaponry innovations, 432, 441
Tools and toolmaking: Aboriginal tools, 17; Acheulian tools, 9, 9f; in Africa, early humans, 2; in Asia, early humans, 3; fossil discoveries, 6f; *H. sapiens*, 11, 12, 13, 18, 28; in India, 10; Levallois tools, 8, 11f; Neanderthals, 23; Oldowan tools, 8–9; Paleolithic tools, 9
Tordesillas, Treaty of, 461f
Torricelli, Evangelista, 501
Toumaï, 2, 6, 7
Toussaint Louverture, François-Dominique, 665–6
Trade activities: Abbasids, 285; Afghanistan, 72; Africa, 622; Africa, Mediterranean, Indian Ocean (1415-1498), 461m; Afro-Eurasian global system, 296–8; Aksum, 155; Aksum Kingdom, 155, 405; Alexandria, 318; Americas, 622; Anatolia, 46; Argentina, 690; Athens, 184; Australian Aborigines, 16, 17; Brazil, 530, 695; Caral-Supe valley, Peru, 129; Caribbean Islands, 659; Carolingians, 285; central Asia, 71–2, 108–9, 147; Chichén Itzá, 434; China, 160, 318, 622, 624, 631–3, 840; early humans, 11–12; East Africa, 155, 159–60, 405, 835; Egypt, 46, 65; England, 460; Ethiopia, 153; Eurasia, 346m, 724; Europe, 318–19, 319m, 335–6; Great Britain, 690, 789, 834; Greece, 54; Harappan civilization, 65, 71–2; Hispaniola, 543–4; India, 217, 219, 222, 225, 228, 231–5, 318, 345, 350; India, Indus Valley, 71; Indonesia, 141, 159–60, 345, 571, 623–4, 845; Inuit, 136; Iraq, 404; Japan, 350, 387, 624, 636, 652f, 725f, 738–9, 745, 749, 791; Korea, 387; Latin America, 711–12, 713; Mali, 421, 563; Mapungubwe Kingdom, 414; Mayan Kingdoms, 431m; Mediterranean trade, 319; Meroë Kingdom, 151–2, 160; Americas, 431m; Mesopotamia, 37, 46; Middle East, 350; Morocco, 52, 561; Mughal Empire, India, 608–9; Muslims, 222, 296; Northeast Africa, Middle East (80–1200 CE), 404m; in Nubian Kingdom, 37, 402–4; Parthian Persia, 160; permanent port developments, 160; Persian Empire, 182, 296; Philippines, 387; Phoenicia, 52, 54; Portugal, 473m, 530, 567–8; Ptolemaic Egypt, 160; Roman Egypt, 160; Roman Empire, 296; Sasanian Persia, 160; Scotland, 789; sea trade networks, 460; Songhay Empire, West Africa, 561–2; Spain, 318, 840; Sri Lanka, 160; Swahili city-states, 413; Syria, 46; Tang Dynasty, 350; Timur Empire, 594–5; Toltec culture, 432; Trans-Saharan trade route, 156, 461m; 2008, global balance of trade, 965m; United States, 789; Vietnam, 394–5; West Africa, 567–8, 834; world commercial revolution and, 622–3; Yangzi River system, 255; Yemeni, 159–60; Yuan Dynasty's prototype free trade zone, 356. *See also* Maritime trade; Silk Road trade network
Trade unions, 802
"Trail of Tears" (U.S. Native Americans), 679
Transatlantic radio message (Marconi), 787f, 795
Trans-Atlantic slave trade, 124, 543
Transcontinental railroad (U.S.), 787f, 790
Transoceanic cables, 795
Trans-Saharan trade routes, 461m
Trans-Siberian Railroad, 778
Treaty of Kadesh, 49
Treaty ports (China), 727–34, 729f, 735f, 735m
Tres Zapotes settlement (Olmec culture), 136
Trinitarian Byzantine Christianity, 275
Trinitarianism, 275
Tripitaka (Buddhist texts), 227, 378
Triple Intervention against Japan, 723, 741, 778
Trotha, Lothar von, 836
Trotsky, Leon, 869
Truman, Harry S, 891
Truman Doctrine, 891
Trump, Donald, 974
Tsetse fly, 158, 418, 568
Tughluq Dynasty (India), 348
Tula (capital of the Toltecs), 432
Tunisia, 763; Arab Spring protests, 960–1, 981; Bouazizi's self-martyrdom in, 981; Charles V's campaigns in, 472; Fatimid rebellion in, 281; founding of, 766; France as protectorate of, 831–2; independence gained by, 891f; Islamist party electoral victory, 981; Ottoman conquests of, 763; ouster of Ben Ali, 981; PLO forced relocation to, 949; trade activities, 188, 561
Túpac Amaru burial site (Peru), 428–9
Turkestan, Arab-Persian conquest of, 275f
Turkey: ascent of, 979; early agricultural settlements, 31; Erdoğan's leadership, 979–80; failed coup in, 963f; mass exodus of refugees, 975; secularization of, 856f. *See also* Anatolia
Turner, J. M. W., 683f
Turner, Nat, 587
Tutenkhamen, 49f, 62
Tutu, Desmond, 953
Twelver Shiism, 766–7
Twelve Tablets (Roman law), 195
Twitter, 961, 984–5
Twitter Revolution, 985

Ubaid culture (Mesopotamia), 35, 56
Ukraine: Chernobyl nuclear accident in, 930; Eastern Christianity in, 285; Golden Horde occupation of, 356; migrations across, 282; political unrest in, 963f; pro-Russian rebellion in, 971; Putin's land grab, 971; Russia's campaigns in, 869; trade activities, 24, 102; in World War II, 876; Yanukovych's presidency, 971

Umayyad Dynasty: Abbasid Revolution, 276, 318; eastern and western conquests, 275–6, 276m; empire building by, 273; religious developments, 275; timeline placement, 275f
Unction ceremony (defined), 310
Union of German Women's Organizations, 805
Union of Soviet Socialist Republics (USSR). *See* Soviet Union
United Nations (UN): African "nations" with seats, 986; "blood diamonds" scheme, 987; Charter of the United Nations, 669, 889, 915; China's bid for a seat, 942; Darfur crisis intervention, 968–9; environmental conferences, 990–1; feminism report, 939; Iran sanctions, 978; Iraq-Iran war hostage crisis intervention, 950; Iraq weapons inspections, 967; Korean intervention, 894–5; Lumumba and, 920; Mali preservation program, 424f; middle-income countries survey, 963; Non-Aligned Movement and, 914–15; Palestine independence question, 908; peacekeeping in Rwanda, 968; regional peace efforts, 967–9; Syrian withdrawal from Lebanon, 949; Yom Kippur war ceasefire, 948
United Nations (UN) General Assembly, 894, 939
United Nations (UN) Security Council, 894, 967, 978
United States Steel Corporation, 806–7
United States (U.S.): Afghanistan invasion by, 967; African American voting rights, 677–8; Al-Qaeda attack on, 849f, 963f; Alt-Right movement, 974; atomic bombing of Japan, 889, 890f; Berlin Airlift with Britain, 893; boycott of 1980 Summer Olympics, 929; buffalo herds, destruction of, 679; Bush, George W., presidency, 966–7; capital investments in Latin America, 719; capitalist democracy in, 848; Carter's presidency, 929, 948, 950, 955; challenges of slavery in, 755; China's treaty port opened with, 729m; CIA, 891f, 893–4, 894m, 897, 904, 919, 954–5; citizens emigration to Mexico, 702–3; Civil Rights Act, 934; civil rights movements, 933–7; Civil War, 677, 704–5, 790; Clinton's presidency, 965–6; collapse of détente with Soviet Union, 929; Confederate States of America, 677; conquest of Philippines, 819f; constitutional development, 676–7; containment policy vs. Soviet Union, 891; Cuban Missile Crisis, 849; Declaration of Independence, 653, 658, 761; dollar regime in, 964; dual economic recessions, 973; early industrialism in, 790; economic recession, 849f; Eisenhower's presidency, 933; era of détente with Soviet Union, 849, 925, 926–7, 927f; European emigration to, 798; expansion (1900), 678m; fiscal discipline advocacy, 962; free trade advocacy, 962; gay rights movement, 935, 935f; GI Bill for African Americans, 900; Gilded Age, 679; global crisis and recovery, 970; global financial crisis, 849f; and globalization, 965–6; globalization offensive by, 965–6; Great Depression, 837, 848f, 849, 851, 853f, 861–2, 970; Great Depression (U.S.), 853f; Great Society programs, 934; Harlem Renaissance, 860–1; imperialism in Southeast Asia, 839m; as import sinkhole, 964–5; Indian Removal Act, 679; influence on Japan, 723; Iraq invasion by, 963f, 966–7; Japan's studies of commerce in, 745–6; Johnson's presidency, 927f, 934, 945–6; Kennedy's presidency, 898, 899, 917, 926, 934; Korean War involvement, 895; Kuwait invaded by, 963f; Latin American exports to, 713; leisure and sports activities, 806; limited fulfillment of peace missions, 967–9; Louisiana Purchase, 665–6, 678; lynching of African Americans, 677–8, 859f, 860; Marshall Plan, 891, 893, 900, 904; Marxism opposed by, 954; McCarthyism in, 895; Mexican-American War, 738; military dominance of, 966; Monroe Doctrine, 704; Montgomery, Alabama bus boycott, 933f; nation-state building, 677–8, 678m; New Deal, 853f, 862; 1970s, 1980s economy, 937; nuclear agreement with Iran, 963f; Nuclear Test Ban Treaty, 849f, 899, 925, 927f; Obama's presidency, 966, 973–4; onset of "scientific–industrial society," 785; Philippine-American War, 842; plantation slavery in, 712; post-Civil War Reconstruction era, 677–8; post-Revolution early years, 658–9; post-WW I, anti-immigration, anti-communist hysteria, 860–1; post-WW I, business and labor, 859–60; post-WW I, high artistic creativity, 858–9; post-WW I unfolding of modernity, 856, 858; post-WW II, mass consumption culture, 900; post-WW II artistic achievements, 900–1, 901f; Progressive era, 679; railroads, railroad construction, 787f, 790; Reagan's presidency, 929, 937, 954; resistance to adaptation, 653; Roaring Twenties, 858, 861–2; September 11, 2001, terrorist attack, 967; Seven Years' War and, 665; Sino-Japanese War and, 735–6; Smoot-Hawley Tariff, 862; Social Security Act, 862; space race with Soviet Union, 897; stock market crash, 848f, 853f; student demonstrations, 936–7; summer of love, 936; Tea Party movement, 973–4; technological renewal and globalization, 965–6; trade activities, 789; training of dissidents in Latin America, 897–8; transcontinental railroad, 787f, 790; transnational economic integration advocacy, 962; Trump's candidacy, presidency, 974; 2002 military budget, 963f; 2016 presidential campaign, 974; U.S.–Mexico War, 703–4; Vietnam War involvement, 944–6; voting rights, early, 658–9; Voting Rights Act, 934; Washington's presidency, 658; women's suffrage movement, 804–5, 858; Woodstock music and art festival, 936f; in WW I, 855–6. *See also* Colonial North America; Native Americans
Universal Negro Improvement Association, 861
University of Paris, 311f
Upanishads (Hindu religious texts), 67f, 85, 87, 224
Upper class society (nouveau riche), Europe, 799
Urban II (Pope), 289, 324
Urbanization: in the Americas, 118, 129–34; in the Andes, 129m; in Caribbean Islands, 903m; in East Africa, 159–60, 411; in Europe, 320, 797; in India, 79, 83, 225; in Japan, 644; in Latin America, 903m; in Mexico, 868; in Ming Dynasty, 622; in Teotihuacán Kingdom, 161; in West Africa, 149
Urban VI (Pope), 334
Uruguay, 690, 691–2
Urukagina of Lagash (King), 42, 44
Uruk city-state (Mesopotamia), 33f, 37–8
U.S. Bureau of Indian Affairs, 934
U.S. Department of Commerce and Labor, 680
U.S.–Mexico War, 703–4
USSR. *See* Soviet Union
Utamaro, Kitagawa, 648

Vajjian Confederacy (India), 79–80
Vansina, Jan, 152–3, 157, 159
Vanzetti, Bartolomeo, 860
Varna social structure (India). *See* Caste system
Vedas (Indian sacred texts): Bhagavad Gita, 81, 82; composition of, 67f; criticism of rituals, sacrifices, 224–5; four *varnas* of, 76–7, 82–3, 85; *karma-samsara* concept in, 86; Mahabharata (poem), 80–1; oral transmission of, 84–5; Puranas, 81; Ramayana, 80–1, 83; *Rig-Veda* text, 74, 76, 77–8, 88; Upanishads, 67f, 85–6, 224
Vedic society (India): ahimsa doctrine, 219, 225–6; asceticism path, 85, 85f, 225; caste system, 67f, 76–7, 82–6, 88; chiefly assemblies tradition, 421; domestication of animals, 74; northern India, 75–9; religion, 57, 67f, 74–8, 80–1, 83–8; rice cultivation, 78–9; Upanishad reformers, 217f; visionary reformers in, 223–9
Velvet Revolution (Poland), 931
Venezuela: caudillo rule in, 699–700; Creoles in, 696–7, 696–8; democracy in, 903; independence gained by, 689, 699–700; populist regime in, 904; railroads in, 700; state-church issue, 711; state-church issues in, 711
Verbiest, Ferdinand, 631
Versailles Treaty, 848f, 853f, 856, 866
Viceroyalty of La Plata, 690, 691, 696–7. *See also* Argentina; Bolivia; Paraguay; Uruguay
Victor Emanuel II (King of Italy), 675
Vietnam: adoption of written Chinese, 243; Black Death origination, 331; bride-price, 392; Buddhism in, 270, 344, 373f, 392, 395–6; China's occupation of, 373f, 393, 940, 946; Cold War proxy war in, 849; Confucianism in, 262; cultural, political conflicts, 394; economy of, 394–5; France's conquest of, 819f; French conquest of, 842–4; gender equality in, 377–8; Ho Chi Minh's leadership, 916, 917, 925, 937; independence gained by, 393, 911; Le Dynasty, 373f, 393, 396;

Neo-Confucianism in, 607; Neolithic culture in, 391–4; politics, labor, trade, 394–5; Qianlong's military campaign against, 629; repeated invasions of, 393; repulsion of Mongol invasions, 271f, 373f; resistance to sinicization, 393; rice in, 391–2, 394; survival of communism in, 971; Tran Dynasty, 373f, 393; "tribute missions" to China, 625; Trung sisters revolt, 373f; village society, 392; war, communist rule in, 944–5; women in, 395; writing developments, 396
Vietnam War, 849f, 927f, 936, 944–6, 945m
Vijayanagar state (India), 271f, 345–6, 345f
Vikings, 285, 312, 466
Villa, Pancho, 701f, 707–8
Vita Kimpa, Dona Beatriz, 558–60
Vivaldi, Antonio, 494
Vlad III Dracul of Wallachia, 468, 469f
Vladimir I (Grand Prince of Kiev), 284
Voodoo religion, 584–5
Voting Rights Act (1965, U.S.), 934
Voting rights/suffrage: of African Americans, 677–8, 934; in Argentina, 692–3; in Athens, 184; in Brazil, 693; of Creoles, 698, 710; in England, 802; for women, 804–5, 858, 934

Wafd Party, 866
Wagadu (Ancient Ghana), 401, 418–19, 421, 422
Waldseemüller, Martin, 496, 497f
Walesa, Lech, 928–9, 929f, 931
Wang Anshi, reforms in China, 354–5
Wang Chong (Chinese astronomer), 265
Wang Mang, Red Eyebrow Revolt (Han ruler), 252–3
Wang Wei (Tang poet), 354
Wang Yangming, 365
Wang Zhihuan, 91
Wari (South America): adobe houses, 449; agriculture in, 443; disintegration of, 441; frontier, 437–8; geographic features, 443; map, 437m; Nazca influenced by, 173; origins and expansion, 436, 437, 453; ruling class of, 429; timeline placement, 431f
War of a Thousand Days, 700
War of Independence (Mexico), 701–2
War of Liberation from Spain, 493f
War of the Pacific (Chile, Peru, and Bolivia), 700, 720
Warring States period (China), 103, 105, 242, 243, 245f, 246–8, 253, 262, 269
Warsaw Ghetto (1940–1943), 886
Warsaw Pact (1955), 893, 928m
Washington, George, 658
Washington Naval Treaty, 879
Water frame, 787
Watt, James, 652f, 787f
Weaponry innovations: in the Americas, 120; in Asian agrarian centers, 3; in Aztec Empire, 441; bow and arrow development, 15; in China, 476, 629, 636; 1830s–1860s period, 795–6; in France, 506; in Hittite Empire, 47; of *Homo sapiens*, 22; of the Incas, 444–5; in India, 611; in Mali Empire, 421–2; Maxim's automatic machine gun, 787f; Meroë Kingdom, 152; in the Middle East, 476; in North Africa, 476; of Paleolithic Africans, 150; Persian Empire, 180–1; of steppe peoples, 3; of the Toltecs, 432, 441
Wedgwood, Josiah, 627
Weimar Republic (Germany), 872–3
Well-field land division system (Zhou Dynasty, China), 107–8
Welsh nationalism, in Great Britain, 680
Wen (Zhou King), 245
Wesley, Charles, 554
Wesley, John, 554
West Africa: agriculture in, 155; Ancient Ghana Kingdom, 417–19, 420m; archaeological discoveries, 156–7; Benin Kingdom, 424; chiefdoms in, 151f, 156; conquest and resistance in, 834–5; gold fields, 461m; Ife Kingdom, 270f, 403f, 422–3, 424; inland delta urbanism, 156; Islamic imperial traditions in, 401; Islam religion in, 834–5; Jenné-jeno city-state, 151f, 155–6, 160, 418, 422, 561; Mali Empire, 271f, 403f, 420–3; Muslim invasions, 560; pastoralism in, 155; plant domestication, 156–7; Portuguese exploration, 561f, 564–5, 567; private merchant interests in, 565; rain-forest settlements, 155–7, 403f; Saadids invasion of, 469; Swahili city-states comparison, 411; terra-cotta pottery of, 156f; trade activities, 567–8, 834; urbanization in, 149; village farming, 157; West African savanna, 155–7. *See also* Mali Empire
West African savanna, 155–7
Western Christianity, 270, 271; age of early global interaction, 491; Battle of Tours, 276; Charles V's rule of, 470; growth in developing states, 350; post-Black Death recovery, 505; scholastic Middle Ages in, 492
Western Zhou Dynasty (China), 93f, 104, 114
West Germany, 895, 898, 937
What Is the Third Estate? (Sieyès), 660
What Is to Be Done? (Chernyshensky, Lenin), 779, 782–3
Wheel, development of, 128, 143, 144
White Huns (Hunas), 222
White Nile slave trade, 404
White Revolution, 949–50
Wilhelm I (King of Germany), 675–6
William I (French Duke), 321
William I of Aquitaine (French Duke), 321
William of Ockham, 338
William of Orange (King of England), 838
William the Conqueror, 308m
Windmills, 317
Wireless telegraph, 795
Witchcraft, 159, 553–4, 559
Women: in ancient Egypt, 41; in China, 109–10, 260–2; in Creole culture, 548; in democratic Athens, 212–13; Empress Wu, 349–50, 353, 354f.368–9, 2526; in India, 83–4; industrial era jobs, 804; in Korea, 377–8; in Latin America, 718; Married Woman's Property Act, England, 805; rise of modern feminism, 927f; *Roe v. Wade* decision, U.S., 934; role of, early humans, 11, 12, 15, 27; and the sexual revolution, 934–5; suffrage movement, 804–5, 858; in Vietnam, 395. *See also* Feminist movement; Gender roles and divisions
Women Journalists Without Chains, 961
Women's liberation movement, 927f, 938–9
Wong Kon (Korean merchant), 375
Woodstock music and art festival (1969), 936f
Working class society, Europe, 800–1
World Trade Center attack (9/11/2001), 967
World War I (WW I): aftermath of, 851–68; Battle of the Marne, 853; early course of, 853–4; explosives, weaponry used during, 793; France's participation, 853–4; France's postwar direction, 848–9; Germany's participation, 837, 853–4; Great Britain's participation, 853–4; interwar period and, 848–9; Latin America's pre-war development, 715; 1917 turning point, 854–6; Ottoman entrance into, 836–7; Russia's losses in, 781; timeline placement, 848f, 853f; as total war, 851, 852f, 853; U.S. participation, 855–6; Versailles Treaty, 848f, 853f, 856, 866; weaponry, 793, 796
World War II (WW II): Battle of Britain, 876; China in, 848f, 853f; destructiveness of, 889, 890f; Egypt's participation, 866; Europe in, 853f, 878m; France in, 875–6; Germany's participation, 872–7; Hitler's Final Solution against Jews, 848f, 853f, 876–7; Jewish Holocaust, 876–7, 877f, 886, 889; Mediterranean in, 853f; North Africa in, 853f; Pacific campaigns, 882–4, 883m; Poland in, 875–6; rise of new nations and, 849; Stalin's actions in, 868, 875; timeline placement, 848f; turning point, 876, 877. *See also* Nazi Germany
World Wide Web, 984
Wounded Creek massacre (Native Americans), 679, 934
Wright, Wilbur and Orville, 787f, 794–5
Writing developments: Aztecs, 136; China, 91, 93f, 103, 109, 110–13, 115, 250, 264, 371, 381, 386; Chinese characters, 111; clay tablets, Persian Empire, 182; cuneiform writing, 38, 39f; Egyptian hieroglyphics, 44, 44f, 52, 136, 165; Greece alphabet, 53f, 54; India, 65, 67f; Korea, 373f, 378–9; Linear A and B script, 53–4; Mayan glyphic alphabet, 151f, 165–6, 167f; Mesopotamia, 44, 46; Minoans, Linear A script, 136; Nazca geoglyphs, 172–3; Americas, 136, 137f, 143; Phoenician letter alphabet, 52, 53f, 54; *quipu*, in the Americas, 119, 130–1; Teotihuacán Kingdom, 167–8; Vietnam, 396; writing paper introduction, 493
Wudi, the Martial Emperor (Han Dynasty, China), 188, 251–4, 253–4, 259, 265
Wu Ding (King of China), 90–1, 100, 102, 109, 111
Wu (Wu Zeitan) (Empress of China), 256, 349–51, 353, 354f, 356, 368–70
Wu (Zhou King), 245
Wycliffe, John, 335, 337

Xia Dynasty (China): age of myth and, 97–9; archaeological discoveries, 98; chariot origins, 78; Erlitou city and palace complex, 93f, 98, 99, 102; human sacrifices, 113; origins, 94; silkworm cultivation, 97; traditional dates, 93f
X-ray technology, 808

Xuan Zang (Chinese Buddhist pilgrim), 344–5
Xunzi (Chinese philosopher), 246–7

Yalta Conference (1945), 891f
Yamato period (Japan), 371, 373f, 382–3, 386–7, 389, 397
Yangshao culture (China), 93f, 94–5, 98
Yangzi River system (China): agriculture and commerce, 92, 351; British attacks, 727–8; cultural artifact discoveries, 96; Grand Canal project, 257, 351; rice cultivation, 3f, 93f, 96, 254; and Taiping Movement, 729; trade activities, 255; Zhou expansion, 104, 107, 115
Yanukovych, Viktor (Ukrainian President), 971
Yayoi period (Japan), 373f, 380–1, 386
Yellow fever, 666, 833
Yellow River cultures (China), 68, 91–9; climate and geography, 92, 93m, 94; Grand Canal project, 257, 351; historical background, 91–2; Neolithic settlements, 91, 93f; Yangshao communities, 93f, 94–5, 98
Yeltsin, Boris, 932–3
Yemen, 13, 32, 33, 152, 153; Arab Spring protests, 960–1, 981; Saudi military intervention in, 963f
Yi Dynasty (Korea), 373f, 376–8, 396
Yom Kippur/Ramadan War (Arab-Israeli War), 927f, 937, 947m, 948
Yongzheng (Qing Dynasty Emperor), 628, 636
Yoruba confraternity *(cabilde),* in Cuba, 697
Young Ottomans (Young Turks), 653f, 757f, 762–4, 769
Yrigoyen, Hipólito, 693
Yuan Dynasty (China): administrative needs, 358; creation of, 356–7; as "darkest time" for China, 358; overthrow of, 359, 376, 594; prototype free trade zone, 356; timeline placement, 345f
Yugoslavia: anti-Nazi resistance, 891; civil war, ethnic cleansing in, 849f, 963f, 975–6; as Eastern Bloc country, 898; ethnic nationalist groups in, 975; Tito's presidency, 975

Zacatecas silver mine, Mexico, 541
Zacuto, Abraham, 504
Zaghlul, Saad, 866
Zagwe Dynasty (Ethiopia), 403f, 406–7
Zapata, Emiliano, 707
Zarathustra (Zoroaster), 199
Zen Buddhism (Japan), 375f, 385, 389–90, 398–9
Zeng Guofan, 731f, 734
Zeppelin, Ferdinand von, 794
Zhang Heng (Chinese astronomer), 265, 266f
Zheng He, naval expeditions of, 345f, 623f, 727
Zhou Dynasty (China): agricultural innovation, adaptation, 107; Confucianism's influence, 245; decline of, 104–5; Eastern Zhou, 93f, 104–5; economy, 107–9; *fengjian* system, 104, 384; feudalism government in, 104–5; folk culture in, 114; grain cultivation, 96; historical background, 102–5; iron casting technology, 114; literary achievements, 98, 102–3, 109–10, 114; Mandate of Heaven, 103–4, 116; map, 103m; merchants and *shi* class, 108; political crises in, 80; Qin conquest of, 248–9; references to Korea, 372; rural society, 107; social, political tumult in, 243; society of, 107–10; Warring States period, 103; well-field land division system, 107–8; Western Zhou, 93f, 104, 114
Zhuang Zhou (Chinese philosopher), 248
Zhu Yuanzhang (soldier-Buddhist monk), 359, 376
Zimbabwe, revolution in, 951–2
Zimbabwe African National Union (ZANU), 952
Zimbabwe African People's Union (ZAPU), 952
Zionism, 865
Zoroastrianism: face-off with Christianity, 179; Islam's origins and, 278; Jewish adoption of elements of, 147; origins of, 199–200; Persian Empire adoption of, 193; as Persia's preferred religion, 182f
Zwingli, Huldrych, 510